Contents

Authors' Acknowledgements

A book like this involves the work of a whole army of people of whom the nine mentioned on the cover are really only the tip of the iceberg. While those nine are the ones who take full responsibility for the book, they would not be in that position without the help, support, advice and encouragement of a lot of others.

First the team would like to thank Sue Walton and her editorial team at Heinemann, namely Jane Tyler, Rob Bircher, Nicola Haisley and Sophie Williams, for their support for the project and the expertise and assistance in seeing it through. Roger Parker, Heather Serjeant, Fiona Barr, Sandra Stafford, Trish Stableford, Victoria Ramsay, Melanie Gray, Helen Maxey and Rachel Caldin also contributed with their particular forms of expertise.

Our first attempts were kindly read by a group of academic sociologists and their extremely helpful comments and advice were much appreciated. We would therefore like to thank Bob Blanchard, David Booth, Phil Brown, Stephen Edgell, Helen Fawcett, David Gillborn, Lesley Hoggart, Kate Nash, Alan Scott, John Solomos, Merl Storr, Bill Sugrue, Steve Taylor, Kenneth Thompson, Frank Webster and John Westergaard and the reviewer from OCR. It is important to stress that none of these bears any responsibility at all for the final book, but we would like to thank them and let them know their comments were both incisive and helpful, an extremely useful combination.

Writing a book like this requires reference to an enormous amount of material and it is therefore appropriate to thank the various libraries and library staff who always proved invaluable in assisting us in locating such material.

We would also like to thank all those who contributed to this book by designing it, typesetting it and printing it. Your skills mean the book looks good despite the material we provided you to work with.

Finally we would like to thank our families and friends for putting up with our obsession, and our students for humouring our early attempts and for re-creating the correct atmosphere of humility in the team members.

Individually, members of the team would like to offer their thanks as follows:

John Barter – Thank you to Janet, Joe and Becky for supporting me with this project. Love, John.

Tanya Hope – Thanks to all sociology students at Wheatley Park School Sixth Form, 1990–1995.

Warren Kidd – Thanks to my parents, Joan and Eddie, for their continued support.

Also thanks for a great deal of conversations, resource swapping and other such support from Dave King

Mark Kirby – Thanks to students at Amersham & Wycombe College. Also thanks to Jo Edwards, Carol Forster and most of all Frances Newman.

Alison Kirton – Thanks to Professor Jannette Elwood and Dr. David Gilborn.

Francine Koubel – Thanks to Jim

Nick Madry – Thanks to Julie, James and Anna and also to my mother.

Paul Manning – Grateful thanks to Winnie, Dan, Peter and Michael.

Karen Triggs – Thanks to Alan White and Merl Storr

The authors May 2000

Introduction to study

Chapter outline

1.1 The OCR specification   page 1
This section explains how the OCR specification is organized and how each module will be assessed.

1.2 Assessment objectives   page 2
To gain a good grade in your Sociology A level, you will need to show competence in two 'assessment objectives'. These are laid down by government bodies and are therefore contained in the OCR specification. This section of the chapter explains what the assessment objectives mean, how they are measured, and how you can show competence in them.

1.3 Developing skills for success in sociology   page 6
This section shows how you can develop your skills both as a sociologist and as a student. It makes suggestions for improvements in: (1) time-management/action-planning, (2) active learning, (3) note-taking, (4) essay writing questions, (5) structured questions, (6) data response, (7) revision, and (8) examination techniques. The argument running through this section is that when you become an *active* participant in your learning – rather than expecting everything to come from your tutor – you can develop your full potential and get the grade you are truly capable of.

1.4 How to use this book   page 19
This section contains an explanation of the structure of *Sociology in Perspective*, and shows how to use its key features to best effect.

1.1 The OCR specification

The OCR specification is divided up into eight modules. If you are studying for GCE Advanced Subsidiary (AS) then you will need to study modules 1 and 2 and either 3 or 4. For the full A level you will in addition study modules 5 and 8 and either 6 or 7. All modules are examined by written examination except for modules 4 and 7: the coursework modules.

The AS modules

Module 1 (Unit 2532)

In this module you study two sections: *Introducing the individual and society* and *Culture and the formation of identities*. This module is examined by answering one structured question from a paper of two such questions.

Module 2 (Unit 2533)

In this module you will study at least one topic from either *Family* or *Mass media* or *Religion* or *Youth and culture*. This module is examined by answering two two-part structured essay questions, chosen from the same or different options.

Module 3 (Unit 2534)

In this module you study *Sociological research skills*. This module is examined by answering one data response question.

Module 4 (Unit 2535)

This module is a coursework module. You are required to produce a Research Report of no longer than 1000 words. This will be marked in accordance with procedures laid out by OCR in the subject specification.

The A2 modules

Module 5 (Unit 2536)

In this module you study either *Crime and deviance* or *Education* or *Health* or *Popular culture* or *Social policy and welfare* or *Protest and social movements*. This module is examined by answering one unstructured essay question from a choice of two (there are two questions on each of the six topics).

Module 6 (Unit 2537)

In this module you study *Applied sociological research methods*. This module is examined by answering two compulsory structured questions.

Module 7 (Unit 2538)

This module is a coursework module. You are required to produce a Personal Study that should be no longer than 2500 words. This will be marked in accordance with procedures laid out by OCR in the subject specification.

Module 8 (Unit 2539)

In this module you study *Workplace inequality, poverty* and *explanations of inequality and difference*. This module is examined by answering one from two multi-part data response synoptic questions.

1.2 Assessment objectives

In the OCR subject specification for sociology there are two 'assessment objectives' (AOs), called AO1 and AO2. You must demonstrate 'competences' (abilities) in these two assessment objectives in order to pick up the marks that will determine your final grade. Given that you will first be working at GCE Advanced Subsidiary Level (specification number 3873), and perhaps then going on to full GCE Advanced Level (specification number 7873), the work will not be easy. However, if you follow the advice given in this chapter and by your tutors you can make the task much easier.

Activity

Think of the skills that you have now, such as walking, talking, reading or writing. Perhaps you excel in music or sport or art. Think about how you have developed such skills. Unless you are unique, you were not born with these skills. Was their development smooth and straightforward? Ask your parents or other family members for their comments on this.

C3.1a

Your thinking and discussions have probably told you that your skill development in any area of life

was not without a few hiccups, but through practice and perseverance you reached the high level of competence that you have today. Studying sociology at post-16 level will prove to be equally challenging, but it is also possible for you to become highly competent. Read on to find out more!

In the OCR specifications marks are awarded for competence in relation to two assessment objectives as follows:

	AS Level	A2 Level	Advanced Level
AO1	54	46	50
AO2 a	26	27	26.5
AO2 b	20	27	23.5

With the exception of Personal Study (Unit 2538), which is only available in June each year, all units will be available in both January and June each year from 2001 in the case of AS units (2532, 2533, 2534, 2535) and from 2002 in the case of A2 units (2536, 2537, 2539). The introduction of January and June assessment points facilitates the accumulation of marks throughout the one or two year programme.

Learning a new skill is not without a few hiccups

Assessment objective 1: Knowledge and understanding and presentation and communication

To gain marks for this assessment objective you will need to show that you can accurately recall (or remember):

- the names of sociologists
- the major details of their theories
- the important concepts (key ideas or terms) they use, plus accurate definitions
- the main pieces of evidence they use to support their theories
- the methods of research they used to gain their evidence, and the reasons for their selection.

You will also need to communicate your knowledge and understanding in a clear and effective manner. You will initially be studying for the GCE Advanced Subsidiary (AS), an entirely new qualification which exists as a discrete entity designed to be more conceptually challenging than GCSE, but less challenging in terms of depth and detail than Advanced level.

For GCE Advanced Subsidiary (AS) you need meet only the standard expected of the notional (or average) 17-year-old. At GCE Advanced Level (A level) you must meet the standard of the notional 18-year-old in examination conditions. At A level these standards are worked out through comparison with previous years' students to ensure (despite what you read in some newspapers) that a grade A when you sit your exams will be at the same standard as a grade A in years gone by.

To obtain all the available marks for AO1, you need to be able not only to recall the details listed above, but also to show that you have grasped the significance of what you are writing and can communicate that to the examiner. Particularly in longer questions, you will need to do this by developing a structured or logical argument to answer the question set. This is where you will be showing that you understand the ideas and details that you have memorized. In the examination this will also be apparent in answers that concentrate on selecting *relevant details only*, so avoiding 'everything I know about ...' responses. Consider this quotation:

In the time available under examination conditions ...

it is not possible to put on paper all that one knows on the topic. ... Therefore the selection and planning of the presentation of knowledge is vitally important.

(Sugrue, 1996, p. 30)

Activity

Draw a diagram to show the main features of 'knowledge and understanding' as you have understood them. Ask a friend or your tutor to check it.

C3.2, C3.3

Bill Sugrue argues that a secure knowledge base is 'an essential precondition' for the development and demonstration of the other required skills. These combine to form the second assessment objective, AO2.

Assessment objective 2(a): Interpretation and analysis

To gain marks for this assessment objective you will need to show that you can *use* your knowledge and understanding of sociology.

This suggests that you can see *trends* in data given to you. You can 'identify' the significant things. You can also pick out relevant information for the question set from your own knowledge and understanding of sociology:

Interpretation

One cannot, in the limited time available to answer a question under examination conditions, include all the points, findings, studies, concepts and theories that could be seen as having some form of relevance to the set question. In short ... you will have to interpret – that is, select – from your body of knowledge ... the 'bits' or version that best suits the set question.

(Sugrue, 1995, p. 24)

As you will discover, sociology has a language of its own. It develops concepts of its own (e.g. moral panics – see Section 6.2), and sometimes uses words in a different way from other people (e.g. secularization – see Section 7.4). Your job is to 'translate' those ideas or words simply so that ordinary people could understand, much as you might translate French or German into English so that it could be understood.

Analysis

To gain marks for analysis you will have to break down information to its essential or basic component parts. You will make sociological sense of arguments, data or sources to draw relevant conclusions.

Assessment objective 2(b): Evaluation

Evaluation requires you to consider the strengths and weaknesses of a theory or piece of research. This could be called 'asking awkward questions' (Moores, 1995) or not taking things for granted.

If you develop this skill well, you might find that you frustrate your family and friends because you constantly demand 'Who?', 'When?', 'Why?', 'Where?', 'How do you know?', 'How can you be sure?', and such like, when they tell you something. Such questions may also be awkward for other sociologists, but they allow you to get beyond the surface of an issue, helping you to get nearer to the 'truth' (whatever that might be!).

In sociology, five key *evaluation questions* you can ask are:

1 *How was the evidence gathered?* (Could better evidence have been collected by another method?)

2 *When was the research carried out?* (Will research from the past explain the present? Does it provide indicators?)

3 *Can the evidence be checked?* (Could it be repeated? If yes, would the same results be produced?)

4 *Does the writer have a theoretical bias?* (In other words, have his/her conclusions been influenced by their sociological perspective or standpoint?)

5 *Are ethnicity, class and gender taken into account?* (in the evidence or conclusions.) (The questions are taken from *S-Magazine*, September 1998, p. 38)

Answers to these questions should help you to determine the usefulness of a theory or piece of research.

Remember that good evaluation, although sometimes called '*critical* sociology', looks at the good and bad points of a theory or piece of research. It is not just a matter of criticizing the sociologist.

Generally speaking, for an evaluative stance, take on the role of 'judge and jury' – hear competing claims, consider the evidence put forward by each. Which do you believe to be the most convincing and why? Then produce your 'verdict' giving clear justifications for your choice.

(Mukerjee, 1994, p. 26)

Activity

Read the short passage 'Middle-class youth: conformity and rebellion'. What are the strengths and weaknesses in the research? (Answers are provided on page 22)
Source: *S-Magazine*, September 1998, p. 38.

C3.2, C3.3

Middle-class youth: conformity and rebellion

Recent research has investigated many aspects of the lives of young working-class males and, more recently, young women and youth from ethnic minorities. The study of middle-class youth, however, remains relatively underdeveloped and it is this gap in our understanding which is addressed in Peter Aggleton's 1987 study, *Rebels Without a Cause*.

Aggleton conducted a three-year study in which data were collected through a combination of participant observation and semi-structured interviews. The sample consisted of 27 students on A level courses at a college of further education in southern England. The students came from households defined as 'new middle class', a category defined by 'new left' political interests such as the environment, animal rights, feminism and so on, as well as liberal views on social issues such as sex and drugs.

The study examines the reasons for the educational under-achievement of young people from 'new middle-class' families. In a similar way to Paul Willis, in *Learning to Labour*, young people's experience of education is considered in relation to other aspects of their lives so that the social factors which cut across these different areas can be analysed.

Source: Adapted from Penna, S. 'Middle class youth: conformity and rebellion', in Warde, A. and Abercrombie, N. (eds), '*Family, Household and the Life-Course*', Framework Press, 1994.

Synoptic Assessment

The synoptic module, *Social Inequality and Difference*, will be the final module taken by those studying for the full A level. In this module students will be required to demonstrate their ability to connect issues of methodology as well as social inequality across the whole specification. Therefore, whatever options you take you must ensure that you make note of possible links to the synoptic module.

OCR explain that assessment on the synoptic module will test your understanding of the connections between sociological thought and methods of enquiry as they apply to the study of social inequality and difference. They go on to argue that you should take every opportunity to include references to aspects of social inequality that you have studied throughout your course.

This means that issues and material studied in both the AS and A2 modules can be referred to in the synoptic module. To help you draw such links we have used the following symbol:

on the chapter outline page of each chapter against sections where we feel the content is particularly relevant to the synoptic unit in order to remind you to note these synoptic links. We suggest you make notes for the synoptic module from these sections under the heading of 'Social inequality and difference in the context of [chapter title, e. g. *Social Policy and Welfare*]'.

We have also included, at the end of the synoptic chapter (Chapter 17), a table which includes a list of all the sections which we feel contain material relevant to the synoptic module. This includes AS chapter sections as well as A2 chapter sections.

We hope this will help you in preparation for tackling the synoptic unit.

Combining AO1 and AO2

Your final grade in sociology will be determined by how well you develop AO1 and AO2. The weightings of each assessment objective in relation to your overall qualification under the *OCR Specification* (2000, p. 6) are as follows:

- *GCE Advanced Subsidiary*
  AO1: 54 per cent
  AO2: 46 per cent

- *GCE Advanced Level*
  AO1: 50 per cent
  AO2: 50 per cent.

The levels of attainment necessary for A, C and E grades are as follows (*OCR GCE Sociology Specification*, 2000, p. 21):

- *Grade A*
  'Candidates display a detailed knowledge and understanding of a range of sociological theories, concepts and methods, and of the links between them. They demonstrate a well-developed ability to select and interpret different types of evidence from a range of sources, and make detailed and valid evaluations of evidence and arguments from a variety of contexts. They show a well-developed and refined ability to organize material from diverse sources, where appropriate, and use it to present and sustain sociological arguments of some complexity.'

- *Grade C*
  'Candidates display a good knowledge and understanding of some sociological theories, concepts and methods, and some recognition of the links between them. They demonstrate the ability to select and interpret different types of evidence from a range of sources, and are able to show some evaluation of evidence and arguments from different contexts. They show some ability to organize material from diverse sources and use it to present a sociological argument.'

- *Grade E*
  'Candidates display an outline knowledge and understanding of sociological theories, concepts and methods and the links between them. They demonstrate a basic ability to select and interpret evidence presented in different formats, and they are able to make a partial evaluation of evidence and arguments. They show an ability to organize material and present a basic sociological argument.'

The Unified Mark Scheme

All units will be allocated either 90 or 120 marks. This is necessary to ensure grade compatibility with units that are repeated. Your teachers will have received more information about this from OCR.

Opportunities to develop key skills through the study of sociology

As well as gaining an AS or A level qualification in sociology, you may find that there are opportunities throughout your course to produce portfolio evidence of your competence in *key skills*. As part of their reforms to the curriculum, the government has introduced national qualifications in certain key skills. There are six of these:

- communication
- information technology
- application of number
- working with others
- improving own learning and performance
- problem-solving.

It is possible to signpost opportunities for the first three using the *activities* contained in this book.

Communication

To provide evidence for *communication* you need to show that you have read material (C3.2), written material (C3.3), discussed issues with others (C3.1a), and presented material to others (C3.1b). There are plenty of opportunities to undertake communication during a GCE AS/A level sociology course, and the specific way you can evidence this to provide material towards a key skills unit should be discussed with your tutor.

Information technology

For *information technology* (IT), you need to show that you have planned and selected information (IT3.1), developed this information using IT (IT3.2), and presented the information using IT (IT3.3). You might provide evidence in relation to this key skill by completing and presenting a finished piece of coursework if you follow units 4 and/or 7, which are centre-assessed.

Application of number

For *application of number*, you are required to present evidence that you have planned and interpreted information (N3.1), carried out calculations and interpreted the results (N3.2), and presented the findings (N3.3). Clearly this key skill is really applicable only to the quantitative side of sociology; but if your coursework involves quantitative data, this is again an ideal opportunity to provide portfolio evidence of this key skill. It is, however, possible that there will be other opportunities to provide evidence in relation to this key skill, and you should consult your tutor about the possibility of this.

Key skills opportunities in this book

The OCR specification for AS/A level sociology contains the following statement:

Particular sections of the specifications can provide opportunites to develop candidates' key skills and to generate key skills portfolio evidence.

(OCR, 2000, p. 42)

In this book we have signposted activities (in the bottom right-hand corner) where we feel they may offer the potential opportunity to develop evidence for the key skills of communication, application of number and information technology. The codes used refer to the specifications contained in the key skills units, so you will need to refer closely to these to ensure that any evidence produced is in accordance with the requirements.

Further information on the key skills units can be found at www.qca.org.uk

1.3 Developing skills for success in sociology

Time-management/action-planning

Vocational Advanced level students get a lot of tuition early on in their courses about their personal use of time. It is sometimes assumed that GCE students can already organize their time, so tutors may give them less help. If you fall into this category, you need to teach yourself. If you can plan your available time sensibly and keep to the plan, you should find that you meet your academic deadlines (developing confidence in your ability as a learner) and still have time for all the other things you want to do.

An old study of American university students (Dole, 1959; referenced in Pauk and Fiore, 1989,

p. 7) found that they spent 49.3 hours per week sleeping, 10.7 hours eating, 18.7 hours in classes and labs, and 19.8 hours doing extra study. This left 69.5 hours (almost 10 hours per day) unaccounted for. The danger of leaving time unaccounted for is that it gets wasted. Once it's gone you can never get it back. You are left with thoughts of 'if only'. The answer is to avoid future disappointment by planning your time usefully from now on.

Pauk and Fiore (1989, p. 5) suggest the idea of '*scheduling*' – mapping out each day/week according to the time available and the action to take place within it. This would develop from a '*master schedule*' produced in discussion with your subject tutors for the whole term. It would set targets for achievement in that time period. Detailed *weekly and daily schedules* could be built up from there. Pauk and Fiore argue that:

... although some people believe it's a waste of time to make a schedule, planning actually saves time and energy. Sure, it takes time to schedule time, but the time you spend making a schedule is returned to you several times over when you work – and relax – according to your schedule.

(Pauk and Fiore, 1989, p. 7)

In terms of individual study sessions it is probably useful not only to have a good idea about what you want to achieve in the time available, but also to ensure that you have all the materials necessary for completion of the task. Failure to do this may mean hunting around for them, increasing your stress level and wasting time. Thus you need to set aside some time for this too.

As a good 'critical' sociologist you have every right to question the truth of these arguments. The only way to come to an informed answer is to try them for a few weeks. Do they work for you? Do you get more done? Are you meeting your deadlines?

Once you have decided to 'schedule' or manage your time in order to get your sociology (and your other studies) done, you must decide *how* you will work within that time in the most efficient way. The rest of this chapter offers many suggestions – some will work for you, others may not. You are advised to try them out in order to find the ones that do work. Rowntree (1997, p. 2) argues that you, as a student, should beware of 'the myth of the super-student' – the one who gets *everything* done *perfectly* and *to deadline*, whilst still having a full and exciting social life. There are few, if any, of these kinds of student;

comparison with such an ideal is likely to leave you feeling inadequate and demoralized. Instead you need to develop a sense of proportion, setting *your own* targets according to *your own* circumstances. At the same time you need to develop some appropriate study strategies, and this chapter will help with that.

Active learning in sociology

Think back to the assessment objectives; they require not only straight memorization of facts but also understanding of sociological theories, concepts and evidence, and an ability to identify, analyse, interpret and evaluate them. Such a range of skills requires a range of study techniques. Deakin (1998a, p. 11) argues that they require 'active learning strategies' which 'involve you in a creative way'. They engage you and enable you to 'play with ideas' rather than just 'recall them'. In his interesting articles (1998a,b) he offers guidance on a number of strategies you could use, including:

1 exploring sociological themes through the design of posters

2 cutting out and storing interesting photographs from magazines and newspapers so that you can analyse them when you cover an area related to the topic

3 writing out a number of statements about an issue like divorce (perhaps with the help of family and friends) and then ranking them from 'most' to 'least' effective explanations

4 mapping out timelines of sociological explanations so that you can ensure a greater understanding of how sociological arguments have changed and developed.

Further strategies

You could also try some of the following strategies. Several would fit into your ordinary lifestyle without having to change it too greatly. They could make life much more fun! You would become an active sociologist in your own right.

Observing

Watch people on the bus, in town, anywhere (without being too obvious about it). Ask yourself what they are doing, what their lives are like, and whether any sociological theories you know would explain these circumstances. Would the situation 'disprove' other theories?

Reading

Read a broadsheet newspaper to keep up to date on current affairs (the *Guardian*, for example, has lots of articles about social issues). Local newspapers are also very useful. Cut out articles on social issues from newspapers and magazines and file them in appropriate sections of your folder. You could evaluate the truth of the arguments and evidence within them. You might also build up ideas for coursework and you will already have some evidence to help get you on your way.

Viewing and listening

You can continue to watch your favourite TV programmes, but with a critical eye. For example, when watching soaps, ask yourself how 'real' the presentations of family life and other issues are. How do these presentations relate to the sociology on that area?

Do the same for 'factual' programmes like the news and documentaries. The latter are required to be fair and balanced, but are they? Is anything missing? If so, what does that tell you about the media? What do you learn about the sociological issues?

The Internet

Many students nowadays have access to the Internet at their institution or at home. Why not use it to make learning sociology fun?

Activity

The websites below might be a good place to start.
- Exam boards:
  http://www.aqa.org.uk
  http://www.ocr.org.uk
- Government statistics:
  http://www.ons.org.uk
  http://www.statistics.gov.uk
- Website provider portals:
  http://www.yahoo.com/social_science/sociology
- Annual reviews related to sociological topics:
  http://anurev.org/soc/home.html
- Leicester University social science resources:
  http://www.le.ac.uk/education/resources/socsci:/femach.html

- Social Science Gateway and other gateways to a multiplicity of sociological sites:
  http://www.sosig.ac.uk
  http://www.sosig.esrc.bris.ac.uk
  http://www.pscw.uva.nl/sociosite
  http://www.studyweb.com
  http://www.socio.com
- School, college and individual sites:
  http://www.hewett.norfolk.sch.uk/curric/soc/theory.htm
  www.sociology.org.uk
  http://www.wakcoll.ac.uk/line1/a-level/sociology

The following are sites related to particular specification topics.
- Culture and the formation of identities:
  http://www.ccccs.ac.uk
- Family:
  http://www.trinity.edu/~mkearl/family.html
- Mass media:
  http://www.bbc.co.uk
  http://www.guardianunlimited.co.uk
  http://www.ft.com
  http://www.itv.co.uk
  http://www.magicdragon.com/EmeraldCity/Nonfiction/socphil.html
- Religion:
  http://www.coe.org.uk
  http://www.islam.org.uk
- Sociological research skills:
  http://www.sosig.ac.uk/iriss/papers
- Crime and deviance:
  http://personal.tmlp.com/ddemelo/crime/index.html
  http://www.statistics.gov.uk
- Education:
  http://www.dfee.gov.uk
  http://cem.dur.ac.uk
- Health:
  http://www.doh.gov.uk
- Social policy and welfare:
  http://www.mistral.co.uk/connect.pub
  http://www.dss.gov.uk
- Protest and social movements:
  http://www.greenpeace.org.uk
  http://www.conservativeparty.org.uk
  http://www.libdems.org.uk
  http://www.labour.org.uk
- Theory:
  http://www.hgx-hypersoft.com/clothilde/home.html
  http://eddie.cso.uiuc.edu/Durkheim

http://msumusik.mursuky.edu/~felwell/http/
weber/home.html
http://www.anu.edu.au/polsci/marx/marx.html
http://paradigm.soci.brocku.ca/~lward
http://www.socio.ch/sim
http://weber.u.washington.edu/hbecker
http://www.uta.edu/english/apt/collab/
baudweb.html
http://www.csun.edu/~hfspc002/foucault/
home.html
- Social inequality and difference:
  http://www.bath.ac.uk/~mamwns/ethnicit.htm
  http://www.abacon.com/list/sso603.html
  http://www.gre.ac.uk/~j.hoodwilliams

Always read the pages on these sites with a 'critical' eye!

IT3.1, C3.2

Keep up to date with new Internet sites of interest to sociologists by reading 'Eyes on the net' in *Sociology Review*. If you locate any good sites yourself you can send them to Philip Allan Publishers for inclusion in this feature of *Sociology Review*.

Creating a personal dictionary

A practical method of developing your basic knowledge of sociology might be to use an exercise book to make up your own sociology dictionary. Every time you come across a new term or an everyday word used in a specialized way, you can enter it under the appropriate letter with a simple definition that you learn. You might want to get your tutor to check it through to make sure the definition is correct before you commit it to memory.

If you prefer learning in a social environment, most if not all of the above activities could be done with a friend or small group, but make sure you do not get sidetracked! Try encouraging your tutor to organize a sociology field trip. You could organise a Sociology Society at lunchtimes to help students with essays or coursework. You can organise presentations or seminars to students who are not sociologists. Try challenging a few of their common-sense notions. Encourage them to ask some awkward questions!

Whatever active learning methods you adopt, aim to keep to your learning schedule. If you find other useful ways of learning, why not share your ideas with others by writing to one of the sociology journals for students and/or their teachers?

What is there to read?

As you are already finding out, reading is an essential element of studying sociology. For some students this can prove tiresome. However, there are ways of making your reading productive and satisfying. You should, firstly, be aware that there are different types of reading matter available to you.

Textbooks, like this one

These tend to be 'second-hand' reviews of the work of sociologists. They may cover the whole specification, be written for pre-university students and contain activities to make you think/do. They tend to be the best place to start on a topic.

Topic books

These are a step up from textbooks. They are concerned with one topic only – such as 'gender' or 'education' – and cover it in more detail. Again they tend to be written for pre-university students, have activities and are quite accessible.

Journals

Journals, such as *Sociology Review*, are written for pre-university students and usefully they have articles written by examiners about revision, study skills and so on. They also have simplified accounts of research, or commentaries on theories or concepts.

Readers

These are collections of essays or short segments from the work of particular sociologists, written in their own words. This is 'first-hand' sociology at its most accessible. Many of these books have been compiled for undergraduates so are harder to understand (but well worth attempting); others, like *Readings in Sociology* (Kidd *et al.*, 1998), have been edited specifically with pre-university students in mind.

Primary texts

These are books containing the work of one sociologist (or a team) in his or her own words. They can be very difficult but some are extremely accessible (and enjoyable!). Your tutors will be able to point you towards the most useful ones.

Particularly accessible primary texts are Michael Young and Peter Willmott's *Family and Kinship in East London* (1957), William Foote Whyte's *Street Corner Society: The Social*

Structure of an Italian Slum (1981), and Andrea Dworkin's *Life and Death: Unapologetic Writings on the Continuing War Against Women* (1997). In general, do not aim to read whole books – look for the preface/introduction, the conclusion and one or two of the chapters that seem most interesting.

Unit 4 of the OCR specification requires you to report on a short piece of sociological research you have chosen. The specification stresses that this should be a straightforward piece of research.

By following advice to read primary tests, you can gain credits towards your AS/A level. The authors feel that articles summarize the books mentioned above may be suitable for this, but would stress that you must discuss this issue with your teacher or lecturer.

How should you read to make best use of your time

This might seem rather an odd heading. You've been reading for many years now, starting at the top left, following each word in turn! This method assumes that every word is worth reading, but at this level of sociology you may have a specific purpose and a short time-scale, so not every word *is* worth reading. You may find it useful to begin by skimming over the section, chapter or essay that you think will be useful, to determine where the relevant elements are to be found. You could mark these with a pencil. Once you have completed this you could read over the indicated paragraphs in more detail.

However, active learning strategies involve you in a creative way, so you must do more than just read. You must *interact* with the text you are reading to maintain your interest, develop all the skills in the assessment objectives and, psychologically speaking, transfer material to your long-term memory. Rowntree suggests:

Once you have embarked on your reading, then you may find it helpful to: pause from time to time; close the text; tell yourself the main ideas you have met so far.

(Rowntree, 1997, p. 90)

He goes on to say:

Don't just think your re-call. Write down the key points. Make brief notes of the main ideas and any details that seem important to you.

(Rowntree, 1997, p. 91)

Exploring the best way to make notes

Personalize your approach

Brown offers important advice:

Try to experiment with techniques until you find one which matches the way your own mind works. The best technique for you may not necessarily be a straightforward written form. It may be that making use of diagrams, charts, lists and colours to highlight the main points suits you better.

(Brown, 1997, p. 26)

She also suggests that you try to save time by abbreviating key terms. You could try 'func'ism' for functionalism, 'sec'z' for secularization or 'sctn' for socialization. Try to develop abbreviations of your own for concepts or other sociological words that you use often.

A suggested approach

Rowntree (1997) suggests three basic note-taking forms:

- summary notes in straight prose
- skeleton outlines
- patterned notes/spray diagrams/spider charts.

Example of summary notes

Andrea Dworkin (1997) argues that women are in most danger in their own homes. In the USA, 4000 women/year are killed in their own homes by men who are supposed to love them (not by strangers).

She believes that the expressions of anger and frustration that lead to such murders are normalized and excused by society. The violence men use to control women is similar to methods used in prisons by politically repressive societies.

A woman's self-esteem is destroyed by such violence because she can't control it. She doesn't know how or when it will happen. She believes it's her fault.

The woman will find it difficult to talk about it. Who will she tell? Can she trust them? Will they believe her?

Example of a skeleton outline

1 *Andrea Dworkin (1997): women – most dangerous place is their home. In USA 4000/yr killed by partners (not strangers)*

2   *Cause of the murder – men's anger and frustration – is excused/normalized*

3   *Violence similar to that used by prisons in repressive societies*

4   *Violence destroys victim's self-esteem – too unpredictable – 'Is it my fault?'*

5   *It is isolating – 'Who can I rely on?'*

Example of a spider diagram

A spider diagram covering the same area could look like Figure 1.1.

Activity

a Which method do you now think would be best for you, and why?

b Could you adapt one of the forms (or combine them) to suit you better?

c Talk to other students. What methods do they use?

C3.1a

The method of note-taking you adopt will depend on the task/purpose and/or your own preferred style. Try a few different styles before you settle on a specific one.

Most reading you do will be aided by note-taking. It makes you reflect on the important bits. It also provides you with useful summaries for essays and revision.

Assessment in the OCR specifications

We will now look at the type of questions you will face in the OCR units. The table below provides a quick summary of the type of question you will face in each unit:

Unit number	Level	Type of question	Number to be answered
2532	AS	Structured	1 from 2
2533	AS	Structured essay	2 from 8
2534	AS	Data response	1 from 1
2535	AS	Research Report	–
2536	A2	Unstructured essay	1 from 12
2537	A2	Structured	2 from 2
2538	A2	Personal Study	–
2539	A2	Data response	1 from 2

You will therefore confront structured questions (units 2532 and 2537), data response questions (units 2534 and 2539) and also essay questions, both structured (unit 2533) and unstructured (unit 2536). If you are studying for the AS level, you may only need to deal with structured questions and structured essay questions (and possibly data response questions if you do not take the Research Report option). If you are studying for, or go on to study for, the full A level you will be meeting all the styles of question listed above. We will therefore consider each of these styles of question in turn.

Approaching structured questions

These will be the first type of question you will confront and they are likely to seem familiar to you since they are similar in style to the GCSE questions you have just finished. This similarity is deliberate: the idea is to allow you to gradually work your way up the AS and/or A level ladder.

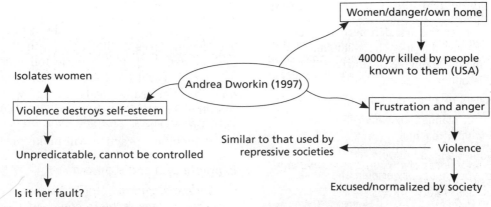

Figure 1.1 Example of a spider diagram
Source: Adapted from Rowntree (1997, pp. 134–6)

The 'structure' in structured questions comes from the fact that they are multi-part questions with the early parts being more approachable than the later parts, where higher level skills are required. The structure is therefore an incline of increasing difficulty, starting off relatively easy. So for instance in a structured question on Unit 2532 the early parts will ask you to briefly explain something and this will only require AO1 skills, while the later parts of questions will test both AO1 and AO2. Equally, the first parts of questions on Unit 2537 will be less involved than later parts, which will require you to demonstrate skills in both AO1 and AO2. These questions will all have stimulus material included and so you will need plenty of practice to make sure that you are familiar with the sorts of material likely to be included in questions in the exam, and how to approach them. Your teacher will be able to provide more advice on this.

As with data response questions, the wording of the question gives you clues as to the type of skill being tested, so read each one carefully. You will also need to read closely for the issue/topic that you must respond to. Do not make hurried assumptions; be sure that the question actually does say what you initially think it says.

You must also take notice of the marks (indicated in brackets at the end of the question) that are available for the answer. Few marks indicate a short answer. Seven or more marks indicate the need for a longer answer, with a series of points (including analysis and evaluation). You would be advised to do a quick plan or brainstorm before you write your answer, to ensure that you don't forget anything and that your points are structured logically.

Approaching data response questions

While structured questions have one item of material to respond to, data response questions have more than one, usually two. That data might be a paragraph or two from a sociology textbook, a novel, a newspaper or magazine. It could be a photograph, a small table of statistics or a diagram. The OCR specification provides more detail on the variety of data response questions you may encounter. You might be asked to:

- show knowledge or understanding by defining a key word
- identify a specific element or trend
- analyse/interpret the data
- evaluate the worth of the data.

Activity

Ask your tutor to show you copies of past or sample questions so that you become familiar with the type of questions you could be asked.

C3.1a

The wording of the questions on the exam paper gives you clues as to the type of skill being tested and the type of answer required. Read the questions carefully, working out what you will be required to do, before going on to read the information sources or 'items'. As you read you ought to highlight or underline elements relevant to the questions being asked. You can return to these when you begin your answer.

The available *mark*, usually in brackets after a question, gives a vital clue as to the length of answer expected. If you write too much on one answer, you will not have enough time left for a question that really needs a lengthy answer. On the other hand, if you write too little you will not earn full marks.

Remember, practice will make perfect.

Activity

Ask your teacher for copies of past examples of structured questions.

a For two questions explain how the questions are structured.

b Rewrite them so the first part becomes the last and the last the first. This will require you to think about the degree of structure involved in one question.

c Plan answers to all parts of one question.

d Discuss your planned answers with classmates and your teacher.

e Revise your planned answers.

f Write out your final answer plan and present it to your classmates.

C3.1a, C3.1b, C3.2, C3.3

Activity

a Practise writing answers to past or sample data response questions. Ask your tutor to make comments on your answers and bear these in mind when you write the next ones.

b Practise marking answers written by your friends. Have they answered questions as you would? What are the answers worth? Discuss the marks you have awarded them.

c Put yourself even more firmly in the place of the examiner by designing your own data response questions when you complete a topic. Choosing appropriate data items can be good fun. Wording the questions so that they cover the range of skills and both assessment objectives can be harder. Ask your friends to have a go at answering your questions and then mark them. Set them a clear target for improvement with the next piece of work that they do. Afterwards discuss the data, the questions, the answers, the marks awarded and the target set.

N.B. In marking the exercises, remember that examiners do not subtract marks, they add them as they are earned. Also remember to be positive and helpful if you are writing comments.

C3.2, C3.3

Approaching essay writing

Types of essay questions

Structured essay questions

In the OCR units you will come across two types of essay question. Unit 2533 contains structured essay questions. What this means is that each question contains two parts. The first will ask you to *identify and explain* something and will test the AO1 skill only. The second will ask you to *outline and discuss* something and will test both skills, AO1 and AO2.

Unstructured essay questions

The more 'conventional' essay questions are known as unstructured essay questions. They occur in Unit 2536. Unstructured essay questions have only one part to each question. You will be asked to outline and assess something and the question will test both these skills.

Because both types of essay question, structured and unstructured, require long prose answers, it is necessary to give more thought to their planning.

Planning and writing essays

Your sociology tutor is likely to set you quite a few essays throughout the length of your course. This is partly because you will have essays to write if you go on to do GCE A level, but also because the research and thinking involved help you develop skills in AO1 and AO2. As Rowntree (1997) reminds us:

There is nothing like the writing of an essay to make us question our ideas, weigh up our impressions, sort out what information is relevant and what is not – and above all, come up with a reasoned viewpoint on the topic that we can feel is our own.

(Rowntree, 1997, p. 149)

So how should *you* approach the writing of the essay? This obviously depends on whether it is to be done under examination conditions or in your own time; however, the general principles are the same. In your own time you will have time to read, take notes and to think a good deal before writing. Under examination conditions you do not have this luxury, but if you have done your revision properly (see pages 15–18) and have practised your examination techniques (see pages 18 and 19) you will have the necessary ideas in your head.

Planning your response

At this point, in both cases, you will need to plan your response to *the question set*. Examiners stress these three words because weaker candidates often see one or two words in the question – perhaps ones they hoped would turn up – and write a response to a question that is out of their imagination. If they had taken the time to read the question properly, understanding key terms in the question, they might have realized that a different response was required.

Reading the question

So, careful reading of the essay question is the first part of the planning process. Look out for *action words* (those telling you to 'assess', 'critically evaluate', 'discuss', etc.), all of which indicate that the full range of assessment objectives need to be covered. Look out too for *topic words* (such as 'deviance', 'social class' or 'Marxism'), which indicate the area of knowledge that you need to draw from. Think about the relationship between the words and what the examiner is expecting from you.

Jotting down your main ideas

Put a few ideas down on paper, and then try to put them in a logical order – this becomes *your plan*, one which will allow an argument to follow.

Remember that every issue in sociology involves a 'debate' – different sociologists put forward opposing viewpoints. So even if the question asks you explicitly to assess Marxist arguments about deviance and social class, it will also require acknowledgement and some discussion of other sociological perspectives in order for you to weigh up (evaluate/assess) how good the Marxist arguments are. Your plan could be a list of bullet points indicating the topic of each paragraph, or more like a spray or spider diagram (as in Figure 1.1). Use the method which most suits you.

Activity

Practise reading through past essay questions (perhaps together with a friend) and deciding who the debates in each would be between. What are the key ideas you would need to cover? Which are the best ones? If you do this with a friend you may find you have different ideas and the debate comes alive.

C3.1a, C3.2

Starting writing

When it comes to writing essays you will already know from past experience in English and in other subjects that they need a beginning (introduction), middle (main part) and end (conclusion). It is no different in sociology!

The introduction

This needs to 'set the scene'. In a paragraph you need to set out *briefly* who the debate in question is between, the central arguments, and an indication of what your response to the question is. Aim to explain the meanings of key topic words in the question. Avoid doing this in a dictionary style – aim to make any definitions part of a flowing sentence or paragraph.

Activity

Practise writing introductions to answers to the past exam questions at your disposal. Try to keep them to between five and eight lines. Get your tutor or a friend to make comments on them. What could you do to improve them?

C3.3

The main part of the essay

This should aim to add the flesh to the skeletal argument set out in the introduction. Ensure that each paragraph covers a separate point.

Remember that you must show evidence of Assessment Objectives 1 and 2.

- To gain marks for AO1 you will need to select relevant theories, concepts and evidence. You will need to describe (only) the essential details accurately.
- To gain marks for AO2 you will need to be able to comment on the theories, concepts and evidence selected. Why are they relevant to the question set? How do they compare/contrast with theories, concepts and evidence previously mentioned? Are there examples from current affairs which illustrate the points? What are the strengths and weaknesses of the theories, concepts or evidence? How useful does this make it?

Ideally each paragraph will contain both AO1 and AO2 type statements.

Activity

Before you hand in an essay for marking, read all the way through it. Check that you are close to the ideal with every paragraph.

C3.2

The conclusion

This should refer back to the question and emphasize your response to it. Aim to justify your views and do not be afraid of supporting or criticizing a particular notion expressed in the question if you feel that your view is more accurate. If you feel that no one particular theory, concept or piece of research referred to in the question is better or worse than those used to oppose it, explain why.

Activity

If the essay is one that your tutor marks, take good note of the comments he or she writes. If you don't understand them or need clarification, ask. Your tutor will have spent quite a lot of time marking the essay and will want you to benefit. They will not be upset if you want to go over something. Once you are clear, build on that advice when you write the next essay. If you have time in the future, rewrite the original essay. It will help your revision and help you develop your essay technique.

C3.2, C3.3

Approaching revision

Revision is the re-learning of material in preparation for an examination. If you have followed the advice on action-planning and active learning, you will now be in an excellent position to begin it. You will have learnt more, at a deeper level, and will have developed the skill of organizing your learning. Even if you have not done this so far, following these techniques will help. The advice is as simple as possible, dealing with the 'why', 'what', 'when', 'where' and 'how' of revision. We hope that it will be informative and help to keep you organized and, therefore, as stress-free as possible. Good luck!

Source: *How to do Better in Exams*, reprinted by permission of the AEB/Barclays Bank

The WHY? and WHAT? of revision

The WHY?

You should be able to answer this easily. By the end of your AS or A level Sociology course you will have built up a file or more of notes and handouts. Unless you are unique, it is unlikely that you know everything word for word. Even if you do, it is less likely that you will understand all of it or be skilled in identification, analysis, interpretation and evaluation. As the exams approach, you will need to learn as much relevant sociology as you can *and* practise using it. This is what is meant by the process of revision.

The WHAT?

You need to find out what you need to learn for each exam paper. In essence the specification offers you an element of choice (see page 1) but pressures of time or an emphasis on doing fewer topics in greater detail may have led your tutor

to cover less than the highest possible number. So:

1 Check the specification (ask your tutor for a copy if you don't have one) and consult your tutor about it.

2 Find out how the questions will be assessed – structured questions, data response questions or essays (see pages 11–14).

3 Check on the skills being tested. Do you know exactly what they are and what the terms mean? – See pages 2–4.

The WHEN? – Setting revision targets

It has already been suggested that continuous action-planning and active learning will help your skills development. However, there comes a time when you need to increase the number of hours you spend studying sociology. But you will also need to balance this with time spent studying other subjects – there is no point in doing well in one subject and failing the rest. Only you can decide how much you need to do and how early. Six weeks is probably a good length of time for intensive revision. Your tutor, who has a good deal of experience in getting students through their exams, will be a good person to consult.

Once you have a specific time period you will then need to break this down into weekly timetables. Firstly, include normal lesson and tutorial times, part-time job(s) (would you be better off giving up work for this period, or at least reducing your hours?), and regular social commitments (remember that you will need short but regular periods of rest and relaxation). Once you have done this there should be lots of gaps. You ought to assign equal time-slots to each of your subjects.

Using the sociology time-slots

Now you are in a position to divide out the separate topics you have done in sociology to the separate time-slots available for sociology revision. Set yourself targets for achievement in each.

The length of time-slots

Too much in one go will lead to tiredness and inefficient use of time. Keep revision sessions to one hour, and then take a 10–15 minute break. Do not lose track of time – that will put you behind schedule.

Realistic and achievable targets

There is no point setting yourself the task of learning this textbook, word for word, in an hour. First, that is a pointless task because you do not need to know it all. Secondly, it is impossible in the time-frame. If you work to hourly slots, it may be possible to go through a section from one chapter, perhaps two, in one hour. Only you know what you are sensibly capable of doing in that hour. Setting yourself an over-ambitious target will lead to incompletion of the target, disappointment and stress: so don't do it!

Measurable targets

One way of ensuring realistic and achievable targets is to make them measurable. Then you know how much more you have to do, when you've completed it and when you can have a rest/reward! The latter is essential for the avoidance of stress. You can go out with your friends, without feeling guilty, if you know that you have completed the targets you set yourself.

Flexiblity

Do not fill up every slot over the revision period. Earlier in the chapter we mentioned Rowntree's 'myth of the super-student'. There are times when you cannot get everything done. Don't worry. If you have built some flexibility (some empty slots) into your revision schedule, you will be able to do it another time.

Confidence

Lastly, remember that your friends might not always tell the truth about what they are doing. Some may claim not to be doing any revision at all, whilst others claim to be working all the time. The truth is probably somewhere in between. Don't be influenced by their claims – stick to your carefully worked schedule, with slots of work and relaxation, and success will come your way.

The WHERE?

Again, everyone is different. Unless you have built in a revision slot with a friend, it is probably best to revise in a quiet place with few people around to distract you. Sit in a comfortable chair to reduce back-ache. Ensure that you have the right books, papers, pens and other necessary equipment. Be within easy reach of refreshments and toilets. If you need music to help to drown out peripheral noise, try to ensure that it does not also have lyrics – then you won't end up singing along and forgetting the revision!

The HOW?

As with the other study skill strategies discussed in this chapter, revision techniques are highly personal. What works for another student may not work for you (and vice versa). Listed below are a number of different techniques. The only way to find out whether they work for you is to try them.

Pre-checking

Start by checking that you have covered all of the work you need. Did you miss any lessons? Did you fail to catch up? Are you missing any handouts? With a friend, go through your folders. Do the contents tally? Make a note of the things you are missing and need to catch up on. If you are missing handouts, ask your tutor for them (or photocopy your friend's).

Reading and note-taking

Many people begin their revision with an intensive period of reading and note-taking (particularly if they never really got around to this before). Given the time-scale for revision, you would probably be wise to stick to a textbook (like this one) containing activities, to help you develop all the skills and not just knowledge. Topic books with activities would possibly suit the more ambitious.

Whenever you make notes, break your sessions down into small units. For example, make notes for 20 minutes, then spend 5–10 minutes recalling what you have done, orally or on paper. Do this at the end of the session too. A. Smith (1999), an expert in learning, argues that 80 per cent of new knowledge is lost within 24 hours without some sort of review. Regular recall strategies will make your note-taking sessions even more efficient in terms of learning.

In sociology each topic is broken down into a series of debates (or sociological arguments). For example, 'The family' is broken down into debates like:

- Is there a typical family structure in the UK?
- What is the typical division of labour within the family?
- Do families have a dysfunctional 'dark side'?
- Is marriage an out-dated institution?

So, whatever method of note-taking you choose for yourself, aim to make the debates the central feature of that process. Try to work out the key debates within the topics you have studied (there are often about five or six). Compare your ideas with a friend's. Get your final lists checked by your tutor to ensure that your revision will be on the right track. Using past (or sample) papers, note how closely the questions relate to the key debates.

Making your notes more user-friendly

Reading and note-taking will help to develop your knowledge, and following the set activities will help you to develop the other necessary skills. However, you will probably need to change the notes into another form if you are to develop your skills further still. Students follow a number of different options:

- Condense the notes into *summary bullet points* that are easier to scan.
- Build on this by highlighting a key word from each bullet point and then taking the first letter of each highlighted word to form a *mnemonic*. A mnemonic is a word or phrase formed to help you remember something. The more silly or rude it is (keep it to yourself!) the easier it will be to remember. An example is 'Richard Of York Gave Battle In Vain', to help you remember the colours of the rainbow.

- At your present level of study you will need to do more than remember the key words, so you should aim to recall them and then the bullet point that stems from them. Such re-call could be done on paper or in your head as you take a walk.

- Some students like to condense information on to index cards, possibly colour-coding them by topic. From the condensed notes, they aim to recall the other associated information. Again, the recall can be done anywhere.

- Some students, preferring to listen rather than read, transfer important notes to an audio tape. They then listen on a personal stereo, aiming to learn the notes by a kind of brainwashing. However, you must also aim to recall points orally or on paper if this method is to work.

- Some students prefer visual stimuli to aid their learning. They convert their notes into spider or flow-diagram form. They aim to reproduce these and recall associated points.

Study guides

When revising, many students welcome the support of one of the study guides available in bookshops. There are several available. *Sociology Magazine* (1999, no. 3, pp. 36–9) got some students to trial some of the better known books. If you decide to invest in such a guide it would be a good idea to consult that article.

Using timelines

Deakin (1998b, p. 15) suggests the idea of developing 'timelines' for studying debates or topics. By entering different theories, studies or events on to the timeline at the appropriate year, you can see how and why the sociology of that area developed. This will help you to identify trends, analyse possible reasons for them, and evaluate the worth of various sociological explanations.

Using situation cards

Another method of study suggested by Deakin is the drawing up of 'situation cards' which detail events – such as a march against hunting or a rise in football hooliganism:

Take each card in turn and consider how different social scientists would explain the situation, what their policy suggestions would be, which key ideas they adopt, which other perspectives agree or disagree with them, their strengths and weaknesses, what the public feels, what the political views are, etc.

(Deakin, 1998b, p. 15)

Perhaps you can think of other 'games' to make your revision more fun. If they work, tell your tutor and fellow students.

Testing yourself

After each hour of revision and at the end of each day you should attempt to recall what you have learnt. If at first you don't get it right, keep trying until you do. Initially, if you cannot recall everything, go back to your source to help you. However, try to rely on this less and less.

After some time on a topic you should be ready for a higher level of testing. You ought to try some of the following:

- Write plans and/or introductions to longer data response questions or essays.

- Write answers to past or sample questions, *under timed examination conditions*. There is, ultimately, no substitute for replicating what you have to do in the exam.

- Set small tests for a friend who is revising the same topic. Get them to do the same for you. Discuss answers you get wrong.

- If revising with a friend, you could try taking up two different positions (e.g. functionalist and Marxist–feminist) in a mock debate about whether, for example, domestic tasks are shared. Having taken notes and revised the key points of the theory/research you have looked at, the two of you can hold a debate in role. Another friend could act as observer noting down the two sets of arguments. At the end you can discuss who seemed to win the argument, and why. Do, however, keep the debate at a sociological/professional level, avoiding personal comments that could offend deeply at this stressful time.

Final tips

Students sometimes try to build up their confidence by spending most time on the areas they know best. In contrast, Tony Lawson (1993a) suggests that you should spend most time on the areas in which you are *weakest*. The realization that you are getting better at these areas will help your confidence a great deal.

Try to spend some time every day reading a broadsheet newspaper. Failing this, try to watch one news broadcast in the evening. This will give you up-to-date knowledge of events that you can use to illustrate points made by sociologists – helping you gain marks for AO2.

Good students can be their own worst enemy. They work hard all year and then aim to convince themselves that they cannot do exams. If you have worked hard and followed advice given in this textbook, there is no reason why you should not do well. Even if your marks have not been that good up to now, there is every chance that you will do well on the day. Remember, athletes tend not to run world records months before a major event – they have trained to peak on the day; so have you! Keep a positive focus.

Finally, do take time out of revision for relaxation. Stop working at least an hour before you go to bed, so that you have 'wound down' and will sleep well. Exercise and a good diet will help. Pills and other artificial stimulants will hinder. Meet friends, watch television. See these as a reward for your hard work during the day – you deserve it!

Dealing with examination day

A checklist

Check that you:

- are certain what paper is being examined

- know where the exam room is (and where the nearest toilets are)

- know the time when you have to be in the exam room, and be there in good time to avoid a stressful panic

- take the necessary equipment

- have a watch with the correct time in case the clock in the exam hall is difficult to see

Handling stress

Do not worry about feeling stressed. In fact some stress is a good thing because it shows you care, and it will help you to perform.

Outside the exam room there is *always* one student who claims to know everything (or nothing). Avoid him or her. Concentrate on what you know personally. Be mentally focused.

Checking the paper

Before you are allowed to turn over the front page of the exam paper, read the details (the rubric) on it one more time. Be clear about the instructions.

Getting started

When you do get to start:

- Remember that there are no prizes for being the first person to begin writing.

- Skim the whole paper to decide which questions look best for you. Read the selected questions and items carefully (as suggested on pages 13 and 14).

- Check that they are the questions you thought they were when you started skimming. Remember to plan your longer answers; it is essential that the material you put down is relevant to the question set.

- Even though you may start writing later, you will probably write more because you will not have to keep stopping to think of the next point. Your answers will definitely be much more focused on the question set, and therefore likely to earn more marks.

- Plan your time question by question. Once you have spent the appropriate amount of time on a question, force yourself to move on; you can always go back to it later if there is time. The first half of the available marks are always easier to pick up than the second half.

Final comments

Remember that the examiners mark positively, so do not worry about forgetting something or getting it wrong. Concentrate on what you do know and what you are doing well. Too much stress can hinder your memory. If you forget an important detail take a couple of deep breaths to calm yourself. If you still cannot remember, leave a space and move on. It may come back to you later.

See the exam as a game or an athletics competition. You know the rules. You have 'trained' hard. You have practised over and over again. Not everyone can set a record score, but you are certainly ready to achieve a personal best on the day. Nobody can ask more of you. Good luck (although you don't need it!).

1.4 How to use this book

The chapters

The chapter headings in *Sociology in Perspective* follow the unit by unit structure for GCE AS and A level specifications produced by OCR. The content of each chapter is designed to cover the requirements of the relevant section in the OCR specification.

Reading the chapters

Many of the units in the OCR specification offer a choice of topics for study (see page 1) so you will not study all the topics in this book. We cannot know which elements of the book you will use, so we have tried to ensure that each chapter is self-contained while at the same time providing cross-references to other sections in the book to allow you to consider the links that exist between topics.

One of the key elements of the skill of application is the ability to select and use relevant material, and this can mean looking at parallels which cross the boundaries of the specification areas. We would therefore encourage you to follow up these cross-references to deepen your sociological knowledge and understanding and allow you to apply material where you think it is relevant.

Each chapter is numbered, as are the sections within it. So, for example, a cross-reference to Section 4.5 refers to the fifth section of Chapter 4.

The content of the chapters

Each chapter begins with an outline which gives details of the main debates covered, to help you find the section most relevant to your needs. The cross-references that are included are mostly to sections rather than chapters.

Within each chapter we have tried to cover both classical theoretical and empirical material and recent developments, including the most recent material available to us, while also drawing out the links between the 'old' and the 'new'.

We have included a considerable number of quotations so that you can learn about the work of sociologists in their own words. Full page references are given to facilitate ease of access to the quoted material. A date in brackets appears after each author – for example, McRobbie (1994) or Eldridge (1993). The date refers to the year of publication of the piece of work referred to. Full details can be found in the bibliography at the back of the book.

Because sociology, like every other subject, has its own terminology and concepts, the meaning of sociological debates may seem obscure and confusing at first. In order to aid your reading (and to help prevent any feelings of confusion!) we have added a glossary of useful terms at the end of each of the AS level chapters. The words in these glossaries are printed in bold the first time they occur in the unit.

Activities in the chapters

Although the idea that it is best to 'learn by doing' has been around for a long time, it is only relatively recently that textbooks have begun including activities which encourage this. In *Sociology in Perspective*, each chapter includes a number of activities. These are highlighted with the following symbol:

Activity

We have tried to make the activities intrinsically interesting things to do, and we have tried also to use them to help you to develop the skills approach which is now a standard requirement of all sociology specifications.

The activities in this book are based around the development of skills required by assessment objectives 1 and 2 (AO1 and AO2), usually by requiring you to engage in some form of written work. We highlight where we feel activities offer possible opportunities to collect portfolio evidence towards the key skills qualification.

However, since sociology is at its most enjoyable when it involves discussing the state of society today, throughout *Sociology in Perspective* discussion points are included to form the basis for class discussions and discussions among students away from class. These are each highlighted using the following symbol:

Discussion point

As far as possible these relate to contemporary events. There is no right answer to these discussion points (it follows logically that there is no wrong answer), and you should therefore not feel too intimidated to become involved. Recognize that your experiences and views are as valid as anyone else's. Discussion in a friendly and supportive atmosphere is one of the best ways to learn. So get involved and enjoy your sociology: make it meaningful to you. Engaging in discussions can also provide evidence towards the key skill of communication, since this is the essence of element C3.1a.

Exam questions

Your tutor will be able to provide you with past exam questions, and probably also the comments of Chief Examiners and the mark schemes for those exam questions. They should also be able to provide you with practice materials from the *Teachers' Resource File* which accompanies this book. You should also regularly consult the 'Examinations matters' section of *Sociology Review* for advice on tackling exam questions.

Further reading

It is important that you engage actively with the material in your sociology course, and we hope that *Sociology in Perspective* offers a sound foundation to enable you to do this. However, we must stress that you will need to read widely so that discussions and written work are informed by a high level of sociological knowledge and a detailed understanding of it. For this reason, we have included some suggestions for further reading at the end of each chapter. Most of these should be readily available, while others might form the basis of detailed reading if you find yourself drawn to a particular topic, perhaps for your coursework.

They are not intended to be exhaustive and you should of course consult your tutor and the various suggested reading lists provided by the exam board for other sources of material on particular topics. *Sociology Review* is particularly useful here and the back copies of this (and its predecessor, *Social Studies Review*) provide a wealth of useful information both on substantive sociological debates and articles aimed more specifically at developing your skills in sociology.

Using the bibliography

The bibliography is there to help you to locate the exact source of the material referred to. For instance, in the bibliography you will find that the references quoted in the section on the content of chapters above (see page 18) relate to:

- McRobbie, A. (1994) *Postmodernism and Popular Culture*, London: Routledge.
- Eldridge, J. (1993) 'News, truth and power', in Eldridge, J. (ed.), *Getting the Message: News, Truth and Power*, London: Routledge.

If there is more than one publication by the same author in any one year – or two or more publications in the same year by authors with the same surname – this is indicated by the use of letters to differentiate between the two. For example, Fiske (1989a) and Fiske (1989b) refer to:

- Fiske, J. (1989a) *Understanding Popular Culture*, London: Unwin Hyman.
- Fiske, J. (1989b) *Reading the Popular,* London: Unwin Hyman.

The use of dates in the text will allow you to be aware of the broad period when work was produced, and therefore to contextualize the ideas being discussed. You would expect ideas about popular culture to be different in the 1950s and 60s from those in the 1990s, and this can help you make that connection.

This approach also provides a format or template which you can use yourself, for example in the presentation of your coursework. It is similar to the format adopted by many books.

Where the date of publication is misleading – for example where books by long-dead sociologists have been reprinted in recent years – the original date of publication is given as well to avoid confusion.

Using the indexes

To find out where the writers referred to above are discussed in this book, you should refer to the index at the very back of the book. There are two indexes, one based on subject topics and one based on authors' names. The authors mentioned above can be located in the author index and you will find that the page numbers referred to fall largely in Chapters 6 and 13.

Equally, if you are considering the changes in the way we look at the world – for example the move from religion to science as the key basis of knowledge – index entries will take you to Chapters 7 and 16; and if you then go on to look at the statistics produced by this new scientific method you will find important debates in Chapters 10 and 12, as well as Chapter 9. Indexes can therefore help you draw out the links between topics.

They can provide a quick way of finding cross-references, since all other references to a particular author or a particular subject area will also be listed in the index. You should therefore use this as a way of finding other references to the particular author or subject you are discussing or working on.

Conclusion

This introduction has given a brief flavour of what sociology is about and what you will be looking at while you study the subject, as well as suggestions to approach your study in an active way. We would underline one final piece of advice, which is that you should *use the book in conjunction with advice from your tutor*. This will ensure that you follow a course of study designed to achieve your maximum potential.

Good luck, we hope you enjoy sociology.

Further reading

Books aimed at helping to develop skills needed for A level sociology are:

- Kidd, W. *et al.* (1998) *Readings in Sociology*, Oxford: Heinemann Educational.
- Lawson, T. (1993) *Sociology for 'A' Level: A Skills-Based Approach*, London: Collins Educational.

Books designed to help with coursework are:

- Barrat, D. and Cole, T. (1991) *Sociology Projects: A Student's Guide*, London: Routledge.
- Harvey, L. and MacDonald, M. (1993) *Doing

Sociology: A Practical Introduction, London: Macmillan.

- Howe, N. (1994) *Advanced Practical Sociology*, Walton-on-Thames: Nelson.
- Langley, P. and Corrigan, P. (1993) *Managing Sociology Coursework*, Lewes: Connect.
- Williams, L. and Dunsmuir, A. (1991) *How To Do Social Research*, London: Collins Educational.

The following are summary and revision guides:

- Harris, S. (1994) *Sociology Revise Guide*, London: Longman.
- Selfe, P. (1995) *Work Out Sociology*, London: Macmillan.

The following are dictionaries of sociology:

- Jary, D. and Jary, J. (1991) *Collins Dictionary of Sociology*, London: HarperCollins.
- Marshall, G. (ed.) (1994) *Concise Oxford Dictionary of Sociology*, Oxford: Oxford University Press.

Answers to the activity on page 4

Strengths

- Successfully identifies gap in our knowledge
- Methods likely to produce an in depth view of people's views and feelings (researcher could be an interactionist)
- Findings could be useful in helping schools combat underachievement

Weaknesses

- Pretty out of date, a lot has happened since 1987
- Methods used unscientific
- Sample size very small and from limited geographical area

Introduction to sociology

2.1 Approaching sociology

What is sociology, and is there a need for it?

On one level the answer to this question is that sociology is a subject you have chosen to study with the aim of obtaining a qualification. You might need such a qualification to obtain a job or to go to a university. It may well be that this subject is new to you.

The OCR specifications for AS and A level sociology contain the following introductory comments which seem to us to provide a very reassuring entrance to the subject and we therefore quote them at length here:

These specifications build on but do not depend on the knowledge, understanding and skills specified in the GCSE criteria for the Social Sciences, which include Sociology.

However, candidates following a course based on these specifications do not require prior sociological knowledge. Candidates may enrol without any prior learning or attainment in sociology. However, it would be helpful if they had achieved a GCSE at grade A*-C in at least one subject requiring continuous written work under controlled examination conditions, particularly English. PSHE programmes at KS4 may also form a useful introduction to some of the subject matter of sociology.

Sociology may be of particular interest to candidates who are members of minority groups and/or are mature students returning to study, whose life experience may contribute particular insights to their study of sociology.

(OCR Specification Summary, Sociology, 2000, p. 1)

In our experience as teachers of sociology, it is indeed the case that the vast majority of students come to sociology at AS or A level without having formally studied the subject before. This requires us to ensure that this book is accessible enough to require no prior knowledge and in this introductory chapter we try to outline some basic concepts and themes in sociology. The following chapters covering the *Individual and society* module also follow up these themes to provide a basis for you to begin to explore this key sociological theme of the relationship between individuals and social structures in society.

The study of society

The literal meaning of the word 'sociology' is the 'science of society', and it is one of the most popular social sciences concerned with understanding human behaviour. This tells us it is an '-ology' – a science, but again this can be said about many other subjects dealing with human beings, such as biology and psychology. To justify the need for sociology it must be possible to show that its knowledge provides something more than, and arguably superior in some respects to, these other worthwhile disciplines.

Society

The obvious difference is the 'socio-' bit of the word, meaning the study of society. However, this leads us no further than to ask the obvious question: 'What is society?' and here we begin to get a feel for a real debate. There are those who would deny that such a thing as society exists.

The individual

Margaret Thatcher, when Prime Minister, once declared that 'there is no such thing as society, merely individuals and their families' (Kingdom, 1992, p. 1). But if this is true then there is clearly no need for a science to study society – no need for sociology.

Does society exist?

A number of points can be raised to question the validity of this notion. First, Margaret Thatcher was able to make her statement and to communicate it to others because of the existence of language that prescribes certain rules for communication. Which individual invented this language? It is impossible to answer, for the simple reason that the existence of language is proof that we do not exist merely as individuals but as social animals interacting with others. If we lived as individuals why would there be any need for language, or indeed any other form of communication? If an individual wanted to invent their own language, what language would they use to think it up?

Secondly, it can be asked, who invented the family? Why should individuals suddenly all decide (as individuals) to invent a particular way of living found in 250 societies of widely differing types (Murdock, 1949) and call it a family? (For an outline of Murdock's argument and the critical debate that followed, see Section 5.1) Furthermore, even if one individual did decide, by what method did he or she get the rest of humanity to adopt this way of acting?

Thirdly, who invented the concept of the 'individual'? While they are biological and psychological entities, individuals have not in all societies and at all times been seen as the key basis of society. Arguably the 'individual' was only really invented by the rise of ideas in the seventeenth and eighteenth centuries, which in many ways reversed older ways of thinking and set in train major changes in society, including the invention of sociology.

It is this idea that there are forces beyond the overall control of any one individual that allows us to reject Margaret Thatcher's pronouncement, since it is this that we see at the heart of notions of society and sociology.

The social patterning and determination of individual action

Patterns are often evident in human behaviour. Why, for instance, is it likely that a sociology class will be composed predominantly of females, something it is likely to have in common with a class of biology students? In contrast, if you visit a physics or computing classroom why are you likely to find a predominance of male students (see Section 8.8)? No one (presumably) forced them to choose these subjects, and as individuals they did make a choice – yet year after year, and in institution after institution, these patterns are evident.

> ### 🗨 Discussion point
> To what extent does the regular occurrence of such patterns undermine notions that we are all individuals able to exercise free choices?
>
> C3.1a

It is this kind of regularity which suggests that there is something beyond the individual (and therefore beyond psychological aspects of humanity) which causes these patterns (see Section 3.1). It is possible to argue that it is biology that causes men and women to behave differently, but this would require that all men behaved in a certain way and all women behaved in a certain different way, and this can be shown to be false (see Sections 4.1 and 17.8). Although a majority of candidates for A level sociology are female, it is far from being exclusively a subject studied by females.

The conclusion seems to be that there are certain forces which go beyond the individual and which are not biologically programmed into us – forces that tend to make us act in certain non-random ways, even if we think we are all acting as individuals. It is this non-random social patterning of behaviour that is the basis of the idea of society, and therefore the subject matter of sociology. (See also Sections 3.2 and 3.3.)

Human creativity and action

It would be wrong to suppose that people are all puppets controlled by unknown forces, since the

authors of those forces are none other than ourselves. Individuals and social groups find themselves subjected to forces beyond their control,
but also help in the construction of these forces
and the maintenance and reproduction of society. Sociology does not treat us all as robots
(although some approaches may run close to
this), because if society exists then people must
have built it – and people can, if they wish, try
to change it.

In order to decide whether some aspect of
society should be changed, it is first necessary to
understand how it operates – and this is precisely
the purpose of sociology. One of the most emi-
nent contemporary British sociologists has
explained the purpose of sociology as follows:

*Sociological thinking is a vital help to self-under-
standing, which in turn can be focused back upon an
improved understanding of the social world.*
*Studying sociology should be a liberating experience:
sociology enlarges our sympathies and imagination,
opens up new perspectives on the sources of our
own behaviour, and deepens a sense of cultural settings different from our own. In so far as sociological
work challenges dogma, teaches appreciation of cultural variety and allows us an insight into the workings of social institutions, the practice of sociology
enhances the possibilities of human freedom.*

(Giddens, 1989, p. 2)

So not only does studying sociology give one a
chance to gain vital points towards university
entrance, the subject also offers the chance to
develop self-understanding, to enlarge one's imagination and enhance human freedom. Not many
subjects can offer this intoxicating combination of
benefits. Since sociology does, you should grasp it
and dive into it with great enthusiasm.

Okay, it may not always seem like that on a
wet morning in February when you haven't quite
got to grips with a particularly stubborn concept
and an essay is two days overdue. But like anything else that is new it takes time to develop
your understanding, and explanations sometimes
become complex. However, everything is understandable if one takes the time and effort. Your
tutor or teacher will positively encourage discussion about anything that is unclear, and in sociology there are lots of opportunities to debate
issues and the society we all live in. Everyone can
contribute since they are part of society and
therefore part of the subject matter of the topic.

One example of such a debate concerns the
place of sociology itself. It is certainly the case

that some right-wing political and social thinkers
have shown great hostility to the subject. Roger
Scruton, professor of philosophy at the University
of London, declared:

*I suspect a lot of people feel this about sociology,
that there are certain matters which should not be
pried into, least of all by half-baked lefties from
universities. … I would say also because of this
relentless questioning of human institutions and
human realities it may be inappropriate for young
people to study it.*

(Scruton, 1991)

💬 Discussion point

To what extent do you agree that there are certain things that it may be inappropriate for
young people to study? What sort of things
might they be?

C3.1a

The usefulness of sociology

Reading all this, one is in danger of being left
with the thought that sociology either studies a
non-existent subject and is therefore pointless or
alternatively is positively dangerous to impres-
sionable young minds! The charges outlined
above are serious. However, they do introduce
you to the notion that sociology is a controversial subject in some respects. Before you are put
off studying sociology, we would want to argue
that the charges are wrong, for the following
reasons.

Human societies are fantastic things because
they result from the interaction of countless numbers of highly creative and active beings. This
raises questions about how societies should be
and how humans should treat each other. While
some might find this threatening, sociologists do
not. We are all part of society and we all want
to live meaningful and fulfilled lives, and consider
the best way this can be achieved. Studying society is therefore partly about studying oneself and
one's experiences, and you should have some
views on that. This questioning leads to new
insights and ways of looking at the world. As a
leading professor of sociology, Zygmunt Bauman,
puts it:

*As long as we go through the routine and
habitualized motions which fill most of our daily
business, we do not need much scrutiny and*

analysis. When repeated often enough, things tend to become familiar, and familiar things are self-explanatory; they present no problems and arouse no curiosity. In a way, they remain invisible. ... In an encounter with that familiar world ruled by habits ... sociology acts as a meddlesome and often irritating stranger. It disturbs the comfortingly quiet way of life by asking questions no one among the 'locals' remembers being asked, let alone answered. Such questions make evident things into puzzles: they defamiliarize the familiar. Suddenly, the daily way of life must come under scrutiny. It now appears to be just one of the possible ways, not the one and only, not the 'natural' way of life.

(Bauman, 1990, p. 15)

In this respect you should question everything, considering what you once saw as natural as now problematic, and asking questions such as why, how and for whose benefit did the things you took for granted come about. We would argue that this is not a threatening or destructive act, but allows one to develop insights and understanding. This is of course a continuing process, a point also made by Zygmunt Bauman:

Sociology is an extended commentary on the experiences of daily life; an interpretation which feeds on other interpretations and is in turn fed into them. Sociological thinking does not stem, but facilitates the flow and exchange of experiences. ... The great service sociology is well prepared to render to human life and human cohabitation is the promotion of mutual understanding and tolerance as a paramount condition of shared freedom.

(Bauman, 1990, pp. 231–2)

While studying sociology, you are also part of that flow and exchange, and are helping to construct, challenge and think about how the society that you are living in will develop. So get stuck in!

2.2 Sociology: Century 21

The twenty-first century

For a long time, A level sociology was based around sets of ideas developed and elaborated in the period roughly covering the 1930s to the 1950s. Exam questions sometimes still tend to be framed around these ideas.

As we enter the twenty-first century, this framework is increasingly beginning to show its age and arguably can no longer be adapted to either the reality of the world around us or even the reality of sociology around us. Some have suggested that we quickly electrify the tracks to allow for the speedy transmission of currently fashionable notions and theories, such as the theory of post-modernism.

It seems to us inappropriate to jump directly from the 'old' sociology to the question of the validity and usefulness of the post-modernist world viewpoint, since this merely creates a dialogue of the deaf. But, equally, we sometimes wonder whether it is still useful to continue to present, as contemporary explanations, ideas from the 1930s and 40s as explanations for the world of the 21st century. What is the point of teaching students, in detail, ideas which no longer inspire or relate to the world around them? The time for the 'Talcott Parsons, boo! hiss!' (to use a notable phrase of Aidan Foster-Carter) version of A level sociology is over. The world (and sociology) has moved on.

Building bridges

However, the world did not simply move on by rejecting the 'old' theory of functionalism and jumping into the warm embrace of post-modernism. Things happened in between which we feel need to be included. These are the bridges which link the 'old' to the 'new'. Our aim is to build such bridges, and to illuminate them in the hope that this will help you to see with greater clarity how today's debates have come about. We hope it offers a richer, deeper version of what sociology is.

We have tried to give what we see as a good coverage of the main elements that constitute sociology today. In order to do this, we have consulted a wide variety of sources and have undoubtedly been influenced by them. As far as possible the sources are mentioned so that you can be aware of where the views originate. We hope we have done this fairly and have interpreted what others say accurately. The aim is to throw light on what these others say, and to encourage you to follow these up by seeking out some of the references quoted.

A discursive subject

Sociology should, if it is to have any meaning, shed light on the real world. In this book, contemporary case studies are used to illustrate certain ideas and themes. The skill of identification in A level exams requires the presentation of relevant examples, so you should be inspired to seek out your own.

Sociology is inherently a discursive subject – best approached through discussion and active learning. In this book, activities are designed to enable you to reflect, interpret, identify, analyse and evaluate the theories, ideas and evidence presented. In our teaching, we have found these very useful instruments, but with one potential weak spot. Given activities to complete, it is sometimes the case that students work only as individuals and silence fills the room. We strongly believe in the importance of discussion, so 'discussion points' appear throughout the book to encourage people to discuss ideas. In a supportive environment, this is what learning is all about: talking and discussing with others, where all contribute and all gain. These discussion points are purposely intended to encourage maximum discussion, and it is of course entirely up to you and your colleagues where such discussions lead.

We have tried to make this book as up to date as possible, both empirically and theoretically. But sociology is a dynamic subject, and things keep changing all the time. This makes it exciting but also means you need to keep up to date through your reading.

We hope this book provides you with a good basis for your studies and we hope you enjoy your sociology. Good luck with your course!

Further reading

The following book is aimed at helping to develop skills needed for A level sociology:

- Lawson, T. (1993) *Sociology for 'A' Level: A Skills-Based Approach*, London: Collins Educational.

Books designed to help with coursework are:

- Barrat, D. and Cole, T. (1991) *Sociology Projects: A Student's Guide*, London: Routledge.
- Harvey, L. and MacDonald, M. (1993) *Doing Sociology: A Practical Introduction*, London: Macmillan.
- Howe, N. (1994) *Advanced Practical Sociology*, Walton-on-Thames: Nelson.
- Langley, P. and Corrigan, P. (1993) *Managing Sociology Coursework*, Lewes: Connect.
- Williams, L. and Dunsmuir, A. (1991) *How To Do Social Research*, London: Collins Educational.

The following are summary and revision guides:

- Harris, S. (1994) *Sociology Revise Guide*, London: Longman.
- Selfe, P. (1995) *Work Out Sociology*, London: Macmillan.

The following are dictionaries of sociology:

- Jary, D. and Jary, J. (1991) *Collins Dictionary of Sociology*, London: HarperCollins.
- Marshall, G. (ed.) (1994) *Concise Oxford Dictionary of Sociology*, Oxford: Oxford University Press.

The individual and society
Introducing the individual and society

Chapter outline

3.1 **Introducing the individual and society**   *page 28*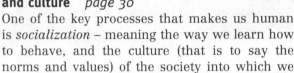

For sociology to exist, it must be necessary to argue that we cannot analyse human behaviour solely by looking at individuals. This section defends the need for a sociological outlook to explain human behaviour.

3.2 **Socialization: norms, values and culture**   *page 30*

One of the key processes that makes us human is *socialization* – meaning the way we learn how to behave, and the culture (that is to say the norms and values) of the society into which we are born. This process also affects our individual identity. One key element of sociological theories is therefore the attempt to explain the process of socialization and the importance of culture in human life.

3.3 **Learning social roles**   *page 35*

This section considers further the relationship between the individual and society, mediated by culture, and the way that cultures and structures act to regulate social life. It introduces the key dichotomy of social structures and social actions in sociological thinking.

Glossary   *page 42*

Words in bold in the text are explained in the glossary at the end of this chapter.

3.1 Introducing the individual and society

The relationship between the individual and society

It is initially difficult to get a grasp on this notion since you cannot point to **society** because it is an abstract concept. This often leads to the view that individuals (who are concrete and we can point to) are the only real things or entities that exist. Logically if this is the case then we should all become psychologists and sociology could become redundant. However, it is a mistake to argue that we can look at human behaviour only either in terms of individuals or in terms of societies. In fact, sociology argues that we need to look at both, since they offer different views on human behaviour and complement each other.

The link between the individual and society

If we are all seen as unique individuals then this implies that we have no commonality (meaning we have nothing in common with others), or at least that any such commonality is accidental and the result of millions of people independently making the same choice. However, it is relatively easy to demonstrate that we do have commonalities. For example, all the people reading this (or at least the vast majority of them) are interested in or are actually studying sociology at some level. If they are studying for AS or A level they will be working towards qualifications offered by a limited number of exam boards, rather than writing out their own sociology certificate. Equally, all the people reading this share the commonality of being able to read and understand English, a language they as an individual did not invent.

Cultural rituals

An individual person cannot be said to have chosen to speak their first language. It is a presence in whatever **culture** they are brought up in, along with other cultural **rituals** and **social institutions**, that make up the social life of each particular society. So, for instance, rituals surrounding food, clothing, religion and even love cannot easily be said to be freely chosen; instead they are something in a sense you are born into. Equally one cannot choose to be born a man or a woman, this is decided for you.

Sociologists point out that since these things exist our lives cannot simply be explained on the basis of the choices we make, since some things exist that have an important effect on our lives but which are not freely chosen by us. We need to understand how these things operate and why they exist. This is the arena of the social and the reason for the existence of sociology.

The sociology of breakfast

In order to illustrate this notion, let us take one rather mundane event, namely breakfast. Now of course it is possible to understand this in terms of individual choice. People may decide to have breakfast or not have it, they may decide to have a fry-up, or muesli, or toast and marmalade. Equally they may choose to have coffee or tea. Is this all that is needed to explain breakfast? If we focus on individual choice, it might seem to be; but what if we consider the economic and social links that need to be in place to enable those choices to be made? We therefore begin to build up a more complex picture enabling us to see breakfast choice as a social and therefore sociological phenomenon. Nigel Harris (1983) provides the following example of this:

For people in London the corn that has gone into the breakfast cornflakes was harvested in Tennessee or Brazil. The wood for the table was cut in Malaysia. The sugar, the tea, the coffee, the Formica tabletop – each detail concludes such an enormous and complex world division of labour that no single person

can comprehend it. The world economy is not some external phenomenon, it is present in each kitchen.

(Harris, 1983, p. 9)

To enable you to have your breakfast, **structures** and institutions exert effort around the globe and it is these that are of interest to sociologists and mean that no one person is an island. Remember to think about this next time that you have breakfast.

Activity

Draw a diagram on a map of the world to show the links that had to be in place for you to eat your breakfast.

C3.2, C3.3

The sociology of coffee

Anthony Giddens (1997, p. 4) highlights another aspect of social behaviour when he looks at what he calls the sociology of coffee. He argues that coffee-drinking possesses **symbolic value**. When we meet for coffee we engage in set rituals and forms of interaction, all of which are of interest to the sociologist. Secondly, although it is a drug it is not restricted in our culture, whereas some drugs such as marijuana and cocaine are. However, Giddens points out that there are societies where coffee consumption is frowned upon. Again this offers scope for sociological investigation.

Thirdly, he argues that drinking coffee requires and builds upon a whole set of economic and social relationships around the globe, and in this he echoes the comment of Harris above.

The sociology of love and romance

Another area where it is assumed that individual choice is sufficient to explain human behaviour is in relation to the choosing of love partners. The suggestion from romantic literature that love traverses all boundaries seems not to be backed up by sociological evidence. Peter Berger argued that this picture of love was flawed:

As soon as one investigates which people actually marry each other one finds that the lightning shaft of Cupid seems to be guided rather strongly within very definite channels of class, income, education, racial and religious background.

(Berger, 1966, p. 48)

C3.3

Activity

Draw up a spider diagram to show the extent of and limits to choice you have about your sociology course.

Hint: You are not your own exam board. Did you choose this specification? Did you choose options?

The levels of society

All this leads us to the conclusion that, while we do have choices, we cannot explain human behaviour solely on the basis of notions of individuals making choices. There are clear patterns and regularities which suggest that our choices are constrained or enabled in certain fairly consistent ways, and sociologists seek to identify these forces and explain how they affect human behaviour. This means we have to analyse society at a number of different levels. Table 3.1 tries to illustrate this notion.

Sociologists seek to study the links between these various levels and the way one level impinges on and affects other levels. It is this endeavour that has provided sociology with a raft of basic concepts which, however, are the subject of continuing debate as there are conflicting viewpoints, or perspectives about how this all works.

Table 3.1 Levels of society

Level of analysis	Example	Concepts
Global	Food production Television	**Globalization**
Society	United Kingdom	**State** Society **Community**
Structures	Family Money	Structure of family **Capitalism**
Institutions	Education Health	Schools/colleges The NHS
Culture	Masculinity Femininity Popular culture	**Socialization/ norms/values**
Individual	A person	Choices/actions

3.2 Socialization: norms, values and culture

What would human beings be like without society? We know from the rare cases in which children have been denied access to human company for long periods that interaction with other people is a vital ingredient in human development.

The wild boy of Aveyron

The 'wild boy of Aveyron' was found wandering from a wood in Southern France in 1800. He had apparently spent most of his eleven or twelve years on his own in the wild. He was unable to communicate, other than through shrieking; he was fearful of other people, lacked social skills and took no interest in personal hygiene. Although after some time he learned to dress himself and became toilet-trained, he was never able to learn more than a few basic words.

Genie

In a much more recent case in California a quarter of a century ago, a baby girl was locked away in a closed room by her father who was ashamed of her hip defect. Genie spent several years away from human company, being fed by her father but denied any social interaction with others. Her father refused to talk to her and communicated merely by growling at her. After escaping with her mother, Genie received extensive help from doctors and child development experts but it was clear that permanent damage had been done. While she learnt to walk, to dress herself and became toilet-trained, she remained introverted and was never, even as an adult, able to master language beyond the level of a four-year-old.

In the case of both Genie and the 'wild boy', it appears that the absence of social interaction had severely stunted human development. Some psychologists believe that there is a crucial stage in psychological development at which point children learn language and, perhaps, other social skills extremely rapidly. The cases of Genie and 'the wild boy' suggest that if this crucial stage is missed then the acquisition of language and social skills becomes much more difficult. In other words, **social interaction** with other human beings is crucial to the process of becoming fully human.

Socialization and identity

Sociologists call the process through which we learn how to fit into society 'socialization':

Socialization is the process whereby the helpless infant gradually becomes a self-aware, knowledgeable person, skilled in the ways of the culture into which she or he is born.

(Giddens, 1993a, p. 60)

The family, the **peer group**, the community and, in modern societies, the formal education system and the **mass media** all contribute to the process of socialization in which we acquire the beliefs, habits and skills necessary to play an appropriate role in society. Socialization does not end with childhood but continues through life as we adjust to new situations and enter new communities (for example, changing jobs or moving to new neighbourhoods). Someone entering middle age may reflect on memories of what they were like when they were young and almost feel they are looking at a different person. This is because the human personality develops throughout life. This is how our sense of our own **identity**, or who we feel ourselves to be, is constructed.

Table 3.2 Types of socialization

Type of socialization	Description	Main agencies involved
Primary socialization	Process of learning values, norms and rules of behaviour appropriate to a particular human society. Process of becoming social.	Family Primary education
Secondary socialization	Continuing process of learning the (possibly changing) values, norms, ideas, rules of society and of particular roles within it.	Education Peer group Mass media Religion Family Workplace

Primary and secondary socialization

In relation to socialization, sociologists distinguish between **primary socialization** and **secondary socialization**.

Primary socialization

As its name suggests, primary socialization means the first form of socialization that occurs. This is usually centred on the family and involves the child learning from the parent or guardian. However, it is clear that the early stages of formal education also play a role in this process of primary socialization. It is precisely because of the importance of this stage that psychologists study child-rearing practices and sociologists study the processes that go on within families. Within this phase of primary socialization, children learn basic communication and the language of the society into which they are born.

Secondary socialization

Secondary socialization is, in contrast, that form of socialization which follows after primary socialization and which continues throughout the life of the individual concerned. There are a multiplicity of agencies concerned with secondary socialization including the education system, the mass media, peer groups, the workplace and religion. While the general rules learned during primary socialization are still important, here other more specific rules need also to be learnt and applied. Given that roles and rules may change throughout life, this process of secondary socialization continues as we grow older. Since socialization contributes to the process of identity formation, this also means that this process of identity formation will continue throughout a person's lifetime.

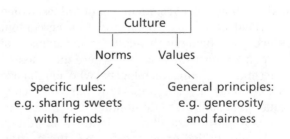

Figure 3.1 Culture, norms and values

Culture, norms and values

What precisely is learnt through socialization? Sociologists distinguish between *values* and *norms*.

Values

Values are the fundamental beliefs underpinning a community or society and providing general principles for human behaviour. Some values are formalized as principles of law and are enforced through the formal agencies of social control. Others remain as general organizing principles for life and are fostered through the agencies of socialization.

Values are essentially the ethical principles by which a particular group of people or a society chooses to live their lives. They therefore consist of a series of beliefs about what you should and should not do. The Ten Commandments would be a clear example of a set of values for many Christians, or the Sharia law derived from the beliefs of Islam for many Muslims.

The fact that we as humans do seem to have consciences allows us to act as moral beings, that is, to adhere to some sort of code of right or wrong. However, one important issue is whether that code is an individual one or a social one based on similarity with other individuals. It is this notion of social values that is central to sociology.

This does still leave us with a further question. Do people adhere to the same set of values because they agree with them or because one person or group is powerful and is able to make other people adhere to the values they want them to adhere to? This brings us into the realm of **power**. Sociologists who emphasize that society is characterized by agreement or consensus are talking about an agreement about values which is arrived at through open and free agreement by everyone (usually through the mechanism of voting in democratic elections where the outcome is accepted by all). Sociologists who emphasize that conflicts are an important part of society argue instead that dominant individuals or groups impose their views and values on others.

An alternative approach to both these arguments is to suggest that in fact there is no society-wide consensus on values, because society is fragmented into many groups, each with their own set of values, which may or may not overlap with the values of other groups.

Norms

While values operate as general principles, norms are specific rules that govern human behaviour in particular situations. Once again these may vary widely from society to society and from community to community. Examples include appropriate behaviour whilst eating (in some societies belching loudly is regarded as good manners, in others as rather vulgar); rules governing courtship and 'going out'; rules governing behaviour in public places, and so on (see Figure 3.1, page 31).

Table 3.3 Values and norms

Name of concept	Definition	Examples in contemporary UK society
Values	General principles of behaviour which provide a framework within which to exist in society.	• honesty • tolerance • generosity • fairness • democracy
Norms	Specific rules for behaviour in specific circumstances derived from the general principles contained in the values of the society in which people live.	• Do not vomit in public. • Do wear clothes in public. • Do help others to cross the road. • Don't hit others unless you are acting in self-defence. • Don't lie to your teachers/parents about not completing your homework.

Activity

a Take a simple routine situation which is familiar to you, such as eating breakfast with your family or sitting in the canteen with friends. In a five-minute period make a list of all the values and norms you think are governing behaviour.

b Construct a spider diagram of the norms and values associated with 'dating' in contemporary society.

C3.3

Culture

The fact that norms and values vary across different human societies and across different time periods is an important pointer to the role of culture, or learned behaviour as opposed to the role of biology and genetically determined behaviour. Since all humans are virtually identical biologically, something else must explain the variations in human behaviour. That 'something' includes the human capacity to choose and to change, and that leads to the idea that we have some degree of free will about our behaviour. Haralambos and Holborn (1995) cite one very good example of this:

Two individuals, one from North America, the other from South America, are conversing in a hall 40 feet long. They begin at one end of the hall and finish at the other, the North American steadily retreating, the South American relentlessly advancing. Each is trying to establish the 'accustomed conversation distance' defined by his culture. To the North American, his South American counterpart comes too close for comfort, whereas the South American feels uneasy conversing at the distance his partner demands. Often it takes meetings such as this to reveal the pervasive nature of culturally determined behaviour.

(Haralambos and Holborn, 2000, p. 3)

It is these things that are learnt through the process of socialization. Clearly some institutions in society play an important role in socializing us, amongst which can be mentioned the family, the education system, and perhaps religious institutions and the mass-media institutions of TV and radio.

Sociologists are interested in exactly how these norms and values are transmitted through socialization, and how the *content* of these norms and values stays the same or changes.

While we have mentioned the key institutions associated with socialization as including the family, the workplace, the education system, the workplace, religion and the mass media, it is important to recognise that individuals should not merely be seen as the passive products of a top-down socialization process, but instead as being active in the pursuit of their own identity formation and therefore judging for themselves whether to accept or reject the norms and values of pre-existing society. This provides one basis for social and cultural change in society as new generations modify or reject the values and norms of old generations.

Culture and biology

Learnt behaviour

When sociologists refer to the *culture* of a society they include all behaviour learnt through socialization, rather than simply that governed by instinct. Culture includes the norms and values of a society, together with behaviour which is governed by a sense of tradition, shared history and common identity. Culture is expressed through routine behaviour and through language, visual work (painting, design, etc.) and other forms of symbolic representation. When sociologists use the term 'culture' they are normally referring to 'a whole way of life' within a society or smaller community. This is an important point because sometimes in other intellectual traditions it is used in a much narrower sense to refer just to 'great' works of art, music or literature.

Culture or biology?

There is a continuing debate about just how much of our behaviour as human beings is learnt or shaped by socialization and just how much is determined by instinctive patterns and governed by genetic inheritance.

Clearly, both genes and socialization contribute to human behaviour – but in what proportions? This, of course, is the heart of the debate over 'nature' (biology) or 'nurture' (culture). It is a crucial issue which has very important implications for our understanding of such topics as gender roles and sexuality, criminal behaviour, performance at school, differences between ethnic groups, and so on.

Discussion point
Are we the products of culture or biology?

C3.1a

However, it is worth noting that in recent years the weight of 'popular opinion', as measured by media discussions and newspaper articles, has been shifted significantly towards the biological view by advances in genetic science. Geneticists can now understand much of the genetic code to be found within DNA. It is now possible to identify and manipulate certain genes which regulate particular functions within the human body.

Most sociologists remain sceptical of the most ambitious of these claims. While they acknowledge the importance of genes, they question whether genetic theory can really explain the enormous variations in human behaviour between different cultures. It is one thing to point to the influence of instinct in shaping human wants for food, shelter, sex, comfort, and so on; it is quite another to try to explain all the ways in which such wants are expressed in purely biological ways. Our biology tells us to eat but it does not tell us to choose McDonald's rather than a French bistro. Both men and women may have sexual appetites that are genetic in origin, and this may be nature's way of ensuring the evolution of the human species; but we do not spend all day trying to jump into bed with each other. There are important values and norms operating to regulate sexual conduct, and lending it a special meaning or significance for us. This is clearly the influence of culture.

Activity

a Describe briefly your own sense of identity. Who do you think you are? Where do you belong and what makes you the person you are? To what extent do you think your own identity has been shaped by culture and socialization? To what extent do you think your own identity has been shaped by biology and genetics?

b Now share this information in small groups. On the basis of the information provided by the members of your group, discuss the conclusions you can draw from this exercise about the respective importance of biological, genetic and cultural influences on your identity.

c Compare your conclusions with those of the other groups.

C3.1a, C3.1b, C3.3

Technology, culture and the Internet

Technological determinism

What makes culture change? For some writers technological innovation is one of the most important forces for cultural change. Think, for example, of the way in which inventions such as television or the automobile have stimulated developments in culture.

In the post-war period, television became a hugely important element in culture: we talk about what we saw on television last night, and from it we get ideas about books, fashion, music and film. So television likes to be associated with new developments in popular culture (for example, 'youth TV'). The automobile is equally embedded in our culture. We may dream about owning an expensive car; we judge others by the type of car they drive; and until recently we designed our towns and cities to maximize the use of cars. Now the negative effects of mass car ownership provide an equally important theme for novelists, movie makers and cultural commentators.

On the face of things, then, it is tempting to see technological innovation as a key determinant of cultural change. This approach to explaining change through technological innovation is not without critics. Theories which place an important emphasis on technological innovation leading to other changes in society are sometimes seen as examples of technological determinism.

Criticism of technological determinism

Raymond Williams (1990) sounds a warning note against technological determinism. He argues that technology in itself does nothing; rather, it is how we as social actors *choose to use* technologies that is important. In other words, the use of technology is decided by social relationships, not the other way around.

The Internet

The rise of the Internet provides an excellent example of how culture changes, which is now being studied by a number of cultural theorists and sociologists (Smith and Kollack, 1998; Shields, 1996).

The Internet started as an American communications technology devised for military purposes. However, it began to be used by civilians who had access to computers and enjoyed communicating with each other through a cyber network. It has now grown into a huge and uncontrollable global phenomenon. Although commercial interests have tried to steer the use of the Internet in particular directions, it remains a technology which develops largely as particular individuals or social groups find new uses for it. Thus, there are websites, bulletin boards and chat rooms to support almost every conceivable cultural activity – following a particular football team, listening to music, cooking dinner or finding someone to fall in love with.

Internet cultures

As Shields (1996) and Smith and Kollack (1998) demonstrate, use of the Internet has encouraged the development of new vocabularies, and new etiquettes or social rules governing interaction between users. For example, it is considered by some to be rude to send messages in capital letters in an e-mail – this is equivalent to shouting at someone. If culture is made up of language, customs and rules, we can say that new cultures are developing in association with the Net and electronic communication systems.

Nevertheless, we could still agree with Raymond Williams that it is not necessarily the case that the Internet is determining these newer cultures; rather, Internet cultures develop as social actors interact with others using the technology. It is the people, not the technology, who generate new cultures. Argyle and Shields (1996) provide an example of bulletin-board use:

If a user types,
 handshake Kitty
as another user named Rubber did to me, everyone would see:
 Rubber is shaking hands with Kitty
while I would see,
 Rubber is shaking hands with you,
and when I return the handshake, I type, 'handshake Rubber', and I see,
... shake, shake ...
and I type, 'grin Rubber' to introject not just words or a command but a gesture ... The screen responds
 Smile
And I spontaneously do.

(Argyle and Shields, 1996, p. 61)

This is a new culture – an example of 'Net culture' – but it is very much a product of human, social interaction and not just technology.

Activity

a Give three examples of technological innovations that have had an important impact upon culture.

b Explain in your own words what is meant by the term 'technological determinism'.

c Explain in your own words why Raymond Williams is critical of technological determinist arguments.

d Can you add your own examples of 'Net culture'? Do you agree or disagree with the view that it is not technology but social relationships which shape the cultures associated with new technologies? Explain the reasons for your views.

C3.2, C3.3

3.3 Learning social roles

We now need to consider the ways in which culture, created in the process of human interaction, works to regulate social roles and the nature of society. Sociologists have devised many theories to explain the way in which the life of individuals is somehow regulated either by cultural norms and values or by longer-standing entities such as institutions or social structures. In this section we will introduce the main theories you will encounter and focus on what they have to say about this issue of the link between the individual and society and the regulation of social life.

Structural functionalism

Society as an interlinked whole

Sociologists known as *functionalists* use an **organic analogy** – biological models of the body – to explain how society works.

We can of course identify parts of the body, such as the heart, liver and kidneys, and identify the function that each plays in the maintenance of the whole body. We can also understand that if any one element breaks down the whole body is threatened, showing that there must be interlinks between organs of the body.

So, functionalists argue, the various institutions in society all fulfil different functions, and all need to work together if society is to function harmoniously. They argue that if there is a disruption to one institution in society, this threatens the stability of the whole. Therefore, to understand the role or function of anything in society – such as the family, the education system, the mass media, religion or the welfare state – we have to consider its function in relation to the whole of society.

The structure of society

In order to do this, *we need to have a picture of how everything fits together*. This requires more than simply a list of the various institutions in society and the roles they play. It requires also an understanding of the links between them and the way changes in one area affect others. Sociologists use the term **social structure** to refer to these links.

The social structure is generally thought of as existing somewhat independently of the individuals and institutions that act within it for a time. Thus money can be thought of as part of the social structure. We as individuals do not decide to live in a society operated with a money economy, but this is there when we are born and affects our lives. Lack of money can constrain our actions and choices, just as earning money can provide us with opportunities to enable us to act out our choices. In either case, we live within certain relationships determined by the existence of money.

If you doubt this at all, imagine the differences in your life if there were no such thing as money. For one thing, you certainly would not be able to get a Saturday job working on the tills in a supermarket.

The functions of existence

Functionalism derives its name from the belief that everything that exists does so for a reason – *it serves a function*. Functionalists believe that if something served no purpose at all, it would cease to exist.

Furthermore, for functionalists the most important thing is to consider the role or function that any institution or act plays in the *maintenance* of society.

One of the key sources of later functionalist thinking were the ideas of the nineteenth century French sociologist Emile Durkheim. Emile Durkheim's analysis of crime provides one example of this. While crime is often thought of as a negative thing, Durkheim pointed to its role – or

rather the function of its punishment – as showing us the difference between right and wrong and allowing society periodically to test its norms and values. Thus debates today – such as those about whether to legalize the recreational or medicinal use of cannabis, or the ethics of genetically modified food or views about artificial fertility – allow society to engage in *moral debates*. These may lead to changes in the norms and values of society as seen in the law of the land.

This is an important point because it suggests that laws are made and changed as the shared views of society change.

The value consensus of society

Durkheim believed that the content of the law was an important indicator of the norms and values of a particular society at a particular time. Since the law is essentially a prescription of norms and values, there is something to be said for this view. Later functionalists used this argument to suggest that the law is the result of a *value consensus*. This is a version of a theory that believes that societies are democratic. The people have their views and these views are represented in government and the law. If opinions change, so does the law. Everyone has equal power to affect the content of the law and therefore the consensus of public opinion is the most powerful force in society.

Consensus

The early part of this section spent some time considering the functionalist view that society is based on a value consensus, where everyone has a say (it is therefore democratic) and what happens results from agreement (or consensus) about the fundamental norms and values by which the society is to be run. Leaders are responsive to the ideas of the people and therefore they simply reflect that consensus in their actions.

Functionalism and consensus

The most important example of this sort of thinking in sociology is functionalism. For functionalists the key basis of society is agreement over the basic moral and behavioural guidelines in society. Because these are viewed as being agreed, their enforcement through the law is seen as the government implementing the will of the people. Thus society is seen as democratic since the government acts on the wishes of the people.

This view was dominant in sociology in the 1950s, but it had difficulty in accounting for the upsurge in social conflict around the world that happened in the late 1960s.

However, it is the case that the falloff in overt social conflict around the world in the 1980s and early 1990s could be cited as evidence in support of the existence of agreement or consensus.

Criticisms of the functionalist tradition

There are two major criticisms of the overall functionalist viewpoint. Firstly, if the laws, norms and values of a society are the result of a value consensus, why would there ever be any need for change? This is important since it is relatively easy to demonstrate that changes do happen.

For instance, take views on the position of women in society. Women in the UK were not able to vote in public elections until 1918, and there were legal restrictions on their employment and their right to own property. Nowadays, there are no legal impediments to equality between men and women. This does not of course mean that equality has been achieved, but it does point to the tremendous change in attitudes towards, and the position of, women in the UK. What is now to explain this change if the previous situation was the result of a value consensus, something about which everyone agreed?

The second criticism of functionalism argues that not everyone is equal – some groups have more power and influence than others, so that society is not characterized by consensus. Instead there is a *power structure* in which the views and influence of some count for more than those of others. Thus, it is argued, society is riven by fundamental *conflicts of interest*, which lead to continual arguments and battles over the nature and direction of society.

This approach rejects the idea of society as a consensus and instead sees it as based on the continually changing outcomes of conflicts between different groups. This type of approach is known as 'conflict theory'.

Conflict

There is a group of alternative views in sociology which start instead from the proposition that society is riven by conflicts of interest, which sometimes lead to actual conflicts. Examples include:

- **Feminist** sociologists tend to argue that there is a fundamental conflict between men and women and that men oppress women.
- **Marxist** sociologists tend to argue that there is a conflict between classes in society, whereby the ruling classes exploit the working class.

There are therefore lots of theories stressing that conflict between groups in society is wide-ranging and to be expected. In this section we explore these important positions by looking at the implication of arguments which start out from an analysis of power and inequality and the way it leads to conflict in society.

Conflict, power and inequality

In contrast to some views which see **consensus**, or agreement, as the key basis of society, other sociologists argue that the key basis of society consists of **conflicts** between different social groups. This influences the nature and direction of society, and the outcome of these conflicts provides the basis of the social structure.

Whilst sharing an emphasis on the importance of conflict, the actual nature of the conflict is thought of in different ways by various perspectives within this approach. Marxists, for example, argue that the key conflict in society is between classes – that is the owners and the non-owners of units of economic production. Feminists, on the other hand, tend to argue that conflict between men and women is a much more fundamental aspect of society.

Marxism and class conflict

Marxists argue that workers are not paid the full value of what they produce. They are therefore exploited, because the owner (a 'non-worker') benefits from the effort of the workers. The implication of Marxist theory is that this will cause conflicts in the economy which will, over time, lead to economic and social change through, for instance, the formation of trade unions.

Feminism, patriarchy and female oppression

Feminists agree that there is conflict, but argue that historically and in contemporary terms the potential and actual conflict between men and women is more important, and somehow more fundamental to human existence. Feminists use the concept of **patriarchy** to describe how all structures, ideas and cultures of society are male-dominated or act in the interests of males. They argue that this leads to the oppression of women, either:

- *legally* through differential requirements or limits placed on the activities of women; or
- *politically* through the restriction of voting rights for women, or inequalities in voting rights for men and women (women did not get the vote on an equal basis to men in the UK until 1928); or
- *economically* through unequal pay; or even
- *physically* through domestic violence, sexual assaults and rape.

Symbolic interactionism and consensus

Another sociological approach that tends towards acceptance of the notion of consensus is *symbolic interactionism*. Here the argument is that there is agreement about the meaning of symbols such as language. It is argued that in order for conversations to take place each party has to have a shared understanding (in simple terms, speak the same language) or else interaction cannot take place. Another example cited is traffic lights, which act as a signal and the meaning of which is commonly understood and accepted by people in society.

Both functionalism and symbolic interactionism therefore share an emphasis on the existence of consensus in society, although they do differ in other respects.

Structure and social action

Structural or macro sociology?

The views considered so far are often classified as structural in nature – meaning that they tend to talk in terms of large groups such as society, classes or genders. This is sometimes known as the **macro** *approach*. Other sociologists have argued that it is the level of power involved, rather than the simple numbers of people, that should determine whether we are looking at the macro rather than the micro level.

One potential problem with such structural

approaches is that they sometimes give the impression of describing only things being done *to* people. They thus present individuals and social groups as passive puppets of society without any choice or ability to affect events.

The social action approach

The rigid structural approach is rejected by those sociologists who advocate what has become known as the *social action* approach.

Their starting point is precisely to say that society is the result of human activity, and that in order to understand society we need to consider how people act, think and feel. In some versions of this approach reality is understood as whatever people subjectively feel is real – whether it is or not. So, for instance, if people believe in God this will presumably affect their behaviour, even though we can find no evidence to prove that God does exist.

Subjectivity and society

This version of sociology thus starts from a consideration of how people see themselves and society. It investigates in great detail the notion of social identities – meaning the way people feel and think about themselves, how they present themselves to the outside world, and how the reactions of the outside world can have an effect on the way they view themselves.

For instance, one individual could see himself primarily as a man, as a working-class person, as a black British person, as a young person and/or as bisexual. All of these may be elements of his personality and identity. But it is possible for two people who share all these identifying characteristics nonetheless to see things in different ways, because they view different things about their identity as the most important.

Subjectivity and identity

This issue of the multiple aspects of our personality and identity leads on to the question of whether we each exist as coherent individuals or as fragmentary persons inhabiting several social worlds all at the same time. It also leads to the question of whether we all live in the same society, or instead inhabit different social spaces and therefore effectively different societies.

Symbolic interactionism

Symbolic interactionists are less inclined than

Weber to emphasize the *permanence* of the social structures which emerge as individuals act on the cultural definitions or meanings which guide them. Instead, they tend to describe a more *fluid* process in which social actors interact to construct particular ways of living (cultural arrangements) – but the emphasis is on the ways in which such cultural arrangements can change, depending on the nature of particular patterns of interaction. Culture is generated, then, through social interaction and the exchange of meanings or interpretations.

One of the originators of the symbolic interactionist approach to notions of the self and society, Charles Cooley (1864–1929), argued that the 'self' (an individuals picture of themselves and the image they portray to the world) was in fact a 'looking-glass self' since we tend to think of ourselves through our thoughts and feelings about how others see us. This idea highlights the importance of the social in concepts of identity. We may have some idea of how we see ourselves and we may think that it is a purely personal projection of our own individuality, but in fact it involves a clear element of social interaction since it is a 'looking-glass self'.

Mead: the 'I' and the 'Me'

Mead argues that the way we make sense of the world is through language, which is inherently social in nature, and this underlines the need to embrace the social as a fundamental element of human life. His most famous distinction is between the 'I' and the 'me'. What he meant by this was the distinction between the real inner self ('I') and the public front, the social image we present of ourselves ('me').

Both of these are creative and active but the 'me' is a reflection that our behaviour is affected by others, that we are social. We sometimes abstain from doing things we might wish to do because we fear the negative reaction of others. Mead recognized that we do not know everyone we meet, but they have a potential effect on us since, through our knowledge that others will react to what we do, we construct a generalized notion of the 'other' which is contrasted to our notion of 'me'. He also points out, however, that some others will have more of an effect on us and our notion of self and therefore our behaviour. He called these 'significant others'.

Erving Goffman and dramaturgy

The most influential development of the symbolic interactionist tradition can be found in the work of Goffman, who has developed what has been called a 'dramaturgical' approach. Goffman starts from the premise that the expectations that others have of us are the basis of roles, and that these expectations form a kind of script that we then act out. Social life is really therefore all an act, it is a drama (hence dramaturgical) during which we play different roles and all the time strive to manage our performance.

Goffman did fieldwork in the Shetland Islands for his book *The Presentation of Self in Everyday Society* (1971) and found that the people there often let the appearance of their cottages decay so that the landlord would not put up their rents. They were presenting themselves as poor to achieve this effect. This can be called impression management. Craib points out the implication of this:

That 'impression management' is going on all the time, as if we were all advertising agents. We use our physical surroundings as props and maintain areas of privacy 'backstage' where we can relax from our performances (the toilet, for example).

(Craib, 1992, p. 89)

This distinction between the performance and the relaxed artist backstage is in effect a reworking of Mead's 'I' and 'me'. However, Goffman develops this insight to the point where it might be argued that everything we do is an act and it is not clear whether a real coherent self is ever present.

Goffman conducted a number of famous studies in developing this dramaturgical approach. In *Asylums* (1968) he studied the way in which the routines employed in asylums for the mentally ill are actually manipulated to effect change in people's self-identity as a way of enforcing social control over them.

Activity

Goffman's work does essentially define interactions as being face-to-face.

a How might phone conversations or communication by letter be considered on this basis?

b Goffman saw phone conversations and letters as reduced forms of real interaction. What do you think is reduced in this form of interaction and what remains?

c What are the implications for the future of symbolic interactionism bearing in mind the growth of electronic forms of communication such as email?

d How real is virtual reality on this basis?

Interaction and identity

Symbolic interactionism is committed to charting the ways in which identity can change as patterns of interaction change and individuals are exposed to new cultural environments. Social identity is not fixed or permanent but fluid, changeable and dynamic.

Becker's 'classic' study of dance or jazz subcultures and marihuana use in the 1950s illustrates this very well. Individuals may come to see themselves as 'part' of the dance subculture and, perhaps, as 'marihuana users' – but this depends on how much they interact with other members of the subculture and the nature of the symbolic meanings that are exchanged (Becker, 1973).

Structure or action

Sociologists who believe that the structure of society shapes a great deal of our lives and places limits on the choices we can make (functionalist and Marxist approaches tend to share these assumptions) argue that the account of cultural behaviour the interactionists provide is incomplete unless there is also a consideration of how structure, power and history impact on and limit the development of culture and identity.

In turn, interactionists point to the lack of attention in structural sociology to the importance of the processes through which identity is constructed via small-scale, everyday interactions between social actors. For example, contemporary urban dance music could be understood as the product of hundreds of small-scale interactions between clubbers, DJs and those involved in particular clubs or events. It may not be shaped by any larger sociological structure such as social class.

Case study: Imagining ourselves

The work of George Herbert Mead has been extensively used in thinking about identity because he offered useful insights into the link between how we see ourselves and the ability of human beings to imagine how others might see us (Mead, 1934).

Think about it this way. Imagine you have an interview for a job. You think about the interview before the 'big day' and consider what to wear. You want to look smart but perhaps that new suit would be too hot and you would end up feeling, and looking, very uncomfortable, especially if the heating was turned up high. Maybe you should try not to look so formal? What is going on here?

In order to make a decision about what to wear you have to imagine yourself, to look at yourself from the outside. Mead argued that it is the capacity to imagine how others would see us and our capacity to carry images in our head which is an important distinguishing feature of human beings. This is best illustrated in our use of language, where words operate as symbols. Pictures, images and gestures are also symbolic in that they too represent something else. A symbol stands for something else. Symbols and representations are important in the production of identities. This is how we signal our identities to others and how we know which people we identify with and those who are distinguished as being different. How we speak, the clothes we wear, badges, scarves, uniforms or flags all offer symbols of identity. Judith Williamson describes choosing an identity in the following way:

When I rummage through my wardrobe in the morning I am not merely faced with the choice of what to wear. I am faced with the choice of images. You know perfectly well that you will be seen differently for the whole day, depending on what you put on.

(adapted from Woodward, 2000, pp. 12–13)

Sociology: the individual and society

In this chapter we have sought to consider the nature of the relationship between the individual and society and the various ways that sociologists have thought about that relationship.

It is clear that one of the key divisions in sociology is between those who view individuals as the product of society either in the form of structures which pre-exist the individual and which he or she has little or no choice over. It is this tradition that tends to emphasise the way that individual and social life is regulated by the construction of various roles embedded in cultures, institutions and structures. This approach is clearly seen in the functionalist tradition.

However it is clear that at least some versions of Marxism and feminism also hold to a largely structural view of the relationship between the individual and society. A key difference is that these sociologists view society as riven by conflicts either between classes or between the sexes and therefore the creation of these structures, institutions and cultures is not the result of a societal consensus as functionalists believe, but instead reflects the imposition of values, norms, laws and other structures on the majority by a ruling group of some sort or other.

In contrast to this top-down view of society, social action sociologists tend to emphasize the active nature of individuals and social groups in the construction of the society around them. In this view individuals are not seen as either powerless puppets or happy robots but instead as active creators of their own identity and the world around them. Clearly this approach places less emphasis on the determination of social life and more on individual freedom. It is however true that here again we can identify divisions between social action theorists who believe society is constructed on the basis of consensus, largely symbolic interactionists, and those who believe that the construction of society by individuals involves some degree of conflict, notably **phenomenology**.

These key concepts of social structure, social action, consensus and conflict will reappear throughout your sociology course and it is therefore important that you grasp the meaning of them early on. We hope this chapter has helped introduce you to these notions in a relatively painless way.

Drawing together some basic concepts

Table 3.4, below, has been constructed using the two continuing dichotomies in sociology, namely (1) social structure or social action and (2) consensus or conflict. You can see that they remain concepts that lead to debates and arguments in sociology. This is because sociology is composed

Table 3.4 Theoretical approaches and dichotomies in sociology

Theoretical approaches	Emphasis on social structures	Emphasis on social action
Consensus views	Society is seen as a set of structures and institutions that have been created by individuals in the past but which still impact upon and constrain the lives of individuals today. The best example is the law. This approach believes that the basis of society is agreement about the general principles or values of society. This is best effected through democracy where everyone can have their equal say, and the law thus represents the views of all. E.g. functionalism	Society is seen as being the intended and unintended results of the actions and interactions of all the individuals who make up that society. It is therefore constructed by individuals. In order to interact together, individuals have to be able to communicate with each other and they must therefore have some sort of agreement about the meaning of words, or the names of things. Thus their interactions are based on communication. E.g. symbolic interactionism
Conflict views	Society is seen as a set of structures and institutions that have been created by individuals in the past but which still impact upon and constrain the lives of individuals today. This approach believes that the basis of society is that the powerful use force to dictate how everyone else is to live their lives. Since those subject to force are unlikely to like this, there is conflict potentially always waiting to break out. E.g. Marxism, feminism	Society is seen as the result of the intended and unintended result of the actions and interactions of all the individuals who make up that society. It is therefore constructed by individuals. The meanings which individuals construct are the result of actively trying to make sense even in situations which have no sense or of some people being able to get their interpretation of events seen as the truth. There is therefore potential conflict over whose view is accepted as truthful E.g. phenomenology

of many differing approaches, known as perspectives. By studying sociology you will see the views of many different perspectives on what is wrong with society (if anything) and how we might go about putting it right (or counter those who want to change it). This might help you to think about your own views on these subjects. In developing your own views it is certain that you will be using the same basic set of concepts as your first building blocks that the other sociologists who have gone before you have used.

Sociology will make you think about such fundamental concepts as society, the individual, socialization, power, inequality, conflict, oppression, exploitation, conflict and consensus.

Activity

Basic sociological concepts

the individual	power	social
society	inequality	inequality
socialization	class	differentiation
social	gender	social structure
Institutions	ethnicity	social action
culture	oppression	conflict
identity	exploitation	consensus

a Using the index of this book and the glossaries contained at the end of the first nine chapters to help you, write your own explanation of the basic sociological concepts listed here. You might find a sociological dictionary helpful, too.

b Divide into five groups and pick one of the following terms: society, social structure, social action, consensus or conflict. Then draw a spider diagram with the chosen term in the centre and make as many connections as you can to the other words in the basic sociological concepts list. You could include examples from your own life to make it meaningful to you, if you so wish.

c Discuss your findings with other groups and amend your diagram in the light of those discussions.

d Present your finished diagrams to the rest of the class, explaining what they show.

e Pin your finished diagrams up on the wall to remind you of these key concepts.

C3.1a C3.1b, C3.2, C3.3

It is these themes and concepts that underpin all sociological debates and you will therefore find yourself returning to them whichever particular sociological topics you study as part of your course. In adding your own thoughts you are engaging in the sociological process in a creative and proactive way, something that is central to being human. Studying sociology does therefore allow of the expression of human creativity.

Further reading

- Abbott, D. (1998) *Culture and Identity*, London: Hodder & Stoughton.
- Jenkins, R. (1996) *Social Identity*, London: Routledge.
- Taylor, P. (1997) *Investigating Culture and Identity*, London: Collins.
- Back copies of *Sociology Review* (and its predecessor *Social Studies Review*) also contain articles on these topics and others.

Glossary of useful terms

Capitalism   An economic system based on production for individual profit with goods being bought and sold in a market. Often associated with private property but can also exist with public or state owned property.

Community   A group of people who have close social bonds that seem to bind them together.

Conflict   Some sociologists argue that there are fundamental conflicts of interest between different groups in society and that these result in the outbreak of open struggle between these groups from time to time. They also see these conflicts and their resolution as providing the main basis for social change in societies. Thus the principle of Marxism is that there is conflict between classes, while the principle of feminism is that there is conflict between men and women. Phenomenologists are also conflict sociologists in that they argue that we come into conflict with each other over the meanings of things. Functionalists and symbolic interactionists, however, see society as largely characterized by consensus, not conflict.

Consensus   The view that society is characterized mainly by agreement or consensus. Thus functionalists talk about the existence of a value consensus in society, expressed through the law being the embodiment of the views of the people. Symbolic interactionists also emphasize the way that we can only interact through signs or symbols having the shared meanings that allow interactions to take place and society to function. Feminists, Marxists and phenomenologists are critical of this approach, instead seeing society as largely characterized by conflict.

Culture   Used by sociologists in a number of ways but most importantly to describe the whole way of life among groups or in a particular society. Thus we could talk about the culture of the UK or youth culture, and in each case we would be looking to say something about how these groups of people live their life. Culture is often also considered more changeable than institutions or structures, and therefore more associated with choice.

Femininity   Social and behavioural characteristics associated with being biologically female.

Feminism   Feminism is based on the idea that there are fundamental conflicts between men and women. It stresses that for centuries men have oppressed women in a number of ways ranging from paying them less than men, restricting their employment or property-owning rights, through to physical oppression through violence and rape. Feminists use the word patriarchy to mean this male power of oppression.

Functionalism   Functionalist sociologists see society as being based on agreement, or consensus, expressed in the values of that society and enshrined in the laws of that society. They also argue that everything that exists does so for a reason because it serves a purpose of function, hence functionalism.

Global   This term is used to refer to events or processes that have an impact across the whole world.

Globalization   Refers to the perception that the lives of people in different societies across the globe are becoming more closely connected. It is a controversial process, with some sociologists seeing it in broadly positive terms, while others see it as a process having negative consequences.

Identity   Sum total of who you think you are and also sum total of how other people think of themselves.

Individual   A human being, a person able to make choices.

Institutions   Areas where behaviour is limited by rules and where there are therefore clear expected patterns of behaviour. There are numerous examples of this ranging from schools, hospitals, workplaces, courts, football games to the institution of marriage. The process whereby social actions move from being random and not rule-controlled to rule-controlled is known as institutionalization

Macro   A focus on large scale events or structures in society.

Marxism   Marxism is based on the idea that there are fundamental conflicts between classes in society, notably between those who own the means by which things are made but who do no work in actually making things, and those who do not own the means of production and have to sell their labour to stay alive. Marx argued that profit was derived from paying the workers only a fraction of the full value of the goods they produce and this he called exploitation.

Masculinity   Social and behavioural characteristics associated with being biologically male.

Mass media   'Media' means methods of delivering a message, so the mass media are methods of delivering messages to a lot (mass) of people: TV, radio, newspapers, magazines, the Internet.

Micro   A focus on small scale interactions between groups or individuals.

Norms   Rules about expected behaviour in specific circumstances. What is normally expected of one.

Organic analogy   The argument that society is like (analogous to, hence analogy) the human body (an organism, hence organic). So just as everything in the body serves a purpose and is linked together to form a whole, so everything in society has a function and is linked together to form society.

Patriarchy   Originally meaning 'the rule of the father', it is now a term used by feminists to describe the situation where males have power over females.

Peer group   Group of people who are close to you (especially in age and social setting) and are therefore influential in your thoughts, feelings and actions.

Phenomenology   The study of the 'commonsense' understandings (as opposed to 'scientific' or 'academic' explanations of things) that people have about their lives and the importance of these for interaction and for society. The study of the process through which people create their consciousness.

Popular culture   Term used to counter the idea of mass culture. Mass culture suggests we are all the same and we have become dulled and unthinking through culture. In contrast the concept of popular culture suggests that instead we can comment on and think about the cultural products around us which are popular such as TV programmes, pop music and fashion and these can be used in a potentially subversive way. Culture is therefore not seen in purely negative terms.

Power   The ability to get others to do or think something. Can be seen as enabling action or constraining action. Often used by conflict-oriented sociologists in discussions about who has power over whom and whether that is seen as right or not. Thus feminists emphasize the way that men have power over women and this is unjust and leads to the oppression of women. However, more consensual views of power stress that it is a resource for getting things done.

Power structure   The concept of power is central to conflict theories which tend to stress the way one group has power over others. This is not usually through one individual being literally stronger than another, but instead through the power they weild through positions or roles they fulfil in the social structure. For example, teachers have the power to set students homework, but students do not have the power to set teachers homework.

Primary socialization   The first stage of socialization undertaken by the family and the early part of schooling.

Rituals   Actions of social significance undertaken repeatedly by individuals or groups. This concept is seen as important particularly in Durkheim and his analysis of how rituals help to bond us together.

Role   Pattern of behaviour associated with a particular position or status and therefore expected of individuals who fill that role. The fact that these expectations are known creates the potential for stability and social order.

Secondary socialization   Coming after primary socialization, this concept stresses that we are continually learning new things and confronting new situations in our lives.

Social   Clearly this is the key term for sociol-ogy: the study ('logos') of the social, of society ('socio'). This term is used to distinguish those features of an individual that might be explained by biological or psychological processes from that which needs to be explained by reference to the thoughts, feelings or actions of others. It therefore stresses the centrality of other people in our lives. We do not live as isolated individuals but as social animals.

Social action   The argument that society is constructed by the interactions of individuals and is nothing more than the result of the sum of all these interactions. Used by symbolic interactionists and phenomenologists.

Social interaction   Term covering all the ways in which individuals mix with each other and in the process impact on the thoughts, feelings and actions of others.

Socialization   The process of learning appropriate roles and behaviour.

Society   Used by sociologists to describe the sum or totality of all relationships, with the suggestion that these are important in the lives of people considered members of that society. Therefore people may talk about British society or even European society. Sometimes considered to be simply the result of the sum of individual social actions but some sociologists include notions of the impact of institutions and structures.

State   The total of governmental institutions that have the power to influence people's lives: e.g. by taxation, legislation (passing laws), military force, etc.

Structural   Structural sociologists are those who emphasize structures as an important element in sociology. This can include Marxists, feminists and functionalists.

Structure   One of the key terms in sociology. It signifies the existence of relatively permanent elements in social life. The term structure is used to signify things that are more than social interactions between individuals. If you try to think of things that are beyond your control you will think of structures, for example the existence of money, the law as a structure requiring you to go to school till you are 16. Structures impact on people's lives without them necessarily having any say in their direction. They exist before you are born and they will exist after you die. Therefore they persist in time longer than the life of any individual. Some sociologists deny they exist and they are called post-structuralists ('after-structures'). Key examples of sociological views arguing for the importance of structures are Marxism, functionalism and feminism.

Symbolic interactionism   A social action type of sociology that stresses the way that we interact with others through the use of symbols. The most notable example of this is language, which is a series of symbols which when put together in a certain way have a meaning. Symbolic interactionists suggest that the meaning of these symbols is commonly understood and it is this which allows society to function.

Symbolic value   The suggestion that something has value not for what you can do with it but instead for what it stands for. Thus while both non-brand and brand trainers can be used to walk or run in, certain brands are purchased for their label and the social status is therefore based on them as a symbol. This type of analysis is mainly associated with social action type sociologists such as symbolic interactionists and phenomenologists.

Values   Views about general ways of behaving which express something about how people feel they and others should behave.

4

The individual and society
Culture and the formation of identities

Chapter outline

4.1 Gender identities

Individuality and identity

What does it mean to be a man? What does it mean to be a woman? On a biological level we can at least attempt to answer this question with some degree of certainty by stating that only women can bear children and only men can produce sperm and impregnate women.

However, as sociologists, we are more concerned with the way that there are certain behavioural and attitudinal traits which are seen as associated with males and/or females.

What does it mean to behave like a woman? And are there multiple variations on behaving like a woman?

Identity and the way that our culture affects the formation of identities is a key element of the link between individuals and society. In relation to this, Burkitt and Tester (1996) define some key terms, as follows:

In everyday usage, the term identity is frequently used more or less interchangeably with the words individual and individuality. Yet identity and individu-

ality are not the same from a sociological point of view.

The word individual can be taken to refer to the continuous sense of being different and distinctive from others. I am an individual because I know that I am not you. ...

*However, the word identity has different meanings. Whereas the word individual refers to what we are in contemporary society, the word identity refers to who we are. Our identity is what is learnt and taught to us through processes of **socialization** and through our place and participation in social relationships. Identity is tied up with such things as our families, our names, what we do, what we look like, what we wear and so forth.*

(Burkitt and Tester, 1996, p. 2)

So, if we try to answer the question, 'Who am I?', we are dealing with issues of **identity**. If we try to relate that to the existence of social relationships and **social networks**, we are talking about social identity. This issue is potentially complex quite simply because of the multitude of possible identities embodied in any one person. In relation to gender, for instance, you may identify yourself as a man, as a woman, as a person or even as something else. However, on top of this there is the possibility that gender may not seem the most important to you and instead you may choose to emphasize your age, your ethnicity, your class, your nationality, your sexuality or even your regional background as the key basis of your identity.

Activity

a Think about your own identity. How do you define yourself? What aspects of yourself are most important in the way you see yourself?

b Discuss your findings with your friends. See what commonalties and differences you find among this group of people.

C3.1a, C3.2, C3.3

We are now going to look at some of the debates surrounding gender identity, and the rest of the chapter will then go onto look at other aspects of identity. We separate them for the purpose of analysis, but it is important to remember that they are all possibly present in each individual. At some points in a day, a person might define themselves as a woman or as a man, at other points being black or white might be the most important aspect of that person's identity, and at another being heterosexual or homosexual may be the most important element.

Gender role socialization

While gender is therefore not the only basis of identity, it is clear that it does form an important element.

In *Frogs and Snails and Feminist Tales*, Davis (1989) looks at the way young children reacted to books which were designed to avoid gender stereotyping. In one a princess rescues a prince, but the story ends with the words 'they don't get married'. Although this book was an attempt to undermine stereotyped roles, the children themselves did not like it.

She argues that this occurs because gender identity and the idea of very different roles being assigned to the two genders of male and female are central to young people's notion of identity. Being male or female and being clear about what this means and how you behave is a fundamental aspect of human identity. This point was also illustrated by Davis' research with the negative reactions of children to a girl who looked and behaved like a boy.

Clearly, gender identities are an important way children begin to make sense of the world and locate themselves in it. People who do not fit into the pattern of behaviour of their biological sex may be ostracized or attacked in some way. Girls who behave in ways which are seen as associated with males may be called 'tomboys' and boys who behave in ways seen as associated with females may be attacked even more. As the article on page 48 shows.

Discussion point

Read the article 'Oliver prefers to play with girls'.

a How might this punishment be overcome?

b How is sexuality and sexual identity depicted in this incident?

C3.1a

Questioning what is 'natural'

The problem with these examples is that the processes reinforcing gender identities as conventionally understood are so strong that we might simply begin to assume that they are somehow natural.

Oliver prefers to play with the girls. So the boys call him gay. Why?

DAVE HILL

Oliver is a 12-year-old boy who likes to hang around with girls. And why not? Girls, Oliver reckons, are more fun. He thinks other boys are idle, immature and only interested in football. …

And the girls, for their part, like talking to Oliver. He says, with satisfaction, that when he is around them they 'treat me like I am a girl.' The only trouble is that the other boys make Oliver pay a price. They tease him by walking past when he's with his female friends and sneering: 'All right, girls?' Oliver hates that: 'It feels really rotten to be called a girl.' And maybe other things they call him make him feel more rotten still. Do they also call him 'gay'?

Oliver went silent when the question was asked. It was a silence that said 'yes' more eloquently than the word itself and, furthermore, exposed a dimension of homophobia's power that has been barely acknowledged in the section 28 debate. The point about Oliver is that he has probably never experienced homosexual desire, let alone acted on it. He likes having girls as friends, but if one of them wanted to become his girlfriend, he wouldn't mind at all.

Indeed, he relates the one romantic relationship he has had with a girl, how he'd asked her if she'd mind if he bought some condoms, and even when might be a good time for them to try intercourse. Oliver's crime in the eyes of other boys is not a suspected attraction to boys, but being attracted to girls in the wrong way. For this, Oliver must be punished by being designated 'gay'.

Source: Adapted from *Guardian*, 2 February 2000

It is therefore very important that, as sociologists, we begin to question this. Why, for instance, do we only have two possible identities in terms of gender – male or female? It is for this reason that Riley (1988) pointed to the importance of stating that although we always are either male or female (biologically speaking), this is not always at the forefront of our identity. Sometimes we may see ourselves as persons, and sometimes we may identify ourselves by other criteria. We therefore need to question what it means to be a 'woman' or a 'man'.

'What is a woman?'

Are men and women different? There are anatomical differences, of course. But does this mean that men and women will behave differently in everyday life? And if they do seem to think and behave differently at times, how can this be explained? Are men and women biologically programmed to act in certain 'masculine' and 'feminine' ways? Or does their respective behaviour arise through a process of **gender-role socialization**?

Biologically determined or socially constructed?

What is a man? What is a woman?

While 'What is a man?' and 'What is a woman?' might at first seem like silly questions, they are not. We can, of course, refer to anatomical differences and point out that a man is a physical being with certain distinguishing biological characteristics (notably having a penis and testes), as is a woman (notably having a womb, a vagina and breasts). However, beyond these it is difficult to come up with any arguments that are not open to question. Does the fact that some women can give birth indicate that all women have a 'natural' inclination to care for children and carry out associated domestic tasks? Does a woman have particular mental processes and thoughts which lead her to behave in certain ways?

Some sociologists and other thinkers have argued that women are natural, 'stay-at-home' carers. This rather traditional view sees child-rearing and housekeeping as logical extensions of their innate domesticity.

However, this view of women's life role has been strongly challenged, particularly by **Marxists** and **feminists**. French feminist philosopher Simone de Beauvoir has summed up the challenge in her book *The Second Sex* (1972; orig. pub. 1953), stating: 'One is not born, but rather becomes a woman'. It was not the case, said de Beauvoir, that women were naturally inclined to housework or to childcare, as had been previously supposed. But rather that females were generally constrained by their upbringing, or by social and cultural expectations of them, or by the limited educational and job opportunities open to them. All this effectively forced them to marry – 'love' or not – for 'respectability' and for some measure of financial security.

Sex and gender

Many sociologists who have questioned the social relationships between women and men have distinguished between 'sex' and 'gender'. They have used the term 'sex' to refer to the biological and anatomical differences between men and women, and 'gender' to refer to men's and women's social and cultural roles. They argue, after Stoller (1968), that there is no necessary correlation between 'sex' and 'gender'. For example, it is not always the case that a boy will behave in a 'masculine' way, or a girl in a 'feminine' way.

Some contemporary sociologists have taken Stoller's argument one step further, suggesting that this shows 'femininity' and 'masculinity' are more like a set of socially imposed rules than natural preferences. In this way it becomes possible to suggest that women have generally shouldered the bulk of domestic responsibilities in any given household because that is seen as culturally appropriate feminine behaviour, and not because they are biologically inclined to do so. The same goes for men, who have tended to do household jobs like DIY that are perceived to require physical strength, traditionally a male preserve.

Social scientists debate sex and gender

Sociologist Ann Oakley separated 'sex' and 'gender' in her ground-breaking studies on women and on housework (1972, 1974a). She argued that the numerous social scientists who claimed it was 'natural' for women to take a caring role in the family – and thus to look after children and perform household tasks – had been tricked by their own prejudices into assuming what it meant to be a woman.

In particular, Oakley took issue with the work of anthropologist George Peter Murdock (1965; orig. pub. 1949), with **functionalist** sociologist Talcott Parsons (1959) and with psychologist John Bowlby (1965).

Murdock had argued that the biological dif-

ferences between men and women underpinned the sexual division of labour – the allocation of social and economic tasks by gender – in society. His survey of 224 societies from around the world appeared to show that women and men undertook different social and economic duties – women gathering vegetables, cooking and caring for children, and men hunting and mining. He claimed that as men were in the main stronger, and as women in the main bore children, it was only logical that a society should organize tasks in a manner which recognized this. Oakley disagreed, however, showing that some of his examples were flawed.

Oakley dealt similarly with the work of Parsons and Bowlby. These influential thinkers had suggested that women were best suited to the role of giving emotional support and socialization to children. Bowlby, in particular, has argued that a child primarily cared for by someone other than its mother would not thrive. Oakley's work showed, on the contrary, that it was perfectly possible for a woman to give care of her child to others for significant periods with no ill-effects for the child. She pointed to the Indonesian Alor islanders. In this society women, who grew and harvested vegetables, generally gave over the care of their children to a member of their extended family about two weeks after giving birth.

Oakley's early conclusions

Oakley's studies found that the social role that has been ascribed to women – that of wife and mother – existed for the convenience of men. Male theorists like Murdock, Parsons and Bowlby, she argued, conducted research which reflected their own claim to dominance over women. Thus it is not surprising that their work simply reinforced traditional ideas about the social relationships between men and women.

Oakley argued that 'gender' is a cultural phenomenon, not necessarily linked to 'sex'. She claimed that it is human nurturing, rather than biological nature, that is the key determinant of gender identities, whilst gender-role socialization is a more important factor in creating 'masculine' men and 'feminine' women than any genetic traits which men and women might be discovered to have.

Oakley's later conclusions

Oakley has developed these ideas in her more recent work. In an essay 'A brief history of

'Maternal deprivation'

What is believed to be essential for mental health is that an infant and young child should experience a warm, intimate and continuous relationship with his mother (or permanent mother-substitute – one person who steadily 'mothers' him) in which both find satisfaction and enjoyment. It is this complex, rich and rewarding relationship with the mother in early years, varied in countless ways by relations with the father and with the brothers and sisters, that child psychiatrists and many others now believe to underlie the development of character and of mental health. A state of affairs in which a child does not have this relationship is termed 'maternal deprivation' … A child is deprived if for any reason he is removed from his mother's care …

[This] book…does [not] treat in detail the child's relationship with his father. The reason for this is that almost all the evidence concerns the child's relationship with his mother, which is without doubt in ordinary circumstances by far his most important relationship during these years. It is she who feeds and cleans him, keeps him warm, and comforts him. It is to his mother that he turns when in distress. In the young child's eyes father plays second fiddle and his value increases only as the child becomes more able to stand alone.

Nevertheless, as the illegitimate child knows, fathers have their uses even in infancy. Not only do they provide for their wives to enable them to devote themselves unrestrictedly to the care of the infant and toddler, but, by providing love and companionship, they support the mother emotionally and help her maintain that harmonious contented mood in the atmosphere of which her infant thrives.

Source: Adapted from Bowlby (1965)

Activity

a Read the excerpt 'Maternal deprivation'. List the parts of Bowlby's argument with which you feel Oakley would disagree.

b Do you agree with any of Bowlby's ideas?

C3.2

gender' (1997) she argues that, just as 'gender' is a cultural phenomenon, so too is 'sex'. She proposes that, to date, feminists and other social scientists researching 'gender' have wrongly assumed 'sex' to be a unassailable 'fact of nature' when, in truth, it is as much a variable as 'gender'.

Developing the work of sociologist Thomas Laquer, Oakley proves that prior to the seventeenth century male and female bodies were seen to be the same. Women and men were said to have the same genitals, with women's simply being an inside-out version of men's. It was only after the Enlightenment that perceptions changed and women and men began to be seen as anatomically and sexually distinct from one another.

Subsequently it has generally been assumed that just as there are two sexes, male and female, there must be two corresponding genders, masculine and feminine. Whilst sociologists have investigated 'gender', questioning assumptions about the basis for distinct masculine and feminine behaviours, 'sex' has been the province of **natural scientists**. Some natural scientists and other theorists have ignored gender research like Oakley's and continued to make claims about the fixed behaviour of men and women. This has only been possible because social scientists have tended to understand 'sex' and 'gender' as opposites, in the same way as do natural scientists. Oakley writes:

The social construction of sex/the body is different for the two genders, with women's bodies/sex seen as being much more controlled by hormones than men's and therefore as fragile and altogether less stable biological products.

(Oakley, 1997, p. 50)

A case of mistaken identity

HELEN MATHER did not suspect she was any different from other women her age. But two factors worried her. At 19, she'd never had a period. And penetrative sex had always been impossible.

Mather went for tests at the Elizabeth Garrett Anderson Hospital for women. Here it was discovered that she did not have a vagina, or uterus, fallopian tubes or ovaries. She was told she had a rare genetic condition called androgen insensitivity syndrome (AIS). She would have been born a boy, but an insensitivity to androgens, or male hormones, caused the foetus to develop along female lines. Tests showed that she was biologically male and had XY chromosomes, but in every outward way, she appeared female.

"It would be grotesque to suggest I'm anything other than female," says Mather, now 46. "I wouldn't know how to be a man."

There are around 500 women in Britain with AIS. The condition shows physically in the reproductive organs and ranges from complete AIS (completely female genitalia in appearance, although the vagina is usually short or absent) to partial AIS (almost completely male).

Her mother considered her condition so embarrassing that she swore Mather to secrecy – presumably unaware that AIS is mostly inherited via the maternal line. Her father was simply never told. "At times I felt fearful and lonely. If you have chickenpox, you can tell people about it. You can't with AIS. The hospital didn't offer me counselling to cope with the psychological effects. It just wasn't considered then."

Philippa Blackman was diag-nosed as having AIS at 16. Her doctor told her nothing of her condition, only that she'd need surgery to remove her "ovaries". This was a medical euphemism for a gonadectomy, or the removal of the testes, which occur in all women with AIS and which were undescended and not visible in Blackman's case. However, her condition and the surgery were not mentioned again beyond that day.

Blackman, like Mather, was registered female at birth and reared as a girl. Unlike Mather, however, her vagina developed to a normal length and penetrative sex was possible, although in fact she remained celibate for 10 years.

At 28, she produced a documentary on women with AIS and, listening to them talking, realised that she couldn't have children either. Then, when being examined by an osteopath following an accident, she admitted she'd never had a period and didn't know why. Going to a GP for the first time in 12 years, she was diagnosed as having AIS. "I remember the female doctor saying: 'You can consider yourself female, if you like.' I'd never thought of myself as anything else."

Reassurance came from Howard Jacobs, professor of reproductive endocrinology at Middlesex Hospital. "He told me I am completely female, but my genes are male. That was the first time my condition had been explained to me. I had always felt like an outsider; the one who didn't have periods. I'd spent years wondering: will anyone want me?" They did: Blackman plans to marry her long-term boyfriend next year.

Naomi Walters certainly wishes there had been more honesty in her case. When she was a child, strangers would stop her mother in the street and say: "What an adorable little girl." She looked female, but Walters had been registered male at birth, as she was born with male genitalia (albeit smaller than average). From three years old, she underwent many surgical operations to augment her "maleness".

She was never comfortable as a boy, she recalls. "My best friends were girls. I leaned naturally towards female behaviour." Her confusion about her gender was exacerbated in her teens by the non-appearance of male sexual characteristics, such as facial and body hair, a deep voice and muscles. Then she discovered painful "lumps" in her chest. "I was terrified. I thought, boys don't develop breasts, do they?"

It wasn't until her mid-twenties that Walters found the courage to live as a woman. After consulting a psychiatrist, she began surgery, including a vaginal reconstruction using a section of her bowel, and hormone replacement therapy. Switching gender roles was no problem for her – she'd always been mistaken for a female anyway – and her mother, she says, coped with it well.

She is currently taking time out from her career in agriculture to have her first counselling sessions and "to discover who I really am. I've never had a relationship. I know I could have a sex life now, but I don't feel any sexual attraction to anyone, male or female. I have the stigma of having male on my birth certificate and as I have XY chromosomes, I can't get that changed. I envy someone born with AIS now. People are so much more realistic and open today."

Source: Guardian, 29 August 1996

Activity

Read the article 'A case of mistaken identity'. With reference to that piece and your other reading, answer the following questions.

a Briefly explain what you understand by the term Androgen Insensitivity Syndrome.

b Identify and briefly explain what you understand by 'female behaviour' and 'malevers'.

c Outline and comment on the statement by the doctor that 'You can consider yourself female if you like'.

d Discuss the view that doctors are making people into females and that this shows that gender is constructed rather than being natural.

C3.2, C3.3

The sociology of gender is a space in which to debate the academic distinction between 'sex' and 'gender'. This distinction has been crucial to feminist sociology (and to feminism itself), because it has important implications for the life-choices of men and women. Once women and men were freed from the biologically based assumptions that governed their social behaviour, they could begin to justify any attempts that they made to behave differently. Feminists have made much of this possibility.

If, for example, it is no longer 'natural' that women should take on the bulk of domestic responsibilities, then there are grounds for arguing that household tasks should be shared. If it is no longer 'natural' that women are the 'weaker sex', and it is apparent that they can perform work tasks as well as a man, then by implication they should be paid the same rate for the job. (Until the 1970s employers were legitimately able to pay a woman less for a job, simply because she was female.) Thus, distinguishing between 'sex' and 'gender' in the abstract has an important knock-on effect – that of, challenging existing *power* relationships between women and men.

The construction of femininity

As we have seen, the construction of gender roles and notions of correct masculine and feminine behaviour starts very young in life. It does, however, carry on in many institutions and arenas throughout a persons life.

Sociobiologists argue that these differences reflect underlying biological differences and are therefore justified. However, as we have seen, the sociology of gender has grown up by opposing such biologically based views, even moving to the position that biological notions of sex are themselves social constructions, and therefore we need to concentrate on culture in order to understand the way different roles for men and women are created.

Joan Smith – *Different for Girls*

One contemporary account of this process of the construction of gender roles is provided by Joan Smith (1997). In her book *Different for Girls*, she points to the way that culture makes females 'different' from men, allegedly on the basis of biological differences. But like other feminist writers, Smith does not find this a convincing basis for these distinctions and instead argues that they are culturally and socially constructed.

She argues that the nature of femininity and the way that gender identities are assumed to flow from natural biological differences can be summarized as follows:

1 men and women become 'different' because they are treated differently

2 difference between men and women is believed to be normal yet evidence suggests it is not and that socialization and upbringing are more important basis of these distinctions than nature

3 being defined as a 'woman' is not solely about biology but also involves moral judgements about how you should behave

4 religious values and other theories about male and female 'difference' such as medical theories are used as 'evidence' of the difference between men and women

5 sex or biology is given great importance and as a result all women are seen to be fundamentally different from men, and similar to all other women.

Most sociologists would argue that biological notions of sex are as likely to be social con-

Figure 4.1 Jane Couch, female boxer

Feminism and gender identity

Activity

What model of femininity is portrayed by the women pictured? Discuss what other possible models of femininity there might be.

C3.1b, C3.2, C3.3

Figure 4.3 Margaret Thatcher, British Prime Minister, 1979–90

Figure 4.2 Melinda Messenger, Page Three model and TV presenter

Figure 4.4 Geri Halliwell, former Spice Girl

structions as ideas about gendered behaviour. Therefore, biological notions are just as much the result of gendered thinking as are notions of masculinity and femininity.

Gender and popular culture

Discussion of popular culture, including the products of the mass media such as magazines, music, books, TV programs and films, leads to consideration of the way that men and women are represented in popular culture and the role that this plays in reproducing or transforming gender roles and identities.

Angela McRobbie (1982) argued that magazines aimed at female readers helped define their identities and expectations from childhood onwards. In her study of *Jackie* magazine, she focused on the way the magazine constructed a female world around notions of romance, fashion and pop music and how this pushed the message to young women that their primary task was to get a man and that their primary identity would be based on getting a man. All else was secondary.

In a later study, Ferguson (1985) pointed to the rather restrictive notions of female imagery given in the pages of magazines aimed at women. She argues that they pushed the 'cult of femininity' and concentrated on providing advice on cooking, housework and childcare which were seen as the main roles of women and which clearly defined female identity as centred around housework and childcare.

She argues that while there has been some change in the particular way in which this message is pushed from the 1940s to the 1980s (the period of her study) nonetheless, what is constant is the construction of a notion of femininity around housework and childcare.

In slight contrast to this argument, Winship (1986) argued that in fact there were important differences between magazines such as *Women's Own* and *Cosmopolitan* in the way they constructed notions of femininity. While *Cosmopolitan* offered new possibilities of freedom and identity for women, it also in a sense placed new pressures on them. The creation of the idea of the independent, strong woman created a new model of femininity which did include its own pressures.

Girl power

One recent innovation has been the emergence of the concept of 'girl power', which came to popular attention through the highly successful pop group, the Spice Girls. The fans of this pop group seemed to be mainly girls in the 10–14 age range and it is suggested that the promotion of the notion of girl power provided a positive identity and set of expectations for these girls as they reached for models of femininity.

However, it might be argued that the whole girl power concept, and indeed the Spice Girls themselves, was constructed by male record producers, and that the overt sexuality of the Spice Girls represented the masculinization of femininity. Alternatively, it could represent the end of restrictions on female sexuality.

It is clear that the 1990s saw the emergence of a model of female identity which became known as the 'ladettes'. This encompassed media figures such as Zoe Ball, Sara Cox and Denise Van Outen. Again, a debate arose as to whether this was a positive new identity which young females might adopt or merely a backward step as women aped the worst traits of males.

What is clear is that sexuality has become a much more openly discussed and displayed element of identity leading to discussion of sexuality itself as a basis for identity.

Gay and lesbian identities: queer theory

Until recently there were very few sociological studies of same-sex behaviour and the cultures associated with gay and lesbian relationships. However, since the 1960s western societies have grown more tolerant of same-sex relationships and lesbian and gay activists have publicly campaigned against 'homophobia' – a term coined in 1973 by the American psychiatrist Weinberg, as the dread of being in close quarters with homosexuals (Weinberg, 1973, quoted in Macionis and Plummer, 1997, p. 376). As lesbian and gay relationships have become more visible in society, so also during the last decade more sociological attention has been devoted to gay and lesbian experiences. There is now a considerable range of sociological research and theorising about non-heterosexual cultures and experiences, much of it produced by lesbian and gay writers. In the 1990s, this was often referred to as queer theory.

Early assumptions about sexuality

Until recently, sociological approaches to the topic of sexuality tended to uncritically accept a number of 'common sense' assumptions about heterosexual and homosexual identities. For example, it was often assumed by sociologists and the wider public that sexuality was something that was primarily driven by biological processes, though some writers, following Freud, believed that early experiences in childhood also played a part in determining sexuality. In the past, therefore, sociologists tended to ignore the question of homosexual identity, leaving research in this area to biology or psychology.

Secondly, sociologists and the wider public usually approached the matter of sexual behaviour and sexual identity as if they were the same thing. In other words, if someone engaged in an act of homo-erotic behaviour this meant that they were 'homosexual'. It was assumed that an individuals' sexual behaviour provided the most important key to understanding their 'essential' natures.

Thirdly, in much sociological writing until very recently heterosexuality was equated with 'normality' and by implication all forms of non-heterosexual behaviour were understood to be 'abnormal'.

Finally, sexuality was often seen as something potentially dangerous that had to be controlled and managed by society. Examples of the kind of sociology which made these assumptions can be found in the writing of early functionalists, such as Parsons, Davis and Murdock on the sociology of the family (see Chapter 5).

Discussion point

Should gay and lesbian identity be based on trying to gain equality in a legal and social sense or in creating a space where they can celebrate the fluidity of their sexuality?

C3.1a

Queer theory and the history of sexuality

More recently each of the assumptions above has been challenged by **queer theory**. Jeffrey Weeks (1986), drawing upon his own historical research, demonstrates that sexuality cannot be understood as one, essentially biological, process which takes the same form in every society and at different times in history. He argues that the

Table 4.1 Approaches to gay and lesbian identity

Approaches to gay and lesbian identity	Gay Liberation	Queer Nation
Aim	Equal civil rights with heterosexuals	A space in which to be themselves
Strategy	Stressing similarities Respectability	'In your face' queer identity Heteros need to deal with their problems if they are prejudiced
Examples of groups based on this form of identity	Gay Liberation Front Stonewall	Queer Nation Outrage

concept of sexuality in modern western societies is a 'historical construction' which brings together a number of elements which, in other societies or periods in history, are not necessarily related. These include ideas about gender identity (how women and men 'should' behave), specific forms of sexual behaviour, reproduction, desire, and sexual fantasies. In contemporary western societies, all these elements are joined together in the modern concept of sexuality. But, for example, in ancient Rome there was a preoccupation with *how* people had sex but far less emphasis upon the question of *who* they had sex with and whether this was hetero or homosexual.

Erotic life has always been a topic of enthusiastic conversation, he argues, but the idea that sexual behaviour some how reveals the 'essence' or 'true nature' of individuals is a relatively recent and western approach. Weeks (1986, pp. 32–4) identifies three developments in the history of ideas about sexuality which explain how this has happened in Europe.

Early Christianity

With the collapse of Roman power and the spread of early Christian teaching, the 'sins of the flesh' came to be seen as a constant temptation. The Christian Church began to teach that the primary purpose of sex was reproduction rather than pleasure.

Established Christianity

In the twelfth and thirteenth centuries, with the

authority of the Church firmly established in Europe, more elaborate rules were developed by theologians and clergy to regulate marriage and sexual relations. More detailed distinctions began to be made between legitimate and sinful forms of sexual behaviour.

The rise of secular regulation

In the eighteenth and nineteenth centuries new forms of secular or non-religious regulation emerged. This is when discourses to do with science, medicine, and psychology begin to distinguish the 'normal' from the 'abnormal', and different forms of 'perversion' and 'sexual degeneracy' were listed and classified, using new 'scientific' methods. By the early twentieth century, sexology had emerged as an academic discipline to study sexual behaviour and homosexuality was understood as a '**pathology**'.

Discourses of sexuality and homosexual identities

Following Foucault (1979), Weeks argues that the concept of a homosexual identity is actually a product of these new 'scientific' **discourses**. The term 'homosexual' only came into common use in the 1860s. From the middle of the nineteenth century onwards more and more effort was invested in trying to explain this 'pathological' behaviour. Foucault argues that all languages or discourses reflect power relations. In this case, power was being exerted, through the discourses of science and sexology, to regulate sexual behaviour. But Foucault also insists that as discourses are developed, individuals will try to resist the power which is being exerted over them. Weeks (1986, p. 34) suggests that this is how the modern homosexual identity emerged – through a struggle against the prevailing norms and discourses which prohibited such sexual behaviour. In other words, as individuals were subjected to the pressures and controls associated with the discourses of 'pathology' and 'perversion', they began to see themselves in terms of a 'homosexual identity'.

Lesbian and gay identities: a symbolic interactionist approach.

Symbolic interactionists are interested in the way in which our identities are constructed through social interaction with others. Much of how we see ourselves, they argue, is shaped by how we think others see us. There are two important implications for the study of sexual identity here.

Firstly, what this approach suggests is that identities may not be fixed but may change as we interact with different groups. Secondly, labelling by agencies of social control (see Chapter 10) may be very important in shaping how see ourselves and in shaping our identities.

For nearly four decades, Ken Plummer has used a symbolic interactionist approach to study sexual identities. In his early work (1975, 1984), he too, like Weeks and Foucault, rejects the idea that sexuality is determined by biology or that it is 'fixed in stone'. On the contrary, he argues that our sexualities are much more fluid than might be supposed and can change as our patterns of social interaction change. While he does not dismiss the influence of biology or psychology, he argues that individuals may experience a process of sexual socialization through which they come to see themselves as gay or lesbian as they interact more within homosexual communities. He also notes that all societies impose rules about sexual behaviour – 'who' and 'how' restrictions. Interactionists argue that whenever rules are applied, new forms of deviancy emerge. Plummer argues that this applies to sexual behaviour, too. As labels to do with sexual deviancy are applied, so the 'victims' of labelling come to see themselves more strongly in terms of the label.

Discussion point

Is Ken Plummer correct in suggesting that society is becoming more and more fascinated by other people's sexual stories? If so, why do you think this is?

 C3.1a

In his most recent work, Plummer (1995) has noted that society is increasingly fascinated with other people's sexual stories. In books, magazines, television shows like *Oprah*, and so on, people are invited to explain their 'narratives of the intimate life' which may include everything from the problems of heterosexual love, to the experiences of coming out as 'gay' or 'lesbian'. Plummer argues that the telling of such sexual stories is a process of symbolic interaction involving the story tellers, those who coax or coerce the storyteller (for example, Oprah or journalists undertaking an interview) and those who like to consume these stories. When people tell 'sexual stories' on television this provides others with a vocabulary to begin to understand or

A 'Gay Pride' march

explain their own sexual experiences, including the experience of coming out as gay or lesbian.

Judith Butler: gender trouble and the instability of sexual identities

Judith Butler also rejects the idea that gay or lesbian experiences can be 'explained' in terms of essential qualities or biological differences. However, she is critical of theories which treat the concept of lesbian or gay identity in too simplified a fashion. She argues that all terms or concepts such as 'gay', 'lesbian' or 'heterosexual' bring with them expectations or pressures regulating how individuals should behave.

She argues that many of the images, ideas and discourses generated in society promote a 'compulsory heterosexuality' (1993, p. 313). In other words, there is considerable pressure exerted through the mass media, education, friends and family to conform to heterosexual norms. But in practice most individuals find it impossible to conform to the expectations of the heterosexual norm – women want to escape from the expectations associated with traditional gender roles and men are often uncomfortable playing traditional 'macho roles'. This is why gender 'performances' are always likely to be unstable. A limited number of gender identity labels cannot capture the complexity of the behaviour involved.

However, Butler applies the same analysis to terms like 'lesbian' or 'gay'. These terms can never capture the full range of experiences through which individuals define themselves. In fact, when people speak of themselves in terms of 'gay' or 'lesbian identities', they are really engaging in a kind of identity talk which is, itself, a particular kind of 'performance', rather than a comprehensive description of what they are really like as people.

Activity

a Make a list of the reasons why sociologists do not believe that gay and lesbian identities are mainly shaped by biology.

b Explain in your own words why Judith Butler has reservations about the use of gender identity categories.

C3.2, C3.3

Gender and identity: difference and equality

Feminist social scientists have argued that it is possible for women to be equal to men, without becoming *like* men. These feminists want a share in what they see as men's exclusive privileges. At the same time, they want to retain the way in which women and men are seen to be different from one another, each possessing a distinct set of qualities. Their arguments are summarized here.

Should women become more like men?

Gilligan (1982) has suggested that women and men have different moral viewpoints. She argues that women's moral viewpoints are based on an 'ethic of care' which is produced through their concern with the nurture and moral development of children. Hence women tend to conceive morality as an understanding of relationships and responsibilities towards others. Men, on the other hand, tend to conceive morality in terms of 'fairness' and 'justice', focusing on the construction and maintenance of a system of 'rights' for individuals.

An ethnic of care

Gilligan seems to suggest that an 'ethic of care' or an inclination for peace are somehow 'built in' to women. Her arguments have been taken up, for example, by feminist peace activists or 'eco-feminists', who have used them to support their claims that women are essentially more peaceable than men, say, or more conscious of the relationships between human beings and their natural environments. If attaining 'equality' involves becoming 'like men', contend these feminists, women would be forced to emulate men's war-mongering and environmental destruction. Instead it is better for women to concentrate on preventing war and devastation. Thus 'difference' is emphasized, although it is assumed that 'equality' between men and women can emerge when men disarm and turn away from war, or consider 'green' claims about pollution.

 Discussion point

Do you think that women are naturally more peaceable than men?

C3.1a

Gender identity and motherhood

Kathryn Woodward (1997) argues that one important suggested source of identity for women is the notion of motherhood. This is seen to be stable and rooted in biology and fits in with the notion of women as natural carers. It is also something everyone can respond to since everyone has a mother and everyone has some notion

of the meaning of the concept of motherhood.

However, Woodward points out that it is clear that, in reality, motherhood is not natural at all since today conception can also occur through artificial insemination, surrogate motherhood and lesbian motherhood, none of which involves engaging in what passes for 'natural' conception.

Secondly, Woodward points out that the concept of motherhood involves more than just conception since it also involves the notion of child care. She argues that although it is often assumed that women make natural mothers, this is not the case: there are good mothers as well as bad mothers, largely because the tasks involved are so complex and difficult. If being a mother is so natural, why the variation and why the difficulty?

The myths of motherhood

The ideas that Woodward calls the 'myths of motherhood' serve to identify an expected role for females which justifies them being brought up differently from a very early age. These gendered upbringings remain despite the fact that levels of childbirth are going down and for many women the skills they are taught for motherhood will not be relevant. Woodward argues that one important facet of these ideas is the notion that being a good mother involves sacrifice and giving up your own identity. This leads to the situation where women are defined not by who they are, but by who they look after. This is one key example of the way in which gender identity creates distorted notions of the roles of women and, indeed (by their absence), men.

Gender and other identities

Feminists who argue that the differences between men and women are historically produced have taken issue with claims that women might be 'naturally' more caring or peaceable than men.

Spelman, in her book *Inessential Woman: Problems of Exclusion in Feminist Thought* (1990), has suggested that not only is it incorrect to imbue women and men with 'natural' qualities, when those qualities are assumed but never explained; but furthermore it is impossible to speak of 'gender' – of differences between women and men – without also speaking of other differences such as 'race' and class.

Spelman points out that if the experience of being a woman is different for black women and white women, working-class women and middle-class women, then gender identity itself becomes a problem:

[Do] we have gender identity in common? In one sense, of course, yes: all women are women. But in another sense, no: not if gender is a social construction and females become not simply women, but particular kinds of women.

(Spelman, 1990, p. 113)

The problem of equality

Whilst differences currently produce inequalities they also produce cultural richness and diversity. So even as black people experience racism, they may want to hang on to their sense of themselves as 'black', and construct a positive identity out of it, such as in the phrase 'black is beautiful'. In the same vein many women derive a great deal of satisfaction from performing their traditionally ascribed roles, particularly caring for children, and might suggest that their rich experiences of mothering are not something they feel can be shared beyond the level of giving responsibility for particular tasks to a partner at particular times (see Section 5.7).

Is equality desirable?

While it seems that 'equality' between men and women and between women is desirable, 'difference' currently acts as an apparently insurmountable stumbling block to its attainment. Alternatively, one might argue in this case that the existence of 'difference' undermines the notion of 'equality'. If men and women become equal in the sense that the notion 'equality' describes, then women may lose what is precious to many – a particular sense of their relationships to others. But if they emphasize their differences from men, suggesting that these are in some way 'natural', they fall prey to traditional ideas about women's cultural roles.

'Equal worth'

Pateman (1992), a feminist theorist, has pointed out that it is very difficult for feminists to argue they are different from and yet equal to men. She has called the attempt to think through the argument that women are different from men, and yet the same as men, 'Wollstonecraft's dilemma', after the eighteenth century feminist writer Mary Wollstonecraft who grappled with the same issue.

Equal worth and citizenship

Pateman speaks of 'equal worth', arguing that 'equality' can flexibly accommodate both a predisposition in women towards motherhood, and a desire for equal status that relates only to the potential similarities between women and men, and between women.

She invokes the notion of 'citizenship' – social, political and economic participation – to frame her argument, suggesting that women must be free to make life-choices for themselves. She argues:

*If ... women's citizenship is to be worth the same as men, **patriarchal** social and sexual relations have to be transformed into free relations. This does not mean that all citizens must become (like) men or that all women must be treated in the same way. On the contrary, for citizenship to be of equal worth, the substance of equality must differ according to the diverse circumstances and capacities of citizens, men and women.*

(Pateman, 1992, p. 29)

Men and women, while making a claim to the right of self-determination of each, might thus conceive of themselves as having the potential to be 'differently equal' and 'equally different'.

Studies of men and masculinity

Perhaps unsurprisingly, feminist sociologists and theorists have tended to concentrate their efforts on putting across women's points of view. Thus, until very recently, relatively little attention was paid to the manner in which social constructions of masculinity operated to make men powerful. Of late, however, feminists and male theorists, taking their cue from feminism, have begun to develop perspectives on male attitudes and behaviour. At the same time, male theorists who are 'opposed' to feminist arguments have also made an entrance into the field of study.

- The first group considers that without knowledge about masculinity, studies of gender may tend to construct men as 'gender-neutral' while regarding women as inherently gendered beings.

- The second group – those 'opposed' to feminist arguments – take a different view. This latter group includes men's rights activists, as well as the followers of US men's movement leaders like Robert Bly, who lay emphasis on the supposed spiritual qualities that constitute the basis of masculinity.

The second group consider that feminists are wrong when they call men 'oppressors'. In reality, they say, men are as oppressed as women have claimed to be. For example, it has been traditionally expected that men will work long hours to maintain a family. After separation or divorce, custody of children is usually awarded to women, and men are granted only restricted rights of access. The theoretical basis for the claims of both groups is considered below.

Male theorists working alongside feminisms

Feminists have always understood the necessity for wholesale changes in male behaviour and attitudes and have argued, like Segal, that:

We want to see an end to the self-centredness, arrogance and insensitivity which accustomed privilege and authority bring to so many men when simply functioning within the day-to-day rituals which simply confirm their relative superiority to women. We want, most urgently, an end to the fear of men's violence towards women (and other men) in which their affirmations of a perhaps precarious sense of masculinity become one and the same as their expressions of fear and contempt for 'femininity'.

(Segal, 1989, p. 16)

Some men, broadly in agreement with these views, have subsequently been involved in a rethinking of aspects of male behaviour – taking the position that men must listen to women and take note of their prescriptions for change, as well as proposing their own vision of a reworked masculinity. These men have sometimes been involved with men's groups, akin to feminist consciousness-raising groups. One such group has intermittently produced a men's magazine *Achilles Heel*, which has carried articles on men and parenting, on domestic violence, and on men's use of pornography, for example. (See also Sections 5.7 and 5.9.)

Theorists of masculinity

Hearn (1987) has described men as the oppressors of women and of other men. Questions as to the genesis of male domination of women and other men, and the social and emotional costs of men's dominant behaviours – to men and to women – emerge from a perspective such as this.

Seidler (1989) has argued that, while the traditional, dominant western model of masculinity is often perceived to be 'natural' to men, it has developed only comparatively recently.

Rationality and emotionality

Seidler explains that in western cultures the male mind and masculine ways of thinking are characterized by logic, rationality and objectivity, while masculine identities are strongly linked to the public rather than the private sphere. Men's restricted association with the private sphere means that they may have less of a chance than women to develop emotional skills that would allow them to address the needs of others. At the same time men are discouraged from expressing their emotional needs by a socially constructed dominant masculinity which emphasizes aggression and competition, and are forced to 'prove' their masculinity by competing with other men. This need to prove one's 'manhood' spills over into male sexuality and sexual behaviour.

Masculinity and sexuality

Rutherford (1988, 1997) links 'dominant' conceptions of masculinity to ideas about sexuality. He argues that masculine identity is tied to particular dominant forms of *heterosexuality*. These forms are 'white' constructs. They are also constructed within a patriarchal tradition. But recently, as these dominant forms of heterosexual masculine identity have been challenged by gay men, by women and by black men, individual white heterosexual men have, of necessity, begun to reassess their masculinity.

Those who have done this, and as a consequence have begun to change their behaviour – attempting, for example, to more freely express an emotional side of themselves – have been dubbed 'new men' by the media. But does the 'new man' really exist? Rutherford draws on sociological evidence to suggest that, while some appearances may have changed, men are still taking a great deal less responsibility than women at home, for example.

> **💬 Discussion point**
> Does the 'new man' exist, or is he simply a media construct? Are younger men more likely to be 'new men'?
>
>

Anti-feminist backlash?

Some men have responded with a degree of hostility to the criticisms of conventional masculinity raised by feminists. Taken as a whole their responses might be characterized as an anti-feminist 'backlash'.

US journalist Susan Faludi (1992) has catalogued the evidence for such a backlash in her book of the same name. She writes:

[The] last decade has seen a powerful counter-assault on women's rights, a backlash, an attempt to retract the handful of small and hard-won victories that the feminist movement did manage to win for women.

(Faludi, 1992, p. 12)

Faludi argues that the anti-feminist backlash is occurring on a number of fronts as men attempt to regain the power and status that they perceive themselves to have lost to women. In the USA it is also manifested, for example, in the angry condemnations of women's independence by New Right politicians, or the fire-bombing of women's clinics by anti-abortion protestors.

Faludi on men

In a further attempt to understand why some men resist equality for women, Faludi set out to investigate the lives of men and to conduct interviews. The result is *Stiffed* (1999), a book that considers what has gone wrong for men and how this has led them to react in certain ways.

Faludi argues that since the 1970s the lives of men and women have changed out of all recognition and that, for the men, this has included the redundancy of traditional male skills and growing unemployment. Since paid work has been central to identity and roles, this loss is felt very deeply. They hark back to a golden age for men of the 1940s and 50s when women did not compete for jobs.

This uncertainty has led some men to fear the emergence of the independence of women, but the portrait Faludi paints is hardly of the all-powerful males portrayed in notions of patriarchy. Instead, some of the men seem also to be victims. This offers the possibility of adding to the debate about whether men are the oppressors of women, or whether they can be their potential allies.

 Discussion point

Do all men oppress all women?

C3.1a

The 'seesaw effect'

Kaplan, a feminist theorist, likens women's gains and setbacks to a 'seesaw effect' which allows women to succeed in one or two spheres, but suffer a backlash in other areas. She argues, for example, that in a society where women are well represented in politics, it is less likely that they will be so 'equal' in their personal relationships with men. Alternatively, in a society where women are able to conduct reasonably 'equal' personal relationships with men, their economic status may be lower.

Men maintain their dominant social position as a consequence of the operation of capitalism, rather than because they have all deliberately, as a group, sought to undermine gains made by women. That is not to say, of course, that some men have not actively sought to maintain the system as it stands.

The men's movement

Some men have attempted to imitate what they understand to be feminist 'successes' and have explicitly characterized themselves as part of a men's movement – stating the need to 'reclaim' what it means to be a man. US poet and writer Robert Bly has been seen at the forefront of this initiative.

Masculinity as a spiritual state

In his book *Iron John* (1991), Bly argues that the dominant western model of masculinity is out of touch with 'true' masculinity, a spiritual state connected to the idea of natural male 'instincts'. In order that men can get in touch with their 'real' masculinity – a wild, primitive and deeply hidden part of themselves – Bly and others like him organize workshops and country weekends where men participate in what is essentially group therapy, exploring their emotions through the enactment of rituals.

Clearly, Bly and his supporters believe that masculinity and femininity are to some extent 'natural' and given – although men also naturally have a feminine side, and women a masculine one. But at the same time Bly claims a relationship to the feminist movement, arguing that his position is not anti-feminist, but rather pro-men.

Men's rights?

Bly himself is keen to keep his distance from men's rights activists who contend that feminism

Figure 4.5 Paul Gascoigne, footballer

Figure 4.7 Gary Rhodes, celebrity chef giving advice on cooking

Figure 4.6 Tony Blair, British Prime Minister. 1997–present

Figure 4.8 Cary Grant, Hollywood actor

has 'gone too far', affecting men and devaluing masculinity. These men claim the necessity for 'men's rights' to be addressed in the law and social policy – citing, for example, the Child Support Agency as an institution that constructs them as absent fathers, while family courts are simultaneously restricting their access to the children they are supporting.

Activity

One example of such a men's rights organization is the group Families Need Fathers, based on the Internet at www.fnf.org.uk. Visit their website and see whether you agree with what they say.

IT3.1, C3.2, C3.3

'Campaign for the Feminine Woman'

Discussion point

Do you agree that men are suffering oppression at the hands of traditional social and economic expectations? Are they suffering oppression at the hands of the feminist movement? To what extent are 'men's rights' already enshrined in the law?

C3.1a

Masculinities

Is it correct to characterize men as conforming to one masculine stereotype or another? Or could it be argued that there are many different forms of masculinity? While the behaviour of some men is undoubtedly in keeping with images of dominant masculinity, most men's behaviour is like this only sometimes, while some individual men do not behave 'like men' at all.

Just as some women are more powerful than others, so masculinity too is modified by 'race', class and sexuality, making some men more powerful than others. Is it more appropriate, then, to refer to 'masculinities' rather than the singular 'masculinity'?

Being a man

Weeks (1986), a theorist of gay masculinity and sexuality, has argued that what it means to be a man or a woman in contemporary society is, in fact, always contradictory:

[We] learn early on in our particular society that to be a man is not to be a homosexual. Male homosexuality has been stigmatised through several centuries as effeminate, an inversion of gender, precisely unmanly. Yet we also know that many 'real men' do see themselves as homosexual and that the 1970s saw a general 'machoisation' of the gay world. Here conventional views about what it is to be a man conflict with sexual desires and (probably) sexual activities: yet for many gay men the two are held in tension.

(Weeks, 1986, pp. 58–9)

To argue that there are many ways to 'be a man' suggests that it is more correct to refer to 'masculinities' than 'masculinity'. However 'masculinities', too, act to affirm dominant forms, and to oppress women. Issues of masculinity bring us to a consideration of how gender identities are constructed through culture.

Activity

What model of masculinity is portrayed by the men pictured opposite? Discuss what other possible models of masculinity there might be.

C3.1b, C3.2, C3.3

4.2 National identities

This is a relatively new topic in sociological study. According to Mears (1994), the reason for this is that in the years following the Second World War it was believed that nations had stabilized and that **ethnic enclaves** had either been **assimilated** or accepted for their 'charming' difference. It is now clear that national stability has not developed into a long-term trend and that nationalist desires are being expressed, turning to bitter conflict in several areas of the world. Sociologists have been keen to find explanations.

Nations: imagined communities?

Anderson (1983), from a **neo-Marxist** perspective, argues that we could define a nation as 'an imagined political community – and imagined as both inherently limited and **sovereign**' (p. 6). 'Imagined' is used because people of a nation cannot possibly know each other and therefore cannot know if they think and behave in the same ways – they have to believe or imagine that they do. 'Limited' is used because the nation is seen to have physical boundaries; 'sovereign' because national citizens believe they are free and safe under their leaders and give them authority to lead; and 'community' because comradeship is emphasized over inequalities and divisions.

Anderson links the advent of nationalism to the development of print and literacy. Thereby the ideas of the élite were more easily geographically transferable. The empires of the nineteenth century were also given credit for this phenomenon. Nationalist vocabulary made reference to kinship in order to inspire beliefs of naturalness and the safety of home. 'Collective amnesia' helped the 'nation' to forget aspects not fitting the necessary formula, and particular records were kept to remind people of the parts to be remembered, helping to create the required identity.

The functions of nationalism

Hobsbawn (1990), a **Marxist** historian, also sees nations and nationalism as invented, but believes it more useful to begin looking at nationalism than the physical entity of the nation:

Nationalism comes before nations. Nations do not make states and nationalisms but the other way round.

(Hobsbawn, 1990, p. 10)

He sees nationalist beliefs changing in quantity and quality within any given nation, and reminds us that although people have nationalist beliefs they may also have other beliefs that override them. He also argues that, although states may hold 'official ideologies', we cannot be sure that these are held by its citizens. These are important points which many other sociologists have emphasized.

For Hobsbawn, nationalisms are not new and their effects have been overrated. He illustrates this by looking at recent developments that are claimed, incorrectly in his view, to be caused by nationalism. The break-up of the USSR, he claims, was due rather to *glasnost* (political 'openness') and internal political changes, and the reunification of Germany was due to unforeseen external circumstances. Thus he argues:

... nationalism, however inescapable, is simply no longer the historical force it was in the era between the French Revolution and the end of imperialist colonialism after World War II.

(Hobsbawn, 1990, p. 169)

Where it did arise it was due to uncertainties of modern global phenomena.

Gellner: nationalism as society worship

Gellner (1983) has a more **Durkheimian** view of nationalism, seeing it taking over the role of religion in allowing society to worship itself. (See Section 7.8 for a discussion of Durkheim's views on religion.) Like the previous two theorists, he argued that it had an imagined quality:

The cultures it claims to defend and revive are often its own inventions, or are modified out of all recognition.

(Gellner, 1983, p. 56)

It was found in the modern world because modernity required a homogeneous culture (which, like Durkheim, he thought would be taught in schools). Social and geographical mobility meant that people would need to communicate in a variety of contexts, and culture would be the connecting process. Nationalism, he argues, was not the only process.

Nationalism and globalization

Globalization is the process by which societies, communities and individuals become increasingly *interconnected* around the world (McGrew, 1992). Many social commentators have, for example, pointed to the spread of US culture – 'Americanization' – across the globe through media, advertising and industry.

A future cyberstate: communities beyond nation?

The theorists associated with globalization and nationalism have tended to see the latter as a response to the former.

But what form will this new world order take and what will become of the nation state? Angell (1995) and Mooney (1996) both predict the death of the nation-state, with the 'new city state' and the 'cyberstate' (respectively) taking its place, emphasizing how information technology has taken power away from national governments. Angell argues that:

It will be inevitable that nation-states will fragment: rich areas will dump the poor areas. ... One inevitable consequence of global trade will be the rise of the New City State at the hub of global electronic and transport networks.

(Angell, 1995, p. 4)

Discussion point

a Both Angell and Mooney were writing for the Libertarian Alliance, an organization campaigning for total freedom for the market and the individual, so their ideas might be considered wishful thinking rather than reality. What do you think?

b Films such as *Independence Day*, *Bladerunner*, *Mad Max*, *Escape From New York* and *Escape from LA* have offered views about the future of communities and nations. The sociologists cited in this section have also discussed their points of view. However, we don't have a crystal ball and our opinions are just as valid as those of the film-writers, if not the sociologists. Discuss the following issues.

- What is the future of the nation-state?
- Might it be torn apart by nationalist conflicts or the developing 'cyberstate'?
- Could a new global political order develop? What form might it take?
- If a new global order developed, could the nation-state find a place in it?

- Several of the films mentioned above see society breaking down and relationships being fragmented. What is the future of nations and society?

C3.1a

Perhaps we are already seeing evidence of this transformation in cities such as Los Angeles and London. If nation-states have a role, Angell believes it would be by acting as a 'corporation-state', providing market-based corporations with staff of the necessary expertise, and a stable economic and political environment in which to operate. If they don't they will be left behind and crumble.

Mooney (1996) sees the future in the 'cyberstate', where the world is governed by commerce (rather than politics) via information technology:

On the ground, people will organize themselves into small regional states and control their own local affairs.

(Mooney, 1996, p. 6)

Globalization

Where Hobsbawn simply hinted towards the role of globalization and its resulting uncertainties creating a need for nationalism to provide a sense of safety, many other sociologists have considered this process in greater depth.

Giddens defines globalization as:

... the intensification of world-wide social relations which link distant localities in such a way that distant social happenings are shaped by events occurring many miles away and vice versa.

(Giddens, 1990, p. 64)

This process, as far as he is concerned, has been caused by the world capitalist economy, the nation-state system, the world military orders and industrial development. Robertson (1992) adds to these structural factors by promoting individual actions as a factor contributing to globalization. He argues that global conditions can be seen to destabilize identities. The result is that individuals, perhaps through collective collaboration, re-assert themselves to enforce their 'common humanity'. Such a collective response via anti-globalist or new social movements could be in terms of a nationalist manifesto; however, it could be organized around others' doctrines. Whatever the doctrine, the aim was:

... the 'restoration' of their own social communities to pristine condition with the rest of the world being left as a series of closed communities posing no threat to the 'best community'.

(Robertson, 1992, p. 81)

The political and the cultural

A similar stand is taken by Held (1991), emphasizing the 'political' rather than the 'cultural'. He suggests that citizens of nation states are led to believe that they can participate in choosing their country's future, but globalization has affected the ability of a nation to be autonomous in its decision-making. Likewise, decisions made within a nation-state, such as whether to build a nuclear power station, affect the autonomy of other nation-states. This can result in a desire to recapture political autonomy and nationalism can become a consequence:

Globalization is frequently portrayed as a homogenising force, eroding 'difference' and the capacity of nation-states to act independently. ... Yet ... the age of the nation-state is by no means exhausted. ... The importance of the nation-state and nationalism, territorial independence and the desire to establish or regain or maintain 'sovereignty' does not seem to have diminished.

(Held, 1991, p. 210)

In particular, he notes how non-nuclear powers and peoples have tried to re-assert themselves in the light of the knowledge that nuclear powers will be unlikely to use their full arsenal to stop them.

Post-modern identity

National identities in a '**post-modern**' global age have been the concern of Hall (1992), a post-Marxist. For him the '**post-modern subject**' is constantly open to new influences. Identity therefore has:

... no fixed, essential or permanent identity. Identity becomes a 'moveable feast': formed and transferred continuously in relation to the ways we are represented or addressed in the cultural systems which surround us.

(Hall, 1992, p. 277)

As a result, Hall says the '**post-modern identity**' in terms of individuals or, importantly, collectivities (such as nation-states) can be 'dislocated' or lacking stability and a single point of reference.

This can be negative by disorientating identity, but also positive by challenging individuals or collectivities to re-appraise their identities. The usefulness of the 'post-modern subject' in terms of globalization and nationalism is apparent when considering the weakening of the autonomy of nation-states:

The erosion of the nation-state, national economies and national cultural identities is a very complex and dangerous moment. Entities of power are dangerous when they are ascending and when they are declining ...

(Hall, 1991, p. 25)

This is illustrated by considering the concept of 'Englishness' through the rise and fall of the British Empire. The ascendance of Englishness is seen in the rise of 'The Empire', allowing the English to place themselves in a superior position relative to all other people's – an obviously racist and nationalized condition. This offers them stability and reassurance in their own identity. However, Hall notes the decline in more recent times of the UK as one of the world's leading economies, putting an end to the 'old logics' and discourses of identity. Thus with economic decline the air of superiority is difficult to sustain and an instability in terms of identity is created.

Globalization and national identity

We have considered some of the ways in which our identity may be linked to nationality. However, one key process we have also begun to look at, namely globalization, could be seen as undermining nationality as a potential basis for identity in that much of the food we now eat, the clothes we wear and the goods we buy come from all around the world.

Malcolm Waters (1995) provides the following example of how consumer culture and therefore the identities signalled by what we consume has undergone dramatic shifts:

In the 1930s the German car industry built a Wagen for its own Volk and the Model T and the Austin 7 were similarly conceived of as cars for the people of their respective nations, but now manufacturers build and market 'world cars', the latest from Ford appropriately called 'Mondeo'.

Waters, 1995, p. 141

Activity

Consider the following brands:

Benetton	Castlemaine	Rolex
YSL	XXXX	Luis Vuitton
DKNY	Pizza Hut	Chanel
Nike	Pizza Express	OCR
Reebok	McDonalds	Perrier
Levi	KFC	
Fosters	Birds Eye	

a Identify where these brands come from originally and briefly explain the image they present in terms of identity.

b To what extent are identities now produced by drawing on goods from around the world?

C3.2, C3.3

The link between consumption and identity is made very clear in the following extract from Raymond Williams (1983):

There was this Englishman who worked in the London office of a multinational corporation based in the United States. He drove home one evening in his Japanese car. His wife, who worked in a firm which imported German kitchen equipment, was already at home. Her small Italian car was often quicker through traffic. After a meal which included New Zealand lamb, Californian carrots, Mexican honey, French cheese and Spanish wine, they settled down to watch a programme on their television set, which had been made in Finland. The programme was a retrospective celebration of the war to recapture the Falkland islands. As they watched it they felt warmly patriotic, and very proud to be British.

(Williams, 1983, p. 177)

Activity

a Briefly explain what point you think Williams is making.

b Comment on how representative you think the situation he describes is.

c Draw up a spider diagram indicating the national cultural influences in your life.

d Present your findings to the rest of your group.

e Discuss how important you think national identity is to your own identity.

C3.1a, C3.1b, C3.2, C3.3

While the previous examples might suggest that globalization could be undermining nations as a basis of identity, it could also be argued that the process of globalization and the threat that this implies to traditional national identities will make people cling onto national identities even more fiercely. It is therefore a matter of debate as to how the rise of globalization will impact on national identities. We will consider in greater detail some of the arguments surrounding this development.

4.3 Ethnic identities

Ethnicity refers to the beliefs, customs, religious practices and understanding of belonging which give individuals their senses of identity. Culture and identity are inextricably bound up with ethnicity.

Migration and first-generation experiences

For the first African–Caribbean and southern Asian families coming to settle in the UK in the 1950s and 60s, the experience of **migration** had a powerful impact on their senses of identity and culture. Contrary to some of the myths about the UK which circulated in former colonies, on arrival many immigrants faced open hostility in the response of whites and experienced discrimination in labour markets, housing and education. Several researchers have discussed the impact of these experiences on first-generation immigrants.

Frequently, the response to racism was to find ways in which ethnicity could be re-asserted as a form of protection against the hostility of white society. Cashmore and Troyna (1990) show that the inclination to 'turn inwards', to seek support from within the migrant community was reinforced by employment and housing market patterns which encouraged a concentration of migrants within particular parts of each town.

Amongst West Indians, Cashmore and Troyna point to the growth of **Pentecostalism** and other forms of Christian worship quite separate from the Church of England, as examples of a turning inwards, away from white society. Ken Pryce's famous study (1979, 1986) of the African–Caribbean community in the St Paul's area of Bristol confirms the importance of religion for first-generation migrants. In a similar process of 'turning inward', Cashmore and Troyna suggest (1990, pp. 152–3), first-generation migrants of southern Asian origin set about the task of recreating in the UK the institutions and organizations (temples, mosques, business networks, cinemas, shops, etc.) necessary to re-affirm and reinforce important cultural traditions within new settings.

So for both southern Asian and African–Caribbean families in the 1950s and 60s, the response to racism and harsh economic conditions was a strengthening and re-affirmation of traditional forms of ethnicity and identity, but often in ways which sought to accommodate rather than openly challenge white society.

Political and subcultural responses

Winston James (1993) suggests that the experience of racism actually unified the culture and identity of African–Caribbeans in the UK. In the West Indies, blacks were often divided by differences of culture and tradition between islands and by the hierarchy of colour which was imposed by colonialism (individuals were ranked according to the darkness of their skin, with the lighter coloured enjoying a higher status). However, in the UK, James argues, racism regarded all West Indians, whatever their island of origin or shade of skin, as blacks:

Although island loyalties still remain, the people of the Caribbean have been brought together by London Transport, the National Health Service, and, most of all, by British racism to recognise their common class position and common Caribbean identity.

(James, 1993, p. 240)

Black identity

This experience had the effect of drawing African–Caribbeans together; in the eyes of whites they 'were all the same'. As a response, James argues, a shared oppositional culture began to grow amongst African–Caribbeans living in the UK which organized around the label 'black'. Some younger political activists within the southern Asian communities also argued that the common experience of racism in the UK meant that southern Asians should unite around the label 'black'. Despite obvious differences in

tradition and culture, Asians and African–Caribbeans should develop a common political identity.

Cultural resistance

The 1970s and early 1980s was a period in which evidence of **cultural resistance** by minority communities to racism and the culturally oppressive aspects of white society became much more visible. At its most dramatic, this took the form of rioting and street disorder, but cultural resistance was expressed in other ways, too.

Rastafarianism

Cashmore and Troyna (1990), argue that **Rastafarianism** appealed to young African–Caribbeans because of their experience of racism and discrimination in capitalist labour markets. It represented a way of asserting a black identity and a critique of an oppressive system (referred to as 'Babylon').

Young black street culture

Similarly, Hall *et al.* (1978) linked the spread of young black street culture to the impact of the way in which British capitalism directed young blacks towards low-paid work or the industrial reserve army. Young blacks attempted to resist by adopting a range of street 'survival strategies' and social networks, forming a young black subculture.

Black values and identity

Pryce (1979) describes the same process in Bristol through which black 'teeny bobbers' and 'hustlers' survived discrimination in labour markets and conflicts with the police by developing distinct and separate subcultures, based on the assertion of black values and identity.

Activity

a How did ethnicity help first-generation African–Caribbean and southern Asian migrants to Britain in the 1950s and 60s?

b How did notions of ethnicity change amongst ethnic minorities in the 1970s? Explain why such changes occurred.

C3.2, C3.3

Migration and the concept of diaspora

The myth of the culture clash

It was sometimes supposed that the children of migrant families might face a 'culture clash', being educated in British schools, mixing with white children, learning English and yet experiencing pressure to retain traditional customs within the migrant home and community. Early research exposed this view as an over-simplification. Ballard (1979) was able to show that, even in the 1970s, young southern Asians did not feel they had to choose between two cultures. Rather, they devised a variety of ways to negotiate between the culture of their community and the values of the wider society, producing their own synthesis of Asian and British values.

Diaspora

More recently, sociologists have returned to questions of ethnicity and identity as central research themes. Rather than picturing immigrant cultures as passive and subject to dilution, the new approach recognizes the dynamic processes that can develop when different cultures interact. The term '**diaspora**' is used to refer to this process of cultural dispersal.

Thus, sociologists are now interested in the impact and influence of the southern Asian diaspora, the black diaspora, the Irish and Italian diaspora, and so on. The rising status of black working-class fashion and music within western popular culture now has an enormous influence in many parts of the world. This is partly because black populations have been dispersed to so many different societies, and partly now as a consequence of the global reach of the mass media which highlight particular aspects of black style, music and fashion.

As Paul Gilroy (1993) argues, the spread of such cultural influences through the influence of global media and communication networks actually undercuts nationalist value systems (for example, 'the English way of life'); although he also notes that this can sometimes produce a violent counter-reaction in which some groups strongly reassert nationalist values.

The influence of other diaspora is now highly significant and is reflected, for example, in the popularity of 'world music' or the spread of different styles of cooking.

Activity

There is a wealth of evidence in the actions of English citizens, politicians and the media to re-assert the superiority of 'Englishness'. Make a list of these actions, and explain and evaluate the consequences of their use.

C3.3

White tribes and white English ethnicities

While there have been a number of studies of the identities of ethnic minorities and the various processes and structures that contribute to these identities, we have not often seen as sociologists, an analysis of white people in ethnic terms. There is therefore a paucity of information about white identities.

One reason for the emergence of these as an area of study is concern over the effect of ignoring the construction of white identities, namely that unless they are somehow incorporated into society, they will drift towards extremist racist notions of white identity.

Darcus Howe set out to examine some aspects of white identity in a series of TV programmes broadcast in early 2000 under the title *White Tribe*. The executive producer of the programme explained what they saw as the purpose of the programme in the article quoted on the next page.

Discussion point

a How far do you agree that we are living in a pick-and-mix culture?

b What might a positive, proud, non-racist white identity consist of?

C3.1a

White English ethnicities

Anoop Nayak (1999) studied white ethnicities in the north-east of England, using semi-structured interviews with students aged 10–17 at two multiethnic schools.

He examines the variety of models of whiteness that exist. Nayak argues that the anti-racist policies of the schools can sometimes lead to a reaction by white students feeling that it is unfair. However, another aspect is that white students do not seem to have any cultural heritage to draw upon:

alongside the opinion that anti-racism was 'unfair' to the needs of white youth ran an overwhelming feeling that black students had an identifiable culture that they could draw on which was denied to English whites. Moreover, the positive expression of black ethnicities could be experienced by sceptical white youth as a broader exclusionary device.

(Nayak, 1999, p. 187)

Nayak goes on to argue that there is a clear danger of a potentially racist backlash in this and that there is a need to devise strategies for engaging in white ethnicities and identities in a positive way. One example of this might be considering the diversity of meanings attached to Englishness over time and the ways in which it has changed. Another might be to consider the diversity of white ethnic identities that exist and the way these contribute to multiculturalism. Linking anti-racism to local histories and lived culture is a way to ensure that it is seen to engage with all identities.

Look on the white side

NARINDER MINHAS

Across hours and hours of television output, 'white' and 'English' are words that are rarely heard. It's even rarer to see them together. And yet the white English are the biggest group in Britain, the silent majority. They have become a race that dare not speaks its name. Could it be that in our politically correct culture we're ignoring the ethnic majority and actually not making enough programmes about how white people feel?

I wanted to send Darcus Howe around Britain in search of the White Tribe – a tribe lost and, in some cases, even ashamed to be English. But it took a long time to get the idea off the ground. ...

White Tribe, for me, is a radical format. For centuries the white man has gone to the dark continent to investigate the strange rites and rituals of a black tribe. This time we've reversed that and sent a black man to England to meets its ethnic majority, the whites.

Our real intention was to re-define what multicultural television should be in the new century. There's no reason why multicultural programmes should focus only on people with dark skin and life in the ghettos. ...

In *White Tribe*, Englishness gets the Darcus treatment. He argues that the English are lost, demoralised and even ashamed to admit who they are. He confronts a tribe that prefers vindaloo to fish and chips, chooses coffee rather than tea, but still blames the rest of the world for its slow demise. It's a world in which to be white and proud is contradiction in terms. Even the future king looks like a wigger – a white nigger – with his baseball cap back to front.

One example reveals some of the difficulties of making this type of television. On one occasion we filmed Darcus moving cautiously through the grey, rundown streets of an Oldham housing estate, looking left and then right. He was the only black man for miles. This was a white space, do not disturb. Asian families have tried living here but have not lasted long.

Darcus was visibly shocked by the views of the residents who consider themselves an ethnic minority in a town where they make up 90% of the population. ...

The argument that we might be providing a platform for the far right was taken seriously, but ultimately dismissed.

The reason? Well, I wanted to see whether it was possible for people in places like Oldham to be white and proud but not racist ... but sadly there is a thin line between English nationalism and racism.

People struggle to describe their Englishness in positive terms ... [and] this country has been completely transformed by immigration and globalization. We're no longer so sure who the victims are, what black and white means, and ultimately what it means to be English. We're in a state of flux, living in a pick-and-mix culture. In this new landscape, multicultural no longer needs to be dull and worthy or confined to ghetto subjects. We have to move it in to primetime. We're all multicultural now.

Source: Adapted from *The Guardian*, 10 January 2000

The new ethnicities

Ethnicity and cultural politics

Rattansi (1994) argues that the use of images of ethnicity by advertising agencies and the mass media produces a very important change in our understanding. It becomes obvious that ethnicity is not fixed. On the contrary, we must now understand ethnicity as much more fluid, subject to change and a product of the ability of individuals to synthesize or create new cultural identities from the influences around them, including the mass media and popular culture:

... ethnicities ... are products of a process to be conceptualised as a cultural politics of representation, one in which narratives, images, musical forms and popular culture more generally have a significant role.

(Rattansi, 1994, p. 74)

Rattansi acknowledges a debt to an important and influential essay by Stuart Hall called 'New ethnicities' (1992b). Hall was concerned specifically with black cinema, but his arguments are regarded as possessing a wider significance.

Black film-makers

Hall argues that in the 1970s black film-makers faced two fundamental tasks: first, to open up access to cinema and television for black artists; and secondly, to counter the negative images of blacks in mainstream film and television. In these conditions, the cultural umbrella label 'black' was used to unite artists and cultural producers from a variety of ethnic backgrounds who shared a common interest in opposing racism.

However, Hall senses that in the 1980s important changes occurred. There grew an awareness of the importance of different kinds of ethnicity and the ways in which ethnicity intersects with class, gender and age. It is now acknowledged that it not only makes a difference if you are black or white, but also whether you are, for example, a young male or a young female from a Punjabi family, or a middle-aged middle-class Indian in a professional occupation, or a working-class Bangladeshi from a rural village background. And all these different ethnicities intersect with the idea of Britishness: it is possible to be black and British, or young female southern Asian and British, and so on.

Recent films and television programmes have begun to explore the complexity of ethnicity and the variety of ways in which ethnic identity is constructed. Films like *My Beautiful Launderette*, *The Buddha of Suburbia*, *Bhaji on the Beach*, *East is East* and *Mississippi Masala*, which all achieved mainstream success, reflect these themes. These films strike a chord, particularly with young people, because they discuss the process through which identity is actively constructed through the influence of popular mainstream culture, the continuing importance of minority cultural traditions, and the synthesis of different ethnicities.

Activity

Try to watch all or some of the films mentioned above. Draw up spider diagrams showing the issues about identity which emerge in each film.

C3.2, C3.3

This is reflected in other popular cultural forms, too. The musician Apache Indian, for example, has used a mixture of American rap rhythms and southern Asian Bhangra styles, to sing about themes which relate directly to the experience of young southern Asians living in the UK. He has enjoyed significant mainstream success, including a stint as a BBC Radio 1 disc jockey. Apache Indian provides an example of what Stuart Hall refers to as 'cultural hybridity' – the process through which a variety of cultural influences are synthesized to produce new cultural forms.

Fragmented cultures and spaces

Tony Sewell, writing about black youth culture, identifies a similar process in which hard-and-fast ethnic and cultural divisions are beginning to blur and fragment:

The big shift in African–Caribbean youth culture during the mid-eighties was the break with the big tribes of soul and reggae. The confidence that has come with understanding and taming Britain has generated the freedom to have a whole range of diverse cultural expressions. There is now the courage for fragmented cultures and spaces ... It is now virtually impossible to tell junglists, ragga boys and girls, and those from the hip hop nation, apart in terms of their badges of identity and the clothes they wear.

(Sewell, 1997, p. 159)

Black hairstyles

Sewell takes developments in black hairstyles to illustrate the process of cultural cross-fertilization which is now producing complex or hybrid cultural identities. Afro and dreadlock styles were first adopted by young blacks in the 1970s in order to symbolize their refusal to embrace white expectations in terms of appearance. Afro and dreadlock styles were understood to be more 'natural' and regarded as a re-affirmation of a sense of belonging to Africa and one's roots. However, as Sewell notes, it was not long before both styles were 'depoliticized and incorporated into the mainstream', becoming 'a fashion statement in which Afros and dreadlocks became just another form of artifice' (1997, p. 162).

Modern-day Africans regard such hairstyles – although devised as a way of reminding young blacks of their African roots – as coming from abroad. It was the Jamaican reggae music of Bob Marley which first made dreadlocks fashionable amongst African youth. Now, of course, both young black and young white people may adopt dread hairstyles, in almost every part of the world. Such hairstyles, then, further illustrate the idea of cultural hybridity because they are products of a black diaspora, shaped first by the desire to express political opposition to white authority, but then also reproduced by commercial mainstream fashion, and transported via music and popular culture around the world.

Case Study – Television, ethnicity and identity in Southall

Marie Gillespie (1995) conducted research into the ways in which young Punjabis in Southall, West London, drew on the traditional culture of their community, their sense of Englishness and the influence of popular culture, including television soaps and McDonald's, to construct distinct identities. Gillespie worked as a teacher in a local school and used **ethnographic methods**, supplemented by **quantitative** data gathered through a social survey (see Section 9.5).

Gillespie describes how parents and grandparents in Southall use communication technology to reaffirm a commitment to Punjabi culture and tradition. Such media also help to reinforce Hindi and Punjabi language skills. As Gillespie notes:

Language ... is a potent symbol of collective identity and often the site of fierce loyalties. In the context of a British society which constructs linguistic difference as a problem rather than as a resource, the desire to defend and maintain one's linguistic heritage becomes strong.

(Gillespie, 1995, p. 87)

The pull of traditional culture

On the whole, Gillespie shows, young southern Asians in Southall are still strongly committed to the traditional culture of their communities. However, there is evidence of gradual change and young people are critical of some aspects of the culture and traditions which their parents uphold. *Izzat*, or family honour, is of prime importance to families in Southall, and this can place quite severe restraints on young people. The fear of provoking gossip within the community and endangering the *izzat* of one's family acts as a significant mechanism of social control, and this is sometimes resented by young people who feel that they are under continual surveillance by the community.

The mix with other cultures

At the same time, young Punjabis mix with white and black students at school and college and are attracted to some aspects of young white and African–Caribbean culture. Whilst often retaining a commitment to the idea of the traditional Punjabi marriage, many young Punjabis now form romantic attachments, with boys and girls 'going out' together, sometimes without the approval of their parents. The mix of traditional Punjabi and non-traditional attitudes is reflected in the survey data. These showed that, although 58 per cent of Southall's youth aged between 12 and 18 thought that 'going out with a boy or girl was normal', 67 per cent thought that 'parents should be more understanding about it', and 75 per cent thought that 'people should be free to marry whom they liked', almost half the sample still indicated that they would prefer to marry within their culture (Gillespie, 1995, p. 210–19).

Secrecy can add to the sense of romance but also heightens the risk of gossip. Gillespie shows that young people in Southall use the resources provided by popular culture to open up more space for themselves. While there are no fast-food outlets in Southall, a trip to McDonald's in a neighbouring area provides an opportunity to meet members of the opposite sex, free from community surveillance, and a change from the parentally approved diet of the home.

The popularity of soap operas

Gillespie spent a considerable time exploring the consumption of television with the young people she knew. Television soaps were hugely popular – particularly *Neighbours*, which is a little surprising, given that it concerns mainly white Australian middle-class families living in the suburbs. Gillespie shows that young Punjabis can identify with the programme precisely because it revolves around gossip and family life. Just as *izzat* can place pressures on young people in Southall, so the gossip-mongers in *Neighbours* generate problems for young people in the soap storylines. One Punjabi girl compared an aunt, who reported her flirting with boys to her family, with the notorious Mrs Mangel in *Neighbours*:

... when you think of a soap you think of that woman and that's why you begin to hate that person in the soap, like when they show Mrs Mangel and Madge is having a go at her and then I think of this aunt on my road that I really hate cos she's an old gossip and it makes you feel good and you wish you could have a go at her yourself.

(Gillespie, 1995, p. 152)

Soaps also provide a way of talking about problems. By discussing the plots of soaps with their friends, young Punjabis can indirectly talk through a lot of the problems they have to deal with regarding family and personal relationships.

Convergence of black and southern Asian diaspora

Black and southern Asian diaspora converge in Southall. African–Caribbean music and dress styles enjoy a very high status, particularly amongst Punjabi boys. Black slang, expressions and gestures are sometimes incorporated into young Punjabi street style, though Punjabi parents do not always approve of these developments, and young Punjabis also draw strongly from the styles, traditions and history of their parents.

Activity

a Explain what is meant by the term 'diaspora'.

b Explain what is meant by the term 'ethnicity'.

c What is meant by Hall's phrase 'the new ethnicities'?

d Provide some of your own examples of the influence of black or southern Asian diaspora in Britain.

e In your own words explain how Gillespie's study of young Punjabis in Southall illustrates the way in which ethnicity, gender and age all intersect to produce a sense of cultural identity.

C3.2, C3.3

Critical points

Critics of the literature on cultural diaspora and 'new ethnicities' make a number of points. Mahmood (1996), for example, makes two points:

- It may be a mistake to over-emphasize the novelty of the process of cultural synthesis and the emergence of hybrid cultures. The merging of cultures is as old as the process of migration and military conquest.

- Secondly, there are dangers in becoming so preoccupied with the process through which individuals construct cultural identities, that we forget that cultural change is frequently driven by the exercise of political power, often in ways which are oppressive to minorities.

Similarly, Cathy Lloyd comments that we should not allow a fascination with the growing diversity of culture and identity to distract attention from issues of inequality and power, both within particular societies and between the different regions of the globe (Lloyd, 1993, p. 227).

Activity

Make a list of the various cultural influences which shape your own lifestyle. Think about food, clothing, music, holidays, sport, television and film, and anything else that might be relevant. To what extent does your experience confirm the emergence of 'hybrid identities'?

C3.3

4.4 Class identities

Twenty years ago the American sociologist Herbert Gans argued that, while there were always exceptions, it was possible to relate culture and taste to social class (Gans, 1974). He pointed out, for example, that most people from upper socio-economic groups liked classical music and most people from lower socio-economic groups did not.

Drawing the same kind of distinction between the culture of social classes today is much more problematic:

1 First, the mass media have now made the '**high culture**' of cultural élites much more accessible to a wider audience, so it is no longer an intellectual minority who enjoy opera.

2 Secondly, the relationship between culture and social class appears to vary widely around the world. Samba, for example, is regarded as a music of the young working-class within Brazil while heavy rock is popular amongst the young wealthy and privileged strata of Brazilian society. And yet, in Europe and north America, samba music is regarded as an exotic form of 'world music' popular with educated élites (Lull, 1995, p. 69).

3 Thirdly, and perhaps even more significantly for sociology, the debates over the changing nature of the class structure make the very concept of a 'class culture' problematic.

There are several different ways of defining the differences between social classes in sociology. If sociologists cannot agree about the concept of social class, what do we actually mean by 'working-class culture' or 'middle-class culture'? And yet, in our daily lives we do still recognize cultural signals – in terms of language, fashion, shopping, even television viewing – which tell us about the class of the people we meet.

Working-class culture

Affluence and the working class

In the 1950s it became fashionable to argue that rising living standards were changing the nature of working-class culture. Zweig (1961) argued that a new affluent worker was emerging who was becoming middle class in lifestyle and political attitudes. Certainly, sections of the working class enjoyed access to a range of cultural goods and commodities for the first time, including family cars, washing machines, televisions and holidays abroad.

Richard Hoggart, for example, saw the arrival in the UK of American cultural products – rock and roll, juke boxes, American movies, etc. – as part of the creation of a society in which important traditions of working-class culture were being washed away.

The values of working-class culture

Hoggart himself came from a working-class background. In *The Uses of Literacy* (1958) he devotes the first half of the book to detailing the richness and vitality of pre-war culture in the homes, churches, pubs, and other organizations of working-class communities. Working-class people faced a life of permanent insecurity, never being sure that their jobs would last or their rented housing would be permanent. Accordingly, working-class culture emphasized a certain frivolity – living for the moment rather than planning ahead, and taking fun while the chance was there.

Nevertheless, Hoggart insists, traditional working-class culture also stood for certain values which he strongly approved of: a sense of responsibility for others in the community, tolerance, 'a goodwill-humanism' (1958, p. 142), a commitment to political involvement, and a sense of decency or knowing right from wrong.

In the second half of his book, Hoggart describes the ways in which he feared traditional working-class culture was being eroded by the arrival of mass entertainment designed to appeal to all classes. Radio, for example, made it no longer necessary for working-class people to meet together to sing their own songs. Hoggart felt something important was being lost:

No doubt many of the old barriers of class should be broken down. But at present the older, more narrow but also more genuine class culture is being eroded in favour of mass opinion.

(Hoggart, 1958, p. 285)

Critics of Hoggart pointed to the nostalgic flavour of his account of pre-war working-class culture and his inclination to ignore the tougher and more brutal aspects of living in such communities.

Perhaps a more important criticism is that, while Hoggart stressed the inventiveness of pre-war working-class culture, he fails to recognize that exactly the same process might be at work 20 years later in the reaction of working-class people to commercial culture (Storey, 1993, p. 47). In other words, rather than passively absorbing a 'poorer', 'classless' commercial culture, working-class people might still be adapting and using 'bits' of the commercial culture to create new equally rich forms of working-class culture.

Culturalism and working-class culture

The Centre for Contemporary Cultural Studies (CCCS) is strongly influenced by neo-Marxist **hegemony** theory or 'culturalism'. They have produced accounts of working-class culture which try to point to the ways in which it expresses 'resistance' to the dominant culture within capitalist societies. This contrasts with the rather pessimistic account provided by Richard Hoggart.

Cultural resistance

Writers at the CCCS identify local **subcultures** within what they term a 'parent' working-class culture. Phil Cohen (1972), for example, describes how working-class communities in the East End of London developed patterns of class cultural resistance to forces which threatened them, such as the decline of the local docks and the redevelopment of the East End. Richard Johnson (1979) traces the ways in which working-class adults attempted to organize their own education in the nineteenth century. Paul Willis (1977) conducted an ethnographic study of a group of working-class boys actively engaged in resistance within a Midlands **comprehensive school** (this is discussed in more detail in Section 8.7). Each study stresses the active and varied ways in which the **dominant culture** of **capitalism** can be resisted by working-class people.

Discussion point

Have working-class people lost control of sports such as soccer which were formerly part of 'their' culture?

C3.1a

Popular culture or masculine culture?

A frequent criticism of the work of the CCCS is that it seems preoccupied with masculine culture, so that there is insufficient recognition of the ways in which class intersects with gender and ethnicity to shape distinct cultural patterns.

Bourke (1994) has used a variety of historical sources to demonstrate the importance of *both* class *and* gender in the development of working-class culture. For example, a preoccupation with physique and the body became common amongst working-class men in the 1930s. Increasing numbers joined the League of Health and Strength, formed in 1906 to counter the danger of French and German men becoming fitter than their English counterparts. Bourke suggests that this was in part a response to rising rates of male unemployment which undermined men's 'traditional authority'. Their response was to try to reaffirm their masculinity in other ways.

Working-class women, on the other hand, had a different cultural agenda to address. Cinema and popular fiction in the 1930s had begun to offer to women suggestions of a greater openness and freedom in terms of their sexuality. However, the boundaries of working-class female sexuality were still strongly defined by the fear of unwanted pregnancy, 'lost' reputation and the spectre of the 'amateur prostitute' raised by middle-class commentators. Working-class women in their day-to-day lives had to find a way through this difficult cultural minefield.

Middle-class culture(s)

The idea of 'middle-class culture' is very familiar. The term is used to denote particular tastes in food, books, cinema, leisure activities and even furniture and interior decor. And yet, it is hard to define precisely in sociological terms what is meant by the term.

Surveys of attitudes tend to suggest that there are a number of different groups, all of which could be termed 'middle class'. It may not be possible to speak of a single middle-class culture, but there is a relationship between cultural taste, social class and power which appears still to give an advantage to people from middle-class backgrounds.

Cultural taste and power

Drawing on both Marx and Durkheim, the French sociologist Pierre Bourdieu (1993b) has developed an account of the relationship between cultural taste and power. Bourdieu insists that it is possible to link particular cultural tastes to social class, although he does not believe that class background is the only determinant of these things.

Habitus

According to Bourdieu (1993), in approaching culture, whether it be a work of high art or an edition of topless darts on cable television, individuals operate according to a *habitus* which involves particular responses and particular evaluations of what is offered. The *habitus* is the result of inculcation or socialization since early childhood, which makes second nature or almost instinctive the adoption of particular 'positions' on matters of cultural taste.

Bourdieu argues that a *habitus* will reflect the social conditions in which it is inculcated – and, in particular, social class background will leave a strong impression. Bourdieu argues that it is possible to distinguish between the *habitus* of different social classes.

Cultural capital

Just as there exists an 'economic field' in which the possession of economic capital gives to one class an advantage, so Bourdieu argues there is a cultural field in which the possession of 'cultural capital' allocates an advantage. By 'cultural capital' Bourdieu means the particular cultural skills and knowledge required to 'appreciate' or 'understand' cultural products which enjoy high esteem – in other words, the 'code' that is necessary to decipher a painting or understand the particular significance of a novel.

The cultural field

The cultural field in a society is made up of the institutions and agencies that deal with the discussion and evaluation of culture – the review pages of newspapers, television programmes which discuss culture, museums, galleries, educational institutions, and so on. Just as there is competition in the economic field for resources, so in the cultural field there is competition between social groups for cultural prestige and authority. The *habitus* of those from high socioeconomic or middle-class backgrounds provides them with skills and knowledge – cultural capital – which allows them to compete successfully. They will, for example, possess the vocabulary and knowledge of art history required to engage in a discussion of the latest exhibition or a new 'art house' movie. The *habitus* of the working-class does not automatically pass on such cultural capital.

Just as Bourdieu believes that schools operate 'rituals of humiliation' to legitimate the under-achievement of working-class pupils, so he argues that cultural institutions continue the process in which bourgeois or middle-class culture is awarded status and authority, and the *habitus* of the working-class is defined as lacking cultural worth.

Museums provide a good example. Bourdieu argues that museums may not charge an admission fee, but this is a 'false generosity' (1993b, p. 237) because only those with sufficient cultural capital can enter and derive benefit from this 'free' opportunity. Free entrance to museums may appear to be a democratic policy which offers access to culture and art for all, but given the distribution of cultural capital between social classes, museums in practice operate like schools:

It is not infrequent that the working-class visitors explicitly express the feeling of exclusion which, in any case, is evident in their whole behaviour. Thus, they sometimes see in the absence of any indication which might facilitate the visit – arrows showing the direction to follow, explanatory panels, etc. – the signs of a deliberate intention to exclude the uninitiated.

(Bourdieu, 1993b, p. 298)

Discussion point

Museums and 'heritage centres' have changed quite a lot over recent years. Do you agree with Bourdieu's view of museums, or do you think they are now more accessible to people from a wide range of backgrounds?

C3.1a

Thus, through the way exhibitions are presented – the language used, the knowledge of culture assumed, the layout and atmosphere of the museum – the experience of visiting an art gallery or museum is mystified, so that only those with cultural capital can make sense of it all. Those without are made to feel that it is their own *inadequacy* which makes them incapable of decoding what is going on.

Criticisms of Bourdieu

Bourdieu provides an illuminating analysis of the reasons why 'high art' often remains the exclusive preserve of an educated bourgeois élite, but there are some important criticisms.

- The mass popularization of opera in recent years suggests that the barriers to 'high art' can sometimes be rapidly broken down.

- James Lull points to the development of 'black gold' or 'popular cultural capital' – the rising status of black American working-class culture as it receives growing recognition amongst a wider audience of young people, partly as a consequence of media and advertising imagery (Lull, 1995, p. 81).

- Some theorists, particularly post-modernists, question whether it is in the interests of capitalist and capitalism to restrict access to 'high' art and culture. They point to the way in which commercial energies break down the barriers between 'high' and 'popular' culture in the pursuit of profit: everyone, these days, can buy a Picasso T-shirt.

Activity

a Why was Richard Hoggart pessimistic about the development of post-war working-class culture in Britain?

b Summarize briefly, in your own words, the approach of the Centre for Contemporary Cultural Studies to the study of working-class culture.

c What does Bourdieu mean by the terms '*habitus*' and 'cultural capital'?

C3.2, C3.3

4.5 Social change and identities

Nationalism, globalization and self-identity

By 'globalization', sociologists usually mean the process whereby societies, communities and individuals are increasingly *interconnected* around the world (McGrew, 1992). Social processes in one part of the world impact on those in other parts. The cultural implications of globalization have been of particular interest. (The sociological arguments about globalization and its implications are also explored in Section 4.2.)

Globalization

Globalization is sometimes portrayed as a process in which the individual is helpless; a process through which the multinational cultural

conglomerates come to dominate popular culture across the world in a relentless way.

Critics would argue that this is, indeed, happening. Cultural homogenization (the wiping out of regional and local cultures) will accelerate as the same fast-food outlets, the same cola advertisements, the same fashions, the same satellite television shows, and the same popular music, proliferate around the world. After all, Rupert Murdock, owner of News Corporation, with huge media interests in America, the UK, Europe and Asia, has indicated that his strategy is to find the cultural common denominator that will allow him to market the same cultural commodities through all the parts of the globe in which he has an interest. The common formula, he thinks, is sport plus rock music.

Three scenarios on the effect of globalization

In considering the relationship between national identity and globalization, Stuart Hall (1992b, p. 300) identifies three possible scenarios:

1 *Cultural homogenization.* National identities and culture are eroded by the impact of global cultural industries and multinational media.

2 *Cultural resistance.* National and local cultures may be strengthened if members of nations and local communities consciously resist the impact of cultural globalization. The French state, for example, passed legislation intended to reverse the creeping Americanization of its language and culture. In most parts of the globe there are cultural resistance movements of one kind or another, each struggling to preserve a sense of national, regional or local identity.

3 *The emergence of 'new identities of hybridity'.* Globalization may encourage a circulation of cultural elements and images which allows local communities to create new 'hybrid' identities. Gillespie's study of Punjabi youth in Southall (see the case study in Section 4.3) demonstrates clearly the impact of global influences in the process of constructing a new youth subculture, but they are fused with strong traditional influences as well.

Cultural homogenization, or cultural resistance?

A number of writers favour the cultural homogenization thesis and there is considerable evidence to support their views.

In 1997, Tunstall pointed to the global dominance of American culture. More recently, the experience of Canada has prompted writers to conclude that global communication systems make it very difficult for nation states to protect national cultural identities even when they use state legislation (Perlmutter, 1993; Collins, 1985). Canada has been anxious to limit the impact of US media on Canadian cultural life but it has been unable to prevent a steady movement of audience away from the Canadian national broadcasting system towards US satellite stations which reach across the border, or the dominance of Canadian cinema by US-based multinationals. This is despite the efforts of the Canadian government in encouraging national cultural projects.

In Europe, similar fears are now being expressed about the dominance of multinational media conglomerates and their impact on national cultures, particularly since many European governments have deregulated to allow market forces a greater influence in media markets (Petley and Romano, 1993; Blumler, 1992a).

However, there are some important criticisms of the cultural homogenization model which encourage a more optimistic interpretation, and the idea of cultural resistance. As Robins (1991) points out, even if multinational media conglomerates enjoy an increasing influence, *this may not necessarily lead to the eradication of cultural differences*. He argues that successful global conglomerates will exploit local cultures and identities commercially, rather than try to eradicate them. This is what Sony, the Japanese electronic and media corporation, calls 'global localization'. The Coca Cola Corporation describes itself as 'multi-local', rather than multinational.

Case Study – MTV in Europe

Further evidence to support Robins' thesis is provided by a study of MTV in Europe (Sturmer, 1993). MTV, the television rock music station, was launched in 1981 when it reached 1.5 million households. By 1991 it reached 201 million households in 77 countries, across five conti-

nents. Given the global reach of MTV and the nature of popular music, this example might be regarded as a good illustration of the cultural homogenization thesis.

However, as Sturmer shows, the situation is more complex. The European branch of MTV (MTVE) is based in London but broadcasts to the whole of Europe, including Scandinavia and eastern Europe. It is largely independent of its US parent company; its choice of videos and programming strategy represent a conscious attempt to avoid Americanization. There is a strong emphasis on European music, such as 'Euro pop' and 'indie', while attempts are made through audience request shows to establish a relationship with European audiences.

Sturmer does note, nevertheless, that the uneven distribution of wealth and living standards within Europe means that MTVE's marketing strategy is oriented more towards northern Europe, with less attention given to the local cultures and identities of young people in southern and eastern Europe.

Perhaps the most important evidence concerns the response of audiences. Are they embracing a 'Euro-culture'? The varying degree of success of MTVE suggests that local cultural differences are still very important in determining audience responses. MTVE is hugely popular in Sweden but less successful in Italy. Most interestingly, MTVE's rap programme *Yo!*, which *is* imported from the USA, has enjoyed a very mixed response. While it is one of the more popular shows across Europe as a whole, it is much less successful in the UK and France where there are very strong indigenous rap and jungle music scenes. This may indicate that in certain circumstances local culture can resist global influences. For Sturmer:

The differing reactions to Yo! *in Germany and the UK, or to the channel as a whole in Sweden, Poland or Italy, indicate that as MTVE strives to build its European profile it is at the same time reflecting and helping to create a range of diverse and surprising 'imaginary continents' for and with its young audience.*

(Sturmer, 1993, p. 65)

New identities of hybridity

The third possible scenario identified by Hall is the emergence of 'new identities of hybridity'. Hall points out that globalization through the spread of western cultural influences around the globe is as old as colonialization and certainly not a new phenomenon. What was new was the volume of migration from one society to another in the second half of the twentieth century. By 1990, one in every four Americans came from an African–American, Asian–American or American–Indian background.

In Europe, migration has brought strong cultural influences from, for example, North Africa, Turkey, Senegal, Zaire, the Caribbean, Bangladesh, Pakistan, India, Kenya, Uganda and Sri Lanka. These are the new post-colonial diaspora (dispersions of peoples and cultures). In this way, globalization has made the issue of national identity much more complex: there is now a 'pluralization of national cultures and national identities' (Hall, 1992b, p. 307). The simple existence of *different* cultures within one nation makes the concept of a 'national culture' much more problematic but it also makes the emergence of new cultural identities possible through a process of cross-fertilization.

However, Hall makes it clear that the emergence of new hybrid cultures is not inevitable. First, local communities may respond to the influence of globalization through a fierce reassertion of tradition and fixed ethnicity (he points to the rise of national and religious fundamentalists around the world). Secondly, cultural exchange is never an even or equal process. The cultures of minority communities will also reflect the experience of racism, and the opportunities for creating new subcultural identities will be constrained by the continuing dominance of white mainstream culture in schooling, the mass media, and so on.

Activity

a Stuart Hall identifies three possible consequences of globalization. Identify and explain each one.

b Summarize briefly some of the evidence which points to:
(i) growing cultural homogenization,
(ii) continuing cultural resistance,
(iii) the emergence of cultural hybridity.

C3.2, C3.3

Anthony Giddens: globalization and self-identity

In *Modernity and Self-Identity*, Anthony Giddens stresses the interplay between global structures and self-identity:

The self is not a passive entity, determined by external influences; in forging their self-identities, no matter how local their specific contexts of action, individuals contribute to and directly promote social influences that are global in their consequences and implications.

(Giddens, 1991, p. 2)

Choices and consequences

For Giddens, one of the defining features of living today is that the cultural choices we make always have global consequences. In buying a new pair of trainers, for example, we reinforce an economic relationship between a multi-national sportswear company and low-wage workers thousands of miles away.

Speed, space and identity

At the same time, the structural changes bound up in the process of globalization have important consequences for our self-identities. The speed of modern transport means that time is no longer a powerful determinant of our experience of space or distance – we climb into a jet and travel hundreds of miles in a relatively short period of time.

Distance and experts

Secondly, Giddens refers to 'disembedding mechanisms'. In the past, social relationships were rooted in tangible, concrete settings. For example, in the past factory workers would receive a pay packet at the end of each week which would be physically handed to them by a clerk within the factory office. Now most wages and salaries are paid into bank accounts directly by computer transfer; the social relationship of payment has been removed from the local context. Similarly, we increasingly depend on 'experts' (financial advisors, health experts, therapists, scientists, etc.) for guidance in social life.

What all this means is that we depend on globalized systems, far removed from our own local control. We have no choice other than to trust the 'expert systems' on which we depend.

Activity

Make a list of the global influences and experiences of 'time–space distanciation' in your own life. Think of things like using banks and building societies, going on holiday, shopping, leisure activities, travelling, the food you eat, who your parents work for, etc.

C3.2, C3.3

Globalization and identities

So far we have looked at the ways in which globalized structures intrude on the experience of the individual, but Giddens is at pains to emphasize the interplay between individuals and the global structures. Giddens argues we are more aware of our own identities and more self-conscious about the ways in which identity can be socially constructed: 'The self becomes a **reflexive** project' (p. 32) – a project in which we self-consciously relate personal change to wider social changes. Giddens points to the ways in which individuals rebuild their lives (and their identities) after the traumatic experience of divorce, as an example. The greater **reflexivity** of the self in the modern world is related to the faster pace of change in personal and social life (rising divorce rates, for example) and is assisted by some of the 'expert knowledge' systems which are available. Thus, individuals may employ counselling, therapy, even sociology, to try to make sense of their lives and build their own sense of identity.

Risk society

The risks posed for the individual in personal and social terms should not be under-estimated, but the arrival of late modernity also allows a new freedom to contemplate and explore new forms of self-identity. Modernity 'balances opportunity and potential catastrophe in equal measure' (Giddens, 1991, p. 34).

Wallerstein (1991) also notes the political dimension with regard to globalization and nationalism, arguing that the state is able to define the 'national culture'. However, just as state boundaries in capitalism allow the free movement of capital commodities etc., they also allow free movement of ideas and cultural expression. Thus:

At the very moment that one has been creating national cultures each distinct from the other, these flows have been breaking down the national distinctions.

(Wallerstein, 1991, p. 97)

He goes further in suggesting that, just as there is a dialectical relationship between global and national cultural identities, there can be:

[simultaneously created] homogeneous national cultures and distinctive ethnic groups or 'minorities' within these nation states.

(Wallerstein, 1991, p. 98)

This relates to the movement of peoples in the world economic system and the formation of minority enclaves. Thus we have a situation whereby a multitude of identities is being created and re-created by different camps related to global contexts and consequences.

Class culture in the post-modern world

Some writers use the term postmodern to indicate that many societies have moved through very significant changes in the last thirty years. Some theorists question whether it still makes sense to talk of a unified class culture, either working-class or middle-class, given recent changes in the nature of capitalism.

Claus Offe (1985a) argues that fewer and fewer individuals share a common, unifying experience of full-time work – the experience which used to shape the culture of social classes. The very high rates of unemployment, casualized, part-time and temporary working, mean that wage labour grows less and less important in shaping people's lives. There will be ever-widening differences in culture and lifestyle between social groups, depending on their position in relation to work. Some skilled 'core' workers will continue to develop a culture around full-time work, but many other groups, on the periphery of the labour market, will develop much more varied lifestyles and identities.

Lash and Urry (1987) argue that in the post-modern world there is a progressive weakening of the relationship between social class and culture. This is because the commercial drives of capitalism, the use of globalized media images in advertising and fashion, the emphasis on 'spectacle' in the mass media rather than serious social commentary, all encourage individuals to detach their identities and lifestyles from older social contexts. With so many images and symbols floating around in a 'media saturated' society, there is a decreasing connection between individuals' cultural tastes, fashion choices, or senses of their own identities, and their social class background.

Activity

a Note down a list of points which support the view that class culture continues to be influential.

b Then note down points which support the view that class is no longer the most important determinant of culture and identity.

You will find it helpful to re-read this section as you proceed.

C3.2, C3.3

Gender, postmodernism and feminist post-structuralism

Feminist post-structuralism argues that there is a need to move beyond the notions of identity that are based on pairs of opposites (male/female, black/white, straight/gay). This rejection of binary oppositions comes from the work of Derrida (1977, 1978), who argues that such categories do not allow for the diversity of human identity and existence.

These ideas have been taken up in the work of Donna Haraway (1990) who argues that talking about male also tells you about female since it is the other to male. However, in such binaries one side is always seen as inferior and there is also a suppression of alternative identities.

For Susan Bordo (1990) this argument rests on the proposition that there are no more absolutes any more and therefore gender identities are fluid and diverse. There are therefore many ways of 'doing woman'. Judith Butler (1990) (see Section 4.1) also argues that we should no longer talk in terms of masculinity or femininity as these are now hopelessly plural and diverse as to be meaningless terms.

The obvious key implication of this is that the idea that every woman has something in common with every other woman (which was the key basis of the feminist movement) begins to be undermined by these arguments.

Discussion point

a Is femininity diverse today?

b How many versions of femininity can you identify?

C3.1a

Difference and diversity – towards individualism

One potential end point of talk of identity is to arrive at the proposition that we are all individuals in that we each have a unique set of social relationships contributing to the way we see ourselves.

The extent to which there is still a 'social', an arena which we share in common, is therefore something which can be questioned.

Linda Nicholson (1999) illustrates the way this tension exists in relation to sex and gender. She argues that while most feminists rejected the idea that a woman's (or man's) behaviour was determined by their biology, they nonetheless assumed that all women as a group shared something. She suggests that this statement is made when feminists argue that all women have something in common, since she argues that since their cultural behaviour and their gender identities are different in each society, the only thing they have in common is their biology, and the fact that this is different from men.

The point of her argument is to emphasize that it is not only arguments about class or ethnicity that divide women, as in the arguments about whether the women's movement was dominated by white middle-class women who did not represent black and/or working-class women. As well as these sources of difference, there are differences in gender terms, since there are many ways to be a woman.

This does indeed lead to debates about whether we are witnessing the end of the social or the rise of the multiplicity of social worlds and the fluidity and plasticity of identity, meaning that you can be as many persons in a day as you want to be. These debates are still continuing.

Those who have done this, and as a consequence have begun to change their behaviour, have been dubbed 'new men' by the media. But does this 'new man' really exist?

A survey by Social and Community Planning Research (SCPR), reported in the *Guardian* (20

November 1991), found them very elusive. The researchers argued that men were the main reason why women with children did not have paid employment. Although the number of women citing problems with finding suitable hours and the cost of suitable childcare is higher than those citing the attitude of their husband or partner, the authors nonetheless argue that men's attitudes in general support the notion that the prime responsibility for looking after children should be that of the mother. It is this general attitude to women's role in society, rather than the specific attitude of a man to his wife or partner working, that is seen as heavily influencing the actions of mothers of children under 12. The authors argue that there is a need to make considerable changes to the way that flexibility in the workplace is seen to be introduced to primarily enable women to fit their childcare and domestic work as their primary responsibility and therefore argue for flexible working arrangements and paternity leave. The authors suggest this reflects the continuing belief that work and employment is the man's primary responsibility. Thus the new man is seen as very elusive.

Bernardes (1997) does point out that there have been some changes in attitude recently in that it is now seen as acceptable for men to find work in the caring professions such as teaching and nursing, and it is also the case that Russell (1983) has shown that men can competently care for children:

That men take up paid work and provide at least the major part of family incomes should not be belittled, it is an important and valuable aspect of fatherhood. What has happened, however, is that the primary commitment of men tends to be to continuous paid employment. The primary commitment of women, however, tends to be motherhood and childcare with paid employment coming second. What this does is to ensure that men's interest in employment overrides any commitment they may have to parenting.

(Bernardes, 1997, p. 170)

Bernardes therefore suggests that there will not be substantial change until commitment to the family is put first, over and above commitment to paid employment. This would mean making male occupational carers like those of female occupational carers. While there are changes occurring to the laws and attitudes relating to paternity leave (an issue talked about considerably in the media due to the arrival of a new child in the household of the Prime Minister, Tony Blair

in 2000) the situation is far from being as described by Bernardes.

Rutherford draws on sociological evidence that, while some appearances may have changed, men are still taking a great deal less responsibility than women at home, for example.

Further reading

- Abbott, D. (1998) *Culture and Identity*, London: Hodder & Stoughton.
- Jenkins, R. (1996) *Social Identity*, London: Routledge.
- McRobbie, A. (1994) *Postmodernism and Popular Culture*, London: Routledge.
- Taylor, P. (1994) *Frontiers of Identity: The British and Others*, London: Collins.
- Taylor, P. (1997) *Investigating Culture and Identity*, London: Collins.
- Woodward, K. (ed.) (2000) *Questioning Identity: Gender, Class, Nation*, London: Routledge.

Glossary of useful terms

Assimilation   The idea that ethnic migrants should seek to adopt the norms and values of the society into which they have moved: i.e. that they should 'fit in'.

Capitalism   An economic system based on production for individual profit with goods being bought and sold in a market. Often associated with private property but can also exist with public or state owned property.

Comprehensive school   A school which does not use academic selection as a criteria for pupils' entry: a school which will take in everyone from a particular area.

Cultural resistance   Theory, popular with neo-Marxists, that it is possible to resist capitalism and other oppressive systems through cultural actions, such as making music, films, plays. Can also be applied to the way that certain lifestyles embody a culture of resistance, e.g. skinheads.

Diaspora   A term meaning people who are not geographically resident in an area or nation but who nonetheless have cultural and emotional ties to that area or nation. Its original use was to describe the Jewish population of Europe in the centuries before the recreation of a Jewish nation (Israel). Irish diaspora and African-Caribbean diaspora would be two more examples. Origins are an important part of identity for such groups.

Discourse   A set of ideas that together form a coherent whole. Religion may be considered a discourse, as may science. Different discourses present different ways of seeing and understanding the world.

Dominant culture   Idea used by Marxists to suggest that some ideas are dominant in a society: e.g. the idea of making profit is dominant in a capitalist society.

Durkheimian   In the spirit of the ideas of Emile Durkheim, the nineteenth century classical sociologist.

Ethnic enclave   A term used to describe a geographical area viewed as being separate or isolated from its surroundings due to its containing a high proportion of people of a minority ethnic group.

Ethnographic methods   The study of particular ways of life ('ethnos'). It is a method originally developed by anthropologists studying other societies but is now used widely in sociology. It encompasses methods such as participant observation and unstructured interviews.

Feminism   Feminism is based on the idea that there are fundamental conflicts between men and women, based on male exploitation of women.

Feminist   A person who adheres to the beliefs of feminism.

Functionalism   The belief that society is based on consensus (agreement), as expressed in the values of society and enshrined in its laws, and that everything that exists does so for a reason because it serves a purpose of function: hence functionalism.

Functionalist   A person who adheres to the beliefs of functionalism.

Gender role socialization   The process whereby individuals are taught to behave in ways seen as appropriate to their gender.

Habitus   Concept associated with Bourdieu who uses it to talk about the way certain patterns of thought and behaviour are acquired by people almost by habit. This habitus is one key element in the culture which links individuals and social actions to social structures.

Hegemony   A term used by neo-Marxists to signify the way that some ideas play a dominant role in society. These ideas are said to be hegemonic.

High culture   A term used to describe that type of cultural product seen by some social groups as the highest form of human achievement: e.g. opera, Shakespeare.

Identity   Sum total of who you think you are and also sum total of how other people think of themselves.

Marxism   Marxism is based on the idea that there are fundamental conflicts between classes in society, notably between those who own the means by which things are made and those who have to sell their labour to live.

Marxist   A person who adheres to the beliefs of Marxism.

Marxist theory   The work of, or theories derived from the work of, Karl Marx, who argued that class conflict was the most fundamental element in society, and derived from the exploitation of workers by bosses.

Migration   Moving from one area to another, usually in the context of moving from one nation to another.

Natural scientist   Term used to describe physicists, chemists, biologists: those who use the scientific method to study the natural world. Used in contrast to social scientists, e.g. sociologists, economists, psychologists, who may use the scientific method to study human behaviour.

Neo-Marxist   'Neo-' means 'new', so neo-Marxist describes Marxists who have changed 'classical' Marxist theory so much that it justifies being called a different name. Neo-Marxist theories place much more emphasis on culture and ideology and less emphasis on economics than classical Marxists.

New Right   Used to distinguish the views of right-wing political parties in recent times from earlier conservative views: notably the views of the British Conservative Party from the premiership of Margaret Thatcher onwards and the US Republican Party from the presidency of Ronald Reagan onwards. The most notable difference is the New Right's emphasis on the benefits of the free market and individual freedom.

Pathology   Study of disease.

Patriarchal process   Process that reinforces patriarchy.

Patriarchy   Originally meaning 'the rule of the father', it is now a term used by feminists to describe the situation where males have power over females.

Pentecostalism   Christian religious movement in which speaking in tongues, divine healing and ecstatic experience of the Holy Spirit of God are central. This movement has become popular amongst African-Caribbeans, where it stresses the need to integrate African elements into Christianity.

Post-Marxist   The term means literally after Marxism and this means a sociologist who holds that belief. It has emerged largely since the fall of the Soviet Union and the eastern Europe self-styled socialist states in 1990.

Post-modern   Post-modern literally means after modern or following the death of the modern. In sociological terms the modern means trying to arrive at a scientific objective understanding through research and developing theories. Post-modernists argue that these are just big stories or meta-narratives and that none of them is any more true than any other. Therefore instead of trying to search for the truth you should choose those theories that appeal on other grounds.

Post-modern condition   A term used to describe the way that living in post-modern times leads to a lack of certainty and thus uncertainty which can also be seen as giving choice to individuals to decide how to live their lives since there are no longer any complete notions of right and wrong.

Post-modern identity   The idea that in post-modern times we can draw upon multiple sources for our sense of social identity or we can construct a multiplicity of identities for ourselves.

Qualitative data   Data in the form of words.

Quantitative data   Data in the form of numbers or statistics.

Queer theory   Set of ideas adopted by some in the gay and lesbian movement to try to make the term 'queer' a positive term rather than a term of abuse.

Rastafarianism   Religion based on ideas of a return to Africa. Emerged in the Caribbean as black descendants of slaves who sought a way to understand their situation and racial oppression through religion. A famous Rastafarian was Bob Marley whose reggae music brought the ideas to a wider audience.

Reflexivity   The idea that we monitor and think about our own behaviour and modify it according to our reflections. Knowledge does not therefore exist outside or separate to the person who holds that knowledge.

Socialization   The process of learning appropriate roles and behaviour.

Social networks   The links between individuals, which together create a network of links that are a key part of social interaction with others.

Sociobiologists   A group of thinkers who believe that the behaviour of all social animals, including humans, can ultimately be explained on the basis of biological processes.

Sovereign   The institution or person that has supreme power, usually in the context of a nation.

Subculture   A social group in society which does not completely conform to the norms and values of the society as a whole but has its own set of values and norms. Associated with specific groups in society such as youth, who may hold very different norms and values while not totally rejecting the society they live in.

Culture and socialization
Family

Chapter outline

5.1 Family concepts and definitions

The family is often considered by non-sociologists to be one of the few 'natural' institutions in society. People often express concern about its 'health', regarding healthy families as good for society and being fairly sure that they know what a 'healthy family' is. It is considered 'ideal' that the family should consist of two parents of different sexes and one or more children – preferably their own.

This model of the ideal family is shared by some sociologists. However, other sociologists tend to see this model of the ideal family as the 'cereal packet' family – a dream promoted by advertisers to sell other products or an ideal designed to produce a stable concept of society which ignores the variety of family life both throughout the world and within our own society. At the heart of this debate are very differing definitions of some key terms such as 'family' and 'household'. We will therefore start by examining this debate and considering some of the implications that flow out of it.

Defining some basic terms

There are a number of key basic terms used in the study of the sociology of the family. Firstly it is important to distinguish between the term 'family' and the term 'household'.

'Family'

Whilst there are debates about the precise definition of the word 'family,' as a starting point we can say that the term 'family' refers to a unit consisting of people who are related to each other; they can be related either biologically by blood ties or legally (for example by marriage).

Such a commonsense definition would allow us to distinguish family relations from more general social relations – for example, friendship – while not really saying anything as yet about the *quality* of those relationships between people who form the family unit. Fulcher and Scott (1999) argue that families have two things in common:

[1] *The closeness of family relationships. There is a sense that relationships are closer within a family than with people outside it. There is a boundary around a family, a sense of family identity that separates it off from other people.*

[2] *A sense of obligation and responsibility. Members of a family give higher priority to each other's needs than those of other people. Family responsibilities are not fixed and are continuously negotiated by family members, but there is, none the less, something distinctive about them which makes family commitments different from say, those to friends.*

(Fulcher and Scott, 1999, p. 355)

Activity

Which of the examples below would you consider to be families and which not? Give reasons for each answer. Suggest other forms of living arrangements that might be defined as a family.

a man and woman married for ten years without children

b man and woman married for six years, both children at boarding school

c man and woman cohabiting (living together) for three months with his daughter aged four

d 16-year-old girl living with her mother and her mother's boyfriend

e man and woman, married and living with their four children, under age 10

f woman cohabiting with her male partner and three young children from his marriage

g woman cohabiting with her female partner and three young children from her marriage

h two men cohabiting with an adopted son

i man and woman cohabiting with an adopted son

j man living with his two children, his wife died last year

k man and woman with a child, but living separately due to work

C3.2

'Household'

A household consists of people living at the same address and sharing meals and/or living accommodation. A household is therefore a unit of accommodation which might contain a number of different social arrangements – some of which might be considered to be families while others might not.

Families do live in households (for at least part of their lives) but there are other examples of households. For example, an increasing number of households consist of single people and it is certainly debatable whether these households contain a family. Another example might be students or young people who are unrelated but sharing a flat. It is therefore the case that, as Lawson and Garrod (1996, p. 124) point out: 'most families live in households, but not all households are families'.

Discussion point

Is someone living on their own part of a family?

C3.1a

'Kinship'

The social notion of a family is based on the idea that our relationships with, and obligations towards, people we identify as *part of our family* will in some way be different from (and often, by implication, closer than) other relationships such as friendships. Sociologists use the term 'kinship' to refer to how relationships by blood or marriage contain and create *expectations* and lay down certain notions of *how we should behave* to people in the family.

'Kinship' also refers to the way we construct notions of relationships within families through ideas such as *family trees*, which again might contain expectations and responsibilities – for instance about who might inherit family property or take over family businesses or social responsibilities.

Debates about definitions of the family

The definitions above are purposely simplistic, to provide a basic starting point. *However, one of the very first lessons one needs to learn in sociology is that the meanings of virtually all key terms are contested in sociological debate.* Thus all debates about the family at some point hit upon the whole question of exactly what we mean by 'family'.

We will therefore now look at some of the issues in the debate about this term. Differing definitions are related to different theoretical positions in sociology. For example, we can con-

sider the following two contrasting definitions, one provided by the **functionalist** *sociologist* George Peter Murdock, and one provided by the **neo-Weberian** *sociologist* Anthony Giddens.

Murdock (1949) defined the family in the following way:

The family is a social group characterized by common residence, economic co-operation and reproduction. It includes adults of both sexes, at least two of whom maintain a socially approved sexual relationship, and one or more children, own or adopted, of the sexually cohabiting adults.

(Quoted in Haralambos and Holborn, 2000, p. 504)

However, a more inclusive view is taken by Giddens, who suggests this definition:

A family is a group of persons directly linked by kin connections, the adult members of which assume responsibility for caring for children.

(Giddens, 1993a, p. 370)

We can begin to see that accepting either of these two definitions will have a great influence on the extent to which we consider people to be living in families today.

Activity

Think about the two definitions of the family provided above. Consider whether those authors would consider the following arrangements as constituting a family:

a married couple with their own biological children

b cohabiting couple with adopted children

c cohabiting couple with no children

d lone-parent family with three children

e a cohabiting gay couple living with the biological children of one of the adults.

Look up the latest statistics you can find on the composition of households in the UK. You could try looking at www.ons.org.uk. This should contain a section on statistics on families and households. Alternatively you could look at the latest copy of *Social Trends* you can find.

Work out the proportion of households that contain families *in relation to each of the two definitions of the family given above.*

C3.2, C3.3, IT3.1

Debating the structure and function of the family

Sociologists do not debate definitions of the family merely to nit-pick. They do so because this is the starting-point of further debates about what makes up a family, the nature of relationships within it, the role or function of the family, and sometimes even notions of what an 'ideal family' might look like. We will therefore now move on to consider some of these debates in more detail, focusing particularly on functionalist, **Marxist** and **feminist** views. As you will see these offer contrasting insights.

Functionalist views on the family

Classical functionalists see traditional family structures as necessary for the maintenance of society – and the transmission of any social group's culture to the next generation. Functionalists believe that a family which is made up of a caring mother, and a father who provides economically for his wife and children, is the most sensible and stable way for people to live in society. Therefore this type of family is both:

- universal (found everywhere), and
- functional (effective).

The family as a universal institution

Much of the evidence of a universal family structure comes from the work of Murdock (1949). As a functionalist, he sought to show that some form of family structure was the basis of all societies – that is that the family was universal.

He argued that the family performs three key functions, and society would disappear if they were not served:

- it stabilizes sexual behaviour and reproduction
- it provides basic economic requirements such as food and shelter
- it serves the function of **socialization** of the next generation into the norms, values and other aspects of culture in that society.

Discussion point

Is the family needed everywhere?

C3.1a

The functions of the family

Most sociologists who support a traditional family structure (such as that outlined by Murdock) argue that the family is universal because it serves particular functions for society and for all its members. Not all functionalists agree totally on which functions are essential. Parsons (1959) argued that in modern societies there are only two 'basic and irreducible' functions:

- **primary socialization** of children.
- stabilization of the adult personality

Primary socialization of children

Once a couple have children they have to be taught how to behave. They need to learn how to socialize. The first (primary) stage of this process of socialization occurs largely within the family.

Stabilization of the adult personality

The key here is the way that marriage and family life provides emotional security for couples and helps them deal with stresses in other areas of their life.

Murdock and Parsons agree that a family structure is essential for the maintenance of society, and that this will always be the case. The family is universal because its functions cannot be performed by any other institution.

The basic functions of reproduction, satisfying sexuality and the rearing and caring of children are necessary to ensure society's survival. The most efficient way of achieving these ends is the nuclear family.

(Muncie et al., 1995, pp. 11–12)

By examining families from a number of different societies – O'Connell (1994) suggests that the family can only be defined by its functions. She claims that:

While there is no universally applicable definition of the family, there is a broad consensus about the role of the family in society and the functions it should perform, namely, procreation, socialization, providing affection and emotional support. In particular the family has a central role in the education, socialization and care of children.

(O'Connell, 1994, p. 1)

Activity

a Identify and explain two functions undertaken by the family.

b Outline and discuss the view that the family performs a positive role in society.

C3.2, C3.3

Critical views on the family

Whilst functionalists argue that the family is functional for society as a whole – and indeed provides a happy and stable environment for all its members – other more critical views on the family do exist. While agreeing that the family fulfils certain functions in society, and plays a role in its maintenance, other sociologists argue that contemporary society is *not* harmonious but is ridden with conflicts. In this view, the family both contributes to the reproduction and maintenance of society and is itself an institution ridden with conflicts and negative effects on some or all of its members. This approach is best seen in Marxist and feminist accounts of the family.

Marxist views on the family

In a book first published in 1884, **Marx's** colleague Frederick **Engels** (1972; orig. pub. 1884) demonstrated how the family arose in response to the development of private property and the need for men to pass on their property to their own offspring. *Thus he saw the main function of the family as the reproduction of the capitalist system.*

Beechey (1977) argued that housewives perform major functions for capitalism; (a) by providing free care for current and future (male) workers, and (b) as a cheap '**reserve army of labour**', easily returned to the home in times of recession.

Marxist–feminist views on the family

From a **Marxist–feminist** perspective, Barrett and McIntosh (1991) suggest that the nuclear family is an *ideological instrument*. This means that the 'typical' nuclear family of two parents and their children is presented as an ideal for all of us to aspire to. This makes the concept of the family 'anti-social', as it implies that other forms of family life are inferior.

Thus, single or homosexual and lesbian par-ents can be presented as deficient, while unmarried people are often to be pitied. Barrett and McIntosh believe that this ideological view of the family allows the state to stereotype and scapegoat alternative family structures.

Other feminist views on the family

Radical feminists suggest that *patriarchal ideology* (the concept of male domination, which comes from the superior role of the men in the family) leads to the tyrannization of women and children, both within the family and within the wider society. Rape and sexual assault are seen as evidence of male power, and the family is the key site of its maintenance.

Liberal feminists blame neither men nor capitalism for the unequal treatment of women and children in the family. They have argued for legal changes in order to ensure *equality of opportunity*. The most important pieces of legislation relating to equal opportunities for women are the Equal Pay Act 1970 and the Sex Discrimination Act 1975, although they mostly affect women in the public arena rather than in the home. Of more consequence for women in the family have been the legal changes that outlaw rape within marriage and a greater awareness of the nature of domestic violence.

Activity

a Identify and explain two legal changes which have attempted to ensure women and children are treated as equal to men.

b Outline and discuss the view that the family is anti-social.

C3.2, C3.3

Defining the family – feminist views

As Leonard and Hood-Williams (1988) point out, a lot of the problems involved in this debate relate to how the family is defined. To define it as just a mother and her offspring is clearly too inclusive; but as soon as we try to incorporate the idea of two adults, then the definition does not allow for diversity between social groups or even within them.

However, there is a political dimension to the debate which is probably unavoidable in such an emotive issue. The promotion of the ideal family does have important implications, suggesting the inferiority of other family types. There is a further important question to be asked here – who does the defining?

The ideology of the family

Diana Gittins (1993) argues that the ideology of the universal nuclear family is more important than the reality, as this ideology has major consequences for our view of society. She demonstrates how a number of aspects that we tend to take for granted as 'natural' are in fact very different in different social conditions and are therefore *socially constructed*.

For example, the view of marriage as a binding contract between one male and one female is challenged by the existence of **polygamy** (several spouses) in many societies, and by the popularity of **serial monogamy** (marriage, divorce and remarriage) in western societies today. The idea that marriage has always been (and is) based on love and mutual attraction was not only uncommon in many societies, but is not always true in our own.

However, Gittins concludes that *some sort of definition of the family is important if we are to debate issues within it*. She believes that relationships between people can be extremely varied, but that the ideological view of the 'good' family is based on long-term heterosexual relationships which always incorporate childbearing. Although this may be an ideal *in our society*, it does not make it either universal or natural.

It appears that the ideology of the family is becoming stronger than ever as different forms of family life appear to be on the increase. Despite larger numbers of people choosing to cohabit or live alone, the ideal of the family is promoted ever more strongly.

 Discussion point

What are the advantages and disadvantages of living alone?

C3.1a

Like Gittins, Barrett and McIntosh (1991) do acknowledge the popularity of 'familialism' (the promotion of family life), and admit that most alternatives are often perceived as unsatisfactory. They propose three ways in which *familialist ideology* could be undermined so that people

would be free to choose their lifestyles more freely:

- encouraging variety – e.g. communes, single households, same-sex pairings
- avoiding oppressive relationships – giving support to those who find family life oppressive and may wish to escape from it
- avoiding domesticity – basic domestic chores to be carried out equally by all members of the household, so that the living arrangements of each person serve their own needs rather than those of society. (See also Section 3.6.)

 **Discussion point**

How do you think these aims might be achieved within your own or your ideal family arrangement?

C3.1a

Family – household or family plurality?

Households

As we have seen, there is no agreement about how the term 'family' should be defined. While some sociologists may continue to try to convince others of the rightness of their particular definition, others are now arguing that perhaps the term 'family' is no longer really appropriate for describing the way we live our lives. It may be more accurate to incorporate more inclusive terms such as 'households' or 'household units', as suggested by Nik Jorgensen (1995).

Family plurality

Alternatively, we may wish to follow Diana Gittins (1993) in arguing that there are so many different types of family that to try to use one overarching definition does not reflect reality, merely the ideological biases of whoever is doing the defining. She argues instead that we should talk of '**family plurality**', the way in which different structures exist giving a choice of ways of living.

Everyday notions and choice

This notion of choice is also emphasized by interactionist-inspired writers such as David Morgan (1996). He argues that we need to take note of how people use the term in their day-to-day living. Such an approach would not try to reach one overall definition of the family, but instead catalogue and understand how ordinary people understand the term.

Family practices

David Cheal (1993) also argues that we need to understand the way in which the family is constructed through the social practices of individuals.

Instead of having a fixed notion of the family, such an approach emphasizes the *diversity* of family structures, as well as the *fluidity* of any particular structure.

Despite these problems of definition, for the purposes of this textbook we shall continue to use the term 'family', as it remains such an important social institution and basis for social practices, even if its exact nature is increasingly varied, flexible and diverse. As will be seen in later sections, often moral pronouncements are made which blame many of our social ills on the 'decline of family life'. Debates about the family (or family structure) are thus hugely important.

Alternative family structures

To underline the problems that exist with definitions, we must also consider the fact that sociologists have claimed to find 'families' in all societies.

If we accept that the meaning of the term 'family' can and does vary between societies and at different times, we need to provide some terms to distinguish these different types of structures – all of which are encompassed within the term 'family'. The following are the most commonly used expressions:

- *The nuclear family.* This is used to cover family arrangements consisting of an adult male and an adult female living with their biological offspring or adopted children. It is often thought of as the basic family unit in contemporary times, particularly by functionalist sociologists.
- *The extended family.* The meaning of this term in contemporary times can vary. Firstly it can be used to describe wider family relations, including grandparents, aunties, uncles and cousins. Secondly it can be used to describe situations where a household consists of family members but extends beyond the nuclear family. In this case, with common residence involved, we might more properly refer to it as an extended family household.

- *Monogamy.* When considering sexual relationships, sociologists distinguish between arrangements that limit a person to one sexual partner at a time and those that do not. Monogamy is the name given to the former. Here we must also distinguish between the original meaning of monogamy – as in 'marriage for life' –and the more recent emergence of 'serial monogamy', whereby someone has one sexual partner at a time but has more than one partner in their lifetime.
- *Polygamy.* This describes structures where family arrangements permit and/or encourage people to have more than one sexual partner at any one time. Murdock (1949) found that this type of arrangement was operative in about 80 per cent of the societies he studied. Within this arrangement we can distinguish between *polygyny*, whereby men are allowed to have more than one wife, and the more uncommon but still existent *polyandry*, whereby women are allowed to have more than one husband.
- *Patrilineal.* This describes societies in which family lines, and often notions of inheritance, pass down the male line.
- *Matrilineal.* This describes societies in which family lines, and often notions of inheritance, pass down the female line.

Activity

Draw up your own 'family tree'. Decide who to include and who to leave out. Think about the criteria you use to define who is a member of your family and who is not. What sort of family do you come from (nuclear/extended/ reconstituted etc.)? Compare your family tree with other people you know, to identify similarities and differences.

Comparative examples of alternative family structures

A few examples of familial structures from various places and times will provide comparative evidence of the diversity of family structures, helping us to avoid seeing any one model of the family as universal, ideal or normal.

The Nayar

Gough (1972) studied the Nayar tribe in Southern India to show a picture of their family life. Girls were married before puberty, but men did not live with their wives. Either party could end the marriage or relationship at any time. Women shared the care of children, and the paternity of the child was not relevant. In a matrilineal society like the Nayar, what little property there was descended through the female line. Males also made little economic contribution to their children's upbringing, and this role was played mainly by brothers and sisters who tended to form an economic unit along with their children.

Activity

On the basis of the definitions of the family used by Murdock and by Giddens, did a family exist among the Nayar? (The definitions are on page 87 in this section.)

C3.2

Haralambos and Holborn (2000) provide the following description of some of the practices surrounding family life among the Nayar which may seem unusual to anyone used to family life as defined by contemporary UK norms – particularly those which stress an ideal conventional family. However, it is important to remember that for the Nayar this is normal and no doubt our way(s) of doing things would seem strange to them:

Before puberty all Nayar girls were ritually married to a suitable Nayar man in the tali-rite. After the ritual marriage had taken place, however, the tali-husband did not live with his wife, and was under no obligation to have any contact with her whatsoever. The wife owed only one duty to her tali-husband: she had to attend his funeral to mourn his death.

Once a Nayar girl reached or neared puberty she began to take a number of visiting husbands, or 'sandbanham' husbands. The Nayar men were usually professional warriors who spent long periods of time away from their villages acting as mercenaries. During their time in the village they were allowed to visit any number of Nayar women who had undergone the tali-rite and who were members of the same or lower caste as themselves. With the agreement of the woman involved, the sandbanham husband arrived at the home of one of his wives after supper, had sexual intercourse with her, and left before breakfast the next day. During his stay he

placed his weapons outside the building to show other sandbanham husbands he was there. If they arrived too late then they were free to sleep on the veranda, but could not stay the night with their wife. Men could have unlimited numbers of sandbanham wives, though women seem to have been limited to no more than 12 visiting husbands.

(Haralambos and Holborn, 2000, p. 504)

Discussion point

To what extent would you like to see a family structure such as that of the Nayar become part of contemporary UK family life?

C3.1a

The Oneida community

Founded in 1848 by a Christian preacher, John Humphrey Noyes, the aim of this community was to establish complete spiritual, economic and sexual equality. They set up a system of economic cooperation and group marriage in which everyone contributed equally to the group. As well as the system of group marriage, the community introduced a programme of **eugenic breeding**, whereby only those considered suitable were allowed to reproduce, while other, controlled forms of sexual activity were allowed among other members where both parties agreed. After early care by the mother, children were raised communally and treated equally by community members.

The Kibbutz

In Israel in the 1940s, collective settlements were set up based on a system of collective ownership and childrearing. While marriage was monogamous (one spouse), children lived in collective dormitories and were raised by a number of child caretakers or educators. Children would spend an hour or so daily with their parents, but their sibling group was effectively made up of all the children of a similar age. Parents and children did not comprise an economic unit as all worked for the good of the kibbutz and needs were provided for collectively.

Spiro (1968) argued that this system of childrearing cannot fit into Murdock's definition of the family, although the Kibbutz could be seen as a form of extended family. Communes established in the 1960s also adopted a similar form of collective childrearing, although they generally tended to be short-lived.

The 'new world' black family

In many parts of the Caribbean and among black families in the United States, families – based on mother, children and grandmother – make up a larger than average percentage of the population. Herskovits (1958) suggested that this reflected traditional family structures in West Africa, from which many black African–Americans and African–Caribbeans had originated before being captured and enslaved.

It has also been suggested that mother and child formed the basic family unit under slavery, as the father was often sold separately, perhaps to allow sexual access for white slaveowners to black female slaves.

Other writers such as Liebow (1967) argued that most black men were so poorly paid that they were unable to maintain a family, so it made economic sense for the woman to receive sexual favours and economic contributions from a number of different fathers.

Other alternative family structures

Taylor *et al.* (1995, p. 234) provide the following examples of family life in other societies:

- The Lakker of Burma do not see children as having any blood relationship to their mother.

- In Tahiti, young women who do not consider themselves ready to settle down often give their children to their own parents or other kin members to look after.

- The Ashanti in West Africa trace their family lines through the female line (a matrilineal society), and the father has no legal authority over the children. As a result couples often live apart, and only a third of married women actually live with their husbands.

Activity

a Identify and explain two family models which could be seen as alternatives to the traditional nuclear family.

b Outline and discuss the view that no one model of the family is universal.

C3.2, C3.3

The family and industrialization

Many sociologists have argued that the coming of the industrial revolution brought about huge changes in society, including changes to the structure of family and kinship networks.

Families before the industrial revolution tended to be involved mostly in subsistence production, selling some of their surplus (if any) in the marketplace. All members of the family were involved in the production process and they usually lived near each other. There were some relatively wealthy families who owned larger amounts of land. Often there was a system of rights and obligations between landowner and the peasants who worked on his land. Land was, for most people, the only form of wealth, and production was mostly for personal consumption. The family was the main *unit of production*.

Although the process of industrialization varied in terms of class, region and throughout different periods of time, the industrial revolution brought important changes to the way families were structured and how their members related to each other.

Functionalist views of families and industrialization

Pre-industrial societies

Functionalists stress the relationships between institutions in society and how changes in one aspect of society – for example, the economy – will bring changes in other institutions, including the family. They therefore see the family as changing and responding to the needs of society, before, during and after industrialization. Functionalists argue that the nuclear family developed mainly as a *result* of industrialization.

Industrialization

Fletcher (1966) argued that the long hours of work required by early industrialists meant that family members rarely saw each other, apart from a few hours for eating and sleeping. Low wages and poverty ensured that the home was often poorly furnished and uncomfortable. Arguably this led to high levels of deprivation and all forms of vice, including drunkenness and incest.

Then, with the further development of industrialization, especially improved systems of transport, people were more able to move away from their family of origin (their own parents). This often allowed them to live in more pleasant, suburban surroundings. As a result of this increased geographical mobility, the *isolated **nuclear family*** developed. Increased prosperity also gave people greater economic independence from their family of origin.

Fletcher therefore concluded that industrialization led to a move from extended to nuclear families. He also believed that, as a result, family members became closer to each other and more supportive than they were before industrialization or during the period of early industrial production. In this view, the nuclear family today is not evidence of decline, but of a growth in family ties.

🗨 Discussion point

What are the advantages and disadvantages of living in either extended or nuclear families?

C3.1a

Challenges to the functionalist view

Evidence has been used to challenge functionalist views of family structure. Michael Anderson (1971) studied the 1851 Census records in Preston, which was then at the centre of the cotton industry. Here he found evidence of extended family networks among nearly a quarter of all households. Anderson suggested this was due mainly to the hardship and uncertainty experienced by workers at the time. The only way in which families could survive was within a system of reciprocal support which benefited all parties. Those who could work did so, while others cared for the children – and in many cases the orphans – of the workers.

📝 Activity

Draw up a map to show the distribution of your immediate family members. Does it show that your family is geographically isolated from the rest of your relatives? Speak to parents, aunts, uncles and grandparents to identify whether any changes have taken place over the past 50 years or so.

C3.3

The functionalist view has also been challenged by some social historians. Laslett and Wall (1972), for example, used evidence from a study of parish registers in the seventeenth century to show that families in much of pre-industrial northern Europe were most likely to consist of a more nuclear family structure of adults and their dependent children and siblings.

Laslett argued that the average size of families in western Europe had stayed constant over the period of industrialization, at 4.75 persons. He said that one reason why some sociologists argued that the size had reduced during this period was that they included servants and other non-family members in their calculations. In effect these household members were not really family members; therefore, while the average size of the household may have declined, the average size of the family had not. This point further underlines the importance of distinguishing between the two terms, family and household.

🗨 Discussion point

What problems do you think might arise when trying to study family structures of hundreds of years ago?

 C3.1a

Industrialization and the family – a summary

It is clear that there is no agreement amongst sociologists about the effect of industrialization on the structure of the family. It is possible to distinguish at least three contrasting positions:

- Sociologists such as Ronald Fletcher argue that the process of industrialization led to a shift from the dominance of the extended family to the dominance of the nuclear family, and therefore a fall in the average size of the family.

- In contrast, the work of Michael Anderson suggests that the early period after industrialization saw pressures which led to an increase in the extended family.

- A third view, associated with Peter Laslett, suggests that there was no noticeable change in the average size of the family as a result of the process of industrialization.

Families in industrial society

The conjugal family

Goode (1963) argued that the nuclear or *conjugal family* developed in a variety of ways, but to some extent these did have to suit the 'needs' of an industrialized system.

The conjugal (or nuclear) family establishes its own household, largely ignoring ties of wider kinship. Most importantly, the family of origin often no longer assists its younger members in gaining jobs or finding partners, so that contact with wider kin is much reduced. The close ties between conjugal family members also provide **emotional satisfaction**.

An example – family and marriage in East London

Young and Willmott (1975) argued that industrialization led to a change in relationships *between* family members. They showed how the family moved from the pre-industrial unit, working largely as a 'team', to far more *segregated conjugal roles* during industrialization. Husband and wife then tended to work and socialize in largely separate social spheres. These writers believed that **conjugal roles** (those of husband and wife) became far more *symmetrical*, with the family sharing social and leisure time and both adults contributing similarly to the running of the family unit.

Young and Willmott's study of East London in 1957 showed extensive evidence of close-knit, kinship-based communities in Bethnal Green among working-class families in the 1950s. Such groups were mainly mobilized by women, incorporating grandmother, her daughter and the daughter's children. Young and Willmott also found, in a follow-up study in 1973, that slum clearance of the East End had largely diminished these communities (and changed relationships between spouses), although some older parents would follow their children into the suburbs when possible.

Activity

Draw a spider diagram to identify which members of your family you see, how often you see them, and how near or far away they live. You may wish to consider various forms of contact, such as telephone calls, letters or e-mails.

C3.3

5.2 Recent demographic change

Patterns

In the UK at the beginning of the twenty-first century, we seem to have more varieties of family types that ever before. There are two-adult families where both partners work, one partner works or neither partner works – all with or without children. There are more **lone-parent families** (usually headed by women) than previously, although that is far from a new phenomenon. We see more people living alone, **cohabiting**, divorcing and remarrying, as well as many different types of extended families and a whole range of 'nuclear' families, some more 'isolated' than others. This section will provide an overview, using statistical material, of recent trends in these and other aspects of family life.

Statistical patterns in family life

Table 5.1 shows that the nuclear family (married couple with dependent children) made up only about 23 per cent of households in the UK in 1998. Approximately 28 per cent were single-person households and over half were made up of adults only.

Before considering the data in this table it is important to be aware that we are here looking at the *number of households*, as opposed to the number of persons in households. If you discover a table giving figures on the basis of percentage of persons, a different picture will emerge. This is because the number of people in a household varies by household type. There will always be more people in a household containing a couple with two children than in a household containing a lone parent and two children, or alternatively a single-person household.

As an example of this, the *General Household*

Table 5.1 Types of household: 1961–98

Household type	Percentage of households of each type				
	1961	1971	1981	1991	1998
One person: under pensionable age	4	6	8	11	14
One person: over pensionable age	7	12	14	16	14
Two or more unrelated adults	5	4	5	3	3
Single-family households: couple no children	26	27	26	28	28
with 1–2 dependent children	30	26	25	20	19
with 3 or more dependent children	8	9	6	5	4
non-dependent children only	10	8	8	8	7
Single-family households: lone parent with dependent children	2	3	5	6	7
non-dependent children only	4	4	4	4	3
Multi-family households	3	1	1	1	1
All households = 100% (million)	*16.3*	*18.6*	*20.2*	*22.4*	*23.6*

Sources: ONS (1998) and *www.statistics.gov.uk*

Survey 1994 (ONS, 1995) showed that, while only 24 per cent of households contained couples with dependent children, such households contained 41 per cent of the whole population. When interpreting the trends shown here, be aware that the statistics presented relate only to percentage of households.

Activity

a Summarize the patterns and trends shown in Table 5.1.

b Look up the latest statistics at *www. statistics.gov.uk/statbase*. See if you can identify current figures for the percentage of persons. What difference does this make to the picture of the family in contemporary Britain?

C3.2, C3.3, IT3.1

Table 5.1 includes a number of family structures in households as identified by the government. The remainder of this section considers recent trends in relation to some of these family structures. In particular we need to consider the changes in relation to marriage, divorce, cohabitation, single-person households, same-sex couples and lone-parent families.

Marriage

Because marriage is a legal contract, comprehensive statistics are available that allow sociologists to track trends. Sociologists refer both to the *absolute number* of marriages in one period

(and consider how it changes), and the *marriage rate* which is calculated by the number of marriages per 1000 eligible persons. This allows us to compare the popularity of marriage between countries with radically different population sizes. To illustrate this, Table 5.2 cites statistics for EC countries.

If we restrict ourselves to consideration of the marriage figure for the UK, it is relatively high but certainly not the highest. In fact the figure

Table 5.2 Marriage and divorce rates: EC comparison, 1981 and 1993

	Rates per 1000 population			
	Marriages		Divorces	
	1981	1993	1981	1993
United Kingdom	7.1	5.9	2.8	3.1
Denmark	5.0	6.1	2.8	2.5
Finland	6.3	4.9	2.0	2.5
Sweden	4.5	3.9	2.4	2.5
Belgium	6.5	5.4	1.6	2.1
Austria	6.3	5.6	1.8	2.0
Netherlands	6.0	5.8	2.0	2.0
France	5.8	4.4	1.6	1.9
Germany	6.2	5.5	2.0	1.9
Luxembourg	5.5	6.0	1.4	1.9
Portugal	7.8	6.9	0.7	1.2
Greece	6.9	6.0	0.7	0.7
Spain	5.4	5.0	0.3	0.7
Italy	5.6	5.1	0.2	0.4
Irish Republic	6.0	4.4	–	–
EC average	6.1	5.3	1.5	1.7

Source: Eurostat, *Social Trends* 1996

reached an all time peak in the period 1960–70 and has since declined. However, it must be remembered that the marriage rate today remains higher than that in Victorian times. The trend was therefore for marriage to rise in popularity, particularly quickly after World War II, and since 1970 to decline.

According to the government statistical office, the Office for National Statistics (ONS, 1999), the number of marriages fell 2.3 per cent between 1996 and 1997 to 272 536, and this figure can be compared with 351 761 in 1987.

The average age at which people marry has also been rising. In 1997, men married at an average age of 29.6 years (26.4 in 1987) and women married at an average age of 27.5 (24.3 in 1987).

The *way* in which people marry is also changing. Civil (as opposed to religious) ceremonies are becoming more prevalent. In 1997 nearly 61 per cent of couples had a civil ceremony. Another area of increase is marriage in 'approved premises' – for example, some pubs and hotels. These are premises licensed by law as acceptable venues for marriage. There were over 22 000 such unions in 1997.

Divorce

People are now divorcing in greater numbers and earlier in their relationship than previously.

As Gittins (1993) points out, large-scale divorce is a relatively recent phenomenon, being an expensive luxury until 1857. Even then, the Matrimonial Causes Act required the husband to be at greater fault than the wife in order for a divorce to be granted.

However, the continuing popularity of divorce, in most western industrialized societies at least, has been a subject of much sociological debate. Statistics for separation and cohabitation are a lot less reliable than divorce statistics, but not all couples can or do choose to divorce even if they are unhappy; many maintain what are known as 'empty-shell marriages', with limited joint social interaction.

Activity

a Identify the trends in divorce shown in Tables 5.3 and 5.4 on page 98.

b With reference to Figure 5.1, to what extent are the grounds for divorce given by men and women different?

C3.2, C3.3

England, Wales & Northern Ireland

Percentages

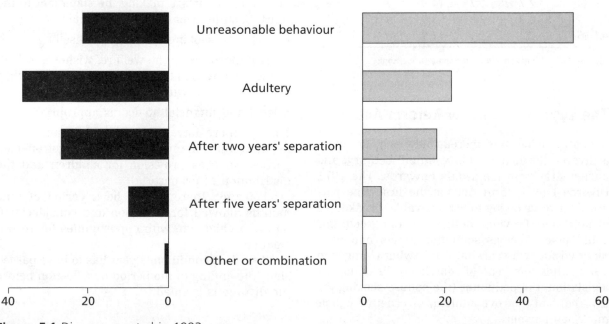

Figure 5.1 Divorces granted in 1993
Sources: OPCS; General Register Office (Northern Ireland); *Social Trends* 1996

Table 5.3 Divorce in the UK from 1961 to 1996, by duration of marriage (percentages)

Duration of marriage	1961	1971	1981	1991	1993	1996
0–2 years	1	1	2	9	8	9
3–4 years	10	12	19	14	14	13
5–9 years	31	31	29	27	28	28
10–14 years	23	19	20	18	18	18
15–19 years	14	13	13	13	12	12
20–24 years	0	10	9	10	10	9
25–29 years	21	6	5	5	5	6
30 years +	0	9	5	4	4	5
All divorces (=100%) (thousands)	*27.0*	*79.2*	*155.6*	*171.1*	*180.0*	*171.7*

Sources: OPCS; General Register Office (Scotland); General Register Office (Northern Ireland); *Social Trends* 1998; *www.statistics.gov.uk*

Table 5.4 Divorce in England and Wales, per 1000 of the married population

	1961	1971	1981	1991	1996
Males					
16–24	1.4	5.0	17.7	25.9	26.3
25–29	3.9	12.5	27.6	32.9	29.9
30–34	4.1	11.8	22.8	28.5	28.6
35–44	3.1	7.9	17.0	20.1	21.6
45+	1.1	3.1	4.8	5.6	6.3
All 16+	*2.1*	*5.9*	*11.9*	*13.6*	*13.5*
Females					
16–24	2.4	7.5	22.3	27.7	28.3
25–29	4.5	13.0	26.7	31.3	31.2
30–34	3.8	10.5	20.2	25.1	26.7
35–44	2.7	6.7	14.9	17.2	18.9
45+	0.9	2.8	3.9	4.5	5.0
All 16+	*2.1*	*5.9*	*11.9*	*13.4*	*13.4*

Source: *Social Trends* 28, ONS, Stationary Office, 1998

The 1971 Divorce Law Reform Act

Arguably, it became increasingly easy to obtain a divorce throughout the twentieth century, and particularly from the 1960s onwards. The 1971 Divorce Law Reform Act for the first time permitted divorce owing to 'irretrievable' breakdown of marriage. Provided both partners agreed, this could take effect as soon the couple had been married for two years (and following changes in 1984, after one year of marriage). Prior to this legislation, the petitioner (the spouse seeking the divorce) had to prove adultery or cruelty by their marriage partner.

The 1996 Family Law Act

The 1996 Family Law Act, which came into effect in 1999, was passed to try to make divorce a more carefully considered and less confrontational experience – especially as divorce was often seen as highly damaging for any children involved. Petitioners wishing to have their marriage dissolved have to obtain a divorce order from the courts. However, to get the court to issue this order, a number of circumstances have to be met.

Firstly, a statement has to be made that the marriage has broken down irretrievably. Secondly, there has to be an information meeting between the petitioner and his or her solicitor not less than three months before making the statement to the court. Such information has to include:

- advice on seeking marriage counselling
- the importance of the welfare, wishes and feelings of any children involved, and how they can best cope with a divorce
- legal and financial advice as appropriate.

Thirdly, there have to be agreed arrangements for the future financial arrangements of affected parties, such as provision for children and the distribution of property.

Fourthly, there has to be a period of nine months allowed for reflection and consideration on the breakdown, with opportunities for reconciliation.

As a final condition, a year has to have passed since the ending of the period of reflection before the divorce is granted.

Activity

a Do you think it is too easy to obtain a divorce? How might the Family Law Act change this?

b Carry out an opinion survey to collect the views of other people. Can you detect any differences between the views of males or females, or between older and younger people?

C3.1b, C3.2 ,C3.3, N3.1, IT3.1

Recent trends in divorce

ONS (1999) points to the 6.6 per cent fall in the number of divorces granted in England and Wales between 1996 and 1997 (157107 in 1996, 146 889 in 1997). This can be compared with the figure of 189 864 for 1992 provided by Jorgensen (1995). Whether this reflects the change in the law in 1996, or a more general trend towards fewer divorces, remains to be seen. Whatever the underlying reason(s), it is an important new trend which at the very least shows that the number of divorces has levelled off.

It is, however, still the case that there are concerns over the *impact* of divorce, particularly with regard to children of the divorcing parents. Sociologists are therefore interested in debating the causes and consequences of marital breakdown.

Causes of marital breakdown

Writers such as Dennis (1975) claimed that the family had fewer functions than previously, and consequently fewer things to tie people together. The modern isolated nuclear family is rarely a unit of production (although it may still act as a unit of consumption). The lack of other functions leads to the *affective* **relationship** becoming central. In other words, if people are no longer in love, they have nothing else to keep them together and so they decide to divorce. This reflects the sort of family structure required by industrialized society, and high divorce rates are therefore seen as a consequence of industrialization.

Some writers feel that divorce is now too easily obtained, and these sentiments arguably contributed to the introduction of the 1996 Family Law Act. However, it is also important to remember that other changing attitudes – for instance, **secularization** (the decline in religious belief and practice) – means that divorce is no longer taboo.

Hart (1976) argues that the increasing divorce rate reflects the conflict generated by contradictory demands on women to be both economic and domestic workers. Women, when they can, work to provide the increasing material demands of many families; but they are not fully supported in the domestic or emotional field by their husbands. She believes that the major cause of conflict leading to marital breakdown is the result of the increasing demands on women without enough male support.

Discussion point

What do you think are the main reasons why people get divorced? How are different members of the family likely to be affected?

C3.1a

Births

Jan Pahl (1999) makes the point that a glance at the age structure of the UK population shows that there were rises in the number of births in the late 1940s ('the baby boomers'), and another 'bulge' in the late 1960s, when large families were in fashion.

The **total period fertility rate** peaked in the UK at 2.95 in 1964, and fell to 1.69 in 1977. There were a number of reasons for this, notably:

- smaller size of families as effective birth control was introduced
- greater numbers of women remaining childless
- women working in employment in greater numbers, and leaving childbirth till later
- marriage occurring at later ages.

Social Trends 1998 (ONS, 1998) show that childbirths are still tending to occur later in adults' lives. Fertility has been falling among women in their twenties, but rising among women in their thirties.

Van Every (1995) suggests that increasing numbers of people are choosing to remain childless voluntarily. This increasing phenomenon of childlessness was also referred to by Giddens (1997), who pointed out that:

A survey carried out by the British Family Formation Survey in 1976 found that only 1 per cent of married women at that time did not want to have children. A recent report of the Office of Population Censuses and Surveys, by contrast, predicted that 20 per cent of women born between 1960 and 1990 will remain childless – by choice.

(Giddens, 1997, p. 158)

In the UK, births have gone down from around 2.5 births per woman in 1960 to 1.5 births per woman in 1990. Despite this general downward trend in the level of births, *Social Trends* 1998 (ONS, 1998) reported that there were 649 000 live births in England and Wales in 1997, a rise of 1000 compared to 1996. They also point out that this was the first rise in the annual number of births since 1990. Whether this represents a turning point in trends remains to be seen.

Despite this, it is clear that if we look at the period since the end of the Second World War, the large fall in the birth rate has affected the structure of the family.

More recent debates concern the variety of family and household structures within which children are raised. (See Section 5.6 and 5.8).

An ageing population

'Bulges' in the birth rate in the 1940s and 1960s (referred to in the section on births previously) will over time also affect the number of older persons in the population. The 'baby boomer' generation, and those born in the late 1960s when there was another 'bulge', will be coming up towards retirement. This means that older people will reach their highest proportion in the population in 2030, unless there is a dramatic shift in the birth and death rates.

One area where this has caused concern is over provision through the welfare state. It is argued that the number of people being supported by the welfare state will rise dramatically as older people live longer and increase in numbers, while falls in the birth rate since the late 1960s mean that the number of people working and paying tax to support the welfare state will have fallen. Johnson *et al.* (1989), writing from a New Right perspective, have argued that this might lead to conflicts between workers and pensioners, though Vincent (1995) sees this as an attempt to provide a justification for cutting back the welfare state in the way New Right policy suggested while in government.

In contrast, Will Hutton (1996) has argued that the financial burden imposed by older people will not increase substantially, and that by raising tax by 2.3 per cent of GDP by 2030, we will be able to retain the real value of the pension at its current level.

The impact on the family is two-fold. Firstly, one effect of an ageing population is the rise of the 'new grandparenting'. Pahl (1999) argues that with an increasing level of young mothers in paid employment, grandparents, and more particularly grandmothers, will play a larger role in looking after children. The longer life expectancy of people means that grandparents will be able to fulfil this role for longer and longer periods of time.

Secondly, it is clear that concerns over the cost to the welfare state have led to initiatives to push more and more of the burden of care of the elderly back onto families, and more specifically, onto women within families (see Section (5.7).

In the past, married women may well have remained out of the sphere of paid employment for some considerable time due to childcare commitments. Today, due to falling birth rates, it is possible that the time spent on childcare has fallen, but the time spent on familial care overall may have stayed the same or even risen, as many families choose to look after sick or elderly relatives at home, rather than opt for residential care.

The impact of divorce

Divorce may have a different impact on each family member. It is still rarely an easy option, particularly for many women. Gittins (1993) suggests that many men benefit financially from divorce and often find it easy to attract other (often younger) women as new partners. However, divorced men do tend to experience higher levels of ill-health than married men.

Women, especially if they have custody of their children (which most of them desire), may find it difficult to obtain appropriate work or be limited to low-paid casual or part-time employment. As women still tend to earn only about 72 per cent of the level of male earnings, even full-time employment reduces their standard of living.

Many more divorced men remarry than women, despite the higher economic and social necessity for many divorced women to do so. It could be argued that this reflects women's greater independence – they probably feel less in need of another relationship, or they feel disillusioned with the very idea of marriage.

5.3 Social policy and the family

As Gittins (1993) shows, the expansion of the state in modern industrial society has resulted in an ever-growing body of legislation which, in different ways, affects families and the individuals who live in them.

How such legislation affects individuals depends very much on both their sex and their social class. One law may act to the detriment of one member of the family while another law may benefit another member of the same family. Legislation on sexuality, marriage, divorce, child-care, abortion, birth control and mothering crucially affect families in different ways.

The family is generally represented as a private institution in society where individuals have a great deal of freedom from state intervention. However, this is something of a myth, as the state has always intervened in family life.

This point is underlined by Muncie and Sapsford (1995):

... social policy not only has a caring welfare objective but also carries with it notions of 'normality' to which families are directed to conform.

(Muncie and Sapsford, 1995, p. 29)

The family and the state

State supports

While the state provides a number of support mechanisms for families, such as **child benefit**, the state education system and **income support**, it does not do so without families meeting certain criteria and without certain assumptions underlying the systems that are developed.

Public policy therefore shapes the way we live our supposedly private lives. The key question to ask is whether the way public policy shapes an idea of 'normal' family life is a true reflection of the way people *actually* live their lives, or whether it is a reflection of the beliefs of certain groups of people or interest groups about how we *should* live our lives.

The enforcement of normality

Given that states generally do have the power to enforce their will, the view of normality which is presented to us might affect our individual autonomy and supposed privacy. Certainly the enforcement of such normality might lead to certain individuals losing out to others. An important point made by feminist sociologists such as Gittins (1993) and Abbott and Wallace (1992) is that imposing a particular family structure through social policy can contribute to the continued oppression of women and their dependence on men within family structures.

Assumptions underlying social policy

The most important developments in social policy in relation to the family were arguably the series of pieces of legislation passed in the late 1940s which created the **welfare state**. These changes were identified in the Beveridge Report of 1942 which set out a blueprint for the welfare state and laid the foundations for this legislation.

Beveridge and the family

The main form of provision in the Beveridge Report was for a system of 'national insurance' which would provide financial assistance to those who were unemployed or sick, and pensions for people in old age. This was to be paid for through contributions collected from both employers and employees. It is here that the main problem arises, since it does not consider how those *without* paid employment could make a contribution, and therefore whether they would be entitled to the benefits available through this scheme.

In fact this became the basis on which married women were largely excluded from many of the benefits available, since it was assumed that their husbands would look after them. In effect, this meant that married women were made economically dependent on their husbands. This reflected Beveridge's ideas about what normal family life was like, and his view that women, on marrying, should cease to be employed outside the home. Married women were seen as mainly being provided for by men and generally not employed in paid work, and so required restricted entitlement to benefits.

Beveridge's mistake

Muncie and Wetherell (1995) point out that, even at the time, this was a somewhat less than an accurate reflection of reality. In 1943, 40 per cent of married women were in employment, and after World War II the number of women in employment increased rather than decreased as Beveridge had expected. Today, the majority of married women work in paid employment for a considerable portion of their lives.

The assumption about how people lived their lives was therefore never a reflection of reality, simply a particular view about how people *should* live their lives. Nonetheless, despite its lack of link with reality, the assumptions held by Beveridge continue in some respects to underlie the benefits system, often leaving women worse off than men.

New Right policy and the family

It appears that the family remains central not just to debates about family life, but also to policies concerning familial arrangements. Smart (1991) points out that, although aspects of family structure have dominated state policy for years, the recent focus on the family has been unprecedented.

Much of this, she suggests, was due to the **New Right**'s desire to cut support for lone mothers. She argues that a number of policies can be seen to be combined into a singular attack on lone mothers.

These include the Social Security Act 1986, which stressed the need to support the 'responsible family'.

One area, that of divorce and the pension entitlements of a divorced wife, still remains problematic. Changes in unemployment allowances and benefits have also made it increasingly difficult for lone parents to take paid employment, despite recent changes.

Smart points out that the taxation and benefits system is so complex that the implication of such changes for the family are difficult to assess. However, it is clear that people receiving benefits will be disadvantaged as *means testing* widens. Examples are the loans which replaced the Social Fund payments in 1991. Undoubtedly, this will not act in the interests of single parents, who find it more difficult than most to find the type of work that makes using childcare services financially viable.

Formal and informal caring

The push towards more private family care and the move away from large-scale institutionalized care has indeed led to more pressure on women

to care for elderly relatives. Claire Ungerson (1995) has argued that the traditional distinction between formal (paid) and informal (unpaid) care tended to assume that unpaid care was done 'for love'. However, she points out that changes to the care system mean that now both formal and informal caring contain elements of labour and love. This is owing to the development of 'waged care' in the form of 'paid volunteering':

The payments that they make look very much like wages, in the sense that the payments are conditional on evidence that specific work has been undertaken and successfully carried through.

(Ungerson, 1995, pp. 33–4)

It could be argued that this is a partial recognition of the work done predominantly by females in a family setting. However, it has sparked off another debate because it can also be argued that this money constitutes an extra pressure on women, by pushing them into traditional stereotyped roles.

Activity

a Identify and explain two forms of caring that take place within the family.

b Outline and discuss the view that engaging in unpaid care creates an unfair burden on women.

C3.2, C3.3

5.4 Recent trends in family life

The trends in choices about family living considered in this section contribute to the greater diversity of family structures which now exist in British society (see Figure 5.2).

Cohabitation

Many people are marrying later in life, and this often initially involves a period of unmarried cohabitation. In the 1960s, **cohabitation** was often called 'trial marriage', perhaps to give the term respectability. Now, a considerable number of people seem to marry only after the birth of a child, while many choose not to marry at all. A considerable proportion of people cohabiting will

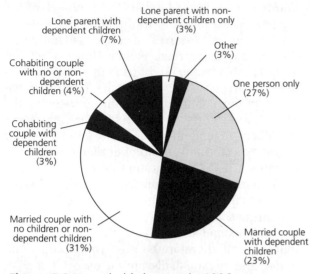

Lone parent with dependent children (7%)

Lone parent with non-dependent children only (3%)

Other (3%)

Cohabiting couple with no or non-dependent children (4%)

One person only (27%)

Cohabiting couple with dependent children (3%)

Married couple with no children or non-dependent children (31%)

Married couple with dependent children (23%)

Figure 5.2 Households by type in 1996
Source: ONS (1997a)

include at least one partner who is separated or divorced from someone else (see Table 5.5).

Table 5.5 Cohabitation in Great Britain (combined years 1995/96 and 1996/97) (percentages)

	Single	Separated without marrying	Divorced	Widowed	All non-married
Males					
16–24	9	–	–	–	9
25–34	37	20	50	–	37
35–49	22	22	36	–	27
50–59	7	17	28	7	17
Total 16–59	*20*	*20*	*36*	*10*	*22*
Females					
16–24	18	9	–	0	17
25–34	34	9	35	–	32
35–49	23	9	27	6	22
50–59	9	7	18	5	12
Total 16–59	*23*	*9*	*27*	*6*	*22*

Sources: ONS (1996) and *Social Trends* 28, ONS, Stationary Office, 1998

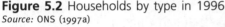

Activity

Summarize the key trends to be found in Tables 5.5 and 5.6. Explain how the following social trends may have caused cohabitation to rise: contraception, decline in religion, rise in divorce, changing norms and values concerning sexuality.

C3.2, C3.3

Table 5.6 Percentages of people who agreed with the statement that living together outside marriage is always wrong, by gender, 1994

Year of birth	Males	Females
1960–1978	7	6
1950–1959	10	8
1940–1949	16	14
1930–1939	23	22
Before 1930	40	34
All	*17*	*16*

Sources: British Household Panel Survey; ESRC Research Centre on Micro-social Change; *Social Trends* 1996

It is often assumed that many cohabiting couples eventually marry or (in many cases) remarry. This also means that there are a number of **step-families**. Therefore cohabitation and remarriage are not usually seen as evidence of family decline in the way that lone-parenting is sometimes presented.

McRae (1993) carried out a postal survey of new mothers in 1988. From the replies received, she found that about 7 per cent were cohabiting. Her follow-up study of this group found a number of interesting differences between them and married mothers.

As most women marry before or soon after the birth of their children, this group offered an example to investigate why some people with children reject marriage despite quite strong societal expectations that parents should marry. Her research identified a number of interesting trends.

Cohabiting mothers tended to be younger than married mothers. They tended on average to have more children (some from previous relationships of themselves or their partners). Their family income tended to be markedly lower than for married couples, partly owing to their lower involvement in paid employment. However, cohabiting mothers are usually considered as less of a 'problem' for themselves or society as a whole, than single mothers who have divorced or have never married and who are living without a partner.

Discussion point

What are the advantages and disadvantages for men, women and any children in a cohabiting household?

C3.1a

Reconstituted families

Although many divorced people become single-headed families for a while, large numbers remarry to form **reconstituted families**. This means that many children are growing up with step-parents and, in some cases, step-siblings as well. *Social Trends* 1998 (ONS, 1998) found that in 1991 there were 500 000 step-families with dependent children in Britain. The children living in such households numbered one million, both step-children and biological and adopted children of both adults. In 84 per cent of cases step-families contained a step-father, in 12 per cent a step-mother, and in four per cent both.

The greater number of step-father families probably results from the tendency for children to stay with their mother in divorce cases. Chester (1985) argues that, despite these changes, most people are now brought up in what he terms a **neo-conventional family**, where there are two parents, a small number of children and long-term commitment. The main difference between this and the conventional 'isolated nuclear family' is the number of married women who are now economically active outside the home, although often working part-time while their children are very young. Table 5.7 shows the percentages of different types of these families.

Table 5.7 Features of step-families with dependent children in Great Britain, 1995[a,b,c]

Couple with child(ren) from the woman's previous marriage	86%
Couple with child(ren) from the man's previous marriage	10%
Couple with child(ren) from both partners' previous marriages	4%

[a] Dependent children are people under 16, or aged 16–18 and in full-time education, in the family unit, and living in the household.
[b] Family head aged 16–59 [c] Includes previous cohabitations.
Source: ONS (1996)

Remarriage and step-parenting

Although it is difficult to generalize about those who remarry, it is argued by many writers that the popularity of remarriage demonstrates the strength of family values for most people. Although Gittins argues that, at least for women with children, remarriage is an important financial consideration, writers such as Fletcher and

Murdock point to remarriage as evidence of the high value we place on traditional family life.

This trend towards a cycle of marriage, divorce and remarriage is sometimes described as *serial monogamy*, and this is the pattern identified by writers such as Fletcher (1966) as evidence of our commitment to the nuclear family. This view suggests that although more marriages are likely to end in divorce, owing to greater longevity and (until recently) earlier marriage, it remains a popular institution.

Remarriage is usually considered to be the best option for the children of divorced parents. It is argued that step-parents may offer a 'new' (possibly extended) family for these children and that they will therefore be less prone to the emotional and personal disruption associated with lone-parenting. However, a report produced in 1995 by the National Child Development Study suggests that girls in particular tend not to benefit from step-parenting.

More children in a step-family leave school at 16, leave home at 18 after family arguments, get poorer educational qualifications and marry younger than do those from lone-parent households. There is also evidence that girls are more vulnerable to sexual abuse from step-fathers than from any other family member, although this problem is clearly not found in all step-families. (See Section 5.9 for a fuller discussion of this issue.)

Discussion point

What are the main advantages and disadvantages for the children, mother and father if their parents remain together, divorce, remarry, etc.? Consider factors such as the age and gender of the children, the number of siblings and the economic situation.

Single-person households

An important recent trend is the large growth in households consisting of only one person. While there have always been a number of these comprising the elderly (mainly women since women live longer than men), it is now becoming much more a phenomenon associated with younger age groups. (See Table 5.1 on page 86)

Richard Scase (1999), in a report for the Economic and Social Research Council entitled

'Britain towards 2010', highlighted this as one of the key trends in UK society. He argued that by 2010 single-person households will be the predominant form of household in the UK. However, he also points to the fact that the experience of living in a single-person household varies greatly by gender. Single men in their thirties and forties tend to be more socially isolated and suffer from loneliness, while single women in their thirties and forties tend to have well-developed social networks of friends and involvement in a wide range of social and cultural activities.

This difference was somewhat overstated in a report in the *Observer* (17 October 1999), where it was argued that the gender differences will be reflected as follows:

Profile of the single man in 2010
Watches *Terminator VII* at home
Eats takeaway Chinese
Surfs the Net
Has one-night stands
Plays five-a-side
Goes to strip clubs
Enjoys playstation
Drives a BMW
Shops at Next and The Gap

Profile of the single woman in 2010
Goes to book club with friends
Eats organic pasta
Stretches at yoga class
Practises serial monogamy
Does Feng Shui
Attends Shakespeare plays
Does meditation
Drives a Renault
Shops at Agnès B and French Connection

Discussion point
How convincing do you find the portrait of clearly gendered single lives in the UK in 2010? Is there any evidence of this today?

C3.1a

Same-sex families

We tend to assume that people who have relationships with others of the same sex are unable or unlikely to have children. While some may choose not to do so, as do an increasing number of heterosexual couples, there is a small but growing number of same-sex parents.

Some women leave a heterosexual relationship to live with another woman, taking their children with them. This is often not an easy task, as there have been instances when charges of lesbianism have been used to suggest that a woman is unfit to be a mother, although there is no evidence to support this. It appears that the only disadvantage suffered by children brought up in lesbian households was the response of others to their situation.

Plummer (1976) argued that homosexuals are less likely to establish long-term relationships because of social disapproval of homosexuality which makes it more difficult to meet potential partners. Furthermore, existing norms among some gay men tend to stress transient rather than long-term relationships. Nor can homosexuals marry or have children in the conventional ways that heterosexual couples tend to do.

However, Plummer also argues that many homosexuals seek the ideal of a life-long partnership despite these discouragements, although many homosexual and heterosexual people do not seek such a relationship. The idea that two homosexual men can bring up a 'normal' child is often considered unacceptable, and lesbian mothers are often seen as deficient in some way. Such prejudices do not appear to be supported by any evidence of greater levels of **dysfunction** among same-sex families. (See also Section 4.1.)

Discussion point
Read the story from the *Guardian*, 'Gay couple will be legal parents' on page 107. What sociological issues about the structure and function of the family does this case raise?

C3.1a

Current social policy seems to stress the advantages of traditional family structures. Whilst other options have always been adopted, there appears to be something of a backlash against certain forms of households, especially same-sex arrangements.

Weeks (1977) pointed out that, although the legislation relating to homosexuality was liberalized in 1967, the number of convictions for homosexual offences has actually increased.

Despite this, there is some evidence of change. In October 1999 a number of court cases led to significant decisions. These included a ruling that a homosexual couple in a stable relationship *could be defined as a family*; a separate decision allowing two gay men both to be registered on the birth certificates of their children (see page 107); and the ban being lifted on homosexuals in the armed forces. In July 1999 the Children's Society lifted its oppositon to gay and lesbian individuals adopting or fostering children.

The government plans legislation to reduce the age of consent for gays to 16, bringing this into line with the law for heterosexuals. Plans are also underway to reappeal Clause 28, a controversial ruling which made it illegal for teachers to promote homosexuality in schools. Finally, the Trades Union Congress (TUC) has called for discrimination on the grounds of sexual orientation (to be made illegal) in the workplace.

Single-parent families

According to the *Living in Britain General Household Survey* (ONS, 1996), since 1971 there has been a marked increase in the proportion of families with dependent children headed by lone parents, in particular those headed by single mothers. The latter rose from 1 per cent of all families with dependent children in 1971 to 8 per cent in 1993. Since then there has been no increase in the proportion of families headed by single mothers. The proportion of lone father families has remained at 1–2 per cent since 1971.

Particularly noticeable is the increase in the number of mothers who have never married (see Table 5.8 on page 107). Although many of these women were involved in a stable relationship with both parents' names on the birth certificate and often lived together, this group is seen as the most problematic for government. Many of them are teenagers, who are least likely to have a well-paid job and so are reliant on state benefits. Young, never-married mothers are often portrayed as 'welfare scroungers'.

Moral panics about lone-parent families

In an extensive article in *Community Care* magazine, Burghes and Roberts (1995) suggest that politicians and the media have generated the rise in the number of lone parents into a '**moral panic**'. They argue that in the 1990s single parents were presented as a major social problem. Policies such as the introduction of the Child Support Agency were designed to stress the indi-

vidual responsibility of parents (both fathers and mothers) towards their children.

One attempt to gain public support for this move was a concerted media attack on lone parents by (among others) a number of Conservative cabinet members in the 1980s and 90s.

The Labour government elected in 1997 has also introduced legislation to encourage more single mothers to enter (or re-enter) the employment market, although many would apparently prefer to be at home to bring up their children.

The Institute of Economic Affairs produced a study called *Families without Fatherhood* (Dennis and Erdos, 1992).

Reasons for moral panic

Burghes and Roberts (1995) point out that the reality does not support the idea that lone parents are a major social problem, although their numbers have increased. They claim that the main reason for the development of such a moral panic (see Section 6.2) was to reduce state spending on lone-parent families, who are certainly disproportionately reliant on benefits. This is especially the case for less well-educated women who find it difficult to gain paid employment that covers both living expenses and childcare costs. This meant that single mothers face particular problems in escaping dependency on welfare and state support.

However, the implicit argument was that the breakdown of the family was leading to a decline in morality and this could therefore also explain rising levels of crime, delinquency and drug-taking, particularly among young people. In response to this many people would argue that there is a problem with the growth of lone-parenting, whether it is one for the state, the mothers or the children themselves. If this is the case, were the politicians not right to panic? Burghes and Roberts conclude that:

... they were absolutely right to be concerned but seriously wrong in how they went about it, the way they initially attributed causes and effects, and therefore, their analysis of the policy options. Most of all, they were wrong to play to the media gallery, to go for the quick social security fix and so encourage a panic.

(Burghes and Roberts, 1995, p. viii)

Gay couple will be legal parents

JULIA HARTLEY-BREWER

Two gay men from Essex made legal history yesterday when a US court gave them both the right to be named on birth certificates as the parents of surrogate twin babies.

Barrie Drewitt, 30, and Tony Barlow, 35, from Chelmsford, are to become the legal parents of the boy and girl due to be born in December to an American woman, after the ruling by a Los Angeles superior court judge.

The couple, wealthy businessmen who have been together for 11 years, have spent £200,000 on the surrogate birth after their application to adopt was rejected by Essex social services four years ago.

They went to a surrogacy agency in Los Angeles that advertises on the Internet and specializes in providing children for gay men. They paid for four donor eggs to be implanted after fertilization in Rosalind Bellamy, 32, a married mother of four, using sperm from both men. A separate egg donor was used to ensure that neither woman involved would have a claim on the children after birth.

However, both the surrogate and the biological mother, Tracie Matthews, will be godparents to the children, whom the fathers plan to name Aspen and Saffron Drewitt-Barlow.

The ruling is the first of its kind involving a European surrogacy, although two fathers have been named in a handful of American cases. Previously, only the biological father has been named on the birth certificate as the legal father, with the surrogate mother named as the legal mother. A second 'father' could be named later only as a 'second parent'.

Yesterday's ruling, which will be legally binding in the UK, means that for the first time the partner who is not the biological father will also have the right to have his name on the birth certificate.

The men have had DNA tests to discover who is the real father of the twins but have declined to reveal the result.

They have a holiday home in Beverly Hills, California, and plan to fly to America next month in preparation for the birth, returning to the UK in the new year.

They have interviewed for a nanny and plan to provide the twins with a brother or sister in a few years using more eggs from Mrs Matthews.

Mr Drewitt, a former nurse, said: 'We are celebrating a legal victory. The nuclear family as we know it is evolving. The emphasis should not be on it being a father and a mother, but on loving, nurturing parents, whether that be a single mother or a gay couple in a committed relationship.'

Mr Barlow, a dermatologist, added: 'This ruling affirms that gay couples are entitled to the same fundamental procreative freedoms as heterosexual couples.'

Source: Guardian, 28 October 1999

Table 5.8 Families with dependent children, and marital status of lone mothers, 1971–95 (GB, percentages)

Family type	1971	1974	1981	1984	1991	1993	1994	1995
Married/cohabiting couple[a]	92	90	87	87	81	78	77	78
Lone mother	7	9	11	12	18	20	21	20
single	1	1	2	3	6	8	8	8
widowed	2	2	2	1	1	1	1	1
divorced	2	2	4	6	6	7	7	7
separated	2	2	2	2	4	4	5	5
Lone father	1	1	2	1	1	2	2	2
All lone parents	8	10	13	13	19	22	23	22

[a] Including married women whose husbands were not defined as resident in the household.
Source: ONS (1996a)

Activity

Using the previous material and the statistical information presented in Table 5.8 and elsewhere from the ONS, summarize arguments for and against the view that lone mothers are a problem to society.

C3.2, C3.3

Dependence on the state

There has also apparently been an increase in the number of fathers who do not support their children. The Child Support Agency (CSA) was established in 1991 to ensure that absent fathers paid maintenance for their offspring. This initiative is an interesting example of the kind of policies that are being applied to reduce the 'burden' of lone-parenting, and the dependence of lone parents, on the state.

Lone-parenting as a choice?

Dallos and Sapsford (1995) point out that being a lone parent can take a variety of forms, although in most cases lone-parent families are headed by the mother who takes prime emotional (and often financial) responsibility for the offspring. They also found from talking to lone mothers that a period of initial doubt and anxiety was often followed by feelings of increased self-confidence and the enjoyment of independence and autonomy. They conclude that in many cases lone parenthood reflects the choice of at least some women. This is supported by evidence such as the decline in the popularity of marriage and rising rates of births outside marriage (see Figure 5.3).

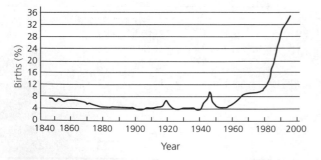

Figure 5.3 A sign of the family in crisis? Births outside marriage in Great Britain between 1840 and 1999 (percentages)
Source: Social Trends (1999)

5.5 Dimensions of diversity

We now need to consider sociological arguments as to the basis of the diverse family forms considered in the previous section.

Types of diversity

The apparent diversity of family structures in modern industrial societies has been the subject of much sociological debate. Functionalists argue that the nuclear family is still most common or has been replaced by a similar type of 'reconstituted' family structure (incorporating step-parents and step-children). Others accept that family life is certainly changing, but regard this as a sign of moral decay – this can be seen for example in the New Right's call for a return to traditional family values, or the '**ethical socialist**' concern with the effects of absent fathers. Others, especially some feminist writers such as Gittins (1993) and Barrett and McIntosh (1991), welcome and celebrate the diversity of family structures in modern societies.

Such diversity can be divided into groups, although these, too, are only models. These can be classified as:

• organizational diversity
• cultural diversity
• class diversity
• regional diversity
• lifecycle diversity
• cohort diversity.

Organizational diversity

Organizational diversity is the term used to describe the variety of family structures that can be found in the UK. There are, for example:

• dual-income families
• non-employed families
• same-sex parents
• single-parent families
• reconstituted families (formed after divorce and remarriage).

These last two appear to be increasingly numerous in British society and there is also an increasing number of families in households consisting of three generations of a family as elderly parents move in with their children and children-in-law (see Section 5.8).

It appears that the traditional 'cereal packet family' no longer makes up the majority of households in the UK. Oakley (1974a) defined this as the advertisers' ideal family with the mother at home with a child of each sex and the father obviously leaving the happy home (and breakfast) to go off to work. Figure 5.2 on page 103 shows clearly that in 1996 only about 23 per cent of households consisted of a married couple with dependent children – and few of these now contain only the one male breadwinner.

Cultural diversity

Cultural diversity refers to the way groups in society have different lifestyles or cultures and one aspect of this may be over the way they construct families.

One of the major advantages of living in a multi-ethnic society like the UK is the contributions different ethnic groups make to diversity in society. There are a number of culturally specific family structures, but you need to be aware that these are generalizations and that many people from the ethnic groups outlined here do not live in the family structures identified (see Table 5.9).

One of the problems for sociologists looking at cultural differences is the tendency to produce stereotypes, and all students of sociology need to be aware of this pitfall. The three groups explored here are South Asians, Cypriots and African–Caribbeans.

One of the problems with seeing the nuclear family as the norm is that other family structures are judged to be inferior. Dallos and Sapsford (1995) warn strongly against this form of *ethnocentrism* (seeing your own culture's social arrangements as superior to those of other social groups):

In thinking about ... other cultures it is important not to be trapped into a Eurocentrist perspective. Afro-Caribbean families, for example, may be different in many ways to white, British nuclear families, but it would be a mistake to regard these differences as an attack on family life. In fact the reverse could be argued: there is often a strong sense of family life and respect for it, and moreover the family can represent or offer a 'haven' for black people from the racial prejudice they may experience in white society.

(Muncie *et al.*, 1995, p. 146)

South Asian families

Ballard (1982) draws some generalized findings from his studies of migrant families from the Punjab, Gujarat and Bengal. Such families are usually **patriarchal** and ideally all the family live together and all contribute to the domestic and wage-earning tasks. Although the work of women and men is usually highly differentiated, Ballard found increasing numbers of women needing to work outside the home. Often extended families were split into smaller, more nuclear family units. Some British-born Asians have rejected the traditional family authority structures. He found that many children co-existed in two cultures, conforming largely to peer expectations outside the home and parental demands within the home.

Cypriot families

Oakley (1982) found extended family patterns among Cypriot families, most of whom migrated

Table 5.9 Ethnic group of head of household, by household size, spring 1995 (GB, percentages)

	One person	Two people	Three people	Four people	Five people	Six or more people	All (=100%) (thousands)
White	28	34	16	15	5	2	22 548
Black[a]	31	29	20	12	4	4	379
Indian	9	17	20	26	16	12	265
Pakistani/ Bangladeshi	8	11	14	21	15	31	163
Other[b]	28	23	20	19	6	5	239
All ethnic groups	28	34	16	15	5	2	23 594

[a] Includes Caribbean, African and other black people of non-mixed origin.
[b] Includes Chinese, other ethnic minority groups of non-mixed origin and people of mixed origin.
Source: Labour Force Survey, Central Statistical Office in *Social Trends* 1996

to the UK after World War II, although some came earlier. He found strong connections between married children and their parents, with considerable emphasis on family support rather than external agencies. Children, as in many South Asian families, were expected to contribute to the family businesses. Similar patterns can also be seen in closely-knit Italian migrant communities, for example in Clerkenwell in London.

African–Caribbean families

Barrow (1982) identified three types of family structures found in the Caribbean:

- conventional nuclear families found among religious and/or economically successful groups
- **common-law families** where less well-off unmarried couples cohabit and raise children who may or may not be their own biologically
- the 'mother household' where the mother (or sometimes grandmother) is head of household, adult males contribute to childrearing, but are often transient and most support comes from the wider female kinship group.

There is evidence of all these sorts of structures among African–Caribbeans in the UK, although women are more likely to be the main breadwinner in many households. There is less opportunity for input from other female family members, but many African–Caribbean women have extensive female support networks in areas of high black population. According to Barrow, this form of mother-headed family (commonly found in Jamaica) offers alternative family arrangements both in the Caribbean and for some women in the UK. Women in Jamaica have always been strong, both in the home and in public life such as teaching and politics. Single women have problems of unemployment or, if employed, finding childcare. Formal nurseries are one solution, but in more rural areas this role usually comes from within the extended family.

Working mothers will often find that their mothers and sisters can offer informal childcare, either within Jamaica if they have to migrate to find work, or within the UK. This suggests that many white British people often have little understanding of the importance of the role of the grandmother in African–Caribbean society, which is to provide support and strength for her daughters and nurture for grandchildren. This also provides a useful role for older women in society, something which is rarely found among many British families. Barrow attributes the

cause of this family structure to slavery, as nuclear families were not encouraged by slave-owners. One positive outcome of this has been the tradition of mutual support found between women in a largely matriarchal (mother-headed) society.

Activity

a Indentify and explain two examples of cultural diversity in family life in the UK.

b Outline and discuss the views that ethnicity has little consistent effect on family and household structure in the UK.

C3.2, C3.3

Class diversity

This refers to the way people in different social classes may have different family structures. The argument here arises from the material inequalities behind class divisions and the effect these have on the family. Eversley and Bannerjea (1982) argued that there were a number of ways this could affect family life. Firstly, it is well known that the amount of income is related to the type of housing one is able to choose, and therefore to the type of material and social environment the family exists in. Secondly, the amount of income has an effect on the social life of the family, affecting anything from the likelihood of experiencing overcrowding to whether the family have holidays or other leisure expenditure.

Young and Wilmott (1975) see class as an important factor in the emergence of what they called the 'symmetrical family' (see Section 5.7). They argue that it emerged first in the middle class and then moved into the working class. This meant the relations between the two adults within families differed by class.

Middle-class families

The above argument was somewhat countered by the work of Stephen Edgell (1980). He studied husbands and wives in 38 professional couples and considered how they made decisions. Specifically he looked at who made the decisions varied both in terms of the frequency of decision required and the perceived importance of the decision.

His findings were that wives controlled frequent decisions which were not seen as important while the husbands controlled the important but less frequent decisions. This clearly suggests a gendered approach to decision-making and undermines the argument of Young and Wilmott that middle-class families were in the forefront of moves towards gender equality in family households.

The working-class family in the 1990s

O'Brien and Jones (1996) returned to the parts of East London studied by Young and Willmott in the 1950s and 1960s to see what, if anything, had changed. The main pattern they observed was one of diversity in family and household composition. There were far more one-parent households and higher levels of divorce, remarriage and cohabitation compared with the 1950s. In fact these family structures appeared to be more common in their study than in the population as a whole. There were also more dual-income households and greater ethnic diversity than found either in the 1950s or in many other parts of the UK.

Such changes clearly reflect the increase in divorce rates, as well as changes in the roles of women – the majority of whom are now in paid employment – and in the ethnic composition of the UK. Although they found considerable differences in family composition in the 1990s compared with the 1950s, they also identified patterns that had shown little change. One striking example was the persistence of 'matrilocality' – that is, married women whose own mother (and father) still lived in the area. The maternal grandmother remained a particularly popular and important figure in the family household.

Social and geographical mobility were comparatively low in the area, suggesting a link between close family ties and low educational achievement. However there was also evidence of higher aspirations among younger people, who also generally expressed a greater desire for equality in the home between men and women. Overall, though, O'Brien and Jones found surprisingly little change in kinship patterns in East London, despite a variety of household structures and lifestyles and higher educational and occupational aims among large numbers of people in the area – especially women.

Regional diversity

According to Eversley and Bannerjea (1982), different patterns of family life can be found in certain parts of England. Many southern coastal regions have large numbers of retired couples and single households. Two-parent families are more commonly found in the south east, while inner-city areas tend to have higher levels of single-parent families and ethnic minorities. Strong kinship networks are maintained in most highly rural areas. Particularly in areas of high unemployment, adult children may remain living with their parents to the age of 30 and beyond.

Activity

Carry out either primary research in your own school or college, or secondary research at a local library, to identify and categorize cultural differences between Welsh, Irish and Scottish families. Produce a report summarizing the differences and similarities between them.

C3.1b, C3.2, C3.3, N3.1, IT3.1

Table 5.10 Birth statistics for the UK and constituent nations, 1996

	No of live births (000s)	Mean age at child-birth (years)	Births outside marriage (%)
United Kingdom	733.4	28.6	35.5
Great Britain	708.8	28.6	35.8
England	614.2	28.7	35.5
Scotland	59.3	28.4	36.0
Wales	34.9	27.8	41.2
Northern Ireland	24.6	28.8	25.9

Source: Birth Statistics 1996, ONS, Stationary Office, 1998

Activity

Table 5.10 shows some variation among the nations making up the UK.

a Explain the difference between the United Kingdom and Great Britain.

b Identify the nations with the highest and lowest percentage of births outside marriage.

c Write down your own ideas about reasons for the variations shown in the table.

 C3.2, C3.3

Evidence of family diversity appears quite convincing, but it is equally true that these are only snapshots of a society at a particular time. Over the last 20 years, trends related to increased cohabitation and, probably more importantly, never-married single parenting, have been at the heart of the debate not only about the family but about the morality and structure of society itself. We could also cite examples of different family structures in the constituent parts of the UK as an example of a combination of cultural and regional diversity.

Lifecycle diversity

What is meant by lifecycle diversity is the idea that we go through various stages of our life. For instance we may start life as children in a household with one or more adults and then we move on to being adults ourselves. We may get married, may get divorced, may stay single or later on may be widowed. Clearly the stage at which you are at in your life will therefore have an effect on the type of family structure you are likely to be part of.

Cohort diversity

Groups born at different times tend to live in different ways. Cohort diversity refers to the way the time you were born may affect family arrangements. One example is the way in which cohabitation has become much more popular among groups born in the last 25 years than it was among groups born prior to this. As time goes on the question arises as to whether cohabitation remains a preserve of the young and is seen as a temporary staging post to marriage, or whether groups born later will begin to adopt this as an alternative to marriage even into their 50s and 60s.

5.6 Explanations of family diversification

By considering recent trends in family life and the diversity of family structures, we can begin to gather evidence relating to what is probably the most controversial debate about family life. This concerns the question of how we are to interpret these trends. If we look at the falling rate of marriage, rising and then stabilizing rates of divorce, rising rates of cohabitation, rising rates of births outside of marriage and rising rates of lone-parent families, we can see that the conventional nuclear family, which is often pre-

sented as a norm in the ideology of the family, is most certainly statistically not the norm.

Two contrasting positions

There are two reactions to this.

- One is to argue that the family is in decline and, given its central role in socialization, this usually extends into an argument that dire social consequences will follow.

- A second contrasting argument suggests that these trends are merely evidence of an increasing diversity of family structures as people feel they have more freedom and choice about the ways they 'do' the family. This argument leads to the conclusion that there is greater choice, which is a good thing, and that no one family type is better than another or suits all people and circumstances.

While this debate is central to the sociology of the family and to debates by politicians and media commentators, it does essentially also boil down to exactly what we mean by the family (leading us back to the definitions covered in Section 5.1). Secondly, since this debate is about change over time, it depends crucially on what starting point you choose for your comparison with today.

The family: continuity or change

Is the family in decline? Those who think it is are particularly associated with functionalism and the New Right, but it can also be seen in elements of **New Labour** thinking about the family. A key issue, however, is what *is* the past when we want to make comparisons.

The most common chosen starting point is the 1950s and 60s. Among some commentators this represented a golden age of the family before the permissive 1960s began to undermine it. Statistics comparing the family in the 1960s/1970s with today do indeed provide a picture of a decline of the conventional nuclear family as a proportion of all households. This is seen as a negative thing.

However, if we take a longer time span and compare the 1990s with Victorian times (the mid 1860s, for example) we get a radically different picture. The conventional family is arguably stronger today than it was in Victorian times.

Lorraine Harding (1996) points out that the main decline in marriage occurred from around 1970, and she puts this down to greater levels of unemployment since that time. However, national Census figures also show that a greater proportion of the population were married in 1991 than in 1861, and that the rise in marriage occurred particularly after World War II when state benefits were used to promote the family.

On this basis it could be argued that it is not the decline of the conventional family since 1970 that should need explaining, but rather its unusual popularity between 1945 and 1970. Furthermore, since the 1970s were historically unusual do they represent an appropriate starting point for comparisons with today?

One trend that has aroused much comment is the rise in lone-parent families. Again, if we take a longer time span, this appears to be more a matter of explaining their relative scarcity in the period 1945–70 than of explaining their growth from the 1970s to today. Millar (1989) shows that in 1981 the proportion of families with children headed by lone-parent families was 8.9 per cent, while the equivalent figure for 1861 was 8.1 per cent.

It is therefore crucially important when debating trends to consider the starting point used as a basis for comparisons, and whether this affects the picture that develops.

Despite this reservation, it is clear that there has been a debate about the supposed decline of the family, so this section will now move on to consider some contributions to the debate.

Political positions on 'the family' in the 1997 general election

The family is the most important institution in our lives. It offers security in a fast-changing world. But the family is undermined if governments take decisions which families ought to take for themselves. ... Conservatives believe that a healthy society encourages people to accept responsibility for their own lives ... we want families to help themselves.

Conservative Party Manifesto, 1997

We will uphold family life as the most secure means of bringing up our children. Families are the core of our society. They should teach right from wrong. They should be the first defence against anti-social behaviour. The breakdown of family life damages the *fabric of our society. ... Yet families in Britain today are under strain as never before.*

Labour Party Manifesto, 1997
(Quoted in Kidd, 1999, p. 13)

Discussion point
Discuss the differences and similarities in the implied structure and functions of the family contained in the above two manifesto extracts.

The New Right and the family

[The] New Right in both Britain and the USA has long seen itself as developing a 'new' morality through its approach to sexual and family matters. Its particular emphasis has been on redefining women's place within the family, especially as mothers. This focus on the family is central to New Right ideology.

(David, 1986, p. 136)

The New Right have had most influence in the UK on the Conservative Party, which had a continuous period in government in the UK in the 1980s and 1990s. Central to the ideas of the New Right is a negative view of the state.

This had clear implications for the idea of a welfare state. This was seen by New Right thinkers as creating a culture of dependency which encouraged laziness, leading to economic decline. The structure of the family was also central to this theory of economic decline. The New Right believe in the notion of the stable nuclear family as the bedrock of society. Paul Johnson provided an example of this:

The ideal society must rest upon the tripod of a strong family, a voluntary church and a liberal minimal state. Of these, the family is the most important.

(Paul Johnson, *Observer*, 10 October 1982)

A further development of this line of argument is that state welfare payments encourage people to engage in 'deviant' family structures, leading to moral decline and a lack of personal responsibility. This view is the intellectual basis of the attack on lone-parent families. They cause concern also because they are supported mainly by welfare benefits, leading to a rise in welfare expenditure in most cases.

The New Right, the family and women

This view has particular implications for women. The attempt to rein back the welfare state has not in fact led to the disappearance of the social problems that the welfare state sought to deal with. Instead, the New Right has attempted to privatize these problems by seeking to push responsibility back to the family unit. Within this family unit it is clear that it will be largely women who are expected to assume the traditional role of unpaid carer.

Abbott and Wallace (1992) make this point clearly, as well as exposing the mythical nature of the New Right vision of the family:

The appeal of the New Right is one of nostalgia for a lost past when children respected parents, the crime rate was low, marriage was for life and the streets were safe for everyone to walk in. What is concealed when this image of the past is invoked is that it was never a reality but an ideal, a middle-class dream ... the lost society is not a 'golden age' but one that secured the interests of capitalism and patriarchy at the expense of the working class, of women and of children. Indeed, this is what many in the New Right would appear to want to recreate.

(Abbott and Wallace, 1992, p. 6)

Discussion point

To what extent do you think that most people have a nostalgic view of families and society in the past?

C3.1a

The New Labour agenda

Fathers and families

In *Families without Fatherhood*, Dennis and Erdos (1992) argue that the riots which terrorized both Chicago in the USA and North Tyneside in the UK in the early 1990s could not be attributed to poverty alone. In fact, despite the problems of poverty and inequality which persist in those areas, the standard of living has improved for all but a tiny minority of working-class people. Far more hardship was endured by working people in the 1930s and 1950s, with far less social upheaval or unrest.

This suggests that economic deprivation alone cannot explain social unrest. However, Dennis and Erdos set out to investigate whether the changes in family life (including rising divorce and increasing lone-parenting) were causally related to declining civil life and commitment to community.

Writing from a perspective defined as 'ethical socialism', Dennis and Erdos (1992) argue that a number of factors can be identified as contributing towards the decline of moral standards they found among some groups in society.

- First, they suggest that most professional welfare workers no longer believe that they have any right to comment on the behaviour of others. Dennis and Erdos argue that such moral apathy may not always benefit society.

- They argue that we should help the 'deserving poor' who are unlucky, but not the 'undeserving poor' who are immoral and work-shy.

- Furthermore, they claim, most respectable working-class people agree with them. However, in relation to the family, sociologists have traditionally sympathized more with the single mother on benefit than with the woman who struggles at home on a limited income, either alone due to widowhood or trying to keep her husband in work and her children clean, well-fed and out of trouble.

Until the 1960s, there was a distinction that prevailed between the widowed mother and the never-married single mother in terms of both moral views and welfare entitlements. However, by the 1970s, the marital status of the mother and the legal status of the child had become irrelevant. If a women could not or did not work she was entitled to benefits for herself and her child. No one – not even the Church – was entitled to make moral judgements about the sexual behaviour of anyone. As a result, many children were being raised largely without a father for much of their lives.

Discussion point

To what extent do you think that young, unmarried mothers – and fathers – have done something immoral?

C3.1a

Against lone-parent families

Dennis and Erdos attack the view (which they see as one commonly held) that single parents are just as successful as those where both parents bring up the children. They argue that boys in fatherless families in particular grow up without the restraints on their behaviour that a father might impose, and without any expectations that they should take any responsibility for their own children when they become fathers themselves.

Boys (especially) brought up without a father do less well at school and are more likely to gain a criminal record than those with two parents, even when class and income are allowed for. Their evidence comes from a study of 1000 children born in Newcastle in 1947, who exhibited a greater statistical chance of having poor physical health, low intelligence quotient (IQ) scores and a criminal record if they were in an 'unfathered' or 'poorly fathered' group.

So far, many of their views seem similar to those expressed by the New Right; but while their ideas about the cause of social problems seem similar, they suggest different solutions to the problem.

The New Right argue that the **free market** and the rolling back of state support available to single parents will immediately wean people from their dependence on welfare. On the other hand, Dennis and Erdos suggest that the 'free market' has become part of the thinking of many young males, who deny any **social responsibility** for the children they produce. The views of Dennis and Erdos are shared by many of the most influential family policy-makers in the New Labour government. While accepting the need for some social support for families with problems, the New Labour agenda also stresses the individual responsibility of parents and the importance of traditional 'family values' in people's lives.

Activity

Outline and discuss the view that our society is suffering from moral decline as a result of family disintegration. Use the material in the accompanying pieces from the *Observer* and *Guardian*, the sections above, and any other sociological arguments with which you are familiar.

C3.2, C3.3

Post-modern views of the family

In trying to explain how **post-modern** thought affects our view of family life, Cheal (1991) argues that:

Postmodernist theorists have begun to grapple with the possibility that many of the features of social life that were taken for granted for a long time will have to be rethought.

(Cheal, 1991, p. 145)

He suggests that the key aspects of **postmodernism** are *pluralism*, *disorder* and *fragmentation*, and these concepts can be seen to be particularly relevant for a description of family life in many societies today. The post-modern view of family life is very different from seeing the family as the entity which more or less defined our gender roles – female as mother and carer and male as father and breadwinner – throughout the past 200 years at least.

From this view, lone parents, surrogate mothers, lesbian households or gay couples, for example, are not seen as problematic, although many people in our society still consider them to be so.

Most feminists argue that there are still different expectations about working mothers and working fathers. Women who work outside the home (as the majority now do) are often expected to combine this with taking on most of the responsibility for childcare and domestic work. As a result of this, most children still grow up expecting their mothers to do more in the house than their fathers, and women see domestic responsibilities as their own.

This debate about the domestic division of labour is explored more fully in Section 5.7; but from this point of view, traditional two-parent families can be seen as reinforcing the gendered division of labour in our society.

'PROMOTING MARRIAGE'

Labour is to support proposals by a group of right-wing Tories to teach all schoolchildren the importance of heterosexual marriage. In a late change to the Education Bill now going through Parliament, the Conservative family values campaigner, Edward Leigh, has tabled a clause to promote marriage and parenthood in maintained schools. The proposal would mean rewriting the national curriculum to include lessons about the positive aspects of marriage and heterosexual parenthood.

Source: Extracted from an article on promoting marriage, *Observer*, 26 January 1997

Back to the 1950s

LARRY ELLIOTT

Now it looks as if the 1950s are coming back: or rather, one bit of the 1950s. What we are *not* getting is the full employment, the progressive taxation and the determination of an interventionist state to use active welfare policies to reduce the gap between rich and poor.

What we *are* being offered instead is social authoritarianism; a crack-down on law and order and discipline in schools; a willingness to tell people how they should conduct their relationships and bring up their children.

This combination of the free-market economics of the 1980s and the social policy of the 1950s is being sold as a cure-all solution to society's ills. But this is not a social policy, nor even a moral policy. It is a policy of cut-price containment – a cheap way of coping with the middle-class fear that a burgeoning "underclass" is out of control.

Women should be aware that the emphasis on family values and the need for parents to teach their children the difference between right and wrong is by no means the whole agenda. There will be pressure for tougher laws on abortion, and before long almost certainly calls for the ideal family unit to be made up of one male breadwinner and a wife who stays at home to care for the children. Just like the 1950s.

Stand back a second from the sense of moral panic that the politicians have stirred up, and what we see is not the inheritance of the permissive society but the inevitable consequence of an economic system built around exclusion, alienation and greed. As the American writer E. J. Dionne puts it in his new book: "It's [the moral crisis's] roots lie deeper, in a society built on individualistic and market values that steadily cut away the bonds of solidarity, morality and trust."

The particularly harsh variant of free-market capitalism championed over the past two decades has led to the widest income distribution since records began. More than that, workers have found that the consumer society cuts both ways: they themselves are now commodities to be bought and sold in the flexible labour market.

This is in stark contrast to 40 years ago. Then, it was taken as read that the government should use demand management to create jobs, and that progressive taxation should redistribute income. The result – not just in Britain but in the whole of the West – was rising real incomes, a narrowing of income differentials and a stable society.

Of course, this won't be tried. Higher taxation for the rich is not on the agenda, because as we have been

told countless times over the past two decades, it is bad for the economy and bad, ultimately, for the poor themselves. There is absolutely no evidence, even in the United States, that cutting taxes, either on rich individuals or on wealthy corporations, leads to higher investment or stronger growth. On the contrary, American growth rates were strongest when the top rate of tax was above 80 per cent.

It's a nice idea that cutting taxes for the rich makes everybody better off by unleashing a new wave of entrepreneurial activity. But in reality, all it has done is make a lot of rich people a whole lot richer and left a hole in the finances that has had to be filled either by raising taxes on the less well-off or by borrowing at damagingly-high rates of interest.

Ultimately, the question is whether compulsory parenting classes, minimum sentences and bans on guns and knives can fill the gap where economic policy used to be. Some of these reforms might be desirable; some may have a limited impact. But the experience of the US, where the crackdown on the poor is already well advanced, suggests otherwise.

Source: Adapted from *Guardian*, 31 October 1996

Morgan (1996) argues that marriage is still seen as the central domestic relationship for most people. We may accept some reduction of gender differences in marriage, but expectations about the sexual roles (and sexual orientations) of married couples remain important. There are expectations now that many women will seek to combine a job or career with marriage (and often with children), while men are generally expected

to contribute far more to the parenting of their children than was previously the case.

Late-modern views on the family and risk society

Another approach tending to celebrate rather than decry the diversity of contemporary family structures is based on the notion that we now live in a risk society (Beck, 1992), in which we have to consider carefully the choices we make and the consequences they might have. However, it is also argued that choices can be liberating as well as constraining, and that this position gives greater emphasis to individual freedom and the ability of people to adapt structures to their own personal circumstances and beliefs.

Warren Kidd (1999) argues that the work of Anthony Giddens fits into this category:

*Giddens suggests that divorce offers the individual both challenges and opportunities to rebuild one's sense of self in **reflexive modernity** – to contemplate as an individual, rather than to take for granted, the nature of relationships, the future direction of our life, the nature of the family and of society.*

(Kidd, 1999, p. 14)

The complexity of family life

It appears that a more varied and complex set of domestic arrangements is becoming acceptable to many people. However, certain common sense assumptions remain about marriage, including one that both partners are exclusively heterosexual and that they marry with the intention of staying together.

There still seems to be a general rejection of the idea in our society that people should marry for money, or to help someone stay in the country or to suit the wishes of their parents and other family members. Clearly, post-modern views consider diversity in family life to be largely acceptable and desirable, but not all sociologists or politicians share this view. Indeed, the current debate about the decline of morality and the lack of stability in society is what many people see as characteristic of a post-modern (or at least changing) society.

5.7 The distribution of power between men and women in the family

How power is distributed in the family can be studied by examining various factors, including the allocation of housework, childcare and care of the elderly; who controls decision-making and money; and emotional tasks. We are used to considering the family as a very positive institution in society, based on ties of kinship or emotional and sexual attachment. It is certainly the case that everyday visions of the family project this image.

Functionalist views on the family

Such a positive image was behind early sociological visions of the family, seeing in it the ultimate basis for the consensus and harmony that exists in the rest of society.

As an example of this we can quote the work of Shorter (1977):

The nuclear family was a nest. Warm and sheltering, it kept the children secure from the pressures of the outside adult world, and gave the men an evening refuge from the icy blast of competition. And as the nuclear family rose in the nineteenth century, women liked it too, because it let them pull back from the grinding exactions of farm work, or the place at the mill, and devote themselves to child care.

(Shorter, 1977, p. 279)

In the passage quoted from Shorter we are presented with a vision of the nuclear family as a structure that benefits all members. However, there are many assumptions about the roles of family members contained within the passage. It suggests that a division of labour exists whereby men go out to work and expect emotional and material comfort from the family, while women stay at home looking after the children. It also assumes that everyone enjoys this division of domestic labour. Such assumptions have been widely challenged.

Activity

What assumptions does Shorter make about the roles of men and women, both in society and in the family?

The changing role of women in the family

Feminists have particularly noted that industrialization affected men and women differently.

Oakley (1974a,b) showed how women moved from being equal partners when the family was a pre-industrial unit of production, to being increasingly constricted and confined to the home by industrialization and factory legislation. She suggests that these changes, resulted in the 'mother–housewife' role becoming the dominant one for women in industrialized societies.

Hall (1982) extended this analysis to show how, as men became increasingly identified by their work, the separation of work and home became more important. Men and women increasingly operated within separate spheres – men with business and politics (the public domain) and women with the home and children (the private domain). Men whose wives went out to work were considered inadequate providers, while waged females such as mill girls were notorious for their independence and cheekiness.

However, O'Day (1983) argues that the roles of males and females were often quite separate even *before* industrialization. Davidoff (1979), meanwhile, suggested that many women earned money from within the household. Both these writers suggest that the separation of home and work was neither so dramatic nor so complete as writers such as Oakley and Hall contend.

Whatever the reasons, it can be seen that the idea of the male breadwinner and the female domestic carer was well established by the end of the nineteenth century. Hartmann (1981) argued that this was due largely to an alliance between capitalist employers and working men to ensure high profits for the former and reasonable wages for the latter. This view has been challenged by Humpheries (1977), who regarded the fight for a family wage as a form of resistance by working-class people against capitalist exploitation.

Activity

Explain in your own words the different views amongst feminists of the influence of industrialization on the working-class family.

C3.2, C3.3

The feminist critique of 'happy families'

The rise of feminist thinking in sociology has led to a questioning of the idea of the family as a harmonious unit. The view that family structures can lead to the oppression of women by either men and/or capitalism, depending on the variety of feminism, has led to analysis of family units in terms of relationships involving unequal power struggles. As a result, the vision of the family produced by feminist writers is very different from the one quoted above from Shorter. For example:

The family-household system of contemporary capitalism constitutes not only the central site of the

oppression of women but an important organizing principle of the relations of production and the social formation as a whole.

(Barrett, 1980, p. 211)

The reasoning behind feminist analysis was the experience of women in family life. Emerging evidence of domestic violence, marital rape and other very negative parts of family life was at the root of the rise of the women's movement and feminist analysis. (See also Section 5.9.)

The domestic division of labour

It is clear that the rather cosy views of family life presented by the early functionalists (see page 88) would not be endorsed today. However, the question of whether the family is evolving towards structures that do at least allow a degree of equality and freedom to all parties, or whether they still represent patriarchal oppressive structures, is central to the debate about the domestic division of labour.

The start of this debate can be traced to the mid-1970s with the publication of two books with radically different conclusions on family life and relationships within it.

The 'symmetrical family'

In 1975, Young and Willmott published a book entitled *The Symmetrical Family*. It was based on historical evidence plus work from their earlier studies of family life (Willmott and Young, 1971) and outlined their views on the way in which family life was changing.

Central to this was the notion of changing roles for men and women in society in general and the family in particular. They argued that families have gone through a pattern of change leading to the emergence of the 'symmetrical family' in late industrial society, moving towards a balance or symmetry between the roles of males and females inside families.

This can be seen in the increased tendency for women to engage in paid employment outside the home, and the increase in the amount of work males do around the house (domestic labour). In line with their more general views on evolution and the principle of **stratified diffusion**, Young and Willmott argue that these developments occurred first in middle-class households and were later being adopted in working-class households. Their view of the 'symmetrical family' was therefore something of a prediction about the future at the time it was written as well as a description of how some middle-class couples lived.

The sociology of housework

In Ann Oakley's book on housework (1974a), she argued that the idea of 'symmetry' discussed above was a myth. She supported this criticism by pointing out that Young and Willmott's own statistics showed that only 72 per cent of husbands 'helped' their wife in some way. She also asserted that this was a very loose notion and, more importantly, the idea that husbands 'help' their wives showed that the prime responsibility for domestic labour was still seen to lie with women.

One important influence on Oakley's work was the series of studies of the frustrations faced by male assembly-line workers, such as Blauner's (1964) study of work and **alienation**, and Goldthorpe and Lockwood's affluent-worker study (1968). Oakley set out to analyse housework using similar categories to underline her argument that it should be treated as real work. Some of her findings in this regard are presented in Table 5.11.

Table 5.11 The experience of monotony, fragmentation and speed in work: housewives and factory workers compared (percentages)

Workers	Monotony	Fragmentation	Speed
Housewives	75	90	50
Factory workers	41	70	31
Assembly-line workers[a]	67	86	36

[a] The assembly-line workers are a sub-sample of the factory workers.
Source: Oakley (1974a, p. 87)

 Activity

a Identify and explain two aspects of feminist critique of families.

b Outline and discuss the view that housework is monotonous and oppressive.

C3.2, C3.3

Furthermore, Oakley's research indicated that, far from males becoming more involved in domestic tasks – although middle-class males helped slightly more than working-class males – most support was related to childcare rather than to general housework duties. Overall she rejected the notion of progress implied by the idea of the development of the symmetrical family, since it could be found only in a minority of households.

She argued that the construction of the housewife role should be analysed on the same basis as the construction of predominantly male employment and that housework should be viewed as work. This was not in fact the case, despite the fact that some women spent up to 77 hours per week on domestic work.

According to Oakley, the oppression of women occurs through this role since:

The characteristic features of the housewife role in modern industrialized society are

(1) *its exclusive allocation to women, rather than to adults of both sexes;*

(2) *its association with economic dependence, i.e. with the dependent role of the woman in modern marriage;*

(3) *its status as non-work – or its opposition to 'real', i.e. economically productive, work; and*

(4) *its primacy to women, that is, its priority over other roles.*

(Oakley, 1974a, p. 138)

 Discussion point

In the above passage Oakley makes a number of statements about the situation of housewives. Discuss whether each of these is still valid today.

C3.1a

Decision-making and power inequalities in the family

Further criticism of the notion of increasing domestic equality came from Stephen Edgell's (1980) study of middle-class couples. Given that the theory of *stratified diffusion* suggested that this was where most equality would be found, his conclusion was that in fact no such equality was present:

In contrast to certain optimistic theorists who claim that the nineteenth-century patriarchal family has been superseded by a more democratic type ... the present study provides abundant evidence of the survival of patriarchalism.

(Edgell, 1980, p. 105)

Recent developments in the debate

The control of finance in households

Research on this issue has mushroomed since the 1970s. Pahl (1989) found that, while there were some instances where women controlled the family finances, in these cases the women used their budgeting skills to provide goods for their husbands or children, often themselves going without in the process. Therefore even when women gained some control, ultimately it was men (and others) who benefited from this.

She suggests that there are a number of factors that contribute to decisions over the control of money within marriages. She found that there were four main ways in which family finances could be organized: control by wife, control by husband, or pooling arrangements controlled either by the wife or the husband.

In later work, Pahl (1993) also found that the way finances were organized seemed to make a significant difference to the level of marital happiness expressed in the families she studied (see also Table 5.12 below):

Table 5.12 Marital happiness by control of finances: wives' answers (husbands' in brackets)

Marriage described as:	Wife control	Wife-controlled pooling	Husband-controlled pooling	Husband control
Happy/very happy	13 (13)	23 (25)	37 (35)	13 (16)
Average/ unhappy	1 (1)	4 (2)	2 (4)	9 (6)

Source: Pahl (1993)

So the way in which a couple organize their finances reflects the resources which each brings to the relationship and affects the quality of the relationship. An ideology which stresses the sharing of resources helps to conceal the structurally weak position of those who do not earn. An ideology of separateness in financial matters strengthens the position of those who earn compared with those who do not.

The control and allocation of money in marriage has proved to be an exciting new area of sociological enquiry. In the past, the 'sociology of work' was largely separate from the 'sociology of the family'. Now we can see that the broader socio-economic context shapes the control of money within the household, which itself shapes the experience of individual members of households. Asking about money offers a revealing way of exploring the differences between 'his' marriage and 'her' marriage.

(Adapted from Pahl, 1993)

Activity

Summarize Pahl's main findings about the relationship between financial control in families and marital happiness.

C3.2

Money, the family and recession – a case study of Hartlepool

Also considering financial resources within the household, Lydia Morris (1987, 1993) conducted a case study of family relationships in Hartlepool, looking at the effects of recession and unemployment on family decision-making.

She concluded that, while changes in the economic structure had led to the decline of the male as an exclusive breadwinner for the whole family (owing to the rise of unemployment, which had reached 27 per cent in Hartlepool by the time of her fieldwork in 1986), in relation to gender roles, this has not led to a great deal of change.

Most employment opportunities for women with children remained part-time, and when women took such jobs their household roles were not largely taken over by husbands but predominantly by female relatives and friends. Therefore, even when men were unemployed, gender roles remained 'traditional' and women still undertook most household tasks, even if that meant a network of women rather than one individual woman. In relation to finance, however, Morris argues, the effect of the recession and the growth of male unemployment and consequential low household incomes had meant some greater influence for women in budgetary matters.

Generally, the wives of unemployed men are themselves more likely to be unemployed than the wives of employed men, largely because the social security benefits system doesn't make it worth their while. So women gain greater control, but over smaller amounts of money – merely giving them a greater say in poverty. A more detailed summary of this piece of research can be found in an excellent article in *Sociology Review* by David Abbott (1994).

Money, control and male unemployment

A similar study by Wheelock (1990) looked at what happens when the husband is unemployed and the wife still has paid employment. For a number of reasons this is an unusual scenario, since most studies show that when the husband becomes unemployed the wife is very likely to become unemployed as well. However, it does provide a situation in which it is possible to test out whether men would adopt domestic duties if their wife were indeed working.

Wheelock studied 30 such families in the north east of England. Although the women in the study still retained primary responsibility for core household tasks, the men did become more involved in various activities. However, their involvement remained limited. The amount of help in domestic work given by husbands did seem to vary in line with the number of hours of paid employment the wives were doing.

Negotiations around family responsibilities

Finch and Mason (1993) looked at the ways in which families tended to negotiate family responsibilities. This involved various expectations about obligations to family and wider kin. They found that there was no general agreement about the level of help and obligation one should feel towards family members. They therefore argue that we should talk about guidelines rather than rules in this respect, as what is expected within families seems to be so varied.

It is here that the importance of negotiation becomes apparent. The lack of clear rules leaves room for discussion, taking the form of negotiations about the type and amount of help to be given or expected. In particular this is the case in relation to looking after elderly relatives, often provoking discussion and negotiation between the children of the elderly person and also between their children and their spouses.

A number of studies (e.g. Elliot, 1996; Hicks, 1988) have shown that much domestic care for the elderly seems to be delegated to daughters and daughters-in-law. However, men and women

equally provide care for a spouse, and both male and female carers experience similar problems in acquiring the levels of support they need.

Emotional labour in the family

The 'second shift'

In *The Second Shift*, American sociologist Arlie Hochschild (1989) investigated the role of caring in the home and how this affected men and women's engagement with paid work. This contribution moved the debate about the domestic division of labour on to new terrain, with discussion of the division of **emotional labour** in the household.

She studied 52 couples with children under 6 years of age, looking particularly at how men and women managed their emotions and whether there were any differences. She argued that, despite rhetoric about the move to equality in this respect, there had been a stalled revolution, with women taking much greater responsibility for childcare and men being reluctant to get involved in this 'second shift'.

Hochschild argues that emotions are an important element in the way households connect and interact, and that this division between paid work and the 'second shift' of caring for the family has impeded the movement towards gender equality.

The 'triple shift'

Morgan (1996) suggests that discussions about emotional labour in the family are part of the increasing analysis of 'emotions' within sociology, a concept that has traditionally been associated with the notion of (ir)rationality.

While analyses of emotional labour have looked mostly at the preponderance of women in the 'caring' professions, Marsden and Duncombe (1993) argue that the biggest part of the emotional work in families is done, unpaid, by women. These views draw on the concept of the 'expressive' role attributed to women by Talcott Parsons in the 1950s. However, the increasing number of women working outside the home, plus evidence of their continuing contributions towards domestic care, suggest two outcomes:

• women are being exhausted by what Marsden

and Duncombe call the 'triple shift' of paid, domestic and emotional labour

- men are expected to contribute more, not just to the domestic but also to the emotional labour required to maintain family life.

Morgan also points out that children and elderly relatives as well as men need to contribute some emotional labour, even if they are the ones being cared for.

Noddings (1984) discussed the concept of 'caring' as a relationship, but one that is changing within existing social contexts. One consequence of this emphasis on changes in emotional relationships in the family is the phenomenon of the so-called 'new man'.

A recent report on fathering published by the Family Policy Studies Centre and the Joseph Rowntree Foundation suggests that, just as many women feel overburdened by the 'triple shift', many men feel trapped by the double burden of providing for a family and living up to expectations of the greater involvement expected from fathers in domestic and childcare. There is a further problem in that many men still want to be the chief provider and consider women as the more skilled at parenting. Furthermore, many women share these views while still wanting more emotional involvement from their partners.

🗩 Discussion point

How are boys and girls and men and women expected to behave within the family and in other emotional relationships? Do you think these expectations have changed? Who does most of the emotional labour in your family? Give examples. How do you think fathers could be encouraged to become more emotionally involved with their families?

C3.1a

5.8 The relationships between parents and children

As well as considering relationships between adult men and adult women within families and households, sociologists discuss relationships based on age differences – notably that between parents and children, but also between adults and their elderly parents.

Households and family groups

Household size

During the 1970s, 1980s and 1990s, there was a gradual reduction in the average (mean) size of households, from 2.91 people in 1971 to 2.51 people in 1989 and to 2.40 people in 1998. This reflected a combination of:

- the gradual ageing of the population
- a decrease in the number of births
- an increase in the proportion of one-person households
- a reduction in the proportion of large households (5 or more persons)
- an increase in the proportion of lone-parent families.

Family groups

In 1995, the types of family most frequently found in private households were (ONS, 1997a):

- couples (married or cohabiting) with no dependent children (36 per cent)
- persons living alone (28 per cent)
- couples (married or cohabiting) with dependent children (24 per cent).

Two more commonly identifiable trends are towards smaller family size and greater longevity of its members.

Children in families

The onset of industrialization

Industrialization is seen as changing the role and position of children in the family and beyond. The social historian, Philipe Ariès (1973), showed that industrialization almost completely changed the position of children. He argues that, before industrialization, most children were seen as mini-adults. They dressed much like their parents and did much the same work, mainly in the fields or the home. Like their parents, most children received relatively little formal education and learned the skills they needed from parents and older siblings.

In contrast, industrialization has led to what Ariès sees as an obsession with the physical, moral and sexual problems of childhood. Children are now expected to undertake at least

10–12 years of formal education, often learning things their parents have no knowledge of. Modern families are often seen to be 'child-centred', partly because couples tend to have fewer children and partly because they have more leisure time to spend with their offspring.

Although Ariès is right to identify the increasing emphasis that families place on children in contemporary society, he has been criticized because:

- he tends to ignore the brutality of many children's lives in pre-industrial times

- he also tends not to look at the serious issues of child abuse in some families (see Section 5.9).

Children, social control and the state

Ariès' identification of childhood as being largely socially constructed (rather than merely biological) is an extremely important insight. However, we also need to look at how industrialization has led to greater state controls over children and their parents, and the support networks that many children need to avoid serious difficulties like poverty and abuse. Charities such as Childline and the National Society for the Prevention of Cruelty to Children (NSPCC) seek to raise awareness of these issues, which were largely ignored in pre-industrial times. (See also Section 5.9.)

Many commentators identified the twentieth century as the century of childhood. Perhaps the twenty-first century will be increasingly child-centred, in the affluent west at least. There are various reasons for suggesting this:

- children are becoming an increasingly small proportion of the population, giving them rarity value

- rapid technological changes place an emphasis on up-to-date knowledge, which is epitomized by youth

- youth is associated with health, beauty and desirability (and even capability), as the growth in plastic surgery for healthy adults testifies.

Socialization

Clearly, some form of social network is required to introduce children to their own culture. They need to learn the culture of their own society if they are to exist within it in any acceptable way.

Evidence from feral (wild) children and those not socialized by their parents (see Section 3.2) shows that skills like speaking, affection, toilet control, tolerance and patience do need to be learned – they are not given at birth.

What people eat, wear, believe in, aspire to and reward, as well as how they behave, has to be learned from someone. This process is often called *socialization* by sociologists.

Socialization, then, is the way in which the culture of a society is passed from one generation to the next. This means that we have to learn the **norms** and **values** attached to particular roles or positions in society – such as how to be a student, a shopworker, a teacher, a friend or a parent.

Families are sometimes described as 'the agency of **primary socialization**'. They are usually the first group in which we meet our cultural norms, although we continue to learn new roles and values throughout our lives. We also learn through many other socializing agencies, such as school, friends, work, partnerships, religion and the mass media.

Some writers who promote the traditional model of the family suggest that children who are not brought up in a 'normal' family might become **deviant** – so anything that changes the 'normal' structure (such as single mothers) is seen as a sign of social decay.

The legal status of children

As discussed previously, Phillipe Ariès (1973) famously suggested that prior to the fifteenth century and the early stirrings of industrial society, there was no real conception of children, and that the people we today call 'children' were treated as miniature adults. Although this argument is debated, it is clear that it suggests that what we mean by 'childhood', and the rights and responsibilities (or the lack of them) that go along with it have considerably changed over time.

Stephen Moore (1993) points out that the 1908 Children's Act was the first time that children were legally treated differently from adults in the UK. Today, the notion of 'childhood' does have a clear meaning in our society, although the age at which this period ends is somewhat unclear, with contradictory periods cited in various laws. For instance, although you can get married (with your parents' permission) when you are 16, and might therefore become a parent yourself shortly afterwards, you cannot vote until you are 18, and you cannot apply for a licence to run a pub until you are 21. These restrictions may now be somewhat contradictory in the way they have developed, but their existence serves to show that we do now use age to delineate a period known as 'childhood' when different legal criteria apply.

In essence, children are considered unable to make mature decisions themselves, and therefore need guidance from adults. However, they are also considered in need of protection, since they are unable to fend for themselves. A key problem is that these two demands may sometimes be in conflict with one another: for instance, in the case of child abuse, parents who are supposed to protect a child are in fact harming it.

In looking after their own children, parents are subject to the laws that concern children in general. In particular, they are required to ensure that they attend school full-time between the ages of 5 and 16, unless they can show that they can provide a satisfactory alternative. Families are, however, also given support by the state to assist with the costs of children, in the form of 'child benefit'.

Recognising that children are in need of protection, and that this is not always automatically provided by adults, led the United Nations to adopt the 'Convention on the Rights of the Child' in 1989. As Marsh *et al.* (1996) report;

The Convention has 54 articles covering the following broad areas of rights: survival, protection, development and participation. As well as defining the social, economic, cultural, civil and political rights of children, the Convention outlines the duties and responsibilities of governments and other adults to children and their families.

(Marsh *et al.*, 1996, p. 422)

The Childrens Act 1989

In the same year in the UK, the government passed the 1989 Children's Act. The key shift underlying this act was a shift away from parental rights to parental responsibilities, and the paramount concern with the welfare of the child.

Clearly, the impact of this is to provide a legal basis for other agencies to be used to protect children when their parents are not protecting them, or are actually harming them. The assumption that parents automatically knew and acted upon what was in the best interests of the child has been replaced by legal rights for children to

'divorce' their parents in certain cases. Children can now have a say in which parent they live with following a divorce, and they can even bring to the attention of the court instances of where parents have not properly discharged their responsibilities to them (Marsh *et al.*, 1996). It is also the case that under the Child Support Act 1991, absent parents are required to contribute to the financial cost of providing for the child, and the parent with immediate parental responsibility is required to cooperate with the Child Support Agency to assist in this process. This agency was somewhat controversial, and is examined in more detail on page 126.

Following the 1989 Act, the wishes of the child must be taken into account when deciding on what is in his or her best interests. Children are therefore no longer passive objects of the law and their parents, but have legal rights, and a voice that must be taken into account.

However, one other effect of the changing conception of children can be seen in debates about whether children under 14 know right from wrong. It is assumed they do, this would suggest that in some ways 14 year olds should be treated as adults, and this opens up the debate on the exact status of children, and at what age this status ends.

Debates about parenting

The Labour government elected in 1997 changed the tax legislation (for the purposes of tax relief and social assistance) to produce a shift away from dividing the population into those who are married and those who are not, towards those who are parents or not. This reflects a greater concern with parenting and a move away from seeing marriage as the only acceptable route to parenting. Clearly it is possible for marriage and parenting to be separated.

Activity
Suggest family structures where marriage and parenting go together, and family structures where they are separated.

C3.1a, C3.2

Forms of parenting

Table 5.13 shows the distribution of dependent child into different family types. As can be seen, the 'cereal packet' image of the family consisting of two parents and two children covers only just over a third of all children, and is only just over twice as likely to happen as lone-parent families. This table illustrates the wide diversity of family structures in which today's children will grow up.

Table 5.13 Dependent children living in different family types in Great Britain (percentages)

	1972	1981	1986	1992	1997	1998
Couple families						
One child	16	18	18	17	17	17
Two children	35	41	41	37	37	37
Three or more children	41	29	28	28	26	25
Lone-mother families						
One child	2	3	4	5	5	6
Two children	2	4	5	7	7	7
Three or more children	2	3	3	6	6	6
Lone-father families						
One child	–	1	1	–	–	1
Two or more children	1	1	1	1	1	1
All dependent children	*100*	*100*	*100*	*100*	*100*	*100*

Source: Social Trends 1998, ONS (1998) and www.statistics.gov.uk

Activity

Summarize in your own words the trends in child-rearing patterns shown in Table 5.13.

C3.2, C3.3

Parenting and the well-being of children

The National Childrens Homes (NCH) Action for Children (1997) studied family life using a survey of 1000 parents and 250 children. They report that children today are worried about violence, whether at home or at school in the form of bullying.

The NCH survey also revealed that parents are worried about their children. The main concerns here were alcohol and drug abuse, and the lack of job prospects for the young. However, fears about bullying and violence in the home were also high on the list of concerns.

Figures from Childline seem to back this up. In their annual review, Childline (1998) reported that bullying was the most common problem cited by children phoning them for advice, and that this problem covered 17 per cent of all calls to them. A further 13 per cent of calls concerned family relationships, 11 per cent concerned physical abuse and 8 per cent concerned sexual abuse.

Parenting and employment

One aspect of New Right thinking stresses the importance of the caring role of the mother. However, Ferri and Smith (1998) could find little evidence of full-time employment by both parents leading to the erosion of family life. This is significant given Labour governments emphasis on employment as a key route out of poverty, and the ensuing debate about whether this would undermine the quality of care being offered by parents to their children.

Divorce and separation

A key area of concern over the rising rate of divorce (see page 97) has been its effects on children. Rodgers and Pryor (1998) reviewed the findings of 200 studies on the impact of divorce and separation on children. They found that, while divorce and separation were associated with short-term distress for the children, in the longer term this usually fades and children develop into a 'normal' pattern of development.

They point out, however, that there are some studies pointing to longer-term adverse effects on children. These include a greater tendency to show behavioural problems and perform less well in school, the likelihood of subsequently living in a household with low income, and an increased likelihood to cohabit, have children earlier and outside of marriage.

Does this mean that the government should act to make divorce harder, or simply provide greater support for families going through divorce, placing greater emphasis on the needs of children in divorce settlements? This is an ongoing debate arising out of concerns over the effect of divorce and separation on children.

Lower and later childbirths

Figures from *Social Trends* 1998 (ONS, 1998) show that childbirths are tending to occur later on in adults' lives. While fertility has been falling among women in their twenties, it has been rising among those in their thirties.

One concern has been infertility, particularly among men. This has led to debate about the provision of infertility treatments, and the question of whether these will enable men and women to overcome the 'biological clock' in relation to parentage.

Adoption

One area of parenting that seems to have declined in recent years is adoption of children. In 1996 there were 5700 adoptions in England and Wales, representing a 1 per cent fall on the figure for 1995 but a substantial fall from the peak of 25 000 in 1968.

> ### Activity
> Explain how the following social trends may have caused adoption rates to have declined since 1968: abortion, fertility treatment, surrogacy, decline in mortality rates, contraception, decline in birthrates.
>
> **C3.2, C3.3**

Step-families

Along with the increasing numbers of divorces and remarriages has come an increase in the proportion of reconstituted and step-families.

Ferri and Smith (1998) investigated the experience of step-families by studying 878 people in their thirties bringing up children in this type of household. They found that family activities involving all members was just as common in step-families as in conventional families. However, these families tended to have lower average incomes, and there was a greater polarity between high income and low income families.

The Child Support Agency

The Child Support Agency (CSA), established in April 1993, was charged with the task of assessing and collecting maintenance payments from absent parents.

The CSA uses a standard formula to assess levels of child maintenance based on the ability of both parents to contribute. This approach assumes that parents have just as much responsibility for children conceived through a previous relationship as they do for children of any current relationship. It differs from the approach adopted earlier by the courts, which used discretion in individual cases when determining the level of child maintenance.

When the parent with care of a child is on welfare benefits, successful enforcement by the CSA will result in considerable savings for the state. The reported concentration of the agency's efforts on relatively well-off absent parents, whose former partners are currently on welfare benefits, has attracted the strongest criticism.

Surveys show strong support for the *principle* that maintenance payments should come from absent parents according to what they can afford. Ninety-four per cent agree that a divorced father should pay maintenance to support a primary school-aged child of his who remains with the mother. Ninety-one per cent agree that the amount of that maintenance should depend on the father's income. However, there is some disagreement over where paternal responsibility should come to an end. A substantial majority (about two-thirds) think that the amount of maintenance should depend on the mother's income too – in other words, that questions of need as well as biological responsibility are relevant. When asked to consider what should happen if the mother remarries, only about two in five say maintenance should definitely continue, while a similar number say it should depend on the new husband's income.

While in opposition the Labour party criticized the Child Support Agency. Now in power, New Labour have sought to reform rather than disband it to make it more efficient while at the same time emphasizing the responsibilities of fathers for the maintenance of their offspring.

> ### Activity
> Identify the aims of the Child Support Agency. Outline the advantages and disadvantages for:
> (a) children; (b) fathers; (c) mothers;
> (d) the state.
>
> **C3.2, C3.3**

Childlessness and the family

Van Every (1995) suggests that increasing numbers of people are choosing to remain childless voluntarily.

> ### Discussion point
> Discuss reasons why an increasing number of couples may choose not to have children. Do they still constitute a family?
>
> **C3.1a**

Despite this trend towards fewer people wanting to have children, *Social Trends* 1998 (ONS, 1998) reported statistics of population trends showing 649 000 live births in England and Wales in 1997, a rise of 1000 compared with 1996. It goes on to point out that this was the first rise in the annual number of births since 1990.

5.9 The dark side of family life

Despite numerous criticisms, the family is still usually considered one of the most significant social institutions in society, linked closely with notions of love and caring. It can therefore be something of a shock to find out that there is a dark side to family life. Sociologists need to consider the reality of the ways people live their lives in contemporary society. They therefore seek to understand some of the activities within the family which constitute a threat to some or all of its members. It is important to discover whether darker aspects of family life such as domestic violence and child abuse are exceptional acts committed by deviant people, or whether they are at least partly the result of the private nature of family life itself.

Violence against women

The extent to which women face domestic violence came to prominence as one of the key campaigning issues of the **women's liberation movement**. The rise of feminism has led to continuing sociological concern about this.

Domestic violence in Scotland

The largest study of domestic violence is that by Dobash and Dobash (1980), who analysed crime statistics in Scotland. These researchers came to the rather frightening conclusion that 25 per cent of all serious assaults were committed by husbands on their wives.

When one takes into account their view that the study, if anything, underestimates the extent of 'wife-battering' (because this type of offence is not always recorded in crime statistics), it shows the rather dangerous prospects that women face in conventional heterosexual partnerships. However, instances of domestic violence have also been recorded between same-sex couples and by women on men. While such occurrences often receive a lot of publicity, male violence on women is by far the most frequently recorded aspect of domestic violence.

In this study, one of the major factors precipitating assaults was the husband's perception that the wife was not performing her domestic duties to his satisfaction. Insofar as our society still accepts a domestic division of labour which allocates the majority of domestic duties to the female, this leaves women vulnerable to this sort of criticism, and possible subsequent assault.

However, the problems go deeper than that. Since domestic labour is unpaid and most women are in poorly rewarded jobs when they do work outside the home, many females are left economically dependent on male wages.

Dobash and Dobash also found that, although most women who were assaulted left their homes, many were forced to return. This was largely owing to their economic dependency, but also because of the stigma surrounding the break-up of marriage. Many radical feminists argue that this stigma is based on the idea of heterosexual coupling as the normal form for family life.

The UN Women's Conference and Domestic Violence

A document produced for the Fourth UN Women's Conference held in 1995 implies that this problem has not disappeared. It alleges that a quarter of the world's women suffer domestic violence; five women are burned to death in dowry disputes in India every day; more than a million newborn girls are murdered or left to die every year; and 90 million girls have endured genital mutilation. Women still do two-thirds of the world's work, earn one-tenth of the world's income and own less than one hundredth of the world's property. There are twice as many illiterate women in the world as men, with wages between 30 and 40 per cent lower than those of men.

Activity

a Identify and explain two aspects of violence that occurs in families.

b Outline and discuss the view that families are violent and unsafe.

 C3.2, C3.3

Social versus individual explanations for domestic violence

Cheal (1991) argues that feminist and Marxist theories have allowed sociologists to understand more about the problems that occur within families. These perspectives examine the *structural causes* of problems, rather than accepting individual explanations for behaviour within what had always been thought of as a private institution.

Psychologists tend not to identify the relationship between the private and public aspects of family life. This has resulted in the 'invisibility' of battered women. Cheal argues that such isolation is not a purely individual phenomenon. It has its roots in the social isolation experienced by many women living in private families.

Discussion point

To what extent do you agree that problems between domestic partners are largely a private matter?

C3.1a

Problems such as 'wife-battering' (now more commonly included under the phrase 'domestic abuse') have largely been ignored by police and courts, who have traditionally been reluctant to intervene in family disputes. Such views are linked to the idea that families are private institutions.

Cheal points out that the belief that external groups should not intervene in domestic matters highlights three key notions we have about the family.

- One notion is the idea that the family is a private institution to which the public has limited access – and therefore incomplete knowledge of the true circumstances.

- Another is the idea that individuals can act as free agents – so that women ought to be able to simply leave the abusive relationship if they want to.

- Finally there is the concept of 'interests'. The private interests of the individual woman are seen as being subordinate to her position in the family – she should be acting for the whole family group.

Discussion point

How free are men, women and children to act as individuals within their own family?

C3.1a

Rape within marriage

Until 1991, a women in England who was forced by her husband to have sexual intercourse against her will had no recourse in law. This reflected, partly, the notion of the wife being at the disposal of her husband – summed up in the phrase 'conjugal rights'. Although the law in this regard has been amended, it is still rare for a woman to bring a dispute to court, especially if she still lives in the same household as her husband.

In a survey of practices in a number of countries, Connors (1992) found that few societies penalized rape in marriage, while some still excused a man who killed his wife if he suspected adultery. For most feminists, rape within marriage is an extreme example of violence found – and accepted, or at least tolerated – in many patriarchal families.

Connors also found that women throughout the countries she studied experienced considerable mental and psychological oppression alongside their physical abuse. However, things were beginning to change.

Responses to domestic violence

Connors (1992) suggests that, for domestic violence to be controlled, women must be assured that legal advice is freely available. Changes in attitudes among the police and the judiciary are also required.

In many cases, the most effective action has been taken by groups of women themselves. The Women's Aid movement has set up refuges in America, the UK and a number of other countries. This sort of action appears to be more effective when combined with educational programmes, such as those now operating in Papua New Guinea and Australia.

Child abuse within the family

The nature of the problem

It is important to look at the way child abuse within the family has been examined over the past twenty years or so. In fact, many sociological explanations of violence within the family tend to attribute similar causes to the abuse of women and of children. There have been some very emotive debates in recent years.

The issue of sexual abuse of children came to prominence in the 1980s. There were a number of media stories about the actions of social workers in Cleveland, who had taken the drastic step of removing children from their parents because of suspicions of abuse. The whole incident provoked debate not only about the power of social workers, but also about whether parents could really be capable of abusing their own children. The issue culminated in a number of media stories in which the picture of child abuse became mixed up with images of satanic rites, such as events reported (and subsequently disproven) in the Shetland Islands.

Gittins (1993) argues that the topic of child abuse – or more precisely, child sexual abuse – has become increasingly important to debates about the family. She claims that it is predominantly males who abuse children sexually, and she adopts a radical feminist argument which suggests that children are endangered by males in the home. This seems to imply that it might be better to bring children up in a male-free environment.

Marxist–feminist critics of that position, such as Elliot (1996), point to the way in which the issue of child abuse is one example of how middle-class social workers seek to stigmatize and control the lives of working-class parents in order to enforce a dominant code about parenting.

They also argue that the radical feminists' concentration on child *sexual* abuse is not actually giving the full picture, since women too are sometimes abusers of children in other ways. Although it can be argued that sexual abuse is worse than other forms of abuse, it is also difficult to maintain that a male-free environment leads inevitably to a completely safe domestic environment for all children.

Elliot (1996) suggests that there are three main explanations of domestic violence: psychopathological, sociological and feminist. Psychopathological debates come mainly from psychologists and mental health therapists, who focus on individual pathology where domestic violence is viewed as both rare and deviant. Here we concentrate first on sociological explanations of child abuse, before going on to look at the feminist perspective on domestic violence in general.

Sociological explanations of child abuse

Non-feminist sociological approaches to child abuse often link it to economic deprivation and the development of a particular set of sub-cultural beliefs. Poverty, overcrowding and poor educational and occupational opportunities lead to frustration and repression, which may result in abusive behaviour where men seek to establish power over at least some aspect of their lives.

In this view, abuse of children is apparently accepted in some families, and this acceptance is transmitted to the next generation. The behaviour is also enhanced through the number of lone mothers, with their alleged tendency to have numerous sexual relationships with men.

Structural explanations, too, tend to regard deprivation as the key to understanding child abuse, as violence and inappropriate sexual behaviour can be seen as 'normal' responses to blocked opportunities. Stress, conflict and violence are seen as constant aspects of working-class life, so that structured age and gender inequalities can be viewed as explanations of domestic violence – even if sexual abuse is harder to understand.

While these explanations move beyond simplistic notions of individual pathology, Elliot shows that they, too, can be widely criticized. First, there is an assumption that child abuse – and other forms of violent and sexual abuse – takes place only in deprived families, whereas this has been shown not to be the case. It also ignores gender differences in patterns of abuse, and there is also a tendency to treat the statistics relating to child abuse as unquestionable.

The validity of child abuse statistics

Debates about the causes of abuse in the family often focus on the problems of defining and measuring the phenomenon. By its very nature, domestic abuse – and especially the sexual abuse of children – is a secret act that is deliberately hidden. While the number of recorded cases of child abuse has increased in recent years, there is a debate about how much this reflects changes in patterns of behaviour and how much it reflects changes in awareness and reporting.

Defining 'parental abuse' is not without its problems. Even the definition of 'sexual abuse' is complex, as one of the key features of the parent–child relationship is cuddling and showing affection. The level of child abuse, therefore, depends to a great extent on the definitions used – whether certain actions are included or excluded. The widest definitions tend to suggest that a large proportion of children experience some form of sexual abuse, mainly in the home with someone they know, quite often a relative or friend of the family.

Table 5.14 shows a wide variety of abusive behaviour experienced by children.

Table 5.14 Experiences of sexually abused children[a]

Abuse by a stranger	51%
Abuse by a known person	49%
Abuse by a family member	14%
Non-contact abuse	51%
Contact abuse not involving intercourse	44%
Abuse involving intercourse	5%
One incident involving one person	63%
Repeated abuse	23%
Multiple abuse	14%

[a] Based on a random national survey of 2019 women and men, using a wide definition of abuse that included contact and non-contact experiences.
Source: Baker and Duncan (1985), quoted in Elliot (1996)

Elliot quotes a study by Russell which shows that recorded child abuse quadrupled between 1900 and 1970. Girls are more likely to be abused than boys, especially within the home and incestuously, while the great majority of abusers are men. However, it is important to remember that *the majority of men as well as women find abuse of children both unthinkable and unacceptable*. Furthermore, some feminists tend to ignore the small but significant level of child abuse by women.

Child abuse is clearly a growing problem, not just for sociologists but for social workers, family therapists and psychologists as well. We do need to be cautious, however, about seeing it as a 'new' phenomenon. There are no statistics to illustrate its occurrence in Victorian times, for example, but it is quite possible that there is less child abuse today. In those times child prostitu-

tion was common and children were considered the possessions of their fathers. One of the key benefits of the greater equality of power between parents and children – resulting partly from feminist challenges to patriarchy – is to empower children to challenge abuse by adults in ways that they could not do in the past.

Recent statistics on child abuse

The charity Childline has published figures for children who telephoned their confidential advice lines during 1998/99 (see Table 5.15). These statistics highlight the significance of the abuse problem. However, it is important to remember that the figures have to be interpreted with caution.

Table 5.15 Childline statistics

Age of phone caller	
11 and under	21%
12–15	62%
16–18	16%
Gender of phone caller	
Girls	78%
Boys	22%
Five most common problems children call about	
Physical (11%) and/or sexual abuse (9%)	20%
Bullying	17%
Family relationships	13%
Worries about others	8%
Pregnancy	6%

Source: Childline's *Annual Review* (1999, pp. 8, 10 and 11)

Childline also provided figures on the perpetrators of sexual abuse against the children who phoned them about it (over 10 000 in 1998/99); these are given in Table 5.16.

Table 5.16 Perpetrators of sexual abuse

Person responsible	Against girls	Against boys	Total	(%)
Father	2222	1027	3249	30
Male acquaintance	853	126	979	9
Step-father	648	94	742	7
Mother	145	536	681	6
Male school child(ren)	505	56	561	5
Stranger	419	81	500	5
Teacher	353	139	492	5
Total (overall)	7968	2941	10909	

Source: Childline's *Annual Review* (1999)

Discussion point

In what ways can such statistics contribute to debates about the reality of family life and the experience of children in the family?

C3.1a

Social policy and child protection

Stephen Moore (1993) reports that the neglect of children first became an offence in 1868, when the Poor Law Amendment Act made it illegal not to provide for one's child.

While at first sight this provides positive legal protection for children, Moore (1993) points out that one purpose of this legislation was to ensure that demands were not made on local authorities to provide for children.

Following the more positive notion of welfare introduced in the early part of the twentieth century, various measures for the protection of children were introduced, allowing local authorities to receive children into their care when their parents were not able to look after them. Later on, local authorities and their social services department were also given powers to investigate suspected cases of cruelty or neglect of children.

Social workers now have the power to put children on an 'at risk ' register when they are concerned that a child may be being abused. The aim is to ensure close surveillance of the conditions of all children on these registers.

The work of local authority social services departments is also supplemented by the activities of voluntary and charitable organisations in the field of child protection, such as the National Society for the Prevention of Cruelty to Children (NSPCC) and Childline.

This alliance has provided some legal redress against parents who are no longer automatically assumed to know what is best or have the interests of the child as their prime concern. Evidence which shows the effect of this is cited by Kirton (1999), who points out that while in 1970 about two-thirds of children in care were there voluntarily, by 1980 only a quarter of children in care were there voluntarily. The rest were there under a statutory order issued by a court. The key reason for this change was the re-emergence of concerns over child abuse, starting in the 1960s.

Child abuse inquiries

The death of seven-year-old Maria Colwell in 1973 at the hands of her stepfather led to concern over the need for greater intervention by social workers to prevent this sort of event. In turn, this led to more pressure for social workers and others to intervene and protect children.

However, this pressure turned to anger at social workers and other professionals in the famous case of accusations of child sexual abuse in Cleveland. Beatrix Campbell (1988) points out that, in this case, over 120 children were diagnosed as having been abused, and their families came under suspicion.

Campbell (1988) also points out that in the Cleveland case, middle-class families came under suspicion of abusing children for the first time. Previous cases of abuse had been overwhelmingly linked to deprivation and poor families. (Pringle, 1995).

As a result of the Cleveland enquiries, the pressure was reversed. Social workers were now seen as too ready to get involved, and there was public outrage at the removal of children from their parental homes, although as Campbell (1988) points out, only one fifth of the children removed were later determined to have been wrongly diagnosed.

Alcock *et al.* (2000) summarizes the turnaround in pressures on social services departments as follows:

In the 1970s and early 1980s, a series of scandals involving the death of children brought the issue of physical abuse to the attention of the public. In the late 1980s, the cases in the public eye more often concerned child sexual abuse, and the debate began to shift from outcry at parental neglect and the failure of social workers towards a concern at the invasion and over-policing of the private family.

(Alcock *et al.*, 2000, p. 275)

The Department of Health produces statistics on child protection investigations, and the figures for 1995 are as follows:

Table 5.17 Child protection investigations

Categories of suspected abuse	%
Physical abuse	44
Sexual abuse	28
Neglect	25
Emotional abuse	3

Source: Department of Health, 1995, p. 69

Kirton quotes research showing that in 1992 there were 160 000 child protection investigations, of which 40 000 led to **case conferences**, and later 24 500 additions to the **child protection register**, but that only 4 per cent of cases led to children being removed from the home under a legal order.

This suggests an ambivalence about the need to protect children, but also a desire to keep the family together, as a result of conflicting political pressures and the legacy of the moral panics outlined above.

The 1989 Children's Act ensures that the paramount concern in relation to child protection is the welfare of the child, and does provide legal redress if necessary against parents.

However, in relation to this issue of what to do with children, the options have remained broadly the same in the post-war period – namely providing care in a residential childrens' home, providing foster parents, arranging adoption or trying to keep the family together and intervening within that unit.

The conflicting pressures on social workers both to intervene and to respect the privacy of individuals and families also remains, which adds to the complexity of child protection.

As Alcock *et al.* (2000) point out in relation to cases of child abuse:

What such cases have highlighted is that families do not always represent safety for those within their private world, and that constructing policies and delivering services which are neither overtly intrusive nor unable to properly protect children is very difficult indeed.

(Alcock *et al.*, 2000, p. 277)

Feminist explanations of domestic abuse

Although they differ widely in their approaches, feminist writers tend to focus on the male domination of society as the key cause of abuse of both women and children – and even of older people – within the family. Elliot argues that this is based on two linked arguments:

- First, there is the assumption that all male domination is, in the last resort, supported by physical force.
- Secondly, there is an equally persuasive assumption that male sexuality is both powerful and irresistible; i.e. that men simply cannot help their actions.

Elliot goes on to say:

Feminist discourse suggests that aggression and abuse are inherent in this construction of masculinity and seeks to show that wife-battering and killing, date-rape and marital rape and child sexual abuse are extreme forms of the sexual aggression which women and children routinely experience.

(Elliot, 1996, p. 178)

Feminists, too, suggest that such a construction of masculinity puts women at constant risk of sexual harassment, that male sexual fidelity is all but impossible, and that children are at risk of sexual abuse unless men are regularly 'serviced'. Some feminists also claim that male sexual violence receives institutional support from the law, judges and the media. This implies that the dark side of the family is, in fact, the most common picture of family life.

This highly negative picture of family life has also received considerable criticism. Not surprisingly, on an individual level, most men reject the image of themselves as inherently violent, potential (or actual) abusers of women and children with no control over their sexual feelings and desires. Many men, indeed, regard the sexual or physical abuse of women and children as abhorrent deviant behaviour, and imprisoned child abusers usually have to be kept apart from other prisoners for their own protection. Some women, too, agree that the argument removes all blame from those men who choose to attack or abuse.

The radical feminist approach also fails to explain women's abuse of children, men and other women, which – although apparently far less common than abuse by males – appears to be a growing phenomenon. Nor does it really explain violence in homosexual and lesbian relationships, or abuse of people by others of the same sex both within and outside of the family (often discussed as a form of 'bullying'). It also ignores the age-related physical and emotional abuse by both men and women of elderly parents within the household.

Activity

Summarize the various explanations of child abuse (both sociological and feminist) discussed in this section of the chapter. Say which view you agree with, and give your reasons.

Black feminism and the family

Elliot (1996) points out that **black feminist** perspectives – from writers such as b. hooks (1982) – offer some interesting insights into our understanding not only of ethnicity but also of family structure.

They argue that feminist ideas of universal male oppression and violence tend to ignore racial oppression in society. Arguments about abortion and contraception are very different for black women in poor countries, where contraception is often imposed upon them rather than their being offered much option about their fertility. Their arguments do not deny instances of male oppression of women within black families, but they do highlight the fact that inequalities exist in more than the one dimension that some radical feminists seem to suggest.

This view once again demonstrates the varied nature and perceptions of the family, which – for all its faults – seems to offer many of us some escape from the perceived stresses and problems of the world outside.

It is important therefore to remember that, while many families do have their darker aspects, most people gain considerably from family relationships.

While critics of the family tend to stress the dark side, and supporters stress its caring and supportive role, the diversity of family structures tells us that the concept of one family type, structure, relationship or household is probably less useful for explaining family life than it has ever been.

Further reading

- Abbott, P. and Wallace, C. (1992) *The Family and the New Right*, London: Pluto Press.
- Abercrombie, N. and Warde, A. (eds.) (1994) *Family, Household and the Life-Course*, Lancaster: Framework.
- Barrett, M. and McIntosh, M. (1991) *The Anti-Social Family*, 2nd edn, London: Verso.
- Gittins, D. (1993) *The Family in Question*, 2nd edn, London: Macmillan.
- Jorgensen, N. (1995) *Investigating Families and Households*, London: Collins Educational.
- Leonard, D. and Hood-Williams, J. (eds.) (1988) *Families*, Walton-on-Thames: Nelson.
- Morgan. D. H. J. (1996) *Family Connections*, London: Polity Press.
- Muncie, J., Wetherell, M., Dallos, R. and Cochrane, A. (eds.) (1995) *Understanding the Family*, London: Sage.

Back issues of the periodical *Sociology Review* (formerly *Social Studies Review*) also contain many articles on this field of sociology and many others.

Glossary of useful terms

Affective relationship   Relationship based on love and affection.

Alienation   This is a Marxist concept where Marx talks about the way that things humans produce then seem to have power over us. It is also used to refer to situations we find unpleasant such as jobs or household tasks.

Black feminist   Set of ideas and groups of women who emerged out of the feminist movement, arguing that the specific issues and relationships involved in being black meant there was a need for a specific set of ideas that recognised this, leading to black feminism.

Case conference   Where various professionals get together to talk about a particular child (a case) and their needs.

Child benefit   Benefit provided to all mothers to help with the cost of raising children.

Child protection register   Register which professionals can put children on if they are concerned for their safety or fear that are being abused.

Cohabitation   A couple living together in a sexual relationship without being married.

Cohabiting   Living together in a sexual relationship without being married.

Common-law family   Where a couple live together in a sexual relationship but are not married. In certain circumstances they can be considered legally a couple.

Conjugal family   Family consisting of husband and wife or in today terms, partners.

Conjugal roles   The roles performed by husband and wife within the family.

Deviant   Straying from the norms of society or a group.

Disorder   A lack of order resulting either from

a lack of agreement or the imposition of one groups views on another.

Dysfunction Something that does not contribute to the maintenance of society, but instead may positively harm it.

Emotional labour Idea that keeping everyone happy (emotionally stable and satisfied) is a job requiring effort and is largely done by women.

Emotional satisfaction The idea that we gain happiness or fulfilment and this emotional issue is something people seek to get out of families. Notions of love and sexual pleasure are also linked in here.

Engels Co-founder, along with Karl Marx of what today is called Marxism.

Ethical socialist Brand of socialism based on morals and living your life the right way. Very pro-conventional family life.

Eugenic Set of ideas based on the notion that we need to improve the quality of the population. This means encouraging high quality people and discouraging low quality people. Generally associated with policies to promote reproduction in some groups and to deny or discourage it in other groups.

Familial ideology Idea devised mainly by feminist writers that one particular form of the family (namely the conventional nuclear family with some degree of role separate for male and female) is presented as normal and pressure is applied to get everyone to live this way. Such a way of living is presented as the ideal or the best, stigmatizing potential other social relationships.

Family plurality The idea that there are a number of different ways of living in families, none of which is superior to the others.

Feminist   A person who adheres to the beliefs of feminism.

Fragmentation Splitting into or already existing in many different forms or varieties.

Free-market Where goods are offered to buy and sell and there is minimum interference from the state so the market is free from outside intervention.

Functionalist   A person who adheres to the beliefs of functionalism.

Ideological Means pertaining to the realm of ideas. In contemporary terms it is used to refer to the way that ideas people have affect the way they behave and therefore there is an ideological

struggle going on trying to win peoples minds to particular views.

Income support Benefit which supplements income to ensure that all families have a certain level of income.

Liberal feminists This group of feminists tend to argue that the oppression of women is due to ignorance and bigotry which can be removed through education and changes in the law.

Lone-parent family Family with only one parent. In 90% of cases this will be the mother.

Marx Karl Marx was the founder of what today is called Marxism.

Marxist A person who adheres to the beliefs of Marxism.

Marxist-feminism Argued that Marxists and Socialists need to fight not only for an end to exploitation, but also for an end to the oppression of women. Emphasized that this could possibly be done through traditional socialist strategies and allowed the idea that men and women might together seek the liberation of women.

Means testing System where benefits are only made available to those whose income (means) falls below a certain limit.

Moral panic Exaggeration or invention of a problem usually through sensationalist stories in the media.

Neo-conventional family Idea which suggests that although the structure of the family may vary today, the functions they fulfil are the same as the conventional family and also that most people at some point in their lives will live in this 'conventional' way.

Neo-Weberian Sociologists who are followers of the work of Max Weber but who have made sufficient amendments or changes to his ideas to mean that they become different or new. 'Neo-' literally means 'new'.

New Labour Term used to describe the Labour Party under Tony Blair and emphasizing the difference between this and 'old Labour' (pre-Blair).

New Right Used to distinguish the views of right-wing political parties in recent times from earlier conservative views: notably the views of the British Conservative Party from the premiership of Margaret Thatcher and the US Republican Party from the presidency of Ronald Reagan onwards. The most notable difference is the New Right's emphasis on the benefits of the free market and individual freedom.

Norms   Rules about expected behaviour in specific circumstances. What is normally expected of one.

Nuclear family   Seen as the basic unit of the family today, consisting of two adults with their biological children.

Patriarchal   Ideas or structures which support the oppression of women or the power of men.

Patriarchal ideology   A set of ideas that endorses or supports male power and the oppression of women.

Patriarchalism   System where ideas of male dominance are in force thus oppressing women and distorting the views of men.

Pluralism   Set of ideas based on there being a multitude (plural) of possible factors that affect things.

Polygamy   Having more than one spouse.

Post-modern   Post-modern literally means after modern or following the death of the modern. In sociological terms the modern means trying to arrive at a scientific objective understanding through research and developing theories. Post-modernists argue that these are just big stories or meta-narratives and that none of them is any more true than any other. Therefore instead of trying to search for the truth you should choose those theories that appeal on other grounds.

Postmodernism   The belief that life today is characterized by plurality and a multiplicity of possible options. Therefore there is no longer a right and wrong way of living your life.

Postmodernist   Someone who believes in the ideas of postmodernism.

Primary socialization   The first stage of socialization undertaken by the family and the early part of schooling.

Public policy   Wider than social policy since it also includes issues of industrial policy and economic aspects of life which impact on issues of social policy.

Radical-feminist   Approach within feminism that is opposed to any co-operation with men since they are seen as the oppressors of women. Radical-feminists tend to talk about the system of patriarchy (male control) and the way males physically threaten and control women.

Reconstituted families   Families formed from previously existing families through remarriage or cohabitation where at least one partner has had previous family relationships. Most issues of concern surround step-parenting.

Reflexive modernity   Idea linked to Anthony Giddens which stresses that today we think about the consequences of our actions and feel the need to justify what we want to do. Tradition and doing it because it has always been done are no longer acceptable reasons for any given course of action.

Reflexivity   The idea that we monitor and think about our own behaviour and modify it according to our reflections. Knowledge does not therefore exist outside or separate to the person who holds that knowledge.

Reserve army of labour   Marxist concept used to describe the unemployed whose existence keeps others in work from making too many demands since they can always be replaced by the reserve army.

Secularization   Process of the declining influence of religion and the corresponding rise in importance of non-religious (secular) influences on life.

Segregated conjugal roles   The set up where husband and wife have very different roles within the family. Traditionally the male went out to work to earn money (breadwinner) and the female stayed at home and looked after children (housewife role).

Serial monogamy   Having a sexual relationship with only one person at a time (monogamy), but through your lifetime you may have many of these, one after the other (serial).

Social authoritarianism   Term used to describe those who believe there is a right way to live your life and seek to persuade or force all others to live their lives that way.

Social fund payments   Introduced under the 1988 Social Security Act, these were repayable loans which replaced non-repayable loans and as such were seen as controversial.

Socialization   The process of learning appropriate roles and behaviour.

Socially constructed   Term associated with social action approaches which emphasizes the way things are made up by human action rather than being 'natural' phenomena waiting for us to notice them.

Social policy   This is policy relating to certain areas of life, notably the family, education, health and other caring areas of society. It however does also include policies in relation to crime and imprisonment. Policy to do with people and their lives.

Social responsibility   Deciding on a course of action not simply on the basis of how it will affect you personally but in terms of thinking about the consequences on others.

Step-families   Family where the adults are not the biological parents of all the children in it. Usually when a person with children remarries or cohabits.

Stratified diffusion   Theory that change and the spread of ideas through groups and society (diffusion) occurs unequally such that some groups change first and then others later.

Structural   Structural sociologists are those who emphasize structures as an important element in sociology. This can include Marxists, feminists and functionalists.

Symmetrical family   Type of family where the roles and jobs performed by husband and wife are mirror images of each other. Thus both partners have paid work outside the home and both share the housework and childcare.

Total period fertility rate   A measure devised by the Office for National Statistics (ONS) which measures the average number of children born to each woman if the birth rates in the period being considered persisted throughout her child-bearing life.

Values   Views about general ways of behaving which express something about how people feel they and others should behave.

Welfare state   This refers to help provided through the state, notably in the arena of health, education, support for the unemployed, support for families and also the homeless.

Women's Liberation Movement   Group who emerged in the late 1960s and 1970s based on the idea that women needed to be freed from the oppressive attitudes and behaviour that existed.

Culture and socialization
Mass media

6.1 Theories of media content

The mass media has an increasingly large role in contemporary advanced industrial societies. Very few households do not own televisions or music systems of varying degrees of sophistication, and very few people do not have daily access to television, radio or print news. Among the young in particular, rapidly advancing home and personal computer technologies take up a large space in patterns of leisure consumption in day-to-day life.

Defining the mass media

Before starting to analyse any social phenomenon it is important to be clear on some important key terms – the media is no exception to this.

- *Medium* refers to a single source of information or technique of passing on information.
- *Media* is simply a collection of more than one medium.
- *The mass media* is a term used to refer to more than one source of information designed to reach out to many people – a mass audience.

Studying the mass media

The mass media itself is of interest and concern to many members of, and groups in, society, some of whom are involved in the media, or use the media to gain publicity for their particular opinions, causes or **ideologies**.

Activity

a List the groups in society who might have an interest in, or who might express concern over, how the media presents its stories, etc.

b What issues might these groups be interested in or concerned about, and why?

C3.3

As with any topic in sociology, it is possible to apply a number of different theoretical perspectives in attempting to understand the role of the media in contemporary society, in order to help us think critically about the role of the media in society.

Discussion point

Why is it important to be able to think in a critical fashion about what the media does in society?

C3.1a

What follows in this first section is a brief introduction to ideas and research which form the background to more recent discussions and debates.

Classical Marxism

Marxists treat the media as an agent of **ideological control**, in much the same way as they would view the operation of institutions such as the education system or a religious belief system (see also Section 7.7).

False class consciousness

The idea of false **class consciousness** is suggested as a way of explaining why working class people sometimes believe in and support policies or ideas which are not in their interests. For example, it could be argued that racism is not in the interests of working class people, since it creates divisions among the working class. However it is clear that some working class people do nonetheless express racist sentiments in varying degress.

Marxists believe that the media creates false class consciousness – to take the minds of the masses away from the harsh realities of **capitalist** society. Through deliberate manipulation and censorship the media contains images and messages which are seen by this perspective to amount to little more than propaganda.

The **classical Marxist** treatment of the issue of false class consciousness comes from Marx and Engels' *The German Ideology*, written originally between 1845 and 1846. In this work, Marx and Engels state:

*The ideas of the **ruling class** are in every epoch the ruling ideas, i.e. the class which is the ruling material force of society, is at the same time its ruling intellectual force.*

(Marx and Engels, 1974, p. 64)

Here Marx and Engels illustrate their belief that ideas in society flow from the top of the wealth and power structures downwards to the masses. The masses are seen as victims in this war of ideas: the most popular ideas, values and attitudes in society come from the ruling class. In this respect, some modern-day Marxists claim that the media has taken over from religion as a prime source of ideological control.

Criticisms of Marxism

The classical Marxist account of the role of the media as an agent of oppression in the class struggle has its criticisms.

1 Some commentators suggest that the idea of a **dominant ideology** simply fails to take into account the wealth and diversity of ideas that exist in society, both pro-establishment and anti-establishment (subversive). Abercrombie *et al.* (1980) believe that there is a lack of a dominant ideology in contemporary western capitalist nations.

Discussion point

Are the dominant ideas always those of the dominant class?

C3.1a

2 Another criticism made against the classical Marxist account of the role of the media is that it treats people as passive robots.

Discussion point

Are people able to replace or resist media messages with those of their own?

C3.1a

Neo-Marxist approaches

There are many different ways to read and interpret Marxist sociology, and the so-called 'classical account' is but one. Other commentators commonly referred to as new or **neo-Marxists**, suggest that individuals are capable of resisting these media messages, yet these messages do nevertheless exist.

Neo-Marxism and hegemony

The newer or neo-Marxisms are often described as being *hegemonic* theories. The concept of **hegemony** was introduced to sociology by Antonio Gramsci (1971) and is used to represent a state of physical and mental control where one ruling class dominates another subject class.

Coercion, or physical force, is effective in society, but for only a little while. However, ideological control – the domination of the minds of the masses – is more effective and longer lasting (see also Section 2.2).

Discussion point

Can the media really shape the ideas of those who watch/read/listen to it?

C3.1a

What is 'hegemony'?

Hegemony refers to the success of a nation-state or ruler in controlling or dominating another. In its contemporary sociological use, the concept is used to refer to the control of a **subject class** through their own participation and consent. Modern-day Marxists believe this to be one of the functions of the media.

Gramsci argues that before a revolution can occur, even if the necessary economic conditions are in place, class consciousness has to be ready too. A lack of revolutionary potential could be explained by the ideological battle waged against the masses through the media.

Activity

Study the following list of points.
- Modern society is based on class conflict.
- The mass media contributes to false consciousness in society.
- Whereas the ruling class own the media, managers control the day-to-day running.
- The ruling class rule as the controller of ideas.
- Bias does exist, but it is not a deliberate capitalist conspiracy.
- The media is the mouthpiece of the ruling class.
- The ruling class own and control the media.
- The purpose of sociology is to expose ideological rule in society.
- The nature of media ownership has changed since the death of Marx.
- The media contributes to hegemony in society.

Some of these ideas are associated with the classical Marxist perspective, some with the neo-Marxist perspective, others with both.

Rewrite the list, dividing it into three sections, one each for the three combinations above.

C3.2, C3.3

The Glasgow University Media Group

This group (GUMG, 1976, 1980, 1982) presents an attempt at the hegemonic analysis of bias in television news coverage on a variety of news events such as elections, strikes, warfare and health issues.

The GUMG asserts that bias is not the result of deliberate or conscious conspiracy by members of the ruling class, but is instead part of the day-to-day process of how news is made by professionals working within a culture which presents a pro-capitalist viewpoint as normal and natural while excluding or ignoring other views. Thus the media creates a hegemony or total dominance of one viewpoint.

Pluralism

The **pluralist** perspective in media sociology stems from an analysis of the range of sources of power in what are seen as contemporary western democracies. Pluralism is a belief in competition *within* compromise and consensus.

The pluralist view of the media

Pluralists believe that, although bias exists, it does so in order to represent the interests of the buying public who have purchasing power and exercise a *free choice* over where to give their custom. Audiences do have the power to make one media product successful, while closing down another owing to lack of demand – this is democratic.

💬 Discussion point

Does shareholding and privatisation increase public power, or is this situation nothing more than an ideological invention?

C3.1a

Pluralists claim also that a dominant ideology does *not* exist through enforced ideological control and the manipulation of the media by a ruling class élite, since *every* taste and political view is represented in the media. The most popular of these is bought by the public and becomes the most successful.

💬 Discussion point

Does the audience 'have the power' or does the media have the power over the audience?

C3.1a

📝 Activity

Study the two newspaper front pages in Figure 6.1 (opposite), produced on the day of the 1992 general election in the UK. How are they biased, if at all? Whose interests do they represent? Using the three theories of classical Marxism, neo-Marxism and pluralism, try to think through the eyes of these theories. How would they interpret these front covers? Write one detailed paragraph per theory.

C3.2, C3.3

Feminism

The **feminist** analysis of the media, sharing many similarities with the Marxist analysis, looks towards the media as an agent of ideological control. The media is a source of the **socialization** of traditional gender roles (masculinity and feminity) and constructs an ideological femininity to be followed by girls and women alike (see also Section 2.2).

The central concept in any feminist analysis of power in society is **patriarchy**, or rule of the father. This concept is used by feminists as a means by which aspects of everyday life can be labelled critically as contributing to the inequalities between the sexes. The media is seen by this view to portray women in a very limited way.

💬 Discussion point

Does the media support 'patriarchy'?

C3.1a

The audience: active or passive?

A key feature of the debates between most sociological perspectives concerns the role of the audience. We can ask a number of questions here:

- Do individuals or even groups believe media messages?
- Is it realistic to speak of 'the masses', or are audiences all different?

Figure 6.1 Front pages of the *Daily Mirror* and the *Sun*, 9 April 1992
(© News International Newspapers Limited, 9 April 1992)

- Are media audiences complete victims of ideological influence?

In presenting this key issue of sociological debate, a simple answer would be to create a dichotomy of extreme positions: either audiences are active and able to interpret from the many media messages on offer; or audiences are passive and able to be tricked by manipulated messages which may support a ruling-élite view of the world.

As we can see, the issue of bias in the media and the issue of the effect of the media on society are closely related. Contemporary sociological approaches to these problems try to treat different audiences differently. Some may be affected by what they hear, see or read, but others will not.

Case Study – Teenage girl audiences and *Jackie* magazine

Angela McRobbie illustrates through her research that magazines aimed at a young audience contain highly ideological messages. McRobbie (1983) takes as an example *Jackie* magazine, aimed at pre-teen girls, and through content analysis demonstrates the existence of **patriarchal ideology**.

She claims that this *ideology of adolescent femininity* attempts to define, for young girls, how they should live their teenage and adult lives. Magazines like this contain articles, problem pages and photo-stories all of which are concerned with a limited number of themes – the importance of romance in a girl's life, the importance of finding a good boy, and the importance of looking good.

Is there a media effect?

McRobbie does not assume that readers of these magazines are necessarily influenced by them in a passive fashion. She suggests that sociological research into the content of the media needs to take a two-sided approach:

- it needs to identify bias and whose interests are represented by such bias;
- equally, it needs to demonstrate the extent to

which audiences read this bias in a critical fashion.

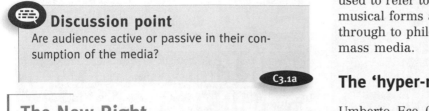

Discussion point

Are audiences active or passive in their consumption of the media?

C3.1a

The New Right

The **New Right** is not so much a sociological perspective as a set of political ideas that have become influential in British society since 1979 with the arrival of the first Thatcher Conservative government.

The New Right view on the media can be summarized as follows:

1   Of central concern are the issues of ownership and censorship.

2   Like those of pluralism, New Right ideas are influenced by a belief in the fairness of a **free market economy** to meet the needs of the public/consumers/audiences in a democratic fashion. The public have freedom of choice and demonstrate this through their patterns of consumption.

3   Among those who believe in New Right ideas, there are often **moral panics** (see Section 6.2) created concerning the content of the media and its perceived potential to corrupt the morality of society.

Post-modernism

Contemporary approaches to the study of culture in all of its forms include increasingly popular ideas on **post-modernism**. This concept, despite its wide variety of meanings and definitions, is used to refer to many aspects of social life – from musical forms and styles, literature, and fine art through to philosophy, history and especially the mass media.

The 'hyper-real': Eco and Baudrillard

Umberto Eco (1987), an Italian **post-modernist** philosopher and literary figure, defined something called the 'hyper-real' as that which seems more real than real.

In his essay entitled 'Simulations', Baudrillard (1983a) attempts to explain the differences between one reality as lived by individuals in their day-to-day life, and the so-called reality portrayed by the media. Baudrillard contends that everyday reality and media reality have become blurred. Individuals obtain what they experience as real knowledge about the real world from the media, but this is actually reproduced knowledge about an entirely simulated or reproduced world. This he also calls the hyper-real.

Audiences live their lives through the simulations of reality given by the media. Thus, the knowledge and experience **social actors** believe they have of real life becomes indistinguishable from that given to us by the media.

Raymond Williams

From a neo-Marxist stance, cultural critic Raymond Williams (1990) has suggested that television has not so much shaped contemporary times and the contemporary audience, as been itself shaped by the times. We therefore need to be very careful when attributing a cause or effect to any social phenomenon:

Activity

With the theories of media content covered in this section in mind, copy and complete the following grid. This should help you to understand these theories and act as a summary for your notes.

	Classical Marxism	Neo-Marxism	Pluralism	Feminism	New Right
View of society					
Key concepts					
View of the role of the media in society					
View of bias in the media					

C3.2, C3.3

It is often said that television has altered our world. In the same way, people often speak of a new world, a new society, a new phase of history, being created – brought about by this or that new technology: the steam-engine, the automobile, the atomic bomb. Most of us know what is generally implied when such things are said. But this may be the central difficulty: that we have got so used to statements of this general kind, in our most ordinary discussions, that we can fail to realize their specific meanings.

(Williams, 1990, p. 9)

Rather than the shape of contemporary social life being caused by television, Williams argues that the form and content of television could be seen as a product of contemporary social life.

Activity

There are a great deal of different theories on the content of the media:

classical Marxism	neo-Marxism
pluralism	feminism
New Right	

To help you make sense of these ideas, create the following lists:

- theories believing that there is bias in the mass media
- theories believing there is no bias

Summarize the views of each theory.

Are there any important differences between theories within the lists you have created? What are they?

C3.2

Defining culture and assessing quality

Raymond Williams (1961), in an important early study of the development of modern culture, identifies three different approaches, each of which defines culture in a distinct way. These approaches are:

- the 'ideal'
- the 'documentary'
- 'social definition'.

The 'ideal'

The first definition is termed by Williams the 'ideal'. Writers employing this definition assume that culture is a 'state or process of human perfection' (1961, p. 57). Only the very best in intellectual and artistic endeavour would be included as examples: the greatest literature, most moving opera and drama, most skilfully constructed poetry, most beautiful painting, and so on – in other words, what is often termed **high culture** rather than **popular culture**.

The study of culture, according to this approach, involves the application of universally agreed criteria or rules (which apply at all times across all societies) for assessing the quality of particular examples. It is assumed that it is possible to apply universal rules for separating the 'good' from 'bad' because human experience – the range of human emotions – is also universal and great art successfully describes the 'truth' of this human condition.

With its insistence on including only the very 'best' in human creative endeavour, the ideal definition can be regarded as narrow. It is assumed, for example, that only a small minority of creative artists or intellectuals actually make culture. This is an important point: Williams argues that such narrow definitions of culture were 'selective' in the sense that they served to exclude large numbers of people and secured a privileged position only for those with the 'instincts' or 'skills' to appreciate fine artistic or intellectual work.

The 'documentary'

A second way of defining culture is termed by Williams the 'documentary' approach (1961, p. 57). This is a slightly broader definition which considers not just artistic or intellectual products which satisfy the criterion of near-perfection, but all those works which represent 'the body of intellectual and imaginative work' a society has produced. In other words, writers employing the 'documentary' definition consider not only the very best in art and intellectual activity, but all examples which represent or 'document' the 'culture' of a society.

Recently the British government, in its approach to the schools curriculum, has appeared to embrace this kind of approach, with policies encouraging a concentration on 'English' literature and 'English' history. Ministers have argued that all school pupils should have an appreciation of their English heritage in terms of art and history.

This definition is slightly broader but the focus remains on art and intellectual work, created again by a minority of artists and intellectuals within particular societies.

Williams argues that frequently, even with this definition, there remains an assumption that universal aesthetic or intellectual criteria can be applied in order to assess what counts as 'culture'. Shakespeare *is* counted as culture but the television show *Blind Date* is not.

'Social definition'

Williams identifies a third approach as the 'social definition' (1961, p. 57). Whereas the first two approaches are most closely associated with traditional teaching in art and English as academic disciplines, this approach owes its origins to early anthropology and sociology. Although an English academic by profession, Williams himself, together with Richard Hoggart, can be credited with developing the argument for embracing this much wider definition of culture. Williams argues that the term 'culture' can also be taken to mean 'a particular way of life' and that the study of culture could also include:

... certain meanings and values not only in art and learning but also in institutions and ordinary behaviour. [It] will also include analysis of elements in the way of life that to followers of the other definitions are not 'culture' at all.

(Williams, 1961, p. 57)

In other words, culture could be understood as:

... a whole way of life, material, intellectual and spiritual.

(Williams, 1963, p. 16)

This is a much broader definition. Not only artists and intellectuals but all members of society are engaged in the process of making culture, on a daily basis, as part of their ordinary lives. Culture is no longer understood as 'separate' from ordinary people: it is something made and consumed by everyone – in local communities, on local streets, inside families and pubs, as well as in opera houses and 'serious' theatres.

Taking popular culture seriously

This radical break with previous definitions allowed researchers and academics to begin to take popular culture seriously, and for cultural

studies to evolve as a discipline in the 1960s. However, there is an important implication regarding the assessment of the quality of culture. If 'culture' is part of ordinary life and all are involved in its production, it is still possible to distinguish between the 'good' and the 'bad'? The implication appears to be that all cultural work, irrespective of its worth, has to be treated with the same degree of critical respect.

- The first two definitions above assume that there exist *universal* and *absolute* criteria for assessing the value of a cultural product. These criteria are timeless and unchanging.

- The 'social' definition, on the other hand, seems to imply a *relative*, rather than absolute, approach. Cultural standards are understood as being relative to particular societies at particular times.

Discussion point

a To what extent do you think it is possible to make objective judgements about the quality of cultural products?

b Is it important to distinguish between 'good' and 'bad' television, books, films, etc., or should we simply allow consumers to make their own choices without imposing any concept of 'cultural standards'?

c Recently, several classical musicians have been angered because their recordings of 'lighter' musical pieces (for example, songs taken from Hollywood musicals) have been banned from the United States' classical record chart. This implies the imposition of an absolute judgement. What do you think? What *is* the difference between pop/rock and classical music?

C3.1a

It is interesting to note that neither Williams nor Hoggart were entirely comfortable with **relativistic** approaches. Although each writer wished to broaden and democratize the study of culture, neither wished to abandon entirely the insistence on 'standards' and 'quality'. Indeed, Richard Hoggart continues to campaign actively against the influence of **relativism** in contemporary cultural discussion (Hoggart, 1996).

Methods of media analysis

It is possible to draw a distinction between:

- techniques that involve the analysis of media content, and
- those involving the analysis of audience responses to media content.

This section discusses two main approaches to studying the content of the media:

- content analysis
- semiology.

Content analysis

Principles

Content analysis is a highly successful technique used by a number of sociologists to investigate the content of the media. Since the media comes ready-made, it is relatively easy to gain access to the required broadcast or publication and relatively cheap to build up a sample.

 Discussion point

How can sociologists investigate and expose the hidden messages in the media?

C3.1a

Content analysis allows a researcher to measure or simply add up the frequency of a given message. Provided the method is agreed by a team of researchers beforehand, and clearly discussed in published research, replication of this type of counting is possible.

- For example, feminist researchers may be interested in counting the frequency of so-called traditional gender roles in a whole variety of media products – children's books, shopping catalogues, television advertisements and other sources.
- Marxist-orientated sociologists may wish to study the frequency with which a pro-establishment viewpoint occurs in the media.

Using a 'coding scheme'

When conducting content analysis, researchers often use coding schemes – lists of categories to look for. Thus, when coding-up a piece of media

Mad dogs and Englishmen

We have	**They have**
Army, Navy and Air Force	A war machine
Reporting guidelines	Censorship
Press briefings	Propaganda

We	**They**
Take out	Destroy
Suppress	Destroy
Eliminate	Kill
Neutralize	Kill
Decapitate	Kill
Dig in	Cower in their foxholes

We launch	**They launch**
First strikes	Sneak missile attacks
Pre-emptively	Without provocation

Our men are ...	**Their men are ...**
Boys	Troops
Lads	Hordes

Our boys are ...	**Theirs are ...**
Professional	Brainwashed
Lion-hearts	Paper tigers
Cautious	Cowardly
Confident	Desperate
Heroes	Cornered
Dare-devils	Cannon fodder
Young knights of the skies	Bastards of Baghdad
Loyal	Blindly obedient
Desert rats	Mad dogs
Resolute	Ruthless
Brave	Fanatical

Our boys are motivated by	**Their boys are motivated by**
An old-fashioned sense of duty	Fear of Saddam

Our boys	**Their boys**
Fly into the jaws of hell	Cower in concrete bunkers

Our ships are ...	**Iraqi ships are ...**
An armada	A navy

Israeli non-retaliation is	**Iraqi non-retaliation is**
An act of great statesmanship	Blundering/Cowardly

The Belgians are ...	**The Belgians are also ...**
Yellow	Two-faced

Our missiles are ...	**Their missiles are ...**
Like Luke Skywalker zapping Darth Vader	Ageing duds (rhymes with Scuds)

Our missiles cause ...	**Their missiles cause ...**
Collateral damage	Civilian casualties

We ...	**They ...**
Precision bomb	Fire wildly at anything in the skies

Our PoWs are ...	**Their PoWs are ...**
Gallant boys	Overgrown schoolchildren

George Bush is ...	**Saddam Hussein is ...**
At peace with himself	Demented
Resolute	Defiant
Statesmanlike	An evil tyrant
Assured	A crackpot monster

Our planes ...	**Their planes ...**
Suffer a high rate of attrition	Are shot out of the sky
Fail to return from missions	Are zapped

Source: Guardian, 23 January 1991

text (be it a picture, text, or a TV advert) the research uses a pre-arranged set of codes or categories and simply measures the frequency of occurrence of these codes.

Language bias

One popular starting point for media research among sociologists is to analyse the type of language used. Does the media contain words or phrases that may contain a biased, one-sided viewpoint? A clearly identifiable example of this type of bias can be seen in newspaper headlines – especially in the tabloid press, where bold statements are often necessary to capture the public's attention and persuade them to purchase today's big story. (See also the chart, '*Mad dogs and Englishmen*', reproduced from the *Guardian*.)

The selectivity of editorial decisions

News items, be they transmitted or published through radio, television or print, are based on and created by a process of selection (editing). The construction of the news involves decisions made by media personnel as to the relative merits and importance of each story or item. At some points in the year, most notably the so-called 'silly season' during the summer parliamentary recess, a few stories are given attention they would not merit at other times – except perhaps as the short, light-hearted item at the end of a broadcast.

Scheduling

The decision as to what item is most important is reflected in the order of the scheduling of the items. In television and radio broadcasts, the priority of a story is reflected by the brief headlines often used as an introduction to the longer programme. Audiences share a common-sense understanding that these items are the most important since they come first. Equally, newspaper front-page headlines serve the same function.

The frequency of stories

A simple method of conducting content analysis into the biased and selective decisions made by media personnel is to measure the frequency of particular types of news stories, and where they are scheduled in an overall broadcast or publication. Over a period of time it should be possible for the researcher to see any patterns, if they exist, in the type of items given precedence over others.

Newspaper content analysis

By far the easiest and most accessible form of content analysis is the measurement in newspapers of biases in language, pictures, and use of space and headlines. In analysing a daily newspaper, the sociologist would expect to:

- measure the sizes of headlines and surface areas of stories to see which type of story are given most coverage
- measure the frequency and type of words used to see whether they are biased or emotive
- assess the images used in pictures
- assess the order in which stories are presented from front cover to back cover
- study the content of political comments, editorials and news stories for openly one-sided views.

As the chart '*Mad dogs and Englishmen*' (see page 145) demonstrates, the language used in the media can often contain bias that is not always obvious until it is presented in a different form, in this case side-by-side. The vocabulary relates to news coverage of the Gulf war.

Problems and limitations of content analysis

A major problem with content analysis is that the coding scheme used is almost invariably open to personal interpretation. These codes are sometimes guided by the ideological and personal values of the researchers themselves. *It is quite possible to see what you think is bias if you go looking for it in the first place.*

Furthermore, in turning the essentially **qualitative** (images, words, order, etc.) into the more **quantitative** (frequencies, figures, etc.), the subtlety of biased messages may be lost. It is important to remember with content analysis that *the whole of the product is greater than its parts*. Thus the overall effect of a biased piece of reporting may be lost in pulling it apart in order to represent it as a series of figures.

Nevertheless, content analysis does tend to be more reliable than semiology, which is discussed next.

Semiology

Semiology can be defined – by the literal meaning of the word – as the scientific study of signs. Semiology as a technique or academic discipline developed from linguistics – the concern to study the meanings, origins and uses of language, and how humans communicate in a shared way through language.

Looking at the meaning of 'signs'

Semiology takes as its starting point the view that language is a series of learnt or socialized codes, a series of messages or meanings. In semiology, codes or signs are studied for the meanings they communicate, but these codes are believed to exist in all human life, not just language.

For example, in order to establish in the first few seconds of a film that a character is a business person, we would probably be given an image or a sign of that person with a smart suit and briefcase. This sign would represent a cultural image which is socialized into the minds of members of western Europe and communicates a common-sense message.

Deconstructing signs

In studying the signs in a piece of media text, researchers using semiological methods seek to read the text in such a way as to pull apart and uncover each of the codes to establish the meaning being communicated. Semiologists believe that audiences of the media, and social actors in day-to-day life, deconstruct the signs around them.

Some signs communicate codes that could be seen as being ideological. For example, a television advertisement featuring an apron-clad woman in a kitchen could be seen to contain patriarchal ideology.

Problems and limitations of semiology

Semiology is unrepresentative and often subjective. It is not true that the audience and the researcher share a common meaning of a sign, nor is it correct to assume that fixed meanings will exist over time. Again, this takes us back to the debate concerning the participation of the audience of the media with the signs and ideology contained in the media.

Do audiences accept signs and dominant meanings pre-constructed for them; or are they free to re-create meanings and to read the media in a subversive way, rejecting ideology?

6.2 The role of media professionals

Hegemonic sociologists such as those working at the Glasgow University Media Group (GUMG), who adopt a neo-Marxist orientation to the media, have made a major contribution to the sociological study of the media by asserting that news productions are inevitably and normally the result of selection, interpretation and therefore bias. This is an important point to realize when starting to think critically about the creation of news stories and other programmes.

Is the news 'value-free'?

News as a production

News is not a neutral, objective reality which exists in a vacuum ready-made and separate from those in the media who report it. News simply would not exist without the media. As Figure 6.2 illustrates, news (or any media product for that matter) is not made away from outside influences.

Neo-Marxist sociologists, however, point out that reported events are considered important by the public only if they are presented by the media as being important news in the first place.

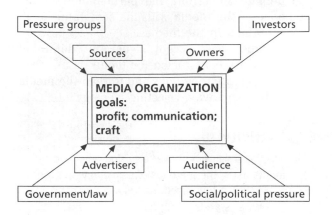

Figure 6.2 The media organization sources of demand and constraint
Source: McQuail (1983)

We can identify a number of influences on the media in the process of the creation of news programmes or publications.

News values

'News values' are the decisions guiding the overall look or feel of a newspaper or television news programme, and the values they follow concerning what types of stories to concentrate on at the expense of others. The existence of these values shows that news is not created in a totally neutral way – it involves decisions and selection.

Activity

a Identify and explain two aspects of news production.

b Outline and discuss the view that news is a manufactured product.

C3.2, C3.3

As we can see from the example in Figure 6.3, a news programme typically goes through many stages in its production. (Some processes in the figure will have been modified in the light of technological developments.) A number of groups and

individuals come into contact with what will be the finished news item.

Setting the agenda: the 'gatekeepers'

Many sociologists see the groups of editors and journalists as 'gatekeepers' who set the news agenda. The media personnel control, regulate and oversee what information or biases are given to the buying public – and what are not. Media organizations and institutions thus set the agenda for audiences.

Although pluralist sociologists would argue that audiences are given what they want because they have the power to purchase on the media marketplace, Marxist sociologists and others critical of the role of the media in society would suggest that audiences are given a very limited selection of ideas and views to choose from in the first place.

The act of agenda-setting is, however, a very complex one involving many different stages, processes and influences from both within and without the media organization in question. As Figure 6.4 on page 150 shows, the media does have the potential to affect or shape the public agenda, but the media is itself shaped by the agenda of the public and the government of the day.

Professional culture

The GUMG have highlighted the existence of a professional culture among media personnel. Upon entering the profession, media workers at a number of different levels undergo a process of **secondary socialization** where they learn the culture and values (see Section 3.2) of the particular organization they have joined. The GUMG argue that this professional culture is essentially based on white, European, male, middle-class, middle-of-the-road values.

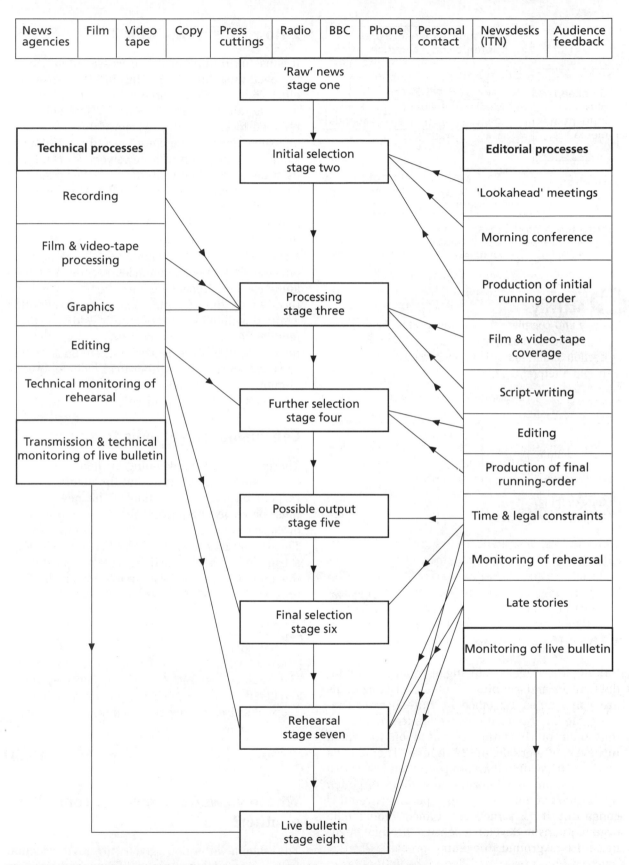

Figure 6.3 The daily evolution of television news (in this case Channel 4)
Source: Blanchard and Morley (1982)

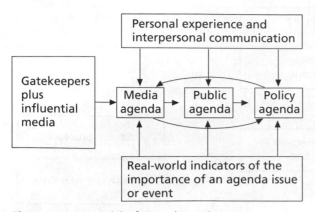

Figure 6.4 A model of agenda-setting
Source: E. M. Rogers and J. W. Dearing, in J. Anderson (ed.), *Communication Yearbook*, Vol 11, 1987

 Activity

Copy and complete the following table. This should act as a summary of the ideas in this section so far, indicating how perspectives would interpret them.

	Definition	Classical Marxism	Neo-Marxism	Pluralism
News as a production				
News values				
Gatekeeping/ agenda-setting				
Professional culture				

C3.3

1 The office routine

Galtung and Ruge (1976) suggest that the day-to-day set-up and running of media organizations are constrained by office or bureaucratic routines. Media organizations are limited by the fact that their office culture is based on the rapid turnover of periods of 24 hours. The outside world is more often than not presented as a series of sudden, unrelated events, sometimes forgotten by the start of the next 24-hour period. Given this constraint it is sometimes difficult for media organizations to develop a sense of gradual build-up and background to events.

2 How does news 'flow'?

It is useful to think of the processes of gatekeeping/agenda-setting, and the influences of the office routine, professional culture and news values, as all working together. This could be referred to as 'shaping the news flow'.

News flow can be complex and multi-dimensional. The creation of a newsworthy event, and its transmission between different news sources – international, foreign, regional, community, etc. – can best be seen as a chain or flow. After the initial event the piece of news in question is passed from journalist to journalist, each time in a shortened or slightly modified form depending on how these media agencies see the intended audience – the 'receiver'. Once the news has been received by the audience it may be transmitted again, this time by word of mouth, and once more modified as this process occurs. Finally, the reaction of the receiver is transmitted back to the original source through critical debate, public opinion polls, audience complaints, letters to media organizations, and so on.

Conclusion: Hegemonic theory

The concepts of gatekeeping/agenda-setting and news values may suggest that the media is solely responsible for the creation of the news. But it must be remembered that the news is a product of bargaining between many different groups. This bargaining does not, however, take place on a truly level playing field – some groups such as the government do have more power, but not necessarily all of the time.

 Activity

Using copies of the *Sun* and the *Guardian* newspapers *from the same day*, write a list of the news values each has. Explain how they are different, and how you can judge this from the use of space, running order and the other issues raised above.

C3.2, C3.3

Whose views? The owners, controller or other?

The media attention given to environmental issues, like all other news, is frequently subject to the definitions of those who put the news together as to what is current or topical and what is not; or, to put it another way, what is important or of significance and what is not.

Taking the environmental movement Greenpeace as an example, Hansen (1993) contends that for some social movements, media publicity, and its effective use, is the key to getting its message across to the public, and hence gaining popular support. The successful use of media coverage through organized publicity stunts enables these groups to reach a wide audience, and in doing so, to embarrass those they are protesting against – such as those hunting endangered species, dumping waste, etc. However:

It is one thing for environmental groups to achieve massive media coverage for a short period of time and in relation to specific issues. It is quite a different task to achieve and maintain a position as an established, authoritative and legitimate actor in the continuous process of claims-making and policy-making on environmental matters.

(Hansen, 1993, p. 151)

In trying to identify and explain the nature of the press coverage received by Greenpeace, Hansen conducted a content analysis of five years' worth of two British newspapers, the *Guardian* and *Today*, between January 1987 and December 1991.

Frequency analysis

Although Greenpeace is one of the more successful environmental groups to have developed in the 1980s (based on its membership figures, and especially considering it started as one of the very smallest), it nevertheless trailed behind Friends of the Earth in the volume of coverage received during the period of this study. For the period 1987–91 the numbers of articles were:

- Friends of the Earth – 1031
- Greenpeace – 896
- World Wide Fund for Nature (WWF) – 304
- Royal Society for the Protection of Birds – 328.

Only 120 articles mentioned both Greenpeace and Friends of the Earth together.

Hansen notes that these two groups have not allowed their rivalry to play a significant part in their press coverage. Rather than fighting against each other to the benefit of the press, they have concentrated on the issues they wish to put across, and on taking and directing the media agenda, rather than being directed by it.

Range of issues

A simple count of the frequency of being mentioned in the press does not, however, tell us much about the nature of that coverage, nor how successful each group has been in getting its ideas and causes into print. Hansen notes, in response to this, that Greenpeace is able to obtain press coverage on a wide range of issues. For example, the ten highest mentioned issues were (as percentages of all articles):

- *nuclear power/arms/waste – 21.5*
- *exploitation of natural resources – 11*
- *waste disposal/management – 11*
- *conservation/endangered species – 10*
- *sea/beach pollution – 7*
- *air pollution/acid rain – 5*
- *ozone layer/global warming – 5*
- *discussion of governmental environmental policies – 4*
- *the Rainbow Warrior affair – 3*
- *other environmental groups – 3.*

(Hansen, 1993, p. 157)

Conclusion

This indicates that Greenpeace is relatively prominent in media coverage, and is relatively successful in getting its own agendas across; or, to put it another way, in shaping the news, in shaping the agenda-setting process.

In this way, Greenpeace has been able to project an image of a legitimate or expert party on its chosen subject (environmentalism), and in this respect is a credible source for the media to turn to. It has been successful in making itself appear an authoritative voice, largely through the use of a scientific legitimation claim, whereby it appears expert because it has a number of scientists who speak on its behalf, but also by using its own opinion poll research and environmental testing which it makes accessible to the media.

This increases the likelihood that it will be contacted by journalists seeking an easy source of information. In this way, unofficial sources sometimes do have the ability to shape the agenda-setting process.

Moral panics and the media

In the competition to sell to their audiences, the media not only simplifies but also exaggerates: sensational stories are popular and sell well. What follows are some key terms.

1 Moral panic

This is a term coined by sociologists to refer to an exaggerated fear or outrage by the media and the audience, over an issue that has been blown out of proportion by the media in the first place.

2 Folk devil

This is a group targeted by a moral panic, fictional or not.

Activity

There have been many contemporary media moral panics. Compile a list of all those you can remember and their respective folk devils. It might be useful also to ask other people of differing ages which ones they can think of. (If you do this you must give them clear definitions of a moral panic and a folk devil.) Finally, decide whether there are any common links between the entries on your list.

C3.3

3 Moral crusader

The media can take it upon itself to speak for the morality of society and for public opinion in condemning the supposed actions of various groups in society. It adopts the mantle of crusader.

4 Amplification

Far from always reporting some events neutrally, the media can amplify acts of **deviance**. It can:

- exaggerate these acts to report an apparent rise in **deviant** actions

- arouse increased public concern which may have an effect on crime figures based on public reporting

- actually increase particular deviant acts by making such appear interesting to an audience, or by labelling individuals as deviants.

Discussion point

How do audiences respond to moral panics?

C3.1a

Case Study – The creation of mods and rockers

A classic example of a moral panic is provided by Stanley Cohen in his book *Folk Devils and Moral Panics* (1980), first published in 1972. Cohen reported research on the disorders in 1964 by mods and rockers at British seaside towns, most notably during Easter bank holidays at Clacton. He illustrates the extent to which media sensationalization can have an effect on audiences, including the public, police and the government. (See also Section 10.2)

How did the media exaggerate reality?

Cohen demonstrates that the newspaper accounts of these riots tell stories of horrific terror, chaos and large-scale rioting. Clacton was pictured as being at the total mercy of rival gangs who, through mob behaviour, destroyed property, intimated the public and fought with each other.

Although these images may have become more and more familiar on subsequent occasions, they were by no means a true account of the first mods and rockers disturbances. Cohen argues that there were no opposed rival gangs until after the media moral panic had begun. There were minimal numbers of motorbikes and scooters used by these young people – their so-called main symbol of group membership – and the most serious offences originally committed were threatening behaviour and minor vandalism.

Self-fulfilling prophecy

Owing to over-reporting, a self-fulfilling prophecy had been created whereby more members of the public became worried, police activity was increased as a response, and young people themselves created and joined these gangs that had been presented to them by the media as a fashionable and exciting lifestyle option.

Case Study – Ethnicity and moral panics

The Centre for Contemporary Cultural Studies (CCCS) at Birmingham University has produced a range of material focusing on the representation of ethnicity in the British pro-capitalist media. Stuart Hall *et al.* (*Policing the Crisis*, 1978) aim to explain media prejudice, racism and the creation of the mugging moral panic within the context of a crisis in **capitalist legitimation** since the 1970s.

The crisis of capitalism

Classical Marxist sociology suggests that the 'inevitable' break-up of capitalism will occur owing to periodic crisis points, at which time capitalism will be seen by the masses as no longer able to deliver what it promises. Rising unemployment, a declining standard of living and a rising cost of living will lead to the development of true consciousness. Then the working classes will change from a class *in* themselves and become a class *for* themselves, this being the forerunner to any mass revolutionary action. Such economic crisis leads to a legitimation crisis, which is considered by Marxists such as Gramsci to be an even more serious threat to capitalism.

Antonio Gramsci was an Italian Marxist who placed great emphasis on the way that rulers maintained their position by making ideas that were favourable to them seem like common sense. These ideas would then become popular or hegemonic. Gramsci's vote led to research interest in ideas or ideology rather than on simply economic processes.

The media and hegemony

A legitimation crisis, or a crisis in **hegemonic control**, occurs when the ruling class, through the state, is no longer able to win over the hearts and minds of the general population. The very authority of the ruling class is challenged. Hall and colleagues argue that this very situation occurred in the first half of the 1970s in the UK.

Hall and colleagues argue that the British mass media served the interests of the state at this time of crisis, and acted to divert public attention away from the problems of capitalism. A moral panic was created aimed at the scapegoat or folk devil of the black mugger. In doing this, the media – especially the British press through sensationalism and exaggeration – turned the problems faced by a capitalist economy on to an outsider. Thereby mugging was defined as a new crime imported from violent America, and sweeping the country like a plague.

Does 'mugging' really exist?

It was noted, however, that the crime of 'mugging' is merely a catch-all phrase for a number of different violent street crimes that were by no means new to the UK. In defining the mugger as a black and creating a widespread moral panic, the media helped to develop racism. However, this too served the interests of the state, since while the white and black working classes are divided the possibility of collective mass revolutionary action remains small.

Primary definition and the role of official sources

• Hall *et al.*'s *Policing the Crisis* has proven to

be of great importance for subsequent media analysis, especially concerning the issue of **primary definition** – the claim that official sources will dominate over non-official sources in most reporting of events. The concept of primary definition suggests that official sources will be the first that people turn to, thus making them the source of the first (or primary) definition of any event. This tendency for official sources to create the common or primary definition of a social situation through the media is seen as further evidence of hegemony in society – ruling-class definitions of events rule, but without direct action taken by the ruling classes themselves.

• Recent work within the Glasgow University Media Group (GUMG) has taken issue with this claim. It is suggested that journalists, pressure groups (and other examples of non-official sources) and official sources are in competition and negotiation with each other, and news reporting is a product of the interaction of these agencies. This idea can be clearly seen in the work of Paula Skidmore, a member of the GUMG, who has researched the issue of whether there has or has not been a moral panic in the media over sexual abuse of children in recent years. (See also Section 3.9 on child abuse.)

Case Study – Media reporting of sexual abuse of children

Paula Skidmore (1995) argues that, rather than seeing a moral panic over sexual abuse of young people, we have witnessed a moral clampdown – an altogether different process aimed at the social work profession.

Methodology

A content analysis of all references to this type of abuse in newspapers and on television in 1991 in England – sponsored by the Economic and Social Research Council's (ESRC) Child Sexual Abuse and the Media Project, based at Glasgow University – shows some 1668 press items and 149 TV news items. Skidmore notes that of these items, 71 per cent of the press items and 83 per cent of the TV items were what she terms 'case-based' – that is, based on the reporting of an event or incident, rather than a more general piece discussing intervention, protection, etc. Therefore, the media coverage of this issue can be seen to be reactive rather than proactive. It becomes a newsworthy subject only once a scandal breaks, and not beforehand.

The effects of moral panics

Of these case-based news items, positive representations of the social work profession were rare. When discussing the effects of this reporting on the audience, Skidmore contends that the audience:

... remembered, in general terms, social workers being wrong, parents fighting for their rights and police as goodies. ... However, people were often less anti-social work and recognized negative media coverage as not being true of the profession as a whole. Participants often believed social workers were being scapegoated.

(Skidmore, 1995, p. 22)

This observation is vital. It suggests that, although social workers were portrayed in a negative light, the audience did not necessarily accept this image even though they did remember it. As Skidmore further comments:

There is evidence therefore that audiences deconstruct and resist dominant media constructions around CSA [child sexual abuse]. People draw on personal and professional experience, their different structural positions within society, and diverse political frameworks in order to challenge or reinforce media accounts and develop alternative explanatory frameworks.

(Skidmore, 1995, p. 22)

How do the media use official sources?

Skidmore's research could be seen to throw some doubt on Hall *et al.*'s assertion that official sources are more likely to take dominance in news reporting. In the case of reporting issues of child sexual abuse, the media is presented with a problem of specialism – it is unclear which journalists should cover the story in-house since child abuse experts do not professionally exist (there has not been a call for them until recently). More often than not these stories are reported in a similar fashion to crime stories. The journalists are thus dependent on any information, official or otherwise, and the creation of a common-line-of-media-enquiry is based very much on the negotiation of a number of different agendas from a number of organizations and sources.

Interestingly, this research also notes that the media is currently faced with what might be called 'child-abuse fatigue' – a growing feeling that too much reporting has already taken place and a reluctance to spend more time on these stories.

Conclusions

What appears to have taken place in the reporting of cases of child sexual abuse, after the initial sensationalism, is not a moral panic but the reverse – an inability (or an unwillingness) to consider this practice as potentially as widespread as claimed by social workers and some feminist groups. Instead of a moral panic, then, we see an attempt by the media to scapegoat the social work profession: to suggest that these cases are not widespread, but are falsely started owing to the incompetence of social workers to detect cases correctly:

Instead of just the abuser as a deviant folk devil we often see the social work profession scapegoated for their inadequate or incompetent intervention to protect children. This has often focused on an expressed belief that there cannot be the level of abuse of children that child protection professionals or feminist groups suggest. Social workers are therefore portrayed as zealots looking for abuse where none exists. In this sense, instead of a moral panic about child sex abuse in the media, we have increasingly seen a moral clampdown.

(Skidmore, 1995, p. 22)

Case Study – The politics of HIV/AIDS reporting

An understanding of the media sensationalization of some stories and the trivilization of others often provides the sociologist with a keyhole view into the news values of the particular media product or organization under study.

David Miller and Kevin Williams (1993), while working for the GUMG, focused their research into HIV/AIDS reporting and the interaction between the news media and the sources of information used in reporting, in particular government official sources.

News as a negotiated product

Miller and Williams suggest that news is not simply a manufactured product based solely and always on the dominant assumptions of media personnel which support and justifies a ruling élite. Instead, news is created through a process of negotiation between reporters, other media personnel and the sources of information themselves:

The interaction between the news media and the social institutions they report is a key issue for the sociology of journalism. What appears in the news is the outcome of a process of negotiation between the reporter and the source of information. In the dance between reporters and official sources some see the officials as leading, while others argue that reporters do. However, this dance is subject to a number of agendas, personal, organizational and political, that are brought to bear on the reporter and the source within their own organisation.

(Miller and Williams, 1993, p. 126)

HIV/AIDS media coverage has often been factually misleading, politically motivated and sensationalized. In this respect, it is similar to many other news stories. However, Miller and Williams are highly critical of what they see as the mistake made by other sociological research. It is not possible nor desirable to treat the mass media as a machine or unified whole. It is equally undesirable to assume that the media always takes the side of dominant social élites.

Do 'offical sources' always get their own way?

Official sources of information do not always have a smooth access to the media, and often fail to set the news agenda as previously assumed by some. The opposite is also true: alternative or limited resourced groups and opinions do sometimes gain access where and when official sources are unable to do so. In the case of HIV/AIDS reporting, Miller and Williams focus on the work since 1987 of the Health Education Authority (HEA).

The aim of the HEA was to promote messages of safe sex and safe drug-use through the media, focusing in particular on the issue that anyone can be at risk regardless of their sexuality. However, the HEA met with many problems when trying to use the media as a form of public education.

- The HEA workers were largely distrustful of journalists and so failed to develop good working relationships.
- The HEA failed to produce good quotable material that the media could use.
- Health education has a relatively low status in the eyes of journalists.

These factors combined to limit the space and air time given to the official viewpoint, and this study serves to illustrate the fact that the media does not always blindly follow the official line.

6.3 Media stereotypes

Many groups and organizations in society are interested in, and concerned about, the potential the media has for spreading political bias and propaganda. These interested groups include, of course, sociologists, but also pressure groups, governments, governmental watchdogs and political parties. Sociologists have been concerned with bias in the media since the very beginning of a sociological interest in the subject of the media in general.

Discussion point
Why is it important for sociologists, and other interested parties, to be able to identify possible bias in the media?

C3.1a

Case Study – Politics and public belief

Greg Philo (1994), a neo-Marxist member of the Glasgow University Media Group, contends that the dominance of a New Right Conservative government in the UK since 1979, and the electoral failures of the Labour party, could be explained by the success of Conservative administrations in using the media as an effective campaign tool:

To understand public beliefs about politics we must analyse how political parties have used the media. The crucial issue is how successful they have been in establishing strands of political belief which make sense and work with voters.

(Philo, 1994, p. 46)

Philo suggests that although sometimes the media gives a biased account of the world to the audience – which they may or may not believe – at other times the media is a resource or campaigning tool over which the political parties fight, each trying to give a good impression to an audience.

Repetition of key phrases
He suggests that the Conservative government's use of key phrases time and time again in the media – through speeches, interviews, party political broadcasts and other forms of political advertising – placed Conservative policies firmly into the public consciousness. These popular political phrases included:

- 'there is no alternative'

- 'a share-owning/home-owning democracy'
- 'popular capitalism'
- 'enterprise culture'
- 'the miracle economy'.

Some of these phrases not only acted as shorthand for Conservative policies, they were also used to attack and discredit in an effective manner Labour ideas and previous Labour governments:

- 'the winter of discontent'
- 'picket-line violence'.

Using advertising techniques to project 'image'

The importance of the mass media for politicians and politics is perhaps best illustrated by the fact that the advertising company Saatchi & Saatchi were employed by the Conservatives as image gurus. Political broadcasts since 1978/79, based on Saatchi & Saatchi ideas, used music and images in dramatic ways much more than previous campaigns. According to Philo, electoral success was the result of the careful manipulation of these phrases or media messages.

However, Philo also suggests that although the media presents a ready-made world, the audience is sophisticated enough to reflect on this world and to compare it with experience already gained.

Shifting alliances

It is also important to recognize that not all of the mass media in the UK supports the Conservatives all of the time. As illustrated by the front pages of the *Daily Mirror* reproduced in Figure 6.5, sometimes the tables are turned.

Activity

It has been argued by some that the *Daily Mirror* has in recent years moved away from its traditional support for the Labour party. Build up a collection of contemporary *Daily Mirror* front covers and editorials. Do they support the Labour party more than other parties, or not? How can you tell?

C3.2, C3.3

Representations of gender in the media

Feminism is concerned with how women (and men) are portrayed by the media. Feminist

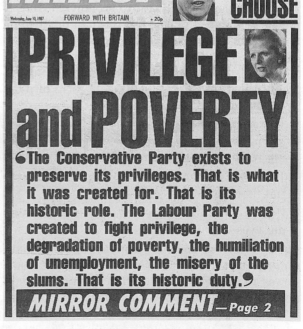

Figure 6.5 Front pages of the *Daily Mirror*, 1 June and 10 June 1987

research has been occupied with the goal of exposing bias against women in the media for the same reasons, and using the same methods, as Marxists are concerned to demonstrate a pro-capitalist bias. Both these two sociological traditions are built on a belief in *political action*. Deconstructing what they see as false ideas in the media can form the basis for a rejection of traditional socialization patterns by both women and the working classes alike. A concern with false representations in the media is a concern, by these perspectives, to establish true consciousness in the minds of the traditional victims of the media – the subordinate in society.

Discussion point

To what extent are men and women portrayed differently in the media?

C3.1a

Varieties of feminism

It is possible to draw a distinction between three types of feminist views on the role of the media in contemporary society:

- **liberal feminism**
- **radical feminism**
- **Marxist/socialist feminism**.

As Liesbet van Zoonen (1991) comments:

Classifying feminism in three neatly separated ideological currents is certainly at odds with the present fragmentation of feminist thought. ... Also, feminist theory and practice is often rather eclectic, incorporating elements from different ideologies as circumstances and issues necessitate. ... However, taken as ideal types ... they are indicative of various ways in which feminists perceive the media.

(van Zoonen, 1991, p. 35)

Liberal feminism

Within the liberal strand of feminist thought, stereotypes and **gender socialization** are seen to be the reason for the inequality of power between men and women. In this context the mass media, like education, is responsible for the continuation of these prejudices and stereotypes through the representations of femininity it creates and reinforces. Liberal feminism suggests that, by removing these images and replacing them with positive images of women, socialization can be

changed and power differences in society ultimately addressed. Full equality, however, must also exist through the law.

Radical feminism

For radical feminists, female oppression and subordination are the direct result of a male-dominated social system. Such a **patriarchal society** is built on men's desire to control women ideologically and, in the extreme, through violence and force. Radical feminism often leads to the political/sexual choice of lesbianism – women must be free of men, otherwise inequality will always continue. Radical feminists advocate use of the media, by feminists, as a tool against patriarchy: to set up alternative media which can be used to recruit women to the feminist cause:

Technological developments in print and audiovisual media made the proliferation of feminist writing, newsletters, magazines, radio and TV programmes, video and film groups possible. A host of feminist ideas would otherwise have not received a public forum.

(van Zoonen, 1991, p. 37)

Marxist/socialist feminism

Socialist or Marxist feminism has attempted to combine accounts of gender discrimination in society with those of class. Recently, (dis)ability, ethnicity and sexuality have also been added.

Discussion point

To what extent are capitalism and patriarchy a similar source of inequality and social control? How may the media reinforce and reproduce these?

C3.1a

The mass media is seen to be a key institution in the process of cultural reproduction – of continuing the capitalist and patriarchal systems through hegemony. Like the liberal and radical feminists they wish to reform the existing media, while in the meantime creating socialist media of their own. Ultimately, however, inequality can only be solved by a change in the class system in society.

Women's magazines

Marjorie Ferguson (1983) has provided feminist sociology with an analysis of magazines aimed at older women. Her sample of magazines was drawn from issues of *Woman*, *Woman's Own* and *Woman's Weekly*. Ferguson first looked at a random sample of magazines between 1949 and 1974 and then, in order to determine whether the content of these magazines changed over time, she drew a second sample between 1979 and 1980. In addition to this content analysis, Ferguson conducted interviews with media personnel in an attempt to understand the day-to-day decisions made by those who put these magazines together.

The cult of femininity

Ferguson identifies a number of dominant concerns shared by all three magazines across her first sample. These dominant themes included:

- overcoming misfortune
- getting and keeping a partner
- being a good wife
- keeping a happy family.

Ferguson suggests that these concerns, taken together as a whole, make up a cult of femininity.

Although the content of some of these themes had changed between the first and second sample periods, what remained the same was the magazines' atmosphere of instruction. These magazines were judged as teaching or instructing women and girls how to behave as a 'normal' member of society. They socialize their audience into a cult of femininity.

Utopian solutions

Ellen McCracken (1993) has argued that, despite the male-gendered nature of ownership and control changing in American womens' magazines during the 1980s, they still reflect the underlying ideological structure identified in Ferguson's analysis – the use of utopian solutions such as the perfect lover, dress and job as the ideal goal for women. McCracken argues that women are encouraged to feel part of a utopian community by these magazines.

Activity

a Identify and explain two ways in which women's magazines represent women.

b Outline and discuss the view that women's magazines no longer create a cult of femininity.

C3.2, C3.3

Case Study – Does sex change the way a newspaper thinks?

In 1995, the non-profit-making organization Women In Journalism (WIJ) was formed, its aim being to promote women's work in the media industry while monitoring the portrayal of women in magazines and newspapers. The WIJ group, whose committee members include some female editors and MPs, have conducted a number of content analysis studies to investigate what they see as the unfair representation of women in national newspapers and magazines in the UK. They comment:

To place the coverage of women in the news in context it is important to note two things. One is that most news decisions are taken by men. For the past two years the WIJ survey of the news and comment pages has shown that 80 per cent of those at news conferences are men. This is not to say that women do not play key roles in news rooms, including that of editor on several papers. But news and comment are still male dominated and, at the moment, the ultimate decision-maker – the Editor – is a man on 18 of our 19 national daily and Sunday newspapers. The other factor is that most news is about men. Previous research has shown that, on the whole, the news pages are dominated by male figures and, in this way, it reflects the reality of our public society. Unlike men, who appear in news columns in any and all roles, women who make the news tend to fit into certain categories, namely politicians, actresses, members of royalty, crime victims, wives and women of achievement.

(WIJ Research Committee, 1996, p. 1)

Methodology

The WIJ group took the 1995 political scandal of the crossing of the floor in the House of Commons by Alan Howarth (from Conservative to Labour) and by Emma Nicholson (from Conservative to Liberal Democrat). To cross the floor in the Commons means to switch political allegiances. This is very unusual and is done when the MP in question feels she or he is unable to continue to represent a party on a point of policy.

Alan Howarth announced his decision to leave the Conservatives on Saturday 7 October, and Emma Nicholson did likewise on Friday 29 December. The WIJ group compared the newspaper coverage of these two similar events to see whether media coverage was similar, or whether it differed owing to the difference in gender of the two MPs.

The WIJ group studied five days' of newspaper coverage, looking at ten newspapers: the *Sun*, *Daily Mirror*, *Daily Mail*, *Guardian*, *Daily Telegraph*, *Times*, *Mail on Sunday*, *News of the World*, *Observer* and *Sunday Times*. Both qualitative and quantitative methods were used. The result was that Howarth and Nicholson received about the same amounts of coverage:

- 60 articles for Nicholson, 67 for Howarth
- 999 paragraphs for Nicholson, 861 for Howarth
- average length of a story – 17 paragraphs for Nicholson, 13 for Howarth.

There are some signs here, perhaps, that a bit of extra interest was given to Emma Nicholson. However, differences showed up when looking at the *tone* of the pieces. In terms of the bias behind the stories the results reported were:

- *Emma Nicholson* (out of 60 stories)
  favourable 12
  unfavourable 19
  neutral 29
- *Alan Howarth* (out of 67 stories)
  favourable 13
  unfavourable 20
  neutral 34.

Analysis: Language
The language used, in both the text and the headlines, pointed to the frequent use of sexist and stereotypical images for Emma Nicholson. The *Observer* frequently (about 50 per cent of the time) referred to Nicholson as Emma but never referred to Howarth as Alan. Overall, no reference was made to the appearance of Howarth, yet Nicholson's appearance and domestic situation were frequently reported. Also, while Howarth was described as:

- 'intelligent and independent-minded'
  'an honourable man'
  'a principled man'
  'intelligent and committed'

Nicholson was described as:

- 'an admirable woman but not a serious politician'
  'frightful bitch'
  'at an emotional age'
  'something to do with the menopause'

(WIJ Research Committee, 1996, p. 4)

Analysis: Masculine and feminine stereotypes
From looking at this brief snapshot of headlines we can see a difference in how the two MPs were represented. Alan Howarth was described as a man, as if tough decisions were the things that characterized being a man; whereas Emma Nicholson's femininity is used to create an image of an irrational women not quite in control.

This work of the WIJ group is useful in highlighting the differences between the representations of gender and sexuality created in the national press.

Problems for feminism

Proving gender bias in media representations is one thing, but saying that these representations might have an adverse influence on men and women in society is altogether a different argument.

Brown (1990) even suggests that popular culture, such as soap operas and situation comedies, can actually be used as a weapon against **patriarchal hegemony**. Thus women might be able to use popular culture in a subversive fashion, questioning dominant and traditional notions of gender.

Activity
Watch a popular comedy programme featuring women comedians. Does this sort of TV challenge gender roles in any way?

C3.1a

Representations of ethnicity

Traditionally the sociological treatment of 'race', ethnicity and disability in the media focused on issues of under-representation and negative images. Although many would still argue that non-white ethnicity and disability are portrayed in a limited fashion, the argument can now be made that – in cinema and television at least – conscious steps forward are being made in the creation of positive representations.

Discussion point

Does the media create and reinforce racist images?

C3.1a

Pluralist viewpoints

Hartmann and Husband

An important and now classical contribution to the debate about the existence of racist ideology in the mass media is provided by Hartmann and Husband (1974, 1976). This research focused on two aspects of media research:

- content analysis of British daily newspapers between the years 1963 and 1970
- audience research directed at a sample of children in schools – both those of a multi-ethnic and a relatively single-ethnic nature.

Hartmann and Husband concluded that, during the time span of their content analysis, the British press contributed to racist ideology by portraying a specific stereotypical image of black people. They did this by focusing on stories and issues that emphasized racial problems and the strange cultural attitudes of new immigrants.

This suggests that black people are portrayed in the media as a threat to the smooth-running of white British society. They are portrayed as criminals, illegal aliens and much else besides.

These images and representations also manipulate racist ideas and create moral panics in wider society.

Hartmann and Husband also contended that such stories and racist images had a very limited *reinforcing effect* on the audience – especially on those who lived in areas and went to schools that were not especially multi-cultural:

Mass communications regarding race will be interpreted within the framework of meanings that serve to define the situation within any social group. At the same time the way race-related material is handled in the media contributes towards this definition of the situation. Attitudes and interpretations prevailing in a community are therefore seen as the result of the interplay between the on-the-ground social situation and the way race is handled by the media.

(Hartmann and Husband, 1976, p. 273)

The work of Hartmann and Husband illustrates a pluralist perspective. They claim that the media is shaped by the values and attitudes of society.

There is an interplay between the media and the audience. Thus, media images will change, in time, only when social attitudes themselves become less racist:

The way the media define the situation is seen as resulting from the definitions prevailing in the general culture and from institutional factors that stem from the media themselves.

(Hartmann and Husband, 1976, p. 274)

Stuart Hall and colleagues

Stuart Hall *et al.* (1978) suggest that ethnic groups are frequently 'defined' in the British media as social problems, as criminals around which we often find moral panics constructed. This view of the media is shared by other commentators. For example, although the media is controlled by legal and self-policing professional codes of conduct, informal racism can be created by under-representing black and Asian people in all other aspects of the news and popular drama programmes, except as social problems.

Ethnicity and moral panics

Hall and colleagues see a link between the economic conditions in society and the significance of moral panics – in this case the creation of a mugging moral panic (see Section 6.2) around young black males in the 1970s.

In their view, the British press contributed to the dominant hegemony of capitalism by creating racist images which divided the white and black working classes at a time of insecurity for the capitalist rulers in society.

Racism and the press

A recent example of content analysis of the representations of 'race' and ethnicity in newspapers is to be found in Van Dijk's *Racism and the Press* (1991).

Van Dijk studied the headlines in five newspapers – the *Times, Guardian, Daily Telegraph, Daily Mail* and the *Sun* – between August 1985 and January 1986, looking at the stories related to 'race'. He records that the two most frequently used words in such stories were *police*, which was used 388 times, and *riot*, used 320 times. This illustrates the negative context in which 'race' issues were raised in the press.

Van Dijk's research illustrates the point that news issues involving members of ethnic minorities are usually based around ideas of racial tension or crime problems which, as suggested by Hartmann and Husband (1974, 1976), identifies members of racial groups as a problem for white society to deal with.

However, for Van Dijk this racist ideology is seen to go further:

[It] is not limited to news reports, but also characterizes background articles and editorials. Indeed, the editorials clearly show the dominant ideology at work in the media account of the ethnic situation. In the right-wing press, ethnic events are primarily evaluated as a conflict between us and them, against the background of a conservative ideology that prominently features such concepts as order, authority, loyalty, patriotism, and freedom.

(Van Dijk, 1991, p. 246)

Pluralist criticisms

A pluralist perspective would argue that under-representation has indeed occurred, and still does occur, but is slowly being challenged in various ways. For example:

- British and American television companies are producing more self-conscious black-issues programmes.
- Independent black television companies are beginning to have their product exposed to mainstream audiences.
- Black and Asian actors are being cast more in popular dramas.

Activity

Using a copy of a weekly TV listings guide, answer the following questions:

a Roughly what proportion of programmes on the mainstream channels are aimed at an ethnic audience?

b How many of these programmes are comedies? Does this tell us anything?

c Among the programmes that are *not* comedies, at what time of the day or night are they scheduled, and on which channels? Does this tell us anything about the scheduling decisions made?

C3.2, C3.3, N3.1

Reporting of famines and aid issues

An increasingly frequent occurrence in the western media is a concern for charitable events,

causes and relief. From Band Aid-style global music and media events, through to telethons and celebrity Christmas records, public attention is often turned towards good causes that merit attention.

Whilst not wishing to devalue the worth of such causes, some sociologists are concerned with the charitable events, organizations and issues that do not have access to public attention through media exposure, and those seeking to create funds by using what could be described as racist images.

Defining 'natural disasters'

As a critic of the ways in which the media reports natural disasters, Jonathan Benthall (1995) suggests that disasters and emergencies become defined as disasters only by the world's media. So powerful is the media in swaying public attention and attitudes that the media itself has the power, through an act of *endorsement*, to define what constitutes a worthy cause or dangerous situation:

Disasters do not exist – except for their unfortunate victims and those who suffer in their aftermaths – unless publicized by the media. In this sense the media actually constructs disasters.

(Benthall, 1995, p. 27)

Selectivity

Coverage of suffering and disasters is so selective and arbitrary, argues Benthall, that media endorsement of one particular cause inevitably occurs at the expense of another. Benthall says that this media hallmark is often a prerequisite for the involvement of many world powers.

On the other hand, governments may use media coverage and public attention turned towards one part of the globe as the ideal time to perform actions in another part of the world they may not wish to be scrutinized too carefully.

Racist photographic images

Benthall takes issue with what he sees as potentially racist photographic images presented by the western media. Images of Africans and Asians in the western media either appeal to romantic stereotypes so as to continue tourism in these areas, or we are presented with images of women and children as passive victims, dependent on others for help. As Benthall argues:

Figure 6.6 (next page) The need for sensitive choosing of pictures
Source: Adapted from an Oxfam leaflet

Which picture?

You won't find Oxfam using harrowing pictures of starving children in its appeals – although some charities think such pictures are an effective way of fundraising. Why?

Behind the picture

In 1985, during the worst of the Sudanese famine, a UN representative set out on a tour of the famine zone. In tow was a film crew.

They arrived at a camp near Port Sudan where hill-dwelling Hadenowa had come to seek help. Everyone was in a desperate state. The men had all gone to find work – and money – in Port Sudan. The only people left were the old, and mothers with their children.

A guide picked up a child sitting motionless under a makeshift shelter and placed the child on the parched soil. He was being helpful, showing the visitors what was happening. "Here," he said "look at this child" and the TV crew took their pictures.

It is a familiar image of famine – one that says very little about what is really going on. But step back, as the photographer Wendy Wallace did, and the picture is very different.

Why do pictures matter to Oxfam?

Pictures have power. They can convey information and emotion. They can provoke a response and leave a lasting impression.

The right pictures can mobilize people and change the course of events. It's a power that can be used for good or bad.

Are pictures true or false?

We like to think that photographs are a piece of reality, captured on film. But they are not neutral. They have one particular view point, which can distort as well as reveal.

In Oxfam's experience the pictures we see from developing countries are an example of distortion. Harrowing pictures of starving children still feature in some charity advertising, and news from outside Europe and North America is dominated by famine, disaster and poverty.

We are being given a begging-bowl image of the Third World – which is at odds with people's actual lives.

Is Oxfam saying famine doesn't exist?

No – only that disasters and famines are the exception not the rule. And even in these situations the pictures of exhaustion and hunger we are used to seeing don't do justice to people's struggle to stay alive.

Is it always wrong to use pictures of famine?

No – but show it like it is. This means begging-bowl pictures of starving children aren't enough. Who is this picture of? What's their story? What happened to cause this suffering?

Hang on, didn't Oxfam use pictures of starving children?

In the past Oxfam – and other aid agencies – ran fundraising campaigns showing starving pot-bellied children. They were relatively successful in raising money, at least for a short time.

But we've learnt from our mistakes. Such poster campaigns were counter-productive. They gave the impression that people sat and waited for food – or death, and that they did nothing for themselves. It was as if Oxfam was saying the response to famine should be pity – when it should be a demand for justice and action.

How does Oxfam try to use pictures?

Pictures used well can challenge prejudice – about race or about stereotypes of men and women. They can either give people dignity, or take it away. They can help to provoke a positive and appropriate response or they can mislead.

When Oxfam uses pictures it tries to take this into account. We try to tell the story behind the picture. We try to use named people and give some idea of their lives. We try to use pictures that reflect Oxfam's practical experience, which is that people don't want hand-outs, but help so that they can help themselves.

Photography and the ensuing technologies of film and television – though in principle they can be, and sometimes are, adapted for all sorts of liberating purposes – are in practice often used to reinforce stereotypes which have a controlling function in our society.

(Benthall, 1995, pp. 186–7)

Many charities are now conscious of the way in which photographs and the media in general can be used in an ideological fashion to create an image of suffering, weakness and pity designed to raise more money for a particular cause. As the Oxfam leaflet reproduced in Figure 6.6 demonstrates, each picture used in such campaigns must be used and chosen with extreme care. The image created must be a true reflection of the lives of those individuals, not just a snapshot which reinforces stereotypes and prejudice.

Gender and cultural definition

Christine Gledhill (1997) argues that the ranking of 'high culture' above 'popular culture' as more 'serious' or 'worthwhile' often betrays a masculine approach to defining culture. This is partly because men still occupy more of the positions of power within cultural industries, universities and schools.

Cultural forms or genres associated with femininity are taken less seriously while 'serious' cultural forms are understood in masculine terms, even if women participate in their production. Gledhill produces a table to illustrate the gendered hierarchy which she believes underpins the way in which society defines 'serious' and 'popular' culture (see Table 6.1).

Table 6.1 A gendered hierarchy

Femininity	Masculinity
[Mass culture/entertainment]	[High culture/art]
Popular genre conventions	Realism
Romanticized stereotypes	Rounded characters
Glamour	Severity
Emotions	Rational thought
Expressive performance	Underplaying, understatement
Talk about feelings	Taciturnity, decisive action
Fantasy	Escapism
Private domesticity	The public world
Pleasure	Difficulty (intellectual challenges)
Soap opera	The Western

Source: Adapted from Gledhill (1997, p. 49)

Gledhill suggests that this table summarizes the gendered framework underpinning the way in which high and popular culture has been distinguished. She points out that while soap operas, enjoyed by mainly female audiences, are still frequently dismissed as lacking serious content, Clint Eastwood can receive an Oscar award for directing *The Unforgiven*, an example of the Western genre which Gledhill regards as the male equivalent of the soap opera.

Gledhill acknowledges that these distinctions are not set in stone, and that in recent years shifts in the gendering of cultural forms have occurred more frequently. For example, growing numbers of men enjoy television soaps such as *EastEnders*, while certain masculinized forms of 'action' television, such as *The Bill* and *London's Burning*, succeed partly because they develop characters and plots involving human relationships in much the same way as the soaps. Gledhill explains these changes in terms of the struggles which those involved in television, film and publishing have undertaken to break down the gendered nature of cultural production.

 Activity

a In relation to Table 6.1, provide one example of a masculine cultural feature and one example of a feminine culture feature.

b According to Gledhill, what is the difference between the way in which soap operas are regarded by society and the way in which Westerns are regarded?

C3.2

Mass media and disability

The representation of disability in the mass media

In an outline of the way disabled people are represented in the mass media, Anne Karpf (1988) argues that there are two consistent themes involved. Firstly, she points to the way in which the media are interested in miracle cure stories and secondly, she argues that the disabled also only appear on telethons where children, in particular, are portrayed almost like victims.

She argues that medicine is seen as offering a cure and charity is seen as offering help. We are therefore encouraged to pity or praise disabled people for their fortitude in the face of suffering.

Cure stories are the favourite media stories. The disability movement feels that they celebrate disabled people, but that the media celebrate people who somehow overcome or are cured of their disability.

Karph argues that telethons such as 'Children in Need' do indeed raise valuable funds but that in America, in particular, telethons have been accused of perpetuating damaging stereotypes of disability. In order to get money some feel that telethons have to humiliate disabled people on television and to allow them to be presented as poor, unfortunate cripples. A second point in relation to telethons is that in the UK they invariably focus on children. Thirdly, Karpf argues that we need to ask in whose benefit such telethons are made. Arguably, their main benefit is to give cheap advertising and a whiff of worthiness to business sponsors: suggesting the main beneficiaries could be able-bodied corporation executives.

Finally, she argues that there is the sin of omission whereby disabled people are rarely asked to contribute to discussion on issues such as abortion or prenatal screening. When disabled people feature in mainstream programmes it is purely because of their disability, as if this is all that defines them.

Recent improvements?

O'Sullivan and Jewkes (1997) accept most of the arguments made by Karpf but argue that things may have improved slightly since she was writing. In particular they argue that since 1998 representations of the disabled in mainstream television have become more common. They cite films such as *My Left Foot, Children of a Lesser God, The Piano, Born on the Fourth of July* and *Rain Man*, all of which featured characters with disabilities.

Even accepting this improvement, however, the other points made by Karpf still seem to have a ring of truth about them.

6.4 Trends in the ownership and control of the mass media

The media and its freedoms and constraints in contemporary social life are of great significance for politicians, media workers and sociologists, as well as for the public as audience members

and possibly as pressure group members. Even if you are simply engaged with the media as a reader of a newspaper or a viewer of television, issues of freedom, choice, control and quality affect your life.

Two issues will be discussed in this section:

- Do free-market policies lead to freedom of choice for the consumer?
- Does market competition lead to erosion of the quality of broadcasting?

Discussion point

To what extent do you think the mass media is the most significant technological development of the present age?

C3.1a

Broadcasting

Public and commercial broadcasting

Debates over media policies in the late 1990s included analyses of the nature of, and differences between, public and commercial broadcasting.

The term 'broadcasting media' usually refers to media transmitted through the air – terrestrial TV, satellite TV and radio. To be technically correct, cable TV is not a form of broadcasting by this definition because it is not transmitted through the air but received via cables. For the sake of convenience, however, cable and digital TV are often included in definitions of broadcasting, especially since many programmes for cable TV are produced originally by traditional stations and production houses for broadcast.

Broadcasting can be further subdivided into public and commercial:

- *Public broadcasting* in the UK refers to the BBC. The audience pays a licence fee, which notionally acts as a funding mechanism. The top positions at the BBC are government-appointed.
- *Commercial broadcasting* is sometimes referred to as independent broadcasting. Traditionally, this concept was used to refer to regional companies which transmitted via the Independent Television (ITV) network. Recently the independent sector has grown owing to the intro-

duction of Channel 4, Channel 5, satellite, digital and other technologies.

The widening of choice?

To what extent have free-market policies led to a freedom of choice in the public's consumption of broadcast media? There has been much contemporary debate about whether consumer choice has been increased by the widening of independent broadcasting.

Discussion point

How much real choice does the audience have in its media consumption?

C3.1a

Two basic responses to this issue can be identified:

- VIEW one: *Widening media products increases the freedom of consumer choice and therefore the power of the audience*. This 'free-market' position argues that developments in technology bring an ever-increasing choice of products into the home. This view is based on a belief in an ideal future of broadcasting where the audience enjoys an almost unlimited choice.

- VIEW two: *Freedom of choice cannot exist when the public can consume only what they can afford to buy*. Some commentators – including Marxists and Socialists, but also increasingly some pluralists – have suggested that this is not a democratic situation, far from it. Additionally, there will be only a very limited choice as more and more stations buy products from similar sources – products that are increasingly similar in nature and content. With a rather pessimistic tone, these commentators see a future where audiences are exposed to repeats of cheap, poor-quality programmes, where ultimately there is no choice.

Activity

a Identify and explain two approaches to the widening of choice in the consumption of mass media products.

b Outline and discuss the view that widening media products increase consumer choice.

C3.2, C3.3

Activity

Try to determine just how much choice there is for the audience of non-fee paying TV – e.g. channels like BBC1, BBC2, ITV and Channels 4 and 5. Look at a TV guide for a whole week.

a How many programmes are there of a political nature which might encourage people to think critically? At what time are they on? Are people encouraged to watch them because of their scheduling?

b How are programmes aimed at 'minority views' scheduled?

c How much choice does the audience really have?

d How would Marxists and pluralists interpret your answers to the questions above?

C3.2

The mass culture debate

With the development of a system of mass communications, sociological thinkers, since the early 1900s onwards, have been concerned to chart, describe and evaluate the artistic or intellectual nature of the media. This analysis of the artistic or intellectual value of modern-day cultural products is commonly referred to as the '**mass culture** debate'. There are four basic issues:

1 What effect has the creation of a mass communications system had on the quality of media products?

2 What effect has the quality of media products had on the audience?

   or, in a more critical (and perhaps pessimistic) fashion:

3 Have modern cultural products suffered from lack of intellectual, artistic and creative value owing to their mass production as commodities to be bought and sold?

4 Has the creation of the mass media led to a mass culture where the media audience is an uncritical, unintellectual mass unable to value truly artistic achievement?

What characterizes this debate is a confusion of terms, all of which sound similar. Theorists in this debate discuss mass society, mass culture, popular culture, high culture, low culture, etc. The following are some key terms and their meanings:

- *Culture*. This commonly used concept has two definitions, both of which are important in this debate:

  a the highest artistic and intellectual achievements of a society

  b the way of life of a group.

- *Mass communications*. This is the development of a widespread system of communications (the mass media) where a vast array of technologies and media products are on offer to the consumer or audience.

- *Mass culture*. With the development of a mass communications system, some argue that the media products on offer in today's society lack the intellectual and artistic value of previous times: that the large-scale production of the media lowers its value – it is only a throwaway, temporary product to be consumed.

- *Popular culture*. This is a term often used as a replacement for mass culture.

- *Mass society*. Those critical of mass culture also contend that we have seen, or are seeing, the rise of a mass society where the audience has become a faceless, uncritical, apolitical mass open to all worthless media products, controllable by the media and the ruling class without question or criticism.

- *Low culture*. Mass culture is also seen, by those critical of it, as a low culture. It is made simply for money and immediate consumption, not for lasting artistic value.

- *High culture*. This is the opposite of low culture. High culture is believed by some to be a thing of the past – truly critical, artistic and intellectual cultural products.

Activity

a Identify and explain two aspects of high culture.

b Outline and discuss the view that mass culture has destroyed high culture.

The Frankfurt School

The **Frankfurt School** have claimed that contemporary societies are mass societies. By this they mean that social community has been lost and, with the rise of mass communications, the media has become worthless. The media contains no genuine attempts to express critical thinking regarding the social condition, and in failing to do so stands in the way of revolutionary changes in the consciousness of the masses.

Herbert Marcuse

Marcuse (1966), a member of the Frankfurt School, refers to individuals in a mass society as one-dimensional. By this he means that membership of contemporary society is based on socialization through the culture industry and a loss of free-thinking, intellectual curiosity and critical thought.

Marcuse suggests that these mass societies are characterized by the paralysis of criticism – the inability of the masses to engage with critical, enlightened and revolutionary thought. A new post-war affluence, combined with this loss of criticism, leads to the continuation of false class consciousness in society.

Adorno and Horkheimer

Adorno and Horkheimer (e.g. 1993), like Marcuse above, operate with an image of the mass media (or in their words, the 'culture industry') which sees the media feeding crass, commercial low culture into the minds of the willing masses – who are tricked and duped into thinking that media entertainment represents a free and active choice.

Liberation from capitalism

Liberation, the end-goal of the project of critical theory, can in this view be achieved only by waging a war on consciousness – of showing the masses that they do have the ability to achieve critical thought. But to do so they must give up the comfort and security of the mass culture delivered by the modern system of mass communications.

The Frankfurt School condemn this mass culture. Media products are seen to deliver low culture as a commodity to be bought and sold for capitalist profit, rather than concentrating on genuine expressions of taste, art and intellect. This low culture, characterized by its essential sameness, is consumed by the masses who in turn lose individuality.

The Frankfurt School take this idea to its logical conclusion. They place their hope of revolutionary change for society in the hands of high culture.

Criticisms of the Frankfurt School

Critics of the School point out that, whereas they wish to achieve a Marxist revolution of the masses, they put their hopes for this in the hands of a non-working class, cultural élite.

As a warning against these pessimistic and critical theories which claim that social life has been characterized by the development of a mass society, Raymond Williams (1963) notes that the concept of 'masses' is highly problematic – it means many different things to many different theorists:

The masses are always the others, whom we don't know, and can't know. Yet now, in our kind of society, we see these others regularly, in their myriad variations; stand, physically, beside them. They are here, and we are here with them. And that we are with them is of course the whole point. To other people, we are also the masses. Masses are other people.

(Williams, 1963, p. 289)

Williams claims that whereas 'we' are always able to think for ourselves, the 'masses' are always other people who cannot. In fact, the concept of 'masses' is so general it is meaningless, and certainly not capable of being measured:

There are in fact no masses; there are only ways of seeing people as masses.

(Williams, 1963, p. 289)

💬 Discussion point

Do popular television programmes stop critical thought – or might they encourage it?

C3.1a

Alan Swingewood

Swingewood (1977) argues, in accordance with the title of his book, that we are witnessing *The Myth of Mass Culture*. Mass culture, he asserts, is neither good nor bad, revolutionary nor exploiting. Actually, it is not real – it does not exist. It is simply an ideological phrase used by some groups to win intellectual arguments while devaluing all other viewpoints.

6.5 The relationship between ownership, control and production

The traditional battleground for debates over the level of democracy in the media, especially between pluralist and Marxist viewpoints, is often referred to as *the ownership and control debate*.

💬 Discussion point

Who owns and controls the media and in whose interests?

C3.1a

The classical Marxist perspective

The classical Marxist view on media ownership (as an example of the ownership of *any* of the means or **forces of production**) starts from the observation that it rests in the hands of a narrow group. This is the 'ruling class' – so defined by their very ownership of media interests. Marxists argue that this leads directly to media bias: the ruling class own the media *and therefore are able to control its output.*

Marxists are especially critical of the development of large-scale multimedia conglomerations, such as News Corporation owned by Rupert Murdoch depicted by the graphic in Figure 6.7. Marxists perceive the development of media oligopolies (where control of a market is in the hands of a few large companies only) as serving ruling-class interests.

The media audiences of contemporary western societies, it is argued, are subjected to a limited range of opinions, given that a limited number of key individuals still have ultimate control. Share-holding does not benefit working-class democratic ownership of the media, in view of the vast sums needed to hold a majority share.

Pluralism

Pluralists take issue with the classical Marxist view, which they see as simplistic and naive. Pluralists would argue that, with the rise of joint-stock companies (i.e. share-holding), control has become divided or dispersed. Although a narrow élite may own a majority holding of a media company, these owners are forced to employ controllers (i.e. managers) to run the organization on a day-to-day basis.

Pluralists believe that a **managerial revolution** has occurred. The classic example of this argument came from James Burnham (1945), who claimed that the rise of the professional manager was an indication of increased democracy in the workplace. Professional managers

The whole world in his hands?

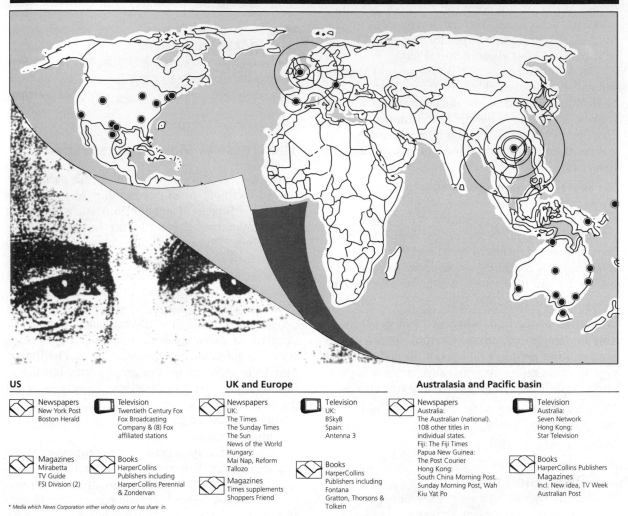

US

 Newspapers
New York Post
Boston Herald

 Television
Twentieth Century Fox
Fox Broadcasting
Company & (8) Fox
affiliated stations

 Magazines
Mirabetta
TV Guide
FSI Division (2)

 Books
HarperCollins
Publishers including
HarperCollins Perennial
& Zondervan

UK and Europe

 Newspapers
UK:
The Times
The Sunday Times
The Sun
News of the World
Hungary:
Mai Nap, Reform
Tallozo

 Television
UK:
BSkyB
Spain:
Antenna 3

 Magazines
Times supplements
Shoppers Friend

 Books
HarperCollins
Publishers including
Fontana
Gratton, Thorsons &
Tolkein

Australasia and Pacific basin

 Newspapers
Australia:
The Australian (national).
108 other titles in
individual states.
Fiji: The Fiji Times
Papua New Guinea:
The Post Courier
Hong Kong:
South China Morning Post.
Sunday Morning Post, Wah
Kiu Yat Po

 Television
Australia:
Seven Network
Hong Kong:
Star Television

 Books
HarperCollins Publishers
Magazines
Incl. New idea, TV Week
Australian Post

* Media which News Corporation either wholly owns or has share in.

Figure 6.7 A snapshot of Rupert Murdock's developing media 'empire'
Source: Guardian, 2 August 1993

are, in theory at least, left to do their jobs by owners and investors, who can come from all aspects of the social system.

This is very much the image of the share-owning democracy supported by the New Right, as illustrated by increased privatization of British industry since the 1979 general election.

A neo-Marxist perspective on ownership and control

Modern-day Marxists, such as those who adopt the neo-Marxist or hegemonic approach, contend that the development of share-owning and the arrival of professional managers, although highly significant, does not mean that ruling-class inter-

ests are any less represented in the media. Also, it has to be questioned whether professional managers do in reality have ultimate freedom from their share-holding, élite owners.

 Discussion point

Do the media audience (the public) have the power to control the content of the media; or are they simply exposed to whatever media bosses wish them to consume?

C3.1a

Ownership and control: Feminist views

There are two dominant interpretations of the ownership and control of the media within the feminist perspective: that the vast majority of owners and decision-makers are men, and that programming has a bias towards male interests.

Senior media personnel

It seems to be a fact that the majority of media moguls are men, as are the higher post-holders within these media empires (see Figure 5.8). Thus it can be argued that media institutions are male-dominated: they present a male view, a patriarchal ideology, both within the organization and within the content of their own products.

An estimate produced by the group Women In Journalism (WIJ) suggests that, in 1995–96, only 20 per cent of positions of significant decision-making power in newspapers were held by women (WIJ Research Committee, 1996).

Activity

Study Figure 6.8 on page 170 and interpret this from the viewpoint of feminism. What does this *suggest* about women's role within the BBC, and possibly in the media in general?

C3.2, C3.3

Playing the male game

The second interpretation of ownership and control is that even those women who are able to reach the higher levels within a media organization may have to play the male game in order to get there – that is to continue to organize programming based largely on male understandings of what female audiences like.

Sex objects

Laura Mulvey (1975) argues that the representation of female bodies in films has contributed to the patriarchal stereotype the media uses when displaying what is defined as 'femininity' in contemporary society. She believes that the cinema industry operates from an overwhelmingly male viewpoint. For example, female bodies are depicted as playthings for the male audience. This argument suggests that women in general in the cinema take on passive and subservient roles, and are often treated as sex objects.

The image of femininity

Wolf (1990) refers to the way in which women are portrayed in the media as 'the beauty myth'. By this she means that the media presents a particular physical image of femininity as the normal body image for women to have, even though this image may well be unobtainable (or even not wanted) by many women.

Discussion point

How are female bodies used by the media to sell and make popular, commercial products?

C3.1a

Female fear

In her book *Misogynies* – meaning women-hating – Joan Smith (1989) explores a similar theme to Mulvey. Smith is concerned with the use (or, in her terms, misuse and exploitation) of the female fear of violent assault as a basis for film plots. Female fear is used as a commodity, being marketed and sold to audiences. But these films add to the stock-of-fear which already exists in wider society. In this way, the cinema industry contributes to male dominance by reinforcing an image of femininity which defines women as victims of the superior strength of the male – weak, vulnerable and in need of protection:

Female fear sells films. It's a box-office hit. In 1960 the shower scene in Hitchcock's Psycho ... shocked audiences who had never seen anything like it on their cinema screens; today such scenes are ten a penny. Terror, torture, rape, mutilation and murder are handed out to actresses by respectable directors as routinely as tickets to passengers on a bus. No longer the stock in trade only of pornographers and video-nasty producers, they can be purchased any day at a cinema near you.

(Smith, 1989, p. 16)

Activity

Watch any popular Hollywood crime film. How are the female characters portrayed – what do they wear, how do they act, and so on? How might the film exploit or play up to female fear? How might the film represent women only as victims?

C3.1a, C3.3

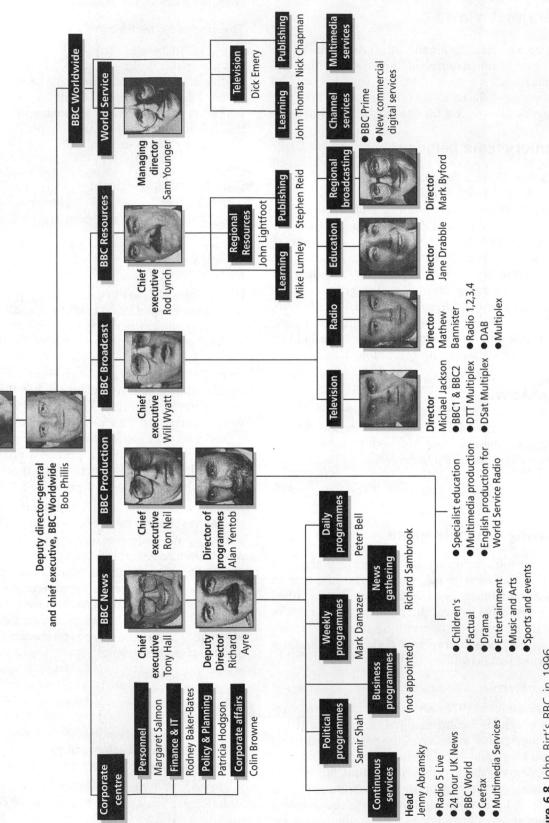

Figure 6.8 John Birt's BBC in 1996
Source: Guardian, 22 July 1996

6.6 Ownership and trends in production and consumption

Broadcasting in the 1980s: public choice and deregulation

Channel 4 was launched in 1982 to provide for minority tastes, away from the mainstreams of BBC1 and ITV (as, indeed, was BBC2, which started broadcasting in 1964). This was intended in practice to mean a move away from light entertainment, towards educational programming, programmes directed at issues concerning community or marginal groups, British-sponsored drama and arts/cultural broadcasting. At their respective conceptions there were commonly held views that BBC2 and Channel 4 were supposed to be the 'arts' channels.

The Peacock Report

The Peacock Committee, set up in 1985 by the Conservative government to look into the issue of deregulation, suggested that it should occur. Its *Report of the Committee on Financing the BBC* (1986) recommended that an alternative to the licence-fee method of funding the BBC should be sought. The argument was that if the BBC was to become simply one of many channels in a new free-market, openly competitive, deregulated system – seen by the Conservative government as encouraging freedom of public choice – then the compulsory purchase of a licence fee for a channel that people may choose not to watch would no longer make sense. The Peacock Committee saw the future of television with a pay-per-programme or pay-per-channel funding mechanism.

Discussion point

Do television audiences have a real choice; or just the illusion of choice?

C3.1a

Broadcasting in the 1990s

Following on from the recommendations made in the Peacock Report was the publication in 1988 of the White Paper *Broadcasting in the 1990s*. Included in the recommendations of this White Paper were:

- replacement of the ITV network with a new Channel 3 based on regional franchises
- creation of a Channel 5 (and a Channel 6 if possible) whose franchises would be auctioned
- introduction by the BBC of a pay-as-you-watch subscription service in the future.

More than any other previous media legislation, the 1988 White Paper clearly illustrated New Right free-market ideas at work. However, many years on from its publication, several of its ideas and recommendations are yet to be developed, or are still in an infant stage. For example, ITV – now referred to as Channel 3 – saw franchises given to four new licence-holders:

- Carlton, which took over the old Thames Television network
- Meridian, which replaced TVS
- Westcountry Television
- GMTV, which replaced the TV-AM breakfast slot.

Channel 5, as set out in the 1988 White Paper and launched in March 1997, was to provide further diversity of tastes by offering yet another channel – and thus supposedly increasing the freedom of the audience. We might hold a pessimistic view of this, considering how much cable and satellite broadcasting has arguably *not* widened choice but simply allowed increased exposure to repeated programmes. MTV coverage, Sky sports coverage and CNN news coverage are accessible through a wide variety of other mechanisms.

Activity

Either watch some Channel 5 television or look in a TV guide to find out what is on offer (bearing in mind that even TV guides may not be entirely independent and unbiased).
Has the introduction of Channel 5 widened public choice? Explain your answer.

C3.3

Deregulation: should we bury pluralism?

With deregulation gaining momentum, a number of sociologists have begun to re-appraise the future of media democracy.

When pluralism was first developed, the

media was in the hands of an élite who competed with each other for audience attention over their limited media products. Curran suggests that since this situation has changed it is time to reject orthodox pluralism: to recognize this and move on from its dated values:

The result is a legacy of old saws which bear little relationship to contemporary reality. ... it is time that they were given a decent funeral.

(Curran, 1991, p. 82)

The media at times of war

The role of the media at times of national and international conflict is a much debated political, as well as sociological, issue. In recent times the television viewing public have been presented with so-called instant or as-it-happens media coverage of conflicts such as the Gulf war.

The war in the Arabian Gulf

Two main issues of concern for sociologists came out of the media coverage of the Gulf war:

• the new developments in so-called instant news coverage

• the use of language in reporting.

Discussion point

Why are audiences fascinated by so-called as-it-happens news events?

C3.1a

Instant coverage

Philip Taylor (1992) is highly critical of the claims, by some sections of the media, to instant coverage of the events in the Gulf war. In particular, the 24-hour news station in America, Cable News Network (CNN), presented its images as first-hand real events as they happened. These images and reports were often used by other news organizations, including the BBC and ITN, the British independent news provider for commercial television. Taylor shares the concern of other sociologists, such as John Eldridge, in questioning the role of CNN in the war.

'News pools'

The Gulf war has been interpreted by some as a staged media event in order to create pro-American capitalist propaganda. Rather than the coverage being instant, true, direct and totally real, Taylor points to the existence of news pools controlled and organized by the military. Journalists were put into Media Reporting Teams which combined reporters from a wide number of organizations. The reports created by these teams were then made available to all other journalists – out of the 1500 journalists in the region, only 200 places in the pools had been created.

How much censorship was there?

Taylor and Eldridge comment that, since the Gulf war, reporters have complained that the activities of these pools were controlled by the military, defining for them what information to have from official sources, where they were allowed to go, and which other journalists could and could not benefit from the information created by these pools. The exclusiveness of these pools resulted in direct competition between journalists, which may well have hindered the collection of information if based on more equal and co-operative grounds.

Did we see it 'as it happened'?

Regarding the claims by satellite and cable news organizations to instant, reality-as-it-happens reporting, Taylor asks:

But what exactly had they seen? ... audiences could indeed be forgiven for thinking that they were participating in historic events as they were unfolding. But the excitement of the occasion, when people not directly involved in matters of life and death felt that they were actually a part of what was going on, raises a number of questions about the relationship between war and the media. Was this a new variation of total war in which the gap which had previously existed between soldier and civilian had been substantially narrowed by television? Or was it something else? Were people seeing a war in which nations resolved their disputes for the benefit of their publics ... were they, in other words, being manipulated into believing that they were part of something they were not ... ?

(Taylor, 1992, p. 33)

Activity

In April 1991, *New Statesman and Society* in conjunction with Channel 4 published a list of songs that were banned from BBC radio stations during the Gulf war. The list is reproduced here as Figure 6.9. Write one paragraph interpreting the BBC's intentions from each of the following points of view: pluralism, classical Marxism, and neo-Marxism. (See Section 6.5.)

C3.2, C3.3

Baudrillard: did the Gulf war really 'happen'?

The popular French thinker Jean Baudrillard (1995) came to even more popular and public infamy during the Gulf war when he claimed that the conflict did not actually happen.

Many of Baudrillard's critics point out that claiming the war did not happen is to offer little comfort and great insult to the thousands of ordinary citizens and military personnel who were killed or injured, and to their families.

The point Baudrillard wishes to make, however, in characteristically dramatic fashion, is that for many – including many of the journalists and military personnel who were actually there – the Gulf war existed only as flickering images on a TV screen. It is an example of what Baudrillard refers to as *simulacrum* – simulated images of reality which appear so direct, instant and clear, they define what we think of as reality.

Post-modernists refer to this situation, where media-reality becomes blurred with reality, as hyper-real: more real than real. As Paul Patton comments:

At the time, the TV Gulf war must have seemed to many viewers a perfect Baudrillardian simulacrum ... Fascination and horror at the reality which seemed to unfold before our very eyes mingled with a pervasive sense of unreality as we recognized the elements of Hollywood script which had preceded the real ... occasionally, the absurdity of the media's self-representation as purveyor of reality and immediacy broke through, in moments such as those when the CNN cameras crossed live to a group of reporters assembled somewhere in the Gulf, only to have them confess that they were also sitting around watching CNN in order to find out what was happening. Television news coverage appeared to have finally caught up with the logic of simulation. ...

ABBA   Waterloo; Under Attack
AKA   Hunting High and Low
ALARM   68 Guns
ANIMALS   We Got to Get Out of This Place
ARRIVAL   I Will Survive
JOAN BAEZ   The Night They Drove Old Dixie Down
BANGLES   Walk Like an Egyptian
BEATLES   Back in the USSR
PAT BENATAR   Love is a Battlefield
BIG COUNTRY   Fields of Fire
BLONDIE   Atomic
BOOMTOWN RATS   I Don't Like Mondays
BROOK BROS   Warpaint
CRAZY WORLD OF ARTHUR BROWN   Fire
KATE BUSH   Army Dreamers
CHER   Bang Bang (My Baby Shot Me Down)
ERIC CLAPTON   I Shot the Sheriff
PHIL COLLINS   In the Air Tonight
ELVIS COSTELLO   Oliver's Army
CUTTING CREW   I Just Died in Your Arms Tonight
SKEETER DAVIS   End of the World
DESMOND DEKKER   Israelites
DIRE STRAITS   Brothers in Arms
DURAN DURAN   View to a Kill
JOSE FELICIANO   Light My Fire
FIRST CHOICE   Armed and Extremely Dangerous
ROBERTA FLACK   Killing Me Softly
FRANKIE GOES TO HOLLYWOOD   Two Tribes
EDDIE GRANT   Living on the Frontline; Give Me Hope Joanna
ELTON JOHN   Saturday Night's Alright For Fighting
MILLIE JACKSON   Act of War
J HATES JAZZ   I Don't Want to be a Hero
JOHN LENNON   Give Peace a Chance; Imagine
JOHN LEWIS   Stop the Cavalry
LULU   Boom Bang a Bang
McGUINNESS FLINT   When I'm Dead and Gone
BOB MARLEY   Buffalo Soldier
MARIA MULDAUR   Midnight at the Oasis
MASH   Suicide is Painless
MIKE AND THE MECHANICS   Silent Running
RICK NELSON   Fools Rush In
NICOLE   A Little Peace
BILLY OCEAN   When the Going Gets Tough
DONNY OSMOND   Soldier of Love
PAPER LACE   Billy Don't Be a Hero
QUEEN   Killer Queen; Flash
MARTHA REEVES   Forget Me Not
B A ROBERTSON   Bang Bang
TOM ROBINSON   War Baby
KENNY ROGERS   Ruby (Don't Take Your Love to Town)
SPANDAU BALLET   I'll Fly For You
SPECIALS   Ghost Town
BRUCE SPRINGSTEEN   I'm on Fire
EDWIN STARR   War
STATUS QUO   In the Army Now; Burnin' Bridges
CAT STEVENS   I'm Gonna Get Me a Gun
ROD STEWART   Sailing
DONNA SUMMER   State of Independence
TEARS FOR FEARS   Everybody Wants to Rule the World
TEMPTATIONS   Ball of Confusion
10CC   Rubber Bullets
STEVIE WONDER   Heaven Help Us All

Figure 6.9 Songs banned from the airwaves by the BBC during the Gulf war

... It was not the first time that images of war had appeared on TV screens, but it was the first time that they were relayed live from the battlefront. It was not the first occasion on which the military censored what could be reported, but it did involve a new level of military control of reportage and images ... what we saw was for the most part a clean war, with lots of pictures of weaponry, including the amazing footage from the nose-cameras of smart bombs, and relatively few images of human casualties, none from the Allied forces ... the Gulf war movie was instant history in the sense that the selected images which were broadcast worldwide provoked immediate responses and then became frozen into the accepted story of the war.

(Quoted in Baudrillard, 1995, p. 2 and p. 3)

6.7 The effects of the mass media on audiences

Discussion of the effects of the media is of great importance to the sociological study of the media as a whole. Theories of bias and one-sidedness are often based on an interest to demonstrate how ideas in the media may control the audience. Media effects can be as simple, or even as important, as socialization, whereby individuals learn the norms and values of their culture; or they may be perceived – depending on the perspective of the researcher – as negative and harmful, a source of social control used to suppress the masses by a narrow ruling élite.

💬 Discussion point

To what extent does the media control the audience, or can the audience fight back?

C3.1a

Sociological and psychological models of media effects often spill over into the minds of public consciousness. Moral panics (see Section 6.2) related to violence on television, video-nasties and computerized pornography often contain simplified versions of academic ideas. However, it is important that sociologists keep an open mind when discussing these issues, because it is all too easy to be drawn into an unsociological discussion, lacking any theoretical or **empirical** basis.

Media effects can be intended or unintended, and short-term or long-term. This makes the study of effects a complex process. The easiest way to approach the issue is to understand how sociological ideas have changed over time.

Five main models of media effect can be identified:

1 the hypodermic syringe model (Classical marxist)

2 the two-step flow model (pluralist)

3 the uses and gratifications approach (pluralist)

4 the post-modern view

5 cultural effects theory (neo-Marxist).

Direct effects: the hypodermic syringe model

Models of media influence used at the beginning of the twentieth century assumed a direct effect on the audience. The media was likened to a hypodermic syringe, capable of 'injecting' bias, violence, ideology, etc. into the mind of an audience. The audience was seen as relatively passive, unable to resist media messages.

The hypodermic syringe model has come to inform popular and current media and public debate. The ideas of Mary Whitehouse (a campaigner for Christian values and morality in broadcasting), among others, demonstrates the concern some individuals and groups have with media violence and the influence it may have on a passive audience.

The Frankfurt School

An example of this type of model came from the Frankfurt School. Modern societies were characterized by the decline of individual, creative and critical thought, and replaced by media mass culture. These mass societies produced indoctrinated victims of ruling-class ideology unable to resist or to reject.

This relatively simplistic model of media effects is still used today by some sociologists and behavioural psychologists. They suggest that humanity is the victim of external stimuli in the environment and that all human social action is the product of these determined responses, not of free will or consciousness.

Indirect effects: the two-step flow model

The idea of the media having direct effects on a passive audience has many criticisms. It treats the audience as little more than absorbent robots, unable to think critically about the world around them. Media influence is assumed to be direct and unstoppable.

Lazarsfeld and colleagues

The work of Lazarsfeld *et al.* (1944) in America provided sociology with another model, this time emphasizing the social context of media viewing. In their study *The People's Choice*, these workers identified the existence of key individuals who were responsible for transmitting ideas, originating from a media source, to a social group. Through interaction, these opinion leaders (or as they are sometimes known 'molecular leaders') take ideas from the media in an active fashion and then pass them on through discussion.

In this model, media influence is *indirect or mediated*. The audience are no longer passive victims of external stimulus, but are shown to be consuming the media within a social context – viewing takes place with others, and ideas can be rejected.

The two-step flow model and pluralism

The two-step flow model fits within a pluralist conception of the mass media. Democracy is preserved because individuals are not passive victims.

Marxist criticisms of this model point to the fact that no reference is made to the existence of a narrow ruling élite in society. The pluralist model fits the American dream well – élites exist, but they do so not through ideological control, since the audience has power.

Discussion point

To what extent is it useful to think of media consumption as a collective or social activity and not just an individual one?

C3.1a

The uses and gratifications approach: how does the audience use the media?

Taking the idea of a conscious, critical audience further, Blumler and Katz (1974) suggested that the important issue when discussing media effects is not to ask how the media influences its audiences, but rather to focus on how the audiences use the media to their own ends.

This model, the uses and gratifications approach, takes even further the pluralist notion that audiences are not blank sheets of paper on which the media writes, but are capable of using the media to secure personal goals.

For example, the same television programme may be used by audience members in a variety of ways. Audience members have goals or motivations for their patterns of media consumption: some may seek information, others escapism, others yet more uses:

... it is clear that the need to relax or to kill time can be satisfied by the act of watching television, that the need to feel that one is spending one's time in a worthwhile way may be associated with the act of reading, and that the need to structure one's day may be satisfied merely by having the radio on.

(Blumler and Katz, 1974, p. 24)

Blumler and Katz (1974) identify five key elements in the uses and gratifications model:

1 The audience is seen to be active.

2 The audience has the power to exercise choice over his/her consumption of the media.

3 The needs satisfied by the media compete directly with other sources of need-fulfilment in society.

4 The goals of media consumption can be identified by the audience themselves in a reflective process.

5 The researcher should suspend all value-judgements regarding the relative and specific worth or merit of these audience goals.

The uses and gratifications approach has implications for media policy-makers and programme designers:

... instead of depicting the media as severely circumscribed by audience expectations, the uses and gratifications approach highlights the audience as a source of challenge to producers to cater more richly to the multiplicity of requirements and roles that it has disclosed.

(Blumler and Katz, 1974, p. 31)

In other words, since the audience is shown to have multi-dimensional needs that are gratified in various ways – often differing from one individual to the next – the media must cater for these needs by producing a wide variety of media products. Free choice, as argued by the pluralist influences on this perspective, is essential to ensure that all members of the audience can and will have their needs met.

The post-modern view

Potentially a far more harrowing account of the audience is provided by post-modernist Jean Baudrillard (1983b). In his book *In the Shadow of the Silent Majorities; or, The End of the Social*, he paints a picture of the contemporary audience as a silent, uninterested, apolitical mass.

Baudrillard refers to the media as part of the 'simulacra' – images or pictures which simulate reality for the audience whose meaning and knowledge of the world is dependent on these 'simulations' and indistinguishable from their real experiences. This situation is also referred to as the 'abyss of meaning'.

Cultural effects theory

In his book *Seeing and Believing*, Greg Philo (1990) attempts to develop a new approach within which to understand the issue of media influence on different types of audiences.

Philo suggests that, although the media does contain preferred ideological messages, the audience does not necessarily simply reject or accept these. It is possible to talk of the cultural effects on the audience – in some cases, some members of the audience will take on media images in an uncritical fashion, in other cases individuals will be able to understand the biased message, but to resist it. Rather than the media being an all-powerful controller of society, Philo would rather understand it as a struggle or battle-site where the audience and media-makers fight over dominant meanings.

Thus, the audience does not exist as a silent mass with a collective identity, but as active, thinking, reflective and creative *audiences* who share cultural experiences in common:

... the news may offer a preferred view of events, but we cannot assume that its audience will all accept this interpretation.

(Philo, 1990, p. 5)

The methodology of cultural effects

Taking the 1984 miners' strike as an example, Philo's methodology was to ask audience members, in groups, a year later, to write their own media stories based on photographs. The respondents were shown pictures of violence and asked to put together a news item. This was then followed up by interviews where the respondents were given the opportunity to explain their thinking.

Philo found that many of the audience members produced very similar stories, focusing on the violence of the picket-lines (which Philo suggests was a source of ideological bias in the news at the time) and on the phrase 'drift back to work' – as used at the time to suggest (again, wrongly according to Philo) that the strikes were failing and the miners were returning.

Passive or active audiences?

Taken at face value this would seem to suggest that the audience were all passive victims of the media, as the hypodermic syringe model suggests. However, through interviews, Philo discovered that the respondents were perfectly able to create stories in the style of a biased media, while not actually believing these stories. The key factor in whether the audience was affected (or not) lay in the cultural and class background and experiences of the individuals themselves:

The consensus [in the media] that violence is wrong is not likely to be matched by a common agreement on who should be blamed. For example, attitudes on whether police or pickets are more likely to start trouble may vary between different groups in the society (as between groups of working-class trade unionists and middle-class professionals). Such differences within the audience may affect the way in which information from the media is received.

(Philo, 1990, pp. 5–6)

Life histories

This new effects model aims to show that individuals have a personal life history or biography which is the sum of all their cultural experiences so far. Individuals use this biography to interpret the media, and those who lack direct experience of the issue presented by the media may be more likely to believe it than others.

As Figure 6.10 opposite demonstrates, the meaning that a programme or item may have for any one member of the audience is based on the interplay and interrelationships between the message of the text in question, the ideas of the audience member (how she or he responds to the text), and ideas which already exist in reality as experienced by the individual.

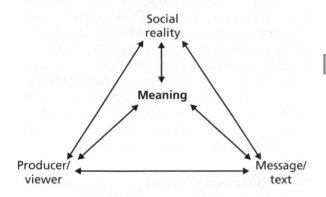

Figure 6.10 An interactive model of how meaning is constructed
Source: Hart (1991) after Fiske (1990)

6.8 Media effects and censorship

Public power or mass culture?

The recent concern with the widening of the availability media products in society throws up problems with a great deal of orthodox Marxist, pluralist and New Right thinking. As a result these positions are currently re-inventing their traditional ideas in the light of the changes.

The key issue, then, is whether this widening of availability leads to increased public power through consumer choice, or to increased levels of mass-culture (see also Sections 6.1 and 6.4), poor-quality, uncritical, unintellectual programming that hinders the powers of the audience to reflect critically about society.

Amongst those holding the latter, more pessimistic view – that this so-called wider media choice will lead to negative outcomes – are sociologists who would usually or traditionally be opposed to each other. They share what appear to be similar views although they have often arrived at these views through very different theoretical assumptions and routes.

For example, some Marxists and neo-

Marxists may find themselves aligned with some pluralists and members of the New Right in expressing concern over the quality of the media. An equally odd combination are the feminists and New Right theorists who both condemn the alleged increase in pornography from satellite and cable TV, and CD–ROM and Internet mediums.

The New Right

It is worth noting that what we have come to refer to as the New Right in sociology is a combination of two, perhaps contradictory, beliefs.

1 Some New Right thinking, especially since the beginning of the Thatcher Conservative administrations in 1979, has openly supported the economic mechanisms of the free market in society. This is seen as providing greater individual choice and therefore contributing to an increase in the democratization of social life.

2 Another slightly older ingredient in New Right thinking is a desire to return to traditional morality or values, to re-emphasize religion and the family as the source for moral well-being and social stability. This could be seen in former Prime Minister John Major's 'back-to-basics' campaign.

The second tradition blames rising crime, and other indicators of a decline in moral standards, on the increase in single-parent families, the supposed lack of moral authority and discipline in schools, and the increase of undesirable products in the media which contain violence, swearing and sexually explicit materials.

The role of the media during wars

Periods of warfare are generally considered as times when governments both censor the media and use it as a tool of propaganda. Under the legitimation of a 'national emergency', some information is labelled as state secrets and subsequently controlled. Journalists are often dependent on government agencies for information or news, and both formally and informally information can be withheld, made open or leaked as misinformation, all in the name of national security.

💬 Discussion point

Is it justifiable to have censorship at times of war?

C3.1a

World War II

Philip Schlesinger (1992) suggests that there is a long-established myth of independence surrounding the BBC's role at times of war. For example, during World War II the government had the legal power to commandeer the BBC, and at times such a policy was advocated by the famous wartime British Prime Minister, Winston Churchill. Although it did not do so, this is not to say that the BBC was allowed to go totally unrestrained:

Instead, the BBC was politicized by making it into an emergency service, and incorporating its top echelons into the government information machine ... there was nothing so crude as planting a censor in the makeshift newsroom. It simply was not necessary as Reith and his staff knew what had to be done, and moreover, fully accepted its propriety.

(Schlesinger, 1992, p. 18)

The government of the day did not need to control the BBC overtly because the corporation, under the control of its Director-General Lord Reith, controlled itself in line with the government as a matter of course.

The war in Vietnam

The relationship between government and media at times of war was a much debated issue during the Vietnam conflict, fought between the USA and communist-dominated North Vietnam. Some believe that the exposure of the American people to violent scenes from the battlefield led to public pressure to end the war. Others go further and claim that this is evidence of a democratic media free from government interference and state control, allowing the audience to make up their own minds.

Kevin Williams (1993) of the GUMG takes a very different side to the argument. He claims that the American government of the day controlled the reporting of the conflict through the selective use of information given to journalists, and in doing so was able effectively to set the agenda. Whereas some argue that the media was actively biased against the American war effort – and in effect lost the war for the American government by lowering public morale and support through graphic and violent news coverage – Williams' research attempts to prove the opposite.

Williams suggests that rather than the media shaping public consciousness, the reverse is true. It is more correct to operate with a model of the audience which sees the audience or public as able to influence media coverage. The media only began to question governmental policy after public opinion had already begun to swing this way. The swing in public consciousness is seen by Williams to be a direct result of the inability of the White House itself to avoid internal confusion and disagreement regarding the war.

The Falklands conflict

During the Falklands conflict between the UK and Argentina, many serious questions were raised concerning the problems presented for governments by the British mass media at a time of national emergency. The BBC in particular came under heavy criticism from the government, and from some of the pro-establishment press such as the *Sun*, *The Times* and the *Daily Mail*.

In *The Times*, columnist John Page criticized Peter Snow, a BBC *Newsnight* presenter, for his superior tone of super-neutrality which so many of us find objectionable and unacceptable. So the problem with the BBC for some people was that it was *too neutral*: as the nation's public TV broadcasting organization should it not have supported the British government in order to build up public morale at a time of crisis?

Also criticized was a particular showing of the BBC's *Panorama* programme. Some Conservative MPs at the time complained that this programme, like *Newsnight*, represented little more than treason. The Prime Minister, Margaret Thatcher, at Question Time in the House of Commons, responded to such criticism of the BBC:

I know how strongly many people feel that the case for our country is not being put with sufficient vigour on certain – I do not say all – BBC programmes. The chairman of the BBC has assured us, and has said in vigorous terms, that the BBC is not neutral on this point, and I hope his words will be heeded by the many who have responsibilities for standing up for our task force, our boys, our people and the cause of democracy.

(Quoted in Eldridge, 1993, p. 9)

Activity

Use the previous extract from Margaret Thatcher's speech as a basis for the following task. Choose any one theoretical perspective and write a critical report detailing why the BBC should be neutral or pro-government, depending on the beliefs of the perspective you choose. Then team up with another student who has used a different, contradictory perspective. Make a short list combining and summarizing both sides of the argument.

C3.2, C3.3

6.9 Mass communications and globalization

The modern world – the era of modernity – emerged through the rise of the Industrial Revolution, the spread of urbanization, and the growth of capitalist markets. This happened in the second half of the eighteenth century and throughout the nineteenth century.

With urbanization came the creation of large groups of people – *the masses*. Concerns about the instability and irrationality of the masses, their propensity for disorder and unruly behaviour, and the associated problem of how to 'civilize' or integrate them socially, is a preoccupation to be found in the sociological work of Tönnies and Durkheim and in the writings of nineteenth-century philosophers and cultural critics such as the philosopher John Stuart Mill (1806–73) and the author Matthew Arnold (1822–73).

Civilizing culture and the danger of the masses

The thinking of Mill and Arnold has to be placed in the context of the debate over whether or not to extend the political franchise to working-class men in the 1870s. In principle, Mill supported the concept of democracy, but he wondered whether the masses would use the right to vote in a responsible way. Mill pictured the masses as a large group of isolated individuals, no longer regulated by the close-knit ties of the rural community. Without the social controls of the pre-industrial rural community, isolated urban individuals could be swayed or manipulated by skilful orators, music hall, or the other mass media of the day. Mill was cautiously optimistic that a programme of universal education could 'civilize' the masses through the elevation of their cultural standards. Only then could they be relied on to use political rights responsibly.

Matthew Arnold made the link between 'high culture' and civilization even more explicit. In *Culture and Anarchy*, he defined culture as 'the study of perfection', or:

... the best that has been thought and said in the world.

(Quoted in Billington *et al.*, 1991, p. 8 and Storey, 1993, p. 21)

He regarded as anarchic the habits and pastimes, or culture, of the urban working-class masses – not only without cultural worth but actually dangerous because they often degenerated into social disorder. Arnold, like Mill, believed that the urban masses – who he described as:

vast miserable, unmanageable ... raw and uncultivated

posed a potential threat to the stability of society, particularly after the Second Reform Act of 1867, which extended the electoral franchise. The only hope was to use cultural education as a civilizing force

to minister to the diseased spirit of our time

(Quoted in Storey, 1993, p. 22; orig. pub. 1868)

Both Mill and Arnold can be said to belong to the tradition of 'mass society' theorists because they assume that society is divided between an educated and cultured élite, on the one hand, and the uncultured masses on the other. Both also picture the masses as unsophisticated, easily swayed and vulnerable to political and commercial manipulation.

Globalization and the future of mass communications

Traditionally, the largest unit for **macro sociology** has been individual societies themselves, or the nation-state. Recent theoretical developments in sociology, however, have attempted to study social life on a much wider, global scale. Theories of globalization suggest that sociology should now concern itself with the relationships *between* societies.

The global village

Cultural and media critic Marshall McLuhan (1964), famous for his early discussions of the likely impact of information technology, predicted that individuals would live in a kind of global village.

The implications of this idea are enormous. Individuals would be able to share cultural experiences in time and space, where before inter-action was often unlikely and in some circumstances impossible owing to geographical separation.

Cyberspace and globalization

The areas on the Internet available for linking individuals are known collectively as 'cyberspace' (see Section 3.2). The development of this system of telecommunication came primarily from eco-nomic transactions on global stock-markets and from weapons research. Increasingly, it is possi-ble for individual homes to use this new tech-nology. Many homes now subscribe to cable or satellite television services.

🗫 Discussion point

Have contemporary media technologies changed significantly the face of global broadcasting? Have we witnessed a global media revolution?

C3.1a

A global culture?

It would be naive to assume that a truly common culture is developing across the globe, simply because people are watching the same or simi-lar television programmes. Nevertheless there is a *degree* of globalization occurring in the media.

For example, countries across the world now share common images through the buying of pro-grammes by one television company from another; charity rock events can be shown simul-taneously worldwide; and events considered newsworthy – such as warfare, elections and nat-ural disasters – are transported into our homes 'as they happen'. Malcolm Waters (1995) amongst others suggests that this is evidence of globalization, though not as yet to the degree first predicted by McLuhan.

Globalization and consumption

A major theme in the analysis of the development of new technologies across the globe is the emphasis given to the development of a global consumer culture. The media acts as a giant shopping catalogue where, as Featherstone (1991b) argues, individuals are able to define themselves through consuming particular lifestyles and products.

'Americanization' and global imperialism

Pluralists have embraced the idea of globaliza-tion as a positive development towards a democ-racy in which individuals are free to select the goods they wish to consume from the media from a vast range. Other commentators are more scep-tical, claiming that globalization represents a process of 'americanization' or 'westernization': the expansion of capitalist ideas and values to the rest of the globe.

Sklair (1991) suggests that the direction of globalization, through the mass media, flows from the western world outwards. The process is of the expansion of western trading for economic gain into new global markets. As Waters com-ments:

Not only the programme producers but the advertis-ing agencies and news agencies as well as the com-panies that manufacture consumer products are owned in advanced capitalist societies.

(Waters, 1995, p. 148)

🗫 Discussion point

Is the 'traffic' in cultural values all or mainly from the western world outwards? Can you think of cultural themes that have travelled *into* the western world from elsewhere? Have they had a significant impact on western life?

C3.1a

Further reading

Accessible A level standard texts designed to introduce the key debates in this field include:

- Barrat, D. (1990) *Media Sociology*, London: Routledge.

- Dutton, B. (1986) *The Media*, London: Longman.
- Trowler, P. (1996) *Investigating the Media*, 2nd edn, London: Collins Educational.

Further texts designed to provide more detail include:

- Abercrombie, N. (1996) *Television and Society*, Cambridge: Polity.
- Sorlin, P. (1994) *Mass Media*, London: Routledge.

A good, general 'reader' covering many classic and contemporary writings in this field is:

- Eldridge, J. (ed.) *Getting the Message: News, Truth and Power*, London: Glasgow University Media Group/Routledge.

Important studies which are accessible and of theoretical and empirical significance include:

- Cohen, S. (1980) *Folk Devils and Moral Panics: The Creation of the Mods and Rockers*, Oxford: Basil Blackwell.
- Philo, G. (1990) *Seeing and Believing: The Influence of Television*, London: Routledge.

Back issues of the periodical *Sociology Review* (formerly *Social Studies Review*) also contain many articles on this field of sociology and many others.

Glossary of useful terms

Capitalist   A person who makes their living through engaging in capitalist accumulation. This means that they own some means of production and therefore earn dividends or profits.

Capitalist legitimation   The process whereby capitalism is presented as the only way to run an economy and therefore a society, and in this sense is seen as the only valid form of organization. This idea would be contested by radical sociologists.

Class consciousness   Having an awareness of your own class position and feeling this is an important part of your identity.

Classical Marxist   Those who followed in the vein of Marx and Engels, who placed much emphasis on economic and political struggle. Used to distinguish certain Marxist approaches from neo-Marxists who place more emphasis on ideas (ideology) and culture.

Deviance   Behaviour that strays from set standards in society, its norms and values; deviance can be seen as positive, but it is usually negative.

Deviant   Straying from the norms of society or a group.

Dominant ideology   A Marxist idea which suggested that the ruling or dominant class who own the means of production will also dominate politically (be the ruling class) and also in the realm of ideas (the Dominant Ideology).

Empirical   Means that the assertion is based on research findings and is therefore more than simply ideas and speculation.

Feminism   Feminism is based on the idea that there are fundamental conflicts between men and women. It stresses that for centuries men have oppressed women in a number of ways ranging from paying them less than men, restricting their employment or property owning rights, through to physical oppression through violence and rape. Feminists use the word patriarchy to mean this male power of oppression.

Feminist   A person who adheres to the beliefs of feminism.

Forces of production   Marxist term for the basic tools and resources needed to engage in production.

Frankfurt School   A group of Marxist thinkers who emerged in the 1930s and sought to combine Marxism with influences from psychoanalysis and Freud, and thus be able to come up with a theory of the whole person. They rejected positivism seeing it as too complicit with an oppressive society and instead called themselves Critical Theorists. Main members include Adorno, Horkheimer and Marcuse.

Free market economy   Where goods are offered to buy and sell and there is minimum interference from the state so the market is free from outside intervention.

Gender socialization   The process whereby individuals are taught to behave in ways as appropriate to their gender.

Hegemonic   Means having or achieving political and/or ideological dominance over a certain group or over society.

Hegemonic control   Exercising control by influencing the way people think.

Hegemony   A term used by neo-Marxists to signify the way that some ideas play a dominant role in society. These ideas are said to be hegemonic.

High culture   A term used to describe that type of cultural product seen by some social groups as the highest form of human achievement: e.g. opera, Shakespeare.

Ideological   Means pertaining to the realm of ideas. In contemporary terms it is used to refer to the way that ideas people have affect the way they behave and therefore there is an ideological struggle going on trying to win people's minds to particular views.

Ideological control   This term is used to suggest that through controlling the ideas in society, and therefore in people's heads, you can in effect control what they think and consequently how they are likely to behave. Seen as a more stable form of control than merely using force. Advertising and persuasion might be key examples of this.

Ideologies   Sets of ideas or world views (often false) which for feminists and Marxists constrain and limit the truth of exploitation.

Liberal feminism   This type of feminism tends to argue that the oppression of women is due to ignorance and bigotry which can be removed through education and changes in the law.

Macro sociology   Approaches, such as Marxism, that adopt a structural view of society, in that they examine the large-scale social structure and the way it influences the individual.

Managerial revolution   Idea associated with James Burnham that suggested that the fact that most industries were not owned by an individual proprietor but instead by large numbers of individual shareholders meant the number of owners declined and power now rested with managers in organizations.

Marxist-feminist   Argued that Marxists and Socialists need to fight not only for an end to exploitation, but also for an end to the exploitation of women. Emphasized that this could possibly be done through traditional socialist strategies and allowed the idea that men and women might together seek the liberation of women.

Marxists   People who adhere to the beliefs of Marxism. That is the belief that there are fundamental conflicts between classes in society, notably between those who own the means by which things are made and those who have to sell their labour to live.

Mass culture   This is the effect that the production of large-scale media products, which are of a lower artistic and intellectual value than in previous times, has had on society. It implies culture is about money rather than lasting artistic value.

Moral panic   Exaggeration or invention of a problem usually through sensationalist stories in the media.

Neo-Marxist   'Neo-' means 'new', so neo-Marxist describes Marxists who have changed 'classical' Marxist theory so much that it justifies being called a different name. Neo-Marxist theories place much more emphasis on culture and ideology and less emphasis on economics than classical Marxists.

New Right   Used to distinguish the views of right-wing political parties in recent times from earlier conservative views: notably the views of the British Conservative Party from the premiership of Margaret Thatcher onwards and the US Republican Party from the presidency of Ronald Reagan onwards. The most notable difference is the New Right's emphasis on the benefits of free market and individual freedom.

Patriarchal   Ideas or structures that support the oppression of women or the power of men.

Patriarchal hegemony   A situation where women are oppressed by patriarchal ideas that stress the dominance of men. The idea also suggests that this comes about through some people, at least, accepting this situation rather than through force.

Patriarchal ideology   A set of ideas that endorses or supports male power and the oppression of women.

Patriarchal society   A society where men oppress women.

Patriarchy   Originally meaning 'the rule of the father', it is now a term used by feminists to describe the situation where males have power over females.

Pluralists   People that adhere to pluralism. That is the set of ideas based on there being a multitude (plural) of possible factors that affect things.

Political action   Action designed to change the balance of power in a situation or a state.

Popular culture   Term used to counter the idea of mass culture. The concept of popular culture suggests that we can comment on and think about the cultural products around us which are popular such as TV programmes, pop music and fashion and these can be used in potentially subversive ways. Culture is therefore not seen in purely negative terms.

Post-modernism   A theory that denies the possibility of there ever being a truth, because there are no objective links between symbols (language, words, ideas) and the objects in the real world they are meant to represent.

Primary definition   The idea here is that there is potentially more than one way of defining many things such as crime, freedom, justice and terrorism. It is suggested that those whose definition is accepted (the primary definers) will thus be seen to be in line with common sense and will have an easier time getting their views accepted.

Qualitative data   Data in the form of words.

Quantitative data   Data in the form of numbers or statistics.

Radical feminism   A feminist approach that is opposed to any co-operation with men since they are seen as oppressors of women. Radical-feminists tend to talk about the system of patriarchy (male control) and the ways males physically threaten and control women.

Reinforcing effect   The idea that the effect of the media may not be to directly change people's ideas but instead to reinforce ideas they picked up elsewhere from peers or friends.

Relativism   A belief in knowledge being partial and existing only in relation to a person's position in the social structure, which means there are no absolute truths.

Relativistic   The idea that no set of ideas are ultimately an absolute truth and that therefore the value of all ideas is relative to other ideas. Connected to social action and more recently post-modern approaches.

Ruling class   A Marxist term meaning those who own and control the means of production in society.

Secondary socialization   This concept stresses that we are continually learning new things and confronting new situations in our lives.

Social actor   A person involved in a situation through interaction.

Socialist feminism   See Marxist-feminism.

Socialization   The process of learning appropriate roles and behaviour.

Subject class   A term sometimes used to refer to the group of people who are oppressed by the dominant class.

Culture and socialization
Religion

Chapter outline

7.1 **Church, denomination, sect and cult**

Whereas philosophers are interested in whether God exists, sociology is concerned less with what God may or may not be and more with the social effects and the social consequences of religious belief and practice. It is important to be clear on this distinction; early on, there are some questions which are beyond the remit of the sociologist to answer.

The study of religious effects and consequences is fundamental to the birth of sociology in western Europe in the nineteenth century. Early sociology was the sociology of beliefs. Or, more specifically, early sociology was concerned with explaining, charting and predicting the replacement of a **religious world view** by a scientific and rational one.

Activity

Using material in this section and any other material you are familiar with, answer the following questions:

a Identify and explain two aspects of a religious world view.

b Outline and discuss the view that we now live in a society where science, not religion, is dominant.

Definitions and measurements of religion

We have yet, however, to define what we mean by 'religion'. This is a fundamental question of sociological enquiry. We must be able to identify the characteristics of religion before we can attempt to explain its role – past, present and even future – in social life. A starting point is often to make the observation that a wide variety of beliefs called 'religions' exist, some of which are older than others, some similar, some influenced by others. Figure 7.1 illustrates the large number of major world religions.

The problems of definition

Defining 'religion' presents sociology with a number of problems:

1 There is no single, commonly held definition of religion. This may well increase debate within sociology as to what religion *is*, but, equally, it constrains debate on the issue of what religion *does*. It is difficult (though not impossible) to discuss the possible functions of religion until we understand what it is we are discussing.

2 The secularization debate – the belief that religion has declined or will decline – is severely hampered by the lack of a shared definition of religion. Broad definitions tend to lead to a conclusion that religion has not declined, whereas more narrow definitions often lead to the opposite conclusion. (See also Section 7.4)

3 Many of these definitions of religion contain an element of function about them. That is, they are based on the role or service provided by religion. Given this, it is sometimes quite difficult to separate the points at which sociologists disagree. Do they disagree over the characteristics or the functions of religion?

4 This lack of a definition may well invalidate the sociological study of religion. Does the debate and argument, at the end of the day, come down to a question of definitions? Are we simply studying competing definitions and nothing more?

Despite these problems, the study of religion is a popular sociological topic area, for students and sociologists alike. While the definition of religion is sometimes left to one side, it is important to remember that it is a very real problem.

Discussion point

Why is it important for sociologists to be as clear as they can on definitions?

Early definitions

Tylor

In 1871, Edward Tylor approached the definition of religion via animism: the belief that all things, human, animal, plant and other objects, have a soul. Tylor defined religion as humanity's attempts to understand the soul, both their own and others. It was a belief in 'spiritual beings' (Berger, 1990).

Emile Durkheim

The nineteenth century French sociologist, Emile

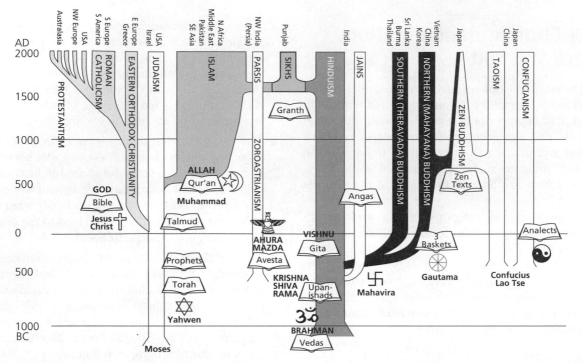

Figure 7.1 The world's religions, their symbols and sacred texts.

Source: General Studies Review, September 1991, p. 33

NOTES: The leading prophet or founder of a religion is in lower case letters. The God (or the name given to 'God') worshipped by the followers is in block letters. Judaism, Islam and Christianity are usually spoken of as monotheistic religions; and Hinduism and its derivatives – notably Buddhism – as polytheistic religions. The more learned among Hindus, however, would say that Vishnu, Krishna and others are not themselves gods, but are revelations (avatars) of the one spirit, Brahman. Certain other religions, significant in numerical terms (Shintoism, Bahai, Animism) do not feature in the diagram. The denominations and sects within (and beyond) Protestantism require a diagram of their own.

Durkheim provided the following definition of religion – the ***sacred*** as opposed to the ***profane*** – and this has proved highly popular and influential amongst his contemporaries, and equally amongst contemporary sociologists.

Turner (1991) considers that Durkheim's idea of 'the sacred' was of ground-breaking significance at the time. It marked the end of a concern with 'gods' or 'beings', and the development of an emphasis on the importance of religious *practice*. For Durkheim, religion is:

... a unified system of beliefs and practices relative to sacred things, that is to say, things set apart and forbidden beliefs and practices which unite into one single moral community called a church, all those who adhere to them.

(Durkheim, 1988, p. 224; orig. pub. 1912)

Durkheim's definition has three main advantages over previous definitions:

1 It concentrates on religious practice as a central ingredient.

2 It allows comparison to take place between societies and their different sacred practices.

3 It does not consider or question the truth of religious beliefs.

As Durkheim comments:

All [religions] are true in their own fashion; all answer though in different ways, to the given conditions of human existence.

(Quoted in Turner, 1991, p. 243)

Phillip E. Hammond

Hammond (1985) wishes to see religion defined as 'the sacred', following the ideas of Durkheim. Hammond is highly critical of the problems previous definitions of religion have created for sociology. As a result, definitions of religion which are far too narrow have been inherited by contemporary sociology. They fail to take into consideration the revival, renewal and persistence of the 'sacred' in social life.

The mistakes of definition

Hammond believes we have mistakenly related religion and the sacred together, as if they are one and the same category. Instead, he wishes to understand religion as a smaller sub-category of the sacred. For example, we could point towards nationalism and science as possible examples of modern-day 'sacreds', which are nevertheless non-religious:

We cannot blame the founders. A sensitive reading of them makes clear the distinction they drew between 'sacred' and 'religion', so that, if secularization meant the decline of religion, it did not necessarily mean as well the disappearance of the sacred.

(Hammond, 1985, p. 3)

Golden Becks proves a match for the deity in Bangkok

DANIEL TAYLOR

First there was Eric Cantona depicted as Jesus, then Ronaldo posing as Christ the Redeemer. Now David Beckham has joined the exclusive list of footballers who could be suffering from delusions of deity.

Resplendent in Manchester United kit but completed, alas, before the £300 'short Beck and sides', this sculpture of Mr Posh himself has taken pride of place in one of Thailand's most popular places of worship.

At a spot usually reserved for angels, Beckham has been immortalized by the sculptor Thongruang Haemhod at the foot of Buddha in Bangkok's Pariwas Temple.

'Football has become a religion with millions of followers,' says the temple's senior monk Chan Theerapunyo, 'so to be up to date, we have to open our minds and share the feelings of the millions who admire Beckham.'

He still has some way to go before moving in the same mysterious ways as the previous incumbent of Manchester United's No 7 jersey.

An eight-foot, luridly coloured Cantona (or Le Dieu, as the Gallic genius may prefer to be known) sparked an unholy row at Manchester's City Art Gallery in Michael Browne's interpretation of Piero della Francesca's 'Resurrection of Christ' and Andrea Mantegna's 'Julius Caesar on his Triumphal Chariot'.

Ronaldo, Brazilian by birth but sometimes (when not injured) lending his feet to football miracles in Milan, confirmed his divine qualities by posing as Christ not in Rome but above Rio de Janeiro. 'The phenomenon', as he is known in Italy, was advertising Pirelli tyres.

Source: Guardian, 16 May 2000

Activity

Using the ideas of Durkheim, Hammond contends that the sacred still exists in modern society, but in a new, modern form. Create a list of all those aspects of contemporary life, such as beliefs, that may have become 'sacred'.

For example, could we argue that football merchandise or counselling have now become sacred and almost new religions?

The sacred: an evaluation

Although a useful and popular definition, Durkheim's use of 'the sacred' is recognized to have some problems. Turner (1991) identifies what he considers to be the two most fundamental of these.

First, hidden in Durkheim's work is the **ethnocentric** evaluation of other cultures: the belief that western science ultimately is more advanced than, and therefore better than, primitive religions.

Thus, sociological **positivism** represents the 'truth' which will evaluate the less truthful views of other cultures. This is a stance Turner and many others find politically and academically objectionable.

Secondly, Turner also objects to Durkheim's lack of understanding of the subjectivity of the individuals involved in religion. He fails to look, in a detailed way, at individual consciousness.

Max Weber

Whereas Durkheim failed to study individuals' subjective ideas about their existence, Weber concentrates fully on this aspect of sociological study. Using the concept of **verstehen** – meaning 'to see the world through the eyes of those involved' – Weber believes the point of all sociology should be to understand the meanings and motives of social actors.

Weber suggested that the definition of religion, should be attempted by a sociologist only at the end of a piece of research. The sociologist should never impose his or her own categories on the understanding of the actor.

Bell and Berger: phenomenological approaches

Many contemporary definitions seek to:

* discuss the 'sacred'
* understand individual subjectivity
* not impose their own understanding on that of people they are researching.

Two examples of this approach to defining religion can be identified in the work of Daniel Bell (1977) and Peter Berger (1990).

For Bell:

Religion is a set of coherent answers to the core existential questions that confront every human group, ... the celebration of rites which provide an emotional bond ... and the establishment of an institutional body to bring into congregation those who share the creed and celebration.

(Quoted in Turner, 1991, p. 244)

For Berger:

Religion is the human enterprise by which a sacred cosmos is established. ... By sacred is meant here a quality of mysterious and awesome power, other than man and yet related to him, which is believed to reside in certain objects of experience.

(Berger, 1990, p. 25)

Solutions?

Contemporary solutions to the problem of the definition of religion appear to be either to ignore the problem as much as possible and get on with the job of doing sociology, or, as with Turner, to attempt to bring different approaches together. As Berger comments:

Definitions cannot, by their very nature, be either true or false, only more useful or less so. For this reason it makes relatively little sense to argue over definitions.

(Berger, 1990, p. 175)

Glock and Stark

Glock and Stark (1965, 1968) recommend that all sociological research on religion – its beliefs, practices and functions – should meet five criteria (or, in their terms, five 'dimensions'). Thus, all sociological study of religion should meet a requirement to:

1 study individual's and group's levels of religious belief

2 understand the amount of involvement an individual has in acts of religious worship and celebration

3 investigate feelings of supernatural, sacred and spiritual contact amongst individuals and groups

4 measure the amount of understanding and knowledge people hold of their religion

5 see how dimensions 1–4 influence the day-to-day action and interaction of these people.

Glock and Stark contend that a full sociological understanding of religion will be possible only if we study all these aspects.

Activity

Design a piece of sociological research which investigates religion as defined by the five dimensions suggested by Glock and Stark.

C3.2, C3.3, N3.1, IT3.1

Activity

Copy the chart below and complete the information in order to summarize the main features of the six different ways of defining religion (as discussed previously).

	Key concepts	Strengths	Weaknesses
1 Tylor			
2 Durkheim			
3 Hammond			
4 Weber			
5 Phenomenological			
6 Glock and Stark			

C3.2, C3.3

Religion and religious beliefs can vary in the way they are practised according to each individual. For some, being religious involves some sort of formal, public worship whereas for others the emphasis is on personal, private belief. It is thus possible to be religious in one's own mind without joining a religious organization or being part of a group.

Typologies and classifications

On making this observation, sociologists have become increasingly concerned with the process of classifying types of religious organizations. How can we identify and explain the different ways in which groups of religious people join together in more or less public services? In answering this question sociologists have drawn a distinction between types of religious organizations.

The act of classification, of creating a **typology**, is a central process in much sociology. Classifications can be extremely helpful in allowing sociologists to think about the social world and specific aspects of it. However, it is important to remember that not all typologies are exact, that they do not all perfectly mirror society. The value of typologies is that they can be compared to social life and then modified, changed and discussed.

The basic distinction to be explored in the next few pages is between the following four types of religious organization:

• church

• sect

• denomination

• cult.

Ernst Troeltsch

Ernst Troeltsch (1981) was one of the first thinkers in the early 1930s to attempt to classify different types of religious organizations. The distinction Troeltsch draws between church and sect has proved to be long-lasting and highly influential in more contemporary sociological discussions of types of religious practice.

The church

The church can be seen as the original and institutionalized form of religion in a society – dominant, and widely integrated into mainstream culture. The church is an extremely large-scale organization, drawing membership from all sections of the population, although it is particularly related to the culture of the ruling or upper social groups. Although members can join, or be baptized into, a church, the majority of members are born into it, following the practices of their family.

Churches are based on strong hierarchies and often have specialist priests arranged in a heavily bureaucratic system of power relations to one another and to their followers. Churches are often related to the state, so they are by nature protective of the existing role of social life and attempt to promote the ideas of a long-established ruling group in the interests of social stability. Hence, they are often a conservative force.

Sects

Sects are smaller, more radical protest movements set up in opposition to a dominant mainstream church. They are less traditional than the church, and less hierarchic, having an emphasis on community and fellowship. Troeltsch suggests that while churches are a source for the integration of all of society, sects appeal to very specific types of people, the marginal lower classes who may be opposed to the state.

Sects typically place high demands on those who do join, in some cases asking their members to withdraw from the mainstream world. Some examples include:

- the Divine Light Mission
- the Unification Church
- the Church of Scientology
- the Children of God
- Hare Krishna.

Activity

Using a library, research any one of the examples of sects listed above. Explain briefly their aims, and why they could be classified as sects.

C3.2, C3.3, IT3.1

Denominations

In response to Troeltsch's distinction between church and sect, others have added a third type – that of the denomination. Often associated with H. R. Niebuhr (1957), the denomination is usually thought of as an organization more like a church than a sect. Being larger than sects and much more mainstream, denominations tend to be conservative and hierarchic. However, unlike churches, denominations are not necessarily supportive of the state, and they often do not claim to hold a universal truth but are tolerant of the existence of many other religious ideas.

Rather than control the lives of members in a communal, sometimes world-rejecting, fashion, as is the case with some sects, the emphasis within a denomination is on the creation of a lifestyle based on freedom of decision for the individual. They are focused on behaviour in this world, not salvation in the next.

Case Study – The making of a Moonie: choice or brainwashing?

Eileen Barker

This classic study in the sociology of religion was published by Eileen Barker (1984).

The Moonies were founded by the Reverend Sun Myung Moon in 1954 under the name The Holy Spirit Association for the Unification of World Christianity. Also known as the Unification Church, this religious group has been the subject of much media, public and government attention.

Just another moral panic?

Barker conducted her study in the light of a media moral panic (see Section 6.2) about the so-called 'brainwashing' activities of this sect. Her research focus was the explanation of how and why people decided to join the Moonies, and to attempt to explain what sort of people they were:

This book is concerned primarily with an attempt to clarify an answer to the question with which it started: Why should – how could – anyone become a Moonie? For many people it seems so incredible that

Table 7.1 The differences between church, denomination, sect and cult.

Church	Denomination	Sect	Cult
• Large Membership. Conversion is encouraged. Inclusive. • Bureaucratic. Clear set of authority and responsibilities. • Professional clergy arranged in complex hierarchy of paid officials. • Acceptance of wider society. Often seen as the 'establishment' view. • A monopoly view of the truth. Strong use of ritual. No emphasis on arousing emotional response from people attending rituals.	• Large inclusive membership. All accepted who wish to join. • Bureaucratic but smaller than that of church. • Professional clergy but lacking the complexity and bureaucracy of church structure. Use of lay preachers. • Acceptance of wider society. But not part of any formal political structures. Seen as a basis of radical or nonconformist views. • No monopoly view of the truth. Less emphasis on rituals but clear emphasis on emotional fervour.	• Small exclusive membership. Believe themselves to be the elect of the elite. • Total commitment. Members are expected to be completely loyal and can be expelled. • No professional clergy. Lacking in any bureaucratic structure. • Some opposition to wider society. Try to protect members from influence of the secular world. • Charismatic leader/founder, claiming divine inspiration. • Do claim monopoly on truth. Aim to re-establish fundamental truths.	• Small and typically very short-lived and therefore lacking in any bureaucratic structure. • Individualistic. Not necessarily based on membership. May be based on common interest or provision of service for a fee. • Mystical. (eg) astrology and meditation. Often advocate behaviour seen as bizarre. Leads to conflict with state and society. • Pragmatic. No clearly defined ideas. Borrow from various sources. • Informal. Very few examples of public worship.
• **Key examples in the UK:** 1. Anglicanism 2. Anglo-Catholics 3. The Church of Scotland 4. The Church of England 5. The Roman Catholic Church 6. The Orthodox Church	• **Key examples in the UK:** 1. Baptists 2. Methodists 3. Congregationalists 4. Pentecostalism 5. Evangelical Protestants	• **Key examples in the UK:** 1. Mormons 2. Quakers 3. Jehovah's Witnesses 4. Salvation Army 5. Christian Scientists	• **Key examples in the UK:** 1. Scientology 2. Moonies 3. Spiritualism 4. Transcendental Meditation 5. New Age ideas 6. Yoga

Source: Adapted from Bird (1999), Bruce (1995), Selfe and Starbuck (1998)

anyone should choose to become a Moonie that the simplest resolution of the question is to deny that such a choice is ever made. The assumption is that Moonies are brainwashed ... since no one, in his or her right senses would want to become a Moonie. Becoming a Moonie must be the result of something that others do to the victim, rather than something that a convert himself decides to do.

(Barker, 1984, p. 6)

We must understand Barker's research decisions in the context of this media moral panic at the time, created by 'scare' stories of kidnapping and 'brainwashing', perpetuated by the popular press in both the UK and the USA. Examples of newspaper headlines of the time are:

Parents fight brainwashing by bizarre sect
Rev. Moons plot to rule the world today
Moonie cult faces probe by MP into brainwashing
Mass suicide possible in Moon church
Moonies have captured my son
Tragedy of the broken families

(Barker, 1984, p. 2)

Research objectives

Barker had two main research objectives.

1 The first was to explain and discover the process and pattern of Moonie recruitment.

2 The second was to classify who is recruited: are Moonies a similar or specific type of person?

Methodology

Heavily indebted to the work of Max Weber,

Barker can be seen to attempt *verstehen* in this work:

- to understand the world through the eyes of those involved
- to investigate the motives and meanings of becoming a Moonie, rather than to rely on a media produced picture of the world.

Barker used **participant observation**, **in-depth interviews** and **questionnaires** (see Section 9.5). Although there are a number of ethical problems involved in participant observation, notably in this case the need to take on the role of a Moonie, Barker states:

I never pretended that I was, or that I was likely to become one. I admit that I was sometimes evasive, and I certainly did not always say everything on my mind, but I can't remember any occasion on which I consciously lied to a Moonie.

(Barker, 1984, pp. 20–21)

Conclusions

1 Barker's research illustrated that the Moonies are highly inefficient in holding on to interested new members.

2 The low rate of recruitment and high pattern of dropout after relatively short periods suggest that particular types of people become full Moonies: they are not 'brainwashed', and not everyone who shows an initial interest has an equal chance of joining.

3 Barker suggests that Moonies come from very happy and secure family backgrounds, which are usually respectable middle-class homes, with parents whose jobs involve some sort of commitment to public service – doctors, teachers, police, etc.

4 She concludes that individuals join the Moonies because they are offered a solution to their needs. At times of crisis in these individuals' lives, often in early adulthood, the warm family atmosphere of the Moonies offers support and comfort.

5 Equally, the community of the Moonies offers these individuals a chance to commit to a group of people and serve the community with them – as their parents did in wider society.

Discussion point
Why are cults such controversial aspects of society?

7.2 New religious movements

Although the three-fold typology – church, sect, denomination – has its uses, especially as a starting point to encourage the sociological study of religious groups, the reality of social life is always a little more complex. A vast number of different types of religious groups exist in society, a fact which has lead some commentators to conclude that some groups defy classification as so far developed by sociological study.

More contemporary sociology has identified a fourth religious type, the cult. They are usually less rigid as an organization than the other types.

Roy Wallis: Elementary forms of the new religious life

Another way to discuss smaller, contemporary religious organizations is to use the concept of new religious movements. Perhaps the most detailed use of this broad concept is provided by Roy Wallis in his 1984 study *The Elementary Forms of the New Religious Life*.

Discussion point
What different relationships to wider society might small religious movements have?

C3.1a

Wallis draws a distinction between three types of new religious movements, as based on the relationship of the movement to the social world they exist in. Although the first to note that some movements do not fit readily into this typology, Wallis identified three main relationships a movement can have with the outside world:

- rejection
- accommodation
- affirmation.

Movements that reject the world are often sects, movements that accommodate the world are denominations or offshoots from denominations, and movements that affirm the world could be seen as cults. (See also Section 7.1.)

World-rejecting groups
These groups are largely hostile to the world around them. They ask of their members a total commitment, which usually involves leaving the

world behind. In practice, the process of joining a group such as this would involve the giving up of past ties, material objects and often one's name – to be given a new identity by the new community once joined.

Limited contact with the outside world may be allowed for recruitment, publicity or fundraising purposes. As a result, these movements vary in size from very small one-off communities to more national and even international communities. Many media, public and government **moral panics** (see Section 6.2) exist around these groups. They are seen as **deviant**, and are sometimes accused of brainwashing their members.

These groups are very much introverted and seek to isolate themselves from the wider world. The key examples cited by Wallis (1984) include ISKON (the International Society for Krishna Consciousness), The Children of God, The Moonies, The People's Temple and the Manson Family.

World-accommodating groups

Rather than being openly hostile to the world, these movements accommodate it; or rather, they ignore it and concentrate on more spiritual matters such as their faith, and how to practise it in the most successful fashion. Although these groups will have traditional social contact and traditional social roles such as jobs and families, they are not concerned with creating or building a new or alternative community. These beliefs may help them in their day-to-day mainstream lives, but are not designed solely for this purpose. Instead, these groups place great emphasis on seeking **enlightenment**. They are tolerant of others and of other faiths.

These groups place great emphasis on spiritual and emotional matters so while they do not reject the world around them, it is not really seen as crucial to a person's identity. They are the sects most like denominations since they realize that the world outside themselves does exist. The key examples cited by Wallis (1984) include Neo-Pentecostalism and groups based on speaking in tongues.

World-affirming groups

World-affirming groups, similar to cults, are often not actual organizations at all, but simply a loose collection of like-minded individuals. These groups often lack collective public worship, a meeting place and even a fully developed set of ideas.

However, these groups do offer individuals something vital in their lives, a source of spiritual power. They seek not to ignore or reject the world but to make the world better; not by building a new society but by helping the individuals of this one become more successful, happy and able to cope with life.

They are largely tolerant of other faiths and do not demand too much commitment from their members. They recruit from as wide a group of people as possible and often sell training courses or workshops based on a particular technique aimed at unlocking the hidden spirituality in each person (such as by meditation).

These groups place great emphasis on spiritual renewal by the individual. This is more often influenced by notions of psychotherapy than conventional religion and therefore these sects are similar to the various New Age cults. The key examples noted by Wallis (1984) include Scientology (which he himself studied), Transcendental Meditation (which has also a political angle in the UK in the form of the Natural Law Party) and EST (Erhard Seminar Training). Steve Bruce (1995) points out that the later spin-offs from this group include Psychosynthesis and Insight.

🗨 Discussion point

What image do the mass media give of new religious movements? How are they portrayed? Why do you think this is?

C3.1a

The difficulty of classification

As indicated in Figure 7.2, Wallis recognizes that some groups in modern social life defy classification because they occupy a middle or intermediate space between two or more of these types. These movements include:

- the Jesus People
- Meher Baba
- the Divine Light Mission.

Stark and Bainbridge

Rodney Stark and William Sims Bainbridge (1985) are highly critical of all attempts to classify religious types, organizations or movements. They claim that all typologies are not an actual list of identified characteristics, but an assumed list of possible criteria which movements may or may not possess.

Figure 7.2 Orientations of the new religions to the world.
Source: Wallis (1984)

Instead, Stark and Bainbridge seek a genuinely useful method to compare and distinguish movements from one another. They suggest this could be conducted through an analysis of the levels of conflict between a movement and wider society.

Activity

a Identify and explain two problems in classifying some religious sects.

b Outline and discuss the view that any attempt to classify religious movement is bound to fail.

C3.2, C3.3

Some commentators suggest that an alternative method of classification could be developed, based on the religious ideas and beliefs from which these new religious movements have developed. It would be possible, in this way, to classify movements as being Hindu-orientated, Christian-orientated, Buddhism-orientated, etc.

However, once more, this typology would not allow us to classify all modern movements. As Roy Wallis and Steve Bruce (1986) argue, some religious movements are based on attempts to improve the person, to unlock human abilities through the mastery of techniques aimed at increasing ones spirituality – such as meditation, some forms of dance, some martial arts, massage, Yoga, Tai Chi, etc.. These groups are often not derived from a clearly identifiable past reli-

gious source but are part of what some call the 'human potential movement', and as such present problems for classification in the above manner.

The human potential movement is concerned precisely with that – with improving the potential of its followers, with enabling them to grow in various ways. The use of the word movement is significant – it is not a group as such, although one could join a smaller group which was a part of the overall movement. Many are members of the movement without being a member of a group or sect *per se*, just a follower or interested individual practitioner of a number of spiritual practices.

7.3 The appeal of religious institutions

A great deal of the sociological discussion of the role of different types of religious organisations in society focuses on the idea that different types of religious institutions appeal to people of differing social characteristics.

Bryan Wilson

Wilson (1970) notes that since the work of Troeltsch, the task of defining sects has become more difficult. Even when very general ideal types have been drawn up to describe the nature of sects, we still must not assume that these so-called essential characteristics will not change over time. As Wilson also comments:

In actual sects we must expect that each of these general attributes will show some variation from the formulation. Sects undergo change, both in response to changes in the external environment, and by a process of what might be called mutation. Consequently, some attributes may be receding in importance, and others growing, at particular times in a sects life history.

(Wilson, 1970, p. 28)

Typology of sects

Wilson draws a typology or ideal-type of sects which emphasizes eight central characteristics, which may be more or less important at different times in the history of any one sect:

1 *Voluntariness*
   Sects are based mainly on voluntary membership, but Wilson nevertheless identifies the

growing trend for children of sect members to join the same sect as their parents.

2 *Exclusivity*
Sects are often seen by their members to be based on a sense of exclusivity where those who have joined are part of the few who show their commitment by great allegiance.

3 *Merit*
Over long periods of time, Wilson suggests that some sects may offer membership on the basis of some act or proof of merit, of suitability for belonging to the group.

4 *Self-identification*
Sects, like other social groups, are a source of self-identification for those who make them up. They use a more or less flexible or rigid categorization of them and us depending on the sect in question.

5 *Élite status*
Some sects define themselves and their members as social élites, as a chosen people.

6 *Expulsion*
As well as tests for membership, some sects often have rules, the breaking of which might lead to expulsion. Having said this, Wilson also notes that over time, with increased life, sects may take these rules less strictly than before.

7 *Conscience*
Many sects operate on a day-to-day basis by relying on the individual conscience of their members to live a worthy life however this might specifically be defined.

8 *Legitimation*
No sect, or any other religious or social movement, new or otherwise, exists without a set of ideological values which give its practices and rulers legitimacy in the eyes of its followers.

The response to the world by sects

Wilson (1985) develops a typology of seven different types of sect, in order to aid comparisons between them based on their response to the world:

1 *Conversionist sects*
These are evangelical or fundamentalist Christian sects, suggesting that the outside world is corrupt because humanity is corrupt. In order to change the world, humanity must be changed, or saved. These sects tend to engage in mass meetings and public preaching rather than door-to-door recruiting.

2 *Revolutionary sects*
These desire to change the existing social order: a time will come when change will become necessary, whether by force and violence or through other means. The members of these sects believe they will become powerful, in this world, after this revolutionary change, through their status as representatives of God.

3 *Introversionist sects*
This type desires not to convert the population, nor to overturn the world, but rather to retire from the world: to cut themselves off in order to find a more personal spiritual experience.

4 *Manipulationist sects*
These are groups claiming that they have access to a specialized form of religious knowledge, which they must use to improve the existing goals of society, which they accept. They are after what they see as improvements in this world, and are less concerned with what might happen in the next – which will simply be an extension of the happiness found in this one, using the correct sources of knowledge.

5 *Thaumaturgical sects*
These groups seek personal messages from spiritual sources. They believe it is possible for humanity to experience the supernatural dimension. So-called miracles or magic healing are seen as further examples of the existence and power of the supernatural.

6 *Reformist sects*
These are based on having changed their nature from an original early revolutionary orientation to the world, slowly moving towards an introversionist type. They associate with the world, but at the same time they are concerned to maintain some distance from it.

7 *Utopian sects*
These partly withdraw from the world, yet partly wish to improve on it. They seek to remake the world along **communitarian** lines, often on a global scale.

Wilson stresses that sects tend to undergo changes in their history, and so these types should not be seen as fixed, but open to movement and reinvention.

Table 7.2 Typology of sects

Type of Sect	Key examples
Conversionist	Salvation Army
	Jehovah's Witnesses
Revolutionary	Rastafarianism
	Christadelphians
Introversionist	Mennonites
	Amish
Manipulationist	Salvation Army
	Scientology
Thaumaturgical	Christian Science
	Spiritualism
Reformist	Quakers
Utopian	Shakers
	Oneida Community

Source: Adapted from Bird (1999), Selfe and Starbuck (1998)

The rise and functions of new religious movements

As well as measuring and labelling religious movements, sociologists are interested in the functions these movements perform, both for the individual and for wider society. In many respects, these issues of classification and function are related: the function of a movement is often used as part of a classification scheme.

Thomas Luckmann

While making a similar point to some other sociologists such as Bellah, Luckmann (1967, 1996) describes contemporary society as based on the processes of the transformation and **privatization of religion**. He suggests that although large-scale institutional religious practice has declined, it would be a mistake to make the assumption that religion has declined or will decline:

... even thirty years ago it was obvious that [institutional religions] dominance and pervasive social reach had come to an end. The widespread view that this meant the end of religion seemed erroneous to me. Even in the heyday of secularization theories, there were signs that a new, institutionally less visible social form of religion was emerging, and that it was likely to become dominant at the expense of the older form.

(Luckmann, 1996, p. 73)

As Luckmann comments, although religion may have declined in the public sphere of life, it has still lived on in the private sphere – at the level of private belief and individual practice. This new religious world, or newly transformed, privatized social consciousness, will still have its religious expression:

The new, basically de-institutionalized, privatized social form of religion seemed to be relying primarily on an open market of diffuse, syncretistic packages of meaning.

(Luckmann, 1996, p. 73)

Spiritual shopping

Individuals are free to shop around for a set of religious meanings and values which suits them so they are not dictated to by a rigid, set, institutionalized form of public worship. This privatization of religion is seen by Luckmann to be a liberating consequence of differentiation in wider society.

Religious transformation

The arguments above suggest that the 'sacred' has not declined, it has changed or transformed. Religions' emphasis has moved away from institutionalized public practice towards individual personal belief; away from collective rites and ceremonies towards a personal search for meaning. This leads to a situation of **religious pluralism**, evidence not of the break-up of religion but of its continued expression. (See also section 7.5.)

The Christian New Right in America

Recently we have seen the rise of evangelical Protestantism within the USA, in the late 1970s and the 1980s. Known by the label the New Christian Right, or the Christian New Right, this movement has attempted to reunite Christian religious beliefs with political life. Peter Beyer (1994) refers to the Christian New Right as a 'religio-political movement'. It is an example not only of a new religious movement, but also, in a much wider sense, of a new social movement. It seeks to mobilize popular public support through the use of techniques such as '**televangelism**', in order to have its nominated candidates elected at the political ballot box.

Showing some resemblance to the **New Right** in British and American politics, the Christian New Right is a return to what is seen to be traditional morality. There is, on occasions, some overlap between the political New Right and the religious New Right.

Core values of the Christian New Right:

- family values
- sexual discipline
- censorship of corrupt views through television, censorship of pornography
- a condemnation of homosexuality.

While members of the Christian New Right would, we can assume, see their project as the start of the moral regeneration of America, the evidence suggests that the membership and influence of this movement is not yet large enough to make a significant difference on the national or global stages. It does, however, suggest that religious values in the West do still exist, even if they are often combined or used in conjunction with other sources of power.

Activity

a Identify and explain two core values of the Christian New Right.

b Outline and discuss the view that the evangelical religion is seeking a return to traditional morality.

C3.2, C3.3

Max Weber: marginalization

Weber provides an explanation for the rise of religious movements by looking at the functions they perform for the individuals who join them. He notes that religion is not necessarily a conservative force, and so sects and cults could offer the oppressed and marginal a sense of hope, status and dignity: an alternative search for that lost in mainstream culture.

Weber argues that new religious movements are joined by the marginal – those on the outskirts of society, those not fully integrated into the dominant cultural values of society, or those not able to achieve success in society.

The marginalized include the poor, exploited and disadvantaged. In western societies, we could identify members of some ethnic minorities, the under-educated and the working class to represent the marginalized. They often turn to small religious movements and groups offering them a chance for political and radical struggle against those in society who are seen to oppress and exploit in society. Religion can be a major political motivating force.

An example of religion acting in this fashion

is the Nation of Islam, a group of political activists in the USA in the 1960s, among whom was Malcolm X. This group, referred to as the Black Muslims, preached salvation for American black peoples from white oppression through revolutionary struggle.

H. R. Niebuhr: deprivation

It is often suggested that new religious movements offer the marginal an answer to their deprivation. They are given the chance to replace what is lacking from their lives by an alternative religious source separate from the mainstream.

Niebuhr (1957) originally applied the concept of deprivation solely to economic matters. He contended that working-class, economically unsuccessful individuals joined sects as an answer to their economic deprivation. Through their emphasis on hard work, these sects raised the economic status of their members.

Niebuhr also suggests that sects are inevitably short-lived. If their members are economically successful as a result of their work ethic, the sect changes to reintegrate members back into mainstream culture.

The social composition of the religious

Steve Bruce (1995) makes the point that in Pre-Industrial Europe, there was both widespread superstition and Christian faith. However with the **Industrial revolution**:

formal involvement in structured religion declined, that decline seemed to affect some classes and regions more than others ... the least religious people were those closest to industrial production: working-class adult males living in towns and cities.

(Bruce, 1995, p. 42)

The question arises of whether in contemporary society the same sort of divisions are evident in relation to religious practice and belief. In particular, we need to consider the evidence available about attendance at religious events in relation to the social factors of class, age, ethnicity, gender and nation.

Class

The British Social Attitudes Survey 1991 contained a number of questions relating to religious behaviour, and these statistics provide the basis of evidence about contemporary society. In relation to social class, these figures suggest that the middle class are more involved in religious practice than the working class.

Table 7.3 Social class and church attendance, Britain, 1991 (%)

Attendance	Non-manual	Manual
Fortnightly or more	16	12
Monthly – once a year	29	24
Less than once a year	3	4
Never	48	57
No answer	3	3

Source: 1991 British Social Attitudes Survey quoted in Bruce, 1995, p. 44

However, if we widen the category out to religious belief, the relationship between belief and social class seems to be the reverse of that between attendance and social class. Middle-class people are less likely to call themselves religious, and more likely to call themselves non-religious than their working-class counterparts.

Table 7.4 Overall religious commitment (%)

	Low	Low–medium	Medium	Medium–high	High
AB	22	23	17	18	20
C1	25	24	16	14	21
C2	23	24	19	18	17
DE	17	24	15	23	21

Source: Abrams, Gerard and Timms, 1985, p. 70

Nation

As can be seen from the figures presented above, Northern Ireland is the most religious of the nations which comprise the UK, followed by Scotland, then Wales leaving England as the least religious of all.

There are, however, also distinctive differences in the religious elements in each nation.

In Northern Ireland, religion has become involved in political and national questions of identity, and the two main religious groups are the Roman Catholics and the Protestants. Wallis and Bruce (1986) argue that Ulster (along with South Africa) is an example of the impact of conservative Protestantism. These religious divisions have their echos in Scotland and also certain cities where there was Irish emigration – Liverpool for instance – and this has been reproduced in football loyalties as well, particularly in Glasgow and Liverpool.

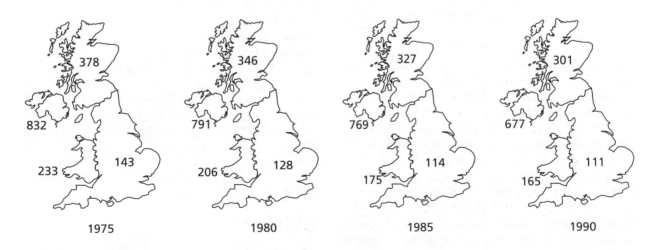

Figure 7.3 National variations in church membership, 1975–90. The figures show total church members per 1,000 of the adult population.
Source: Davie, 1994

In Wales there is a strong strand of **non-conformist religion** linked to a degree of political radicalism. The notion of justice contained in religions such as Baptism and Methodism can be the basis of people beginning to arrive at political arguments about the need to change society. In particular there are strong Baptist and Methodist traditions found in the country. Martin (1990) argues that the Welsh chapels are an important element of local identities, but they also contribute to politicization.

In Scotland, the national Church (kirk) of Scotland remains important, and provides an element of Scottish identity. Northcott (1993) points out that there is a tradition of Presbytarian Protestantism, but also a Catholic area in the south-west of Scotland. Davie (1994) makes the point that the Scottish Calvinists also have links to their spiritual families in Europe, notably in Geneva.

In relation to England, Davie (1994) includes an interesting discussion of the regional differences. For example, in the south west, non-conformity and in particular Methodism was very strong, while in the north west, the Roman Catholic church is relatively strong.

Age

There is a clear impact of age on religious commitment, namely that the older you are, the more likely you are to be religious. This may be because issues of death are closer to your mind as you get older than when you are a teenager. It is not therefore all that surprising to see the patterns shown in the tables below.

Table 7.5 Age and religious self-image, Britain, 1991

Self-image	Age		
	18–24	25–59	60+
Religious	26	37	60
Undecided	31	35	25
Non-religious	42	28	14

Source: 1991 British Social Attitudes Survey, quoted in Bruce, 1995, p. 52

Table 7.6 Overall religious commitment (%)

Age	Low	Low–medium	Medium	Medium–high	High
18–24	39	27	15	11	9
25–44	24	31	16	16	14
45–64	14	21	19	20	27
65+	14	11	18	28	28

Source: Abrams, Gerard and Timms, 1985, p. 70

There is, however, a debate about whether this is in fact an age factor or a generation factor. If it is age, then all people would expect to see a change in their level of religious commitment as their age changes. However, on the other hand if this is a generational factor, then it is clear that later generations are less religious than earlier generations, and this would point to the dying out of religion over time. Time will of course be the judge of this.

Gender

Women seem to be more religious than men. Steve Bruce makes the following comments in relation to this:

What is known about the social characteristics of contemporary church-goers? First, they tend to be women. Whereas the sexes are pretty evenly balanced in the general population (51 per cent female to 49 per cent male), 63 per cent of Scottish church attenders in 1984 were women. Of English church attenders in 1979, 55 per cent were women, in 1989 it was 58 per cent.

(Bruce, 1995, p. 42)

While a lot of attention has been given to the question of why men dominate in the ministry and other positions in the Church (leading to the campaign for women priests) there has been less attention paid to the reasons why women dominate in the congregation.

One possible factor is age, since women live longer than men, and studies show that the older you are the more likely you are to be religious (although not necessarily attending).

A second possible factor is social class, since women are more likely to hold non-manual jobs, and are also more likely to have no paid employment. According to figures gathered by Abrams *et al.* (1985), this distinction between employed and non-employed among women seems to have an effect on their religious commitment. It also confirms the general point that women seem to be more religious than men.

Table 7.7 Overall religious commitment (%)

	Low	Low–medium	Medium	Medium–high	High
Male	27	25	18	14	15
Working female	18	23	17	23	20
Non-working female	15	23	14	22	26

Source: Abrams, Gerard and Timms, 1985, p. 70

Grace Davie (1994) has her own explanation of why this might be:

Very few women give birth without any reflection about the mysteries of creation and very few people watch someone die (especially a close relative) without any thought at all about why that person lived or what might happen to them after death. … But the giving of birth remains, despite everything, one of the most profound experiences of a woman's life, even if she is in hospital at the time, and women are still disproportionately involved in the caring roles of our society; in the care of the elderly and the dying as well as in the nurture of children.

(Davie, 1994, p. 120)

Ethnicity

One key basis of ethnicity is religion, and the contemporary UK includes members of a large variety of religions, partly due to the legacy of immigration which has occurred over time.

Some of the variations within the Christian Church in different parts of the UK were examined on p. 190. So in this section we will restrict ourselves to considering of religious beliefs originating among the ethnic minorities of the UK. In doing this, we will rely on information contained in Steve Bruce's 1995 book *Religion in Modern Britain.*

One of the earliest religious communities to emerge as an alternative to the Christian tradition in the UK was that of Judaism. Steve Bruce points out that there were 30 000 Jews in England in 1800 and that figure had risen to 100 000 by 1905 with migrations from Europe.

In the 1990s, there were about 300 000 Jews in the UK, with around a third located in London.

The other immigrant communities in the UK emerged largely as a result of immigration post-WW2, and this has led to the rise of Pentecostal religions in the UK because of the number of African–Caribbeans who adhere to them. Bruce points out that their participation in religion is much greater than the host population, particularly among males and the young.

Among people from the Asian sub-continent, there are a variety of religious differences, some of which also assume political significance on the sub-continent itself.

The majority of Pakistanis and Bangladeshis are Muslims, and this gives a Muslim population of between 1 million and 1.3 million. They tend to congregate in certain areas, notably Bradford and Manchester, and are hardly present at all in Wales and Scotland. Islam is however undoubtedly the fastest-growing religion in the UK.

Many of the people from India are Hindus, and it is estimated that there are about 400 000 Hindus in the UK today. They come mainly from the Indian states of Gujarat and the Punjab. There are large concentrations in Birmingham, Leicester and London.

Finally, there are the Sikhs, who also mainly come from the Punjab, in a region now contested between India and Pakistan. Bruce estimates their numbers to be around 400 000 in the UK, with a large community in Southall in London, but also in Coventry and Leicester.

7.4 The secularization debate

Central to the sociological study of religion is the area of intellectual activity known as the secularization debate. A very important part of the debate is the question of definition (see Section 7.1). Like the definition of religion itself, many sociologists do not agree on the term secularization. Equally, there is little agreement amongst the vast secularization literature, once we decide what the concept means, as to whether or not it has happened, will happen, and whether its existence or otherwise is a cause for celebration or disillusionment.

What is 'secularization'?

To attempt to deal with the fundamental problems of definition through the course of this section, a basic definition will serve: *secularization is usually referred to as the decline of religion, or the loss of the religious in society.*

Classical views for secularization

Early sociological activity was the sociology of secularization. Early sociologists, in particular Comte, Weber and Durkheim, emphasized the character of sociology as a rational intellectual activity, quite unlike the irrationality of the religious thinking preceding it. The industrial age was the dawn of a new, higher human history. No longer did human societies lie in the dark shadows of nature, controlled by its forces; instead, humanity mastered the world around it. Science became the new-found guiding principle behind social change. Religion was believed to be in decline, and this was seen as a good thing.

The birth of sociology: Auguste Comte

The origins of sociology are generally considered to lie with Auguste Comte, the founding father of **positivism** and the first to use the name sociology in 1838 to describe his scientific analysis of industrialization. Comte, and others of the era – Condorcet – proclaimed that sociology was the ultimate achievement of human science (Kumar, 1986).

> ### 💬 Discussion point
> Is scientific thought always necessarily opposed to religious ways of thinking?
>
> C3.1a

The scientific society

Comte claimed the aims of sociology were the same as all other sciences. Thus, sociology – the scientific study of society – was to predict the future path of history, a path considered to represent the rise of scientific thought at the expense of religious explanations of the world.

Positivism and the law of three stages

Positivism became the general term used by all those who believed in a general, universal scientific method shared by all sciences, social and physical or natural.

In taking an evolutionary image of social change, where each epoch or stage of history grew naturally and logically from the one preceding it, Comte suggested that positivism was the highest intellectual human achievement, the third and final stage of history – the positive stage:

1 *The theological stage*
Society and social events are understood in terms of magic, superstition and religion.

2 *The metaphysical stage*
The development of abstract concepts to explain society and to replace superstition.

3 *The positive stage*
Where science develops, based on experimentation and observation.

In taking this image of history, Comte believed science developed at the expense of religious explanations. Therefore, sociology is by nature a counter-religious or anti-religious explanation of the world. It was the highest achievement of the last stage in human and social intellectual development. The existence of sociology for Comte naturally leads to secularization – the decline of religion, the erosion of the supernatural.

> ### 💬 Discussion point
> Is sociology opposed to religion? Why might this be so? Is it possible to be both religious and sociological?
>
> C3.1a

Modernity and religion

Comte had an image of modernity central to his sociological ideas. The modern age, or modernity, as opposed to the pre-industrial or traditional social epoch before it, would represent the final development of a number of great social changes. Modernity, the scientific age, would be characterized by:

- the decline of community
- urbanization
- the rise of technological methods of production
- an increasing reliance on scientific knowledge
- rationalization
- the rise of bureaucracy
- a decline in traditional forms of religion.

The founders of sociology wrote the majority of their sociology with these processes in mind, although many of them differed in their interpretations of these events.

Discussion point

Has religion lost its social significance? If so, how can we tell, and how can we measure this loss?

C3.1a

Max Weber

Max Weber was one of the few founding fathers of sociology to view secularization in a slightly less than positive light. For Weber, rationality and bureaucracy would rise to prominence in modernity, but at the expense of earlier ways of thought. The modern world may control nature by science, but humanity, for Weber, would also suffer under its hands (Kasler, 1988; Kumar, 1986).

Weber outlined a number of elements in the general trend towards secularization:

- desacralization
- disenchantment
- rationalization
- the 'iron cage'.

Desacralization

One element was the desacralization of the world view, used to explain events in society. The 'sacred' or supernatural was believed to be in decline, in favour of scientific explanations.

Disenchantment

Along with desacralization, Weber identified the process of disenchantment, or rather, the loss of enchantment from social thought. Traditional society was believed to be characterized by a general belief in the reality of magic. Myth and folklore played a central part in the social life of the past, but would fade out, giving way once again to scientific rationality and reason.

Discussion point

Are contemporary ways of thinking different to those of the past?

C3.1a

Rationalization

By this Weber means that modern social action would be based on rational motives rather than magical ones. Rational motives are those where means, ends and goals are *calculated*, rather than relying on supernatural forces. Weber was somewhat disillusioned by this process, regretting the loss of the enchanted.

For Weber, then, secularization is a process of increasing rationalization (see also Section 7.9). Weber's idea of rationality was as a process, whereby precise calculation is introduced into areas of social life. Rational thinking is based on the systematic breaking-down of an object for study, into smaller parts, all of which can be classified and analysed. In this way, all areas of modern life can be seen to have become rational, from health (systematic classification of the body and disease) to music (systematic classification of notes, scales, etc.).

Discussion point

Has the rise of 'rational thinking' eroded religious practice?

C3.1a

The 'iron cage'

Weber believed that along with the rise of rationality comes the rise of bureaucratic systems of management. Once again, Weber did not see this necessarily as a positive contribution to modern social life: bureaucracy is seen as an iron cage, limiting human individual freedom and controlling and constraining action.

Activity

Take each of Weber's four key concepts opposite and think of two examples from modern life which might illustrate that these predictions have happened in contemporary society.

C3.2, C3.3

Contemporary arguments for secularization

Activity

Study the statistics in Table 7.8, which represent modern trends in church membership. Write a paragraph describing what these figures appear to suggest for the idea of secularization.

C3.2, C3.3

A number of sociologists have adopted the idea of secularization and have applied it to contemporary forms of society.

Table 7.8 UK church membership[1] (millions)

	1970	1980	1992	1994
Trinitarian churches				
Roman Catholic[2]	2.7	2.4	2.1	2.0
Anglican	2.6	2.2	1.8	1.8
Presbyterian	1.8	1.4	1.2	1.1
Methodist	0.7	0.5	0.4	0.4
Baptist	0.3	0.2	0.2	0.2
Other free churches	0.5	0.5	0.6	0.7
Orthodox	0.2	0.2	0.3	0.3
All Trinitarian churches	**8.8**	**7.4**	**6.6**	**6.5**
Non-Trinitarian churches				
Mormons	0.1	0.1	0.2	0.2
Jehovah's Witnesses	0.1	0.1	0.1	0.1
Other Non-Trinitarian	0.1	0.2	0.2	0.2
All Non-Trinitarian churches	**0.3**	**0.4**	**0.5**	**0.5**
Other religions				
Muslims	0.1	0.3	0.5	0.6
Sikhs	0.1	0.2	0.3	0.3
Hindus	0.1	0.1	0.1	0.1
Jews	0.1	0.1	0.1	0.1
Others	0.0	0.1	0.1	0.1
All other religions	**0.4**	**0.8**	**1.1**	**1.2**

[1] Adult active members
[2] Mass attendance

Source: Social Trends 26 (1996); original data from Christian Research

Bryan Wilson

Like Comte and Weber, Wilson believes that religion has made way for scientific thought, reason and rational calculation. He contends that religious practice and religious thought have both declined in western societies:

Religious thinking is perhaps the area which evidences most conspicuous change. Men act less and less in response to religious motivation.

(Wilson, 1966, p. x)

Wilson suggests that modern consciousness has indeed become disenchanted. The modern 'mind' is based on the ideologies of science, not magic. He also suggests that the social significance of religion, in all its forms, has declined. Religious ideas, consciousness and explanations no longer inhabit the human mind, no longer dictate human action. Equally, religious practices no longer take up the time of the individual.

Will Herberg

In his book *Protestant, Catholic, Jew*, Will Herberg (1956) suggests that although the USA has significantly larger church attendance figures than, for example, the United Kingdom, this should not immediately lead us to assume that people are more religious in America than elsewhere, or even that those individuals and groups who attend church services are more religious than those who do not. Attendance figures do not give the whole picture, and in particular they do not give an indication of the reasons or motives for attendance.

Herberg suggests that church attendance in the USA is largely an indication of a commitment to a wider community, not necessarily an indication of religiousness. Many people attend church services out of a sense of duty to their family and neighbourhood.

> **Activity**
> The work of Wilson and of Herberg offers modern sociology very different interpretations of the process of secularization. Whereas Wilson focuses his argument on the increasing rationalization of social life, Herberg is more concerned to investigate the purposes or functions of religious services and rituals. Make a list of the key similarities and differences between these two approaches.
>
> **C3.2, C3.3**

Objections to secularization

Far from following Wilson or the earlier founders, many sociologists are highly critical of the idea that religion has declined. These sociologists claim that secularization is a myth.

David Martin

David Martin (1978, 1991) is highly critical and skeptical of the term secularization. He suggests that it has become almost meaningless in recent sociological debate owing to the inability of sociologists to agree on a precise definition.

Martin suggests that the concept of secularization should be made redundant. It is a myth that does not take sociological debate forward, but hinders it. It should be dropped from sociological analysis.

Religion and individual consciousness

Many modern-day **phenomenologists** are concerned with illustrating how religion continues to play an important function in society, especially in the consciousness of individuals. In direct contrast to Bryan Wilson, thinkers such as Robert N. Bellah and Thomas Luckmann claim that institutionalized religion may be on the decline and church attendance may have dropped, but private individual belief still continues. It is a mistake to assume that the analysis of church attendance figures, can allow us to achieve a realistic understanding of the meaning and motives of private belief.

💬 Discussion point

Was there really a 'golden age' of high religious commitment in the past?

C3.1a

Many secularization theories are based on a highly unrealistic notion of a golden age of religious commitment in the past. Phenomenologists are keen to reject this naive image of the history of religion. Whereas the decline in church attendance figures does not necessarily mean an end to religious belief, past high church attendance figures do not immediately indicate that all those who attended believed to the same level or extent. It may well be that the past was a time of *forced participation*, whereas the present allows more individual freedom of choice.

💬 Discussion point

How valid are discussions about the past which rely upon notions such as thoughts, feelings etc? What evidence might we use and how reliable might it be?

C3.1a

Robert N. Bellah and Charles Y. Glock

Bellah (1970) and Glock (1976) both suggest that it is a mistake to assume that religion has declined simply by looking at declines in its public and communal forms. Instead, Bellah claims that a process of individuation has occurred. That

---

Unhappy people losing faith in God and their leaders, poll finds

JULIA HARTLEY-BREWER

People are losing faith in God and are less happy than they were a decade ago, but most are still proud to call themselves British.

These are among the findings of one of the most comprehensive surveys of values and beliefs. It also found that half the population believes that Britain is 'heading in the wrong direction', while 45% believe that the decline of traditional religion has made this country a worse place to live.

The poll, commissioned by the BBC for a TV series, *Soul of Britain*, revealed that Britons are becoming uncertain about their personal moral judgements and are losing confidence in the country's moral and political leadership.

The results of the survey, conducted by Opinion Research Business, among a representative sample of 1,000 people, found that 49% feared the nation was going in the 'wrong direction'. People are also less happy with their lives than they were 10 years ago, when 38% of people said they were 'very happy'. That figure has now fallen to 29%, with a corresponding increase in the proportion describing themselves as 'quite happy'. The same proportion of people described themselves as 'unhappy' in 1990 and 2000.

The poll also found that 62% of people believe in God, down from 76% in 1980, yet only 23% of people have attended a religious service in the past month – the same figure as a decade ago.

Most people retain their faith in family values and the institution of marriage, although there has been a move away from organized religion, with those regarding themselves as belonging to a particular religion falling from 58% in 1990 to 48% today, the Church of England suffering the biggest drop, from 40% in 1990 to 35%.

About 27% described themselves as 'spiritual' rather than 'religious', with 25% believing in reincarnation and 55% in fate. And despite the finding that 45% of Britons never attend church, 69% of the population believe they have a soul – up from 64% 10 years ago. The survey also found that just over half the population believes in an afterlife, up from 44% a decade ago.

Although the belief in a personal god has consistently fallen over the past 40 years, from 41% in 1957 to 32% in 1990 and to 26% now, a larger proportion, 32%, still believe in the Devil. While 52% profess to believe in Heaven, only 28% are convinced that Hell exists – figures that have changed little over the past 20 years.

A spokesman for the Archbishop of Canterbury said the survey results 'seemed to go against the ideas that religion is dead'. He added: 'Religion is far more important to people than a lot of commentators think.'

Source: Guardian, 29 May 2000

is individuals are free to search for their own religious and spiritual meanings, unconstrained by a repressive church.

Activity

Read the article on page 203.

a Identify and explain two poll results that point to people losing faith in God.

b Outline and discuss the view that religion is dead.

C3.2, C3.3

7.5 Religious fundamentalism and the search for certainty

Globalization and religion

Examples of fundamentalism in the contemporary world

Case study: Protestant fundamentalism in the USA

Fundamentalist Protestantism has existed in the USA since the nineteenth century when it rejected changes in the theology of other Protestant denominations. Since that time it has come to prominence through the rise of the evangelical movement and more recently, the involvement of fundamentalist Protestants in the political arena, notably the Republican Party (see also Section 7.3).

Its origins as a movement lie in the end of the nineteenth century and splits in the Church over whether the Bible was seen as literal and therefore whether Christians should insist that events referred to in the Bible, such as the virgin birth and the resurrection for example, did actually happen. There was also the clash over the emergence of scientific explanations and whether Christians should reject Darwin's theory of evolution and insist instead that the earth was wholly created by God in seven days (the idea known as 'creationism'). In relation to both these important questions, conservative fundamentalist Protestants argued that the answer should be 'yes'. Thus the Bible was to be understood literally and the world was created by God. Interpretations of the Bible and Darwin's theory

of evolution were thus both potentially seen as anti-Christian.

In the early part of the twentieth century, fundamentalists created a number of bible institutes which spread rapidly. The movement achieved world-wide infamy when in 1952 the American State of Tennessee banned the teaching of evolutionary theory and took a teacher, John Thomas Scopes, to court for refusing to comply with this order. This trial became famous through the media and known as the 'monkey trial' due to the central argument in Darwin's theory – that humans are descended from monkeys. At the end of the trial Scopes was found guilty of corrupting children. He was fined $100 and although the outcome was later reversed on a technicality, the actual Tennessee law was not repealed until 1967.

Although the acceptance of scientific notions led to the demise of fundamentalism, the crisis of confidence in science and other ideas has seen the re-emergence of such movements often using the media through televangelism. Fundamentalists and evangelicals have created alternative conservative groupings of churches and have sought to gain influence through both the media and through influencing political parties. They have often focused on issues such as abortion (to which they are opposed) and education (where they argue over how science should teach about the origins of the world).

Many fundamentalist groups have websites where their long connection with media outlets finds another outlet. For instance, there is a 'Dial-a-Ministry' service who claim to:

stand on the sole authority of the King James Bible, offer a free bible course and also provide a 666 Watch which gives information on questions and answers about the number 666, such as 'Is "www" equal to "666" in Hebrew?' and 'Can someone "innocently" or "accidentally" receive 666: the Mark of the Beast?'

(www.av1611.org)

Activity

You can look up 'Dial-a-Ministry' on www.av1611.org/

They also provide you with links to other sites to enable you to gain information about this type of religious approach. We would suggest you look at some sites in a spirit of scientific enquiry. However, we would also strongly remind you not to get involved with any religious organization or group and not to provide any such group with your name, address, email address or any other details.

IT3.1, C3.2

Much more recently, the media have refocused on fundamentalism in the USA because of the decision in October 1999, by the Kansas State Board of Education, to remove Darwin's theory of evolution from the core curriculum which provides the basis for state-wide education assessment tests. There is clear popular pressure (though not compulsion) to replace evolutionary theory with notions of creationism (the idea that the world was made by God, or an 'intelligent design' as God is known).

According to a report in the *Guardian* (3 October 1999) 44 per cent of Americans accepted the Creationist account and only 10 per cent believe God played no part in evolution. Publishers have altered the text of some proposed books.

Activity

You can check out information about the Kansas decision on various websites:

• An article in the *Guardian* by Ed Vulliamy (3 October 1999) was headlined 'Anti-Darwinism makes a monkey out of Kansas'. It can be found on www.guardianunlimited.co.uk/Archive/

• At the same site you can trace a review of 'Inherit the wind' (2 September 1999) and an article by Salman Rushdie headed 'And the metaphor was made flesh – in Kansas' (19 September 1999).

• The *Topeka-Capital Journal* is a Kansas newspaper whose reporting of this debate can be found on their site at http://cjonline.com/stories/

In particular you can find an article headed 'Suit looms over science teaching' in their issue of 8 November 1999.

Read these and other articles and present a summary of the controversy.

Set up a debate in your class with pupils taking individual roles for and against the decision of the Kansas School Board.

IT3.1, C3.1a, C3.1b, C3.2, C3.3

The BBC reported this issue in an article entitled 'Kansas rejects theory of evolution':

Opponents of Charles Darwin's theory of evolution have scored a victory in the United States after the board of education in Kansas voted to drop evolution as a subject in the science curriculum.

The State School Board approved by six votes to four a new curriculum that eliminates the teaching of evolution. It offered a compromise instead, endorsing the theory of micro-evolution – which explains changes within a species – but rejecting evolution as a way of explaining the origin of species.

The decision is being seen as a victory for supporters of creationism who believe the world came into being more or less as described in the Bible and who refuse to accept Darwin's teaching as scientific fact . .

. . . Evolutionists gave a hostile reaction to the decision, saying it would diminish the credibility of the Kansas curriculum.

The heads of all six state universities had earlier written to the Board chairwoman, saying the proposal would set Kansas back a century. Charlie Pierce, who has taught biology at Hutchinson High School for eighteen years, said before the vote: 'We're going back to the 1880s. It does make us look to the people of the rest of the country that we're a bunch of hicks'. But creationists argue that the theory of evolution is not proven and that to tell students that it is a science is a deception.

Kansas is one of a handful of states – including Arizona, Alabama, Illinois, New Mexico, Texas and Nebraska – where school boards have attempted in recent years to take evolution out of state science curricula or reduce the emphasis on evolutionary concepts.

Source: Adapted from BBC News report, 11 August 1999; http://news.bbc.co.uk

Since the decision, there has been a flurry of debate and threats of lawsuits echoing the arguments surrounding the trial in Tennessee in

1925. Late in 1999, a new version of the play *Inherit the Wind*, which dramatized the 1925 trial, opened in London immediately becoming topical again.

🗨 Discussion point

The play *Inherit the Wind* was written in 1955 in response to McCarythite 'Witch hunts'. Does its relevance today in the 21st century indicate that we are now entering a new dark age?

C3.1a

Case study: Islamic fundamentalism

While there has been a resurgence in interest in American Christian fundamentalism in the 1990s, there is no doubt that for most of the 1980s the term was applied most usually to various elements of Islam. Undoubtedly the most notable event that led to this was the Iranian revolution in 1979 led by the Ayatollah Khomeni which brought radical Shi'a Islam to the world stage and by confronting America came to be portrayed by Western media as a threat to society.

However, the use of the description 'Islam fundamentalism' has been seen as controversial since fundamentalism, as applied to Protestant groups in the USA, meant the belief in the literal truth of the Bible, and the groups to whom the label 'Islamic fundamentalist' is most usually applied do not believe that all truth resides simply in the Qur'an. Instead there is a debate inside Islam as to the meaning of and identity of prophets and also of the extent to which church and state should be divided (not at all, according to Shi'a Islam, and not a great deal according to Sunni Islam).

Because of this the Islamic movements which have grown up since the 1980s have been very overtly political and the label fundamentalism has most often been attached because of their perceived traditionalist and conservative social views on issues such as women, the family and sexuality.

Islam is divided into two broad traditions, the majority Sunni and the minority Shi'a. The rise of Shi'a Islam to some degree of prominence has been based on their radical refusal to bow down before the West and their view that many Sunni Islam leaders are not really following a true religious path and have become intertwined with the West (the Sunni leaders of Saudi Arabia seem arguably the best example of this). Because of the importance of Sunni Islam countries and leaders, these statements have often led to conflict in the Islamic world notably the Iran-Iraq War (Iraq is led by Sunni Muslims, and Iran was led by Shi'a Muslims), and more recently conflicts of a religious nature in a number of states, notably Yemen.

While for many liberals in the West, the fairly traditional and (to their view) reactionary attitudes of militant Islam seem like the oppression of women and others who follow non-traditional lifestyles, there are also arguments that dislike of Islam is merely an example of Orientalism (Said, 1985) by which he means the way Western writers have misunderstood and misinterpreted non-Western societies.

🗨 Discussion point

To what extent do you agree that arguments against Islam are examples of Orientalism and ethnocentricity?

C3.1a

Studies by Charlotte Butler (1995) and Helen Watson (1994) suggest that the portrayal of the treatment of women by Islamic religions is somewhat wide of the mark. Butler argues that Asian women in Britain are finding a new place for themselves, including working as professionals, but that they also reaffirm their commitment to Islam as a part of their new identity since they still see Islam as a key spiritual and cultural guide to life.

Helen Watson (1994) points out that the concept of personal modesty is central to Islam, but that this has been interpreted differently for men and women. Although this means that in some senses it could be argued that patriarchal practices inside Islam have contributed to the oppression of women, she also argues that in some instances, Muslim women view the return of the veil as a positive thing, freeing them from worries about sexual harassment. Veiling is seen as a reaction to the growing importance of Western culture in the world as a result of globalization and thus as an attempt to reassert some kind of local identity. The one key problem with this study is that it is based on interviews with only three women and this clearly leads to concerns over its representativeness and therefore its validity.

Despite these arguments, it is however clear that there are still objections by some to the practices of Islamic fundamentalism and fears and concerns about their activities in the UK. For example, Peter Tatchell, writing on the Outrage website, recognizes the existence of a liberal compassionate side to Islam, but argues that the global threat of Islamic fundamentalism represents the 'New Dark Ages'. He goes on to outline many instances where he feels individuals have been persecuted by religious fundamentalists. He cites the example of Iran where, since 1980 , over 4,000 lesbians and gay men have been executed. However, it is clearly not only Iran, as Tatchell also cites the following examples:

- The Bangladeshi writer, Taslima Nasrin, had to flee to exile in Sweden in 1994 after she was condemned to death by Muslim fundamentalists for advocating the revision of Islamic law to protest the rights of women. Issuing a fatwa against Nasrin, they offered a bounty to anyone who would kill her.
- In neighbouring Pakistan, an illiterate 14-year-old boy, Salamat Masih, was sentenced to die in 1994 for allegedly writing words offensive to the prophet Mohammed on the wall of a mosque. Although saved by a last minute reprieve, he was forced to seek refuge in Germany after Islamicists threatened to hunt him down and kill him. [...]
- The Algerian Islamicists have a particular hatred of women who refuse to confirm to the Muslim tradition of subservience and modesty. Women who work instead of staying at home and waiting on their husbands, or who study at university rather than looking after children, risk death. [...] Any female behaviour deemed 'scandalous' by the militants can have lethal consequences, as 16-year-old Katia Bengana discovered. She was shot dead on her way home from school for refusing to wear a veil.

(www.outrage.cygnet.co.uk/isl_dark.htm)

Discussion point

To what extent do you agree with the view expressed by Peter Tatchell or the view expressed by Helen Watson in relation to Islamic or more broadly fundamentalist religious movements?

C3.1a

Some religions, especially Islam and Christianity, are seen as major contributors to the process of **globalization** (see also Section 4.5). With their emphasis on the conversion of non-believers,

they have both become world-religions, stretching across traditional geographical and cultural areas.

Fundamentalist forms of religion are seen by Lechner (1990) as providing an answer to the chaos of the contemporary world, and in doing so they flourish well under such global conditions.

As Waters (1995) comments, contemporary global life is not so much a new world order as a new world disorder. Increasing levels of globalization produce chaos, a lack of meaning; in fact, too much diversity of meaning. This is because globalization involves the unification of many diverse ideas, ideologies, beliefs, faiths and other cultural practices, into a chaotic shared culture to which everyone is exposed.

Lechner sees fundamentalism as a *response* to this global chaos. Religions such as Islam seek to unite together, back into a common and shared set of meanings, all those peoples alienated by and anxious about the diverse array of cultural ideas they have suddenly become exposed to. As Lechner comments, fundamentalist religions are:

a socio-cultural movement aimed at reorganizing all spheres of life in terms of a particular set of absolute values.

(Quoted in Waters, 1995, p. 130)

The continuing influence of Durkheim

A return to the sacred

In discussing the idea that religion has become transformed in modern society, many commentators have returned to the ideas of Emile Durkheim. They claim, following Durkheim, that the 'sacred' lives on, but in an altered form. The central idea is that the sacred is a much wider category than just institutional religion. In his classic text, *The Elementary Forms of the Religious Life*, Durkheim (1982) suggests that:

... the former gods are growing old or are already dead, and others are not yet born ... But this state of uncertainty and confused agitation cannot last for ever. A day will come when our societies will again know those hours of creative ferment in the course of which new ideas and new formulas are found which will serve for a time as a guide to humanity; and when these hours have been once experienced, men

will spontaneously feel the need of reliving them from time to time in thought, that is to say, of keeping alive their memory by means of celebrations which regularly reproduce their products.

(Durkheim, 1988, p. 244; orig. pub. 1912)

and:

There are no gospels which are immortal, but neither is there any reason for believing that humanity is incapable of inventing new ones. As to the symbols with which this new faith will express itself, whether or not they will resemble those of the past, or be more adequate for the reality which they seek to represent, this is a question which goes beyond the human capacity to predict.

(Durkheim, 1988, p. 245; orig. pub. 1912)

Activity

a Identify and explain the two approaches to understanding entitled rationalism and romanticism in the article below.

b Outline and discuss the view that religion and the sacred is necessary to stop science destroying the planet.

C3.2, C3.3

The transformation of the sacred

As we can see, Durkheim believed that the role performed by religion – the sacred – was so great,

Prince courts controversy as he places the nature of God above the god of science

JAMES MEEK

Prince Charles's twin ambitions to cast himself as defender of the natural world and defender of Britain's many faiths have long been an open secret. But in tonight's Reith lecture, to the dismay of scientists and unease of some within the religious mainstream, he explosively brings the two ambitions together.

He declares that love of nature and faith in an unspecific deity he calls the 'creator' or 'sustainer' are one and the same thing, and that over-dependence on scientific rationalism has become the enemy of the nature-god.

The spread of genetically modified foods is clearly the spur for the prince's concern, but the lecture comes across as an attack on science in general.

The prince's nature-god beliefs are unlikely to be greeted with enthusiasm by all traditional religions. Protestantism, with its traditional acceptance of capitalism, and Catholicism, with its abhorrence of birth control, have not been traditionally environmentally friendly.

The prince's religious views seem closer to a blend of Buddhism, Islam and Orthodoxy, with a strong streak of neo-paganism.

John Durant, Professor of public understanding of science at Imperial College in London, said he agreed with the prince that there had to be a proper balance between head and heart, between reason and moral intuition. The difficulty was, he said, in knowing whose moral intuition was right. 'In me, the balance of head and heart seems to have led me to judge that it's right to take heart valves from pigs and put them into human beings to save lives. If it's right to do that, which doesn't seem like going with the grain of nature, I think we need to look at other areas of science and technology and be very careful about ruling them out because we could be doing the world a great disservice.'

The clash between the prince and scientists is an echo of the great ideological clash between Enlightenment Rationalists and Romantics which began two centuries ago and has never quite died down. The Rationalists wanted to tame nature and analyse the mechanics of the human mind. The Romantics preferred nature and human emotions in their raw state.

The difference now, to the prince's alarm, is that science has become much more powerful – capable not simply of taming nature but of altering it.

Excerpts from the speech:
- If literally nothing is held sacred any more – because it is considered synonymous with superstition, or in some other way 'irrational' – what is there to prevent us treating our entire world as some 'great laboratory of life', with potentially disastrous long-term consequences?
- Part of the problem is the prevailing approach that seeks to reduce the natural world, including ourselves, to the level of nothing more than a mechanical process.
- It is all too easy for us to forget that mankind is a part of nature and not apart from it.
- We should show greater respect for the genius of nature's designs, rigorously tested and refined over millions of years. This means being careful to use science to understand how nature works, not to change what nature is, as we do when genetic manipulation seeks to transform the process of biological evolution.
- Do you not feel that, buried deep within each and every one of us, there is an instinctive, heartfelt awareness that provides – if we allow it – the most reliable guide as to whether or not our actions are really in the long-term interests of our planet and all the life it supports?
- It is only by employing both the intuitive and the rational halves of our own nature – our hearts and our minds – that we will live up to the sacred trust that has been placed in us by our creator.

Source: Guardian, 17 May 2000

that when an old sacred expression died, another would, in time, be born.

Civic religions and rituals

Many sociologists have suggested that a re-definition of the concept 'religion' is needed, in the light of the claim that there has been a transformation of the sacred in modern life: the category 'sacred' is seen to be a much wider category than religion, which was used quite narrowly by the majority of the founders (but not all, as the work of Durkheim illustrates) to represent almost exclusively institutional religious practice and beliefs. As one commentator, Robert Bocock (1985), comments:

Many people, including some sociologists, define modern western societies such as Britain as being secular. In the sense that such modern societies are no longer dominated by religious institutions in the way the Catholic Church dominated life in the Middle Ages in Europe, then it is possible to say that they are more secular. However, such a description can overestimate both the role of the Church in the past and the decline of the influence of religious groups on many people in present day societies. So some definition of religion and the secular is needed which allows for these complications in a way which the notion of secularization fails to do.

(Bocock, 1985, p. 208)

One of these new definitions, to explain the continued existence of the sacred, focuses on what are called 'civic religions' or 'civic rituals'. Whereas a religious ritual is an organized event around a religious figure or occasion, a civic ritual is an event organized around a head of state, or a date of significance such as a day of independence or a coronation. These civic rituals celebrate citizenship in a nation-state.

Although civic rituals and religious rituals are different in focus, many have indicated how, in practice, these two types of rituals are quite similar. Bocock suggests that civic rituals could be a new expression of the 'sacred' as defined and discussed in the work of Durkheim. Such modern-day civic rituals could include:

- coronations
- royal weddings
- remembrance days
- state funerals
- independence days
- celebrations of revolutions
- ceremonies based around wars or battles.

Discussion point

Has religion declined or been transformed?

C3.1a

Many commentators suggest that the civic rituals shown in Figures 7.4–7.7 have a common 'sacred' character with more so-called 'traditional' religious practices and rituals. In this way, the annual celebration of the French revolution was considered by Durkheim as an example of a nationalist-based civic ritual, which indicated the presence of the sacred in a supposedly 'secular age'.

Equally, the old Soviet Union (USSR), despite formally banning religion, could still be seen to have its sacred expressions – particularly in the way that the revolution was celebrated annually by parades in Red Square, and statues of Marx, Lenin and other important historical figures were erected as focal points for celebration and other national activities.

Activity

Suggest how coronation and remembrance parades could be seen as examples of civic rituals.

 C3.2, C3.3

Timothy Crippen

Crippen (1988), following the ideas of Durkheim, suggests that the secularization thesis, whereby religion will slowly decline in the contemporary world, is an unrealistic way to understand the nature of modern-day religious belief and commitment. Instead, according to Crippen, we have witnessed a transformation of previous sacred symbols. He argues that 'the sacred' is a human universal, so it is present in every society, but not necessarily in an identical or common form:

Decaying commitment to supernatural forms of explanation in combination with an increased reliance on technorational explanations of experience represents a transformation in the way that the 'sacred' is constructed.

(Crippen, 1988, p. 320)

Crippen suggests that modern sacred symbols are based on scientific (or, as he defines them, 'technorational') images. The sacred has not declined or decayed, but the 'old gods' have been replaced by 'new gods'. For him, these are based around nationalist identities; the most sacred symbols,

Figure 7.6 A remembrance parade

Figure 7.4 A celebration of the French Revolution

Figure 7.5 A coronation

Figure 7.7 Celebration in Red Square, Moscow

along with many modern-day rituals, are those based on the **sovereignty** of the nation-state:

... the nation-state represents the most dominant, extensive, and inclusive boundary of moral identity in modern societies. Thus, it is no surprise that so many scholars remark that nationalism is the dominant form of modern religious consciousness ... the emblems and shrines that identify and commemorate the nation are among the principal sacred objects in the modern world and correspond to the dominant organizational form of sovereignty.

(Crippen, 1988, p. 325)

Discussion point

Is science the complete opposite of religion or merely its modern equivalent?

C3.1a

Activity

Create a list of other 'modern sacreds' not listed on these pages. What sort of collective rituals surround these aspects of social life?

C3.2, C3.3

Resistance to civic rituals

Bocock (1974, 1985) warns that even if civic rituals are identified as exising in society, we should not immediately assume that they are valued and accepted by all, or even that those who attend such occasions accept that they are involved in a form of 'sacred' ritual.

For example, coronations and royal weddings may not be seen as being legitimate sources of norms and values (see Section 3.2) by anyone outside of the higher social classes, and may be actively resented by some working-class members and political activists.

Discussion point

Do all members of society follow the religious and secular rituals of society with an equal degree of acceptance and deference?

C3.1a

Uncertainty and changing morality

The New Right see religion as a vital source of morality. The possible present or future decline of religion is not so much a consequence of social instability, but rather the cause of it. For example, New Right theories on crime and deviance (see Section 10.6) in society often blame the rise of moral degeneration of society, especially amongst the young, for rising rates of crime. The rise of single-parent families (see Section 5.4) is seen as the result of a society lacking values from a religious source.

Discussion point

How might a lack of religious values lead to moral degeneration and an increase in deviance? Do you think this is a fair picture of modern society?

 C3.1a

A phenomenological approach

While **functionalists** and the **New Right** see religion as a form of social 'cement', and **Marxists** and **feminists** see religion as social 'opium', there is another perspective on the role of religion in society: the belief that religion *contributes to the consciousness of the social actor*:

- it provides meaning to social life
- it legitimates norms, values and élites
- it can provide the marginalized with a set of ideas that can advocate social action to create change.

This emphasis on consciousness and meaningful social action is more of a phenomenological interpretation of the role of religion in society. It is concerned with how religious beliefs create or contribute to a **socially constructed** reality.

Berger and Luckmann

Berger and Luckmann (1967) see social actors as *symbolic actors*: they create, construct and develop reality by searching for meanings in individual events, and in doing so make sense of the world around them through common sense thought. In order to act in this world, individuals need to have a sense of stability. Common sense knowledge provides stability by giving meaning and by legitimating the world.

Building a meaningful reality

Berger (1990) suggests that religion contributes to this construction of a meaningful world by building what he terms '*nomos*'. In following Durkheim, Berger uses *nomos* to refer to a situation opposite to *anomie* (see Section 10.1). For Durkheim, *anomie* means 'meaning*less*ness', while for Berger *nomos* means 'meaning*ful*ness'. Religion has the potential to help to build *nomos* by offering a particular script that actors can adopt in order to act and interact.

Threats to meaningful stability

Berger argues that, although religion provides a 'socially constructed reality' with shared meanings, there are still periodic threats to such a meaningful stability – most notably when death occurs within the social group (a similar point is made by functionalist thinker Malinowski, see Section 7.8).

Marginal situations

Berger refers to death as a 'marginal situation'. These marginal situations push social actors to the margins or boundaries of stability. They represent moments in an otherwise stable world where commonsense understandings are called into question and doubt:

Death radically puts in question the taken-for-granted, 'business-as-usual' attitude in which one exists in everyday life.

(Berger, 1990, p. 43)

Although a phenomenologist, Berger believes that religion functions to help people cope with challenging situations (as did Durkheim and Malionwski).

Religion then, maintains the socially defined reality by legitimating marginal situations in terms of an all-encompassing sacred reality. This permits the individual who goes through these situations to continue to exist in the world of his society ... in the 'knowledge' that even those events or experiences have a place within a universe that makes sense.

(Berger, 1990, p. 44)

Anthony Giddens

Continuing the theme of the relationship between religion, stability and marginal situations, Anthony Giddens (1991, 1993b) is also concerned with death and self-identity in modern society. Giddens argues that the social consequences of death are highly problematic – much more so than in early-modern or traditional eras of society. Giddens suggests that one of the consequences of high-modernism is to profoundly change how individuals cope with death.

Activity

Using a library, research any two of the following four figures. Write a brief report explaining how their lives and religious work show that religion can be used as a political force to change the status quo, not to protect it: *Gandhi, Malcolm X, Archbishop Desmond Tutu, Martin Luther King.*

IT3.1, C3.2, C3.3

The transformations involved in modernity are more profound than most sorts of change characteristic of prior periods ... they have come to alter some of the most intimate and personal features of our day-to-day existence.

(Giddens, 1993b, p. 4)

By the process of secularization – the decline of religion – associated with high-modernity, death is no longer made meaningful by religion. Instead, it has become a problem which individuals attempt to cope with by adopting lifestyles aimed at creating a self-identity based on health. Death is no longer explained by religion, but avoided by lifestyle.

7.6 Religion and control

Feminism and religion

Feminists are interested in the way religion is used as a source of social opium – to control women. Whereas the New Right would regard social control as a positive function of religion (as too would functionalism), feminists regard religion as an instrument or source of patriarchy – male domination over women.

Religion has been used, historically, to:

- control feminine bodies by labelling some women as deviant
- deny feminine sexuality, seen as a threat to social stability
- support the family – another agent of patriarchy.

Feminists are critical not only of society, but also of the way in which female thinkers have been ignored and thus devalued within academic study – including some areas of sociology. Until recently the role of religion as a source of control of women has been largely ignored by mainstream sociology. Feminists refer to the invisibility of women in sociology as 'malestream' – illustrating the inadequacies of dominant male sociology to deal with gender issues.

Simone de Beauvoir identified the **patriarchal** content of religion, especially in relation to the family. As she comments:

Christian ideology has contributed not a little to the oppression of women ... [Women] could take only a secondary place as participants in worship, the deaconesses were authorized to carry out only such tasks as caring for the sick and aiding the poor. And if marriage was held to be an institution demanding mutual fidelity, it seemed obvious that the wife should be totally subordinate to her husband.

(Quoted in Turner, 1989, p. 119)

Feminism identifies a strong relationship between religious ideology, **familial ideology** and the control of feminine sexuality. Religious ideology is seen to contain an ideology of the family, as the above quotation from de Beauvoir illustrates. Religious ideology presents the family structure – and women's subordinate place within it – as normal and natural (see also Section 5.7). It could be argued that the family is vital for the continuation of capitalism. For example, Weber, although not a feminist, describes how humanity needs to be organized, disciplined and controlled in society to aid capitalist production and its efficiency. The body and its sexual desires need to be ordered and regulated to avoid chaos which could disrupt capitalist organization. Religion deals with this problem of sexuality for capitalism through the development and enforcement of strict moral codes.

Case Study – Witchcraft

An example of a feminist-style analysis of religion – or at least an analysis of religion which could contribute to a feminist debate – can be drawn by looking at the rise of witch-hunting in western Europe in the sixteenth and seventeenth centuries.

Alan Anderson and Raymond Gordon

Alan Anderson and Raymond Gordon (1978, 1979) provide an historical interpretation of witch-hunting, which can be seen to fit into a

feminist perspective on religion and its role in society. They contend that:

*Witch persecution had a **misogynous** ideological basis which reflected the low status of women at that time.*

(Anderson and Gordon, 1979, p. 359)

They argue that, with the exception of England, in the sixteenth and seventeenth centuries women were a credible target to be singled out, labelled and controlled by this moral panic (see Section 6.2) because they were seen to be an instrument of the devil–weak and open to satanic temptation if not controlled by society. Viewed in this way, witch-hunting by the Christian church can be seen as an attempt to control female sexuality.

However, in England, although some witch scares did occur, they were of a significantly lower rate than in other countries. This is interpreted by Anderson and Gordon to be due to the influence of a Puritan form of Protestantism, which raised the status of women relative to other European societies.

Bryan S. Turner

A second, but complementary interpretation of European witch-hunts is provided by Turner (1989, 1990). He locates witch-hunting within the history of the exclusion of women from medical practice. Turner contends that the male-dominated Christian church scapegoated as witches wise women who practised herbal medicine and midwifery at a local village level. By focusing the already existing fear of female satanic temptation on these women, the newly developing medical profession within the church was able to win an important battle over clients and credibility.

Religion and liberation

One way in which religion can create meaningful lifestyles, around which social action and interaction can take place, is by offering people a source of revolutionary or radical potential. Using the ideas of Max Weber, who believed that religion can offer the oppressed a source of liberation, some sociologists are concerned to illustrate examples of this phenomenon in the contemporary world.

Rastafarianism

Stuart Hall (1985) argues that religion means something for both the rulers and oppressed in society. Claims made by religions may not be empirically correct, but they can nonetheless create a stable sense of meaning for those who subscribe to their ideas. In this way, Hall argues that religion can be ideological, but he also suggests that it is not simply nor always a matter of **false class consciousness**.

In turning to the example of religious meanings in Jamaica, Hall notes the existence of religious **discourses** or sets of meanings which are used by their followers as an act of rebellion or resistance, both from within Jamaica, and for young blacks in the UK in the 1970s and 1980s.

The history of Jamaican culture is dependent on a varied mixture of a number of cultural influences: the Spanish occupation which almost destroyed the indigenous culture; the establishment of the slave trade and plantation economies; and the merging of the so-called dominant white culture of the colonial rulers and administrators with the colonized blacks originally from West Africa, into a single coloured population. Hall notes how, over time, non-slave or free coloureds became the Jamaican middle class, while the descendants of the slave populations became the lower-class members, all of which shared, to greater and lesser extents, the creole Jamaican culture.

Hall suggests that in this context of oppression and colonial rule, religious meanings were used as an act of resistance by some, against the white colonial invaders. Since the movement towards independent nationalism for Jamaica, the Rastafarian movement, in particular, has shown great resistance against outside ideas, beliefs and practices.

Within the Rastafarian movement, identified by Hall as a mixture of religious, political and nationalist ideas, the emergence of the Ras Tafari brethren, based on the ideas of evangelical preacher Marcus Garvey in the mid 1920s, can be seen as a militant opposition to White Babylon, promising to deliver its black members to a world free from slavery, oppression and exploitation in all forms.

Taking Emperor Haile Selassie I of Ethiopia as the reincarnation of Jesus, and believing that the Rastas were originally a lost tribe of Israel who would be delivered back to a promised land, many members of the Rastafarian movement

Figure 7.8 A member of the Rastafarian movement

have been harassed by the police in Jamaica for their non-conformist ideas, and in particular the taking of ganja (marijuana) which is believed to increase spirituality.

In terms of cultural style and identity (see Section 4.3), Rastas wear their hair in dreadlocks – an interpretation of the Bible's instruction not to cut their hair. Equally, through identification with Haile Selassie, they wear the colours of Ethiopia – green, yellow, red and black.

With its emphasis on the liberating force of religious belief, Rastafarianism has proved popular not just in Jamaica, but also in the UK, with some young blacks adopting these ideas (suggests Hall) as a means by which to resist a racist society.

Liberation theology

'Liberation theology' is a present-day general term given to a version of South American Roman Catholicism that uses Christian religious ideas as a political motivating force to create social change. As the name suggests, liberation theology believes that Christ was a revolutionary figure who practised the liberation of people from slavery, poverty and oppression. Liberation theology explains third-world poverty and deprivation to be the result of governmental corruption and exploitation, which must be challenged directly, through political and violent means if necessary.

Liberation theology offers a set of ideas based on ending privilege and oppression and as such, in Weber's terms, is used by the marginal to challenge the status quo and change society.

The examples of Rastafarianism and liberation theology serve to suggest that far from being the opium of the people, religion can often be used as a force for radical and political social action and social change.

Religion as discipline and control

Medicalization and secularization

A contemporary topic of sociological enquiry charts the growth of common ground between the sociologies of religion and medicine. For theorists such as Shilling (1993), Bull (1990) and Featherstone (1991), the synthesis between these areas of study is an inevitable consequence of the changes taking place in late-capitalist societies in western Europe and America.

Bryan S. Turner

Medicalization is a term used by Turner (1982, 1985) and Bull to refer to the increasing dominance of the medical profession, medical personnel and medical knowledge in areas of society previously controlled by other institutions such as religion. Medicalization, then, is seen by some as a process of secularization. Religion has lost or is losing the battle for control over morality, sexuality and diet. Religion is losing or has lost control over the human body and how the body is to be disciplined.

Discussion point

To what extent has medicine taken over from religion as a source of social control?

C3.1a

Contemporary society is often described as having a consumer culture, in which individual self-identity is something to be bought as a lifestyle package (see Section 4.5). The claim is made by Turner that religion has lost the ability to define, dictate and control this consumer culture of the healthy body, so it has lost a cultural battle to medicine.

Discussion point

Why are people in society more inclined to believe and obey something if it can convince them of its scientific nature?

C3.1a

According to Turner (1989, 1990), religion has been taken over by medicine. Medicine, with its claims of being a science, offers a source of morality that can control the body. Sickness is no longer the result of a sinful life, instead it is the result of an unhealthy life, an equally amoral lifestyle:

Put simply, the doctor has replaced the priest as the custodian of social values.

(Turner, 1990, p. 37)

Michel Foucault

In *History of Sexuality* (1990a, 1990b, 1992) and *The Birth of the Prison* (1979), Michel Foucault discusses the ways in which religion controls the body, and in particular the female body.

Foucault identifies a number of mechanisms of control which operate on the human body, and which benefit the way in which the capitalist economy of the West operates. Looking at a critical history of education, the prison, the hospital, the mental asylum and religion, he argues that the body is subjected to diet, timetable, surveillance, and physical punishment, distributed by these different institutions at different times in the history of the social body and the individual body. In particular, these mechanisms of discipline and punishment operate to create, mould and constrain the self-identity and the sexuality of the individual, creating a self ready to be controlled by capitalist production methods.

7.7 Religion, ideology and conflict

Sociologists are concerned with the role religion plays in society. A number of interpretations of this role have been presented within sociological debate. Briefly, these can be summarized as:

1　religion bonds social groups together

2　religion contributes to social control through ideology

3　religion is a form of discipline which controls the human body

4　religion stops social change

5　religion creates a meaningful reality in which social actors can act

6　religion offers the marginalized hope, status and a force through which radical social change can take place.

As can be seen from this brief list, sociologists disagree on the role religion performs. It may well be the case, though, that religion has performed, does perform and will perform all of these roles at different times and in different locations. Debate focuses on two vital issues:

* Does religion contribute to the status quo?

* Does religion encourage or hold back social change?

When interpreted by different theoretical perspectives, these two issues lead to the full range of possible interpretations listed above. It is important to remember that each perspective has its own associated political ideology which forms a framework or window through which these issues are discussed. While Marxists, functionalists and feminists may all agree at one level that religion does support the status quo, at another level they will disagree on whether this situation is positive or negative for the individual and for society.

Religion as social cement

Some perspectives regard religion's role, or function, as contributing to social harmony. The term 'social cement' is usually associated with theories that see harmony as a normal, natural and positive state for society.

Functionalist theorists such as Durkheim and Malinowski believe that religion bonds social groups together into a moral community. Talcott Parsons also shares this interpretation. He stresses religion's function as an agent of **socialization**: it contributes to the internalization of shared **norms** and **values** (Holton and Turner, 1988).

Discussion point

To what extent does religion operate as 'social cement'?

C3.1a

Religion as social control

Conflict theories such as **Marxism** and **neo-Marxism** tend to stress the control functions of religion. Religion is seen as another agent of ideology which performs a similar role to the education system and the mass media.

It is important to recognize the connections between these institutions and others in social life. Marxism, neo-Marxism and feminism, like any other theories, would not see one of these institutions as providing all of society's ideological control (see Section 3.2). They may well focus on some as more significant than others, but the nature of social life is such that all institutions operate together in a structured form. Thus, working-class subordination from a Marxist perspective is a result of both ideological and repressive controls. The working classes are controlled by all social institutions – religion being a smaller, but significant, part of a larger system of discipline. The same is true of a feminist analysis of female subordination.

Discussion point

To what extent does religion operate as a form of social control?

C3.1a

Marxism

Perhaps the best-known and most widely cited Marxist views on religion come from Marx's *Toward the Critique of Hegel's Philosophy of Right* (1984b), first published in Germany in 1844. This essay is concerned with the theme of self-alienation. Marx formed the idea that ideological control is sometimes a form of self-delusion: the subordinate in society can keep themselves subordinate by ideological means. The concept of 'alienation' was used by Feuerbach to refer to situations where humans create intellectual forces, or ideas, in their consciousness, but then let themselves be ruled over by these ideas. Alienation means to be ruled over by the products of one's own labour. Viewed in this way, religion represents a set of ideas created by humanity, but which humanity lets rule over them. Religion is a form of self-delusion which holds back revolutionary consciousness. As Marx commented:

The basis of irreligious criticism is: Man makes religion, religion does not make man. Religion is the self-consciousness and self-feeling of man, who either has not yet found himself or has already lost himself again ... This state, this society produce religion, a perverted world consciousness, because they are a perverted world.

(Marx, 1984, p. 303; orig. pub. 1844)

For Marx, then, religion is not a form of social cement but of 'social opium'. Although he agrees that religion supports the status quo and stops change, he goes further and suggests that it is ideological since it supports, hides and legitimates capitalist exploitation:

[Religion is] the opium of the people. ... Religious distress is at the same time the expression of real distress and the protest against real distress.
Religion is the sign of the oppressed creature, the heart of a heartless world, just as it is the spirit of an unspiritual situation.

(Marx, 1984, p. 304; orig. pub. 1844)

Marx, while recognizing that religion provides hope and dignity for those who are suffering in society, asserts that these are a false hope and a false dignity because they hide the true nature of society and the true causes of suffering: an oppressive class-based economic system. Religion creates false consciousness. It stops revolutionary feelings by promoting reward in an afterlife for compliance with the rules of this one.

Friedrich Engels

In his essay *On the History of Early Christianity* (1984), first published in Germany in 1894, Engels (a close colleague of Marx) discussed similarities between early religious movements and early socialist movements. Engels notes that the history of Christianity, for example, is very similar to the sort of communist ideas both he and Marx were involved in:

Both Christianity and the workers' socialism preach forthcoming salvation from bondage and misery; Christianity places this salvation in a life beyond, after death, in heaven; socialism places it in this world, in a transformation of society.

(Engels, 1984, p. 209; orig. pub. 1895)

However, the points of comparison, for Engels, can only be made this far. He regards religion (as does Marx) as a false search for equality and an end to suffering, since it is alienated and leads to false consciousness. It gets in the way of true consciousness, which would be brought about by socialism.

Internal debates within Marxism

Since the death of Marx in 1883, great debate has taken place concerning the 'real' meaning of his ideas. Various sociologists have taken what is called a 'neo-Marxist' stance: they believe in a general Marxist sociology but with some reservations, alterations and new ideas – often brought about by combining Marxist thoughts with those of other thinkers.

Discussion point

Over 100 years on, can we still use Marx's ideas successfully to explain the contemporary world?

C3.1a

This issue concerning the real meaning of Marxism can be divided into two branches or camps of Marxism:

- One branch emphasizes the materialistic reading of Marx. Concentrating on his later mature work, they interpret Marx as a scientist studying the universal, inevitable laws governing history.

- The second interpretation is regarded as humanist. Concentrating on Marx's early work, these sociologists focus on Marx's concerns with consciousness, subjectivity and ideology.

These two readings have led to two interpretations of his sociology of religion.

Dominant ideology

As stated in *The German Ideology*, Marx and Engels (1977, originally written in 1845) believed that the dominant ideology of every social epoch was invented, distributed and controlled by the ruling class of that epoch. From this idea, religion could be seen as yet another weapon in the class struggle, used, but not necessarily created, by the ruling class to control the masses.

Criticisms of Marx

However, Abercrombie and Turner (1978) are highly critical of this dominant ideology interpretation of Marx. They contend that, in feudal times, although Christianity was a major part of ruling class culture, it was largely ignored by the peasantry and had little effect on their lives. The ideas of the ruling classes could not therefore control a population if they did not share these same ideas. Abercrombie and Turner suggest that economic and repressive control were used far more effectively than religion as a means for gaining the compliance of the population. This criticism leads to the second interpretation of Marx's ideas.

Discussion point

Which theoretical interpretation on the role of religion in society do you find most convincing and why? – Marxism or functionalism?

C3.2, C3.3

Religion and class distinctions

The second interpretation is that religion has an economic character: it is related to different socio-economic classes and used by these groups in different ways.

Using the work of Engels, Turner (1991) argues that in each epoch there will develop two ideological positions, one each for the subordinate class and the ruling class. Religion does not simply bond the whole of society together into a unified whole based on a ruling class ideology of which everyone is a victim in a passive fashion. Instead, it contributes to individual class solidarity. Different classes can get different functions from the same religion:

... it is argued that religion satisfies the need of the dominant class to feel that its privileged social position is legitimate; however, the same religion, or some version of it, gratifies the need of subordinate groups, for comfort on this world or revenge in the next. As a narcotic, religion is the expression of human misery, but it is also a reaction against human suffering.

(Turner, 1991, pp. 79–80)

Max Weber

Max Weber was highly critical of the idea of an all-controlling dominant ideology – the idea that religion is a weapon always to be used to control subordinate classes. He believed religions provide society with a 'theodicy' – a set of abstract ideas and beliefs which explain both the existence of God or gods and evil. Weber drew a vital distinction between:

1 theodicies of privilege
2 theodicies of non-privilege.

Ruling groups have a theodicy of privilege in which they have no need for ideas of salvation from poverty: they have, after all, no poverty to be saved from! However, subordinate groups develop a very different theodicy, which is one of non-privilege as a response to their lower socio-economic position. These groups use religion to justify their pain and suffering. Sometimes a theodicy of non-privilege can have a revolutionary nature – a major criticism of Marx's idea that religion was always a 'social opium'.

7.8 Religion, stability and consensus

Early functionalist studies

Early functionalist and functionalist-based theories of the role of religion in society developed through the use of fieldwork and the study of small-scale non-western societies. The theoretical justification for the study of such small-scale pre-industrial societies is given through a use of evolutionary images of history. The so-called advanced western world was seen to have progressed further along the historical path towards science, reason and rationality than these other, slower developing societies. Sociologists could therefore understand more of their own culture by spending time researching societies in those traditional stages of development believed to have come before modernity.

For the functionalists, it was undeniably a simpler task to study the interrelationships of harmony and consensus between social institutions on a small-scale, than in an industrializing and changing western European society.

A common belief shared by these anthropological or ethnographic pieces of research was the importance of *ritual* or collective ceremony to bond society together with a set of norms and values.

We will look at two functionalist approaches to the study of collective religious worship, those of Emile Durkheim and Bronislaw Malinowski.

Emile Durkheim

Durkheim uses a wide definition of religion encompassing many different sets of beliefs and practices. In a similar fashion to W. R. Smith, he places high value on the importance of religious rituals – which function to bond society together.

The role of the sacred in society

Durkheim defines religion as the 'sacred' rather than the 'profane': religion is any set of practices and beliefs which are treated as sacred – set apart, special, not treated as part of the ordinary, mundane and profane world.

Given the importance of the integrative function which the sacred performs, Durkheim believed this distinction was a human universal. All societies, irrespective of their place along the path of historical development, had their sacred forms. This is because Durkheim places great stress on the need for moral element in society to keep the society together and functioning harmoniously. Precisely what he meant by the integrative function of religion.

What is religion?

What is especially interesting about Durkheim's definition of religion is his insistence that religion is not solely a belief in a God or gods. Religion is characterized more by what it does, the function it performs, the collective practices it encourages.

Religion and magic

Durkheim draws an important distinction between 'religion' and 'magic':

- Religion bonds social members together – it gives a group unity through the sharing of a common faith. In this sense, religion has what Durkheim calls a 'church' – a set of shared practices which are communal and collective in nature.
- By contrast, magic has no 'church' – it has no general, collective ceremonies which bind individuals together into a conscience collective: magic may well have rituals and ceremonies, but its bonds are not lasting.

The socialization of norms

With the case of religion, the bonds or collective norms and values are socialized through public ritual, but are internalized and carried around in the consciousness of individuals. In this manner, even on their own, individuals are never individuals – they are always part of a shared collective.

Looking at crowd behaviour

Durkheim borrows from the work of Gustave Le Bon. In his discussion of collective public rituals, Le Bon conducted research into the psychology of crowd behaviour in the late 1800s. Durkheim places great importance on the public or crowd nature of religious ceremony. Socialization occurs through integration with others. (See Section 3.2)

The problem of social order

Durkheim's work – especially on religion – is often presented as an attempt to answer what is known as the 'Hobbesian problem of order'. Thomas Hobbes, a seventeenth-century English philosopher, posed the question 'how is order possible?' For Hobbes, the basis of human activity was competition, which led to a 'nasty, brutish and short life'. Given this state of nature, how is society possible? How is the greedy individualistic will put aside for the good of the collective?

Talcott Parsons, a later American functionalist, interpreted Durkheim's work to address this problem, by arguing that the external constraint of a social group and the institutions of society lead to an internal control within the individual body, whereby moral codes are internalized via rituals and rites.

Totemism

In his classic text *The Elementary Forms of the Religious Life*, originally published in 1912, Durkheim (1982) uses the example of totemism as practised by Australian aborigines to illustrate how religion contributes to the conscience collective.

Totemism (the practice of worshipping a totem) simply means to take an object – usually from the natural world, a plant or animal – as a symbol of group membership. It is the method by which clans are able to identify insiders and outsiders.

The totem also fits into Durkheim's definition of a religion: it is a sacred object, not a profane one. The practice of totemism also involves the development of a shared moral unity designed to integrate and contribute to the conscience collective. Since these social bonds are long-lasting, totemism is considered to have a 'church'.

Durkheim contends that in religion, the real object of worship is not a God or gods with special or supernatural powers, but rather the group itself. The totem is a sacred symbol of group life, of belonging to a collective. The function of religion is to give social members a concrete symbol of group life around which they can organize public group-enhancing rituals.

Activity

a Re-read the ideas of Emile Durkheim and create a list of the functions of religion from this perspective.

b Do you think that religion still performs these functions? If not, which ones have declined, and what might have replaced religion instead?

C3.2, C3.3

Bronislaw Malinowski

Malinowski (1954), too, believes that the function of religion is to bond a moral community together. Using research from the Trobriand Islands – another small-scale non-western society – Malinowski's work both complements and criticizes Durkheim's.

Social solidarity

In agreement with Durkheim, Malinowski believes religion contributes to social solidarity by reinforcing a value consensus (see Section 3.3). However, Malinowski believes that collective religious ceremonies operate to create solidarity only when such cohesion is threatened. Therefore, religion does not involve the worship of a symbol which stands for society; rather, it is a powerful mechanism of stability used at times of disruption, anxiety and crisis.

Religion and uncertainty

Uncertainty and a loss of meaning are powerful sources of social disruption for group life. The loss of a clear, stable understanding of the meaning of life, by those involved in such, would be dysfunctional for the smooth functioning of the group.

The function of religion is to create public rituals which reinforce collective norms and values at times when they are threatened. A good illustration of this argument would be death and marriage. Both these events could harm the status quo of society, albeit in different ways. By creating public rituals around these events, and thereby pulling individuals together, stability is reinforced and collective life can continue.

The Trobriand Islanders

Malinowski applies his ideas to his fieldwork in the Trobriand Islands. At times of sea-fishing, group members are tense and anxious. Normally, for most of the year, fishing in their protected lagoon offers a safe environment. However, the sea – a potentially hostile, dangerous and hazardous environment – offers many opportunities for fear and tension amongst the group. This tension, although potentially a threat to social solidarity, can be combated via collective ritual. In this way, religion operates at times of life crises.

Activity

a Identify and explain the views of Malinowski and Durkheim on the functions of religion in society.

b Outline and discuss the view that religion acts as a basis of stability in society.

C3.2, C3.3

Non-functionalist theories of religious ritual

Claude Lévi-Strauss: a structuralist approach

A contrasting anthropological treatment of small-scale non-western societies is provided by structural anthropologist Claude Lévi-Strauss (1989), whose work has proved highly influential on modern-day social theories, such as the development of post-structuralism.

Lévi-Strauss' work was popular in the late 1950s and 1960s and represented the beginnings of an interest in structural philosophy in French academic thought.

What is 'structuralism'?

'Structuralism' refers to the general belief that specific aspects of social life, although appearing perhaps on a surface level to be unrelated, can in fact be interrelated at a more hidden level (or structure) beyond, above or behind the level of mere surface appearance. Social life is therefore patterned, regulated or structured in much the same way that language is thought to be.

The structures of tribal life

Lévi-Strauss sought to analyse the patterns or structures inherent in human life – kinship patterns, myths, totemism, the classification of the natural world and religious customs. He believed that a common structure united all societies despite the apparent uniqueness of such societies.

The Savage Mind

In his text *The Savage Mind*, first published in 1962, Lévi-Strauss (1989) argues that the 'scientific mind' of western societies and the so-called 'savage mind' of 'primitive cultures' are not simply different points along a shared historical path, one lesser developed than the other. Instead, the savage mind is as capable of 'scientific' thought as the western mind. They are both united by a deep structure.

Criticisms of Malinowski

As a point of departure, Lévi-Strauss takes the work of Malinowski, of whom he is highly critical. Malinowski, although believing totemism provides vital functions which enhance social stability, nevertheless believes (as does Durkheim) that it is a pre-scientific mode of thought. We are given the impression that totemism is a basic or 'primitive' mode of thought incapable of seeing the world 'how it really is'.

Lévi-Strauss believes that the work of Malinowski has created an illusion of understanding so far as the real meaning of totemism is concerned. At a surface level, totemism may appear distinct, but at a deep structural level it uses the same categories and methods of thought as 'modern man'. The (not so) 'savage mind' uses a vast and complex system of classification for the natural world, in a similar way to western science. Equally, the telling of myths and stories of totemistic religion illustrates individuals relationships to the world around them.

7.9 Religion, social action and social change

Although for very different reasons, with different interpretations, Marxism, functionalism and feminism all believe religion is a **conservative** force.

Max Weber

Using the work of Max Weber, however, it is possible to present an alternative understanding of this issue. Far from always stopping change and always supporting the status quo, historical analysis provides sociology with a number of instances where religion has, on the one hand, led groups to cause unintended change, and on the other, to actively seek social change using religion as a political force.

> **Discussion point**
> Does religion stop change or contribute to it?
>
> C3.1a

The Protestant Ethic and the Spirit of Capitalism

Weber's ideas on historical and social change can best be described as a conversation with the ghost of Marx. Weber's influential 1920s study, *The Protestant Ethic and the Spirit of Capitalism* (1930; orig. pub. 1905), can certainly be read as a critique of Marx's ideas on **historical materialism**.

For Marx, history was divided into stages or epochs. Borrowing from Hegel, Marx contended that conflict produced social change. All history is based on class struggle, which moves history along the path towards communism – towards a classless society – and therefore the 'end of history', since there would be no more conflicting classes to produce revolutionary changes.

Weber, in contrast, offers a very different image of social history and the origins of capitalist development. In doing so, he provides sociology with a criticism of the idea that religion is a conservative force. In effect, Weber argues that a very particular form of Protestant religion, Calvinism, created the social conditions which made society ready for a capitalist economic system.

Frank Parkin

Frank Parkin (1986) is critical of simplistic interpretations of Weber's work which lead to the conclusion that religion created capitalism. Parkin emphasizes that Weber's intention was to study the ideas and beliefs which lead to a capitalist spirit – the values of capitalism – but not actually directly to a capitalist economic structure itself. This was not a universal or inevitable development but an unintended consequence of Calvinist belief.

Calvinism: the Protestant ethic

Calvinism rejected what it saw as the decadence of Roman Catholicism. Calvinism was based on an idea or theodicy known as 'the elect': it was believed that, at birth, some individuals were predestined to go to heaven. These 'elect' few were chosen by God, irrespective of their conduct in this world. However, in order to cope with feelings of anxiety, the Calvinists believed that a sign of God's favour, an indication that one was a member of the elect, was success at one's 'calling' – the career an individual adopted. The Calvinists believed that hard work was a virtue. If an individual worked hard and became successful, God was thereby praised; and in turn, God would give the elect few a sign (success) of their predestination. This is known as the 'Protestant (work) ethic': a lifestyle based on religious beliefs which lead to a very specific form of social action – economic activity. Other aspects of the Protestant ethic included condemnation of time-wasting, idleness, laziness and gossip.

The spirit of capitalism

Weber suggests that the meaningful social action produced by the Calvinist's 'work ethic' leads to the 'spirit' of capitalism, the essential ideology of profit-seeking and profit reinvestment at the heart of the subsequent capitalist economic system. Capitalism was thus not an inevitable outcome of scientific forces as identified by Marx, but the unintended consequence of specific religious meanings and motives.

Discussion point
To what extent can religious meanings cause unintended changes in society?

C3.1a

Religion and political conflict

Weber's ideas described above serve as an example of religion not being a conservative force. Rather than holding back change, religion has created the conditions necessary for change on a major scale and of great historical significance, even if this change was largely unintended.

Other historical examples suggest that social actors can use religion and religious ideas in a self-conscious political fashion to achieve radical and often revolutionary social movement and change.

Discussion point
Can religion act as a political force in creating revolutionary struggle?

C3.1a

Case Study – The ghost dance cult

The Ghost Dance Cult of the Sioux North American Indians can be seen as an example of a religious movement which actively sought social change through religious ideas. This movement preached salvation from the bondage and exploitation of the white settlers (Brown, 1991).

The Ghost Dance is an example of a 'millenarian movement', a social movement which preaches salvation from suffering due to coming great natural changes (floods, volcanoes, etc.) and a return to a glorious past, free from misery. Millenarian movements are intimately related to Christianity and normally develop among the poor and marginal either in the western world, or amongst Christian colonized areas in the non-western world.

The Ghost Dancers believed that Christ supported the plight of Indians over the settlers and that Christ had returned to encourage Indians to fight for their freedom once more. This indicates how the religion of colonial invaders often influences and becomes combined with native religions.

The Ghost Dancers represented a major political threat to the American government of the time. Conflict escalated until, in December 1890 at the Battle of Wounded Knee, the Ghost Dancers were stopped. An estimate puts those killed amongst the Sioux as nearly 300 men, women and children (Brown, 1991).

Although ultimately unsuccessful as a revolutionary movement, this example serves as another indication that religious belief can act as, to use Weber's term, a theodicy of non-privilege.

Further reading

Accessible A level texts designed to introduce the key debates in this field include:

- Bird, J. (1999) *Investigating Religion*, London: Collins.
- Bruce, S. (1995) *Religion in Modern Britain*, Oxford: Oxford University Press.
- Selfe, P. and Starbuck, M. (1998) *Religion*, London: Hodder & Stoughton.
- Thompson, I. (1986) *Religion*, London: Longman.
- Thompson, K. (1986) *Beliefs and Ideology*, London: Tavistock.

Further texts, designed to provide more detail, include:

- Hamilton, M. B. (1995) *The Sociology of Religion: Theoretical and Comparative Perspectives*, London: Routledge.
- Turner, B. S. (1991) *Religion and Social Theory*, 2nd edn, London: Sage.

A good, general 'reader' covering many classic and contemporary writings in this field is:

- Bocock, R. and Thompson, K. (eds.) (1985) *Religion and Ideology*, Manchester: Manchester University Press.

Back issues of the periodical *Sociology Review* (formerly *Social Studies Review*) contain many articles on this field and many others.

Glossary of useful terms

Communitarian   A world view based upon the belief that the good of the community is better than that of the individual: a desire to be 'bonded' with others.

Conflict theories   A mixture of Marx and Weber that arose as a reaction to the emphasis on consensus in the functionalist approach, concentrating on the fundamental conflicts in society.

Conservative   Term used to describe the attitudes of fundamentalist religious groups. Can either be interpreted as a desire to preserve the past or backward-looking.

Deviant   Straying from the norms of society or a group.

Discourse   A set of ideas that together form a coherent whole. Religion may be considered a discourse, as may science. Different discourses present different ways of seeing and understanding the world.

Enlightenment   The period in the second half of the eighteenth century which saw the rise of reason and science and the challenge to religion as the way to explain things. This was described as a process of throwing light on to a period later characterized as the Dark Ages.

Ethnocentric   This term is used as a criticism suggesting that people should not judge other societies using the norms and values of their own society as the yardstick.

False class-consciousness   A Marxist concept which states that ideas originate with the ruling class and filter down to the subject class.

Familial ideology   Idea devised mainly by feminist writers that one particular form of the family (namely the conventional nuclear family with some degree of role separate for male and female) is presented as normal and pressure is applied to get everyone to live this way. Such a way of living is presented as the ideal or the best, stigmatizing potential other social relationships.

Feminist   A person who adheres to the beliefs of feminism.

Functionalist   A person who adheres to the beliefs of functionalism.

Globalization   Refers to the perception that the lives of people in different societies across the globe are becoming more closely connected. It is a controversial process, with some sociologists seeing it in broadly positive terms, while others see it as a process having negative consequences.

Historical materialism   Method devised by Marx. He believed that to understand society you needed to look at real events (materialism) and see how things change over time (historical).

In-depth interviews   These are interviews designed to gain as much detail as possible and are based on a series of linked open questions.

Industrial Revolution   The period when Europe swapped from being a primarily agricultural society to one based on industry. This took a long time to spread across Europe and is still arguably spreading across certain parts of the globe.

Marxism   Marxism is based on the idea that there are fundamental conflicts between classes in society, notably between those who own the means by which things are made and those who have to sell their labour to live.

Marxist   A person who adheres to the beliefs of Marxism.

Moral panic   Exaggeration or invention of a problem usually through sensationalist stories in the media.

Misogynous   Women-hating.

Neo-Marxism   Approaches that have derived from the many works of Marx and include: Evolutionary Marxism (socialism will result from logical discussion); Revolutionary Marxism (Marxist thinkers who stick to the notion of a need for revolution to free the oppressed masses from capitalism); Western Marxism (a reaction to events in the West after WW2); and Hegelian Marxism (knowledge comes from action in the social world, by understanding the historical context).

New Right   Used to distinguish the views of right-wing political parties in recent times from earlier conservative views: notably the views of the British Conservative Party from the premiereship of Margaret Thatcher onwards and the US Republican Party from the presidency of Ronald Reagan onwards. The most notable difference is the New Right's emphasis on the benefits of the free market and individual freedom.

Non-conformist religion   This is a term used to describe Christian religions not part of the establishment that is the Anglican Church. Notable examples include Methodism and Baptism. Such religions are also seen to have a slight radical political edge.

Norms   Rules about expected behaviour in specific circumstances. What is normally expected of one.

Participant observation   Key sociological research method where the researcher participates in the group in order to observe their activities.

Patriarchal   Ideas or structures which support the oppression of women or the power of men.

Phenomenological approaches   Those who use phenomenology.

Phenomenologist   A person who adheres to the ideas of phenomenology.

Phenomenology   The study of the 'common-sense' understandings (as opposed to 'scientific'

or 'academic' explanations of things) that people have about their lives and the importance of these for interaction and for society. The study of the process through which people create their consciousness.

Positivism   An approach that believes that sociology should be scientific and precise in nature, favouring quantitative data.

Privatization of religion   The replacement of large-scale institutional religious forms with an individual, small-scale search for the personally spiritual: the creation of private and intimate religious feelings.

Profane   A term used by Durkheim to refer to the everyday things and occurrences in life.

Questionnaires   A primary research tool that discovers information about a population through an organized list of questions, which can range from one-word responses (closed) to detailed answers (open-ended).

Religious pluralism   The development of a culture characterized by a wide-spread diversity of religious expressions and views having more than one religion at the same time.

Religious world view   Using religious ideas and beliefs to understand the world and society around you.

Sacred   A term used by Durkheim to represent all things that are distinct from everyday life.

Socialization   The process of learning appropriate roles and behaviour.

Socially constructed   Term associated with social action approaches which emphasizes the way things are made up by human action rather than being 'natural' phenomena waiting for us to notice them.

Sovereignty   The institution or person that has supreme power, usually in the context of a nation.

Televangelism   Meaning using television to get across an evangelical message. Often associated with conservative fundamentalists Protestantism in the USA.

Typology   A classification of types of religions.

Values   Views about general ways of behaving which express something about how people feel they and others should behave.

Verstehen   Seeing the world through the eyes of those involved.

Culture and socialization
Youth and culture

Chapter outline

Youth culture and subcultures

8.1 Youth culture and youth subculture   *page 225*
This section looks at the meaning of the terms culture and subculture and examines some of the debates surrounding these terms as applied to youth.

8.2 Youth and class, gender and ethnicity   *page 229*
This section considers the way accounts of youth subcultures have incorporated notions from other social divisions such as class, gender and ethnicity.

8.3 Theories of youth subcultures   *page 232*
This section looks at some of the theories which have emerged in the 1990s, including those looking at the emergence of urban dance culture.

Youth and deviance

8.4 Delinquency   *page 234*
This section looks at the evidence of youth involvement in delinquent behaviour and considers this in a historical context. It also asks whether youth resistance is a thing of the past.

8.5 Gangs   *page 239*
This section considers material relating to the existence and behaviour of juvenile gangs and sociological accounts of their behaviour.

8.6 Theories of delinquent subcultures   *page 242*
In this section sociological accounts of deviance and delinquency are outlined. Such theories were first developed in relation to the study of adolescents in the USA.

Youth and schooling

8.7 Experiences of schooling
page 248
This section considers the interactionist-inspired accounts of the way schools operate and the experience of schooling from a pupils perspective, drawing on a number of studies relating to different divisions and identities.

8.8 Femininity, masculinity and subject choice   *page 253*
This section highlights the way expected behaviour is constructed differently for males and females in the process of schooling and the way this affects the subjects pupils choose to study.

Glossary   *page 259*
Words in bold in the text are explained in the glossary at the end of this chapter.

8.1 Youth culture and youth subculture

Culture/subculture

By youth culture, sociologists mean the fashions and tastes associated with 'youth' and young people. However, by youth subculture, sociologists usually mean the distinctive and often rebellious styles associated with particular groups of young people who seek to separate themselves out within society (e.g. skinheads, punks, rastas).

The category of youth has suddenly become much more important to government and policymakers. All sorts of government initiatives and projects are now aimed at tackling the 'problem of youth' – Millennium Volunteers, the New Deal, anti-drugs campaigns, homework clubs, citizenship education, youth offender teams – not to mention the Crime and Disorder Act.

From the Thatcher period when ministers denied in the House that there was any such category as youth, to the situation now when there appears to be nothing except the social priorities of youth, we have moved from studious neglect to potentially chaotic over attention.

(Nicholls, 1999, P. 49)

Activity

Divide into groups of three or four. Nominate a leader for each group. Discuss the following task and assign specific duties to each individual.

a Using library or Internet sources, identify and explain two government initiatives on youth.

b Outline and discuss the effectiveness of these in meeting young people's needs.

c Write a report on your findings and present these to your class.

IT3.1, C3.1a, C3.1b, C3.2, C3.3

What government and policy-makers (and of course marketing agencies) all assume is that the category of 'youth' has a real existence – that young people as 'youth' have a distinct set of interests, tastes and problems that governments can 'deal' with and advertisers can 'appeal' to. However, as we shall see, while older sociologists assumed that it did make sense to approach young people as a separate social group, perhaps with a distinctive subculture, recent sociological approaches have begun to question this.

The concept of 'youth subculture' was used by sociologists to refer to the particular values, styles, cultural tastes and behaviour of young people, which separated out their culture from that of their parents. Youth subcultures certainly have a history which can be traced back at least to the second half of the nineteenth century (Pearson, 1983); but, as we shall see, some sociologists now question whether the cultural behaviour of young people can still be described in such terms.

Is 'youth' still a useful sociological category?

Not only do some writers question the concept of 'youth subculture'; some sociologists take the view that the very concept of 'youth' as a separate sociological category no longer makes much sense.

Jeffs and Smith (1999), for example, argue that there is little mileage left in the study of the sociology of youth. They point out that:

- The older literature in the sociology of youth used to deal with themes that were believed to be particular problems for young people. For example, the literature regarded the transition from childhood to adulthood as an important problem for young people.

- Older approaches attached a great deal of importance to theories of psychological development which suggested that young people were on a psychological journey travelling through a series of stages to reach adult psychological maturity.

- Young people were regarded as being particularly vulnerable in terms of 'risk-taking behaviours', ranging from early sexual experience to alcohol and drug abuse.

- Finally, young people were assumed to identify with 'youth subcultures' which were often associated with social disorder.

A more complicated view of transitions

In terms of each of the above areas, Jeffs and Smith wonder whether it still makes sense to think in terms of 'the problems of youth'. 'Transitions' are now much more complicated. 'Transitions' can be interrupted, delayed or reversed, and this can happen at most stages of the life-cycle after childhood.

For example, some adults return to full-time study as mature students at university and frequently take up with enthusiasm the 'lifestyle choices' and 'risk behaviours' of their younger counterparts. And yet, in areas of continuing high unemployment, some young people are not given the opportunity to make the 'transition' to adulthood, if this is defined in terms of getting a full-time job. The increasing rate of divorce and family break-up also contributes to the interruption of 'transitions' because marriage and parenthood are no longer such stable and permanent markers of adult status:

Transitions that were previously linked to youth are frequently no longer the sole property of a particular age group. Back tracking, revisiting, revising and the reversing of earlier decisions regarding lifestyle and content are a growing feature of life.

(Jeffs and Smith, 1999, p. 54)

Jeffs and Smith are equally sceptical of the view that young people experience particular emotional stresses as a stage in psychological development towards adulthood. There is little evidence to suggest that 'adolescents', in the main, cope any less well than 'adults' with the stressful issues of identity (who am I?) and attachment (where do I belong?). Adults experiencing a divorce or 'mid-life crisis' are likely to demonstrate the same signs of emotional trauma as young people leaving home for the first time or breaking up with a boy or girl friend. Evidence regarding risk-taking behaviour, Jeffs and Smith claim, also fails to justify the use of a separate category of 'youth':

The literature is full of discussions of the various risk-taking behaviours that young people are allegedly more prone to, for example, with regard to drug usage and sexual behaviour. There can be no denying that some young people experience problems in these areas but the question is whether the problem is better approached as a 'youth question' or as an experience shared by people across a span of ages.

(Jeffs and Smith, 1999, p. 55)

Youth as a category of social control

It is not only young people who expose themselves to the risks associated with drugs and alcohol. The experience of homelessness is traumatic whether one is young or old; and many of those arrested for violent offences associated with football have long said goodbye to their teens. According to Jeffs and Smith, these are problem behaviours but not necessarily specifically related to 'youth'.

If, as these sociologists argue, there is little that is intrinsically unique about youth, what can explain the fascination amongst politicians, policy-makers and academics with the category of 'youth'? Jeffs and Smith suspect that the answer to this has a great deal to do with *control*. 'Youth' is a convenient category around which to organize social control initiatives including, for example, youth offender schemes, policing strategies and the employment of youth workers.

Activity

a List three reasons why Jeffs and Smith believe that the category of 'youth' has lost much of its usefulness to sociologists.

b What points might sociologists make in favour of retaining 'youth' as a sociological category?

C3.2

An alternative view

Jeffs and Smith provide a useful critique in underlining the extent to which 'youth problems' are actually shared by adults as well. However, some sociologists argue that the very fact that so much importance continues to be attached to the category of 'youth' by politicians and social control agencies means that it should continue to be of interest to sociologists. In other words, so long as it remains an important category for organizing and controlling groups of people in society, the term will continue to be of interest to sociologists.

Discussion point

To what extent do you agree with the statement that youth subcultures are now dead?

C3.1a

The end of youth resistance?

Absorbing resistance

For some writers, we now live in a **post-modern** rather than **modern world**. In other words, these writers believe that certain key changes have occurred which made life in the 1990s fundamentally different from the way we experienced the social world in the middle of the twentieth century. A central feature of the post-modern world, according to Baudrillard (1988), is the speed at which images, signs and symbols are incorporated by the 'agencies of signification' (media, marketing and advertising).

Dick Hebdige (1988) applies this argument to developments in music and youth culture. He points to the way in which advertising and the media can 'absorb' even the most subversive **cultural products** to sell new **commodities**. For example, songs once made famous by The Clash, a punk band with a left-wing views, are now used in advertisements to sell jeans. Television makes even the most rebellious youth subcultures familiar and less threatening. In this way, the agencies of signification deny young people the power to shock.

Style over substance

Secondly, post-modern writers argue that another consequence of living in a 'media saturated' world is that symbols and elements of subcultures are removed from their original contexts and recirculated. Subcultural dress becomes a matter of surface style; it can no longer have a deeper meaning. For example, Dr Marten boots used to 'say something' about young working-class life, with a bit of menace thrown in. Now, removed from this context, they simply represent a surface style, used for a variety of fashion statements. This view is very similar to the arguments of Bennett and Willis discussed above.

The mass media and definitions of authenticity

Thornton (1995) also points to the importance of the mass media in influencing young people's judgements about the quality of particular kinds of music, arguing that the music press and fanzines have an important influence in defining what is regarded as 'authentic' and 'progressive' – or, on the other hand, 'trivial' or 'too commercial'. In other words, even our understanding of 'authenticity' is actually influenced by the mass media.

Through the mass media, particularly television stations such as MTV, young people have access to the 'back catalogue' of previous forms of music and subcultural styles. They can engage in parody and pastiche, using earlier subcultural styles in a mocking or humorous way to play around with subcultural identities. A 'bit' of punk can be mixed with a 'bit' of mod or teddy-boy style. This is one illustration of what some post-modern writers, such as Jameson (1991), mean by the end of history – the historical context for particular subcultural styles is forgotten and the **oppositional** messages associated with them are forgotten, too. Everyone, young or old, middle-class or working-class, can 'play' with subcultural styles but they will not actually 'mean' very much.

The end of cultural resistance?

This is a rather bleak view of the future of youth culture. All hope of meaningful cultural activity is denied; young people face a future in which any genuine radicalism is quickly incorporated into the commercial marketing system and used to sell more products. Even our efforts to separate the good from the bad in music are shaped by the mass media.

Some writers influenced by **post-modernism** present a more optimistic analysis. Dick Hebdige, for example, points to the way in which the technologies of the post-modern age permit more democratic or participatory forms of music to emerge. Samplers and computers allow many more young people to make music in cheaply built home-made studios. Nevertheless, Hebdige does not expect the return of the spectacular forms of cultural resistance associated with the 1960s and 1970s, such as the mods, rockers or skinheads.

Activity

a Explain in your own words what Paul Willis means by the phrase 'symbolic creativity'.

b Explain why Andy Bennett is critical of the use of the concept 'youth subculture'.

c Write a paragraph summarizing the reasons why sociologists such as Willis and Bennett believe that the concept of youth subculture can no longer be applied to the cultural behaviour of young people in contemporary societies.

C3.2, C3.3

Is there still some resistance?

However, there are also some reasons to question the view that young people's subcultural resistance is a thing of the past. Steve Redhead (1993) points to the rise of 'rave' as a subculture which clearly did develop an oppositional approach in the late 1980s. Through the music which represented a clear break with 'guitar music', the use of illegal drugs, the organization of large parties on unauthorized land, and the use of all sorts of costumes to heighten the fun, 'rave' looked suspiciously like a genuine youth subculture. As Redhead describes, it represented a sufficient degree of cultural resistance for the state to respond with new laws and tougher policing.

A similar point can now be made about the varieties of dance music and 'jungle'. Although some forms of jungle have been **incorporated** and are now to be heard within the commercial mainstream (jungle now provides the beat for many television advertisements, BBC Radio 1 now has a jungle evening), it is also the case that some forms of jungle form a **non-incorporated** 'underground' in less well-known dance clubs with flourishing independent record and fanzine producers. Perhaps the future for youth subcultures is not quite so bleak.

8.2 Youth and class, gender and ethnicity

The 1950s and the emergence of youth subcultures

The approach of sociologists writing from a **functionalist** perspective in the 1950s was to argue that youth subcultures could be regarded as functional both for industrial societies and young people, for a number of reasons.

Functionalists such as Eisenstadt (1956) or Parsons and Bales (1956) noted that the concept 'youth' and the status 'teenager' appeared only in advanced, industrialized societies. In other kinds of society, the transition from child to adult was managed much more quickly, often through a single initiation ritual which announced to the community that an individual had become a full adult. This is not possible in advanced industrialized societies because the transition between childhood and adulthood takes longer – it has been 'stretched' by the need to educate and train young people. Youth subcultures help young people to manage this 'stretched' period between childhood and adulthood. Through membership of a wider but close peer group, young people can gradually grow more independent of their parents and accomplish the transition to adulthood in a relatively smooth way.

Moreover, membership of a youth subculture can help young people to cope with the pressures and stresses they are likely to face, particularly those generated by the education system and the need to get qualifications. If the education system introduces young people to the pressure of competition and universalistic criteria (all being judged according to the same performance indicators), the subculture offers a more relaxed world where friendship and particularistic criteria still count (being valued for who you are rather than how you perform) (Parsons and Bales, 1956).

Functionalism and social divisions

One of the most important contributions of **functionalism** was to highlight the point that age categories such as 'youth' are not fixed biologically but are *social constructions*: different societies quite clearly organize age categories in different ways.

Criticisms of functionalism

There are, however, several criticisms of early functionalist approaches to youth.

1 One important point is that youth subcultures did not always appear to function in a way which managed tension, either for young people or for society. Some youth subcultures were associated strongly with social disorder – British teddy-boys were happily ripping up cinema seats in the 1950s, at the time Parsons and Bales published their work in the USA (1956).

2 It is clear that position in the class structure makes a difference. Working-class young people face different problems and respond in different ways from their middle-class peers.

3 The 'gender blind' nature of most sociology written in the 1950s and 1960s meant that the important differences in the position of male and female teenagers were ignored. (This issue is discussed also in Section 8.8.) For example, the vast majority of the studies on youth subculture were on groups of males; females only tended to feature as girlfriends of male group members.

Activity

a Explain what is meant by the term 'youth subculture'.

b According to functionalists, what purposes do youth subcultures serve in advanced industrial societies?

c Using your own words, write a paragraph summarizing the strengths and weaknesses of the functionalist approach to the study of youth subcultures.

C3.2, C3.3

Culturalism and working-class subcultures

Functionalism made connections between the position of young people in the social structure and their cultural behaviour. However, functionalism was not very interested in the styles and fashions associated with particular youth subcultures. It was preoccupied with the functions but not the meanings of subcultures (Frith, 1984, p. 8).

The CCCS and youth subcultures

The early work of the Centre for Contemporary Cultural Studies (a group whose work is based on the **neo-Marxist** view of the work of Antonio Gramsci and his concept of **hegemony**) shifted the theoretical focus towards making connections between social structure and what particular youth subcultural styles were communicating. What messages were being communicated when somebody cropped their hair, put on a Ben Sherman shirt and a pair of Dr Marten boots?

Cultural resistance

One example of this, the famous skinhead subculture took elements of traditional working-class culture – industrial boots, braces, an emphasis on masculinity and toughness – and turned these into a style that communicated a 'two finger' message to teachers, social workers, the police and the institutions which exerted control over their lives. The mod obsession with the latest fashions and chrome-styled motor scooters conveyed the message that they considered themselves at the top rather than the bottom of the status hierarchy. In each case, according to the CCCS team, working-class youths were finding ways of expressing, through culture, their rejection of the role assigned to them by **capitalism**.

At the same time, it was argued, each style also reflected the particular social circumstances in which working-class young people found themselves. Each subculture offered a 'magical' or symbolic solution to problems which capitalism generated but which, in reality, young working-class people were powerless to do anything about.

Skinheads first emerged from the East End of London where traditional working-class communities were being destroyed by the decline of the London docks and by housing redevelopment. The skinhead subculture was an attempt to re-create the working-class community in symbolic form, through the strong emphasis on collective loyalty and defence of territory against rival mobs. Similarly, mods could not in reality solve the problem of being locked into low-status work, but the mod style of dress provided them with a symbolic or 'magical' way of claiming higher status.

The early **'culturalist'** approach of the CCCS team combined the neo-Marxist interest in hegemony theory with an interest in what the selection of items of clothing, hairstyles, music and symbols actually 'signalled' to society. Their argument was that through the construction of particular styles (skinhead, teddy-boy, and mod) the young working-class were developing a form of **cultural resistance** to the **dominant ideology** of **capitalism** (Hall and Jefferson, 1976).

Is a structural approach useful?

Sociologists talk in terms of structural approaches and cultural approaches. Broadly what is meant by these are as follows:

1. A structural approach would emphasize the way things outside of the control of the individual, and therefore not open to choice by them, affect their lives. The notion of structure suggests some degree of permanence such as the law or money or capitalism.

2. In contrast, culturalist approaches tend to emphasize the more fluid changing nature of society and its way of life or culture. Culture is in part made by the choices people make and cultural approaches tend to place more emphasis on social action and the choices people make.

The early CCCS approach was extremely influential and inspired the development of what is now known as **culturalism**. However, subsequently a number of important criticisms of this approach emerged and these highlight, amongst other issues, the question of whether structural approaches can be applied to the study of culture.

Interactionist criticisms

Stan Cohen, drawing on **interactionist** ideas, developed a sustained critique of the CCCS approach (Cohen, 1980). He made three main points:

1. He first pointed out that the CCCS team were preoccupied with the most spectacular and glamorous examples of youth subculture; the

most highly visible. But, Cohen argues, even at the height of the mod and skinhead eras, reality looked at from the point of view of most working-class youngsters was much more mundane.

2. The class structure does not simply determine the behaviour of young people in a straight-forward way. Many young working-class people did not become mods, skinheads or teddy-boys. Equally important, there were a number of middle-class youngsters who did do so, once each style had received media coverage.

3. Cohen goes on to insist that we should not lose sight of the subjects' views of reality in developing our analysis – a key symbolic interactionist idea. Did skinheads see themselves as engaging in an ideological struggle against the hegemony of capitalism; and if not, does this invalidate the CCCS approach? The problem of the status of the subjects' own points of view is something that continues to surface again and again in approaching culture and identity.

The complexity of subcultures and bricolage

Although studying at the CCCS, Hebdige (1979) developed a theoretical approach which moves away from the early work of the CCCS team. Hebdige insists that the influence of black culture and music on white working-class subcultures cannot be ignored. In the teddy-boy, mod, skinhead and punk subcultures there is a large debt to black styles, particularly through music. This prompts Hebdige to develop a theory that abandons the attempt to simply analyse youth subcultures in terms of the social class position of those involved.

1. Hebdige suggests that subcultures are actually much more complicated and involve the mixing and matching of previous subcultural styles to create new ones.

2. Further to this, Hebdige argues, they involve the process of *bricolage*, a term he borrows from anthropology to describe the way in which cultures re-use ordinary objects or commodities to create new meanings. For example, punks assembled safety pins, dustbin liner bags, chains, and other household commodities, together with items taken from entirely different contexts, such as bondage gear, to create a new subcultural style.

3. Hebdige shifts the focus of enquiry. He is interested in the way elements of culture, signs and symbols are used and reworked, rather than the links between culture and social structure.

Activity

a In what ways did the CCCS culturalist approach differ from earlier functionalist approaches?

b What did the CCCS team mean when they suggested that youth subcultures provided 'magical solutions' to structural problems? Give an example.

c Summarize in your own words the main criticisms that sociologists have made of the CCCS approach.

C3.2, C3.3

Feminist approaches to youth subcultures

The CCCS account of youth subcultures devotes very little attention to the position of girls. The picture we are presented with is one in which boys react to social structure by developing masculine cultural styles.

McRobbie and sexual bias

According to Angela McRobbie, who began her career at the CCCS, the early work of the Centre was blind to a number of key issues which a feminist re-reading of its work sharply highlights (McRobbie, 1991b).

The sexist nature of much of the culture and language of boys was ignored. There was a failure to consider the ways in which such language degraded girls and contributed to their subordination. The fascination with masculine and visible subcultures meant that the Centre ignored the important distinction between public space (the streets, the youth club, the shopping centre) and private space (the home and the bedroom). McRobbie argues that boys were able to colonize public space and marginalize girls – hence the need for 'girls' nights' at many local youth clubs.

A feminist perspective

A feminist approach would attach more importance to the domestic sphere and the politics of the family. It would explore the connections between female adolescent culture and the ways in which the family contributed to the subordination of women. McRobbie wanted to explore how young women might develop forms of cultural resistance, not only to the roles allocated to them by capitalism but also to the **patriarchal ideology** reproduced through the home, the school and the media.

McRobbie's work remains culturalist in that she draws on the theory of hegemony used by neo-Marxists, but she insists that the dimension of gender must be added to that of social class when considering patterns of cultural resistance. While McRobbie's early work focused mainly on the 'culture of the bedroom' and the ways in which young women resisted subordination within the home, her more recent work reflects important changes in the position of young women and the cultural space they have claimed.

For example, she points to the way in which black 'ragga girls' can use sexually explicit dancing in a way that ridicules male sexism and re-asserts female control over sexuality (McRobbie, 1994, pp. 183–4). According to McRobbie, despite the sexism of the lyrics in some ragga music, it is now possible for young black women to use this music to open up public cultural space for themselves.

Discussion point
Do you think that contemporary youth culture continues to be 'sexist'?

C3.1a

8.3 Theories of youth subcultures

Paul Willis and 'symbolic creativity'

In the 1980s, following the decline of punk, there appeared to be a fragmentation of youth culture. Many new cultural patterns emerged, associated with certain styles of dress and particular kinds of music, but nothing that appeared to involve young people on such a widespread and spectacularly visible scale as in the 1960s and 1970s. New romantics, goths, casuals, two-tone and mod revivalists did not seem to have the same kind of cultural power as the original skinheads, teddy-boys and punks.

The end of youth subcultures?

Paul Willis (1990) argues that the age of spectacular youth subcultures has gone for good. This is because there are now so many 'style and taste cultures' which offer young people different ways of defining identity – there is too much diversity for any single youth subculture to dominate society. The growth of capitalist culture and leisure industries has meant that almost all young people now have access to the cultural resources they need to engage in **'symbolic creativity'** in their leisure time (Willis, 1990, p. 16).

Willis draws on **unstructured interviews** (see Section 9.5) with groups of young people in the Midlands to explore the variety of ways in which they use language, clothes, music, media products, even their own bodies, to create new cultural meanings. The elaborate designs and symbols created through blacks' hair-styling provide one example. Consumption, for Willis, does not involve manipulation of a passive audience but a creative process in which young people are the active agents, often rejecting the frameworks offered by the fashion industry and using its products in highly original, even subversive ways:

If it ever existed at all, the old 'mass' has been culturally emancipated into popularly differentiated cultural citizens through exposure to a widened circle of commodity relations.

(Willis, 1990, p. 18)

Criticisms of Willis

Willis' work underlines the point that the old accounts of youth subcultures are in need of substantial revision if they are to be applied to the world of the 1990s and beyond. However, critics point to weaknesses in Willis' approach, too.

He is anxious to emphasize that everyone, not just artists, makes culture. But this leads him to work with such a wide definition of 'symbolic creativity' that almost anything could be included. He even includes the account of one young Midlander who 'jumped into the canal pissed' as an example.

His approach seriously under-estimates the extent to which powerful capitalist media and leisure conglomerates can exercise control over consumption, while over-estimating the extent to which we can seize opportunities to be creative or subversive, assuming we want to be.

Youth subcultures or neo-tribes?

The fragmentation of youth subcultures

The view that fashion and musical styles adopted by young people are too fragmented to be described as subcultures is shared by a number of sociologists who studied developments in the 1990s (Bennett, 1999; Hetherington, 1998).

Bennett shares the views of those who pointed to important flaws in the youth subculture literature of the 1960s and 1970s. The link between social class and particular youth subcultures was not confirmed by hard evidence, he believes, and often the ways in which young people, themselves, thought and talked about style, music and attitudes were overlooked. However, for Bennett, the most serious weakness associated with the concept of youth subculture is highlighted by the development of urban dance music culture in the 1990s.

Bennett conducted research in Newcastle in the early 1990s, interviewing large numbers of young clubbers, together with DJs, and others involved in the urban dance music scene in the North East. One of the most important conclusions Bennett draws from this research is that the concept of youth subculture must be rejected since the actual lives of young people may:

... be rather more fleeting and, in many cases, arbitrary, than the concept of subculture, with its connotations of coherence and solidarity, allows for.

(Bennett, 1999, p. 603)

The fluidity of dance music identities

In other words, on the dance music scene young people mix with other people from a wide range of backgrounds and musical tastes; they draw upon a number of musical and fashion influences at the same time, and do not necessarily identify with just one lifestyle and set of attitudes in the way that, perhaps, the mods or skinheads of the 1960s did. The concept of subculture, Bennett argues, suggests that young people become 'mods', 'skinheads', 'hippies' or whatever, and fiercely identify with these identities to the exclusion of other influences.

Now, he suggests, cultural identities are much less stable and much more fluid. Young people do not have such fixed commitments to just one set of cultural influences and tastes. Urban dance music, Bennett argues, contributes to this fluidity because, in its production, DJs and producers often sample a very wide variety of beats, riffs and snatches of previous tunes. The ecclectic nature of the music encourages an ecclectic approach amongst young people to dress and lifestyle. A particular preference in terms of type of music does not necesarily imply a particular visual style or appearance.

Neo-tribes

In the work of Bennett, Hetherington and other recent writers, a key difference from earlier subcultural approaches is that they reject the view that the cultural behaviour of young people is shaped or determined by social structures, such as social class.

Hetherington (1998), for example, in a study of New Age travellers, found that they came from a wide range of backgounds and certainly not from just one class position.

Both Bennett and Hetherington emphasize the element of choice in young people's cultural behaviour. Young people choose particular lifestyles, rather than being pushed into patterns of cultural behaviour by social structural influences. In Hetherington's study, for example, it was the attraction of a nomadic life, felt to be more 'authentic' than routine life in an industrial society, which encouraged young people from a variety of backgrounds to choose New Age lifestyles.

Bennett argues that a new term is required to replace 'youth subculture' in order to emphasize the elements of choice and fluidity in contemporary youth lifestyles. Drawing on the work of Maffesoli (1996), Bennett argues that we should think in terms of 'neo-tribes' rather than youth subcultures. By 'neo-tribe' Bennett means a social grouping or association with a much looser structure than implied by the term 'subculture', organized around lifestyle themes, and consumer choices, rather than a shared position in the social structure. Members of a 'neo-tribe' share a common mood or state of mind, rather than class position. Style tribes, Bennett argues, are bound up with the emergence of a mass consumer market for young people in the post-war period. He argues that even in the 1950s, 1960s and 1970s, often regarded as the 'golden age' for youth subcultures, young people were already actually exercising much more complicated choices in music, visual style and taste, than the youth subculture literature acknowledges.

8.4 Delinquency

Delinquency: a phenomenon of youth?

Gender

Bob Coles (1995) makes the following point about criminal offences:

Of those offenders who are identified by the courts or the police, four out of five (80%) are male, and almost half (47%) of the offences are committed by those under the age of 21. As far as the police and the courts are concerned, therefore, crime is predominantly an issue to do with young men.

(Coles, 1995, p. 176)

Statistics tend to suggest that youth delinquency is an activity structured by social class, gender and ethnicity. If we look first at gender we can see that delinquency is overwhelmingly a male phenomena. If we start by looking at Home Office statistics relating to custody for the period 1980–95 (Table 8.1), we can see a pronounced gender imbalance.

This would suggest that when we talk of youth delinquency we are more properly talking

Table 8.1 Young persons sentenced to immediate custody 1980–95

Year	14–16 Males	14–16 Females	17–21 Males	17–21 Females
1980	7600	100	20500	700
1985	6100	100	25700	800
1990	1700	50	1700	400
1995	2400	100	15800	500

Source: Criminal Statistics, CCJU (RDS), Home Office

Table 8.2 Ratios of male to female offenders

Crime	Male : Female Offender ratio
Serious motoring offences	30:1
Burglary	25:1
Robbery	20:1
Violence against the person	10:1
Theft and handling	3:1

Source: Moore, 1988, p. 94

of *male* youth delinquency. Youth is clearly a gendered category. Moore (1988) points out that the peak age for female crime is 13–15 while for males it is 14–18.

He goes on to provide the following ratios of male to female offenders in relation to various criminal acts, as shown in Table 8.2.

Feminist writers have however suggested that the extent of female delinquency is somehow masked (see also Section 10.4). In order to research this Campbell used self-report studies on a sample of young girls and found a ratio of 1.2:1 (males opposed to females) instead of a 7:1 ratio of offences committed.

Critics of this research did however point out that when less serious offences were removed, the clear gender differential reappeared. Committing serious offences does therefore seem to be a male phenomenon. However, males are also more likely to be victims of crime. The typical offender is someone who goes out drinking and gets involved in fights. This is however also the profile of the typical victim.

Frances Heidensohn (1985) has also suggested that the lack of female involvement may reflect the lack of opportunity to commit crime and the greater surveillance juvenile females have to face. As a result, one effect of the lessening of controls on young females may be an increase in involvement in crime and juvenile delinquency.

It is also the case that although there remains much less likelihood of women being prosecuted and convicted for crime, the rates of imprisonment are increasing and the periods for which women are being imprisoned are increasing.

Ethnicity

Black and Asian youths are much more likely to get stopped and arrested by the police than white youths. For many people this has led to the allegation that the police are in some way racist and deliberately target ethnic minorities. This view gained considerable support after the MacPherson report (1999) labelled the Metropolitan Police as 'institutionally racist' in relation to its failure to arrest and prosecute the murderers of the black teenager Stephen Lawrence.

Ruggiero *et al.* (1995) argue that the **'Fortress Europe'** policy of strict immigration controls ('Fortress Europe' refers to the fact that while the borders between member countries of the EU are becoming more relaxed, the external borders of the EU have been greatly strengthened) has led to greater controls being applied over ethnic minorities. This has also led to heavier policing and imprisonment of groups whose lifestyles are seen as a threat to order and stability. In particular, they claim, greater attention is now being paid to immigrants, asylum seekers, guest workers and foreigners.

In relation to offending and ethnicity, Tarling (1993) reports on a study by Ouston in the mid-1980s relating to young people attending schools in inner London. He found that by the age of 17, 28 per cent of boys with parents born in the UK and Eire had been either cautioned or convicted, while 39 per cent of boys born in the West Indies or of West Indian parents had been cautioned or convicted. Equivalent statistics for other ethnic groups include 24 per cent for those of Indian or Pakistani descent and 21 per cent for those of Cypriot descent.

However, Tarling (1993) goes on to point out that once factors such as social class and educational achievement are taken into account, the ethnic differences virtually disappear.

It is clearly the case that the over-representation of ethnic minorities in certain statistics relating to delinquency has led to something of a debate about the possible reasons for this. Racism on the part of the police and the **criminalization of the black community** have both been suggested as reasons for this in the work of Hall *et al.* (1979), Paul Gilroy (1982) and more recently John Solomos (1993). (See also Section 10.4.)

Class

There have been a number of studies considering the class background of offenders. Coles (1995) summarizes the findings of some of these, arguing that they point to a clear link between **material** and **social deprivation** and levels of offending. Serious offending is seen to be more prevalent among sons of manual workers and among those who live in big families. Unemployment and ill-health are also seen as factors likely to be associated with higher levels of offending and these factors are also known to be more prevalent in lower income areas than in higher income ones.

One interesting question, asked by Tuck (1993), was why young working-class males do not undertake crime in rich areas where the pickings would be much better. The research gives

no clear answers as to why they do not do this, but does suggest that notions of class justice (taking from the rich) do not seem to play a part in such proceedings.

Such findings lay open to question the usefulness of statistical **correlation** in explaining juvenile delinquency and Coles argues we need to focus much more on the process of decision-making concerned with becoming a delinquent, rather than simply looking at the social background of offenders.

The treatment of youth delinquents

Derek Kirton (1999) argues that the treatment of youth delinquents over the last thirty years is full of paradoxes, none more so than the Conservative governments of the 1980s who emphasized the need for greater and harsher punishment. But in fact during this time the number of young people in custody fell sharply, as seen in Table 8.3.

Table 8.3 Sentencing and custody rates for young offenders, 1985–95

Year	Males (10–17) Numbers sentenced (thousands)		Females (10–17) Numbers sentenced (thousands)	
	Total	Custody	Total	Custody
1985	87.2	11.5	9.8	0.2
1990	40.8	3.6	5.1	0.1
1995	37.2	4.2	5.0	0.1

Source: Criminal Statistics for England and Wales, 1995, Home Office quoted in Kirton, 1999, p. 398

Table 8.3 emphasizes the gap between rhetoric and reality in the 1980s. At the same time as **New Right** politicians were talking of the need to get tough, there was a greater use of diversionary tactics to keep youth away from the **criminal justice system**. What this meant was an increase in the number of police cautions and a desire to avoid the label of criminal being attached early in someone's life. As Kirton (1999, p. 399) put it:

Diversion was for the most part pursued away from the public gaze and stood in sharp contrast to the 'get tough' rhetoric of politicians. It was, however, sufficiently successful to underpin the Criminal Justice Act 1991's emphasis on custody only as a last resort, albeit with the quid pro quo of tougher 'punishment in the community' sentences.

Really getting tough

However this approach soon gave way to the real emergence of tough responses. A number of factors contributed to this including the re-emergence of **moral panics** about youth in terms of stories about joyriding and the persistent young offender. However, undoubtedly the most important event was the murder of James Bulger by two adolescent boys. This led to wholesale questioning of the notion of childhood innocence.

These pressures led to longer and tougher sentences and the introduction of Secure Training Centres for persistent offenders aged 12–14 and there was also talk of the introduction of US-style 'bootcamps'.

Moral panics around youth

Eadie and Morley (1999), writing from a **criminological perspective**, also note the importance of moral panics in relation to youth and delinquency. They point to the way this trend was clearly identified in the work of Pearson (1983, see below) and summarise the re-emergence of moral panics in the late 1980s and early 1990s as follows:

The deepening of the recession from the late 1980s coincided with official crime statistics published at the beginning of 1993 which showed figures for the previous year as being the second highest on record. An already disillusioned electorate sought a scapegoat. Crime, particularly that of young people, was back on the agenda. Tabloid newspapers ran stories on 'bail bandits', 'ram raiders' and 'twockers' ...

The tragic death of a 2-year-old at the hand of two truanting 10-year-old boys convinced the public that children and young persons were out of control and 'something had to be done'. The then Home Secretary, Kenneth Clarke, swiftly announced a package of measures, including the introduction of a secure training order for 12- to 14-year-old persistent offenders and a restriction on cautioning young offenders. ...

Just as the response to young people's offending in the 1960s had been to impose more treatment, the response in the 1990s was to impose more punishment.

(Eadie and Morley, 1999, p. 454)

Offenders or victims?

This trend to greater toughness reflects a partial acceptance of the notion that juveniles are responsible for the choices they make and should be held responsible. It also reflects acceptance of the notion of an **underclass** with a distinct culture as espoused by the cultural version of the underclass thesis. This can be seen as the latest in a long line of such approaches. As Kirton (1999) points out:

The last hundred years have seen a continuing debate about whether young offenders are criminals deserving punishment, or the victims of deprivation who need social care.

(Kirton, 1999, p. 397)

The argument that they are victims can be clearly seen in accounts which look at what has happened to the social context in which young people grew up in the 1980s and 1990s. The transition from school to work has become more problematic with the massive rise in youth unemployment. Ashton (1986) points out that using the **ILO** definition of unemployment, the rate for those under 25 rose from 4 per cent in 1960 to 5.9 per cent in 1970, 12.2 per cent in 1979 and 21.4 per cent in 1981, and Finn (1987) shows that in the late 1970s, while overall unemployment grew by 40 per cent, for those under 20 it grew by 120 per cent.

The problems of unemployment and deprivation, which became a feature of the 1980s and 1990s in the UK, thus seem to have hit young people hardest in many ways. Faced with this, and in the face of all the deprivation and exclusion faced by young people and particularly the continuing problem of homelessness it seems more logical to ask:

not why are there so many crimes committed in inner-city areas; it is, rather, why aren't there more? It says something extraordinary about the English character that these armies of young people sit peacefully to beg. They similarly make extraordinary attempts to keep clean. They queue quietly in supermarkets to get their sliced white bread and margarine and then walk peacefully away. Some drink. It is amazing they don't all want to stay drunk all the time. It is equally amazing that most of us shuffle past them in embarrassment.

(Field, 1993, p. 72, quoted in Jeffs and Smith, 1995, p. 69)

This places questions about youth much more clearly on the plane of questions about the conditions and causes of their condition, rather than the behaviour they may sometimes engage in.

Despite this, the concern over juvenile offending remains.

New Labour and toughness

This new rhetoric about crime and youth offending became **common ground** when **New Labour** refused to be outclassed by the Conservatives on law and order and adopted the slogan 'tough on crime, tough on the causes of crime'. This approach can be seen, Kirton (1999) argues, in the Crime and Disorder Act 1998. This Act included provisions to remove the presumption that children under 14 did not know right from wrong and replaced the system of cautions with a system based on two warnings only. It also allowed curfews for children under 10. Youth offending teams, including social workers, probation officers and police officers, were to be created in local areas and a National Youth Justice Board set up.

The fall in juvenile offences

It is in this context that it is possible to understand the sometimes despairing tone of those who argue that things are getting better. For instance, Jeffs and Smith (1998) argue that:

Given the general air of despondency enveloping this topic [young people, crime and control] and tenor of public debate it is often difficult to convince many that the available evidence indicates things are getting better rather than worse. Certainly the number of young offenders aged 10 to 17 known to have committed **indictable offences** *in England and Wales has declined in recent years. In 1993, 129,500 young offenders aged 10 to 17 were cautioned or found guilty of indictable offences compared with 204,600 a decade earlier. The fall in the number of young offenders during this period far exceeded the decline in the relevant population cohort which was only 19 per cent. Interestingly, whereas politicians and the media previously accepted as accurate the statistical evidence collected on the same basis when it confirmed their belief juvenile offending was escalating out of control, they now refuse to do so.*

(Jeffs and Smith, 1998, p. 66)

This is an example of the way that moral panics around youth continue to be constructed. This in itself is not a new phenomenon, as an investigation of the historical dimension will reveal.

Violent youth: an old or new fear?

Imperfect memories?

According to Pearson (1983), what the fears of rising crime illustrate is the temptation for each generation, especially those of the post-middle-age bracket, to look back through rose-tinted glasses and with nostalgia at the past: to see society before the present unruly age to be a golden age where all was at peace and harmony reigned.

When viewed in this fashion, current trends in criminal statistics immediately take on new possibilities and interpretations. Do they represent not so much a genuine increase in the amount of crime, but rather the increased reporting and awareness of crime – the result of fear of the present age, reflected in and reinforced by the media?

Moral panics and hooliganism

Pearson comments that modern-day fears of football hooliganism are nothing new, and in fact date back to at least the mid-nineteenth century. Pitch invasions, attacks on referees and players and conflicts between rival fans were a regular feature in local newspapers of the time.

Pearson dates the word 'hooligan' back to the summer of 1898 (as illustrated by the pen and ink drawing from *Punch* that year), when it was used in newspaper headlines to describe the activities of youths during the August Bank Holiday. Pearson suggests that the word may have been first popularized within the music halls in the 1890s.

Is delinquency 'normal'?

Whereas we frequently read stories in the tabloid press regarding the 'mindless' anti-authority behaviour of young people, it is important to try to take this behaviour seriously and to try to understand it, rather than just a knee-jerk, politicised reaction to this behaviour. Sociology has been seriously attacked by some – especially from the New Right (see Section 2.1) – for what is seen as its 'dangerous' and 'anti-authoritarian' bias: sociology is seen to be dangerous to young minds, contributing to a general decline of discipline and moral standards in society.

Sociology is often seen to side with the **deviant** too often, finding academic explanations

A REMEDY FOR RUFFIANS
Hooligan. 'What are you up to, Guv'nor!'
Policeman. 'I'm going to introduce you to the
"harmless, necessary Cat"!'
Source: *Punch*, 10 September 1898

for behaviour which is sometimes dangerous, violent and which frequently causes great distress in society. Although some sociologists might be guilty of such 'romanticization' of the delinquent and the gang member, it is still important to note that understanding does not necessarily mean supporting or glamorizing.

David Matza

For David Matza (1964) delinquent activity is a 'normal' and very usual aspect of youthful behaviour. It does not indicate a criminal tendency, nor does it mean that the individuals involved will become 'hardened criminals' later in life. Instead, he describes young people as 'drifting' both in and out of delinquent behaviour on a periodic basis. Delinquents are not unusual – they are not a separate or specific type of person. Those defined and labelled as delinquents by police, schools and social services are simply those who have been identified and caught. Many other teenagers also engage in this behaviour as a 'normal' part of teenage life.

Matza draws a distinction between two types

of values, which young people hold at different times:

1 the 'normal', dominant values of a society
2 the **subterranean values** – those that lead to delinquency.

It is not the cases that individuals have either one set of values or the other. Instead, teenagers drift in and out of both. They have 'normal' moments and also 'deviant' moments. This observation in fact makes the whole notion of 'deviant' a problem since if it is commonplace and normal then it simply cannot be 'deviant' in the first place!

Matza is interested in how these 'normal' delinquents are able to justify their behaviour to themselves and others – given that they drift in and out of different patterns of behaviour. These methods of self-justification are described as 'techniques of neutralization', meaning that once the individual drifts back into 'normality' he or she is able to make sense of the deviant behaviour by writing it off as 'an unusual incident' or even that 'everyone else does it'.

Marxist explanations of delinquency

A common theme that runs throughout a great deal of **Marxist** discussions of crime and deviance in general – including delinquency itself – is the idea that one can only be judged (or labelled) as 'deviant' according to a set of standards that themselves are regarded as normal. This reflects the observations of Howard Becker who notes that deviance, as such, is not the actual action one performs, but rather the social reaction to the initial action.

Marxists note that delinquency is a term used to refer to working-class youthful acts, rather than to middle-class 'high spirits'. This argument is further reflected in the Marxist observation that working-class men are more likely to appear in the crime statistics because the law enforcement agencies are more likely to define them as being a problem in the first place. Thus, working-class boys are more likely to be 'caught' and charged as 'delinquents' since this fits in with the cultural class-based stereotypes used by police officers to make their job meaningful.

8.5 Gangs

Like delinquency, youth sub-cultures and 'neo-tribal membership' gang culture is seen to provide a meaningful worldview and a stable sense of reality for those involved. Membership of such groups might be based upon **'deviant values'** but such membership still offers a sense of community, togetherness and a way of making sense of the world around and one's place within such a world.

Again, like delinquency and sub-cultural membership in general, gang membership and culture is often the source of moral panics. As noted by Pearson (1983) earlier in this chapter, violent crime has been a feature of society for a very long time – it is not a recent phenomena.

Discussion point

a Identify and explain two moral examples of moral panics in reltion to gangs.

b Outline and discuss the view that concern about the activities of gangs is merely a moral panic.

C3.2, C3.3

Activity

Read the article below.

a Identify and describe two problems arising from the activities of child gangs.

b Outline and discuss the view that teenage criminals create no-go zones.

C3.2, C3.3

Gangs of mods and rockers

A classic example of a moral panic is provided by Stanley Cohen in his book *Folk Devils and Moral Panics* (1980), first published in 1972. Cohen's research of the 1964 mods and rockers disorders at British seaside towns, most notably during Easter bank holidays at Clacton, illustrates the extent to which media sensationalization can have an effect on audiences, including the public, police and the government.

Council acts to bust teen gangs

WILL WOODWARD

Nottingham Council is set to become the first in Britain to hire police officers full time in a new effort to break up youth gangs which are plaguing city estates. Its 'gang-busting' team will tackle the groups, which include children as young as six.

A 14-year-old from the Bulwell estate, nicknamed Dangermouse, recently became the youngest person in the country to be placed under an anti-social behaviour order after being arrested more than 100 times, and convicted 55 times, for offences including assault, burglary and threatening behaviour.

Nottingham's problems are no worse than those of comparable cities, the council said, but complaints about child gangs are on the rise, accounting for nearly half the complaints about anti-social behaviour in the city.

Two police officers will join the council to work full time, mainly in plain clothes on surveillance work. The council wants to prosecute ring-leaders and prevent other youngsters from being drawn into gangs.

Assuming, as expected, that the plan receives backing from the full council, the police officers will join a 12-strong group disorder unit.

'It shows our faith in the police. Other councils have gone down the route of private security but we want the real thing and people with real powers,' the council leader, Graham Chapman, said. 'We don't want to end up with housing estates that are no-go zones because of teenage criminals.'

The unit will extend the use of anti-social behaviour orders and curfews. It will work with the local youth crime reduction agency, which involves council departments and voluntary organisations. The scheme adds £120,000 to the city's £382,000 budget for tackling anti-social behaviour.

Lawrie Heighway, the council's anti-social behaviour team leader, said the police were committed to dealing with teenage gangs but numbers were stretched. The new scheme would guarantee police who could work exclusively on the problem.

Adapted from The *Guardian*, 11 January 2000

Figure 8.1 Mods, Clacton, 1964

Figure 8.2 Rockers, 1960

Media moral panics

Cohen demonstrates that the newspaper accounts of these riots tell stories of horrific terror, chaos and large-scale rioting. Clacton was pictured as being at the total mercy of rival gangs who, through mob behaviour, destroyed property, intimated the public and fought with one another.

Although these images may have become more and more familiar on subsequent occasions, they were by no means a true account of the first mods and rocker disturbances. Cohen argues that there were no opposed rival gangs until after the media moral panic had begun. There were minimal numbers of motorbikes and scooters used by these young people – their so-called main symbol of group membership – and the most serious offences originally committed were nothing more than threatening behaviour and minor vandalism.

Amplification of gangs

However, owing to over-reporting, a self-fulfilling prophecy had been created whereby more members of the public became worried, police activity was increased as a response, and young people themselves created and joined these gangs that had been presented to them by the media as a fashionable and exciting lifestyle option.

Girl gangs

Kenneth Thompson (1998) notes that there has been a rise recently in media moral panics con-

cerning 'girl gangs'. We can locate this panic within a general media concern with so-called 'rising female violence' and with an increase in the media – and in films in particular – of images of strong, violent women, so-called 'shebos' after the 1980s action character 'rambo', and with the 'feminist' film *Thelma and Louise*.

Mary Kearney (1998) locates the rise of girl gangs – and in particular the mainly American 'Riot grrrl' subculture – as a reflection of postmodern times. What this means is that girl gangs – as political movements and forms of symbolic cultural resistance – are a product of the decline of class-based politics and rise of 'lifestyle politics' often associated with the rise of new social movements.

In such a post-modern world, identity is freed from a limited number of sources (such as class, gender, nationality) and instead we have a plurality of rapidly changing identities. The creation of how one lives one's life, one's sexuality and even what and how one consumes becomes a matter of free political choice. We come to define who we are by how we live. Within this context, membership of girl gangs offers post-modern teenagers the chance to resist previous patriarchal limited forms of identity: to define who they are afresh and often by incorporating previously 'male' forms of behaviour. (See also Section 4.1.)

The arguments of Kearney reflect those made by the CCCS previously – and of Hebdige in particular. These ideas have been found to be particularly useful in discussing gang membership since they locate such struggles into ideas of symbolic resistance and see the creation of these lifestyles as an active, self-aware process on behalf of the individuals themselves.

Discussion point

Many sociological studies of gangs use the method of participant observation. Why do you think this might be the case?

C3.1a

Activity

Read the article below.

a Identify and explain two ways in which young people have been involved in local schemes to improve their area.

b Outline and discuss the view that youth are much better at dealing with crime in their local area than adults.

C3.2, C3.3

STREET-WISE TEENAGERS FIGHT YOUTH CRIME
We know what gangs get up to, say youngsters masterminding estate projects

MARTIN WAINWRIGHT

An effective antidote to youth crime is given in a report on recruiting teenagers to turn round localities blighted by their contemporaries' vandalism, violence and theft.

Two years of pilot schemes have found that local young people, unemployed and many without school qualifications, can reach disaffected gangs and broker deals with adult authorities on their behalf.

Crime and fear of crime have dropped in districts ranging from Swansea to Bradford, according to the independent Local Government Information Unit, after the formation of youth action groups, funded by a range of charities and other agencies but run by under-25s. On a vandalized Bradford estate, emergency calls have dropped from more than 10 a week to nil after a youth team spent six months working with a gang that had targeted a parade of shops.

The key to success has been recruiting street-wise young people and genuinely taking their advice and acting on it, said the report, *Taking Part*, published by the information unit and the National Association for the Care and Resettlement of Offenders.

'The central complaint of most children and young people who have had difficult experiences is that they were not listened to or involved,' said the report. Chris Bosley, the youth worker heading the Bradford project, called the five young women and seven youths in her team 'incredibly clear headed and effective'. She said: 'We adults have a habit of saying "God, I don't believe that goes on", but these kids are out there and they know that it does, and why it does. And that's a start in dealing with it.'

The findings are the first national response to the 1997 Crime and Disorder Act, encouraging 'young people and children to take part in deciding how to tackle crime at local, community and neighbourhood level'.

Hilary Kitchin of the information unit toured experiments where teenagers had become policymakers and an informal community police force. 'These examples show how you can bring about a change in attitude if you listen to what young people have to say. They set out guidelines that are the opposite of the old idea young people should be seen but not heard.'

In Wolverhampton there are 'primary school parliaments' and in Swansea there is a teenage 'action against crime squad'. Common to schemes, said the report, was a recognition young people knew about street life and were much more credible as problem solvers to their contemporaries.

The report, sent to all local councils, pointed out young people were far more likely to experience violent crime – affecting 21% of 16 to 24-year-olds in 1997, compared with 5% of the general population, but the public persistently focused on youth involvement in crime, possibly deterring policy-makers from consulting young people in finding solutions. 'Adults appear to make strong connections between crime, young people and the disintegration of the community,' it said. 'It is important to be clear on the facts of youth crime, and to avoid these assumptions which feed negative views of young people and what they have to offer.'

The report highlighted the hidden ingredient of such youth schemes which emerged when word had spread on the streets that young people played more than a token role, and that trust was genuinely devolved from adults.

Team members also benefited themselves, with nine of the 13 members of Bradford's first group taking university degrees in social work or specialist teaching after doing A levels on the two year project.

Source: adapted from *Guardian*, 30 May 2000

8.6 Theories of delinquent subcultures

Subculture is a central concept in many sociological analyses of deviance – and in particular delinquency. This concept has been adopted by functionalist, Marxist and **interactionist** theorists and refers to the existence, within society, of smaller groups with their own identities, some of which are compatible with wider social values, others of which can be seen as being antagonistic.

The Chicago School

The Chicago School refers to what was the first large-scale and lasting Anglo-American sociology department, opened in 1892 and based at the University of Chicago. The first chairperson of the School, Albion Small, modelled the department along the lines of a typical German university: the lecturers employed were required to conduct many research programmes in the surrounding areas and to give regular seminars.

The School was thus not just a sociology department *in* Chicago, it was a sociology department *of* Chicago. Its members were encouraged to investigate their surroundings. Given that these were the city of Chicago, and its associated subcultures of criminality and deviance, there was a rich, full and easily accessible source for these beginnings in organized criminology. The School was made up of a wide diversity of academics with varying interests, united by one common goal – the understanding of deviant subcultures in Chicago.

Park: 'urban ecology'

A central, early approach to the study of deviant and delinquent subcultures is known variously as the 'ecological perspective' or 'urban ecology'. This is often associated with Robert Park, a student at the Chicago School in the late 1800s and later its head. Park borrowed the idea of ecology from biology: the idea that in the natural world plants, animals and other lifeforms exist in a pattern with each other. Some crops grow better when nearer to others, some insects develop in habitats in which others die. The land is seen as a giant set of connections and interrelationships – an ecological system.

Concentric circle model of the city

This idea of a system was certainly in keeping with functionalist ideas of a social system which were developing at about this time. Park took the idea of ecology and applied it to the hidden and inner workings of the city. He contended that the city could best be understood as a series of concentric circles or zones. Around the outside of a city we have at the periphery the commuter belt or outer suburbs, then the middle-class residential suburbs, then the working-class housing district, and finally the inner city, part of the zone of transition (see Figure 8.3). This label was chosen to reflect the rapid flux of people moving in and out of the central area. At the very centre of the city, in the middle of these concentric circles, is the central business district.

The members of the Chicago School concentrated their research into deviance in the zone of transition, supposing it to contain the highest amounts of deviant, criminal and delinquent activity. The slum-style cheap housing and rapid patterns of migration and immigration were imagined to contribute to a lack of community feeling in this zone. This lack of community was in turn thought to contribute to increased levels of crime.

A return to functionalism?

In many respects, this theory represents a return to the idea of *anomie*: the lack of clear norms

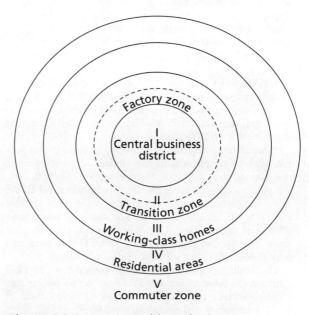

Figure 8.3 Burgess' zonal hypothesis.
Source: Barak (1994)

and values in the inner city is seen to be to blame for deviance. *Anomie* exists in the centre of the city because the rapid turnover of the population does not allow ties to be established.

Discussion point

a In what ways are cities like living, growing entities?

b How and why are cities more prone to deviance than other areas?

C3.1a

Sutherland: 'differential association'

Edwin Sutherland, another member of the Chicago School writing in the early to middle 1900s, studied the higher levels of deviance in the central zone. He suggested that much deviance could be explained by 'differential association' – the contact with others already involved in criminal activities. In this way, young people learn the ways of crime by copying and joining in with the activities of older and established criminals.

Criticisms of the Chicago School's position

A number of criticisms can be raised. Principally, the idea of the zone of transition does not explain what is known as 'white collar' crime, which by definition would not take place in working-class areas. Moreover, a number of the School's ideas are based on the proposition that crime is a response to social disorganization, but we could argue that some criminal activities are very organized.

Merton: strain theory

Functionalist-based ideas such as *anomie* had an effect also on the work of Robert Merton. Writing in the mid-1930s, Merton understood crime and deviance to be a response to the inability to achieve **cultural goals**. This is often referred to as a 'strain theory' of crime, since Merton highlights a tension or strain between:

- the cultural goals of a society
- the legitimate or institutionalized means to achieve these goals.

Merton's work can be seen to be influenced by the 'American Dream': provided one works hard, successes such as a good job, money, a good house and a luxurious lifestyle can be yours. Merton argued that while most poeple fully accepted the norms and values of American society, in reality many lacked the realistic possibilities to achieve the American Dream, and as a result, feel a tension in their lives. A **dysfunction** of this strain is deviance.

Discussion point
How is it possible that society causes problems or tensions for some of its members?

C3.1a

Varieties of deviant responses

Merton suggested the following five main ways (the last four of which are deviant) in which individuals may respond to the strain between goals and the means of achieving them in society:

1 *Conformity*. Even though the goals may be accepted but the means to achieve them are unavailable, the rules of society are still followed. This is therefore not a deviant response.

2 *Innovation*. An individual accepts the goals but is unable to achieve the means. Instead, the goals are sought through alternative, illegitimate (deviant) methods such as robbery.

3 *Ritualism*. Some individuals, although aware that they will never achieve the goals despite having some of the means, continue to work within the system, but never aspire to reach any higher or to develop any further. These people simply go through the motions, in a job for example, and lose sight of the goals. Merton classifies this as a deviant response.

4 *Retreatism*. Those who lack the means and have not accepted the goals may drop out of (retreat from) society, possibly becoming recluses or turning to alcohol or other drug abuse.

5 *Rebellion*. Some individuals reject the dominant social goals and the means to achieve them, but then replace these with their own set of values. This could explain acts of politically motivated terrorism or freedom fighting.

Merton is highly critical of driving social values in western societies, based as they are on what he sees as competition and greed. He suggests that this encourages individuals to break the law:

Criticisms of Merton's position

Although Merton develops many different

explanations of deviant behaviour, he treats deviant responses as exclusively the actions of individuals. He therefore fails to take into consideration the highly communal aspects of some deviance. He ignores the evidence that deviant subcultures exist. These subcultures may well respond to the world along similar lines to those outlined by Merton, but they must be seen as *collective* responses.

Activity

a After thinking about Merton's ideas of the strain between the goals of a society and the means to achieve them, compile three lists as follows:

(i) the dominant goals of contemporary society in the UK

(ii) those groups who may lack the means to achieve the goals you have identified

(iii) contemporary groups who fit one or more of Merton's four deviant responses to social situations.

b Does the idea of strain help to explain the criminal activities of some groups in society?

C3.2, C3.3

The influence of Merton

Other American sociologists, especially within the middle to late 1950s, have taken issue with Merton's emphasis on deviance as an individual's response. Cohen (1955) and Cloward and Ohlin (1960), for example, understand deviance to be a collective solution by like-minded and like-situated individuals to structurally imposed problems. By this they mean that deviance – and especially delinquency – is the result of groups being excluded from the goals of society because of their position in the social structure – usually a class position. Therefore, these writers equate a lower class position with crime and delinquency.

Cohen argues that, although groups of working-class youths may originally accept the wider social goals, their growing awareness of their inability to achieve the goals leads to the development of status-frustration, where the goals are ultimately rejected. Instead, new and deviant goals are created and a delinquent subculture is formed.

Cloward and Ohlin take these ideas further. They contend that as well as legitimate opportunities varying for the successful achievement of wider social goals, illegitimate opportunities also differ. Thus, some young people are able to join a local gang, or to take up a life of crime, but others lack even these choices. These individuals become double-failures and often retreat into a life of violence, drug-abuse, etc.

Marxist theories of youth subcultures

As we have seen, the concept of subculture was first developed to explain the rise of distinctive behaviour among young people by functionalist sociologists. The functionalist argument was that the period of youth represented a time of transition when young people were allowed more freedom by society to try out various identities. This was a subcultural force propelling them to behave in certain ways leading to the creation of distinctive subcultures. However, the key explanations of deviance using subcultural theory still assumed that these subcultures shared some important norms and values of mainstream society.

The meaning of youth working class style

The structural approach characteristic in functionalist analysis (from where classical subcultural theory emerges) was shared by Marxists who felt that something more than the individual or group motivations of individuals was needed to explain deviant behaviour. However, they did not wish to see individual people merely as puppets of wider structural forces and as such took on board insights developed by interactionist sociologists and the Chicago School.

This led to the development of theories which emphasized both the wider social and structural context in which youth deviant behaviour took place but also the meaning attributed to certain forms of behaviour such as styles of dress, music or criminal activities by the participants. These meanings could then be interpreted by sociologists to provide a coherent explanation of youth deviant subcultures.

Hegemony and conflict

The key development leading to the emergence of Marxist subcultural theory was the setting up of the Centre for Contemporary Cultural Studies (CCCS) at Birmingham University. This group sought to distance themselves from notions that the working class had been brought off with a dominant ideology and had been turned into a passive mass addicted to bingo, sex, alcohol and TV.

They utilized the work of Italian Marxist Antonio Gramsci who argued that all of us have contradictory ideas in our head, some of which push us to follow the conventions of the rulers of society and some of which push us to do what we feel to be right. He argued that this led to a struggle over ideas and behaviour in society that was fought over in the cultural arena. Those ideas and cultures that became influential were said to have achieved hegemony and his argument led to the conclusion that Marxists and the working-class could and should engage with popular culture to develop cultural resistance and struggle against capitalism.

This insight led to sociologists from and influenced by the CCCS going out to explore working-class subcultures using the CCCS ideas of seeing popular culture as a form of resistance to capitalism, shown particularly in the book *Resistance through Rituals* (Hall and Jefferson, 1976.) Because they were Marxists, social class was seen as the most important factor and so they emphasized the need to study working class culture.

The freedom of youth

One way in which it was suggested that the working-classes had been bought off was by the rise of affluence and consumerism. Theories of the mass society did not present it as an unpleasant phenomenon, but on the contrary as consisting in cheap package holidays to Spain, more sport on TV and home ownership. However, the commitment to mortgages and credit payments also tied people into the system and made them afraid to rebel. Marx said that workers had nothing to lose but their chains, but some now maybe felt that in fact they had their houses, their cars and their holidays to lose.

However, this did not apply to youth who had not reached the stage when these issues were important. They therefore also remained free of the chains created by mortgages and regular credit payments. It is for this reason that youth were seen as the group least affected by the hegemony of ruling-class ideas and were therefore the groups most likely to rebel against capitalism.

The problem of youth and resistance

The life of youths was not one long party, however. The period of transition when they were relatively free as identified by earlier functionalist writers did have some validity. However, this period was originally written about in the 1950s when the economy was booming and there were plenty of jobs to go around. As such, although the transition from youth to adulthood took a long time, a central element in this transition, namely that from school to work, was relatively unproblematic.

By the 1970s, mass youth unemployment had arrived and a job could no longer always be easily found. Mass youth unemployment fuelled the resentment of young people at being excluded from 'the good things' in life but also maybe made them less likely to rebel since getting a job was now no longer so easy. Young people had to cope with this reality as well as making some statement about how they felt. It is at this point that Marxist writers argue that their creation of various subcultures through dress, style and music also represent a form of resistance to capitalism. Such resistance can also include deviant and criminal activities.

Hebdige (1979), in *Subculture: the meaning of style*, particularly argues that working-class culture is about both coping with the situation and also actively resisting capitalism, through showing disdain for the dominant values of society. Such deviant and criminal behaviour as is involved in this can thus be analysed as part of the class struggle. One key example of this would be the skinhead culture that developed in Britain; and could also characterize the punk movement of the early 1980s in such a way.

Phil Cohen and East Enders

One key example of the study of youth utilizing the neo-Marxist approach first developed by the CCCS was the study of East End culture by Phil Cohen (1972). He argued that there had been a fantastic level of change in the East End of London through various factors, such as:

• the loss of jobs on the docks,

• the decline of the extended family networks,

• the redevelopment of large areas leading to the removal of old 'slums' and the construction of large numbers of tower blocks.

All of this was taking place at the same time as large-scale economic changes in the 1960s led to greater levels of affluence. This provided the

Figure 8.4 Skinheads

basis for people to consume goods in a way that had not been possible before for working-class people

Skinheads and mods

Cohen argues that the two key subcultures that arose out of the working class, the skinheads and the mods, represent contrasting reactions to this situation. The mods based themselves on looking good with sharp suits and shiny bikes with lots or mirrors and accessories. The image created suggested they wanted people to know they now had money. In contrast, the skinhead sub-culture was based on the industrial clothing found in the world of employment that no longer existed. This subculture was therefore more a reflection of the feeling of a loss of community.

Stanley Cohen and the interactionist approach

The key interactionist work looking at youth sub-cultures was Stanley Cohen's *Folk Devils and Moral Panics*. In this book and in other work he is highly critical of Marxists who go around inter-preting all forms of youth behaviour as part of the resistance to capitalism and the class struggle. Instead he argues that their behaviour should be explained in their own words, a method he sought to demonstrate in his *Folk Devils and Moral Panics*.

This book and the dialogue it created between Marxist and interactionist writers has had an impact since many of the CCCS writers have taken over elements of the interactionist account presented by Stanley Cohen. One key example of this is the work of Stuart Hall and others on the way that policing in the 1970s could be said to rely on the development of a moral panic about mugging allowing a much more aggressive style of policing to attempt to legitimate itself.

Mugging: hegemony and ideology – the work of Stuart Hall et al.

Hall and his colleagues, in their book *Policing the Crisis: Mugging, the State, and Law and Order* (1978), criticize what they see as the exaggerated and at times racist reporting of black criminality in the British popular press. In taking the exam-ple of an apparent dramatic increase in mugging in the 1970s, Hall *et al.* suggest that official crime figures can be used as political weapons at times of economic crisis to justify a failing capitalist economy. In this way, a myth or illusion of black street crime has been created to act as a scape-goat, to draw the publics attention away from the real social problems of the time: unemployment, inflation, etc.

The mugging moral panic

We are concerned with mugging but as a social phenomenon, rather than as a particular form of street crime. We want to know what the social causes of mugging are. But we argue that this is only half, less than half, of the mugging story. More important is why British society reacts to mugging, in the extreme way it does, at that precise historical conjuncture – the early 1970s. If it is true that muggers suddenly appear on British streets – a fact which, in that stark simplicity, we contest – it is also true that the society enters a moral panic about mugging. And this relates to the larger panic about the steadily rising rate of violent crime which has been growing through the 1960s. And both these panics are about other things than crime, per se. The society comes to perceive crime in general, and mugging in particular, as an index of the disintegration of the social order, as a sign that the British way of life is coming apart at the seams.

(Hall *et al.*, 1978, pp. vii–viii)

As this extract illustrates, a moral panic (see Section 15.5) developed in the UK in the 1970s, sponsored or created by the media, government and police, regarding a new form of crime from America, previously unheard of in Britain – mug-ging. This developed into a moral panic con-cerning the safety of our streets, which ultimately led to a widespread belief that a previously golden age of law and order had come to an end.

Hall and his co-writers suggest, however, that mugging is simply a new name for a very old crime, that of street robbery with violence. As Pearsons' *Hooligan: A History of Respectable Fears* (1983) illustrates, violent crime has a long history in Britain, whatever its name might be. (See Section 8.4)

The crisis of capitalism

What is particularly interesting, notes Hall and colleagues, is the particular time when this moral panic occurred – it coincided with a period in the UK's economic history that they describe as a *crisis*. These two factors are seen to be linked: rising economic problems and rising so-called new street crimes are, in the media, blamed on the black population – so avoiding a more serious crisis in confidence in capitalism amongst the white British population.

> ### 🗩 Discussion point
>
> **a** Why does capitalism lead to periods of crisis?
>
> **b** How might capitalism deal with these periods of crisis?
>
> C3.1a

Crisis and hegemony

A legitimation crisis is avoided: the government's right to rule, and more significantly the ruling élite's capitalist economic policies, are preserved. Hall *et al.* do not suggest that this antagonism amongst the white working-classes against the black working-class is deliberately created – it does, however, serve well the purposes of the ruling economic élite at this crisis time.

These writers note that the moral panic has resulted in ever-increasing military models of policing where we see a shift from a community-based approach towards a reactionary police force, capable of responding with speed and force to violent situations, yet largely invisible to the general population and increasingly trusted less. This is a model of modern policing that has alienated both the white and black sections of the working classes.

Feminist views on youth subculture

One major criticism of all approaches to explanations of youth delinquency based on subcultural ideas was that it ignored gender, that it developed theories in which either women were invisible or alternatively in which studies of male youth were presented as if they were studies of all youth.

This was seen as being as true of the Marxist-inspired work of the CCCS as of the earlier functionalist inspired work. Not surprisingly, this led to feminist criticism of the subcultural approach and the development of a distinctly feminist approach to youth delinquency.

Angela McRobbie and the criticism of the subcultural approach

It is the work of Angela McRobbie (1978) which has probably done most to underline the absence of a consideration of women from the work of the CCCS and other neo-Marxist writers. She started out by considering the reproduction of gender inequalities, utilizing some of the ideas developed by Paul Willis but also being critical of him.

Willis' classic study (1977) specifically sought to study the resistance of the 'lads', a group of working-class boys in a secondary school in the Midlands. He asked the question 'How do working-class kids get working-class jobs?' (what he meant in fact was boys!).

Willis showed that the resistance these lads displayed to schooling came from their working-class culture which prized manual over mental labour. Despite the fact that the lads enjoyed bunking off and making teachers' lives difficult, their resistance was ultimately reproductive as they ended up in manual jobs as a result of the absence of qualifications.

The cult of femininity

McRobbie (1978) carried out a similar study of working-class girls in a youth club. She found that these girls also regarded school as a place to celebrate their culture of femininity by smoking, gossiping about the boys they fancied, playing up teachers (sometimes using their sexuality). They dismissed successful middle-class girls as 'swots' or 'snobs' with whom they could compete academically but chose not to. Their response to schooling both liberated and trapped them by reproducing gender and class relations. Their future roles as wives, mothers and low-paid workers loomed large in their lives. McRobbie did report that feminist teachers could have a role in challenging the inevitability of such futures.

Willis has been criticized for ignoring girls, and for celebrating the 'lads'culture' of masculinity despite its sexism and racism. He also ignored the conformist boys in the study – the 'earoles'. Clearly the second criticism echoes the interactionist criticisms of Marxist inspired work, while the first points to the feminist criticism that studies of youth were in fact only studies of boys.

Females as a civilizing influence

As well as arguing that there was a need to study female youth groups as well as males, researchers on youth crime have also wanted to consider the interactions between women and men, and the impact this has on criminal activity.

Janet Foster (1990) argues that women are very much a civilizing influence on men. While women do want a good education and a job, they also want good relationships and are arguably much more influenced by this desire than are young men. However insofar as young men do want to have relationships with young women, then the creation of such stable relationships may often be the transition which makes young men cease to engage in criminal activities. Women in this instance therefore act as a civilizing influence on young men, and place clear limits on their criminal activities. Clearly this suggests that gender relationships may have a role to play in explaining the extent of youth delinquency. It further undermines the usefulness of studies of youth delinquency that were based solely on the activities of males, without taking into account in any detailed way their relationships with women, and the way this can impact on male behaviour.

8.7 Experiences of schooling

Eearly studies in the sociology of education and studies of adolescents in an educational context sought to explain events on the basis of structures external to the school, notably the family and class background of pupils. However, interactionist inspired accounts argued for the need to try to understand the way that interaction between teachers, pupils and pupil subcultures affected the experience of schooling. This section considers some recent studies outlining the experiences of schooling of diverse groups of pupils.

Cultural reproduction, resistance and accommodation

One key concern with the experiences of pupils in schools is their reaction to school rules and order. Do they accept these or reject them? Marxist-influenced writers tend to suggest children should reject them since they see them as preparing children for the world of work. Rebellion at school therefore might be seen as **resistance** to capitalism. However, merely rebelling might ensure you get no qualifications and therefore end up in a poorly paid job. Such actions could therefore be said to end up reproducing the existing structure of capitalism. In some instances people may rebel and also fit in to some degree to try to gain their own ends, such as qualifications. This would be called resistance with **accommodation**. These three terms: resistance, **reproduction** and accommodation, are therefore used to refer to different ways that pupils react to schooling and the effects of their reactions. Paul Willis and Angela McRobbie provide evidence of reproduction occurring in schools, while Jean Anyon adds the concept of accommodation and Paul Aggleton talks about resistance among middle-class pupils. These studies are considered in detail below.

Paul Willis

Willis' classic study (1977) specifically sought to study the resistance to schooling of the 'lads', a group of working-class boys in a secondary school in the Midlands. He asked the question: 'How do working-class kids get working-class jobs?' (what he meant in fact was boys!). Willis showed that the resistance these lads displayed to schooling came from their working-class culture which prized manual over mental labour. Despite the fact that the lads enjoyed bunking off and making teachers' lives difficult, their resistance to order was ultimately **reproductive culturally** of the capitalist hierarchy and order, as they ended up in manual jobs as a result of the absence of qualifications.

Angela McRobbie

McRobbie (1978) carried out a similar study of working-class girls in a youth club. She found that these girls also regarded school as a place to celebrate their culture of femininity by smoking, gossiping about the boys they fancied, and playing up teachers (sometimes using their sexuality). They dismissed successful middle-class girls as 'swots' or 'snobs' with whom they could compete academically but chose not to. Their response to schooling both liberated and trapped them by culturally reproducing gender and class relations. Their future roles as wives, mothers and low-paid workers loomed large in their lives. McRobbie did report that feminist teachers could have a role in challenging the inevitability of such futures.

Both the foregoing studies were very important in identifying the complex and contradictory nature of **social** and **cultural reproduction**. Willis has been criticized for ignoring girls, and for celebrating the lads' culture of masculinity despite its sexism and racism. He also ignored the conformist lads in the study – the 'earoles'. It would have been interesting to compare their destinations with those of the lads to see whether conformity and qualifications made a difference.

Ethnographic approaches

Using **ethnography** (see Section 9.5) was very productive. The **ethnographic data** produced a richly detailed picture of working-class children's experiences of schooling, giving them a voice. This work has inspired further study and the development of social and cultural reproduction theory – in Australia the work of Connell *et al.* (1982), and in the USA that of Anyon (1983).

Anyon added the useful concept of 'accommodation'. Her study of girls in five elementary schools found that the girls' responses were complex when faced with two ideologies of femininity, one passive and nurturing, the other confident and competitive. The way they responded was complex and depended on their social class and home background. She considers that neither acceptance nor rejection describe accurately what occurs – it is much more a process of simultaneous accommodation and resistance.

These concepts were later used by Mac an Ghaill (1988) to describe the responses of a group of black A level students, the 'black sisters', who practised resistance with accommodation. They adopted subtle forms of resisting the institutional demands of the school, such as by being late for lessons, but they were in favour of education. Qualifications were highly prized as they provided the opportunity to escape traditional black working-class 'female' work.

> ### Discussion point
> Do you ever resist following the rules in school or college? If so, how far do you go, and in what ways do you do it?
>
> **C3.1a**

Pro-school and anti-school cultures

Modes of challenge and resistance

Middle-class pupils and disaffection

Peter Aggleton (1987) was interested to discover whether the potential to transform society lies with the traditional working class, or whether disaffected middle-class groups had revolutionary potential.

Building on the studies outlined above, he developed social reproduction theory by refining the concept of resistance and introducing a much more finely tuned account of modes of student challenge. He undertook an ethnographic study of 27 students taking A levels in a college of further education. His central concern was to discover the reasons for their educational under-achievement despite their privileged middle-class backgrounds. Related to this was the question of whether this under-achievement was resistance to schooling and had the potential to transform society. He studied these students at home, at school and college, and in their sub-cultural world.

Progressive parents and authority

The parents of the students in Aggleton's sample tended to be members of the '**new middle class**'. Their progressive values led students into conflict with the values of their schools. They objected to the way in which their schools attempted to regulate their personal dress and appearance, the boring routines, the lack of creativity, and teachers whom some of them regarded as illiterate. College, they felt, would allow greater degrees of personal autonomy:

[Tom] 'I went to college because I thought that I wouldn't have to come across authority. I hated having to do things like go to assembly, being there to register, having to be in school at lunch hours, that sort of thing.'

(Aggleton, 1987, p. 68)

The cultural élite

At college these students regarded themselves as a cultural élite. They tried to negotiate their educational experiences with teachers and chose subjects like fine art, communication and theatre studies in order to display their creativity, originality and culture. Other students who pursued courses considered unfashionable, such as industrial training, building or engineering, and those who worked hard, were looked down on:

[Ric] 'They're all so macho those engineering "lads" (sneer). All they ever do is go around getting pissed and trying to pick up secretaries ... They're sort of really thick and brutish and boring.'

(Aggleton, 1987, p. 71)

Hard-working females

Similarly, female students who worked hard and conformed to conventional notions of **femininity**, usually following vocational courses, were looked down on by female respondents:

[Norma] 'And it (the common room at college) was taken over by other sections, people from the other side, secretaries, they rather took it over.'

[P. A.] 'What was wrong with that?'
[Norma] 'We didn't want to be associated with them.'
[P. A.] 'Why not?'
[Norma] 'Well, we looked down on the secretaries and catering students. They were only doing it to get jobs which were really boring. They're going to go and get some shitty job which pays £30 a week and that's it. I think we felt that we were more liberated than them, and that our horizons were wider. And they were all so feminine.'

(Aggleton, 1987, p. 75)

Outside college the rebels spent a lot of time in a public house called the Roundhouse. As was the case in college, their major concern was to gain control for themselves over space, time and meaning. These places were central to their subculture and were valued because exciting people in exotic clothes met there, political discussions took place and gossip was exchanged. The rebels also engaged in what Aggleton calls 'displays to be observed', such as arriving at the benefits office in a taxi and dressed in a cocktail dress with your boyfriend dressed like something out of the colonial stories of Somerset Maugham, or causing a disturbance at midnight Mass on Christmas Eve.

Discussion point

Are there students in your school or college who regard themselves as a cultural élite? If so, what are their 'displays to be observed'? Do these relate in any way to their educational achievement?

C3.1a

Insignificant consequences?

The academic under-achievement at college of Aggleton's Spatown rebels did not have such dire consequences for them in terms of employment as would be the case for, say, the 'lads' of Willis' study:

Fifteen out of twenty-seven students in the present study left Spatown college with no qualifications other than those they had possessed when they enrolled. Six years later, however, at a time of high national youth unemployment, such under-achievement was found to have relatively insignificant consequences for students' employment. Every student was in paid employment at this time – working as theatre staff, video and film technicians, servers in cocktail bars and chic restaurants, or as personal assistants to those in the worlds of fine and media arts.

(Aggleton, 1987, p. 135)

This indicates that something other than educational qualifications was instrumental in their employment. Possibly the network of contacts through their parents and their possession of **cultural capital** helped. Aggleton concludes that the children of the new middle class are not interested in transforming society, and thereby losing the privilege which their class position provides.

Resistance and contestation

Aggleton provides a useful if rather complex grammar of modes of challenge (meaning the ways of challenging authority) by developing and refining the concept of resistance. He distinguishes between resistance and contestation. Resistance is the mode of challenge to structural relations of power, and contestation refers to struggles against control in a particular social practice or site, as in the case of the rebels, to win personal autonomy and reject the dominant ethos of schooling, within existing class relations.

Aggleton's study has been praised as an excellent ethnographic study that includes young men *and* women, which adds to our understanding of middle-class students' under-achievement. But it can also be criticized. The strongest of these would be to ask the question why he thought such privileged young people might be resistant to wider power structures or interested in the transformation of society. He also neglects to address the transition of these young people from school to work – which the title of his book suggests – or to compare them with any other groups, either achievers or under-achievers, who come from similar backgrounds.

Ethnicity in school: the work of Gillborn

The focus of Gillborn's study was the ways in which ethnic differences influence how teachers perceive their pupils. He found that African–Caribbean pupils, both male and female, received a disproportionate amount of punishment and criticism from teachers. Even where pupils from different ethnic groups were engaged in the same behaviour, it was the African–Caribbean pupils who were singled out for criticism. Gillborn gives an example of this from his classroom observations:

Paul Dixon (Afro-Caribbean) and Arif Aslam (Asian) arrived seven minutes late for a mixed ability lesson that I observed. ... almost half an hour into the lesson most of the group were working steadily and, like the majority of their peers, Paul and Arif were holding a conversation while they worked. The teacher looked up from the pupil he was dealing with and shouted across the room: 'Paul. Look, you come in late, now you have the audacity to waste not only your own time but his (Arif's) as well.'

(Gillborn, 1990, p. 31)

Racial discrimination

Paul is blamed whereas Arif is regarded as a blameless victim. But was this just an isolated incident? Gillborn asked pupils in his two case-study classes to answer some sentence completion items, such as '..... is picked on by some teachers'. Half the pupils nominated African–Caribbean pupils, yet they constituted only 10 per cent of the age group. This was supported by data from interviews with pupils:

Gillborn: 'Do you think the teachers particularly like or dislike some people?'
James (a white pupil): 'I think some are racialist.'
Gillborn: 'In what ways would you see that?'

James: 'Sometimes they pick on the blacks. Sometimes the whites are let off. When there's a black and a white person, probably just pick on the black person.'

(Gillborn, 1990, p. 31)

Teachers and racism
Many teachers were unconscious of their behaviour. The source of this conflict was often in the teachers' responses to the pupils' sense and display of their ethnicity, such as styles of speech, dress and manner of walking. This was considered by some teachers as a challenge to their authority, which Gillborn calls 'the myth of the black challenge'. He is careful to point out that this process is complex.

Labelling
Often work in the symbolic interactionist field is accused of claiming that once a person is 'labelled' he or she will automatically internalize that judgement and act accordingly by committing further deviant acts. Instead Becker identified several factors which may lead to the development of a 'deviant career'. Among the most important is when those in authority – in this case teachers – go on to constantly reinforce the initial negative judgement in subsequent interactions. By analysing official disciplinary procedures, such as report cards, detentions and exclusions, Gillborn found that this was the case: report cards were a possible source of the reinforcement of 'deviant' labels. With such cards the total number given was small, but a much greater proportion of African–Caribbean pupils received at least one report card – 37 per cent compared with 6 per cent of pupils of all other ethnic origins. Similarly with detentions – 68 per cent received at least one senior management detention during the research period. This was true for both sexes and unique to pupils of African–Caribbean origin. A majority of these went on to have a total of four or more such detentions. In this way their 'deviant careers' begun in classroom interaction were developed and continued through the school's disciplinary procedures.

Pupil responses
How did these pupils respond to such conflictual relationships with their teachers? Gillborn outlines two forms of response at each end of a range of different styles and subcultures. He focuses on three lads, Wayne, Barry and Roger,

who formed a subculture but who were not anti-school: theirs was not a counter-school culture. Nevertheless, increasing conflict with the school led to their educational failure – one expulsion and no exam passes. This subcultural group's responses were compared with those of another African–Caribbean pupil, Paul, who avoided conflict by playing down his ethnicity in order to succeed academically against all odds. He carefully distanced himself from other pupils who were regarded as trouble and from teachers with whom he was likely to come into conflict.

Complex interactions

Gillborn does emphasize the complexity of interactions: he says it is not an either/or question of 'resist' or 'accommodate', but rather a spectrum of possible responses. He also studied the experience of South Asian male pupils in the school and found it different from both their African–Caribbean and white peers. He found that teachers' stereotypes of Asian culture and traditions did not mean that all of their assumptions operated against the pupils' interests, as it did with African–Caribbean boys. Asian pupils were much more likely to have positive relationships with teachers, who tended to regard them as hard-working and from homes where education was highly valued.

Weaknesses of Gillborn

Gillborn focuses on male experience and ethnicity. The influence of gender, though mentioned in his book in relation to other ethnographic research, is not explored fully. This is a pity, especially as he found that black male and female pupils experienced the same level of conflict with teachers but he studied only the male response. This raises an interesting issue about whether it is possible for male researchers to develop the rapport and interaction with female pupils necessary in this kind of research.

💬 Discussion point

What problems do you think may be encountered, by either male or female researchers, in schools or colleges when carrying out research on students of the opposite sex?

C3.1a

Female teachers and nursery school pupils

As early as 1981, Walkerdine's research in two nursery schools showed that both female teachers and small girls have identities which in terms of power are constantly changing; at one moment they are powerful at another powerless. She describes a teacher aged about 30, sitting at a table with a group of children aged 3 and 4:

The children are playing with Lego; there are three children: a 3-year-old girl, Annie, and two 4-year-old boys, Sean and Terry. The teacher's name is Miss Baxter. The sequence begins when Annie takes a piece of Lego to add on to a construction she is building. Terry tries to take it away from her to use himself, and she resists. He says: 'You're a stupid cunt, Annie!' The teacher tells him to stop, and then Sean tries to mess up another child's construction. The teacher tells him to stop. Then:
Sean: 'Get out of it Miss Baxter paxter.'
Terry: 'Get out of it knickers Miss Baxter.'
Sean: 'Get out of it Miss Baxter paxter.'
Terry: 'Get out of it Miss Baxter the knickers paxter knickers, bum.'
Sean: 'Knickers, shit, bum.'
Miss B.: 'Sean, that's enough, you're being silly.'
Sean: 'Miss Baxter, knickers, show your knickers.'
Terry: 'Miss Baxter, show your bum off.' (they giggle)
Miss B.: 'I think you're being very silly.'
Terry: 'Shit Miss Baxter, shit Miss Baxter.'
Sean: 'Miss Baxter, show your knickers your bum off.'
Sean: 'Take all your clothes off, your bra off.'
Terry: 'Yeah, and take your bum off, take your wee wee off. Take your clothes, your mouth off.'
Sean: 'Take your teeth out, take your head off, take your bum off. Miss Baxter the paxter knickers taxter.'
Miss B.: 'Sean, go and find something else to do please.'

(Walkerdine, 1981, pp. 14–15)

This transcript illustrates how small boys can take away the adult power of a woman teacher. Their power comes from their refusal to be powerless objects in *her* **discourse**, and in the way that they recast her as the powerless object of *their* own discourse. She hasn't stopped being a teacher, but she has stopped *signifying* as one. In this discourse both the adult teacher and the small girl Annie are reduced to sex objects.

8.8 Femininity, masculinity and subject choice

One of the key concerns of studies of youth and youth subcultures concerns the way that the notions of masculinity and femininity are constructed, changed and contested through the experience of these subcultures. One of the key ways this can be seen is in the differing experience of schooling of male and female pupils and the way this impacts on the subjects they take at school. This section will look at the notions of masculinity and femininity and link this to gendered subject choices.

Mac an Ghaill's male peer groups

Mac an Ghaill (1994) identified a range of male peer groups at Parnell School. He outlines four different groups:

- the Macho Lads
- the Academic Achievers
- the New Enterprisers
- the Real Englishmen.

These groups, with the exception of the Real Englishmen, contained white, African–Caribbean and Asian students.

The Macho Lads
The Macho Lads were into the three F's – fighting, fucking and football. Their responses to school were very similar to those of Willis' lads (1977), equating academic work with effeminacy (see also Section 8.7). According to one of them, they spent their time

Gilroy: '... acting tough by truanting, coming late to lessons, not doing homework, acting cool by not answering teachers, pretending you didn't hear them; that gets them mad. Lots of different things.'

(Quoted in Mac an Ghaill, 1994, p. 57)

Teachers policed this group carefully – especially their clothes, footwear, hairstyles and earrings, which were often banned from the school.

The Academic Achievers
This second group, who were mainly Asian or white students from skilled working-class homes, were like the conformist 'earoles' (Willis, 1977) who saw academic qualifications as the route to upward social mobility. (See also Section 8.7.) They were severely ridiculed and punished by other male students for their interest in 'feminine' arts subjects, especially music and drama. According to one:

Andy: 'A lot of the kids take the piss out of us. But it's different with different groups. With the low-set boys, they're more physical and say bad things you get used to. They're dickheads really. But with the middle class ones, it's more difficult. They're real snides. When they are all together, they can put you down bad and what can you do? They've got all this alternative humour. I don't even understand it, using big words and all that business.'

(Quoted in Mac an Ghaill, 1994, p. 63)

The New Enterprisers
This third group are a product of the vocationalization of education, with its emphasis on technology and business studies. These students placed high value on work experience, the computer club and mini-enterprise schemes, which they felt prepared them well for their futures. One commented:

Wayne: 'In class you just sit there in most lessons as the teacher goes on and on, but in business studies and technology you learn a lot, you're really doing something, something that will be useful for your future.'

(Quoted in Mac an Ghaill, 1994, p. 64)

The Real Englishmen
The individuals in this group regarded themselves as superior to other students especially in their 'effortless achievement' and rejection of the work ethic. One said:

Robert: 'They're [the teachers] just guardians of mediocrity. They've this idea that you have to work all the time, slog, slog, slog to pass exams.'

(Quoted in Mac an Ghaill, 1994, p. 67)

Male dominance

The 'effortless achievement' of Mac an Gaill's Real Englishmen was also noted by Power *et al.* (1998) in their study of young men identified as 'academically able'. Middle-class boys were under pressure to achieve, but their achievement had to look as if they weren't really working.

Connell (1987) coined the useful term '**hegemonic masculinity**' to describe the dominant form of masculinity. This form of masculinity is characterized by heterosexuality, authority, power, aggression and technical competence.

Such masculinity is defined as dominant in relation to other subordinated forms of masculinities. There is no corresponding form of femininity to hegemonic masculinity as it rests on the single structural fact of the global dominance of men over women. The hegemonic masculinity of the Real Englishmen required them to ridicule other 'inferior' masculinities. It was also part of their collective identity, reflected in their choice of name, cynically to criticize their middle-class parents' left-wing political correctness. According to one:

Daniel: 'Like my dad he's anti-sexist and feminist and all this. You know he goes out shopping and takes the baby out on his back, any fucking baby will do.'

(Quoted in Mac an Ghaill, 1994, p. 79)

They felt the need to protect themselves from the heavy issues placed on them by their parents, such as having to feel responsible for racism and sexism, having to be 'new men' and to endure comprehensive schools whereas their parents went to grammar schools. They felt their feminist mothers had robbed them of their masculinity.

Masculinity and its effect on female and gay male students

Mac an Ghaill also focuses on how young women and young gay male students at Parnell School experienced both teacher and student masculinities. He did not find equivalent female peer groups except for a group of black and white working-class young women who called themselves 'The Posse'. They were a very visible group whose behaviour was considered the worst in the school. They had a reputation for standing up to both boys and teachers. They felt very strongly that male teachers and the New Enterprisers manoeuvred to exclude them from career opportunities offered by the new vocational curriculum. Under-represented in business studies, technology and computer studies, such girls were encouraged into low-level caring courses:

Smita: 'Teachers keep on about all the money spent on the place. Well we haven't got anything out of it. It's just the same for us in the low classes. They say it's our behaviour. We are too bad to be allowed into the high classes ... when we ask if we can use the new computers they say no because we have the wrong attitude.

(Quoted in Mac an Ghaill, 1994, p. 117)

The centrality of social class

Mac an Ghaill's research adds to our understanding of educational under-achievement for both young men and women. It reasserts the centrality of social class as both the Macho Lads and The Posse consisted of male and female working-class students of different ethnicities. Schools and colleges are being encouraged to change anti-school masculinities in order to produce the 'right kind of boys' – i.e. academic ones. Even if this is desirable or possible, such masculinities are the product not only of schools but also of the interaction of such factors as the economy, families, the media and peer networks.

> **Discussion point**
>
> Mac an Ghaill uses the typologies of the Macho Lads, the Academic Achievers, the New Enterprisers and the Real Englishmen in an exploratory way.
>
> **a** How do they correspond to masculinities in your school or college?
>
> **b** Are there equivalent femininities?
>
> C3.1a

Femininity and schooling

Are single-sex schools better for girls?

Throughout the 1980s, feminist teachers made a good case for single-sex groupings for girls, especially in maths and science. Some girls' schools were valued as havens where feminist teachers could develop anti-sexist strategies and courses, girls' groups and women's groups relevant to the needs of girl pupils and women teachers. Female teachers had better career prospects in girls' schools. However, there were some criticisms of those who defended single-sex schools for girls – that this promoted an image of girls as the problem, of 'passive' girls who couldn't stand up to the boys, of not challenging mainstream practice.

As a result of the kind of research and activities mentioned above, there was an assumption that single-sex education was better for girls. But was the case proved? As early as 1978 Byrne outlined the multiple forms of inequality suffered by less able, lower social class girls in rural areas, whom she considered to be 'quadruply disadvantaged' in the education system. She claimed that unequal facilities and resources – especially in single-sex girls' schools – went some way to explaining this disadvantage. At this time many girls' schools did not have good science laboratories or equipment or workshops for practical subjects like metalwork and woodwork. Some girls' schools were chosen by parents for religious reasons and they sometimes had the effect of reinforcing traditional notions of femininity and restricting girls' choices.

Much of this research conducted was small-scale, focusing on classroom interaction, making generalizations about the benefits of single-sex schools difficult. The only large-scale study was undertaken by Dale (1969, 1971, 1974) who interviewed pupils and teachers and came down in favour of mixed schools on the basis that they promoted 'optimal adjustment to life for all students'.

A problem in claiming definitively that girls' schools are better for girls is that there are so many other variables to take into account, such as type of school, location and social class. This was summed up by Bone (1983):

... the subject mixes taken by girls, their academic results and the responses of their schools to their more personal needs have been conditioned far more by the type of school they attend (comprehensive, grammar, modern or independent) and by the style of school (traditional or not) than by whether their school was single sex or mixed. The repeated absence of a strong indication in favour of either a girls-only environment or a mixed environment through the great variety of research reviewed, supports the conclusion that this aspect of schooling on its own has not been crucial.

(Bone, 1983, pp. 1–2)

Boys' single-sex schools?

Making a case for single-sex schooling also means that boys have to be educated in single-sex schools. In areas where girls' schools are popular then there may be a gender imbalance in the co-educational schools. This could possibly put girls in such co-educational schools at a disadvantage. Some educationalists also feel that working with boys, changing their attitudes and assumptions, is vital if the bad effects of sexism which affect both boys and girls differently are to be countered.

Some recent research has focused on the need to provide single-sex groupings and spaces for both boys and girls *within* co-educational settings. This is not a new idea and single-sex groupings for maths, science and sex education have been established practice in some schools since the 1980s. Epstein (1995) describes how in her primary classroom complaints from three girls about boys dominating the use of bricks led to a discussion of this with the whole class and a solution in the form of specific times for each group to have access to the bricks:

... gradually other girls also began to take the opportunities offered them to play with the bricks. ... Within their domestic play, girls could adopt 'feminine' roles which had reference to future heterosexual expectations of marriage and motherhood. At the same time they could and did build complex structures with the bricks. Girls could, then, at one and the same time position themselves firmly as feminine and do the 'masculine' activity of building – thus giving lie to the notion that 'girls don't do bricks' and to the idea that they must be 'boys' if they wanted to play in this 'inappropriately' gendered way.

(Epstein, 1995, p. 64)

In interesting research in Denmark, Kruse (1992) describes how she divided pupils into single-sex groupings for the benefit of withdrawn and shy girls but found that boys also benefited. She found that more teachers are employing sex segregation because of repeated incidences of conflict between boys and girls. She states that the reason for employing sex segregation is that co-education renders power relations invisible. **Sex segregation**, she claims, helps to expose this power because of the absence of the other group. This helps pupils to relate and act differently, to become owners of their own learning. She says this power becomes clear to pupils when embedded, hidden knowledge is uncovered.

Gender and subject choice

The nineteenth century

In the early days of state education it is quite clear that very different curricula were laid out for boys and girls, which related to assumptions about their future roles as breadwinners (boys) and housewives (girls). For instance Burgess (1985) quotes the following rules for a girls school in the 1880s:

The Mistress is required to teach the girls every kind of plain needlework, making, smocking and plain knitting, stocking, darning. The afternoon of each day is allowed for Needlework.

(Burgess, 1985, p.1 5)

These subjects would not appear in the required list of subjects to be studied by boys and the fact that the curricula were so different also meant that the two sexes had to be taught separately, that is that there needed to be separate schools for boys and girls.

The twentieth century

This separation of the sexes continued well into the twentieth century and could be seen in schools where the girls would study domestic science and the boys would do woodwork or metalwork. Equally, girls tended to shine at subjects like English and the languages while boys did better in physics and maths.

Discussion point

a Why was 'domestic science' so-called?

b Was this an attempt to give cooking an academic gloss?

c Was it an attempt to certify complex knowledge held largely by females?

C??

The National Curriculum

The introduction in 1988 of a National Curriculum to be followed by the vast majority of pupils ended many of the most overt forms of providing different educations for girls and boys. However, whenever there are choices to be made about which subjects are to be studied, these choices continue to occur in gendered ways, leading to classes looking in many ways very sim-

Table 8.4 Entry figures for eight major A level subjects by gender, 1970–90

Subject	Sex	1970	1980	1990	Percentage differences 1970–80	1980–90
Biology	Male	10 235	17 232	17 938	68.4	4.1
	Female	9 463	20 662	28 517	118.3	38.0
	Total	19 698	37 894	46 455	92.4	22.6
Chemistry	Male	23 385	24 836	27 427	6.2	10.4
	Female	7 385	12 408	18 769	68.0	51.3
	Total	30 770	37 244	46 196	21.0	32.1
Physics	Male	35 045	35 752	35 300	2.0	−1.3
	Female	6 501	9 406	10 029	44.7	6.6
	Total	41 546	45 158	45 329	8.7	0.4
Maths	Male	52 364	50 238	47 096	−4.1	−6.3
	Female	12 017	15 775	23 867	31.3	51.3
	Total	64 381	66 013	70 963	2.5	7.5
French	Male	9 822	7 456	7 445	−24.0	−0.1
	Female	16 103	18 640	19 799	15.8	6.2
	Total	25 925	26 096	27 244	0.7	4.4
English Lit.	Male	21 257	20 229	14 621	−4.8	−27.7
	Female	34 736	45 371	32 345	30.6	−28.7
	Total	55 993	65 600	46 966	17.2	−28.4
Geography	Male	19 421	20 714	23 524	6.7	13.6
	Female	12 347	14 360	18 146	16.3	26.4
	Total	31 768	35 074	41 670	10.4	18.8
History	Male	18 145	18 898	19 845	4.1	5.0
	Female	16 811	21 196	23 962	26.1	13.0
	Total	34 956	40 094	43 807	14.7	9.3
All subjects	Male	189 674	195 355	193 196	3.0	−1.1
	Female	115 363	157 818	175 434	36.8	11.2
	Total	305 037	353 173	368 630	15.8	4.4

Source: Elwood (1995b)

ilar to the time when certain subjects were enforced on girls and boys over 100 years ago.

One thing that remains abundantly clear is that there are still clear differences in terms of the subjects that are likely to be studied by boys and girls. These choices may be both the result of existing notions of masculinity and femininity and also the basis of the continuation of these gender stereotypes into adult life.

Explaining gendered subject choices

As can be seen from the table opposite, in 1990 there were roughly twice as many girls as boys choosing to study biology, French, English literature. In the same year there were roughly twice as many boys as girls choosing to study chemistry, physics (over three times as many in the case of this subject), maths. The distribution of students in humanities A levels such as history and geography was not so clearly gendered though geography shows a slight male majority while history shows a slight female majority.

What sociologists are interested in are the reasons why these patterns exist even though individuals have free choice over the subjects they study at A level. They are also interested to know whether these patterns change over time or whether they remain consistent.

Factors explaining individual choice

Why do boys and girls choose different subjects to study? The possible factors cited include biology, school and parental expectations and the existence of ideologies of masculinity and femininity that include notions of appropriate jobs for girls and boys and therefore appropriate subjects to study.

Biological explanations

Theories which assume that men and women are biologically different in ways which impact upon their brain and therefore their school life have been used to try to explain gendered subject choices. It was suggested that females had greater verbal and reasoning skills and this would explain their tendency to gravitate towards language-based courses. On the other hand, it was suggested that males had better innate spatial ability and that they would therefore gravitate towards maths and science type subjects that put these skills at a premium.

Such arguments have been heavily criticized by sociologists. Kelly (1982) argued that the dif-

ferences in spatial and verbal reasoning skills was more to do with socialization practices and the kinds of toys that children were allowed to play with than any innate difference. One key issue is that if there have been any changes in the type of subjects chosen or the proportion of males and females in each subject then this would undermine biological notions, since biology has remained constant and cannot therefore explain changes in subject choice. There is evidence of such a change since if we look at Table 8.4 we can see that between 1980 and 1990 the number of males taking A level maths fell by 6.3 per cent while the number of females taking that subject at A level rose by 51.3. Unless the biological differences between males and females changed dramatically between 1980 and 1990 this would undermine biological explanations for gendered subject choice.

Statham et al. (1991) in a study of subject choices at A level also point out that while between 1970 and 1985 the most common A level combination taken by boys was maths, physics and chemistry, this was not the case with girls. In 1970 the most common A levels taken by girls were English, history and French but by 1985 this had changed to English, biology and maths. They do point out, however, that while this shows some narrowing of gendered choices at A level the evidence from higher education suggests that at that level the gendered curriculum choices remain firmly embedded with men taking science, engineering and technology courses while women take language and literature courses.

Socialization explanations

One key areas investigated by sociologists of education was the effect of gender socialization on subject choice. Sue Sharpe (1976) argued that it was the differences in socialization that generated notions of masculinity and femininity that included presumptions about which subjects children should study. Magazines aimed at teenage girls created a notion of femininity based on domesticity and marriage that influenced subject choices.

Challenging gender socialization

Undoubtedly the most dramatic social changes of the last century included the changing situation of women and this also includes the changes in attitudes towards women's education and employment. These changes have undoubtedly been brought about by the emergence since the

1960s of active feminist campaigns that have been successful in changing notions of what it is to be a woman. They have thus prepared the ground for more and more women to consider careers in previously 'women-free' areas and this has further impacted on the subjects they choose to study.

Motherhood and work

This changing situation is reflected in the work of Riddell (1992). The girls in this study were not passive about their subject choices but they retained a dual consciousness that impacted on their subject choices. While they did take into account employment possibilities in the local area, they also said that their expectations that they would become mothers and therefore notions of care and domesticity still played a part in choices in the education system.

Patriarchal ideologies

Despite these changes in the position of and ideas about women in the last thirty years, it is clear that there are still some elements of patriarchal ideology about which are seen by feminists to support the interests of men and to continue to oppress women. In the 1980s and 1990s the key examples of this were the New Right ideologies about the family and the importance placed on the conventional family in terms of gender roles. These attempts to reinforce notions of traditional femininity were however rebuffed. Arnet (1992) argues that the key reason for this was that feminism had given women enough confidence to be able to resist these ideas.

Teachers' expectations

There has been a long tradition of analysis considering the impact that teachers have upon their pupils. One key element in this was the suggestion that boys and girls are treated differently. For example Sadker *et al.* (1991) found that while boys were criticized more than girls in classrooms, they were also more heavily praised. This would only really matter if teachers' comments, attitudes and expectations were seen to have an impact on pupils and this is the general consensus of such studies. It is therefore possible that teachers may influence pupil subject choice. Spear (1985) found many male science teachers hostile to girls in their subjects and held rather traditional views on the place of women in society. However, initiatives to improve the proportion of science qualifications going to females

seems to have been relatively successful even in the face of this, so we need to remember that there are always a multitude of factors present and they will have counterbalancing effects in some instances.

Activity

a Outline the gender segregation in subject choice outlined in Table 8.4 above.

b Read the material on masculinities and femininities.

c Use this material to explain the patterns of gender segregation in subject choices shown in table 8.4.

d What other factors might explain these patterns?

C3.2, C3.3

Further reading

Two books which consider the topic of youth in contemporary society are:

- Bates, I. and Riseborough, G. (eds.) (1993) *Youth and Inequality*, Buckingham: Open University Press.
- Coles, B. (1995) *Youth and Social Policy*, London: UCL Press.

The following books contain discussion of youth in the context of wider structures:

- Modood, T. *et al.* (1994) *Changing Ethnic Identities*, London: PSI.
- Phillips, A. (1993) *The Trouble with boys*, London: Pandora.
- Redhead, S. (1993) *Rave Off: Politics and Deviance in Contemporary Youth Culture*, London: Avebury.
- Willis, P. (1990) *Common Culture*, Buckingham: Open University Press.

Back issues of the periodical *Sociology Review* (formerly *Social Studies Review*) also contain many articles on this field and many others.

Glossary of useful terms

Accommodation   Behaviour which is an accommodation to the perceived dominant norms and values in an institution or in capitalism.

Anomie   A term first used by Durkheim to represent a stage where people may not be properly integrated into society after a transformation in society.

Capitalism   An economic system based on production for individual profit with goods being bought and sold in a market. Often associated with private property but can also exist with public or state owned property.

Commodities   Goods which are brought and sold in the marketplace.

Common ground   Where there is an overlap between two views.

Correlation   A situation where two variables seem to be linked to each other.

Criminalization of the black community   A term used to suggest that the effect of racism in the police is to target black people leading to the criminalization of the black community. It also suggests that cultural differences are not accepted and are instead seen as deviant and threatening.

Criminal justice system   The system of the courts and associated institutions which administers justice and criminal procedures in this country.

Criminological perspective   Criminology studies crime with the aim of coming up with policy prescriptions to help solve the problem of crime. A criminological perspective therefore draws upon sociology and psychology but is nonetheless distinct.

Cultural capital   The skills, knowledge, language, manners and style of the dominant culture. (Possession of cultural capital places middle-class children at an advantage in the education system.)

Cultural goals   Goals about how you want to live your life.

Culturalism   Belief that the culture of a society is the most important element in affecting peoples lives.

Culturally reproductive   Actions which have the effect of reproducing the existing way of life, usually unintentionally.

Cultural products   Products of the cultural industries. Examples would include newspapers, artistic products, music, ballet, opera, dance and media products.

Cultural reproduction   The process of reproducing the existing ways of living.

Cultural resistance   Theory, popular with neo-Marxists, that it is possible to resist capitalism and other oppressive systems through cultural actions, such as making music, films, plays. Can also be applied to the way that certain lifestyles embody a culture of resistance, e.g. skinheads.

Culturist   Someone who adopts the culturalism approach.

Deviant   Straying away from the norms of society or a group.

Deviant values   Values which are seen to be different and potentially subversive of the dominant norms and values.

Discourse   A set of ideas that together form a coherent whole. Religion may be considered a discourse, as may science. Different discourses present different ways of seeing and understanding the world.

Dominant ideology   A Marxist idea which suggested that the ruling or dominant class who own the means of production will also dominate politically (be the ruling class) and also in the realm of idea (the Dominant Ideology).

Dysfunction   Something that does not contribute to the maintenance of society, but instead may positively harm it.

Ethnographic data   Data produced by ethnographic studies.

Ethnography   Means the study of a way of life. This usually involves participant observation. It builds upon the anthropological tradition where researchers went to live with the group they were studying. Therefore it involves participation in the lives of those studied.

Femininity   Social and behavioural characteristics associated with being biologically female.

'Fortress Europe'   Term used to point to the strengthening of the external borders of the EU, making it very difficult for immigrants from outside the EU to enter it.

Functionalism   Functionalist sociologists see society as being based on agreement, or consensus, expressed in the values of that society and enshrined in the laws of that society. They also argue that everything that exists does so for a reason because it serves a purpose of function, hence functionalism.

Functionalist   A person who adheres to the beliefs of functionalism.

Hegemonic masculinity   A term used to describe the power, heterosexuality, authority and aggression of the dominant form of masculinity.

Hegemony   A term used by neo-Marxists to signify the way that some ideas play a dominant role in society. These ideas are said to be hegemonic.

ILO   International Labour Office. A body that conducts research on work and employment.

Incorporated   Taken in to the dominant ideology of consumerism. Sold out or brought off.

Indictable offences   This term is used to refer to those offences which were recorded by the police. The term was used until 1979 and was then briefly replaced with the term 'serious offences'. It has now become 'notifiable offences'.

Interactionist   Sociologists who adopt the perspective of interactionism.

Marxist   A person who adheres to the beliefs of Marxism.

Material deprivation   Lacking material wealth or income, being in poverty.

Modern world   The term 'modern' refers to the period dominated by science which replaced the dark ages dominated by religion. The modern world is therefore the one created by science and knowledgeable humans.

Moral panic   Exaggeration or invention of a problem usually through sensationalist stories in the media.

Neo-Marxist   'Neo-' means 'new', so neo-Marxist describes Marxists who have changed 'classical' Marxist theory so much that it justifies being called a different name. Neo-Marxist theories place much more emphasis on culture and ideology and less emphasis on economics than classical Marxists.

'New middle class'   A term used by various writers to refer to the new professionals who may behave in different ways to the old middle class of bankers, civil servants and business people.

New Right   Used to distinguish the views of right-wing political parties in recent times from earlier conservative views: notably the views of the British Conservative Party from the premiership of Margaret Thatcher and the US Republican Party from the presidency of Ronald Reagan onwards. The most notable difference is the New Right's emphasis on the benefits of the free market and individual freedom.

Non-incorporated   Actions which have not been taken into the commodity culture. Therefore they retain an oppositional element.

Oppositional   In opposition to the dominant norms and values of society, notably the value of capitalism.

Patriarchal ideology   A set of ideas that endorses or supports male power and the oppression of women.

Postmodernism   The belief that life today is characterized by plurality and a multiplicity of possible options. Therefore there is no longer a right and wrong way of living your life.

Reproduction theory   Theories which stress the way that people acting in a certain way may end up unintentionally reproducing the very things they are protesting about.

Resistance   Action which resists the dominant values of capitalism.

Sex segregation   Separation into males and females.

Social construction   The idea is associated with social action type approaches and more particularly with phenomenology and postmodernism. It suggests that there is nothing outside of perception and that everything that exists is made up by people.

Social deprivation   Being poor.

Social reproduction   Process whereby structures and behaviours characteristic of the present society are reproduced.

Subterranean values   Values which exist but are sometimes hidden. Kept out of the light.

Symbolic creativity   The way people use their creativity to make symbols or ways of living.

Underclass   A group of people with similar norms, values and lifestyles who have the lowest position in the stratification system.

Unstructured interviews   Interviews which provide qualitative data. They are very much like a conversation and informality is used to place the respondent at ease.

Sociological research skills

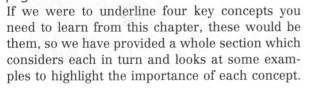

Chapter outline

This chapter looks at the basic concepts and issues involved in research design. This is a central issue in any sociological debate because arguments and conclusions rest on the quality of the evidence supporting them – which means the accuracy of the data supplied. All sociology must be judged in terms of its methods as well as its theories and concepts. In particular, we need to pay attention to the ethical and practical issues affecting the choice of research method, and be aware of the practicalities, strengths and limitations of the main research methods used.

Basic concepts in research design and aspects of data collection

9.1 Reliability, validity, representativeness and generalization
page 262

If we were to underline four key concepts you need to learn from this chapter, these would be them, so we have provided a whole section which considers each in turn and looks at some examples to highlight the importance of each concept.

9.2 Identifying causes and effects
page 270

This section considers some methodological debates, notably the difficulty of moving from links or correlations between variables to making cause and effect statements. It relates this into various methodological approaches.

9.3 Ethics in the research process
page 279

How research should be conducted, and its potential effects, need to be considered as an integral part of any research proposal.

9.4 Sampling   *page 280*

With the exception of the official national Census, social research is conducted via a sample of the population under consideration. The sample must be selected correctly. This section looks at different sampling procedures, populations and response rates and considers the basic concept of representativeness.

9.5 Collecting primary data
page 285

The sociological research methods of questionnaires, interviews and observation each have their strengths and limitations. This section looks at what each method entails and then moves to consider these strengths and weaknesses.

9.6 Sources of secondary data
page 291

This section looks at different sources of secondary data such as life documents, offical sources, libraries and the Internet and considers the basic concepts of reliability and validity.

Interpreting and evaluating data

9.7 Interpreting and evaluating data and reporting research results   *page 301*

This section looks at different ways of interpreting and evaluating quantitive and qualitative data. It also considers how to interpret and evaluate secondary sources and gives advice on how to report research results.

Glossary   *page 308*
Words in bold in the text are explained in the glossary at the end of this chapter.

9.1 Reliability, validity, representativeness and generalization

Interpreting and dissecting findings

The world is full of findings and statements. Some of these are true and some are not, or, alternatively, some people may feel that one view best represents how they feel or experience the world and others may disagree. The issue of interpreting research findings, however, aims to arrive at an objective (a meaning independent of any person's views or feelings) about research findings and we therefore need some tools to enable us to measure claims made. In this way we can try to ascertain those claims which should be taken seriously and those which should not.

It should be said at the outset that this is a relatively easy thing to explain (and hopefully to understand) but an extremely difficult thing to actually do. It is therefore vital for you to gain plenty of practice in thinking about these concepts and applying them to studies and data you have come across. This chapter will contain examples of research and commentary upon it so you can see this type of dissection of findings in actual sociological studies. We will look at each concept in turn and explain its meaning and then provide examples of it, allowing you to think through the implications.

Key concept: reliability

The key idea here is repeatability and consistency. A method of research is said to be reliable if it can be repeated and if the repeated research conducted under identical conditions would lead to identical results. One example of this might be the system of centimeters and millimeters and the construction of rulers, which allow us to measure things. If the ruler is solid and kept at a constant temperature, every student in your class should come up with an identical result if asked to measure the height of this book. But if the ruler was made out of rubber and could stretch, then no such confidence would be justified and in fact very different measures might be reported depending on how much each person stretched the ruler.

Pat McNeill (1990) defines reliability as follows:

If a method of collecting evidence is reliable, it means that anyone else using this method, or the same person using it at another time, would come up with the same results. The research could be repeated, and the same results would be obtained.

(McNeill, 1990, p. 14)

However, we still need to explain why reliability is important. On one level we know that it is since we know that researchers often repeat their research. In doing this, clearly one important consideration is to check if their method of research is reliable. But why do they do this? Mel Churton (2000) explains the importance of this concept as follows:

Reliability is important if generalizations are to be made. If researchers can establish that their research is reliable there is less risk of their taking a chance pattern or trend exhibited by their sample (the group being studied) and using it to make inferences or assumptions about the population as a whole.

If research has been completed twice under the same research conditions and the results are not similar it is dangerous to generalize. If research has only been completed once and there is no verification (double check) of the findings, it is unwise to use the results to make inferences or assumptions. However, given the pressure on sociologists to complete their research quickly and economically many do in fact do this.

(Churton, 2000, p. 157)

Harvey and McDonald (1993) suggest that we can distinguish between internal reliability and external reliability as tests of the consistency of a measure. Internal reliability is concerned with whether responses to survey questions are internally consistent. The way to measure this is to split your sample of answers in half randomly and compare the answers on the two samples. If the sets of answers largely agree this is evidence in support of the idea that the questions are reliable.

External reliability is measured by repeating the survey at a different time. The problem here is that the actual people completing the survey the second time around will most likely be different from those in the first survey. It is possible to minimize this problem by being careful about sample selection and therefore ensuring that both samples are representative (see below).

Harvey and McDonald (1993) do, however, point out the following shortcoming of reliability as a measure: 'Reliability is not enough in itself though. A questionnaire, for example, may be consistent, but it may be consistently measuring the wrong thing.'

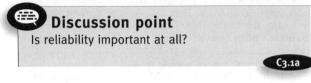

Discussion point
Is reliability important at all?

C3.1a

Key concept: validity

Pat McNeill (1990) defines validity as follows:

Validity refers to the problem of whether the data collected is a true picture of what is being studied. Is it really evidence of that it claims to be evidence of? The problem arises particularly when the data collected seems to be a product of the research method used rather than of what is being studied.

Suppose that we were making an enquiry into people's leisure habits. If we designed a questionnaire to ask people what they did in their free time, how would we know whether the answers we received gave us a true picture of how they spend that time; or a picture of what they will say to a researcher when they are asked the question? This is not just a matter of people telling lies. They may genuinely believe what they are saying, but actual observation of what they do might well produce a different picture.

(McNeill, 1990, p. 15)

Mel Churton (2000) explains the importance of validity as follows:

Validity is important if researchers are seeking to obtain an in-depth insight into individuals, small groups or situations. If researchers can establish that their research is valid, they can be confident that their findings really do portray the uniqueness of the issue being studied. If the research lacks validity, this means that the researchers cannot guarantee that their findings reflect the truth.

(Churton, 2000, p. 159)

In essence, the concept of validity tells us whether findings are really showing us what they claim to being showing us. One good example of this are the sex surveys that appear frequently in our magazines and Sunday supplements and claim to tell us about how many or how much or how many times various people are doing various things with various other people.

For instance the following findings appeared in the *Observer Magazine* in 1991:

Table 9.1 Number of sexual partners in lifetime

Age	Male	Female
16–24	7.12	3.20
25–34	7.88	3.40
35–44	8.57	3.16
45–54	5.64	1.66
55–64	3.39	1.29

Source: *Observer Magazine*, 16 June 1991

What do these findings claim to tell us?
- They claim to tell us the number of sexual partners people have in their lifetime.
- They claim to tell us that all groups have more than one sexual partner in their lifetime
- They claim to tell us how this varies by gender and age: namely that males have more sexual partners than females and that the 25–34 age group had the most sexual partners among men and women.

What problems might there be with these claims?
- Are all the people questioned likely to have told the truth about such a personal matter? There seem to be good reasons to doubt this.
- We know there is a problem since in actuality the number of sexual partners for men and women should be about equal. (Otherwise with whom are they having sex – assuming gay men and lesbians cancel each other out statistically?)

What do the findings nonetheless tell us?
- It tells us what people are willing to reveal about their images of sexuality
- It tells us that either men overstate their partners or women understate them or a combination of both these is going on. As a result it tells us about cultural expectations of sexual behaviour in UK society and therefore something about this society's notions of masculinity and femininity.

Would I lie to you honey?

You are in bed with your partner, who asks you how many previous lovers you have had. What do you say? Very possibly you lie; or at least you aren't fully frank. Among the reasons that you might not tell the whole truth are: you don't want to describe your sexual past in any detail, or can't remember; you want the other to think you have had more, or fewer, sexual experiences than you really have; you are bisexual, homosexual, or heterosexual, but wish to keep this concealed from the other.

It is disturbing to think we may not be able to trust even our nearest and dearest. The issue does not only concern individuals. Knowing who does what to whom, how, and how often, matters to society at large. Without such knowledge, the epidemiology of AIDs and sexually transmitted diseases cannot be determined. Government, the medical profession, social workers and similar agencies depend upon such information for policies in the health field and other areas.

Yet can we ever know the truth about the sexual behaviour of others? It almost always happens in private, nor is there a clear independent criterion against which to compare what people say they do with what they actually do. The meeting point of sex and truth is the sex survey. Last month's *Cosmopolitan* magazine [February 1996], for instance, faithfully recounted the proportion of women in 29 countries who masturbate, cheat on spouses and use sex toys.

But how do these responses relate to actual sexual behaviour? There is no way of judging from the survey, which was based upon readers' responses to a questionnaire. We can't judge how truthful the respondents were. Moreover, they could have been a distinctive group – sexually more adventurous, say, than non-respondents.

Probably few, including its organizers, would take this survey too seriously. It is meant to titillate as much as inform. Other sex surveys, however, take themselves, and are taken very seriously indeed. If they are 'scientific', they make strenuous efforts to cope with the problems just mentioned. Take for example an investigation recently carried out in the US by sociologist Edward O. Laumann with 220 interviewers producing a book of more than 700 pages littered with statistics and graphs.

It came up with strikingly different findings from the work of Alfred Kinsey which shocked many Americans in the 1950s. Kinsey had uncovered large differences between public expectations about sexual behaviour and the conduct reported to his interviewers. More than 90 per cent of males, and 60 per cent of females, had masturbated, even though 'self-abuse' was widely regarded as wholly unacceptable. Sixty per cent of men and women had practised oral sex, although it was illegal in many states. And 37 per cent of men reported a homosexual experience to the point of orgasm – this when homosexuality was still seen in many manuals of psychiatry as a form of mental illness.

Since Kinsey, the public sexual climate would seem to have become much more liberal. One would expect higher numbers of people now to engage in the various sexual practices he analyzed.

Yet Laumann reported that the sexual lives of Americans now are mostly staid and confined. Only a small proportion, for example, had engaged in homosexual acts. Was Kinsey wrong? Have Americans altered their characteristic sexual behaviour?

Laumann's research produced something of a collective sigh of relief. Moral decay has after all been kept at bay: people are much more restrained than most may have believed.

But are they? Last year, Richard Lewontin, a Harvard biologist, wrote a highly critical review of Laumann's work in the *New York Review of Books*. His critique centred precisely upon the question: how can we ever know if people are telling the truth when they respond to sex surveys? Lewontin's blunt answer – which outraged the researchers – was that we can't.

Nearly 20 per cent of people refused to co-operate and we have little idea about how truthfully the others responded. The only check we have is the internal consistency of their answers. And here some strange things did emerge. Discounting homosexual encounters, men reported having many more partners than women. Yet this cannot be so: the average numbers of sex partners reported by each sex must be equal. An unknown proportion of respondents, Lewontin concluded, must have been untruthful. If they are lying in one of the only instances where we have any way of telling, he asked, why should we take seriously any of the other results? The point is not that most people lie, but that for the most part we can't be sure if they do or not. I think Lewontin's arguments are conclusive. We don't know how far people tell the truth about their sexual behaviour in surveys.

Should we mark down the sex survey as a failure of sociology, or perhaps even a failure of science? To do so would be to misunderstand what such surveys are really all about. Beginning in the late nineteenth century, the attempt to investigate and categorize sexual behaviour, as Michel Foucault pointed out in his *History of Sexuality*, serve to give an entirely new importance to the domain of the 'sexual'.

The sex survey, one could say, served to constitute what it was about, creating that very 'sexuality' it set out to investigate. It was both a signal and a sparking-point for that absorption with sex which is so characteristic of our society today. It is an absorption, as Foucault has noted, which links prudes and libertines. The Mary Whitehouses of this world are as preoccupied with sexuality as those they oppose. Just as much as anyone else, perhaps more, they help provoke constant debates about sex and its central importance. A direct line of connection runs from Havelock Ellis, the English pioneer of 'scientific sexology' to Shere Hite and from there to Oprah Winfrey. Hite cloaks her surveys with a mantle of science and quotes percentages. Yet, like Oprah, her work is above all focused upon disclosure: sex as a means of revealing the self and its possibilities. 'To discuss sex', she says, 'is to discuss our most basic views of who we are, what we want life to be, and what kind of society we believe in.'

In the end that's what sex surveys are all about. Sex for us exists in and through the very ways in which we survey it, talk about it, publicly and privately sift through it. It is no longer a given, a phenomenon of reproduction. Sex has become plastic: we discover, mould, create our sexuality through the very modes of talk which allow us, and also force us, constantly to delve into what we are as sexual beings. Sex surveys, and all the other sexual fodder with which we nourish ourselves – including articles such as this – help to shape our sexual behaviour and supply sources for the dialogues, the endless worries and debates which are an essential part of what sexuality has now become.

Source: Anthony Giddens, *The Observer*, 31 March 1996

Activity

a Read the article and study the table that precedes it, both from *The Observer*.

b Identify and explain two problems with sex surveys.

c Explain and discuss the view that dismissing sex surveys would be a mistake.

C3.2, C3.3

Key concept: Representativeness

Sociologists spend a lot of time and energy constructing samples for their research. Sampling itself is covered in much more detail in Section 9.5, and here we will outline the reasons why sociologists take so much care over sampling. The key issue is that of ensuring that their findings are representative. Again, Pat McNeill (1990) provides a clear and concise definition of what this term means:

Representativeness. This refers to the question of whether the group of people or the situation that we are studying are typical of others. If they are, then we can safely conclude that what is true of this group is also true of others. We can generalize from the example we have studied. If we do not know whether they are representative, then we cannot claim that our conclusions have any relevance to anybody else at all. Careful sampling methods have been devised to try to ensure representativeness in survey research, but many other methods do not involve systematic sampling, and there must always be a question as to the representativeness of their findings and conclusions.

(McNeill, 1990, p. 15)

If you do a piece of research on what students think of the school or college that you are studying at, and you simply ask this question to four of your friends and then report the findings as if they are the views of the whole student body, this would be a problematic claim and one nobody should accept. It is highly unlikely in this case that four people could have all the characteristics and views to be able to stand in as representatives for the whole student population.

Instead, if we wished to conduct such a piece of research we would need to draw up a sample that was representative in important respects. For instance, we would want to know that the characteristics of the sample were the same as that of the student population in relation to social characteristics considered to have some significance, such as social class, gender, ethnicity and perhaps age. In order to construct such a sample you would need to know detailed information about the student population in terms of these characteristics. You would then need to construct or obtain a complete listing of the student population from which you would then select your actual sample. Such a list is known as a sampling frame.

In reality, one key problem many sociologists have with sampling is that sampling frames often do not exist. People do not wait around on lists for sociologists to select them and often these lists do not exist. This point is made clear by Devine and Heath (1999), who pointed to the considerable difficulties in constructing a sample faced by Phizacklea and Wolkowitz (1995) in their study of the extent of homeworking (meaning paid work at home). This is just one example of a group for whom there is no list, no sampling frame, and so sociologists have to think carefully about how they might go about constructing a sample.

Case study–Sampling hidden populations

Sampling issues, especially the difficulties of sampling minority populations, also arise in Phizacklea and Wolkowitz's Homeworking Women, *which was published in 1995. Homeworking – paid work at home – is one way in which women combine employment with child-care and domestic commitments and is especially prevalent among ethnic minority women. That said, Phizacklea and Wolkowitz wanted to look at all types of homework undertaken by different groups of women. In order to capture this diversity, they employed a variety of research methods including a postal questionnaire included in the women's magazine* Prima, *in-depth interviews with white and Asian women homeworkers in Coventry, and a series of case studies of organizations which had developed teleworking schemes. Their use of a readership of a women's magazine for a postal questionnaire elicited a limited response from a highly select group of women derived from an already skewed group of readers, while they also encountered considerable difficulties in generating a sample of homeworkers for their in-depth study. An initial attempt to contact homeworkers via adverts in the local press met with limited success, especially with regard to Asian women homeworkers. A second strategy of contacting them through community workers proved somewhat more successful in generating a sample of white women in a range of manual and non-manual occupations and a smaller number of Asian women homeworkers. It was nonetheless disappointing that they achieved only a small sample of Asian women homeworkers, based only in manual occupations. Their research therefore highlights the considerable difficulties of generating a sample from a relatively small and hidden workforce. That said, their intensive case study research powerfully captures the diverse experiences of working-class Asian women homeworkers performing low-skilled tasks for which they were paid very little, as against the experiences of white middle-class women teleworkers undertaking high-skilled work for which they were well remunerated.*

(Devine and Heath, 1999, p. 12)

Activity

Read the extract on the work of Phizacklea and Wolkowitz above.

a Identify and outline two ways in which they attempted to select samples for their study.

b In your own words, briefly explain the concept of representativeness.

c Identify and explain the main strengths and weaknesses of the research design adopted by Phizacklea and Wokowitz.

C3.2, C3.3

A new research tool that is being discussed and used in some quarters is the Internet (see also Section 9.6). Although this does offer new possibilities of reaching people for research purposes it is possible that there may be representativeness issues when using this approach. The following newspaper article outlines some information about internet usage which is relevant to this issue.

Activity

Read the following newspaper article.
How might this article make us think about the representativeness of any research conducted using the Internet as a delivery mechanism?

C3.2, C3.3

Villagers bypassed on computer highway

JEEVAN VASAGAR

Rural communities are falling behind in online buying despite hopes that the Internet could compensate for the decline in village shops, a study reveals.

One in 10 Britons shop online with well-heeled urban commuter types being, as ever, the most sought-after customer while older people living in out of the way places are more likely to be unfamiliar with buying on the net.

The research, compiled by market analysts CACI using 30m lifestyle records, shows that Reading is the online consumer capital with nearly 18% of adults regularly surfing the web for holidays, books, CDs and other goods and services. London and Cambridge follow close behind.

In these and other online boom towns such as Chester, Southampton and Brighton, internet shopping poses a real threat to those businesses with little or no web presence.

But wide swaths have been left almost untouched. In the north of England, Scotland and Wales only 16% of adults are online and less than 6% are frequent online buyers while rural and remote counties such as Cornwall or Orkney show the greatest reluctance to take up shopping on the web.

Lower computer literacy was partly to blame for the slow uptake of internet shopping in rural areas, the authors suggest. 'A lot of people have access to the Internet at work, and those kinds of white-collar jobs tend to be more concentrated in urban areas,' said Paul Winters, head of market analysis at CACI.

The urban centres at the bottom end of the scale are predominantly in poorer northern areas, with Liverpool having only 16.6% of the population online and just 5% as frequent online purchasers.

The report highlights not only a clear north-south divide, but also a sharp distinction between rich and poor despite the lower prices online.

Source: Adapted from the *Guardian*, May 30, 2000

Key concept: Generalizability

Representativeness refers to the extent to which a sample has the same proportions of important social characteristics as the whole population being studied. This is clearly related to the sampling procedures undertaken. The aim of having a sample as representative as possible is to enable you to make claims about the whole population being studied on the basis of actually only studying the sample. Generalizing from your sample is thus an important aim and object of representativeness and having a representative sample is one important way of ensuring your research is generalizable. However, more is involved in this concept, as Devine and Heath (1999) explain:

Methods of sampling and the effective use of different sampling frames – pre-existing lists from which one can select a sample, such as membership lists or registers of various kinds – crucially affects two key issues. These are the representativeness of the sample (the degree to which the sample accurately reflects the characteristics of the broader population, whether that population consists of all British citizens, all ferret owners, or all flower pot factories) and the generalizability of the research findings (the degree to which one can say with confidence that the findings from one setting are likely to apply to similar settings).

(Devine and Heath, 1999, p. 10)

The point here is that it is not always enough simply to ensure that your sample is representative to claim that your findings are generalizable. A representative sample can allow you to make statements about the population from which that sample is drawn. However, we may wish to consider whether the study tells us something about populations other than those studied. Here we need to consider the role of research that purposely sets out not to be representative but does nonetheless claim to be useful in terms of helping us to generalize about populations other than those directly studied or sampled. This is the terrain of the critical case study. The term 'case study' refers to the detailed study of one particular example of whatever it is the researcher is trying to study. Clearly, the sample cannot therefore be representative (except accidentally) and in many cases it will purposely be chosen not to be average or representative.

Case study–Critical case studies

Conventionally, it is assumed that generalizations cannot be made from case studies as they are 'one-off' studies. However, some researchers use case studies to test hypotheses. They do so by developing what are called critical case studies (sometimes also called theoretical case studies). These are case studies that are selected so they are as favourable as possible to confirming a hypothesis. The case study is then examined and if it does not support the hypothesis then it is taken as refuting the theory that underlies the hypothesis.

For example, John Goldthorpe et al (1969) used a critical case study to examine the embourgeoisement thesis. The embourgeoisement thesis argued that capitalism, in the second half of the twentieth century, had led to a breakdown in the division between working class and middle class. In particular, highly paid workers in factories characterized by new technology no longer exhibited working-class tendencies or attitudes. Instead, they were adopting middle-class attitudes and values, had become like the bourgeoisie, and no longer identified with the working class. Such well-paid workers, it was argued, had become embourgeoised. To test this out Goldthorpe et al selected an area of the country that as far as possible showed all the characteristics of the new embourgeoised worker. They chose Luton and studied workers living there who worked in three factories that paid high wages and were characterized by new technology. The case study was thus selected so that it was as favourable as possible to the embourgeoisement thesis. They selected a sample of workers, carried out two formal interviews with them (one at work and one at home) and observed the work situation. What they showed was that the workers did not exhibit middle-class tendencies. The embourgeoisement thesis did not hold up. If it did not apply in Luton where the circumstances were favourable they argued, it was unlikely to apply elsewhere.

(Harvey and McDonald, 1993, p. 226)

> ### 💬 Discussion point
> To what extent do case studies allow us to generalize from unrepresentative samples?
>
> C3.1a

Types of data and key concepts

The four key concepts examined above are to be applied to all research findings to allow you to consider whether these findings should be seriously considered as sociological knowledge or not. There are thousands of findings presented as the truth every day. Your job as a sociologist is to consider whether these claims are accurate using the concepts outlined above.

Activity

a Carefully consider each finding set out below. Discuss with other members of your group.

b Elect one member of your group as lead reporter in relation to each finding

c For each finding, discuss and write down your answers to the following:

1. What does the finding claim to tell us?

2. What problems are there with this claim?

3. Does the finding actually tell us anything?

C3.1a, C3.1b, C3.2, C3.3

Example 1

The age of the American hero is dead and most Americans can no longer tell right from wrong, according to a new survey.

Based on 1800 question interviews with 2000 Americans held simultaneously at 50 locations, with privacy and anonymity guaranteed, 'The Day America Told the Truth' found that 91 per cent of Americans lie regularly both at work and at home.

Source: Guardian, 2 May 1991

Example 2

Violent Britain: 109 Murders and it's still only Feb 28

Headline from *The Sun*, 28 February1994

1. If we convert this to an annual rate by multiplying by 6 we get 654.
2. Figures from *Social Trends* 1993 show there were a total of 694 homicides in 1991.

Example 3

True crime is a difficult concept. It represents the total amount of crime which takes place in the country whether or not it is recognized as crime and whether or not it is reported to and recorded by the police. The crime figures quoted in the media most often [...] do not show the true amount of crime. They are simply statistics of recorded crime: i.e. crimes which have been reported to the police or discovered by them and which they regard as genuine. These figures are the most readily available and they form the basis of the regularly published statistics.

(Lewis, *Social Trends 22*, 1992)

Types of data used by sociologists

The main types of research tool used by sociologists include the questionnaire, the interview, observation and the analysis of secondary material. (These will be examined in more detail in Sections 9.5 and 9.6)

The type of data they produce can be divided into **quantitative** data, which are data that are based largely on numerical or statistical material, and **qualitative** data, which are data in the form of words.

These two types of data result from using different research methods. In order to obtain numerical or quantitative data, you need to be able to classify people so you can turn the responses into percentages, for instance. (See also Section 9.7.)

Only certain methods will yield qualitative data, namely closed questionnaires, structured interviews, structured observation and official statistics.

Qualitative data is useful for allowing people to speak in their own words and for avoiding the problem of having to put them into a 'pigeon-hole'. Certain methods will allow you to collect qualitative data, namely open-ended questionnaires, unstructured interviews, participant observation, non-participant observation and the analysis of personal or life documents.

One key issue we need to be aware of when using these methods is their characteristics in terms of reliability, validity, representativeness and generalizability. The methods that will yield quantitative data are said to have a high degree of reliability since they will generally obtain the same answer to an identical question if asked later or by a different person. However, since we cannot predict people's answers we do not necessarily find it possible to come up with detailed data that will enable us to consider our findings a valid picture. Quantitative methods therefore are said to have a low degree of validity.

Alternatively, methods which provide us with qualitative data are said to have a high degree of validity because they allow the researchers to probe and clarify answers allowing an in-depth picture of reality to be built up. However, it is clear that due to their lack of any structure or consistency, such methods would not provide a very reliable method of undertaking social research.

	Reliability	Validity	Representativeness	Generalizability
Questionnaires	With closed questions the reliability should be high. With open-ended questionnaires, the reliability is lower			
Interviews				
Observation				

Activity

From the material in this section and from other material you are familiar with, complete the table above. One section has been done already

C3.2, C3.3

Using more than one method: triangulation

Triangulation refers to the use of more than one method in order to try to counter the weaknesses of one particular method by combining it with another that is strong in that area. Structured interviews might be combined with participant observation, for example. It is also possible to use both structured and unstructured interviews, the logic behind doing so being to try to gain the highest levels of both validity and reliability.

The classical exposition of this approach is in Barkers' (1984) study of the Unification Church, better known as the Moonies. In her study, Barker used participant observation, questionnaires and interviews. Information from the participant observation (which lasted six years) and from the interviews (which consisted of 30 interviews lasting between six and eight hours) was used to gain a detailed picture of the Unification Church, and this information was then used to enable the researcher to draw up more detailed hypotheses for later investigation using questionnaires.

Barker argued that by combining these methods her study of the Moonies gained greater validity and reliability than would have been the case if she had conducted the study using only qualitative or only quantitative methods. Since research methodology allows us to be fairly sure about the relative strengths and weaknesses of the various techniques, and since this information is now widely available, more and more sociologists are seeking to use triangulation, or 'methodological pluralism' as it is sometimes called.

It is clear that triangulation can offer real benefits and is leading to more and more sociologists adopting the principles that lie behind it. Case studies focusing on specific issues but using more than one method have risen in popularity in sociology recently. While this might put a spotlight on the issues of validity and reliability, it could also impact on the issue of representativeness. For instance, the famous study by Goldthorpe and colleagues, *The Affluent Worker* (1968), chose to study workers in Luton, not because they were representative, but because this seemed the most likely place to find 'affluent workers'. In this sense an extreme case was picked rather than a representative sample. So here although not representative, it is nonetheless a finding that allows us to generalize.

C3.2, C3.3

Activity

Write your own short paragraph containing the words: reliability, validity, representativeness, generalizability, quantitative, qualitative.

9.2 Identifying causes and effects

Methodological theories and choice of method

The techniques sociologists use to obtain research data are just that – techniques. So why do researchers choose to use one particular technique rather than another? One key aspect to an answer is that it depends on their view of how they see the world operating, and in particular whether they believe it is possible to make statements about the causes of something or the effects of something. It is here that the relevance of theoretical and methodological debates becomes clear:

In a sense, methods are a-theoretical and a-methodological (meaning, independent from methodology). Interviews, for instance, like observation, experiments, content analysis etc., can be used in any methodology type, and serve any chosen research purpose. The same methods can be used in the context of different methodologies, and the same methodology can employ different methods. ... Nevertheless, although methods are in general a-methodological, their content structure and process are dictated by an underlying methodology. Although interviews, for instance, can be used in a qualitative and a quantitative methodology, the former employs an unstructured, open or in-depth interview, while the latter normally opts for a standardized interview. In a similar vein, participant observation is used in qualitative studies while structured observation is employed in quantitative studies.

(Sarantakos, 1993, p. 33)

Theoretical and methodological outlooks will play a large part in deciding which particular technique to use in the research process. This is as it should be; otherwise all the arguments which rage in sociological theory about the nature of society, and all those which rage in relation to

methodology about how or whether we can know the reality of a situation, and whether sociology should or can be a science, would be utterly pointless. People spend time on these arguments because they matter. This point further underlines the fact that there can be no separation between theorizing and empirical research, since in either case this would lead to pointless and useless activity.

Theories, methods and types of data

The terms quantitative and qualitative have an important meaning in this context. Both words refer to types of data.

1. Quantitative refers to data that are largely numerical in form or contain large amounts of numbers and/or statistical data.

2. Qualitative refers instead to data which consist of words – that is, verbal or written descriptions based on words.

While it is important to note that all sociologists may produce evidence in all forms of data, there is a link between theoretical outlook and the likelihood of producing a certain type of data.

1. Positivist sociologists (who believe that sociology should be scientific and precise in nature) tend to be more likely to want evidence in the form of quantitative data and therefore to use methods which would provide such data.

2. Phenomenologically inclined sociologists (who believe the job of sociology is to report the way people see and understand the world) are more concerned to understand the point of view of the people they are researching and this leads them to report their respondents' views in their own words, leading to a desire for qualitative data and the use of methods which would provide such data.

Positivism, quantitative methods, causes and effects.

The positivists' desire for quantitative data arises from their belief that humans are in essence subject to the laws of society. Their view of humanity means it does not really matter what people think, since this can have no real influence on the direction society will take, and this leads to a concern with delineating the structures of society.

Their belief in the superiority and precision of the scientific method is a further factor influencing them to move in the direction of quantitative research, since this will lead to the production of data in the form of numbers – essentially statistics which can then be easily manipulated to consider trends over time or differences between various social groups according to certain criteria.

This leads them to seek connections – and ultimately causal connections – between variables.

Cause and effect: the problem of correlation and causation

Demonstrating a link (correlation) between two variables is merely evidence that there might be a relationship between them. It is important to remember that it is *not* evidence that one *causes* the other. Unfortunately, demonstrating a link is often the basis for dubious interpretations of statistical findings. For example, in looking at the statistics relating to number of marriages and number of wedding rings purchased one would expect to find that they were linked – when one rises, so does the other. However, it would be foolish to argue that the reason people get married is because they have bought a wedding ring. Clearly some *other* factor is here causing a change in people's behaviour such that they (a) buy a wedding ring and (b) get married. It might be said that the causal factor was 'falling in love', or 'a baby due to be born'. Here a third factor – which can be debated – causes changes in the first two factors.

An important example of this is the doctrine of monetarism. On the basis of studies of the American economy, monetarist economists noted that there was a link between the rise in the level of money in circulation and the rate of inflation. They demonstrated that the two variables were correlated. However, monetarists then went on to argue that this was a causal link whereby increases in the supply of money in circulation were the cause of inflation. This argument is hotly disputed by other economists, but it was this economic doctrine which underlied much of the economic policy of the New Right in the 1980s and 90s.

It is important not to assume that two variables that change in the same direction are necessarily causing one another, although they may be interrelated. For example, over the past five years, girls overall have achieved higher GCSE grades than boys. Over the same period the frequency of soap operas on TV has risen (correlation). Does this mean that watching soap operas on TV makes girls more intelligent (causation)? The answer is obviously no.

In summary, never confuse *correlation* with *causation*. One does not prove the other, and one should always be careful to check that this slippage is not occurring when reading accounts of sociological research.

Strengths of quantitative methodology

1. Statistics play an important role in sociology because they do allow us to consider trends over time. Since numbers provide a common currency with which to compare social groups in relation to certain issues, quantitative research remains very popular.

2. Quantitative data can easily be analyzed using statistical techniques, and this attractive feature has been enhanced in recent decades by the availability of computers that can process data very quickly. This allows sociologists to obtain findings from social surveys with large samples with relative ease.

3. Computers also permit researchers to re-analyze data easily, so sociologists can go back and re-use primary data that have been collected many years before.

Problems with quantitative methodology

1. Those influenced by phenomenology and hermeneutics would suggest that at the heart of all their problems with quantitative methodology is the nature of humanity espoused by positivism, namely the way humans are viewed as puppets subject to forces and laws external to themselves. The construction of questionnaires and interview schedules often reveals this problem, with a limited number of options being offered and no space being given to allow people to explain in detail the reasons behind their choices. This reflects the positivists belief, but

it is of course rejected by phenomenological sociologists who argue that it is precisely in the process of interaction and the construction of meaning that humans not only have choices, but make the choices that make the world the way it is. This is central to sociology, they argue, and it is largely missed out in quantitative methodology, which instead imposes its own framework of meaning on those being researched.

2. It is therefore argued by phenomenologists that, although quantitative methods can be shown to be reliable (in the sense that if repeated they will produce the same result), this reliability is of no use because the findings, although constant, are not valid. Rather, they represent the 'reality' imposed on people by the researcher. Furthermore, it is this that also accounts for the data's reliability, since the findings are a reflection of the methodology used rather than the superiority and accuracy of the method.

Those who criticize quantitative methods therefore say they lack validity, in that the findings do not really represent the reality of those being studied.

The belief that facts are value-free and theory-free is at the heart of the empiricist approach that underlies positivist methodology, and this is, of course, rejected by those who argue that facts only make sense in the context of theories. The danger is of generating reams of 'facts' without any coherent theoretical framework with which to make sense of it all.

Phenomenological approaches, qualitative methods and interpretive theories

For research sociologists, the central defining aspect of the qualitative, phenomenological, or interpretive methodological approaches is that reality is the result of human interactions, and the way people interpret their world and try to construct meanings out of it.

So the key concern in such methodological approaches is a wish to describe and analyze how people interact; although it is possible to do this using quantitative methods, these are largely rejected because they impose a frame of meaning on the subject being researched.

For example, a questionnaire framed to elicit quantitative data will allow only responses picked from a preselected number of alternative answers. People might be forced to place themselves within a category that does not really represent their true situation, and it is also possible that two people with widely differing views might end up in the same statistical mass. For instance, in a survey asking people whether they are a) impressed or b) unimpressed with the current leader of the Labour Party, the group of responses in the second category might include Conservatives, Liberal Democrats and left-wing socialists. This category would thus include a very diverse range of people who made their choice for divergent reasons. Conservative Party supporters might be unimpressed because they see the Labour leader as a socialist, while left-wing socialists might be unimpressed because they see the same person as not enough of a socialist.

To explore more deeply the meanings and attitudes behind responses like these requires the asking of further questions, and this leads towards a qualitative methodology. Those adopting a qualitative methodology argue that research should be approached without any preconceptions or structures, and that people should be treated as conscious, active subjects in order to capture the full depth and detail of how people interact meaningfully to create the world. This reality, they say, is far too complex to be captured by pigeon-holing people into the categories associated with quantitative methodology.

Strengths of qualitative methodology

1. The key advantage claimed for qualitative methods is that they allow a deeper – and therefore more valid – picture to emerge of the particular set of social relationships under investigation. By focusing on interactions, they allow sociologists to look at the dynamic and fluid nature of society, and by focusing on the meanings people construct they concentrate on the active nature of humanity.

2. In so far as social researchers wish to view people in this way and to focus on the cultural and social processes by which they live their lives, then this approach has clear advantages over the more static fixed pictures which emerge from quantitative methods.

3. This is seen as much more important than defining so-called objective variables which

are merely seen as the imposition of researchers on a somewhat more fluid, subjective reality. Ultimately, the advantages of qualitative methods are related to the methodological theories out of which they flow, and if one disagrees with the theories then the approach will seem subjective and unreliable. Justification of such criticism relies on a more positivistic view of the world than those undertaking qualitative research will accept.

Problems with qualitative methodology

1. The key criticism, resting implicitly on positivistic notions, is that qualitative approaches are subjective. The implied charge in this is that data produced using such approaches should not ultimately be taken too seriously. Sometimes this criticism is extended to say that qualitative methods tend to be applied towards the more trivial aspects of life, but this obviously depends very much on your point of view.

2. A potentially more serious criticism made of qualitative methods is that they are unreliable. This means that a second researcher repeating the research using the same techniques – or even the same researcher repeating the research at a later date – will not be guaranteed to achieve the same results. While it is clearly the case that techniques such as participant observation do rely very heavily on the personal characteristics and skills of the researcher – and therefore another researcher is unlikely to be able to repeat the research precisely – this may be missing the point:

It might be that the positivist's research tool consistently and reliably measures the variables but if what is being researched is invalid then the whole process is rather pointless. ... For example, intelligence tests are reliable measures of intelligence quotients but whether this has anything to do with intelligence is debatable.

(Harvey and MacDonald, 1993, p. 188)

In other words, a method that consistently measures things inaccurately or wrongly in some sense can still be considered reliable, but ought to be considered rather pointless and arguably dangerous in certain contexts.

3. A final criticism of qualitative methods is that,

since they build on theories that tend to deny the existence of any social structures beyond those constructed at the level of interpersonal interactions, their approach is deficient in considering the whole ensemble of relations that make up society.

Theories, methods and types of data

The terms *quantitative* and *qualitative* have an important meaning in this context. Both words refer to types of data:

- Quantitative refers to data that are largely numerical in form or contain large amounts of numbers and/or statistical data.
- Qualitative refers to data consisting of words – that is, verbal descriptions.

Whilst it is important to note that sociologists of all persuasions may produce their evidence in terms of both types, there is a link between a particular theoretical outlook and the likelihood of producing a certain type of data. For example:

- Positivist sociologists (who believe that sociology should be scientific and precise in nature) tend to be more likely to want evidence in the form of quantitative data – and therefore to use methods that provide such data.
- Phenomenologically inclined sociologists (who believe the job of sociology is to report the way people see and understand the world) are more concerned to understand the point of view of the people they are researching – and this leads them to report their respondents' views in their own words, leading to a desire for qualitative data and the use of methods that provide such data.

Positivism, quantitative methods causes and effects

The positivists' desire for quantitative data has several roots.

1. They hold the belief that humans are in essence subject to the **laws of society**.

2. This vision of humanity implies that it does not really matter what individual people think, because their views can have no real influence on the direction society will take. This

leads to a concern with delineating the **struc-tures of society**.

3   Their belief in the superiority and precision of the **scientific method** is a further factor influencing them to move in the direction of quantitative research. This will lead to the production of data in the form of numbers – essentially statistics that can then be manipulated easily to consider *trends over time* or *differences between various social groups* according to certain criteria.

4   This in turn leads them to seek *connections* – and ultimately causal connections – *between variables*.

Cause and effect: the problem of correlation and causation

Demonstrating a link (correlation) between two variables is merely evidence that there *might* be a relationship between them. It is important to remember that the link is *not* evidence that one *causes* the other. Unfortunately this is often the basis for dubious interpretations of statistical findings.

For example, in looking at the statistics relating to number of marriages and number of wedding rings purchased one would expect to find that they were linked – when one rises, so does the other. However, it would be foolish to argue that the reason people get married is because they have bought a wedding ring. Clearly some *other* factor is here causing a change in people's behaviour such that they (a) buy a wedding ring and (b) get married. It might be said that the causal factor was 'falling in love', or 'a baby due to be born'. Here a third factor – which can be debated – causes changes in the first two factors.

Another important example of this is the economic doctrine of 'monetarism'. On the basis of studies of the American economy, monetarist economists noted that there was a link between the rise in the level of money in circulation and the rate of inflation. They demonstrated that the two variables were *correlated*. However, monetarists then went on to argue that this was a *causal* link whereby increases in the supply of money in circulation were the cause of inflation. This argument is hotly disputed by other economists, but this economic doctrine was behind much of the economic policy of the **New Right** in the 1980s and 90s.

In summary, *never confuse correlation with causation* – one does not prove the other. When reading accounts of sociological research, always be careful to check that this confusion of thought is not occurring.

Strengths of quantitative methodology

Statistics play an important role in sociology because they do allow us to consider trends over time. Since numbers provide a common currency with which to compare social groups in relation to certain issues, quantitative research remains very popular.

Secondly, quantitative data can be analysed quite easily using standard statistical techniques. This attractive feature has been enhanced in recent years by the availability of computers and software that can process data rapidly, allowing sociologists to derive findings from social surveys with large samples with relative ease.

Computers also permit one to re-analyse data easily, so later sociologists can go back and re-use **primary data** that was collected earlier.

Problems with quantitative methodology

Those influenced by phenomenology would suggest that at the heart of all problems is the nature of humanity espoused by positivism – namely the way humans are viewed as puppets subject to forces and laws external to themselves.

The construction of questionnaires and interview schedules often reveals this problem, with a limited number of options being offered and no space being given to allow people to explain in detail the reasons behind their choices. This reflects the positivists' belief, but it is rejected by phenomenological sociologists. The latter argue that it is precisely in the process of *interaction* that humans not only have choices, but make the choices that determine the world the way it is. This is central to sociology, they argue, and it is largely missed out in quantitative methodology, *which instead imposes its own framework of meaning on those being researched*.

It is therefore argued by phenomenologists that, although quantitative methods can be shown to be reliable (in the sense that if repeated they will produce the same result), this reliability is of no use because the findings, although constant, are not valid. Rather, they represent the 'reality' imposed on people by the researcher. Furthermore, it is this which also accounts for the data's reliability, since the findings are a reflection of the methodology used rather than the superiority and accuracy of the method.

Those who criticize quantitative methods thus say they lack *validity*, in that the findings do not really represent the reality of those being studied.

The belief that facts are value-free and theory-free is at the heart of positivist methodology, and this is of course rejected by those who argue that facts only make sense in the context of theories. The danger is of generating reams of 'facts' without any coherent theoretical framework with which to make sense of it all.

Phenomenological approaches, qualitative methods and interpretive theories

For research sociologists, the central defining aspect of methodological approaches is that reality is the result of human interactions, and the way people interpret their world and try to construct meanings out of it.

So the key concern is a wish to describe and analyse how people interact. Although it is possible to do this using quantitative methods, these are largely rejected because they impose a frame of meaning on the subject being researched – as explained above.

For example, a questionnaire framed to elicit quantitative data will allow only responses picked from a preselected number of alternative answers. People might be forced to place themselves within a category that does not really represent their true situation, and it is also possible that two people with widely differing views might end up in the same statistical mass.

For instance, in a survey asking people whether they are (a) impressed or (b) unimpressed with the current leader of the Labour party, the group of responses in the second category might include Conservatives, Liberal Democrats and left-wing socialists. This category would thus include a very diverse range of people who made their choices for different reasons. Conservative supporters might be unimpressed because they see the Labour leader as a socialist, while left-wing socialists might be unim-

pressed because they see the same person as not enough of a socialist.

To explore more deeply the meanings and attitudes behind responses like these requires the asking of further questions, leading towards a qualitative methodology. Those adopting a qualitative methodology argue that research should be approached without any preconceptions or structures, and should treat people as conscious, active subjects in order to capture the full depth and detail of how people interact meaningfully to create the world. This reality, they say, is far too complex to be captured by pigeon-holing people into the categories associated with quantitative methodology.

Strengths of qualitative methodology

The key advantage claimed for qualitative methods is that they allow a deeper – and therefore more valid – picture to emerge of the particular set of social relationships under investigation. By focusing on interactions, they allow sociologists to look at the dynamic and fluid nature of society; and by focusing on the meanings people construct they concentrate on the active nature of humanity.

Secondly, in so far as social researchers wish to view people in this way and to focus on the cultural and social processes by which they live their lives, then this approach has clear advantages over the more static fixed pictures emerging from quantitative methods.

This is seen as much more important than defining so-called objective variables that are seen merely as the imposition of researchers on a somewhat more fluid, subjective reality.

Ultimately the advantages of qualitative methods are related to the methodological theories out of which they flow, and if one disagrees with the theories then the approach will seem subjective and unreliable. Justification of such criticism relies on a more positivistic view of the world than those undertaking qualitative research will accept.

Problems with qualitative methodology

The key criticism, resting implicitly on positivistic notions, is that qualitative approaches are subjective. The implied charge is that data produced using such approaches should not, ultimately, be taken too seriously. Sometimes this criticism is extended to say that qualitative methods tend to be applied towards the more trivial aspects of life – but obviously this depends very much on your own point of view.

A potentially more serious criticism made of qualitative methods is that they are unreliable. By this is meant that a second researcher repeating the research using the same techniques – or even the same researcher repeating the research at a later date – will not be guaranteed to achieve the same results. While it is clearly the case that techniques such as observation as a participant do rely very heavily on the personal characteristics and skills of the researcher – and therefore another researcher is unlikely to be able to repeat the research precisely – this may be missing the point:

It might be that the positivist's research tool consistently and reliably measures the variables, but if what is being researched is invalid then the whole process is rather pointless. ... For example, intelligence tests are reliable measures of intelligence quotients but whether this has anything to do with intelligence is debatable.

(Harvey and MacDonald, 1993, p. 188)

In other words, a method that consistently measures things inaccurately or wrongly in some sense can still be considered reliable, but ought to be considered rather pointless and arguably dangerous in certain contexts.

Positivistic research uses preset categories of answers. However, one criticism of this is that respondents are forced to pigeonhole themselves into answers imposed by the researchers. Proponents of qualitative research claim that it overcomes this **imposition problem**. Ray Pawson, however, argues that there is nonetheless an imposition problem involved in qualitative methods. As an example he cites the large amount of material generated by Ann Oakley in her study of the experiences of motherhood (see also Section 5.7), which involved 233 interviews and produced 545 hours of tape-recorded data. It is clear that not all of this material appears in the final report of her research project. (This is a general problem with all research that produces qualitative data.) In the final report, the data are represented by quotations from the material, but not by production of the whole data set. The problem with this is outlined by Pawson:

The phenomenological schools as a whole have traditionally been very tough on quantitative methods for imposing meaning. ... This very familiar anti-positivistic missile has now been trained inwards and applied to participant observation. 'Field research' in general, and by its very nature, tends to produce findings which are anecdotal and massively selective in terms of the ratio of events reported to those witnessed. In this process of the selection and packaging of evidence, the possibility of imposition of meaning again looms large.

(Pawson, 1989, p. 161)

> ### Discussion point
> To what extent do you agree with the argument that both positivist and phenomenological approaches suffer from the imposition problem? Do they suffer from it in exactly the same way, or differently?
>
>

Using more than one method (triangulation)

Triangulation refers to the use of more than one method, to try to counter the weaknesses of one particular method by combining it with another that is strong in that area. So, for example, **structured interviews** might be combined with **participant observation**. It is also possible to use both structured and **unstructured interviews**, the logic behind doing so being to try to gain the highest levels of both validity and reliability.

Eileen Barker – The Moonies

The classical example of this approach is in Barkers' (1984) study of the Unification Church, better known as the Moonies (see the case study on page 280). In her study, Barker used participant observation, questionnaires and interviews. Information from the participant observation (which lasted six years) and from the interviews (which consisted of 30 interviews lasting between six and eight hours) was used to gain a detailed picture of the Unification Church, and this information was then used to enable the researcher to draw up more detailed hypotheses for later investigation using questionnaires.

Barker argued that by combining these methods her study of the Moonies gained greater validity and reliability than would have been the case if she had conducted the study using only qualitative or only quantitative methods.

Since research methodology allows us to be fairly sure about the relative strengths and weaknesses of the various techniques, and since this information is now widely available, more and more sociologists are seeking to use triangulation – or 'methodological pluralism' as it is sometimes called.

Pierre Bourdieu, *Distinction*

As another example we can look at the points made by Pierre Bourdieu when being interviewed about his book *Distinction* (Bourdieu, 1984):

Q: I'd now like to turn to the question of the relationship between sociology and the neighbouring sciences. Your book Distinction *opens with the sentence: 'Sociology is rarely more akin to a social psychoanalysis than when it confronts an object like taste.' Then come statistical tables, and accounts of surveys – but also analyses of a 'literary' type, such as one finds in Balzac, Zola or Proust. How do these two aspects fit together?*

A: The book results from an effort to integrate two modes of knowledge – ethnographic observation, which can only be based on a small number of cases, and statistical analysis, which makes it possible to establish regularities and to situate the observed cases in the universe of existing cases. So you have, for example, the contrasting description of a working-class meal and a bourgeois meal. ... On the working-class side, there is a declared primacy of function, which appears in all the food that is served: the food has to be 'filling, body-building' ... to give strength (conspicuous muscles). On the bourgeois side, there is the primacy of form, or formality, which implies a kind of censorship and repression of function, an aestheticization, which is found in every area, as much in eroticism, functioning as sublimated or denied pornography, as in pure art which is defined precisely by the fact that it privileges form at the expense of function. In fact, the analyses that are described as 'qualitative' or more pejoratively, 'literary', are essential for understanding, that's to say fully explaining, what the statistics merely record, rather like rainfall statistics. They lead to the principle of all the practices observed, in the most varied areas.

(Bourdieu, 1993a, p. 14)

Problems and solutions

While it might be seen that this approach can allow research strategies to be developed that avoid the problems associated with using only one method, it should be noted that it does not eliminate these problems – it merely covers them over by utilizing other methods with strengths in the areas of weakness in the first method. Rather than a unified overall methodology, it is a form of using complementary methods. As Tim May has pointed out:

While triangulation might appear attractive, it is not a panacea for methodological ills.

(May, 1993, p. 90)

(A panacea is a cure-all so clearly May feels triangulation cannot solve all problems.)

Nonetheless it is clear that triangulation can offer real benefits and is leading to more and more sociologists adopting the principles that lie behind it. Case studies focusing on specific issues but using more than one methodological technique, or even methodology, have risen in popularity in sociology recently. While this might put a spotlight on the issues of validity and reliability, it could also impact on the issue of representativeness.

For instance, the famous study by Goldthorpe and colleagues, *The Affluent Worker* (1968), chose to study workers in Luton, not because they were representative, but because this seemed the most likely place to find 'affluent workers'. In this sense an extreme case was picked rather than a representative sample.

Whether a unified methodological toolkit can be devised which would go beyond triangulation remains to be seen.

Most of the sections in the remainder of this chapter contains extracts from sociologists talking about their research, and more than one method was used in many instances.

Further factors impacting on the research selection process

This part of the chapter would be redundant if we lived in a world where sociologists were allowed to put forward their theoretical arguments (positivism *versus* phenomenology *versus* realism) and then choose research methods solely on that basis. Of course, we do not live in such a world. Structures of power exist, and these impinge upon – and are created by – sociologists in the world of sociology just as in every other sphere of society. These structures therefore have an impact upon how research is done.

Obvious constraints are *money* and *time*. Funding is not always easy to come by, and awarding bodies may require the sociologist to undertake research using specific methods as a condition of their funding. Equally, if a research report is required in four months one is unlikely to have the luxury of choosing in-depth participant observation. Lawson (1986) has provided a useful summary of possible constraints on researchers (see Figure 9.1).

Lawson points to how the subject matter itself can constrain choices:

Interactionists are likely to be highly disposed towards observational techniques. But if you are a fifty-year-old female sociologist interested in football hooliganism, it is going to be difficult to perform a participant observation study of that topic! Similarly, if you are a positivist wishing to investigate illiteracy, a written questionnaire is not an option you can easily take.

(Lawson, 1986, p. 41)

Activity

Suggest *two* examples of your own of how
(i) the nature of the subject matter, and
(ii) practical constraints such as time and money, may serve to affect choices over research methods to be employed.

C3.2, C3.3

The points made above about resources serve as a reminder that sociological research (as opposed to reading about it) operates in a world where the people with power might not care much for your preference for qualitative methods. They might want just the bare statistics, and they could withdraw funding if they do not get their way. Of course, it is likely that such a project would be entrusted to a sociologist already quantitatively inclined, but this would leave our qualitative sociologist without a grant and therefore possibly unable to do research. The nature of what is researched, and how it is researched, would therefore still be influenced.

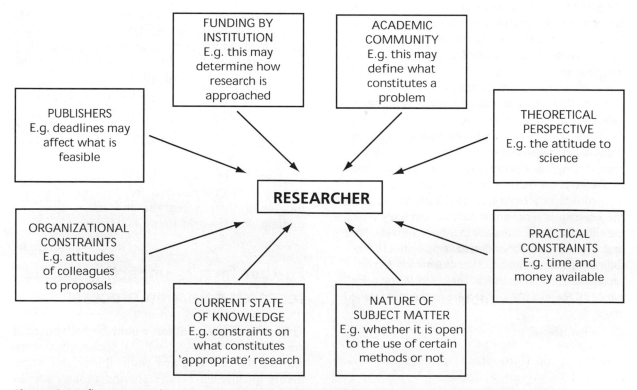

Figure 9.1 Influences on the researcher's choice of method
Source: Lawson (1986, p. 40)

9.3 Ethics in the research process

Sociologists conduct research to try to understand the world, and possibly to try to influence policy decisions. This research can have real effects on the lives of people. Sociologists need, therefore, to think about the ethical issues – before, during and after their research.

The ethics of research relationships

At the heart of the way sociologists treat respondents in research is the notion of 'informed consent'. All people should be participants out of free choice, rather than face pressure of any sort to take part. It follows from this that they should be aware of the fact that the researcher is doing research, and something about the nature of that research.

Once the sociologist has collected data, there is still a responsibility towards the respondents. Information gained in the process of research should be treated as confidential, and people should be granted anonymity when the findings are published. This is not always easy. For example, if a researcher is doing research in a school, omitting someone's name while identifying them as a head of department might make it possible for that person to be identified. On the other hand, to leave this information out might not provide a full context in which to consider that person's statements or actions.

So, although it is relatively straightforward to think about these issues and to outline some general principles, the application of the principles in research is sometimes difficult and involves sociologists in ethical and professional dilemmas. This section looks at two actual sociological studies as a way of considering how ethical issues arose and how sociologists tried to deal with them.

Case Study – Tearoom trade

With regard to **covert observation** of participants (see Section 9.5), one of the most famous cases is that of Laud Humphreys' study (1970), which he called *The Tearoom Trade*.

In this research he observed gay sexual encounters in public rest-rooms. He wished (a) to explain how such encounters, and the social structure they required, worked; and (b) to investigate the rules and meanings attached to the encounters by the participants. In order to do this he engaged in **covert participant observation**, but also later used follow-up interviews (see Section 9.5).

Humphreys became an accepted part of the gay scene in Chicago by visiting gay bars and attending balls. He adopted the role of 'watch-queen' – meaning a lookout, but also someone who got satisfaction from watching others engage in sex. Publication of the study attracted some controversy.

Discussion point

To what extent do you think controversy over the methods used by Humphreys was related to the subject matter of his research?

C3.1a

Humphreys noted 134 car number-plates and, using contacts with the police force, obtained the addresses of the owners. He later got 100 of these addresses included in a survey on health he was involved with a year later. In that year, having changed his appearance, he called on the 100 people in the guise of the health survey to conduct further research. May (1993) recounts the details of the response to this research:

The reactions to the publication of his study were variable. As Humphreys notes in a postscript to the book: 'several have suggested to me that I should have avoided this research subject altogether' (1970: 168). He was accused of deceit, the invasion of privacy and increasing the likelihood of the sample's detection by the police force. One account suggests that some faculty members at Washington University were so outraged 'that they demanded (unsuccessfully) that Humphreys' doctoral degree be revoked' (Kimmel 1988: 23). On the other hand: 'The research was applauded by members of the gay community and some social scientists for shedding light on a little-known segment of our society, and for dispelling stereotypes and myths' (Kimmel 1988: 23). ... In this sense, the means justified the end. He brought into the public domain an understanding of an issue which American society had done so much to repress. To his critics, however, the means can never justify the ends: 'Social research involving deception and manipulation ultimately helps produce a society of cynics, liars and manipulators, and undermines the trust which is essential to a just social order.' (Warwick 1982: 58).

(May, 1993, p. 46)

Activity

In your own words, explain (i) the case for supporting Humphreys' research methods, and (ii) the case for opposing his methods.

C3.2, C3.3

Case Study – The Moonies

Another example of the issue of ethics in social research can be found in Eileen Barker's study in 1984 of the 'Moonies', members of the Unification Church. She argues that conducting the study seemed difficult or impossible without gaining access and becoming a member of the church, but she was unwilling to do this, partly because of ethical questions:

It seemed unlikely that I would be able to obtain much information unless I was to pretend to become a member myself. This was out of the question for a number of reasons. First, I would have been unhappy about the deception on purely ethical grounds; secondly, I had no desire to give up my job; and thirdly, even if I were to have joined, I would not have been able to go around asking questions on any sort of systematic basis without arousing suspicion.

(Barker, 1984; quoted in Dunsmuir and Williams, 1991, p. 60)

Activity

With reference to both the studies by Humphreys and by Barker, consider the following questions:

a To what extent do you support the notion that social researchers should never lie in their research?

b To what extent do you support the notion that social researchers should never invade people's privacy in research?

C3.2, C3.3

Barker eventually became an ***overt* participant observer** (see Section 9.5), following an invitation from the Unification Church itself. Although this clearly did not involve the deception she had worried about, which had led her to abandon

covert observation, this method was itself not without problems, as she recounts:

The people I was studying could be influenced by my presence because I was studying them. ... There were several occasions on which I mediated between a Moonie and his parents. ... These interventions ... I undertook with an awareness that what I was doing could affect the situation. There were also numerous occasions on which my influence was unintended. ... One occurred while I was on a 21-day lecture course at which the participants were expected to deliver a lecture. The subject I was allocated was 'The Purpose of the Coming of the Messiah'. I did not exactly enjoy this aspect of my research, but participant observation does involve participation, so I gave the talk, carefully punctuating its delivery with phrases such as 'The Divine Principle teaches that ...' or 'According to the Principle ...'. When I had finished, a member of the audience declared that she had been extremely worried about this particular part of the doctrine, but now she understood it, and she fully accepted that the Reverend Moon was indeed the Messiah. I was horrified. 'But I don't believe it,' I insisted, 'I don't think it's true.' 'Perhaps not,' interrupted the Moonie in charge, 'but God has used Eileen to show Rosemary the truth.'

(Barker, 1984; quoted in Dunsmuir and Williams, 1991, p. 62)

9.4 Sampling

The one instance in which an individual's participation in social research is not optional is the national Census of the whole population (see Section 9.6). People are legally required to fill in a questionnaire and can be fined if they fail or refuse to do this. The Census costs so much to conduct that it is done only every 10 years. The resources needed to conduct research on this scale are unavailable to other sociologists, who are therefore required to fall back on the use of *samples* of the population for their studies. However, this is problematic since most pieces of research will want to draw conclusions about the UK as a whole.

How are sociologists to select people to be studied, and how are they to get them to agree to participate?

Representativeness

The first thing to be clear about is the population

to be studied. 'Population' in this context does not refer to the population of the whole country, but to all those people in the group to be studied. Thus a study of the effects of unemployment might have as its population all those who lived in households where at least one member is unemployed.

While this may suggest that deciding on a population is relatively straightforward, that is deceptive. While the suggested population does not limit itself to individuals who are unemployed, it does limit itself to households and it can be argued that the effects of unemployment spread much wider than that.

For instance, shopkeepers in an area with a large number of unemployed people might be affected, while not being unemployed themselves. Equally, given the known links between unemployment and ill-health, it is possible to argue that levels of unemployment would have an impact on demand for health services, and thereby affect the length of time employed people have to wait to see their doctor. It is also the case that since the level of unemployment affects the costs of social security, and has an impact on the level of economic output of the economy, it could be said that unemployment affects every person in the UK – even if they as an individual are not unemployed and do not have an unemployed person as a member of their household.

So, identifying a population to be studied requires much reflection on the nature of the problem at issue, and the possible aspects of it that might need to be considered.

Generalization

Despite the fact that a population in this sense contains a much smaller number than the whole of the population of the UK, it still may involve impracticably large numbers. So sociologists seek to select a sample to *represent*, or stand in for, the population they wish to study. In order to be able to make general statements about the whole of the population they are studying, they need to ensure that the sample selected is indeed truly *representative* of that population. This introduces the important concept of 'representativeness':

This refers to the question of whether the group of people or the situation that we are studying are typical of others. If they are, then we can safely conclude that what is true of this group is also true of others. We can generalize from the example that we have studied. If we do not know whether they are representative, then we cannot claim that our conclusions

have any relevance to anybody else at all.

(McNeill, 1985, p. 13)

The procedures used to ensure that any sample is representative are known as 'sampling techniques'. They involve several stages, issues and choices which are examined in this section.

Discussion point

What problems might arise in trying to define a population to study the effects of a school opting-out of local education authority control and becoming grant-maintained?

C3.1a

The sampling frame

The first problem (and an extremely important practical one) is how to obtain a complete list of the names of the population to be studied. This is known as a 'sampling frame' because it provides the list from which the sample will be selected. Sometimes people seem to assume these just exist, but this is a misconception.

Lists that are openly available are those making up the electoral registers, compiled for the purposes of checking eligibility to vote. These are by polling district and are available at local reference libraries. They contain the names and addresses of all people eligible to vote in that particular district. Since a roll is updated every year, it will provide an up-to-date list.

The Post Office General Address File lists all the addresses in the UK, and if one were trying to select a sample based on households rather than individuals this would provide a possible starting point.

Various professionals, such as doctors, have lists of people in their area and it might be possible to try to utilize these. However, the issue of confidentiality may lead to access to these lists being denied. Howard Newby (1977) points to some problems he faced in his study of agricultural workers in Suffolk:

I sampled farms rather than farm workers, since I believed I could obtain a reliable sampling frame of farms (mistakenly, since the Ministry of Agriculture refused to co-operate and I was forced back on to Yellow Pages) and then contact the workers via an employer. This was not only an administrative convenience, but probably also an administrative necessity. However, the result was that, in common with so many other sociological studies, I was taking the easy option of homing in on a captive set of respondents.

(Newby, 1977, pp. 114–15)

Activity

a What problems did Newby encounter in the construction of a sampling frame?

b Explain why he described his sample as a 'captive set of respondents'.

c Suggest reasons why he did not sample farm workers.

C3.2, C3.3

This example illustrates the point that it should not be assumed that existing data will automatically be made available to sociological researchers.

A further problem might be that no potential sampling frame exists covering exactly the population one wishes to study. If, for example, one wished to study relations between parents and young children, school lists would not include those under school age, and an electoral roll does not include children aged under seventeen or eighteen.

All this serves to emphasize that populations do not simply exist nicely lined up in alphabetical order on sampling frames waiting for a sociological researcher to turn up! Constructing a usable sampling frame might in itself involve a considerable amount of work.

Sampling procedures

Once a researcher has managed to obtain or construct a sampling frame, he or she is in a position to select a sample from it. There are a variety of ways of doing this. These can be divided into *random* and *non-random* sampling methods

Random sampling

The idea behind truly random sampling is that everyone in the population has an equal chance of appearing in the sample, so ensuring that the sample is not biased. This 'equal chance' is based on **probability theory**, and random sampling is sometimes known as *probability sampling* for that reason. The technique is therefore not haphazard, as its name might suggest, but based on clear scientific principles.

Simple random sampling

The most basic form of random sampling involves selecting people through the use of a random-number generator on a computer. This selects numbers randomly and adds the names and addresses corresponding to those numbers on to the researcher's population list, up to the required amount to form a sample.

Alternatively one can scan the population list and select every tenth, twentieth, etc. name, depending on the sample size required. Lee Harvey and Morag MacDonald call this 'systematic random sampling' and they explain its potential pitfall:

There is a possibility that this process might give an unrepresentative sample if the lists are ordered in a particular way. For example, if the list was an address list in house number order then every tenth house might generate only even numbers that would (in Britain) lead to the houses selected all being on one side of a street. It is possible that this might generate a sample with an unrepresentative housing class.

(Harvey and MacDonald, 1993, p. 118)

Stratified random sampling

This method divides the research population into a number of **strata** based on what are seen as significant variables – for example, gender, ethnicity, class, age. Samples are then randomly drawn from each of the strata and combined together to form the final sample. Decisions about the precise way the final sample is to be made up can be made on the basis of the respective importance of the substrata in the population as a whole. For example, men and women each comprise roughly 50 per cent of the population so a final sample based on gender would be 50 per cent male, 50 per cent female. However, since the ethnic minority population is 5 per cent, only 5 per cent of ethnic minority members would appear in a sample based on ethnicity.

Stratified sampling allows the researcher to ensure that all potential target groups within a population are represented in the final sample, and that all variables considered potentially important (or in which they have a special interest) are covered.

Cluster sampling

This method can be used when no sampling frame is easily available. It is based on identifying a number of clusters in the population, such as schools or classes within schools, and then selecting individuals from within these clusters. While this allows the construction of a sample in a much quicker way than would be possible if it were necessary to construct a sampling frame and construct a simple random sample, it is also problematic in that it can be biased. In selecting clusters before individuals are selected, not every individual has an equal chance of being selected, and the overall sample might therefore not be representative of the population under study.

Multi-stage random sampling

Here the selection of a sample goes through various stages. Each stage involves the selection of a sample from the previous sample chosen, until the researcher arrives at a list of individuals. This method was employed, for example, by Marshall *et al.* (1988) in their study *Social Class in Modern Britain*:

A three stage design was employed. This involved the selection of parliamentary constituencies, polling districts, and finally individuals. ... One hundred parliamentary constituencies, then two polling districts from each sampled constituency, were selected with probability at both stages proportionate to size of electorate. ... Nineteen addresses from each sampled polling district were then selected by taking a systematic sample through the list of elector names and noting the address of the elector on which the sampling interval landed.

(Marshall *et al.*, 1988, p. 288)

The main potential drawback with this method is that, if parliamentary constituencies have differing total numbers of electors, then the chances of individuals being selected at the final stage become unequal. This issue explains the concern in the extract above with ensuring that probability was proportionate to size of electorate, but this entails careful attention to the detail of the sampling.

Panel studies

While all the above methods relate to one-off samples, the idea of a panel study is to conduct research on the same sample over a period. Such an approach is important when one wishes to consider changes over time. The original sample can be constructed using any of the above methods.

Key problems are, first, convincing people to agree to be questioned on more than one occasion; and secondly, keeping in contact with the original sample if, for example, they change residence. Because of these problems such studies tend to have relatively high drop-out rates which may make the sample progressively less representative.

For example, Himmelweit *et al.* (1985) selected a sample of 450 men who were 21 years old in 1959 and considered their voting behaviour through to the October 1974 general election. By 1974 the sample numbered only 178 and all were now middle-aged. Since their sample was also overwhelmingly non-manual workers, their findings were criticized as not being representative.

Spatial sampling

If it is required to study the participants at a particular event, then one can choose respondents randomly from within a group of people gathered together in a certain space (hence 'spatial'). This is random in so far as it selects people randomly from within a *given* population.

The method might be employed to study people on a demonstration, or at a concert, since they will be gathered together for only a short time and this means more conventional methods are inapplicable.

Non-random sampling

While it is often thought that a sample should always be representative of the population, this is not in fact the case. There are instances when one might purposely wish to select a sample that is not representative. It is not therefore a criticism of these approaches to say that they are not representative since they do not aim to be, neither do they claim to be. As with random sampling there are a number of forms this type of sampling can take.

Accidental sampling

Here the researcher studies all individuals he or she comes into contact with over a given period – for example from 3 pm until 4 pm on a Tuesday in a shopping centre. Such an approach tends to be associated with qualitative research, or for the pilot stage of quantitative research where the main aim is to test the usefulness of a questionnaire.

Such an approach does not yield a representative sample. For example, a researcher in the high street on Tuesday afternoons is unlikely to obtain responses from those with full-time employment working traditional hours.

Purposive sampling

Here the researcher selects people on the basis that they are likely to be relevant to the subject being studied. This of course means that the sample reflects judgements made by the researcher which may be open to question. However, it does allow researchers to include significant individuals within their research.

Volunteer sampling

In this method, people volunteer to be studied. It has its limitations:

Ien Ang's (1985) study of viewers' attitudes to Dallas [an American TV soap] was based on a volunteer sample of people who responded to her advertisement in a Dutch magazine. Volunteer samples are thus self-selecting and usually biased as they are a subgroup of a population who are prepared to be involved in the research. Sometimes researchers have to resort to volunteer samples as there is no other way of reaching sufficient numbers of people to build up a sample.

(Harvey and MacDonald, 1993, p. 120)

Activity

Suggest two potential research topics where researchers might have to 'resort to volunteer samples'.

C3.2, C3.3

Quota sampling

Quota sampling is similar in some respects to stratified sampling. Instead of choosing randomly from strata within the population, the researcher sets a quota precisely outlining the number of individuals meeting certain criteria that are to be included in the sample.

An interviewer might therefore be told to ensure that the sample comprises 10 men over 40 years, 10 men under 40, 10 women over 40 and 10 women under 40. The interviewer would be left to select individuals who fit these criteria.

The first stage is to decide on the important variables, and then investigate how they are located in the population as a whole, probably by consulting the national Census. For example, according to the 1991 Census 56 per cent of the economically active population were in non-manual employment and 44 per cent in manual employment, so these proportions could be used as the basis of a quota instruction. The final sam-

ple would then fit the population as a whole on this criterion. There is, however, the problem that the interviewer is left to decide which individuals are to be questioned, out of all the possible ones who fit the criteria. This can lead to problems:

Problems of abuse and bias caused by the interviewer, who may turn to the first available, convenient or least resistant person, are hard to avoid. However, quota sampling normally is not meant to be a random procedure, and should not be expected to provide random data.

(Sarantakos, 1993, p. 139)

Snowball sampling

Here researchers start with very few people and ask them for recommendations of further people to interview who fit the criteria of the study. When interviewing these people the same procedure is applied and gradually a sample is built up.

A sample can be constructed when no sampling frame is available, and when studying a close-knit group of people who, however, do not necessarily appear on any lists. Roseneil (1995) used this method to construct a sample for the interview stage of her study of feminist activists at Greenham Common.

This is a method often associated with participant observation. The links between individuals that such approaches reveal can unveil important insights, as well as providing one with a sample.

Sampling errors and response rates

The key purpose of sampling is to enable social researchers to make generalizations on the basis of questions asked of only a few people. In order to be able to do this, they need to be sure that their sampling techniques have been properly applied to enable them to do this. There are three key sources of potential error in sampling.

Firstly there is sampling bias. This term is used to refer to a situation where a sample is not drawn at random. Clearly, all non-random sampling methods are open to this problem, although these methods exist because it is not always possible to produce a random sample.

Secondly there is sampling error. This refers

to a situation where, by chance, the sample is not truly representative. The way to rectify this error is to make your sample as large as possible since it is suggested that increasing the sample size will eliminate the chance errors of sampling error. However, it is also suggested that once the sample reaches about 2500 no great improvements will occur by increasing it more. This size therefore represents the logical maximum size for sampling research.

The third problem is the response rate. We can spend time constructing a wonderful sample ensuring it is free from sampling bias and sampling error, but it still remains a list of *potential* respondents only. If you have a perfectly constructed sample and you only get 10 per cent of these to answer your questions, your research might then be worthless.

While it is probably impossible to achieve a 100 per cent response rate, it is clear that the greater the response, the more likely the final results are to be representative and therefore generalizable. Any sociological research with a response rate of less then 60 per cent would generally be seen as problematic. The desire to obtain a high response rate may be a factor in deciding which method of sampling to use (see Section 9.2).

9.5 Collecting primary data

Questionnaires and social surveys

The term 'social survey' refers to a study which aims to gain data from large numbers of people, generally through the use of various types of questionnaire and interview methods. A questionnaire, which is a list of organized questions, is the primary research tool in much sociological research.

The basic questionnaire method involves providing respondents with a printed list of questions to be answered. If, on the other hand, the questions are asked verbally by the researcher, then this situation becomes an interview. Many interviews involve some kind of questionnaire and must take into account the methodological rules devised for drawing up, administering and analysing questionnaires.

Questionnaires are most commonly used when there is a desire to gain information from a large sample of people. There is a minimum number which must be reached if the sample is to stand a chance of being representative – though this is a necessary but not sufficient basis for representativeness.

The validity of findings from a social survey using a questionnaire is related to the actual wording of the questions, so extreme care must be taken at the stage of designing and wording the document. If questions are ambiguous, or if the instructions on how to complete the questionnaire are unclear, it might be that the answers given do not reflect the true situation. The design of a questionnaire and its testing through a *pilot study* are therefore very important.

Piloting a questionnaire

A pilot study is a small initial study conducted with an early draft of a questionnaire. Its sole aim is to test whether it is worded clearly and contains questions that are both understandable and answerable. At this stage it is hoped that any sociological jargon will show up, and any questions that remain unclear can be rectified.

In a pilot study, therefore, respondents may be asked to comment on the questionnaire itself. On the basis of this study, careful consideration must be given to any possible need to rewrite or reorder the questions.

This stage is important because once questionnaires have been issued it is unlikely that they can be reissued if any problems emerge. The finalized questionnaire must be clear of any technical blemishes.

Administering a questionnaire

There are a number of ways of asking people questions, and consideration must be given to the choice of method of administration of a questionnaire. There are four main methods:

• respondents' self-completion
• delivery by mail
• delivery by telephone
• administration by an interviewer.

In the first two cases the questionnaire will be completed by the respondents, so there is a particular need for the wording of the questions to be as clear as possible. Instructions on how to complete the questionnaire have to be drawn up and attached to the front.

The other two forms of administration involve the researcher, or interviewers working on his or her behalf, filling in the answers. Here, careful training is needed to ensure that the interviewers apply the questionnaire in a standardized way and record the answers accurately. There is a degree of personal interaction, and so issues relating to interviewing technique are involved.

Closed versus open-ended questions

Closed questions allow only a limited number of possible responses. Often these responses are written on the questionnaire, where a space or box is allocated for a tick or a cross. Another variety of closed question is that attempting to elicit the attitudes of people by providing them with a set of scales – ranging from, say, 'strongly agree' to 'strongly disagree'. Other scales are possible.

Alternatively, questions may be open-ended. Here the respondents are provided with spaces in which they can construct their own answers.

Some questionnaires contain a mixture of closed and open-ended questions, with closed questions used to identify the person on a set of social variables such as gender, occupation (and thereby class), age, and locality. If statistical information is needed then it is likely that the vast majority of the rest of the questions will also be closed.

Aspects of closed questions

By limiting the number of possible responses, closed questions allow the data to be produced in quantitative form, which is ideal for statistical analysis. The advent of computers has meant that large amounts of data can be compiled into statistical tables and graphs easily and quickly. This has to some extent led to a resurgence in interest in quantitative social surveys.

The main criticism of this type of question is that, since the researcher constructs the possible answers, this forces people to pigeon-hole themselves, and the possible responses may not in fact cover all possibilities. Further, the meanings of the possible responses may vary between respondents, and so what looks like a homogeneous

block of people who all respond in the same way might in reality not be such. Sociologists influenced by the phenomenological approach therefore argue that closed questions do not reveal in-depth insights into the people being studied.

Aspects of open-ended questions

Open-ended (or simply 'open') questions are designed to avoid the problems of closed questions. By allowing respondents to speak for themselves, they are not limited in their possible responses.

However the great problem with this is, of course, that it becomes extremely difficult to make comparisons between the answers because there is no way of ensuring that all respondents interpret the questions in exactly the same way. There is no guarantee that there will be any overlap in their answers which would allow comparisons. In effect, results can be reported only by quoting the comments of the people who have responded.

Can it be claimed that the conclusions are valid if in reality only a sample of all the answers is quoted in the final report or book, and the decision over which bits to include lies with the researcher? Questionnaires conducted using open-ended questions can therefore be criticized over their validity and representativeness, unless all the answers are included in the final research report (which is unlikely).

Interviews

While all research involves asking questions in some way, if a questionnaire is administered face to face then this becomes an interview. The design of the questionnaire remains important, but many other issues arise from the fact that an interview involves interpersonal interaction. The relative importance of these issues varies according to the type of interview conducted.

Types of interview

All interviews involve communication between people, but the way in which this occurs can vary. One key issue is the degree of *structure*, leading to three different types of interview: structured, unstructured and semi-structured.

Structured interviews

These occur when the interviewer is not allowed to deviate from the wording of the questions, nor the order in which they are asked. The aim is to *standardize* the experience so that variations in the answers given reflect real variations. Since this type of interview is used mainly by those interested in obtaining quantitative data, the questions will usually be of the closed type.

Structured interviews were used by Marshall *et al.* (1988) in their study of social class in modern Britain. The methodological issues surrounding this piece of research are considered in detail later in this section.

Unstructured interviews

These occur when there is no rigid format imposed on the interviewer, although there will almost certainly be a checklist of topics to be covered. The interviewer may thus decide the order in which questions are asked, and indeed may modify the questions themselves to suit the flow of the interview. It is unlikely that a detailed list of questions would be drawn up beforehand. Instead the researcher uses interviewing skills to frame questions to cover all chosen areas.

The questions are likely to be much more open than those used in structured interviews. The aim is to try to make the interview feel as natural as possible, almost like a conversation. The lack of structure permits the interviewer to react to the actual answers given by the respondent.

Semi-structured interviews

As their name suggests, these fall in between the above two extremes. The questions are not set down in detail beforehand, thus allowing the interview to proceed in a natural way. The interview will focus on certain predetermined topics, but without preset questions. Alternatively it could be that some questions *will* be preset, especially those relating to the social characteristics of the interviewee which the interviewer has deemed to be possible significant variables. This allows consideration of the way responses might vary according to these social characteristics, whilst also ensuring that the overall sample is representative of the population to be studied in respect of the social variables identified.

The extent of the structuring of the interview will be affected by the general methodological beliefs of the researcher. The more structured interviews are likely to be part of social surveys aimed at producing quantitative data, whilst less structured interviews tend to be favoured by those seeking qualitative data and looking for a more natural interview process.

The interview process

An interview is similar to (though not the same as) a conversation in that it involves interaction between at least two people. In order to make an interview work it is necessary to build up some form of relationship with the person being interviewed, if only to encourage them to participate. The role of the interviewer also involves making contact with potential interviewees and gaining their co-operation. The interview process clearly involves the use of interpersonal skills.

The interviewer effect

A problem may arise over *objectivity* if the personality of an interviewer intrudes into the research process. This is particularly true if more than one interviewer is used, since the intrusion of their *different* personalities will mean that the interview experience varies between the interviewees. Then the actual experience of the interviewees will not be the only variable involved, so the research experience will not have been standardized. This would place a question-mark over the reliability of the research findings.

This issue has been investigated by looking at the outcome of interviews conducted with variations in the characteristics of the interviewers. May (1993) quotes a study of the levels of satisfaction of black Americans with their social, economic and political lives, showing that the answers given differed according to whether respondents were interviewed by white or black interviewers. Given that the interviews were conducted in the southern US state of Tennessee, it is likely that the overall context of racial relations there had an effect, but it was manifested in variations in response according to the social characteristics of the interviewer.

Labov (1973) found that black children responded very differently when interviewed by white or black interviewers. In this case the findings from the sessions with white interviewers had been used to define the black children as linguistically deprived, and such a conclusion was the basis of special programmes of education for them. Labov clearly showed this finding to be invalid; instead the interviews reflected the extent to which black children in a country with high levels of racism would respond openly to white people.

That is a clear example of what is called the 'interviewer effect'. The characteristics and behaviour of the interviewer can be hugely important factors affecting the answers that respondents give. It is in order to minimize this problem that surveys using more than one interviewer often involve training (sometimes of many days' duration), covering in detail how the interviewers are to approach their task. This issue is of extreme importance if the research findings are to be used for practical social reform.

The interview problem

When choosing both interviewers and the location of the interviews, researchers must be aware of the potential for these to affect the research findings. This can be called the 'interview problem'.

Oakley (1979) highlighted this by pointing out that an interview is an artificial situation. It is therefore likely that, however hard the interviewer tries to create a naturalistic environment, respondents may choose not to reveal certain things. This is particularly true of any questions relating to sensitive issues. Thus we can be fairly certain that an interview reveals only what respondents are willing to say – which may not be the same as what they actually think or say in other circumstances.

Evaluating interviews as a research method

In essence, the advantages and disadvantages of interviews depend on the degree of structure imposed.

Structured types

Advantages
One advantage here is that it is possible to make *direct comparisons* between the responses given by interviewees, given the commonality of questions asked and the attempt to standardize the interview experience. In so far as this is done

successfully, such interviews can be said to have a high degree of reliability.

In this respect they are similar to self-administered closed-question questionnaires. However, an advantage they have over those is the fact that there is someone present to clarify the meaning of any confusing questions. Also, the response rate from social surveys using the interview method tends to be much higher (around 65–80 per cent) than is the case with mailed questionnaires.

Disadvantages
A disadvantage of this method is that the structure of the interview is preset, and it is argued – particularly by qualitative researchers – that this precludes the respondent providing full and detailed responses. This results in a lower degree of validity than would be achieved by, for example, an unstructured interview.

Unstructured types

Advantages
Here, since respondents can respond in their own words, it is argued that this provides a more in-depth valid picture of reality. The interviewer can follow up issues arising in the course of the interview. The more naturalistic setting is also likely to make the respondent relaxed and willing to continue participating.

Disadvantages
The key disadvantage is that there is no guarantee there will be any great level of comparability between interviews within a research project. It is possible for two interviews which start at the same point to go off in different directions, making comparisons difficult if not impossible. This lack of similarity undermines the reliability of the approach.

Interviews of all types

Interviews as a whole tend to gain a greater response rate than mailed questionnaires, but they also tend to be roughly twice as expensive to conduct. This will affect the number of people it is possible to interview.

Time constraints also limit the number of people it is possible to interview, and therefore the size of the sample in interview programmes tends to be smaller than in mailed questionnaires. In particular the sample size in unstructured interviews tends to be between only 30 and 150, which means that careful consideration needs to be given to the sampling procedure to ensure that something approximating a representative sample is achieved. The smaller the actual sample, the more difficult this is.

Finally, with all interviews the skill of the interviewer is paramount. The selection and training of interviewers must be undertaken carefully to minimize the 'interview effect'. All of this adds to the time and cost of the method.

Nonetheless, conducting interviews remains a very popular method of social research, with the potential to provide both qualitative and quantitative data.

Observational methods

Participant and *non-participant* observation are two important methods in sociology which arise from the ethnographic methods developed by anthropologists. The term 'ethnography' refers to the study of small-scale communities. It derives in particular from researchers such as Bronislaw Malinowski who, in order to study the Trobriand Islanders, actually lived in their society as a member and a researcher. He observed while participating. (See also Section 7.8).

While the term 'ethnography' is strictly wider than participant observation and includes a number of other possible approaches, such as interviews and document analysis (see Section 9.6 on Hey's research), it is undoubtedly true that participant observation is the most important legacy of ethnography in sociology.

The central idea is to study life 'as it really is', and to observe the interactions people engage in. In order to do this, it is argued that the best way to obtain the most natural and most valid picture is to use a naturalistic setting, observing life in as undisturbed a way as possible. What differentiates it as a sociological research method from purely journalistic descriptive accounts of lifestyles is that it is used to develop and test theories in a systematic way.

The key aim behind observational methods is to avoid the construction of an artificial research environment, which would occur if one approached somebody with a clipboard or even sent a questionnaire through the post. The latter methods provide only a static snapshot of social reality, and as a result miss out the most impor-

tant fact about societies – namely that they consist of people interacting in a dynamic way.

Non-participant observation

This involves a sociologist observing without actually participating in the events being studied. The method is used both to capture the reality of a dynamic situation without affecting it by intrusive research situations (such as conducting structured interviews), because it is believed that any such intrusion would actually affect the situation being observed. It is therefore a non-obtrusive method.

The most obvious way to observe something without affecting what happens is to do it from a distance or from behind a barrier such as a two-way mirror – then those being observed are not aware of their status. This is to avoid the infamous 'Hawthorne effect' (discussed earlier in Section 9.5). That effect was observed in an example of a 'field experiment' in which variables were changed systematically, and the results observed were explained on the basis that workers responded in a certain way precisely *because* they were being watched – they knew the experiment was taking place. Unobtrusive measures seek to avoid this drawback.

This may mean that researchers choose not to be visible to the group being observed; or alternatively not to announce that they are conducting research.

The most famous examples of this type of research are the various interactionist-inspired studies of education. In David Hargreaves' (1967) study, for example, observation occurred by the researcher sitting in on classes, and there is some evidence that his presence affected what subsequently happened. Some teachers and pupils clearly modified their behaviour whilst under observation.

However, although this method has been used, one of its key drawbacks is the virtual impossibility of eliminating totally any trace of the Hawthorne effect. It is for this reason that participation is considered as a cover for the observation. Such research then becomes a form of participant observation.

Participant observation

There are a variety of possible approaches to

participant observation, reflecting the level of participation involved and whether or not the group being observed is made aware of the research being undertaken. Any one study may involve a variety of these subtypes, though it is usual for one to predominate.

The degree of involvement

It is possible to envisage either complete participation in all the activities of a group, or only partial involvement. Ned Polsky (1971), for example, in his study of poolroom hustlers, was involved in their activity in the poolroom (where his prowess as a pool player helped him) but was not involved in other activities of the group. In contrast, William Foote Whyte (1943) lived as a lodger in an Italian house with the group he was studying, even becoming a member of their street gang.

Is total participation possible?

One important consideration concerns the extent to which total participation is possible. Clearly in order to participate the researcher has to share some particular social characteristics of the group. It would not be possible, for example, for a male middle-aged sociologist to engage in complete participant-observation research of the Girl Guides, nor would a white sociologist be able to join the Black Panthers as a participant.

It also tends to place a limit on the type of groups than can be studied by this method. One obvious thing that is characteristic of researchers is that they are adults, and this limits the extent to which they can become complete participants in the activities of youths and children. Since the method has been popular in the study of juvenile delinquents, this issue has frequently surfaced, and the general response has been to try to achieve an accepted status which means that one can hang around and observe.

Paul Willis' (1977) study of male subcultures in a school environment (see Section 8.7) might fit into this category, since as an adult he clearly could not be a complete participant but was allowed to hang around with the youths. Similarly, Howard Parker (1974), in his study of juvenile delinquents in Liverpool, used his position as a community worker to hang around and therefore observe.

Safety issues

Even if it is possible to participate, it might be decided against on the grounds of personal safety. As mentioned, many studies have used this method to study juvenile delinquents who engage in illegal activities. Clearly to be a complete participant involves the danger of being called upon to participate in such acts.

'James Patrick' (1973) found this was the case with his study of a juvenile gang in Glasgow: he was eventually forced to flee and abandon his research when he refused to carry a weapon and turn up to a gang fight. Another member of the gang, at that time in prison, threatened him with retaliation and the researcher was forced to leave and change his name – with the result that the real name of the author of *A Glasgow Gang Observed* is not known and he is referred to as 'James Patrick'.

Laud Humphreys (1970) was on occasions arrested by the police during his study of gays, and Michael Haralambos (1974) recounts episodes of being threatened with a gun several times while researching music and culture in Chicago.

It is essentially because of these dangers that Polsky argued against *covert* participant observation when studying criminal groups, since he believed that such observers would invariably be found out and would then face violent retribution.

This leads on to the question of whether the researcher should inform the subjects of what is going on, and thereafter engage in *overt* participant observation, or whether covert observation is the better choice. It might be argued that unannounced (covert) observation is the only effective way to engage in research on certain activities because some groups are unwilling to be observed openly. This is, of course, particularly true of any activities of a sensitive or criminal nature, and why therefore the research by Humphreys and 'James Patrick' illustrate this point so well.

Ethical issues

Again, even if it is possible to participate, it might be decided against on ethical grounds. There is clearly an ethical question surrounding *covert* participant observation. Should sociologists *ever* engage in research on people without their knowledge, since this involves a breach of privacy?

This method of research receives special mention in the British Sociological Association's (1991) ethical guidelines:

There are serious ethical dangers in the use of covert (or secret) research, but in some circumstances covert methods may avoid certain problems. Covert methods violate the principles of informed consent and may invade the privacy of those being studied. Participant or non-participant observation in non-public spaces or experimental manipulation of partic-ipants without their knowledge should be resorted to only where it is impossible to use other methods to obtain essential data. Inexperienced researchers are strongly advised to avoid covert research. ... Covert researchers should: (1) safeguard the anonymity of research participants, and (2) ideally obtain consent to the research after it has been concluded (prior to publication).

(BSA, 1991, p. 2)

Activity

a Explain in your own words the principle of informed consent.

b Suggest some problems that covert methods might avoid in certain circumstances.

c To what extent do you agree with the view that this method should be resorted to only where it is impossible to use other methods?

C3.2, C3.3

Structured observation

As well as forms of observation that allow the researcher to collect qualitative data, there is also a form of observation that allows you to collect quantitative data. This is known as structured observation. It works as follows. The researcher will observe a group of people inter-acting and will make a note of who speaks, who speaks to whom, and how many times each person speaks. The data can then be con-structed into a diagram that shows the fre-quency of involvement in discussion and the level of contact between each individual.

This method is often used to analyse small-scale interactions between groups of people, such as a classroom or a committee meeting, for instance.

9.6 Sources of secondary data

Life documents

Sociology seeks to consider social relationships, so the ways in which those relationships are thought about and communicated can become an important source of information. This leads to a consideration of the use of *life documents*. The term refers to documents created by individuals which reflect their own personal experiences of various events or reflect their feelings about certain things.

Historical evidence

Life documents can be particularly useful when considering historical events, since the authors themselves may no longer be around but it may be possible to gain access to their feelings through documents they have written. The letters and diaries of soldiers killed in war can, for example, still give some insight into what the experience was like, and how social relationships within the army worked.

There is no reason why such documents should not inform research about the present. One famous example of the usage of life docu-ments is W. I. Thomas and F. Znaniecki's (1919) study, *The Polish Peasant in Europe and America*. In order to try to understand the expe-rience of migration for Polish peasants to America, they made use of an extensive collec-tion of documents – including diaries, 764 letters and articles from newspapers.

Ken Plummer (1983) identifies a number of other studies that have made use of life docu-ments, including Oscar Lewis's (1961, 1968) studies of poverty in Mexico and Puerto Rica, and Clifford Shaw's (1931) life histories of delinquents in Chicago in the 1920s. Plummer says of this approach:

All this research is characterised by a lack of pom-posity and pretension about methods: the researcher is merely there in the first instance to give 'voice' to other people; in some circumstances the voices may then be interpreted. Such studies rarely get bogged down in the abstract methodological and theoretical debate which characterizes so much social science today.

(Plummer, 1983, p. 1)

💬 **Discussion point**

To what extent do you think it is a good thing to get away from the 'abstract methodological and theoretical debate which characterizes so much social science today'?

C3.1a

The sheer variety of source materials identified by Plummer as falling under the category of 'documents of life' is quite staggering:

The world is crammed full of personal documents. People keep diaries, send letters, take photos, write memos, tell biographies, scrawl graffiti, publish their memoirs, write letters to the papers, leave suicide notes, inscribe memorials on tombstones, shoot films, paint pictures, make music and try to record their personal dreams. All of these expressions of personal life are hurled out into the world by the millions and can be of interest to anyone who cares to seek them out.

(Plummer, 1983, p. 13)

Reliability and validity

One of the key issues in considering the use of historical and contemporary anecdotal data is a concern over its reliability and validity. People keep diaries, but does the content of these always and completely reflect the reality of their lives? On the other hand, what they say in their diary *is* a reality in itself, and this recalls W. I. Thomas's dictum that if people believe something to be real then it is likely to be real *in its consequences*. This is because beliefs impact on actions whether they are true or not.

The use of life documents reflects this *interactionist approach* to the study of society, and therefore seeks to consider the interpretations people make of events as valid data.

Plummer points to the Polish peasant study as perhaps the best example of this type of research, and its popularity as a method seems to have risen and fallen with the star of interactionism – he sees its most influential period as being the 1920s to the 1950s. Since then the tradition of oral histories and life stories has seen something of a re-emergence as a popular research tool.

Plummer makes the further point that the lack of regard shown to this method reflects the desire to adopt a scientific method as a frame-

work for research. He quotes this view of Nisbet who laments the fact that sociology did not choose the arts as a discipline on which to model itself as the basis of a 'humanistic' sociology:

How different things would be ... if the social sciences at the time of their systematic formation in the nineteenth century had taken the arts in the same degree they took the physical sciences as models.

(Nisbet, 1976, p. 16; quoted in Plummer, 1983, p. 5)

💬 **Discussion point**

How different do you think sociology would now be if this had been the case? Should sociology be a science or an art?

C3.1a

Plummer argues that life documents offer a richer, more in-depth, picture of the way people feel and act than is generally possible with social surveys and quantitative research, and he therefore sees them as having great validity. He accepts that there may be a problem with reliability, but is quite clear that this is of less importance than validity:

Validity should come first, reliability second. There is no point in being very precise about nothing! If the subjective story is what the researcher is after, the life history approach becomes the most valid method.

(Plummer, 1983, p. 102)

Case Study – The study of girls' notes

An interesting variation on the use of life documents was adopted by Valerie Hey (1997) in her study of girls' friendships in two London schools. Although the principal method used was participant observation, she also gathered girls' notes and examined their diaries. The study therefore combined a number of methods which result in qualitative data. She explains the collection and importance of the notes as follows:

In the course of my time in the schools I got to know about 50 girls reasonably well, 20 of these girls very well and three sufficiently well to have been invited to their homes and to have invited them to mine. One girl even sent me a note during a lesson. Others kept up communication after I left the schools, updating me on their present situation. ... Yet other girls sent me notes which they had stored away; others offered me diaries to read. I offered mine in return. ...

In so far as teachers noticed girls' extracurricular activities they called girls' notes 'bits of poison' or 'garbage'. Girls referred to them as 'bits of silliness'. As far as I was concerned they were sociologically fascinating because they were important means of transmitting the cultural values of friendship.

It emerged that not only did these writings constitute visible evidence of the extensive emotional labour invested by girls in their friendships, they also comprised a 'pocket ethnography' of girlfriend work.

(Hey, 1997, p. 50)

Activity

a Explain in your own words why Hey feels the notes were important.

b Apart from notes, suggest two other life documents which might be used in a study of friendships.

C3.2, C3.3

Official statistics

The term 'official statistics' refers to numerical data produced by government departments. They are official because they are produced by the state apparatus. As Martin Slattery (1986) points out, the word 'statistics' derives from the German word meaning facts and figures for the use of the state.

All of this information exists primarily for the purposes of government administration. There are data produced in the course of administering government policy, such as figures on the number of people receiving various benefits. Surveys are conducted with the aim of allowing policy to be formed on the basis of clear information – an example being the ten-yearly national Census. Their production in a political context is therefore something which should always be borne in mind.

There are a vast quantity of such statistics, and for sociologists this represents a mine of potentially useful information, easily and cheaply available. Official statistics are kept in reference libraries and university and college libraries. Production of the figures is co-ordinated by the Office for National Statistics (ONS) – formed in April 1996 by a merger of the Central Statistical Office (CSO) and the Office of Population Censuses and Surveys (OPCS). This section of the chapter concentrates on the most important sources from a sociological point of view.

The national Census

Undoubtedly the largest survey, in terms of the amount of data produced, is the ten-yearly national Census, produced at some considerable cost. Slattery (1986) points out that the 1981 Census cost £45 million and involved the employment of 129 000 people.

The Census involves questionnaires being delivered to every household in the UK, with assistance being available to help people fill it in if necessary. It has been a regular feature of UK statistics since the middle of the nineteenth century and is clearly the most representative survey in existence since it involves everyone. The Census Act 1920 made completion of the form compulsory, and although there are some who refuse to fill it in, the threat of a £400 fine is sufficient to ensure that almost everyone complies. Slattery says that, in 1981, out of 54 million people only 6000 refused to fill it in and 700 of these were prosecuted.

The cost of the 1991 Census was £135 million, and the increasing cost is leading to debates about whether the present format should be changed so that Census forms are sent out by mail rather than given out door-to-door.

Discussion point

Do you agree that a shift to a mailed census is a good idea?

C3.1a

The 1991 Census

For the first time in 1991 a question was included on 'ethnicity'. Such a question had been planned for the 1981 Census but was eventually dropped after protests and debate in Parliament. The questions in the 1991 Census cover the following categories:

- Type of accommodation
- Amenities in household
- Type of household tenure
- Sex and age of people in household
- Marital status
- Household relationships
- Country of birth

- Ethnic group
- Long-term illness
- Work status
- Hours worked
- Occupation
- Journey to work
- Educational and professional qualifications

Activity

a The Census' main aim is to provide reliable information for the government to facilitate policy planning and administration. Suggest ways in which information collected using the categories listed above might be useful to the government in this respect.

b What other areas, if any, which are not presently included do you think should be included?

C3.2, C3.3

Criticisms of the 1991 Census

Although the Census is generally considered reliable and representative, and as such is often used by sociologists as the basis for checking whether their sample is representative, the 1991 Census cannot be said to have achieved this level of accuracy.

The reason for this is the existence of the 'poll tax' at that time. This extremely unpopular tax led to people avoiding payment, and in order to avoid detection they did not fill in any official documents. Recognition of this problem led to after-the-fact adjustments being made to the population figures derived from the Census.

There were further complaints following the 1991 Census, both about the Census in general and the 1991 one in particular. Some complained that the forms were difficult to understand and fill in and demanded a very high level of literacy. Also there were complaints from those administering the survey about the difficulty in contacting some people. Although there were attempts for the first time to attain a census of the homeless, the extent to which this was successful is a matter of debate.

In relation to the specific questions to be included on the 1991 Census form, there were debates over the inclusion of a question on ethnic origins, and on the issue of work which was defined in such a way as to exclude the work done by women as unpaid housewives. Both these debates reflect the fact that definitions used in official statistics do not always reflect sociological ideas in the areas they cover.

The 2001 Census

Additional categories are under consideration for inclusion in the 2001 Census (Garrett, 1996). These embrace religious affiliation, levels of voluntary care provided to relatives and friends, access to a garden, and the highest level of qualification gained after leaving school.

Activity

Research the questionnaire to be used in the 2001 Census. What differences are there from the 1991 form?

C3.2, C3.3, IT3.1

Undoubtedly the most important possible additional category, however, relates to income, which has never been included on the Census form.

While these additional categories would undoubtedly provide useful information for sociological research in the future, there is also the suggestion that the inclusion of the question on income reflects commercial pressures. Such information, when cross-referenced to the other information from the Census, would give companies free (but very valuable) market-research information. Debate has therefore focused on the inclusion of the income question:

The ONS says that in 2001 such a question would be used to help government departments target areas of low income. But others suspect its inclusion has more to do with the ONS ... becoming more commercial, possibly as a precursor to privatisation.

(Garrett, 1996, p. 2)

Other government surveys

For sociologists, probably the most important of the rest of the surveys are the *New Earnings Survey*, the *General Household Survey* and the *Family Expenditure Survey*. Many of the results of these surveys can be found in the annual publication *Social Trends*, which is an extremely useful source of information for sociologists.

New Earnings Survey

As its name suggests, the *NES* covers income and is compiled using a 1 per cent sample of employers operating within the pay-as-you-earn (PAYE) tax system. It provides information on earnings, broken down into various categories, and allows comparison by class (manual/non-manual), gender and locality. It is therefore one of the most important secondary sources in relation to income.

However, this survey is not without its problems. First, since it is collected using the PAYE tax data, those who do not earn enough to be liable for National Insurance or income tax are excluded from the statistics. This has a particular impact on the gender distribution on earnings, since the vast majority who fall into this category are women, and mostly part-time workers. Faludi (1992) estimates that the earnings of roughly three million people, mainly women, are excluded on this basis.

Secondly, the survey excludes the self-employed, and those elements of people's earnings which accrue from self-employment, even if they are employed as well. This is likely to affect the higher-paid categories.

As a result of both of these factors, it is likely that the *New Earnings Survey* considerably under-estimates inequalities in the distribution of income.

The Inland Revenue also publishes statistics on wealth, but these too are likely to be less than accurate since the information derives from their estimate of the value of the estates left by those who die. This ignores the many ways in which estate duty can be avoided, thereby under-estimating wealth. It also ignores the fact that in some cases there are disputes over the actual estimates of the value of estates.

Since Inland Revenue statistics are collected from data whose primary purpose is the administration of taxation – and given that many people wish to minimize their liability of being taxed – they must be treated with extreme caution. The survey is, however, easily available and allows sociologists to consider some trends in the distribution of income.

General Household Survey

The GHS was started in 1971 and is based on interviews with 10 000 households. It covers such issues as household composition, population trends, health and illness, employment and education, all of which are of immense potential interest to sociologists. The usefulness of this survey is further enhanced by the fact that it has a very high response rate, with the latest estimate

being 82 per cent. Early in 1997 this survey was at the centre of controversy when the government announced plans to suspend it. In response Anthony Giddens wrote an article defending it:

... dumping of the GHS is a symbol of a much larger and disturbing trend. It is a symptom of a society which is turning away from self-knowledge towards an ostrich-like inability to face up to a new and rapidly changing world. ... One wonders whether Social Trends will be the next to fall under the axe. The 1997 version of Social Trends is due to appear this week. As with previous editions, it will be full of material produced by the GHS. It's hard to see where this information will come from in the future.

(Giddens, 1997)

This points to the important way in which political decisions can affect what information is readily available and what is not.

Activity

If you have access to a quality newspaper on CD–ROM, look up newspaper reports from January 1997 to follow up this issue.

C3.2, C3.3, IT3.1

Family Expenditure Survey

The *FES* comprises a diary completed for a fortnight by a sample of 11 000 households. It covers income as well as expenditure and considers expenditure under headings such as food, clothing and entertainment. One problem with this is a relatively low response rate of 67 per cent.

This survey has also been at the centre of controversy over government changes in presenting statistics on the poor (see Section 7.6). The new measure 'Households below average income' is based on data from the *FES* and has been criticized because such figures are based on households, not individuals. Critics point out that it is perfectly possible for an individual to be poor in a household which is not, but the government response is that it assumes households share their assets. It is this assumption that has been most criticized, precisely because it is an assumption rather than a fact, and one which has been shown to be not always true according to studies of household budgeting.

Problems with government statistics

The political context

Given that the government funds the production of official statistics, it is open to the suspicion that they might be manipulated for political purposes. The government might decide not to collect certain statistics or not to publish others.

For instance, the famous Black Report on *Inequalities in Health* was originally published as only 260 photocopied reports on an August Bank Holiday Monday. This, it was thought, was an attempt to avoid drawing attention to a document critical of the government's policies on the health service.

The availability and accessibility of official statistics has been the subject of much debate. In essence, they were started because the government wanted to be actively involved in the administration of many services (notably the welfare state), and there grew a feeling that the general public should be informed about the state of the nation as a key basis of an enlightened democracy where people make choices on the basis of facts and figures. Although the ideas of the New Right have led to it being questioned whether the government should be responsible for producing all the official statistics, critics fear that any move to commercialize the collection, publication and distribution of statistics might lead to a reduction in their availability. The Rayner Reviews on government expenditure in the early 1980s considered this possibility, and at one time threatened the existence even of *Social Trends*. Subsequently the introduction to that publication was changed to stress its usefulness to the government, without any reference to the general public.

Although there was a trend to more openness in the 1990s, and *Social Trends* is now seen as being aimed at the general public as well as the state, nonetheless there are still concerns. A particular row erupted over the claim by Muriel Nissel, the first editor of *Social Trends*, that her proposed introductory article to the 50th issue of *Social Trends* had been 'blatantly suppressed' (Phillips, 1995). The article was rejected by William McLennan, Director of the Central Statistical Office, because it was seen as too political. The article was critical of the pressures put on statisticians by the Rayner Reviews of Official Statistics. This incident led to a debate in which the second editor of *Social Trends*, Eric Thompson, also intervened:

Impartial statistical information is not only needed to help make, manage and monitor government policies; it is also essential for informed public debate about those policies. Integrity in government statistics is essential for democratic debate. ... As I had succeeded Mrs Nissel as editor in 1975, she let me comment on drafts of her article. I thought it a balanced review of the history of Social Trends ... though I regretted that she had felt it necessary to pull her punches when commenting on government statisticians' self-censorship after the post-Rayner attacks on government statistics in the early 1980s. This incident reinforces Mr McLennan's call for a UK Statistics Act to place the independence of government statistics on a statutory footing. Government statisticians should serve Parliament and the public as well as ministers.

(Thompson, 1995, p. 9)

Definitions in official statistics

The definition of various things is an issue in relation to official statistics. Clearly, the government can decide on the definitions to be used, and it is not always the case that the definitions actually adopted will correspond to general sociological views, or even those held by the general public. Since the data are not collected by sociologists, there is little they can do about this. There are a number of notable examples of this problem.

Class

The most commonly used measure of social class, until recently, was the Registrar General's measure of occupations. This was based on the relative prestige attached to various occupations, and in many ways it is therefore a measure of *status* rather than social class. Certainly there is no *direct* link between the social class on the Registrar General's scale and level of earnings; and it is also the case that those without an occupation are not included, this most notably excluding the capitalist class. Since capitalists live off unearned income in the form of share dividends, they do not have employment and so do not appear in occupation-derived measures.

Unemployment

The official definition of unemployment is in fact a measure of those eligible for certain benefits, and so changes in the administration of the benefits system will lead to changes in the total number recorded as unemployed – regardless of whether the employment status of those affected has indeed changed.

The definition of unemployment in this context has in fact changed over 30 times since 1979, and all but one of those changes resulted in a fall in the number classified officially as unemployed.

Health expenditure

Another example is the way in which expenditure on the National Health Service can appear differently if the definition of a nurse is changed:

The number of nurses and midwives has risen, but the size of the increase is a matter of hot dispute. This is because in 1980 nurses' and midwives' contract hours were reduced. Because so many work part-time, they are usually counted in terms of 'whole-time equivalents' – in other words according to the proportion of the full week worked. When the hours were reduced, a nurse working the same hours became a larger whole-time equivalent overnight, so, according to the Radical Statistics Group, the 63,000 extra nurses and midwives featured in the Conservatives' 1987 election advertising would have amounted to only 32,000 if the change in definition had been acknowledged.

(*Guardian*, 15 March 1989)

The examples considered in this subsection serve to underline the need for sociologists to check the definitions in official statistics to see whether there have been any (perhaps subtle) changes.

Other sources of statistics

Bodies such as trade unions, charities and independent research organizations conduct research and publish statistical information. For example, the Rowntree Foundation produces a wealth of data on income distribution, poverty and the welfare state which is of course potentially useful to sociologists. Harvey and MacDonald suggest that the name 'unofficial statistics' should be given to this body of data:

This should not be taken to mean that 'unofficial' are any less correct than official statistics. The distinction is simply that official statistics are the ones that 'officially' the government agencies collect and use.

(Harvey and MacDonald, 1993, p. 62)

Libraries

So far in this section we have considered the wide variety of secondary material that is available to the sociologist. One key advantage of this material is that it already exists waiting for you to come along and collect it. However, it is true that you have to (a) be aware of its existence, and (b) know where to find it.

We now need to ensure that you know where to find this material and the possible sources are wider than ever today. For most purposes, however, you will be using the services of various libraries or learning resource centres and you may have access to the Internet.

Different types of libraries

School or college libraries

Your school or college library should contain a selection of sociological material. There are two principal forms of library indexing. Depending on which is used in your institution, you will find sociology books beginning at either 300 or HM51.

Books in the form of this and other textbooks are the first sort of secondary data you are likely to come across and you can use the references and the bibliographies in the back of these to try to locate other relevant material.

Of course, the best information source about secondary resources available in your library is likely to be your sociology teacher. He/she will be aware of what is available and probably where it is. Alternatively, the library staff will also be able to help you in locating material and indeed in using any specialized search equipment available.

It is also likely that other material will be available in your school/college library, such as journals like *Sociology Review* for sociology students and back copies of newspapers. It may also have more dated back copies of newspapers on CD-ROMs. These allow you to search for relevant articles using a keyword search facility. Newspapers are a good source of basic information if what you are looking for is likely to have been discussed in them, although, as everything, they should be approached critically.

Public libraries

A second potential source is public libraries and public reference libraries. Most local libraries will have a selection of sociology books available. If there is nothing on the shelf, you should ask the library staff about availability since it may be that the item is held at another branch and could be transferred. It is also possible to obtain material on inter-library loan (although it is likely you will be charged for this). Since the British Library has a copy of every book published in the UK, you should ultimately be able to obtain a copy to borrow (though you might have to wait, so do allow plenty of time for any inter-library loans).

Public reference libraries

There may be a reference section attached to your local library or alternatively a local reference library in your area. These hold books and other material which can be read on the premises but not taken out. They are usually a very good source for government statistical material. Copies of the latest Census reports are likely to be held there, as are the latest copies of reports of interest to sociologists such as the *New Earnings Survey*, the *Family Expenditure Survey* and the *General Household Survey*.

Reference libraries also often have archives of material related to the local area. So if the work you are doing is in any way connected to your locality, this may be a good source of material.

Higher education libraries

Higher education libraries will be attached to the local higher education institution. Although you have no entitlement to use them, and cannot therefore demand access to them, you can at least ask whether it would be possible for you to use the library on a reference basis. It may be possible for your teacher to arrange such access with staff at the higher education institution.

Higher education libraries will have a much greater range of material available, although it is important to note that these are designed to help people on degree level courses so not all the material will be at an appropriate level or possibly accessible to you. Nonetheless it is worth investigating as a possible source of relevant material.

Working in a library

In all libraries, the most important thing is to be focused and aware of what you are looking for. While you may occasionally get sidetracked as you turn up something interesting which was not on your original list, this must be the occasional

happening and not the entire library visit.

You need to consider the purpose of your research and what use you will be putting the material to. Judith Bell (1993) puts this point well when she says:

We all think we know how to use libraries, and certainly it would not take any of us long to get to grips with the system operating and the stock held by small branch libraries. Finding the way round and discovering what stock is held in main public and specialist libraries in universities and colleges is quite another matter. They can seem like Aladdin's caves for students and researchers. They hold treasures that dazzle; but caves can be dangerous. It is easy to get lost and to become so anxious not to leave any treasures behind that it becomes impossible ever to leave. All this is rather fanciful, but many a research project has foundered because the investigator had not defined the area of study sufficiently clearly and so extended the range of reading far beyond what was necessary. Large libraries are complicated places, and library staff at the information desk will do their best to help you to come to grips with the way the stock is organized – but first, you need to know exactly what you are looking for.

(Bell, 1993, pp. 40–41)

Search resources to use in libraries

First of all ask the librarian if there are any available guides to the library. For example, these may well include an explanation of how to conduct computer searches in the library. You will find large stocks of government reports and statistics most often in the reference section of libraries. For up-to-date material you are best to start with journals and other specialist publications.

There are a number of abstracts produced of articles contained in journals. For instance, the British Education Index lists periodicals and journals concerned with education and details on how to locate them, including the names of publications and their library classification. You could also try looking at the relevant section (by subject area) of the British National Bibliography which details books, some journals and government publications. The British Newspaper Index covers newspaper articles. Using these can mean that you do not spend an inordinate amount of time merely surfing the library.

Look out for any microfiche readers or CD-

ROM players which will allow much quicker electronic searching.

One new innovation quickly being introduced into public libraries is access to the Internet via payment for a set period of time. The Internet is, of course, the new big thing in relation to obtaining information.

The Internet

Even in the mid-1990s, use of the Internet was fairly rare in the UK. People had possibly heard about it, but actually using it was a different matter. Today, however, the Internet seems to have come of age in terms of mass access. Surveys of Internet use in the UK such as CommerceNet/Nielsen (Nielsen Media, 1999) show that over a quarter (27 per cent) of adults in the UK are now regular users of the Internet, having used it in the last month. This mounts up to 12.5 million people. However, at the other end of the spectrum, 1.6 million people have never heard of the Internet.

Internet use in the UK

Some statistics on Internet use in the UK, October 1999:

- 12.5 million (27 per cent of population) have used it in the last month
- of these, 44 per cent log on every day, 38 per cent are women and 11 per cent are over 50 years old.

Of those with Internet access:

- 72 per cent use the Internet for work-related activity
- 69 per cent use the Internet to research travel destinations
- 60 per cent use the Internet to check sports and entertainment news
- 52 per cent use the Internet for international news
- 40 per cent use the Internet to access information about the local community
- 27 per cent have purchased goods online whereas 49 per cent have used the Internet to compare the price of goods and services.

Source: CommerceNet/Nielsen Media Research Internet and eCommerce Survey (UK) based on a sample of 4700 respondents and reported in Nielsen Media (1999)

Using the Internet

It seems likely, therefore, that you will probably already have heard of the Internet and are likely to have access to it at school or college and possibly also at home. If you do not, increasingly public libraries are providing access to the Internet for a set time for the payment of a small fee. Equally there are now a number of cybercafés where you can access the Internet on a pay per hour basis. A full list of cybercafés can be obtained by sending an email to internet.cafes@computing.emap.co.uk/. The amount of information available is quite simply staggering and vast amounts of time could be whiled away aimlessly surfing the Internet.

In order to use it usefully for sociological purposes you need to know how to track down useful sites and how to remember where they are. Obviously the possible technical permutations available in relation to the Internet are enormous, so we will not pretend to offer detailed technical information. There are a number of books available which provide detailed technical and practical advice in relation to getting onto the Internet, such as Holland (1999).

However, it is likely that you will access the Internet via one of two browsers, namely Internet Explorer or Netscape Navigator. These are the bits of software that enable you to connect to the Internet, along with hardware such as a PC and a modem. (The modem is there to connect to the phone system, so remember when on line you are running up the phone bill!).

Search engines

Assuming you have managed to work out how to get connected, you will need to conduct a search of the Internet to find sociology-related sites. This requires the use of search engines. These have addresses on the Internet like everything else. Under the 'File' menu, click on open and a box will appear where you can type the address of the site you wish to visit. Since you will be searching for sociology sites it is handy to have a pen and paper ready as backup to write down any addresses you find.

Some examples of search engines and their addresses include the following:

AltaVista	www.altavista.digital.com/
Ask Jeeves	www.askjeeves.com/
Infoseek	www.infoseek.com/
Yahoo	www.yahoo.com/

Bookmarking

As you use the Internet more you will undoubtedly find more search engines and more sites of sociological interest. It is impossible to remember the not-always-user-friendly addresses and fortunately you don't have to. If you are using Netscape Navigator you can create bookmarks so your favourite site addresses are automatically remembered. In Internet Explorer the similar process is known as adding to your favourites. Always bookmark your favourite sites since otherwise you will undoubtedly lose their addresses.

Hot links

One good thing about the Internet is the existence of hot links. These are words which are underlined and usually initially appear in blue. If you click on these they will take you to the site described. Most Internet sites have such links allowing you to arrive at any site via any number of possible routes.

We have tried to include some useful Internet website addresses in the introductory chapter to this book (see pages 8–9) and as soon as you yourself get searching you will no doubt find your own way round. However, to get you in we suggest you visit the following and use the links provided at these sites to take you further:

Sociology Central:
www.sociology.org.uk
ATSS:
www.atss.org.uk/
Sociology Online:
www.sociologyonline.f9.co.uk/
Dead Sociologists Society:
www.runet.edu/~Iridener/DSS/DEADSOC.HTML/
Sociology Ring (with 198 sites):
www.markfoster.net/sociology/socring.html/

Mailing lists and newsgroups

As well as websites there are two other sources of information on the Internet. These are mailing lists and newsgroups. There are examples of both related to sociology. You can get information on mailing lists at www.listserve.com/ and information on newsgroups at www.deja.com/. Accessing newsgroups requires the use of a newsreader. An email programme such as Outlook Express will also serve as a newsreader.

Examples of using the Internet for social research purposes

As the Internet becomes more widely available, sociological researchers are beginning to discuss the possible use of the Internet not only as a source of secondary material but as a medium through which primary research can be conducted.

Social surveys on the Internet

One example of social surveys being carried out over the Internet is that of Coomber (1997) who considers the way it may be possible to use the Internet for social survey research. Coomber had previously studied the topic of drug usage and drug dealing through 31 interviews and a review of forensic evidence. This led to the conclusion that most drugs were not adulterated. Further research was conducted by posting a questionnaire on the World Wide Web and this eventually led to some 80 replies. This example shows that actual research can be carried out using the Internet as a delivery and response medium. However, in relation to methodology, the author states:

Whilst the Internet and WWW does offer new and exciting prospects for sociological research, in many respects the methodological issues which it raises are by and large not new. The key issue that any survey research conducted via the Internet will have to contend with, as with non-Internet based surveys, is that of sampling bias. At present this is more acute than it is likely to be in the future because contact can only be made with those who can and do use the Internet and the WWW, and all that implies in terms of background, education, gender and resources.

(Coomber, 1997, p. 1)

This research can be accessed at: www.socresonline.org.uk/2/2/2.html

Activity

Explain the meaning of the problem of sampling bias. Is there any recent evidence in relation to Internet use which suggests this may be becoming less of a problem?

C3.2, C3.3

Another survey conducted using the Internet is that of Bonchek *et al.* (1996) who were interested in looking at the way people used email and the

Internet to access government documents in the United States as published by the White House electronic publications service. This survey aimed to consider the effect of this innovation on democracy and, in order to conduct the survey, they used email and the Internet to deliver surveys to 18 000 subscribers to the service. The 1472 people who responded were then sent further surveys based on their initial responses. This survey highlights the importance of email as a new research tool:

Survey recipients could either respond to the email instruments or connect to our Web server and reply through an HTML interface. 79 per cent of the respondents chose email, while 21 per cent replied via the Web.

(Bonchek *et al.*, 1996, p. 2)

This article can be accessed at www.w3j.com/3/s3.bonchek.html/ and the White House electronic publications can be accessed at www.whitehouse.gov/.

Ethnographic research using the Internet

It should not be thought that it is only quantitative researchers who are considering using the Internet. Paccagnella (1997) outlines the way that it is possible to conduct ethnographic research on virtual communities constructed through the Internet:

Cyberspace constitutes a wonderful example of how people can build personal relationships and social norms that are absolutely real and meaningful even in the absence of physical touchable matter.

(Paccagnella, 1997, p. 2)

Her study was concerned with Italian cyber communities and the way that people create on-line worlds which may not correspond with off-line worlds. For example:

What is really happening, for example, when SweetBabe, a regular participant in IRC channel#netsex and one of the hypothetical cases from our survey sample, tells us that her real name is Mary, she's thirty years old and she worked as a secretary?

It is wise to suppose that, more than providing us some (if any) actual information about Mary's real life, such an answer could help to understand better SweetBabe's symbolic universe, her on-line self-representation, her social values and relationships.

(Paccagnella, 1997, p. 5)

The main method of research was participant observation by virtue of becoming a member of this particular cyber community:

In order to gain an intimate understanding of the culture and the symbolic system of the conference, the author has been a participant observer for 18 months. All the messages have been recorded and archived every month in a separate file, for a total of nearly 10 000 messages and 400 users involved.

(Paccagnella, 1997, p. 10)

Permission to publish these messages was not sought.

Paccagnella goes on to argue that using the Internet to conduct ethnographic research may be easier because it may be possible to observe naturalistic behaviour (at least naturalistic in cyberspace) without having the problem of the watched being affected by the presence of the watcher. The Hawthorne effect (see Section 9.5) may well be dispensed with in relation to cyber research according to this author:

While this obviously urges us to take into consideration new ethical issues [this will be discussed further on], at the same time it reduces the dangers of distorting data and behaviour by the presence of the researcher.

(Paccagnella, 1997, p. 6)

Cyber participation opens us new possibilities for non-intrusive methods and Paccagnella goes on to argue that computer software may be useful in the interpretation and presentation of qualitative data.

Discussion point

What new ethical problems might the author of this study be referring to and what old ethical problems might apply?

If you want to locate the discussion referred to in the quote above, access this article at http://jcmc.huji.ac.il/vol3/issue1/paccagnella.html/

9.7 Interpreting and evaluating data and reporting research results

The data you will be looking at in sociology comes in two forms, quantitative data and qualitative data.

Quantitative data is in the form of numbers and therefore includes statistics presented in various ways, including tables and graphs. You need to be able to effectively and accurately interpret this data and also come to an evaluative conclusion about its validity and representativeness.

Qualitative data is in the form of words and therefore includes all the books and articles you will read as you study the course. It also includes accounts of research done using participant observation or unstructured interviews, for instance. Again, you need to effectively and accurately interpret this data and also come to an evaluative conclusion about its reliability, validity and representativeness.

In this section we will outline issues concerning this process of interpretation and evaluation in relation to both types of data.

Quantitative data

Sociologists use statistics a lot. If you flick through this or any other sociology textbook you will find lots of statistics presented on various topics in a number of different ways, notably tables, graphs and charts. These statistics originally derive from research undertaken using the social survey methods of closed questionnaires and structured interviews. It is also possible they may emerge from the use of **structured observation**.

Quantitative data will be reported in the form of a table or graph and it is important that you spend time considering in detail exactly what information is being relayed and what, if anything, may be obscured.

Looking at tables of data

When considering any data one of the first issues to think about is the way concepts have been operationalized. Durkheim developed the concept of *anomie* (see Section 10.1) but this is an abstract concept and you certainly could not ask people 'How anomic are you feeling today?' Durkheim, just like everyone else, had to try to find **indicators** for this concept and he used, for example, the levels of industrial unrest, crime and suicide.

Equally, work or poverty are areas where the definition of what they mean is very much open to debate. Therefore, if you come across a table giving figures for the percentage of people in poverty in the UK you need to know how poverty is defined to really consider the significance of the figures given.

In order to consider the issue of looking at tables, we will use Table 9.2 as an example. This will provide a few pointers on how to interpret tables. Table 9.2 shows information relating to work in Great Britain.

Table 9.2 Economic status of people of working age: by gender and ethnic group, (GB, percentages, spring 1995)

	White	Black[1]	Indian	Pakistani/ Bangladeshi	Other[2]	All ethnic groups[3]
Males						
Working full time	72	49	65	41	51	71
Working part time	5	8	7	8	8	5
Unemployed	8	21	10	18	12	9
Inactive	15	22	18	33	29	15
All (=100%)(thousands)	16,993	273	306	216	224	18,017
Females						
Working full time	38	37	36	12	30	38
Working part time	29	15	19	6	16	28
Unemployed	5	14	7	7	8	5
Inactive	28	34	38	75	46	29
All (=100%)(thousands)	15,420	296	279	191	238	16,428

[1]Includes Caribbean, African and other black people of non-mixed origin.
[2]Includes Chinese, other ethnic minority groups of non-mixed origin and people of mixed origin.
[3]Includes ethnic group not stated.

Source: Labour Force Survey, quoted in *Social Trends*, (1996, p. 83)

The title

Firstly you need to look at the title of the table to see what subject it is discussing and to see what other information is contained there. In Table 9.2, for instance, we are told that it is about economic status, but also that it only covers people of working age (therefore excluding both those above retirement age and those below 16). We are also told that it covers Great Britain and not the United Kingdom (what this means is that Northern Ireland is not included).

The title also gives you a time period for the figures so you can see how up to date they are.

The source

The second thing you should look at is the bottom of the table to consider the source. Here this table was taken from *Social Trends* but the original source of the data is the *Labour Force Survey* which is a government survey, telling us that this table is an example of official statistics. You can look up the *Labour Force Survey* to see if there are any issues about it which you should take into account when evaluating the table overall.

Footnotes

Equally, you need to look at the footnotes. These include information of importance (otherwise why are they there?) and if you ignore them you might misinterpret the figures. In this case, they act to clarify the exact meaning of the ethnic group titles used in the table. Again, it is possible there may be debates about the usefulness of these categories and you can only decide on this by considering the actual way they are constructed.

The table headings

You can now look at the actual table and firstly consider the headings. Do you understand what they mean? For instance, do you know what the difference between unemployed and inactive is? The answer is that someone who is unemployed is looking for a job while someone who is inactive is not. Do they seem like sensible divisions to you? What is the distinction between working full time and working part time and does it matter?

The figures

You then need to look at the figures. These read across (rows) and down (columns). Looking at the columns we can see that there are figures given

first for whites. The title tells us that these are percentages rather than raw numbers. But if we look at the row starting 'All' at the end of the section on males or at the end of the section on females, we can see that this is given in figures. Here the authors are saying that the whole sample (100 per cent) had the following numbers in it (in thousands).

We can now consider whether there are any important differences in economic activity by ethnicity (by reading respective rows). For instance, looking at the row for unemployed males tells us that this experience is much greater among black and Pakistani/Bangladeshi groups than among whites.

We might then want to consider the gender angle and compare the position of females. Looking at the relevant row (Females, Unemployed) tells us that the difference between black and white females is even greater, but that there is not such a significant difference between Pakistani/Bangladeshi females and white females as was evident with the males.

If we wanted simply to consider the effect of gender differences on one particular ethnic group we could look down the relevant column. So, for instance, looking at Indians tells us that males are much more likely to be working full time than females, but females are more likely to be working part time or inactive than males. If we want to see whether this pattern is distinctive to this ethnic group we compare this column with others.

Sociological explanations

Table 9.1 does not tell us why these patterns exist and we therefore need to consider sociological explanations (in this case for the patterns of economic activity by gender and ethnicity) for the phenomena we are looking at. However, the table and its interpretation does provide the basis for understanding what evidence shows or what trends are evident if the table considers data over time (which Table 9.2 does not).

One thing to be aware of when looking at graphs such as line graphs, which allow comparisons over time, is the start and end period. Are these logical or have they been chosen to illustrate a certain trend? If you come across figures about the decline of the family that start at 1971 you should be suspicious since 1971 was the highpoint of marriage and therefore the **conventional family** and if you looked at earlier data this might provide a somewhat different picture.

Validity of data

It is important always to evaluate tables and graphs since you need to consider the validity of the figures that are being presented to you. One obvious example of this is surveys on people's sex lives which appear occasionally in the newspapers. These tend to show that males have more sexual partners than females. However, these figures should be roughly the same, so we should ask a lot of questions about such data and indeed not rely on its accuracy in this case. Sex surveys are an obvious example because of the very personal nature of their subject matter, but it is important to remember to consider this in relation to any data you use.

Presentation of data

Equally, the way data is presented, including issues such as the scale or the timescale, has important consequences for the picture you are presented with. This point is illustrated well in relation to two depictions of changes in crime statistics (example given in HMSO's *Social Trends* for 1992, Figure 9.2).

Activity

What problem do the two diagrams in Figure 9.2 illustrate?

C3.2, C3.3

Producing your own quantitative data

No data will be of any use unless its collection adheres to the principles of social research associated with the various methods which have been outlined in the earlier sections of this chapter. This section therefore rests on the assumption that this has been done.

Assume you have decided to collect quantitative data for your coursework and are now sitting at a desk confronted by 60 completed questionnaires. What steps need to be taken to ensure you present your results properly?

Creating a summary sheet

Firstly you need to create summary sheets for each question so that the answers from each of the 60 questionnaires can be transferred onto them. This allows you to get an overview of your results from one sheet. Bell (1993), using the example of a study looking at qualifications students held before enrolling on an access course, provides the example of a completed summary sheet and how this can be used to construct a basic but informative table (see Figure 9.3).

Notice that the questionnaire and therefore the summary sheet and the table include an 'Other' category. You should ensure that the contents of this are fully explained in your report.

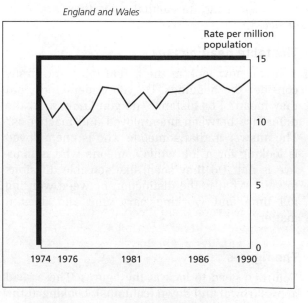

DEATH TOLL: How the murder figures have soared

Source: Lewis (1992), *Social Trends* 22 (HMSO) p 20

Figure 9.2 Murder: up or not?

QUESTION 1 QUALIFICATIONS BEFORE ENTRY				
None	O level/GCSE	A level	Access/Return to Study	Other
卌 ǀ	卌 卌 卌 卌 卌 ǀǀǀ	卌 卌 ǀǀ	卌 卌 卌 卌 卌 卌 ǀǀ	卌 卌 卌 ǀ
6	28	12	32	16

None	O level/GCSE	A level	Access/Return to Study	Other
6	28	12	32	16

Figure 9.3 Bell's summary sheet and table

Equally as Bell says:

The full list of 'Other' qualifications will need to be recorded on a separate sheet and if categories of qualification emerge, then reference can be made to them in the commentary.

(Bell, 1993, p. 129)

Using tables and graphs to present your data

Once you have a picture of the data your research has thrown up, you need to decide how to present it. The first thing to say (and it is something the authors have often found themselves having to say in relation to A level coursework) is that any table or graph does not stand on its own. It needs to be commented upon and explained in the text so that the reader knows what you are trying to show with this data and how it helps you to answer the research question you selected.

There are a number of choices on how to present material. Material can be presented as a table or as a graph. In the case of the latter you can also choose whether to present the data as a line graph, a bar graph or a pie chart. Figure 9.4 includes examples of these types of presentation.

It is important to notice that these tables and graphs use various shades of grey to distinguish between categories. This will allow you to distinguish between them if you are printing in black and white. Using different patterns for each category is an alternative way of doing this.

Legends or keys are added to some of the graphs while, on others, the category titles are placed directly onto the graph. Each includes a source showing where the data comes from and

if you use any secondary data in your study you will need to do this also. The use of gridlines in the bar chart in Figure 9.4 makes it easier to compare the various categories in the chart.

Fulcher and Scott (1999) contains an excellent section on presenting data and provides a summary of the rules for constructing tables outlined in Chapman (1986):

- *Round all numbers to two effective digits wherever possible*

- *Put the numbers to be most often compared with each other in columns rather than rows*

- *Arrange columns and rows in some natural order or in size order*

- *Where possible, put big numbers at the top of the table*

- *Give column and row averages or totals as a focus*

- *Use layout to guide the eye*

- *Give a verbal summary of the main points of the table.*

Source: Fulcher and Scott, 1999, p. 104 summarizing Chapman, 1986, p. 39

Using spreadsheets to present your data

As spreadsheet packages become more widely available and student ICT abilities become enhanced, more and more examples of the use of spreadsheet programs, such as Microsoft Excel, to generate graphs and tables, are seen in sociology coursework. These packages are good tools but it is important to remember that is all they are. As Stephens *et al.* (1998) put it:

If you use spreadsheet/graphics packages, it's essential that the information contained in your graph is related directly to your hypothesis and objectives. Fancy, coloured diagrams have little relevance unless they're analysed. You're interpreting the information, and applying it to your study.

Sociology teachers should not and will not be impressed by your ability to produce colourful diagrams if this is not backed up with anything else, although experience suggests that this is still a myth believed by some students.

For those intending to use such packages they mostly now have chart wizards which allow you to construct a whole variety of tables or graphs from a set of data you have entered. Once you have constructed your chart you need to ensure that you add on elements such as the key, the source of the data, the title of the chart and any

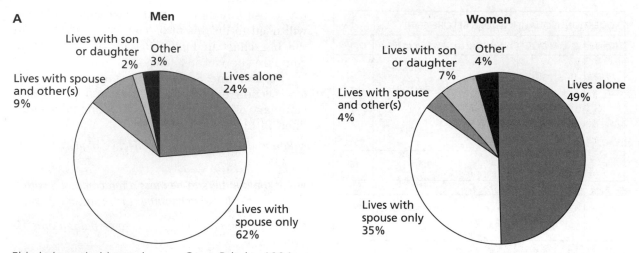

A

Men

Lives with son or daughter 2%
Other 3%
Lives with spouse and other(s) 9%
Lives alone 24%
Lives with spouse only 62%

Women

Lives with son or daughter 7%
Other 4%
Lives with spouse and other(s) 4%
Lives alone 49%
Lives with spouse only 35%

Elderly household type by sex: Great Britain, 1994
Source: Living in Britain 1994, General Household Survey Preliminary Results 1996 (ONS 1996)

B

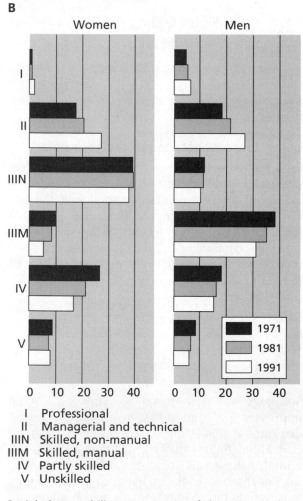

I Professional
II Managerial and technical
IIIN Skilled, non-manual
IIIM Skilled, manual
IV Partly skilled
V Unskilled

Social class mobility: percentage of the UK population by social class and sex
Source: Census/The Guardian, 25 february 995

C

Region	Male manual	Male non-manual	Female manual	Female non-manual
South East	£310.70	£506.30	£208.50	£326.10
East Anglia	£283.30	£402.70	£175.30	£264.00
South West	£276.50	£410.00	£178.00	£267.30
West Midlands	£285.20	£410.20	£186.40	£264.20
East Midlands	£282.40	£395.80	£177.20	£262.80
Yorks & H'side	£285.50	£390.60	£176.20	£259.30
North West	£290.40	£414.40	£182.00	£270.60
North	£286.40	£385.40	£180.30	£258.70
Wales	£284.40	£386.80	£185.40	£264.90
Scotland	£284.50	£413.20	£186.00	£272.70

Average gross weekly pay for full-time workers on adult rates whose pay was not affected by absence
Source: New Earnings Survey, 1995

D

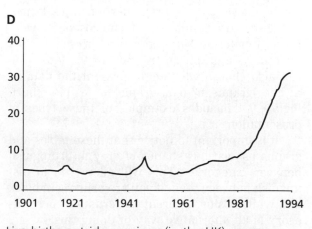

Live births outside marriage (in the UK) as a percentage of all births
Source: Office of Population Censuses and Surveys/Social Trends 1996

Figure 9.4 Different ways of presenting data: **A** a pie chart; **B** a bar chart; **C** a table; **D** a line graph

other features you feel are necessary. Advice on the use of these packages in coursework is provided by Tony Lawson in an article in *Sociology Review* (Lawson, 1993) which we strongly suggest you consult.

A final warning in relation to these programs and the presentation of quantitative data more generally is contained in Bell (1993), where she says:

Do not get involved with complicated statistics unless you know what you are doing.

(Bell, 1993, p. 69)

Qualitative data

Qualitative data is used to present material in greater detail than is often possible using the tables and graphs used in quantitative data. One key side effect of this is that the sample size of studies done using methods that yield qualitative data tend to be smaller, leading to question marks over their representativeness (see Section 9.4). However, they are used to provide detailed information in the words of the respondents. They are therefore felt by some sociologists to have greater validity, though it is important to remember that in all likelihood the qualitative data you will get will be that which the researcher has selected for you to see and this is unlikely to be the total amount of data collected.

Reading qualitative data

You need to consider the source of the data. That is to say, who constructed it, when and for what reason. This is important since you need to consider the accuracy or more strictly the validity and reliability of the data you are presented with. This is especially true of historical data since, for instance, people's diaries may not always be entirely truthful. It is also the case that with historical data it is impossible to retest the statements being made (except by reference to other secondary material) and in some instances this material will be all that is available.

We need to know what the original purpose of the material was and we need to know whether there is anything else that the material tells us. This can be called the witting and the unwitting content of the material.

If you are dealing with material collected in primary research by a sociologist then you need to consider the material in the context of the

research method employed. Was it conducted by unstructured interviews using a tape recorder or alternatively by participant observation with the researcher writing up their notes every night and relying on their memory? Whose words are we reading – the respondent's or the researcher's?

In this form of research, there is often an attempt to present an ethnographic approach, that is, writing about people and their particular way of life. The question needs to be considered whether this style of research does actually allow people to get closer to the respondents and present a more accurate detailed picture of their life. This also involves consideration of the extent to which the nature of conduct of the researcher will have an impact on the respondents and therefore the findings. This is also clearly affected by the subject matter of research so if the data you are looking at considers a particularly sensitive topic (for instance, crime or sexuality) then you need to be aware of the possible effects of this.

It would also be useful to know how much material was collected and how much of this you have been presented with. This often requires access to the published research report so you can look at the methodology section.

Recording qualitative data

The first thing to consider if you are intending to conduct research to collect qualitative data is how you are going to record it. Making notes while conducting an interview may not provide an accurate summary of the content of what someone is saying unless you are expert at shorthand. It may be possible to tape the interview, thus allowing for perfect recall of what was said. However, you then need to get this transcribed and if you are doing it yourself it will probably take between 10 and 15 hours to transcribe one hour of an interview.

If you are considering engaging in observation studies, tape recording or overt notetaking of any sort may not be possible so you will need to devise methods which allow you to record your findings at intervals which do not stretch the credible memory length of an average human being.

Presenting qualitative data

Assuming that you have managed to actually collect your data and now have a mass sitting in front of you, you need to consider how best to present it.

Qualitative data is most often presented in the form of lengthy quotes or extracts from replies given to the researcher. Since the point is to try to put answers in the words of the respondent so as to present a picture of the world as they see it, you will need to include several such quotations with an explanation of who is saying what. Comparison between different respondents then becomes possible.

It might also be useful to indicate what proportion of your total data is actually included in the report and to explain the basis on which you selected material for inclusion. If you are including extracts from interviews, it might be useful to include some complete transcripts to enable readers to judge for themselves the representativeness of the selections you have included.

Stephens *et al.* provide the following advice (in the context of looking at A level coursework):

Students often use unstructured interviews and observation to obtain qualitative data. If you have permission of the respondent to tape-record your interview, it will probably take you at least ten times the length of the actual interview to transcribe it verbatim. Another option is a summary transcription which includes key verbatim quotes. You could also devise a system to transcribe accurate notes as the interview proceeds. An interview schedule will help to structure the information under subheadings, but it's likely that some of the conversation will be misrepresented or forgotten.

There are different ways of presenting the dialogue:

- *You could include a complete transcript of the interview and place this in an appendix. You could then refer to particular aspects of the interview which relate specifically to your objectives. The organisation and presentation may be clearer if you use sub-headings for each objective.*

- *You could include 'snap shots' of the interview within the content section. This may include direct quotations from the interview.*

It won't be enough just to present the transcripts. It's essential that you analyse all the material as you present it.

(Stephens *et al.*, 1999, p. 39)

Final point

Whatever data you are presenting, it is important to remember that it does not speak for itself and that you have to relate it to what you are studying. You also need to ensure that you are careful to interpret and evaluate any data in any sociological exercise, including answering data questions, structured questions or writing essays.

Further reading

The following are two useful introductory texts:

- Chignall, H. (1996) *Theory and Methods*, Lewes: Connect.
- McNeill, P. (1990) *Research Methods*, 2nd edn, London: Routledge.

A clear and comprehensive overview of the social research process can be gleaned from:

- Kidd, W. *et al.* (1999) *Readings in Sociology*, Oxford: Heinemann Educational.
- May, T. (1993) *Social Research*, Buckingham: Open University Press.

The following book is comprehensive and packed with original extracts. It is of immense use to those wishing to consider methodological debates:

- Harvey, L. and MacDonald, M. (1993) *Doing Sociology: A Practical Introduction*, London: Macmillan.

Back issues of the periodical *Sociology Review* (formerly *Social Studies Review*) also contain many articles on this field and many others.

Glossary of useful terms

Conventional family A term used to describe what was seen as the norm in family structure, namely the nuclear family with two married parents and their biological children.

Covert observation Where the people being observed do not know that they are being observed.

Covert participant observation A research method where observation is facilitated by being a participant. However, since it is covert, all or most of the group being observed will be unaware that they are being observed.

Imposition problem   This is the idea that by providing people with alternative answers in closed questionnaires/ structured interviews, the researcher forces a person to pigeonhole themselves and thus imposes an answer upon them. It occurs in relation to more qualitative orientated research by the selective use of quoted material gathered in interviews or observation.

Indicators   Observable things which can stand in to indicate something else. Notably Durkheim used suicide rates as indicators of anomie.

Laws of society   Idea associated with positivism that suggests that the world is determined by some force beyond the individual.

New Right   Used to distinguish the views of right-wing political parties in recent times from earlier conservative views: notably the views of the British Conservative Party from the premiership of Margaret Thatcher onwards and the US Republican Party from the presidency of Ronald Reagan onwards. The most notable difference is the New Right emphasis on the benefits of the free market and individual freedom.

Overt participant observation   A method where people are observed while the person doing the observing participates in whatever they are observing. However, since it is overt, the people being observed are aware that they are being observed.

Participant observation   Key sociological research method where the researcher participates in the group in order to observe their activities.

Primary data   Data collected by the sociologists themselves.

Probability theory   One basis of sampling is the idea that we can establish the likelihood or probability of something happening. The science behind this is known as probability theory.

Qualitative   Data in the form of words.

Quantitative   Data in the form of numbers or statistics.

Scientific method   Being scientific means basing your thoughts on evidence and on systematic collection, testing and re-testing of ideas using evidence and theories.

Secondary data   Used by sociologists but not actually collected by them. The best example is official statistics; this is data actually collected by the government which sociologists make use of.

Strata   The idea that society can be divided up into layers of people either by class, gender, ethnicity or other significant variables.

Structured interviews   Interviews where the wording of questions and the order in which questions are asked remains the same for all respondents.

Structured observation   This is associated with sociologists who have a structural approach. It suggests that more than individual choice and decision-making is needed in order to explain how society functions. The more needed is some notions of structures, as long-lasting things which are not easily changed.

Unstructured interviews   Interviews which provide qualitative data. They are very much like a conversation and informality is used to place the respondent at ease.

Power and control

Crime and deviance

Chapter outline

The social nature of crime and deviance

10.1 Defining crime and deviance

Deviance is an often exciting and popular area of investigation for sociology and sociologists. To start, we can draw a distinction between:

- sociological problems – those concerned with getting adequate knowledge about the social world
- social problems – aspects of social life that are a worry or cause of concern for those within it.

Deviance, and more significantly that specific form of rule-breaking known as crime, is not only a *sociological problem* – it is also defined by some, especially ruling groups, as a *social problem*.

💬 Discussion point

Why might deviance – people going against the normal way of behaving in society – be defined as a social problem by ruling groups in positions of power?

C3.1a

Whereas some see that the purpose of sociology is to explain and describe human behaviour in a detached fashion, others working within this topic area often wish to use sociological insights to produce social policy that limits the effects of crime and helps policy-creators and decision-makers to reduce or limit the amount of so-called 'undesirable' activities.

In 1993, the then prime minister John Major said of crime that we should *condemn a little more and understand a little less*. This has important implications for the pursuit of a sociological understanding of crime and deviance. Are sociologists guilty of supporting the activities of deviants in society by not condemning their activities, or must understanding come before society can genuinely attempt to solve or reduce social problems?

💬 Discussion point

To what extent does sociology side with the underdog too often to make the insights produced by sociologists of value?

C3.1a

Before we can discuss, analyse and evaluate some of the theoretical and empirical contributions made by sociologists and sociological thought to an understanding of crime and deviance, we must be clear on our use of these terms and of others central to this topic area.

1 Crime

'Crime' is usually associated with behaviour that breaks the formal, written laws of a given society. The punishment of crime is likely to be more serious than the punishment of deviance in general but, obviously, different crimes and different laws are treated in varying ways.

2 Deviance

To deviate means, literally, to move away or to stray from set standards in society. Deviance, then, is a much more general category than crime, and is used by sociologists to refer to behaviour that, while being different, is often not controlled legally.

It must be made clear, however, that to distinguish between crime and deviance like this is to do a disservice to the complexities of these concepts. It is of more value to think of deviance as a wide category, of which crime is a smaller part. Thus, all crime is deviance, but not all deviance is crime.

To deviate from social standards, however, is not to say that the deviant in question has performed a negative act (as defined by the standards of a given society). Although crime is usually associated with negative action, it is perfectly possible for one to deviate in a positive fashion: one could be held in high social regard, for example, for contributing outstanding and original knowledge in the sciences.

3 Norms

As the name suggests, norms are the normal ways of behaving in society. A norm refers specifically to a given behavioural pattern. This is what we do in our everyday lives to behave *normally*. As with the relationship between deviance and crime, all laws are norms but not all norms are laws. If one breaks a norm one is considered as deviant. Sanctions or punishments against one who breaks norms depends on the severity of the norm and the public nature of the norm-breaking action. Such sanctions can range from a disapproving stare to, on extreme occasions, social exclusion from a group.

4 The social construction of deviance

Norms are the products of social construction. Behaviour can vary in being normal or abnormal depending on the situation a social actor is in. Norms also vary across both time and space – they vary within a society historically, and between societies. (See also Section 3.2.)

5 Values

A value has a special relationship to a norm. Values are the specific cultural goals towards which norms are directed. Whereas a norm prescribes actual behaviour, a value justifies that behaviour – it is the reason why some actions are approved of more than others.

Activity

Using the following examples of cultural styles, describe how these normal ways of behaving vary across both time and space:

men's earrings	women's tattoos
men's ponytails/long hair	women's shaven/ short hair

C3.1a, C3.1b

The problems of a 'sociology of deviance'

The term 'sociology of deviance', as an overarching theme for this chapter, has its problems. Whereas some sociologists investigate deviance in its everyday, general sense, others almost exclusively study the specific form of deviance known as 'criminality'. In the literature, these two terms have also become associated closely with one another; so much so that what is called the sociology of deviance contains a vast and complex array of different theories, terms and interests. As Downes and Rock comment:

The very title of the discipline which we shall describe, the sociology of deviance, is a little misleading. A singular noun and a hint of science seem to promise a unified body of knowledge and an agreed set of procedures for resolving analytic difficulties. It suggests that the curious and troubled may secure sure answers to practical, political, moral, and intellectual problems. And, of all branches of applied sociology, the demands placed on the sociology of deviance are probably the most urgent. Deviance is upsetting and perplexing and it confronts people in many settings. Turning to sociology, enquirers are

rarely given certain advice ... They will not be offered one answer but a series of competing and contradictory visions of the nature of people, deviation, and the social order.

(Downes and Rock, 1995, p. 1)

Activity

a Why do Downes and Rock suggest that enquirers are rarely given certain advice from the sociologists of deviance?

b Why might this be a problem for the public and governmental perception of sociology as a subject?

C3.2, C3.3

Discussion point

To what extent do you think it is a serious problem if sociologists cannot agree on the role of deviance in society? Why do you think this is?

C3.1a

Durkheim and the sociology of suicide

Suicide as a topic has become popular in sociology largely through the efforts of Durkheim. In his now classic text *Le Suicide*, published originally in France in 1897, Durkheim (1979) wished to explain his sociological method. He chose what he considered, at the time, to be this most individual and personal act and attempted to illustrate how it was really the product of social collectivity (see also Section 13.2).

Pre-sociological views of suicide

Prior to the work of Durkheim, the topic of suicide had already received much intellectual attention, with various theories developed to explain how suicide rates varied over time, and between societies. These pre-Durkheimian theories sought to explain patterns of suicide through reference to:

- biological factors such as heredity and racial predisposition
- psychological factors such as the suffering of an individual from an unstable mind
- meteorological and cosmic factors such as climate, temperature and the movement of the planets.

For Durkheim, rather unsurprisingly, these explanations were inadequate. Instead, he focuses in particular on the bonds of solidarity through which a social group is drawn together.

The methodology of Durkheim

Durkheim chose the topic of suicide as a challenge: it represented a great test of the claims of scientific knowledge made by positivists such as himself and Comte before him. He used a comparative method, studying the rates of suicide between different societies at different times. Vital for Durkheim is the belief that social reality exists outside of the individual consciousness and will:

Sociological method as we practise it rests wholly on the basic principle that social facts must be studied as things, that is, as realities external to the individual.

(Durkheim, 1979, pp. 37–8; orig. pub. 1897)

Four types of suicide

By focusing on the official (coroners') suicide records for a number of societies, Durkheim identifies four types which he relates to the degree of solidarity experienced in society:

- *Egoistic suicide* occurs when the bonds or ties which usually unite a group together weaken and increased individuality occurs.

- *Altruistic suicide* occurs when the bonds or ties which usually unite a group together are so strong that over-integration occurs. Individuals sacrifice themselves for the good of the group.

- *Anomic suicide* occurs when the individual is not regulated by the norms and values of the group or by the social order.

- *Fatalistic suicide* occurs when the individual is regulated too much – when the norms and rules of a society are so rigid they stifle the individual and oppress too much.

Egoistic and altruistic types of suicide occur owing to too little or too much integration, whereas anomic and fatalistic suicide occurs owing to not enough or too much regulation. Egoistic and anomic suicides were seen by Durkheim to be particular problems of industrial societies.

Suicide and religion

For Durkheim, suicide rates and the types of suicide involved were directly related to the religious practices in the wider society. For example, he noted that Roman Catholics had a much lower rate of suicide than Protestants. He explained this by suggesting that Catholics were more strongly bonded to the social group than Protestants, given the Catholic emphasis on collectivity.

An interactionist critique

Using the methodological insights of phenomenology, a number of commentators have attempted to develop a critique of Durkheim's original research into suicide. This interactionist approach suggests that social facts do not exist: reality does not exist outside of an individual, but rather, individual consciousness is reality in society. Suicide, like any other aspect of social life, deviant or not, is thus a product of social construction: it does not create or mould the individual, but rather, individual action creates the social reality.

Applied to the deviant act of suicide, this interactionist critique turns its attention to what its supporters see as the unreliability of official suicide rates. Like official crime statistics, suicide rates are seen as a social construction: they tell us more about the activities and ideas of coroners than they do about the actual nature of death or suicide itself. They tell us about the interaction between doctors, the family, coroners and the police – and the attempts each of these groups make in defining the real meaning of the death, through the search and classification of so-called indicators of suicidal intent such as a note, etc.

Viewed in this way, suicide statistics are created and shaped through strong social and cultural forces. Thus, Catholic societies may well have a lower rate of officially measured suicide than Protestant societies, but this is not the same thing as a real or objective rate of suicide. It might just be the case, as argued by Atkinson (1977), that Catholic coroners and coroners in Catholic societies are less inclined, for religious reasons, to record a death as a suicide.

Social construction and the relativity of crime and deviance

This section started with a distinction between social problems and sociological problems. Let us look at this again:

- Social problems are those defined by society itself – problems such as crime, delinquency, civil unrest, etc. that are seen by either the majority by consensus, or by the ruling élite from above, to represent aspects of behaviour considered to be undesirable.

- Sociological problems are much wider, including issues of theories, methodology, etc. Social problems can also *become* sociological problems – objects of sociological measurement, definition and study.

Whereas some sociologists claim that sociology should be the study of social problems and accept these problems without question, others – especially Marxists and interactionists – question social problems: in whose interests does it serve to define an aspect of society as a problem? Marxists and other radical sociological positions suggest that definitions of crime and deviance and laws and social rules tend to benefit those in powerful positions in society.

'Correctional criminology'

Hester and Eglin (1996) suggest that criminology is a practical or applied branch of sociology. They refer to both sociological and criminological theories, and to theorists who seek practically to solve crime and deviance as *correctional*. Hester and Eglin, adopting what they refer to as a subversive approach to the study of crime using symbolic interactionism, ethnomethodology and conflict structuralism believe it is a mistake for sociology to set out to solve the problems of society, for three main reasons.

1 The problems of positivism

Hester and Eglin believe that such correctional research is often forced to adopt positivistic approaches to the study of crime. It ends up as an exercise in the measurement of criminal frequencies. More seriously, they believe that ultimately this type of sociology does little more than serve the state. It becomes the mouthpiece of governmental political power. They note that at the extreme this positivistic approach becomes

untheoretical, dealing only with measurement and its associated issues while failing to use or explain more deep-rooted issues of *cause*. This becomes what Jock Young refers to as *administrative criminology*.

2 Crime is meaningful

Secondly, Hester and Eglin are critical of the assumptions about human nature used in so-called 'correctional criminology'. They believe that this type of explanation fails to understand that crime, like all social action, is socially meaningful to those involved and to those who react to it. This level of meaningful analysis is absent from most correctional criminology. Thus, humans are treated as objects or passive victims of the environment rather than creative actors.

> ### 💬 Discussion point
> Why is it valuable for sociologists to see crime and deviance as 'meaningful'? Why might politicians be wary of such ideas?
>
> **C3.1a**

3 The definition of a social problem involves power

Thirdly, Hester and Eglin suggest that correctional criminology fails to recognize that crime, like all so-called social problems, is defined by society. It is not an innate, static or objective phenomenon but the product of political, cultural and historical forces.

David Matza

Matza, in *Becoming Deviant* (1969), identifies the five key components of a correctional criminology of which, like Hester and Eglin above, he is highly critical:

1. Sociological problems are all those defined as social problems within society itself. They are identical.

2. Sociological concerns should come solely from wider social concerns.

3. The purpose of sociology is to solve such wider social problems.

4. The main focus of investigation is the causes (aetiology) of criminal behaviour at the expense of a study of the process of power and ideology involved in the construction of the rules, the breaking of which defines crime.

5 The methodology is derived from positivism).

From the above critique of what we will from now on refer to as 'correctional criminology', a number of key issues are raised – seemingly from within something approaching a Marxist and/or interactionist theoretical framework.

Marxist interpretations of crime and deviance

We can suggest that within a Marxist framework, any study of crime and/or deviance must take into account the process of power involved in the creation of rules in society. Attention must be given by the sociologist to the activities of the ruling class in using laws and rules to support their activities.

> 💬 **Discussion point**
>
> To what extent should sociology be used as a means through which to change the world?
>
> **C3.1a**

Interactionist interpretations of crime and deviance

From an interactionist stance, we can take the position that crime and/or deviance can be understood successfully only by seeing it as a meaningful activity created by society, since rules must exist for deviation away from the rules to be possible.

Sociological and non-sociological theories of crime and deviance

Sociologists are not the only academics to study crime and deviance. The specific study of crime – criminology – is itself made up not just of sociological ideas, but also other non-sociological ideas.

Within criminology roughly three types of explanation for crime can be identified:

- sociological
- psychological
- physiological.

Many researchers and theorists have used some sort of combination of these theories. Our interest in them, though, is only fleeting – an attempt to understand the sociological approach better through a comparison with other approaches. As a rough guide, the following distinctions can be drawn:

- *Sociological* theories locate deviance and crime as a *response to the society* in which they occur.
- *Psychological* theories locate deviance and crime *within the psyche or mind of the individual*: the product of inborn abnormality or of faulty cognition processes.
- *Physiological* theories locate deviance and crime *within the biological make-up of the individual*.

> 💬 **Discussion point**
>
> To what extent do you think that criminals are born as such? What do sociologists believe, and what implications might this have for social policy?
>
> **C3.1a**

As Hester and Eglin (1996) comment, non-sociological theories have offered a whole range of interpretations in order to explain the criminality of the individual:

- biological 'inferiority'
- extreme extroversion
- chromosome abnormality
- body shape
- nutritional deficiency
- extreme introversion
- a dominant sexual drive.

> ✏️ **Activity**
>
> The non-sociological explanations for criminal behaviour listed above are in a random order but contain examples of both psychological and physiological thinking. Sort the list into these two categories.
>
> **C3.2, C3.3**

It is useful to remember that ideas very rarely become extinct. They are often dormant for periods of time, sometimes decades, only to reappear at a later time, renamed and suddenly popular once more. Sociologists are equally as guilty of following the crowd or jumping on the bandwagon as they are of producing original and highly imaginative theories. Although some ideas, especially those dating back in time, may appear dated or even ridiculous to the modern reader, many still have their current expressions.

Cesare Lombroso: classical physiological theory

Italian army doctor Cesare Lombroso is considered by many to be the founder of the scientific biological school of criminology. Lombroso's now infamous work *L'Uomo Delinquente* (1876) first developed the idea of the *atavistic criminal*.

Are criminals 'throwbacks'?

Atavism, a term originally used by Charles Darwin, suggests that in the process of human evolution some individuals can represent a genetic throwback to a previous stage in the history of human growth. Darwin commented:

With mankind some of the worst dispositions which occasionally without any assignable cause make their appearance in families, may perhaps be reversions to a savage state, from which we are not removed by many generations.

(Darwin; quoted in Taylor *et al.*, 1973, p. 41)

Taking up this idea, Lombroso contended that the criminal individual was born so. Physical indication of criminal potential could be identified through specific bodily characteristics, all of which suggested that the bearer was a throwback to a more primitive age. These physical characteristics included abnormal teeth, extra nipples, extra or missing toes and fingers, large ears, and overly prominent jaw bones.

Solutions to crime?

The logical, and quite frightening, conclusion of this idea, from a social policy point of view, is that criminal *types* can easily be identified and therefore action can be taken against them even *before* they commit crime! Since criminality, for Lombroso, was inborn, action against crime would have to involve exclusion from society, or indeed capital punishment.

Criticisms of Lombroso's position

1 Those identified in society as criminals may be so identified owing to how they look physically, rather than their physiological characteristics actually having a causal effect.

2 Although those in prison may be more typical of a specific physical type, it may be that this is the effect of social or environmental factors – such as diet and access to fitness – and therefore associated with class and occupation (manual work) and subculture, rather

than with a biological predisposition towards criminality.

Hans Eysenck: psychological theory

A well-known author who has adopted the psychological approach to studying crime and deviance is Hans Eysenck. In his work *Crime and Personality* (1970), Eysenck attempts to correlate (to demonstrate a link between) criminal behaviour and the personality type of the individual. He claims that criminality is the result of genetic and largely inherited predisposition: some individuals are more likely to become criminals given the sort of person they are. In adopting what he would see as a scientific or positivistic approach, Eysenck claims that tests conducted in prison on inmates indicate that prisons have more extroverts amongst their populations than the population does at large. Therefore, he asserts, extroversion is the inherited psychological basis of criminality.

Introverts, extroverts and crime

Eysenck claims that extroverts are more likely, given their genetic make-up, to be under-socialized, and therefore to lack the internalization of norms and values that guide the rest of the population. He draws very specific differences between the two personality types of introversion and extroversion, suggesting that all human personality types exist along a continuum somewhere between these two points. At the extremes of this continuum:

The typical extrovert ... craves excitement, takes chances, acts on the spur of the moment, and is generally an impulsive individual ... He prefers to keep moving and doing things, tends to be aggressive and loses his temper quickly; his feelings are not kept under tight control and he is not always a reliable person.

(Eysenck; quoted in Taylor *et al.*, 1973, pp. 56–7)

It is interesting to note that some of the above characteristics are remarkably similar to modern-day definitions of hyperactivity and attention-deficit disorder (ADD). On the other hand:

The typical introvert is a quiet, retiring sort of person, introspective, fond of books rather than people: he is reserved and reticent except with intimate friends ... He does not like excitement, takes matters of everyday life with proper seriousness, and likes a well-ordered mode of life. He keeps his feelings under close control, seldom behaves in an aggressive manner, and does not lose his temper easily.

(Eysenck; quoted in Taylor *et al.*, 1973, p. 57)

Criticisms of Eysenck's position

A number of sociologists, especially Taylor, Walton and Young (1973), have taken issue with the ideas of Eysenck on both methodological and theoretical grounds. These criticisms can be summarized as follows:

1   Research in prison on inmates is not necessarily the same thing as research on all criminals in general. Many criminals are not caught, or are not imprisoned, and some people who are innocent are wrongly imprisoned.

2   Perhaps Eysenck is measuring the effects of imprisonment on the person's personality, and not the characteristics which led to imprisonment.

3   Those who have the characteristics identified as being extrovert by Eysenck, although not committing more crime than introverts, may be stopped by the police, arrested and sentenced more because their behaviour is of a more obvious nature.

4   Some commentators, such as Miller (quoted in Downes and Rock, 1995), have associated immediate pleasure-seeking behaviour with working-class subcultural values. It may well be the case, as argued by Box (1981, 1995), that the working classes are more likely to be arrested and imprisoned owing to stereotypes which operate amongst the courts and police concerning what a typical criminal is like.

Modern physiological and psychological theories

There have been a number of recent science-based research programmes into the biological and psychological sources of criminal and other antisocial behavioural characteristics (Moir and Jessel, 1995). These research programmes, mainly funded within American and British university departments, seek to find a medical cure for crime, based on the assumption (shared with Eysenck) that criminality can be treated biologically. These medical-based modern explanations for criminality include:

• various mental health explanations, such as schizophrenia

• the existence of a medical condition described as episodic dyscontrol: a condition similar to an epilepsy-type explosion in areas of the brain

• a dramatic inactivity of brain functions in the prefrontal area of the brain, the areas usually associated with making plans and strategies

• explanations based on a version of hyperctivity or, as it is sometimes called, hyperkinesis.

 Discussion point

Why might sociologists be critical of the use of physiological and psychological theories to explain crime? What alternative views might sociologists suggest?

C3.1a

A sociological criticism of medical models

Cohen (1977) is highly critical of the types of explanation for criminality offered by non-sociological sources. In particular, he is suspicious of those theories based on a medical model of the criminal the suggestion that criminals, or deviants in general, are pathological, ill or sick, and that they therefore require help or treatment.

Cohen suggests that such approaches, while appearing to be based on a desire to care for or help and rehabilitate the individual, are actually based on strong and powerful mechanisms of social control, and are often the justifications given by the state for repressive activity against so-called deviant minorities: individuals or groups which have the potential to embarrass the state unless hidden, controlled or condemned.

Cohen advocates a sceptical stance, a left-of-centre, Marxist and interactionist influenced approach. Within this sceptical approach, what Cohen terms *official criminology* – or psychological and/or medical models of criminality – is to be mistrusted. This supports the state and highlights the differences between the normal and the abnormal. It fails to discuss the vital question, *normal according to whose definition?*

Violent crime: an old or new fear?

Rose-tinted nostalgia?

According to Pearson (1983), what the fears of rising crime illustrate is the temptation for each generation, especially those of the post-middle-age bracket, to look back through rose-tinted glasses and with nostalgia at the past: to see society before the present unruly age to be a golden age where all was at peace and harmony reigned.

When viewed in this fashion, current trends in criminal statistics immediately take on new possibilities and interpretations. Do they represent not so much a genuine increase in the amount of crime, but rather the increased reporting and awareness of crime – the result of fear of the present age, reflected in and reinforced by the media?

Violence of the past

Social historians Hay and colleagues, in their work *Albion's Fatal Tree* (1988) which drew on a wide variety of sources, went to great lengths to illustrate the violent and dangerous nature of the past – in particular the eighteenth century in England. They point to a whole range of crimes and criminal activity widespread in those times, including smuggling, street robbery, highway robbery, theft of wood, poaching, anonymous and threatening letter-writing, forgery, arson and, of course, murder.

This suggests that crime did not experience a dramatic increase since the eighteenth century, but rather that the creation of the law, run in favour of a ruling élite for the protection of their property, criminalized the actions of the poor – actions which had always existed.

Activity

From the ideas presented above by Pearson and Hay *et al.*, write a Marxist interpretation of the role played by law in society.

C3.2, C3.3

Nineteenth century moral panics

In looking at moral panics closer to our own times, Pearson comments that modern-day fears of football hooliganism are nothing new, and in fact date back to at least the mid-nineteenth century. Pitch invasions, attacks on referees and players and conflicts between rival fans were a regular feature in local newspapers of the time.

Pearson dates the word 'hooligan' back to the summer of 1898 (as illustrated by the pen and ink drawing from *Punch* that year), when it was used in newspaper headlines to describe the activities of youths during the August Bank Holiday. Pearson suggests that the word may have been first popularized within the music halls in the 1890s.

Sociology and common sense

Cohen goes further and suggests that the medical/psychological models of criminality fit easily within society's commonsense understandings of deviance. Over time, through the mass media in particular, the ideas associated with these theories ideas such as criminality representing sickness, mental ill-health, a response to disturbing childhood experiences, etc. have become part of the lay person's or public's frame of reference, which makes them difficult to resist.

Discussion point

Why is sociology so critical of commonsense thought? What makes sociology a better way of viewing the world?

C3.1a

Some commonsense, non-sociological theories on crime, however, do mirror quite closely the ideas of sociologists. Although lacking in the key characteristics of a sociological approach – namely, research and a theoretical perspective – the public sometimes (and politicians often) come close when discussing the social causes of crime. For example, as Tony Blair, when he was Shadow Home Secretary in 1993, commented:

Any sensible society acting in its own interests as well as those of its citizens will understand and recognise that poor education and housing, inadequate or cruel family backgrounds, low employment prospects and drug abuse will affect the likelihood of young people turning to crime. If they are placed outside mainstream culture, offered no hope or opportunity, shown no respect by others, and unable to develop respect for themselves, there is a greater chance of their going wrong.

(Quoted in New Statesman and Society, 1993, p. 5)

Activity

Use the quotation above from Tony Blair and the ideas of Stanley Cohen to answer the following questions:

a What are the causes of crime identified by Blair?

b Which of the points identified by Blair are sociological and which are psychological?

c Can you think of any other sources of criminality in the modern world? Explain your examples.

d Referring to the ideas of Stanley Cohen, why might it be comfortable for the public to identify the sources of criminality to be somewhere 'out there'?

e Why might the same be said for governments?

C3.2, C3.3

10.2 Social reactions to crime and deviance and their consequences

A significant development in the sociology of deviance is labelling theory, a term often given to the symbolic interactionist perspective. Central to this is the wish to study the meanings and motives of the actor, and the meanings his or her actions have for society.

There are some problems associated with the term 'labelling theory'. In certain respects many different sociological theories are theories of labels because they deal with negative or stigmatized labels and how they affect the individual. However, the phrase 'labelling theory' will be used here to refer to the particular branch of interactionist sociology concerned with how deviant labels are created, imposed and resisted through interaction.

Becker: action and reaction

The key to understanding labelling theory is to draw a distinction between social *action* and social *reaction*. Becker (1973) makes the point that deviance is not a quality inherent within an act, but is defined by a label or reaction to an act by society. No actions are by nature criminal or deviant – it depends on the norms of the society,

and the reaction of members of society in different situations and contexts. As Becker states:

All social groups make rules and attempt, at some times and under some circumstances, to enforce them.

(Becker, 1973, p. 1)

In his now classic text, *Outsiders: Studies in the Sociology of Deviance*, Becker asserts that:

... social groups create deviance by making the rules whose infraction constitutes deviance, and by applying those rules to particular people and labelling them as outsiders ... the deviant is one to whom that label has successfully been applied.

(Becker, 1973, p. 9)

Within that short sentence we have the basic tenets of the whole labelling theory approach: deviance is about public or social reaction, and not the initial individual action. Deviance is only deviance if publicly labelled as such, through the process of interaction in which meaning is established.

Labels

Deviance, then, is considered a matter of labelling, a social judgement. Or, to use other terminology, it is a stigma – a reaction which judges the behaviour of an individual or group, and in so doing comes to define the nature of that person's subsequent actions. If the labelling process is complete, then one may become an outsider to the mainstream society:

Since deviance is, among other things, a consequence of the responses of others to a person's act, students of deviance cannot assume that they are dealing with a homogeneous category when they study people who have been labelled deviant. That is, they cannot assume that these people have actually committed a deviant act or broken some rule, because the process of labelling may not be infallible; some people may be labelled deviant who in fact have not broken a rule. Furthermore, they cannot assume that the category of those labelled deviant will contain all those who actually have broken a rule, for many offenders may escape apprehension and thus fail to be included in the population of deviants they study.

(Becker, 1973, p. 9)

This approach takes us away from a sociological study of why people commit crime, or why they act originally in a deviant fashion, and turns its attention to why and how people become *seen* as a deviant by others. It is not important if the outsiders concerned have actually committed a deviant act – deviance is not about what you do, but about how others perceive and react to what they think you have done.

The deviant career

Becker sees the path a person follows in becoming a fully fledged socially defined deviant as a deviant career: a number of stages one has to pass through before the label has any lasting effect. He makes the point that those who ultimately end up as deviants in the eyes of society are not the only ones who think about committing a deviant action. Perhaps, he notes, we should ask why people conform, rather than why people deviate, since the impulse to deviate is seen to be within us all.

Deviance as a learnt experience

The concept of a deviant career allows Becker to discuss the idea that deviant behaviour may be so labelled, but it is also learned: deviance is a product of interaction with others, through which deviance becomes meaningful, and understood by those involved. One of the most valuable ideas to come from the interactionist perspective is this emphasis on the shape of interaction associated with each crime, and the emphasis given to the face-to-face and learnt nature of criminal activity.

External and internal control

Becker also raises the possibility that the initial labelling process which leads to a deviant career may come from *within* the individual so labelled, rather than from others. Since we are all socialized into the culture of our society, it is possible that we can police ourselves: we can act as our own public reaction, and know we are doing wrong even if the wider social reaction is absent:

... even though no one else discovers the nonconformity or enforces the rules against it, the individual who has committed the impropriety may himself act as enforcer. He may brand himself as deviant because of what he has done and punish himself in one way or another for his behaviour.

(Becker, 1973, p. 31)

The self-image

Central to this labelling theory, as to all symbolic interactionist sociology, is the concept of the self.

The self or self-image refers to that aspect of human consciousness through which we interact with others, define social situations and strive for meaning. Thinkers such as Charles Horton Cooley describe the self as a *looking-glass* – it is the product of others' reactions to us, created through interaction. As social actors, therefore, we reflect back to others their thoughts about us.

If an individual is defined as a deviant by social reactions, he or she may well begin to act out this career and learn how to become a better deviant to find such behaviour meaningful. This is known as a 'self-fulfilling prophecy' and is a key concept in the labelling theory's approach to crime. Perhaps some individuals who are relatively powerless in society are put on paths towards deviant careers as a result of increased social reactions, over a period of time, defining for them their understanding of their self.

Discussion point

To what extent are individuals controlled against their choice by labels?

C3.1a

Lemert: primary and secondary deviance

For Lemert (1989a,b), another leading interactionist figure writing originally in the 1950s, an essential distinction can be drawn between two types of deviance:

- *primary deviance* refers to an initial action committed by an individual
- *secondary deviance* refers to the social reaction to the initial action.

Secondary deviance is the true reality of deviance for the labelling theorists. *Deviance is not the act, but the reaction.* Owing to social reaction, the individual accepts the label and starts the deviant career. Lemert suggests that there are a number of stages or processes which lead from primary deviance to secondary deviance and the acceptance of the social judgement:

1 primary deviance

2 social penalties

3 further primary deviance

4 stronger penalties and rejections

5 further deviation, perhaps illustrating resentment against those doing the labelling

6 crisis reached by those doing the labelling – formal action taken by the community

7 strengthening of the deviant actions as the label is applied

8 finally, the ultimate acceptance by both the individual and the wider community of the deviant's status.

Lemert appears to suggest, then, that primary deviant acts are not necessarily defined as deviance by those who commit them. Equally, primary deviance can be committed, but if no social reaction follows then the individual involved will not pass on to the second deviance stage – will not accept the label.

Lemert further suggests that the definition of oneself as a deviant, once the label has been applied by a wider social source, is often a sudden and dramatic change in the self-image:

Self-definitions or self-realizations are likely to be the result of sudden perceptions and they are especially significant when they are followed immediately by overt demonstrations of the new role they symbolize.

(Lemert, 1989a, p. 196; orig. pub. 1951)

Criticisms of Lemert

Many have been highly critical of what could be seen as the determinism in this labelling approach. We can contend that the labelling process or the deviant career must not be seen as fixed or inevitable. It is possible that social actors are able to resist labels, and to fight back against them. (See also Section 8.7.)

Activity

Using all the ideas and key concepts of labelling theory, as presented in this section, write a short piece explaining how they could usefully describe anti-school behaviour in the classroom.

C3.2, C3.3

Case Study – Deviance amplification

In his classic essay, 'The role of the police as amplifiers of deviancy, negotiators of reality and translators of fantasy', Jock Young (1977) provides an excellent example of the processes known as 'deviance amplification'.

Police stereotypes of criminality

Young was interested in explaining the ways in which the police influence labels of criminality.

Taking a group of marijuana smokers in Notting Hill, London, between 1967 and 1969, he conducted an observational study (see Section 9.5). Young suggested that, owing to increasing segregation between members of the police force and members of the public, the police had come to rely much more on stereotypes of criminals and criminality as produced through the police force's cultural values. These stereotypes guided police actions on a day-to-day basis and informed the definitions of criminal situations within which the police operated.

Stages of deviant amplification

Young suggested a three-stage process through which deviant stereotypes were created within the police cultural world view, and the labelling effects these could have for those who came under the police's professional gaze.

1 *Translation of fantasy*

First, he said, police officers *translate the fantasy* (exaggerated stories) of the media:

... the policeman [sic], because of his isolated position in the community, is peculiarly susceptible to the stereotypes, the fantasy notions that the mass media carry about the drug-taker.

(Young, 1977, p. 27)

2 *Negotiation of reality*

Next, police officers *negotiate the reality* of what they see in everyday situations according to the stereotypes they have accepted from the media:

... in the process of police action particularly in the arrest situation, but continuing in the courts, the policeman because of his position of power inevitably finds himself negotiating the evidence, the reality of drug-taking, to fit these preconceived stereotypes.

(Young, 1977, p. 27)

3 *Amplification*

Finally, through the process of arrest and conviction, drug-takers become labelled and their self-image comes to accept this label, leading possibly to more deviance. Thus the police play the role of *amplifying* deviance:

... in the process of police action against the drug-taker changes occur within drug-taking groups involving an intensification of their deviance and in certain important aspects a self-fulfilment of these stereotypes. That is, there will be an amplification of

deviance, and a translation of stereotypes into actuality, of fantasy into reality.

(Young, 1977, pp. 27–8)

Amplification and moral panics

At times of media moral panics (see Section 6.2) an amplification of original deviance can occur if deviant labels are accepted into the self-images of those so labelled. Young, in adopting a symbolic interactionist stance, identifies the police as a key agent in this labelling process.

In terms of the behaviour of the middle-class, so-called hippy drug-takers of Notting Hill who formed Young's sample, their deviant actions intensified once the police action against them also intensified. As Young notes at the beginning of his essay:

The starting point of this article is W. I. Thomas' famous statement that a situation defined as real in a society will be real in its consequences. In terms, then, of those individuals whom society defines as deviants, one would expect that the stereotypes that society holds of them would have very real consequences on both their future behaviour and the way they perceive themselves.

(Young, 1977, p. 27)

10.3 Measuring crime and the fear of crime

Of great concern in the literature associated with the sociology of crime and deviance is the validity of criminal statistics. Whereas some, especially those involved in aspects of social policy creation, view criminal statistics as a good indication of the nature of crime and criminal behaviour in society, others are more critical. Most sociologists, however, believe criminal statistics to be of value, but for some, the value of statistics lies in the opportunity it presents to demonstrate how unrealistic and fabricated such statistics actually are. The issue of the usefulness of official statistics more generally is discussed in Section 9.6.

The contemporary pattern of crime

According to Reiner (1996), a brief survey of current crime figures then pointed to a number of clearly identifiable patterns:

- Between the two world wars the level of crime, according to the statistics, remained relatively constant.

- *Recorded* crime has increased sharply since then. In 1950, for example, 500 000 crimes were recorded, a figure that rose to 5.7 million in 1993.

Reiner asserts:

In the last 40 years, we have got used to thinking of crime, like the weather and pop music, as something that is always getting worse.

(Reiner, 1996, p. 3)

The commonsense and media-hyped picture of criminal statistics is often found unsatisfactory by sociologists. The key to the sociological criticism of official crime statistics is based on the inadequacies of a measurement of crime based on *recorded* levels. Clearly not all crime is discovered, and not all crime is recorded. This is a key point we will return to later.

The historical dimension of social problems

Although some sections of the mass media, and some statistics on crime, would have us believe that today's society is characterized by rising and ever-more-violent crime, it must be remembered that deviance is a feature of every society and crimes of this nature have always existed.

Politicians, especially those of the Right who are traditionally strong on law-and-order policies, have with great relish debated the so-called 'rising crime' problem, trading media-friendly sound-bite politics. As Sir Keith Joseph warned in 1977:

For the first time in a century and a half, since the great Tory reformer Robert Peel set up the Metropolitan Police, areas of our cities are becoming unsafe for peaceful citizens by night, and some even by day.

(Quoted in Pearson, 1983, pp. 4–5)

In a similar vein, also in 1977, the Chief Constable of Merseyside proclaimed:

... the freedom and way of life we have been accustomed to enjoy for so long will vanish ... what we are experiencing is not a passing phenomenon but a continuing process of change in our way of life ... our customary ways of behaving and our traditional values are being radically modified.

(Quoted in Pearson, 1983, p. 5)

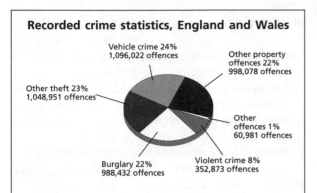

Recorded crime statistics, England and Wales

Vehicle crime 24%
1,096,022 offences

Other property offences 22%
998,078 offences

Other theft 23%
1,048,951 offences

Other offences 1%
60,981 offences

Burglary 22%
988,432 offences

Violent crime 8%
352,873 offences

- In the the twelve months to March 1998, 91 per cent of offences recorded by the police were against property; 8 per cent were violent crimes.
- Offences of violence against the person rose by 5 per cent, sexual offences rose by 6 per cent, but the number of robberies fell by 13 per cent.
- Vehicle crimes fell by 12 per cent, with falls in all but one police force area.
- Domestic burglary fell by 14 per cent, with non-domestic burglary falling by 11 per cent. The number of recorded burglaries fell in all but one police force area.

Figure 10.1 Notifiable offences recorded by the police, April 1997 to March 1998

Source: Home Office Statistical Bulletin, 13 October 1998, 22/98

Activity

From Figures 10.1 to 10.3 summarizing Home Office announcements on recorded crime, describe the trends they suggest in recorded crime in recent years.

C3.2, C3.3

Recent changes in the recording of crime statistics

According to an article in the *Guardian* towards the end of 1999, quoting the latest release of Home Office statistics, the figures for recorded crime for 12 months up to the end of March 1999 showed a fall (see Table 10.1).

Changes in the method of counting recorded crime statistics

The decline is all the more notable when bearing in mind that, during 1998–99, the method of counting crimes known to the police changed, the effect of the change being to add around 600 000 offences to the statistics and cause an increase in the headline figure of crime of 14 per cent.

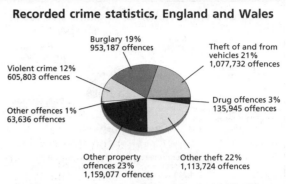

Recorded crime statistics, England and Wales

Burglary 19%
953,187 offences

Theft of and from vehicles 21%
1,077,732 offences

Violent crime 12%
605,803 offences

Drug offences 3%
135,945 offences

Other offences 1%
63,636 offences

Other property offences 23%
1,159,077 offences

Other theft 22%
1,113,724 offences

- In the the twelve months to March 1999, 84 per cent of offences recorded by the police were against property; 12 per cent were violent crimes.
- Offences of violence against the person showed a 10 per cent fall; however sexual offences rose by 2 per cent and robberies increased by 6 per cent.
- Both theft of vehicles and theft from vehicles fell by 2 per cent.
- Domestic burglary fell by 6 per cent, with non-domestic burglary falling by 2 per cent.
- 29 per cent of all crimes, including two thirds of violent crimes, were cleared up during 1998/99.
- Half of all detected crimes were cleared up using a charge or summons, whilst less than one in twelve were cleared up by interviewing a convicted prisoner.

Figure 10.2 Notifiable offences recorded by the police, April 1998 to March 1999

Source: Home Office Statistical Bulletin, 12 October 1999, 18/99

The details of the changes are as follows:

1   The idea is to try to reflect more accurately the number of *victims* of crime and therefore in some way bring it into alignment more with the British Crime Surveys (see below). This has meant that recorded crime figures now involve counting the number of victims involved, rather than the number of offences. One example given is that if a thief breaks into six cars in a car park this will now be recorded as six crimes rather than one.

2   Some offences are included in the crime figures for the first time. The statistics now include all crimes that can be tried in a crown court. Specifically this adds for the first time: possession of drugs (112 000), common assault (151 000), assault on a police officer (21 510), cruelty to children (2300), vehicle interference (48 000) and dangerous driving (4500).

Recorded crime statistics, England and Wales

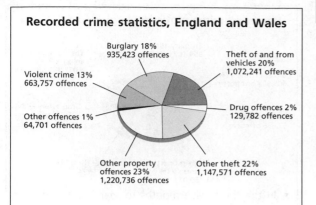

- Burglary 18%
  935,423 offences
- Theft of and from vehicles 20%
  1,072,241 offences
- Violent crime 13%
  663,757 offences
- Other offences 1%
  64,701 offences
- Drug offences 2%
  129,782 offences
- Other property offences 23%
  1,220,736 offences
- Other theft 22%
  1,147,571 offences

- In the the twelve months to September 1999, 84 per cent of offences recorded by the police were against property; 13 per cent were violent crimes.
- Domestic burglary fell by 5 per cent, with non-domestic burglary falling by 3 per cent.
- Offences of violence against the person showed a 5 per cent rise, sexual offences rose by 2 per cent and robberies increased by 19 per cent.
- Theft of motor vehicles fell by 2 per cent and theft from vehicles fell by 1 per cent.

Figure 10.3 Notifiable offences recorded by the police, October 1998 to September 1999

Source: Home Office Statistical Bulletin, 18 January 2000, 1/00

Despite this move to a more 'victim-centred' count, the total figure for recorded crime of 5.1 million for 12 months up to the end of March 1999 is dwarfed by the 20 million shown in the British Crime Surveys.

Discussion point

a This change in the method of recording crime will lead to an increase in the 'headline' figure for crime. How do you think politicians and the media will react to this?

b Do you agree that someone breaking into six cars should be classified as six crimes rather than one?

Recorded and unrecorded crime

Many commentators claim that the reason why official crime statistics are potentially so invalid is due to the problems of recording crime. Official governmental and police records recorded by and for the Home Office represent only those crimes *known to the police*. It is, however, ridiculous to claim that all crimes committed in society are known to the police. It is worth noting that the police have access to only three, interrelated sets of figures:

- crimes detected
- crimes reported
- criminals apprehended (crimes 'solved').

Box (1995, 1981) from a Marxist perspective, and Heidensohn (1989) from a feminist perspective, amongst others, have commented on the reasons why many crimes go unreported. To summarize:

- The public may fear the consequences from the criminals themselves if they turn to the police for help.
- The public may fear the police themselves, or may not believe that the crime will be solved: 'there's nothing the police can do' might be the stance taken by members of working-class communities.
- In cases such as rape, sexual assault or domestic violence the victim may feel embarrassed, or fear that the police will lack sensitivity.
- In some close-knit communities, there is a tendency to deal with criminality 'within the community, by the community' and not to involve the police.
- Some crimes may be seen as too trivial to report.
- Some victims may not even be aware they are a victim. This is especially true in the case of fraud.

Table 10.1 Home Office crime statistics

	To end March 1999	Change since March 1998	Percentage change
Total violent crime	331 843	−21 030	−6.0
Total property crime	4 086 694	−44 789	−1.1
Total all offences	4 481 817	−63 520	−1.4

Source: Quoted in the *Guardian*, 13 October 1999

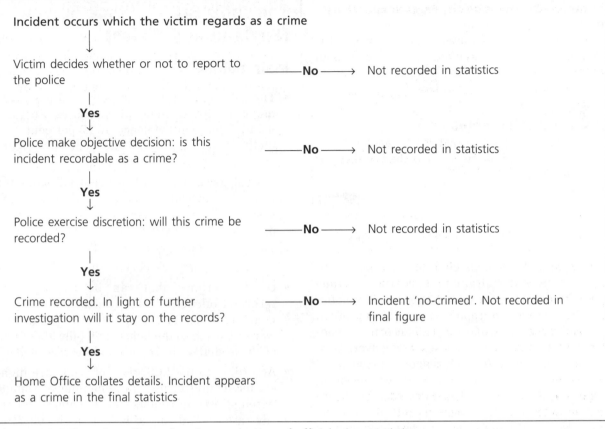

Incident occurs which the victim regards as a crime
↓
Victim decides whether or not to report to the police ———**No**———→ Not recorded in statistics
|
Yes
↓
Police make objective decision: is this incident recordable as a crime? ———**No**———→ Not recorded in statistics
|
Yes
↓
Police exercise discretion: will this crime be recorded? ———**No**———→ Not recorded in statistics
|
Yes
↓
Crime recorded. In light of further investigation will it stay on the records? ———**No**———→ Incident 'no-crimed'. Not recorded in final figure
|
Yes
↓
Home Office collates details. Incident appears as a crime in the final statistics

Figure 10.4 Flow chart illustrating the production of official crime statistics
Source: Sanderson (1994)

Activity

Using the flow chart in Figure 10.4, write a description of the process through which official crime statistics are created. Then address the following question: How can the construction of official crime statistics be open to the interpretation of various different groups?

C3.2, C3.3

The 'hidden figure' of crime

The recorded figure of crime does not by any means cover all crimes committed. This has massive implications for the usefulness of official criminal statistics: if they do not give a valid picture, then what use are they? Many would claim that they tell us more about the construction of crime statistics than about the rate of crimes.

We can best understand the problems and limitations of official crime figures with reference to Figure 10.5, which is based on an estimate from the British Crime Surveys that some 70 per cent of all criminal activity goes unrecorded. The

30 per cent of crime recorded is just the tip of the iceberg: it is visible, but more important is the undisclosed or hidden figure. This can have profound implications for the crime rates for any particular year, because an increase in recorded crime may not represent a real increase in the rate or total of all crime – it may well be that people are reporting more. Equally, a decline in the crime rate may not indicate that less crime is occurring, but that instead much less crime is reported and recorded.

Official crime statistics are further made problematic by the fact that crime, by its very

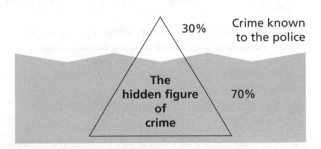

30%   Crime known to the police

The hidden figure of crime   70%

Figure 10.5 The 'hidden figure' of crime

nature, is often secretive. Thus, although offences are recorded, not all offences are solved: without knowing who committed a particular crime, it is very difficult to begin to make assumptions about types of criminals and the crimes they may or may not commit.

Discussion point

Are official statistics as valid as they are pre-sented? How can sociologists use them, if they do not show the whole picture?

C3.1a

Moral panics and official statistics

Moral panics (see also Section 6.2) and police ini-tiatives can have a dramatic effect on the crime rate. If a particular issue is exaggerated, the pub-lic may be led to report it more, out of an increased but artificial or unrealistic sense of con-cern. Thus, the rate increases and government and the police may well respond to such an increase in order to be seen to tackle the prob-lem in the eyes of the public. Further police atten-tion may lead to more arrests and, once more, the crime rate rises! This process is known as 'deviance amplification'.

The British Crime Surveys (BCS)

The British Crime Surveys (BCS) are a response by the Home Office to the problems of recorded and unrecorded crime which influence and to some extent raise problems with the 'Notifiable Offences' crime statistics.

1 The BCS are large-scale face-to-face surveys of adults living in England and Wales.

2 The 1998 BCS was based on a sample of 14 847 people from the age of 16 upwards.

3 The face-to-face interviews for the BCS take place in the household of the individuals in the sample.

4 The response rate for the 1996 survey was 83 per cent and for 1998 it was 79 per cent.

5 The sample is based upon the postcodes of the households.

(*Source*: Mirrlees-Black and Allen, 1998)

The BCS ask respondents about crimes they have experienced and their fears of crime. The 1998 findings are summarised below.

The 1998 British Crime Survey (England and Wales)

Main points

- The BCS shows a fall between 1995 and 1997 in nearly all the offences it measures. Burglary fell by 7 per cent; violence by 17 per cent; and thefts of vehicles by 25 per cent (see Figure 10.6 on page 327).

- Overall there was a 14 per cent fall since the last BCS, covering crime in 1995. This is the first time the survey has recorded a fall. It con-firms the downward trend in recorded crime.

- There were four times as many crimes against private property, as violent ones.

- Of BCS crimes that can be compared to recorded offences, just a quarter ended up in police records. This is because less than half were reported to the police, and only about half of those that were reported were recorded.

- According to the BCS, risks of crime are high-est for: young people; the unemployed; single parents; private renters; those living in inner-city areas and in areas of high physical disorder.

Findings from the 1998 British Crime Survey

Key points

- People tend to over-estimate the crime prob-lem:
  - although crime fell between 1995 and 1997 according to both police recorded crime and the BCS, only 9 per cent of people are aware of this
  - the BCS shows that about a fifth of crime is violent but 58 per cent of respondents believe that violent crime accounts for half or more of the total.

- However, there are signs that people are less concerned about crime than in 1996. There has been a fall in the proportion of people who:
  - think crime is going up
  - believe they are likely to be a victim of bur-glary or mugging in the next year
  - are worried about being the victim of bur-glary or car crime.

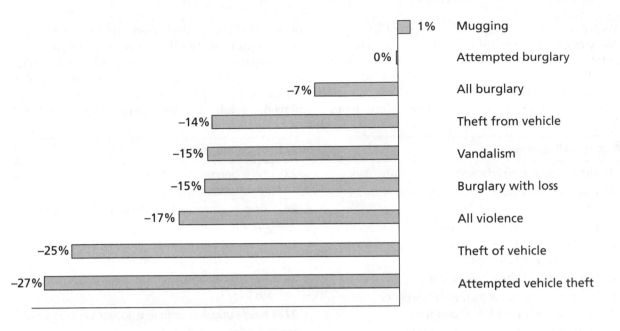

% change 1995 to 1997

Figure 10.6 Percentage change in BCS crime between 1995 and 1997

Source: Home Office Statistical Bulletin 21/98, 1998

- Women worry more about all crimes, except vehicle crime, and they are particularly worried about violent crime. 31 per cent were very worried about the possibility of being raped.

- There is little difference in worry about burglary and mugging according to age, though the young worry more about vehicle crime and violence. It is only in relation to safety after dark that the elderly register noticeably high concern. For instance, 31 per cent of women aged 60 or over say they feel very unsafe out alone after dark.

- Concern about crime is linked to people's beliefs about their chances of becoming a victim, and how vulnerable they feel. People who live in the higher risk inner cities, and those who have been victims, tend to express most most concern.

- 8 per cent indicated that the fear of crime had a substantial effect on the quality of their lives. Half said it had no or little effect.

Source: Home Office Research, Research Findings No. 83, 1999

Victimization studies

The British Crime Surveys are based on a research strategy known as the 'victimization survey'. Rather than focus on crimes known to the police, instead the emphasis is given to crimes known to the victim. Members of the public are asked to discuss crimes they have been the victim of in a given time period. This technique is particularly effective in getting at the hidden figure since it does not rely on the public to report specific instances of criminal behaviour, nor does it accept official measurements uncritically.

Problems with victimization studies and the BCS

The major drawback of victimization studies is that they miss recording those crimes regarded as 'victimless crimes' by respondents. Crimes such as drug selling/taking and vandalism against unowned/public property are known as victimless. Who, for example, is the victim, and in some cases is it possible to separate the victim from the criminal? Are not the drugs pusher and taker both criminals, and equally as unlikely to report the crime to either the police or a researcher?

Activity

Draw up a list of other examples of victimless crime.

 C3.2, C3.3

A second problem concerns the extent to which the victimization studies do in fact manage to obtain a nationally representative sample. Elliott and Ellingworth (1997) considered the issue of the representativeness of the sampling of the 1992 BCS. They found that there were types of social factors that were under- and over-represented in the BCS sample. Those over-represented included two-pensioner households, owner-occupier households and 16–24 year olds. Those under-represented included male unemployed, adult females and single-pensioner

Acts of delinquency

1 I have ridden a bicycle without lights after dark.
2 I have driven a car or motor bike/scooter under 16.
3 I have been with a group who go round together making a row and sometimes getting into fights and causing disturbance.
4 I have played truant from school.
5 I have travelled on a train or bus without a ticket or deliberately paid the wrong fare.
6 I have let off fireworks in the street.
7 I have taken money from home without returning it.
8 I have taken someone else's car or motor bike for a joy ride then taken it back afterwards.
9 I have broken or smashed things in public places like on the streets, cinemas, dance halls, trains or buses.
10 I have insulted people on the street or got them angry and fought with them.
11 I have broken into a big store or garage or warehouse.
12 I have broken into a little shop even though I may not have taken anything.
13 I have taken something out of a car.
14 I have taken a weapon (like a knife) out with me in case I needed it in a fight.
15 I have fought with someone in a public place like in the street or a dance.
16 I have broken the window of an empty house.
17 I have used a weapon in a fight, like a knife or a razor or a broken bottle.
18 I have drunk alcoholic drinks in a pub under 18.
19 I have been in a pub when I was under 16.
20 I have taken things from big stores or supermarkets when the shop was open.
21 I have taken things from little shops when the shop was open.
22 I have dropped things in the street like litter or broken bottles.

Acts of delinquency

23 I have bought something cheap or accepted as a present something I knew was stolen.
24 I have planned well in advance to get into a house to take things.
25 I have got into a house and taken things even thought I didn't plan it in advance.
26 I have taken a bicycle belonging to someone else and kept it.
27 I have struggled or fought to get away from a policeman.
28 I have struggled or fought with a policeman who was trying to arrest someone.
29 I have stolen school property worth more than about 5p.
30 I have stolen goods from someone I worked for worth more than about 5p.
31 I have had sex with a boy when I was under 16.
32 I have trespassed somewhere I was not supposed to go, like empty houses, railway lines or private gardens.
33 I have been to an '18' film under age.
34 I have spent money on gambling under 16.
35 I have smoked cigarettes under 15.
36 I have had sex with someone for money.
37 I have taken money from slot machines or telephones.
38 I have taken money from someone's clothes hanging up somewhere.
39 I have got money from someone by pretending to be someone else or lying about why I needed it.
40 I have taken someone's clothes hanging up somewhere.
41 I have smoked dope or taken pills (LSD, mandies, sleepers).
42 I have got money/drink/cigarettes by saying I would have sex with someone even though I didn't.
43 I have run away from home.

Figure 10.7 Example of a self-report study
Source: Campbell, 1981

households. Although the owner-occupiers were the most inaccurately sampled – and so we cannot simply say that relatively deprived groups tend to be the most inaccurately sampled – they do tend to be under-sampled.

Elliott and Ellingworth go on to argue that the response rate diminishes as crime rates rise, meaning that in high-crime areas the surveys get a low response. They suggest that living in a high-crime area is a key causal factor leading to low response.

This suggests that the BCS itself, in under-sampling from high-crime areas, might be under-stating the amount of crime. This would if anything lead to a widening of the gap between BCS figures and recorded crime figures.

💬 Discussion point

Why does it matter if the BCS sample is not representative? What does this suggest about the figure for 'true' crime?

C3.1a

Self-report studies

Another technique open to sociologists keen to uncover the hidden amount of crime is self-report studies (see the example in Figure 10.7). These work in much the same way as victimization studies but ask the respondents to admit, quite literally, to crimes they have committed within a given time period. Such studies tend to be slightly invalid: working-class youths, for example, may exaggerate in order to gain prestige within their peer group, whereas others may not trust the researcher and so lie.

✏️ Activity

a Consider applying to yourself the survey in Figure 10.7. What are the problems of some of the questions asked? How might these problems be overcome?

b Originally this questionnaire was applied to girls, so what changes might have to be made for it to be suitable for boys?

C3.2, C3.3

The political nature of the crime debate

Law and order has always been a traditional vote-winner in British politics. Every year, and in particular at every election campaign, we hear from politicians that they wish to be 'tough on law and order', or that they will 'win the fight for law and order'. However, many different politicans make the same figures on crime mean different things at different times.

The 1995 figures (Travis, 1996a) showed a 10 per cent fall in recorded crime since the 1993 measurement. The Home Office responded with the claim that the government was 'turning the tide in the fight against crime' – a claim difficult to disprove, but equally difficult to substantiate given the fundamental problems with the official figures as outlined above. It is interesting to note that whereas the Conservative government hailed a success in the falling rate of crime, the Labour party pointed out that, within the overall decline in reported and recorded crime, street robberies had apparently *risen* by 14 per cent and violent crime by 2 per cent since the previous year.

The inadequaces of crime statistics

It has become increasingly difficult to attempt to analyse in any meaningful way what the official statistics show. It has been suggested by some commentators that official statistics are interesting from a sociological point of view, but only for providing us with an understanding of the social and political processes involed in their construction, not as an absolute or real measurement.

✏️ Activity

a Write about 500 words to explain how interactionists (see Section 10.5) would view the nature and usefulness of official crime statistics.

b What criticisms might be made of the interactionist view?

C3.2, C3.3

10.4 Patterns of crime and victimization by social profile

Crimes of the rich and powerful

Criminal activities that are conducted by the powerful in society are often missed by official and many sociological measurements of crime (Pearce, 1976). A distinction can be drawn between:

- *crimes of the powerful* – largely those committed by ruling groups, élites and governments
- *white-collar crime* – crimes committed by professional people, such as tax evasion, business fraud, industrial espionage, insider-trading
- *corporate crime* – crimes committed not so much by individuals but rather by boards, chairpersons, etc., including the breaking of the Health and Safety at Work Act.

Steven Box, writing from a Marxist perspective, comments:

… it might be prudent to compare persons who commit other serious but under-emphasized crimes and victimizing behaviour with those who are officially portrayed as our criminal enemies. For if the former, compared to the latter, are indeed quite different types of people, then maybe we should stop looking to our political authorities and criminal justice system for protection from those beneath us in impoverished urban neighbourhoods. Instead maybe we should look up accusingly at our political and judicial superiors for being or for protecting the real culprits.

(Box, 1995, p. 3)

This view by Box (and shared by Pearce) – that the real criminals are those who make and even enforce the rules – is a good example of a Marxist critique of official definitions and measurements of crime. Whereas, under capitalism, working-class criminality is emphasized and working-class activities and localities policed on a regular basis, others are ignored and allowed therefore to continue in their criminal ways. For Marxism, the real issue is not whether the crime rate is high or low, real or unreal, but why some actions and groups are over-represented by official measurements.

Looking at 'police crime'

Box adds a fourth category to the crimes of the powerful, that of police crime. He suggests that beating-up suspects, arresting the innocent, intimidation, blackmail, bribery, fabricating and ignoring evidence are all routine in the dirty business that is the reality of law enforcement. It is, however, difficult to substantiate this claim. As Box recognizes, although it is common sense that all these activities exist in higher numbers than the odd bad apple exposed by the media on an infrequent basis, proving this through evidence is a different matter.

Case studies of the powerful in society and the criminal world

Politicians and the mafia

In 1994, Italian society was shaken by revelations of links between top political leaders and the mafia. Stille's (1997) book on the subject reveals the intricacies of the links between Salvatore Riina, a top mafia boss, and Salvatore Lima, a former mayor of the city and a finance minister in Prime Minister Andreotti's government despite numerous mentions in an anti-mafia commission. In 1999 an Italian court found Andreotti innocent of personal involvement in mafia affairs. However, it is clear that some of those around him had at least some links to known mafia figures.

In what appeared to be a warning to top political contacts to respect the mafia's code of 'omerta' or silence, Lima was murdered in March 1992. It is also suggested that certain journalists critical of the Christian Democrats were removed from the scene. In return, it is alleged, the mafia benefited from numerous government contracts through front companies. Stille points to £50 billion in extraordinary aid between 1986 and 1990 which seemingly disappeared into projects without any apparent benefit to the local population.

Police accused of dirty tricks war on BA passenger

In 1994, various newspapers carried articles recounting the bizarre events surrounding accusations of police dirty tricks. The article opposite from the *Daily Telegraph* is an example.

Activity

Suggest into which of the categories devised by Pearce and by Box the two case study examples above relating to allegations about criminal behaviour might fit.

C3.2, C3.3

Studying gender and crime

Has there been a surge in female crime?

Box (1995) suggests that any fear of a surge in female crime is largely a media moral panic (see

Tricks of the trade

MICHAEL SMITH

A file on allegations that Metropolitan Police officers at Heathrow took part in a sustained 'dirty tricks' campaign against a British Airways shareholder who made a complaint against the company is to be sent to the Crown Prosecution Service.

Scotland Yard said results of the police complaints unit investigation were being sent to the CPS and the Police Complaints Authority. BA also confirmed that it had handed Scotland Yard its internal files on allegations by John Gorman, 37, a former police officer, that he was the victim of a sustained campaign of dirty tricks following his complaint. Mr Gorman told BBC's *Newsnight* programme that on a BA flight from London to New York in January last year he swallowed broken glass in an in-flight drink.

Staff on the aircraft apologized, but when, after having expensive medical treatment for the injuries caused by the glass, he sought compensation, BA accused him of being a Virgin stooge. Mr Gorman took this to be a reference to the airline's battle with Richard Branson's Virgin Airlines over alleged dirty tricks, but he says he has never had any involvement with Virgin.

Three months after Mr Gorman lodged his claim, seven officers from Heathrow police station, accompanied by a senior BA investigator, raided his home and arrested him for conspiracy to defraud British Airways.

Mr Gorman alleges that he was subsequently subjected to a vicious campaign of dirty tricks involving hate mail, telephone threats and an attack by two men who burst into his home. They sprayed him with gas, banged his head against the wall and said: 'This is what you get when you mess with British Airways.' They also took documents referring to the compensation claim, which were subsequently returned to Mr Gorman by a BA lawyer who said he was unaware they were stolen. Some of the telephone threats, including one in which the caller said: 'We'll get you next time', were allegedly traced by BT to British Airways' Heathrow offices. Another, in which Mr Gorman was told: 'Any morning now, nice and early, we are going to arrest you' was allegedly traced to Heathrow police station.

Mr Gorman, a former member of the Metropolitan Police anti-terrorist branch, was forced to retire after the Brighton bombing because of the effects of asbestos he inhaled while digging victims out of the rubble. He now lives on his police pension and disability allowance.

A statement from British Airways said: 'The John Gorman matter is in the hands of the police with whom British Airways has co-operated fully from the beginning. Neither the police nor British Airways has been able to determine who may have been responsible for any of the acts about which Mr Gorman complained. Those matters are the subject of continuing police investigations. British Airways has made available to the police all the information it has regarding Mr Gorman's allegations. We take them very seriously.'

Source: Daily Telegraph, 31 August 1994

Section 6.2) designed to discredit feminist thinking. He does note that as groups become increasingly more economically marginalized in a society – through unemployment and inadequate welfare benefits (see Sections 7.4 and 8.6) – there is an increase by this group in property offences, although often minor. Therefore it may not be liberation which leads to an increase in female crime, but rather the opposite – an increased economic marginalization of women owing to economic policies based on the free market in both the UK and the USA. Even if this were not the case, and liberation did lead to an increase in minor property crime, as Box puts it, it would be 'well worth it in comparison with the price paid now by powerless women' (Box, 1995, p. 200).

Women as victims

We should not view women exclusively in terms of being victims who are helpless against the stronger male. To do so would be to reinforce much malestream sociological analysis of the past, when women were discussed only in the crime chapter of textbooks in this context. However, crime against women in society is a legitimate area for investigation. Again we can quote Heidensohn:

One of the most important gender issues raised in recent years has concerned the sex of the victim and of the perpetrator of violent crime. By and large ... the feminist critics have not succeeded in directly putting gender into the main currents of criminological thought. But if the academy has been slow to respond, the polity and public opinion have reacted more rapidly and considerably. Campaigns to promote awareness of and to seek help for battered wives and rape victims, and more recently the victims of sexual abuse in the family and of sexual harassment at work, have all met with some degree of public response and even policy changes.

(Heidensohn, 1989, p. 98)

Making gendered crime visible

A large part of feminist sociology is to make visible otherwise invisible gendered crime. Heidensohn uses the concept 'gendered crime' to refer to that in which women are victims of men – such as domestic violence, rape and harassment. Such crimes are frequently invisible in the official crime statistics because they are characterized by a reluctance or fear to report. Many of these crimes are hidden away not just from the records, but from public attention, being located within the family or home.

Crime: the 'dark side' of social life

The increasing attention of feminist analysis paid to these areas has massive implications for other sociological topic areas, and not just crime and deviance. For example, research into abuse and rape within the home has highlighted a dark side which makes traditional images of the caring–sharing or symmetrical family problematic. (This issue is also discussed in Section 5.9.)

The starting point for a feminist analysis of crimes against women is to assert that violence against women, particularly of a sexual nature, cannot necessarily be understood through reference to sexuality alone. Traditional accounts of rape, for example, locate the act within a faulty sexuality or a damaged masculinity. Heidensohn suggests, however, that these are not expressions of sexuality – faulty or otherwise – but of *power*. These acts can be seen to represent on a small scale the exercise of male power over women in society in general. As Wilson comments:

Rape is an act of violence against women. It is a hostile and sadistic act. It is a violation of a woman's autonomy and a negation of her independence.

(Wilson; quoted in Heidensohn, 1989, p. 106)

Or, from a radical feminist perspective, Brownmiller suggests that:

... rape and fear of rape are used as a weapon of control by men over women as a conscious process of intimidation by which all men keep all women in a state of fear.

(Brownmiller; quoted in Heidensohn, 1989, p. 108)

Studying 'race', ethnicity and crime

The relationship, if any, that exists between ethnicity and crime is another popular topic for study by sociologists, especially since the so-called inner-city riots of the 1980s when issues of marginality, deprivation and criminality came to the attention not just of academics, but also of the general public via the media (see also Section 6.3). This section will identify three basic positions on the relationship between ethnicity and crime.

Gilroy and Hall

The first position is associated especially with Gilroy (1982a,b) and Hall *et al.* (1978), writing at the neo-Marxist Centre for Contemporary Cultural Studies (CCCS) based at Birmingham University. They suggest that higher levels of criminality amongst the British black population are mythical, the illusion being largely the result of distorted media attention and inadequate official statistics.

Paul Gilroy

The second position, also connected with Gilroy, goes further to suggest that crime by blacks, especially antagonism to police authority, is a legacy of colonial struggle, the origins of which are located in West Indian history and associated with the Rastafarian movement. (Rastafarianism is discussed in more detail in Section 7.6) From this perspective, although blacks do not commit more crime, they do commit crime of a revolutionary and political nature. Gilroy also suggests that the over-representation of ethnic groups in the official figures is a result of selective police practices arising from police racism.

Lea and Young

The third position, from a New Left realist perspective, is adopted by Lea and Young (1993). They suggest that, although anti-colonial political struggle, media exaggeration and police racism may all exist, this does not adequately explain the over-representation of some ethnic groups in the official figures – especially young, working-class African–Caribbean males. Instead, the increased levels of social deprivation and marginalization experienced by this group explain their use of crime as a response to their situation.

Hall *et al.*: mugging, hegemony and ideology

Hall and his colleagues, in their book *Policing the Crisis: Mugging, the State, and Law and Order* (1978), criticize what they see as the exaggerated and at times racist reporting of black criminality in the British popular press. In taking the example of an apparent dramatic increase in mugging in the 1970s, Hall *et al.* suggest that official crime figures can be used as political weapons at times of economic crisis to justify a failing capitalist economy. In this way, a myth or illusion of black street crime has been created to act as a scapegoat, to draw the public's attention away from the real social problems of the time – unemployment, inflation, etc.

The mugging moral panic

We are concerned with mugging – but as a social phenomenon, rather than as a particular form of street crime. We want to know what the social causes of mugging are. But we argue that this is only half – less than half – of the mugging story. More important is why British society reacts to mugging, in the extreme way it does, at that precise historical conjuncture – the early 1970s. If it is true that muggers suddenly appear on British streets – a fact which, in that stark simplicity, we contest – it is also true that the society enters a moral panic about mugging. And this relates to the larger panic about the steadily rising rate of violent crime which has been growing through the 1960s. And both these panics are about other things than crime, per se. The society comes to perceive crime in general, and mugging in particular, as an index of the disintegration of the social order, as a sign that the British way of life is coming apart at the seams.

(Hall *et al.*, 1978, pp. vii–viii)

As this extract illustrates, a moral panic (see Section 6.2) developed in the UK in the 1970s, sponsored or created by the media, government and police, regarding a new form of crime from America, previously unheard of in Britain – mugging. This developed into a moral panic concerning the safety of our streets, which ultimately led to a widespread belief that a previously golden age of law and order had come to an end.

Hall and his co-writers suggest, however, that mugging is simply a new name for a very old crime, that of street robbery with violence. As Pearson's *Hooligan: A History of Respectable Fears* (1983) illustrates, violent crime has a long history in Britain, whatever its name might be. (See Sections 8.4 and 10.1.)

The crisis of capitalism

🗩 Discussion point

Why does capitalism lead to periods of crisis? How might capitalism deal with these periods of crisis?

C3.1a

What is particularly interesting, note Hall and colleagues, is the particular time when this moral panic occurred – it coincided with a period in the UK's economic history that they describe as a *crisis*. These two factors are seen to be linked: rising economic problems and rising so-called 'new' street crimes are, in the media, blamed on the black population – so avoiding a more serious crisis in confidence in capitalism amongst the white British population.

Crisis and hegemony

A hegemonic or legitimation crisis is thus avoided: the government's right to rule, and more significantly the ruling élite's capitalist economic policies, are preserved. Hall *et al.* do not suggest that this antagonism amongst the white working classes against the black working class is deliberately created. It does, however, serve well the purposes of the ruling economic élite at this crisis time.

These writers note that the moral panic has resulted in ever-increasing military models of policing where we see a shift from a community-based approach towards a reactionary police force, capable of responding with speed and force to violent situations, yet largely invisible to the general population and increasingly trusted less. This is a model of modern policing which has alienated both the white and black sections of the working classes.

As illustrated by the article 'London muggings rise despite £13m campaign', street crime is still equated largely with young black men.

Gilroy: the Empire strikes back

Another text from the CCCS, *The Empire Strikes Back: Race and Racism in 70s Britain* (1982), is devoted to a detailed study of the nature of this topic.

Amongst the contributors to that volume is Gilroy, who claims that black criminality is a political struggle against the racism and capitalist economics of British society. Gilroy's position has a point in common with that of Taylor *et al.* in *The New Criminology*. They too suggested, within a neo-Marxist framework, that working-class crime can often be seen as a response to poor social conditions and to political marginality – that some working-class crime is political in nature because it is a product of capitalist inequality, yet at the same time, it strikes out against capitalist society.

Gilroy contends that:

Police theorization of alien blackness as black criminality shows where the filaments of racist ideology disappear into the material institutions of the capitalist state.

(Gilroy, in CCCS, 1982, p. 145)

Gilroy suggests that police racism is to blame for the over-reporting of black criminality within the official figures. He goes on to claim that, in recognizing this as a day-to-day problem and a major feature of the black experience, especially for those living in the inner cities, we can begin to understand why some black crime is a political and revolutionary response to capitalism and racism.

Activity

Study the cartoon below from the May 1981 issue of the magazine *Police*. Describe what messages this sends out concerning the nature of potential police stereotypes of black criminality in the early 1980s.

C3.2, C3.3

London muggings rise despite £13m campaign

ALAN TRAVIS

SCOTLAND Yard's £13 million Operation Eagle Eye campaign against street robbers has had only a limited impact in its first year, according to the Metropolitan police annual report published yesterday.

The official London crime figures show there were 4,000 more street robberies, a rise of 14 per cent, in the year to the end of March 1996.

The campaign, launched in August last year, drew strong criticism because it appeared to be targeted mainly at young black men.

But the commissioner, Sir Paul Condon, yesterday defended it, saying it had capped the increase in snatch thefts and robberies of personal property which had been increasing by 20 to 30 per cent a year.

He cited figures showing street muggings had fallen between November 1995 and June 1996 by some 5 per cent. Detections also doubled, to 19 per cent of street robberies being cleared up.

"Not only have we capped street robbery, but we are bringing it down dramatically," he said. Police figures show that 69 per cent of those arrested for street robberies as a result of Operation Eagle Eye have been young black men. After the launch of the operation, Sir Paul said that in some parts of London most muggers were black.

Source: Guardian, 31 July 1996

'If I'd not been told this wasn't a race riot but only their way of getting rid of frustration, I would be really worried.'
Source: Police, May 1981

Victimization: age and region

The 1998 British Crime Survey (BCS) provides statistics on the relationship between age and the types of crime experiences as a victim, as the following table indicates:

Table 10.2 Proportion of households victims of burglary and vehicle-related theft, and proportion of adults victims of violence, by age of head of household

Age of head of household	Burglary	All vehicle thefts	All violence Age of victim	
			Male	Female
16–25	15.2	21.0	20.9	8.8
25–44	6.5	19.7	7.0	4.6
45–64	4.8	15.2	3.0	2.0
65–74	3.5	7.8	0.2	0.8
75+	4.1	5.5	1.0	0.2

Source: Home Office Statistical Bulletin 21/98, tables A5.2, A5.8, A5.12

Activity

What trends regarding the age of the victim do these figures indicate?

C3.2, C3.3

A key theme of the BCS is the idea of 'unequal risks' – in other words, figures that present victimization as a percentage likelihood of all crimes fail to take into consideration the fact that some people – according to, for example, age and sex – are more likely to be victims of some crimes than other people. Equally, the region and area where one lives will affect the likelihood of being a victim of crime – and of certain sorts of crimes rather than others.

That crime varies according to region and location can be seen in the official crime statistics from the Home – the police recorded crime figures – in Figure 10.8 and Table 10.3 below (from September 1999). It must be remembered, however, that the data in this diagram is based upon recorded crime and will therefore not necessarily show the whole picture.

The BCS also provides figures on victimization according to both region and by what they call 'area type' (see Table 10.4).

The BCS also breaks victimization down further and looks in a detailed fashion at the types of people who are victims of certain crimes – it looks into other characteristics such as household type – as illustrated in Table 10.5.

Activity

What trends and patterns in victimization are illustrated by Tables 10.4 and 10.5 on page 338?

C3.2, C3.3

Victimization and 'ACORN'

In order to analyse the patterns of victimization according to household types, the BCS have adopted a slightly modified version of what is known as the ACORN system of classification, which seeks to try to understand differences in 'locality' and 'neighbourhood' (ACORN stands for 'A Classification Of Residential Neighbourhoods'). The ACORN classification system was developed from the 1991 Census and contains 54 types of local social environment. The BCS has adapted these 54 types into a 17-fold scheme, as indicated in Table 10.6.

10.5 Theories and explanations of crime and deviance

Sociologists' concern with the study of deviance, like many other ideas, issues and concepts, can be traced back to the thinking of Durkheim. But perhaps now we should ask whether a functionalist analysis is still of value to sociologists. As Downes and Rock note:

At times, a package deal is presented in which functionalism, positivism, empiricism, evolutionalism, and determinism are collectively linked with a consensus approach to social problems and a conservative approach to their solution.

(Downes and Rock, 1995, p. 90)

In other words, much functionalist sociology has been found wanting in its explanations of society in recent years. It has become a *routine conceptual folly for students to demolish before moving on to more rewarding ground*, to use the words of Downes and Rock once more.

Yet despite this trend towards functionalist bashing, its role in the history of sociological thought is firmly secured. Equally, its linkage with modern liberal- and conservative-based approaches such as neo-functionalism and the New Right means that its history and heritage is still of relevance to the contemporary sociology syllabus.

Discussion point

How would sociology be worse off without functionalism?

C3.1a

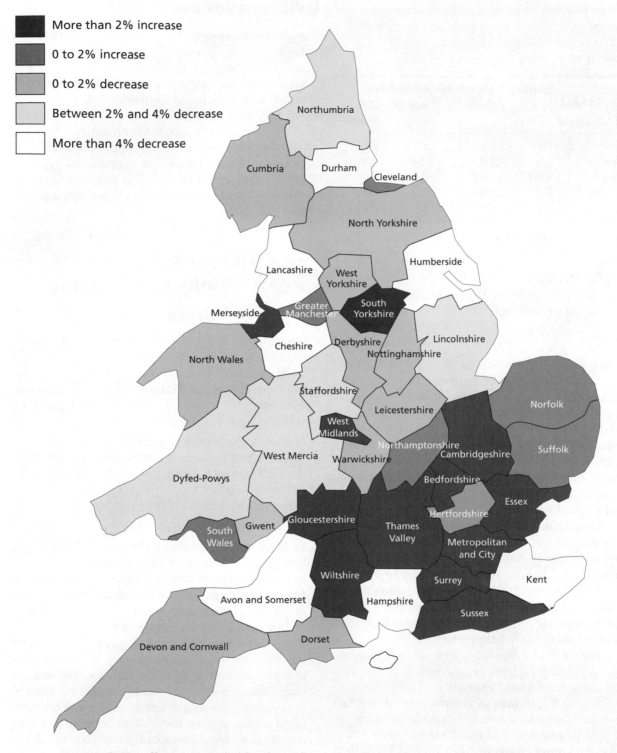

Figure 10.8 Notifiable offences recorded by the police
Source: Recorded Crime Statistics England and Wales, October 1998 to September 1999, HMSO

Table 10.3 Notifiable offences by police force and offence – 12 months ending September 1999

England and Wales

Police force area	Total	Violence against the person	Sexual offences	Robbery	Burglary	Theft and handling	Fraud and forgery	Criminal damage	Drug offences	Other offences	Vehicle crime[1]
Avon and Somerset	149,123	12,017	765	2,176	28,982	72,647	8,621	20,613	2,201	1,101	48,104
Bedfordshire	52,480	5,109	392	585	7,946	24,034	4,813	7,939	1,111	551	16,385
Cambridgeshire	68,872	5,678	460	528	12,712	32,391	2,676	12,267	1,174	895	20,143
Cheshire	62,852	6,229	499	429	12,287	26,407	2,008	11,476	2,187	1,330	16,738
Cleveland	66,462	3,016	372	836	16,476	30,668	2,606	10,956	1,083	449	18,524
Cumbria	39,775	5,644	221	95	5,653	15,825	1,425	8,612	1,735	565	10,194
Derbyshire	86,170	9,310	567	546	16,275	37,043	4,878	14,675	1,597	1,279	24,706
Devon and Cornwall	111,444	12,378	904	484	17,381	49,889	6,909	18,290	3,877	1,332	31,877
Dorset	51,781	3,071	316	212	8,869	23,578	5,884	8,122	1,238	491	15,308
Durham	49,180	5,402	253	187	9,623	19,754	1,309	10,540	1,329	783	14,217
Essex	99,815	9,098	970	571	15,292	45,470	4,753	19,746	2,455	1,460	30,120
Gloucestershire	50,666	3,876	348	282	10,409	23,649	3,104	7,105	1,295	598	11,000
Greater Manchester	365,972	38,512	2,301	8,116	76,000	144,781	17,038	69,855	5,080	4,289	116,017
Hampshire	127,306	13,988	1,031	658	18,648	55,724	5,002	25,871	4,344	2,040	34,986
Hertfordshire	50,130	3,361	368	324	8,244	22,727	2,687	10,636	1,249	524	18,411
Humberside	127,253	9,307	723	855	33,331	55,516	3,787	21,042	1,794	898	35,167
Kent	127,233	12,466	912	780	21,459	54,843	6,796	23,803	3,775	2,399	37,942
Lancashire	112,472	9,896	771	993	22,420	47,426	4,037	21,834	3,605	1,490	32,051
Leicestershire	93,795	10,892	804	987	16,260	37,416	8,480	15,313	1,438	2,205	24,879
Lincolnshire	46,708	4,037	357	157	10,508	19,354	2,442	8,190	1,089	574	10,896
London, City of	7,868	548	26	42	501	4,608	1,154	401	445	143	667
Merseyside	143,207	13,480	975	2,549	25,914	60,073	4,246	28,856	5,488	1,626	42,351
Metropolitan Police	1,000,380	148,814	8,942	30,670	125,907	406,318	94,203	145,870	28,408	11,248	242,260
Norfolk	56,603	6,165	456	267	10,149	25,686	3,063	10,640	1,567	610	14,837
Northamptonshire	64,702	5,017	291	461	11,982	28,347	4,415	12,121	1,275	793	20,896
Northumbria	145,735	12,793	910	1,353	28,626	59,821	5,051	30,847	4,309	2,025	42,566
North Yorkshire	55,187	5,069	295	182	11,290	24,795	2,579	8,633	1,641	703	13,934
Nottinghamshire	137,018	13,371	988	1,503	28,024	60,839	5,730	22,841	1,999	1,723	36,899
South Yorkshire	135,138	7,253	666	1,112	34,335	56,836	4,894	24,855	4,040	1,147	42,087
Staffordshire	92,379	11,015	621	603	18,962	38,149	4,054	15,950	1,905	1,120	25,884
Suffolk	40,696	4,356	369	197	5,980	17,322	1,951	8,325	1,522	674	9,953
Surrey	44,767	4,856	521	155	6,983	18,280	3,471	8,130	1,593	687	11,207
Sussex	134,894	16,199	960	911	20,535	59,165	8,504	24,970	2,232	1,418	38,555
Thames Valley	184,991	12,564	945	1,421	31,234	93,553	12,880	27,042	3,851	1,521	63,447
Warwickshire	36,079	2,095	172	202	8,108	17,857	2,518	7,061	691	375	12,928
West Mercia	82,900	7,844	571	356	14,445	36,124	3,976	16,330	2,170	1,084	23,178
West Midlands	353,035	40,033	2,404	8,810	71,255	136,717	23,706	57,959	6,685	5,466	101,978
West Yorkshire	268,767	16,941	1,834	3,139	65,832	113,744	11,621	46,961	6,046	2,649	83,490
Wiltshire	39,622	4,682	407	218	6,309	17,366	2,048	6,896	1,175	521	10,071
Dyfed-Powys	24,235	5,216	332	38	2,288	7,539	1,325	4,448	2,176	873	4,185
Gwent	60,731	12,396	430	201	8,474	20,846	2,506	12,583	2,191	1,104	15,671
North Wales	44,561	5,358	369	148	6,958	17,677	1,719	9,935	1,830	567	12,063
South Wales	136,318	12,070	674	504	22,557	59,018	7,191	30,046	2,8987	1,371	52,930
England and Wales	5,234,211	551,442	37,492	74,843	935,423	2,219,812	312,151	908,585	129,782	64,701	1,489,702

[1]Vehicle crime includes theft of a vehicle, theft from a vehicle, aggravated vehicle taking, vehicle interference and tampering and criminal damage to a vehicle.

Source: Recorded Crime Statistics England and Wales, October 1998 to September 1999, HMSO

Table 10.4 Proportion of adults who were victims of burglary, vehicle theft and violence, by region and area type (% of victims once or more times)

	Burglary	All vehicle thefts	All violence
Region			
North East	8.6	15.4	4.4
North West	6.8	18.9	6.4
Merseyside	6.7	17.2	4.3
Yorkshire/Humber	8.3	20.0	4.6
East Midlands	5.6	14.7	4.8
West Midlands	5.9	16.0	4.2
Eastern	3.1	15.2	3.9
London	5.7	15.6	5.6
South East	4.3	13.8	4.4
South West	4.4	13.5	4.4
Wales	4.8	14.2	4.2
Area type			
Inner city	8.5	23.7	6.8
Urban	5.9	16.2	4.9
Rural	3.4	12.0	3.3
Council estate area	8.1	18.7	5.9
Non-council estate area	5.1	15.2	4.5

Source: The 1998 British Crime Survey (England and Wales) *Home Office Statistical Bulletin 21/98*, tables A5.3, A5.4, A5.9, A5.10, A5.14, A5.15, HMSO

Table 10.5 Proportion of adults who were victims of violence, by household characteristics

	% victims once or more				
	All violence	Domestic	Acquaintance	Stranger	Mugging
Head of household under 60					
Single adult & child(ren)	11.9	6.9	3.0	1.4	0.9
Adults & child(ren)	5.6	1.0	2.4	1.5	1.0
No children	6.0	0.8	3.0	1.8	1.0
Head of household over 60	1.2	0.1	0.5	0.3	0.4
Household income					
<5k	6.6	1.9	2.5	1.4	1.5
5k<10k	2.9	0.9	1.1	0.6	0.6
10k<20k	4.1	0.9	2.0	1.0	0.6
20k<30k	4.7	0.4	1.9	1.9	0.9
30k +	5.1	0.6	2.6	1.3	0.8
Tenure					
Owner occupiers	3.2	0.4	1.4	1.0	0.5
Social renters	6.3	1.8	2.6	1.4	1.2
Private renters	9.4	2.1	4.2	2.5	1.4
Accommodation type					
Houses	4.5	0.9	2.0	1.3	0.6
Detached	3.1	0.5	1.4	0.7	0.8
Semi-detached	4.1	0.9	1.8	1.2	0.4
Mid terrace	5.9	1.1	2.7	1.8	0.7
End terrace	6.3	1.4	2.3	2.2	1.5
Flats/maisonettes	6.4	0.9	2.8	1.3	1.9
All adults	**4.7**	**0.9**	**2.1**	**1.3**	**0.8**

Source: The 1998 British Crime Survey (England and Wales) *Home Office Statistical Bulletin 21/98*, table A5.13, HMSO

Table 10.6 Proportion of households victims of burglary and vehicle-related theft, by ACORN, and proportion of adults victims of violence, by ACORN

ACORN	Burglary	All vehicle thefts	All violence
Thriving			
Wealthy achievers, suburban areas	3.7	14.6	3.7
Affluent greys, rural communities	3.3	11.9	3.0
Expanding			
Prosperous pensioners, retirement areas	4.3	13.8	2.4
Affluent executives, family areas	4.2	18.5	4.8
Well-off workers, family areas	3.8	17.7	4.3
Rising			
Affluent urbanites, town and city	9.9	20.2	8.4
Prosperous professionals, metropolitan areas	5.1	17.3	4.8
Better-off executives, inner city areas	8.7	20.1	6.4
Settling			
Comfortable middle agers, mature home owning areas	4.8	14.0	4.3
Skilled workers, home owning areas	5.8	20.5	5.0
Aspiring			
New home owners, mature communities	5.2	18.1	4.8
White collar workers, better off multi-ethnic areas	7.9	18.5	5.9
Striving			
Older people, less prosperous areas	7.7	19.4	5.8
Council estates, better off homes	9.8	23.0	6.5
Council estates, high unemployment	6.0	24.6	6.8
Council estates, greatest hardship	13.2	24.3	6.9
Multi-ethnic, low income areas	10.1	26.9	8.0

Source: Derived from Tables A5.2, A5.8 and A5.11 in Mirrless-Black, C., Budd, T., Partridge, S. and Mayhews, P., The 1998 British Crime Survey, England and Wales, Home Office Statistical Bulletin 21/98

Unlike other major theoretical perspectives such as Marxism, interactionism and feminism, no specific functionalist criminology exists to speak of, with its own individual interpretations of crime statistics, the source of criminality and potential policy solutions. Rather, functionalism takes a passing look at the issue of deviance in general, rather than crime in particular, while in the process trying to explain whole social trends and patterns. The explanation of deviance is vital to this macro analysis, but it does not contain the seeds of a break-off into the distinctive field of criminology in its own right. According to Downes and Rock:

Being peripheral and ad hoc, [modern-day] functionalist criminology may be represented as a somewhat piecemeal accumulation of arguments. It is not integrated, organized or coherent, and it has not been the subject of lengthy debate. Others may have criticised what it has done, but those who have been attacked have not usually turned round to amend, defend or clarify their work.

(Downes and Rock, 1995, p. 97)

Can we really ignore Durkheim?

While functionalist criminology, especially in contemporary times, does not have a large, organized or particularly popular voice, this is not to say that within the work of Durkheim the concept of deviance has been ignored. Far from it. Equally, this is not to say that functionalist analyses have not informed and shaped the development of non-functionalist perspectives within criminology, since the idea of *anomie* had a great influence on many American and British subcultural studies from the 1920s to the 1950s.

It must be recognized that Durkheim's work, as an individual, does not represent the totality of functionalist belief, and equally, the totality of functionalist belief does not recognize necessarily all that Durkheim wrote.

The historical context of Durkheim's work

Durkheim's major concern was with the analysis of social order: how stability is created and how the collective will is maintained in the face of individualism. These concerns are hardly surprising if we consider the specific socio-cultural context within which Durkheim worked. Sociologists, like artists, musicians and scientists, are shaped by the world they live in, even if their object of study is this world.

Durkheim's image of modern society needs to be understood within the changing times in which he lived.

Changing times and changing problems

Durkheim's sociology, like Comte's before him, was an attempt to engage with the problems of the era – so solutions can come only after understanding and reflection. Durkheim's concern with order and consensus is not, then, one of presumption. He does not assume that consensus is unproblematic; on the contrary, his sociology is concerned to understand how order is possible in times which may lead to disorder, in times where rapid social, cultural and economic changes throw into darkness the previous sense of order.

Deviance, crime and disorder were thus vital for Durkheim's explanations of the future of social life at his time of writing.

The functions of deviance

Development of the morality of the future

For Durkheim, *deviance is functional for society*, provided its social expression is not too much or too little. At first glance this claim may appear to contradict much of functionalist thought concerning the importance of social *stability*. However, Durkheim recognized that all societies experience some level of deviation from norms and values, and in periods of social change – not unlike

those he experienced in France during his own lifetime – new moral codes develop. During their creation the newer rules may be out of step with the old ones for a time. As Durkheim explains:

A society can only survive if it is periodically renewed: that is to say, if the older generations cede place to new ones. Therefore it is necessary for the first to die. Thus the normal state of societies implies the illness of individuals; a certain rate of mortality, like a certain rate of criminality, is indispensable to collective health.

(Durkheim, 1988, pp. 106–7; orig. pub. 1886)

The reinforcing of norms and values

Moreover, for Durkheim a small amount of deviance can have a reinforcing function in bonding society together against the common enemy. This point has been made by functionalists concerning the amount of air-time given to crime in the mass media (see also Section 5.5). We are shown how *not* to behave and thus have our collective sentiments enhanced:

Never do we feel the need of the company of our compatriots so greatly as when we are in a foreign country; never does the believer feel so strongly attracted to his fellow believers as during periods of persecution. Of course, we always love the company of those who feel and think as we do, but it is with passion, and no longer solely with pleasure, that we seek it immediately after discussions where our common beliefs have been directly attacked. Crime brings together honest men and concentrates them. We have only to notice what happens, particularly in a small town, when some moral scandal has just occurred. Men stop each other on the street, they visit each other, they seek to come together to talk of the event and to wax indignant in common.

(Durkheim, 1988, p. 127; orig. pub. 1886)

The 'balance' between control and disorder

Thus, Durkheim suggests that too much crime and deviance will lead to instability, yet too little does not allow a social group to bond together. Equally, deviance is often a forerunner of a new set of collective sentiments: the criminal may be before his time.

Activity

Draw up a list of historical and contemporary figures who might fulfil the forerunner role suggested by Durkheim, i.e. who might be said to have been *before their time* (e.g. Jesus of Nazareth). Should these people be considered as criminals?

C3.2, C3.3

Durkheim's definition of crime

For Durkheim, crime is a category that can be defined only by reference to the specific social norms and values of the society in which it occurs. Durkheim does not regard some actions as deviant *absolutely* – he recognizes that given the whole total of human social experience, actions accepted in some societies are condemned in others. Crime is that which contradicts the collective sentiments of the social group:

... an act is criminal when it offends strong and defined states of the conscience collective ... we must not say that an action shocks the conscience collective because it is criminal, but rather that it is criminal because it shocks the conscience collective. We do not condemn it because it is a crime, but it is a crime because we condemn it. As for the intrinsic nature of these sentiments, it is impossible to specify them; they have the most diverse objects and cannot be encompassed in a single formula.

(Durkheim, 1988, pp. 123–4; orig. pub. 1886)

Too much crime and deviance – or rather, too little collective sentiment and order – becomes a problem for society: individuality rises and the status-quo breaks down. This situation is referred to as *anomie* by Durkheim: the loss of shared and dominant guiding principles or normlessness. In these situations, social actors have the potential to behave in an unrestrained way, ignoring the group and its rules:

Thus we can understand the nature and source of this malady of infiniteness which torments our age. For man to see before him boundless, free, and open space, he must have lost sight of the moral barrier which under normal conditions would cut off his view. He no longer feels those moral forces that restrain him and limit his horizon.

(Durkheim, 1988, pp. 173–4; orig. pub. 1886)

Durkheim suggests that the rise of *anomie* is the principal concern for the industrial age, given the wide-ranging and rapid social changes that have occurred. This concept is of great value, both within functionalist sociology (particularly in Durkheim's own analysis of suicide) and as taken up by other writers since Durkheim's death.

Criticisms of Durkheim's position

This section considers briefly three main criticisms of Durkheim's analysis of deviance, and of his functionalist position in general. We will focus on three main criticisms here.

1 As Cohen (1968) has illustrated, Durkheim's ideas on crime and deviance are *teleological*: they suggest that there is a purpose to the existence of all social phenomena, the necessary purpose of deviance being to bond the social group. This is difficult to imagine because it treats society as a living thing, an object which forces individuals to follow, like sheep or robots, the wider social pattern.

2 As Downes and Rock argue, it is difficult to test the functionalist theory of crime. It seems to be a 'have your cake and eat it' theory, where crime may invalidate the functionalist's claims of social stability, but is seen to really function to create such stability by showing people how *not* to behave. Thus, functionalists are able to prove stability in life, even where conflict is shown to exist instead!

3 Functionalism fails to provide an adequate answer to the question 'functional for whom?' Crime may be defined as that which goes against the good of the community, but who decides what the good of the community is? It is at this point that Marxist analysis suggests that functionalism supports the ideological interests of the ruling group in society.

Marxist criminology: the old and the new

The basis for a Marxist analysis of crime and deviance, as in other fields, is the social conditions (or social structures) leading to the creation of deviance – the political economy. Marxist views on deviance adopt a conflict–structuralist stance.

Marxist political economy

As identified by Marx, the economic base or the infrastructure is seen to determine the precise nature of the superstructure. In other words, the ways in which the economy is organized shape all other aspects of that society, including its culture, normative system and what does and does not become defined as deviant.

Deviance in a capitalist society

Classical Marxists contend that:

- capitalism is itself a crime, and
- it also causes crime.

Capitalism is, they say, based on oppression and economic exploitation of the majority. It creates a competitive, dog-eat-dog world in which greed, violence and corruption – which are the only means of survival for some – flourish.

The most basic question is 'deviant for whom?' Marxism suggests that deviance means *to stray from the norms and values of the ruling classes* since they control the means of production, and are therefore the intellectual rulers in society. They have the power to define working-class activities as deviant, and in doing so, to control them.

Marxism and the neo-Marxisms

Marxism as a theory is by no means homogeneous: within Marxism itself there is a great deal of internal conflict and debate. It is possible to identify the existence of two very general camps, classical and new (neo-).

Classical Marxism

Classical Marxism assumes that the ruling classes use their power to control, fight against and punish the working classes. In the case of deviance, the legal system and the police are weapons or tools in the class struggle to be mobilized against those who step out of line.

Bonger (1916) provided a very early interpretation of Marxist ideas on crime and deviance. Bonger shared with Marx himself a belief that, by nature, humanity is altruistic and not competitive – a very different idea from that of modern right-wing control theories. Bonger suggested that capitalism itself, as a form of economic organization, makes humanity greedy and selfish.

Quinney (1973, 1977), in common with

Bonger, also argues that under capitalism the law is used to oppress the working classes. He suggests that what we now regard as criminal will disappear only once capitalism itself has disappeared. He contends that there will be no greed and profit-seeking under socialism; also, the ruling class will not exist to use the law as a weapon to define as deviant those working-class activities they do not wish to allow.

Neo-Marxism

While not rejecting the ideas of the more classical approach, neo-Marxists take this analysis further, often by suggesting fruitful ways of evolving the development of Marxist sociology by combining it with other ideas – especially those from interactionism and, more recently, feminism.

Within this neo-Marxist camp there are further subdivisions, of which the following are but two examples:

- *New criminology.* In 1973, Taylor, Walton and Young published a book entitled *The New Criminology: For a Social Theory of Deviance.* In this they advocated the development of a fully social theory of deviance: in other words, to expand on and to elaborate existing ideas while borrowing heavily from interactionism.
- *New Left realism.* Aiming an attack against what they saw as the excesses of both right-wing and left-wing theories, in 1993 Lea and Young (having moved further on from *The New Criminology*) suggested that we should become realistic about crime and deviance. We should understand that crime is a harsh reality for many working-class people and not something to be glorified in a 'Robin Hood' way.

 Discussion point

Why are there so many different varieties of Marxist theory?

C3.1a

Despite offering many different ideas and exploring many different research interests, the two neo-Marxisms outlined above do agree on a vital issue: *crime is the product of inadequate social conditions.* In making this claim, they reflect the original ideas of traditional or classical Marxists such as Bonger and Quinney.

A new criminology?

The book *The New Criminology*, published in the early 1970s, was seen by its writers, Taylor, Walton and Young, to mark both a new beginning and an end in criminology. No longer were functionalist or even the non-sociological approaches of psychology or physiology seen as acceptable theoretical paradigms within which to work. Instead, a new theory was required – Marxist in orientation, open to interactionist ideas, but firmly rooted in the orthodox Marxist concerns with political economy, with the social and economic conditions within which crime occurs. Taylor and his co-writers argued that they have:

... redirected criminological attention to the grand questions of social structure and the overweening social arrangements within which the criminal process is played out. We are confronted once again with the central question of man's relationship to structures of power, domination and authority – and with the ability of men to confront these structures in acts of crime, deviance and dissent we are back in the realm of social theory itself.

(Taylor *et al.*, 1973, p. 268)

To move criminology on into the future of new criminology, Taylor and colleagues drew on some very old criminology and some (in their day) quite recent criminology. They recommended that all explanations of crime and deviance should address seven basic issues or levels:

- the wider origins of the deviant act
- the immediate origins of the deviant act
- the actual act
- the immediate origins of the social reaction
- the wider origins of the social reaction
- the outcome of the social reaction on the deviant's further action; and finally
- the nature of the deviant process as a whole.

According to Taylor and his colleagues:

A criminology which is to be adequate to an understanding of these developments, and which will be able to bring politics back into the discussion of what were previously technical issues, will need to deal with the society as a totality. This new criminology will in fact be an old criminology, in that it will face the same problems that were faced by the classical social theorists.

(Taylor *et al.*, 1973, p. 278)

In the establishment of this new criminology they wished to advocate a change in social conditions, to achieve a revolutionary change in socialism.

Activity

Consider the seven points identified by Taylor *et al.* in *The New Criminology*, and make a note of the other ideas and theorists you have come across so far who make a similar point, or have raised a similar issue. Then answer these questions:

a How new is/was the new criminology?

b How is this mixing of approaches useful in contemporary sociology?

 C3.2, C3.3

Studying gender and crime

A great deal of feminist sociology is concerned with reinstatement of the female voice in sociology. Regarded as 'malestream', the discipline is seen to reflect largely the achievements and interests of male academics while concentrating on men as the object of study. This is why the non-feminist sociology of crime and deviance has contributed to the invisibility of women.

Discussion point

Is sociology male-dominated? Why has the work of women researchers been undervalued?

 C3.1a

Heidensohn: The invisibility of women

Heidensohn (1989, 1996), amongst other recent feminist and feminist-influenced commentators, has made the popularization of a feminist interpretation of crime a major priority. She offers three reasons for the invisibility of women in criminology:

1 It may be felt by male sociologists that crime traditionally associated with women, such as shoplifting, lacks the same excitement and interest as male crime.

2 Since it is often assumed that male crime is of a more violent and dangerous type, women's crime is ignored since it is of no real social threat.

3   Since the official figures tend to show marked differences between male and female crime, the latter is often ignored and the compliance of women with laws and norms is often assumed.

For Heidensohn, all three of these factors have contributed to the exclusion of a detailed and well thought-through feminist analysis of crime, until recently. As she comments:

Not so very long ago, students searching textbooks on crime for references to either gender or women would find few or none. That is no longer so, although there has been no comprehensive revolution; criminology has not yet been born again.

(Heidensohn, 1989, p. 94)

Heidensohn suggests that although the female voice is now being recognized, this trend has yet to develop fully into a truly detailed use of feminist criminology in mainstream or orthodox thought. At present, the issue of women and crime is still not of central importance and has been tackled only superficially:

* by the lengthy analysis of official crime statistics
* as an add-on, a sociological added extra, but still not of central value (Heidensohn refers to this as the 'cosmetic touch approach').

Conformity and non-conformity

Criminologists and even the more broadly interested sociologists of deviance have been uncomfortable with the study of female criminality because, logically, it leads to the superficially dull topic of conformity and not to the excitements of deviance.

(Heidensohn, 1996, p. 12)

In opposition to her male traditional criminological counterparts, Heidensohn suggests that the lower levels of recorded rates for female crime do not make it less interesting as an object of study but more so:

I simply want to point out that, paradoxically, an examination of female criminality and unofficial deviance suggests that we need to move away from studying infractions and look at conformity instead, because the most striking thing about female behaviour on the basis of all the evidence considered here is how notably conformist to social mores women are.

(Heidensohn, 1996, p. 11)

Taking female conformity seriously

Heidensohn says that sociologists should be asking why women conform more, rather than why they deviate less. By asking the question in the reverse sense to the traditional sociological approach to crime and gender, Heidensohn hopes to place women firmly centre-stage in the sociological debate.

In adopting the feminist strategy advocated by Heidensohn, we should take female conformity seriously. This has implications for our interpretation of official crime statistics. Are we to believe the official figures which suggest that women commit less crime than men? Or, alternatively, are explanations which rest on a chivalry factor more convincing? Do women commit crime, but of a certain sort? As in other issues in the sociology of crime and deviance, women's criminality rests on two different interpretations of the official crime statistics:

* view ONE: *The official figures are incorrect*. Women do commit a large proportion of crime, although not necessarily of the same type as men. However, they are often treated leniently.
* view TWO: *The official figures are correct*. Women conform more than men.

'Women commit crime but are treated more leniently'

Pollack (1961) suggests that a chivalry factor operates to protect women from becoming labelled as criminals. The argument is that the largely male-dominated police force and Crown Prosecution Service (CPS) are more likely to informally caution women than to officially prosecute. For Pollak, women's invisibility from official crime figures has contributed to a myth of female criminality. In this view, women do commit crime, but it is not reported, recorded or prosecuted as often as for their male counterparts. The official crime figures are therefore an illusion.

A similar point is made by Steffensmeier (cited in M. Leonard, 1995) who suggests that women tend to be treated more leniently by the courts and therefore do not end up in prison. The argument is that judges are reluctant to separate a mother from her children, whereas prison is more suitable for men since they are not seen to adopt the caring role.

Allen (1987) illustrates how mental health explanations for female criminality often reduce the punishment given to female offenders, both in terms of the length of time of imprisonment and the format of their custodial care. For example, women are often given psychiatric care as an alternative to prison since it is believed by the courts that women are more emotional than men and therefore more prone to emotional crisis.

Leonard (1982), however, suggests that this chivalry factor is itself an illusion. If women are treated with more leniency, we must also look at how gender differences relate to, and operate with, other factors such as ethnicity, class and age. It is unrealistic to assume that these are separate, as in fact they combine to make up the life chances of the individual. Women are, in fact, sometimes treated more harshly by the courts than men would be.

Abbott and Wallace (1990) suggest that adolescent girls are more likely to be put into care for their own protection. There is a tendency to sexualize the crimes of girls and to protect girls from their own promiscuity, whereas teenage boys are viewed by society as needing to 'be a lad'.

'Women commit less crime and conform more'

Box (1981, 1995) suggests that women have less power and less opportunity to commit crime, given the manner in which they are socialized, protected by their parents during adolescence, and employed in jobs that exclude opportunities for risk-taking and deviance given their service and/or caring nature, such as nursing, teaching, secretarial work, etc.:

[Girls'] potential autonomy is hedged in by parental close supervision; they have fewer legitimate opportunities through which they might obtain some escape from this manifestation of patriarchal control. ... the sex-differential in rates of delinquency/crime can be accounted for by the fact that in comparison with their male age peers, adolescent girls are relatively less powerful and this crucial social-difference persists into adulthood.

(Box, 1995, p. 187)

Box goes on to suggest that women find it difficult to reach the upper levels of the crime world. There are few employment opportunities in organized gangs, unless through taking on a role associated with the deviant expression of sexuality – such as prostitution.

A similar point is made by Smart (1976), who contends that women and girls do commit significantly fewer crimes and acts of delinquency because they lack the means and opportunities. While their brothers are allowed out in the evening, girls are forced to adopt a bedroom-orientated culture by having friends to visit. They have restrictions placed on their behaviour and movements.

Familist ideology

In adulthood, childbirth and marriage provide further mechanisms of control, restriction and surveillance:

Marriage and domesticity provide powerful controlling mechanisms to ensure the good behaviour of adult women. They are all the more powerful since they can largely be imposed with the willing, even eager, acquiescence of women themselves.

(Heidensohn, 1996, p. 180)

This familist ideology provides a powerful source of social control in all stages of life. (This issue is discussed in more detail in Section 5.6.)

10.6 Social control and the role of law

Within the field of deviance and crime, sociologists and criminologists are interested not just in individual and collective deviant behaviour but also in how the state responds.

Durkheim: the functions of punishment

Discussion point
What role or function might the public punishment of crime have for society?

C3.1a

For Emile Durkheim, crime represents those actions which go against the collective sentiments of a society. Durkheim recognizes the relative nature of crime and deviance: an act is not criminal because of its inherent properties, but rather because it breaks the collective rules.

Like many other social theorists, Durkheim charts a change in systems of discipline, freedom and punishment in modern social types. He notes that modern societies are supposedly based less on essentially revengeful repressive punishments for criminality, and more on dispassionate necessity. Crime is punished, according to modern-day commonsense wisdom, out of a need to preserve the best interests of the group – not through an emotional response:

Today, it is said, punishment has changed its character; it is no longer to avenge itself that society punishes, it is to defend itself. The suffering which it inflicts is in its hands no longer anything but a methodical means of protection. It punishes, not because chastisement offers it any intrinsic satisfaction, but so that the fear of punishment may paralyse those who contemplate evil. It is no longer anger, but a well thought-out precaution which determines repression.

(Durkheim, 1988, p. 124; orig. pub. 1886)

Durkheim himself is sceptical of this commonsense image of the change in forms of punishment in modern times. He would rather point to the continuing similarities between the past and the modern social types with regard to the functions of discipline and punishment:

The nature of a practice does not necessarily change because the conscious intentions of those who apply it are modified. It might, in fact, still play the same role as before, but without this being perceived ... There is no radical division between the punishment of today and yesterday, and consequently it was not necessary for the latter to change its nature in order to accommodate itself to the role that it plays in our civilised societies. The whole difference derives from the fact that it now produces its effects with a heightened awareness of what it does.

(Durkheim, 1988, p. 125; orig. pub. 1886)

Durkheim goes further to suggest that modern punishment is often based on the need or desire for vengeance. The reason for this, he says, is that crime hits at the most important aspect of social stability, which is morality; and if morality is attacked on a frequent basis then the social order will soon collapse. Durkheim appears to imply that the social group does have the capacity for revenge if what it holds most dear is threatened – the identity of the group itself.

A radical interpretation of social control

The Durkheimian perspective on the nature of punishment is of value because it attempts to re-evaluate commonsense thought. It is essentially debunking – it pulls apart what we might imagine to be the case, and examines social life more deeply. Thus, Durkheim claims that there is a difference between what society may say or conventionally believe about punishment and what actually occurs. In this case, Durkheim claims that modern-day punishments are not very dissimilar from older punishments and that they both perform the same functions.

Activity

On 2 March 1757, Damiens, the regicide, was condemned 'to make the amende honorable before the main door of the Church of Paris', where he was to be 'taken and conveyed in a cart, wearing nothing but a shirt, holding a torch of burning wax weighing two pounds'; then, 'in the said cart, to the Place de Grève, where, on a scaffold that will be erected there, the flesh will be torn from his breasts, arms, thighs and calves with red-hot pincers, his right hand, holding the knife with which he committed the said parricide, burnt with sulphur, and, on those places where the flesh will be torn away, poured molten lead, boiling oil, burning resin, wax and sulphur melted together and then his body drawn and quartered by four horses and his limbs and body consumed by fire, reduced to ashes and his ashes thrown to the winds.'

(Foucault, 1977, p. 3)

The extract above describes a public execution in 1757 in France. Taking a Durkheimian perspective, describe how this type of punishment might be considered functional for the social group (that is, the French people).

More recent commentators have also attempted to debunk or critically investigate apparent distinctions between modern-day and older forms of punishment and discipline. Amongst these, of particular interest are Stanley Cohen and Michel Foucault. Although offering quite different accounts of modern systems of discipline and punishment, they can be seen as similar in one important way. Whereas Durkheim believed modern punishment, however ordered or whatever its relationship to the past, was essentially positive since it performed a number of bonding functions, Cohen and Foucault are much more sceptical: they see punishment as largely repressive and often determined in the interests of ruling élites. They therefore offer us a far more critical or radical interpretation of punishment. They share a concern to highlight previously hidden mechanisms of social control which, they contend, operate in contemporary society.

Cohen: visions of social control

Sociologists, philosophers and historians are becoming increasingly interested in facets of discipline and punishment in society which may not be obvious at first glance. In his book *Visions of Social Control: Crime, Punishment and Classification*, Cohen (1994) attempts to expose these facets and classify contemporary forms of control.

Activity

Social control is a central concept in much sociology, especially within the sociology of crime and deviance.

a Define social control. Use a dictionary of sociology if you wish.

b For each of the three perspectives, Marxism, functionalism and feminism, write a paragraph describing how the perspective interprets the role of social control in society. Include a reference to the value-dimension implicit within these perspectives – that is, whether they would interpret social control as negative or positive. Give reasons for your answers.

C3.2, C3.3

When thinking about the concepts of discipline, control and punishment, many of us may first imagine scenes of imprisonment or torture. Although these are very well established methods used in various societies for controlling so-called deviants, they are not by any means the only methods. The more radical thinkers wish to point to other forms of control, many of which are part of our everyday life and experiences. These hidden systems of control may include the following:

• *Specialist language*. A number of commentators such as Cohen and Foucault (but from different theoretical orientations) have illustrated how language performs a controlling function. It shapes thought and therefore dictates action. The specialist knowledge of élite groups such as doctors, psychologists, scientists, etc. is seen to contain its own language, unintelligible to others. In this way the medical profession, for example, is able to control patients and to justify an élitist position in society.

• *Systems of classification*. Both Cohen and Foucault also recognize that classification plays a part in social control. For example, in the classroom – especially in secondary years – teachers put children into ability sets. In doing this, individuals stop functioning as individuals and instead take up a place in an overall classification of ability. Such labels may subsequently dictate how others react to these social actors, and ultimately, what these social actors may think of themselves.

• *Timetabling*. Actions are very often controlled by the use of schedules and deadlines. In factories, hospitals, schools – virtually everywhere – individuals' and groups' activities are determined and controlled.

Discussion point

a How might 'language' contain power and the ability to control some groups?

b How might the use of timetables control the body and stop deviance from taking place? In what social areas might this happen?

C3.1a

Punishment: the why? and the how?

In conducting his re-mapping of the terrain of social control in contemporary life, Cohen engages in penology (the study of prisons). He, like others, is highly suspicious of the official state-sponsored forms of social control such as imprisonment, and he is especially concerned to re-evaluate or to rewrite the history of penology. Like Foucault, Cohen suggests that the official reason given for policies of incarceration and decarceration are not all they might seem to be. He wishes to revise the history of punishment:

We will have to move continually between the realm of words and the realm of deeds. The relationship between these worlds is a problem for the student of social control no more nor less than it is in any other area of social inquiry ... This is what is meant in the debates, respectively, about motive and ideology. What is perennially at issue, is how surface reasons can differ from real reasons, or how people can say one thing, yet be doing something which appears radically different. ... Perhaps such gaps between appearance and reality, or between words and action, exist because people cannot ever comprehend the real reasons for their actions. Alternatively, they understand these reasons only too well, but use words to disguise or mystify their real intentions. Or perhaps the stated verbal reasons are indeed the real ones, but because of the obdurate nature of the world, things somehow turn out differently.

(Cohen, 1994, p. 11)

The 'master patterns' of social control

Cohen argues that the master patterns, or the major changes, that have occurred in the history of state-sponsored social control are not necessarily those that appear to have been made. He suggests that our commonsense understanding, and the state-validated image of historical changes in punishment, imprisonment and social control, are of an illusory nature. In putting this critical notion forward, Cohen is attempting to create a revisionist history of punishment. Four principal changes or developments are supposed to have taken place in the history of punishment up to the present day:

1 The increased influence of the state in social control through the creation of police forces, laws, prisons, etc., plus the increased use of state-sponsored care or treatment of deviants.

2 The specialization of agencies of deviance control: the separation into separate categories or classifications of the sick, the mad and the dangerous and the creation of separate bodies of knowledge to deal with them.

3 Segregation of these various deviant types themselves into different geographical spaces – such as hospitals, prisons, asylums, etc.

4 Finally, at the end of the great first transformation, the decline of public physical punishment in favour of a much more so-called humane treatment of the deviant individual.

These changes are well documented; but Cohen argues that other, less visible, changes are taking place that are not so well documented or publicized.

Decarceration

The great second transformation in the history of punishment is the increasing process of decarceration in the western world, especially in the UK. The tendency is to close down prisons, asylums,

etc. as part of a great reform – an enlightened and liberated method of dealing with and controlling deviants.

Putting aside the obvious economic factors that may lead the state towards a policy of decarceration, Cohen suggests an altogether more suspicious function. He detects within the so-called enlightened policy of decarceration, not a truly humane or liberal reasoning, but the desire to increase the marginalization of traditionally non-deviant groups: to widen and blur boundaries of legitimate state-sponsored social control.

Blurring and widening the boundaries

Cohen contends that with decarceration and the development of a care-in-the-community policy, the traditional boundaries between deviant and non-deviant behaviour will become blurred. With the increasing use of the medical profession, social workers and educational professions as state agents of social control, more and more individuals can be controlled, since the traditionally deviant and traditionally non-deviant interact and live side-by-side.

Moreover, along with blurring occurs the widening of social control. More and more people become subject to these contemporary mechanisms of discipline. Social control moves out widely across more of society.

The sociology of punishment

One key practical issue of social control is exactly how we decide to punish offenders. Clearly there is the argument over whether people commit crimes because they are somehow intrinsically evil or bad, or alternatively because they are placed in poor environments. This issue is then about whether we should punish or reform society as a method of trying to solve crime.

💬 Discussion point

Should criminals be punished or seen as victims of society?

C3.1a

Talk of punishment however, presumes that the person about to be punished has committed an act which is punishable and is responsible for their own actions and such actions cannot be explained by their situation.

It is a common misconception that punishment has gone 'soft' in the UK and that people consistently underestimate the actions taken by the courts.

Alan Travis, writing in the *Guardian*, 9 May 2000, made the following point in relation to this:

The public [...] believes courts are far softer than they are – half the public, for example, thinks that more than 40% of adult rapists are not jailed when the actual figure is less than 1%. Some 80% of people still think that judges are out of touch.

(Alan Travis, 2000)

Clearly since there are so many myths about, it is important for sociologists to consider the actual nature of punishment and who gets punished, and also to consider the reasons for and the effectiveness of various forms of punishment.

Activity

Conduct a quick poll among other students to see if the misperceptions outlined in the above quote from Alan Travis are also found among your peers.

C3.2, C3.3

The shift in punishment policy

Eadie and Morley (1999) point to the shifts in policy in terms of punishment from 1970 onwards. They argue that in the elections of 1970, 1974 (both) and 1979 there were clear differences in the political approach of the two main parties to law and order questions. The Labour party sought to locate getting rid of crime within notions of removing inequality, poverty and racial bigotry. Clearly the implication of this view is that crime is due to social and environmental factors and in this sense, people arguably do not choose to become criminals but are influenced by their background. The solution is to change their background.

In contrast, in elections in the 1970s, the Conservative party sought to argue that crime was the result of policies adopted by the government, specifically Labour party policies. The attempt to portray Labour as the criminals friend seemed to have some impact and encouraged the Conservatives to continue in this vein. In the 1979 election the Conservatives were elected on a clear

'law and order' approach. What they meant by this was the belief that the solution to crime was in reforms to the police and their operation and also to sentencing policy. This was the start of the 'get tough' policies that have in effect continued to this day.

This approach came into fruition in the 1990s. The prison population which rose until 1985, but then fell in 1992, rose again afterwards. Since 1993 it rose very rapidly, notably among women. Since 1993 the rate of increase in imprisonment for women has been twice that of men.

Activity

Use the Internet to look up the current policies on law and order of the main political parties. What are the similarities and differences?

C3.2, C3.3, IT3.1

The New Right and the 'get tough' approach

The person most notably associated with the Conservative 'law and order' agenda was Michael Howard, who served as home secretary from 1993 until 1997 when the Conservatives were removed from government. Eadie and Morley (1999) quote the following examples of the meaning of this approach to law and order:

... the Conservative administration was heavily influenced by New Right thinking in the USA that regarded crime as an inevitable part of modern life and its management more important than discovering its causes. Management of crime focused on incarcerating serious and repeat offenders on the basis that 'wicked people exist. Nothing avails them except to set them apart from innocent people' (Wilson, 1975). In Britain, these sentiments were reflected in Michael Howard's statement to the Conservative Party Conference in October 1993 that 'Prison Works' (Howard, 1993), and John Major's statement that 'we should condemn more and understand less' (Major, 1994).

(Eadie and Morley, 1999)

New Labour: 'Tough on crime and tough on the causes of crime'

Despite being slightly sceptical of the New Right approach and the Right realism from which it came, it is clear that the Labour party wished to shift its policy on crime, law and order. The most influential person in this respect was the new leader of the Labour party (previously the Home Affairs spokesperson, therefore responsible for policy on crime), Tony Blair, who became famous for coining the phrase 'Tough on crime, tough on the causes of crime'. This is in essence a practical application of the ideas of New Left Realism associated with Jock Young. As Eadie and Morley (1999) point out:

Labour, desperate to rid itself of its 'soft on crime' label, joined the debate with the soundbite 'Tough on crime and tough on the causes of crime', an imaginative compromise of matching the Tory rhetoric of toughness while holding on to its own beliefs in crime being linked to societal and structural inequalities. Since Labour's victory in May 1997, the home secretary, Jack Straw, has stated that securing the safety of the public is his overriding priority. 'Tough on crime' is reflected in the implementations of mandatory sentences for certain offences, set out in the Crime (Sentences) Act 1997, and the Crime and Disorder Act 1998, to address youth crime.

'Tough on the causes of crime' is reflected in the government's 'Welfare-to-Work' programme for the young and long-term unemployed which the home secretary hopes will reduce 'both the temptation and the opportunity for crime'.

(Eadie and Morley, 1999, p. 456)

Activity

Obtain up-to-date figures for the prison population and see which of the predictions outlined in the following article comes true.

C3.2

It is also clearly the case that the potential cost of imprisoning large numbers of people is something that has great implications. Eadie and Morley (1999) report the following figures of the cost of various responses to crime:

Cost per month in 1995/6:
Adult male prison	£1,776
Supervision order	£180
Probation order	£190
Community service order	£140

(Eadie and Morley, 1999, p. 457)

Clearly sending people to prison is extremely expensive compared to other approaches and

---

Crackdown may mean 15 new jails

JULIA HARTLEY-BREWER

Fifteen new jails must be built to house the thousands of extra offenders who will be imprisoned each year under tough sentencing to be brought in by the Home Office, probation officers will warn today.

There could be about 60,000 additional offenders each year as a result of the legislation, the National Association of Probation Officers warned.

The criminal justice and court services bill, which received its second reading yesterday, aims to tighten penalties for offenders breaching community sentences and to crack down on drugs offenders.

But probation officers predicted the legislation would require 15 new jails and cost £210m per year. Napo said that up to 40,000 offenders who breached community sentences, as well as 10,000 offenders denied bail because they tested positive for Class A drugs on arrest, would be jailed. And the prison population could be increased by up to 7,500 offenders each year who breached curfews and orders to attend drug treatment centres.

Napo's assistant general secretary, Harry Fletcher, said: 'The majority of this group need treatment and assistance, not punishment.'

The Home Office dismissed Napo's figures as 'nonsense', estimating that 15,000 people breaching orders under the new rules would be jailed.

A spokeswoman said: 'We have calculated that, as a result of the enforcement proposals, around 2,000 extra prison places will be required.'

Source: Guardian, 28 March 2000

---

there are concerns that the cost of the current governments 'get tough' approach may be very large indeed, both in financial and indeed in human terms. The second fear is also based on the belief that prison does not work. This became the basis of a debate in 1998 when the *Guardian* printed articles showing that prison does not work.

Activity

Read the following article.
Outline the arguments for and against imprisonment contained within the article.
Hold a class debate about whether there should be more or less use of prison to deal with crime.

C3.2, C3.3, IT3.1

Crime need not pay

Sunshine finally broke through the dark scowling clouds of rhetoric that have blocked an intelligent debate about crime. Belatedly, Labour honoured the second half of its famous law and order promise yesterday: 'tough on the causes of crime'. In a bold move, it published a research report which demolished the most common myths about crime control. The simplistic solutions propagated by the Howard school of populist policies – more prisons, longer sentences, more bobbies on the beat – do not work. Crime reduction needs a far more focused approach.

It is not just the Conservatives who should be cringing from the blunt facts – drawn from national and international studies over the last 40 years – but Labour, too. They were equally guilty of distorting the debate by ducking crime's complex causes in their search for simplistic solutions and votes. Remember Jack Straw's 'zero tolerance', even with the squeegee merchants, winos and beggars? Forget it, if you mean 'tough policing'. All that will achieve is an alienated community, which will reduce the effectiveness of the police.

Yesterday the home secretary repented. Just as the health service needed to aspire to evidence-based medicine, so the Home Office should pursue evidence-based policing. The age of rationalism approaches. John Stuart Mill should be alive and watching. His heart would have melted at the press briefing by Chris Nuttall, head of Home Office research, who is still 'stunned' after so many years of his team's work being ignored by the ministerial endorsement of an evidence-based crime reduction programme. It is time for optimists, not pessimists.

We are now entering our third and most promising phase of modern crime control. First came the negative 'nothing works', a demoralizing and fatalistic era which lasted for over two decades. Then came 'prison works', Michael Howard's simple-minded, one-club approach to policy-making, which both major parties embraced, despite the huge cost implications: every one per cent fall in crime needed a 25 per cent increase in the prison population.

Finally, we've arrived at a crime reduction strategy, which incorporates a succession of successful strategies, ranging from early years intervention to literacy programmes for old lags. It is not a soft liberal cop-out. It includes targeting high profile repeat offenders and 'hot spot' criminal areas, and special support for victims. But it also involves long-term schemes, such as the High/Scope Perry pre-school programme in which children and parents are given more support. Prevent a child from dropping out of school through early preparation and not only will there be huge benefits to the child but to society as well.

The researchers are frank. Some findings are firmer than others. American schemes may not be as effective here as over there. But the report is packed with sufficient successful British schemes to give even the most pessimistic sceptic some grounds for optimism. British Safer City anti-burglary drives have achieved up to a 30 per cent reduction in levels of crime at a fraction of the cost of prison. Ensuring all police forces pursue such policies will require both stick and carrot. But at least ministers were unambiguous in their message: the police must become more effective. They will also need the support of other services like schools, housing and social services that will need careful co-ordination. But best of all – why can't we have a bipartisan approach? Here is a hard-nosed, cost-effective package which high Tories, if they're sensible, will endorse.

Source: Guardian, 22 July 1998

Women in prison

One key effect of the 'get tough' approaches which have featured in the punishment policies of the 1980s and 1990s has been the way this has been applied in relation to gender. The rate of increase of imprisonment for women has been twice that of men since 1993. Although women are still a minority of those imprisoned this increase has occasioned great concern and debate about the changing nature of women and how society should respond to this as the article 'Jailed because of their gender' from the *Guardian* on the following page shows.

💬 Discussion point

Read the article on page 352.
Does greater equality for women also mean more women in prison?

Michel Foucault: a post-structural view

Foucault adopts a post-structuralist stance. Like Cohen he is concerned with how modern systems of punishment contain previously invisible or hidden forms of control and are legitimated by the state and others as being humane or liberated.

The birth of the prison

In his key text *Discipline and Punish: The Birth of the Prison* (1977), Foucault charts a revisionist history. Using a historical-based methodology which he refers to as 'archaeological' and as 'genealogical', Foucault wishes to explore and to dig behind the surface layers of the appearance of reality. This is largely what is understood by the term 'post-structuralist' – a desire to investigate social reality at a deep-structural level, to

JAILED BECAUSE OF THEIR GENDER
A record number of women are in prison.
Most shouldn't be there.

ANGELA NEUSTATTER

In the past seven years the number of women in prison has doubled to 3,391, having climbed steadily from 1970, when there were just 988, and through the Thatcher years. Meanwhile, our New Labour home secretary is planning to build two new women's prisons providing 800 more beds, presumably because he anticipates needing to lock more and more women away.

These findings from the Prison Reform Trust's two-year research project, chaired by Professor Dorothy Wedderburn, culminating in a major report called 'Justice for Women: The Need for Reform', may come as a shock to those of us who do not perceive women as an ever-growing threat. Women do not seem to pose the kind of risk that male offenders do – who account for 61,964 convicted criminals, almost a quarter sentenced for violent crimes. But have we got it wrong? Must we conclude from this that women really are becoming more dangerous and deviant?

Luridly detailed press reports of women who set out to get rivals killed or plan the death of a partner to get life insurance suggest so. The image of the teenage girl who will put the boot in and tickle your ribs with a knife as quickly as her male counterpart is over-reported, surely because it brings a sexual frisson in the guise of telling us how bad things are getting.

The truth is rather different. Just 13 per cent of women – around 350 in all – are presently in prison for violent crimes, and they are not, on the whole, smart, sassy dames but women who have responded to their desperate powerlessness by killing violent husbands and partners after years of abuse; or a very few women who, in a state of despair or depression, kill their children.

Less than a third are in for violence, robbery, burglary and drug offences, and fewer still are the other female criminal the media loves – the well-educated, successful career woman, like barrister Carole Winston-Churchill, jailed last week for blackmail and forgery who is held up as proof positive that equality has made women as bad as men. Most women filling cells are there for theft, handling stolen goods, fraud, forgery and motoring offences. Nor are they habitual offenders. Nearly half of those surveyed had no previous convictions.

The more we learn about the women we imprison the easier it is to see how they are being punished as victims of circumstances they have failed to cope with. Sir David Ramsbotham in his 1997 study 'Women in Prison' drew a sad picture. Nearly half of all women prisoners said they had been abused, sexually and physically, and almost half were self-harmers. Over a third had failed at school and more than a quarter had been in care. Trying to cope on their own, many lived in poverty with nearly one in ten homeless before they came to prison, while 70 per cent had no employment and over a third were in debt. Many had mental health problems and were on high doses of medication.

Of course, plenty of men have similarly deprived and wretched life experiences, but it is here that research demonstrates gender differences. Chris Tchaikovsky, the charismatic ex-prisoner and director of the campaigning group Women in Prison, explains: 'Where men react by becoming angry and determined to prove themselves, women do the reverse. They become depressed, unable to function and self-loathing makes them turn anger at their circumstances – which fuels men's violence – on themselves'.

Locking these women away comes at a high price. Each person in prison costs the tax-payer some £25,000 a year, and the majority of the women are young with dependent children who, if there is nobody to care for them, must be taken into state care. According to the Prison Reform Trust, 8,000 children are affected each year.

So why are we seeing ever more women in prison? One reason, as Wedderburn's report suggests, is the tough on crime climate of successive governments which has meant more women being taken to court, more being convicted and longer custodial sentences. Feminist writers such as Ann Oakley and Helena Kennedy in her book *Eve Was Framed*, have looked at how women may be punished more harshly than men when they transgress against traditional ideas of femininity, threatening the investment society has in women being virtuous.

If we believe in equality for women, then they must be punished on a par with men although not excessively. But clearly there are far more cases where women pose far less risk than men and could be punished and rehabilitated in the community keeping their families together and offering them constructive help.

As things stand, we have a female prison population higher than at any time since the 19th century and almost certainly set to rise. The government has put a great deal of thought and money into reforming youth justice, now is the time for it to tackle the destructive injustice meted out to women.

Source: Guardian, 4 April 2000

discuss those rules and regulations that exist behind the surface, usually based on language.

Discourses

Foucault suggests that social life is controlled by what he terms 'discourses' or specialized sets of knowledge. These discourses – such as penology (the study of prisons), medicine (the study of the body and health), pedagogy (the study of forms of education), psychology (the study of the mind), etc. – operate on the human body to dictate and regulate action and shape self-identity. Our understanding of our self – of who and of what we are – is seen as the sum total of all the discourses that have operated on us.

Control over the body

Foucault notes an interesting historical rupture or break where the birth of the prison, the hospital, the asylum, the school and the factory all derive from a method of discipline originally found in the workhouse. All these institutions are seen to be based on the same form of social control which regulates minds and actions by the use of timetables, space, classifications and exercise. Foucault claims (in a similar way to Cohen) that these are the hidden mechanisms of social control – the underlying forms of discipline and punishment which are a key feature of modern social life, even if we are largely unaware of their existence.

The changing nature of policing

It could be argued that government policy is now concerned less with the ultimate solution to crime – if such a thing actually exists – and more with what is called 'target-hardening' (Reiner, 1996). By this is meant that anyone likely to be a potential victim of crime – individuals, families, companies, local councils – must undertake better crime-prevention measures. We are asked to move crime away, by making ourselves more of a hard target. Reiner describes this as a 'burgle my neighbour' approach – criminals are moved on to softer targets.

The policy of target-hardening amongst the New Right is referred to in the sociological literature as 'Right realism'. This can be seen as an alternative claim to that of Lea and Young's 'New Left realism' already described above. Right realism points the finger of responsibility at the individual: if you are the victim of crime, it says, you may well have yourself to blame.

Case Study – Inner-city riots

The inner-city streets of the UK witnessed serious mob violence in, *inter alia*:

- the St Paul's district of Bristol (in 1980)
- the Railton Road area of Brixton in South London (1981)
- Southall in West London (1981)
- Toxteth in Liverpool (1981)
- the Lozells Road area of Handsworth, Birmingham (1985).

Three perspectives

John Benyon (1986), in summarizing the main sociological interpretations of these riots – largely, but not exclusively, linked by the media and police to the activities of young black and Asian youths – identifies three main approaches:

- the *conservative* view, which suggests that collective violence is needless and without justification (this view was held by much of the media and the government of the day)
- the *liberal* perspective, which suggests that collective action is often a last-hope response to inadequate social conditions such as deprivation
- the *radical* response, which sees collective action as purposeful, meaningful and politically motivated.

Using this distinction, we can suggest that whereas Gilroy adopts a radical approach, New Left realists such as Lea and Young adopt a more liberal approach. What is interesting to note is that both would regard themselves as influenced by Marxism. That shows us just how wide a perspective this is.

Underlying causes

Benyon suggests that we should, in our analysis of these events, draw a distinction between the sparks and the tinder. The tinder is the underlying cause of a riot, the sparks being a specific event or set of events that set off the tinder. (See also Chapter 17.) Benyon identifies eight characteristics that were common to the 1980s riots – the underlying causes or tinder. He claims that these riots can be understood only with these underlying causes in mind. They were:

- high unemployment
- widespread deprivation
- racial disadvantage
- racial discrimination
- political exclusion
- powerlessness
- distrust of the police
- hostility towards the police.

As Matthews (1993), an advocate of the New Left realist perspective, has noted: crime, in all its varieties, is a complex social phenomenon, not easily attributable to one factor (see Figure 10.9). He comments:

... crime is, in an important sense, a socially-constructed phenomenon. Its meaning is profoundly influenced by considerations of time and space. Its construction is based on the interaction of four key elements – victims, offenders, the state and the public. These four dimensions constitute what realist criminologists have termed the square of crime.

(Matthews, 1993, p. 28)

In a similar vein, all crime (not solely that committed by or against members of ethnic groups) can be seen as a complex form of behaviour – a multi-dimensional process of meaningful intended and unintended action, interaction and labelling. In this sense, as Figure 10.9 illustrates, crime is a product of interaction between the state, the offender, the victim and the informal mechanisms of social control which operate in society.

In more recent times, many have noted how members of ethnic minorities may be disadvantaged and discriminated against, not just by the activities of police and criminals, but within the wider criminal justice system.

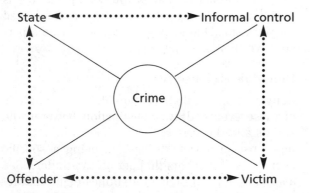

Figure 10.9 The square of crime
Source: Matthews (1993)

Control theory and policing

Control, prevention and victimology

The New Right realist camp have adopted what has become known as a control approach to crime. This approach attempts to limit the frequency of crime by a policy of target-hardening – moving potential law-breakers on towards harder targets in the hope that the effort involved in this will deter them altogether.

Crime as a 'rational choice'

Control theory operates with a view of criminal nature as being essentially rational: crime is committed when the chances are highest of getting a maximum reward with the minimum of risk. This has implications both for crime prevention and for policing. Does it mean, to use a popular media image, that policing cannot stop the 'rising sea of crime'? Control theory also has implications for those of us in society unfortunate enough to become victims. Does it mean that those who have experienced crime have an individual responsibility to target-harden, or should this be a collective or community responsibility?

Solving or reducing crime?

Discussion point

Has crime got out of hand? Will we ever be able to reduce and solve crime – or just find different ways to manage it?

Increasingly, the concept of crime prevention has become an important reality for many people, especially those who are defined, whether rightly or wrongly, as vulnerable and in fear of crime – such as women and the elderly, and those who have experienced the majority of total crime committed in the UK in recent times, in urban areas and inner cities. The desire to prevent crime has developed as a response to a crisis of confidence in the ability of governments, the police, the courts and social workers to reduce it.

Control theory

Control theory is based on the idea of the 'reasoning criminal'. Human actions are seen as the response by an individual through calculated reasoning to the situations around him or her. It is often referred to as 'situational control theory' because it emphasizes that crime occurs only if it is allowed to in specific situations. Crime is not a universal action; it is not always committed for the same reasons, but is specifically related to the ease, opportunity and absence of risk of detection that each situation presents.

Philosophical roots

Control theories of one type or another have an intellectual heritage which travels back in time, through Emile Durkheim to Thomas Hobbes (a seventeenth-century English philosopher) and Jeremy Bentham. These control theories are therefore influenced by functionalism.

Hobbes believed that human nature was greedy and competitive. Humans were only communal because they could profit from not living in a constant war of all against all. This is referred to as a 'social contract' – order, harmony and social stability are possible only by the creation of rules and moral laws (the contract) which groups follow because they are in their best interests. If the rules are broken, chaos will be created.

Bentham founded what is known as utilitarianism. This philosophy suggests that human nature is concerned with the search for pleasure and the avoidance of pain. The individual constantly takes stock of, or reflects on, his or her actions, situation and choices. The individual is seen as a calculating being who assesses the sum total of pleasure and pain in every situation before acting. If a given action will lead to a surplus of profit or pleasure, then this will be the path to take.

Crime deterrents

Contemporary control theory similarly has an image of the *criminal* as seeking reward, while avoiding situations where the dangers of being caught, arrested, identified or having time wasted which could be spent on another crime are obvious from the outset. Thus, so the idea goes, highly visible car locks, burglar alarms on houses and bars on windows will deter the rational criminal who will look for another target.

CCTV: Big Brother is watching you

Perhaps the biggest investment in recent years, based on control theory lines, is the development of closed-circuit television (CCTV) monitoring in large urban areas. Initial research appears to indicate that these schemes, while not reducing

Parents face delinquent bill

JAMES MEIKLE

LABOUR yesterday backed suggestions that affluent parents should pay for the behaviour of their delinquent offspring.

It endorsed measures to tackle youth crime being considered by the Audit Commission, the public spending watchdog, even as the commission stressed it had yet to develop an official view.

Alun Michael, Labour's home affairs spokesman, said: "Given that the burden of crime has increased so massively over recent years, it is right that a share of that should come from those who contribute to it."

Speaking on GMTV's Sunday programme, he said the commission, "which has done a very serious piece of work on this", had understood and analysed the point Labour had been making – "that there is a need to nip things in the bud to reduce youth offending".

Labour is keen to capitalise on the idea that prevention is better than cure for juvenile crime. It plans to try out curfews for young children on housing estates, and will welcome any report that suggests the present system is not working.

Simon Hughes, the Liberal Democrat spokesman on urban affairs and youth issues, said early reports of the commission's study sounded encouraging. "Parents should take more responsibility for anti-social acts committed by their children," he said.

"Youth provision should be properly co-ordinated but, above all, the teaching of good parenting to all youngsters before they leave school, nursery education for all three and four-year-olds, and activities for all young people outside school hours, including a nationwide expansion of youth services, will all make a difference." Punishment regimes had been shown to have failed badly.

According to the *Sunday Times*, the commission paper finds existing arrangements "expensive, inefficient and ineffective", and criticises punishment-led regimes such as boot camps which have led to a 25 per cent rise in reoffending.

Estimates of between £5 and £10 billion have been put on the cost of damage and replacement caused by juvenile crime. A further £1 billion is spent by police, the Crown Prosecution Service, the courts and local authorities on dealing with young offenders.

The commission is said to propose the creation of a single agency for the custody of young people and a national strategy to promote good behaviour. Parents should be made to accept their responsibilities to their children.

"Social services agencies which have to help and support children because their parents refuse to house them, for example, should have powers to recover some of the costs from parents."

While the paper concedes these powers would be of limited relevance to poor parents, it adds parents should be required to pay compensation for the consequences of anti-social behaviour and vandalism by their children. There is also backing for parenting lessons, of which a number already exist with different levels of formality.

Source: Guardian, 19 August 1996

the number of crimes committed, have had an effect on arrest rates and clear-up rates (Travis, 1995; Campbell, 1995c).

A new generation of theorizing

Control theory based on 'right-wing' tenets, and the 'left-wing' counterpart New Left realism, developed out of what Rock (1989) described as a 'theory bottleneck' – the theoretical stalemate reached within the sociology of deviance during the 1970s and 80s. From the late 1980s the expansion of criminology, both theoretically and in terms of university posts and research places, slowed to a halt. There has been no new generation of upstarts eagerly fighting with the old order for their place in the limelight in the sociology of deviance. As Rock comments:

Over time ... people get tired of rehearsing the same intellectual criticisms over and over again. ... The charms of theoretical debate decline, especially when the debate is between members of a group who have known one another for a very long time and can predict what the others will say and how they will reply in return. The outcome has been a decline in the rate of intellectual innovation. To a large extent, the sociology of deviance is preoccupied with an agenda that was established in the 1970s.

(Rock, 1989, p. 3)

💬 Discussion point

Why does sociology have so many different types of theories? How is this of value?

C3.1a

However, this intellectual bottleneck, this lack of interest in debate or theorizing, has recently been overcome. Contemporary debates concerning the merits of right-wing control theory versus New Left realism place the sociology of deviance firmly back into the heated debates and intellectual innovation which characterized its growth through the 1960s and 70s.

New Right realism

New Right realism, in adopting control theory, has attacked what it sees as the liberal and left-wing ideology of many sociological accounts of crime, law and order. Right realists accuse social theorists of providing not a reason but an *excuse* for criminal behaviour while engaging in unnec-

essary abstract theorizing.

New Right ideas became popular in many quarters in the UK during the Thatcher Conservative administrations, and simultaneously in the USA in the Reagan years. They are frequently linked to political and economic free-market policies which seek to reduce the welfare state and put social responsibility firmly on to the individual's own shoulders. These ideas are expressed clearly in the works of Wilson (1975) and Van den Haag (1975).

Tame (1991) notes that, in popular usage, especially in politics and the media, the term New Right has:

... of late been once more applied to a very real phenomenon, the rise of schools of thought and writers whose common characteristic is a rejection of, or critical stance towards, the dominant worldview of socialism/Marxism in myriad forms, of doctrines of social determinism and social engineering, and of state interventionism in personal, political and economic life.

(Tame, 1991, p. 27)

The central features, or emphasis, of a New Right policy on crime and law and order, according to Tame, are the concepts of freedom, justice and responsibility. Although in a very general sense we could argue that most political ideologies have something to say about these concepts, the approach offered by the New Right is distinctive because it is made up of two traditions: liberalism and conservatism.

In the case of policing (or rather, of establishing law and order), New Right theorists such as Van den Haag suggest that strong and public punishments are necessary. To echo a famous slogan of the British Conservative party, these New Right theorists wish to be 'strong on law and order' – to show criminals and the wider population that disorder will not be tolerated and will be treated accordingly. Added to this idea is the concern that rehabilitative measures do more harm than good: they are ineffective and as a result encourage criminals to commit even more crime. Social workers in particular are seen as being too soft on the perpetrators of crime.

Case Study – The call for a children's curfew

Interestingly, many social ideas and policy suggestions from the Labour party in the mid-1990s were based on a similar call for individual and family responsibility, giving them common ground with the New Right realists.

Embracing what is broadly a control theory of crime, New Labour advocated the adoption of a children's curfew, with children being asked to stay indoors unless accompanied by an adult after a certain time in the evening. This idea places the responsibility for juvenile criminal activity and delinquency firmly in the hands of the parents – it is up to the family to police itself and is possibly a recognition that the police force can no longer be reasonably expected to afford the time to patrol the streets as a visible presence.

This idea, that families must face up to their shared responsibility for curbing delinquency, adopted by those on the Left and the Right for different reasons and to different extents, is reflected in the article on page 355, 'Parents face delinquent bill'. (See also Section 8.4.)

10.7 Solutions to the problem of crime

Not all fears of crime are equally realistic. Crime is not an equal opportunity predator. The chance of becoming a victim will vary according to where you live, how you live, who you are, and who you know.

(Reiner, 1996, p. 4)

At the time of the first British Crime Survey in 1983 (based on data from 1981), the government claimed that it was irrational to fear crime: the public's concern over burglary and assaults was the product of media sensationalism which in turn resulted in more reporting, and so on (Jenkins, 1991).

Lea and Young: New Left realism

In response to the Home Office's claim that it was irrational to fear crime, the mid-1980s saw the rise of a new approach to law and order by left-wing thinkers. The New Left realist approach developed by Lea and Young (1993), and popular amongst some London councils, suggested that some citizens, particularly the urban working class, *should* fear crime. Lea and Young claimed that the majority of crime was committed by working-class people, yet the majority of victims of such crime were also working class – often from within the same communities.

As a response to what they saw as the inadequacies of official figures on crime, Lea and Young conducted the Islington Crime Survey, based in a small area of London. This revealed that the working-class residents were thoroughly rational to fear crime.

Understanding black crime

Lea and Young are critical also of some neo-Marxist attempts to politicize black working-class crime. They suggest that such idealistic approaches to crime ignore the fact that for many – including many black members of urban areas – crime is an unpleasant and harsh day-to-day reality. Lea and Young do largely accept the official crime statistics and the trends in relation to ethnicity that they show. They suggest that poor economic conditions, inadequate housing in ghettoized areas, unemployment and wider social racism result in more crime committed by people living under such unacceptable conditions.

Political ideology and media exaggeration of crime

Lea and Young are critical, too, of political, media and sociological treatments of crime from both left-wing and right-wing ideological assumptions:

We are caught between two opposing views on crime: the mass media and a substantial section of right-wing opinion are convinced that the crime rate is rocketing, that the war against crime is of central public concern and that something dramatic must be done to halt the decline into barbarism. The left, in contrast, seeks to minimize the problem of working-class crime; ... [it has] spent most of the last decade attempting to debunk the problem of crime. It has pointed to the far more weighty crimes of the powerful ... It sees the war against crime as a side-track from the class struggle.

(Lea and Young, 1993, p. 11)

Lea and Young criticize what they term the 'Left idealists' – those who seek to understand working-class crime as a stylized fight against the rich and powerful, a tactic in the class war. Instead, they recommend that a New Left realism about crime must seek to navigate between these two currents.

Victimology

Victimology is the name given to the sub-field of criminology that is concerned with the study of the victims of crime. It has been developing since the late 1940s and has been responsible for the British Crime Surveys. Victimology seeks to understand crime by trying to assess why those who are victims of crime were chosen as targets by criminals: to search for an underlying logic and order behind what are frequently seen as random or illogical events.

Walklate (1994) identifies the three main ingredients of 'realist victimology' which highlight the differences between this and the approach described above:

1   the wish to understand real-life problems as experienced by people

2   the wish to investigate the relationships between crime and the age, gender, class and ethnicity of both the criminal and the victim

3   to use local community-based victimization studies (such as the Islington Crime Survey) as a means of influencing local council policy.

What is to be done about law and order?

The ideas of Lea and Young, outlined in their publication *What is to be Done about Law and Order? Crisis in the Nineties* (1993), and the work of several others, has refuelled the contemporary criminological stage with argument, theorizing and debate. The New Left realists are unhappy about what they see as the crisis of explanation reached in modern British criminology, what they refer to as the 'aetiological crisis' – a lack of adequate explanations for the causes and prevention of crime. They have approached this crisis in two ways:

1   At a theoretical level, they wish to address the dominance of state-sponsored right-wing control theories, which they see as wholly inadequate in their attempt to simply move crime on through a policy of target-hardening.

2   At a methodological or research level, they have conducted and supported numerous small-scale victimization studies in Islington, Merseyside, Fulham and other places, in order to attack what they see as the inadequacies of the British Crime Surveys.

Considering themselves to be orientated towards the left in politics, the New Left realists are critical of what they see as the dominance of left idealism in contemporary British sociology.

However, Lea and Young suggest that to see all working-class crime as a fight against capitalism in the wider class struggle, as they claim the idealists do, is to fail the working classes. They argue that the working classes *do* commit the most crime, particularly street crime; but equally, they *suffer* from the largest amount of crime, living as they do in inner-city and other urban areas (see Figure 10.10).

Realism concerning the victims of crime

Lea and Young accuse the Left idealists of suffering from a contradictory position over crime: on the one hand the latter criticize crimes of racism and crimes against women (largely carried out in urban areas by the working classes), but in the same breath support working-class crime as a form of redistribution of wealth. Lea and Young argue that the Left idealists cannot have it both ways.

Realism concerning the causes of crime

The New Left realists do not wish to reject totally the notion of crime as a politically motivated activity. They understand that the motivation for some crime is, particularly in urban areas where the difference between the wealthy and the poor is so marked, from a sense of deprivation; but they also recognize that this is a thoroughly inadequate and ineffective start for any socialist style struggle against capitalism.

For Lea and Young, on the other hand, the causes of crime are manifold:

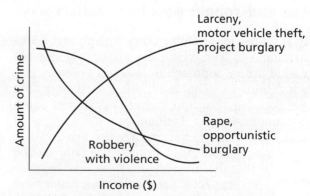

Figure 10.10 Types of criminal victimization by income
Source: Lea and Young (1993)

- *Social deprivation.* Low incomes, poverty, unemployment and poor living conditions lead to crime.

- *Poor political representation of the working classes.* Frustration at the inability to solve problems through political channels leads to an increasing sense of hostility against the establishment.

- *The nature of working-class subculture.* Developed out of a sense of frustration, the lifestyles chosen by some working-class people to solve their problems of living in a capitalist society often emphasize antagonism – against the police and authority in general.

Realism concerning the policing of crime

Lea and Young offer a number of solutions to crime, but stress that, ultimately, a radical socialist transformation of society is needed because the problems of day-to-day life as experienced by the working classes are largely a response to a divisive class society. We can identify three areas of interest here:

- community policing
- police involvement
- looking at social change.

Community policing

They advocate a return to community policing, in contrast to recent moves towards a military-style approach that they blame for the growing number of riots in inner-city areas from the 1980s onwards. Local community policing is needed to encourage members of working-class areas to stop seeing the police as the enemy, to start trusting the police once more and to report crime on a regular basis:

The causes of the shift towards military policing in the inner cities and peripheral housing estates we saw as a combination of economic decay and rising crime, police racism and the stereotyping of young people from these areas as criminals tout court, and developments in police technology which put more officers in cars and fewer on foot patrol, with a resulting decline in contact with the community.

(Lea and Young, 1993, p. xix)

The point is made that distrust of the police and under-reporting leads to a general fear of crime because nothing appears to get done about it.

This fear of crime in turn can lead to an increase in actual criminal acts (see Figure 10.11).

In keeping with this idea, Lea and Young also argue that police marginalization from the community over trust will also result in more crime. Criminals are less at risk of being caught, and the police themselves, frustrated with a lack of support and information, may need to break normal legal operating procedures in order to make arrests. In doing so, they could appear to the community as even less trustworthy (see Figure 10.12).

Minimal police involvement

Lea and Young advocate a return to consensus policing, whereby the public are encouraged to go to the police for help, asking them to become involved in the community – in contrast to the trend towards armed and rapid-response patrolling.

Social change

Finally, Lea and Young make the point that, however much police reform is advocated or

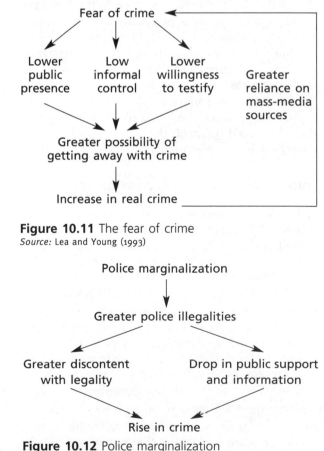

Figure 10.11 The fear of crime
Source: Lea and Young (1993)

Figure 10.12 Police marginalization
Source: Lea and Young (1993)

attempted, no real progress can be made without adequate social change of a long-term variety:

As long as the basic combination of economic decay, rising crime and lack of local democratic control over policing persist in the inner cities and poorest areas, then a shift towards consensus policing is a utopian dream. Whatever the training programmes say, the pressures generated by the ghettoised police subculture to stereotype ethnic groups, working-class young people and inner-city areas will continue.

(Lea and Young, 1993, p. xx)

The female fear of crime

What the official measurements of crime, such as the British Crime Surveys, show is the marked difference between the male and female fear of crime, especially amongst the elderly, and in inner cities.

Heidensohn suggests that a paradox exists in how traditional criminology treats the female fear of crime. In placing an emphasis on the female fear of *street* crime, conducted by a stranger to the victim, little attention is given to the fact that crime against women is greatest in the home, between husband and wife, or mother and son.

Stanko (1988) suggests that, in emphasizing the fear of impersonal crime against women – that committed by a stranger – the ideology of the family is once more reinforced. It is seen as a universally warm and safe place, ignoring the discipline and control the family traditionally exerts on its female members.

Implications for policy formation

Heidensohn comments that women's fear of crime, highlighted by sociological and criminological research, feminist or otherwise, has had an effect on recent policy formation – especially the attention given by local councils in the inner cities to adequate street lighting, women-only registered taxis, self-defence classes and closed-circuit television (CCTV) monitoring. Although such policies are still only piecemeal, they do represent a growing concern with women's issues unlike anything seen before. Feminist sociology, suggests Heidensohn, has to be thanked for this, but the fight against gendered crime is far from over.

Further reading

Accessible texts designed to introduce the key debates in this field include:

- Aggleton, P. (1991) *Deviance*, London: Routledge.
- Lawson, T. and Heaton, T. (1999) *Crime and Deviance*, London: Macmillan.
- Marsh, I. (1986) *Crime*, London: Longman.
- Moore, S. (1996) *Investigating Deviance*, 2nd edn, London: Collins Educational.

Another text, treating the subject in some depth, is:

- Heidensohn, F. (1989) *Crime and Society*, London: Macmillan.

Important studies which are accessible and of theoretical and empirical significance include:

- Lea, J. and Young, J. (1993) *What is to be Done about Law and Order? Crisis in the Nineties*, London: Pluto Press.
- Pearson, G. (1983) *Hooligan: A History of Respectable Fears*, London: Macmillan.

Back issues of the periodical *Sociology Review* (formerly *Social Studies Review*) also contain articles on this field and many others.

11

Power and control
Education

Chapter outline

Education, socialization and identity

11.1 Education and socialization   *page 362*
This section considers theories of education that consider the way education functions in relation to socialization. It goes on to consider processes of cultural transmission and cultural reproduction. In particular it considers theories in the functionalist and Marxist traditions.

11.2 Institutional processes in education   *page 367*
This section considers those theories that look at the role of educational institutions themselves and the interactions within them, including the role of the hidden curriculum and of streaming and labelling processes, to try to explain the way in which education functions in society. In particular, it considers theories in the interactionist and post-structuralist traditions.

Patterns and trends in educational achievement

11.3 Social class and educational achievement   *page 374*
This section looks at the trends in terms of educational attainment by social class over time and goes on to investigate whether recent educational reforms have opened up or reduced opportunities.

11.4 Ethnicity and educational achievement   *page 380*
This section looks at the rise of multi-cultural and anti-racist education and more recently of post-structuralist critiques of these developments. It also looks at some of the evidence on the debate about black under-achievement.

11.5 Gender and educational achievement   *page 384*
This section looks at arguments about the differential educational achievements of boys and girls. It goes on to consider debates about single-sex schools and whether such schools are affected by the marketization of education.

11.6 Educational participation and the implications for policy and provision   *page 391*
This section considers a range of debates surrounding notions of participation including the emergence of IQ testing, the concern with special educational needs and the rise of inclusive education, and the emergence of New Labour's 'Third Way' approach to education.

Power, control and the relationship between education and the economy

11.7 Education and training: the vocational and academic curriculum   *page 403*
This section considers the emergence of concerns about the link between education and employment, and the rise of the marketization of education. It also considers some of the arguments about vocational education including the effect of the new vocationalism on the shifting power in education between the central and local state, employer, parents and teachers.

11.8 Theories of the transition from school to work   *page 414*
This section considers some of the theories which have looked at the transition from school to work, the changing nature of this transition and the implications of this for young people today.

11.1 Education and socialization

This section considers the role that education plays in the process of socialization. Sociologists distinguish between the processes of primary and secondary socialization. Primary socialization largely occurs within the context of the family and is concerned with the process of cultural learning relating to the acquisition of norms, values, attitudes, beliefs, language skills and other skills necessary to begin functioning in society. It is also the case that this early process of socialization is linked into the beginning of the development of personal identity. Since the early years of education are also concerned with these processes they also could be said to form part of the process of primary socialization.

Secondary socialization refers to the later stages of socialization beginning in the later stages of childhood and identity formation and continuing throughout a person's life. The key agency of secondary socialization is undoubtedly the education system but there are also other influences at work here, notably that of the peer group (also important in relation to the experience of education), the mass media, religion and the possible continuing role of the family.

Overall, therefore, socialization refers to the process whereby the norms and values of society are taught to new members of that society, and the way that this process contributes to the construction of personal identity. Since the education system plays a central role in this, education is therefore part of the cultural transmission process and various sociologists have commented on this role of function of education. This has also led to debates about the place of education in the culture of society and whether it encourages cultural reproduction or cultural resistance. These concepts will all be considered in this section.

Functionalist theories of education and socialization

The sociology of education: Basil Bernstein and his influences

Emile Durkheim

Emile Durkheim (1858–1917) has been very influential in the sociology of education, especially in the work of Basil Bernstein. Bernstein constantly acknowledges the influence, particularly as he feels Durkheim rather than any other social theorist is a source of what the term 'social' means. Bernstein explained the importance of Durkheim to him:

[I read] Durkheim and although I did not understand him it all seemed to happen. I did not care that he was a naughty functionalist with an over-socialised concept of man, that he neglected the institutional structure and the sub-strata of conflicting interests, that his model of man contained only two terms, beliefs and sentiments. In a curious way I did not care too much about the success of his various analyses. It was about the social bond and the structuring of experience.

(Quoted in Atkinson, 1985, p. 21)

Education and socialization

These concerns about the 'social' became central to Bernstein's sociology. What did Durkheim have to say about education? Durkheim emphasized the moral force of education, the way in which children internalize the values and beliefs of society to become 'social' beings. So for Durkheim, the main function of education was the development of social solidarity through the transmission of a collective culture, not just a family culture based on kinship. Primary socialization was carried out by the family and secondary socialization by education and the schools. The main problem was to resolve the divisions of modern industrial society, especially reconciling individualism and social solidarity. This meant the need to reconcile the construction of personal individual identities with the maintenance of a stable society where norms and values are internalized by all members. The role of the education system was centrally concerned with both these functions, thus providing education with a somewhat difficult balancing act.

The division of labour

Bernstein was particularly drawn to Durkheim's work on the division of labour, the distinction between mechanical and organic solidarity – mechanical solidarity characterizing pre-industrial societies with a simple division of labour, and organic solidarity characterizing industrial society with a complex and interdependent division of labour. Durkheim used them to characterize whole societies, but Bernstein uses them to look at principles of differentiation within societies. Specifically he looks at the nature and consequence of the change from mechanical to organic solidarity on education systems. This is clearly seen in his work on the organization and transmission of school knowledge. Durkheim's work and his influence on functionalism generally are also discussed in Sections 3.3, 7.8 and 10.1.

Mary Douglas

The notion of boundaries between subjects is a key theme in Bernstein's work, and this brings us on to another influence. Traditional forms of knowledge are regarded as sacred and have strong boundaries. Newer forms of knowledge have weaker boundaries. This work on boundary maintenance between subjects is partly the result of the influence of Mary Douglas, a structural anthropologist. Her work (1966) focuses on why some things – particularly food – are considered polluting and dangerous. This is because they break systems of classification.

Discussion point

For Douglas, matter out of place breaks classification systems and is considered dangerous. What other areas of social life could this be applied to?

C3.1a

Bernstein and the classification of school subjects

Bernstein applied this notion to the classification of school subjects. Classification is the organization of knowledge into curricula – what is thinkable and what is not. Strong classification means that the curriculum is highly differentiated and separated into traditional subjects, and weak classification means that the boundaries are fragile. 'Framing' refers to the degree of control teachers and pupils have over the selection, organization, pacing and timing of the knowledge taught and learnt. The curriculum, the teaching methods and evaluation are three message systems. Underlying these message systems are codes, rather like Bourdieu's *habitus*, a regulating grammar. (This is like the grammar in a language which tells you which words you can or cannot put together, and how to do so.) These codes were developed into two ideal types which

Table 11.1 Collection code and integrated code

Collection code	Integrated code
Strong classification and framing	Weak classification and framing
Highly specialized, pure forms of selection and combination	Flexibility of control of knowledge
Hierarchical relationships	Horizontal relationships
Authoritarian control	Self-regulatory control
Visible pedagogy	Invisible pedagogy
Traditional academic	Progressive
Sacred	Profane
Pure	Polluting
Examples: physics, maths, English, Latin, history	*Examples: integrated humanities, media studies, women's studies*

do not exist in pure forms – integrated code and collection code (see Table 11.1).

Bernstein looked at the way in which the change from collection code to integrated code represents the change from mechanical to organic solidarity. The curriculum is the message system of the school which privileges middle-class pupils because they come to school with access to the codes. Working-class pupils, on the other hand, are not able to meet their requirements. In this way the message system reproduces within schools the social class inequalities of the society. There is a link between the codes of the school and the families that they serve.

Conflicts between the 'old' and 'new' middle class were reflected in the debate over progressive education in the 1970s: the integration code was favoured by the new middle class and the collection code by the old middle class. More recently there have been conflicts over the curriculum: vocational education emphasizing skills is favoured by neo-liberals, and traditional subjects are favoured by neo-conservatives. (See Section 11.7.)

Bernstein's work is difficult to understand and largely theoretical. It does provide a useful theory of the 'how' and 'what' of the curriculum and the relationship between power and knowledge. The curriculum is seen as a codified reflection of societal and ideological interests. In this way Bernstein's work sits firmly in the French structuralist tradition.

Activity

a Why might certain subjects in the curriculum be considered dangerous or polluting? Use Table 11.1 to help you answer this question. Has this affected the subjects' status or popularity?

b What is the relationship between production, the needs of employers and the curriculum in schools and colleges?

c Where pupils have some control over the selection, organization, pacing and timing of the knowledge taught and learnt, is this to their advantage?

C3.2, C3.3

American functionalist views on education and society

Functionalism was developed by American sociologists like Talcott Parsons and Davis and Moore between the 1930s and 1960s (see also Section 3.3). Central to this work was an analysis of the ways in which the educational system functions in society. If talent is unequally distributed, then the education system plays a central role in the allocation of the most talented to the occupations that are functionally most important for society. This implies a meritocratic model in which everyone has an equal chance to be unequal.

Discussion point

Are a meritocracy and an equal society the same thing?

C3.1a

Functional importance is decided by the length and specialist training required for particular occupations. It is claimed that to be a brain surgeon, for example, takes much more talent, education and training than to be a nurse. Therefore in order to ensure that people are prepared to undertake long and expensive training the rewards offered must be substantially greater for surgeons than for nurses:

A medical education is so burdensome and expensive that virtually none would undertake it if the MD did not carry a reward commensurate with the sacrifice.

(Davis and Moore, 1945, p. 244)

Inequality is therefore functionally necessary. If everyone had the same levels of pay and status no one would be prepared to take on the more difficult and responsible jobs, it is argued.

Criticisms of functionalism

There are many criticisms of this position on the role of education.

1 It assumes firstly that all pupils start from the same point – a level playing-field – whereas in fact some children start with large amounts of cultural capital in the form of language, attitudes, confidence and manners that privilege them in schools. Parents pass on such advantages to their children. Looked at closely it may not take a lot more training, education and skills to become a surgeon rather than a nurse. This difference may be a mechanism to protect the privileged position held by the minority in the top jobs.

2 It also assumes a value consensus where everyone agrees about the most important jobs and shares the same values to be transmitted through society by schools.

Activity

'The best people get the best jobs because they have received the best education.' Evaluate this statement by drawing up three arguments *for* the statement and three *against*, using a functionalist perspective on education.

C3.2, C3.3

Functionalism is not a dominant perspective in sociology at the moment, but some of the ideas in crude form seem similar to New Right ideas (see Section 6.3 for a discussion of this).

Marxist views on education and society

In the sociology of education there are a variety of 'Marxisms', all drawing on different interpretations and developments of the work of Marx. It can be useful to divide them into structuralist and humanist Marxisms. (See also Section 3.3.)

Marxists like Bowles and Gintis, Bourdieu and Althusser come from the structuralist perspective within sociology. The term 'structuralist' has two meanings. Firstly it means theories that put emphasis on the structure of society as a system of functioning institutions as their starting point. The second meaning is quite difficult to understand but important to do so in order to understand post-structuralism. Structuralism has been influenced by anthropology, mainly the work of Lévi-Strauss: it means that language defines social reality for us. The structures of society are internalized in us through language, a social system of signs and symbols which we use when we think and speak. We only know the meanings of things because we can name them. This theory signals the death of the 'subject'. We are determined, our stories are written for us. (See also Sections 13.2 and 16.1.) This is the opposite of social action theory where social actors create their social worlds:

Althusser rejects completely the idea that humans can be 'subjects' – creative agents ... in charge of their lives and worlds. For him, human life is always entirely structured. ... Althusserian Marxism thus sees itself as heir to the late Marx – to writings produced towards the end of Marx's life, when he tried to build a scientific analysis of the structure of capitalism – as opposed to the work of the 'young' or early Marx whose heirs are humanist Marxists like Gramsci.

(Jones, 1993b, p. 63)

Humanist Marxists give much more power to human agency as a means of change.

Structural Marxism

Althusser: the role of education in society

Althusser (1971b) identified three levels in class society:

• the economic
• the political
• the ideological.

Although the economic determines the other levels in the last instance, the ideological and political have 'relative autonomy' and are not directly or crudely determined.

Althusser looked at the way in which the state exercises power through repressive state apparatuses like the courts, army, police and law. The state also rules through ideology, using ideological state apparatuses, like the media, culture, religion and education.

Education has now replaced religion as the main ideological state apparatus. In schools children receive the ideology that prepares them for their role in capitalist society. This includes the rules of good behaviour, skills and knowledge needed by capitalism. Althusser has been criticized for the similarities between his analysis and functionalism. His theory leaves little room for struggle or contradiction.

Discussion point

How is education ideological?

C3.1a

Bowles and Gintis: schooling and cultural transmission in capitalist America

Bowles and Gintis (1976) were influenced by Althusser in their study of the relationship between the education system and the economy. They stated that the roots of inequality in the USA are in the class structure, and the school system is one of the institutions that perpetuates this inequality. Despite educational reforms and claims that the USA is a meritocracy, educational achievement is just as dependent on parents' socio-economic background as it was 30 years before. The association between the length of schooling, ability and how much you earn is dependent on factors other than ability. Parents' social class, and the fact that ability improves the longer you stay in school, are crucial factors. The 'intelligence quotient' (IQ) is evenly distributed in society, but power and income are not. The use of IQ to justify inequalities of outcome places the blame for educational failure on the students themselves:

The predatory, competitive and personally destructive way in which intellectual achievement is rewarded in US schools and colleges is a monument not to creative rationality, but to the need of a privileged class to justify an irrational, exploitative and undemocratic system.

(Bowles and Gintis, 1976, p. 107)

They claim that schools reflect the hierarchical division of labour in the economy through a correspondence between the social relations of production, school and family. This is transmitted through the values and organization of the school, in grades, fragmentation, alienation because of a lack of control over the curriculum, and discipline. Working-class schools are authoritarian whereas middle-class schools are more open and democratic, in the same way as workplaces. This correspondence allows the education system to produce an amenable and fragmented labour force.

💬 Discussion point

To what extent does daily life in your school or college correspond to that in the workplace?

C3.1a

Bowles and Gintis conclude that the creation of an equal and liberating school system requires a revolutionary transformation of economic life. They encourage teachers to become effective subversives by teaching the truth about society, encouraging a sense of collective power and fighting ideologies of privilege like racism and sexism.

Criticisms of Bowles and Gintis

1 Bowles and Gintis have been criticized for ignoring the role of the state and its mediation between education and the economy.

2 They are seen as being over-deterministic in that they see students as somewhat passive receivers of ideology (this is a criticism also made of Althusser).

3 They also ignore what is transmitted by schools – the content of the curriculum.

Bourdieu: cultural reproduction

Bourdieu (1977), another neo-Marxist, looked at the way in which schools in France reproduce social and economic inequalities. (See also Section 16.1.) He examined the relationship between the culture acquired in the family, in the school and that of the ruling class. Central to this are three concepts:

• cultural capital
• *habitus*
• relative autonomy.

Cultural capital

Through their families, children of the dominant class acquire cultural capital. Their culture is similar to that which permeates education. They have the right manners, accent, confidence and know-how. This is the same culture as the teachers who teach them. They have the right language (linguistic capital) to unlock the categories used in formal education. Possession of cultural capital means the ability to engage with the high culture so prized in traditional academic education. Education is a message system: possession of cultural capital privileges middle-class children who arrive at school equipped with the code to decipher the message of the dominant culture.

Habitus

These underlying rules, like grammar in a language, are what Bourdieu calls *habitus*, the rules of the game to succeed.

Relative autonomy

Bourdieu also uses the concept of 'relative autonomy'. This means that schools have the appearance of being independent of the economy, which makes them appear neutral and fair.

The sum of these processes, according to Bourdieu, is the social reproduction of the dominant class. The main function of the education system is not to transmit knowledge but to select, to differentiate, to categorize. This is achieved by making socially acquired linguistic and cultural competencies appear natural in those students who succeed. Bourdieu recognizes, however, that some working-class children do break the code and succeed against the odds.

Criticisms of Bourdieu

Bourdieu has been criticized for the same reasons as Bowles and Gintis and Althusser. He sees only one culture, that of the dominant class, and students are cultural dupes who passively accept their failure. Such theories are also very abstract and not rooted in the complexities and contradictions of real classrooms and schools. However, they have been very influential in the development of further research by sociologists. Their real importance lies in exposing the power relations at work in educational systems that appear neutral and fair. They also help to account for the persistence of working-class under-achievement.

Transformation

The foregoing studies of social and cultural reproduction have led to interesting debates by Marxists about the role of education in society, and particularly how teachers as organic intellectuals can change society. Organic intellectuals are those workers who attempt to develop a socialist political consciousness in those with whom they work.

The American sociologists Apple (1986) and

Giroux (1989) have focused on the possibilities for counter-hegemonic struggles in schools and the development of radical pedagogy. Radical pedagogy means developing in students the ability to act and think critically so that the true nature of class society is uncovered and possibly transformed. The terms hegemonic and organic intellectuals come from Gramsci, a humanist Marxist. (See Section 13.2.) Hegemony helps to explain how the ruling class hold on to power over subordinated groups in society. They do this by winning the consent of subordinated groups to the existing social order in a way that this order is taken for granted, seen as natural and normal. This has to be constantly fought for and is done by taking seriously some of the interests of subordinate groups. Schools are possible sites for counter-hegemonic struggle, rather than merely passing on dominant meanings and values according to Giroux.

These ideas have recently come under attack from feminist post-structuralists like Ellsworth (1989) and Lather (1991). They are particularly critical of the notion of radical pedagogy which they feel speaks in an abstract and disempowering way about all classrooms, all teachers, all stu-

dents. They find it arrogant and prescriptive – 'what we can do for you! – which disempowers the very people it seeks to empower. They say it hides such educators' own positions as wielders of power in education. Education itself is regarded by feminist post-structuralists as fundamentally a paternalistic project.

11.2 Institutional processes in education

For a long time, consideration of the role and effectiveness of education was concerned with the extent to which it reproduced the cultures and inequalities of the wider society in which it was located. The key here was the relationship between the home and the school and the key variables on school performance were seen to lie outside the school.

Newer approaches argued that what happens inside educational institutions is actually an important element in itself in determining the effect of education. This led to an emphasis on processes such as labelling, streaming, the hidden curriculum and debates about what counts as knowledge inside the classroom. The key theoretical inspirations behind these newer approaches was a concern with interactions and the work of symbolic interactionists played a large part in ensuring these issues became part of the agenda of the sociology of education.

Symbolic interactionism: labelling theory and the self-fulfilling prophecy

Symbolic interactionism covers a range of different approaches and traditions but is associated mainly with the Chicago School. It has its roots in the work of John Dewey, George Herbert Mead and Herbert Blumer. In relation to education, some of the most interesting work in this perspective has been produced by Howard Becker. His work on labelling and the self-fulfilling prophecy, sub-cultures, educational careers and the ideal client has been very influential in the work of sociologists studying education. Ethnographic studies of schools which originated from within this perspective also have an established place in sociology.

Activity

Working in small groups, discuss the following statements and sort them into 'agree', 'disagree' and 'don't know'. Report back to the whole group.

- Teachers working as organic intellectuals is the same as indoctrination.

- Teachers are relatively powerless to change society.

- Any attempts at radical pedagogy are now impossible because of the National Curriculum.

- The idea of schools as sites for counter-hegemonic struggles is totally unrealistic in the twenty-first century.

- Students are interested only in good grades, not in transforming society.

- New Right ideas are dominant in education because of the failure of socialist educational reforms.

- Some small gains can be made by the collective action of teachers, parents and students.

C3.1a, C3.1b

Labelling theory and the self-fulfilling prophecy

Becker

Labelling theory was developed by Becker (1951, 1963) in relation to the study of deviance and was later applied to the study of teachers' interactions with pupils. Two classic studies illustrate this work well.

Rist

In Rist's (1977) ethnographic study of an elementary school in a black community of St Louis, USA, a teacher made children sit at tables according to her evaluations of their academic ability. These were based on social class. The poor children whose parents were on welfare became known as the 'clowns' by second grade, and sat at one table; the working-class children, the 'cardinals', sat at another; and the 'tigers', the middle class, sat at a third. Rist followed these children through first and second grades and found that the initial labels had stuck. What had begun as subjective evaluations became objective ones as the school continued to process the children on the basis of the initial labels.

Rist measured how the teacher operationalized her expectations of these groups of children by the amount of time she spent with them, and her use of praise. He then applied the concept of a self-fulfilling prophecy. He reminds us of the central premise of this:

If men [sic] define situations as real, they are real in their consequences.

(W. I. Thomas, 1909)

So if the 'clowns' accepted the false initial definition of their ability and performed on the basis of it over a period of time, then it has become a self-fulfilling prophecy.

Rosenthal and Jacobson

A second study, the controversial *Pygmalion in the Classroom* by Rosenthal and Jacobson (1968), also illustrates early work in this area. They found that when teachers were told that some pupils whom they had randomly chosen were 'intellectual bloomers' (i.e. bright) this caused the teachers to treat them differently, and they performed better at the end of the year. This study received a great deal of criticism, mainly about the methods used as they had not actually observed changes in expectations and behaviour. They

analysed pre- and post-test data (IQ scores) but not what happened in between. This led Rist to reiterate when evaluating these studies that teachers' expectations are *sometimes* self-fulfilling.

> ### 💬 Discussion point
> To what extent do you agree that students disregard the labels teachers attach to them because 'teachers are not significant'?
>
> C3.1a

Labelling theory has been used to investigate deviance in schools through the social typing of pupils. Hargreaves (1967), amongst others, has looked at subcultural development in a secondary school through the labelling of pupils. Ball (1981) studied the banding of pupils in a comprehensive school moving to mixed-ability teaching. He analysed the ways in which teacher expectations affected the academic performance and behaviour of pupils in different bands. (Labelling theory is also discussed in Section 10.5.)

Case Study – The work of David Gillborn

A study by Gillborn (1990) aimed to understand the experiences of African–Caribbean and South Asian pupils in a comprehensive school in the English Midlands. It was strongly influenced by Howard Becker (1951). Gillborn drew especially on Becker's work on teachers' notions of the 'ideal client', a construction drawn from their own lifestyle and culture:

Professionals depend on their environing society to provide them with clients who meet the standards of their image of the ideal client. Social class cultures, among other factors, may operate to produce many clients who, in one way or another, fail to meet these specifications and therefore aggravate one or another of the basic problems of the worker–client relation.

(Becker, 1952; quoted in Gillborn, 1990, p. 149)

Research aims

The focus of Gillborn's study was the ways in which ethnic differences influence how teachers perceive their pupils. He found that African–Caribbean pupils, both male and female, received a disproportionate amount of punishment and criticism from teachers. Even where pupils from different ethnic groups were engaged in the same behaviour, it was the African–Caribbean pupils who were singled out for criticism. Gillborn gives an example of this from his classroom observations:

Paul Dixon (Afro-Caribbean) and Arif Aslam (Asian) arrived seven minutes late for a mixed ability lesson that I observed. ... almost half an hour into the lesson most of the group were working steadily and, like the majority of their peers, Paul and Arif were holding a conversation while they worked. The teacher looked up from the pupil he was dealing with and shouted across the room: 'Paul. Look, you come in late, now you have the audacity to waste not only your own time but his (Arif's) as well.'

(Gillborn, 1990, p. 31)

Paul is blamed whereas Arif is regarded as a blameless victim. But was this just an isolated incident? Gillborn asked pupils in his two case-study classes to answer some sentence completion items, such as '..... is picked on by some teachers'. Half the pupils nominated African–Caribbean pupils, yet they constituted only 10 per cent of the age group. This was supported by data from interviews with pupils:

Gillborn: 'Do you think the teachers particularly like or dislike some people?'
James (a white pupil): 'I think some are racialist.'
Gillborn: 'In what ways would you see that?'
James: 'Sometimes they pick on the blacks. Sometimes the whites are let off. When there's a black and a white person, probably just pick on the black person.'

(Gillborn, 1990, p. 31)

Findings

Many teachers were unconscious of their behaviour. The source of this conflict was often in the teachers' responses to the pupils' sense and display of their ethnicity, such as styles of speech, dress and manner of walking. This was considered by some teachers as a challenge to their authority, which Gillborn calls 'the myth of the black challenge'. He is careful to point out that this process is complex.

Often work in the symbolic interactionist field is accused of claiming that once a person is 'labelled' he or she will automatically internalize that judgement and act accordingly by committing further deviant acts. Instead Becker identified several factors which may lead to the development of a 'deviant career'. Among the most important is when those in authority – in this case teachers – go on to constantly reinforce the initial negative judgement in subsequent interactions. By analysing official disciplinary procedures, such as report cards, detentions and exclusions, Gillborn found that this was the case: report cards were a possible source of the reinforcement of 'deviant' labels. With such cards the total number given was small, but a much greater proportion of African–Caribbean pupils received at least one report card – 37 per cent compared with 6 per cent of pupils of all other ethnic origins. Similarly with detentions – 68 per cent received at least one senior management detention during the research period. This was true for both sexes and unique to pupils of African–Caribbean origin. A majority of these went on to have a total of four or more such detentions. In this way their 'deviant careers' begun in classroom interaction were developed and continued through the school's disciplinary procedures.

How did these pupils respond to such conflictual relationships with their teachers? Gillborn outlines two forms of response at each end of a range of different adaptational styles and subcultures. He focuses on three lads, Wayne, Barry and Roger, who formed a subculture but who were not anti-school: theirs was not a counter-school culture. Nevertheless, increasing conflict with the school led to their educational failure – one expulsion and no exam passes. This subcultural group's responses were compared with those of another African–Caribbean pupil, Paul, who avoided conflict by playing down his ethnicity in order to succeed academically against all odds. He carefully distanced himself from other pupils who were regarded as trouble and from teachers with whom he was likely to come into conflict.

Conclusion

Gillborn does emphasize the complexity of interactions: he says it is not an either/or question of 'resist' or 'accommodate', but rather a spectrum of possible responses. He also studied the experience of South Asian male pupils in the school and found it different from both their African–Caribbean and white peers. He found that teachers' stereotypes of Asian culture and traditions did not mean that all of their assumptions operated against the pupils' interests, as it did with African–Caribbean boys. Asian pupils were much more likely to have positive relationships with teachers, who tended to regard them as hard-working and from homes where education was highly valued.

Gillborn focuses on male experience and ethnicity. The influence of gender, though mentioned in his book in relation to other ethnographic research, is not explored fully. This is a pity, especially as he found that black male and female pupils experienced the same level of conflict with teachers but he studied only the male response. This raises an interesting issue about whether it is possible for male researchers to develop the rapport and interaction with female pupils necessary in this kind of research.

> ### 💬 Discussion point
>
> What problems do you think may be encountered, by either male or female researchers, in schools or colleges when carrying out research on students of the opposite sex?
>
> C3.1a

Internal selection: streaming and setting

The issue of whether to separate children into groups by ability and the potential effects of this were a key issue in early studies of the sociology of education. Studies by David Hargreaves (1967, *et al.* 1975) showed the importance of the way teachers classified their pupils and this information led to the idea that teachers' views could have an important influence on the educational career of the pupils. One clear way that this could occur is that teachers' views were most important in distributing pupils to different streams. Streaming was designed to ensure that pupils of differing talents were given an appropriate education. However, the labelling theory suggested that the actual process of streaming could in itself affect the actual performance of pupils.

This idea was clearly proven in the work of Rosenthal and Jacobson (1968). They conducted research by informing teachers that certain pupils who had been selected at random were very able as measured on some tests they had conducted. The key fact was that this selection was not based on the tests but was truly random. The idea was to test the effect of teachers being informed that some pupils were very able on the way the teachers treated them and consequently on the educational success of the pupils. The conclusion of this study was that the teachers had high expectations of these pupils and this had an effect on the actual students' performance, lead-

ing to the finding that the teachers' expectations of pupils actually do have an effect on pupil performance.

Since 1988 there has been a return to internal selection by ability in many schools. This takes the form of either streaming, which is allocating pupils to classes for all subjects on the basis of ability, or setting, only for certain subjects (usually mathematics or modern foreign languages). Factors which sociologists claim have contributed to this trend include:

- pressure to re-structure pupil groupings to deal with the demands of prescribed National Curriculum content assessed by SATs (Standardized Assessment Tasks)
- tiered entry for GCSE examinations
- larger class size, making mixed-ability teaching more difficult.
- increased competition between schools arising from published league tables making methods of improving the A–C grades in GCSE examinations a priority
- lobbying by middle-class parents, whom schools are eager to attract, who make the assumption that their children will be in the top sets and that this is a way of protecting from them less desirable and badly behaved pupils in the lower sets.

(The above evidence is summarized from research by the following: Ball, Bowe and Gerwitz, 1996, Crozier, 1997 and Reay, 1998.)

What does the evidence about internal selection tell us?

The evidence for and against streaming is often complex and contradictory. Accumulated research (Hallam and Toutounji, 1996) suggests that streaming tends to improve the achievement of those in the top bands but to suppress the achievements in the lower sets having a detrimental effect on self-esteem. Schools generally justify their moves to grouping by ability as being beneficial to the highest achievers.

However, recent research (Boaler, 1997, 1998b) into teaching mathematics using different forms of internal selection has challenged this assumption. Boaler found that significant numbers of students, particularly young women, were disadvantaged by their placement in the highest ability groups. Their achievement was seriously diminished by the pressure they felt, the fast pace of the lessons and the mechanistic nature of the work they were given. The ablest students taught in mixed-ability classes attained significantly higher GCSE grades than those taught in top sets. A follow-up study (Boaler, 1998a) found that students taught in the top sets were the most negative about their learning experiences in the whole study. The study also found that students taught in lower sets were severely disadvantaged and described their experiences as dominated by boring, low-level work, and being labeled as failures. Further research is needed before these findings can be generalized to subjects other than mathematics and different types of schools.

Debates about classroom knowledge

A key element in debates about educational institutions was a consideration of the type of knowledge that they valued and considered important to pass on. This debate was crystallized with the publication of *Knowledge and Control* in 1971, edited by Michael Young.

In this book, Young outlined what he argued was a radical new approach to debates about education. He argued that the 'old' sociology of education had been too ready to accept the arguments of teachers and politicians in terms of explaining the failure of some groups in education, notably the relative failure of the working class.

He himself argued that it was important to consider the notion of classroom knowledge and the various processes through which what is considered important knowledge is decided.

Young and his colleagues therefore set out to consider and discuss why it was that we teach what we do teach and why some particular forms of knowledge are valued above other forms of knowledge. They argued that what is considered good knowledge in classrooms actually reflected the particular views of an élite upper-middle-class grouping in society whose views were not necessarily reflective of other views, but were nonetheless dominant. The development of the curriculum and the syllabus therefore reflected a particular middle-class viewpoint and not surprisingly middle-class pupils were better able to work with and achieve high standards in this knowledge.

In this sense the success of the middle-class is not surprising since schools value the knowledge associated with the middle-class, and work-ing-class students who do not have this knowledge are disadvantaged.

The criticisms of this position were that it has relativist implications since it criticizes those who seek to consider some forms of knowledge as more important than other forms of knowledge. This view is rejected by those who believe in the notion of high and mass culture and this view has been influential in devising the National Curriculum. It has also been argued that the recommendations of Young *et al.*, namely that we should value all forms of knowledge, would lead some people to be unable to get jobs since they would not possess the knowledge which employers and other influential groups in society deem important.

Debates about the impact of teachers and classroom knowledge

One key form in which the important factor of teachers' expectations of pupils could be quasi-publicly announced was in the process by which pupils were allocated to streams. Stephen Ball (1981), in his study of streaming at a comprehensive school, makes the clear point that the process of streaming in the secondary school is crucially based on reports on the pupils completed by primary school teachers. Ball showed that non-academic factors, such as social class background, played a role in this allocation process. Once pupils were in different streams they were treated differently by the teachers, thus reinforcing the original division. This led the pupils in the top stream to improve and those in the bottom stream to deteriorate, thus increasing the inequality of attainment between the different streams.

A further study of streaming undertaken by Nell Keddie (1973) also included consideration of the construction of classroom knowledge. She argued that one of the key issues that affected the way teachers evaluated the performance of pupils was by holding a view on what knowledge they considered important. Abstract rather than concrete knowledge was seen as superior. This led to those students able to express themselves in abstract terms being seen as more intelligent and therefore given greater encouragement, which reinforced and widened any initial inequalities that existed. This study confirms the importance of issues of classroom knowledge and debates about it for the actual achievements of pupils in the classroom.

This whole issue of the construction of

classroom knowledge led to a greater focus on exactly what was considered knowledge and how such decisions are reached. In their critique of the idea of knowledge and control, Young *et al.* precede and anticipate in their relativist stance the later arguments of post-structuralists and post-modernists.

Post-structuralism

It has been argued that there has been something of a crisis in sociology generally with the development of new perspectives, namely post-structuralism and post-modernism.

Post-structuralism is a sociological perspective which developed out of structuralism, whereas post-modernism is a much broader term. Sometimes the two terms are used interchangeably.

Post-modernism describes a movement which encompasses architecture, the arts and sciences as well as sociology. Post-modernists are critical of the Enlightenment period, which began in the seventeenth and eighteenth centuries, when science replaced religion to explain social phenomena, capitalism replaced feudalism, and rationality replaced superstition. Events in the twentieth century, such as the use of science for war and destruction, the demise of the Soviet Union and the continuation of sexism and racism, have led post-modernists to question grand theories like Marxism, as well as the products of rationality and science. (See also Sections 16.9 and 16.10.)

What is post-structuralism?

The central concept in this perspective is *discourse*: specific ways of thinking and talking about aspects of the world. Discourses are forms of knowledge which work like languages. Such languages or discourses have power over us because they define what we can think and say about the world. They are the thinkable and the unthinkable and the yet-to-be-thought. These discourses create us, our identity and subjectivity – they constitute us.

Discursive practices provide a link between thought, knowledge, language and action and are at the root of social life. These ideas come mainly from the French philosopher and historian Foucault. His ideas are difficult because of the language used and because they changed and developed over time. Foucault's work is, nonetheless, becoming very influential in the sociology of education.

Feminist post-structuralism

There are several examples of feminist research in the sociology of education using a post-structuralist framework. It is valued because it allows a move away from former macro-theories of education – grand theories that explain everything, which reduce everything to a single cause, usually either patriarchy or social class – towards much more complex and fluid notions of power:

When girls are seen as multiply located, and not unambiguously powerless, a feminist approach to classroom research must shift away from the 'disadvantage' focus. An interest in the unevenness of power means that ... studies might focus on the ways in which girls are variously positioned in the classroom.

(Jones, 1993a; quoted in Weiner, 1994, p. 69)

Case Study – Frogs and snails and feminist tales

Davies (1989) carried out research in Australia using a post-structuralist framework. She values this perspective because:

If we see society as being constantly created through discursive practices then it is possible to see the power of those practices not only to create and sustain the social world but also to see how we can change that world through a refusal of certain discourses and the generation of new ones.

(Davies, 1989, p. xi)

Her research was inspired by two events. The first was her reading *The Paper Bag Princess*, a feminist fairy tale, to a 5-year-old girl. In the story Prince Ronald is rescued by Princess Elizabeth, but instead of being pleased he is appalled by her appearance. The story ends with the princess skipping off into the sunset and the words 'They didn't get married after all.' Davies realized that the ending was not appreciated by the 5-year-old, and that the story she was hearing was not the same story that the child was hearing.

The second event involved the same child's response to another girl called Penny, who looked and behaved like a boy. The first child was outraged that other children were calling a 'boy' by a girl's name.

These experiences raised the following questions: Why had the child not appreciated the feminist story? Why is it so important to get people's gender right? Why was Penny regarded as a problem by parents and other children?

Davies decided to investigate this in a two-year systematic exploration of children's understanding of feminist stories. She chose eight children aged four and five from varied social class backgrounds and spent hundreds of hours reading feminist stories to them. She also observed pre-school children playing and read them stories so that she could fit children's understanding of the stories to their actions in the everyday world.

Using post-structuralist theory, she found that when children insist on sticking to traditional forms of femininity and masculinity it is because the male–female dualism is so central to the way their human identity is constructed. Children had difficulty with feminist stories because their ideas had already been shaped by the discourses of traditional children's stories in which all the characters are positioned as either male or female. That was what they had come to expect and how they made sense of the world.

Davies hopes that through this kind of action, the reading of feminist stories, children will be able to see masculine and feminine qualities as a range of options rather than two types of behaviour – these types being related to biological reproduction and relatively minor bits of anatomy. She hopes we will come to question how the social world could have been seen in terms of two types of people.

Davies' research can be criticized for not considering sufficiently how her presence may have affected the children's behaviour. She perhaps should also have considered how a child's experience of the world differs from that of an adult, as a framework to discuss their responses.

A critique of post-structuralism and post-modernism in education

Beverley Skeggs (1991) provides an interesting and amusing critique in which she states that her aim is to stop educationalists wasting their time over ideas that are of very little use or have been said before. Here is a summary of her criticisms:

1 Post-modernism is an attempt by disillusioned male academics to win back power and influence in a world where there is a decline in the demand for their services.

2 Theorists like Lyotard claim that one of the purposes of post-modernism is to destroy meta-narratives (grand theories), yet he simply constructs another called post-modernism.

3 The ideas have an exclusive status because only the highly articulate can play confidently with the language.

4 Foucault's ideas are useful for understanding the role of education in the reproduction of techniques of discipline and surveillance, but they cannot explain the effect of the central power of the state. For post-structuralists the state is seen as simply a multitude of local sites of micro power. For example, how can the imposition of the Education Reform Act 1988 be explained in post-modern terms, of a multitude of local sites of micro power alone?

5 Adopting a post-modernist position could lead to political inactivity and conservatism. If subjectivities (identities) are multiple and changeable and power is diffuse, then political struggle is difficult.

Activity

This is an activity to test your understanding of the various perspectives in the sociology of education. It is adapted from 'As if … an introduction to perspectives', in *A Handbook for Sociology Teachers* by Gomm and McNeill (London: Heinemann Educational, 1982). The class should be divided into small groups and each group allocated a 'statement' from the seven choices that follow. Your group should first identify the perspective and then discuss the questions *as if you are sociologists from that perspective* using material from the whole of this chapter. Finally, report back to the whole group.

1 'We would like you to think of the educational system as a means of producing a highly motivated, achievement-oriented workforce. Both the winners (high achievers) and the losers (low achievers) will see the system as just and fair because status is achieved in a situation where all have an equal chance.'
a Identify the perspective.
b How would you explain working-class under-achievement?
c How would you explain the existence of independent (private) schools?

2 'We would like you to think of the educational system as a site of a series of complex interactions between teachers and pupils. Through these interactions teachers label pupils as bright or dull or troublemakers, and these labels become self-fulfilling prophecies with pupils behaving accordingly. These labels are not fixed or unchangeable but are socially constructed.'

a Identify the perspective.

b How would you explain working-class under-achievement?

c Suggest how teachers might improve pupils' educational achievement.

3 'We would like you to think that the main role of the educational system is not to reduce inequalities but to reproduce them. Pupils are prepared for their work roles through a close correspondence between the social relations of the workplace and the social relations of the school. Subordinacy and discipline are rewarded while creativity, aggressiveness and independence are penalized.'

a Identify the perspective.

b How would you explain that the educational system appears to be fair?

c How would you explain teachers who encourage pupils to be critical of society?

4 'We would like you to think of the educational system as a marketplace. Parents and pupils are consumers, education is the product and teachers are deliverers of the curriculum. Through competition and choice the best use is made of educational resources and the wasteful role of local education authorities is minimized.'

a Identify the perspective.

b How would you explain a centrally imposed, statutory, National Curriculum?

c How would the market work for parents with statemented children with special educational needs?

5 'We would like you to think of the educational system as a male-dominated hierarchy with men in most of the powerful positions. In the curriculum, history and literature reflect the interests and activities of white, middle-class males. The main aim of the education system is to prepare young women for a domestic role in the family and that of a flexible worker in the economy.'

a Identify the perspective.

b How would you explain girls' success at GCSE relative to boys?

c How would you explain the improved take-up of places in higher education by mature women returners?

6 'We would like you to think of the educational system as the micro-politics of power relations in different localities. Schools, like prisons and hospitals, have their own histories and techniques of discipline and surveillance. Localized complexity describes such sites rather than any notion of centralized power.'

a Identify the perspective.

b How would you explain educational inequality?

c Explain how discipline is exercised by teachers.

7 'We would like you to see the educational system as a means by which some working-class lads celebrate their culture of masculinity by playing up teachers and being anti-academic. Pupils who conform to school rules by wearing uniform, carrying a briefcase, respecting teachers and working hard are ridiculed by these 'lads'. They think university is for middle-class hippies.'

a Identify the perspective.

b How would you explain working-class boys who achieve academically?

c How would you explain the behaviour of girls who behave in the same way as the 'lads'?

C3.1a, C3.1b, C3.2, C3.3

11.3 Social class and educational achievement

The origins of the sociology of education lay with attempts to consider whether social factors such as class, gender and ethnicity had an effect on the educational performance of pupils. This began a long tradition of research into inequalities of educational achievement, which continues to this day.

Social class inequalities in education

It is interesting that there was very little sociological research on social class and educational attainment in the 1990s, given that this has been the major preoccupation of sociologists of education since the 1960s. In what has come to be known as the 'old' sociology of education, working-class under-achievement, was explained largely by cultural factors outside the school. These were investigated by empirical studies of educational inequality. They were influenced by American functionalism but this was implicit. Karabel and Halsey describe the approach:

British researchers in education were as preoccupied with 'wastage' and 'dysfunctions' as their American colleagues but perhaps more animated by the egalitarian concerns of a country with a long established and politically organised Labour Movement. The attack by British sociologists on inequality of educational opportunity was not only that it was unfair, but also that it was inefficient.

(Karabel and Halsey, 1977, p. 10)

Their approach has been called 'political arithmetic', derived from social mobility studies and aimed at calculating the chances of reaching different levels in the educational system for pupils of different social class origins. The 1944 Education Act opened up educational opportunities to working-class pupils by making education free and compulsory for all pupils to age 15. Thus financial barriers which may have denied them access to education were removed. Despite this, class differences in educational attainment persisted.

The home and the school

Sociologists such as Douglas (1964) focused on home background to explain the relative failure of working-class children compared with their middle-class counterparts. He conducted a longitudinal study of 5362 children born in 1946, tracking them through primary and secondary schools. Douglas found that children of similar measured ability at age 7 varied a great deal in their educational attainment, and by 11 the gap had widened and these differences related to social-class background. Pupils were also much more likely to stay on at school if they were middle-class.

Douglas claimed that the greatest influence on attainment was parental attitudes. He measured this by the number of times parents visited the school. He also outlined other factors such as family size, early child-rearing practices, health and the quality of the school.

> ### 💬 Discussion point
> What are the factors that might affect the number of times parents visit a school? Is this necessarily a good indicator of their interest in their child's education?
>
> C3.1a

Compensatory education

The old sociology of education has been criticized for focusing on the form rather than the content of education. This was evident in the support for the comprehensivization of secondary education as a reform that would improve educational opportunities. There was also a rather naive belief in educational reform and the power of education to bring about social change or to reduce inequalities.

Studies like Douglas' also gave rise to the idea that working-class culture was to blame for under-achievement. This resulted in compensatory education schemes like educational priority areas established as a result of the Plowden Report (1967) and Operation Headstart in the USA. These schemes attempted to compensate for the perceived cultural deficit of black and working-class pupils.

The old to the new

Challenges to the political arithmetic approach occurred within the sociology of education in the late 1960s. De-schoolers like Ivan Illich began to challenge the content and form of education and the idea that education was a good thing *per se*. Studies began to focus on schools and what happened in them, rather than on the effects of the environment and home background.

Case-study approaches were used by Hargreaves (1967), Lacey (1970) and later Ball (1981) to investigate the ways in which school organization worked against working-class pupils, particularly the effects of selection by the 11-plus examination and streaming. Hargreaves

(1967) used some qualitative methods such as participant observation (see Section 9.5) to investigate social relations in a secondary modern school. He found that working-class boys in lower streams developed an anti-school subculture as a response to their lack of educational success. Not only had they failed to get a place in grammar school, they were also negatively labelled by teachers and placed in the bottom stream. By inverting the culture of the school they produced an alternative value system from which they could derive status.

These studies began a change of focus in the sociology of education, away from explanations of failure in terms of home background towards a focus on school organization, teacher–pupil interaction and the content of the curriculum and school knowledge. This shift was influenced by 'interactionist' perspectives, with sociologists undertaking ethnographic research into classrooms.

The new sociology of education

The 'new' sociology of education had several strands, the two most important being phenomenology and cultural Marxism. These strands did, however, share certain concerns, which were to challenge taken-for-granted assumptions about what counts as legitimate school knowledge, educational success and failure.

They were critical of functionalist explanations of working-class failure. Pupils and teachers were viewed as creators of meaning rather than passive receivers of 'education'. The content of the curriculum and what counts as legitimate knowledge came under scrutiny from sociologists like Young (1971). The assertion that all knowledge is equally valid led to interesting debates about cultural relativism.

The social construction of reality in schools and classrooms was the approach taken by the phenomenologists. The emphasis here was on subjective meanings of how pupils and teachers make sense of their experiences of the culture and knowledge of schools.

Who has benefited from educational expansion?

The political arithmetic tradition in the sociology of education did, however, survive the challenges of the new sociology of education. In 1980, Halsey, Heath and Ridge produced *Origins and Destinations*. Using data from the Nuffield mobility study (1972) of 8529 men born at different times in the twentieth century, they investigated two issues:

• to determine to what extent the educational system had achieved its professed goal of meritocracy.

• to test Bourdieu's theory of cultural capital – that while schools appear fair and meritocratic, in reality they privilege pupils with the requisite cultural attributes. (Bourdieu's work is considered also in Section 16.1.)

They found that despite the expansion of the educational system, relative chances remained the same or in some periods worsened. Before the 1944 Education Act service-class men were eight times more likely than men from the working class to go to university; after 1944 this increased to 8.5 times:

The 1944 Education Act brought England and Wales no nearer to the ideal of a meritocratic society. ... Secondary education was made free in order to enable the poor to take advantage of it, but the paradoxical consequence was to increase subsidies to the affluent.

(Halsey et al., 1980, p. 210)

They found that the existence of private schools structured class chances and built bias into the meritocratic development of the state system of education. The two systems, private and state, remained divided along class lines. They did find a large volume of intergenerational educational mobility, so cultural capital is not an exclusive means of cultural reproduction of social classes. Those from privileged social class backgrounds were more likely to stay on at school (70 per cent of Social Class 1 pupils went on to university). They concluded that qualification inflation could lead to social class inequalities becoming a permanent aspect of education.

Since Halsey et al.'s study there has been very little large-scale research of this kind. Two studies, by Drew and Gray (1990) and Jesson et al. (1992), indicate that while the proportion of pupils entered for examinations at 16 has expanded massively, social class differences in educational performance remain.

A multi-dimensional approach – ethnicity, gender and social class

What *has* increased in recent years is research that considers together the various factors that may affect the educational achievements of pupils, including gender, ethnicity and social class. Such a multi-dimensional approach, though often complex, is extremely important. Pupils do not experience the effects of gender, 'race' and class separately; these work *together* to influence performance at school.

A report from the Office for Standards in Education (Ofsted), prepared by Gillborn and Gipps (1996), focuses on the achievements of ethnic minority pupils. It reviews research on the effects of social class, race and gender, and its findings are interesting and revealing. Some of their findings are reported in Figure 11.1.

Activity

a Study Figure 11.1. What does it tell us about the primacy of social class?

b What does it *not* explain?

c How satisfactory are the categories used for ethnicity?

C3.2

Social mobility: assisted places

Following a promise in the 1979 Conservative election manifesto to provide a ladder of opportunity for academically able working-class pupils, the 'assisted places' scheme was introduced as part of the provisions of the 1980 Education Act.

The scheme was intended to enable academically able pupils whose parents could not afford the fees to benefit from education at an inde-

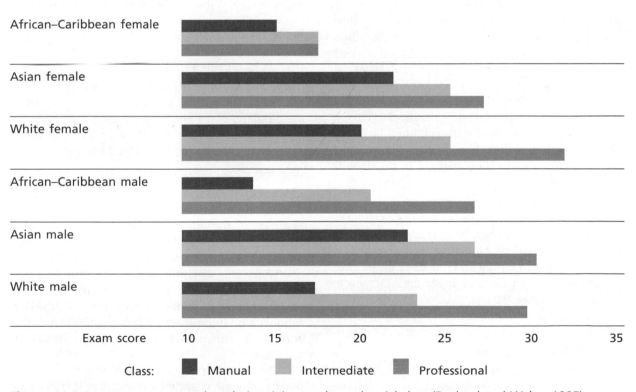

Figure 11.1 Average exam scores by ethnic origin, gender and social class (England and Wales, 1985)
Source: Adapted from Drew and Gray (1990) 'The fifth year examination achievements of black young people in England and Wales', *Educational Research* 32(3), pp. 107–17

pendent school. Between 5000 and 6000 means-tested places were to be made available. This was justified as a way of improving parental choice, rescuing pupils from the 'wreckage' of local comprehensives, necessary as pupils' opportunities had been restricted by the demise of so many maintained grammar schools.

Edwards, Fitz and Whitty (1989) carried out an evaluation of the scheme. Their aim was to look at the political and ideological context and sources for the scheme and to test empirically some of the competing claims being made for and against it. They collected evidence on three levels:

- national statistics on the allocation and take-up of places

- the scheme's implementation in selected geographical areas with high concentrations of assisted places

- how individuals were affected by the scheme (they interviewed 600 pupils in independent and maintained schools and over 300 of their parents).

What is especially interesting here is the social origins of pupils with assisted places. These researchers used the Hope–Goldthorpe classification of eight groups within three broad classes: 'service' (higher and lower grade professionals), 'intermediate' (white-collar workers, small business people, technical foremen), and 'working-class' (skilled, semi-skilled, unskilled). (This is discussed in more detail in Sections 17.3 and 17.7.) They found very few children of working-class parents among their sample of pupils with assisted places:

In the assisted places scheme, it is noticeable that while children from single-parent families constitute the largest category of beneficiaries identified in relation to social 'need', as successive ISIS surveys have emphasised, children from other kinds of family also thought to be widely disadvantaged are either much less prominent (like the unemployed) or conspicuously under-represented (parents in semi-skilled and unskilled manual work, black and Asian families.)

(Edwards *et al.*, 1989, p. 166)

They found a high proportion of service-class occupations and a conspicuous absence of 'unambiguously working-class occupations' amongst the parents participating in the assisted places scheme in their sample. This supported earlier research by Salter and Tapper (1986) who found that a large proportion of the beneficiaries were

relatively impoverished but educationally aware members of the petite bourgeoisie.

Yet head teachers, when asked how they allocated the places, were very keen to emphasize the working-class pupils they recruited:

[Head of Milltown Grammar]: 'I'm trying to decide who will get the last five assisted places this year, and it's awful trying to weigh one up against the other ... but the occupations we are talking about are ... we've got a lorry driver, a British Rail guard, window cleaner, school meals assistant, ... that's a single parent family ... van driver, textile worker, unemployed, and two of these boys are actually ... both sons of first generation Pakistani immigrants who work in textile firms as operatives. So overwhelmingly our application this time is bringing in poor children from inner cities.'

(Edwards *et al.*, 1989, p. 115)

Heads when interviewed cited various reasons for entering the scheme, including helping individual children and serving the local community. Some claimed the school benefited from the improved social mix and that attracting high-fliers helped their exam results and competitive edge. There was some evidence of bright children being talent-spotted in primary school. A matron at one of the prestigious public schools described the effect on the social mix of the school:

[Cathedral College]: 'It's good for them to realise that not everyone has three cars and two houses ... It's the old thing of the nobility freshening their blood by marrying pretty shop girls. I think it's the same principle really. Introducing fresh blood into the school.'

(Edwards *et al.*, 1989, p. 102)

In another school a teacher viewed the assisted places scheme as rescuing the school from *nouveau riche* parents with 'thick' and uncultured children, by providing bright working-class pupils who were preferable.

There was a stereotyped assumption amongst many of the parents interviewed that independent schools were better. However, out of the 470 schools who initially offered places, 200 were discarded as unsuitable for explicitly academic purposes.

The research seems to show that the assisted places scheme, despite its rhetoric of justification, is not drawing in pupils from inner-city neighbourhoods, and is 'saving' middle-class rather than working-class children from comprehensive schools. With potentially their best students creamed off, comprehensives are placed by the scheme in a position of increased competition, and of having to mimic independent schools in order to attract able pupils.

This research has been strongly criticized by John Marks (1991) who carried out an appraisal of the scheme for the Independent Schools Information Service. He used data from a Mori survey of 3475 pupils which found that roughly four in ten assisted places are from working-class backgrounds. This is higher than the findings of the Edwards *et al.* research, which found only one in seven from working-class households.

💬 Discussion point

What type of questions would you ask of both pieces of research in order to evaluate their findings and account for the discrepancies?

C3.1a

By 1995 there were 33 000 assisted places being taken up and plans to double the number – seen as an attempt to put 'clear blue water' between the Conservative government and the opposition parties. It was considered better value than investing in state schools. The Independent Schools Information Service considered the scheme a great success, claiming that 80 per cent of people receiving assisted places had parents earning below the national average wage. Their wish was to extend it to non-academic pupils.

💬 Discussion point

Could the assisted places scheme provide equality of opportunity? Is it meritocratic?

C3.1a

In 1997 the scheme was abolished by the Labour government.

Access to higher education

Eighteen-year-olds today have a nearly 60 per cent chance of going to university, either straight from school or later in life, full or part time. In 1900 it was 1.2 per cent, in 1938 it was 2.4 per cent and in 1962 it was 6.5 per cent (including teacher training).

(Smithers and Robinson, 1995, p. 2)

As we move from an élite to a mass system of higher education, it is interesting to explore whether this has improved relative chances for working-class students.

💬 Discussion point

Will a mass system of higher education necessarily improve the relative chances of working-class students?

C3.1a

Features since 1900

Egerton and Halsey (1993) identify three features in the history of access to higher education since 1900:

- a considerable expansion of tertiary provision
- no reduction of relative social class inequality
- a significant reduction in gender inequality.

They used a sample of 25 000 men and women between the ages of 20 and 50, drawn from the General Household Survey for 1985, 1986 and 1987. (This particular source of official statistics is discussed in Section 6.3.) They included the prestige of the institution and the age of attaining the qualification. Most studies use only academic qualifications as measures of tertiary educational attainment, but type of institution is also important in maintaining or reducing inequalities because the most prestigious institutions may be accessible only to the most privileged groups. The age of attaining qualifications was also considered as there is some evidence that qualifications gained later in life may lead to upward mobility. A three-point version of Goldthorpe's social class schema was used.

Egerton and Halsey found social-class inequalities in access to all educational institutions (universities, polytechnics and colleges): the service class had an advantage over both the intermediate and the manual working class. Absolute access had increased for all, but the service class had maintained its relative advantage in both universities and polytechnics.

They found that students from service-class backgrounds were more likely to take degree courses in universities than working-class and intermediate-class students, who were more likely to take them in a polytechnic or college of further education. This supports the thesis that more advantaged groups tend to dominate more prestigious institutions. They sum up:

The overall picture for social class is of unchanging

service class advantage. The children of managerial or professional families are more likely to gain access to university; more likely to have obtained the most prestigious qualification, a degree, at a university; and more likely to have qualified earlier in life than people from an intermediate or manual class background.

(Egerton and Halsey, 1993, p. 189)

They did find, however, that the expansion in tertiary education has benefited women and it seems likely that women's educational participation will soon be on a par with that of men.

The answer to the question 'Is social class still the most important determinant of educational attainment?' would appear to be yes. Despite the expansion of the education system, relative chances have apparently remained the same.

Discussion point

What data, other than participation rates, would be required to establish that women have equality with men in higher education?

C3.1a

11.4 Ethnicity and educational achievement

It is difficult to understand the position of the ethnic minorities in the education system, particularly African–Caribbean, African and South Asian pupils, without reference to Britain's colonial past. After World War II, immigrants from the ex-colonies – now the Commonwealth – were recruited to meet Britain's post-war labour shortages. We can look at this issue by thinking about how it has developed historically.

The 1950s

By the 1950s there was growing resistance to this immigration amongst the white population. In 1958 a series of attacks by youths led to riots, first in Nottingham and then in Notting Hill in London. This led to a call for action and it was to schools that the policy-makers turned. Before this, black children's needs had been relatively neglected. If black children would take on British traditions, values and mastery of the English language then the process of assimilation would be smooth, it was assumed.

The late 1960s

In 1966 a speech by Roy Jenkins, the Labour Home Secretary, was taken as the turning point in the movement away from an assimilationist position towards a more liberal integrationist phase. He advocated:

... not a flattening process of assimilation but equal opportunities, accompanied by cultural diversity, in an atmosphere of mutual tolerance.

(Quoted in Mullard, 1982, p. 125)

The 1970s and early 1980s

Whereas an assimilationist position meant total absorption, integration made allowances for cultural diversity. This approach resulted in multi-cultural education being developed by teachers, encouraged by some local education authorities in the 1970s and 1980s.

There was also growing concern about under-achievement amongst black pupils. This it was felt was partly explained by the Eurocentric nature of the curriculum. It was felt that the curriculum should draw on the experiences and cultures of all ethnic minorities, and that this should permeate the whole curriculum. Multi-cultural education was interpreted very differently in different locations.

It was heavily criticized by some educationalists. Stone (1981) blamed multi-cultural education for the under-achievement of black pupils. She claimed that black pupils needed more formal methods rather than the child-centred approach implicit in multi-cultural education. Tailoring the curriculum to the needs of black pupils, she felt, was interpreted by teachers as encouraging them in sports and music. They should be encouraged to take academic subjects which would lead to educational success and upward mobility. Multi-cultural education was also parodied unkindly as 'saris, samosas, and steel bands' because of its focus on lifestyles rather than life chances. It was also regarded as ignoring structural racism in the wider society.

The mid-1980s

By the 1980s many teachers had adopted a much more political, anti-racist approach. This represented a move away from the pluralist model of multi-cultural education where all cultures were regarded as equal. It used a socialist or Marxist model of dominant and subordinate cultures, and neutrality for teachers was considered impossible where racism was concerned. Teachers tried to create an atmosphere of trust in classrooms so that 'race' and racism could be discussed openly and honestly.

This position also had its critics. Some multi-culturalists saw it as indoctrination by teachers who should remain neutral. In one school – Burnage in Manchester – it was claimed that a badly implemented policy contributed to the murder of an Asian pupil. The white working-class pupils of the school felt that the way in which the school's anti-racist policy was used ignored their needs and blamed them for racism. Such poorly implemented one-dimensional policies were condemned by an enquiry into the death, the Macdonald Report (1989).

Many schools developed much more comprehensive equal-opportunities policies to address the different and interconnected oppressions faced by pupils. They included 'race', gender, class, disability and learning difficulties, and sexual orientation.

The late 1980s

In the late 1980s there were attacks in the media on schools and LEAs with strong equal-opportunities policies. A more sophisticated version of the old assimilationist position was beginning to reappear. It emphasized the notion of difference rather than superiority or inferiority. The right-wing Hillgate group and academics like Roger Scruton claimed that multi-cultural education was a threat to the British way of life – that ethnic minority pupils should be encouraged to discard their culture and blend in. The Hillgate group were influential in planning the content of the National Curriculum, especially the teaching of English history, English literature and the use of standard English.

The 1990s

By the 1990s it was not just the right who were attacking multi-cultural and anti-racist education. Recently sociologists like Gilroy (1990) and Modood (1989), influenced by post-modernist thinking, criticized some anti-racist policies for their emphasis on 'colour racism', which focuses on the dualism of black and white and ignores other minority groups. Modood claims that religion as part of identity is more important to Muslims and possibly Sikhs and Hindus. Gilroy calls for the end of anti-racism, as presently conceived, to be replaced by the new cultural politics of difference. He accuses modernist accounts of 'race' of being essentialist and reductionist:

- *Essentialism* means deciding who is racist and who isn't on the basis of a set of essential defining properties or dispositions.

- *Reductionism* means reducing everything back to a single cause, such as capitalism or patriarchy.

Celebrating difference, and understanding the complexity of identities, is important for teachers and pupils committed to anti-racism. These 'New Left criticisms' could have a demoralizing effect on teachers and contribute to political inactivity. As Epstein comments:

Essentializing slogans have played a necessary part in the construction of positive identities by people in subordinate groups, and the development of oppositional strategies has often rested on these identities.

(Epstein, 1993, p. 17)

Discussion point

What are the 'essentializing' slogans referred to by Epstein, and how might they be dangerous?

C3.1a

African–Caribbean boys at school

For a long time sociologists have focused on the educational achievement of groups from different ethnic groups. According to Gillborn and Gipps (1996) in an Ofsted report, African–Caribbean boys are over-represented amongst those failing in the educational system (see the article on page 382).

Activity

Read through the extract 'Caribbean boys fall far behind' and answer the questions. You will need to draw on Section 11.2 on interactionism and the information in Figure 11.2 to help you to answer the questions.

a Summarize the evidence that African–Caribbean boys under-achieve at school.

b Is racism to blame? What are the arguments for and against this?

c Is ethnic monitoring of exam results important? Why might there be opposition to this?

C3.2, C3.3

CARIBBEAN BOYS FALL FAR BEHIND

NICHOLAS PYKE

Afro-Caribbean boys are marking up disastrously low scores in the crucial subjects of mathematics and science, according to worrying new studies.

A project by Birmingham education authority, one of the first of its kind, shows Caribbean boys scoring only a third of the male average in technical GCSEs.

The Birmingham analysis, based on 1995 GCSE results, shows only 8.6 per cent of black Caribbean boys getting grades A to C in maths, and 12.4 in science. The comparable figures for other groups of boys are: black African – 14.3 and 28.6; Indian – 34.2 and 44.1; and white – 32.2 and 36.9. Black Caribbean girls did considerably better, scoring 33.3 per cent A to C in maths and 37.5 per cent in science.

Another authority, which did not wish to be named, surveyed 1508 pupils at 15 secondary schools and found that only 10 per cent of black Caribbean children got five grades A to C at GCSE (national average 43 per cent) and that only 7 per cent got any sort of GCSE pass in maths.

Birmingham produced its figures after working with the African-Caribbean Network for Science and Technology, a group of black scientists concerned about the failure of Britain's Caribbean pupils, boys in particular.

"What future will black Caribbean young people have in this Western, numerate, industrialised society?" asked the network's spokeswoman, chemical engineer, Liz Rasekoala. "They're not even qualified for an apprenticeship."

The network condemns the lack of detailed information. "Everybody was telling us there's a general problem. There was a lot of wringing of hands, moaning and groaning. But no one in the mainstream was willing to come out and say exactly what was going on.

"What we want from the government is to have ethnic monitoring made statutory. As a result of gender monitoring there have been major improvements and support for girls. No one, apart from Birmingham, has had the moral courage to come forward with the figures."

Ms Rasekoala, who trained in Nigeria, said that black scientists are so rare they often feel isolated and may be tempted to seek other professions. She has spent her entire career as the only black individual at work and blamed low expectations at school for the failure of many black pupils in science.

Dr David Gillborn, a lecturer in policy studies at London University's Institute of Education, said that Birmingham's detailed figures are the first he has seen from a named local authority.

"Good quality ethnic monitoring is a crucial element in addressing existing inequality. But it must be with categories that are sufficiently detailed and meaningful." So far the government is only proposing to collect very basic information.

Source: Times Educational Supplement, 24 April 1996

African–Caribbean girls at school

The growing gap

There is some evidence that African–Caribbean girls perform better in examinations than their peers, but the data are from small-scale ethnographic studies and therefore not generalizable. Yet recent figures from the London Borough of Brent and from Birmingham show that, while there was an increase in what pupils of each ethnic group achieved, the gap grew between the highest and the lowest achieving groups (Gillborn and Gipps, 1996). This is between Asian and African–Caribbean pupils of both sexes (see also the evidence in Figure 11.1 on page 377).

The difference with black girls

However, ethnographic work shows a very different response to schooling by black girls compared with their peers. Fuller (1980) studied a small group of girls of West Indian parentage who formed a discernible subculture, by virtue of the girls' positive acceptance of the fact of being black and female. These girls, unlike their black male peers, directed their frustrations and anger towards achievement in school through the acquisition of educational qualifications. Their response to racism was to work hard and prove their worth. They were not, however, conforming, 'good' pupils. They were pro-education but not pro-school and had clever and subtle ways of showing their defiance. Teachers' expectations of them were unimportant.

Second-generation African–Caribbean girls

In an ethnographic study of two south London comprehensives, Mirza (1992) found young black girls did better in exams than their peers and that the black girls aspired to careers in social classes 1 and 2. In the sample, 74 per cent of black females expected to find work in social class 1 or 2, compared with only 27 per cent of black boys and 35 per cent of white females. Mirza accounts for the difference by a comparison of second-generation African–Caribbean and Irish pupils. The black girls in her sample rejected the economic dependency desired by the young Irish women. They looked forward to relationships which 'have joint responsibility towards the household' within the context of *relative autonomy* between the sexes which are a common feature of West Indian family life.

Mirza also found that positive attitudes to education and lack of restrictions on the female labour market participation within West Indian families account for high aspirations amongst young black women. This presents an important alternative to pathological accounts of West Indian family life with an emphasis on strong mothers as role models which therefore marginalize black men. (This issue is discussed also in Section 5.5.)

Continued gendered choices

Mirza's study is also a real indictment of careers advice available to young black girls. Such advice does nothing to challenge the gendered choices they make by widening their horizons and offering alternatives to those safe, traditionally female, occupations like teaching and social work. She shows, as do other studies like the Eggleston Report (1986), that the careers service plays a significant role in the reproduction of sexual and racial divisions in the labour market. (Such divisions are explored in more detail in Section 17.2.)

Mirza found that black girls developed strategies to avoid teachers' negative assessments that were often detrimental to their own interests, and had little power to counteract negative outcomes.

Resistance with accommodation

These findings are very similar to those of Máirtín Mac an Ghaill's (1988) study of the 'Black sisters', a group of A level students who responded positively to education. They were pro-education but anti-school. They practised *resistance* with *accommodation*, finding subtle ways of resisting the institutional demands of the school and the racist curriculum, but at the same time succeeding academically. This accommodation came from wanting highly prized academic qualifications and the opportunity to escape from traditional black working-class occupations.

Supplementary schooling

More recently Mirza (1997) has studied black supplementary schools in London which she regards as part of the transformative social movement developed by black women. Such women give up their Saturdays to teach black children what mainstream education fails to provide. Ethnographic research carried out by Mac an Ghaill (1991), in Marcus Garvey, a black voluntary school in the Midlands, suggests how maintained schools might incorporate more positive responses to the black communities they serve. The school was held in a community centre and was based on the values of collective self-help. Most of the black pupils attended local state schools with a majority of black pupils, but they felt them to be white institutions. The teachers lived out of the area. At Marcus Garvey the curriculum did not marginalize black people's culture, literature and history. The teachers were from the same area and were committed to promoting academic achievement through high expectations of their pupils. A positive use of creole was promoted, though there was a strong recognition that good English was also necessary. High priority was given to numeracy and literacy so that pupils could follow high-status academic courses.

South Asian pupils

South Asian pupils would appear to face a different set of barriers and prejudices from their African–Caribbean peers. The work of Avtar Brah (1992) focuses particularly on the position of South Asian girls. Firstly she rejects the assumption that South Asian women should be regarded as a homogeneous group when their country of origin, class, religion, language and gender systems are often different. She rejects 'culturalist' explanations of South Asian girls' under-achievement at school because they pathologize South Asian family life, blaming inter-generational conflict for educational failure. Attention is then diverted from teacher racism and a Eurocentric curriculum. In earlier research she found no evidence that the level of inter-generational conflict was higher amongst South Asian families.

Brah challenges orientalist ideologies that construct South Asian girls as passive. She points to the long tradition of resistance and struggle among South Asian women.

> **Activity**
>
> The following is a summary of the findings of an Ofsted report (Gillborn and Gipps, 1996) in relation to South Asian pupils:
>
> - Indian pupils appear to achieve more highly, on average, than pupils from other South Asian backgrounds.
>
> - Indian pupils achieve higher average rates of success than their white counterparts in some – but not all – urban areas.
>
> - There is no single pattern of achievement for Pakistani pupils, although they achieve less well than white pupils in many areas.
>
> - Bangladeshi pupils are known on average to have less fluency in English, and to experience greater levels of poverty, than other South Asian groups. Their relative achievements are often less than those of other ethnic groups. In one London borough, however, dramatic improvements in performance have been made – here Bangladeshis are now the highest achieving of all major ethnic groups.
>
> **a** Which ethnic groups are included in the term 'South Asian'? Why is the qualification 'South' added?
>
> **b** Offer explanations for the differential achievements of pupils of South Asian origin, drawing on Brah's work described above.
>
> C3.2, C3.3

11.5 Gender and educational achievement

In the media there has been a moral panic about boys' under-achievement at school relative to girls' – Figure 11.2 offers some examples. The idea of a moral panic came from the study of deviance. Folk devils like the mods and rockers were considered a moral threat to society and this threat was sensationalized in the media (see Section 6.2).

> **Discussion point**
>
> Consider the newspaper headlines in Figure 11.2. Are they sensationalizing this problem?
>
> C3.1a

It is working-class boys who are now the folk devils of the education world. Programmes on television have focused on girls' achievement and boys' relative academic decline at all levels of the educational system. Interestingly, girls' success is not celebrated; instead there is a strong concern about boys losing out to 'girls with attitude'. The BBC's *Panorama* programmes ('The future is female', 24 October 1994, and 'Men aren't working', 16 October 1995) compared boys' and girls' attitudes to education and doing well at school. Some of the boys described how being good at school conflicted with their 'culture of masculinity': they claimed 'it just isn't macho to work' and 'boys who work hard aren't boys'.

The popular stereotype of the female under-achiever is now being challenged. This trend of girls doing as well as or better than their male counterparts is also part of a global trend in both the developed and developing worlds. Research

Why flash boys shine at A-level
The Independent, 10 July 1996

Girls excel despite the male culture
TES, 26 April 1996

Male brain rattled by curriculum 'oestrogen'
TES, 15 March 1996

They're falling rapidly behind girls at school. Are boys in terminal decline?
The Independent, 18 October 1994

Go-ahead girls leave experts with a mystery
Sunday Times, 22 May 1994

Anti-school bias 'blights boys for life'
The Times, 6 March 1996

Figure 11.2 Newspaper headlines on gender and educational achievement

conducted in the Caribbean islands of Jamaica, Barbados, St Vincent and the Grenadines found that, while subject choice followed traditional patterns, Caribbean females were outperforming their male peers (Parry, 1996). This has led to similar moral panics about the marginalization of men and men at risk (Miller, 1992).

Is this a new phenomenon?

In the UK, boys' under-achievement is not a new phenomenon. Historical research carried out by Cohen (1998) shows that, from the late seventeenth century to the present, boys have always under-achieved but this has never seriously been addressed. This academic failure, she states, has been made invisible by attributing it to factors external to the boys themselves – for example teaching methods, teachers or the textbooks used. Interestingly she quotes John Locke in 1693 who was concerned about young gentlemen's failure to learn Latin while little girls learnt French so quickly by 'prattling' it to their governesses.

Locke was keen to promote the conversational method for learning Latin, but in focusing on the method as the culprit he explains away boys' under-achievement. Cohen suggests that we re-phrase the question 'Why is boys' under-achievement now an object of concern?' and start by problematizing boys, not girls, and the construction of masculinities.

Why is there a moral panic about boys' under-achievement?

🗨 Discussion point

Below are some of the reasons offered by sociologists for you to explore and discuss:

a It is part of the New Right's attack on feminist teachers and left-wing local education authorities who were seen to promote girls' achievement at the expense of boys'.

b It is a smoke-screen which focuses on gender to hide much more significant and difficult-to-counter under-achievement arising from deepening social class divisions in society.

c It comes from anxieties amongst middle-class parents about the future occupational prospects of their sons. Unless professional employment expands, their sons may lose out to better qualified young women.

d It comes from much wider fears about young males who are regarded as 'bad and dangerous' – resulting from statistics linking truancy, exclusions and crime. The term 'sad' could be added to this if suicide and depression rates are added to the evidence.

C3.1a

Gender and exam statistics

Over the last ten years girls have been out-performing boys in most subjects at GCSE, as Table 11.2 shows. It has been suggested that the coursework methods of GCSE suit girls and account for the differences.

Research was undertaken in 1992 by the University of London Examinations and Assessment Council, in collaboration with NFER, to investigate the causes of differential performance between boys and girls in GCSE English and mathematics. Data were collected by questionnaires from 200 heads of departments in schools and from 3000 examination scripts. This suggested that coursework played only a minimal role in explaining such differences, which were more likely to be a result of experiences that candidates brought with them to the exam and a complex interaction of all the elements within GCSE, including teachers' expectations, entry policies, how coursework is regarded and different emphases in the syllabus (Elwood, 1995b).

Boys catch up at A level

It is interesting that the early pattern of success is reversed at A level, as demonstrated by Table 11.4 on page 389.

Despite its importance as the 'Gold Standard' of education, A level has been left out of the gender and equity debate. Females do not leave post-compulsory education better qualified than their male counterparts, in terms of the percentage of higher grades obtained. What, then, do the statistics tell us?

Activity

Using Tables 11.2–11.4, answer the following questions:

a From Table 11.2, in which subjects were boys ahead of girls in A*–C grades at GCSE?

b From Table 11.2, in which subjects were girls ahead of boys?

c From Table 11.2, in which subjects do the percentages of male and female entry rates at GCSE differ? Offer possible reasons for this.

d Since 1988, GCSE has replaced CSE and O level, the National Curriculum has been implemented, and league tables of exam results are now published. How might this affect teachers' expectations, entry policies, how coursework is regarded and how different syllabuses are viewed?

e From Table 11.3, analyse the change in entry pattern from 1970 to 1995 for A levels. Suggest reasons for these changes.

f From Table 11.4, in which subjects were males out-performing females at A level, in terms of A–C grades achieved? Suggest reasons for the reversal of achievement in some subjects between GCSE and A level.

g Using the sources here and elsewhere, make a list of the explanations for differential male and female success in GCSE and A level exams and evaluate them.

h Evaluate the statistical evidence provided above. What might it *not* reveal?

C3.2, C3.3

Single-sex schools

Primary schools

In the 1970s and 1980s, feminist researchers found that boys dominated co-educational classrooms to the detriment of girls. Researching primary school classrooms, Clarricoates (1978) looked at the operation of the hidden curriculum:

... in particular how teachers tailor the subject content to boys through the ostensibly non-sexist curricula, through the use of linguistic sexism, through preferences of teachers for pupils by sex, and through the link between the criteria for according status and sex appropriate behaviour.

(Clarricoates, 1978, p. 353)

She showed that control and discipline were the central concerns of most teachers. Because of this they spent more time listening to, talking to, and helping boys who were considered more undisciplined than girls.

Her research corroborates evidence from previous studies that girls are more academically successful at primary level in most subjects (Douglas, 1964; Sharpe, 1976). Teachers, however, instead of awarding girls status as a result of this success, tended to see them as boring and conforming. Boys were considered more interesting and challenging to teach. Similar findings resulted from research by Walkerdine and Walden (1982), who found that teachers in primary schools 'explained away' girls' success in mathematics as not really 'success' but rather an ability to be neat, tidy and follow rules; whereas the boys' 'success' was defined as having 'real understanding'. This led them to develop a theory, using the work of Foucault, to find the way different 'truths' relating to girls' failure are constructed.

Discussion point

To what extent is the notion of the conforming, passive, girl a myth?

C3.1a

Secondary schools

Dale Spender

In secondary schools, Spender and Sarah (1980) found that sexism permeated the entire curriculum. Women's contributions to history and science were ignored and more male writers were included in English literature examination syllabuses.

Spender also looked at the reasons for female non-participation in verbal activities in the classroom. She reviewed the research which showed that both sexes regarded talking in class, particularly questioning or challenging teachers, as specifically masculine behaviour. Therefore encouraging girls to take part verbally in class was requiring them to play what was considered an unfeminine role. Spender regarded talk as a powerful tool that teachers should encourage girls to use. She notes, though, that much of the language used then in textbooks and worksheets was sexist, using 'man' and 'he' to cover both male and female activities. This, she felt, was no

Table 11.2 Percentages of male/female entry and grade A*–C results in 1997

Subject	Male entry	Female entry	A*–C (M)	A*–C (F)	Difference A*–C (M-F)
Art/Design	48.4	51.6	52.9	70.8	-17.9
Biology	52.8	47.2	80.6	72.8	7.8
Chemistry	60.8	39.2	86.5	87.3	-0.8
Combined Science	49.7	50.3	49.8	51.0	-1.2
English	50.2	49.8	48.5	64.8	-16.3
English Literature	47.6	52.4	55.3	69.9	-14.6
French	46.5	53.5	43.9	57.7	-13.8
Geography	55.8	44.2	52.3	58.9	-6.6
History	48.7	51.3	54.6	51.7	-7.1
Maths	49.3	50.7	47.4	47.3	0.1
Technology	63.1	36.9	41.1	56.4	-15.3
Physics	63.1	36.9	86.5	85.5	0.7
All subjects	49.3	50.7	50.3	58.7	-8.4

Source: Inter-Group Statistics (1997), SEG Surrey; quoted in Elwood and Gipps (1999)

UNDER-ACHIEVEMENT AMONG BOYS

Boys, particularly from working-class backgrounds, may be experiencing low self-esteem and poor motivation which is having an adverse effect on their educational performance. Research by Harris *et al.* (1993) into the attitudes of 16-year-olds from predominantly working-class backgrounds towards schoolwork, homework and careers, confirms that many boys are achieving below their potential. It was found that girls tended to be more hard-working and better motivated than boys, whilst boys were more easily distracted in the classroom and less determined to overcome academic difficulties. Overall, girls were prepared to work consistently to meet coursework deadlines, whereas boys had difficulties organising their time.

There was a greater readiness among girls to do school work at home and they spent more hours on homework than boys. When thinking about the future, the young women recognised the need to gain qualifications for lives which would involve paid employment as well as domestic responsibilities. Generally, the males had not given much thought to their futures and seemed fairly unconcerned about poor school performance.

The authors relate their findings to the gender 'regimes' which the young people encounter in their homes and communities. Some of the girls, exposed to the image of woman as organiser, responsible for home and family and wage-earning, displayed similar characteristics themselves, i.e. being highly organised with school work and homework. Harris *et al.* argue that the dominant stereotype of the male in the working-class communities they examined was highly 'macho'. Typically, this was characterised by a disregard for the authority of organisational structures and an enjoyment of the active company of other males. Some boys were already fulfilling such a stereotype in their approach to school, showing little regard for working steadily and dissociating themselves from formal requirements.

Source: Clark (1996) *Sociology Review* Vol. 5. No. 4

linguistic accident but a rule intended to promote the primacy of man.

Discussion point

To what extent has the linguistic sexism described by Spender disappeared in schools and colleges?

C3.1a

Sarah, Scott and Spender

Sarah, Scott and Spender (1980) put forward a strong case for single-sex education for girls. There was some evidence at the time that girls did better in single-sex schools, but this was not supported at the time by findings in the ILEA (Mortimore, 1981). However, Sarah *et al.* based their evidence on research in mixed schools where boys received more attention from teachers, where the curriculum was directed towards

They're falling rapidly behind girls at school.
Are boys in terminal decline?

JUDITH JUDD

PAUL CAVANAGH, 17, is honest about why he did less well than he expected in his GCSE exams. "Complacency and arrogance," he says. "After our mock exams, the teacher predicted I would get six As. No trouble, I thought. I don't need to work. So I didn't and I got three As."

He is now in the sixth form at King Alfred's School, Wantage, Oxfordshire, preparing for four A-levels. He says he is working harder to get to a decent university but still not as hard as the girls in his physics group. "The group is mainly boys and they do almost no work at all, especially homework," he says.

Paul, according to national studies, is a typical male student. Girls work harder and are less confident of their ability. Working hard is not "cool" for either sex, but girls are less swayed by their peers' attitude to school work. Alison Francis, 15, another King Alfred's pupil, puts it this way: "Girls do more work at home even if they want to keep up an image of doing no work at school."

Girls' industry has been rewarded. In the days of the 11-plus 30 years ago, they did better than boys in primary schools. Recently they have beaten the boys at 16: more than four in 10 get top grades at GCSE compared with only a third of boys. Even in science and maths, traditionally male strongholds, girls have edged ahead. Last year, for the first time, they had more top grades in science.

A-level has remained the bastion of male achievement but the gap is narrowing. More boys still get the top two grades but girls are cutting their lead. Already a higher proportion of 18-year-old girls than boys gets three A-levels. Male undergraduates do both better and worse – more firsts and more thirds – than their female counterparts, but the difference varies from university to university.

The inexorable march of girls towards better examination performance is not explained just by hard work. It is the result, too, of the equal opportunities revolution of the past 20 years. Girls have been encouraged by a generation of determined female teachers to tackle maths and science, to stay on at school, to go to university and to have careers.

Recently, however, concern has shifted. Experts have begun to suggest that schools, in their eagerness to encourage girls, have neglected boys. They say that, in precisely the same way as teachers in the past failed to interest girls in maths, they are now failing to make boys enthusiastic about English. Recently, Demos, the independent think-tank, suggested that the revolution in girls' education had a price: demoralisation of boys. As girls have become more optimistic, the report said, boys have become so pessimistic that their depression is affecting their academic performance.

If this is so, the pessimism has not yet reached King Alfred's boys. They are neither worried about job prospects nor dismal about the future. Complacency remains. Figures from the Equal Opportunities Commission show that there will be a fall in male employment of 300,000 by the year 2000 and 500,000 new jobs for women, but Paul says: "It's definitely easier for men to get jobs. There are still employers who don't want women because they may go off and have children or because they think they lack a hard-nosed attitude." Jonathan Spinage, another 17-year-old, agrees: "Men think, I'm bound to get a job. I'm a bloke'."

Far from being cowed, Paul and his contemporaries are ambitious. They want to be rich – but they are not sure that better qualifications mean a better job. Matthew Ryland, 17, explains: "Boys are more ambitious. The basic boy dream is to be rich, to have a big car and a nice house. It was always said that to get high up you need lots of qualifications. Now there are other ways of doing it."

Girls, says Kate Douglas, 17, take a different view: "With girls it's about succeeding in whatever they're doing. We're not just interested in the money."

Even when girls and boys dislike subjects, girls still do well. Both boys and girls challenge the view that boys perform less well than girls in English because teachers do not stimulate boys' interest. Girls, too, have difficulty seeing the point of English, one of the subjects in which boys trail farthest behind girls.

Are the boys of King Alfred's, a successful comprehensive with exam results well above the national average, unusually cheerful about their future? Research last year among 30,000 teenagers by John Balding, of Exeter University, suggests not. It shows boys have not sunk into gloom at the sight of girls' educational advance. Although fewer of them expect to continue in education, they are more confident than girls that they will have a worthwhile career and find a job. They also expect to meet less sex discrimination than girls when they are job-hunting.

Michael Barber, professor of education at Keele University, comments: "Ten or 15 years of equal opportunities have worked," he says. "That should be celebrated. But it is possible that we have taken away something from one group and given it to another. It is time to reconsider our equal opportunities strategy." In particular, he believes we need to tackle boys' literacy, which is already behind that of girls by the age of seven.

Yet any plan to redress the balance in favour of boys must be treated with caution. There is no evidence that girls' success has been at the expense of boys, nor that teachers are discriminating against boys. According to research by Peter Mortimore, director of London University's Institute of Education, the latter still dominate the classroom and grab most of the teachers' attention.

Source: The Independent, 18 October 1994

Table 11.3 Entry figures for major A level subjects by gender, 1970–95

Subject	Sex	1970	1980	1990	1995	Percentage differences		
						1970–80	1980–90	1990–95
	M	10 235	17 232	17 938	20 711	68.4	4.1	15.5
Biology	F	9 463	20 662	28 517	31 553	118.3	38.0	10.6
	Total	19 698	37 894	46 455	52 264	92.4	22.6	12.5
	M	23 385	24 386	27 427	23 769	6.2	10.4	-13.3
Chemistry	F	7 385	12 408	18 769	18 523	68.0	51.3	-1.3
	Total	30 770	37 244	46 196	42 292	21.0	24.0	-8.5
	M	21 257	20 229	14 621	17 730	-4.8	-27.7	21.3
English Lit.	F	34 736	45 371	32 345	40 444	30.6	-28.7	24.0
	Total	55 993	65 600	46 966	58 174	17.2	-28.4	23.9
	M	9 822	7 456	7 445	8 169	-24.1	-0.1	9.7
French	F	16 103	18 640	19 799	19 394	15.8	6.2	-2.0
	Total	25 925	26 096	27 244	27 563	0.7	4.4	1.2
	M	19 421	20 714	23 524	23 887	6.7	13.6	1.5
Geography	F	12 347	14 360	18 146	19 567	16.3	26.4	7.8
	Total	31 768	35 074	41 670	43 454	10.4	18.8	4.3
	M	18 145	18 898	19 845	19 490	4.1	5.0	-1.8
History	F	16 811	21 196	23 962	24 306	26.1	13.0	1.4
	Total	34 956	40 094	43 807	43 796	14.7	9.3	0.0
	M	52 364	50 238	47 096	41 199	-4.1	-6.3	-12.5
Maths	F	12 017	15 775	23 867	22 281	31.3	51.3	-6.6
	Total	64 381	66 013	70 963	63 480	2.5	7.5	-10.5
	M	35 045	35 752	35 300	27 231	2.0	-1.3	-22.9
Physics	F	6 501	9 406	10 029	7 571	44.7	6.6	-24.5
	Total	41 546	45 158	45 329	34 802	8.7	0.4	-23.2
	M	189 674	195 355	193 196	182 186	3.0	-1.1	-5.7
All subjects	F	115 363	157 818	175 434	183 639	36.8	11.2	4.7
	Total	305 037	353 173	368 630	365 825	15.8	4.4	-0.7

Sources: University of Oxford Delegacy of Local Examinations Archive, Willmot (1994), Inter-Board Statistics (1990, 1995), Associated Examining Board; quoted in Elwood (1999)

Table 11.4 Percentage differences (M-F) in A–C grades at A level (all GCE groups), 1990–97

Subject	1990	1991	1992	1993	1994	1995	1996	1997	Mean 1990–97
Biology	2.3	1.8	2.4	0.5	-0.6	-2.0	-3.4	-3.5	-0.3
Chemistry	2.0	1.3	2.0	1.5	1.0	0.7	-2.3	-2.5	0.5
English Lit.	2.9	3.5	2.3	1.9	0.9	1.2	1.9	0.6	1.9
French	4.0	3.5	5.2	4.6	3.8	4.1	2.3	0.9	3.6
Geography	-0.1	-3.6	-3.5	-2.9	-4.2	-4.9	-6.0	-7.6	-4.1
History	5.4	5.0	3.6	3.2	3.0	1.8	1.4	2.5	3.2
Mathematics	1.8	1.2	0.9	-0.4	-1.4	-2.3	-2.6	-2.5	-0.7
Physics	0.4	1.0	-1.1	-0.9	-1.6	-1.5	-4.2	-4.3	-1.5
All subjects	2.8	2.3	1.5	0.9	0.1	-0.3	-1.3	-1.2	0.6

Source: Inter-Board Statistics (1990–97), AEB, Guildford; quoted in Elwood (1999)

boys' interests, where 'success' in high-status subjects is defined as 'male success'. In such circumstances girls are at a disadvantage and single-sex education would be desirable:

When girls are educated in a context in which boys are absent, in which they are encouraged to grow and develop their human potential, then they will be in a much stronger position to resist oppression in the wider society.

(Sarah *et al.*, 1980, p. 65)

Michelle Stanworth

Stanworth (1983) found, in her study of A level humanities classrooms in a further education college, that teachers paid more attention to the boys, asking them questions and giving them more help with their work. She also found that teachers held stereotyped views of female students' future careers, for whom marriage rather than a profession was considered appropriate. Teachers also found it difficult to remember their female students, especially the quiet ones. Quiet male students *were* remembered.

💬 Discussion point

Discuss the proposition that if boys and girls are separated into single-sex teaching groups they will never learn to confront unacceptable behaviour from the opposite sex.

C3.1a

Does the market favour some girls' schools?

Recent research on choice of school by parents and pupils in this new age of consumer choice in the education market has also thrown up interesting findings about single-sex and co-educational schools.

As part of a larger study of education markets in practice, Ball and Gerwitz (1997) looked at two related questions:

- how girls' schools position themselves in competition with their co-educational rivals (and how they respond).
- how parents and their daughters perceive, evaluate and choose between single-sex and co-educational schools.

This analysis draws on interviews with parents choosing secondary schooling for their daughters and who particularly expressed views about single-sex schooling. Two over-subscribed state girls' schools, Pankhurst and Martineau, are used as case studies. They are positioned differently in the school market because of their intake, with Pankhurst being decidedly middle-class.

Ball and Gerwitz found that girls are one group who are advantaged in certain respects by the current structuring of educational markets. Single-sexness is now a unique selling point for schools in the marketplace. This is due to their favourable characteristics in the context of school competition, for example in performance in public exams and the positive impression they give about ethos and discipline. Both schools gave considerable attention to their corporate image. Part of this was school colour used as a symbol and identifier in both schools, but Martineau also had a logo, flag, flower and motto:

[Union representative, Martineau]: 'Well ... you see a lot more things like our new sign and that sort of stuff and the colours ... so it's very much more emphasis on presentation and our prospectus is very glossy. I mean it's what you would imagine a public school or university, the style of it, and that sort of thing has become very important, and there's quite a lot of emphasis on style and dress for teachers as well.'

(Quoted in Ball and Gerwitz, 1997, p. 209)

School uniform was part of the complex semiotics of girls' schools: the cloistered, traditional ethos. This was based on the absence of and escape from boys. This traditionalism is often mixed with feminism posing as an equal curriculum, enabling girls to get access to computers, to not be afraid to be clever, to have a career and a commitment to modernism and academicism. Such conflicting messages are summed up:

In all this then, feminism and femininity, traditionalism and progressivism are wrapped up together in a sophisticated and sometimes confusing set of signs and meanings. At Martineau something of both is signalled in the school prospectus which announces the school as a 'Grant Maintained School for Girls', and is emblazoned with the school motto: 'The best education today for the woman of tomorrow'.

(Ball and Gerwitz, 1997, p. 212)

Part of the image or 'presentation of self' was the promotion of dance and drama productions, and especially music. Schools in competition for middle-class parents have to promote the playing of an instrument as an option.

Local co-educational schools in the sample

responded by placing emphasis on the recruitment of girls in their marketing, and some also emphasized girl-friendly strategies such as separate play areas and separate teaching. However, it was made clear that co-educational schools were interested in a particular kind of girl – not all girls, but swots.

Discussion point

How do some girls subvert school uniform to convey a very different image from that of the traditional and respectable?

C3.1a

Activity

a From the evidence offered above, list the advantages and disadvantages, first to girls and then to boys, of single-sex schools. What are your conclusions? Is the case for single-sex education proved?

b Discuss the effects of the marketization of education on single-sex girls' schools and co-educational schools. Who are the losers and who are the winners?

C3.1a, C3.2, C3.3

11.6 Educational participation and the implications for policy and provision

The National Curriculum and cross-curricular themes

Is the National Curriculum new?

To a historian of education like Aldrich (1988), one of the striking things about the National Curriculum is that it is at least 83 years old. He makes a comparison of the subjects included in the syllabus prescribed by the Board of Education in 1904 – following the 1902 Act which established state secondary schools – and those of the 1987 National Curriculum:

1904	1987
English	English
mathematics	mathematics
science	science
history	history
geography	geography
a foreign language	a modern foreign language
drawing	art
physical training (PT)	physical education (PE)
manual work/ housewifery	design and technology
	music

Thus the only subject not included in 1904 was music.

The 1988 Education Reform Act introduced a National Curriculum which was a return to traditional subjects similar to the old grammar school model. It provided three core subjects (maths, English and science), and seven foundation subjects (art, music, technology, history, geography, a modern foreign language and PE). In addition, locally determined agreed syllabuses for religious education were to be taught.

The curriculum for each subject was laid down in statutory orders, with attainment targets, programmes of study and ten levels of attainment defining what a pupil must know, understand and be able to do at each level. Pupil achievement was to be assessed through standard national tests at the ends of four Key Stages: at age 7 (KS1), 11 (KS2), 14 (KS3) and 16 (KS4).

The dismantling of the National Curriculum

No sooner had the Curriculum been established than it became obvious that it would need to be amended. Key Stage 4 (KS4) was the first to be changed.

In 1991 the then Secretary of State for Education, John MacGregor, announced that 'curriculum overload' could be solved by the introduction of short or combined courses at GCSE. Pupils could study either history or geography or a combination of both.

In 1992–93 there was strong opposition to the National Curriculum from parents, employers, the training lobby and teachers. This came to a head with a boycott of Standard Assessment Tests (SATs) by all the teaching unions. The then Secretary of State for Education, John Patten, thus appointed Sir Ron Dearing as chairman of the School Curriculum and Assessment Authority (SCAA), to make recommendations to slim down the Curriculum. Evidence collected during a three-month consultation period from teachers, industry and examination boards, amongst others, indicated that there was widespread support for the *principle* of a National Curriculum, but severe reservations about the way in which it had developed.

The most serious reservations were that it was over-prescriptive and administratively complex – especially regarding the mass of statements of attainment. There was strong feeling that it had been introduced too quickly and that teachers had not been consulted properly. This evidence informed Dearing's final report which recommended that the National Curriculum be slimmed down for 5–14-year-olds to make it less prescriptive, and to free 20 per cent of the teaching time for use at the discretion of the school. At KS4 only English, mathematics, single science, physical education, short courses in a modern foreign language and design and technology, religious education and sex education are now mandatory. To allow scope for vocational options at KS4, a General National Vocational Qualification (GNVQ) was to be developed for 14–16-year-olds with the lead body for vocational qualifications (NCVQ). Their brief was also to investigate whether work undertaken as part of GCSE courses could count towards GNVQ accreditation. (For further information on vocational qualifications, see Section 11.7.)

That the ten-level scale should be retained, but reformed, was also recommended. This was to be done by significantly reducing the statements of attainment and levels of attainment. Also recommended was that no further major changes should be made to the National Curriculum Orders for five years following the review. To satisfy the anti-SATs lobby, Dearing recommended that national tests were to be administered only in core subjects. His recommendations were accepted and he then moved on to a review of the post-16 curriculum.

Cross-curricular themes

These were added almost as an afterthought when it became increasingly obvious that the traditional subject model adopted was not well-suited to the promotion of 'the spiritual, moral, cultural, mental and physical development of pupils at school and of society', and to the preparation of pupils 'for the opportunities, responsibility and experiences of adult life', as required by the Education Reform Act 1988. These cross-curricular themes were: education for economic and industrial understanding, careers education, health education, environmental education and citizenship.

Interesting research by Whitty *et al.* (1994), using Bernstein's theories of the framing and classification of knowledge, analyses the relationship between cross-curricular themes and the core and foundation subjects. This research sought to discover how these themes would be organized and taught in schools. Schools were asked whether their delivery of the cross-curricular themes had changed as a result of the ERA 1988, and to identify how the themes were delivered. Various models of delivery emerged, including permeation through the core and foundation subjects, through personal and social education, through the pastoral system, and through integrated humanities.

Whitty *et al.* found that economic and industrial understanding was the most fully permeated theme. Health education and careers were the least permeated, having instead the status of quasi-subjects. Head teachers, teachers and pupils were interviewed, and classroom observations were conducted. The researchers found that some subject teachers in virtually all the schools visited intimated that they did not believe that they should be asked to teach the themes. During one interview a science teacher rejected his role in health education; he was quite happy to teach about tooth decay, but not the necessity to clean one's teeth:

[Science teacher]: 'It's not our job at all. We do do it, but we shouldn't have to. Parents should do it. Our main aim is to get them through the exam. ... we're not nappy changers ... nannies.'

(Whitty *et al.*, 1994)

It was felt that cross-curricular themes 'polluted' the subject and were potentially threatening to the integrity of science as a subject. Thus the strongly framed and classified collection code of the core and foundation subjects sat uneasily with the weakly framed and classified integrated code of the cross-curricular themes.

One way of making sense of the difficulties of linking subjects and themes is Bernstein's work on different contexts being identified by different recognition and realization rules:

- Recognition rules are the clues that pupils use to determine what is a proper school subject. Does specialist equipment such as books, aprons, and PE kit have to be brought to lessons? Is there written work and homework?
- Realization rules tell pupils how or how not to demonstrate knowledge. What form does written work take, what is acceptable oral communication, activity in PE and what sort of things can be made in technology and art?

Activity

a Develop the description of realization and recognition rules by comparing two subjects, one that is strongly framed and classified and one that is weakly framed and classified. How useful are the concepts?

b Carry out a small investigation into the importance of 'talk' or 'chat' in lessons. Interview students about how they view talk in different lessons. What are the rules that determine the use of talk and its status?

c National Curriculum history, English and geography are criticized by some teachers and educationalists for being Eurocentric and racist. Find copies of the most recent curriculum Orders for one of these subjects in your school or college library. Use content analysis to test the above claim.

C3.1a, C3.2, C3.3

One of the key problems of using subjects to teach themes lies in the rules that relate to the use of talk in different contexts. The researchers found that pupils drew a strong distinction between subject discourses and talk, which they saw as not directly related to subjects. Chat in lessons had an illicit feel to it, associated with being off-task or something to get away with. It belonged to the world outside and was different from subject discourse. This ambiguity about the status of talk across different subjects and the importance of the talk of everyday life in teaching the themes also accounted for difficulties in a permeation model. If subject discourses are differentiated by their distinct recognition and realization rules, it will always be difficult to switch between subjects and themes.

The National Curriculum review

Five years later, the Curriculum is being reviewed by a Labour government. However, what has been proposed is tinkering at the edges rather than wholesale change, intended to be evolutionary rather than revolutionary. The Curriculum has been slimmed down by reducing the prescriptive nature of the content in the ten compulsory subjects, allowing schools more choice about what they teach. In an attempt to cut truancy levels of pupils of 14+, schools will be allowed to 'disapply' two subjects out of science, a modern language and design and technology.

Citizenship and the Curriculum

The most radical proposal is the introduction of compulsory citizenship lessons in secondary schools. According to the Secretary of State for Education, David Blunkett:

Lessons in citizenship will teach children to have more pride in their own culture while respecting the traditions of others. ... We have tended to play down our culture and we need to reinforce our pride in what we have. ... This does not mean jingoistic nationalism.

(Quoted in the *Guardian*, 13 May 1999)

Discussion point

What other motives may the government have in introducing compulsory citizenship education?

C3.1a

Teachers' leaders have expressed fears that the proposed new National Curriculum is unworkable and too overcrowded. If citizenship education takes up 5 per cent of curriculum time, then more needs to be cut from the core curriculum, they claim.

Introducing statutory citizenship and giving more emphasis to social and personal education is perhaps a recognition that cross-curriculum themes have not been a great success.

Intelligence, ethnicity and the IQ debate

There has been a rise in the influence of New Right ideas in education (see also Section 6.1). Some of these have a resemblance to functionalist ideas, though in a rather crude form. An example of this is a book called *The Bell Curve: Intelligence and Class Structure in American Life* by Herrnstein and Murray published in 1994, which became a bestseller. Before the ideas in the book can be understood it is necessary to understand some of the debates about intelligence, intelligence testing and 'race'.

Intelligence, intelligence testing and 'race'

It was Binet, a French psychologist, who produced the first intelligence test in 1905 to identify children with special educational needs. Binet tried to separate out innate ability by using a variety of tasks that did not require reading or writing. This was because he believed that intelligence was too complex to reduce to a single number or score. The aim of his scale was to help children to develop and improve, not to label them as in deficit. Binet would not have approved of the subsequent use of IQ to label, limit and stream pupils.

It was then a German psychologist, Stern, who developed a measure known as an Intelligence Quotient (IQ), which is the ratio of a pupil's mental age to their actual age. This measure was welcomed by some as it allowed the abilities of pupils to be described through a simple number. This was potentially very dangerous. American psychologists then highjacked Binet's measures and called them intelligence tests. They assumed that intelligence was inherited and confused environmental and cultural differences with innate abilities.

In England it was psychologist Cyril Burt who promoted the idea that intelligence is innate, inherited and measurable. He claimed that intelligence, as opposed to knowledge, remains unaffected by teaching or training and can be measured with accuracy and ease. Burt thought that once the intelligence of a pupil was measured this should form the basis of selection to an appropriate type of education to meet the needs of the individual. There was a limited and biologically determined pool of talent and only these talented pupils were capable of academic success in higher education.

The 1944 Education Act

After the 1944 Education Act, intelligence tests formed the basis of the 11-plus examination,

used to decide whether a child should proceed to a grammar, secondary modern or technical school. Within these schools, and in larger primary schools, pupils were also streamed according to ability.

The result of this selection was that most working-class children ended up in secondary moderns and most middle-class children in grammar schools. To some educationalists this reinforced the idea that intelligence is derived genetically, while to others it indicated that the whole basis of selection was unfair. The nature/nurture debate – of whether it is environmental or hereditary factors (or both) that determine educational and occupational success – continued to be waged.

The system of selection at age 11 was challenged by the movement towards comprehensive schools and the abolition of the 11-plus by most local education authorities in the 1960s. In many schools, mixed-ability teaching replaced streaming. This was an attempt to break what was regarded as a socially divisive and unfair system of selection which labelled so many working-class children as failures.

In 1969, arguments about intelligence and 'race' were sparked off when Jensen published a paper in the USA which claimed that Operation Headstart, a compensatory education scheme, had failed to improve the educational achievement of ghetto, mainly black, children – because of the belief that intelligence is genetically determined and cannot be changed by educational reforms. Jensen went on to argue that this justified a different basic education for black children and others with low intelligence quotients (IQs). For his evidence Jensen drew on statistics drawn up by Burt.

Why the use of IQ was discredited

Discrediting of the use of the IQ measure for determining a child's education was based partly on the discrediting of Burt's classic study of intelligence.

- He was found to have increased his sample of twins from less than 20 to more than 50 and to have produced correlations that were statistically impossible. His data on the IQs of close relatives were also found to be fraudulent. Was this carelessness or deliberate fakery? Two of Burt's 'researchers' were discovered not to have been involved in the research. Defenders of Burt claim that the attack on his work was part of a left-wing plot by those supporting an environmental rather than an hereditary position on IQ. Others say that Burt was a sick man.

- A second reason for discrediting IQ tests was that they were usually drawn up by white middle-class educationalists. So, despite claiming to test innate ability and often using non-verbal reasoning, the tests were seen to be still culturally biased.

Discussion point
How similar are Burt's ideas on intelligence to functionalist ideas on education?

C3.1a

- A third reason for discrediting IQ tests was that the scores were unreliable. Performance in the test depends on many variables: where the test takes place, who conducts it, how confident the pupil feels, and so on. This also relates to the ethnicity of those involved in the testing. In 1968, a white psychologist carried out some testing with a black assistant in a south London comprehensive. African–Caribbean pupils were found to score much worse when tested by the white psychologist rather than by his black assistant (Gipps and Murphy, 1994, p. 47).

- Finally, some sociologists would claim that intelligence and intelligence testing are social constructs or discourses which change over time and in different locations, rather than being genetic or biological. They are, however, very political. Kamin (1974) states:

There exists no data which should lead a prudent man to accept the hypothesis that IQ test scores are in any degree heritable. That conclusion is so much at odds with prevailing wisdom that it is necessary to ask, how can so many psychologists believe the opposite?

(Kamin, 1974, p. 1)

He anwers his own question:

The IQ test in America, and the way in which we think about it, has been fostered by men committed to a particular social view. That view includes the belief that those on the bottom are genetically infe-rior victims of their own immutable defects. The con-sequence has been that the IQ test has served as an instrument of oppression against the poor ... dressed up in the trappings of science rather than politics.

(Kamin, 1974, pp. 1–2)

Discussion point
How would you test the IQ of a Martian?

C3.1a

The re-emergence of views based on biological notions of intelligence

Herrnstein and Murray: the Bell Curve in the USA

Herrnstein and Murray's (1994) book, mentioned earlier in this section, argues that socio-economic differences between blacks and whites can be explained by differences in intelligence. Put crudely, what they are saying is that whites are cleverer than blacks, that low intelligence is largely the result of genetic inheritance. This they claim explains most of the problems faced by the USA – namely crime, poverty, dependency on welfare and unemployment. They state that new social policies are necessary which accept that social class and racial inequalities are inevitable. In relation to education they suggest scrapping affirmative action in higher education and shift-ing educational resources to more gifted students. Spending money on less intelligent pupils is a waste of money, they claim.

Affirmative action is rather like positive dis-crimination, and covers a range of measures to redress the balance in favour of under-repre-sented groups. Some higher education institu-tions, for example, require different levels of qualifications for members of ethnic minority groups. One of Herrnstein and Murray's prominent themes is that such egalitarian policies victimize whites and privilege minority groups. Another theme is that IQ tests give a fair and accurate measure of people's abilities for selection to higher education and occupations.

Criticisms of Herrnstein and Murray

The work of Herrnstein and Murray has been heavily criticized by educationalists and sociolo-gists on both sides of the Atlantic. Drew *et al.* (1995) present an excellent critique. This can be summarized in the following points:

- Herrnstein and Murray do not present an objective case. Those criticizing IQ testing are presented as ideologically motivated charlatans whereas its supporters are seen as fair-minded and rigorous.

- They present only one side of the case, quoting only sources that support their position. They use racist sources from academics with poor records of research.

- They use simplistic and unspecified definitions of intelligence, intelligence testing and IQ testing. They substitute cognitive ability for intelligence and assert for general purposes that intelligence is the same as what Americans mean by being 'smart'.

- They claim that IQ tests are not demonstrably biased against social, economic, ethnic or racial groups.

- They ignore the contemporary consensus of those working in the field of intelligence that IQ is not fixed, that many IQ tests are not generally useful, and that there is no basis for the assertion that racial differences in IQ are due to genetics (Sternberg, 1995).

- They almost completely ignore the research on racism and educational and occupational inequalities, apart from a few grudging references to the work of W. J. Wilson, author of *The Truly Disadvantaged* (1987).

- There is very little discussion of gender differences or of the interactions of ethnic, gender and social class interactions in their work.

Drew and colleagues thus conclude:

Despite its user friendly presentation, therefore, The Bell Curve is bad science. It trades on the hard, factual image of statistical data and peddles conclu-

Table 11.5 Myths, mythical counter-myths, and truths about intelligence

Myth	Mythical counter-myth	Truth
1 Intelligence is one thing, g (or IQ)	Intelligence is so many things you can hardly count them	Intelligence is multidimensional but scientifically tractable
2 The social order is a natural outcome of the IQ pecking order	Tests wholly create a social order	The social order is partially but not exclusively created by tests
3 Intelligence cannot be taught to any meaningful degree	We can perform incredible feats in teaching individuals to be more intelligent	We can teach intelligence in at least some degree, but cannot effect radical changes at this point
4 IQ tests measure virtually all that's important for school and job success	IQ tests measure virtually nothing that's important for school and job success	IQ tests measure skills that are of moderate importance in school success and of modest importance in job success
5 We are using tests too little, losing valuable information	We're over-using tests and should abolish them	Tests, when properly interpreted, can serve a useful but limited function, but often they are not properly interpreted
6 We as a society are getting stupider because of the dysgenic effects of stupid superbreeders	We have no reason at all to fear any decline in intellectual abilities among successive generations	We have some reason to fear loss of intellectual abilities in future generations, but the problem is not stupid superbreeders
7 Intelligence is essentially all inherited except for trivial and unexplainable variance	Intelligence is essentially all environmental except for trivial and unexplainable variance	Intelligence involves substantial heritable and environmental components in interaction
8 Racial differences in IQ clearly lead to differential outcomes	Racial differences in IQ have nothing to do with differential environmental outcomes	We don't really understand the relationships among 'race', IQ, and environmental outcomes
9 We should write off stupid people	There's no such thing as a stupid person – everyone is smart	We need to rethink what we mean by 'stupid' and 'smart'

Source: Sternberg (1996)

sions which threaten to exacerbate, not lessen, the social divisions and conflicts which lie at the heart of the 'race' and IQ debate.

(Drew *et al.*, 1995, p. 25)

Sternberg (1996), concerned about the media attention to debates about IQ, attempts to outline the current state of knowledge and to avoid extreme positions. Table 11.5 lists the myths, counter-myths and what he believes to be truths about human intelligence.

Activity

1 James Tooley (1995) took up the arguments from Herrnstein and Murray in relation to education in an article in *Economic Affairs* entitled 'Can IQ tests liberate education?' Below are some quotes from the article in which Tooley espouses a New Right position on intelligence. Making use of the information in Table 11.5, evaluate each of the quotes.

   a 'IQ is a better predictor of work productivity than any other single measure.'

   b 'IQ stabilizes at about ten years of age.'

   c 'IQ tests are more efficient than sorting pupils by GCSE or A levels.'

   d 'Low-scoring children will need to be warned that certain employment is likely to be out of reach.'

   e 'Low-scoring pupils can be provided with education that does not involve humiliating public examinations; the child can approach education for whatever intrinsic delights it holds.'

   f 'Telling pupils that they can do well is rather like telling a boy who is short that, if only he will exercise enough, he can play in the top basketball team.'

   g 'If students do not want to partake of the riches of the curriculum offered to them, then they should be allowed to refuse ... and take with them educational credits to be used when they want to avail themselves of learning opportunities.'

2 Draw up a chart of the similarities and differences between New Right, functionalist and Marxist ideas on education and intelligence. You will need to draw on the appropriate sections of this chapter.

C3.2, C3.3

Debates and concerns about inequalities in educational participation and achievement and barriers to greater levels of participation have always been a central element in debates about the sociology of education. They have also formed an important backdrop to educational policy decisions and the actions of governments. In this section we will consider various issues about educational participation by various social groups in society.

New Labour's 'third way' approach to educational policy

The election of a Labour government in May 1997 ended nearly two decades of Conservative rule. A key question is whether the government's policies on education are substantially different from those introduced by the New Right and the neo-Conservatives?

The 'third way' favoured by the Prime Minister, Tony Blair, rejects both the marketization of education favoured by the New Right and the over-centralized state control of the Old Left. Some of the values of the left – such as social justice, community and solidarity – are re-worked to meet the needs of a new global, post-modern world. Labour's election promise of 'education, education, education' has resulted in a number of new educational initiatives – for example, teachers can now be nominated for special 'oscars'; the assisted-places scheme has been abolished; literacy and numeracy hours are in place in primary schools; the National Curriculum has been reviewed, and compulsory citizenship education introduced in secondary schools, as discussed above.

Educational 'action zones'

These are another government initiative and an excellent example of how the 'third way' approach is intended to work. The least popular schools, produced by the quasi-market in education and which have been 'named and shamed' by school inspectors, are being rescued as educational 'action zones'. These zones consist of about twenty schools, typically feeder primaries with one or two secondaries. They are run by a forum of 'partners' including representatives from schools, local councils, central government and local businesses. These businesses have contributed £250 000 in cash or kind, with the remaining £750 000 from central government. The zones do not have to teach the

National Curriculum so that they can focus more on basic skills such as literacy and numeracy.

Arguments in favour of action zones

- Energy and money are being ploughed into disadvantaged areas.
- Parents, teachers, governors, local community groups and businesses will work together and have more say in education.
- Realistic targets will improve standards.
- Their new exciting, innovative approach could benefit the whole educational system.

Arguments against action zones

- Funds are too small to make a significant difference.
- Failing schools could become even more cut off from the rest of the education system and their pupils labelled as failures.
- They are simply a re-working of Educational Priority Areas of the 1960s. They cannot compensate for the social disadvantages that pupils face in health and housing as well as education.
- The involvement of business could mean that the power of locally elected councils is bypassed. This could result in another layer of unaccountable bureaucracy.

> ### 💬 Discussion point
> How do educational action zones illustrate a 'third way' approach in education?
>
> C3.1a

New Labour, 'race' and the inclusion agenda

In seventeen years of Conservative rule, successive governments derided the discources of equal opportunities in favour of 'choice', 'quality' and 'standards.' New Labour is to be applauded for at least putting equality and social justice back on the policy agenda. Evidence of these concerns are the high-profile reports *Excellence in Schools* (DfEE, 1997), *Truancy and Social Exclusion* (1998) and more recently *Excellence in Cities* (1999).

The first two reports offer evidence of 'race' inequalities and suggest that schools and teachers often contribute unintentionally to this prob-

lem. However, Gillborn *et al.* (1999) offer a critique of the approach. This can be summarized as follows:

- Labour's approach to social justice is simplistic and limited to equality of provision rather than outcome.
- 'Race' and ethnic diversity are just 'added on' features rather than being an integral aspect of policy.
- Research findings (Hallam and Toutounji, 1996) indicate that setting, streaming and selection, as well as tiering in GCSE examinations, work against the attainment of black and working-class pupils. Yet the reports mentioned above support such pupil groupings as a solution to low attainment. Use of such selection by schools is likely to deepen existing inequalities.
- New Labour has adopted a type of naïve multiculturalism instead of robust 'race'-specific targets for levels of attainment or reductions in exclusions.

Educational participation – the example of special educational needs

A sociology of special education

Tomlinson (1982) makes a strong plea for a sociology of special educational needs which she says has been marginalized in the sociology of education for too long:

Over the last thirty years, sociologists have devoted much time and energy to demonstrating the inequities of selection by 'brightness' in education while ignoring the progressive removal of more and more children from normal education on the grounds of defect, dullness, handicap or special need.

(Tomlinson, 1982, p. 9)

Tomlinson makes a case specifically for a sociology of special education rather than its dominance by psychology, which tends to consider individuals as divorced from wider social contexts. Sociology, she claims, would view it as a public issue, a social process with the categories used as socially constructed and ripe for some de-mystification. Drawing on C. W. Mills' concept of a sociological imagination, she says:

The promise of the sociological imagination is to help people understand the interrelationship between his-

tory and individual lives, between the so called private and the public. This imagination is urgently needed in special education to examine the way in which the private trouble of having produced, or being, a child with special needs, and the resultant referral, assessment, labelling and diagnosing, is related to the wider social structure, to processes of social and cultural reproduction, and to the ideologies and rationalisations which are produced to mystify the participants, and often to perplex the practitioners.

(Tomlinson, 1982, p. 25)

Since those words were written in 1982 the position of pupils with 'special educational needs' (SEN) and the language used to categorize them has changed considerably, in part due to legislation. This will be considered in detail, but first some historical context is necessary.

A brief history of special education

Tomlinson (1982) provides a sociological analysis of the social origins of special education. She points out that there are two main interpretations of the history of SEN provision. One regards it as fuelled by the motives of benevolent humanitarianism, and the other by social, economic and political interests. The former has been disputed as the motive by sociologists like Barton (1988):

... the view that concern for the handicapped has developed as a result of progress, enlightenment and humanitarian interests is totally unacceptable. The experience of this particular disadvantaged group has generally been one of exploitation, exclusion, dehumanisation and regulation.

(Barton, 1988, p. 276)

Let us look briefly at the historical evidence.

The 1870 Education Act

Full state provision for all children began in 1870 with Forster's Education Act. State provision for special education in England and Wales dates from 1874 when separate classes for deaf pupils were established by the London School Board.

The 1893 Elementary Education (Blind and Deaf Children) Act

This 1893 Act required local authorities to provide separate education for deaf and blind children. In the early 1890s the first classes and schools were set up in London and Leicester for Special Instruction for 'Defective' Children, and so the term 'special' entered educational discourse.

Before the 1870s education was dominated by churches, especially the Anglican church, who showed no interest in the education of the handicapped. It was individual businessmen with the profit motive in mind who saw an opportunity to exploit them. In early schools for the deaf and blind, commercial interests dominated. This was justified as an attempt to save pupils from 'idleness'. In these schools trade and vocational training took place. This emphasis became more pronounced after the introduction of state education:

... the blind, deaf, dumb and the educable class of imbecile ... if left uneducated become not only a burden to themselves but a weighty burden to the state. It is in the interests of the state to educate them, so as to dry up, as far as possible, the minor streams which must ultimately swell to a great torrent of pauperism.

(Egerton Commission, 1889; quoted in Tomlinson, 1982, p. 38)

Education and the mentally handicapped

There was also a political motive in the social control of groups who may prove troublesome. Links had been assumed between defect, moral depravity, crime and unemployment. This was also true for the mentally handicapped for whom separate provision developed in the late nineteenth century. Contemporary echoes of this debate are examined in Section 12.6.

At this time the medical profession, struggling for professional recognition, also had a vested interest in the education of people with mental handicap. They claimed the right to oversee their education. Moves to segregate pupils with mental handicap stemmed from fears about possible dangers to society, especially the hereditary nature of such 'defects'. The moves were also intended to allow normal schools to operate smoothly. Throughout the twentieth century the stigmatization and separation of children with special needs continued. In the 1920s another group of professionals entered the arena – psychologists. Cyril Burt, then considered a progressive, initiated the use of intelligence tests to decide whether pupils had learning difficulties.

The 1944 Education Act

The 1944 Act stated that local education authorities were required to meet the needs of pupils suffering from any disability of mind or body. This transferred responsibility from the medical domain to the educational one. For most children this meant education in special schools because, despite the stated intention of the Act to teach the less seriously handicapped in ordinary schools, this did not happen.

A change of approach in the 1980s

In the Warnock Report and the 1981 Education Act, it was stated that, in planning appropriate services, it should be assumed that about one in six children at any time and one in five at some time in their educational career will need some form of special educational provision. Such children will need one or more of the following (Warnock, 1978, 3.19):

- provision of special means of access to the curriculum through special equipment, facilities or resources, modifications of the physical environment or specialist teaching techniques
- provision of a special or modified curriculum
- particular attention to the social structure and emotional climate in which education takes place.

In the 1981 Education Act that followed the report, special educational needs are defined in terms of:

- significantly greater learning difficulties than the majority of children of the age group
- having a disability which either prevents or hinders a child from making use of the educational facilities generally available in schools.

The Warnock Report

The Warnock Report and the legislation that followed it contained some important and radical changes in the approach to special education. The first of these was that special educational needs were to be seen as a continuum from those with severe and enduring needs to those with milder and more temporary needs. Such children were not to be seen as discrete and separate from the rest of the school population; and of the approximate 20 per cent with special needs, 18 per cent would be taught in mainstream schools and 2 per cent would continue to be taught in special schools.

Secondly, learning difficulties were to be seen as interactive – a result of complex interactions of the social and cultural and learning environment rather than a deficit in the pupils themselves. The social construction of special needs was recognized. As a result of this the system of categorizing children was to be abolished:

We believe that the basis for decisions about the type of educational provision which is required should not be a single label 'handicapped' but rather a detailed description of special educational need. We therefore recommend that the statutory categorisation of handicapped pupils should be abolished.

(Warnock, 1978, 3.25)

The decision about who was to qualify for this special provision was to be decided within a partnership between members of the various educational services and parents. There would be an assessment procedure in which the needs of the pupil and how the local authority would meet these needs would be stated. This became known as 'statementing'.

Discussion point

Are special educational needs socially constructed?

C3.1a

A mixed response

The 1981 Act was met with a mixed response. For some it was a welcome extension of the rights of parents and children, a move towards the flexible integration of pupils with special educational needs and away from the stigmatizing labels attached to them. Some critics of the changes pointed to the composition of the Warnock committee: the fact that no 'handicapped' person was a member, and that there was no ethnic-minority member, despite the fact that a disproportionate number of black children were referred to schools for what were called then the 'educationally sub-normal' or 'maladjusted'.

Another criticism was that the funding implications were not addressed, and without considerably more money the 18 per cent of children might be neglected. Yet another was that the concept of educational needs and integration also hides institutionalized discrimination.

A study by Croll and Moses (1985) of the incidence of special needs in ordinary schools found that, in terms of behavioural problems, boys outnumbered girls by almost four to one. It also appeared that more children from ethnic minority backgrounds are seen to have special educational needs than white children.

Tomlinson (1985) asked why it was that, if all manner of children have special educational needs, the system caters mainly for the children of the manual working-class. Whether the implementation of the Act has led to a real improvement in integration appeared to be influenced by a combination of the traditional practices of the local education authority, politics, and luck (Riddell and Brown, 1994).

The 1988 Education Reform Act

After 1981, further Conservative educational reforms restructured education in fundamental ways that affected provision for pupils with special educational needs. The ERA 1988 set up the National Curriculum and local management of schools (LMS). Since then there has been a debate about whether the effects of these changes have worked against or in favour of the progress made by the 1981 Act.

Assessing the possible effects is a complex matter. There is a sense in which a common curriculum for *all* pupils, including those with special educational needs, can be regarded as real progress – an *entitlement* curriculum. It could mean that discriminatory practices that excluded many pupils with special educational needs from mainstream schools and their curriculum disappear.

However, the effects of the market and LMS may work against progress made by a common curriculum. Bowe *et al.* (1992) looked at the effects of this on SEN policies in the schools in their study of the effects of the 1988 Act on schools. Figure 11.3 maps out the various constraints and possibilities affecting the working of the Act in relation to a school's SEN policy.

Formula funding by local educational authorities means that statemented students have quite high 'price tags', but the other 18 per cent of non-statemented pupils do not (Warnock, 1978). Some schools responded like the one below:

'The deputy head in charge of finances asked me whether I could get more children statemented so that we could get more money for the school.'

This means that pupils with special educational needs are seen not in terms of their needs but in terms of their worth in formula funding. Under the pressures that the legislative changes have brought, schools are then faced with hard choices. Should they attract statemented pupils and risk their school having an image of catering for the 'less able'? Or should they try to attract more able pupils without special needs who are more likely to stay on in the sixth form and therefore attract extra funding?

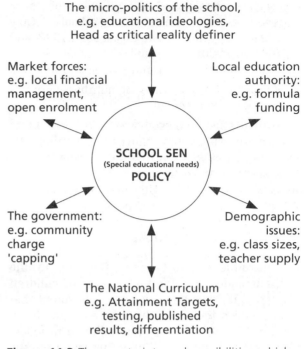

Figure 11.3 The constraints and possibilities which could affect a school's SEN provision
Source: Bowe *et al.* (1992)

LMS and special educational needs provision

Research carried out into the effects of LMS on special educational needs provision between 1989 and 1992 involved three questionnaire surveys to all local education authorities in England (Lunt and Evans, 1994). The findings indicate that, despite the fact that LMS could have led to more openness, accountability, value for money and quality, it has in fact had a negative effect on provision for special educational needs. These negative effects can be summarized as follows:

1 There has been a reduction in centrally provided special needs support services.

2 There has been an increase in the number of pupils seeking statements. This is a result of funding following the individual pupil rather than schools being allocated a budget that allows them to cater for a wide range of both statemented and non-statemented pupils (thus threatening the Warnock notion of a continuum of needs).

3 There has been a trend towards more placements in special schools. The move towards the integration of pupils with special educational needs into mainstream schools initiated by the 1981 Act should have resulted in the closure of

special schools and the transfer of those resources to mainstream schools. Only 100 special schools have closed since 1982, and 100 000 children are still segregated (Swann, 1991; quoted in Lunt and Evans, 1994).

4 There has been a rise in the numbers of pupils excluded from schools.

A positive effect reported was that some LEAs have made substantial moves to monitor the effectiveness of SEN provision. However, LMS does seem to have impacted negatively on the integration of pupils with special educational needs into mainstream schooling.

The 1993 Education Act

The introduction of Parents' Charters in the 1990s included one for the parents of children with special educational needs. This stated that their children had the right to be educated in an ordinary school wherever possible and to follow all the subjects in the National Curriculum to the best of their ability. The rights of such parents were then strengthened by the 1993 Education Act's Code of Practice which imposed on schools a clear procedure for the identification of special needs provision and a programme and timetable for each child as to how these needs were to be met. The responsibility for meeting these needs now lies with the ordinary classroom teacher supported by a team and SEN co-ordinator.

Case Study – inclusive education

The term 'integration' has recently come under attack. It can mean that pupils with special educational needs are educated in mainstream schools geographically, while in terms of their experiences they may still be excluded from the mainstream curriculum. More progressive boroughs and schools now prefer to use the term 'inclusive'.

Corbett (1994) explains inclusive education using a definition from Toronto in Canada:

Inclusion means inclusion! It means affiliation, combination ... Inclusion does not mean that we are all the same. Inclusion does not mean that we all agree. Rather inclusion celebrates our diversity and difference with respect and gratitude ... Inclusion is an antidote to racism and sexism because it welcomes these differences, and celebrates them as capacities rather than deficiencies ... Inclusion means all together supporting one another.

(CIEC, 1992, pp. 1–4; quoted in Corbett, 1994)

Such a position seems to recognize other oppressions and to celebrate difference and diversity. What does it mean in practice? The London Borough of Newham provides us with a case study.

For Newham, firstly it meant closing all the special schools in the borough and all the pupils attending mainstream schools. Teachers in special schools were then employed in mainstream schools. The experience of Newham shows that some parents were happy for their children to attend mainstream schools. They wanted them to share the same educational experiences as other children and to avoid the stigma and the often unchallenging curriculum of special schools. Others feared for their children in what they saw as inhospitable mainstream schools and preferred the sanctuary of special schools where specialist staff and small classes ensured a safe environment.

Secondly it was part of an equal opportunities policy developed by Newham teachers and the LEA. Not all teachers supported the move unless there was careful planning, proper funding, resourcing and training. Some were suspicious that it was just a cost-cutting exercise.

Thirdly it meant that the aims of education were the same for all children and they were all to be taught the same National Curriculum.

This policy of inclusive education was a brave move by Newham, a borough that has high levels of poverty, homelessness and racial prejudice. This begs the question of whether progressive educational policies like this one can survive at a time when the introduction of market forces makes competition for scarce resources undermine the notion of working together for social justice.

Researching special educational needs

It is clear that the voice that is missing from all the debates on special educational needs is that of the pupils themselves. Some recent research has given a voice to those previously marginalized.

Armstrong's (1995a) study is part of research undertaken in three local education authorities between 1989 and 1991, into the assessment of children having emotional and behavioural difficulties (Galloway *et al.*, 1994). Armstrong interviewed 47 children forming three sub-samples:

seven in an off-site unit, eleven in two residential schools, and 29 who were being assessed at the time of the study. He found that children felt they had not been allowed to tell their side of the story in their assessment, and that they had been disempowered by the process. An example of this is George's meeting with an educational psychologist:

George: 'I've been visited by someone in school called a socialist (sic). I didn't like seeing her because I thought they were going to take me away. I couldn't talk to them and tell them about what I felt. They kept talking and I couldn't get a chance to speak. If I had the chance to speak I would have said I didn't want to go away. I wanted to stay with my parents and family.'

(Armstrong, 1995b, p. 91)

Recently sociologists have suggested using a Foucauldian framework for researching special needs education:

Foucault (1967) argues that confinement, segregation, stigmatization and exclusion are all ways in which societies at different stages in their history have reacted to those construed as 'other', different and abnormal. Who is categorized in this way, on what grounds, and what happens to them is dependent upon the cultural and economic influences manifest in particular spatial and historical moments. Just as the ways in which society treats its 'deviants' gives us an insight into that society, we suggest that special education can be a particularly informative 'lens' through which to examine the changes occurring in the education system as a whole.

(Evans and Vincent, 1996, p. 102)

This offers insightful possibilities. As Allen (1994) states, Foucault is useful in two respects. His work on medicine, madness, discipline and punishment is relevant to the study of experiences of children with special educational needs. He provides us with a methodology of analysing the discourses of special education. Allen suggests that this analysis can operate on three levels:

- *macro* – what is said in official reports
- *micro* – informal accounts from SEN pupils, their classmates and teachers
- *meso* – what is said about pupils with SEN in statements and reports.

She used this approach to analyse how mainstreaming policies in Scottish schools affected a sample of 16 pupils with a range of special educational needs. Pupils were shadowed and they, their peers, teachers and parents were inter-

viewed. The emphasis was on their conversations with others, rather than attempting to construct their reality of mainstreaming. School documents relating to these pupils were also examined. Handled with sensitivity such research can give a voice to those so absent from much research on pupils with special educational needs – the pupils themselves. As Allen concludes:

It also offers to explore the relationship between the 'prettifying euphemisms', adopted in our current climate of political correctness (Shapiro, 1993), and the ways in which children with special educational needs are spoken about in mainstream schools.

(Allen, 1994, p. 9)

Activity

a Analyse the times in your life when you may have had real difficulties with learning something. Compare this to times when your learning curve has hit the roof. How do these reflections relate to the idea that special educational needs are interactive and socially constructed?

b Analyse the terms used in this section to describe learning difficulties and disabilities from the nineteenth century onwards. How and why has it changed? What are the 'prettifying euphemisms' used? Is this language satisfactory? If not, how could it be improved?

c What does the position of students with special educational needs tell us about the effects of the marketization of education? Use the Evans and Vincent (1996) idea that: 'Special education can be a particularly informative "lens" through which to examine the changes occurring in the education system as a whole.'

C3.1a, C3.3

11.7 Education and training: the vocational and academic curriculum

One of the key effects of the Great Education Debate, which started in the 1970s and continued throughout the 1980s and into the 1990s, was a reappraisal of the key role of education. This was reflected in a move away from notions of education as a cultural activity, whose key role was the development of cultured individuals, towards a more utilitarian view of the role of education as a provider of a trained workforce. This led to debates about the nature and content of education and the rise of vocationally oriented education and training. Central to this debate was the argument that the UK standard of living was suffering due to the decline in the economy, which was seen as being due to the lack of employment related skills taught in education. A greater emphasis on business and employment skills was linked to a greater emphasis on market methods as a way of providing a more efficient and employment-related form of education.

The 'Great Debate' on education

The start of what came to be known as the 'Great Debate' on education can be dated to October 1976 when the then Labour Prime Minister, James Callaghan, made a speech at Ruskin College, Oxford University, in which he was very critical of schools, education and teachers. In particular, he argued that the schools and the teachers were not providing pupils with the skills needed by industry and neither was the education system encouraging pupils to consider careers in industry:

I am concerned on my journeys to find complaints from industry that new recruits from schools sometimes do not have the basic tools to do the job that is required. ...

There is no virtue in producing socially well-adjusted members of society who are unemployed because they do not have the skills.

(James Callaghan quoted in Marsh *et al.*, 1996, p. 439)

This statement points to the way the Great Debate was framed in terms of questioning the role of education and implicitly suggesting that the needs of industry rather than the needs of the individual pupil should be the key determinant of educational success. It was also suggested that teachers were perhaps not the best people to work out and deliver these needs of industry. It is this debate that provided the pressure for the moves to introduce greater levels of vocational training that became known as the 'New Vocationalism'. Despite being started by Labour, these ideas were enthusiastically carried on by the Conservatives when they came to power in 1979. Indeed, their New Right philosophy was even more pro-industry and the New Right held

to a view that the failure of education to provide the skills needed by industry was one of the key causes of the industrial decline of the UK. These ideas led to the introduction of various schemes such as the Youth Training Scheme and later the introduction of NVQs and GNVQs.

One of the key interesting shifts is that in his original speech in 1976, James Callaghan did at least recognize the need for education to mitigate as far as possible the disadvantages to pupils that flow from poor home conditions, leading, of course, to debates about the relative importance of the home and the school in the construction of educational inequalities, and later on the debate about whether education can compensate for society. While this view did, therefore, at least recognize that factors outside the school may have an impact on the educational performance of pupils, the new vocationalism fairly squarely laid the blame for educational failure on the lack of work-oriented curriculum, on the anti-industry biases of the teachers and as a result on the lack of appropriate employment-related skills held by the pupils. The issue of the home background was removed from consideration.

It is also clear that New Labour (see Section 11.6) have adopted a similar stance in arguing that those who talk about the social background of pupils and the effect this has on their performance are in a sense expecting failure and do not have high enough expectations. This reflects a clear shift away from explanations of educational achievement and failure based on factors outside the school to factors inside the school. This shift has seen the emergence of talk of the effective school and consideration of the power of the teaching profession to act as a force for good or not.

Educational professionals and the educational debate

Ever since the advent of interactionist approaches in the sociology of education (See section 11.2), there has been concern about the effect that teachers and other educational professional may have on the outcome of education and training.

EDUCATION – THE GREAT DIVIDE

NICK DAVIES

Today is speech day at Roedean college. ... The headteacher, Patricia Metham, calls the girls up one by one, announcing their awards and their prizes and their exam results. ...

Down the grassy hill, on the far side of the Roedean playing fields, on this October Saturday it is just another morning on the Whitehawk estate. ... Whitehawk is a sprawl of terraced red-brick houses, home to something like 11,000 people, most of them white, many of them out of work. Whitehawk is the poorest estate in Brighton and one of the poorest 10% in the country.

While Patricia Metham is celebrating success, another headteacher is having a very different experience. Libby Coleman spent three long years as the headteacher of Stanley Deacon comprehensive school on the Whitehawk estate. ...

This is a story of two women. ... The two women have never met. The strip of land between Roedean and Whitehawk marks the most notorious division in British society. And yet, for all this separation, the women have this in common: that after several decades in teaching they know what makes schools tick.

A few weeks before Roedean's speech day, Tony Blair appeared on Channel 4 news and talked about this same division. He made clear how passionately he wants state schools to match the results of their private counterparts. You can see why. There are 550,000 children in private schools. They count for a mere 7% of the pupil population and yet provide more than 20% of those who make it to university and nearly 50% of those who go to Oxford and Cambridge. ... In the private schools 80% of pupils pass five or more GCSEs at grades A–C; in the state schools only 43% reach the same standard.

Why is this happening? In government circles, the answer has been agreed for years: teachers in state schools fail to do their job properly. The analysis is alarming: over a period of 30 years, beginning in the 60s, the quest for excellence was undermined by an obsession with equality; student teachers were injected with a theory of child-centered learning that poisoned the heart of pedagogy, allowing the pupil to dictate the pace and direction of teaching; discipline and effort were banned from classrooms where no child might now be accused of failure; whole-class instruction gave way to groups of children ambling along; criticism was replaced by consolation, and achievement was subverted by a poverty of expectation. By contrast, according to this view, private schools were inoculated from this progressive disease by their tradition of competitive achievement.

This perspective was born on the right as a rebuttal to the comprehensive movement. ...Rightwing journalists pursued the same critique with passion and found that, in opposition, Tony Blair's Labour Party had joined their crusade. ...

It is explicit in this analysis that the strength of private schools is not to be explained by their intake of highly motivated children from affluent families, compared with the deprived and demotivated children in some state schools – in the government's words, 'poverty is no excuse.'...

Stanley Deacon was struggling with poverty. Ms Coleman was struck by two things: some 45% of its pupils were poor enough to claim free school meals, and almost all of them were white. ...

Patricia Metham's study is a peaceful place. ... [Roedean] is a place of academic excellence but, more than that, she says, it is a place of breadth, which prizes drama and dance and sport and music. ...

It may be for this reason that although she knows what ministers and conservative journalists say about private schools such as hers, she does not agree with them. Not at all.

Teaching technique comes into their success, but her explanation has almost nothing in common with the government's analysis. It is built, first of all, on a simple foundation: the intake of children. "Those schools that dominate the league table choose, to be, and can afford to be, highly selective," she says. ...

It is no secret why a private school may do more for its children than a state school. Money. "If the government want state schools to offer what we offer, they are going to have to spend on each child something much closer to the fees that our parents pay," Mrs Metham says. Roedean is paid £10,260 a year for a day girl, roughly five times the amount a school like Whitehawk is given for each pupil. ...

If Patricia Metham is right – that this combination of a bright intake and adequate resources is the real foundation of her schools success– there is nevertheless more to her account. There is a third factor that finally defines the division between these two educational worlds. ...

When she was talking to the parents at Roedean's speech day, Patricia Metham warned her audience: "It's not easy being a teacher these days. What other profession is so beset by 'experts' who haven't ever done the job themselves and who wouldn't last five minutes in a real school?" ...

Nobody dictates terms to the teachers in Roedean. They are not answerable to David Blunkett, the education secretary, or his department or the LEA or Ofsted. They are not bound by the national curriculum or SATs or special measures or any of the superstructure of supervision that has settled over the state schools. And that is the third factor in Roedean's success: freedom to teach as its staff think best. ...

The great irony is that David Blunkett sits in his office, lost in admiration for the success of the private sector, entirely failing to understand that the key to that success is his own absence from their school.

Source: Adapted from the *Guardian*, 6 March 2000

Activity

Read the article 'Education – The Great Divide' the *Guardian* reproduced and use this and other material from this section to answer the following questions:

a What is the basis for the argument that 'teachers in state schools fail to do their job properly'?

b What factors other than the role of teachers and schools may account for the differences in outcome highlighted in the article?

c List and discuss the relative importance of the various factors which affect educational outcomes.

C3.1a, C3.2, C3.3

It is certainly clear that part of the context for the 'Great Debate' in education was a desire to promote vocationalism and a belief that teachers were hostile to this and therefore harming the education of children and the future economic prosperity of the nation. This is the clear implication of arguments that there is no point in producing socially well-adjusted pupils who do not have the skills.

This shift away from knowledge-based learning and education to skills-based competency education and training led to an important question: who is to define the skills that are necessary and the ways in which we test whether pupils have competency in these skills? Jones and Moore (1993) have argued that the shift to competence skills based education is part of moves to undermine the liberal humanistic discourse in education and replace it with one more in line with industrial notions of technical rationality. These moves became the context for a long-running and continuing process of shifting influences in the education world which saw moves to remove power from Local Education Authorities, teachers and teachers' unions and to give more power to central government, business and industrial leaders and parents. It is also clear that these views affected education more generally and were not restricted to vocational courses. This point is clearly made in relation to the introduction of the National Curriculum:

The National Curriculum itself can be seen as a form of vocationalism. Though not related to particular skills, it does very much reflect the kind of response given by employers when asked their views about education. With an emphasis on standards and discipline, it is clearly concerned with the kind of model citizen envisaged by many employers.

(Spours and Young, 1990; quoted in Trowler, 1995, p. 79)

Since the ideas behind the new vocationalism were based on an implicit and often explicit criticism of the teaching profession, it was no surprise that the implementation of new vocationalism and the introduction of the National Curriculum and other changes (discussed in more detail in Section 11.6) would be accompanied by attacks on the teaching profession, and also Local Education Authorities who were seen to be promoting the kind of education attacked by James Callaghan and the new vocationalism.

There are a number of specific instances of changes in educational structure and role which reflect this shifting balance. Firstly there was the introduction of grant maintained schools under the 1988 Education Reform Act. These schools were funded directly by national government, thus bypassing the Local Education Authority altogether. There was also the example of the City Technology Colleges. These were initially intended to be funded by private employers reflecting the argument that industrialists know best what is needed in education and also reflecting the somewhat mechanistic belief in the benefits of technology. Employer interests also predominated in the formation of the Training and Enterprise Councils (TECs) which were given the predominant role in vocational training for the unemployed following the demise of the Manpower Services Commission. These employer-dominated bodies survived until finally abolished by New Labour in 2000.

A further example of the rise of employer interests was the Incorporation of Further Education and Sixth Form Colleges, which meant that these institutions (an important element of 16–19 education) were taken out of Local Education Authority control and instead set up as independent corporations. These colleges were originally required to have a majority of employer interests on their governing bodies, a requirement that existed until 2000. These examples point to a pattern of growing involvement by employers and industrialists in the educational structure, often at the expense of involvement by democratically elected local councillors or other representatives of the Local Educational Authority. The TECs became one important example of the non-elected quangos which became such an important part of government administration during the Conservative era of 1979–97 (see Section 15.5).

Stephen Ball (1991) has argued that the attacks on teachers which occurred throughout the 1980s and which can be seen to derive from the debates started in the 1970s could be called a 'discourse of derision'. Clearly it is the case that these professionals were now openly attacked and blamed for educational and economic decline in the UK, and this is a pattern that has been continued with statements by the Chief Inspector of Schools arguing that there are large numbers of incompetent teachers in schools, and furthermore with more recent market-based initiatives such as the introduction by the New Labour government of performance-related pay. This marketization (see also page 408) was a central element of New Right approaches to educational reform.

One key element of this New Right attack on teachers and the public sector was Public Choice theory. This in simple terms suggests that as much power as possible should be given to the public as consumers in a market situation and that this will ensure the best possible outcome. Teachers on this model were viewed as a producer group who did not necessarily act in the best interests of the consumers:

The consequence of Public Choice theory applied to education is that it assumes that middle-class professional, like teachers, have been unjustifiably privileged because they have not been subject to the spurs and sanctions of market disciplines; that is, they are not suitably rewarded when successful, nor are they threatened with unemployment when unsuccessful. Consequently, it assumes that educational expenditure can be contained or reduced if education is deregulated and market disciplines imposed.

(Brown *et al.*, 1997)

Julian Le Grand (1996) has argued that in the period from 1944 to the mid-1970s the education system was characterized by a 'golden age of teacher control' where parents were expected to trust the judgements of the professionals and where equality of treatment of all was a key notion underlining professional actions.

This approach has been challenged by postmodernist inspired arguments about the need for greater diversity as well as by New Right inspired arguments for marketization and attacks on the power of teachers.

Geoff Whitty (1997) has summarized the implications of this change of view:

There has now been something of a move away from the notion that the teaching profession should have a professional mandate to act on behalf of the state in the best interests of its citizens, to a view that teachers (and indeed, other professions) need to be subjected to the rigours of the market and/or greater control and surveillance on the part of the re-formed state. ...

In the current context, control strategies have taken a variety of forms. In many countries the power of the teaching unions has been challenged, both through the dismantling of former 'corporatist' styles of education decision-making and through the decentralization of education systems. In England, the reforms have been accompanied by swingeing attacks on the integrity of the teaching profession in general and teachers' unions in particular.

(Whitty, 1997, p. 303)

As well as more power being given to the central state, there has also been more power given to parents, through such reforms as open enrolment which requires that schools take as many pupils as possible and the publication of league tables as information to help parents decide where to send their children. Since money now flows with pupils, and parents will try to get their children into the best schools, the argument here is that only those schools who provide high-quality education will attract the funding necessary to expand, while those who ignore the wishes of parents, the state or employers will not attract pupils and will therefore lose out (see also Section 11.3). This has led to a greater focus on notions of what makes an effective school, where effectiveness seems to mean meeting the needs defined not by teachers and LEAs but instead by central government, parents and employers' representatives.

A key example of the encouragement of parents was the publication in 1991 of the Parents' Charter. This document, published by the government, aimed to make parents more aware of their rights, presumably in order to encourage them to exercise their rights and therefore encourage more parental power in the educational world.

The idea of increasing parental power was underlined by various articles suggesting ways to ensure your child gets a good education, including this one produced in the *Observer*:

Seven Ways to Make Sure Your Children Get into a 'Good School'

1 Pay.

2 Move to an area which still has the 11-plus and spend a fortune on coaching.

3 Check with estate agents, pay a graphic mapper to get the right address. Mortgage yourself to the eyeballs to pay for it. Alternatively lie about your address.

4 Ensure your kids have special needs.

5 Get to know the governors of a grant-maintained school who can admit your child under 'governors' provisions'.

6 Convert to Church of England/Catholicism/Judaism.

7 Offer to make substantial donations to school coffers.

(The *Observer*, 7 January 1996; quoted in Giddens, 1997, p. 407)

Activity
Which of the ways outlined above to get your child into a 'good school' are equally available to all parents and which are not?

C3.2, C3.3

From meritocracy to parentocracy

Brown (1990, 1997) argues that we are now moving away from the period when the key theory behind educational reform was the notion of meritocracy and instead are entering a period of education characterized by the parentocracy:

... where a child's education is increasingly dependent upon the wealth and wishes of parents, rather than the ability and efforts of pupils.

(Brown, 1997, p. 393)

He argues that the origins of this were in the failure of the education system to meet the needs and desires of the 1960s, leading to the attacks on the education from the 1970s onwards.

This idea can be seen to operate in the New Right period in terms of attacks on so-called trendy teachers and trendy teaching methods which were seen to be based on options of equality and were therefore attacked as undermining the education of the most talented.

Under New Labour, the same sort of approaches have been used to argue that teachers' low expectations are the key cause of work-ing-class under-achievement.

Both approaches legitimated reducing the power of teachers, increasing the power of the state and, in a populist measure, increasing the power of parents. In this sense Brown argues that the Great Debate about education and the new vocationalism that followed it are all to be seen as part of moves to abandon comprehensive education and to replace equality with notions of quality.

Clearly at the heart of this debate remains questions about what we need the education system to do, how and to whom it should be accountable and exactly who is to decide on the answers to these questions.

Discussion point
Who do you think should have the main say in determining what is in the best interests of children as far as their education and training are concerned?

C3.1a

The marketization of education

'Kentucky fried schooling'

Hargreaves (1989) uses the term 'Kentucky fried schooling' to describe the education market as a system of franchises. What does the marketization of education mean in reality? Take, for example, the experience of the school cited in the following newspaper extract:

Commiserate, please, with Barclay School, a 980-seater mixed comp in Stevenage which won't be getting a £100 000 makeover courtesy of Glaxo Wellcome. Headteacher Russell Ball's imaginative scheme to rent the school's Henry Moore bronze (worth £2 million at the last count) to the multinational apothecary's Stevenage depot for four years in return for super new science labs has collapsed at the eleventh hour. Glaxo withdrew from the deal after union protests that it would be spending cash on a school at the same time as it was laying off its own scientists.

(*Guardian Education*, 9 January 1996)

Parentocracy

School management teams spend a considerable amount of their time on budgets and raising money by sponsorship from local firms, or loaning out their Henry Moore sculptures. They have to ensure quality control and keep an eye on the opposition – the other schools in the area. Schools now have to compete for clients or consumers. They 'package' themselves using marketing strategies and by developing a corporate 'image': knowledge is now a 'product'. Parents have the power – 'parentocracy' (David, 1993) – to choose their school. Freedom from central government and local education authorities allows schools to determine how they spend their budget allocation.

Making sense of the marketization of education

It is useful to see the history of English education as a series of compromises between the old humanists, the industrial trainers and the public educators.

(Williams, 1961; quoted in Whitty, 1992)

The old humanists, or the neo-conservatives, represent the interests of the élite: they defend traditional academic education. The industrial trainers, or neo-liberals, defend narrow vocational or instrumental education. The public educators have struggled to develop an education relevant to all pupils in a democratic society. This provides a useful framework for analysing educational reform.

The market and the National Curriculum

Until recently most battles were over the *form* of education rather than the *content*. ERA 1988 and the National Curriculum changed this. It was a victory for the old humanists defending the traditional grammar school curriculum. This was until the Dearing Report intervened and allowed pupils to choose a vocational path at 14 which marked the regaining of ground by the industrial trainers.

Contradictions within education legislation

The 1988 legislation contains within it a powerful contradiction. The National Curriculum that it established prescribed, in law, what subjects and content teachers were to teach and how these were to be assessed. In this sense it was a centrally controlled prescriptive curriculum with very little choice for teachers, parents or pupils in the state system.

This prescription sits uneasily with another part of the legislation which introduced 'the market' into education with the concept of local management of schools (LMS). This makes it a quasi-market. The 1988 Act also introduced other aspects of the market: formula funding, open enrolment, City Technology Colleges (CTCs), opting out, and grant-maintained schools. The introduction of the market was a victory for the New Right or neo-liberals.

What was 'new' about the New Right?

It is using the market in services like health and education that is 'new':

In the UK, the neo-Liberal, Hayekian vision of the market, to which Margaret Thatcher was converted in the mid-1970s, underpinned both the small-business, self-employment revolution in the UK economy in the 1980s and the market reforms being implemented in the education system and National Health Service.

(Ball, 1994, p. 106)

Anti-state provision

Hayek was an Austrian economist, not an educationalist. His ideas are favoured by the New Right because they wanted to move away from monopolistic state provision to make schools more entrepreneurial and efficient, and to provide freedom of choice for the consumers – parents and their children. This was to be achieved by schools operating open enrolment, in which parents could choose the school for their children, causing competition between schools. This, it was claimed, would improve educational standards generally.

Parents not teachers

Schools would be forced to consider the wishes of parents rather than the needs of teachers and the social justice concerns of local education authorities. Schools were to manage their own budgets, free from the bureaucray of local education authorities, with each pupil attracting a fixed sum. Successful schools would then become like successful businesses: cost-effective, with a positive image, responsive to consumer demand. They would produce a product (educated pupils) in line with National Curriculum specifications, though these subject specifications cannot be chosen. The philosophy behind this is a rational choice model in which the self-interested individual's choice will lead to what is in the interests of the whole community.

Marketization across the world

The marketization of education is also an international phenomenon, with the New Right colonizing political agendas not only in the UK but also in the USA, Canada, New Zealand and Australia. The aim here is to make national economies internationally competitive as part of the global economy. Countries must make their economies more productive, efficient and innovative. Education and training are central to this.

Criticisms of education markets

- Critics draw attention to the fact that markets in theory and markets in practice are very different. In practice, schools' selective and economic purposes become more important than their academic, pastoral and citizenship purposes.

- Markets put schools' educative purposes at risk because 'image' becomes more important than substance, the head teacher becomes a business-person, and resources for teaching get diverted into marketing.

- The idea that all children have the right to equal access to good education is lost. Consumers get power but those with the greatest market capacity get the most.

- The market is accountable only to itself and therefore disregards policies and practices in education designed to redress inequalities.

- The whole game is not taking place on a level playing field. Schools in middle-class areas which inherited good buildings and resources are in a much better position than schools in inner-city areas with run-down buildings and poor resources. League tables on which choices are to be made use raw data, making it impossible to compare like with like:

The implementation of market reforms in education is essentially a class strategy which has as one of its major effects the reproduction of relative social class (and ethnic) advantages and disadvantages.

(Ball, 1994, p. 103)

The academic/vocational divide

Vocational education as the poor relation

Why do England and Wales have such a divided system in post-16 education? Vocational education and training have always been the poor relation of the educational system. Skills training has traditionally been the apprenticeship system, developed outside the state system and organized privately by employers and craftsmen. This was 'on the job training' rather than theoretical study.

In the nineteenth century the theoretical study of science and technology was very under-valued in the UK compared with its European competitors. Green (1990) explains this as part of the liberal tradition of *laissez faire* in education:

In part it resulted from the deep penetration within traditional education institutions of those conservative and anti-industrial values of the ruling elite.

(Green, 1990, p. 293)

Education versus training

Liberal educational values stressed the importance of education for its own sake and its importance in relation to individual development. Elitist academic education should remain unsullied by being linked to usefulness in a future career, aiming rather to produce the 'educated' person. Vocational training, on the other hand, prepares people in a narrow way for a specific occupation. Recently this term has been replaced by 'new vocationalism', which seeks to produce trainees with flexible, transferable skills that can be used in a variety of low-skilled occupations – required because of a change in industrial production methods. (This issue is discussed in Section 17.2.)

Selling out on ideals to attract a better class

JUDITH JUDD

Northwark Park in London is a working-class school struggling for survival. It cannot attract enough pupils, and the majority of those it has are from ethnic minorities.

The school's governors and teachers know the answer: it must learn to compete for pupils in a marketplace set up by a government that funds schools according to the number of pupils they recruit, and fosters competition by the publication of exam league tables.

Northwark (not its real name) is committed to the comprehensive ideal, to opening its doors to all pupils whatever their needs, to co-operating with other schools and to teaching mixed-ability classes. Under sentence of death, however, it is rethinking its philosophy.

The story of Northwark is told in a study for the Economic Research Council by Sharon Gerwitz, Stephen Ball and Richard Bowe, researchers at King's College, London. They say the school is typical of those at the bottom of the league tables. Professor Ball suggests that their response is not, as the government hopes, to start a programme of educational improvement, but to try to increase the intake of middle-class children and to reduce the proportion of problem pupils.

The decision to enter the market divides teachers and governors. At Northwark, the governing body, whose chair is an active socialist politician and which has a majority of left-wing members, is strongly opposed to abandoning the comprehensive ideal. The head and her deputy, however, appear to be toying with the idea of a grammar-school ethos and hinting at the attractions of selection.

The head comments: "I'm not saying we're looking for middle-class parents, but we're looking for motivated parents. Ideally, every school wants to be oversubscribed, so it does have some control over who comes in." Her deputy speaks admiringly of a nearby school: "I'm not saying it has lost its comprehensive ideals, but the head has set it up, as near as dammit, to a traditional girls' grammar school ... it's obviously attracted a lot of people."

In the drive for more pupils, the school's tradition of welcoming children with learning difficulties and teaching them in ordinary classes is thrown into doubt. The deputy head thinks special needs should be questioned: "That sort of provision is expensive, and if you're being asked to produce a good set of examination results, then you want as much of your resourcing as possible to be directed in that way."

The head of special needs feels educational considerations are already being subordinated to commercial ones. Staff, she suggests, are worried by the school's reputation for teaching special-needs children because of its effect on parents of more able children.

Much the same is happening over the exclusion of difficult children. The head and deputies are not discussing the educational merits of exclusions but the financial implications and whether or not they bring good publicity. Meanwhile, the school is attracting a large number of excluded 15-year-olds who depress its exam results.

The decision to review the policy of teaching children in mixed-ability classes has divided staff. The science department has begun to "set" children, and modern languages and maths may follow. The head of special needs is resisting the decision.

Researchers believe changes brought about by the marketplace in Northwark Park have implications for all British schools. They reflect a shift to a system that "rewards shrewdness rather than principles, and encourages commercial rather than educational decision-making. Concern for social justice is replaced by concern for institutional survival, collectivism with individualism, co-operation with suspicion and need with expediency."

Source: The Independent, 27 January 1994

The needs of industry: from Fordism to post-Fordism

There has been a move away from Fordism – line production of standardized mass-produced goods – to the requirement of flexible specialization and computerized control of production. (For more detail on this, see Section 17.2.) This new emphasis on style, design and difference goes with what is called post-Fordism. Old proletarian-type industries, manufacturing and mining, have declined and are being replaced with service sector work. This requires a different type of labour force and training must meet these needs.

The Great Debate on education

The fact that industrialists felt that education was not meeting these needs was expressed very strongly in what has been called the Great Debate. This arose from a lecture delivered in 1976 by the then prime minister James Callaghan, in which he called upon schools to respond more to the needs of industry.

Several initiatives followed. For example, the Manpower Services Commission was set up in 1973. Then, in 1980, the Technical and Vocational Education Initiative (TVEI) was introduced to allow schools to bid for money to develop the work-related curriculum for 14–19-year-olds. The Youth Opportunities Programme (YOP) of 1978 was followed by the Youth Training Scheme (YTS) in 1983, to be replaced by Youth Training (YT) in 1990 organized by Training and Enterprise Councils (TECs).

Sociological criticisms of training schemes

Sociological studies of such training schemes have been critical of their aims and their role in social reproduction. They have been seen as a means of covering up unemployment figures and providing a source of cheap labour. If young people went through a training scheme and still failed to find employment, then the responsibility for this was transferred to them. Such schemes were regarded as having a 'hidden agenda' of keeping young people off the streets and 'cooling out' young people who might otherwise turn to crime. Young people have complained about these schemes being a 'con' – not involving good training at all, but rather about them being used as skivvies (Lee, 1990).

Improvements to vocational training

The NCVQ

Since the initiatives cited above, others have followed as attempts to improve the UK's training and industrial performance. The proliferation of vocational courses eventually led to the National Council for Vocational Qualifications (NCVQ) being set up to rationalize them. NCVQ devised five levels of National Vocational Qualifications in which sets of competencies were drawn up to be assessed by observation on the job. These have since been criticized for being expensive to administer, too narrowly defined, and related to the short-term needs of the employer rather than the long-term needs of the learner. They have resulted in an increasing number of certificates in circulation, rather than improving skills.

NVQs and GNVQs

In May 1991 the Department for Education and Employment issued its White Paper *Education and Training for the 21st Century*. It set out the need for a range of general qualifications within the NVQ framework, and this was the beginnings of GNVQs. These were much broader taught courses, relating to wide vocational areas like health and social care or leisure and tourism. They included key skills of communication, numeracy and information technology. Assessment was by coursework and externally set and marked tests. They were designed so that students could combine them with A levels.

Vocational qualifications – still second-rate?

A national survey of school-leavers conducted by researchers at Southampton University (1996) indicates that government efforts to improve the status and value of vocational qualifications have failed. Students still regard such qualifications as work-related rather than leading on to higher education: only a quarter of those taking vocational qualifications were hoping to go on to such education. Students regarded them as second-rate qualifications, citing A levels as the gold standard and the natural route to a degree.

A levels – still the gold standard?

In 1988, the Higginson Report recommended that five subjects should be studied and that syllabuses be streamlined to allow for greater breadth. This is similar to Scottish Highers and the International Baccalaureate. The Conservative government at the time endorsed the general aim of widening A levels but introduced AS levels as a means of doing this. These have not been a success and have not been used to do what they were designed to do. The government also supported the notion of 'core skills' (now key skills) which all young people should acquire throughout the curriculum.

A levels are regarded as the gold standard of our élite system. Only 30 per cent of each age cohort follow this academic track. Taking three or perhaps four A levels is widely regarded as too narrowly specialist. It compares unfavourably with all the UK's major competitors, as do the staying-on rates and achievement post-16.

Defenders of A levels regard them as rigorous, even if they sometimes lack relevance. There are fears that this rigour and depth of knowledge will be lost if A levels are abolished.

In 1990, the Institute for Public Policy Research published interesting proposals for a British Baccalaureate. These suggested a modular, unified system post-16 with three levels. They proposed that the whole of post-16 education should be modularized and include work-based or community-based learning. There would be a system of credit accumulation and transfer so that all students, including part-timers and adult-returners, could undertake a range of modules to build towards an Advanced Diploma. Such modules would be organized within three broad domains of study: social and human sciences; natural sciences and technology; and arts, languages and literature. Students would have to choose from three modules: core; specialist; or work- or community-based. This structure aimed to provide flexibility, choice, and a balance of the intellectual and the practical.

New Labour's reform of post-16 qualifications

When New Labour came to power in 1997 there was a strong expectation that radical reforms to post-16 qualifications would take place. The Dearing review of qualifications for the 16–19-year-olds (1996), and Labour's own opposition policy document *Aiming Higher* (1996), outlined similar proposals. It was agreed that there was a need for a coherent national framework.

Dearing had proposed three distinct tracks – A levels, GNVQs and NVQs – thus offering choice and diversity while attempting parity of esteem between the three tracks. Labour's policy in opposition was more radical. It was a first step towards a unified system with a range of modules so that all students would have a larger common component (core studies) in their curricula with the same grading and assessment systems. The policy suggested that all advanced level education should be recognized by the award of an Advanced Diploma.

This commitment was, however, watered down both in Labour's election manifesto and later in its new policy document *Qualifying for Success*. The single framework is not mentioned, neither is an Advanced Diploma or a unified system. Since coming to office New Labour has become more cautious. The goverment is adopting a more staged approach to educational reform that cannot be interpreted as a threat to A levels and which will not alienate middle-class supporters.

Discussion point
Suggest reasons why changes to A level might be considered so politically sensitive.

C3.1a

Labour's proposed changes

A levels

From September 2000, A levels have been split into two blocks, AS and A2, with three units in each. This is intended to address the criticism that A levels are too narrow. Students can take five AS units in their first year of study instead of three A levels. They cannot be compelled to do so, though, so many might choose to do three units for AS followed by three units for A2. The standard for AS is below that for an A level.

There are proposals to split GNVQs into similar unit blocks so that students can combine A level and vocational blocks. All vocational qualifications are to be strengthened through greater standardization and more external assessment. This is aimed at proving their credibility and bringing them closer to other qualifications.

Key skills

Key skills for all learners post-16, not just those taking GNVQs, is another part of this reform. Three key skills are given prominence – Communication, Application of Number, and Information Technology at levels 1, 2 and 3. Three others are outlined – Problem Solving, Improving own Learning and Performance, and Working with Others. All specifications will be required to signpost the opportunities to assess these key skills, and points can be awarded in assessments to provide learners with currency in higher education; they will not be mandatory, however.

Criticisms of the changes

Hodgson and Spours (1999) make the following comments on the foregoing reforms:

- They are not a top priority. The prime position on the educational agenda for reform is raising standards in the area of compulsory education.

- The above reforms will be supported by incentives such as inspection criteria, funding regimes and a reformed UCAS tariff, but will this be sufficient for schools and colleges to take them up?

- The 'low-achievement conspiracy' works against institutions' broadening of the advanced level curriculum voluntarily. This is a result of market forces, and includes (a) the fear of making extra demands on students in case they give up their courses or defect to other institutions, (b) a casualized youth labour market which attracts advanced learners from their studies, and (c) less popular higher education institutions being prepared to make low-grade offers.

Compare France

...The French ... have created a more integrated system of general, technical and vocational baccalauréates offered within the lycée system. The qualifications all share the same prestigious title which confers right of entry to higher education; each track has a considerable component of general education, much of which is common to all; and modes of assessment and curriculum design have more consistency across the different tracks. The system has not yet achieved equal status for academic and vocational tracks but it has considerably more potential for doing so than our new system. It has also achieved a level of participation and qualification at 16–19 around 100% higher than our own (48% attain the bac).

Post-compulsory education in France and Britain in the 1970s faced many of the same problems which still face us now. It was highly elitist, not designed for mass participation and vocational routes had very low status. In France it has been improved through decisive and co-ordinated government action and by the adoption of a comprehensive approach to the planning of the whole post-16 sector. To achieve similar results in this country, our own government would need to adopt a similarly resolute and co-ordinated approach. Education and training would need to be brought together under a single department and planned as a whole; SEAC and NCVQ would need to be amalgamated with the new joint qualifications board responsible for creating a single national framework of qualifications. There would be an end to the absurd free-market approach to the setting and awarding of qualifications where over 300 independent bodies currently offer thousands of different certificates, each seeking its particular niche in the market, and in competition with the others.

If the government is serious about giving more choice to students, raising participation and achieving higher and more consistent standards, we need to see a little more rational planning and a lot less free-market dogma. In the meantime teachers will continue to struggle at the local level to make some sense out of the muddle created by myopic ministers and blind markets.

Source: Green (1993)

In 1990, the Institute for Public Policy Research published interesting proposals for a British Baccalaureate. These suggested a modular, unified system post-16 with three levels. They proposed that the whole of post-16 education should be modularized and include work-based or community-based learning. There would be a system of credit accumulation and transfer so that all students, including part-timers and adult-returners, could undertake a range of modules to build towards an Advanced Diploma. Such modules would be organized within three broad domains of study: social and human sciences; natural sciences and technology; and arts, languages and literature. Students would have to choose from three modules: core; specialist; or work- or community-based. This structure aimed to provide flexibility, choice, and a balance of intellectual and practical.

Activity

a Following suitable research, compare the approaches to post-16 education reforms in England and France. What has New Labour to learn from the French?

b Apply Bernstein's theory of the framing and classification of knowledge (outlined in Section 11.1) to the difficulties in bridging the vocational/academic divide.

C3.2, C3.3

11.8 Theories of the transition from school to work

Young people do not simply view work and study in the linear, sequential way implied by the conventional career paradigm ... Images about 'pathways' and linear transitions from school via further study and then into the world of work and an independent adult way of life do not reflect the actual experience of growing up. Young people are establishing different patterns of response which involve complicated mixtures of leaving and returning to the parental home of part-time work and part-time study, of full-time study and part-time work and even full-time work and full-time study.

(Ainley and Cohen, 1999, p. 11)

As this quote indicates, the transition from school to work for young people has changed dramatically over the last twenty years. The process has become much more complex. Below are some of the factors contributing to and resulting from such complexity:

• The globalization of the economy and labour market with the decline in heavy industry and the rise of service sector employment, particularly that associated with information and communications technology. Much employment being casualized, feminized and requiring constant re-skilling.

- Changes to the benefits system in 1988 meant that 16- and 17-year-olds could not claim benefits.

- Young people are experiencing much longer periods of dependency on their parents which has raised the threshold of adulthood and prolonged the period of 'youth'.

- The adoption of market values with an emphasis on individual self-reliance and enterprise rather than social insurance provided by the welfare state.

- An increase in the numbers of young people staying on in full-time education from 50 per cent of all 16-year-olds in 1986 to 70 per cent in 1996, 30 per cent of whom fail to complete their courses (Pearce and Hillman, 1998).

- 7 per cent of 16-year-olds are neither employed nor in education or training. This group of socially excluded, unqualified young people controversially called 'Status Zero' in one study (Williamson in MacDonald, 1997, p. 82) are causing greatest concern to policy makers (Pearce and Hillman 1998).

- The change from an élite to a mass system (at least statistically) of higher education with a participation rate of 40 per cent.

Discussion point

a How have the above changes contributed to young people having to navigate more complex transitions from school to work?

b Are there any other important factors?

C3.1a

Trajectories and transitions

Studies in the 1960s and 1970s, like the National Child Development Study (Kiernan, 1992), allow us to consider the extent to which things have changed for young people. The National Child Development Study tracked all the babies born in a single week in 1958 through the ages of 7, 11, 16, 23 and 33. They reached eighteen in 1976 and more than two thirds had managed the transition to adulthood with relative ease, leaving school and gaining employment. Once these young people became wage earners they were regarded by their parents as 'adults'. This eco-

nomic freedom allowed them to marry and move away from home.

By the 1980s and 1990s, the economic and social factors outlined above changed this pattern with young people being much more likely to experience more complex 'fractured' or 'extended' transitions, finding employment, leaving home and establishing households much later.

Recent studies

More recent studies have focused on how such transitions are experienced differently by different social groups, according to social class background, gender, ethnicity and locality. Interesting research by a number of sociologists (Bates and Riseborough, 1993) on the career trajectories of a range of young people engaged in vocational courses, Youth Training and Youth Enterprise Schemes, as well as A level students destined for university and a group of girls at a private school, revealed deepening social divisions and inequalities rather than improved equality of opportunity. This ethnographic data shows how such young people are active agents in creating their own identities and that their participation was far from passive but involved creative resistance and improvisation.

However, it also shows that those on vocational courses had their initial exciting career aspirations 'cut down to size' by tutors and what was available in the labour market. Not surprisingly, those in the private school had the edge on gaining professional and managerial careers, showing the continuing importance of social class with qualifications earned by age 16 as the single best indicator that a person's career would take. Contributors in Bates and Riseborough (1993) found that gender still determined the type of occupational area likely to be chosen — which confirmed the findings of Griffin (1985) — opportunities vary with locality, and ethnic origin restricted opportunities for some groups.

'Careership'

Research carried out by Hodkinson, Sparkes and Hodkinson (1997) critiques the term 'career trajectory' in favour of 'careership' since the former implies set and predictable channels to pre-determined destinations. They developed the concept of 'careership' from a broad research project which focused on ten young people who were

Training Credits trainees in 1992, and chosen for their gender mix, geographical location and occupational area. They wanted to give a voice to these young people, a voice which is absent in much of the literature on school to work transitions.

They found that career choices taken by these young people were pragmatically rational and constrained and enabled by horizons for action. They could chose only from what was available but also based their choice on their own subjective perceptions as well as the experiences and knowledge of friends and significant others. The stories of these trainees reveal a complex system of negotiation, bargaining and often struggle with the other players in the Youth Training field. Career paths can change or be confirmed and this best characterised by 'turning points' or 'routines', which are influenced by domestic, social as well as educational factors.

An example of this is Helen's story. She secured a place as a trainee in car body repairing. However, before her training was complete, she was made redundant. Her turning point was to change careers and take up a new placement in a record shop. Her view of her own career identity changed and car body repairing became a hobby rather than a career. Hodkinson, Sparkes and Hodkinson (1997) are critical of the New Right emphasis on individualism, choice and market forces in the Training Credits Scheme, which assumes that young people possess the power and influence to make rational choices from an array of options in the education and training market.

Further reading

The following is up to date and includes skills necessary for the A level examination:

- Heaton, T. and Lawson, T. (1996) *Education and Training*, Basingstoke: Macmillan.

A good introduction, with very up-to-date information, is:

- Trowler, P. (1995) *Investigating Education and Training*, London: Collins Educational.

The following, although a teachers' text, is recommended for its coverage of marketization of education, SEN and a post-structuralist approach to educational policy:

- Bowe, R., Ball, S. with Gold, A. (1992) *Reforming Education and Changing Schools: Case Studies in Policy Sociology*, London: Routledge.

The following is very useful and accessible, with good coverage of issues relating to equal opportunities:

- Gillborn, D. (1990) *'Race', Ethnicity and Education: Teaching and Learning in Multi-Ethnic Schools*, London: Unwin Hyman.

A very accessible introduction to all varieties of feminism and their approach to education is:

- Weiner, G. (1994) *Feminisms in Education: An Introduction*, Milton Keynes: Open University Press.

The following is useful for vocational training:

- Lee, D. (1990) *Scheming for Youth*, Milton Keynes: Open University Press.

Back issues of the periodical *Sociology Review* (formerly the *Social Studies Review*) also contain many articles on this field of sociology and many others.

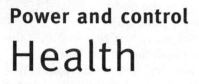

Power and control
Health

Chapter outline

The social nature of health and illness

12.1 The social construction of health and illness *page 418*

This section examines the social construction of health and illness, mental illness and disability. It examines the importance of social reaction, stigma and labelling for the formation of identity in terms of ill health. The treatment of disability as a medical and social issue is explored, as are the implications of the Disability Discrimination Act 1995. It also examines the ways in which definitions and treatments of mental illnesses and mental disability demonstrate such wide differences over time, in relation to different social groups and in different societies.

12.2 Deviance, social control and the sick role *page 429*

This section examines the theoretical basis for viewing sickness as a form of deviance and for seeing society's treatment of the sick as a form of social control.

Trends and patterns in health and illness

12.3 Social class, region and health inequalities *page 430*

This section looks at recent statistical material, and examines the main explanations of health inequalities offered by the Black and Acheson Reports and others to try to identify the causes of class inequalities in health. These studies look at a number of different explanations, in particular stressing the importance of socio-economic factors as a cause of health inequalities in terms of both class and region. The importance of European and international comparisons is identified.

12.4 Gender, ethnicity and health inequalities *page 440*

This section examines the suggestion that women are the greater providers and users of healthcare (both formal and informal), while men generally experience higher rates of mortality than women. Structural and cultural explanations for these patterns are discussed. The arguments about the medicalization of fertility and reproduction and the impact of feminism on our understanding of health and society are examined, as well as the role of women in the 'new' paradigm of health and illness. This section also identifies and seeks to explain differences in the experiences of health, illness and healthcare for different ethnic and cultural groups, including Asian groups, African–Caribbean and other groups. The ideological construction of 'race' and health is explored.

12.5 The establishment of a national health service *page 456*

This section shows how the historical development of the biomedical model of illness and the growing emphasis on scientific explanations of the world led to a desire for comprehensive healthcare. It further examines the political reasons for the establishment of a universal national health service in the UK in 1948. It explores the reforms in 1974 and how they relate to more recent debates about NHS provision.

12.6 Contemporary debates on healthcare *page 459*

This section explores sociological explanations of why the NHS is seen as being in crisis, requiring comprehensive reforms of healthcare provision in the 1980s and 90s. Views about the effectiveness of reforms such as 'care in the community' and the marketization and privatization of the NHS are discussed. Some New Right and New Labour initiatives are discussed.

Medicine, power and control

12.7 Limits to medicine and healthcare
page 465

This section looks critically at the role of the medical professionals and considers the arguments for and against challenges to their expertise. This leads to a discussion about the ways in which doctors may lead us to a passive dependence on them and on other professionals in society. The claim that individuals – and the NHS – are exploited by the powerful drug companies which dominate health treatment in capitalist societies is explored.

12.8 The sociology of the body, mind and sexuality   *page 468*

This section focuses on recent research into the social control and regulation of the body in relation to cosmetic surgery, genetic developments, disability and AIDS. Medical and moral debates on reproduction and abortion are explored. The sociology of death and dying is examined.

12.1 The social construction of health and illness

People often greet each other by asking how they are. The terms 'well', 'healthy' or 'poorly' have commonsense meanings. However, a closer look into the way members of society consider issues relating to health and illness reveals a more complex picture.

Discussion point

Consider some of the problems in defining health by discussing the following questions:

a What does it mean to be unwell or well?

b Is pregnancy a form of sickness? If not, why do women go to a doctor when pregnant?

c If someone goes to a plastic surgeon to change the way they look, should they be considered unhealthy?

C3.1a

Definitions of health

Sociologists and others have distinguished between positive and negative definitions of health. The World Health Organization (WHO), which monitors health throughout the world for the United Nations organization, defined health in a positive way as:

... not the mere absence of disease, but total physical, mental and social well-being.

(WHO, 1955)

It could be argued that this definition means that most of us are unwell for most of the time, since it is an extremely wide definition, particularly in relation to its notion of social well-being. It is also the case that this definition is difficult to test – and therefore apply – when considering changing levels of health. Trowler (1996) asserts that:

In practice the medical profession (and the population at large) tend to define health in a negative way: 'The condition in which there is an absence of disease or disability'.

(Trowler, 1996, p. 2)

Negative definitions of health tend to emphasize the objective lack of disease, but this suggests that we should not feel ill unless we have a physical ailment. Aggleton (1990), a sociologist, argues that this is problematic as we do not always feel pain when we are unwell. It is also the case that such general notions of health ignore the way in which we differ as individuals, and the enormously different expectations of health among social groups.

Health and illness

We need to recognize how the interactions between objective and subjective measures affect the ways in which individuals and social groups react in relation to notions of health.

Discussing the social definition of illness, Field (1976) suggested that we need to distinguish between the objective indicators of disease and the subjective feelings of illness. Since it is perfectly possible to feel ill without actually being objectively unwell, and it is also possible to be suffering from disease or ill-health without feeling ill, the two measures could provide differing views on the extent of health or illness in the population.

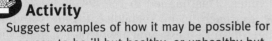

Activity

Suggest examples of how it may be possible for a person to be ill but healthy, or unhealthy but not ill.

C3.2, C3.3

The subjective experience of illness is, in fact, a clear component in the construction of supposedly objective indicators of ill-health. The simple reason for this is the requirement that, to appear on health statistics (at least those compiled by doctors and hospitals), individuals must have sought medical help. Statistics are compiled on the cause of death (mortality statistics) and the prevalence of ill-health (morbidity statistics), but people will not appear on the latter unless they feel subjectively ill enough to consult a doctor, although some conditions may be identified through routine screening.

The clinical iceberg

This leads to the phenomenon known as the 'clinical iceberg', as explained by Michael Senior:

Not all illnesses are reported to the doctor. The morbidity figures only show a small proportion of illnesses. [This] shows how the morbidity figures examine a tip of an illness iceberg. The majority of illnesses are not expressed in the figures because a large number of people do not report every illness symptom to their doctor. The idea that only a proportion of a set of illness is revealed by the morbidity figures is known as the 'clinical iceberg' (Last, 1963).

(Senior, 1996, p. 19)

Although it might be argued that it is impossible to be mistaken about whether someone is dead or not and that therefore the mortality statistics can be considered to be hard evidence, it is important to be aware that it is possible to make mistakes about the main cause of death and therefore there is room for error in relation to these statistics. Senior and Viveash (1998) make the point that the recorded cause of death is not always the underlying disease that has led to death. They point to the way in which many doctors in the early 1980s in New York failed to recognize that many premature homosexual deaths were the result of a single cause – AIDS.

It is also the case that doctors vary in relation to their willingness to classify people as suffering from ill-health (see Section 12.7). This insight is behind *interactionist* views on health that stress the ability of doctors to label people as suffering from ill-health or not, and the different treatment that patients from different social groups might receive.

The idea that health is merely an objective biological category has therefore been challenged. Health, ill-health and illness can be seen as *social constructions* that involve the interaction of doctors and patients – an interaction that includes the involvement of factors other than purely objective measures of health and ill-health.

Sociological aspects of health and illness

A full understanding of the prevalence and distribution of health and illness in a population requires a fully sociological view that goes beyond purely biological and medical knowledge about health and disease. Seedhouse (1986) identifies a number of other definitions of health, which highlight the impact of the social on this area of life.

One example of an early sociological approach to health can be found in the work of *functionalist* sociologist Talcott Parsons (1951). He defined health as the ability to perform expected roles at an optimum level. Parsons also argued that being sick should be seen not merely as a biological phenomenon, but as a specifically defined social role, namely the 'sick role'. (This argument is also discussed in Section 12.2.)

We can also consider the way in which the experience of being ill is experienced by social groups in differing ways. Approaching the issue from a social psychological viewpoint, and based on studies in France, Herzlich (1973) identified three dimensions of health. Aggleton (1990) summarizes her approach as follows:

First, she identified a conception of health as a state of being – the absence of illness. Second, she identified a view of health as something to be had – a reserve of physical strength as well as the potential to resist illness. Finally, she identified an understand-

ing of health as a state of doing – the full realisation of an individual's reserve of health.

(Aggleton, 1990, pp. 13–14)

Changing conceptions of health and illness

It is usually agreed that knowledge, including our knowledge about health and illness, can be separated into three distinct cultural paradigms (or sets of ideas): magic, religion and science.

- *The magical paradigm.* Magic or supernatural forces are sometimes associated with the ability to cause suffering. This may be seen as the punishment of an individual, or sometimes a whole community, for an offence against a god or a powerful individual. The 'cure' was seen as the need to call in the *shaman* or witch-doctor to remove the curse; which obviously gave these individuals considerable power and status in their own society.

- *The religious paradigm.* Religion is often seen as a powerful aspect of illness, and large numbers of people pray when someone is seriously ill. Until fairly recently, mental illness in particular was equated with possession by demons. There is still a strong belief that suffering can be a test of faith. In many societies children with mental handicaps are seen as being the favourites of their god.

- *The scienctific paradigm.* Science in the form of medicine is associated with the rise of *rationalism* and *modernity*. Modern, western medicine, which is based on scientific concepts, can be described as using a *mechanical model of illness*, seeing the body as a machine which sometimes breaks down and requires repairs. This is a highly scientific view of health, where each illness has an identifiable cause and, in time, an effective cure.

Doctor–patient relations

Jewson (1976) has shown how the power relationship between doctor and patient changed with the increasingly medical model of illness. He suggested that in the past, for those few who could afford it, consultation of a doctor was based mainly on the symptoms identified by the patient. It was only in the nineteenth century that hospitalization became commonplace; until that time hospitals were most often avoided whenever pos-

sible because they were seen as places from which people were extremely unlikely to leave! Since then scientific medicine has gone from strength to strength.

However, there are those who argue that we are now living in high-modern or even post-modern times. This has led to the development of a new approach to the sociological understanding of health and illness which will be examined in Sections 12.8.

Criticisms of the biomedical model

Many writers have questioned the assumptions of the medical model – that illness is always caused by an infection, that doctors will be able to cure it, and that preventative measures are highly effective. Such assumptions underpin homeopathic, herbal and other 'alternative' therapies, as well as medical drug-based therapies. The biomedical model assumes that disease is abnormal, that every illness has a specific cause, and it is experienced in the same way in all societies. Medicine is seen as a scientifically neutral way of explaining and dealing with all forms of illness.

Trowler (1996, p. 171) suggests that people are now 'treated as objects to be manipulated by medical technology', although Walker and Waddington (1991) claim that this is no longer true for all illnesses. They show how people with HIV and AIDS, the patients and their pressure groups, often know more about the disease than the doctors, creating a more equal relationship between professional and sufferer.

Turner (1987) points out that the change over the twentieth century from mainly acute illnesses (meaning relatively short-term ill-health, such as pneumonia) to chronic illnesses (meaning long-standing ill-health, such as heart disease and cancer) has two main implications.

- First, stress is now often seen as a major factor in the causation of illness.

- Secondly, sociological skills have become, to some extent, more important than medical skills for many general practitioners (GPs).

One effect of the growing medicalization of healthcare highlighted by Doyal (1995), in her study of gender and health, has been the gradual replacement of mainly female, informal carers (often using herbs and incantations) by mainly male professionals who are seen as experts, offering treatments that many of their patients do not understand.

In a review of sociological models of health suggesting the need to move beyond the medical model, Taylor (1994) highlights five main factors that have challenged this view:

- the replacement of infectious diseases by degenerative diseases as the main killers in society
- the challenges to doctors' claims that they single-handedly improved life expectancy, when writers such as McKeown (1979) have demonstrated the primary importance of improved sanitation
- the evidence that medicine (by way of doctors) causes much illness (e.g. Illich, 1990; see Section 12.7)
- the evidence of widespread inequalities in health and healthcare in many societies
- the social problems encountered by many people with disabilities (see Section 12.2) based on the expectations and assumptions of other people in society.

As a result of these views, sociologists have argued that the social aspects of health and illness have to be an integral part of the overall study of this aspect of society. We cannot simply use the information provided by biology and medicine to analyse health and healthcare; in addition we need to incorporate our knowledge of the experience, roles and distribution of health and illness and the way these are affected by wider social structures and actions.

Individual, social and societal considerations

Turner (1987) argues thus:

Whereas disease is a concept which describes malfunction of a physiological and biological character, illness refers to the individual's subjective awareness of the disorder, and sickness designates appropriate social roles.

(Turner, 1987, p. 2)

He therefore believes that the study of health and illness needs to be explored at three levels: the individual, the social and the societal (see Table 12.1).

Phenomenology and subjectivity

The first of Turner's three levels in Table 12.1 is clearly related to the *phenomenological approach*

Table 12.1 Turner's three levels of health and illness

Level	Topic	Perspective
Individual	Experience of illness.	Phenomenological assumptions about what it means to be healthy or ill.
Social	Cultural categories of sickness.	Sociology of roles, norms and deviance ('sick role').
Societal	Healthcare systems and politics of health.	Political economy of illness (social inequalities in health).

Source: Adapted from Turner (1987, p. 4)

and is therefore based on the insight that it is important to consider the subjective experiences of individuals when considering the distribution of illness.

Since phenomenology extends to the argument that everything is socially constructed (Berger and Luckmann, 1967), the ability of scientists to arrive at any objective notion of health is denied anyway. Studies based on this approach would clearly be critical of the biomedical model which largely excludes the notion of subjective experience.

Such an approach can be criticized by 'realist' sociologists for its denial that social reality exists, and for denying the importance of social structures in society in affecting the distribution of health.

The social construction of mental illness and disability

Definitions of mental illness

Deciding whether somebody is 'mentally ill' requires two judgements:

- Is the individual's behaviour odd enough to be considered outside the scope of normal human functioning?
- Is the reason behind this behaviour 'mental'?

Throughout history and up to the present day there have been problems with establishing concrete criteria for making such judgements. This is partly due to the fact that 'abnormality' is mainly socially constructed: society determines what is abnormal and there are no objective criteria. Therefore what tends to be considered abnormal is that which does not fit in with a particular society's definition of normal.

What is normality?

What exactly is meant by normal? Again there is no baseline; rather 'normality' is defined by a society at a particular time in history, and it is different for different social and cultural groups. Acknowledging that abnormality is socially constructed highlights many problems. It raises further questions such as the following:

- If we are not sure what kind of behaviour is normal, then have we any right to treat or try to change those who we consider 'abnormal'?
- What are the consequences for the individual who we consider to be 'abnormal'?

Discussion point

Discuss the questions raised above and consider to what extent you agree that they pose real problems for social scientists dealing with mental illness or disability.

C3.1a

What causes abnormal behaviour?

A further challenge is deciding what has caused someone's abnormal behaviour. Historically many causes have been identified, including magic, spirits, the devil, demons, lack of conscience and physical malfunctioning. Although modern psychologists lean towards finding physical causes behind mental illness, the influence of psychoanalysis and behaviourism has led many to look for causes in their clients' learning environment or their interpersonal relationships rather than their physiological make-up alone.

It is no longer acceptable to state, for example, that an individual's behaviour is so abnormal as to be considered the result of a mental illness simply because it does not accord with the norms of a current social group or era.

Homosexuality and unmarried motherhood were until quite recently both considered to be symptoms of underlying pathology. Today a number of criteria have to be considered before making a judgement about abnormality, and problems with each criterion need also to be assessed. Over the years a number of criteria have emerged, but none is without problems. Here we consider four: deviation from the statistical norm, deviation from the social norm, maladaptiveness of behaviour, and personal distress.

Deviation from the statistical norm

This suggests that behaviour (such as homosexuality) should be considered abnormal if it is statistically infrequent. However, this criterion does not distinguish between desirable/acceptable behaviour and undesirable/unacceptable behaviour. A person who is extremely intelligent, artistic or happy would be described as abnormal, whereas feelings of depression and anxiety are so statistically common to count as 'normal' under this criterion.

Deviation from the social norm

This criterion implies what people ought or ought not do, with transgressors being labelled 'bad' or 'sick'. But it does not constitute a very reliable or valid definition of abnormal behaviour as abnormality is defined by the norms of that society alone, so we may end up labelling people unfairly. For example, anti-communists in the former Soviet Union were often defined as mentally ill and committed to asylums, whereas in the USA communists have been imprisoned or rendered unable to work. Hence behaviour that is considered normal in one society may be considered abnormal in another.

Maladaptiveness of behaviour

Many social scientists believe that the most important criterion is how someone's behaviour affects the well-being of the individual and/or the social group. Therefore behaviour is abnormal if it is maladaptive in this sense. Some kinds of deviant behaviour interfere with the welfare of the individual (e.g. alcoholism – though this also affects others) whilst other behaviours such as violence are more harmful to society.

Personal distress

This criterion considers the individual's subjective feelings of distress rather than their outward behaviour. People described as 'mentally ill' often feel very unhappy (although not always while in a manic state). Sometimes personal distress is the only symptom of abnormality.

Activity

Looking at the definitions identified above, identify the advantages and disadvantages of each. Can you think of any other or better ways of defining mental illness?

C3.2, C3.3

Emotional well-being

It is clear that none of the above categories provides a wholly adequate definition on which to start categorizing behaviour as normal or abnormal. Jahoda (1958) suggested that most psychologists would agree with the following categories to indicate emotional well-being:

- efficient perception of reality
- self-knowledge
- the ability to exercise voluntary control over behaviour
- feelings of self-esteem and acceptance, the ability to form affective relationships and normal levels of productivity (a chronic lack of energy and feelings of fatigue and lethargy are often symptoms of psychological tension).

Activity

Read the accompanying newspaper report, 'Young poor "have more disorders"'. Summarize in your own words the views expressed about class and gender inequalities in relation to mental disorders.

C3.2, C3.3

Sociological debates about mental illness

Social distribution

Trowler (1996) demonstrates that mental illness is socially distributed, so challenging many of the assumptions of the medical model. More women than men are likely to die while suffering from mental disorders, although this may be due to the fact that they live longer, and the degenerative diseases associated with age. Working-class mothers seem to be more prone to depression than middle-class mothers. Black patients appear to be more likely to be admitted to mental hospitals than white patients with similar symptoms. Males are more likely to commit suicide, but females more likely to attempt it. This suggests that social factors are crucial in understanding mental illness.

Discussion point

Suggest reasons why each of the different patterns in the type and level of mental illness identified above might occur.

C3.1a

YOUNG POOR 'HAVE MORE DISORDERS'

DAVID BRINDLE

Children of poor families are three times more likely to suffer a mental disorder than those brought up in well-off households, a government survey has found. Boys are markedly more prone to mental problems than are girls, according to preliminary results published yesterday. The research was conducted jointly by the office for national statistics and a team from the Institute of Psychiatry and Maudsley Hospital, London.

The survey, the first such large-scale exercise in Britain, covered more than 10,000 children aged 5 to 15. It found that about one in ten suffered a mental disorder sufficient to cause distress or have a 'considerable impact' on the child's day to day life.

Five per cent were found to have a conduct disorder, making them troublesome, aggressive or anti-social; 4 per cent were assessed as having an emotional disorder, such as anxiety or depression; and 1 per cent were rated as hyperkinetic, characterized by inattention and overactivity.

Boys were found to have broadly the same rates of emotional disorders as girls, but were twice as likely to have a conduct disorder and four times as likely to be hyperkinetic.

Children of families classed as unskilled were found to be three times more likely to have a disorder than those from professional households.

Children with a disorder were discovered to be almost twice as likely as others to have no friends. This was especially marked with the hyperkinetic.

Source: Guardian, 26 November 1999

Systemic approaches to mental illness

These include micro-sociological approaches, popularized in the 1960s. Examples are the radical psychiatric views presented by the writer R. D. Laing, and debates about the impact of institutionalization on those defined as mentally ill developed by writers such as Erving Goffman.

Radical psychiatry

The systemic (or 'radical') approach, based mainly on the views of Laing and Esterson (1970), suggests that 'mental illness' is largely the result of faulty interactions between the individual and their family or significant others. Laing and his colleagues demonstrated the 'dark side of the family', whereby family interactions drove a teenager to a state defined as 'schizophrenic'. Laing therefore claimed that it is the world that is mad rather than the individual.

Institutionalization

This approach is also found in the work of Goffman (1991). Writing originally in the late 1950s, he showed that mental asylums – like other *total institutions*, including prisons, convents and military establishments – operate a system which is more likely to create than cure mental problems for the inmates. He showed how the aim of institutionalization is to destroy the personal self-image of the individual and replace it with an institutional self-concept, which makes the inmate more acquiescent and obliging.

Goffman called this *the mortification of the self*, a demonstration of the way that vulnerable people in particular are led to destroy and rebuild their personality by the institutions apparently designed to protect and help them. Although Goffman's ideas were part of the liberal attack on asylums as a way to treat people with mental illnesses, the modern solution, 'care in the community', is not without its critics (see Section 12.6).

Macro-sociological approaches to mental illness

While many of the micro-sociological approaches provide insights into the working of places where people experience problems, they do not really take into account the wider social causes of mental illness. A more 'macro' sociological approach is needed to examine the impact of poverty, social isolation, alienation at work, divorce, unemployment, inequality, racism and the stresses that they cause for the individual.

One of the unfortunate effects of 'care in the community' is that it often returns people to the very stresses and problems that caused their illness in the first place. However, this does not mean that supportive, therapeutic communities cannot work.

Does 'mental illness' really exist?

It can – and has been – argued that there is no such thing as mental illness. Foucault (1973) asserts that the definition of people as being mentally ill developed from the idea of reason and rationality which came to dominate modernist thinking and formed the basis for judging who was and was not 'sane'. Today, people who say very extraordinary things for no apparent reason may be called insane, and even sedated or incarcerated.

Foucault's viewpoint is similar in some ways to that of Szasz (1973). Writing originally in the early 1960s, he suggested that mental illness was a label used to control those who challenged the existing order. It is impossible, he said, to observe symptoms of mental illness (unlike symptoms of physical disease). Various labels are attached to people – such as 'schizophrenic' – if their behaviour does not conform to the dominant ideas in society.

It is important to be aware that, although mental illnesses may be 'just' labels that other people attach to those who suffer panic attacks or see hallucinations, the majority of those who live through such experiences find them very frightening. However, it may also be the case that people find the world they live in – and especially being inside a mental hospital – equally or even more terrifying.

Mental disability

Although more people than ever before are surviving for longer with both physical and mental disabilities, there is relatively little material available on this issue in the sociology of health and illness. While disabled people may reject the label of sickness, they can certainly be seen as disadvantaged within society.

Historical factors and developments

Midwinter (1994) suggests that the rapid population increase in the nineteenth century made society aware for the first time of the existence of a large number of people with disabilities, especially those defined as 'mentally handicapped'.

Mentally handicapped (and chronically sick) people were often placed first in asylums, from where their release only took them into the workhouse, though this was never the intended function of such places. In either place there was little positive treatment, whether the person concerned was classified as 'mad' or 'feeble-minded'.

After World War II, new treatments and programmes were introduced, such as 'token economies' for the mentally disadvantaged and a considerable range of somatic treatments for those defined as suffering from forms of mental illness like schizophrenia. Drugs or electroconvulsive therapy (ECT) remained the preferred treatments for those defined as mentally ill or mentally disabled.

The Mental Health Act 1959 attempted to set up a system of definitions and treatments for the approximately 350 000 people experiencing mental suffering. The Chronically Sick and Disabled Person's Act 1970 identified certain provisions required from local authorities, and this legislation was extended in 1981.

The NHS and Community Care Act

While the foregoing measures all sought – not always effectively – to help the mentally disadvantaged, nothing brought about change quite so dramatically as the National Health Service and Community Care Act 1990. While the aim was to integrate people back into the community, the lack of resources has been a constant reason for criticism, and a survey by the charity MIND suggests that the 'mentally ill' still suffer high levels of discrimination and abuse.

Taylor and Field (1993) assert that it is wrong to act as if all people with a 'mental handicap' have a medical condition rather than a social condition. Although there is quite often an organic or genetic cause for a handicap (e.g. handicaps resulting from Down's Syndrome), they argue that the same cannot be said for all forms of mental handicap:

Mild mental handicap is linked to poverty and deprivation, and its genetic causes are uncertain in most cases. A growing body of opinion suggests that adopting the 'medical model' has serious negative consequences, leading to the infantilization and the inappropriate application of the sick role to people who were not sick, but had learning difficulties.

(Taylor and Field, 1993, pp. 148–9)

'Normalization' and community care

Attempts to introduce a process of 'normalization' for people with a range of mental health problems have included the promotion of positive role models, and practical training for people with learning difficulties. However, the cornerstone to this process has been moves to integrate these people into the 'normal' community. It has to be said that the community may not be all that welcoming in some cases.

Community care has three features that differentiate it from institutional care:

- It takes place outside any institution.
- Individuals are treated as far as possible as other members of the community.
- Support comes mainly from lay carers – especially family members, supported by health and welfare workers (see Section 12.6).

Criticisms of community care

Community support, however, often becomes patchy and there seems to be an increase in the number of people suffering from a range of mental disorders who have effectively been made homeless. As long ago as 1979, Scull argued that some people who 'returned to the community' might not be safe, for themselves or others.

Despite this warning, the 'normalization' approach may possibly reduce the impact of the medical model in the identification and treatment of people experiencing 'mental illness' and those with learning difficulties. To an extent, 'care in the community' seems the best way of supporting people who have problems in coping with living. However, finding a caring community and providing care which is supportive, caring and also safe and secure remains a real challenge for welfare services today.

Realist views of health and illness

The above views challenge a purely biomedical model of health and stress a sociological approach. However, this can sometimes lead to the argument that illness is purely a social construction, especially within phenomenological approaches. Although their critique of the purely objective or positivist view of the biomedical model is an important corrective, there are also problems within the modified approach. Sheeran (1995) comments:

Students of the sociology of health are sometimes asked to explain how taken-for-granted concepts like health and illness are 'socially constructed' rather than biologically determined. ... Sometimes, however, introductory presentations of the 'social construction- ist' perspective encourage the uncritical acceptance of ideas which are in fact the subject of controversy.

(Sheeran, 1995, p. 8)

Taken to its limits, the view that illness is purely a social construction implies that medical science has no objective basis at all. While phenomenol- ogists and interactionists have long argued that phenomena are socially constructed, the lack of any real conception of power and wider struc- tures in their analysis has often led to their views being rejected. However, their 'relativist' con- ceptions are shared by a more recent approach which most certainly does have a conception of power, namely the post-structuralist work based on the ideas of Michel Foucault.

On the basis of Foucault's work, which included detailed analysis of the rise of hospitals and clinics, it is argued that contemporary med- ical science is merely a particular form of power and has no claim to represent any universal truths. Relativist arguments have therefore resur- faced in accounts of health and illness inspired by post-modernists and post-structuralists (see also Section 12.8).

Sheeran concludes that we need a realist view of health and illness. Realist sociologists argue that, although what it means to be ill may depend on different definitions in different social systems, we also need to be aware that there are biolog- ical causes of ill-health – such as bacteria and viruses – which can and should be dealt with through the use of medical treatments.

In other words, even if the way society reacts to a person with cancer or influenza may vary over time and between social groups, there is still some biological malfunction which can and should be treated by a variety of methods, includ- ing those based on scientific principles.

The discourse of medicine

Some of these ideas draw on – and challenge – Foucault's writings. He argued basically that medicine is a form of knowledge whereby differ- ent paradigms of health and illness affect the way people understand, explain and talk about health – what Foucault terms the 'discourse' of medi- cine. However, knowledge cannot be separated from power, so definitions of health and illness depend on who has the power to define the state our body is in.

This surveillance aspect of medicine is not a new phenomenon. Medicine (and sociology) orig- inally developed from the need to supervise and control the large populations which began to develop in towns at the beginning of the indus- trial revolution. What has changed is how recent forms of supervision, control and ways of seeing the world are closely focused on the body and reproduction (see also Sections 12.7 and 12.8).

> ### Discussion point
> To what extent do you think it is acceptable for doctors to monitor the behaviour of their patients and adopt the surveillance role described here?
>
> C3.1a

Loss of faith in the medical model

Nettleton (1996) agrees that there is a loss of faith in the biomedical model, and suggests that there is a new paradigm of health and illness with an emphasis on people increasingly being expected to take responsibility for their own well-being. For example, they should avoid 'risk-taking' behaviours such as smoking cigarettes or drink- ing too much alcohol.

The role of health professionals is increas- ingly one of surveillance, as they monitor and supervise their clients' actions and advise them of the rational course to avoid ill-health. In this way, much illness can be seen as a result of wil- ful self-damage on the part of the patient (or 'client'). This clearly has the potential to marginalize groups who cannot afford the healthy diets and exercise regimes required by the health-oriented in society.

Furthermore, Sheeran argues that the argument based on the social construction of health is often used as a demonstration of the power of sociological explanations. However, it overstates its case by denying any biological component of illness. Realist sociologists reject this view; but since they also reject positivism, they aim for a more sophisticated approach that does not reject the possibility of objective knowledge while still retaining important insights about the subjective experience of illness. Sheeran concludes:

However, many physical illnesses, especially those which result in death, are not simply deviant in some settings and not in others. Neither are they voluntary. In the end they provide an awful finality to social life from which none of us can escape. According to Twaddle (1973), at least some illnesses must therefore have a biological reality and causation which places limits on interpretation, whereas deviance is always a subjective evaluation of a behaviour or condition.

(Sheeran, 1995, p. 9)

Objective measure of health

While the subjective experience of illness may be explained by social constructionist arguments which point to its relative nature, this does not necessarily mean that objective accounts of ill-health should be abandoned. It is perfectly reasonable to assert that the subjective experience of illness and the objective reality of ill-health do not always coincide, and that therefore an approach based purely on a positivist biomedical model is deficient; but this lack of continuity does not *of itself* prove that there is no objective knowledge and that medical science is merely one form of power.

In fact, much of the evidence for the importance of the subjective experience of illness comes from comparing the subjective feelings of individuals with objective knowledge of their condition as defined by 'medicine'. This is an extremely useful insight; but even to argue that only a small proportion of patients who are in ill-health visit a doctor does rely on some objective knowledge of whether people are in ill-health or not for it to have any meaning.

Realists argue that sociologists should therefore seek to use data both from medical science (*objective* information on mortality and morbidity, for example) and *subjective* information on how people *feel*. They need to consider critically the overall validity of any data presented. This does not mean that sociologists have to throw the objective baby out with the positivist bathwater!

The sick role, deviance and social control

Linking individual subjective experience into the notion of the social was most famously undertaken by Talcott Parsons, with his argument that ill-health is in some respects functional because it fulfils a defined role in society – the sick role. (See also Section 12.2.) Parsons (1951) also claimed that the 'sick role' adopted by people who are unwell, performs a specific social function in modern industrialized societies. He suggests that the role is based on a number of assumptions:

- the sick person is exempt from normal responsibilities such as work
- the sick person needs, and must seek, professional medical help
- sick people must demonstrate the desire to get better.

The function of the sick role is to prevent a subculture of the sick developing, whereby the release of responsibilities makes sickness seem like a desirable state. Healthcare in modern industrialized societies, being largely state-sponsored, allows the surveillance and regulation of those workers who are simply trying to get time off work (Turner, 1987, 1989). Thus a person is considered to be legitimately ill if signed off work by a doctor, but if a person simply declares him or herself to be ill without a doctor's 'certification', that person will be considered a deviant as they are not fulfilling their social duty by not working (especially if they are absent from work for long periods of time). As Turner comments:

This social control and regulation of sickness is brought about by what may be termed the sick-role mechanism. The consequence is that in western societies general practitioners are concerned with clinical situations where they are professionally obliged to certify illness in order to explain the patient's failure to comply with social expectations ...

It was for this reason that Parsons classified sickness as a form of deviant behaviour which required legitimation and social control. While the sick role legitimizes social deviance, it also requires an acceptance of a medical regime. The sick role was therefore an important vehicle for social control, since the aim of the medical regime was to return the sick person to conventional social roles.

(Turner, 1987, pp. 40–41)

Criticisms of the functionalist view

Parsons' views have been the subject of a number of criticisms. First, it is clear that the approach suffers from what critics of general functionalist theory have called the 'over-socialized conception of humanity' (Wrong, 1969). In defining the sick role, Parsons tends to assume that everyone will play by the rules and adopt the rights and responsibilities of the role. This, however, might not be the case.

In particular, the contrast in this theory between the active role assigned to doctors and the passive role assigned to patients can be questioned. The rise of AIDS has led to highly active patient groups and knowledgeable patients themselves challenging doctors' arguments. It is also the case that the level of stigma associated with certain forms of ill-health (again AIDS is an example) might lead people to hide their condition.

The consensual nature of society assumed by functionalism tends to obscure the potential for conflict within the experience of ill-health, and this is contained within Parsons' theory of the sick role. He assumes that sickness is a status that can be exploited, but it can also be argued that sick people are themselves exploited – by doctors, medical companies and health insurance companies. In her study of the sociology of health, Hart (1985) points out that this is a very passive view of illness which largely ignores the function of the medical profession as an agent of social control.

The active–passive relationship outlined by Parsons also came into question with later interactionist studies of the doctor–patient relationship. These questioned both the notion of the doctor as a professional working only on objective knowledge, and the idea of the patient as a willingly passive body upon which doctors worked. The issue of the doctor–patient relationship is explored more fully in Section 12.7.

It can also be argued that, while those suffering from acute diseases could be accorded the treatment described by Parsons, this might not apply equally to those suffering from chronic illnesses, who are expected to 'soldier on'. This is important since, as pointed out earlier, the twentieth century saw a gradual shift from acute to chronic ill-health. As time goes by, this might further invalidate Parsons' argument (see Section 12.2).

Marxism and the political economy approach

The basis of the *political economy approach* is the existence of societal structures (for example, capitalism) wider than that contained in the notion of the doctor–patient relationship, and the way these influence social relationships in the field of health and illness. This is most notably associated with Marxist approaches.

Marxists tend to argue that capitalism generally makes people ill, and doctors – especially psychiatrists and psychologists – are agents of social control (see also Section 12.7).

The evidence in Table 12.2 suggests that industrialization vastly improved the health and longevity of the population, although public health initiatives such as the provision of clean water rather than medical developments *per se* are often seen as the key basis of this.

While Marx recognized that industrial society and capitalism produced advances in health compared with pre-capitalist society, he argued nonetheless that much illness is caused by the capitalist system, while its definition and treatment serves the interests of the ruling classes.

It has been argued that capitalist production methods are inherently unhealthy because it is expensive to protect workers adequately. From a

Table 12.2 Percentage reductions in mortality from 1848/54 to 1971 in England and Wales

Condition	Percentage reduction
Conditions attributable to micro-organisms:	
Airborne diseases	40
Water- and food-borne diseases	21
Other conditions	13
Conditions not attributable to micro-organisms	26

Source: McKeown (1979)

Marxist perspective, Pearce (1976) showed in his study of the crimes of the powerful that, despite extensive health and safety legislation, firms are rarely prosecuted. In their study of health from a broadly Marxist political economy viewpoint, Doyal and Pennell (1979) also point out that housework is similarly unhealthy and alienating (see also Section 5.6). Even *not* working makes us ill because unemployment in a capitalist society causes stress and loss of status, with an increased risk of ill-health, depression and suicide (see Section 14.6).

12.2 Deviance, social control and the sick role

Ill-health as deviance

Society has set 'standards' for how its members should behave, and those members of a society who move away or stray from these standards, and the social roles expected of them may be called 'deviant'. Sociologists have long studied such deviance in relation to crime and what societies have considered to constitute criminal behaviour (see Chapter 10). More recently, sociologists have turned their attention to studying ill-health and sickness as a form of deviance.

Mental illness, deviance and social control

Sociologists have also studied the ways in which society views and deals with mental illness as a form of deviance. Attention has been paid in particular to the processes by which society creates definitions and 'labels' for the deviant role of the mentally ill, and how this role has been institutionalized.

Erving Goffman – *Asylums*

In his work *Asylums*, first published in the early 1960s, Goffman (1987) explores the labelling process in what he calls the 'total institution' of the asylum. He identifies a process he calls the 'mortification of the self' through which the outside self of an individual entering the asylum is stripped away and replaced by an institutional self. Goffman defines a 'total institution' as:

… a place of residence and work where a large number of like-situated individuals, cut off from the wider society for an appreciable period of time, together lead an enclosed, formally administered round of life.

(Goffman, 1987, p. 11)

The mortification of the self is largely achieved through rituals, entered into on joining the asylum, aimed at the establishment of a new, deviant and institutional label: for example, individuals may be required to have a medicated shower or bath, to have their hair cut and their photograph and fingerprints taken, and to receive new clothes.

Goffman suggests that the deviant career of an asylum inpatient is fully established once he or she learns to, and accepts the need to, withdraw from the routines of everyday life. Instead, the patient starts to act in ways associated with being mentally ill, features of behaviour learned while inside the institution:

The last step in the prepatient's career can involve his realization – justified or not – that he has been deserted by society and turned out of relationships by those closest to him.

(Goffman, 1987, p. 136)

Michael Foucault – the birth of madness

Michael Foucault (1989a, b) suggests that the creation of deviant labels such as 'mentally ill' or 'mad' can be understood only by comparing them with their opposites: insanity can only be understood by comparing it with sanity, for example. He explains that these two opposite concepts are dependent on each other for their existence – we cannot have one without the other – so it is impossible for madness to exist as a deviant label without there also being something society understands as normality.

Foucault observes that both opposite concepts are born in history at the same time, yet behaviour that may be classified as deviant, like insanity, exists long before the creation of these controlling categories. Before the creation (or birth) of the concepts of madness and its opposite (what Foucault terms 'civilization'), so-called insane behaviour was openly tolerated and accepted on a day-to-day basis.

The birth of madness and civilization, according to Foucault, are linked historically to the creation of total institutions aimed at the exclusion of these deviants from 'normal' society: the creation of architectural spaces in which those labelled as insane, or criminal, or ill, can be placed – the asylum, the prison, the hospital. Before the creation of the asylum and the exclusion of these people labelled as insane, so-called insane behaviour is tolerated, is widespread and is as yet unclassified with a name – and therefore is not controllable. Thus, reasons Foucault, the birth of the asylum (or, in his words, the clinic) gives rise to the birth of insanity. Deviance can exist in the eyes of society only when it has been named and labelled.

12.3 Social class, region and health inequalities

Sociologists and other social researchers have clearly shown that health and ill-health are affected by the social status of individuals. In particular it has been shown that a person's social class, gender and ethnic background will have an effect on their chances of suffering ill-health. However, overall, the most obvious difference is between the rich and the poor – in simple terms between class groups (see Tables 12.3 and 12.4).

Measuring inequalities in health

One of the key problems with identifying differences in health and illness between social classes is the way in which such groups are classified. Different systems may be used which may produce different outcomes.

In an analysis of social class inequalities in health, sociologists from Nuffield College, Oxford University, suggest that different schemes of classification may indicate different patterns of health inequality (Bartley *et al.*, 1996). They argue that the Registrar General's (RG) classification scheme can be seen as 'commonsensical' because it incorporates many people's assumptions about class differences. It is based on the status criterion of 'general standing in the community', although it is not always clear how status is related clearly to skill or income.

Bartley and colleagues propose the use of an alternative schema: the Erikson–Goldthorpe (E–G) system of classification. This system is designed deliberately to examine differences in the work situation of particular occupational groups. The focus is mainly on conditions of employment, level of job security and promotion opportunities. They argue that, because it is based on objective criteria, the E–G classification (which is less widely used) is more accurate.

Table 12.3 Death rates, by occupation

Occupation	Death rate[a] per 100 000	SMR[b]
Relatively low death rates		
University teacher	287	49
Physiotherapist	287	55
Local authority senior officer	342	57
Company secretary or registrar	362	60
Minister, senior government official, MP	371	61
Office manager	377	64
School teacher	396	66
Architect or town planner	443	74
Civil servant or executive officer	467	78
Medical practitioner	494	81
Relatively high death rates		
Coal miner (underground)	822	141
Leather product maker	895	147
Machine tool operator	934	156
Coal miner (above ground)	972	160
Fisherman	1028	171
Labourer or unskilled worker	1247	201
Policeman	1270	209
Deck or engine room rating	1385	233
Bricklayer's labourer	1644	274

[a] Direct age-standardized death rate per 100 000.
[b] SMR is the Standardized Mortality Ratio. Figures below 100 indicate a below-average mortality rate, whereas those above 100 indicate an above-average rate.
Source: Adapted from Townsend *et al.* (1988)

They compared the efficiency of both systems of classification to explain the health experiences of two samples of employed men over a ten-year period (1976–86). Both systems showed considerable health disadvantages for men employed in unskilled and semi-skilled manual work, although the E–G classification also demonstrated a higher risk of death for lower routine non-manual and service workers and a much lower risk of death for agricultural workers.

Bartley and colleagues also confirmed that the class differences in health experiences identified by the RG classification were valid. Therefore, much of the discussion below can be accepted as being based on real inequalities, even if a different schema might make their measurement more accurate.

Table 12.4 Prevalence in 1994 of reported *limiting* chronic sickness in Great Britain, by sex, age and socio-economic group of head of household (percentages)

Socio-economic group of head of household	Males					Females				
	0–15	16–44	45–64	65 and over	Total	0–15	16–44	45–64	65 and over	Total
Professional	6	8	14	34	12	10	10	18	34	14
Employers and managers	7	10	20	34	15	6	10	24	39	16
Intermediate non-manual	9	11	27	34	17	3	12	28	36	18
Junior non-manual	8	10	25	47	16	10	14	21	43	23
Skilled manual and own account non-professional	8	15	31	46	22	5	13	27	43	18
Semi-skilled manual and personal service	8	15	32	45	21	7	15	31	50	24
Unskilled manual	6	20	40	34	23	8	19	34	45	28
All persons	8	13	27	41	18	6	13	27	43	20

Source: Social Trends, 1996

Explanations of social class inequalities

First it is necessary to look at some definitions. *Mortality rates* measure the deaths per thousand of a particular social group who die of that disease at that age. *Morbidity rates* measure the number per thousand of the population suffering from a particular long-term illness such as heart disease or cancer. *Standardized mortality and morbidity rates* (or ratios) compare the number in each group to a figure of 100: therefore a standardized mortality rate (SMR) of 120 would imply a higher than average level of death or ill-health, while anything under 100 shows a lower than average rate.

The statistics in Table 12.5 and Figure 12.1 show quite clearly that mortality and morbidity rates are higher for almost all diseases for people in Classes IV and V than they are in Classes I and II. Interestingly enough, these differences have persisted, despite significant improvements in healthcare (see Section 12.5) for almost all social groups over the past century, and despite the availability of free, universal and high-quality healthcare in Britain since 1948 through the NHS.

The fact that these patterns exist at all suggests that there may be social rather than just biological explanations for the differences.

Table 12.5 Standard mortality rates (SMRs) of males aged 15–64 in England and Wales

Social class in 1971	1971–75	1976–81	1982–85	1986–89
I	80	69	61	67
II	80	78	78	80
IIIN	92	103	98	85
IIIM	90	95	101	102
IV	97	109	113	112
V	115	124	136	153

Source: OPCS, Social Trends 1996

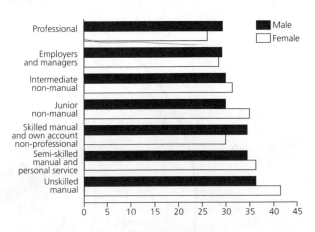

Figure 12.1 Prevalence in 1994 of reported chronic sickness in Great Britain, by sex and socio-economic group of head of household
Source: Social Trends, 1996

The Acheson Report

The most recent study into inequalities in health was the report based on the 'Independent Inquiry into Inequalities in Health' chaired by Sir Donald Acheson in 1998. His findings echoed many of those of earlier studies, such as the Black Report (1980).

Acheson's study found that there are still considerable inequalities in the health of different class groups, with some evidence of growing inequalities in the 1980s and 90s between those at the top and those at the bottom of the social structure.

After looking at considerable evidence of class inequalities, Acheson suggested that there were a number of factors affecting health and illness, as summarized in Figure 12.2. These included:

- general socio-economic factors, cultural and environmental factors
- social and community factors and support networks
- individual lifestyle factors.

Socio-economic factors

The socio-economic factors affecting health outcomes identified by Acheson are depicted in Figure 12.3. They include:

- poverty (both relative and, for some people on or outside the benefit system, absolute)
- inequalities in wealth and income, again especially for those receiving state benefits
- differences in educational provision, especially access to pre-school education
- employment opportunities and stress at work
- housing and environmental factors, such as safe play areas for children, good food and healthy sanitation
- mobility and access to public transport, particularly for the elderly who are most affected by social isolation
- facilities available for older people, mothers, children and people from different ethnic groups
- access to, and treatment in, the NHS itself.

Policies to improve the health of the nation

The Acheson Report finally recommended that policies to improve health should include:

- improved benefits and access to benefits for the most needy
- a concentration on pre-school provision and nutrition in schools
- opportunities for training, re-training and policies to reduce stress at work

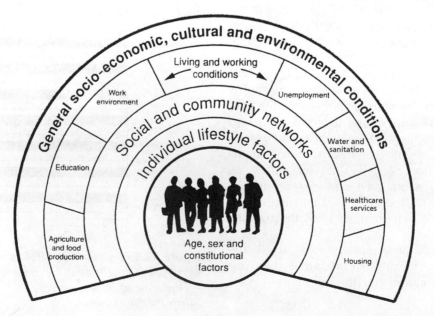

Figure 12.2 Main determinants of health
Source: Dahlgren and Whitehead (1991), reproduced in *Independent Inquiry into Inequalities in Health* (1998)

- better and safer public transport and cycling facilities
- the distribution of surplus food produced in the European Union to poor families
- further policies focusing explicitly on the social and health needs of specific groups such as families, young people (particularly the promotion of sexual health and the reduction of teenage pregnancies among young women and suicide among young men), older people and ethnic groups
- improved access to health services for all these groups.

Acheson therefore proposed an integrated policy which considers all these factors and monitors the effects of all these initiatives on the different groups involved and the inequalities between them.

Criticisms of the Acheson Report

It can be argued that, while the report is extremely comprehensive, it tends not to *prioritize* what should be done, and determine how available funds should be allocated. While he is doubtless right to propose an integrated approach, there is almost too much to be done. What the report does show (as have others) is the complex nature of both the causes of and solutions to, inequalities in health and illness.

Society and community

Acheson also focused on the importance of social and community networks. One of the key policies of the Labour government elected in May 1997 was to deal with the 'social exclusion' experienced by certain groups in society, to enable them to become more involved in their local communities (see Section 14.2). Other studies have focused on the breakdown of the family as a major cause of stress and ill-health, and the importance of stable families in maintaining health and well-being.

Marriage

This view is illustrated in a recent study of marital breakdown and health by One plus One: the Marriage and Partnership Charity. The editor of the study, Fiona McAllister (1995), demonstrates clearly the key points that mortality and mor-

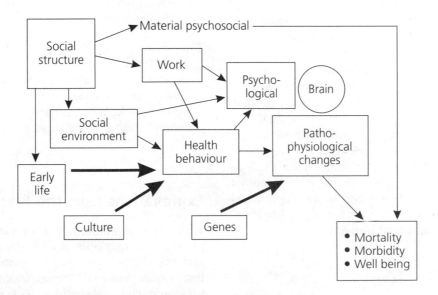

Figure 12.3 Socio-economic circumstances and health outcomes
Source: International Centre for Health and Society, University College London (unpublished, 1998)

bidity rates are higher for unmarried than for married people, especially for men. Married people are less likely than those who are single, widowed or divorced to suffer (or die) from mental illness, suicide (or attempts), accidents, heart disease, strokes and cancer.

Why might the figures suggest that marriage makes us healthier? McAllister argues that there are three main interrelated factors to consider.

- Firstly, people who are physically and mentally healthy are more likely to attract and keep marriage partners, so that in selection terms the statistics are likely to show that marriage partners are more healthy than the general population.

- Secondly, marriage offers the partners protection, support and companionship, thereby reducing the likelihood of the development of unhealthy anxiety, stress and tension.

- Against those two (positive) factors has to be set the negative factor that the break-up of a marriage itself leads to stress, often resulting in more risk-taking behaviour (especially for men) such as drinking heavily, smoking and unsafe sexual practices. Where children are involved, the partner gaining custody (most usually the mother) is less likely to indulge in a more dissolute (unhealthy) lifestyle.

Support networks

Nettleton (1995) also found that working-class people have fewer support networks to help them deal with stressful life events such as loss of a partner or job.

These arguments appear quite convincing. However, it could also be that people's disapproval might lead divorced people into indulging in a more dissolute way of life. It is also assumed that the majority of married people are always stable in their behaviour patterns, happy in their marriages, free from harmful stress and faithful to their partners – a supposition that recent studies of adultery tend to challenge.

There are also some problems with the statistics themselves. As McAllister herself points out, studies of this type need to be longitudinal (following a sample over a period of time) to identify the factors affecting individuals.

Activity

Try to set up a small study of lifestyle behaviour among people you know. What problems might you encounter? How could you overcome those problems?

IT3.1, N3.1, C3.2, C3.3

The Black Report

Lifestyle (diet, smoking, drinking, sexual practices, etc.) is the focus of many magazine and newspaper articles looking at health. However, as Acheson pointed out, lifestyle is just one factor in the identification of inequalities in health. This view has been supported by earlier studies of health and inequality, such as the Black Report (1980) chaired by Sir Douglas Black.

This report (and a number of related follow-up studies) also showed that there was a strong inverse relationship between social class and mortality and morbidity rates, especially in relation to age of death, infant mortality and maternal mortality, and accidents to young people. The report's other findings can be summarized as follows:

- People in lower social classes were in some cases experiencing comparatively worse health than in the 1950s.

- Among working-class people there was under-utilization of the NHS in comparison with need.

- British rates of infant mortality were in many cases higher than those in many other 'developed' countries.

Activity

Suggest as many reasons as you can why people in lower social classes might die earlier and suffer more from disease and ill-health than people in higher social classes.

C3.2, C3.3

Explanations from the Black Report

The report examined four explanations for the patterns of inequality it had identified: the artefact explanation, the social selection explanation, behavioural/cultural explanations, and structural/material explanations. These are similar to some of the points made in the Acheson Report.

The artefact explanation

Artefacts are things made by people. This explanation suggests that class inequalities in health do not really exist; they only appear to exist because of the way class is constructed. There are four important points here:

- The number of people in the lower class groups, especially unskilled manual workers, is in decline, so statistics on health inequalities among the poorer classes are based on fewer people.

- The few workers remaining in lower-class jobs are still experiencing better health than in the past.

- These figures tend to mask the higher levels of degenerative disease among (especially) middle-class women – such as Alzheimer's – as women and middle-class people live longer.

- This explanation also criticizes the classification of people by occupation.

The authors of the Black Report did not find this explanation particularly convincing, as working-class groups have not contracted as much as is often supposed, while poor health affects all manual workers, not just those classified as 'unskilled'.

The social selection explanation

The argument here is that people who experience poor health tend to find it difficult to get good jobs. Therefore they either move into, or remain in, lower-class occupations. This means that people are in lower social classes because of their poor health, rather than their class causing poorer health.

There is some evidence in support of this theory. Based on research on women in Aberdeen, Illsley (1986) concluded that taller women tended to move up an occupational class at marriage while shorter women tended to move downwards. Since height can be taken as an indicator of health, this research tended to support the social selection model. On the basis of data from a National Survey of Health and Development, Wadsworth (1986) found that seriously ill boys were more likely to suffer a fall in social class than others.

However, longitudinal research contained within the National Child Development Survey – following a group of children born in 1958 – also found that while some social mobility was related to health, such differences in health experiences could not explain the degree of class difference in health that existed. Equally a study of 17 000 Whitehall civil servants (Rose and Marmot, 1981; Marmot et al., 1984a) found that, among those with no detectable disease at the start of their career, there were still notably higher death rates among men in the lower grades of the civil service.

The behavioural/cultural explanation

This view tends to blame ill-health on the sufferers because they do not follow a healthy lifestyle. Supporters of this view suggest that working-class people smoke and drink too much, eat the wrong kind of food and take little exercise. This view argues that the prudent would not waste money on cigarettes and alcohol, would live on healthy vegetable casseroles, and would walk everywhere for exercise. The fact that some do not do this suggests a deficient culture and value system.

While the authors of the Black Report accepted that this factor played a role in health differences, like Acheson, they viewed it as less important than structural material factors. However, its high profile in political debates in the 1980s led to the inclusion of questions about smoking-related diseases, notably coronary heart disease and lung cancer, in research on Whitehall civil servants by Marmot et al. (1984a). They found that even with non-smokers the risk of these diseases was still strongly associated with the grade of job held, thereby pointing to the inability of this model to explain most health inequalities. Cultural/behavioural differences can account for only about 25 per cent of social-class inequalities.

The structural/material explanation

This view is favoured by many sociologists and social democratic politicians. The evidence for it was seen as the most convincing by the producers of the Black Report. The point here is that the material situation of the poor is seen as the most important factor in determining their poorer health.

Lower income earners are more likely to live in substandard housing which may be damp, overcrowded and possibly dangerous. Many manual workers experience unhealthy and potentially dangerous working conditions, and statistically they have more accidents at work than non-manual workers. Manual workers often do work that is physically and mentally draining, leaving little energy for relaxation or exercise, while lower income may lead to poor diet and stress, resulting in increased smoking and drinking, for example, with potentially dangerous consequences for long-term health.

Other stress factors for manual workers are also statistically more common. They are more likely to divorce and have a far greater risk of unemployment (see Section 14.6), both of which appear to affect income and health adversely. Finally, working-class people tend to receive less education and information on childcare and healthy eating, etc., as well as having less money to spend on these things.

Wilkinson (1986) found that people in occupations that increased their incomes relative to average earnings experienced a relative decrease in mortality rate, and those occupations experiencing a fall in their earnings relative to the average level experienced a relative rise in their mortality rate. This study provides evidence in support of the importance of material factors in social-class health inequalities.

Summarizing the evidence on the relative importance of the cultural/behavioural and the material/structuralist explanations, Whitehead (1987) argues:

The evidence that health-damaging behaviour is more common in lower social groups continues to accumulate, especially concerning smoking and diet. But can such life-style factors account for all the observed differential in health between different social groups? The short answer is: no. When studies are able to control for factors like smoking and drinking, a sizeable proportion of the health gap remains and factors related to the general living conditions and environment of the poor are indicated. In this context there is also a growing body of evidence that material and structural factors, such as housing and income, can affect health. Most importantly, several studies have shown how adverse social conditions can limit the choice of life-style, and it is this set of studies which illustrates most clearly that behaviour cannot be separated from its social context.

(Whitehead, 1987, p. 304)

The inverse care law

As discussed earlier, it is also argued that working-class people tend to have less contact with, and receive inferior treatment from, the NHS in three key ways. What Dr Tudor-Hart (1971) called 'the inverse care law' operates as follows:

- In poorer areas doctors are less likely to set up practices, so there are fewer doctors to deal with more sick people in, for example, inner-city London than in the leafy suburbs of Surrey.

- Studies on inequalities in healthcare, such as Cartwright and O'Brien's (1978) study of GP consultations, have shown that middle-class people ask more questions of their doctors. Cartwright and O'Brien also found that the average consultation was 6.2 minutes for middle-class patients but only 4.7 minutes for working-class patients.

- Many doctors find it easier to interact with middle-class patients, giving them more time and being more prepared to refer them on for further treatment.

💬 Discussion point

To what extent do you think it possible or desirable to eliminate 'the inverse care law' described above? Suggest policies to reduce each of its elements.

C3.1a

Recent changes in private healthcare

Since the 1970s there has been a massive increase in the provision and use of private medicine, and this is probably one (but certainly not the only) reason why health inequalities continue to widen.

In a study of doctor–patient relationships in private-sector healthcare, Wiles and Higgins (1996) investigated the idea that private patients – most but not all of whom are likely to be middle class – receive better treatment than those using the NHS. Certainly some of the evidence they examine shows better treatment for private patients in both outpatient and inpatient hospital care. Relationships tended to be less formal and patients were treated more as individuals than as 'cases' (see also Section 12.7).

'Time' was the main reason for seeking private healthcare given by the people studied. They were treated more quickly, were given more convenient times for appointments, were allocated more time by their doctors or consultants, and received information back more quickly. They felt they had more right to ask questions and some saw their doctor as a friend. They thought they were entitled to better treatment as they were paying for the time. They also felt entitled to contact the doctor directly if necessary and that there was an atmosphere of mutual respect.

This suggests that although middle-class patients generally get better treatment from their GP, they often seek to enhance their hospital treatment by paying for an experience which they hope will involve mutual respect as well as the ability to buy more professional attention at a more convenient time.

A study by Thorogood (1992) identified a number of black working-class women who were also prepared to pay for private medical treatment. She found that this was usually in order to pay for a second opinion from a general practitioner rather than to gain access to hospital treatment, and concluded that the women in her study used their money:

... to buy back some equality, to regain some power and control in this area of their lives.

(Thorogood, 1992, p. 37)

Thorogood suggests that their use of private medicine was designed to override their inequalities of 'race', gender and class, but it is still rare for white working-class people to use private medicine extensively. She argues that the use of private healthcare by the women she studied was designed to overcome some of the disadvantages they experienced in the NHS.

However, Wiles and Higgins' (1996) study of middle-class people concluded that time was the most important factor for their respondents rather than quality of care.

Regional health inequalities

As well as health and illness being structured in terms of social class, regional differences are also noticeable. It is important for sociologists to examine evidence of regional differences in health indicators.

The regional distribution of health and illness

Regional Trends is published annually by the government. It contains statistical information about a number of different social indicators in different regions of Great Britain. In Regional Trends 34 (1999) statistics showed that the highest death rate in 1997 for both men and women was to be found in Scotland (115) and the second highest

in the North East of England (110). The lowest rates were found in the South East (93), the South West (90) and East of England (92). (The standardised rate is 100.)

Infant mortality rates are a useful indicator of health in any social group. In 1997 the infant mortality rates were highest in the North West (6.8 per thousand live births) and West Midlands (7.1). The lowest rates were found in the eastern (4.8) and south eastern (5.0) regions of England. Despite its high death rates, Scotland had a relatively low infant mortality rate of 5.3 per thousand.

Death is not the only way that health and illness can be measured. Table 12.6 shows that people in the North East are less likely to report their health as good, and this is supported by their high level of morbidity (limiting long standing illness) as shown in Figure 12.7.

Activity

Looking at Table 12.6 and Figure 12.4, identify the regions with the highest rates of self-reported good health. Does that always match their levels of morbidity? Are there any regions where reported health is generally not so good but morbidity levels are quite low?

C3.2, C3.3

Table 12.6 Self-reported general health, 1996–97

	Good	Percentages Fairly good	Not so good
Great Britain	55	33	12
North East	46	37	16
North West	55	31	14
Yorkshire and the Humber	49	36	14
East Midlands	53	36	11
West Midlands	55	32	13
East	59	31	10
London	58	31	10
South East	60	32	9
South West	57	33	10
England	55	33	12
Wales	51	32	17
Scotland	57	31	12
Northern Ireland	56	31	13

Source: General Household Survey, Office for National Statistics; Continuous Household Survey, Northern Ireland Statistics and Research Agency

Figure 12.4 Self-reported limiting long-standing illness, 1996–97

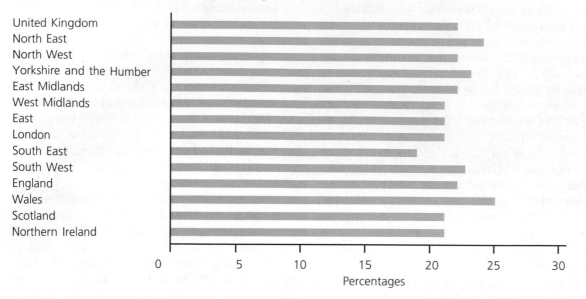

Source: General Household Survey, Office for National Statistics; Continuous Household Survey, Northern Ireland Statistics and Research Agency

Having identified differential regional distribution of both mortality and morbidity in Great Britain, we need to ask two questions: is there evidence of a 'north–south divide', and, most importantly, what causes these differences? The link established above between class and ill health suggests that income inequality might be a major factor.

A north–south divide?

The following article by Jeremy Laurance examines the 'health gap' in some depth. The comparison between one of the poorest parts of Glasgow and the wealthy south-eastern town of Wokingham in Berkshire identifies some notable differences.

Activity

Read the article by Jeremy Laurance carefully and answer the following questions:

a What indicators does the writer use to identify the differences between Springburn and Wokingham?

b Which health indicators does he consider the most important?

c Which new study does he get his information from?

d How do the authors of this study criticise the Acheson Report (see p. 432)?

e Does Jeremy Laurance agree with the concept of a 'north–south divide'?

f What does he see as the most important cause of poorer health and high mortality rates in some regions?

C3.2, C3.3

Another report by researchers at the University of Bristol, published in early December 1999, also confirmed a widening north–south health gap between different areas of Britain. Looking at different parliamentary constituencies, they found that all but one of the 15 unhealthiest constituencies were in the north of England and Scotland and all but one of the 15 healthiest constituencies were in the south of England. Once again, indicators showed wealthy Wokingham as the healthiest place in Britain and a poor area of Glasgow as the least healthy.

However, as we have seen above, indicators of inequality are not always so clear cut. An article entitled 'East of Eden' by Larry Elliott, published in the *Guardian* on 7 December 1999, suggested the situation is far more complex. Some areas of the south, especially Cornwall and south-eastern seaside towns, have high levels of unemployment and poverty. On the other hand, some more northern towns such as Chester and Ludlow (on the Welsh border) are extremely prosperous.

Preventable deaths grow as health gap widens

BY JEREMY LAURANCE

THE HEALTH gap between rich and poor in Britain is the widest on record and is continuing to grow, researchers report today.

Increasing inequality in income, lifestyle, education opportunities and jobs is resulting in thousands of extra deaths in the most deprived inner cities. The death rate among people under 65 is now more than two and a half times higher in the worst parts of Glasgow than in the prosperous southern communities of Esher and Wokingham.

Despite ministerial pledges to narrow the gap, experts from the Townsend Centre for International Poverty Research, at the University of Bristol, say the Government's policies are doomed to fail because they focus on getting people into work or increasing the incomes of those already in work. Most of those living in poverty do not have jobs and could not take them even if they were available because they are looking after children or the sick, or are elderly themselves.

Instead, the authors advocate redistribution, claiming "widespread public support" for measures to reduce poverty in Britain. "It is our firm belief that if health inequalities ... are to be reduced, as is the stated aim of the Government, then policies which actively address the reduction of poverty and of inequality through redistribution [of income and wealth] must be pursued." They add: "The costs would be borne by the rich."

The study, published as a book, *The Widening Gap*, is the most comprehensive since the Black report of 1980, which was updated last year by the Independent Inquiry into Inequalities in Health, chaired by Sir Donald Acheson. The authors criticise the Acheson report for failing to highlight the fundamental role of poverty in creating and maintaining the health gap. It was "lost in a sea of recommendations from traffic curbing to the fluoridation of the water supply", they say.

For the first time, the report compares geographical areas to find the "worst health" and "best health" parts of Britain and reveals a clear north/south divide. If people in the worst areas had enjoyed the same health as those in the best, 71 per cent of the deaths under 65 would not have occurred between 1991 and 1995, a saving of more than 10,000 lives.

The most embarrassing finding for ministers is that those suffering the most sickness and the highest death rates are Labour voters. Of the 100 constituencies with the worst health, 97 are Labour. Of the 100 constituencies with the best health, 81 are Conservative.

The geographical comparisons show the infant mortality rate is twice as high in Salford, one of the worst areas, as in south Suffolk, one of the best, and that 7,500 infants might have been saved between 1991 and 1995 if every area had matched the rate in Suffolk.

The health gap mirrors gaps in income, education and employment levels. The average household income in Glasgow Springburn, one of the worst areas, is £13,697 compared with £24,490 in Wokingham, Berkshire. Average incomes in the worst areas are 30 per cent less than those in the best areas.

The researchers say the gap between rich and poor has widened faster in Britain and that levels of poverty are higher than in much of Europe. The report shows that life expectancy for professional men is now 9.5 years more than for male unskilled manual workers. For women it is 6.4 years more.

Yet in the 1960s and 1970s the gap narrowed. "Just as a gap can widen so it can narrow ... the trends of growing inequality show no sign of abating and the consequences of such a widening gap are dire," the authors say.

Source: The Independent, 2 December 1999

SPRINGBURN, GLASGOW

Chronic illness	155 sufferers per 1,000 population
Infant mortality	67.9 deaths per 10,000 live births
Unemployment*	53.8 per cent
Cars	7,214 (among 30,000 households)
GCSE failures+	7 per cent
Poverty	41 per cent of households

WOKINGHAM, BERKSHIRE

Chronic illness	36 sufferers per 1,000 population
Infant mortality	53.2 deaths per 10,000 live births
Unemployment*	27.9 per cent
Cars	46,195 (among 32,000 households)
GCSE failures+	46 per cent
Poverty	10 per cent of households

*men, aged 16–64, includes sick, early retired and those on government schemes
+defined as not achieving 5 GCSEs at grades A to C

He argues that the growth of new technology companies in East Anglia and the loss of many thousands of manufacturing jobs in large conurbations such as Greater Manchester and areas such as the West Midlands means that there is evidence of a significant 'east–west' divide rather than a gap between the north and the south. This might explain the high levels of infant mortality in the West Midlands. The idea of a north–south (or even east–west) divide has some evidence to support it, but it is probably an over-simplification.

Discussion point

Is there a north–south divide? Give reasons for your answer.

C3.1a

 Activity

Go to your local library (or use the Internet) and identify health indicators for your region. Using this information plus material from this and other sections of the book, write a short newspaper article about whether you live in a healthy and privileged area of the country or an unhealthy and deprived region.

It3.1, C3.2, C3.3

Causes of regional inequalities

Whether or not there is a line dividing the country in any direction, there is no doubt that health indicators are worse for some regions than for others. As with all other elements of inequality, it is important to identify why this might be. The most convincing and frequently presented explanations of health inequality focus on either behavioural/cultural (lifestyle) explanations or structural/material (poverty and social class) explanations.

Behavioural/cultural explanations of regional health inequalities

This view suggests that people who live in regions with poorer health tend to adopt a less healthy lifestyle. This means that people who live in Scotland, the West Midlands and north eastern or south western regions tend to smoke and drink more, take less exercise, eat less healthily and take more risks with their sexual and drug-taking behaviours than do people in the south east or East Anglia. Tables 12.8, 12.9, 12.10, 12.11 and 12.12 look at these behaviours in regional terms.

 Activity

Using the information from Tables 12.7 to 12.10, and Figure 12.5, write a report on lifestyle differences between Scotland and the south east of England for each of these factors. What is your conclusion on the importance of these factors in affecting regional health inequalities?

C3.2, C3.3

Structural/material explanations of regional health inequalities

From this viewpoint, poverty – linked to social class – is the most important factor dividing regions in terms of health. Even if there are lifestyle differences between regions, lack of access to good jobs and a reasonable income is the underlying factor causing both the unhealthy lifestyle choices and poor health. Both the studies discussed by Jeremy Laurance and Larry Elliott take this approach, even though they may disagree about which regions are the most deprived.

The effects of deprivation on health were discussed fully earlier. They include factors such as substandard housing, dangerous working conditions, poor diet, limited exercise, increased stress, high levels of divorce, high risk of unemployment and poor educational opportunities. These factors demonstrate the link between poverty, ill-health and preventable early death. Table 12.11 shows a higher proportion of manual workers and a lower proportion of professionals living in Scotland, the Midlands and northern parts of England than in the south and south east. The article by Jeremy Laurance (see p. 439) shows a number of indicators of deprivation in the least healthy regions. They therefore provide evidence to support the view that material structures such as poverty and class background do have an influence on differences in health rates.

However, we have to be very careful not to over-simplify a complex issue. Other factors such as age, gender and ethnicity all have to be taken into account when looking at both health and regional factors. It is also important to look at inter-European and international comparisons in order to develop a wider understanding of the causes and consequences of inequalities in health and illness within, between and beyond different regions.

12.4 Gender, ethnicity and health inequalities

The paradox of gender, mortality and morbidity

Women are on average likely to live longer than men in all social classes. However, there is a par-

Table 12.7 Contributions of selected foods to nutritional intakes (household food), 1996–7

| | Percentage of fat and energy derived from | | | | | | | | | | | Total intake[1] per person per day | | Percentage of food energy derived from fat[1] |
| | Liquid & processed milk & cream | | Meat & meat products | | All fats | | Fresh & processed fruit & vegetables | | Cereals including bread | | | | |
	Fat	Energy	Fat	Energy	Fat	Energy	Fat	Energy	Fat	Energy	Fat (grams)	Energy (Kcal)	
United Kingdom	10.9	10.2	22.3	14.3	29.2	11.6	8.0	15.0	17.2	35.1	80	1,820	39
North East	10.7	10.2	22.7	14.6	28.2	11.3	8.2	15.1	17.6	34.9	75	1,720	39
North West	11.5	10.8	24.5	15.5	26.5	10.3	7.9	15.1	17.3	34.7	76	1,780	38
Yorkshire and the Humber	10.5	10.1	21.9	14.4	31.2	12.7	7.0	14.4	16.9	34.5	83	1,860	40
East Midlands	10.6	10.3	20.2	13.4	32.2	13.2	8.1	14.8	16.5	34.4	85	1,900	41
West Midlands	10.5	9.8	23.1	14.6	29.9	11.8	7.9	15.0	16.5	34.2	79	1,820	39
East	10.3	10.0	22.5	14.9	29.1	11.9	8.3	15.4	16.9	33.7	80	1,790	40
London	10.8	9.3	20.4	12.4	31.7	11.9	7.7	14.2	16.9	39.5	76	1,840	37
South East	10.7	10.2	21.6	14.1	28.1	11.4	8.3	15.5	17.6	34.2	82	1,830	40
South West	11.5	10.6	21.9	14.2	28.7	11.5	8.0	15.1	17.3	34.0	81	1,840	40
England	10.8	10.1	22.1	14.2	29.4	11.7	7.9	15.0	17.1	35.0	80	1,820	39
Wales	10.9	10.2	22.9	14.6	29.7	11.7	7.9	15.8	17.0	33.8	82	1,900	39
Scotland	12.0	11.0	23.5	15.3	25.7	10.3	8.7	14.9	17.9	35.2	77	1,760	39
Northern Ireland	11.6	10.5	22.4	14.4	31.9	12.8	6.6	14.6	17.4	36.0	83	1,890	40

[1] Total intake from all household food, excluding household consumption of soft and alcoholic drinks and confectionery.
Source: National Food Survey, Ministry of Agriculture, Fisheries and Food

adox. Although women enjoy lower rates of *mortality* than men, they also record higher rates of *morbidity* (limiting chronic sickness) in all but a few specific occupational groups at particular ages (refer back to Table 12.4). Trowler (1996) claims that 14 per cent of women report acute health problems, compared with only 12 per cent of men.

In almost all societies, women tend to live longer than men. According to *Social Trends* 1999, life expectancy in 1997 in the UK was about 79 years for women and 74 years for men. Male babies and children die in greater numbers, and men are far more likely than women to die before the age of 75, whatever other social factors are considered.

This greater vulnerability of male babies can be seen in Table 12.12, which also shows the way age and regional location interact with gen-

der to create health inequalities. For example, although women on the whole live longer than men, in 1997 women in Scotland had a higher standardized mortality rate (115) than males in every region of the UK with the exception of Scotland (117). As with other social aspects of living, gender interacts with other factors and this modifies the overall patterns of health and death rates.

Activity

a Summarize in your own words the patterns shown in Table 12.7.

b How do age and region interact with gender to modify the patterns of mortality?

C3.2, C3.3

Table 12.8 Cigarette smoking among people aged 16 or over, 1996–97

Percentages

	Proportion of smokers having their first cigarette after waking within						Proportion who smoke
	Less than 5 minutes	5 to 14 minutes	15 to 29 minutes	30 minutes but less than 1 hour	1 hour but less than 2 hours	2 hours or more	
United Kingdom	15	18	14	17	13	22	28
North East	23	21	13	16	12	15	31
North West	16	19	13	17	13	21	30
Yorkshire and the Humber	19	20	15	18	14	14	27
East Midlands	17	20	18	17	9	19	26
West Midlands	15	21	13	15	14	22	28
East	10	17	13	19	16	26	26
London	12	15	16	13	14	30	29
South East	10	16	13	21	14	25	26
South West	13	14	12	19	16	26	27
England	14	18	14	17	14	23	28
Wales	12	17	20	12	12	27	27
Scotland	22	18	14	18	10	18	32
Northern Ireland	16	16	17	19	11	21	29

Source: General Household Survey, Office for National Statistics; Continuous Household Survey, Northern Ireland Statistics and Research Agency

Table 12.9 Alcohol consumption[1] among people aged 16 or over: by gender, 1996–97

Percentages and numbers

	Males					Females				
	Consumption levels (units per week)				Average weekly consumption	Consumption levels (units per week)				Average weekly consumption
	Non-drinker	Under 11	11–21	22 or more	(number of units)	Non-drinker	Under 8	8–14	15 or more	(number of units)
United Kingdom	7	43	23	27	16	13	57	16	14	6
North East	9	34	24	33	19	17	55	15	13	6
North West	7	40	22	31	19	11	54	17	18	8
Yorkshire and the Humber	7	41	23	30	17	12	55	18	15	7
East Midlands	6	43	25	26	15	10	59	19	12	6
West Midlands	9	39	24	28	16	16	55	16	12	6
East	7	48	21	24	14	13	59	16	12	6
London	11	45	19	25	15	20	56	12	13	6
South East	5	45	23	27	16	10	57	18	14	7
South West	6	46	24	25	15	9	60	17	13	6
England	7	43	23	27	16	13	57	16	14	6
Wales	6	50	19	25	15	13	56	15	16	7
Scotland	7	41	28	25	16	13	60	16	11	5
Northern Ireland	22	38	17	22	14	31	48	12	8	4

1 Comparative consumption levels are different for males and females.
Source: General Household Survey, Office for National Statistics; Continuous Household Survey, Northern Ireland Statistics and Research Agency

Table 12.10 Exposure category of AIDS cases, cumulative totals to end-1998

	Sexual intercourse			Injecting drug use			Other[3]/ undetermined		Numbers
									Total cases reported to 31 December 1998
	Between men[1]	Between men and women		Injecting drug use		Blood[2]	Other[3]/ undetermined		
		Males	Females	Males	Females		Males	Females	
Region of residence									
United Kingdom	10,606	1,310	1,253	712	291	750	256	164	15,342
Northern and Yorkshire	363	61	41	10	7	100	9	5	596
North West	639	63	45	41	15	91	13	9	916
Trent	275	64	42	27	10	39	8	6	471
West Midlands	262	36	36	9	6	61	9	2	421
Anglia and Oxford	434	72	58	56	16	63	11	6	716
North Thames	4,446	536	510	172	84	99	94	66	6,007
South Thames	2,979	296	369	116	38	115	76	53	4,042
South and West	582	76	43	22	13	73	13	7	829
England[4]	10,033	1,205	1,148	455	189	649	233	154	14,066
Wales	158	22	25	5	3	36	6	1	256
Scotland	371	79	73	251	98	53	16	9	950
Northern Ireland	44	4	7	1	1	12	1	0	70

[1] Includes men who had also injected drugs.
[2] Blood/blood factor and tissue recipients.
[3] Includes mother to infant transmission.
[4] Figures for England include some people living in London whose NHS region of residence was not known (London is split between the North and South Thames regions).
Source: Public Health Laboratory Service, Communicable Disease Surveillance Centre; Scottish Centre for Infection and Environmental Health

Figure 12.5 Drug misuse among 16 to 29 year olds, 1995–96

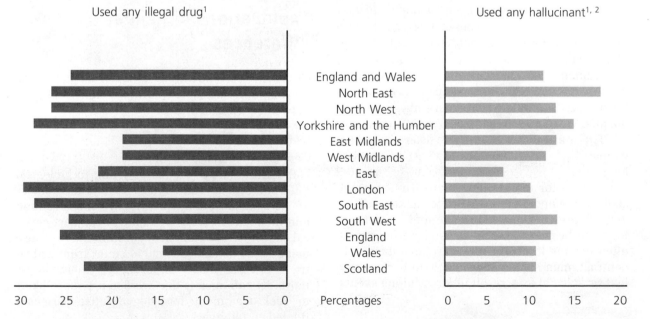

[1] Interviews were conducted between January and April 1996, asking about drug use in the previous 12 months.
[2] Amphetamine, LSD, magic mushrooms, ecstasy or poppers.
Source: British Crime Survey, Home Office; Scottish Crime Survey, Scottish Executive

Table 12.11 Social class[1] of working-age[2] population, spring 1998

Percentages and thousands

	Social class							
	Professional occupations	Managerial and technical	Skilled occupations non-manual	Skilled occupations manual	Partly skilled occupations	Unskilled occupations	Other[3]	Total working-age population (=100%)
	(I)	(II)	(IIIN)	(IIIM)	(IV)	(V)		(thousands)
United Kingdom	5.0	25.2	20.0	17.7	14.9	4.7	12.6	35,807
North East	3.7	19.3	18.8	19.0	16.9	6.3	16.0	1,562
North West	4.4	23.3	18.9	18.4	15.0	4.8	15.2	4,185
Yorkshire and the Humber	4.0	21.6	19.5	20.0	16.6	5.4	12.8	3,064
East Midlands	4.8	23.6	19.1	19.7	17.6	5.2	9.9	2,553
West Midlands	4.2	22.9	19.4	19.6	17.0	4.6	12.4	3,224
East	4.9	26.7	21.9	17.2	14.8	4.4	10.0	3,257
London	6.4	30.5	20.8	13.0	11.0	3.6	14.7	4,457
South East	6.3	30.2	21.6	16.0	12.8	3.9	9.3	4,750
South West	5.0	26.0	21.3	17.9	15.3	4.9	9.6	2,886
England	5.0	25.7	20.3	17.5	14.8	4.6	12.1	29,938
Wales	4.1	21.1	18.3	18.6	17.5	5.2	15.1	1,734
Scotland	5.1	23.2	19.4	18.5	15.1	5.4	13.3	3,143
Northern Ireland	3.4	22.6	17.7	18.4	13.6	5.6	18.8	991

[1] Based on occupation.
[2] Males aged 16–64 and females aged 16–59.
[3] Includes members of the armed forces, those who did not state their social class, and those whose previous occupation was more than eight years ago, or who have never had a paid job.
Source: Labour Force Survey, Office for National Statistics and Department of Economic Development, Northern Ireland

Chronic illness statistics from *Living in Britain* (1994) shows that: (a) women were then more likely to find their illness debilitating (21 per cent of women, compared with 18 per cent of men); (b) women were more likely to see their GP (women six times a year, compared with men's four); and (c) women were more likely to be in hospital (13 per cent compared with 6 per cent).

There are twice as many registered disabled women as men (mainly owing to greater longevity, however); 57 per cent of hospital admissions for mental illness are women, especially for emotional disturbance, anxiety disorders, depression and dementia; and women are found to be twice as likely to suffer from stress, often turning to drink and cigarette addiction. In contrast, men appear more likely to become violent or suicidal as a result of stressful life events.

Explanations of gender differences

Trowler (1996) identified five key explanations for the differences in morbidity and mortality between men and women.

Genetic explanations

Genetic explanations suggest that women suffer from greater ill-health owing to biological differences. They often need to consult doctors about contraception, pregnancy, menstruation and menopause. Only women can contract cervical cancer, while their stronger immune response means they are more likely to suffer from arthritis. Perhaps most importantly, their lower mortality rate means that women are more likely to seek treatment for 'degenerative' diseases related to old age.

However, men suffer (and die from) more

Table 12.12 Age-specific death rates: by gender, 1997

					Deaths per 1,000 population for specific age groups						Rates and Standardized Mortality Ratios[1]	
	Under 1[2]	1–4	5–15	16–24	25–34	35–44	45–54	55–64	65–74	75–84	85 and over	SMR[1] (UK = 100)
Males												
United Kingdom	6.5	0.3	0.2	0.8	1.0	1.6	4.1	11.9	34.0	83.8	192.7	100
North East	6.3	0.3	0.2	0.8	1.0	1.6	4.7	13.9	39.8	92.1	201.6	112
North West	7.9	0.4	0.2	1.0	1.1	1.9	4.7	13.6	37.3	89.3	194.8	109
Yorkshire and the Humber	7.1	0.3	0.2	0.9	1.0	1.4	3.9	11.8	36.0	87.9	191.2	103
East Midlands	6.7	0.4	0.2	0.8	0.8	1.4	3.5	11.4	32.9	83.4	192.0	97
West Midlands	7.4	0.4	0.1	0.8	0.8	1.6	4.2	11.7	34.9	86.9	196.1	102
East	5.1	0.2	0.2	0.7	0.8	1.3	3.3	9.5	29.2	78.0	193.8	90
London	6.1	0.3	0.2	0.6	1.0	1.6	4.4	12.3	32.7	81.0	178.7	97
South East	5.6	0.2	0.2	0.8	0.8	1.4	3.4	9.7	29.2	77.2	193.2	90
South West	6.3	0.3	0.2	0.8	0.9	1.4	3.3	9.8	29.2	75.6	185.6	89
England	6.5	0.3	0.2	0.8	0.9	1.5	3.9	11.4	33.0	82.5	190.9	98
Wales	6.6	0.3	0.2	1.0	1.0	1.6	4.1	12.5	36.3	86.3	192.6	104
Scotland	6.1	0.3	0.2	1.1	1.3	2.1	5.6	15.5	40.3	92.8	201.3	117
Northern Ireland	5.4	0.2	0.2	0.9	0.9	1.6	4.3	13.0	35.9	85.9	187.3	107
Females												
United Kingdom	5.2	0.2	0.1	0.3	0.4	1.1	2.7	7.2	20.7	55.5	154.5	100
North East	5.1	0.3	0.1	0.2	0.4	1.1	2.9	8.8	24.3	61.0	153.2	109
North West	5.6	0.2	0.1	0.4	0.5	1.2	3.0	8.1	23.6	59.3	158.2	107
Yorkshire and the Humber	5.8	0.3	0.1	0.3	0.4	1.1	2.7	7.3	21.6	56.3	150.7	100
East Midlands	4.7	0.2	0.2	0.4	0.4	1.0	2.7	6.9	20.1	54.7	151.4	98
West Midlands	6.6	0.3	0.1	0.2	0.4	1.0	2.7	7.0	20.8	55.9	151.1	99
East	4.4	0.2	0.1	0.3	0.3	0.9	2.2	5.9	17.9	52.5	156.8	94
London	5.5	0.2	0.1	0.3	0.4	1.0	2.6	7.1	20.5	53.8	139.1	94
South East	4.3	0.2	0.1	0.3	0.4	1.0	2.4	6.1	17.5	52.4	158.1	95
South West	5.2	0.3	0.1	0.3	0.4	0.9	2.5	6.1	17.1	50.1	149.6	91
England	5.3	0.2	0.1	0.3	0.4	1.0	2.6	6.9	20.1	54.7	152.3	98
Wales	5.1	0.3	0.1	0.3	0.5	1.2	3.0	7.2	21.8	56.1	154.7	102
Scotland	4.5	0.2	0.2	0.4	0.5	1.3	3.4	9.0	24.3	61.9	173.7	115
Northern Ireland	5.8	0.3	0.1	0.3	0.3	0.8	2.7	7.3	20.6	57.1	177.7	105

[1] Standardized Mortality Ratio is the ratio of observed deaths to those expected by applying a standard death ratio to the regional population.
[2] Deaths of infants under 1 year of age per 1,000 live births.
Source: Office for National Statistics; General Register Office for Scotland; Northern Ireland Statistics and Research Agency

heart disease, at least until about the age of 50. They are the only ones to get prostate or testicular cancer, and more men inherit genetic weaknesses, such as haemophilia. Also, in recent years men in western societies have been more at risk from AIDS-related illnesses and deaths.

Artefact explanations

Artefact explanations look at the way the statistics are constructed. Morbidity statistics are collected from consultations with doctors. In this case the statistics may be misleading because they ignore ethnicity, geography or class, for example. The fact that women tend to have lower status jobs (see Section 17.2), are more likely to take children to the doctor and live longer may be more significant than the fact of their sex.

However, this explains nothing about why women go to the doctor more often. It certainly does not necessarily mean that men are healthier, just that they are less likely to consult a doctor when ill.

Stress explanations

Stress explanations are increasingly considered by doctors and other medical personnel. It is now widely agreed that stress can affect health considerably. Some feminists argue that being a housewife is an extremely stressful experience, owing to the isolation, loneliness, lack of support and status and poor rewards involved (see Section 5.6). However, it also seems to be the case that many women now find the double and even triple shift of paid work, domestic work and emotional work increasingly stressful.

Cultural/behavioural explanations

Cultural/behavioural explanations suggest that men are likely to die earlier overall because they are more involved in risk-taking behaviour such as violence, and are neglectful in terms of their habits and diet. They choose not to consult doctors and so die from the results of these behaviours more than women.

Men have until recently tended to smoke more and drink considerably more alcohol than women, although this is now changing. Class differences, especially in smoking and among young people, are now far more significant than gender differences, with increasing numbers of women dying from smoking-related diseases.

Structural/material explanations

Structural/material explanations emphasize the structural factors affecting the health of women (and men). Most women have to accept the major responsibility for childcare (see Section 5.6) and looking after the health of others – especially with the growth of 'care in the community' (see Section 12.6).

Structural and material issues are the focus of the ideas of most feminist writers on gendered health inequalities. They argue that women also still bear the brunt of domestic labour, the emotional burdens of most relationships, poor pay and conditions at work and more exposure to poverty with poor housing, especially among single women

and single mothers – although some of these factors are changing for middle-class women. However, Nettleton (1995) points out that class differences between women are still less significant than for men (see Table 12.4).

This view also seeks to explain greater female morbidity. The socialization of women means that they accept responsibility for everyone's needs, leading them to suffer greater stress and stress-related illnesses. Although some women choose to do this, it is argued that they are not making a free choice owing to structural constraints and expectations in society. For example, as Hicks (1988) points out, the majority of informal carers in the UK are women, often caring for other women.

Feminist views on health and illness

Women and medical care

As mentioned above, the vast majority of carers – formal as well as informal – are female, although this fact has tended to be ignored or treated unproblematically by many sociologists when looking at the medical profession. Marxist–feminist writers such as Doyal (1995) have shown how the development of the medical profession basically involved the wresting of medical knowledge from women by men. Thereafter women remained as 'helpers' to the mainly male doctors and surgeons (see Table 12.13). However, half the doctors now being trained in England are female.

Table 12.13 Female hospital medical staff in England, 1985

Grade	Proportion of total in grade
Consultant or Senior House Medical Officer	23%
Associate specialist	12.5%
Senior Registrar	23%
Registrar	21%
Senior House Officer	32%
House Officer	39%

Source: Trowler (1996), adapted from *Health and Personal Social Services Statistics for England 1986*, London, HMSO, 1986

Witz (1992) argues that men have used exclusion strategies, such as limiting women's access to medical schools. However, there are still some areas that are mainly closed to men, such as midwifery. Although most obstetricians are still male, the Winterton Report (1992) proposed an enhanced role for midwives.

Feminist critiques of the medical profession

Many feminist writers have criticized the 'medicalization' of childcare. Graham and Oakley (1981) found that women tended to see pregnancy as natural, while obstetricians tended to see it as a medical problem that needed to be organized to fit into the bureaucratic needs of the hospital.

Sometimes births are induced, which might be seen as allowing for babies to be born at a time convenient to the hospital rather than when the babies and their mothers are ready. Using in-depth interviews (see Section 9.5), Oakley (1984) found that many women felt that the (mainly male) doctors they saw denied them much control over their pregnancy and childbirth.

Martin (1989) found that women tended to see their bodies in a medicalized way and so in need of control. It could be argued that this is the basis of many eating disorders which are generally much more likely to affect young women. It is also noticeable that contraception advice is directed far more at women than men, leaving them mainly responsible for birth control. Male-oriented forms of contraception such as condoms and vasectomies have fewer possible side-effects than those for women, such as the pill or coil, yet the latter are far more widely used. Recent developments, such as the male pill and the *femidom* (female condom), have yet to be widely used in Britain.

Women and informal care

In a study of the importance of this type of care in the context of the 'care in the community' initiative, Land (1991) points to statistics from the *General Household Survey* showing that informal care is now an important aspect of healthcare overall. One in seven adults are providing informal healthcare which in total represents some 6 million people, of whom 3.5 million are women. The peak age range for such caring is 45–64, with nearly a quarter of all women of this age acting in such a role.

Women might have to leave a paid job to care for an elderly mother or mother-in-law, while single daughters or those without children are expected to take the chief responsibility for caring for parents. Single women, who are generally dependent on their own income, are often particularly vulnerable to these expectations. Many women find caring for others, and the expectation that they should do so, a further stressful burden on their lives. However, as Hicks also points out, a considerable proportion of carers are men looking after an elderly and often disabled spouse.

Activity

Suggest reasons why women are more likely to visit a doctor than men, even when suffering from the same degree of ill-health.

C3.2, C3.3

Feminism and the body

One of the main developments in the sociology of health and illness has been the attention paid to the body by feminist writers. The ideas of early feminists have been criticized by what Annandale and Clark (1996) call 'feminist post-structuralism', which challenges earlier feminists' views of the way that mainly male doctors have sought to exploit and control women through medical technology.

New reproductive technologies

Nettleton (1995) argues that the medical regulation of bodies, especially female bodies and female sexuality, can be illustrated through the examination of reproduction and, especially, reproductive technologies. According to Stanworth (1987), these include fertility control technologies such as contraceptives, childbirth control technologies such as Caesarean births, screening techniques such as amniocentesis and, most interestingly, conceptive technologies such as fertility treatments, which Nettleton calls 'new reproductive technologies' (NRTs).

Oakley (1984) suggests that the ability for brain-dead women to give birth by Caesarean section means that the mothers are not always seen as autonomous human beings, and this is reflected in many other aspects of NRT.

In an article about *in vitro* fertilization (IVF), Denny (1994) investigates the way debates about this surfaced in radical feminist accounts. While some radical feminist writers, particularly

Firestone (1979), see such techniques as a way of freeing women from the burden of reproduction, others such as Rich (1972) view it as a way for men to gain control of reproduction and therefore undermine women's power in this area. Analyses such as the latter tend to see NRTs as controlling women in two main ways: through pro-natalist ideology, and through men's power and control over reproduction technology.

Pro-natalist ideology

Writers such as Rowland (1985) suggest that 'pro-natalism' (the idea that women are unfulfilled unless they have children) is promoted by the message that infertility is a medical and social disaster for women. While testing this view, Denny found that some of the women she studied did feel pressurized to have children in order to be 'a complete woman', many felt this as a biological urge rather than simply a result of social pressures.

Furthermore, a number of feminist writers (e.g. Stanworth, 1987; Rowland, 1985) have emphasized that the ways in which males control the process of *in vitro* fertilization allows them power over the reproductive processes of women, although Denny rejects the idea that women are so easily duped. She concludes that:

The experiences of individual women have been lacking from most radical feminist literature, women have been portrayed as powerless victims, accepting whatever a male dominated and powerful medical profession offers them. In contrast ... oppression is a very complex process, and one in which women are very rarely totally powerless.

(Denny, 1994, p. 75)

Post-feminist views

Black feminists, such as b. hooks (1982), suggest that women do not have a common cultural experience of oppression due to their sex, and Denny's study supports the view that women experience their bodies in a variety of different ways.

This view is developed by Annandale and Clark (1996) who suggest that radical feminism, with its emphasis on a single female experience, has been replaced – at least in the sociology of health – with a post-structuralist stance which stresses the diversity of women's experience. They look at traditional feminist views on health and illness and suggest that these have now been challenged.

Post-structuralist feminists vary considerably in their views but, according to Annandale and Clark, they share an emphasis on the body as a constructed entity, where gender is only part of the process. This means they look less at the crucial differences between women and men as stressed by earlier feminist writers, and argue that sex and gender are part of a *continuum* of masculinity and femininity, whereby sexual behaviour is not bound by biological sex at all.

Similarities and differences in women's health

Doyal (1995), taking an explicitly feminist stance by focusing specifically on the health of women, points out that women are generally disadvantaged in all areas of sickness in all parts of the world. While there are clearly different experiences between women from a variety of ethnic and class backgrounds, the main difference can be seen among the health experiences of women from the developed and 'developing' countries.

She also argues that the way to understand the gendered experiences of women's health is to examine the inadequacies of biomedical explanations of health and illness. The main factor to look at when assessing the health of women is the impact of poverty and relative deprivation on the health and illness of women, rather than biological or medical differences between men and women. It was really only with industrialization that women seemed to begin to live longer than men, although now the phenomenon is found in most societies apart from very poor countries such as Bangladesh. Far from being the 'weaker sex', females tend to be stronger from birth onwards. The higher mortality of males in industrialized societies seems to be linked to the dangers of many (male) manual jobs and men's more risky leisure activities and patterns of consumption.

Doyal argues that to understand the factors affecting women's poorer health beyond basic biology, we need to look at what makes up their lives in terms of production and reproduction, paid work and domestic work, lifestyle and consumption patterns, and experiences of support and abuse. She concludes that the greater *morbidity* of women in most, if not all societies, shows that many experience economic, social and cultural obstacles which prevent them from fulfilling their physical and psychological needs. She asserts:

Women's right to health and the formulation of appropriate strategies for its realisation must be a central concern, not just in feminist politics, but in wider campaigns for sustainable development, political freedom and economic and social justice.

(Doyal, 1995, p. 232)

A new paradigm of health and medicine?

Nettleton (1996) identifies the shortcomings of the biomedical model which has dominated medical discourse, especially those stressing intervention and cure in healthcare rather than prevention and care. She argues:

We have begun to witness a profound shift in health policy and in the ideological basis of medicine.

(Nettleton, 1996, p. 33)

This change is our loss of faith in the biomedical model and a new emphasis on the prevention of disease. Nettleton suggests that such a model is now increasingly compared with a *socio-environmental model* which, in contrast to the biomedical model, emphasizes how people are increasingly encouraged (and expected) to take responsibility for their own health and healthcare. Such a model has tended to focus mainly on the role of women.

The three key issues at the heart of this new paradigm can be seen as: risk, surveillance, and 'the rational self' (Nettleton, 1996, p. 34).

Risk

The concept of risk medicalizes social activities such as diet and exercise. People are more confused than ever about what to eat, drink or avoid in their diet, but are expected to 'control' their eating, smoking and drinking and sexual behaviour. There is also limited sympathy for HIV sufferers who have admitted to 'unsafe' sex practices. Women tend to be bombarded with advice, often confusing and sometimes frightening, about their health (and that of their children), although men, too, are now sometimes identified as targets by the health industries.

Surveillance

General practitioners are now in the first line of surveillance, and women in particular are expected to have their children vaccinated, themselves checked for various cancers, and their elderly parents injected with anti-flu viruses. Doctors are rewarded financially for achieving vaccination and monitoring quotas for activities like smear tests – which may prove beneficial to women, although the number of scares about mistakes in such testing may reduce its credibility.

There is also surveillance of women's lifestyles as consumers (more women are obese than men); as sexual beings through family planning advice; and, of course, as chief carers for the nation's youth (see Section 5.6). The home is still considered an important arena of primary healthcare where women usually take the main responsibility for the health of all the members of the family.

The rational self

The concept of the rational self within the discourse of medicine – that is the way people talk about health – means that women in particular are expected to act in ways that promote and enhance health because it is rational and sensible for them to do so. After all, not many people wish to follow patterns of behaviour which they firmly believe will damage them physically.

This is an interesting argument and one that is used to dispute the culpability of cigarette manufacturers. On the one hand, the manufacturers argue that cigarettes are not very addictive and so people can make a rational choice about whether to smoke. On the other hand, anti-smoking groups like ASH argue that, knowing the links between cigarette smoking and lung cancer, no rational person would continue to smoke unless it were extremely addictive. However, recent court cases have led to tobacco companies such as Philip Morris publicly admitting for the first time ever that smoking causes fatal diseases and that it is addictive.

> ## Discussion point
> To what extent might arguments about the rational self also be applied to (a) unprotected sexual activity, and (b) the consumption of Ecstasy tablets or other illegal drugs?
>
> C3.1a

So this new paradigm of health and medicine takes the view that all people are expected to be aware of – and do something to avoid – 'risk-taking' behaviours such as smoking, drinking, overeating or lack of exercise. Health professionals increasingly monitor and supervise their clients' actions and advise them of the rational course to take to avoid ill-health. In this way, much illness can be seen as a result of wilful self-damage on the part of the patient.

This view clearly has the potential to marginalize groups who cannot afford the healthy diets and exercise regimes required by the health-oriented in society. Health professionals make judgements as to our suitability for, or our entitlement to, certain types of treatment, again depending on a number of 'rational' criteria. Although everyone is encouraged to monitor their health-related behaviour, Nettleton sees in many of the Department of Health publications issued in the past:

... an underlying assumption that the responsibility for changing health behaviours lay in the hands of women, or more particularly, mothers.

(Nettleton, 1996, p. 37)

Men's health

It is important to recognize that there now also seems to be a growing concern about the health of men. Increases in mortality from male-only diseases, particularly testicular and prostate cancers, may be mainly to do with a lack of knowledge and the reluctance of men to talk about their bodies. Awareness of such issues seems to have been raised by the apparent success of women's health groups in improving female well-being; or it may be that there are now perceived to be a larger number of men without a wife to 'look after' them.

There is also increasing concern about the rates of mental illness, suicide and anorexia among young men. This is often linked to relative lack of achievement among, and limited opportunities for, young males. Girls are now generally doing better in education than boys and often get access to better jobs. It can therefore be argued that the growing interest in the health of males (especially younger men) is due to their changing position in the social structure.

There is some evidence to support the view that there is now more emphasis on the health of men and boys, especially among politicians and in the media. The majority of mens' maga-

zines now focus on health and fitness as well as cars and sex. Furthermore, in May 1999 the Men's Health Forum was set up to investigate and promote a national strategy to improve health among males. A newspaper article linked to the launch of this initiative focused on the nurse who approached men in pubs to discuss any medical concerns they might have and promote healthy practices to encourage early identification of cancers that exclusively affect men.

Ethnicity and health inequalities

Defining 'race' and ethnicity

Aggleton (1990) points out that the problem of defining ethnic origin makes it difficult to measure structural differences between the health and healthcare patterns of ethnic minority groups. So there is a paucity of evidence, but the evidence that does exist is fairly convincing. For example, stillbirths are more commonly found in Britain among mothers born in Bangladesh, Pakistan and the Caribbean than among UK-born mothers (see Figure 12.6).

In a study of mortality rates among immigrants, Marmot *et al.* (1984b) found higher than average SMRs (standardized mortality rates – see Section 12.3) for a number of groups born in Africa, the Caribbean and women from the Indian subcontinent. However, country of birth tells us

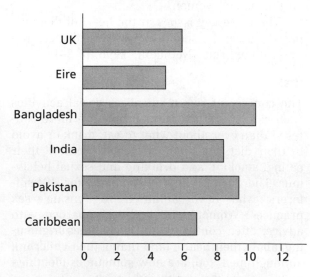

Figure 12.6 Stillbirths per 1000 total births, by mother's country of birth, England and Wales, 1984
Source: Whitehead (1988, p. 253)

little about the health experiences of the children of migrants who are born in the UK.

The ideological nature of concepts of health and ethnicity

Smaje (1996) claims that the concepts of ethnicity used in health research are often applied in discussions about whether poor health among some ethnic groups is due to cultural factors – 'ethnic' lifestyles – or structural factors such as poverty and racism. He argues that such definitions would make more sense in terms of a model based on subjective factors within particular situations. This may prove problematic for much current health research which is based on statistical data collected by epidemiologists who study rates of disease, and clinicians who focus on specific illnesses. Neither type of researcher spends much time analysing the categories they use or investigating the social meanings of their findings.

Most definitions of ethnic membership used by health practitioners are over-simplified and possibly invalid because they focus on either where people were born or their generalized lifestyle. An awareness of the complexities of identities and cultures will also have implications for healthcare practices, such as recognizing and campaigning for the particular health needs of Asian women.

While this debate can be used extensively to criticize ethnic classifications which certainly affect the analysis of health statistics, it is still important to discover whether certain groups have certain needs, and the extent to which they are being addressed or ignored. The lack of hard data gathered on the basis of new theoretical developments requires us to make use of the older data that are available, even though the categories may be challenged.

Patterns of health difference among ethnic groups

In an article considering the debates surrounding 'race', ethnicity and health inequalities, Culley and Dyson (1993) seek to explain why such differences might exist. The majority of premature deaths among, for example, Pakistanis or African–Caribbeans are from heart attacks and cancers, just as among the white population. This does *not* mean that inequalities between racial groups do not exist, although it is not always easy to gain access to such information. African–Caribbeans seem to suffer from higher rates of high blood pressure than the indigenous population, but this measurement tells us nothing about the cause(s).

Although country of origin is recorded in medical records, the increasing number of people who would describe themselves as both British-born and black, for example, makes such a classification less useful. Despite these problems, Culley and Dyson provide us with some interesting information.

African–Caribbeans, Indians, Pakistanis and Bangladeshis are all more likely than the national average to die from liver cancer, tuberculosis or diabetes. Africans and African–Caribbeans are more likely to suffer from strokes and hypertension. Asians (i.e. Indians and Pakistanis) generally suffer more heart disease but fewer deaths from most cancers than the average, while their children are more likely to develop rickets and the adults osteomalacia (brittle bones). Overall, African–Caribbeans and Asians are more likely to be diagnosed as schizophrenic and compulsorily placed in mental institutions. As Trowler (1996) points out, this is despite the evidence which suggests that immigrants generally suffer lower rates of mental illness than average (see also Section 12.2).

Activity

a In Table 12.14, identify one cause of death that has a lower than average rate, and one that has a higher than average rate, for all the ethnic minority groups specified.

b In Figure 12.7 identify the ethnic groups (by mother's country of birth) with the highest and second-highest rates of infant mortality and perinatal mortality. The definitions are as follows: *infant mortality*: deaths of infants under one year of age per 1000 live births; *perinatal mortality*: stillbirths and deaths in the first week of life per 1000 live and stillbirths; *neonatal mortality*: deaths in the first 28 days of life per 1000 live births; *post-neonatal mortality*: deaths at ages over 28 days and under one year per 1000 live births.

C3.2, C3.3

Table 12.14 Causes of death by country of birth

African	*Higher rates:*	Strokes, high blood pressure, violence/accidents, maternal deaths, tuberculosis
	Lower rates:	Bronchitis
Indian subcontinent	*Higher rates:*	Heart disease, diabetes, violence/accidents, tuberculosis
	Lower rates:	Bronchitis, certain cancers
Caribbean	*Higher rates:*	Strokes, high blood pressure, violence/accidents, diabetes, maternal deaths
	Lower rates:	Bronchitis

Source: Culley and Dyson (1993), adapted from Whitehead (1988)

Ethnicity and maternal health

Several indicators suggest poorer maternal health among women born in Africa, the Caribbean and the Indian subcontinent than those born in the UK. Most of the research into poor maternal health has concentrated on women from the Indian subcontinent and has tended to assume poor antenatal and postnatal care rather than deprivation as the main cause of high infant mortality among women from Pakistan or Bangladesh – although Blackburn (1991) has shown significant poverty among many groups of black women in the UK.

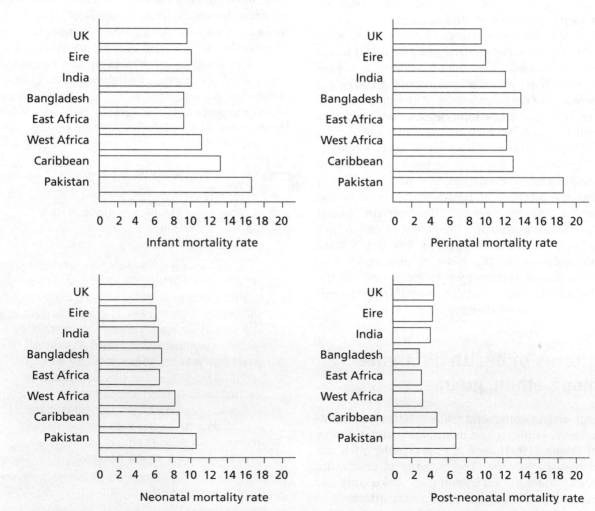

Figure 12.7 Infant, perinatal, neonatal and post-neonatal mortality by mother's country of birth, England and Wales, 1982–85
Source: Jewson (1993, p. 70)

Explaining ethnic differences in health

Although we can identify differential health (and usually significantly poorer health) among ethnic minorities, despite the limited availability of reliable statistics, the explanations have yet to be discussed. Culley and Dyson (1993) propose four possible factors: genetics, culture and behaviour, social class, and racism.

Genetic factors

Genetic arguments focus on the inherited disorders that seem to affect some groups in particular, such as sickle-cell anaemia which is largely found among Africans and African–Caribbeans. Thalassaemia is another blood disorder found in people mainly from the Middle East and the Indian subcontinent. Hunt (1995) argues that such biological differences do need to be identified and suitable screening and counselling facilities made available. It can be seen as a form of covert racism to marginalize diseases which occur mainly among non-white groups, whilst prioritizing wider screening for relatively rarer diseases distributed throughout the whole population.

Cultural factors

Cultural factors include things such as diet, lifestyle and beliefs and attitudes towards healthcare. They are usually stressed by health 'experts' when attempting to explain the high level of particular health problems among certain ethnic groups. Poor attendance at postnatal and antenatal clinics among Asian mothers is seen to explain high rates of stillbirths and infant mortality in this group. However, reasons for low attendance, such as language, transport or educational barriers, are rarely discussed. Again, high rates of heart disease are blamed on the use of clarified butter (ghee) in much Asian cooking, but this tends to ignore structural factors such as stress, isolation, alienation and poverty.

Attempts to explain and deal with ethnic differences in, for example, rates of heart disease have often focused on cultural factors. Culley and Dyson suggest that many of these attempts seem to be misguided, being based on an ideological view of ethnic cultural inferiority rather than facts. Blaming smoking and fat consumption for high levels of heart disease among Asians – when the rate of smoking is slightly lower than the average (especially among women) and fat consumption often far lower than that of other groups – seems to ignore much of the empirical evidence available.

Hunt (1995) also discusses cultural factors, but makes the important point that sweeping ethnic generalizations about health inequalities tend to ignore gender and class differences. The lifestyles of different cultural groups are often seen as strange or inferior. For example, high infant mortality rates among some Asian women was attributed to their ignorance about antenatal facilities, rather than to the assumptions of western medicine which might exclude women who could not be treated by a male doctor or travel alone to clinics.

> ### 💬 Discussion point
>
> Areas where doctors may have limited knowledge of other cultures include diet, religious needs, language, sexual mores, hygiene and death rites. Discuss how doctors might ensure that each of these needs is considered in developing medical care for groups with religious or cultural beliefs different from their own.
>
>
> C3.1a

Social class factors

Social class explanations outlined in Section 12.3 relating to inequalities in health suggest that poor health among many ethnic minority groups is indeed mainly due to class differences. In general, unemployed people suffer poorer mental and physical health, and the ethnic groups with the highest levels of mortality, morbidity and diagnosed mental illness – such as Pakistanis, Bangladeshis and African–Caribbeans – also suffer far higher levels of unemployment than the average (see Section 14.6). As Culley and Dyson point out:

Recruitment patterns of African–Caribbean and Asian migrants mean that they are concentrated in low-paid manual occupations and particularly in industries that are most hazardous to health (e.g. laundry, textiles and clothing industries) and/or have been especially hard-hit by successive recessions (e.g. textiles and footwear industry) (Brown, 1984). Excessive shift-work, lack of job security and fringe benefits, low pay and high likelihood of unemployment are all likely to lead to poorer health amongst black and ethnic communities.

(Culley and Dyson, 1993, p. 26)

The most convincing evidence comes from differences in mortality and morbidity rates between groups. Indians, who suffer relatively low unemployment and social deprivation in the UK, have lower rates than Pakistanis and Bangladeshis, who are more disadvantaged than the average. African–Caribbeans, who are socially and economically disadvantaged on the whole, also suffer higher than average levels of heart disease and high blood pressure.

Racism and ill health

Culley and Dyson (1993) argue that racism affects adversely the health of ethnic minority groups in six main ways.

- It leads to them being concentrated in hazardous, alienating and unrewarding jobs that have been shown to correlate closely with ill-health for all groups. The associated poverty affects diet, and leads to stress and stress-related illnesses such as high blood pressure.

- There is strong evidence to suggest that ethnic minorities are more likely to suffer high rates of unemployment. In recessions in particular, rates of unemployment of black people soar. Rising unemployment has been linked to high suicide rates and higher levels of mortality and morbidity.

- Housing may be an issue. For example, Bangladeshis in Tower Hamlets in East London tend to occupy some of the most overcrowded and low-quality housing in the country. Poor housing has been shown to lead to bronchial problems and other respiratory infections, especially among children. For them, poor health may affect education and future opportunities as well.

- Racism means that black people and Asians are more likely to be attacked and subjected to abuse, and many individuals and families live in constant fear of such attacks. Apart from the physical effects of attacks, psychological problems from abuse and the fear of abuse are common.

- Some ethnic groups experience unequal access to medical care, although this may be mainly due to what might be termed 'institutional racism'. This means that language differences may present a barrier, as may lack of access to a woman doctor for some Asian women. Some doctors may have only limited knowledge of certain illnesses that affect particular ethnic groups. Mares *et al.* (1987) appeared to find that people from ethnic minority groups were more likely to complain of irrelevant and discriminatory treatment.

- Where the NHS can be seen as discriminatory is in the employment of black people. Members of ethnic minorities are widely employed by the NHS, but they are not equally distributed throughout the service. As in most other sectors of employment, black people are disproportionately employed in manual jobs and ancillary work. (See Section 17.2.) They mainly occupy the lower status jobs in nursing and, as doctors, work in the less prestigious sectors such as geriatrics and psychiatric care. Some health authorities have made a determined effort to improve their treatment of black patients and employees, but this is far from widespread, especially with the increasing financial constraints on doctors and hospitals.

As Hunt (1995) points out, the factors which lead to health disadvantages for ethnic minorities are complex. Culley and Dyson argue, however, that material deprivation remains paramount. The high levels of under-employment and unemployment among some ethnic minority groups (especially African–Caribbean and Bangladeshi men) and the consequences of their deprivation continue to underpin all the biological and cultural explanations. To ignore any of the factors identified may be problematic, but to ignore structural and material factors, including overt and covert racism, seems to deny the health realities for many people in our society.

Ideological debates about 'race' and health

Ahmad (1993) argues that research into 'race' and health now forms a large industry in itself, but one that offers few benefits to ethnic minority groups. Most research is based on statistics and draws simplistic conclusions from unrelated factors. Consequently, he argues, much research in this area literally *labels* black people as sick.

Both the terms 'race' and 'biomedicine' are, he says, socially constructed and utilized to legitimize positions of power and authority. He therefore says that the term 'race' was developed to legitimize the colonization (and enslavement, it could be added) of groups defined as inferior. Biomedicine (the 'medical model' of illness) has long been used to restrict and punish deviancy.

Ahmad sees a similarity between images of a good (subservient) patient and a good (docile) black person. Patients are not expected to challenge their doctors, just as black people are not expected to query their status in society. Many migrants to the UK are treated as outsiders, much as 'alternative' medical treatments are marginalized. Therefore, he argues, both concepts are used to strengthen the control of the powerful groups in our society, and rarely can (or will) either be challenged.

In conclusion, it can be argued that there remains within (and beyond) the NHS general assumptions of racial inferiority and 'difference'. While this explains some of the particular problems experienced by black people, their most extreme disadvantages appear to remain a structural combination of disadvantage and racism in the labour market with continuing discrimination in many other sectors of their lives. This does not mean, however, that ethnic minority groups are helpless victims in their own oppression.

As Ahmad points out, there has always been a tradition of black community action, including action on health, and this needs to be extended and expanded to ensure fair access to resources where the needs of all ethnic groups are taken into consideration. He concludes:

Although the scope for reducing racial inequalities in health lie largely outside of the NHS, equity of healthcare provision ... is also of paramount importance. These struggles for equitable health and healthcare are essentially located in the wider struggles for equity and dignity which have been a part of black people's history.

(Ahmad, 1993, p. 214)

Ethnicity, ideology and health

Notions of the way that ideological assumptions and stereotypes about ethnic minorities and their cultural traits, and the way this affects the healthcare offered to ethnic minorities, has been a continuing element of sociological studies. A key example of this is provided in Abercrombie, Warde *et al.* (1994) who point to the:

stereotype of black immigrant, which was widely circulated in the 1960s and early 1970s, as someone who brought disease into the country and who, once here, created a risk of epidemics because of origin and living conditions

(Abercrombie, Warde *et al.*, 1994, p. 401)

One key example of this continuing effect of stereotypes is the way that ethnic minority members, and more specifically African–Caribbeans, are over-represented as patients in the mental health specialisms. Chevannes (1991) points out that we need to look at the way in which there are examples of both high rates of access and low rates of access to medical care. She points out that high access rates for African–Caribbeans in the speciality of mental health might be an example of discrimination, just as the relatively low levels of access seen in the low priority given to screening for sickle cell anaemia (which affects 1 in 400 births among African–Caribbeans), which is not offered to all African–Caribbeans. All mothers, however, are offered screening for phenylketonuria, which affects 1 in 1400 births.

RACE BIAS IN MENTAL HOSPITALS
DAVID BRINDLE

Patients who speak no English are being forcibly treated in mental hospitals without the use of interpreters, checks by the mental health act commission have discovered.

Black and ethnic minority patients were also found to be suffering racial harassment in mental units, most of which had no policies on dealing with the problem.

The commission's findings, to be published this week, are likely to trigger a shake-up in the treatment of black and ethnic minority patients who represent a disproportionately high number of people detained compulsorily under the mental health act. ...

The cases of 534 black and ethnic minority patients were examined.

Research has shown repeatedly that non-white patients, particularly Afro-Caribbeans, are far more likely than average to be detained under the act and given 'physical' treatments, such as drugs and electro-convulsive therapy, rather than psychotherapies.

Of the patients studied, 71% were men and 42% classified as black Caribbeans. Almost a quarter did not have English as a first language and 56 spoke no English, or very little.

Despite this, only 31 patients had been provided with an interpreter. ...

Racial harassment, by fellow patients or staff, was found to have been complained of and recorded in the notes of 11% of all patients surveyed – a figure the commission regards as an understatement.

Source: Adapted from the *Guardian*, 6 March 2000

Grimsley and Bhat (1990), in their study, also pointed to the way in which all black minority groups have a much higher chance of being diagnosed as schizophrenic or suffering from other serious mental illnesses. The key argument here is that such diagnoses are made on the basis of white cultural assumptions about what is rational and irrational behaviour. Cultural differences therefore may be the basis of medical judgements and institutionalization.

While we have here considered gender and ethnicity sequentially, it is of course possible for them to be linked. We can therefore look at the treatment of ethnic minority women. Notions of being educated seemed to be linked to ethnicity in assumptions and instructions given to nurses in a maternity hospital:

Not all women are treated in the same way and not all feel themselves equally powerless to demand information. English-speaking, white, well-educated, middle-class patients are the most likely to obtain information and be given it in straightforward language, while working-class and non-white women may meet condescension. (For example, student nurses relating instructions they received in a maternity hospital, said that if patients seemed educated and 'able to understand', they were told to use terms such as 'internal examination', 'vaginal examination', or 'induction', but where patients were expected not to understand, such terms were replaced with 'examination down below', 'feel inside you', or 'give the baby a push'.)

(Miles, 1991, p. 181)

While these examples do suggest that there are ideological and cultural assumptions made about ethnic minorities which do seem to have an adverse affect on the quality of medical treatment they receive, Sheldon and Parker (1992) have argued that it is important not to overstate the importance of ethnicity. Crucially their point is that the experience of the ethnic minority population is like that population itself – very heterogeneous – and therefore we should be wary of studies which simply talk about ethnic minorities without breaking that down more (see also Section 17.9).

Equally, while such examples point to the continued existence of ideological assumptions, it is also the case that there have been criticisms of some of the conclusions drawn on this basis. It might be argued that the power of the medical profession is sometimes exaggerated in these accounts and the powerlessness of the patients

over-emphasized. Certainly this is the view taken by Williams and Calnan (1996) whose crucial point is that people's capacity to resist such treatment needs to be considered. It is also the case that the rise of AIDS and the fact that the medical profession has so far been unable to find a cure, while patients are often well-informed, provides another example which suggests the power and expertise of the medical profession does not always go unchallenged (see also Section 12.7).

> ### 💬 Discussion point
>
> How might the assumptions and ideological constructions around notions of gender and ethnicity affect the quality of treatment people receive?
>
> C3.1a

12.5 The establishment of a national health service

A brief history of healthcare developments

One cannot hope to understand the development of medical treatment without understanding the structural, historical, economic and political changes that have surrounded such practices. The idea that modern medical practices somehow emerged as a result of certain discoveries by great scientists such as Pasteur or Lister tends to ignore the political dimension of healthcare.

Doyal and Pennell (1979) argued that in pre-industrial societies care of the sick was for the most part undertaken by women. Healing was based mainly on folklore knowledge of herbs and remedies. While this is very different from the biomedical model which dominated medicine throughout the twentieth century, it can also be said that informal care of the sick still remains mainly in the hands of women, and there is considerable interest today in herb-based treatments for many ailments.

Midwinter (1994) reminds us that healthcare in medieval times was haphazard, with whole families and even villages being devastated by plagues and epidemics. A third of the population died in Britain during the Black Death – a virulent form of bubonic plague – between 1348 and

1350, and the plague recurred sporadically until late into the seventeenth century. However, the thinly spread population tended to keep most diseases within fairly local boundaries, and it was only with the growth of towns that diseases due to sewage and water pollution became an extensive problem.

Jewson (1976) suggests that 'scientific medicine' developed through three main stages.

The first stage

In the first stage, from the Middle Ages to the later eighteenth century, medical care was available only to wealthy people who usually retained their own doctor. Diagnostic tools were limited, so the patient's own account of his or her health problem was the most important guide to any treatment.

The second stage

In the second stage, from the beginning of the nineteenth century, hospital medical treatment became more widespread. From a post-structuralist viewpoint, Foucault (1973) identifies this as one of the key aspects of the growth of surveillance in modern society. Doctors became more organized – and more powerful – as a profession, and patients became 'cases' rather than 'patrons'. There was an increasingly biomedical view of ill-health, with the sick body seen mainly as a malfunctioning machine that needed to be fixed. Many diagnostic tools were developed at this time, such as stethoscopes and thermometers, but both diagnosis and treatment remained relatively crude.

Probably the most important developments at this time were in the field of social medicine. The development of the 'germ theory of disease' by Pasteur and Koch, antibiotics by Lister, vaccination by Jenner, and anaesthetics by Wells and Sampson were the main advances in scientific treatment of the sick throughout the nineteenth century. Hospitals were now beginning to be seen as places to be cured in rather than to die in (when they were avoided by those who could afford to do so). Further advances in the treatment of disease can be attributed to social reformers such as Chadwick whose insisted that water must be clean to avoid the transmission of diseases like typhoid and cholera.

The third stage

In the third of the stages set out by Jewson, governments started seriously to consider the health needs of the changing (increasingly urbanized and industrialized) society, most notably through the Public Health Act of 1848.

Introduction of the National Health Service

In 1942 the Beveridge Report (see also Section 14.3) was produced by the wartime government of the day. It identified five 'great social evils' – ignorance, idleness, want, squalor and disease. Its main recommendations were:

- universal secondary education to eradicate widespread 'ignorance' (or poor education) – see Section 11.6
- full employment to deal with the social evil of 'idleness' (or unemployment) – see Section 14.5
- social security benefits to deal with 'want' (or poverty) – see Section 14.5
- new towns and slum clearance programmes to get rid of 'squalor' (or homelessness and bad housing) – see Section 14.5
- a system of universal healthcare to eradicate 'disease' – a national health service.

The National Health Service (NHS) thus came into being with the passing of the National Health Act 1948, with the aim of providing universal healthcare, free at the point of delivery. This occurred with considerable opposition from many doctors and some politicians, who challenged the extra spending required to provide the service. Before this time the majority of the population had had to pay for their healthcare.

Although the change was popular with most of the population, doctors were generally not happy to give up private practice to become employees of the state. Consequently, the Minister of Health at the time, Aneurin Bevan, said he had to 'stuff the consultants' mouths with gold' in order to gain their consent to working within the state medical sector. This left the doctors as independent contractors who were paid a fee to work for the state while still maintaining the right to private practice. A lot of this private treatment was provided within hospitals.

C3.1a

Discussion point

To what extent does the provision of private healthcare within state hospitals breach the principle of equal treatment underlying the NHS?

The structure of the NHS as established in 1948 is usually described as a compromise between:

- the needs of people for local provision and accountability
- the desire of doctors and administrators to remain largely free from the constraints of local authority controls.

The latter meant that general practitioners (GPs) were largely independent of their local health authorities, who nevertheless provided most community and environmental services such as maternity care and health-visiting.

A regional structure was established to supervise hospitals, and this resulted in some areas getting care from doctors, hospitals and local health services with different areas of authority.

This complex set-up of the NHS meant that the universal and collective aims of the welfare state were to some extent undermined by the professional freedom that doctors and hospitals demanded. Doctors made many of the decisions about how money was to be spent on healthcare, especially as they also had considerable representation on the governing bodies of hospitals and other decision-making bodies within the NHS. It was believed that their medical expertise and professional ethos would lead to rational and disinterested policies which would rapidly reduce the demand for their services and improve the health of the nation.

Reorganization of the National Health Service

The structure of the NHS as established in 1948 survived with few changes until 1974. The 'tripartite system', with responsibilities shared by regional hospital boards, specialist authorities and local executive councils, was criticized for being expensive, inflexible and bureaucratic. Morgan *et al.* (1985) showed that political compromises led to growing dissatisfaction with the NHS, on three main issues:

- cost
- administrative inconsistencies
- geographical and sectoral inequalities.

In 1974, the NHS was reorganized into a number of *regional* health authorities, *area* health authorities and *district* health authorities. One major improvement was the alignment of local boundaries, but the medical profession maintained most of their control over primary care and their influence on advisory committees at local, central and regional levels. The main improvements were a closer watch on financial allocation and an attempt to reduce some of the geographical and sectoral inequalities identified in the 1960s.

The reorganization started in 1974 had many critics, and more widespread changes were introduced in the 1980s, establishing a more market-oriented system.

Factors affecting the development of healthcare in the UK

According to Taylor and Field (1993), health and healthcare are intrinsically linked to economic factors. The introduction of the NHS in the immediate post-war period was:

... partly in response to demographic need, consumer demand and medico-technological development, but was made possible by the buoyant national and international economic climate.

(Taylor and Field, 1993, p. 22)

Population changes have also influenced the nature of the NHS. Examples of this are the declining infant mortality, smaller families and increased life expectancy resulting in an 'ageing' population. This places considerable burdens on the NHS, compounded by the growth of 'new' diseases such as cancers and HIV/AIDS, which are expensive to treat and, in many cases, incurable.

One response to this has been an emphasis on 'care in the community'. In order to increase turnover in hospital bed occupancy, hospitals may seek to release patients to what some people consider to be inadequate situations outside of the hospital. Furthermore, as more women enter paid employment there are often fewer of the traditional carers – married women – available to look after the disabled, elderly or chronically sick. It can be argued that this constitutes a crisis, and not only for the NHS and the growing numbers of sick and elderly people in need of care; Hicks (1988) points out that 1.3 million people are left to care and cope, often with little public support.

Modern pressures on the NHS

The ideal contained in the Beveridge Report that the NHS would eliminate disease – one of the 'five giants' of social evil – was shattered by the ever-greater demands placed on it by an increasingly health-conscious and long-lived population. While those who proposed and introduced the NHS can be seen as collectivists in their desire (however reluctantly in some cases) to provide a health service to provide for the needs of all, the collectivist consensus has virtually disappeared owing to a combination of growing financial demands and relative economic decline. According to Taylor and Field (1993), the four main pressures on the NHS are:

- an ageing population
- expensive technological developments
- a highly skilled (and therefore more costly) workforce in the health sector
- rising consumer expectations.

It was believed by those introducing the national health service that improved good health in the nation through NHS provision would result in a drop in demand. It is now clear that demand for healthcare has risen dramatically.

According to *Social Trends* (1999), gross expenditure on the NHS rose in real terms from £24.5 million in 1977/78, to over £32 million in 1994/95, and up to nearly £37.8 million in 1997/98. This means that, even ignoring inflation, spending on healthcare in the NHS has risen by over 50 per cent since 1979, and costs continue to rise.

Although investment in the NHS has continued to increase since the election of the Labour government in May 1997, there are still long waiting lists for many operations. In November 1999, hospital managements were talking of 'a crisis of funding', with the possibility that many of them would run out of money before the new funding round in early 2000.

Activity

Some writers and politicians have argued that the UK can no longer afford a free and universal national heath service. Use information in this section, and other research of your own, to draw up a list of potential reasons why the continuation of a free and universal NHS is seen as a problem. What are the possible solutions to this problem? Do you think any of them can work?

C3.2, C3.3

In the 1980s, critical comments about the welfare state and collectivism generally – especially but not only from the New Right – led to important changes in the perception and organization of the NHS. The main criticisms can be summarized as follows:

- State welfare leads some people to become so dependent on welfare provision that they lose the ability to provide for themselves.
- The welfare state is inefficient and private provision would be better.
- High taxes required to fund welfare are depriving other sectors and reducing money available for private investment.

Although these points are traditionally associated with a 'market liberal' view of healthcare and linked to reforms proposed by the Conservative party in Britain, they also underpinned some of the proposals and policies of the new Labour government in the late 1990s and the beginning of the century (see page 463).

12.6 Contemporary debates on healthcare

The New Right and the NHS

The financial crisis identified within the NHS – and the welfare state generally – was accompanied by a change in views about state healthcare among members of the Conservative administrations between 1979 and 1997, and many of their supporters. The New Right presented a very negative view of the role of the state. Drawing particularly on the work of the economist Milton Friedman and the philosopher Friedrich Hayek, they argued that state provision of medicine and other forms of welfare was bad for the individual and for society. George and Wilding (1985), social policy analysts, summarize the New Right critique of the welfare state as follows:

- The welfare state interferes with individual freedoms.
- Governments are weakened by the incessant demands of pressure groups.
- Large-scale bureaucracy required is wasteful and inefficient.
- More efficient private forms of provision are stifled.
- People become dependent on the state and are therefore unable to take responsibility for their own healthcare.

In the UK, New Right views tend to be expressed by members of the Conservative party, although there is some disagreement about the levels of state healthcare that should be made available. Liberal Democrats and members of the Labour party, although disagreeing on some basic assumptions about the ways in which society should operate, are more likely to adopt a social democratic view of social welfare. This view tends to support the provision of free and universal healthcare as a right for all citizens, as the case was presented in 1948.

Therefore Labour and Liberal Democratic politicians tend to challenge some of the New Right's arguments about the role of the state (see Table 12.15). However, the social democratic view and, in particular, concepts of universal provision, are no longer accepted by many New Labour politicians.

Both the Conservative and Labour parties now agree that funding for the NHS must be controlled in order to keep taxes as low as possible. In April 1999, the deputy leader of the Conservatives, Peter Lilley, argued that they would match New Labour spending on health – suggesting a growing political consensus on health spending. One problem is that people generally want free and universal healthcare when they need it, but some are reluctant to support the level of taxation required to fund it.

Table 12.15 Perspectives on the NHS

Issue	Marxist	Market liberal	Social democrat
Nature of society	Divided by classes with opposing interests	United by common interests	United by common interests and values
Social order maintenance	Coercion and ideology operate to suppress conflict	Self-interest and the common good are the same, therefore social order is maintained by pursuit of self-interest	Humanitarian social policies prevent any conflict which may be engendered by the ill-effects of capitalism
Attitude to NHS	*Anti:* It represents the interests of the ruling class and embodies the class, colour and sex inequalities in society	*Anti:* It impedes the free play of market forces when over-expanded	*Pro:* It alleviates the ill-effects of capitalism, produces political legitimacy and prevents civil unrest
Desired changes to system of healthcare	Must be changed in the context of wider social changes including socialization of NHS	Severe reduction of NHS or its abolition is necessary. It should be replaced by private healthcare	Extension of NHS provision is necessary, especially in such areas as psychiatric and geriatric care
Attitude to private medicine	*Anti:* It is available for the few and is parasitical on state resources. As with other profit-making enterprises, it is detrimental to the general good	*Pro:* It is a source of wealth, leads to better healthcare, improves consumer choice and is beneficial to the NHS	*Anti:* It represents the expression of private interests rather than the general public's interest

Source: Trowler (1985)

Reforms in the NHS

In order to reduce or eliminate many of the problems identified by the New Right, the NHS was reformed by the provisions of the Health and Community Care Act 1990. The key stated aims were to:

- improve institutional efficiency and accountability
- reduce bureaucratic and economic waste
- broaden the choices of patients for their healthcare needs.

There was no stated intent by the Conservative party in the 1980s and early 1990s to replace public with private healthcare, although the private system of enterprise was seen as an appropriate model for the provision of health treatment.

The main changes included an increase in private and voluntary provision to improve competitiveness between private doctors and hospitals and those in the state sector, and a transfer of funds from the secondary sector (hospitals) to primary care (GPs, district nurses, etc.) so that more people could be treated and cared for by community doctors and nurses, either as hospital out-patients or in their own homes. A number of aspects to these changes remain unpopular, as more people tend to be discharged from hospital more quickly than they may have been in the past.

Discussion point

In what way does discharging patients from hospital more quickly benefit (a) hospitals and (b) patients? Are there any groups who might particularly gain or lose out from this?

Activity

a Using Table 12.15 and any other relevant material you have, write short speeches for market liberal and social democratic politicians expressing their views about healthcare provision.

b Which views do you support – and why?

c Is it possible to have policies which bring in some of the views of both?

Economic changes in the NHS

The introduction of market forces

One particularly controversial change to the NHS in the 1980s and 1990s was the introduction of an 'internal market'. Under this, hospitals and other groups offered their services to doctors (many of whom were managing their own budgets) or to district health authority managers. These then chose the best value treatment for their patients from a range of options. This meant that doctors who chose to be 'fundholders' could, in theory, shop around among a number of hospital trusts – the groups that run hospitals – in order to purchase the best and most cost-effective treatment for their own patients.

The general aim was to introduce the managerial practices of the private sector – where the main aim is usually profit – into state health provision in order to improve efficiency and accountability and thus make the NHS more cost-effective. It was considered that the NHS should be able to compete effectively with private and voluntary provision and monitor its own spending.

Some of the problems with these changes came about because many of the aims appear to contradict each other. For example, one of the key aims of the changes was to improve patient choice, but some forms of care in the community (see Section 14.6) seem to restrict choice, at least for some patients. Elderly people, for instance, may find it difficult to get the level of care that they feel they need within their own home.

Rationing of healthcare

There is a suggestion that health needs are increasingly defined in terms of financial rather than purely health criteria. However, there is now much more openness about the need to ration healthcare, although some traditional social democrats, such as the 'Old Labour' MP, Tony Benn, argue that rationing of healthcare is not inevitable.

The majority of politicians from all political parties – and many sociologists – now tend to reject the latter view. In their review of health policy in the UK, Blakemore and Symons (1993) suggested that although spending on healthcare has always been relatively low and well-managed, the fact that it is paid for out of taxation means that governments are constantly under pressure to reduce spending in this area if there is public pressure to reduce taxes. Consequently they suggest that by the 1980s:

Rising expectations of health services coupled with advances in medical treatment and the growing need for treatment from an ageing population have contributed to something of a crisis in healthcare.

(Blakemore and Symons, 1993, p. 195)

Ham (1992), a social policy specialist, also regarded some form of healthcare rationing as almost inevitable for any government owing to the 'crisis' of an ageing population and reduced capability for funding. This problem is shared by most advanced, western economies. With regard to current and future health provision, Ham said in the early 1990s:

The debate about the future has arisen out of concern at the expenditure implications of demographic changes and medical advances. ... With resources for growth likely to be limited throughout the 1990s, whatever party holds office, the rationing of healthcare will become increasingly difficult and controversial.

(Ham, 1992, p. 236)

This view, of course, will hold true for at least the early years of the new century. It can be seen to inform many of the health policies of the Labour government elected in 1997, emphasizing the need for rationalization in the NHS much as as the previous Conservative administrations had done. There is never enough money for all the treatments and drugs available. In October 1999, doctors admitted that cancer patients are sometimes not told of all the treatments available because there is not enough money to pay for the drugs required. All governments now appear to accept the need for targets, rationalization and rationing in healthcare.

Discussion point

One of the most controversial issues raised by the changes in the NHS has been to do with this apparent need to ration healthcare. It has been suggested that some 'treatments', such as tattoo removal, should no longer be available within the NHS. To what extent do you agree that treatment for certain things should not be available? Which services, if any, do you think this should apply to?

C3.1a

The purchaser–provider split

One major change to the NHS introduced by the 1990 legislation was the introduction of a split between purchasers of healthcare (the health authorities and the GPs) and the providers (hospitals and GPs). This change, depicted in Figure 12.8, introduced a market ethos into the system to try to increase economic efficiency.

Blakemore and Symons (1993) explained that:

A system of 'contracts' for providing healthcare was introduced. For example, District Health Authorities must, as purchasers, ensure that they have drawn up contracts with local hospitals to guarantee the supply of a comprehensive range of services and medical operations. Each contract stipulates cost, quantity and quality of the services to be provided over a year. Equally, fund-holding GPs must also draw up contracts with providers.

(Blakemore and Symons, 1993, pp. 196–7)

Trust hospitals and fundholding GPs

An increasing number of hospitals became independent trusts, meaning that they were funded by central government directly rather than by local health authorities. This made them accountable to their own management board rather than to officials appointed by the local authority. A somewhat similar arrangement was introduced for fundholding GPs who, while not being accountable to a board of managers, managed directly the funds they received from their regional health authority. This, too, was an attempt to introduce competition into the NHS with the intention of improving efficiency.

Many of these arrangements have now been removed or amended since 1997 by the new Labour government.

Evaluation of changes in the NHS

Critics of the purchaser–provider arrangements argued that the NHS was already relatively cheap for the nation, and that the outcome would be a two-tier system with better provision for those who could afford to pay. Even without resorting to private medicine, it became clear that some patients were able to get better treatment from

PURCHASERS/COMMISSIONERS

'SELLERS'/PROVIDERS

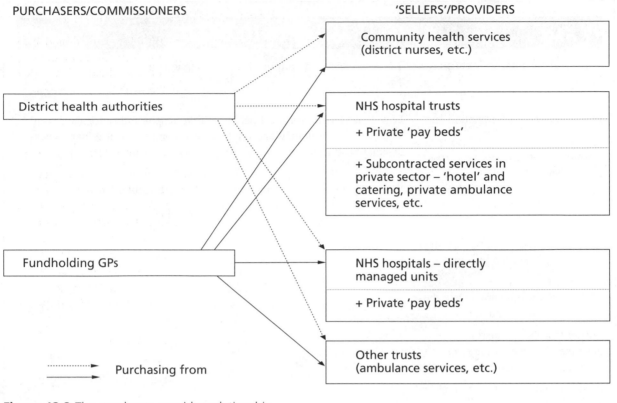

Figure 12.8 The purchaser–provider relationship
Source: Blakemore and Symons (1993, p .197)

their GP than others. This challenges the principle of equality of access, but did improve treatment for some patients.

Blakemore and Symons (1993) queried the ability for the market-style NHS to improve its services to all patients. They were often more rather than less restricted in their choice of treatments as the GP was tied to various contract arrangements. There are also likely to be financial limits on the drugs and other treatments they may be prescribed. Many patients requiring expensive treatments feared that they would be rejected by GPs, but there is no evidence to support this claim.

There was also a fear that there would be an emphasis on the quantity rather than the quality of care – for example the number of patients treated and discharged rather than the state of health they were in when they left hospital.

Finally, there was little evidence that the market-style system was really more cost-effective or less bureaucratic than the system it replaced. However, limitations on the availability of treatments and care provided by the NHS still remained problematic.

New Labour and the NHS

The impact of the reforms have, however, been reduced with the eradication of fundholding and trusts by the Labour government elected in 1997. They have sought to establish a 'contract' between government and population, as outlined in *Our Healthier Nation: A Contract for Health* published in February 1998 (see the boxed item on page 464). This publication argues that there are a number of fixed factors (such as genes, sex and ageing), as well as socio-economic, environmental, lifestyle and access factors, which all combine to affect the level of health in the population.

Health is therefore seen to be the responsibility of individuals as well as of the state. The government has identified a number of targets to, for example, reduce unemployment, improve housing stock, increase public awareness of health factors and improve health and other services for both mental and physical health. It also set up the Acheson Report as part of this commitment to improving the health of the nation (see Section 12.3).

There were a number of initiatives throughout

A CONTRACT FOR HEALTH

Government and national players can:	Local players and communities can:	People can:
Provide national coordination and leadership	Provide leadership for local health strategies by developing and implementing health improvement programmes	Take responsibility for their own health and make healthier choices about their lifestyle
Ensure that policy-making across government takes full account of health and is well informed by research and the best expertise available	Work in partnerships to improve the health of local people and tackle the root causes of ill-health	Ensure their own actions do not harm the health of others
Work with other countries for international co-operation to improve health	Plan and provide high-quality services to everyone who needs them	Take opportunities to better their lives and their families' lives, through education, training and employment
Assess risks and communicate those risks clearly to the public		
Ensure that the public and others have the information they need to improve their health		
Regulate and legislate where necessary		
Tackle the root causes of ill-health		

the late 1990s which demonstrated this approach. In July 1999 it was announced that programmes would be introduced to reduce inequalities in health and target the needs of poor people, the elderly and children. The main focus was on the involvement of local authorities and community systems, with a considerable emphasis on personal responsibility. For example, poorer people were to be provided with help to give up smoking, which remains arguably one of the key reasons for class differences in rates of cancer and heart disease. A further proposal was that people who are overweight or prone to heart disease might be offered access to free exercise facilities at a local leisure centre.

Marxist explanations of inequalities in health and illness

While many social scientists examine the NHS in terms of its ability to provide an effective and affordable service for individuals in an advanced society like the UK, Marxist perspectives tend to

Activity

Look at the proposals in the government's *A Contract for Health*. Draw up a contract for health between yourself, your doctor, your local community and the government for your personal health needs. Make sure you identify your own responsibilities as well as those of others.

C3.2, C3.3

regard the NHS as a tool to help manage the crises of capitalism. This means that the NHS looks after those who cannot maintain themselves adequately in order to be fit as workers. It also legitimates capitalism, by showing how well capitalist societies look after their citizens.

Marxists such as Navarro (1978) suggested that the crisis in the NHS which led to the reforms outlined above was a response to a decline in capitalist profitability in the 1970s. However, Turner (1987, 1992) suggests that this argument ignores the different types of capitalism and health systems found in different societies.

For example, state health provision in the USA was never as widespread as in the UK or Scandinavia. Furthermore, many Marxists do not acknowledge the hard-won benefits that the NHS has provided for workers, despite the inequalities outlined in other sections of this chapter.

In the end, the crucial factor is what money is allocated to healthcare, and how it is distributed. However, there are clearly a number of factors involved which make the issue far more complex. This is and will remain a long-standing political debate – and one that may affect us all at some time in our lives. It also remains at the forefront of much political debate about the way government money should be allocated and the whole complicated issue of the role of the NHS.

12.7 Limits to medicine and healthcare

Doctors as wielders of power

One of the key aims of doctors and, to a lesser extent, nurses is to be accepted as a specialist profession. Doctors in particular enjoy considerable admiration in our society, and this is used to justify their high rewards and status. Their education, skills and expertise lead to them being granted a degree of power. If this is used for the benefit of all, that is fine. However, the power inequalities their position creates does leave open the possibility that medical care is determined for the benefit of the doctor rather than the patient. This possibility is the basis for many critical views on healthcare.

Functionalists believe that we live in a society where the most able people are allocated to the most important roles in society. They therefore argue that doctors are respected and well-paid because their job is so important that only a relatively few extremely able people can do it. Barber (1963) claimed that there are four essential attributes of a professional, which are exemplified by doctors. These are:

- a body of systematic and generalized knowledge with a long period of specialized training
- a concern for the community rather than motivation based on self-interest
- a code of ethics strictly administered by a professional body such as the British Medical Association (BMA)
- generous economic rewards to demonstrate their high standing in the community.

Critiques of the medical profession: the work of Illich

There have been a number of criticisms of the foregoing views from different perspectives, especially from Illich (1990), who argued that professionals are the *cause* of most of the problems in society, and doctors are probably the worst of all. He shows little respect for professionals, especially the medical profession.

Illich argues that although doctors claim to have vastly improved our health and longevity, virtually eradicating such diseases as typhoid, tuberculosis and cholera, most contagious diseases were in decline owing to improved sanitation before the development of vaccinations. He points out that well-fed people are far better able to fight disease than the nutritionally deprived. He also identifies the fact that doctors can do relatively little about the main modern epidemic killers such as heart disease and cancer.

Rather than doctors working in our interest, Illich argues, most medical treatment is useless or, worse still, downright dangerous. Non-infectious illnesses in particular are best treated by prevention and early diagnosis rather than expensive, and often disabling, medical treatment. He goes on to say that medicine is bad for us in four key ways, which he describes as either iatrogenesis or nemesis.

'Iatrogenesis' means caused by itself, so he is talking about medical treatments that make us ill. 'Nemesis' was the Greek goddess of retribution, so here Illich is suggesting that medical treatment finally results in making us sicker as individuals, and as a society. We then need more medical treatment.

Clinical iatrogenesis

This covers the negative effects of medical treatments – the side-effects of drugs, the addiction promoted by tranquillizers, the patient who comes out of hospital sicker than when he or she went in. Examples of this include the thalidomide scandal in the early 1960s. Expectant mothers given tablets for morning sickness subsequently gave birth to children with truncated limbs. It took years of campaigning – most notably by the

Sunday Times – before Distillers, who produced the drug, finally offered their victims compensation. Furthermore, Illich argued, widespread use of antibiotics leads to people (and viruses) becoming resistant, and the World Health Organization is currently arguing for greater restraint in the use of antibiotics for just this reason.

Social iatrogenesis

Even worse, in some ways, is the way in which doctors use the medical model of illness to diagnose and treat reported symptoms of illness. Illich suggests that much illness is actually caused by the boredom, alienation, monotony, materialism and lack of autonomy experienced by most people in contemporary industrial societies. Doctors blame the individual rather than society, and so not only hide the true causes of illness but, unsurprisingly, are unable to treat them.

Cultural iatrogenesis

In an 'over-medicalized' society, people become defenceless consumers of medicine just as they mindlessly consume other products of industrial society. This is instilled by teachers in schools (where we passively consume educational knowledge in order to get the credentials we need) and encouraged by other professionals such as lawyers and advertisers as well as doctors. In this way people become unable to diagnose, treat or deal not only with illness but also with other problems in society. They can no longer respond in a healthy way to illness, death or any other kind of suffering because they always turn to someone else.

Medical nemesis

Illich claims that our lack of autonomy means that we consume medicines and seek help from doctors which ultimately makes us less well, personally, socially and culturally. Medical developments constantly cause problems that lead to the need for 'medical' solutions. He argues that the only way – if it is possible – to restore individual and social health is for people to take control of their own healthcare and wrest it away from the doctors who only make things worse.

Activity

Explain Illich's four concepts in your own words and provide an example of each.

C3.2, C3.3

Other criticisms of the medical profession

Parry and Parry (1976) argue that medical professionals operate mainly in their own interests, limiting entry, criticism and competition to maintain their high rewards and status. However, the autonomy of doctors is not as high in many parts of the world as it is in the USA, where most doctors practise privately. This at least reduces the level of medical lawsuits in the UK in comparison with the USA.

Johnson (1972) argues that many professionals owe their allegiance to their employers rather than their patients. In some cases doctors and nurses have lost their jobs for reporting inefficiencies in the NHS. Doctors also seem to be losing the respect of some members of the public, and a few have been attacked on night visits. However, their response – to suggest that they no longer make home visits at night – was not popular with the public. Doctors are also increasingly open to lawsuits.

Discussion point

To what extent should patients, managers, lawyers or others who are medically unqualified be free to question judgements made by qualified professional medical staff?

Interactionist and Social Action critiques of the medical profession

There is considerable interest in the relationships between doctors and managers and between doctors and patients. A study by Goss (1969) suggested that, in most medical institutions, doctors' views tended to carry more weight than managers'. This debate is increasingly important with the growth of managerialism within the NHS, where these relationships remain problematic.

Doctors are sometimes criticized for their poor communication skills and their inability to interact effectively with patients, especially when there are class or cultural differences. Not only is there the previously discussed 'inverse care law' according to Tudor-Hart (1971), whereby doctors are situated in areas of lowest need (see page 436), but consultation is also class-differentiated. A study by Cartwright and O'Brien (1976) showed that average consultations with middle-class patients tended to be over a minute longer than those with working-class patients, and the doctor seemed to know less about the latter group.

Although evidence suggests that many doctors still tend not to listen to their patients as much as they could, Walker and Waddington (1991) show improved interactions between doctors and homosexual men in the treatment of AIDS. They propose that this is because many homosexual men are actually better acquainted with the medical details about HIV and AIDS than the majority of doctors, who encounter these diseases only rarely. This suggests that interpersonal skills training for doctors and a better-informed public could reduce the professional barrier between doctor and patient, and that this needs to be provided for all members of society.

Nettleton (1995) says that our awareness of many of the above debates suggests that the medical professions and industries may be in decline. There is, undoubtedly, a growing belief in the need for personal control over health and in the use of 'alternative' medical treatments. Sharma (1992) argues that this is evidence of the growing power of consumers – in this case of medical expertise and treatments – in a post-modern society. Bakx (1991) sees it as evidence of a general decline in our faith in the biomedical model.

Furthermore, the autonomy of doctors in the UK is being undermined by the increasing 'managerialism' of the NHS. It can also be argued that people without formal medical training are more involved in the treatment of ill-health, for example as homeopaths, aromatherapists and various types of masseurs. Although the medical knowledge of some lay people is improving, Nettleton (1996) claims that this may be due to the fact that we live in an increasingly medicalized society. Most alternative medicine and self-health groups operate in parallel with biomedical treatments and are often sought only as a last resort.

A report by the British Medical Association (1993) asserts that the medical profession welcomes alternative practitioners, but is keen to lay down their guidelines and to ensure they operate within the biomedical model. In this way challenges to the medical profession can more easily be controlled.

Medicine and capitalism: the profit motive

Some writers argue that there is a link between capitalism and the power of the medical profession. In the USA, McKinley (1977) asserted that the profit motive which drives capitalism has overwhelmed the delivery of healthcare. Even in the UK, it can be argued, healthcare is now more of a commodity than a right.

Rationing of treatments

The arguments about the rationing of healthcare show its increasing commodification. There are now a number of treatments, such as hip replacements and varicose vein removal, which are rarely offered at NHS hospitals, forcing patients to resort to private treatments. It is also now true in the UK that the majority of dentists no longer offer NHS treatment to working adults who join their practice, although in 1999 the Labour government announced a commitment to improve access to NHS dental care.

It seems unlikely that all medical professionals become involved in healthcare purely to make a lot of money, although there are potentially considerable rewards to be had. However, it has been argued far more convincingly by Marxist writers that drug companies and medical equipment manufacturers can, and do, make excessive profits from the production and sale of related commodities.

The drug manufacturing industry

Doyal and Pennell (1979) found that most drug companies justified their high prices and high profits by their claim to be an industry with high research requirements and costs. However, as the writers pointed out, most 'new' drugs are actually slightly modified versions of existing ones, so the main aim is to increase market share rather than produce dramatic improvements. They also note that drugs are aimed at cure rather than prevention of illness, while doctors are bombarded with advertising, so that much of the research and development expenditure goes on marketing. Research into 'real' new drugs is often guarded secretly to ensure that one company makes all the profits.

Ideological control

Navarro (1976) argued that not only do drug and medical equipment companies make huge profits, but medicine itself operates to maintain the ideological control of the ruling classes. The NHS, for example, justifies exploitation and legitimates capitalism by providing a means to keep the workforce healthy and satisfied. Like Illich, discussed above, he claims that the medical model directs attention away from the real (i.e. capitalist) causes of much ill-health.

Medical surveillance and control

Rather than seeing medicine as losing its power, Turner (1987, 1992) argues that the medicalization of society has largely legitimated the increased surveillance of our bodies to the extent that medicine now has control over all our life processes. Drawing on the ideas of Foucault, he suggests that our bodies have been subjected to a process of rationalization and standardization which means that medical professionals have the power to decide what are – and what are not – acceptable behaviours and forms of appearance in our society. He says:

The body has become the focus of a wide range of disciplines and forms of surveillance and control, in which the medical profession has played a critical part. The birth of the clinic and the growth of the teaching hospital have been significant institutional developments in the development of what Foucault has called the medical gaze. This framework provides an organizing principle for looking at the problem of sickness at the level of the individual body, the growth of institutional regulation and control at the level of the clinic and hospital, and finally the emergence of a bio-politics of populations whereby the state through its various local and national agencies constantly intervenes in the production and reproduction of life itself.

(Turner, 1987, 1992, p. 218)

Activity

Turner argues that the medical profession regulates us as individuals, in institutions (such as schools as well as hospitals) and in terms of reproduction. To what extent do you consider your life might be regulated now or in the future by medical limitations imposed by the state in each of these cases?

C3.2, C3.3

12.8 The sociology of the body, mind and sexuality

Social change and perceptions of the body

Lyon (1994) argues that the move towards postmodernity has changed the focus of sociology from production to consumption. Turner (1987, 1992) suggests that we are in fact moving towards a 'somatic society', where the body is the focus of political and cultural activity.

Nettleton (1995) says that changes in society have profoundly changed the way we see our bodies. People tend to be far more knowledgeable about their own bodies than they were even 20 years ago:

The boundaries between the physical body and society are becoming increasingly blurred. In this respect the sociology of the body represents an important and fruitful area of study.

(Nettleton, 1995, p. 100)

Nettleton suggests that there are six key social changes which have made the sociology of the body of increasing importance and significance to an understanding of society today. These include feminist approaches, technological changes, demographic changes, the impact of AIDS, the 'cult of the body', and the growth of 'body fascism'. She develops each of these points as follows.

- There is a growing genre of feminist literature in which women explicitly reject male domination of medicine and control of their bodies (see Section 12.4) and challenge mechanistic views of the body.

- Dramatic technological changes, especially in the sphere of reproduction, have widened the political and ethical debate about, for example, the storage and disposal of frozen embryos that have been produced as a result of fertility treatments. These technological changes lead to a number of medical, religious and ethical debates about abortion, reproduction techniques and euthanasia.

- Demographic changes such as an ageing population and declining fertility rates in western industrialized societies have focused medical and social awareness on the problems associated with ageing and death. Debates about euthanasia are relevant here, as are those about the treatment of medical diseases and the social care of older people.

- The experience of AIDS has led to a reappraisal of health and illness in a number of ways. Not only does it remind us of the limitations of medical technology and professional expertise; it also kills relatively young people in an era when such early death is comparatively rare. However, despite the terrible suffering of many people with AIDS, it has also led to the development of medical self-help groups and provided a model for other sufferers of chronic illnesses.

- The 'cult of the body' (Featherstone, 1991a) now forms an important aspect of the consumerism which structures much of post-modern society. Many people are obsessed by looking fit, slim and young. It is now almost the norm in some parts of America for women to have breast enhancement surgery, while the sale of 'health and fitness' videos (often featuring svelte fashion models) is now big business, as are health clubs, slimming books and magazines and fitness studios.

- The effect of what some people might term 'body and health fascism' on people with chronic illnesses or particular needs in our society – or even the merely overweight – is worthy of sociological debate. Nettleton argues that, because of ageing and other forms of technology, we actually have in our society more people with chronic illnesses and disabilities than ever before.

Activity

a Organize a debate about the sociological issues outlined above, which involve questions about how we (and others) see and treat our bodies. These points also raise important issues of morality in society. Decide first the question(s) to be debated and then use library resources to do research.

b Write your own evaluation and opinion on each of these points following the debate.

C3.1a, C3.2, C3.3

Sociological perspectives on the body

A number of perspectives on the body have been developed over the past few years to place it at the focus of sociological debate. Nettleton outlines recent biological and sociological views which may provide some insights into our understanding of health and illness.

Naturalistic views on the body

Naturalistic views are similar in most ways to the biomedical model of the body. Currently the most popular version is sociobiology, which regards the majority of human behaviour and interaction as a result of our biological (especially genetic) make-up.

For example, homosexuality is presented as the result of a 'gay' gene, as Dr Simon Le Vay terms it, and differences in behaviour between men and women are regarded as mainly a result of genetic needs in terms of mating requirements. However, many of these ideas can be criticized as an ideological critique of feminist arguments that gender roles are determined culturally.

Social constructionist views on the body

Some social constructionists such as Foucault (1976) argue that the body and illness are nothing more than the discourses used to describe them (see Section 12.2). Others, such as Connell (1987) in her study of gender and power, accept the material basis of the body but believe that its structure is largely the result of social expectations. In this case the greater strength of men is built through the expectations (and encouragement) that young males are more physical. In some societies most of the heavy physical work is carried out by women. This weaker relativist view has been developed by a number of writers.

Douglas (1966) argued that parts of the body are classified in different societies according to different systems of purity and pollution. In her introduction concerning our notions of the body, Leder (1992) suggests that we take our bodies for granted until they refuse to work properly (an implicit biomedical model), which is why many sociologists have ignored the importance of human action in relation to the body.

In his influential book on the body and social

thought, Shilling (1993) describes the body as an unfinished biological and social entity which is transformed by the expectations of society. In a society where we often feel at risk, he says, social groups seek to impose more and more control over our bodies in four categories: personally, religiously, medically, and legally.

Activity

Suggest ways in which individuals and social groups seek to control the body in each of Shilling's four categories. To what extent is resistance or conflict involved?

C3.2, C3.3

The regulation of the body

Turner (1987, 1992) complains that discussions about the 'reality' of the body are meaningless; rather it is important to accept that it is both biologically and socially constructed. He focuses on the increasing control and surveillance of the body (and the whole population) by the medical and legal professions, replacing the role of religion. Much of this view develops from the work of Foucault, who wrote a great deal about the control of the body within institutions and by those who judge what is 'normal', such as lawyers, doctors, teachers and social workers.

In a work that has inspired the growth of the figurational approach in sociology, Elias (1978) showed how the processes of civilization from the Middle Ages onwards led to a far more regulated view of the body and shame about many of its functions. Nettleton (1995) argues that this has had a particular effect on nurses, who tend to have to deal with such embarrassing functions. There are rules about the modesty of the patient which are shared by both patient and nurse, who tends to wear a uniform, decide when relatives may stay or leave, and define the rules about what is discussed and in what language.

In summary, the sociology of the body is at the forefront of much academic sociological work. It provides insights into a number of different arguments about health and illness, and illuminates recent sociological theory, particularly post-modernism and problems of relativism. It adds a new dimension to our understanding of debates about people with disabilities and the relationship between gender and health. It also helps our understanding of many of the key ethical and moral debates of the late twentieth and early twenty-first century.

Aspects of chronic illness

Field (in Taylor and Field, 1993) suggests that we need to be aware of the difference between:

- *impairment* – any interruption to the normal functioning of the body
- *disability* – which refers to a loss or reduction of activity
- *handicap* – which focuses on the social problems caused by either of the above.

While finding it difficult to generalize about chronic illness, he notes especially that as age rises so do the numbers of chronically ill in the population. Poorer people from lower social classes are disproportionately affected by such disadvantages, as are women, who also make up the largest group of informal carers for people with long-term illness. However, the most disabling feature of any form of impairment seems to be the negative reactions from many institutions and individuals in society.

The effects of chronic illness

Nettleton (1995), too, identifies a number of important points. Chronic illness usually affects the family and others as well as the sufferer, especially with the move towards caring in the community. Furthermore, the chronically ill are required to adopt a particular attitude in society – as they cannot be expected to get better they should not be too demanding, as they have already challenged aspects of the 'sick role' (see below). She concludes:

Chronic illness can impact upon sufferers' daily living, their social relationships, their identity (the view that others hold of them) and their sense of self (their private view of themselves).

(Nettleton, 1995, p. 69)

The sick role

Writing in the 1950s, Talcott Parsons demonstrated the functions of the 'sick role' as a form of deviance in society (see also Section 12.2). Sick people are allowed a certain escape from normal obligations, but only if they seek to get better. People will tolerate certain behaviour among the sick, but this is only legitimated through seeking medical advice. (A number of studies have shown that the majority of people do not go to a doctor when they feel unwell, in which case legitimation is sought from friends or relatives.) For people with a chronic illness the situation is different. Although they require legitimation (and in many cases may find it very difficult to obtain), they are also usually attempting to maintain some form of social normality alongside their illness.

Non-disclosure

In a large number of cases the chronic illness is not disclosed, particularly for those involving problems which may lead to some sort of stigmatization, such as colostomies. People often have to develop coping strategies to enable them to maintain 'normal' lives. We are also now far more intrusive about medical matters and less trusting of those with any history of medical problems. American presidential candidates are now expected to reveal all details of their medical history, although the two main Allied leaders during World War II, Churchill and Roosevelt, were both chronically sick – a matter that was hidden from the public by a voluntary agreement of the press.

Aspects of disability

How disability is perceived by others

Physical disabilities are often associated with chronic illness. However, Nettleton (1995) argues that disabilities are a result of the way society is organized rather than the true physical capabilities of an individual. We often *define* people as disabled and treat them differently from the rest of the population. For example, Lonsdale (1990), in her study of women and disability, found that women thus afflicted were denied in terms of their sexuality and often encouraged not to have children.

Davies (1994) argues that, despite the relatively large number of people involved, disability tends to be ignored by sociologists. He suggests that this is mainly because:

- few sociologists themselves suffer from a disability
- reactions to people with disabilities tend to be emotional, including embarrassment, guilt and fear – so these groups tend to be ignored
- the medical model of disability tends to mean

that sociologists have regarded it as outside their domain.

However, Davies argues that disabilities are, in fact, socially constructed in a number of different ways. The tendency to define a disability as an impairment or handicap suggests that such people are inferior to, rather than different from, the apparently 'able-bodied'.

Many critics such as Shearer (1981) and Barnes (1992) argue that it is the environment and attitudes of others which set people with disabilities at a disadvantage, rather than their physical or mental impairment. For example, most people would benefit from more ramps or lower steps on to buses.

Loss of self-esteem

Charmaz (1983) suggests that many people with a physical disability lose their sense of self, resulting in them being more suspicious of, and dependent on, others. They often find it difficult to form and maintain relationships, as they are expected to restrain 'negative' feelings about their illness. However, Charmaz also found that re-affirmation and creative living can allow many people with a disability to improve their self-image and interactions with others.

Attitudes

Davies argues that society tends to possess very negative attitudes about those with disabilities – stigmatizing, stereotyping and de-sexing them; a view often reinforced in the media. All this is made worse by the limited interactions between most people with and without disabilities. For many, people with disabilities are seen as deviants, trapped within a medical model and unable to conform even to the expectations of the 'sick role'. Davies concludes that the fight against the stigmatization of, and discrimination against, people with disabilities can be seen as the latest – and possibly the last and most challenging – civil rights battle.

Coping

Field (1993) suggests that people with chronic illness or disability have to learn to cope with and make sense of their 'problem'. Physical and practical management of the condition is important and this will depend on a number of different factors, including the severity of the condition, when it starts to have a limiting effect, how stable it is and how visible it is. The last factor may well affect the level of stigmatization and, very significantly, it can influence confidence and self-esteem as well as occupational opportunities.

Davies (1994) also pointed out that, whereas discrimination on grounds of gender or ethnicity were closely regulated, no law existed specifically to protect those with disabilities from exploitation or discrimination. The Disability Discrimination Act 1995 has introduced a Code of Practice for employers to reduce discrimination against employed people in the workplace. The effects of this legislation on medical (and non-medical) perceptions and treatment of people with disabilities remain to be seen. New Labour legislation to means-test disability allowances as part of Welfare Reform have raised considerable concern and are viewed by some with mistrust.

Social control, reproduction and abortion

The politics of human fertility

In *Sex and Destiny* (1984), Germaine Greer outlined the ways that fertility, reproduction and abortion are regarded differently in different societies. She argued that most western 'developed' nations are largely 'sub-fertile'. This means that the birth rates and death rates in these countries are now so low that they are not increasing their populations. More and more people are choosing not to (or are unable to) have children. In the 'less developed' countries most of the initiatives to reduce population are sponsored and promoted by governments, external agencies or multinational companies. Whereas infertility is one of the major reproduction issues in western societies, many women in countries such as China, India and the South Americas are sterilized or undergo abortions against their will or their best interests.

Discussion point

Suggest reasons why people in less developed (i.e. more rural) societies might prefer to have large or small families.

C3.1a

Greer's argument suggests that fertility is often controlled by outside agencies; she also argues that social norms may affect people's attitudes to children. For example, in a society where both men and women are involved in paid work for most of their lives, having children may be a positive hindrance to social life and career aspirations. In a society where life is less socially and economically demanding, children may offer a source of entertainment and pleasure, as well as security in terms of care for the elderly.

She found that in many societies the barren woman is as much a social outcast as young single mothers are in Britain. This reinforces the view that reproduction and fertility are as much social issues as they are medical ones. However, in most parts of the world levels of fertility are considered part of the health programme and treated as such. Issues such as abortion are seen as legal and moral issues as well as medical ones.

The legal aspects of abortion in Britain

Abortion was made legal in Britain by the Abortion Act 1967. However, the decision as to whether a woman should have an abortion or not was to be taken not by the pregnant woman herself, but by doctors. The 1967 Abortion Act states that:

... a person shall not be guilty of an offence under the law relating to abortion when a pregnancy is terminated by a registered medical practitioner if two registered medical practitioners are of the opinion formed in good faith:

(a) that the continuance of the pregnancy would involve risk to the life of the pregnant woman, or of injury to the physical or mental health of the pregnant woman or any existing children of her family, greater than if her pregnancy were terminated; or

(b) that there is a substantial risk that if the child were born it would suffer from such physical or mental abnormalities as to be seriously handicapped.

(Abortion Act 1967)

Before this legislation was passed any abortion was generally illegal as it contravened the Infant Life (Preservation) Act 1929 (protecting the life of the viable foetus). However, many thousands of abortions did take place before 1967. The fact that they were illegal meant that they were often extremely dangerous, particularly for poor women who could not afford discreet, private medical care.

Changes and trends in abortion

According to *Population Trends* (1997) the number of abortions rose from 1968 to 1972, moderated until 1974, fell until 1976 and since then rose steadily to about 174 000 in 1990 before falling slightly each year. The Abortion Act 1967 was amended by the Human Fertilization and Embryology Act 1990 to reduce the legal time limit for abortion from 28 to 24 weeks, leading to a trend towards more abortions in early pregnancy.

Figures for the 1990s show a slight trend towards fewer abortions, although there was a small rise to 177,871 in 1998.

Table 12.16 Numbers of abortions in Great Britain, 1991–95

1991	1992	1993	1994	1995
167,376	160,501	157,846	156,539	154,315

Source: Population Trends 1990–95 (ONS, 1997)

The issue of selective abortion (aborting one or more foetuses in multiple pregnancies due to fertility treatment) was also addressed by the 1990 Act. These had risen from 33 in 1992 to 46 in 1995. Although very few women are affected, it remains a controversial aspect of abortion. Some of the debates relating to abortion are discussed below, although most people tend to be tolerant of abortion, especially women and people under 30.

Problems relating to abortion

However, just because abortion is now legal and available on the National Health Service, this does not mean that there are no further problems. Two of the main problems are inequality of access to abortion and the moral dilemma of abortion.

Access to abortion

This discussion tends to assume that everyone has access to abortion as and when they need it. However, as the article shows, where you live makes an important difference, especially for women who cannot afford private abortions.

Chances of free abortion 'rely on postcode lottery'

CHERRY NORTON

SECURING an abortion on the National Health Service has become a "lottery" and for hundreds of women depends on age, finances and use of contraception, say researchers.

A survey by the Abortion Law Reform Association, to be published next week, shows that some health authorities are restricting women's access to NHS abortions by using criteria more strict than those set out in the 1967 Abortion Act.

The proportion of abortions that were paid for by the NHS at the 119 health authorities studied ranged from as low as 45 per cent in Solihull to 96 per cent in Northumberland. Seven health authorities admitted to setting additional criteria to encourage women to pay for their own terminations.

"Health authorities are making use of the current law, which is open to far too much interpretation, to avoid offering abortions," said Jane Roe, the association's campaign director. "We don't feel they should be entitled to rewrite the law. They are clearly being judgemental in many of the criteria."

In 1998, 177,871 abortions were carried out in England and Wales, with one-quarter, 45,971, paid for privately.

In Wolverhampton, abortions are offered only to those who have had a failure with an "effective method of contraception," Ms Roe said. "Only women who have been good girls can get an abortion. Those who have not should, as a punishment, be forced to go ahead with a pregnancy," she told the *Nursing Times*.

Walsall health authority will not fund a third abortion and a woman living in Croydon cannot get one until she is more than 10 weeks pregnant.

The East Sussex, Brighton and Hove health authority limits termination of pregnancy to victims of rape, girls under 16, women on low incomes, students, women in refuges, women over 45, homeless women and women having their fourth or more pregnancy. The authority only funds 53 per cent of abortions, and has been criticised by local GPs for applying means-testing criteria.

Steven Ingram, senior performance manager at the authority, said the criteria were in place "to give equitable access of service and as a way of achieving consistency of referral from GPs". In contrast, Somerset imposes no extra criteria and the maximum time a women there waits for an abortion is two weeks.

A patient survey, also published next week, shows that long waiting times is the main reason women opt for private-sector abortions. Half of the 400 women surveyed said they had tried unsuccessfully to get an abortion on the NHS before going private.

Source: The Independent, 2 December 1999

Activity

Look at the article on page 473 and answer the following questions:

a What criteria are each of the different health authorities mentioned in this article using to decide which women are entitled to have an abortion on the NHS? Why might they differ?

b What is the main reason that women choose to have private abortions?

c Do you agree that some women should pay for abortions? If so, in what circumstances should this happen? Should access to free abortion be a 'lottery'?

C3.1a, C3.2

The moral dilemma of abortion

Abortion involves the death of a living organism. It is therefore as much a moral issue as it is a legal or medical one. Moral views on abortion may affect pregnant women and their families, but they also have an impact on the health professionals involved including doctors, nurses, health managers and local health authority staff. Moral opinion may be one of the reasons for the differences in the provision of free abortions discussed in the article from the *Independent*. As the article suggests, decisions may be made on moral rather than legal or medical grounds.

In *Complications of Abortion*, published by the World Health Organisation in 1995, the authors argue that:

The social and cultural environment in which a women lives, the dominant religion, and her own personal beliefs all contribute to the decisions she will make regarding unintended pregnancy and the services she receives. These in turn affect the mortality and morbidity associated with abortion. In addition the socio-cultural perspectives and religious beliefs of health care workers can affect their attitudes towards women who need abortion care.

(*Complications of Abortion*, 1995, p. 29)

This argument suggests that value systems as well as legal and medical factors can have a considerable impact on how people view abortion, including the pregnant woman herself. The reasons for wanting a termination, her socio-economic and marital status and the availability of abortion provision will clearly affect not only access to abortion but also the likelihood that health complications might ensue.

Furthermore, attitudes and beliefs will have a considerable effect on what feelings of remorse or relief a woman might experience. It has been found that relatively few women, whatever their personal attitudes and beliefs about abortion, undergo a termination without some feelings of guilt and regret.

Right to life: right to choose?

The ethics of abortion involve both moral and social issues. Many people believe that life begins at the moment of conception and that abortion is murder. They argue that all children have a right to life, in some cases even at the expense of the mother's health or survival. This view is most strongly associated with fundamental Catholic views espoused by the Life organisation. They have been known to offer financial support to poor expectant mothers to allow them to keep their babies. The more extreme pro-life supporters may picket abortion clinics to try to dissuade those attending.

The alternative view, presented by many feminists, is that a women should have the right to choose what she does with own her body. Pro-choice supporters do not regard a foetus as having the same rights as its mother until it can live outside her body. There is really no solution to this debate because the two sides have fundamentally different views of human life.

Activity

You have probably had talks from one or more of the above pressure groups at your school or college and will have your own views. Set up a class debate to identify the different viewpoints. Do as much research as possible to ensure that both sides are fully informed. After the debate, try to identify the following factors:

a Which sociological perspectives might support each view? Give your reasons.

b Might any particular political beliefs be more closely allied to one or the other side? Give reasons again.

IT3.1, C3.1a, C3.3

Conclusion

Abortion and reproduction are useful issues for looking at the social boundaries of medical treatments in society. They show how much health and medicine are used to control us both formally (through laws, institutions, etc.) and informally through beliefs and values. Even more importantly, they show how these factors might affect our behaviour and our access to certain forms of medical treatment. It is also worth noting that attitudes about, and access to, abortion varies widely between social groups within societies and in different societies. A full understanding of the issues of reproduction, abortion and social control requires us to look at a large range of societies and social issues.

The sociology of death and dying

Caring for the terminally ill

In our medicalized society, the majority of people die in hospitals, hospices or care homes – even though most people say that they would prefer to die in their own home and much informal care is provided to aid this. Support is available for terminally ill people, but respite care for the carers – to give them a break – is often limited and some treatment is less easily managed or monitored outside an institutional setting. Palliative care – the relief and management of pain – is often a major concern for the relatives of people dying from cancer, and this may be particularly difficult to control in a non-institutional setting:

The desirability, and even the possibility, of a 'home death' depends primarily on the human resources available to help both with the control of symptoms and the constant attendance and extra domestic work which such care entails.

(Field and James, in Taylor and Field, 1993, p. 157)

For these reasons, many carers regard hospital or hospice care as preferable for the sick person and for themselves. The levels of community support and input from primary healthcare officials is also important if the aims of 'care in the community' are to be achieved in the care of the dying.

The treatment of the terminally ill remains a key area of concern for health policy in our society, relating to debates about palliative care, euthanasia and the 'right to die' for people with a degenerative disease or terminal illness. One of the main advantages of the promotion of terminal care in the community has been the growth of the hospice movement, where care of the very highest quality is often available for those in the last stages of terminal illness.

Bereavement

Although issues of death, dying and bereavement are profoundly important, relatively few young people experience death as a real personal trauma. This may make it difficult for people to deal with dying and death as natural events later in their life.

Death now appears mainly to be experienced by specific social groups. For example, many elderly people frequently lose family and friends, whilst most young people have limited knowledge of bereavement. Deaths from AIDS are presented – often erroneously – as largely confined to 'gay' men and their friends. In general, people are expected to 'get on with their lives' after a close bereavement and there is little formal time available for mourning. If they find themselves unable to 'cope' with the death of someone, they are advised to try counselling – suggesting that people do need to talk about death but are rarely encouraged to do so informally.

There are few family bereavement rituals available for many people, especially if they have no religious affiliation. However, the growth of the hospice movement allows for dying to be acknowledged and discussed in many cases, a practice which has generally been frowned upon in many hospitals:

It is not uncommon for hospice in-patients to be unaware that they are dying at the time of their first admission. For relatives and hospice staff admission is a clear signal that death is imminent and that now is the time to talk about their prognosis to the person who is dying.

(Field and James, in Taylor and Field, 1993, p. 160)

Kübler-Ross (1970) and Glaser and Strauss (1965) examined how social situations affected the awareness of, and communications with, dying patients. The greater number of people being cared for in the community, and in the hospice movement, may now allow people to speak more freely about dying in a demedicalized context. This could mean that death is no longer a 'taboo' subject in our society. It might also be part of the greater openness between health professionals and the patients (or clients) with whom they deal.

Personal responsibilities for health and illness

In conclusion, we can see that health and illness in particular, and our bodies in general, are key aspects of contemporary sociology. This way of looking at health mirrors the changes in the relationship between the state and the individual that are taking place throughout society.

This change of view is demonstrated in the new 'contract for health' (see page 464) which was defined by the New Labour government in 1998, which suggests that individuals need to take more responsibility for much of their own health along with support from local and national institutions. This new contract expects a far higher level of knowledge and involvement from the individual. This move from the social (responsibility of the state) to the individual (personal responsibility) is found in many other aspects of society and much contemporary sociological study.

Further reading

Both of the following books provide concise and accessible introductions to the sociology of health:

- Aggleton, P. (1990) *Health*, London: Routledge.
- Trowler, P. (1996) *Investigating Health, Welfare and Poverty*, 2nd edn, London: Collins Educational.

More details and some contemporary updates can be found in:

- Doyal, L. (1995) *What Makes Women Sick: Gender and the Political Economy of Health*, Basingstoke: Macmillan.
- Gabe, J., Calnan, M. and Bury, M. (eds.) (1991) *The Sociology of the Health Service*, London: Routledge.
- Senior, M. and Viveash, B. (1997) *Health and Illness*, London: Macmillan.
- Taylor, S. and Field, D. (eds.) (1997) *The Sociology of Health and Health Care*, 2nd edn, Oxford: Blackwell.

Back issues of the periodical *Sociology Review* (formerly *Social Studies Review*) also contain many articles on this field of sociology and many others.

Power and control
Popular culture

13.1 Defining culture

Defining some key terms in the study of culture

Culture can have a number of meanings for sociologists (as the section below on defining culture and assessing quality shows). There are two main approaches. A broad definition would see culture as meaning a whole way of life. The second approach is much narrower and is based around notions of refined behaviour and being aware of and valuing what are seen as key cultural achievements. This second definition would see some aspects of a society's way of life as being 'uncultured'.

This difference reflects very different notions of how we should consider culture. It is certainly the case that debates about culture in sociology have focused around the issue of whether culture should be defined in terms of the highest achievements of humanity in various fields or, instead, on whether it should be based around notions of what is seen as the most popular. It is in essence this debate that leads us into the concepts of :

- high culture
- folk culture
- mass culture
- popular culture.

We will now proceed to offer a definition of each of these and provide a few examples to help you get a grip on these concepts.

High culture

This term is used to refer to cultural and artistic products seen to have very high status. What is considered cultured in this sense is based on those cultural products that represent the highest achievements of humanity. Key examples of these types of cultural products in UK society include the plays of William Shakespeare, classical music, such as Beethoven symphonies, operas by Verdi, classic ballet and art by the great painters: the Mona Lisa by Leonardo da Vinci, for example.

Folk culture

This term is used to refer to the craft skills of 'ordinary' people which developed in the past and which survive to this day in some form. It is seen as genuine and authentic outpourings of creativity. Although worthy of respect it tends to be seen as being less accomplished than high culture. Key examples of this type of culture include folk songs and rural crafts, such as basket weaving, traditional woodworking, traditional recipes, etc.

Mass culture

The term mass culture is always used in relation to something that is disliked. It is a term used by both conservative critics of modern industrial society and by Marxist writers in the Frankfurt School tradition. What they have is common is a belief that much of contemporary culture is manufactured, artificial, plastic, two-dimensional and mass produced rather than reflecting any genuine craft skill or cultural creativity. The key distinction between folk culture and mass culture is really about the distinction between production and consumption. Folk culture was based around producing things using craft skills, whereas mass culture is about the purchase and consumption of cultural products.

Key examples of what might be seen by some as embodying mass culture today could include Sky Sport, soap operas, Hollywood blockbusters, magazines like *FHM* or *Hello*, Coca Cola, TV gameshows, etc.

Popular culture

The type of cultural products talked about as examples of mass culture will, by and large, also serve as examples of popular culture. This points to the fact that the distinction between mass and popular culture is not based on distinctions between different products, but instead distinctions between different ways of looking at the same products. In simple terms, mass culture is a negative term used in relation to something you do not like, while the term popular culture is used in a positive sense to refer to things you feel have a positive quality about them.

Most usage of the term today derives from the neo-Marxist work of the Centre for Contemporary Cultural Studies, which argues that popular culture can be used in a positive and constructive way in contrast to the clear implication of theories of mass culture which suggest that contemporary culture makes us all into unthinking 'couch potatoes'. The term 'popular culture' is also often used by those post-modern writers who argue that the attempt to distinguish between the trivial, shallow entities of contemporary culture and the deep, significant, authentic and meaningful entities of high culture is a mistake. Such writers claim that today everything lacks depth and meaning is really just a matter of opinion, or a power-struggle.

The concepts of high culture and folk culture therefore refer back to a past age and reflect an élite way of looking at society. The élite knew best (in this view) and the proof of this was their ability to talk about and appreciate the best things in life, namely high culture. The peasants, the ordinary people, did not understand this and therefore were in no position to engage in debates about how society should be run or the nature of humanity. However, they still possessed some concept of creativity and developed craft skills through the mastery of the tools they used in their work. This culture was less sophisticated (in the eyes of those with high culture) but was nonetheless an authentic form of creativity.

The suggestion is that both of these forms of culture no longer really exist today and the emergence of industrial production has impacted on the cultural sphere as well making us all into passive consumers of material produced by multi-national capitalism. The term mass culture refers to the way everyone is dealt up the same diet of unoriginal dreary material. The idea is that mass culture is based on entertainment and escapism and not on encouraging thought, since otherwise people might begin to think about the horrible nature of the society they live in and how they need to do something about it.

Theories of mass culture therefore portray most people as totally passive in the face of cultural commodity production. In its Marxist form this is best exemplified by the Frankfurt School and the idea of the 'dominant ideology'.

The concept of popular culture also derives from a Marxist theoretician, the neo-Marxist writer Antonio Gramsci. Gramsci argued that in order for socialism to succeed, it was necessary to intellectually and culturally convince people that it provided a better way of life. This would include engaging in the struggle on a cultural level. Since social change required the agreement of the majority of the population, socialists should aim to make use of popular cultural products and use them to provide notions of a better life. The Italian Communist Party organised operas in this vein.

The idea of popular culture also suggests that we do not passively accept the meaning of anything as suggested by proponents of mass culture, but instead we can be creative and active in its consumption and as a result popular commercial cultural icons can be turned round to make some form of comment on society. Music and dance are probably the area where notions of popular culture have had most effect, but they clearly can also be seen in relation to TV and film.

Defining culture and assessing quality

Raymond Williams (1961), in an important early study of the development of modern culture, identifies three different approaches, each of which defines culture in a distinct way. These approaches are:

- the 'ideal'
- the 'documentary'
- 'social definition'.

The 'ideal'

The first definition is termed by Williams the 'ideal'. Writers employing this definition assume that culture is a 'state or process of human perfection' (1961, p. 57). Only the very best in intellectual and artistic endeavour would be included as examples: the greatest literature, most moving opera and drama, most skilfully constructed poetry, most beautiful painting, and so on – in other words, what is often termed *high culture* rather than *popular culture*.

The study of culture, according to this approach, involves the application of universally agreed criteria or rules (which apply at all times across all societies) for assessing the quality of particular examples. It is assumed that it is possible to apply universal rules for separating the 'good' from 'bad' because human experience – the range of human emotions – is also universal and great art successfully describes the 'truth' of this human condition.

With its insistence on including only the very 'best' in human creative endeavour, the ideal definition can be regarded as narrow. It is assumed, for example, that only a small minority of creative artists or intellectuals actually make culture. This is an important point: Williams argues that such narrow definitions of culture were 'selective' in the sense that they served to exclude large numbers of people and secured a privileged position only for those with the 'instincts' or 'skills' to appreciate fine artistic or intellectual work.

The 'documentary'

A second way of defining culture is termed by Williams the 'documentary' approach (1961, p. 57). This is a slightly broader definition which considers not just artistic or intellectual products which satisfy the criterion of near-perfection, but all those works which represent 'the body of intellectual and imaginative work' a society has produced. In other words, writers employing the 'documentary' definition consider not only the very best in art and intellectual activity, but all examples which represent or 'document' the 'culture' of a society.

Recently the British government, in its approach to the school curriculum, has appeared to embrace this kind of approach, with policies encouraging a concentration on 'English' literature and 'English' history. Ministers have argued that all school pupils should have an appreciation of their English heritage in terms of art and history. (This issue is discussed in more detail in Section 11.6)

This definition is slightly broader but the focus remains on art and intellectual work, created again by a minority of artists and intellectuals within particular societies.

Williams argues that frequently, even with this definition, there remains an assumption that universal aesthetic or intellectual criteria can be applied in order to assess what counts as 'culture'. Shakespeare *is* counted as culture but the television show *Blind Date* is not.

'Social definition'

Williams identifies a third approach as the 'social definition' (1961, p. 57). Whereas the first two approaches are most closely associated with traditional teaching in art and English as academic disciplines, this approach owes its origins to early anthropology and sociology. Although an English academic by profession, Williams himself, together with Richard Hoggart, can be credited with developing the argument for embracing this much wider definition of culture. Williams argues that the term 'culture' can also be taken to mean 'a particular way of life' and that the study of culture could also include:

... certain meanings and values not only in art and learning but also in institutions and ordinary behaviour. [It] will also include analysis of elements in the way of life that to followers of the other definitions are not 'culture' at all.

(Williams, 1961, p. 57)

In other words, culture could be understood as:

... a whole way of life, material, intellectual and spiritual.

(Williams, 1963, p. 16)

This is a much broader definition. Not only artists and intellectuals but all members of society are engaged in the process of making culture, on a daily basis, as part of their ordinary lives. Culture is no longer understood as 'separate' from ordinary people: it is something made and consumed by everyone – in local communities, on local streets, inside families and pubs, as well as in opera houses and 'serious' theatres.

Taking popular culture seriously

This radical break with previous definitions allowed researchers and academics to begin to take popular culture seriously, and for cultural studies to evolve as a discipline in the 1960s. However, there is an important implication regarding the assessment of the quality of culture. If 'culture' is part of ordinary life and all are involved in its production, is it still possible to distinguish between the 'good' and the 'bad'? The implication appears to be that all cultural work, irrespective of its worth, has to be treated with the same degree of critical respect.

- The first two definitions above assume that there exist *universal* and *absolute* criteria for assessing the value of a cultural product. These criteria are timeless and unchanging.
- The 'social' definition, on the other hand, seems to imply a *relative*, rather than absolute, approach. Cultural standards are understood as being relative to particular societies at particular times.

 Discussion point

a To what extent do you think it is possible to make objective judgements about the quality of cultural products?

b Is it important to distinguish between 'good' and 'bad' television, books, films, etc., or should we simply allow consumers to make their own choices without imposing any concept of 'cultural standards'?

c Recently, several classical musicians have been angered because their recordings of 'lighter' musical pieces (for example, songs taken from Hollywood musicals) have been banned from the United States' classical record chart. This implies the imposition of an absolute judgement. What do you think? What *is* the difference between pop/rock and classical music?

C3.1a

It is interesting to note that neither Williams nor Hoggart were entirely comfortable with relativistic approaches. Although each writer wished to broaden and democratize the study of culture, neither wished to abandon entirely the insistence on 'standards' and 'quality'. Indeed, Richard Hoggart continues to campaign actively against the influence of relativism in contemporary cultural discussion (Hoggart, 1996).

Urbanization, modernity and 'mass society'

The modern world – the era of modernity – emerged through the rise of the Industrial Revolution, the spread of urbanization, and the growth of capitalist markets. This happened in the second half of the eighteenth century and throughout the nineteenth century.

With urbanization came the creation of large aggregates of people – *the masses*. Concerns about the instability and irrationality of the masses, their propensity for disorder and unruly behaviour, and the associated problem of how to 'civilize' or integrate them socially, is a preoccupation to be found in the sociological work of Tönnies and Durkheim and in the writings of nineteenth-century philosophers and cultural critics, such as the philosopher John Stuart Mill (1806–73) and the author Matthew Arnold (1822–73).

Civilizing culture and the danger of the masses

The thinking of Mill and Arnold has to be placed in the context of the debate over whether or not to extend the political franchise to working-class men in the 1870s. In principle, Mill supported the concept of democracy, but he wondered whether the masses would use the right to vote in a responsible way. Mill pictured the masses as a large aggregation of isolated and anomic individuals, no longer regulated by the close-knit ties of the rural community. Without the social controls of the pre-industrial rural community, isolated urban individuals could be swayed or manipulated by skilful orators, music hall, or the other mass media of the day. Mill was cautiously optimistic that a programme of universal education could 'civilize' the masses through the elevation of their cultural standards. Only then could they be relied on to use political rights responsibly.

Matthew Arnold made the link between 'high culture' and civilization even more explicit. In *Culture and Anarchy*, he defined culture as 'the study of perfection', or:

... the best that has been thought and said in the world.

(Quoted in Billington *et al.*, 1991, p. 8 and Storey, 1993, p. 21)

He regarded as anarchic the habits and pastimes, or culture, of the urban working-class masses – not only without cultural worth but actually dangerous because they often degenerated into social disorder. Arnold, like Mill, believed that the urban masses – who he described as:

vast miserable, unmanageable ... raw and uncultivated

– posed a potential threat to the stability of society, particularly after the Second Reform Act of 1867, which extended the electoral franchise. The only hope was to use cultural education as a civilizing force

to minister to the diseased spirit of our time.

(Quoted in Storey, 1993, p. 22; orig. pub. 1868)

Both Mill and Arnold can be said to belong to the tradition of 'mass society' theorists because they assume that society is divided between an educated and cultured élite, on the one hand, and the uncultured masses on the other. Both also picture the masses as unsophisticated, easily swayed and vulnerable to political and commercial manipulation.

Mass culture and folk culture

If anything, some cultural critics and intellectuals grew even more pessimistic about the condition of the 'masses' in the twentieth century.

T. S. Eliot

In a famous essay, 'Notes towards a definition of culture' published in 1948, the poet and literary critic T. S. Eliot argues that culture is inevitably stratified, with each social class in society making a distinctive cultural contribution; but he implies that the more sophisticated cultures are developed by the higher social classes.

Eliot appears to mourn the loss of the folk cultures, rich in tradition and custom, which were associated with the era of rural and craft production. Folk cultures served an important function in integrating communities. Now both the 'Englishness' of the higher classes, and the 'folk culture' of lower classes, were in danger of being washed away by the spread of cheap, commercial or mass culture.

F. R. Leavis and Q. D. Leavis

The arguments of two literary critics, F. R. Leavis and Q. D. Leavis, who wrote respectively *Mass Civilisation and Minority Culture* (1930) and *Fiction and the Reading Public* (1932), develop these themes in even bolder terms. According to them, only a small educated cultural élite are capable of understanding and profiting from the descriptions of the human experience contained in great works of art and culture. Only this small cultured élite can pass on this precious inheritance to the next generation, but their position and authority is threatened by the spread of commercial 'mass culture', which panders to the lowest common denominator and undermines cultural standards.

Whilst folk songs and dances, the customs and traditions associated with the rural past, helped to cement social bonds and maintain social integration, the products of mass culture – popular fiction, detective stories, cinema, modern popular music – all debased or coarsened human experience and destabilized the social order.

1940s and 1950s America

In the 1940s and 1950s, the mass society debate developed further in the USA. Given the size of the United States, the power of American capitalism, and the success of Hollywood and other forms of American popular culture, this was inevitable. An important collection of articles, *Mass Culture: The Popular Arts in America* (Rosenberg and Manning White, 1957), set the terms of the debate. Supporters of the mass society thesis made the following kind of arguments:

Folk culture grew from below. It was a spontaneous ... expression of the people, shaped by themselves ... to suit their own needs. Mass culture is imposed from above. It is fabricated by technicians hired by businessmen; its audiences are passive consumers, their participation limited to the choice between buying or not buying ... it is a debased, trivial culture that voids both the deep realities (sex, death, failure, tragedy) and also the simple, spontaneous pleasures.

(MacDonald, 1957, pp. 60 and 73)

The Frankfurt School and mass culture

Whereas the ideas of Arnold, Eliot and the Leavis's can be located within a broadly conservative tradition, the Frankfurt School developed a Marxist analysis of mass culture. The thinking of the Frankfurt School in relation to the role of the mass media is described in more detail in Section 6.7.

The leading writers of the School, including Adorno, Horkheimer and Marcuse, were all clearly influenced not only by their experiences as left-wing intellectuals witnessing, at first hand,

the triumph of Nazism in the 1930s, but also as Marxist immigrants to the USA in the 1940s and 1950s, where advertising and the commercial exploitation of popular culture were most visible and pervasive.

The shallowness and meaninglessness of popular culture

In books like *One Dimensional Man* (Marcuse, 1964) and *The Culture Industry* (Adorno, 1991), a rather pessimistic view emerges of capitalist societies in which the working class has lost its capacity to think critically or to resist its exploitation. The drive of capitalism to make profit produces a form of popular culture which is shallow and meaningless because it is produced to a formula. They refer to:

The assembly line character of the culture industry, the synthetic, planned method of turning out its products (factory like not only in the studio but ... in the compilation of cheap biographies, pseudo-documentary novels, and hit songs).

(Adorno and Horkheimer, 1977, p. 381)

Mass culture and social control

Capitalist culture industries create mass culture. However, unlike earlier mass society theorists, the Frankfurt School did not believe that such a situation reflected the cultural or intellectual inadequacies of ordinary people, but rather the power of advertising and the mass media to shape our consciousness (Strinati, 1995, p. 62).

Mass culture simultaneously helped to stimulate economic demand and maintain social control. The masses were encouraged to develop an appetite for commodities and entertainments – to crave 'false needs' – and the partial satisfaction of these 'false needs' through shopping and mass entertainment fostered docility and an absence of critical thought. In capitalist societies, we become 'one dimensional' people, lacking a culture through which we can express real emotion or feelings, merely the synthetic pleasures derived from the cinema screen and television set.

The function of popular culture

As a response to the pessimism of the mass culture thesis and the Frankfurt School, some writers influenced by functionalism developed a more positive appraisal of the role of popular culture in industrial societies.

Shils (1961) argues that the growing volume

of popular culture (more magazines, the spread of television, the boom in popular music, etc.) does not represent simply more opportunities for commercial exploitation. On the contrary, it proves that the cultural interests of everyone could be catered for in western societies. Popular culture functions in a unifying way, helping to 'incorporate ... the mass of the population into society' (1961, p. 1).

Activity

a What is meant by the terms 'mass culture' and 'folk culture'?

b Why were the theorists of mass culture pessimistic about the future?

c What criticisms can be made of the arguments made by mass society and Frankfurt theorists?

C3.2, C3.3

Global culture

In the late twentieth and early twenty-first centuries, communication and travel have become globalized with links spreading around the world. Some commentators believe that this will generate a global culture as powerful transnational corporations like Coca Cola, McDonalds and Hollywood film companies export their 'culture' around the world. With greater travel and communications between countries we are beginning to share language, customs and even money (many credit cards, for example, can be used in dozens of countries and English can be used to get by in most parts of the world). But at the same time local or regional culture also seems to be becoming more important. Some commentators believe that local resistance to globalization will stop a fully global culture emerging (see Section 15.2).

13.2 Theoretical approaches to the construction and consumption of culture and identity

Some of the fundamental debates within sociology confront us when we explore the range of theoretical writing on culture and identity. As the main theoretical approaches are described below, remember that each one has something to contribute to the following debates.

Marxism and neo-Marxism

Marx and culture

Where do cultural ideas come from? Marx believed that almost everyone had some kind of creative potential within themselves. However, he also believed that we are never entirely free to express our cultural creativity without being influenced by some important constraints. He argued:

Men make their own history but they do not make it directly as they please; they do not make it under circumstances chosen by themselves, but under circumstances directly encountered, given, and transmitted from the past.

(Marx, 1969, p. 360; orig. pub. 1852)

In other words, we do have the capacity to develop new ideas and new cultural approaches and we can use these to make new arrangements or new 'history'; but we have to do this within real, material constraints. These constraints are the social arrangements we always inherit from previous generations. The decisions and actions of one generation will partly set the conditions within which a new generation will have to work.

Human labour and culture

Implicit in Marx's writing is a particular view of human beings and their potential. Although under capitalism work may be an unpleasant experience for many, we are not naturally lazy or reluctant to engage in labour. Quite the contrary, human beings become social through their experience of work and the co-operative relationships involved in making and producing things (see also Section 17.2).

So, according to Marx, the experience of labour is crucial to the development of culture. Language, customs, traditions, and even our sense of ourselves as individuals, are all intimately bound up with the shared experience of human labour. Whereas for Parsons self-identity is forged through the internalization of cultural symbols, or socialization, for Marx the individual develops identity through the experience of labour and relationships in the workplace. The problem, of course, is that under capitalism this is an alienating and frustrating experience.

Discussion point

To what extent do you agree that your individual identity is bound up with the experience of human labour? Have things in this respect changed since Marx's era, or not?

C3.1a

Marx on ideology, culture and power

Marx argued that, because in capitalist societies ruling classes typically own and control the means of mental and cultural production (newspapers, publishing houses, theatres, museums, even music halls), it is likely that ideas and cultural activities reflecting *their* interests and tastes will circulate more speedily around society. Subordinate classes may generate their own alternative and critical ideas, but they will experience greater difficulty in circulating these.

Given the limited circulation of critical or oppositional ideas, subsequent Marxists have suggested that 'the ruling ideas' do, in fact, permeate the consciousness of working-class and other subordinate groups.

Criticism of Marx's approach

One of the most important criticisms levelled at Marx's approach to the analysis of culture is that it is flawed by an 'economic reductionism'.

Some interpretations of his work appear to imply that cultural phenomena, however complex, can be 'explained' simply by referring to the economic processes at work. The criticism is that not all, if any, patterns of social and cultural behaviour can be reduced to matters of economics. There can be many reasons why a film director may wish to produce a particular film, or a writer publish a novel, and there may be an even wider number of reasons why audiences enjoy a particular film or a particular book.

In other places Marx does reject economic reductionism and seems to acknowledge a more complex interplay between social, cultural and economic processes. Theories of hegemony and the work of Antonio Gramsci represent an attempt to save twentieth-century Marxism from the charge of over-simplistic economic reductionism. Further criticisms of Marxist approaches will be considered below.

Activity

a According to Marx, what influences the way in which we produce new cultural ideas?

b According to Marx, why is the experience of work so important to us?

c In Marxist theory, how does a ruling capitalist class exercise control over culture and ideas?

d Explain in your own words the main criticisms levelled at Marx's approach to culture and identity.

C3.2, C3.3

Gramsci and culturalism: theories of hegemony

Hegemony, the ruling class and culture

Theories of hegemony (often referred to as culturalism) take as their starting point the emphasis Marx placed on the capacity of social groups or classes to create culture actively through engagement with the material world, including subordinate as well as ruling classes.

Gramsci, writing from a fascist prison cell in the 1930s, starts by asking why socialist revolutions failed in Germany and Italy after the end of World War I, despite the fact that most of the 'objective conditions' specified by Marx for working-class revolution were present in both countries. The answer, Gramsci argued, had to lie at the level of ideas and culture. Although the economic and political conditions were in place, socialist parties had failed to win the battle of ideas.

Gramsci concluded that the development of class consciousness was never an automatic process simply triggered by the 'right' economic conditions. Rather, the dominant or ruling class in society would engage in a continual struggle to secure support for ideas which actually legitimated its interests. To the extent that it was successful in making its ideas appear like 'common sense', it had secured a hegemonic position. Hegemony occurs when competing ideologies:

... come into confrontation and conflict, until one of them ... tends to prevail, to gain the upper hand, to propagate itself throughout society – bringing about not only a union of economic and political aims, but also intellectual and moral unity.

(Gramsci, 1971, p. 181)

Working-class intellectuals and counter-hegemony

Normally, in a capitalist society the ideas and ideology of the capitalist class would secure hegemony, but it was the task of working-class intellectuals and organizations to try to counter these ideas with alternative perspectives, said Gramsci. Whereas some Marxists seem to imply that ideological indoctrination is a finite process – individuals are indoctrinated once and for all – Gramsci suggests that there is a continual struggle through key cultural institutions in which the dominant class seeks to establish its perspectives as 'common sense' and subordinate classes may more or less resist this. Thus, a capitalist ruling class can never take its hegemony for granted; it has to engage in an active effort to secure and preserve it on a daily basis.

Gramscian Marxism: the Centre for Contemporary Cultural Studies

Interpreting culture as the product of struggles or conflicts between social groups has proved enormously attractive to some neo-Marxists. The Centre for Contemporary Cultural Studies (CCCS) at Birmingham University applied Gramsci's ideas in an attempt to interpret working-class youth subcultures as embryonic class struggles (see Sections 4.4 and 8.2).

Other researchers, extending the idea of social conflict to include the dimensions of ethnicity and gender as well as social class, grew interested in the ways consumers and media audiences might 'resist' the dominant or 'preferred' hegemonic message and, instead, decode or interpret media messages in subversive ways which challenged the perspectives of the powerful (Fiske, 1989a,b; see Section 6.1).

Evaluating Gramscian Marxism

A strength of the culturalist approach is that it reminds us that consumers and audiences are active and less vulnerable to manipulation than is sometimes supposed. However, critics argue that it can go too far in over-estimating the extent to which social groups can 'resist', and for presenting a 'cultural populism' which is little different from the free-market views of the New Right (McGuigan, 1992). The debate over cultural populism is considered further in Section 13.6.

The political-economy approach

The political-economy approach insists that the starting point for a neo-Marxist analysis of culture must lie with the process of cultural production. It must consider:

- the interests of the companies and corporations involved in the cultural industries
- the implications of producing culture through market mechanisms.

If these issues are not explored first, argue political-economy theorists, then it is easy to overlook the important ways in which structures of power shape and limit the ways in which audiences or consumers get access to cultural products.

The structural limits to consumerism

Two leading political-economy theorists, Golding and Murdock (1991), suggest that unless the analysis starts with these issues, the impression is given that consumers are sovereign, freely expressing their cultural wishes in the marketplace. They argue that consumers may consume in different ways but always within limits determined by the structure and working of the capitalist cultural industries.

The evidence on which the political-economy approach bases its argument is discussed further in Section 13.3.

Criticisms of the political-economy approach

Neo-Marxists who draw on hegemony theory are sometimes critical of the political-economy approach, suggesting that – like orthodox Marxism – it suffers from an 'economic reductionism' which over-simplifies and reduces complex cultural patterns to crude economics (Strinati, 1995). The ideas that influence writers, artists, producers or directors originate from a variety of sources, not simply the need to satisfy the 'bottom line'.

Similarly, a political-economy approach, the critics argue, tells us little about the creative and sometimes subversive 'pleasures' consumers and audiences can derive from the culture produced by capitalism.

In their defence, researchers using a political-economy approach acknowledge that consumers are not merely manipulated by the corporations of the cultural industries. Nevertheless, as Golding and Murdock argue:

Consumption practices are clearly not completely manipulated by the strategies of cultural industries, but they are, equally clearly, not completly independent of them.

(Golding and Murdock, 1991, p. 30)

📝 Activity

a According to Gramsci, why had communist revolutions not succeeded in Italy and Germany after World War I?

b What does Gramsci mean by the term 'hegemony' and why can a ruling class never take its hegemonic position for granted?

c What are the main starting points for a political-economy approach?

d Explain in your own words why political-economy theorists do not believe that consumers make entirely free choices in the cultural market place.

e Explain in your own words the main differences between neo-Marxist hegemony theorists and political-economy theorists.

C3.2, C3.3

Feminism

There is not just one tradition of feminist theory but, in fact, several. The most important for the purposes of studying the relationship between culture, identity and society are liberal feminism, radical feminism and neo-Marxist culturalist feminism.

What all feminisms share is, first, the view that popular culture has played an important part in the subordination of women to the interests of men; and secondly that, in failing to identify this fact as a central theme for research and analysis, other theoretical approaches to the study of popular culture contribute to this subordination. For example, many feminist critics have pointed to the way in which popular culture has, at least in the past, strongly associated femininity with the sphere of consumption ('shopping'), non-work and domesticity. Beyond this, however, there are important differences between the main feminist approaches.

Liberal feminism

Liberal feminists point to the importance of popular culture in reflecting the main sexist or 'malestream' values of society, and in reproducing traditional sex role stereotypes. Such stereotypes, particularly in advertising, magazine publishing and television, encourage girls to lower their expectations and to regard male dominance of work and public life as 'normal'. Frequently, liberal feminists used quantitative content analysis (see Section 6.1) to establish the prevalence of masculine images or stereotyped female images in advertising and the mass media (for example, Gaye Tuchman, 1981).

Liberal feminists advocate campaigns to promote women into senior positions within television, advertising, journalism, and so on. They do not believe that either the dominant ideology or the structural arrangements in society make this impossible. Much can be done 'within the system'. Once this happens, the powerful messages helping to construct female identities will change and girls will begin to feel themselves more 'empowered' by popular cultural imagery.

Radical feminism

In contrast, radical feminists argue that the ideology of patriarchy is so all-pervasive that it is unlikely that simply securing more senior positions for women in cultural industries would make much difference. This is because the ideology of patriarchy is related, on the one hand, to deep-seated biological and psychological characteristics in men, and on the other hand to the commercial drives of the culture industries.

Radical feminists point, for example, to the phenomenon of the 'male gaze' (see Section 13.6) to be found in film, television, magazines and even newspapers. Men have a voyeuristic inclination to enjoy the representation of women as 'objects', and the cultural industries – whether controlled by men or by women – will exploit this for profit.

Neo-Marxist culturalist feminism

More recently, feminists drawing ideas from the neo-Marxist culturalist tradition have focused attention on the female audience. Culturalist feminists follow Gramsci in searching for evidence of conflict at the level of ideas within capitalist societies. They believe that such conflicts will flow not only along the dimension of class but also that of gender.

Researchers such as Geraghty (1991), Hobson (1989) and Ang (1985), using audience ethnography, have described ways in which female audiences can derive pleasure, sometimes subversive, from soap operas and programmes which appear at first glance to reinforce sex role stereotypes.

Activity

Explain in your own words the main differences between the three main types of feminist approach to the study of culture and identity.

C3.2, C3.3

Weberian sociology and symbolic interactionism

This section will confine itself to drawing attention to the ways in which some of the 'classic' Weberian and interactionist work can be used to explore themes of culture and identity.

Weber and culture

In *The Protestant Ethic and the Spirit of Capitalism* (1930; orig. pub. 1905) and his other writings on world religions, Weber traces the interplay between economic forces and religion, as a set of cultural ideas. Unlike some Marxists who have argued that protestantism represented an ideology which legitimated and helped to reproduce capitalism, Weber argues that the cultural ideas associated with religion had a force and logic of their own; they contributed significantly to social change and did not merely 'reflect' underlying economic developments or the ideology of a capitalist class.

The rising capitalist entrepreneurs of the seventeenth century, for example, were motivated to develop and expand capitalist trading relations, partly through a desire to organize business in a rational way, and partly because their salvationist beliefs led them to find signs of salvation in business success.

Symbolic interactionism

Symbolic interactionists are less inclined than Weber to emphasize the *permanence* of the social structures which emerge as individuals act on the cultural definitions or meanings which guide them. Instead, they tend to describe a more *fluid* process in which social actors interact to construct cultural arrangements – but the emphasis is on the ways in which such cultural arrangements can change, depending on the nature of particular patterns of interaction. Culture is generated, then, through social interaction and the exchange of meanings or interpretations.

Mead: the 'I' and the 'Me'.

Drawing on the writing of George Herbert Mead and John Dewey, symbolic interactionists have spent a considerable amount of time exploring the relationship between culture, social interaction and identity. Mead's division of the human mind between the 'I' and the 'Me' emphasizes the importance of social interaction with others in the construction of identity (the 'I' monitoring the response of others to the impression 'Me' gives when performing a social role).

Symbolic interactionism is committed to charting the ways in which identity can change as patterns of interaction change and individuals are exposed to new cultural environments. Social identity is not fixed or permanent but fluid, changeable and dynamic.

Becker's 'classic' study of dance or jazz subcultures and marihuana use in the 1950s illustrates this very well. Individuals may come to see themselves as 'part' of the dance subculture and, perhaps, as 'marihuana users' – but this depends on how much they interact with other members of the subculture and the nature of the symbolic meanings that are exchanged (Becker, 1973).

Sociologists who believe that the structure of society shapes a great deal of our lives and places limits on the choices we can make (functionalist and Marxist approaches tend to share these assumptions) argue that the account of cultural behaviour the interactionists provide is incomplete unless there is also a consideration of how structure, power and history impact on and limit the development of culture and identity.

In turn, interactionists point to the lack of attention in structural sociology to the importance of the processes through which identity is constructed through small-scale, everyday interactions between social actors. For example, contemporary urban dance music could be understood as the product of hundreds of small-scale interactions between clubbers, DJs and those involved in particular clubs or events. It may not be shaped by any larger sociological structure such as social class (see Section 13.4).

Foucault and discourse theory

Knowledge, language and culture

In recent years the writing of Foucault has been very influential amongst sociologists trying to understand culture and identity. Foucault is interested in the ways in which knowledge, language and culture operate in society.

Foucault did not believe that social relationships were as stable as earlier sociologists had assumed. Earlier sociologists had tended to picture social class relations, for example, as more or less permanent 'things' which existed 'out there' in the social world. Foucault, in contrast, understands social relationships as much less permanent or stable and influenced very strongly by patterns of language or discourse which he believes organize the ways in which we relate to each other.

The vocabularies or discourses used to describe sexualities have a very profound affect upon the way in which we interact. 'Male', 'female', 'gay' and 'straight' are terms that organize the way in which we approach each other, although they are not entirely stable and change over time. It is now possible, for example, for senior politicians to declare their homosexuality without automatically wrecking their careers.

Power, culture and identity

Foucault seeks to develop an approach to power which departs from the conventional perspectives found in sociology, and this has considerable bearing on his analysis of culture.

Foucault does not believe that power is something owned or possessed by a ruling élite, class or bureaucracy (in contrast to Marxist and Weberian approaches). He rejects the idea that power is always concentrated in central institutions such as the state, financial institutions or large corporations. Neither does he think that power can be analysed through the conscious plans or intentions of powerful individuals (Smart, 1985, pp. 77–8).

Rather, Foucault develops a new approach to the relationship between power and culture. Power is 'relational'; it works through discourse or systems of language and knowledge. Every kind of knowledge brings with it particular power relationships. Thus, for example, the discourse of western medicine implies a particular power relationship between doctors and patients. Students and staff working within contemporary British education institutions have had to become familiar with the discourse of modern business and the power relations associated with it. Thus, talk within educational institutions is now frequently of 'business plans', 'mission statements', 'quality control' and 'marketing', and with this new discourse or 'power–knowledge relation' new patterns of control are established.

Power–knowledge

For Foucault – in contrast to structural sociology – power has to be explored at the micro (or small-scale) level through the various ways in which 'power–knowledge' relations distribute power in varied and specific ways. Foucault does not believe that social actors are always subordinated to dominant structures in society. On the contrary, although 'power–knowledge' relations express power and may coerce, they also generate resistance.

In other words, power can activate responses amongst those it is constraining – prisoners organize 'prison protests'; the inmates of asylums challenge the dominant discourses of psychiatry; and staff and students in a university may find ways to subvert the 'business plan' or satirize the 'mission statement'.

Discources, culture and identity

What does this all mean for the study of culture? Whereas both Marxists and Weberians place most emphasis on tracing interconnections between cultural power and economic structures, for Foucault power exists within culture but in terms of a huge variety of different 'power–knowledge' relations. Culture is shaped not merely by social class or the workings of the state but by lots of different 'power–knowledge relations', or discourses.

Foucault argues that we all find ourselves enmeshed in a complex web of different discourses, each offering particular ways of understanding aspects of our behaviour. Thus, there are discourses which offer ways of understanding our sexuality; there are discourses which offer ways of understanding the way we feel about ourselves as employees, people with ethnic identities, men or women, family members, as hospital users or benefit claimants, even as DIY enthusiasts. Culture is created through the complex web of discourses or 'power–knowledge' relations which are created in society *and* the distinct resistances which each discourse may activate amongst social groups and individuals.

To take the first example, there is now a flourishing lesbian and gay culture which has arisen partly through resistance to dominant discourses which 'normalize' heterosexuality and marginalize other forms of sexuality (Foucault, 1979a). (See also Section 14.1.)

Foucault argues that our sense of self-identity actually comes from the way in which we are positioned in relation to particular forms of knowledge or discourses:

... certain gestures, certain discourses, certain desires come to be identified and constituted as individuals.

(Foucault, 1979a, p. 98)

According to Foucault, one outcome of the spread of 'power–knowledge' relations is the constitution of 'the subject'. In other words, we get our sense of self-identity from the 'power–knowledge' relations within which we operate. For example, discourses about sexuality offer a series of important concepts with which individuals 'position' (or think through) their own sexual identities (Foucault, 1979a). We use the words, phrases and vocabularies of sexuality to actually think about ourselves as sexual subjects. Equally, we use words, phrases and vocabularies of locality, region and nation, to think about ourselves as 'British', 'Scottish', 'a Geordie' or 'a North Londoner'.

Criticisms of Foucault and post-structuralism

Critics of Foucault often argue that the main assumptions of 'modernist' sociology should not be abandoned. They insist that it is still possible to use sociological concepts to move towards a more or less objective understanding of the underlying reality of society.

Poulantzas, for example, a Marxist, argues that post-structuralism ignores the importance of *sources* of power, which he insists are still to be traced to key structures in society such as the organization of capital. In particular, Poulantzas argues that Foucault under-estimates the importance of the state in modern societies: although a variety of political struggles may occur, ultimately power is still concentrated in the institutions of the state, and the state in turn still generally reflects the interests of capital.

Similarly, some feminists are worried by the implication that we should abandon the attempt to analyse the 'truth' of exploitation and patriarchy. While feminists welcome the opportunities Foucault's work suggests for analysing discourses involving gender struggles, there is a reluctance to abandon the assumption that feminist research deals with the 'real' concepts of 'justice' and 'equality' and the 'real' impact social structures have on women's and mens' lives (Hartsock, 1990).

Activity

a According to Gramsci, why had communist revolutions not succeeded in Italy and Germany after World War I?

b What does Gramsci mean by the term 'hegemony' and why can a ruling class never take its hegemonic position for granted?

c What are the main starting points for a political-economy approach?

d Explain in your own words why political-economy theorists do not believe that consumers make entirely free choices in the cultural market place.

e Explain in your own words the main differences between neo-Marxist hegemony theorists and political-economy theorists.

 C3.2, C3.3

13.3 The political economy of culture

Researchers using a political-economy approach, such as Golding and Murdock (1991), insist that before exploring the varied ways in which we consume commodities and construct cultural identities, we should not overlook the capacity of capitalist enterprises to shape the options and resources available to us.

Culture as a commodity

Culture is now more than ever a commodity to be sold in the form of media products, clothes, fashion accessories, leisure opportunities, sportswear and other consumer goods. The media and cultural sectors of most capitalist economies are dominated by a relatively small number of very large companies, often multinationals and with interests in a wide range of media and cultural activities (some examples are shown in Figure 13.1).

Concentration of ownership of media and leisure outlets

Increasing concentration of ownership (fewer and fewer larger and larger companies) is reinforced by the trend towards mergers between already large media companies. Walt Disney, as a huge film and leisure conglomerate, recently took over ABC and Capital, one of the largest US television networks in a $19 billion deal. Time Corporation, the largest publisher in the USA, merged with Warner Communication (records, music publishing, film and television) in 1989 to form Time–Warner, which in turn merged with Turner Communications, to form the biggest media and leisure conglomerate in the world. The size and dominance of these organizations often allows them considerable control over the ways in which cultural markets develop and products are marketed.

To provide just one example, the arrival of digital audio recording technology into western European and American markets, although available in Japan since 1986, was delayed for a number of years because the companies involved wanted to exploit the sales potential of existing technologies and were concerned about the potential for consumers to make high-quality unauthorized recordings (Blake, 1992, p. 14).

Cultural conglomerates

Large cultural conglomerates can also exploit their interests across a range of sectors of cultural production to reinforce and consolidate their power. Rupert Murdoch and News Corporation used the newspapers owned in the UK to promote the image of BSkyB satellite TV, also part-owned by News Corporation. BSkyB purchases a large volume of material from Fox studios, a television production company also owned by News Corporation in the USA. News Corporation's television can be promoted through the listings magazines which Rupert Murdoch owns in various countries. Sony, the Japanese electronics manufacturer, now owns record companies to produce the software to be played on its Walkman and CD players. Sony also has interests in Hollywood to cash in on the use of rock music in films and 24-hour cable television. The process through which a company exploits its interests in one sector to enhance its profits in

another is sometimes described as a process of *synergy* (synthesizing two activities to produce more energy).

As Golding and Murdock (1991) argue, the declining vitality of cultural institutions in the public sector, such as the BBC, local public libraries, and community arts projects, together with the emphasis many governments have put on privatization policies in recent years, have further strengthened the position of the large corporations.

Cultural conservatism

Another point made in the political economic analysis is that the large corporations often have cautious and conservative management strategies which stifle cultural innovation.

Large corporations feel most comfortable sticking to the 'tried and tested' formula with proven commercial success, rather than risking investment in new cultural approaches. Thus, new authors find it increasingly difficult to interest publishers who prefer to invest in guaranteed commercial successes – a Jilly Cooper 'bonk-buster' or a Jeffrey Archer novel. Similarly, new pop and rock bands often struggle to win the backing of the big record companies who can rely on established artists and their back catalogues to keep the profits rolling in. Television production companies find that they more frequently have to work to a commercial formula (for example, costume drama with a leading part for an American actor) in order to interest the large television stations.

Business sponsorship

The large corporations exercise significant influence through their sponsorship of sport and cultural activities, and the importance of advertising revenue thus generated.

When BSkyB bought the rights to televise Premier League soccer in 1991 it had an audience of under one million; by 1996 this had topped five million, built around its coverage of soccer. No wonder it was willing to pay £674 million to secure the rights until the year 2001. The television rights for the 2002 soccer World Cup were sold for $2.2 billion to a German media conglomerate.

BSkyB now exercises considerable influence even over the organization and delivery of sport. Premier soccer is now played on Sundays and Mondays to suit the television schedules, and Rugby League has actually switched seasons from

GERMANY
Bertelsmann
Family planning business built up by unflashy, idealistic Reinhard Mohn into global communications company, rivalling Murdoch and Time–Warner. In 1986 acquired US publisher Bantam–Doubleday (through which it owns Transworld) and the Arista, Ariola and RCA record labels – 14 per cent of the world music industry. Now involved in America Online.

- **Interests**

Publishers in Germany, Spain, UK (Transworld: imprints include Bantam, Corgi, Black Swan); book clubs with 25 million subscribers.
BMG Entertainment: Music publisher/distributor.
Gruner & Jahr: 70 magazines in Germany (including *Spiegel*, *Stern*), France (including *Femme Actuelle*, *Voici*), Italy, Spain, Austria, Poland, Switzerland, UK (including *Best*, *Prima*). Nine newspapers in Germany.
Stakes in four German TV channels (including RTL) and seven radio stations.

- **Connections**

Merged broadcasting interests with CLT in April; already linked (though relations now tense) to Havas/Canal Plus as digital allies and partners in Vox and Premiere. Arch-rival: Kirch.

ITALY
Fininvest
Milan-based vehicle for Silvio Berlusconi, the 'Pope of Television' and short-lived Italian PM. Centred on print, advertising and TV (with 45 per cent of the national TV audience), the empire also encompasses hypermarkets, financial services and AC Milan.

- **Interests**

Italy: Three ad-funded channels. Stake in Telepiu pay-TV (already digital).
Publitalia (ad sales).
Mondadori: Newspapers, 30 magazines (including *TV Sorrisi*, *Panorama*, *Vera*).
Abroad: Stakes in Spanish and German TV stations.

- **Connections**

Kirch has stake in Fininvest's Mediaset (TV and advertising) division, and is fellow shareholder in Telepiu and German sports channel.

UK
News International
British arm of Australia's News Corporation, owning 40 per cent of BSkyB. Benefiting from nerve, ruthlessness and Tory government support in his empire-building, Rupert Murdoch now controls 38 per cent of the UK national press and enjoys complete hegemony in British pay-TV.

- **Interests**

Four newspapers (*Sun, News of the World, Times, Sunday Times*).
Four *Times* supplements.
HarperCollins publishing.
Digi-Media Vision (digital technology).
BSkyB: 10 satellite channels (more in multichannel package).
Germany: Stakes in Vox, Premiere channels.
Holland: Sky radio.

- **Connections**

Linked to Bertelsmann in grand alliance, but now seemingly sulking and semi-detached. Partners Granada in BSkyB, Kirch in Premiere. Murdoch–Berlusconi talks, on acquiring an Italian TV channel, came to nothing.

Figure 13.1 Examples of large multinationals in the cultural industries

Source: Guardian, 8 July 1996

the winter to the summer. Sport is now a major business, with soccer clubs, rugby clubs, horse racing and cricket now fully integrated with television within the commercial leisure industry. (This issue is discussed also in Section 13.5.)

Similarly, in the field of music, both popular and classical, corporate sponsorship is a frequent element in subsidizing productions and 'world tours'.

The unequal access to cultural goods

The political-economy approach points to the way in which the market delivers cultural goods in an uneven and unequal fashion. The consumption of cultural goods is stratified along the main dimensions of social inequality.

Use of new cultural technologies, such as the Internet, depends on access to expensive technology which has to be updated frequently. While, in 1989, over 34 per cent of the highest income groups had access to a personal computer at home, only 0.8 per cent of the lowest income group enjoyed this (Golding and Murdock, 1991, p. 29). Although most households have a television, their access to video recorders, camcorders and even telephones is heavily stratified. As more sporting and cultural events are allocated to pay-TV, this 'problem' will become more acute. This prompts some political-economy theorists to question whether privately controlled media and cultural industries can offer 'cultural citizenship' to all sections of society.

Criticisms of the political-economy approach

Critics of the political-economy approach raise three issues. First, they point to the empirical evidence of diversity and creativity in the ways people – even those in subordinate positions, at the bottom of the social structure – consume and use cultural commodities. The big corporations may be able to control markets but they cannot anticipate all the ways in which people use their products.

For example, Lambretta scooters were originally aimed at housewives but were taken up by mods to become symbols of young working-class freedom and rebellion. Blank audio tapes were supposed to be used for legitimate recording only but are actually used on a daily basis by people around the world to subvert the private ownership of musical rights.

The second criticism of the political-economy approach asserts that big corporations frequently

misjudge markets and so sales figures flop. Consumers resist by simply not buying.

Thirdly, in starting with an analysis of production rather than cultural resistance, culturalists and other theorists argue that the political-economy approach falls back into the trap of economic reductionism (see Section 13.3).

Nevertheless, the political-economy approach is valuable in reminding us that most of the cultural options available to us bear in some way the imprint of multinational consumer capitalism.

Activity

a Using all the evidence presented in this section, write a paragraph summarizing how this supports the political-economy perspective.

b Read the accompanying news report from the *Guardian* of September 1999 describing the proposed merger between Viacom and CBS. What advantages may this merger bring to Viacom and CBS? How do you think political-economic theorists will interpret this report?

c What are the main criticisms of a political-economy approach?

C3.2, C3.3

13.4 Consumption, lifestyle shopping and popular culture

Some sociologists go so far as to argue that it is now consumption rather than production that generates the most important divisions within modern societies.

Saunders (1987), for example, argues that consumption is a crucial issue for people because, in contrast to the world of work where they are often powerless, they can exercise more control over how they consume and can invest a sense of identity in the process – a 'home of one's own' is a common desire.

Critics point out, however, that it is still what occurs in the sphere of production that decides largely what and how households consume. Much depends on whether households contain full-time 'core' workers in secure jobs with higher wages, peripheral workers in low-waged, insecure occupations, or the unemployed (Burrows and Butler, 1989). This debate is explored also in Chapter 17.

Viacom and CBS merger creates £41bn media giant

JANE MARTINSON

A FRESH WAVE of consolidation among the titans of the entertainment and information industry was signalled yesterday as Viacom, the fourth largest media group in the world and CBS, the American television group, unveiled the largest ever media merger.

The combination of Viacom – which owns some of the world's best-known brands including music channel MTV and film studio Paramount – with CBS, which has 15 television stations, will create a company worth more than $66bn (£41.09bn) with annual sales of $21bn.

The group, to be known as Viacom, is expected to set a new benchmark for the media industry with its combination of 34 TV stations, a film studio, cable TV and radio networks, and publishing concerns.

Sumner Redstone, the septuagenarian chief executive of Viacom who will continue at the head of the new company, said: "The creation of this formidable media giant marks the beginning of a new era of explosive growth domestically and around the world. Our future is without limit."

Media analysts welcomed the deal. Several said they expected the new company to expand aggressively in overseas markets such as Britain as well as on the internet.

Jessica Reif Cohen, at investment

The buyer
Viacom

Owns Paramount film studio, television studios including MTV and Nickelodeon, publisher Simon and Schuster, 19 TV stations under UPN and a large stake in Blockbuster, the video rental chain
Market cap:$32.6bn
Sales: $12bn

The target
CBS

Owns 15 TV stations as part of the CBS Television Network, radio through Infinity Broadcasting and King World Productions (pending)
Market cap: $35bn
Sales: $6.8bn

bank Merrill Lynch, said: "They have the financial wherewithal to be aggressive in making more acquisitions."

Yesterday's merger has still to pass competition regulators and some analysts believe the combined group could be forced to sell Viacom's struggling UPN cable TV network.

Under rules set by the federal communications commission, no single group is allowed to own TV stations which serve more than 35% of the American population. Under some calculations the enlarged Viacom will serve 41% of the population. The group is expected to start negotiations with regulators today.

Some analysts also questioned the management structure of the new group, as both Mr Redstone and Mr

Karmazin of CBS are aggressive, hands-on executives. However, both sought to play down any suggestion of future tension.

Mr Karmazin said: "Viacom will be a better company with both of us together." He insisted on his position as chief operating officer being engraved in a three-year management contract. His decisions could still be overturned by Mr Redstone, however, although few analysts believed this was likely.

The landmark deal was prompted by changes to television ownership rules in the United States announced last month. …

Viacom was effectively spun out of CBS in the early 1970s after competition laws limited the amount of programming the TV networks could own.

Source: Guardian, 8 September 1999

Those sociologists who emphasize consumption as being more important than production relations are clearly critical of Marxist and neo-Marxist theories of class and class structure, preferring instead to consider the way in which lifestlyes are much more diverse than the categories that the class structure suggest. They also agree that through the process of consumption people can construct and create lifestyles for themselves.

Consumption, class lifestyles and lifestyle shopping

One of the earliest studies in sociology that considered this issue was that of the notion of embourgeoisement promoted by various sociologists, notably Zweig (1961). G. Zweig argued that large numbers of the working class were on the move towards new middle-class values and middle-class existence. Embourgeoisement of the worker implied a number of related aspects of change within large sections of the working classes, which were described at the time as:

- economic advancement in terms of household income, family expenditure and possessions
- educational advancement
- greater family- and home-centredness
- shift of interest from job to consumerism
- contraction of class consciousness – the idea of class being relegated in the worker's mind to something unimportant.

These changes resulted, it was argued, in the individualization of workers in the sense that they were becoming less committed to the value of solidaristic collectivism – the traditional idea that their common purpose lay in 'sticking together' to advance their collective interests. It was also suggested that the worker became not only deproletarized but also disalienated.

The Affluent Worker study

One of the most influential sociological studies of the 1960s, *The Affluent Worker Study* (Goldthorpe *et al.*, 1969), deliberately sought to test the embourgeoisement thesis by investigating a group of 'affluent' (or relatively well-paid) workers in Luton who might have been expected to be showing signs of embourgeoisement. Their findings, which are presented here very briefly, indicated that while changes were occurring in this section of the working class they did not amount to embourgeoisement. The results may be considered under four headings.

- *Attitudes to work* – Since they were not interested in 'getting on', careers or intrinsic job satisfaction, they could not be said to have adopted the kind of orientation to work traditionally associated with white-collar workers. They had an instrumental attitude to work (primarily motivated by pay).

- *Friendships, lifestyle and norms* – The 'affluent workers' did not associate with white-collar workers outside work nor did they seek middle-class status and had not, therefore, developed middle-class patterns of sociability. However, they had developed a 'privatized' and home-centred lifestyle.

- *Outlook on life and image of society* – They had not adopted a middle-class outlook since they were not concerned with advancement in the 'prestige hierarchy', but were primarily focused on material benefits such as maintaining their relative position in terms of what they perceived to be a hierarchy of income differentials.

- *Political attitudes* – The majority (80 per cent) of the workers in the sample not only voted for the Labour Party but also saw it as 'the party of the working class'. However, they were less aligned to Labour out of a traditional sense of loyalty to their class, than by how they personally might benefit from voting for them. (See also Section 15.1.)

In conclusion, these 'affluent workers' held different views from traditional working-class groups but could not be described as having become middle class. The two respects in which they did differ from the traditional working class were (a) in the sense that they were more isolated from the community in their private family life, and (b) in how they saw trade unions as a way of promoting individual interests. Goldthorpe and colleagues agreed that there had been some convergence between the middle and working classes and that a 'new', possibly prototypical, working class may have been emerging as a result.

The return of notions of embourgeoisement

The Conservative Party's four General Election victories from 1979 onwards (see also Section 15.1) gave a new lease of life to the idea of the transformation of the working class. The Conservatives owed their success in large part to the support from the C2 (skilled manual) segment of the electorate. Once again this was most prevalent in the prosperous regions, and the sobering statistic for the Labour Party in 1987 was that the Conservatives led it by 46 per cent to 26 per cent among the working class in the south of England. This general pattern continued into the 1990s when, according to a MORI poll of 22 727 voters during the General Election in 1992, Labour managed to improve its share of the C2 vote but still only gained two in five of the votes in this group. 'The fact remains that nearly as many skilled manual workers vote Conservative as they do Labour' (Denscombe, 1993, p. 44).

The restructuring of distributional conflict

While there was a consensus of opinion that the 'new' affluent workers were significant in terms of their shifting political allegiances, it was also felt that the term embourgeoisement – and for that matter its twin proletarianization – were unable to explain the complexity of changes that were happening in society. An alternative view was that class conflict had been restructured around new divisions brought about by the economic reorganization associated with global competition. (See also Sections 4.2, 6.9, 15.2 and 17.2 for details about globalisation.)

With more reliance on market forces, less government intervention, increased flexibility of labour, the adoption of microelectronic technology, the decline of the manufacturing sector, and the increasing participation of women in paid work, employment has become insecure and fragmented. These changes are said to have reduced the significance of the manual/non-manual divide. In addition, 'post-modern' culture (see also Section 4.5) has developed in which work is 'decentred' as a source of identity and consciousness, to be replaced by issues of individualist consumption, whether it be housing or state benefits. Work is no longer a way of identifying oneself, more a means of acquiring desirable goals – a tendency which leads to a decline in traditional class politics and the death of the possibility of working-class revolution.

Lukes (1984) identifies a number of divisions emerging in British society which, though related to class, could also be seen as independent of it:

- owner-occupiers *versus* tenants
- waged *versus* welfare claimants
- declining regions *versus* prosperous ones
- secure core workers *versus* peripheral casualized workers.

Activity

a Suggest other sources of division which might be added to Lukes' list.

b To what extent do you agree that these divisions are now more important than social class for the analysis of stratification in contemporary UK society?

The picture that emerged from this theory of restructured class conflict was one of sectionalism, instrumentalism, and privatism:

- sectional in the sense that the monolithic labour movement had been replaced by numerous sectoral interests each resigned, in an era of recession, to the pursuit of its own economic interests
- instrumental in that the workers had embraced the capitalist economic values of an acquisitive society and saw labour organizations as a way of maximizing their level of consumption
- private in view of the tendency of members of the working class to withdraw from class politics into the private world of the family.

Thus it was claimed that the restructuring of distributional conflict had seen a shift from issues of production and class to those of consumption and status.

Marshall (1987) notes the irony of the fact that this analysis of the effects of recession on the working class seems to confirm many of the findings of Goldthorpe's *Affluent Worker* study which, it should be remembered, were conducted against a backdrop of rising prosperity.

In terms of market situation it is probably true that, taken as a whole, the working class enjoys a better standard of living in absolute terms than previously. However, interpretations of this are complicated by a number of factors, primarily the difficulty of generalizing about all members of the working class.

Internal divisions in the working class are potentially created by the large discrepancy in earnings from the top to the bottom of the working class, but the differentials between skilled and unskilled rates of pay have reduced. The most significant source of division is related to the increasing participation by women in paid employment (see Section 17.2). Abercrombie and Warde (1994) surmise that the inferior positions of women and ethnic minorities in the labour market could create deeper and highly visible intra-class divisions.

Working-class lifestyle and culture

Two aspects of changing lifestyle are thought to have eroded working-class solidarity, namely consumption patterns and the tendency to privatism. (See also Section 4.4.)

Consumption patterns

Increasing affluence has seen the spread of consumer durables to the working class and a growth in home-ownership. However, despite an apparent convergence in this respect, consumption patterns remain significantly unequal between classes, reflecting the market positions of the classes.

Despite the fact that these relative class differences in standards of living are still evident, the trend to individualist consumption is thought to be leading to an acceptance of the values of capitalism – creating new divisions around participation in private ownership versus reliance on public services, notably in relation to housing. Abercrombie and Warde, however, argue that it is doubtful whether housing tenure (see also Section 14.5) in itself causes people to alter wholesale other aspects of their behaviour.

Privatism

Privatism refers to a pattern of social life that is restricted largely to the home and the conjugal family. This was held to be another tendency that was reducing traditional working-class solidarity. However, according to Abercrombie and Warde, the extent of conviviality outside of immediate kin relations said to be typical of traditional working-class communities may have been exaggerated, and the privatized pattern of sociability was not unknown in the past. It is true that urban redevelopment and the relocation of industry have led to a more geographically dispersed population, but working-class social contacts remain extensive, though less intense and less centred around masculine roles. (See also Section 13.6.) Furthermore it is probably the case that increased female participation in the labour market has led to a decline in home-centredness on their part.

Saunders (1987, 1990b) rejects the argument that increasing home-ownership has encouraged privatism. The intensity and frequency of neighbourhood relations were more a function of how long people had lived in an area. He also found little difference between home-owners and council tenants in participation rates in leisure activities outside the home. The conclusion that there is little difference between social classes in terms of privatism is supported by both Marshall *et al.* (1988) and Devine (1992). Abercrombie and Warde conclude that 'manual workers are neither obsessed by consumerism nor excessively privatised'. They go on to say that although a few more prosperous regions may exhibit privatism:

. . . *no one has yet demonstrated that there is a systematic structural basis for variation in privatism, or that it has been responsible for undermining solidarism.*

(Abercrombie and Warde, 1994, p. 167)

Explaining patterns of consumption

Marx distinguished between the *use value* of commodities and their *exchange value*. While in terms of practical usage, most of us could manage without a Picasso on the wall or an electric toothbrush in the bathroom, these commodities are often exchanged (sold) for quite high values in the market. This distinction has been developed by some theorists (e.g. the Frankfurt School,

see Section 13.2) into an analysis of consumption which suggests that members of the public are often manipulated by advertising and encouraged to develop 'false' desires for commodities that have little use value.

Conspicious consumption

However, critics of this argue that the manipulative power of big business alone cannot explain the huge growth in demand for consumer goods. They suggest that the meanings and motives which prompt consumers to buy commodities have to be taken more seriously.

An early attempt to do this is found in the work of Thorstein Veblen (1857–1918), an American sociologist, who developed an analysis of the newly wealthy middle class in North America (1953; orig. pub. 1912). Veblen's theory of 'conspicuous consumption' suggests that affluent social groups will use their purchasing power to claim social status through the visible display of commodities which signal high social standing. The North American *nouveaux riches* (newly rich) attempted to copy the consumption patterns of the European aristocracy in an effort to promote their social status. Thus, particular foods and drinks, particular styles of clothing, horse-riding and European holidays all became fashionable during the late nineteenth century amongst this social group.

Working-class affluence

After World War II, 'working-class affluence' brought opportunities for 'conspicuous consumption' to many more people:

By the 1950s, following a pattern already established in the United States, first in Britain, then in the rest of Western Europe, 'mass consumption' ... began to develop amongst all but the very poorest groups. Groups which had to do paid work of various kinds, from mining to typing, unlike [Veblen's] leisure class ... who had to do little if any paid work, became 'consumers', too.

(Bocock, 1993, p. 21)

In analysing post-war consumption, sociologists were tempted to simply elaborate Veblen's original ideas. Thus, Willmott and Young (1973), for example, developed another 'top-down' model in which they argued that lower-middle-class and working-class families aspired to model their consumption patterns on upper-middle-class lifestyles. According to their model of 'stratified diffusion', as soon as incomes permitted, first lower-middle-class and then working-class families adopted middle-class consumption and cultural habits.

Criticisms of models of working-class aspirations

More recently, sociologists have regarded 'top-down' models – which assume that lower socio-economic groups always seek to emulate or copy higher income groups – as over-simplified or even just plain wrong. C. Campbell (1995, p. 109) makes three criticisms:

1 There is little hard sociological evidence to suggest that many lower income groups do consciously seek to emulate middle-class consumption patterns, other than in terms of the simple aspiration to be more comfortably off. Are the cultural patterns associated with middle-class consumption necessarily attractive to other groups? We can see (in Section 16.1) that the French sociologist Bourdieu points to important differences between the *habitus* (systems of taste) of working-class and middle-class groups.

2 Campbell argues that there is some evidence to suggest that consumption patterns which first emerge amongst groups at the bottom (for example, black American working-class styles of dress) can be taken up by mainstream fashion and spread in popularity amongst higher income groups.

3 The arguments presented in these theories are based mainly on conclusions drawn from external observation, rather than the subjects (consumers) themselves. Consumers' own accounts of their purchasing behaviour are not accorded a high priority.

The meaning of consumption: lifestyle shopping

An example provided recently by Dick Hebdige illustrates why some sociologists believe it is important to invest more time in investigating the meanings associated with consumption, particularly from the consumers' point of view:

When I first moved into my present home, I was intrigued by one car in the street – a great spotless Thunderbird, its maroon bodywork and sculptured chromium accessories glistening all year round, irrespective of the weather. This Thunderbird is the single most conspicuous anomaly in the Victorian terraced street in which I live. It is a Cathedral amongst hovels. It is out of scale, out of place (its real home is Detroit or Dallas), out of time (its real time is pre-1974, pre the Oil Crisis). I immediately assumed – drawing on my stock of Hollywood derived cultural stereotypes – that the car belonged to a pimp, a gangster, or a 'big shot' of some kind. ... These assumptions turned out to be unfounded. The car is owned by one of the gentlest, most gracious and modest men I know. Mr H is a slight, mild-mannered Turkish Cypriot who lives with his wife in a run down, sparsely furnished ground floor flat in the house opposite.

(Hebdige, 1996, p. 81)

Hebdige uses this example from his own domestic life to illustrate some of the weaknesses in the theories of consumption discussed so far.

Mr H has lovingly devoted hours to the care and preservation of this car; he spends as much time washing, polishing, tuning and retuning his car as he does in his flat. The car represents a source of pleasure for the owner which goes far beyond a simple attempt to 'copy' the consumption patterns of higher income groups. Indeed, it represents a style and era far removed from the contemporary English middle class. But, at the same time, the car is not an object which can easily be placed within the *habitus* of the London working class, as Bourdieu might expect.

What has to be recognized is that commodities can often provide a very complex source of meanings and pleasures for consumers: they may be pleasurable because they are a source of pride, because they constitute a mechanical or intellectual challenge, because they evoke nostalgic images of earlier eras or distinct cultural influences, and so on. For some cultural theorists, what this suggests is that an analysis of consumption has to *start* with the symbolic meanings associated with sets of commodities.

Activity

Explain what is meant by a 'top-down' model of consumption, and assess the criticisms which some sociologists make of this kind of sociological explanation of consumption.

C3.2, C3.3

Semiology and the symbolic meaning of consumption

During the last two decades, *semiology* has commonly been used as a method through which the meaning of images, symbols and commodities can be explored. Semiology, however, does not employ an interpretative approach like symbolic interactionism. Rather, it depends on the theorist's ability to decode sets of popular symbols (or 'signs' to use the term employed by semiologists). (This issue is explored also in Section 6.1.)

Barthes and the application of semiology

Ferdinand de Saussure (1857–1913) first developed semiology as a method for analysing language as a symbolic system. However, it was Barthes (1915–80) who first applied this approach not only to language but to all aspects of popular culture including photographs, advertisements and actual commodities.

Barthes (1973) believed that all cultural symbols, including commodities, signified (communicated) certain meanings which might combine in a system to create a cultural 'myth'. For example, 'Coca Cola' means more than just a can of soft drink – for many people it *signifies* 'the American way of life' (see Figure 13.2).

First level of signification:	'Coca Cola' (signifier) A fizzy soft drink (signified)
↓	
Second level of signification:	Youth, fun, the American way of life (myths)

Figure 13.2 Levels of signification

Barthes' semiological approach has been used by other analysts to explore, for example, how 'myths' about masculinity, femininity and power have been used in advertisements for cars, deodorants, after-shaves, clothing and chocolates (Williamson, 1978; Myers, 1986). It is still quite easy to find some advertisements attempting to associate particular products with images of masculinity and power, or traditional images of femininity, or suggestions of power and authority.

Many advertisements continue to rework 'myths' about gender, class and power, but advertising is now often considerably more subtle than 20 years ago. Advertisements sometimes portray a 'new man' who is caring, sensitive and willing to do his share of housework and childcare. Some critics suggest that this is yet another 'myth' rather than a reflection of real change.

Case Study – The semiology of Coca Cola

Coca Cola provides an example of the growing sophistication of advertisements. A recent campaign tied its product in with the 1996 European Soccer Championship. 'Eat Football, Sleep Football, Drink Coca Cola' represented a considerable departure from the earlier Coca Cola ads that frequently depicted happy children or young people, 'from around the world', singing an uplifting song, globally united through their common love of the drink. The soccer ad, in contrast, was shot in grainy black and white to emphasize 'documentary realism'; it portrayed scenes of rowdy terrace excitement, used a heavy rock beat, and the slogan of the advertisement, flashed across the screen at repeated intervals. The effect was both striking and a little disturbing. Coca Cola, here, was being associated with something disorderly and unruly – qualities not immediately associated with the bourgeois values of capitalism. But, of course, this is the whole point of the advertisement: to suggest that Coca Cola has an appeal or 'an energy' which transcends classes, cultures and stadium terraces – just like soccer.

🗨 Discussion point

Are television advertisements no longer sexist, or are they now sexist in more subtle ways?

C3.1a

Criticisms of Barthes

Semiology offers one way of beginning to explore systematically the meanings associated with advertising and consumption, but Barthes devotes little attention to two important issues:

1 The meanings or myths associated with consumption patterns clearly do change over time, as we have seen in the case of the representation of gender; but we need to know more about how this occurs.

2 Without conducting research, how can we be sure that audiences 'read' myths in the way Barthes suggests? How can we be sure that consumers derive pleasures from commodities because of the association between product and myth, as argued by Barthes?

In other words, in the absence of thorough audience and consumer research, there is a huge danger that semiology produces an idiosyncratic interpretation which reflects the preoccupations of the researcher rather than widely held, popular myths.

Excorporation and incorporation

Although Barthes recognized that images and commodities could be polysemic (offer multiple meanings), he failed to explore fully the ways in which ordinary people might contest or refute the conventional meanings associated with consumption. Critics argue that he under-estimated the importance of cultural resistance in consumption.

Neo-hegemony theorists or culturalists (see Section 15.2) have been particularly interested in the potential semiology offers for analysing social conflict as it is expressed at the level of culture and ideas. The Centre for Contemporary Cultural Studies (CCCS) has employed semiology extensively in its analysis of dominant and subordinate cultures. However, John Fiske takes the semiological analysis of consumption considerably further.

Lifestyle shopping: subversive consumerism?

Fiske argues that while there is a tremendous energy within capitalist societies which encourages consumption through advertising, marketing and the media, consumers do not always 'consume' in the ways in which capitalism anticipates. They may use commodities in a subversive way. They may engage in semiological guerrilla warfare, creatively employing their own semiology to give images and commodities new meanings. Fiske describes this as 'excorporation' – the process through which commodities produced by capitalism are used in new or different ways (excorporated) by subordinate groups to create oppositional meanings and cultural resistance (Fiske, 1989a, pp. 15–18). Dr Marten boots

were excorporated by skinheads; Vespa motor scooters were excorporated by mods.

This leads Fiske to assert that it is precisely the resistance of oppressed or subordinate groups which *makes* popular culture:

Popular culture is always a culture of conflict, it always involves the struggle to make social meanings that are in the interests of the subordinate and that are not those preferred by the dominant ideology. The victories, however, fleeting or limited, in this struggle produce popular pleasure, for popular pleasure is always social and political.

(Fiske, 1989b, p. 2)

Activity

Is Fiske correct to insist that popular culture always contains expressions of resistance to dominant values? Consider this question with examples and illustrations of your own.

C3.2, C3.3

For Fiske, then, only that which involves consuming commodities to make oppositional or subversive meanings actually counts as popular culture. This is quite a controversial position to take and some of his own examples clearly illustrate why. Arcade video games make huge profits but, according to Fiske, allow people often with little autonomy in their real lives to enter a world they can control using their skill and knowledge. Shopping malls may be symbols of consumer capitalism but the young unemployed can excorporate the public space within, engaging in cultural opposition both by evading security personnel and enjoying the pleasure of window shopping but not buying. Most controversially, Fiske argues that young women can excorporate Madonna as a commodity (her music, films, books, posters, etc.) in opposition to dominant sexist and patriarchal values. This is despite, as Fiske concedes, Madonna being voted number three 'Sex/Lust Object' in a 1985 American magazine. Nevertheless, according to Fiske the 'meaning' of Madonna is a site of:

... semiotic struggle between the forces of patriarchal control and feminine resistance, of capitalism and the subordinate, of the adult and the young.

(Fiske, 1989b, p. 97)

Criticisms of Fiske's position

Do consumers and subordinated social groups really decode or excorporate commodities in the way Fiske claims? Fiske does refer to empirical, usually ethnographic, research on particular social groups to support some of his arguments, but he does not always do this consistently. The great danger is that, once again, the interpretation made by the academic rather than by 'ordinary people' is allowed to shape the semiological analysis.

Also, is Fiske correct in arguing that popular culture is 'always a culture of conflict' involving the subversive rejection of dominant values? It is possible to think of plenty of widely popular cultural activities which do not, on the face of things, appear to involve cultural resistance – going fishing or watching daytime television, for example. If we follow Fiske, either these are ruled out as examples of popular culture, or we have to make the claim that someone sitting at the canal side with a fishing rod is engaged in an act of cultural resistance.

Activity

a Explain what is involved in semiological analysis and how it can be applied to advertisements and other examples of popular culture. Provide some examples of your own.

b Explain what John Fiske means by 'excorporation' and 'incorporation'.

c What criticisms can be made of Fiske's approach to the study of popular culture?

C3.2, C3.3

Lifestyle shopping: post-modernism and consumerism

For post-modernists the dominance of a consumer culture is one of the defining features of the post-modern society. As we have seen (in Section 4.4), Bourdieu believes certain codes or rules shape the way in which social groups consume. He argues, for example, that social class governs taste. The meaning of commodities will signify 'middle class' or 'working class'. However, according to some theorists such as Mike Featherstone (1991a, pp. 18–25), one of the distinguishing features of the post-modern world is that these codes are breaking down. We now all have greater freedom to 'play' with the meaning of commodities and to select commodities from a range of social contexts. Rather than 'inheriting' particular styles and tastes through upbring-

ing and occupation, we can playfully construct our identities by combining permutations of commodities, all signifying in different ways. This commodity stockbrokers may read *The Sun* but shop in Saville Row, while miners may choose Laura Ashley wallpaper but drink in the working-men's club.

Mike Featherstone lists the following reasons. First, in its drive to make profit, consumer capitalism produces more and more of what were formerly 'exclusive' goods, thus lowering the price and thereby making them more widely available. Secondly, the mass media have eroded many of the old distinctions between 'high' and 'popular' culture (see Section 13.1). Thirdly, he points to the proliferation of style magazines and television programmes which now allow a wide range of social groups to acquire knowledge of 'fashion' and 'taste'. Finally, like Bourdieu (Section 4.4) and Mort (Section 13.6), Featherstone points to the role of a particular social group – 'the new cultural intermediaries' – who work in fashion, design, the media, marketing, information and cultural industries. Typically, such workers have been to university or college but are distinct from the traditional middle class. Free from the influence of conventional bourgeois values, they use their cultural expertise:

... to ransack the various traditions and cultures in order to produce new symbolic goods, and in addition provide the necessary interpretations on their use.

(Featherstone, 1991a, p. 19)

Critical thoughts on post-modernism and consumerism

Two critical points developed by Campbell (1995) in a recent review are worth highlighting here. First, there is a danger in:

... treating the attitudes and practices of certain sections of the affluent middle class ... as if they were typical of consumers as a whole.

(Campbell, 1995, p. 114)

The interest in lifestyle, consumption and identity to be found in certain parts of Hampstead and Islington may not be reproduced across all sections of society. Secondly, Campbell suggests, it may not be safe to assume that meanings suggested or signified by different commodities will actually be understood in precisely the same way by all social groups:

... it is rare for anyone to be completely mystified by the goods that others have purchased or by the way that they are being utilized. This is not the same, however, as claiming that all, or even most, members of that society would be in a position to agree on what 'meaning' should be attributed to the fact that a particular individual has purchased a pair of blue jeans or chooses to wear them to go shopping.

(Campbell, 1995, p. 115)

13.5 Leisure and symbolic work

The sociology of leisure developed out of the study of work because leisure was seen as the time available after work was completed. As the amount of time taken up by work declined, owing to the growth in productivity allowed by industrial production, it was therefore assumed that the amount of time available for leisure would increase.

It is in this context that sociologists and other commentators developed notions of the move towards the leisure society which was popular in the 1950s. The post-war optimistic mood of the time contributed to the vision of a society in which work seen as coerced time would gradually reduce, leaving people free to spend more time on leisure activities.

In fact there is little evidence to suggest that the rather rosy picture painted in these early theories ever approached reality. It certainly does not fit contemporary reality where, under the pressure of New Right demands for greater economic efficiency, people are working longer hours, not shorter. Despite this, leisure is now firmly established as an area of sociological study even though the leisure society may not have arrived.

Patterns of participation in leisure

A sociological analysis of leisure starts with the suggestion that, like other forms of human activity, leisure is not something people do in a purely individualistic way. Rather, participation in leisure is structured by the same types of inequalities operative in other areas.

Social class differences in leisure participation

In her study of patterns of leisure, Glyptis (1989) argues that participation in sports and entertainment activities is clearly structured by social class. For instance, she found that 34 per cent of professional workers are involved in indoor sports, compared with only 15 per cent of unskilled manual workers. The reason for this is unequal access to income, since generally charges are levied even when leisure centres are run by public authorities. She also pointed to the importance of car ownership in relation to certain leisure activities, and the fact that this is clearly unequally distributed.

Clarke and Critcher (1985), Marxist sociologists, note the growing importance of the provision of leisure activities as a commercial activity. Again, access to this is dependent on money, which leads to inequalities in access. They argue that leisure needs to be analysed within its social, economic and political context.

Activity

Suggest three ways in which commercialism has increased in the field of leisure provision in recent years.

C3.2, C3.3

Since income is unequally distributed, and has become more so in the 1980s and 90s (see Section 17.1), the kind of inequalities in access to leisure facilities noted by these studies will probably have risen in recent years. This is yet another indicator of the continuing importance of social class as a structure in society, despite the seeming sociological fashion to deny this. As Edgell (1993) comments in his book *Class*:

What needs to be explained is not the presumed demise of class, but the tenacity of class-based patterns of inequality and politics, and much else besides. In the meantime, class rules and classlessness remains a dream rather than a reality.

(Edgell, 1993, p. 122)

While Edgell was there not specifically talking about leisure, his point is nonetheless valid in relation to this topic.

Gender and participation in leisure

If leisure is conceptualized as activities in the time available when all necessary 'enforced' tasks have been undertaken, then it is clear that, in relation to males, this largely means the time after paid work has been completed. This is, of course, true also for women – with the important difference that generally notions of 'necessary activities' for women would also include taking major responsibility for domestic labour. (See Sections 5.6.)

On this basis the number of hours free time per week available to women on average is less than that available to men. In 1991/92, women in full-time paid employment had 3.3 hours free time per day, compared with 4.8 hours free time for males in full-time employment. Even women in part-time employment had less free time than males in full-time employment.

Delphy (1984) argues that this differential is to be explained on the basis of the continuing material context of the position of women in our society, and this round-the-clock responsibility is a structural constraint in their lives which limits the possibilities for involvement in leisure.

Deem's (1990) research on leisure participation in Milton Keynes pointed to the importance of these time constraints on leisure participation for women. She also highlighted another factor, which she calls 'patriarchal control'. What she means by this is the way the extent and type of women's involvement in leisure activities is constrained by the potential reaction of males. This can range from potential harassment of females in pubs, through to discouragement of women going out to places where they might meet men other than their partner, such as a nightclub.

Green *et al.*'s (1990) study of Sheffield came to similar conclusions, and a similar conclusion was reached by Wimbush (1986) on the basis of a study of young mothers in Edinburgh. This notion of the way women's leisure activities are controlled by men thus seems to be a factor commonly found in studies of women's leisure participation.

Discussion point

To what extent do you agree that women's leisure activities are subject to patriarchal control?

C3.1a

Ethnicity and participation in leisure

Because of the greater levels of unemployment suffered by ethnic minorities (see Section 17.2), lower average levels of income will impact on leisure participation in much the same way as do class inequalities. Of course, for some individuals such inequalities interact together.

There may also be cultural or religious norms and values tending to segregate people in terms of leisure activities. However, whether this segregation is a matter of reaction to actual or potential racism or is simply a cultural choice is a matter of debate. It is also clear that young members of ethnic minorities are becoming more adept at creating their own styles of leisure and cultural expression by merging together cultural forms from their ethnic identity with more westernized influences, such as the rise of Bhangra music.

Sivanandan (1990) argues that there is a need to consider how aspects of ethnic minorities' lives have been affected by racism and the colonial legacy, but he goes on to argue that the response to this has often been a form of resistance within which cultural and leisure pursuits feature.

Discussion point

How can you resist culturally? To what extent do you think this happens?

C3.1a

A similar point is made by Gilroy (1987). He argues that cultural identity has been a central element in the resistance to racism, and this has often been expressed through involvement with music, dance, carnivals and sports clubs. In a later work, Gilroy (1993) emphasizes the way in which global cultural styles are mixed together, so that contemporary black cultural forms do not draw upon or feed into notions of fixed ethnic and national roots, but instead point towards a more flexible identity which engages with themes of modernity while not feeling fully integrated within them.

Sociological issues in leisure participation

Proto communities

One of the ways in which sociologists seek to consider the activity of individuals and groups is in the creation of living spaces or communities. The early sociologists approached communities very much in terms of institutions and structures, but more recently a different approach has emerged, which views communities as much more fluid and dependent on social interaction and individual activity. One example of this is *Soft City* by Jonathan Raban (1974). David Harvey (1989) argues that Raban's analysis of city life can be contrasted with earlier analysis of communities and city living because of its optimism and because Raban incorporated elements of post-modernist analysis by arguing that the city is mainly about the production of signs and images. Here cities are composed of individuals engaged in enterprise and individual identity creation through the process of the consumption of possessions and the creation of appearances. The city is seen as being like a theatre, where one can adopt many roles. The communities here are symbolic, created through common purchases or common appearances but also constantly shifting. Studies such as these have led to a greater consideration of the construction of proto communities and symbolic communities.

It has often been suggested that working-class communities, in particular, have offered their members the closeness and support that a collective lifestyle brings. *Writing in Working Class Community* (1968), Brian Jackson offers a romanticized view:

Work, the old poverty cycle, the extended family, this is the settled structure of community. In turn this leads to a style of living which again adds to the structure ... If the community is built up 'vertically' through kinship, where people of different ages – grandchild and great-aunt – are joined together; it is also built up 'horizontally' where people of the same age but different families are joined in a strong social bond. It begins in childhood ...

(Jackson, 1968, pp. 166–7)

In particular the working-class community of Huddersfield, which he was writing about, was seen to be drawn together by economic circumstances – or, more accurately, poverty. This led community members to develop informal support networks and formalized support via friendly societies and trade unions. Young and Willmott (1957) were able to note similar facets of community in Bethnal Green, but both studies suggested that things were changing. Geographical mobility and the decline of traditional industries were having a negative effect on 'community'.

Such views of community have been much criticized for their rather romantic notions, failing to note divisions and conflicts within their subject communities. They have also been criticized for viewing them as socially isolated units without influences from beyond, such as the state or the decisions of multi-national industries.

Sociological studies of contemporary living spaces suggest it is too simplistic to view them as consisting of harmonious and affectionate relationships since they are bound to fluctuate between people within the community and over time. For example, although working-class communities were united in poverty, some individuals would have had more money than others. Although working in the same industry, different people would have different skills and working conditions. Such instances might just as easily have caused 'relative deprivation', where people felt aggrieved at their poverty or lack of skills compared with others they knew, and had the potential for jealousies and conflict. Thus Crow and Allan suggested that:

... the nature of community ties varies with different patterns of physical proximity, differences in longevity of settlements and of people's residence there, different levels of resources (varying according to age, class and gender), and different senses of obligations between people

(Crow and Allan, 1994, p. xviii)

Post-modernism and freedom from oppressive communities

Bauman (1990) is keen to analyse and explain what he sees as a 'post-modern' world. He thinks that the more 'comprehensive' or all-encompassing communities become, the more 'oppressive' they will become as they begin to interfere with a variety of aspects of people's lives. The more oppressive they become, the more tensions will develop. Bauman uses the example of communes, which are most likely to develop according to this schema. Initially they seek to offer liberation from all other claims for living, but in doing so they end up doing the same, forcing members to live in a particular way. As a result he sees them as 'the most fragile and vulnerable of communities' (p. 77) likely to break apart as they become oppressive and fail to live up to the high hopes and expectations of their members. Likewise Bell and Newby (1983) said that in attempting to develop an 'ethos of loyalty' community leaders and members may initiate a framework of rules which infringe upon the freedoms of individuals. Thus we find in communities a contradictory nature:

... community without privacy feels more like oppression. And that privacy without community feels more like loneliness than 'being oneself'.

(Bauman, 1990, p. 106)

💬 Discussion point

To what extent do we need to see community in the black and white form advocated by Bauman? To what extent is there a middle ground? Give examples to justify your answers.

C3.1a

Many have noted how the setting of rules functions to create 'in-groups' and 'out-groups' (Bauman, 1990); 'insiders' and 'outsiders' (Cohen, 1986); 'inclusion' and 'exclusion' (Crow and Allan, 1994). Because communities seek to define who is and who is not acceptable, the result is likely to be potential or actual conflict given that the deviance of the 'unacceptable' group has been focused upon. For Bauman the 'out-group' is 'useful, even indispensable' to the 'in-group', because it 'brings into relief the identity of the in-group and fortifies its coherence and solidarity' (p. 58). However, it is not always clear who is acceptable and who is not. Boundaries are grey and can be threatened by ambivalence from members of the 'in-group' who may not really care if they are acceptable or not, or by people in the 'out-group' who are not members of the 'in-group' but wish to be. An example of the latter might be immigrant groups who, although 'different', want to be accepted as British and to 'play by the rules'. Instead they face discrimination and resulting inequalities as the 'insiders' aim to reinforce their own rules of membership.

Symbolic communities and symbolic boundaries

A. P. Cohen, a post-modernist, has taken ideas of membership and belonging to a new level by introducing the idea of 'symbolic boundaries'. These are 'mental constructs ... boundaries which inhere in the mind' (Cohen, 1986, p. 17) which people use to decide who is and who is not a member of their community. As such they have no factual or accurate quality. They are totally subjective, changing from person to person – an individual may also be completely inconsistent in their application of their own 'symbolic boundaries'. Such boundaries have become necessary because of social changes which have blurred or erased traditional, taken-for-granted boundaries between social groups.

- Geographical boundaries – locally, nationally and globally – have been undermined by industrialization and urbanization, creating uncertainty. We can see the effect of this in the debate over national boundaries and what some see as the increasingly meddling and interventionist European Union aiming to prevent British people living their traditional lifestyle (whatever that is).

- The development of new technology has meant an immediate flow of information from anywhere in the world. Previously communities were relatively sheltered from the outside world, with local opinion leaders reaffirming locally held cultural norms. Now they may have a variety of cultural norms and values thrust upon them, attacking previous certainties.

- Developments in transport have massively increased levels of geographical mobility. Not only do communities face the threat of new cultures via the media, they may meet them face-to-face in interaction too! Geographical mobility and the mass media may, for example, threaten linguistic or dialect differences, creating a national homogeneity in the way people speak. This has been seen by some communities as a major threat to their way of life and has led to campaigns for separate language tuition in schools and for a diversity of dialects in the presenters of television and radio programmes. In Wales it even led to the development of a Welsh language channel, S4C Wales.

- Communities have differing experiences and react to similar events in different ways. This may develop the collective consciousness further but could just as easily divide members.

Unable to assert physical boundaries or to isolate themselves from the threats incumbent in a 'shrinking' world, both in terms of time and space, communities may attempt to develop a distinct or separate identity through reference to symbolic or cultural differences.

Activity

Try to make a list of examples where communities have responded to perceived 'threats' to their language, morals, religion, dress or behaviour patterns. How have they responded and how successful have they been?

C3.2, C3.3

Cohen reminds us that communities will not respond to the same threat or stimulus in the same way. Furthermore, individual members may adopt the symbols created to make their culture distinct but may interpret them differently, but this is necessarily so. If the symbols were too precise and easily open to collective interpretation they would no longer be symbols; instead they would act as structures determining people's behaviour and producing uniformity. The job of the post-modern sociologist becomes a matter of separating the community as it appears to be – 'the community mask' (1986, p. 13) – from the diversity of interpretations held by individual members; i.e. deciding whether what they see is a 'true' representation of the group feeling or just that of a particular person (or persons). In concluding his discussion of symbolic boundaries he says:

Their symbolic character enables their [community's] form to be held in common while also enabling individuals to attribute meanings to them. The symbolism of community thus speaks simultaneously for the collectivity to those on the other side of its boundaries and to each of its members who refract it through their individual sense of belonging.

(Cohen, 1986, p. 17)

Playing out the role

Giddens (1984) makes use of the dramaturgical theory of 'symbolic interactionist' Erving Goffman to suggest that members of communities play a variety of roles, varying with the circumstances in which they find themselves. Goffman suggested

Activity

Consider the reader's letter 'Shearer's goal is to win over Geordies'. When is a Geordie really a Geordie? Is it possible to give an accurate answer? How would A. P. Cohen's concept of 'symbolized boundaries' answer these questions? Was it, as the letter suggests, attachment to the community that brought Alan Shearer back to the North East?

C3.2, C3.3

Shearer's goal is to win over Geordies

THE return to Newcastle of football's £15 million man Alan Shearer, and the fuss made about it, is a reminder that Geordies still take homecomings very seriously.

That this should survive in an era of mass communication reflects the firm attachment to the symbols of regional identity which is just part and parcel of living here.

One element is the continual debate about who does or does not belong to Geordieland. Is birth necessary and sufficient, or can belonging be acquired by sons and daughters after a suitable period of residence?

The exact geography of Geordieland is also unclear and a full research effort into the issue chaired by a trusted outsider (Melvin Bragg would do) is becoming imperative.

The local culture is weighted in favour of the oral tradition. The language is notoriously hard to replicate in print, which may go some way to explain the North East's poor performance in literature compared to its music, sport, painting and its greatest cultural forms, reunions and farewells.

Being a Geordie is a full-time job and it is exiles such as Shearer who have to work hardest to prove the right to continued affiliation.

He will certainly need to allude to legendary number nines, the fervour of local nightlife, the awfulness of beer mugs as opposed to straight glasses, the dangers of the "bad" pint and the frightening possibility that the Metro (a strangely exotic and typically over-ambitious name) may be extended to Sunderland.

Mr Stuart Boyd
Newcastle-upon-Tyne

Source: Daily Express, 31 July 1996

'actors' operate in 'front' and 'back' regions. The 'front' region is their identity as they offer it to people they meet, perhaps strangers. Given that they are afraid to show their 'full hand', only aspects of this cameo are true. The back region is seen as our true selves. Giddens, however, sees a weakness in this schema:

If agents are only players on a stage, hiding their true selves behind the masks they assume for the occasion, the social world would indeed be largely empty of substance.

(Giddens, 1984, p. 125)

Such a situation is likely to cause us as much stress as revealing everything about ourselves. In order to solve this contradiction Giddens offers us the concepts of 'enclosure' and 'disclosure', suggesting that to some people, at some times, in some places, we show more of our true selves. Thus there can be a gradient between 'front' and 'back' regions. These concepts are important when we remember the assertion that living in a community can be oppressive as well as supportive. Individual members of a community may well feel pressure to mask their true feelings in order to accept 'official' versions of truth and action. Some have suggested that the need to follow the 'official' line may be more comprehensive than this, seeing community as a form of prison.

Crow and Allan (1994) quote Damer who described traditional working-class communities as 'effectively prisons for their inhabitants' (1990, p. 89). Communities act like this by making use of an effective social arsenal – tools such as ridicule, threats, or even (as has been the case in Northern Ireland) punishment beatings. It is likely that in a 'strong' community members will be under the surveillance of the watching eyes of their neighbours. In modern society we are just as likely to be under the roving eye of closed-circuit television (CCTV). Such surveillance will be strong enough to ensure that most members adhere to the 'collective' or common will. Those who step beyond the boundaries of acceptability face being the object of gossip, being shunned or ostracized, and possible retribution. For the consensus theorist such actions ensure the smooth running of the community for the good of all.

Activity

How would conflict theorists, such as Marxists and feminists, explain the operation of social control of community members? Do the 'norms' represent the expectations of the 'collective' group as a whole or of powerful sections within it?

C3.2, C3.3

Post-modernity and leisure

Rojek (1985, 1993) argues that it is possible to outline three stages of the development of the sociology of leisure. The first stage comprised the studies focused on the development of leisure provision within local authorities, and arose broadly in the 1970s. The main criticism of this approach was that leisure was viewed in isolation from other aspects of society.

This led to the development of critical studies of leisure based mainly on Marxist and latterly feminist perspectives, concerned with analysing the reasons for the way leisure developed and the structural inequalities which lead to inequalities in access to leisure facilities.

The third phrase he identifies is defined by the rise of debates about post-modernity and the impact of this on leisure activities. This has widened the scope of leisure studies to include concern with social identity and the body, and consumer culture and consumption as forms of leisure participation. Veal (1993) argues that this means that there is a need for theorists of leisure to concern themselves with the ways in which individuals and groups express and construct lifestyles through leisure tastes and activities.

Scraton and Bramham argue that it is possible to analyse how the experience of swimming has been transformed in ways which indicate this shift to post-modernity:

The shift from modernity to postmodernity can be illustrated in many leisure experiences, for instance swimming. Rather than the physical education of 'serious' swimming in Victorian public baths and washhouses, policed by officious baths attendants, swimming has been transformed into water-based fun in leisure pools, with water chutes, slides, wave machines, inflatables, fountains, popular music, aqua-rhythm classes (aerobics in the pool) with laser lights, stylish swimming costumes, casually overviewed by spectators in tropicana restaurants, grazing on fast-foods, whilst drinking diet Cokes.

(Scraton and Bramham, 1995, p. 22)

Activity

a Think of another popular leisure activity and draw up your own summary of changes in recent years.

b Does this support the idea that we are living in post-modern times?

Post-modernity and tourism

Post-modern themes have also been applied to the analysis of tourism. In his book *The Tourist Gaze*, Urry (1990b) argues that Jean Baudrillard's idea that we now live in a world where it is not possible to distinguish between the real and the simulation is applicable to tourism, since package tourism does not provide access to the real authentic experiences of the region being visited, but instead a constructed package of contrived events in an artificial environment.

💬 Discussion point

Is package tourism providing a contrived and artificial environment or a genuine holiday?

C3.1a

However, our desire for tourism also reflects a wish to seek new experiences and create new sensations and simulations. Urry goes on to argue that we may now need to talk of 'post-tourism', since many people actually now play along with the simulations offered by package tours and have given up any attempt to seek out authentic cultural experiences.

Norbert Elias and figurational sociology

Elias developed a particular approach which has come to be known as 'figurational sociology'. This has been applied to the sociology of leisure, and more particularly to sport, in a number of ways.

His notion of the civilizing process and of interactions being part of a wider set of figurations has been applied to sport by the work of Eric Dunning and others at Leicester University. Dunning (1971) argues that sport has developed over time, from folk games where there was a high toleration of physical violence and an emphasis on force rather than skill, to modern sport that is clearly regulated through codified rules and where there is a low toleration of physical violence.

The connections between sport, masculinity and different forms of interdependence were explored in the group's work on football hooliganism (Dunning *et al.*, 1988). The fact that football hooliganism can be analysed within a perspective which talks about the growth of civilization emphasizes how there can be setbacks in this process.

Pierre Bourdieu and cultural capital

A Marxist-influenced approach is more evident in the work of Bourdieu, whose concepts of cultural capital and the *habitus* are applicable to the study of leisure, though can also be applied much more widely in relation to, for example, education (see Section 11.1).

In his book *Distinction*, Bourdieu (1984) applies himself to a consideration of theories of leisure participation. He argues that the choices we make are never totally without constraint, and in effect his argument is that structural constraints are very real.

He argues that while we can most certainly explain inequalities in participation in leisure and cultural activities on the basis of economic inequalities, these factors alone cannot explain all inequalities. When they have been taken into account, there is still a degree of choice in what we engage in. For example, going to watch a Premiership football match costs about the same as a visit to the opera, so the choices people make about which of these to engage in cannot be explained fully by reference to income alone.

It is here that his notion of cultural capital comes into play. Bourdieu suggests that our experiences in childhood and our particular social backgrounds create a *habitus*, a certain set of partially unconscious tastes, preferences and perceptions, which provide the basis for this cultural capital. Members of the dominant economic class can use their power to define their tastes and preferences as superior to others. This has similarities to the debate about the relative merits of high culture and mass or popular culture.

Dominant classes can also use their economic capital to purchase cultural competence in these areas, seen as high status through particular sorts of education such as public schools and Oxbridge. This allows them to develop the level of cultural competence to engage freely with high culture, whose attraction is also partly the fact that those without the cultural competence to appreciate it will in effect be excluded. Cultural capital therefore serves as an exclusion mechanism to shore up inequalities in participation in leisure and cultural activities.

13.6 Femininity, masculinity and the culture industries

A plausible case can be made for the view that changes in gender roles are impacting on both the production and consumption of popular culture. At least four issues can be identified:

1 As women participate more extensively in labour markets (see Section 17.2), so they also should gain more recognition as significant consumers of popular culture. There is some evidence to suggest that this is the case. More magazines, books and television programmes are targeted at key female audiences, and more services are available in the market to support female cultural participation, from women's minicab firms, to pubs with male strippers (see 'John Ball's Diary').

JOHN BALL'S DIARY

THREE lean, mean and clean lads have come up with a novel way of making money.

An advert appearing in this newspaper reads: "Ladies, fed up with those everyday household chores? Now you can have your home professionally cleaned by your own male housemaid. Fully/semi-clothed."

For £15 an hour, Don Russo, Jay James and Nick Jones will cook, clean, iron, polish and scrub, fully clothed in a suit or a maid's outfit or whatever tickles your fancy.

For £22.50 an hour they will do the same while sporting nothing more than a G-string and frilly apron.

When a colleague mentioned that some frustrated women may be looking for hidden extras Mr Russo gasped and said: "Oh no, we are a straight commercial cleaning service and nothing else."

He said: "We think our prices are quite reasonable to go around cleaning a stranger's house with our chests and legs hanging out."

Source: Bedfordshire on Sunday, 29 September 1996

---

2 On the production side, there is some evidence to suggest that women are, at last, securing positions of seniority within the cultural industries. The BBC, for example, set itself the objective of filling 40 per cent of its senior managerial positions with either female staff or staff recruited from ethnic minority backgrounds by the year 2000.

Women's magazines have long represented a sector in which female journalists have occupied a majority of the senior editorial positions.

3 Changes in values and the expectations associated with traditional gender roles have opened up more opportunities for women to participate as creative artists in such areas as drama, music, film and literature. The days when girls were allowed to 'decorate' pop bands as 'singers' but were denied opportunities to write or play music have gone.

4 Changes in gender role expectations have impacted on youth subcultures. Club and dance culture appears to open up more opportunities for girls.

Feminist perspectives

The above points represent the 'good news', but critics argue that there is another side to the story. Within families we know that women do not always share equally in the consumption of goods and services – media and cultural services targeted at men's interests, from sports videos to pornography, still far outweigh the provision for women in the marketplace. Despite recent changes in recruitment patterns, men still occupy most of the controlling positions in a majority of cultural industries – only two national newspapers, for example, are currently edited by women.

The BBC had originally hoped to meet its equal-opportunity targets by 1996 and had to reschedule this to the year 2000. By 1998, 29.1 per cent of its senior executives were women, as were 36.3 per cent of its middle managers and senior professionals (BBC, 1998, p. 82). In 1995, only 20 per cent of the BBC's senior managers were female, so the corporation has made some progress but significant inequalities persist. Every commercial television company is obliged to monitor equal opportunities, but very few have appointed a significant number of women into senior positions (see Table 13.1).

In a recent survey, Thomas and Klett-Davies (1995) concluded that female cultural performers worked more days than men but were paid less per day. And the greater use of part-time, casualized and fixed-term contracts in the cultural industries now is also likely to impede womens' progress. In terms of content, too, critics argue that much of the imagery used to promote pop bands, films and videos continues to use women's looks and bodies in exploitative ways.

Table 13.1 Staffing of commercial TV stations

Company	Female staff (%)	Ethnic staff (%)
Anglia	46.6	2.3
Border	40	0
Carlton	54.2	9.6
Central	40.6	3.8
Channel	46.7	4
Grampian	32.5	0.8
Granada	49.4	3
HTV	48	2
LWT	43.1	8.3
Meridian	44.2	1.9
Scottish	48	1.4
Tyne Tees	43.3	1.3
Ulster	37.1	0
Westcountry	42.9	1.1
Yorkshire	44	2
GMTV	57.6	7.3
Channel 4	57.1	9.4
Channel 5	54.5	7.4

Source: ITC Annual Report and Accounts, 1999

Activity

a From Table 13.1, which TV stations employ the highest and which the lowest proportions of women? From Figure 13.3, in which electronic media areas do men earn more than women, and in which do women earn more than men?

b To what extent does this evidence support the view that women are now securing equal opportunities with men in the cultural industries?

c How would sociologists explain the patterns revealed in these figures? (You may wish to read the rest of this section before answering this.)

C3.2, C3.3, N3.1

Radical feminism

There are important differences between traditions of feminist thought. These prompt different degrees of optimism regarding the possibility for women to enjoy greater freedom in the production and consumption of culture.

Radical feminists are sceptical about the possibility of change. The arrival of women in senior positions within cultural enterprises will make little difference, they argue, for two reasons:

- The imperatives of the commercial marketplace will continue to demand that magazines, films and other cultural products use sex and women's bodies to sell commodities, whether or not women make editorial decisions.

- Patriarchal ideology is so deeply embedded in modern societies that both men and women consume culture through the 'male gaze'. In other words, both men and women simply take it for granted that women will be represented as sexual objects in film and other cultural products, and that it is 'natural' for them to be 'enjoyed' by men in this way.

Criticisms of radical feminism

Critics of radical feminism argue that it has two weaknesses:

- As a theory it encourages an ahistorical approach. In other words it suggests that patriarchy has been dominant throughout most of our recent history and so it fails to address the possible mechanisms of social change which might either modify patriarchal ideology or even replace it.

- Secondly, critics argue that at the empirical level there is actually evidence of change which radical feminism either under-estimates or ignores.

Some feminists develop the ideas associated with Gramsci and hegemony theory (see Section 13.2) to trace the ways in which feminist struggle can challenge the hegemony of patriarchal 'common-sense'. Gamman and Marshment (1988), for example, argue that, while commercialism and patriarchal values continue to dominate a great deal of popular culture, there are opportunities within the mainstream to question patriarchy, if not develop feminist perspectives. They question whether radical feminism is correct in insisting that there are deep-seated psychoanalytic processes within the male mind which always and inevitably lead to culture being constructed through the male gaze.

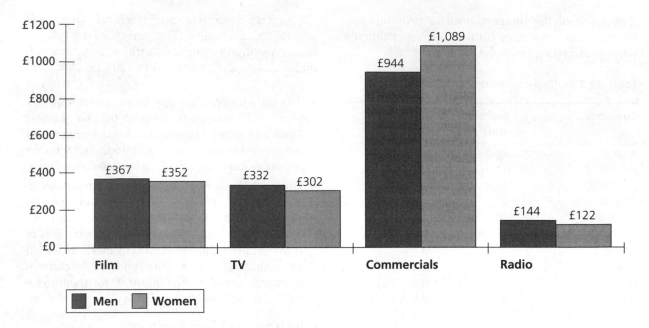

Figure 13.3 Average fee per day for men and women in film, television, commercials and radio in 1993–94 (exclusive of high maximum numbers)
Source: Thomas and Klett-Davies (1995)

Culturalist feminism: watching the detectives

One example of popular culture which has apparently reflected the changes in the construction of gender, discussed at the beginning of this section, is the genre of television 'cop' shows. There have been several series in which the central character has been a female detective. Recently, *Prime Suspect* has proved a particular success in the USA, as well as in the UK, winning top awards for both its acting and writing. However, the prototype for the female cop show is the long-running American series *Cagney and Lacey*. Lorraine Gamman (1988) analyses this show in detail to assess the extent to which it permits a 'feminist' reading (or interpretation) to emerge.

The show features two women who are as effective as their male colleagues in doing their tough work, but not like men in their attitudes or behaviour. The show explores in considerable depth some of the issues which feminists have placed at the top of their political agenda, including rape, child abuse and pornography. The interaction between characters sometimes develops a critique of sexism: male power hierarchies are gently ridiculed.

But, Gammon notes, there appear to be significant constraints on the extent to which a feminist analysis can emerge. The characters Cagney and Lacey are still often portrayed in 'caring' roles; neither character is permitted to stray too far from the conventional expectations associated with female roles. Indeed, one of the actresses was replaced in the second series because she did not look 'feminine enough'. The show has explicitly distanced itself from feminist politics and the leading actresses have publicly disowned feminism.

Despite all this, Gamman argues that, while a full-blown female gaze may not be constructed, the show does offer a variety of 'glances' with 'feminist implications'. In other words, the show touches on or hints at themes which invite a feminist interpretation.

Activity

a Why do radical feminists believe that appointing women to senior positions in cultural industries may not bring about significant change?

b Explain in your own words why Gamman and Marshment believe that signs of a 'female gaze' can be detected in some television shows. Provide some of your own examples.

C3.2, C3.3

Women and romance

Another example of the analysis of popular culture has been shifting conceptions of the importance of notions of love, romance and marriage in the construction of femininity and in popular culture products aimed at women. The classic study which identified the importance of romance to adolescent females was the analysis of *Jackie* magazine carried out by Angela McRobbie (1978, 1983). She saw the stories in the magazines as reinforcing rather conventional notions of femininity which were based on the idea that the prime role of adult women was to be wives and mothers and therefore their key task as adolescents was to find, attract and keep a man. One key implication of this was that young women acted as individuals and in competition with each other over men and this it was argued potentially undermined notions of female solidarity,

Another study of women's magazines was undertaken by Marjorie Ferguson (1983). She also argued that there were constant themes running through magazines aimed at women along the lines of finding and keeping your man. She argues that such magazines encouraged a cult of femininity. This involves a celebration of the way women are different but this also leads to the reinforcement of traditional female roles.

A further study of young women was conducted by Sue Sharpe (1976). Her study of working-class girls found that their priorities were love, marriage, husbands and children and only after these issues of jobs and careers. She focused on the way that girls' education following on from primary socialization reinforced the notion of traditional roles for women.

However, in a later follow up (Sharpe, 1994), she found that there had been some changes with girls much more concerned about careers and much more assertive about claiming their rights on an equal basis to boys and men. It is still the case, though, that the processes of socialization emphasize the future role of women today as being wives and mothers, so Sharpe argues that we are in a rather contradictory period since the world has moved on in some ways but not in others.

As well as the world moving on, sociological views on women, romance and the media have moved on also. Gaye Tuchman (1981) argued that women in the media were normally confined to roles in the home or in sexual or romantic situations. She was making the point that apart from this, women were largely invisible in terms of being represented in the media. This presents these representations involving romance and sexuality as rather limited and limiting.

However, in partial contrast, Ien Ang (1985) argues that the popularity of soaps amongst women television viewers, with their common themes of love and romance, is based on the soap operas portraying many issues, conflicts and dilemmas which are part of women's real lives. Since love and romance are a fair staple of soap operas, this view presents a rather more positive view, emphasizing the uses and gains that audiences can get from programmes such as Dallas. (This issue is also considered in Sections 6.1 and 6.3). More recently, there has been a growth in studies concerned with the increasing sexualization of the male body and debates about the female gaze.

Sexualization of the male body

One quite striking recent development in popular culture is the proliferation of imagery which places the male body in a sexual context. A television advertisement for jeans, in which a young man in a launderette removes all but his briefs, may have started the trend, but it has spread through advertisements, fashion magazines and into the world of pop music. Almost every month brings a new crop of young men, with varying degrees of musical talent, but bodies which are 'fit' enough to be represented in differing states of semi-nudity for publicity shots and music videos. As McRobbie comments:

The beauty stakes have gone up for men, and women have taken up the position of active viewers.

(McRobbie, 1994, p. 186)

Men too, it seems, are being turned into sexualized commodities. This, of course, poses a set of interesting theoretical questions. Is there such a thing as a 'female gaze'? If there is, what does this mean for radical feminist theory which assumed that the male gaze was derived from psychoanalytic processes related to male child development: there was something within the male psyche which turned men into voyeurs. Is the 'female gaze' related to comparable processes within women's psychoanalytic development? But, if this is the case, why has the 'female gaze' found public expression only in recent years?

Discussion point

Is it possible for women now to behave as voyeurs by 'enjoying' looking at men's bodies? Is this evidence of equality between the sexes?

C3.1a

According to Suzanne Moore (1988), in order to approach the sexualization of the male body, we need to move beyond theories which deal only with psychoanalytic processes. We have to recognize that female and male sexual identities (how we see ourselves sexually and how we see others) are no more fixed by psychoanalytic processes than they are by biology. Female and male sexual identities are fluid and can change; women have *learnt* to 'enjoy' male bodies. However, Moore notes that the 'female gaze' is not identical to the 'male gaze'. She argues that it is more subtle. Women do not necessarily enjoy full-frontal shots of men, and early commercial attempts to exploit a 'female gaze' – such as *Playgirl* magazine – failed because they did not recognize that women would not enjoy the crudest forms of erotic representation to be found in *Playboy* (Moore, 1988, p. 57).

Nevertheless, it is clearly the case that cultural producers are keen to satisfy the newly crystallized taste amongst women for commodities which develop more sexually explicit themes. Not all commentators regard this as a further step towards equality between the sexes. McRobbie argues that the commercial exploitation of both male and female sexuality further extends oppressive social relationships, rather than truly opening up new opportunities, either for women or men.

Case Study – Men and fashion

Men are now presented with a proliferation of commodities seeking to cater for them as consumers of fashion. Frank Mort (1996) draws on the work of Foucault in order to explain this new development.

The emergence of a culture which was preoccupied with male fashions and masculine identities in the 1980s was the product of the way in which a number of distinct social groups developed particular forms of knowledge. Power, according to Mort, was exercised within systems of consumption by these social groups: consumption was not determined by the 'power' or 'effect' of 'external' forces, such as the class structure.

A new masculinity

Mort's detailed analysis helps to make this point more clearly. In comparison with the 1950s, he argues, important changes occurred in the way masculinity was represented through fashion and clothes design, advertising and retailing during the 1980s. There was a movement away from traditional masculinity: it became much more acceptable for young men to be deeply preoccupied with image, style and 'the way they looked'. A much wider range of products became available with which men could groom themselves, from deodorants to hair gel. Most importantly, Mort implies, fashion and advertising now offered a much wider range of male identities, many of which departed radically from the respectable image of the heterosexual middle-class white male.

A tangle of alliances

Mort explains this in terms of a 'complex tangle of alliances' between key social groups and individuals who developed new forms of knowledge about fashion and masculinity. Mort uncovers:

... a coalition between independent journalists and designers, photographers, models and urban flaneurs. These experts claimed to provide answers to a set of pressing questions about the disintegration of established consumer patterns and the emergence of new ones.

(Mort, 1996, p. 8)

The thrust of Mort's analysis is to demonstrate that a cluster of separate factors and interests coincided during the 1980s to produce a new understanding of masculinity and fashion. To begin with, a number of factors had already made the issue of masculine identity less clear-cut (see Section 4.1).

The traditional sources of masculine authority, such as lifetime careers, were no longer secure, and the feminist critique of traditional forms of masculinity had also encouraged some men to question their own behaviour. Secondly, a sustained consumer boom developed in the same period; those with sufficient income began to spend more and more on clothes and consumer goods. This helped to stimulate a resurgence in the British fashion industry.

These conditions provided opportunities for 'talented individualists' to develop careers as 'cultural professionals', providing advice and guidance on new trends in consumption, style and fashion. *The Face*, which emerged as an independent magazine in 1980, and later *Arena*, offered such 'cultural professionals' opportunities to disseminate new ideas, which included new ways of representing male dress and design.

Activity

a How does Mort's analysis of fashion depart from earlier approaches?

b According to Mort, how have ideas of masculinity changed between the 1950s and the 1990s?

c What role does Mort believe 'the complex tangle of alliances' played in promoting the new interest in men's fashion?

C3.2, C3.3

The debate over post-modernism

Post-modernism is a slippery term which is used by writers to refer to several distinct things. Featherstone (1991a) points out that the term is variously used to refer to:

- new developments in intellectual and cultural theory (what we shall call the 'theory of post-modernism')

- the suggestion that our subjective experience of everyday life and our sense of identity has somehow changed significantly in recent years ('the post-modern condition')

- the view that capitalist or industrial societies have reached new and important stages in their development (the shift from modernity to post-modernity).

Leading post-modernist writers include Lyotard (1993), Jameson (1991) and Baudrillard (1993, 1998), although there are important differences between them.

The end of meta-narratives and cultural depthlessness

According to Lyotard, the post-modern world is characterized by a spreading cynicism about 'meta-narratives' or general belief systems, including world religions, political ideologies such as socialism or liberalism, and even science and reason itself. We have become disillusioned and no longer expect the world to become a better place. Meta-narratives have partly been discredited because, in an era of global media in which we learn more and more about other peoples' beliefs and lifestyles, it becomes less and less possible to regard one lifestyle or one belief system as the 'true one'. As Lyotard puts it:

Eclecticism is the degree zero of contemporary general culture: one listens to reggae, watches a Western, eats McDonald's for lunch and local cuisine for dinner, wears Paris perfume in Tokyo and retro clothes in Hong Kong; knowledge is a matter for TV games.

(Lyotard, 1993, p. 42)

Discussion point

Have we become disillusioned with *all* meta-narratives and, if so, why?

C3.1a

According to post-modernists, the collapse of meta-narratives is connected with the new 'depthlessness' of culture – 'a new kind of superficiality' (Jameson, 1991). This is because without meta-narratives or fundamental truths, culture cannot claim to offer insights into the 'real' nature of things. Post-modern culture simply 'picks and mixes' in terms of fashion, music, lifestyle and even subcultural belief, whereas in the former modern era culture still 'meant something'. According to post-modern writers, youth subcultural styles no longer express anything more than fashion statements, unconnected to deeper values or experiences.

Similarly, Strinati (1995) suggests that post-modern television and film have become preoccupied merely with surface style and imagery, rather than deeper underlying themes which might relate to 'the realities' of the human condition. Action blockbuster movies dwell on the spectacular special effects rather than strong plots, and television drama departs from the 'realist' plots of the 1960s (which attempted to deal with serious issues like homelessness or poverty) and embraces a surreal world in which 'reality' is often confused; for example, *Twin Peaks*, or more recently *American Gothic* and *The X-files*. Kaplan (1987) identifies pop and rock videos as perfect examples of post-modern culture because they abandon all notion of narrative structure – there is no attempt to 'tell a story', rather the power of a rock video lies purely in the collage of images mixed with music.

According to post-modernists, cultural standards become meaningless (see Section 10.3). Without meta-narratives, it makes little sense to 'judge' the quality of cultural products according to a cultural standard: one cultural standard is as good as any other, all are relative.

The cultural, the economic and the agencies of signification

According to Jameson and Baudrillard, with the decline of engineering and manufacturing in many advanced capitalist economies, the provision of cultural and media services becomes the key economic sector. In the UK, for example, the record industry is one of the leading export sectors of the economy.

Both Jameson (1991) and Baudrillard (1988) argue that Marx failed to appreciate the qualitative transformation which occurs once cultural artefacts, signs and images become the most important commodities in the market. Jameson does not abandon Marx altogether: he acknowledges that it is still the drive for *profit* which leads capitalism to invest in marketing, advertising, public relations and the other cultural or image industries.

Baudrillard, in contrast, moves much more sharply away from Marx, insisting that in order to understand the post-modern society we must develop a 'political economy of the sign' (or image). The trading of signs or images, as opposed to 'things', is now the dominant pattern of market relations and the task must be to explore the 'codes' which govern such exchanges (Baudrillard, 1988, pp. 57–97). It is semiology rather than economics which holds the key to understanding the principles or 'codes' governing such transactions, and it is the 'agencies of signification' – advertising agencies, marketing consultants, public relations firms, and the mass media – which play a crucial role in circulating these codes. For example, the 'designer labels' attached to jeans, shirts and coats all 'mean' something according to a code recognized by most young people.

Activity

Consider the following commodities: jeans, cars, furnishings, food. Write a short summary describing the codes which operate in relation to each example.

C3.2, C3.3

For Baudrillard, we live in a world which is 'media saturated'; a world in which we are bombarded by media and advertizing messages through multi-channel television, globalized electronic and cable networks, a profusion of radio stations, newspapers, and street billboards. Baudrillard argues that the consequences of this are profound. The 'codes' generated by the agencies of signification become our rules for organizing our lives. So powerful are these codes, according to Baudrillard, that we lose the ability to distinguish between reality (for example, the 'real' practical value of a commodity) and its image. We begin to buy images rather than actual 'things'. Thus, for Baudrillard, the post-modern world is a world dominated by 'simulacra' (literally, false or deceptive images) in which we no longer even try to distinguish reality from image, the two blur together.

Post-modern identity

While Baudrillard is pessimistic in his reading of the post-modern world, not all post-modernists share his vision. Hebdidge (1988), who has moved closer to post-modernism in his later writing, and Chen (1992), present more 'optimistic' accounts. We are no longer inhibited by social categories such as class, ethnicity, gender or even age in our choice of styles and fashions. Mixing and matching from a variety of subcultural styles and contexts can be a creative and pleasurable experience. We all now have a detailed knowledge of the history of earlier subcultural patterns, through the work of the mass media in continually providing retrospective accounts, via pop videos, old TV favourites recycled on cable channels, and Hollywood films, so we can select from a huge cultural warehouse of new and retro styles. Post-modern identities, then, are diverse and pluralistic – not shaped by the constraints of social structure. This cultural knowledge which we all possess makes us sophisticated decoders of culture, fashion and mass media. For 'optimistic' theorists, the post-modern condition means having many more cultural options.

However, a more pessimistic picture is presented by others. The semiological power of the cultural codes generated by late capitalism leads Jameson (1991) to doubt whether sustained political opposition to their dominance is possible. Baudrillard goes further: for him, the media encourage a process of 'massification' (Kellner, 1989, p. 69), producing mass audiences and homogeneous patterns of consumption. The only way in which the masses can resist is through passive and silent alienation. They may watch the parade of images and symbols without absorbing any deeper message, merely channel hopping from one television station to another. And even if there were any evidence of resistance amongst the post-modern public, this would quickly be neutralized by the mass media, eager to search out more examples of 'spectacle' as entertainment. Thus, radical demonstrations or protests are represented as 'entertaining' news items without attention to the underlying political issues provoking action. Indeed, the mass media, by bombarding us with so many messages all the time – 'an ecstasy of communication' according to Baudrillard – actually disempower us. We are simply overwhelmed by the sheer volume of information and images. We become immobilized, incapable of discerning the relevant or critical from the mundane.

Gender identities: differences and identities

Feminist social scientists have argued that it is possible for women to be equal to men, without becoming *like* men. These feminists want a share in what they see as men's exclusive privileges. At the same time, they want to retain the way in which women and men are seen to be different from one another, each possessing a distinct set of qualities. Their arguments are summarized here.

Women, femininity and caring

Gilligan (1982) has suggested that women and men have different cognitive processes and that this affects their respective moral viewpoints. She argues that women's moral viewpoints are based on an 'ethic of care' which is produced through their concern with the nurturance and moral development of children. Hence women tend to conceive morality as an understanding of relationships and responsibilities towards others. Men, on the other hand, tend to conceive morality in terms of 'fairness' and 'justice', focusing on the construction and maintenance of a system of 'rights' for individuals.

Gilligan seems to suggest that an 'ethic of care' or an inclination for peace are somehow 'built in' to women. Her arguments have

been taken up, for example, by feminist peace activists or 'eco-feminists', who have used them to support their claims that women are essentially more peaceable than men, say, or more conscious of the relationships between human beings and their natural environments. If attaining 'equality' involves becoming 'like men', contend these feminists, women would be forced to emulate men's war-mongering and environmental destruction. Instead it is better for women to concentrate on preventing war and devastation. Thus 'difference' is emphasized, although it is assumed that 'equality' between men and women can emerge when men disarm and turn away from war, or consider 'green' claims about pollution.

Discussion point
Do you think that women are naturally more peaceable than men?

C3.1a

Analysis of 'different but equal'

Feminists who argue that the differences between men and women are socially constructed and historically produced have taken issue with claims that women might be 'naturally' more caring or peaceable than men, calling them 'essentialist'.

Spelman, in her book *Inessential Woman: Problems of Exclusion in Feminist Thought* (1990), has suggested that not only is it incorrect to imbue women and men with 'natural' qualities, when those qualities are assumed but never explained; but furthermore it is impossible to speak of 'gender' – of differences between women and men – without also speaking of other differences such as 'race' and class.

Ethnicity, class and women

Spelman points out that if the experience of being a woman is different for black women and white women, working-class women and middle-class women, then gender identity itself is problematized:

[Do] we have gender identity in common? In one sense, of course, yes: all women are women. But in another sense, no: not if gender is a social construction and females become not simply women, but particular kinds of women.

(Spelman, 1990, p. 113)

In this argument the existence of inequalities between women demonstrates that there are differences between them. Spelman argues that women must understand their differences in order to be able to tackle inequalities with the eventual aim of equality between all:

[If] the meaning of what we apparently have in common (being women) depends in some ways on the meanings of what we don't have in common (for example, our different racial or class identities), then … attention to race and class … helps us to understand gender. In this sense it is only if we pay attention to how we differ that we come to an understanding of what we have in common.

(Spelman, 1990, p. 113)

In the long term, then, a better understanding of the differences between women may – paradoxically – lead to their erosion. However, if gender, 'race' and class disappear on the road to equality, will they leave us with a world of 'sameness'?

The problem of equality

Whilst differences currently produce inequalities they also produce cultural richness and diversity. So even as black people experience racism, they may want to hang on to their sense of themselves as 'black', as this sense of self mediates and constructs, say, particular family relationships or forms of artistic expression. In the same vein many women derive a great deal of satisfaction from performing their traditionally ascribed roles, particularly caring for children, and might suggest that their rich experiences of mothering are not something they feel can be shared beyond the level of giving responsibility for particular tasks to a partner at particular times (see Section 5.6).

Is equality desirable?

While it seems that 'equality' between men and women and between women is desirable, 'difference' currently acts as an apparently insurmountable stumbling block to its attainment. Alternatively, one might argue in this case that the existence of 'difference' undermines the notion of 'equality'. If men and women become equal in the sense that the notion 'equality' describes, then women may lose what is precious to many – a particular sense of their relationships to others. But if they emphasize their differences from men, suggesting that these are in some way 'natural', they fall prey to traditional ideas about women's cultural roles.

So, for example, if women's and men's differences rest on women's capacities for mothering, then women who choose heterosexual nuclear family-style personal relationships are effectively arguing themselves back into the home. But if differences between women and men are culturally constructed then women have no insuperable claim to staying at home caring for children, which many of them in fact wish to do.

At the 'equality' end of this debate there is, in effect, no way for those women who are mothers to describe and understand their often powerful feelings about motherhood. If men can have those same powerful feelings too – because looking after children must be seen in terms of gender-neutral parenting, rather than gender-specific mothering or fathering – then a feminist vision of womanhood that involves mothering is negated. This presents difficulties for some feminists as many women who are mothers have described the 'realness' of their powerful feelings.

'Equal worth'

Pateman (1992), a feminist theorist, has pointed out that it is very difficult for feminists to argue they are different from and yet equal to men. She has called the attempt to think through the argument that women are different from men, and yet the same as men, 'Wollstonecraft's dilemma', after the eighteenth-century feminist writer Mary Wollstonecraft who grappled with the same issue.

After all, how is this argument different from that made by some anti-feminists who believe that men and women can be equal, but in their separate spheres, 'private' and 'public'?

The answer in this case lies in the very separation of these spheres: there is simply the assumption amongst those who favour separate spheres that equality 'works' between those spheres, when in fact there is no reason why it should do so. Feminists might argue that such assumptions mask the reality – 'public' is more powerful than 'private'. Nonetheless, they are still faced with the problem of rationalizing two apparently opposite concepts.

Pateman goes on to argue that it is the inequalities attendant on 'difference' that present problems, rather than differences themselves (see also Section 17.8). She writes:

[The] meaning of sexual difference has to cease to be the difference between freedom and subordination. The issue in the problem of 'difference' is women's freedom.

(Pateman, 1992, p. 28)

Equal worth and citizenship

Pateman speaks of 'equal worth', arguing that 'equality' can flexibly accommodate both a pre-disposition in women towards motherhood, and a desire for equal status that relates only to the potential similarities between women and men, and between women.

She invokes the notion of 'citizenship' – social, political and economic participation – to frame her argument, suggesting that women must be free to make life-choices for themselves. She argues:

If ... women's citizenship is to be worth the same as men, patriarchal social and sexual relations have to be transformed into free relations. This does not mean that all citizens must become (like) men or that all women must be treated in the same way. On the contrary, for citizenship to be of equal worth, the substance of equality must differ according to the diverse circumstances and capacities of citizens, men and women.

(Pateman, 1992, p. 29)

Men and women, while making a claim to the right of self-determination of each, might thus conceive of themselves as having the potential to be 'differently equal' and 'equally different'.

Tomorrow's women: gender, class, ethnicity and age

Differences and inequalities between men and women and between women framed social relationships between groups and individuals in the twentieth century. Feminist theorists have highlighted the complex links between gender, 'race' and class as stratifying agents. In this vein, Abbott and Wallace have argued that:

... racialised women in Britain suffer discrimination, exploitation and subordination because they are Black as well as because they are women.

(Abbott and Wallace, 1997, p. 80)

They also contend that inequalities can become lesser or greater during the course of a lifetime:

While middle-class women are more advantaged than their working-class sisters, this does not prevent them becoming poor if they become a head of a lone-parent family or from suffering relative poverty in old age.

(Abbott and Wallace, 1997, p. 80)

Hence the inequalities of gender, 'race', class and age which sociologists have identified can act in a compound fashion on particular groups of women, or on individual women.

Gender and 'race'

Feminists writing from a 'black' perspective have attempted to theorize the link between gender and 'race'-related oppressions. This has, how-ever, revealed a number of tensions and contra-dictions within the 'black feminist' perspective. Tang Nain (1991) points out that many black women are ambivalent about feminism:

- On the one hand, black women may be criti-cal of the sexist attitudes of some black men.
- On the other hand, they may feel protective of those same black men, given that those men are seen as already the subjects of racism.

It is temptingly easy for white people and insti-tutions to view black women's criticisms of black men as supporting their claims about the inferi-ority of black people in general.

Black women's ambivalence to feminism

Tang Nain argues (1991, p. 2) that black women's ambivalence about feminism stems from:

- an assessment of feminism as a white ideology and practice which is anti-men
- a sense that it is incompatible with the black struggle against racism and that attention to it will detract from and divide that struggle
- a belief that it does not address issues of rel-evance to black women
- disenchantment over the experience of racism (and/or indifference to it) by black women who were involved in the movement
- the 'race'-blindness of some of the concepts of 'mainstream' feminism
- the insensitivity of some of the practices of mainstream feminism to the experiences of black women and the whole black population.

Controversy has arisen, in particular, over 'white' feminist analyses concerning reproduction, patri-archy, the family, abortion, and male violence towards women. These analyses, it is argued, have not taken the experiences of black women into account.

Tang Nain concludes that, while feminism is necessary for black women in order to understand those aspects of their experiences which are gendered, black feminists could occupy a central role in generating a new feminism – giving equal space to inequalities of gender, 'race' and class. Such a feminism might be called 'anti-racist/socialist feminism'.

How would such a feminism differ from socialist feminism? Most importantly, it would not simply add 'race' to its already existing analyses, as 'socialist feminism' did. Rather, it would generate its analysis directly from black women's experiences and ideas.

Gender and class

The early days of second-wave feminism saw the construction of Marxist and feminist analyses that attempted to understand women's oppression as it was mediated by class. Feminists observed inequalities in the labour market that could not be explained with reference to class alone, as had been previously argued by Marxists. They also constructed an analysis of inequalities between men and women in the domestic sphere, pointing to women's unpaid domestic labour as evidence of oppression and exploitation. One group of Marxist feminists argued that there should be a formally constituted, state-run system of 'wages for housework' (Dalla Costa and James, 1972).

Many years later the British government stated its intention to include an estimate of the economic value of domestic labour alongside its calculations of gross national product, although this figure will not be formally included in the total GNP. In a small way, this represents a recognition, at least, that domestic labour constitutes 'work' or productive labour of some kind (see Section 17.2).

🖭 Discussion point

Do you think women (or men) should be paid wages for housework?

C3.1a

Barrett (1989) writes:

... socialist feminism's influence within feminism as a whole has been steadily declining. ... [The] negotiations of socialist feminism with the issues of men and class have been relatively displaced. ... [The] voices now most effectively addressing questions of class, inequality, poverty and

exploitation to a wider public are those of black women, not white socialist feminists.

(Barrett, 1989, pp. xxiii and xxiv)

Feminism and class

This does not mean that 'white' feminists have nothing further of use to say about class, or do not continue to act around inequalities of class and gender.

In the 1984/85 miners' strike women in mining communities formed Women Against Pit Closures (WAPC), an organization that supported the striking miners but also campaigned on its own behalf. Some male strikers initially reacted adversely to the relatively autonomous activities of WAPC, precisely because the organization gave women a voice of their own. Some women found a new confidence as a result of their involvement with WAPC, and have subsequently been actively involved with reconstructing their economically devastated communities, setting up women's centres and education and retraining programmes. Castleford Women's Centre, in West Yorkshire, is an example of one such centre which offers education to women.

Ethnicity, social class and masculinity

Is it correct to characterize men as conforming to one masculine stereotype or another? Or could it be argued that there are many different forms of masculinity? While the behaviour of some men is undoubtedly in keeping with images of dominant masculinity, most men's behaviour is like this only sometimes, while some individual men do not behave 'like men' at all. This may seem encouraging news for feminists and others who seek to undermine dominant masculine forms, but at the same time it underlines the complexities of the operation of patriarchy.

Just as some women are more powerful than others, so masculinity too is modified and reframed by 'race', class and sexuality, making some men more powerful than others. Given that dominant forms of masculinity are predicated on male power, less-powerful men may express their masculinity differently. Is it more appropriate, then, to refer to 'masculinities' rather than the singular 'masculinity'?

Being a man

Weeks (1986), a theorist of gay masculinity and sexuality, has argued that what it means to be a man or a woman in contemporary society is, in fact, always contradictory:

[We] learn early on in our particular society that to be a man is not to be a homosexual. Male homosexuality has been stigmatised through several centuries as effeminate, an inversion of gender, precisely unmanly. Yet we also know that many 'real men' do see themselves as homosexual and that the 1970s saw a general 'machoisation' of the gay world. Here conventional views about what it is to be a man conflict with sexual desires and (probably) sexual activities: yet for many gay men the two are held in tension.

(Weeks, 1986, pp. 58–9)

To argue that there are many ways to 'be a man' suggests that it is more correct to refer to 'masculinities' than 'masculinity'. However 'masculinities', too, act to affirm dominant forms, and to oppress women. Issues of masculinity bring us to a consideration of how gender identities are constructed through culture.

Gender 'crossover'

In *Freedom's Children*, Wilkinson and Mulgan (1995) argue that as young women have achieved success in the education system (see Section 8.8), and 'male' jobs in the army, manufacturing and construction have dried up (see Section 17.2), there has also been what they call 'a swing away from traditional masculinity' (p. 31). They describe a '"feminization" of men's values' (p. 31) where younger men are professing to want intimacy and emotional honesty, previously seen as the domain of women, as well as wanting more involvement with parenting, and being more prepared to work in 'caring' jobs.

At the same time young women are becoming 'masculinized'. This means that they are more prepared to take risks, but also that they are becoming more attached to violence. This evidence speaks to the documented rise of 'girl gangs', for example. Demos expects these broad trends to continue, and successive generations to take these changes further. (See also Sections 4.1 and 8.5.)

These findings are important because young people's current values, aspirations and experiences contrast sharply with those of previous generations. While this may be an effect of economic trends – the feminization of the labour market, say, or job insecurity – the evidence cited by Wilkinson and Mulgan shows, for example, that while young women still do more housework than young men:

... the ratio of time spent by working women relative to men in cooking, cleaning and doing the laundry has fallen from 3 amongst 35–55 year olds to 2.3 for 25–34 year olds, and just 1.75 for 16–24 year olds. ... Perhaps even more striking is the fact that the amount of time spent by the youngest working women is barely a third of the time spent by the oldest working women. At this rate of change we might expect the gender gap to have disappeared within a decade or so. Perhaps too, despite hi-tech washing machines and hoovers, the young are becoming the dirty generation as masculinised new women accept male standards of cleanliness rather than the other way around.

(Wilkinson and Mulgan, 1995, p. 76)

The end of gender inequalities?

The broad implication of Demos' argument is that if enough people – a *critical mass* – change their attitudes and behaviour, then gender-related inequalities will begin to disappear. At the same time, policymakers in particular will need to address changing social attitudes amongst British people. The UK is a democracy, and so the policy decisions of government and its agencies must generally reflect the will of the people (though see Section 15.1). Thus, institutions like these will be forced to rethink their practices.

This extends to employers too. If employees are generally less prepared to work long hours, then employers – given that they need to employ workers – will be forced to allow for this by building in further flexible working patterns or by changing their 'office culture'.

Demos' trend-spotting points to new prospects for feminists and others interested in promoting equality. If young people are leading a 'genderquake', as Demos have suggested, then those who wish to actively address today's social inequalities must ensure they make room for them to thrive.

Class

The relationship between 'race', ethnicity and class has been discussed in relation to the Marxist and Weberian perspectives. It was noted that racialized minorities occupied mainly the bottom of the socio-economic system, because of the nature of capitalism's class-based colonial roots and post-colonial attitude towards migrant

The African–Caribbean network for science and technology

This group of 60 scientists, mathematicians, medical professionals and engineers was set up [in 1995] in response to growing concerns about the under-achievement of black Caribbean pupils. Based in Manchester but with a national membership, it works with schools; colleges and education authorities by:

- aiming to motivate children's interest by highlighting the achievements of black people in the professions

- providing a mentoring scheme with black scientists and other positive role models

- using a schools outreach service in which black professionals spend time in classrooms assisting multicultural maths and science modules

- making tutorial support available for children and young people from the age of nine through to undergraduates, every day after school, Saturday mornings and during school holidays

- running regular short courses to explain the education system to parents and an information service to help pupils and students who are interested in entering careers in science and technology.

To find out more about the African–Caribbean Network for Science and Technology, contact Liz Rasekoala at 19 Dorchester Road, Swinton, Manchester M27 5PX.

Source: Reva Klein, *Times Educational Supplement*, 26 April 1996

labour. The Rowntree Foundation in 1995 claimed that ethnic minorities are more likely than whites to be part of the poorest fifth of the population, and less likely than whites to be in the richest fifth. However, attention has focused recently on the growing number of black middle-class professionals: self-employment in 1994, for example, was more common among Indian men (23 per cent) than white men (17 per cent), according to the *Labour Force Survey*.

According to Cross (1992), a change in class position for some of the UK's ethnic minorities has raised three issues:

1 *Ethnic difference*. It has been argued by some sociologists that some ethnic groups are 'culturally predisposed' for enterprise.

2 *Ethnic markets*. Do the markets that ethnic minorities serve provide for ethnic groups only, or all consumer needs?

3 *Reasons for enterprise*. Has discrimination *forced* ethnic minorities to start their own businesses because of limited chances in the open labour market? (See also Sections 17.2.)

Cross focused attention mainly on Asian businessmen. However, as demonstrated by the article 'The African–Caribbean network for science and technology', African–Caribbean communities are in the embryonic stages of filtering into the middle class, taking jobs in commerce and other professions.

Two distinct attitudes have emerged towards 'buppies' (black yuppies). The first is that they provide inspiration for other black people, as Richardson nicely summed up:

It could be argued that the success of middle class blacks helps the black community: they create jobs for other black people, they contradict racist stereotypes held by non-blacks, and they provide role models for young black people.

(Richardson, 1996, p. 67)

The second belief is that the black middle class has 'sold out' to the black community and the black working class, being more interested in their own careers than securing improved conditions for black people as a whole (Sivanandan, 1990).

Whichever position is adopted, the stability of this new stratum is presumed. In contrast, Daye (1994) argues that black middle-class workers are highly marginalized and therefore 'it is debatable whether in fact they will form a permanent grouping in the British class structure' (p. 280). Whether this small upwardly mobile group is here to stay remains to be seen.

Post-modernism and post-structuralism

Post-modern and post-structural theories have, according to Bradley (1996), the following elements in common:

1 *A stress on difference and diversity*. Brah (1992) and Madood (1992) argue that each ethnic group experiences different patterns of disadvantage and develops distinctive responses within their own culture and community. For example, Gujaratis and Punjabis are both Asian groups, but have vastly different experiences, histories, etc. Therefore, ethnicity and culture are emphasized rather than

'race'. The UK is seen as a patchwork of heterogeneous groups (Anthias and Yuval-Davis, 1993).

2 *An attack on essentialism.* Donald and Rattansi (1992) argue that various groups and individuals have divergent experiences. 'Race' is a social construction which reveals very little about the group it is trying to investigate. Post-modernists see ethnicity as fluid and complex, thereby guarding against 'ethnic absolutism' (Gilroy, 1987, 1993) which implies that all ethnic groups share the same experiences. It is argued that we are all 'mongrels' because ethnic purity does not exist:

There is no such thing as a 'pure' culture, since all have been inevitably affected by processes of migration, travel and tourism, cultural exchange and communication.

(Bradley, 1996, p. 134)

3 *The analysis of discourse.* Hall (1992a) believes that ideas are perpetuated by various forms of discourse such as the portrayal of white superiority in literary texts. Post-structuralists argue that this helps to embed differences between nations and ethnic groups. Gilroy (1987) traced a discourse of black criminality which had developed since post-war Britain. Black was represented in the media as 'criminal'.

4 *A rejection of the presentation of racialized minorities as victims.* Gilroy (1987) argues that even during slavery African exiles developed their culture and that oppressed and racialized minorities do the same in contemporary society. Black groups are not passive recipients of racism and discrimination, they are active in opposing their own subordination through political and counter cultural forms (e.g. pop music).

Activity

Study the accompanying box 'Sleeve notes', which is a commentary of one of hip-hop artist Paris' record sleeves.

a What images are used?

b How could these images be seen to support a post-modernist perspective?

C3.2, C3.3

Sleeve notes

Controversy? Paris has it oozing from his every creative action. Even the inner sleeve artwork for the new album has got temperatures raised. On one side there is a picture of Paris behind a tree, gat in hand, ready to shoot the president in front of the White House. On the other a collage inscribed with the words "Land of the weak, home of the slave". What's it all about?

"The entire collage is the way that black America destroys itself. You see police violence, domestic violence, a little boy with a gun, a man with Uzis, a drug deal, Colin Powell and Clarence Thomas – those are basically people in allegiance with the oppressor by destroying ourselves. That's what 'Sleeping With The Enemy' is about.

"Originally on that statue it says 'Land of the free, home of the brave' but it's not applicable to us because we're not free and we're not brave. This country is weak and black people are still slaves here, but it's much more subtle now. It's more mind slavery because we don't think freely, we don't do for ourselves. That collage, that shows how a lot of us act as a result of this slave mentality."

Source: Hip-Hop Connection (HHC), February 1993

Identity

All four of Bradley's points discussed above have become evident in one area of post-modernist investigation into 'race' and ethnicity – that of identity.

Post-modern theorists argue that identity was once a concept that people believed to be firm and fixed, but that social change has undermined this. New identities have been created via globalization, which has brought different cultural groups into closer contact, that are both fragile and complex. People adopt different identities to match the diversity in their everyday lives. Individuals no longer identify only with their class position, but with gender, age, disability, 'race', religion, ethnicity, nationality, civil status, music styles, dress codes, etc. (Cohen, 1992). An individual will pick and choose, mix and match, the identity/identities with which he or she feels most comfortable (e.g. 'I am a male Pakistani, black British rapper').

However, identities are fragile or precarious. In a post-modern world where everything is changing, people are no longer *sure* who they are. This can also be used to explain the recent 'revival' of racism, or 'new racism', in terms of worries over identity. Individuals may feel threatened by losing their previously stable sense of identity and search for a more secure identity, which often takes an ethnic form (Hall, 1992b).

Criticisms of the post-modern approach

Criticisms have been levelled at post-modern theory, challenging not only its fundamental basis, but also its application to 'race' and ethnicity (Richardson, 1996):

1 'The idea of post-modernity may yet turn out to be a figment of overheated disappointed radical hopes' (Lyon, 1994, p. 4). It has been argued by some sociologists that today's society is not a radical post-modern departure from the modern world, but a 'reconstituted modernity' (Smart, 1994) or 'late modernity' (Giddens, 1990).

2 'Racial' and ethnic post-modern theories remain under-developed and ambiguous (Hall, 1992a).

3 Post-modernism places too much emphasis on 'new ethnicities' and new identities, which is not an accurate reflection of everyday life for the UK's ethnic minorities who value traditional culture (Modood, 1994). A balance is needed between traditional ethnicity and post-modern identities.

4 Post-modernism ignores socio-economic differentiations between racial and ethnic groups (Sivanandan, 1995). Materially disadvantaged groups cannot participate in post-modern consumer culture in the same way as affluent ones.

5 Post-modernism has been accused of underestimating racism and even reducing it to just another passing 'fad' of a pluralist society (Harris, 1993).

Whether it does or does not progress, post-modernism is a challenging new perspective in the examination of 'race' and ethnic issues in contemporary society.

Ethnicity, the family, black feminism and masculinites

One of the key issues which led to the rise of black feminism was disagreement with what were seen as the predominantly white-based perspectives of the feminist movement over the issue of the family and in particular the power of men and masculinity within the family. While most feminists argued that the family was an oppressive institution, black feminists, such as Hazel Carby (1982), argued that one key difference was that the family is much less a source of oppression for black women, partly because, as also argued by Hooks (1984), the black family is a base of resistance to white racism. However, it is also partly because black males, who also suffer from racism, have less power relative to white males and this undermines the possibility of gender oppression of black females by black males in ethnic households.

Critiques of post-modernism

Post-modernism is important because it represents one attempt to deal with significant new developments in culture and experience in the new millennium. The rapidly increasing number of media outlets and the increasing emphasis on consumption must make a difference to our subjective experience and sense of identity – the way we feel. However, not all sociologists believe that post-modernism offers the most appropriate set of theoretical concepts for dealing with these important developments. The following are five of the most important criticisms.

1 Pessimism

Several critics have argued that post-modernism, particularly in the work of Baudrillard, merely rehearses the old Frankfurt School's 'manipulation theory'. Accordingly, it is vulnerable to the same criticisms. It is too pessimistic and underestimates the capacity of the audience to think critically. Alternative research presents a picture of a much more critical media audience (Morley, 1992; Philo, 1990).

2 Overstating the power of the mass media

As Strinati comments:

... the idea that the mass media take over 'reality' clearly exaggerates their importance. The mass media are important but not that important.

(Strinati, 1995, p. 239)

Baudrillard suggests that the distinction between reality and media image collapses. However, 'modernist' sociologists are often highly critical of this 'extreme relativism'. John Eldridge, of the Glasgow University Media Group, for example, argues that it is one thing to acknowledge the influence which ideology and values have on our attempts to understand the real world; it is quite another to insist that all such attempts are *merely* ideological and equally flawed, or that, as Baudrillard believes, there is no real social world in the first place, merely our ideological perceptions of it. For Eldridge (1993), one of the key tasks of sociology is to continue to test media coverage against alternative, independent measures of reality. He considers that post-modernism's abandonment of this project represents 'intellectual vertigo ... a failure of nerve'.

3 Technological determinism

Kellner (1989) argues that post-modernism rests on a 'media essentialism'. Baudrillard's approach, he suggests, places too much emphasis on the importance of media technology in determining the way in which society develops ('technological determinism') and ignores the importance of social relationships – the ways in which social groups use the media technology. Many sociologists would insist that in order to understand how the mass media work, it is necessary to explore the *social* relationships involved in the ownership and control of the media, or the political connections between media and political élites, or the ways in which audiences can use media, sometimes in ways which resist dominant ideological messages. Without considering social relationships, it is difficult for Baudrillard to explain how signs or images *change* over time. This happens, of course, because far from passively consuming, social groups appropriate signs or symbols and use them to construct new and sometimes, oppositional meanings.

4 Modern or post-modern?

A fourth problem concerns the distinction between the modern and the post-modern (Chen, 1992; McRobbie, 1994). How do we know that we are living in the post-modern, in a qualitatively different kind of society to the modern? Post-modernists are sketchy on this issue and provide different answers depending on whether they are describing changes in social structure or particular forms of cultural production. Giddens (1991) convincingly argues that most of the forces transforming our current subjective experience are essentially the culmination of developments in modernity, not the consequence of a major new historical development.

5 The meta-narrative of post-modernism

Finally, the critics of post-modernism point to its own ideological role. The rejection of all previous meta-narratives is, itself, another meta-narrative. How can post-modernists be so confident in announcing the end of modernist belief systems unless, implicitly, they argue from the vantage point of their own meta-narrative (Strinati, 1995, p. 241)? Critics point to the social context in which post-modernism became fashionable and to the kinds of social groups amongst whom post-modernist ideas seemed to have the strongest appeal. Post-modernist concepts are most popular with cultural experts and academics – designers, creative workers in advertising and marketing, journalists and cultural theorists in university departments – all social groups who are likely to favour a theoretical approach which suggests that their expertise is becoming ever more vital in society. Critics argue that post-modernist ideas, with their emphasis on consumption and image rather than underlying social problems, reflect the priorities of the affluent and a reluctance to confront the less palatable realities of late capitalism (Norris, 1993; Callinicos, 1989).

Activity

Make notes for and then write an essay that evaluates critically the following statement: 'Our identity and cultural experience are shaped by the post-modern condition'. Use sociological arguments and evidence.

C3.2, C3.3

The problem of cultural populism

Avoiding élitism

In recent years, theorists of popular culture have been concerned to avoid what they regard as two great pitfalls. First, writers have sought to avoid the danger of 'élitism'. That is they wished to avoid the 'mistakes' made by, for example, the advocates of the mass culture thesis and the Frankfurt School. Both the Frankfurt School and mass culture critics, like Arnold, Eliot and Leavis, in attacking commercialism in the culture industries, implied that much popular culture was 'inferior' to other cultural forms. Such judgements were criticized for betraying a form of élitism.

Avoiding economic determinism

Secondly, it became unfashionable to present arguments which could be interpreted as examples of 'economic reductionism'. Both Marxist and non-Marxist theorists tried to avoid the 'danger' of economic reductionism by employing theoretical approaches which directed attention to cultural issues (magazine content, tastes in shopping, television audiences, and so on), rather than questions of how the institutions of cultural production were organized. First culturalism and now post-modernism have grown in popularity because they appeared to offer ways in which both élitism and economic reductionism could be avoided.

The danger of culturalist accounts

Harris (1992) argues that those theorists who began to employ Gramsci's ideas in the 1960s and 1970s (culturalists) did so in ways which tended to 'close off', rather than open up, empirical research or theoretical development. Harris argues that other kinds of sociology have been more 'open' in the sense that researchers have been prepared to be 'surprised', or to acknowledge data and historical evidence which did not fit neatly into their theoretical frameworks. It is a little too easy, Harris suggests, to read into audience or consumer behaviour 'evidence' of 'resistance', particularly if qualitative, ethnographic methods are used. The danger is that culturalists 'find' what they assume to be the case at the beginning; and then forms of popular cul-

tural activity which are not compatible with the theoretical and political assumptions of the researchers are ignored. Little attention, Harris notes, has been given to popular but politically less palatable cultural pastimes like blood sports (for example, illegal dog-fighting) or 'consumer pathologies', such as the playground bullying of 'style fascists', who victimize those without designer clothes and trainers.

The collapse into cultural populism

McGuigan (1992) condemns what he regards as a collapse into 'cultural populism'. McGuigan reminds us that the pioneers of cultural studies, including writers like Raymond Williams and Richard Hoggart, were motivated by a desire to see ordinary people's experiences and culture taken more seriously in the curriculum offered in schools and colleges. That is not the same thing as assuming that *any* kind of popular culture should be embraced uncritically simply because it is popular amongst ordinary people. Recent approaches, McGuigan argues, are so eager to avoid the mistakes of old mass society or manipulation approaches that they end up offering an entirely uncritical endorsement of popular culture. This point might be applied to both culturalism and post-modernism. Any kind of popular culture is welcomed because it offers opportunities for 'resistance'. But, McGuigan points out, evidence of 'resistance' is often thin and, at the same time, the mechanisms of real political power are often ignored. Recent approaches, he argues, have also been too anxious to avoid the charge of economic reductionism.

In consequence, the economic aspects of media institutions and the broader economic dynamics of consumer culture were rarely investigated, simply bracketed off, thereby severely undermining the explanatory and, in effect, critical capacities of cultural studies.

(McGuigan, 1992, p. 41)

The need for a political economy approach?

McGuigan suggests that what is required is an approach which tries to relate a political economy of popular culture to a sociology of consumption and identity. In other words, sociologists and cultural theorists should retain an interest in the various and diverse ways in which we all consume commodities and construct identities; but they should not lose sight of the point that many of our cultural options are shaped by the interests of cultural and media conglomerates, the working of capitalist markets, the power of the state, and the routines and professional values of workers inside the cultural industries – artists, producers, film and video directors, journalists, advertising executives, and others.

Too much emphasis on the audience?

Ferguson and Golding (1997) have recently completed a further critical review. They, also, are critical of the extent to which culturalist approaches have focussed too much attention on how audiences consume popular culture and too little attention on the pressures and constraints involved in the actual production of popular culture, whether a television programme or a fashion magazine. In particular, they are sympathetic to those who call for a return to the analysis of culture in the context of social class and structured inequality. We now know a great deal about the diverse ways in which people construct identities and derive pleasures from cultural consumption. Perhaps the next step forward is to return to some of the traditional sociological questions about, for example, the inequalities in cultural resources and power.

Activity

a What is the danger of 'economic reductionism'?

b Summarize in your own words the criticisms made by Harris of research influenced by culturalism.

c Summarize in your own words the criticisms made by McGuigan and Fersuson and Golding. Do you agree?

C3.2, C3.3

Further reading

The following are good introductions to the topic as a whole:

- Billington, R. *et al.* (1991) *Culture and Society*, London: Macmillan.
- Chaney, D. (1996) *Lifestyles*, London: Routledge.
- Corrigan, P. (1997) *Sociology of Consumption*, London: Sage.
- Strinati, D. (1995) *An Introduction to Theories of Popular Culture*, London: Routledge.

The following is an excellent illustration of how research in the area of culture and identity can be undertaken and contains some interesting examples of the application of key theories to a substantive example:

- Du Gay, P., Hall, S., Janes, L., Mackay, H. and Negus, K. (1997) *Doing Cultural Studies; the Story of the Sony Walkman*, London: Sage.

The following book is an excellent example of empirical research which is both accessible and interesting, providing important insights relevant for the study of ethnicity, culture, identity and the sociology of the mass media:

- Gillespie, M. (1995) *Television, Ethnicity and Cultural Change*, London: Routledge.

For those interested in the history of style, fashion and gender images, there is:

- Mort, F. (1996) *Cultures of Consumption: Masculinities and Social Space in Late Twentieth Century Britain*, London: Routledge.

Back issues of the periodical *Sociology Review* (formerly known as *Social Studies Review*) also contain many articles on this field of sociology and many others.

Power and control

Social policy and welfare

Chapter outline

14.1 Defining key concepts in welfare

The issue of welfare is potentially a very large one in society. At its height the welfare state was described as providing care from cradle to grave since the NHS, hospitals and antenatal clinics provided care in relation to childbirth and there were funeral grants available to help with the cost of burying relatives.

The idea therefore was to emphasize the comprehensive nature of the cover provided by the welfare state. Funded through general taxation and the payment of National Insurance contributions, access to the services provided was based not on ability to pay but on need. It is important to realise the quite radical shift in thinking that this occasioned. This is highlighted in more detail in Section 14.3.

In short, the provision of healthcare, education, housing, employment opportunities and unemployment benefits and other social security benefits had up until the 1940s been based largely on work-based or private insurance. This was therefore clearly linked to the ability to pay where differential care or service is available based on how much you can pay. This was replaced by a system where everyone had equal entitlement and where economic inequality was not supposed to make a difference.

Since the 1980s this idea has come under increasing attack. Some of the criticism of this model suggests that such a wide-ranging approach is no longer affordable and therefore we need to reform the welfare model. (See Section 14.3.) Others take the approach that anything to do with the state has largely negative consequences and therefore the welfare state is one of the biggest problems in society. (See Section 14.2.)

These debates have taken place over a terrain littered with its own language. The purpose of this section is to provide a brief introduction to some of the key terms and concepts that will be used in this chapter to enable you to fully appreciate the context of debates covered later in the chapter.

Sociology, social policy and social problems

Firstly, it is important to realise that there is a specialised discipline that considers these issues. This started out as a sub-part of sociology but has now grown into its own specialised subject. That subject is social policy. Those who study social policy purposely set out to consider how various societal problems might best be solved. So, issues relating to how we provide welfare in a society are most certainly the preserve of social policy analysts though of course sociologists may also get involved and the borders between the two subjects are fluid.

Social policy is also concerned with the definition of and the finding of potential solutions to social problems. A problem becomes social when it is something that applies to more than one individual (who may have personal problems, that is problems that apply to them only). In effect, it means problems which are caused by factors beyond the immediate control of any one individual and which are likely to affect more than one individual. For instance, the availability of cheap housing may affect the level of homelessness and homelessness certainly affects more than one person and often people become homeless because they suffer illness or become unemployment, both of which are examples of problems beyond the direct control of any one individual.

There are a whole host of social problems that may be considered. One potential starting point are the 'Five Giants' identified in the Beveridge Report (1942): Disease, Squalor, Idleness, Ignorance and Want. In modern terms these would be described as ill health, homelessness, unemployment, lack of education and poverty. The issues relating to poverty are dealt with in Chapter 17. Equally, debates about access to education are discussed in Chapter 11, and debates about ill-health are discussed in Chapter 12. In this chapter, therefore, we will look at social policy and welfare through the issues of unemployment and the social provision of housing. These issues lead into wider debates about the provision of social security and social services.

Collectivism and individualism

Individualism

Individualism is the belief that an individual has the ability and the right to totally determine their own fate and extends also to the belief that only an individual has the right to control their own behaviour. Those who believe in individualism tend to talk in terms of 'individual freedom'. One of the best outlines of such a viewpoint was that of John Stuart Mill in *On Liberty* (1869). Mill argued that people should be free to engage in any action as long as it did not harm others. What this means is that an individual would have no obligation to help another and it would not be permissible to ban things which were harmful since it would be up to the individual to choose whether they used them or not. From such a position it is difficult to build up a notion of a welfare state, where tax payments made by everyone fund services that an individual may or may not benefit from.

In more recent years, the ideas of individualism underlay the social policies of the successive Conservative governments from 1979 to 1997, with their emphasis on individual choice. This led to greater private provision of services that had been provided exclusively or predominately by the state since the end of the World War II: like train services, buses, pensions, health services, refuse collection services, etc. The Conservative argument was that if, for example, people wanted to pay into private healthcare funds so they could then choose to go into hospital at a time that suited them, then they should be allowed to do so. Such arguments led to the promotion of alternatives to the state in the delivery of welfare, leading to a situation described as welfare pluralism. (See Section 14.4.)

Collectivism

Collectivism, on the other hand, is the belief that a society should be organised so that all are treated equally. In relation to political movements it is the belief that people should join together to fight for benefits and gains that will help all of them, regardless of how it affects each individual. Collectivism is the philosophy underlying the rise of the trade union movement, and, out of that movement, the Labour party.

It is also the set of ideas that lies behind the notion of the welfare state: the original idea was that everyone in society would contribute for the benefit of society as a whole – the welfare state would be paid for collectively through tax and national insurance, based on each individual's ability to pay. Since benefits and services were to be based on need, there would be no guarantee, however, that the value of benefits the individual would *receive* over his or her lifetime would equal the payments *made* over his or her lifetime. Indeed, for most this would certainly not be the case. The original idea was, therefore, that the situation would be equal for everyone, even if it did undermine the individual freedom of those who could afford to queue-jump.

Collective provision is associated with the state and the public sector so it is very much associated with nationalization and with state provision of welfare. It can be contrasted with the market driven notions of individualism, based on free choice and the ability to pay. (See also Sections 14.2 and 14.3.)

Citizenship

Citizenship is a political concept that considers the question of who is to hold the rights and responsibilities in a society, and what these rights and responsibilities are. Not everyone resident in a society may be a citizen of a society. They may not contribute taxation to the government of the society in which they reside and therefore there is the question of whether they should be entitled to the benefits available to citizens of a society. One clear citizenship right is the right to vote. Debates and conflicts can happen in a society about the extension or reduction of the rights of citizens. For example, women only obtained the right to vote on equal terms with men in 1928 in the UK (and not until 1971 in Switzerland).

T. H. Marshall

One of the key sociological theories of citizenship, developed by T. H. Marshall, sought, however, to extend the notion of citizenship beyond this political realm into the arena of the social.

Marshall argued that there were three forms of citizenship, namely civil, political and social. By civil citizenship he meant being treated equally before the law and being allowed to own property. By political citizenship he meant essentially the right to a say, notably through voting rights. All contemporary political parties would see both of these forms of citizenship as necessary and they emphasize an individualist viewpoint on citizenship.

Marshall argued that there was a third aspect to citizenship, which he called social citizenship. By this he meant that people should have, as of right, economic welfare and security and the ability to live the life of a civilized being according to the standards prevailing in society at the time. This idea became an important theoretical basis of the welfare state and the ideas of collectivism, and fed into the more recent issue of international standards of human rights. Contemporary reactions to Marshall's theory affect debates on the extent and nature of the welfare state, how it should be funded and who and how it should benefit people. It is clearly therefore central to an overall consideration of social policy.

State welfare

The term state welfare is reserved for those aspects of welfare that are provided by the state or governmental bodies. People used to use the phrase 'welfare state' at a time when it was the case that welfare provision was largely the preserve of the state. Nowadays, however, we can see that there are many agencies involved in welfare provision, from the family through charities and voluntary organizations to the private sector: the 'welfare pluralism' mentioned above. Therefore we cannot today assume that the term welfare is synonymous with the state and we must therefore distinguish that which is provided by the state. (See also Section 14.4.)

Universal and selective (means-tested) forms of provision

When considering any policy there are two big questions to consider: who pays for it and who benefits from it? The first of these is considered in the section below but here we consider the second of these questions.

Universal benefits are those which are made available to all with no conditions placed on the provision. Key examples of this type of provision are education between the age of 5 and 16, free medical treatment through the NHS, child benefit that is paid to all regardless of the income of the mother.

Alternatively, selective provision is where benefits are only made available to some people. Here systems need to be put in place to determine who is and who is not eligible for the benefit. Usually this involves considering the existing income available to the person or family and therefore looking at the means available to them. If these means fall above a certain predetermined level then assistance is denied. This process is known as means testing.

Progressive and regressive taxation

Who pays for the welfare state – or, more precisely, how is the burden of payment spread? The answer is that it depends on how the tax system is set up. Here we need to distinguish between progressive and regressive taxes. A progressive tax is one that hits the richer harder proportionately than the poor, whereas a regressive tax hits the poor harder proportionately than the rich. Key examples from the UK include income tax that is progressive but not as progressive as it used to be and VAT which is regressive but not as regressive as the now abolished poll tax. The availability of progressive and regressive methods of raising tax income allows governments to decide whether they will hit the

rich or the poor when it comes to raising tax revenue.

Welfare regime

The term welfare regime was developed by the Swedish social thinker Gøsta Esping-Andersen to emphasize that in order to explain the provision of welfare in a society it was necessary to look beyond the narrow confines of the state and to consider the whole social and political culture of a society. In particular, he argues that we need to look at the relationship between state welfare policies, employment and the employment structure, and the general social structure of a society. This term therefore presents a clearly sociological approach to analysing social policy and social welfare. (See also Section 14.5.)

Culture of dependency

The term culture of dependency was developed by New Right thinkers to underline their argument that provision of state welfare has harmful consequences. In effect they argued that people might become 'hooked' on benefits (using the analogy of drug dependency) and in this state they would have no incentive to go out and look for work – they would be able to survive on welfare benefits. New Right thinkers argue that welfare benefits produce lethargy and dependency in those 'on welfare', and that therefore the welfare state, and particularly the provision of universal benefits without any responsibilities attached to them, has negative effects on individuals and on society in general. (See also Section 14.2.)

The underclass

The term 'underclass' is used to describe people who live outside the employment structure. Some sociologists argued that this underclass should not be considered part of the working class since its members did not work and in some versions it was argued that this life existing on benefits led to different attitudes. There are two distinct usages of the term underclass. One group of sociologists, particularly those influenced by New Right thinking, use the cultural version of the underclass thesis, while Weberian thinkers tend to use a more structural version of the underclass thesis. Some sociologists, particularly those influenced by Marxism, reject this term as ideological and not scientific.

We have sought to give purposely brief descriptions here since these terms and their associated debates are all considered elsewhere in this chapter or in this book. Cross-references to these points are provided to enable you to read in more detail about the debates surrounding these terms. (Se also Section 17.6.)

14.2 Ideologies and theories of welfare

George and Wilding (1994) argue that we can identify a number of distinct theoretical approaches to the welfare state, some of which we will consider here, namely:

- the New Right
- social democracy
- the 'middle way' (including consideration of New Labour and the 'Third Way').

George and Wilding (1994) also include information on Marxism, feminism and greenism. Material relating to these three theoretical approaches will be considered in Section 14.6.

The New Right's approach

New Right thinking is based on the belief that a free market is much better than the state at providing economic growth and improved living standards. Similarly, they are very critical of the Beveridge Report for 'discouraging individualism, self-reliance, voluntary organizations and private initiatives' (Marsland, 1992, p. 146).

David Willetts (1992), a New Right theoretician and Conservative MP, makes the further point that centralized planning is impossible owing to the complexity of modern life. The free market should therefore be restored to its role of importance. This in turn means that the cope of the state must be cut back.

The New Right philosopher Friedrich Von Hayek (1944, 1960) argued that any state expenditure threatened individual liberty – since it was financed out of coercive taxation measures – and so in order to defend freedom the state should be kept at an absolute minimum. The idea that the state acts to secure social justice is one that Hayek rejected, seeing it instead as a back-door way to secure moves to socialism and equality.

The welfare state and human misery

Saunders (1995), a sociologist with New Right sympathies, argues that it is possible to see the welfare state as contributing not to a growth in human happiness but to a growth in human misery:

Universal state welfare was established in Britain from the mid-1940s, and both the crime rate and the decline in the conventional two-parent family began to rise a decade or so later. ... This is not to suggest that state welfare directly causes crime and family breakdown, but it is possible that it has enabled these changes to occur. Single parenthood, for example, was not a viable option for most women before various welfare reforms from the 1960s onwards provided financial support for it.

(Saunders, 1995, pp. 91–2)

The dependency culture

By eroding personal responsibility, welfare expenditure is also seen as creating a culture of dependency. Green (1988), a New Right social thinker, argues that this is so in the case of free healthcare provided by the NHS (see also Section 12.6), which he argues has:

... undermined the capacity of people for self direction and spread a child-like dependency on the state.

(Green, 1988, p. 5)

Some people become 'hooked' on welfare benefits like a drug, sapping their will and energy and therefore not helping them at all to fend for themselves.

Policies on poverty

Murray (1984), an American New Right political scientist, has made much the same point in relation to the anti-poverty policies in the USA. He argues that instead of providing more for the poor they have simply provided more poor.

In the UK, Marsland (1996) has given a systematic analysis of the welfare state from a New Right perspective in his book *Welfare or Welfare State?*. He contends that it needs to be substantially contracted, with many of the services it provides coming instead from a free market. In this extract he outlines its negative consequences:

... the welfare state inflicts damaging levels of moral and psychological harm on its supposed

This suggests that the new
as a lazy way out right considers welfare
for people and people need

beneficiaries. It has seduced the British people away from their natural independence of spirit and their traditional commitment to hard work, honesty and high standards. ... It has made of its primary clients – perfectly normal, capable men and women before the state got to work on them – a festering underclass of welfare dependants fit for nothing better than passive consumption of an ever-expanding diet of 'bread and circuses'.

(Marsland, 1996, pp. 6 and 20)

In summary, the New Right believe that state expenditure has negative economic consequences and state welfare expenditure can contribute to negative social consequences. Conversely, a reduction in the welfare state and a greater emphasis on a free market and personal responsibility will lead to a better society.

Discussion point

To what extent do you agree with Marsland that the welfare state has negative moral and psychological consequences for its clients?

C3.1a

Social democratic approaches to welfare

It is perhaps with the broad approach labelled 'social democratic' that the notion of a welfare state is most closely associated. Social democrats believe that the liberal democratic state is the best institutional mechanism to foster democratic control in society, and further that such a state machinery can be used to attain desirable social objectives such as greater equality or equality of opportunity.

Critique of the free market

This trend really came to the fore in the wake of the economic and social crisis of the 1930s which led to the discarding of the ideas of free-market liberalism (the forerunners of today's New Right). The experience of World War II convinced these people that government planning could work. If the government was able to influence the economy to achieve economic ends, then why should not the same methods be applied to social objectives? This is the origin of theories of the welfare state. There is a clear link between economic and social objectives here since one of the key assumptions underlying the Beveridge Report

was that government would seek to achieve and maintain full employment.

Social democracy is based on the belief that free-market capitalism is wasteful, inefficient and unjust. However, the construction of a new society will come not from revolution but from gradual evolution within parliamentary democracies.

Benefits of state welfare provision

George and Wilding (1994), welfare theorists, provide the following list of reasons for social democratic support of the welfare state, showing its economic and social benefits over free-market capitalism:

- It can eliminate want and suffering in society.
- State expenditure on welfare, particularly on education, provides a form of investment in the future, creating greater economic prosperity.
- Education spending also allows everyone to fulfil individual potential. (See also Section 11.6.)
- It can help promote feelings of altruism (willingness to help and consider others), for example through the free giving of blood.
- It can create conditions of social integration since everyone is treated equally.
- Welfare can help compensate for the negative aspects of economic change (e.g. through unemployment benefits). (See also Section 14.5.)

Activity

a Suggest ways in which each of the above aims could be achieved.

b Explain in your own words the meanings of altruism and social integration.

C3.2, C3.3

Social citizenship

The welfare state is therefore seen as a key mechanism to achieve a more ethical, civilized and just society. This notion is encapsulated in sociologist Marshall's (1963) notion of the growth of 'citizenship rights' (see also Section 14.1), which all citizens are entitled to as of right (hence the name). He argued that the meaning of citizenship had developed over time, from:

- *civil citizenship* – meaning individual freedom, essentially freedom of speech, freedom of thought and belief, the right to own property and the right to justice; through to:

to be responsible for themselves

- *political citizenship* – which entails the right to vote and participate in political decision-making; through to:
- *social citizenship* – which involves in addition to the others the right to economic welfare and security, including the right to education, work and healthcare.

As can be seen from this list, the notion of social citizenship essentially entails provision of the services conventionally associated with the welfare state.

Anthony Crosland

The initial success and popularity of the welfare state led some social democratic thinkers in this tradition – notably Anthony Crosland, as a Labour government minister – to argue that essentially the UK was no longer a capitalist or class-divided society. Crosland emphasized the importance of the economic and social reforms introduced by the post-war Labour government as an important element in the construction of the welfare state. Political factors are therefore a central if not the only element in analyses based in this tradition.

Gøsta Esping-Andersen

This can be seen clearly in the work of probably the leading theorist in this approach today, namely Gøsta Esping-Andersen. In a comparative analysis of the rise of welfare states, he argues that the important factor determining the shape of welfare regimes is the nature of class mobilization and of class coalitions in the political structure. (See also Section 14.5.)

The social democratic perspective

A final factor of great importance today is the social democratic support for universal provision of welfare benefits. There are a number of problems associated with means-tested benefits which lead them to take up this position. Among these are the stigmatization associated with the means test, the greater administrative cost of means-tested benefits, the problem of creating poverty traps (see Section 17.4), the generally lowe quality of services provided only for the poor, and the fact that welfare provision intended for everyone is better able to withstand onslaughts on welfare expenditure by the political right (see above).

While undoubtedly the social democratic perspective relies heavily on notions of social justice and ethical considerations of how society should be organized, it is far from clear that the actual welfare states that have grown out of this tradition in fact do very much to make society more just, equal or fair. As George and Wilding point out:

[There is] convincing empirical evidence ... that universal provision does not reduce income inequalities in society.

(George and Wilding, 1994, p. 86)

This has led to criticisms of this perspective from the Left, and an ongoing debate by sociologists about who actually benefits from the welfare state (see Section 14.5). Universal provision has also been attacked by the Right, who argue that to provide benefits for those able to provide for themselves is an expensive waste.

One of the major problems with the social democratic perspective is that it clearly does imply a high level of state expenditure on welfare. This has to rely on improved economic performance by the nation. However, moving towards 'market socialism' and abandonment of the idea of the state playing the leading economic role make such changes more reliant on capitalism. What arises seems to be a much watered-down version of democratic socialism, which places a question-mark over whether democratic socialism is still a step in the transition to socialism:

It is doubtful whether the new brand of market socialism that so many democratic socialists aspire to today poses any real threat to capitalism. The socialism of the future will contain more elements of capitalism than past brands of socialism did.

(George and Wilding, 1994, p. 101)

The 'middle way' and New Labour's 'Third Way'

The election of a Labour government in 1997 brought to an end the dominance of the New Right. This led to expectations of a change in emphasis for the welfare state, although the inclusion of communitarian themes and the development of the notion of the 'third way' by the Blair government also led to the suggestion that the extent of change would not be great. In some ways this 'third way' can be seen to derive from the earlier notion of a 'middle way'.

Against socialism and against the free market

George and Wilding (1994) develop this category of a 'middle way' to capture the point that not all non-socialists are supporters of the New Right. There exists a body of opinion broadly in favour of some kind of welfare state, but opposed to use of it for egalitarian social engineering – as embodied in the social democratic view that the welfare state is a stepping stone to greater equality. While this view would certainly encompass elements of the Liberal Democrats and the left wing of the Conservative party, arguably its most important exponents today are New Labour.

Fairness and equality of opportunity

What unites this approach is opposition to socialism, but a belief that the free market left to its own devices does create certain problems that need rectifying through intervention by the state. This leads to a stress on 'fairness' and 'equality of opportunity', and the way in which the welfare state can help to consolidate society by, for example, promoting policies to make the family unit strong. Underlying this is the idea of a contractual relationship between the individual and the state, leading welfare to operate to promote integration of society as a whole.

Social exclusion

One of the first acts of the new Labour government was the setting up of a unit to combat 'social exclusion'. What this refers to is the way some groups in society have been marginalized through the action of government and others. The welfare state and the assumptions underlying it were seen as a key element in this, and so reforms to this system would play a key role in combating social exclusion.

Ruth Lister (1998) argues that the term 'social inclusion' underlies an important shift in welfare thinking:

From equality to social inclusion effectively encapsulates an important paradigm shift in thinking about the welfare state, and in particular its income maintenance arm, under the new Labour government (new in the sense both of 'New Labour' and a new government). It is a shift which, despite its deployment of the continental language of social exclusion and inclusion, reflects more the influence of the United States.

(Lister, 1998, p. 215)

The shifting notions of welfare under New Labour

Lister argues that there are three important elements to this shift, namely:

- rejection of the promotion of equality for that of equality of opportunity, meaning providing opportunities to work rather than dramatic changes through the tax and/or benefits system
- use of terms like social exclusion/inclusion instead of talking about poverty
- an emphasis on social obligations and responsibilities rather than on rights.

Lister (1998) quotes Prime Minister Tony Blair's speech to the 1997 Labour conference, when he said, as an illustration of these trends: 'A decent society is not based on rights, it is based on duty – our duty to each other. To all shall be given opportunity, from all responsibility demanded' (p. 222).

Analysis of New Labour's approach to welfare

Since the notion of utilizing tax and public expenditure measures was a clear element in 'old' Labour, this came to be seen as a central element in the shift from old to 'new' Labour and one which led to criticism from many academics in sociology and social policy. This culminated in a letter to the *Financial Times* during the 1997 Labour conference, signed by 54 academics (including Ruth Lister) – who came to be known as the 'FT 54'.

The letter argued that the government appeared to have erased the question of *redistribution* from the map altogether. They regretted this since there had been a clear redistribution from poor to rich under the previous Conservative administrations. The implication was that little would be done to reverse the effect of New Right policies, echoing other comments suggesting 'new' Labour was too close to the Thatcherite legacy.

The response to this criticism was that increasing benefit levels does not remove the causes of poverty, it merely alleviates those in it, although the FT 54 argued that no one was suggesting that just increasing benefit levels was enough.

The central focus on education and work

Social inclusion policies focused on education and work, and particularly the latter. Work was seen as the central way to achieve financial independence, as well as producing other advantages. This reflects a partial acceptance of the Conservative notion of the effects of living on state benefits, and the argument about the development of a 'dependency culture'.

The diversity of welfare needs

One argument in defence of the social inclusion approach has come from Andrews (1997), who argues that it is better at addressing the diverse and differing needs of people than was the equality approach – which could be criticized for presenting uniform solutions to diverse problems.

This is one instance of a much wider debate about how to deal with diversity in society. Should we promote equality, or the right to diversity and difference? It has been argued that terms like 'equality' were linked with the class-dominated agenda, and that the rise of notions of difference through consideration of other bases of social inequality (notably gender and ethnicity) has meant that this is no longer theoretically appropriate. (See also Chapter 17.)

The influence of US thinking on New Labour

As Lister (1998) points out, it is clear that one key influence on New Labour welfare policy has been the policy changes implemented in the United States.

Dejevsky (1999) argues that a study of the effect of these changes shows that the poor have in fact become more deprived, not less so. In particular, single mothers have been hardest hit, despite the claim that the reforms were designed to help this group. Research shows that the disposable income of the poorest 20 per cent of the US population rose by $1036 between 1993 and 1995, but since the reforms were instituted their income fell by $577 between 1995 and 1997. The new system provides job preparation and training but also sets a period beyond which assistance will cease. This has led to a fall in the welfare rolls (the number of people on welfare) from 14 million to 7 million.

Recent thinking on welfare regimes

The 1980s, 90s and early 21st century have seen a number of innovative approaches to thinking about the welfare state. This section looks at a few examples.

Post-Fordism and the welfare state

It has been argued (e.g. by Jessop, 1994) that the Keynesian welfare state was the ideal type of the Fordist economic regime (see Section 17.2), with full employment and income support measures to encourage and perpetuate mass consumption. If there is indeed a crisis in the welfare state, it can be seen as an element of the crisis of Fordism. While mass production ensured there were the funds to provide for the welfare state, welfare provision strengthened the working classes and organized labour. This meant that wages grew faster than productivity, which led to a crisis of accumulation. The move towards post-Fordism, with its emphasis on flexibility and divisions within the workforce (between core and periphery), is an attempt to deal with this (see Section 17.2). The effect of this transformation on the welfare state might be characterized as in Figure 14.1.

Activity

Investigate one particular area of welfare state provision and analyse recent changes using the framework suggested in Figure 14.1. Evaluate the extent to which this is a useful way to characterize recent changes in provision.

C3.2, C3.3

	Fordism	**Post-Fordism**
Needs	Mass universal needs	Diversity of individual needs
Provision	Monolithic Bureaucratic Professional-led	Welfare pluralism Quasi-markets Consumer sovereignty Reorganized welfare work

Figure 14.1 The welfare state: from Fordism to post-Fordism?

The key implication of the idea of a post-Fordist welfare state is to move away from mass collective provision, a situation where everyone gets provided with the same and where such provision is justified on the basis of equality. The key potential problem with this is that individual people may have different needs and therefore notions of simple equality do not take these into account. Norman Ginsburg (1998) explains the difference this makes in terms of welfare policy:

Modern social policy was originally founded on the rock of the stable, patriarchal nuclear family in which the male breadwinner brought home a family wage to meet many of the basic needs of his dependants. This has of course been supplanted by the dual-earner family, but by no means entirely.

The basic needs from which modern social policy provides protection are universal and reasonably predictable. Social insurance is the central element of social security and health-care funding. The system is predicted on the continuous and full-time paid employment of the breadwinner(s). The core welfare collectivity is the nation state, which underwrites social citizenship juridically and financially. Delivery of benefits and services frequently devolved to local or regional government and non-governmental organizations. [...]

Postmodernism calls into question every element of modern social policy as summarized above. For postmodernists, socialism, like every other universalizing Enlightenment ideologies, is dead; if socialism is dead, collectivizing social policy is no longer appropriate or needed as a response. Class divisions and the corporatist structures of capital and labour are also no longer central to the socio-political landscape. Diversity and fragmentation of identities, communities and associations in contemporary society is a central feature of postmodernity. The postmodern politics of social policy is radically pluralist, with pressures coming from the new social movements upholding the diversity of needs and associations.

[...] Theorists of post-industrialism and post-Fordism note the standard employment contract is disappearing and that paid employment in the future will be casualized and intermittent, with short-term, temporary contracts and flexitime contracts the norm.

Family structures also appear to be diversifying quite rapidly with the growth of serial monogamy, absent fatherhood, single motherhood and childlessness. Caring responsibilities and obligations are negotiated individually within these structures, often without much support from the state.

(Norman Ginsburg, 1998, pp. 267-8)

This process has seen the emergence of policies based around individual need which, given that potentially these needs are different, mean unequal levels of provision, which do however meet the individuals needs.

For example, we can consider what the needs of a pregnant woman and non-pregnant woman are and whether we should base provision on equality or need. Since there are a number of pieces of legislation which are based on some notion of equality, even if it is equality of opportunity, then shifting the emphasis to need may have fairly dramatic effects.

 Discussion point

Many organizations now have equal opportunities policies. Should these be replaced by policies based on diverse need? What would be the implications of this shift?

C3.1a

While the notion of greater plurality of welfare provision (see Section 14.4) and the greater emphasis on markets are clearly examples of the development of flexibility, seen as characteristic of post-Fordism, there are nonetheless criticisms of the use of the concepts Fordism/post-Fordism to describe the welfare state. These are as follows.

- Ultimately this is an economically determinist type of analysis which attempts to explain changes in the welfare state as deriving from changes in the economy.

- It under-estimates or ignores the importance of political struggle in establishing the welfare state and maintaining it.

- Since the analysis is centred on production it is not really able to take into account social relations other than class. This means that gender and ethnicity in particular are ignored. (On this debate see Chapter 17.)

'Decommodification' and the welfare state

Gøsta Esping-Andersen's concept of decommodification has led to radical new thinking. He argues that we need to consider how the welfare state does more than simply modify existing stratification systems, to understand the way in which it is a stratification system in and of itself. This places welfare right at the heart of analysis of the changing distribution of income and wealth. (See also Sections 14.5 and 17.1.)

Esping-Andersen (1990) analyses the welfare policies in eighteen advanced industrial economies and suggests that we can establish three distinct types of what he calls 'welfare regimes'. The reason he uses this term rather than the more common 'welfare state' is precisely to argue that we cannot analyse welfare simply by looking at the actions of the state; we must root it in a number of factors, in particular the relationships between state welfare policies, the employment structure and the general social structure.

He argues that it is essential to consider the importance of class political mobilization as an explanation for the type of welfare regime. This argument is in line with the social democratic approach which stresses that politics can make a difference. The crucial question is, therefore, the way in which the working classes are mobilized to seek changes to the system. Esping-Andersen thus rejects the idea found in both functionalist and Marxist analyses that the welfare state arises because it is functional for industrial/capitalist society and that this explains its development and character:

To emphasize active class-mobilization does not necessarily deny the importance of structured or hegemonic power. But it is held that parliaments are, in principle, effective institutions for the translation of mobilized power into desired policies and reforms.

(Esping-Andersen, 1990, p. 16)

In the course of developing a comparative picture of different types of welfare regimes, Esping-Andersen introduces the concept of decommodification. What he means by this concept is the extent to which people can survive without having to work for a living:

Decommodification occurs when a service is rendered as a matter of right, and when a person can maintain a livelihood without reliance on the market.

(Esping-Andersen, 1990, p. 22)

For example, in the UK the NHS provides a health service free at the point of delivery (apart from some charges for prescriptions and appliances), and even if you do not have a job there are benefits like unemployment benefit and income support that ensure you survive.

Decommodification overcomes inequality and this creates the basis for social cohesion. The importance of this concept is that it can be used to consider the extent to which a welfare state really offers people a choice about how they live their lives, or whether it forces them to go to work by providing only a minimal safety-net for those totally unable to do so.

Criticism of the decommodification model

Esping-Andersen's views have not been without critics. Most notably his model is criticized for being centred on class divisions while ignoring other social divisions in society, especially those arising from gender and ethnicity, making it difficult to apply to certain policy areas:

The application to family policy of cross-national models such as Esping-Andersen's, derived from examining benefits predominantly for male workers, is problematic to say the least.

(Ginsburg, 1991, p. 83)

Williams (1994), a feminist sociologist, argues that the concept of decommodification can mean different things to men and to women. Decommodification enhances males' ability to enter the labour market on their own terms, but they are also aided in this process by the domestic labour (see also Sections Section 5.7) supplied by women which is also decommodified. In this sense some women may wish for commodification – that is, payment for the work they do – rather than endorsing decommodification.

Discussion point

To what extent do you think diverse social groups would welcome decommodification?

C3.1a

In summary, those writers who are critical of Esping-Andersen's position focus on the centrality of class relations and the labour market in his analysis and the relative absence of other social structures (notably the family), and therefore the invisibility of other social divisions (notably those based on gender).

Activity

Critically evaluate the usefulness of the concept of 'decommodification' in the analysis of welfare provision.

 C3.2, C3.3

Comparative welfare regimes

One of the ways in which we can assess the effect of a welfare state is to look at the social structures and social relations prior to its development. Many studies of the UK contrast the pre-welfare state situation with that prevailing after implementation of the Beveridge Report (see Section 14.3). However, a problem with this type of analysis is that it focuses on one nation-state, which tends to make it appear as if international links have no impact.

Such thinking encourages another way of considering welfare states or welfare regimes, namely that of comparative studies of the operations in various countries. It is useful to consider the extent to which particular societies' welfare regimes are similar or significantly different. Such analyses can therefore also be used to consider the relative importance of international forces and more specifically national factors.

On the basis of his concept of decommodification (discussed earlier), Esping-Andersen divides the eighteen countries he studied into three distinct welfare regimes: the liberal/conservative model, the liberal model and the social democratic model (see Table 14.1). The higher the score the greater the decommodification.

The liberal model

The liberal model is the one where the idea of the importance of the market is strongest, and so the welfare regime tends to involve a weak residual welfare state with mainly means-tested benefits. He argues that the clearest examples of this type of regime are the USA, Canada, Australia and Switzerland.

One example of this type of regime is America. Here, most welfare and social insurance programmes are earnings-related benefits. As a result, overall welfare expenditure appears to be split, with one half going to the poor and the other half going to the well-off. This is a classic element of the liberal model in that there is a desire to avoid any element of redistribution in the way the welfare state operates.

This means there is little desire to impact upon the market which is presumed to provide rational distribution of income. There is therefore, provision for retirement but very little provision for the hazards of working life.

The conservative model

The conservative model arises, he says, in countries where the free market never really caught on. He argues that welfare regimes in these countries are characterized by the relative unimportance of private and occupational welfare as the

state takes a stronger role, to maintain the present social structure. Status differentials in society are maintained and divisions between groups based on occupational categories are reinforced. There is a clear earnings-related method of delivering welfare; entitlements to benefits are therefore unequal, so maintaining old inequalities in the system. Such systems also tend to have a large moralistic element owing to the influence of the Church in these societies. Therefore benefits seek to uphold the traditional family structure as an important element in providing welfare. Examples of this type of regime include Austria, Belgium, France, Germany and Italy.

One example of this type of regime is Italy. Expenditure on health and education in Italy are roughly at the average level for European countries but housing, family allowances and unemployment benefit are all at much lower levels than average for Europe.

This reflects the idea that the welfare state should not interfere with things which are deemed to be the preserve of the family. The proof of this is the low levels of public expenditure on those areas in Italy compared to the European average.

Table 14.1 The rank-order of welfare states in terms of decommodification score

Australia	13.0
United States	13.8
New Zealand	17.1
Canada	22.0
Ireland	23.3
United Kingdom	23.4
Italy	24.1
Japan	27.1
France	27.5
Germany	27.7
Finland	29.2
Switzerland	29.8
Austria	31.1
Belgium	32.4
Netherlands	32.4
Denmark	38.1
Norway	38.3
Sweden	39.1
Mean	27.2

Source: Esping-Andersen (1990, p. 52)

The social democratic model

Esping-Andersen's third model, the social democratic, is one in which the principle of universalism is most fully developed. Here, welfare regimes are based on the idea of citizenship and social rights, and so benefits are made available to all, including the middle class. Welfare is fused with employment via the commitment to full employment in this model. Examples of this type of regime include Denmark, Finland, Norway, Sweden and the Netherlands.

One example of this type of regime is Sweden, in fact the classical example of a social democratic welfare regime. The fact that the social democrats were in power between 1932 and 1976 continuously provided the basis for a country where a high priority was placed on social policy.

Pensions, for instance, represented something like 70 per cent of your earnings, a very high figure. Parental leave was very generous both in terms of time allowed off work and in terms of the amount provided (something like 90 per cent of normal income). All adults had the right to educational leave and immigrants had an additional right to 240 hours leave to learn Swedish.

It is clear that since the 1980s this system which relies on high tax levels has come under pressure and has been eroded to some degree. Nonetheless the differences with other welfare models remains clear.

The United Kingdom

The UK is not easy to classify on this basis according to Esping-Andersen. He says there are few elements of the conservative model here, but there are clear elements of both the liberal and the social democratic model.

Other comparative approaches

Bryson (1992), a welfare sociologist, also adopts a comparative approach in her study of welfare and the allocation of benefits. She argues that advanced capitalist economies were routinely referred to as welfare states but that quite recently this has changed:

We have witnessed a significant change of political direction by both conservative and non-conservative governments. The change involves a stated intention to rely more on the market and to reduce state interventions.

(Bryson, 1992, p. 1)

In this sense the changes of the 1980s and 90s can be understood as a backlash by those dominant groups in society who lost out as a result of the reforms of the 1960s and 70s. These changes occur on a global level. She argues that such global pressures have affected countries differentially. Japan has been the least affected by the pressure to marketize, while the Scandinavian countries have been most affected.

On a comparative level, Bryson argues that a key feature in the 1980s was a movement away from institutional welfare, where the state was seen as the normal first-line provider of welfare, back towards a residual model which sees the state intervening only when other institutions such as the family, the market and private charities fail. This, she says, can be seen most in the USA, Canada and Australia.

 Activity

Figure 14.2 contains summaries of the characteristics of Esping-Andersen's conservative, liberal and social democratic regimes. Using this and information from the section on recent changes in the UK's welfare state, consider how you would locate the UK welfare state. In what direction do you think it is moving?

C3.2, C3.3

Historical and cultural differences

Bryson also asserts that important historical and cultural differences play a part in the way international pressures for change have an effect. While all those countries with a high degree of institutional welfare have a high degree of material wealth, not all wealthy countries have high levels of institutional welfare. Here she cites the examples of Japan and the USA. Japan's system can be explained by an historical cultural tradition of great reliance on the family as the basis of welfare, whereas the USA has had a much greater cultural acceptance of the market. As a result governments in those countries spent less of their economic wealth than countries like Sweden. She argues that by looking at how much the government of each country receives in tax revenue as a percentage of its overall economic production (gross domestic product or GDP), the effects of these differences can be seen. This is illustrated in Table 14.2.

According to Bryson, Australia has a welfare state based largely on securing high wage levels

Conservative welfare regimes
- These see the individual as subordinated to the family or the state.
- They pay large welfare benefits to certain groups such as civil servants to create a class loyal to the state.
- The main form of benefit is of the social insurance type based on contributions made through employment. This creates distinctions based on a person's place in the employment structure and therefore in society.
- Corporatism is used to bind people together but also to recognize status differences between groups.
- They believe in the importance of upholding the traditional family structure owing to the influence of the Church.

Liberal welfare regimes
- These see the individual and individual freedom as most important.
- They believe that the market is the best system for distributing resources and the state should act only in clear cases where the market fails (e.g. short-term unemployment).
- They believe state benefits must not undermine the need for incentives in a market economy, or the work ethic. Therefore benefits tend to be low and means-tested to avoid discouraging people taking paid employment.
- Means-tested benefits are the predominant form, so benefits are only paid to some, notably those with low incomes, creating a selective welfare state.
- They create divisions between those reliant on low benefits and those able to obtain higher remuneration from employment.

Social democratic welfare regimes
- These believe that the equality of democracy needs to be matched with a wider equality in the economic and social spheres.
- Welfare benefits are based on a notion of citizenship and therefore seen as a right.
- This means that welfare benefits need to be available to all, leading to a universal welfare state.
- They believe that such a system can limit inequalities and overcome divisions between the working and the middle classes.
- The welfare state may be an important element in the transition to socialism.
- They are committed to full employment both in principle and because the high level of benefits paid are dependent on it through tax revenue.

Figure 14.2 Features of Esping-Andersen's three types of regime

Table 14.2 Government receipts as a percentage of GDP, 1984–85

Sweden	59.8
France	48.5
Germany	45.4
UK	42.8
Australia	34.1
USA	31.1
Japan	30.3

Source: Adapted from Bryson (1992, p. 74)

and providing residual and means-tested benefits only for those not in work. In the USA she sees a much greater emphasis on private charity through organizations such as the Rockefeller Foundation and the Ford Foundation, and a clear anti-welfare state feeling. This means that although benefits paid through contributions are largely exempt from change, provision for others is minimal and subject to cuts.

She notes that while the Nordic countries developed the most comprehensive universalist model of welfare states, this did mean that a higher proportion of national income went on the welfare state. International market pressures have led them to consider changes in recent years. Since 1976 there have been moves to place greater emphasis on the market, but not without ramifications: the Swedish government fell in 1990 over protests at moves to limit the growth of welfare spending.

Bryson concludes that, while there are important historical differences that are reflected in how welfare states have developed, all have tended to privilege the interests of dominant groups over the rest. All have retained some degree of attachment to a *laissez-faire* notion of a welfare state, reinforced by moves towards free-market doctrines in the 1980s and 90s. The main cause has not been an economic over-burden caused by the welfare state, but resistance by privileged groups to any measures seeking to erode that privilege.

14.3 The development of state welfare in Britain

For the beginning of the welfare state many analyses look to the period immediately after World War II and the implementation of the Beveridge Report. It is possible, however, to see concern by the state for the condition of the population going back much earlier. In particular, we can trace the implementation of the Poor Law of 1601 and its concerns over social disorder due to the rise in vagrancy. This Act divided the poor into the impotent poor (meaning the aged and the disabled), who were to be helped, the able-bodied poor (meaning the unemployed), who were to be sent to workhouses), and finally the persistent idlers, who were to be sent to houses of correction. This categorization betrays the views about the poor and those seeking welfare. The key belief was that the poor were to be divided into the deserving and the undeserving poor, and the suggestion that some poor were undeserving was based on the idea that they had caused their own misfortune either by being lazy or foolish. This categorization of the poor in terms of behaviour becomes a consistent element of categorization, particularly after the 1834 Poor Law Amendment Act (see also Section 14.6), until the late nineteenth century, when ideas about the cause of poverty changed.

Foundations of the modern welfare state

The nineteenth century

By the third quarter of the nineteenth century, ideas about the causes of poverty had changed from those outlined above. There was a realization that poverty was not necessarily the individual's fault. One reason for this was the first major economic recession faced in Britain between 1873 and 1896.

Secondly, since the elderly were people who had worked all their lives, the idea that *their* poverty could be explained by idleness was clearly wrong. Research in the 1890s showed that 40 per cent of the working class aged over 65 were on poor relief and therefore in poverty (Baugh, 1987).

Further important reasons for the change in attitude include the following:

- In 1880, education was made compulsory (see Chapter 11). As a result education authorities compiled evidence on the state of schoolchildren, and many were found to be badly clothed and fed.

- A large wave of strikes hit the nation in the 1880s, leading to awareness of the low wages received by skilled workers.

The shock of poverty

The growth of social science at the turn of the twentieth century was exemplified by two massive surveys on poverty undertaken in London by Charles Booth (1902) and in York by Seebohm Rowntree (1901). Booth reported that the main causes of poverty in London were unemployment and old age. Rowntree found that 28 per cent of the population in York were poor, mainly owing to low wages. (See also Sections 17.1 and 17.4.)

The changing political climate

One important political factor leading to greater concern with poverty and social welfare, which dates from this time, is the rise of trade unionism (see Section 15.3) and socialist movements. The 1867 Reform Act widened the right to vote and meant that working people began to have a say in societal affairs.

Another shift in political philosophy was the

changing definition of liberalism. In the nineteenth century (and again recently since 1979), liberalism viewed the state negatively as an institution which limited individuals' freedom. Oxford philosopher Thomas Green redefined liberalism and argued that the state could act to provide an environment which allowed people to be free. Liberalism as a political philosophy was therefore reconciled with a positive role for the state.

The Liberal reforms of 1905–15

By the time of the election of a Liberal government in 1905, it was clear that changes in relation to social welfare were going to be a major part of their legislative programme. The idea that certain services should be provided by the state – and financed out of a national insurance scheme – were behind this.

A number of pieces of legislation were passed which provided an important basis for contemporary provision, most notably the Old Age Pensions Act in 1908 and the National Insurance Act in 1911. The first of these introduced pensions paid out of taxation to all people over 70. This was because most of the surveys quoted above had shown that the elderly were one group very much at risk of poverty. The second Act introduced health insurance and unemployment insurance.

World War I and the 1930s Depression

World War I massively increased the role of the state in the economy and provided an example of some degree of centralized planning. The free-market ideas of nineteenth-century liberalism were further eroded with the onset of the Great Depression of the 1930s which led to mass unemployment and hardship. This also placed great pressures on the existing system of welfare assistance. The idea behind this system was that people would make payments out of their wages and would in turn receive payments when they were unemployed. It worked on the assumption that unemployment would be fairly rare and short-lived. These assumptions were not true in the 1930s, so that payments into the system declined while demands on it rose.

Continuing poverty

Although wages rose between 1899 and 1936, Rowntree (1937) in a follow-up survey of York found that 4 per cent of the population were still in primary poverty, and he estimated that poverty affected 53 per cent of the working classes at some point in their lives. Old age and unemployment were still the most serious causes of poverty.

The failure of the free-market economy to provide the benefits its proponents claimed it would do led to wholesale revision of economic doctrine, to provide a much more active role for the state in the economy and in the provision of welfare.

The Beveridge Report

The Beveridge Report (1942) pointed to the piecemeal and chaotic introduction of changes into the system and argued for a new comprehensive system.

The Five Giants

Beveridge said that such a system needed to be put into place to cure what he called the 'Five Giants' (see Table 14.3).

Table 14.3 Beveridge's 'Five Giants'

Beveridge terminology (1942)	Contemporary terminology
Idleness	Unemployment/ lack of jobs
Ignorance	Lack of education
Squalor	Poor quality/ inadequate housing
Want	Poverty/lack of money
Disease	Illness, ill-health

State intervention

The report argued for state intervention to ensure that everyone could live without fear of want. The state would guarantee a minimum standard of living for all its citizens. Beyond this, incomes were to be left to the free market, allowing for individual incentive and enterprise. It argued that a comprehensive system of national insurance needed to be introduced, supported by a variety of forms of national assistance.

In order for the system to work (bearing in mind the problems of the 1930s), Beveridge considered that it should be underpinned by full employment, a national health service and a system of family allowances. (See also Chapters 5, 12 and 17.)

- National Insurance was to be unified through payment of contributions by both employee and employer, a system that survives to this day.
- The national health service would reduce illness, and therefore the burden of claims due to illness and disability.
- 'Family allowances' were introduced to help those in poverty from low wages, but also as a conscious attempt to boost the falling birth rate.

Implementation of the Beveridge proposals

The ideas in the report were implemented in a series of Acts, most notably the Education Act 1944, the National Insurance Act 1944, the Family Allowances Act 1945, the National Health Service Act 1946, and the National Assistance Act 1948.

It should be noted, however, that at the time there was much reluctance to enact all the proposals owing to concerns about cost and the principles underlying the notion of welfare. As a result, Beveridge's proposals were never implemented totally, but his ideas served as the clear inspiration for welfare reform up to the 1970s.

Assumptions behind the Beveridge proposals

Full employment

Government economic policy immediately after World War II was influenced by the ideas of the economist John Maynard Keynes (1936). He contended that the government should intervene to ensure that full employment was maintained. (See also Section 14.6.) Full employment was also an important condition for the existence of a welfare state according to the Beveridge Report.

The role of women

Beveridge also assumed that for most of their lives women would not be employed: his report contained the assumption that married women would be full-time housewives. As a result, married women often received benefits only as dependents of men. This raises a number of important implications:

- The system placed women in a position of dependency on men in many respects.
- Overall provision of welfare was based on the assumption that there would be hours of unpaid work by women in the home. (See also Section 5.7.) This, feminists argued, showed that the welfare state operated on a 'familial ideology' (see Section 5.1) and treated women as second-class citizens.

> ### Discussion point
> How valid or acceptable are these assumptions today? What implications does your answer have for the welfare state?
>
> **C3.1a**

The crisis of the welfare state

A universalist (meaning providing provision for everyone) welfare state can operate only on the basis of nearly full employment, since this maximizes tax revenue and minimizes demand for benefits related to unemployment. This position was broadly maintained until the early 1970s in the UK. However, the long-term relative decline of the UK economy led to an economic crisis and rapidly rising unemployment. Mass unemployment returned and has been a continuing phenomenon since that time. (See Section 14.6.) This crisis was to reveal the extent to which a welfare state was dependent on a prosperous economy. This meant in effect that it was reliant on capitalism – rather than overcoming it.

The Welfare State in Crisis

These events were to lead to many social democratic thinkers reappraising their ideas. Mishra produced a book entitled *The Welfare State in Crisis* (1984). He argued that there was a need for much greater integration of social and economic policy owing to their interrelated nature (as the crisis had so clearly demonstrated). This would imply more state control of the economy and the institution of corporatist arrangements, as for example in Sweden and Germany.

Gough (1979) argues that, in order to solve this crisis, capitalism might try to make the workers 'pay' through lower wages and reduced welfare. It might be said that this presents a picture of the effect on the welfare state and welfare generally of the election of a government committed to New Right ideology.

The New Right and the welfare state

The 1979 general election brought to power a government with a radically new approach to public expenditure and the welfare state, leading to a number of changes.

The end of the commitment to full employment

Probably the most important change has been the ending of the Keynesian commitment to full employment. The New Right argued that there was a 'natural level of unemployment' caused mainly by wages being too high, largely as a result of the actions of trade unions (see Section 14.6). The market would therefore solve unemployment by creating downward pressure on wages. However, this also required that the differential between wages and benefits needed to be increased by means of downward pressure on benefit levels and therefore welfare expenditure.

Despite this there was little change in social welfare expenditure until the late 1980s, notably through the 1986 and 1988 Social Security Acts. Arguably 1988 was an important turning point with a much more radical application of New Right thinking to the welfare state after this point.

Welfare provision from the late 1980s onwards

We can summarize some of the main changes to the provision of welfare that have occurred in the period since the late 1980s:

- Grants previously provided to cover costs other than normal weekly expenditure – for example to purchase a cooker – were replaced by payments from a Social Fund which were (a) discretionary and (b) largely repayable loans.

- Eligibility for benefits to 16- to 18-year-olds was removed on the grounds that places on

training schemes were available for all. A lower rate of Income Support payments was introduced for those under 25.

- The value of the state pension was reduced for those retiring early in the twenty-first century by ending the link between earnings and pensions.

- Eye tests attracted charges and there was a much greater use of private charges for dental treatment.

- Some benefits – for example, housing benefit and child benefit – were not increased in line with inflation. This led to real, though not nominal, cuts in the value of such benefits.

- All earnings-related supplements to benefits – such as unemployment benefit – were withdrawn.

- Responsibility for the administration of sickness payments and maternity benefits was shifted on to employers.

- Prescription charges were increased considerably more than the rate of inflation: for example, between 1979 and the late 1980s by 540 per cent.

- 'Right to buy' legislation was introduced, leading to the sale of council homes to their tenants.

Activity

Using the foregoing description of New Right thinking on the welfare state, try to explain how each of the changes noted above might be justified with reference to New Right theories.

C3.2, C3.3

Summary of New Right changes and approaches

All the changes might be summarized in the following way:

1 First, there was a shift from universal provision towards selective provision. The balance between benefits available to all (universal) and those available only to some via a 'means test' (selective) was clearly altered towards greater reliance on selective provision.

2 There was privatization and marketization. This is notable in the case of the sale of council houses, and with the introduction of

market principles into education (see Section 11.6) and the NHS (see Section 12.6).

3   There was a shift towards community care: looking after the elderly, the disabled and the mentally ill has been moved from care in institutions to care in the community. However, it is often pointed out that this effectively means care by the family. (See also Section 12.6.) It is clear that care in the community was considerably cheaper for the state than institutional care.

4   There was a shift away from seeing the state as the sole provider of welfare. The responsibility of the state was reduced by encouraging private provision (notably through the encouragement of private pensions) and by emphasizing the charitable and voluntary sector.

Criticisms of the New Right approach

Hutton (1996), a journalist and economic commentator, asserts that the usual arguments about the need to reduce welfare expenditure in a time of austerity are based on false assumptions. He alleges that cuts are spurred by political ideology rather than by economic need, and that the twenty-first century will see a large rise in the amount of tax revenue available to fund welfare payments. According to Hutton, 'apart from Iceland, Britain runs the meanest, tightest, lowest-cost social security system in the world'. This can be seen by a comparison with welfare expenditure in the EU (see Figure 14.3).

Sally Witcher (1994), Director of the Child Poverty Action Group, states that there is a need to challenge the myths that have created a sense of crisis in welfare provision – particularly the arguments that the UK has a high rate of taxation, and that it is possible to identify a distinction between the deserving and the undeserving poor. (See also Section 17.6.) She argues that these myths have contributed to a situation where it is possible to consider cutting social security. This, she feels, is not based on sound analysis:

[The CPAG does not] accept that underlying growth in social security will exceed future growth in the economy ... expenditure on benefits is largely a reflection of problems or policies elsewhere, like high unemployment, lack of affordable high-quality childcare and deregulation of the housing market. ... Benefits are inadequate, even for the minimalist role of alleviating poverty. An increasing emphasis on means-testing creates poverty traps and work disincentives.

(Witcher, 1994, pp. i–vii)

Discussion point

Talk of a crisis in the welfare state has recently led to discussion about whether the UK can still afford it. To what extent do you think a welfare state is (a) necessary and (b) possible for the twenty-first century?

C3.1a

14.4 Contemporary welfare provision

Because we so often talk about 'the welfare state', it is easy to forget that there are other agencies beside the state which provide welfare. There are private-sector providers in the shape of private schools and medical services and there has also been a greater emphasis on the voluntary sector in recent years. Equally, there has been a greater emphasis on the provision of welfare through families (see also Section 5.3). This situation, where welfare is provided by a multiplicity of possible agencies and institutions, has been described as 'welfare pluralism'.

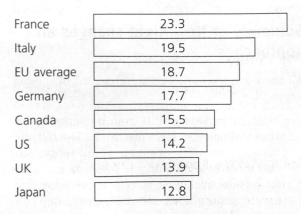

France	23.3
Italy	19.5
EU average	18.7
Germany	17.7
Canada	15.5
US	14.2
UK	13.9
Japan	12.8

Figure 14.3 Social security spending as a percentage of GDP, 1994
Sources: The *Guardian*, 16 October 1995; OECD

Aspects of welfare pluralism

The private sector

Since 1979 there was a number of instances where the UK government sought to encourage private provision of welfare, most notably by encouraging people to take out private insurance plans for their welfare needs. Welfare state theorist, Julian Le Grand (1990), points out that the number of people covered by private health insurance rose from 2.2 to 5.2 million between 1976 and 1986. However, despite the rise, this is still less than 10 per cent of the population.

In the mid-1980s the then government produced proposals to transfer sickness insurance and pension insurance to the private sector, but these were never followed through owing to criticisms and the reluctance of the insurance companies to take up policies for all employees.

In the face of this, the then Conservative government opted instead to try to encourage employees to opt-out of the state pension scheme and transfer to private provision, by providing tax relief for those who chose to do so. However, this scheme received a setback when it was revealed that many of those who transferred would receive less benefit than they would have done from the state pension.

Private welfare – for and against

Supporters of private-sector provision argue that its expanding role in the welfare state is likely to lead to more efficient use of resources and provides some degree of choice to members of the public. Critics often argue that the importance of the profit motive means that private-sector provision will be limited to certain areas, leading effectively to a two-tier welfare state. Fully private provision, they say, would lead to choice for those with money but no choice for the rest.

Burchardt and Hills (1997) estimated that the cost of private welfare insurance for a married man on average pay (about £400 per week, in April 1996) would be £900 per year to cover just three things: mortgage protection, unemployment risk and health insurance. This is equivalent to 6p in the pound on the rate of income tax. Thus, even for someone on average earnings, private provision of welfare is likely to be beyond their means.

The voluntary sector

A number of voluntary organizations provide care – for instance the Salvation Army, Barnados, NSPCC and MIND. These are not statutory bodies set up by parliament but their views are often taken into account since they have a degree of expertise and experience.

In his study of the economics of private and voluntary welfare, Knapp (1989) estimates that the total amount of public-sector support for voluntary organizations between 1983 and 1986 was £3151 million.

Advantages of voluntary provision

To the two advantages of voluntary provision outlined by the former Secretary of State might be added others. For example, voluntary organizations often specialize and can therefore bring expertise to bear. This might lead to innovative provision of services. Since they often use unpaid volunteers, voluntary organizations are often very cost effective.

Disadvantages of voluntary provision

There are also inherent weaknesses in voluntary provision:

- Precisely because it is voluntary it cannot be guaranteed.
- It may be unequally provided across the country.
- It is unlikely to have the monetary resources to contemplate large-scale provision, and thus can exist realistically only as a secondary level of service relying on either state or private-sector provision as the main provider.
- Voluntary services are not directly accountable via democratic mechanisms in the way that state providers are.

The family

The family acted as a key provider of care and welfare before the setting up of the comprehensive welfare state. Now, it may be suggested it plays a smaller role, but does it?

The Beveridge Report and the family

Within the Beveridge Report we have seen that there were assumptions about the continuing role of the family, especially that married women would not seek paid employment because they had another job to do. That, of course, meant the unpaid job of housewife. This clearly provides a largely hidden but substantial subsidy which reduces the cost of state provision, most notably in the case of childcare.

Women and continuing family responsibilites

The 1980s saw attempts to buttress this house-wife role. Families (in effect women within families) were seen as primary carers, with the state and other social services seen as secondary back-up services.

Clarke and Langan (1993) point out that despite this the number of women in paid employment rose over the period of Conservative administrations in the 1980s, which additional role they took on while still maintaining primary responsibility for care within the family. In other words, the burden on women has increased.

Sociological research by Finch and Mason (1993) on family responsibilities showed the continuing importance of family and kinship obligations, even despite the rise of the welfare state. They found that over 90 per cent of their sample had either given financial help to or received such help from relatives, and over 60 per cent had shared a household with an adult relative other than their parents at some time. (See also Sections 5.3 and 5.7.)

Clarke and Langan (1993) argue that one of the major reasons for the increase in the number of patients treated by the NHS is the reduced amount of time people spend in hospital. Recuperative care is effectively transferred from the state to the family – usually women.

Activity

Suggest ways in which the involvement of families in welfare provision has increased in recent years.

C3.2, C3.3

Welfare pluralism and the Third Way

Anthony Giddens – the Third Way and the positive welfare state

Giddens' (1998) book *The Third Way* includes a chapter about the 'positive welfare state' in which he outlines Third Way approaches to welfare. In order to illustrate these ideas we include here a substantial quote from that book and also some critical comments on Giddens from Francis Wheen (2000).

A society of positive welfare

The Catholic unionists saw socialism as the enemy and sought to outflank it on its own ground by stressing codetermination and class reconciliation. Ronald Reagan's view, expressed in 1981, that 'we have let government take away those things that were once ours to do voluntarily' finds a much earlier echo in Europe in the Catholic tradition. Church, family and friends are the main sources of social solidarity. The state should step in only when those institutions don't fully live up to their obligations.

Recognizing the problematic history of the welfare state, third way politics should accept some of the criticisms the right makes of that state. It is essentially undemocratic, depending as it does upon a top-down distribution of benefits. Its motive force is protection and care, but it does not give enough space to personal liberty. Some forms of welfare institution are bureaucratic, alientating and inefficient, and welfare benefits can create perverse consequences that undermine what they were designed to achieve. However, third way politics sees these problems not as a signal to dismantle the welfare state, but as part of the reason to reconstruct it.

The difficulties of the welfare state are only partially financial. ...

Once established, benefits have their own autonomy, regardless of whether or not they meet the purposes for which they were originally designed. As this happens, expectations become 'locked in' and interest groups entrenched. Countries that have tried to reform their pensions systems, for example, have met with concerted resistance. We should have our pensions because we are 'old' (at age 60 or 65), we have paid our dues (even if they don't cover the costs), other people before have had them, everyone looks forward to retirement and so forth. Yet such institutional stasis is in and of itself a reflection of the need for reform, for the welfare state needs to be as dynamic and responsive to wider social trends as any other sector of government.

Welfare reform isn't easy to achieve, precisely because of the entrenched interests that welfare systems create. Yet the outline of a radical project for the welfare state can be sketched out quite readily.

The welfare state ... is a pooling of risk rather than

resources. ... However, the welfare state isn't geared up to cover new-style risks such as those concerning technological change, social exclusion or the accelerating proportion of one-parent households. ...

When Beveridge wrote his Report on Social Insurance and Allied Services, in 1942, he famously declared war on Want, Disease, Ignorance, Squalor and Idleness. In other words, his focus was almost entirely negative. We should speak today of positive welfare, to which individuals themselves and other agencies beside government contribute – and which is functional for wealth creation. Welfare is not in essence an economic concept, but a psychic one, concerning as it does well-being. ... Not only is welfare generated by many contexts and influences other than the welfare state, but welfare institutions must be concerned with fostering psychological as well as economic benefits. ...

The guideline is investment in human capital wherever possible, rather than the direct provision of economic maintenance. In place of the welfare state we should put the social investment state, operating in the context of a positive welfare society.

(Giddens, 1998, pp. 111–117).

Discussion point

a How valid do you think Giddens' criticisms of the old welfare state are?

b In what way is the 'Third Way' different from the New Right or the social democratic approach? (See also Section 14.2.)

c How valid do you think Wheen's criticisms of Giddens and the Third Way are?

C3.1a

The nutty professor

I was invited to the London School of Economics on Monday for a panel discussion with Anthony Giddens. ... Giddens likes to boast that he is venturing 'beyond left and right', ...

During Monday's seminar he said we mustn't hinder the success of entrepreneurs such as Bill Gates. Moments earlier, however, he had insisted that 'we cannot run the world as if it was just a gigantic marketplace' - which is, of course, precisely how Bill Gates does indeed see the world.

On page seven of his book [Giddens, 2000], Giddens warns: 'Companies should not be inhibited from expanding by the existence of too many rules and restrictions.' The absurd qualifier makes the sentence meaningless: even the most unreconstructed old leftist wouldn't propose that we need 'too many' restrictions. But how many are sufficient?

Very few to judge by his comments on page 75: 'Product, capital and labour markets must all be flexible for an economy today to be competitive ... Flexibility does indeed entail deregulation.' But by the time we reach page 143, Giddens is citing Microsoft as the sort of monopolistic corporation which 'left-of-centre governments musn't shirk confronting ... Sometimes the global economy is offered as a rationale for why regulations on monopoly should be relaxed – on the grounds that very large corporations have to compete with others of comparable size in the world marketplace. But the net effect is to project monopoly onto a global scale.'

So then, does the global market require more deregulation or tighter regulation? Both, of course! Like Tinky-Winky's handbag, the third way can accommodate anything. ...

Ralf Dahrendorf describes the third way as a politics that speaks of the need for hard choices but then avoids them by trying to please everybody.

Source: Francis Wheen, *Guardian*, 1 March 2000

14.5 Welfare, social control and stratification

One common image of the welfare state is of an institutional Robin Hood which takes from the rich and gives to the poor. It is certainly the case that many of the social democrats associated with the rise of the welfare state viewed it in such terms, and part of the hostility towards it shown by the New Right is also based on their fear that it involves such a procedure. The question, therefore, of who benefits from the welfare state has been an important and continuing one, in both political and sociological circles. It is also clear that the advent of the New Right to government led to the ending of the notion of the welfare state as a redistributive institution.

In this section we look at arguments surrounding the provision of welfare in the areas of housing, social security payments and personal social security.

What is meant by 'welfare'?

In considering the notion of benefits and social control, we need to think about exactly what is included in the concept of welfare. It is necessary to consider not only the directly observable welfare state – which is aimed at providing *social welfare* – but also fiscal and occupational welfare.

- *Fiscal welfare* means the way in which resources and incomes are distributed through the system of tax allowances and tax rates which clearly affect the disposable income certain groups receive. (See also Section 17.1.)

- *Occupational welfare* is concerned with the existence of large amounts of what are commonly called 'fringe benefits' available to certain people by virtue of their job, such as a company car, a cheaper mortgage, or a subsidized canteen.

All this has an effect on the income and the expenditure needed to maintain a certain lifestyle, so it is important to take it into account when looking at the question of the redistributive effect of the welfare state.

Activity

a Suggest one concrete benefit that might be obtained for each of the three types of welfare outlined so far in this section.

b Explain in your own words why it is important to consider all three forms of welfare in an overall consideration of the effect of welfare.

C3.2, C3.3

The welfare state and social inequality

Women experience the welfare state differently from men. So too do the various classes and people of differing racial and ethnic backgrounds.

(Bryson, 1992, p. 159)

Beveridge referred to the 'five giants' the welfare state was intended to conquer, namely Ignorance, Idleness, Squalor, Disease and Want. In contemporary terms, these refer to education, unemployment and other benefits, housing, health and poverty and personal social services. The issues of education and health are covered in other chapters (see Chapter 11 and 12) so here we will concentrate on the provision of social security benefits, housing and personal social services which covers the provision in relation to the three other 'giants'. We will consider recent debates in relation to each of these areas and look at the way the provision of these services impacts on social stratification since it is clear, as the quote from Bryson above suggests, that there are important inequalities in the way the welfare state is experienced.

Social security

This term covers the wide range of benefits that are available through the Department of Social Security and which consistently top the departmental spending table among government departments.

The idea of social security payments such as unemployment benefit and sickness or incapacity benefits was to provide a safety net, mainly meant as a temporary situation until people could obtain paid employment.

Because of fears over the cost of the welfare state and the argument that benefit levels that were too high might act as a disincentive to work, the original levels set out in the Beveridge Report were reduced by the time it came to be implemented. The actual levels of benefit were therefore set at levels some 40-45 per cent lower than was shown to be necessary to eliminate poverty in Rowntree's 1936 study of York (see also Section 17.4).

There has therefore always been downward political pressure on the level of social security expenditure. This has been combined with moral panics about 'scroungers' to create a belief that this money is somehow wasted and this also places downward political pressure on social security spending.

Social security under the Conservative governments 1979-97

According to Ruth Lister (1989), there were four key themes to the approach of the New Right government to social security between 1979 and 1992. These were:

1 Reducing social security spending.
2 Improving work incentives.
3 Targeting expenditure on those in greatest need.
4 Tackling fraud and abuse.

Reducing social security spending

In line with the New Right belief that state expenditure was bad, social security expenditure was to be reduced. It was a clear priority for reduction since it was also seen as the key contributor to the culture of dependency. Social security payments were said to hook people somewhat like a drug and this had the effect of providing a disincentive to work. In particular, this was done by abolishing the inflation uprating of certain payments. Lister (1989) points to the main changes as follows. The 1980 Social Security Act abolished the uprating link between pensions and average earnings. This meant that prior to 1980 pensions were uprated annually in line with the rise in average earnings, but since then they have only been uprated in line with inflation. Since that time, earnings have generally risen at a higher rate than inflation, so pensioners have lost out.

In the 1980 budget the real value of child benefit was cut by 9 per cent and various earnings-related benefits were abolished. These cuts were however restored in 1983 following pressure from Conservative backbenchers. Lister does however point out that:

about £250 million had been cut by the time of the Social Security Act 1986. The Act has since meant the loss of a further £650 million.

(Lister, 1989, p. 109)

Improving work incentives

Clearly by reducing the real value of social security payments, there was also the aim of increasing the incentive for people to go out to work. This idea rested on the New Right notion that unemployment was voluntary and that people choose not to work. The idea of the various schemes which developed to provide work experience for the unemployed was to provide clear incentives to work and also, because of the belief that the unemployed become the unemployable, the government felt there was a need to get people back into the habit of work.

Lister points out that the rules defining 'availability for work' were considerably tightened up and there was greater monitoring of the unemployed through various schemes. She comments that:

The continued emphasis on work incentives and 'voluntary' unemployment has constituted a classic example of 'blaming the victim'

(Lister, 1989, p. 111)

Targeting expenditure

Ruth Lister (1989) points out that the number of people dependent on social security benefit payments nearly doubled between 1979 and 1987, rising from 4.37 million to over 8 million (1989, p. 116). This was due to the rise in unemployment but also cuts in non-means tested benefits. Changes in the 1980s meant that something like 425 000 claimants were pushed onto reliance on means-tested benefits as cuts in the real value of other benefits took place.

This represents a clear attempt to shift the balance of social security provision towards means-tested benefits on the grounds that this targets expenditure where it is most needed. This is a shift from a universalist philosophy towards a more selective one.

Ruth Lister (1989) makes the following comment:

Means-tested benefits are now explicitly presented as the fulcrum of the system. Many of the reforms introduced in 1988 represent an attempt to rationalise the main means-tested benefits in search of the holy grail of simplification without tackling the underlying problems associated with means-testing. These include the long-recognised problems of low take-up and the poverty trap, which is now ensnaring more poor families than ever.

(Lister, 1989, p. 117)

Stephen Moore (1993) points to studies considering the effect of this targeting. These asked the question of whether this achieved its aim of meeting the needs of the most needy. He points to estimates by the then government showing that there were 3.8 million losers and 2.16 million gainers from the changes to social security payments as a result of the 1986 Social Security Act. However, he also cites a study by the Benefits Research Unit which suggested that 81 per cent of couples and 74 per cent of lone parents would lose out as a result of these changes.

The emphasis on fraud

The Conservative governments have consistently emphasised the need to stamp out social security fraud. An extra 1000 staff were allocated to this after 1980 and the 1983 manifesto of the Conservative party placed a special emphasis on it. Tightening up of regulations followed moral panics about people signing on while holidaying in Spain, the so-called 'Costa del dole'. This led to real restrictions on benefits claims for residential lodgings by young people and it is restrictions from this time that may have contributed to the growth in homelessness.

It is also the case that Gordon and Newnham (1986) report the increased practice of passport checking for ethnic minority claimants. This has been seen to lead to a greater likelihood for ethnic minorities to fail to claim what they are entitled to, further exacerbating income inequalities.

Social security and class inequalities

The most redistributive aspect of a welfare state is the existence of social security benefits. These do distribute income towards the poorest, who would be considerably worse off without them. However, the changes in the 1986 and 1988 Social Security Acts which replaced the system of one-off grants with repayable loans (see Section 14.3) has clearly reduced this effect somewhat. The exclusion of 16- to 18-year-olds from entitlement to income support has also had the same effect. *The Economist* in June 1994 estimated that there were 68 000 people aged 16–18 without any income at all.

Benefit cuts

A second point is that the *real value* of benefits has been cut since the level of supplementary benefit/income support as a percentage of average earnings fell over the 1980s, as can be seen in Table 14.4. Benefit for a single person was equal to 20.8 per cent of average earnings in July 1986, but this fell to 19.1 per cent by April 1988.

Changes in the 1980s therefore seem to have reduced somewhat the redistributive impact of this aspect of the welfare state.

The welfare state, social security benefits and gender inequality

In her comparative study of welfare and the state, Bryson (1992) has separate chapters on men and women – to emphasize the fact that their experiences in a welfare state are very different.

The Beveridge Report, women and entitlement to benefits

The Beveridge Report was clear that the presumed role for married women was in the home,

Table 14.4 Supplementary benefit/income support as a percentage of average earnings

	July 1986	April 1987	April 1988
Single person	20.8	19.5	19.1
Couple	32.1	30.3	28.3
Couple + 1 child	38.5	36.4	32.9
Couple + 2 children	43.1	40.8	37.1
Couple + 3 children	47.2	44.8	41.1
Couple + 4 children	51.0	48.5	44.8

Sources: Department of Social Security; *Guardian*, 12 May 1989

and that they would be provided for via their husbands' earnings. The 'family wage' (see Section 5.3) thus dictated the levels of wages and benefits which were paid mainly to men on the assumption that they were responsible for a wife and children. One vestige of this idea was the married man's tax allowance which survived until 1990.

The principal problem with this idea is that many of the benefits associated with the welfare state are dependent on a certain record of National Insurance (NI) contributions made through paid employment. Women had less involvement in paid employment – in the UK in 1985 only 52 per cent of married women were in such employment. Historically the two main reasons for this were:

- a series of Factory Acts in 1833, 1844 and 1847 which reduced the hours that women and children were allowed to work
- the gendered assumptions contained in the Beveridge Report and consequently enshrined in social welfare legislation.

Patriarchy, the welfare state and the social control of women

Some feminists have seen this as an example of a patriarchal alliance between men of all classes – to exclude women from paid employment and thus increase their dependency on men. Walby (1986), for example, sees the Factory Acts as an alliance between capitalists portraying themselves as concerned with women's and children's welfare, and male workers wishing to exclude women to avoid competitive downward pressure on wages.

While the reforms were seen as progressive precisely because they did appear to remove women from the dangers of factory work – and Bryson argues that in this sense they did improve women's welfare – Walby argues that they reinforced gender inequalities because of their effect on the availability of paid work for women. (See also Section 17.2.)

The benefits of welfare for women

Bryson further argues that, although the welfare state looks after men's interests better than women's, women do nonetheless gain because they are predominant as welfare recipients. This is due to three factors:

- women live longer than men, on average
- parental support is largely given to mothers

- owing to men's superior position in the occupational structure, they are less likely to need the support of the welfare state.

Fiona Williams (1993) echoes the argument that women's experience of the welfare state has been contradictory. She points out that much of the legislation is based on three assumptions about women:

- that their primary role is that of mother and wife
- that they live in heterosexual married relationships
- that they are financially dependent on their husbands.

This creates the following contradictory position:

On the one hand, welfare policies have provided women with material and social improvements: family allowances/child benefit, access to safer childbirth and more reliable forms of contraception as well as employment opportunities. On the other hand the assumptions behind welfare policies have often circumscribed women's lives, with the consequence that many women's needs have been overlooked or marginalised or existing inequalities have been reproduced.

(Williams, 1993, p. 79)

Childcare, social control and the welfare state

Clearly, one important basis of the gendering of the welfare state is about the relative lack of universal provision for childcare facilities – which ultimately requires that at least one partner gives up paid work for some considerable time. The way that the benefits system made assumptions about families and the acceptance of the male breadwinner model with the female housewife role does have the effect of reinforcing or at the very least shoring up the traditional domestic division of labour. The welfare state therefore can act as a form of social control and the way people live their lives and the arrangements couples make for childcare and the domestic division of labour.

Since women are likely to earn less than men, it may in one sense be economically rational for the woman to give up her job in most cases, but this rests on the assumption that the male will share his earnings equally with his family. This assumption has been questioned by research into the field of family finances. Pahl's (1989) study

of family finances and the organization of them has shown that women do not have equal access to, or equal control over, such finances. (See Section 5.7.)

Also, the cost of looking after children – in terms of lost income, mainly by women – is considerable. Bryson quotes the findings of one study done in the UK in 1980 which calculated that the cost in lifetime earnings of a woman bringing up two children was £122 000.

Social security and ethnic inequality

The link to employment

A system of benefits which operates largely on the basis of contributions made through paid employment will place at a disadvantage any groups disadvantaged in the employment sphere. This is clearly the case with ethnic minorities.

A further aspect of this in the case of ethnic minorities is that their employment in low-paid jobs often occurs within the welfare sector itself – particularly the health service – and therefore contributes to the maintenance of services at a lower cost. The cost to society is lowered but at the expense of poorer income for ethnic minority groups. In many ways, all of these points are to a greater or lesser extent also true of women.

Welfare, social control and immigration

One distinctive difference faced by ethnic minorities is the relationship between welfare provision and immigration controls. Studies have shown how many benefits are dependent on a certain period of residence, and the widespread use of passport checking through the Department of Social Security. These restrictions meant, as Williams points out, that while black workers might have been employed to build council houses, they probably were not allocated them; and while they might be employed to clean DSS offices, they probably were not entitled to the benefits they dispensed. The link between residence and entitlement acts as form of social control providing a discouragement for people to immigrate to this country since they would have to survive on their own resources for some time.

The unofficial link to passport checking also acts to discourage some people from claiming benefits to which they are entitled. Consciously or not, such actions lead to a form of social control in restricting access to certain benefits.

The Britishness of the welfare state

A key reason for this was the assumption embodied in much welfare provision that one aim was to produce a British nation that was fit to rule an Empire. This can be seen in the concerns over the fitness of British troops fighting in the Boer War. This led to concerns that the 'national stock' was in decline, and moves to improve it were presented in terms of improving the nation. Since in many ways this talk of 'nation' was conceived in terms of 'whiteness', it created the conditions for the treatment of others differently.

In summarizing the effect of state welfare, Bryson argues thus:

The evidence shows that for societies with either universal or selective approaches, inequality is maintained. This is clearly a bottom line. Benefits from social welfare provisions do deliver assistance, and life is more secure for the needy when such benefits are available. But it is also clear that benefits do not redress inequality.

(Bryson, 1992, pp. 130–1)

Social security and age inequality

The redistributive effects of welfare across the life-course

Hills (1997) argues that there is some evidence that the welfare state through taxation and transfer payments (notably various social security benefits) does redistribute assets from times in our lives when out income is high (notably those aged from early 20s to late 50s) to times when our income is not so high, notably either the very young (largely through child benefits and education) or to the elderly (largely through pensions, other benefits and entitlement to hospital treatment).

Hills points out that this allows different periods of our lives to be smoothed out. He argues that over their lifetime people can expect to receive something like £133 000 in benefits (at

1991 prices). However, what is very different is that those who are income-rich contribute much more to their benefits through self-funding (paying taxes) than those who are income-poor. Therefore over the course of your life the welfare state does have both a degree of a redistributive effect and also creates a degree of stability across periods of your life when your income is not necessarily stable.

However, there is a potential downside to this, as pointed out by Fitzpatrick (1999):

Most of those who are in the poorest 20 per cent of society remain there for extended periods of time. In short, the cash transfer system contributes to the immobility of the poor, providing a safety-net which is also something of a spider's web, and trapping those whom it is designed to help.

(Fitzpatrick, 1999, p. 274)

Pensions

In relation to age and the elderly one of the key changes which has occurred in recent years is changes to the way the level of pensions are calculated. One of the key reasons for this has been the growing concern over the greater numbers of elderly people as a proportion of the population and the potential effects of this on calls on welfare resources. Taylor-Gooby (1991) for example points out that those aged 75 and over use six times as much NHS resources as younger people. However, these statistics should be balanced with the point made by Twigg (1999) which is that most people over the age of 65 do not suffer from health problems which limit their independence.

Pensions used to be uprated in line with changes in average earnings with the aim being to keep the real value of pensions relative to average earnings constant. However, concerns over the cost of this led the Conservative government to end this link in 1982 and instead link changes in pension to changes in inflation. This ended concerns about the potential future cost of pensions and this is now falling as a proportion of the economy. However, it did create a new concern, namely whether the standard state pension would be adequate to survive on.

Because average earnings have risen faster than inflation since, the value of the pension relative to average earnings, and therefore the standard of living of pensioners, has fallen consistently since 1982. Fulcher and Scott (1999) quote figures from Glennerster (1995) who shows that the value of the state pension as a percentage of average male earnings fell from 23 per cent in 1981 to 15 per cent in 1993 and is projected to fall to 10 per cent in 2010. Fitzpatrick (1999) also points out that in the late 1990s the basic pension is worth 15 per cent of average earnings, but by the year 2040 it will be worth only 7.5 per cent of average earnings.

It is figures such as these which have led people to conclude that in the future the basic state pension will no longer be enough to survive on and that therefore they need to consider alternatives. This obviously does suggest that the welfare state no longer provides care from cradle to grave, even though Glennerster (1995) has pointed out that the cost of restoring the value of pensions through restoring the link to average earnings is not great and would require an increase in taxation of only 0.5 per cent per decade.

Social security and debates over disability payments

The payments made to the disabled are conditional benefits, that is they are conditional on meeting certain criteria, usually passing a medical examination or having medical impairment of sufficient nature to qualify for benefits. These requirements and their implementation have often been the cause of disquiet and anger from disabled groups such as the Disability Alliance.

Such payments moved close to the top of the welfare agenda when the amount paid out for various incapacity and disability benefits started to rise dramatically in the 1980s. This was followed by something of a moral panic about the level of payments with attempts continuing under the new Labour government to reduce the amount spent on these payments and to tighten the eligibility requirements. (see also Section 14.6.)

Personal social services

The personal social services are the areas staffed by social workers who look after the needs of various groups such as the disabled, elderly people, the mentally ill and those with learning difficulties. It also covers the area of children in the care of local authority residential care. This area has most certainly been subject to considerable review in the last twenty years since much of its provision is provided and funded by local council authorities, whose budgets and powers were most severely attacked under the Conservative governments of the 1980s.

Competitive tendering and care in the community

The provision of local authority services was subject to competitive tendering and this has led to a greater preponderance of private service providers.

This area was also the subject of the proposals for the Care in the Community initiative which is examined in more detail below.

The attack on institutional care, which combined arguments from the libertarian left in the form of analyses derived from Erving Goffman's book *Asylums* and the libertarian right in the form of arguments against state provision, chimed well with the desire of the then government to cut back on public expenditure.

Disability and care in the community

Those with mental health problems, for instance, were deemed to be primarily the responsibility of the local health authority but it was clear that a number fell between health authorities and social services departments. As a result there were a number of high profile cases where those suffering from mental illness were placed in care in the community with little backup and then suffered a relapse into illness, with tragic consequences:

The dilemma of how to manage severely mentally ill patients who refuse medication was made more acute by a series of high-profile cases that involved killings (the Clunis case) or suicide (one man climbed into the lions' cage at London zoo). In response, in 1994 the government introduced supervisory registers to identify and keep track of mentally ill people who were most at risk to themselves or others and, in 1996, supervised discharge for patients who had been compulsorily detained at some point. Under this, the supervisor – usually the key worker- can require the patient to live in a particular place and to attend for treatment — (Department of Health, 1996). As yet there is no provision for compulsory treatment, though the issue continues to be aired.

(Twigg, 1999, p. 365)

There are also issues over the definition of and

labelling of people as mentally disabled. Showalter (1987) argues that women have often been presented as unstable and irrational and that female sexuality is often seen as the causal basis of this female irrationality when compared to the 'rational' male. In simple terms she suggests that notions of what is rational and irrational tend to denigrate those who are oppressed by the existing order of things, in this case by patriarchal structures in society.

Since there were assumptions about the way women would live their lives which were reinforced by the benefits of the welfare state being based on these assumptions, it can be argued that the Beveridge Report and the welfare state reinforced women in traditional female roles. Since Brown and Harris (1978) showed in their study of depression among working-class women that the key causes were loss of their own mother before the age of 11, having three or more children who were under 14, lacking a confiding relationship (particularly with husband) and finally lacking a full- or part-time job, it is clear that being a woman in a traditional role can indeed make you ill and if welfare regulations reinforce that it can be argued that welfare provision or lack of it makes women ill.

The beneficiaries of social services, housing and other aspects of welfare

Looking at various aspects of the provision of welfare, it seems clear that the affluent benefit much more than the poor. In a famous study on the question of who benefits from the welfare state, Le Grand (1982) investigated the beneficiaries of welfare policy in five areas, namely health (see also Chapter 12), education (see Chapter 11), council housing, public transport and social services. Of these the only one where the poor benefited substantially more than the better-off was council housing.

As can be seen from Table 14.5, annual expenditure on healthcare was 15 per cent greater for the top fifth of income groups than for the poorest fifth. In relation to education, expenditure on the richest 20 per cent was more than 2.8 times that spent on the poorest 20 per cent. This research was conducted in 1978, but later research by Le Grand and Winter (1987) shows that the trends continued.

Housing and the welfare state

Quality of life in urbanity is very much related to the increasingly scarce resource of housing. Sociologists interested in this area have been keen to explain how individuals and households come to live where they do, *and* why they don't live elsewhere. Because squalor was one aspect of the Beveridge Report the provision of housing was centrally involved in plans for the welfare state, primarily through plans to create cheap rented housing which became known as council housing due to its provision through local council authorities.

Definitions of housing type

Sociologists of housing in the UK have identified three key types of tenure:

* *owner-occupied housing* – homes for people who have bought their property or those with mortgages who are not yet outright owners

Table 14.5 Public expenditure (£ p.a.) per household on social services in the UK by income group, 1978

Income group (original income)	Healthcare	Education	School meals, milk and other welfare foods	Housing	Rail travel	All social services
Top 20%	354	444	21	57	25	902
Next 20%	323	400	24	73	11	831
Middle 20%	320	348	26	103	7	804
Next 20%	309	216	22	118	5	670
Bottom 20%	306	156	22	205	2	691
Mean	322	313	23	111	10	780

Sources: Le Grand (1982); CSO

- *public rented housing* – homes rented from local authorities
- *private rented housing* – homes rented from private landlords.

There are distinct changes within and, more importantly, between types of tenure which are seen to indicate varying levels of inequality. The proportions of tenure have also been changing, as Figure 14.4 shows.

Activity

Figure 14.4 shows the changes in these three types of tenure from 1971 to 1993. Describe the trends in the graph and use your knowledge of recent social and political developments to account for them.

IT3.1, C3.2, C3.3

Housing, social policy and the construction of inequalities

It is clear that levels of owner-occupation have increased significantly. Generally such housing has higher status, so we might assume that the increase in stock represents a rise in living standards, particularly when we also note that the number of houses rented from local authorities has declined. Morris and Winn (1990) warn against making such an assumption, noting that

the quality of owner-occupied housing has increasing variation. Instead, they say, government policy – particularly since 1979 – can account for a large part of the change. Policies of Conservative administrations from 1979 were aimed at reducing state involvement in people's lives by developing a wider and more significant consumer market, allowing for more choice, and making individual citizens more responsible for their own destinies. This applied to housing as much as to any other policy area. Such policies, based on political commitments rather than what Morris and Winn identified as the 'realities' of housing needs and availability, had 'led to housing inequality becoming an ever more evident part of the housing system' (p. 14).

Selling off public housing and the creation of rich and poor housing

Policy was deliberately aimed at increasing the levels of owner-occupation and private renting while reducing the amount of publicly owned housing provided by the 'nanny state'. The 'right-to-buy' policy allowed council tenants to buy their homes at a price lower than the market value. It was thought that as private owners they would take much more care of their properties and neighbourhoods, making them more responsible citizens while at the same time reducing long-term costs to the taxpayer. In reality, according to Morris and Winn, it meant that the best homes

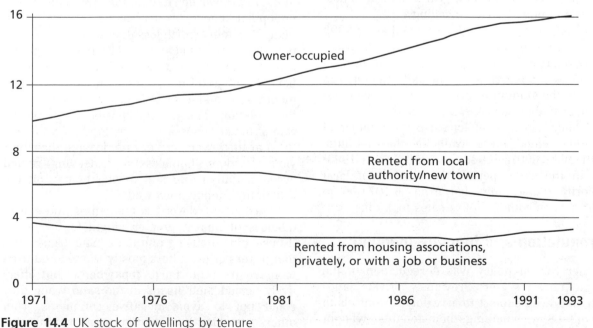

Figure 14.4 UK stock of dwellings by tenure
Source: Social Trends, 1995

in the 'best' neighbourhoods were sold to tenants, leaving local authorities with a stock increasingly located in inner cities and the least popular areas. Councils were left principally with flats and poorly built, experimental homes from the 1960s and 70s which were costly to maintain. They concluded that:

... the right to buy has undoubtedly increased the incidence of housing disadvantages within the public sector and in particular has contributed to the closer correlation between council housing and low income.

(Morris and Winn, 1990, p. 23)

Discussion point

To what extent do you feel that the transfer of council houses to housing associations or the private sector is a good thing?

C3.1a

Housing, privatization and inequality

Local authority homes were also sold 'en bloc' to private (i.e. corporate) or housing association ownership, making them 'privately rented' homes. Winn and Morris believe that this led to short-term benefits such as refurbishment (e.g. newly double-glazed windows) but led to longer-term inequality as rents increased, displacing the poorest tenants who could not afford them. Alcock *et al.* (2000) point out that over the period 1984 to 1994 there was a grand total of almost 1.5 million public sector dwellings.

Alcock *et al.* (2000) also report that by 1993 there were a total of 8 060 000 rented dwelling units available. In the 1980s and early 1990s the then Conservative government had attempted to increase the amount of private rented accommodation available. Alcock *et al.* make the point that this policy had little effect since the number of privately rented units available changed little (from 2 318 000 in 1983 to 2 310 000 in 1993) and in the same period the amount of local authority rented units fell from 6 107 000 to 4 868 000 as council house sales took off.

Deregulation and housing inequality

Another related policy was deregulation of the private rented sector. Previously private landlords had been subject to a variety of controls to prevent them exploiting their tenants, who in turn had various rights which they could use to make their homes safer from interference. The 'New Right' and saw such regulation as 'anti-landlord' and 'anti-market', with the result that people were put off renting their properties to those who could make use of them. The aim of deregulation was to increase the number of homes available to those who wanted the flexibility of renting their homes rather than being tied to one local authority or a mortgage. Morris and Winn suggest that this policy led to an increase in high-rent accommodation, favouring middle-class owners who let their properties to middle-class tenants who chose to rent because it suited their particular needs at the time. This failed to meet the needs of low-income households, resulting in increased homelessness.

The collapse of the housing market and negative equity

Government policy had also been seen to make owner-occupation seem a positive option by offering subsidies to mortgage buyers, and lenders were keen to compete in this newly developing market. This increase in demand for owner-occupied housing – a finite source – led to vastly increased prices and inflationary pressures for the Treasury. The government took steps that had the effect of steadily increasing the levels of interest that mortgage buyers had to pay on their loans. As the Chancellor had hoped, the increase in interest charges reduced demand and eased inflation. However, it had the unintended and unpopular effect of decreasing house prices, many becoming worth less than their owners had paid for them ('negative equity'). Many homeowners were thus caught in a vicious circle of being unable to make their increased repayments, but unable to sell their house to escape the situation. The net result was an increasing rate of house repossessions by lenders, who sold them at the lower market rate, leaving their previous 'owners' homeless and needing rented accommodation and still having to pay off the remaining money borrowed.

Ford (1990) describes the causes and consequences of this at greater length in her essay 'Households, housing and debt'. She argues that non-payers or defaulters mostly wanted and tried to make their mortgage repayments, but effectively buried their heads in the sand when they could not to avoid negative comments from others – making the situation more difficult.

Case Study – The rebuilding of Docklands and the social effects

Deakin and Edwards note how inner-city policy promoted by continuous Conservative administration of the 1980s and 90s was based on the concept of the 'enterprise culture' and links with the private sector. Urban local authorities were seen by ministers as slow, bureaucratic and too mixed up in left-wing ideological commitments, whereas the private sector offered drive, energy and the ability to create jobs. The private sector was the epitome of the 'enterprise culture'. 'Enterprise' incorporated self-interest, confidence, responsibility and a work ethic (compare this with the New Right account of the inner-city 'underclass' – see Section 17.6), all aspects thought to be lacking in the inner city. Allied to revitalization projects it would minimize public costs and be able to do what millions of pounds of public money had been unable to do – bring jobs, create a new culture and end the cycle of deprivation:

... there emerged the new orthodoxy that the root cause of the problems of the inner cities was the collapse of their economic infrastructures brought about by the emigration of firms to out-of-town sites or their death in situ, compounded by the socially selective emigration of their populations. ... What needed to be done was now clear: new industry, new jobs and an economically active population had to be attracted back to the inner areas in order to regenerate their economic infrastructures.

(Deakin and Edwards, 1993, p. 3)

Deakin and Edwards' evaluation of such a policy is based on three case studies: Trafford Park in Manchester; Heartlands in Birmingham; and Docklands in London. We will consider the last case, often seen as the 'flagship' of the Conservatives' urban regeneration policies.

From the East End to Docklands

Deakin and Edwards note how interpretation of the Docklands success in regenerating an area of London's dilapidated East End has caused conflict within the ranks of sociologists. 'New Right' sociologist Marsland was quoted as saying that it was 'the most exciting, positive and potentially profitable (in every sense of that maligned word) development in Europe' (p. 96). Deakin and Edwards conclude that the answer was somewhat more complicated, with benefits and costs requiring consideration.

Docklands and jobs for women

Positively, the Docklands project had brought physical regeneration of the infrastructure, new industry and commerce and new jobs, particularly benefiting women. However, many of the new jobs are not 'new' but due to relocation (bringing in 'old' staff), and when they are new they go to 'outsiders'. The local population do not have the skills required, are not given training and thus unemployment remains high. Formation of the nationally (rather than locally) accountable London Docklands Development Corporation (LDDC) took planning out of local government control, ensuring that local people are not 'stakeholders'.

Deakin and Edwards wonder whether local authorities, with the finance that the LDDC had, might have done a better job. Their feeling is that the question could not be answered, but partnership – allied to a legal commitment from the private sector to live up to its promises – might offer the best way forward. Such an option, however, was not possible in a capitalist world and so all the public sector could do was offer financial subsidies and incentives. The benefits of recent policy, in reality, have been marginal. The assumption had been that new jobs would have a 'trickle-down effect' (see Section 17.1) on other aspects of social deprivation, but there have been few 'new' jobs:

Docklands has neither demonstrated the unquestionable superiority of market-led regeneration and led to the 'death of planning', nor demonstrated the hollowness of claims for the enterprise culture.

(Deakin and Edwards, 1993, p. 249)

The two communities of Docklands

Deakin and Edwards argue that:

... with market-led changes still in full flow and the size and composition of the population altering in response, the risk that the existing population would be squeezed out or at best marginalized was clearly still strong.

(Deakin and Edwards, 1993, p. 112)

Yet they go on to say that:

In the Isle of Dogs, the two communities – the existing East-Enders and the incomers – will have to learn to live with one another.

(Deakin and Edwards, 1993, p. 122)

One wonders how far this is easier for Deakin and Edwards to write than it is for the communities to do – at least in any positive and meaningful sense – especially when one takes the following critical perspective into account.

Crow and Allan (1994) quote Marris who said (in 1987) that the original residents:

... saw themselves threatened by office developers, by an invasion of homeless families herded into huge impersonal Greater London Council estates; by the conversion of the riverside into fashionable, luxury hotels and apartments; and by main roads slashing through what was left of their disintegrating, blighted and economically marginal communities.

(Marris, 1987; quoted in Crow and Allan, 1994, p. 149)

Homelessness

Homelessness became an important issue in the 1980s, but home repossessions were just one factor contributing to this. Other significant reasons were loss of a home previously offered by parents, family or friends, loss of rented accommodation, or separation from a partner.

Youths and homelessness

Hutson and Liddiard (1994) give deeper insights into the causes and consequences of youth homelessness. They suggest that a variety of explanations can be offered, being either structural or personal. In structural terms the following arguments are offered:

- Changes in the labour market led to low pay and unemployment, making the keeping of a home economically unsustainable.

- Changes to the welfare benefits system lowered the level of any alternative income – or even excluded particular individuals from this altogether.

- Changes in the housing market, identified above, meant that there was a lack of affordable housing.

- Demographic changes meant that youths represented an increasing proportion of the population. Combined with a desire to live in single-person households and reduced levels of affordable housing, the result was homelessness.

Among the many personal explanations were the desire to leave home to attain independence; the poor experience of living in care; physical or sexual abuse at home; mental illness; involvement in crime; alcohol and drug abuse. Hutson and Liddiard found that young people were most likely to see their homelessness in one of these terms. For example, a 19-year-old youth said:

I took a lot of bashing because my mother split from my father, yeah, and I stuck with my father. He used to do what he did to my mother to me ... I thought 'I don't want to go through what she's been through! I'm off!'.

Conservative politicians tend to see youth homelessness in terms of personal choice, whereas Labour and other politicians emphazise structural conditions. John Cunningham (Labour) saw youth homelessness in the following way:

The severe shortage of adequate, affordable, fit housing is causing the crisis.

(John Cunningham, *Hansard*, 10 February 1987)

Hutson and Liddiard remind us that political statements are not only to do with ideological commitment but also whether a politician's party is in power or not. It is easier for politicians to espouse a caring attitude if they do not have the responsibility to find the financial resources to manage the problem.

Activity

If your library has a newspaper on CD–ROM, look up the issue of 'homelessness' in the index.

a How does the newspaper explain and evaluate the issue?

b Are there particular biases?

c Are there any contradictions?

d What effect will the stories have on the readers?

C3.2, C3.3, IT3.1

Housing, welfare and inequality

Urban managers and the construction of inequality

Much of this section on housing has considered political policies and economic conditions in explaining inequality of access, but sociologists have also seen causes in other arenas. Pahl's (1975) concept of 'urban managers' is a classic example. He identified them as the people with direct control of urban resources, including housing – estate agents, mortgage lenders, local government officials and councillors, and property developers. All were seen to be guided by their moral and political values.

Morris and Winn (1990) suggest that this concept fell from grace because 'urban managers' was ill-defined, and because power was wrongly ascribed to low-level officials; but they conclude that this work had been overlooked too quickly. The concept had not been fully researched, and a useful addition to it might be the concept of labelling in terms of the interactive setting between managers and clients. Ideas from the sociology of organizations might also be used to evaluate how far officials were constrained by the 'rule book'.)

House price inflation and the creation of inequality

Saunders (1978, 1987), from a neo-Weberian perspective, explained the developing inequalities between owner-occupiers and non-owners in terms of the further financial gains offered by house price inflation, the ability to improve one's property, and gaining extra government subsidies. However, as Morris and Winn note, property may not always gain in value (the 1990s have shown this) and home-owners are an inhomogeneous group with widely different experiences.

Post-Fordism and housing

Ball (1983) criticized the sociological debate over consumption of housing, arguing for a linked assessment of production processes. These include land purchase and development, building of the home, transfer of the completed home to the buyer, and use of the home. A whole range of groups are involved in the processes and there is potential for a variety of conflict situations, which can be assessed sociologically. Until recent times, he argued, land prices had risen so profits came relatively easily for developers. Now, however, they had to think far more widely in their assessment of costs and savings. Savings had been identified by limiting the number of housing types available, offering a blanket design while still marketing homes as 'individually' designed. Recession in the housing market led to building in small batches which had to be sold before the next batch was built. Often the first homes will be built nearest the site entrance as

'show homes' but this was an inefficient process. Small batch production had also led to subcontracting in order to avoid having a wage bill during idle periods – post-Fordism in the sociology of housing!

The homes people live in, or conditions of homelessness, are determined by the complex interaction of a variety of factors. Structural conditions such as the economy, labour market and policy options by 'urban managers' affect the availability of housing and people's chances of entering the housing system. Individual choices such as how much income should be spent on housing or length of stay in one place also affect the type of tenure we find people living in. However, whether macro or micro forces have most influence on housing, it should be noted that there are variations in housing quality according to social class, gender, ethnicity and age, with those least advantaged in other areas of society also least advantaged in housing. Social policy and provision in this areas has at best failed to overcome this and in some instances seems to have been actively designed to exacerbate such inequalties.

Other aspects of welfare provision

In looking at the provision of social security, housing and personal social services, we can clearly see that there are important inequalities which affect inequalities in society. However, it is also important to be aware of the two other aspects of the way welfare is distributed in our society. As well as direct benefits and payments, the amount of money in your pocket can be affected by changes in taxes or tax allowances. This is known as fiscal welfare. Equally if you get a car or occupational pension with your job, this will affect your standard of living. This is known as occupational welfare. Both of these are examined below.

Fiscal welfare and inequality

As has been mentioned already in this section, fiscal welfare relates to a nation's system of taxation. It depends on the balance between taxes that hit the richest hardest (*progressive taxes*, of which income tax is an example) and taxes that hit the poorest hardest (*regressive taxes*, of which VAT is an example). It also depends on the way in which relief from taxation is given to certain activities and the question of who benefits from these reliefs. These reliefs act in effect like benefits, because money that would otherwise flow to the government in taxation payments stays with the individual.

Changes in taxation

In relation to the first of these points, the UK government after 1979 followed a policy of shifting the burden of taxation from income tax to VAT. Overall the tax system does not take from the rich proportionately greater than the poor; if anything it is the reverse and this trend accelerated in the 1980s. Westergaard (1995) points out that if we look at the total net addition to disposable income caused by the tax and benefits system changes between 1979 and 1989, some 46 per cent went to the richest 10 per cent of households and only 8 per cent to the poorest 40 per cent of households.

Tax relief and welfare

The issue concerning tax relief presents a picture of even greater inequality. This is an important form of public expenditure since it constitutes a cost to the government in exactly the same way as do other more direct forms of public expenditure.

Bryson (1992) points out that the cost to the nation of these exemptions and reliefs was greater than in any other heading of public expenditure in 1990/91. Prest and Barr (1985), in a study of the operation of public finance, argued that the effect of this was that the proportion actually contributed to taxation revenues by each income group in the 1980s was roughly the same, despite the apparent progressivity of income tax rates.

It is also the case that fiscal welfare can be received only by those with an income, so women who do not have paid employment lose out.

Occupational welfare and inequality

In the British welfare state the amount of time spent in paid employment has an effect on the state benefits that are available. This has an important effect, owing to the greater likelihood that women's paid employment will be disrupted (by looking after children) and of a part-time nature (see Section 17.2) where the contributions made will be lower. One very important effect of

this is that women are less likely to attain a record of sufficient contributions to qualify for a full state pension.

Benefits provided by an employer

A number of benefits are paid to people by their employer – in common parlance these are called 'fringe benefits'. Obviously it is necessary to be in employment to get fringe benefits, so the unemployed and full-time housewives are excluded. This is another case of inequality in occupational welfare.

However, even among the employed, occupational benefits can serve to reinforce existing inequalities. Oppenheim and Harker (1996), for example, show how the distribution of occupational benefits is clearly gendered, and other research shows that occupational benefits tend to be skewed towards the higher-paid. In a study in Australia, Jamrozik *et al.* (1981) showed that those in the top earnings bracket received 3.8 times the occupational benefits of those at the bottom.

Discussion point

Of all the types of welfare discussed – social, fiscal and occupational – which do you think is the most important and which the least important in contemporary society in the UK?

C3.1a

Social welfare on its own does not seem very redistributive. If we take into account all types of welfare, including fiscal and occupational, it seems that the better-off benefit considerably more than the rest and that the welfare regime serves to reinforce existing class, gender and other inequalities. Much of this extended welfare regime remains hidden, and most media concentration is on the tip of the iceberg – social welfare payments. This serves to protect the main beneficiaries from scrutiny, and the benefits themselves serve to keep certain groups privileged without too many questions being asked.

Welfare regimes as creators of social stratification

Esping-Andersen (1990) suggests that, in order to consider fully the effect of the welfare state on stratification, we need to link consideration of its actions with the concept of citizenship developed by T. H. Marshall (see also Section 15.1). This would allow consideration of the way in which the welfare state actively promotes certain kinds of social stratification:

The welfare state is not just a mechanism that intervenes in, and possibly corrects, the structure of inequality; it is, in its own right, a system of stratification.

(Esping-Andersen, 1990, p. 23)

We have already seen in Section 14.1, that Marshall identified three types of citizenship. He saw the rise of the welfare state as moving towards an era of social citizenship where everyone was entitled to social participation in society. Welfare regimes based on liberal ideology tended to develop residual modes of welfare benefit whereby the state acted merely as a safety-net. This creates a division between those living on benefits, who tend to be poor, and the rest of the population who live off their earnings from employment. The division tends to be large because benefit levels are low to discourage those seen as work-shy from applying. This is further reinforced by the stigma attached to means-tested benefits:

The poor-relief tradition, and its contemporary means-tested social-assistance offshoot, was conspicuously designed for purposes of stratification. By punishing and stigmatising recipients, it promotes social dualisms.

(Esping-Andersen, 1990, p. 24)

Clearly this model fails to ensure that all people are entitled to social participation, and therefore creates inequalities between citizens.

In contrast the conservative model, rooted as it is around social insurance based on workplace contributions, generally contains at least two distinct levels of benefits, since it is designed expressly so that welfare entitlements maintain class and status differentials.

Esping-Andersen argues that because both the liberal and conservative systems were set up explicitly to create or maintain social inequalities, this led to great hostility towards them, particularly from the labour movement. He points out, however, that often schemes promoted by the labour movement benefited only the most organized workers, and excluded others, thereby setting up divisions inside the working classes. (See also Section 17.7.)

In contrast to these approaches, the universalist model of the welfare state seeks to avoid the same problems, and seems at first sight to contain within it the notion of equality. Benefits are to be available to all at the same rate. Everyone is to be treated equally. Esping-Andersen argues, however, that this system can work only when the majority of the population are working class who will accept the modest benefits available. But with the expansion of the middle classes as a proportion of the population (see Section 17.2) this system breaks down – they supplement their state benefits with private-sector provision, thus undermining the equality of universalistic provision.

In this situation the dualistic nature of the social-insurance residual model is re-created. Esping-Andersen points out that one way in which support for the welfare state has been maintained in this situation is to promote higher levels of benefits for the middle classes via the state – by, for example, making the benefits earnings-related. This is what happened in Sweden and Norway. The point is then that the welfare state is maintained but the notion of equality that underpins it has been eroded, although it does remain universal provision.

What is novel in this analysis is the way in which the assumption is avoided that welfare is in some way linked to greater equality. It recognizes instead how welfare regimes developed, some of which were consciously devoted to maintaining inequalities.

 Discussion point

To what extent do you agree (if at all) that welfare regimes have been set up with the aim of maintaining existing levels of inequality?

C3.1a

The government has tried to encourage greater private provision of welfare by giving tax relief on private pension contributions – which tend to be taken up more by the better-off. There are further reliefs available for charitable contributions, which includes many private schools, thus reducing the cost of educating children privately – again something indulged in much more by higher income groups.

In the UK, up to 1990 an allowance was paid to married men exempting some of their wives' earnings from tax. Since 1990 the allowance has been claimable by either men or women in certain circumstances, thus reducing a gender inequality in the system. Westergaard (1995) declares, however, that this change may create more class inequality since it will favour prosperous households at the expense of poorer ones.

It is also the case that fiscal welfare can only be received by those with an income, so women who do not have paid employment lose out.

One illuminating way to show the effect of both social welfare and fiscal welfare was devised by the Child Poverty Action Group in 1991. They showed that the benefits available from fiscal welfare meant that the total benefits paid to someone earning £40000 a year and their family were only £1 per week less than those paid to an unemployed person and their family. This can be seen in Table 14.6.

14.6 The welfare state as social control

Notions of welfare and social control

Although we often think of the welfare state as giving, it is also clear that often it is the case that gifts arrive with strings attached or that gifts are given with the aim of encouraging people to behave in certain ways, or not to behave in other ways. Sociologists, particularly Marxist and feminist-inspired sociologists, have long thought about the way in which welfare benefits were structured to try to control the population in various ways, for instance by making eligibility for benefits dependent on working thus discouraging idleness and providing a strong incentive to become wage slaves. Alternatively, we can look at the way benefits were deemed to be provided to households and largely to men within them as reinforcing patriarchal structures in society.

More recently, the work of Michel Foucault has focused on the way the state operates surveillance on populations and the control mechanism of the state. Foucault is a post-structuralist who is clearly influenced by the work of Nietzche in arguing that power is an omnipresent entity. What is new with Foucault (see also Section 15.6) is his emphasis on micropower and micropolitics, the way that power flows through society like capillaries. In other words we cannot merely consider the central state but we need to consider power relations inside all institutions and relationships. The institutions of welfare are clearly able to be analysed using this model and such a post-structuralist approach has come into fashion of late. In this section we will look at various approaches which have analysed the operation of the welfare state in terms of notions of social control. We will also go on to consider the debate about total institutions and their effects on personal identity. Here we will consider in particular their effect on children, the elderly, single-parent families and the long-term unemployed.

Marxist approaches to welfare

Social control and the reproduction of capitalism

Marxists argue that the welfare state is a mechanism to both stabilize and reproduce capitalism, but also that certain elements of it represent con-

Table 14.6 Benefits for wealthy equal handouts for jobless (£/week)

Married couple with a single earner (aged 44) on £40 000 pa	£	Unemployed married couple with two children aged four and six	£
Married couple's and personal allowance at 40%	13.64	Income support	57.60
			12.35
			12.35
			7.35
Mortgage interest tax relief	33.46	Rent rebate	23.43
Personal pension relief	61.54	Community Charge benefit	10.58
Nat. Ins. personal pension subsidy	8.11	Free school meals	2.85
2% personal pension incentive	6.08	Free welfare milk	2.10
Personal equity plan dividend	4.62		
Total	127.45	Total	128.61

Sources: Child Poverty Action Group; *The Observer,* 17 March 1991

cessions which the working classes have won from capitalism. Perhaps the best example to illustrate this is Marx's idea that legislation to reduce the hours of factory work resulted from centuries of class struggle between workers and capitalists. However, he also argued that it would in the end benefit the capitalists too since their workers would not be so tired and therefore be more productive.

The welfare state as a form of social control

Marxists also argue that reforms are often introduced to head off disruptive action by the working classes. The extent of the class struggle is therefore the key determinant of the nature of any welfare state that develops. However, it is also the case that calculations by the capitalist class will play a part, and this leads on to an analysis that sees the welfare state as a form of social control. With regard to social security, Ginsburg (1991) argues that it keeps wages low by setting benefit levels low; and, by ensuring that able-bodied unemployed are required to work, it seeks to instil and maintain industrial discipline.

The crisis of welfare and legitimacy

A different emphasis is placed on this by O'Connor (1973, 1984). While accepting that the welfare state has to act to maintain the accumulation of capital, he argues that it also has to perform the sometimes contradictory function of legitimating the system. (See also information on Habermas in Section 16.1.) This leads to a crisis because while everyone wants more public services they do not want to pay the necessary extra taxes. He asserts that this may lead to government expenditure exceeding government revenue. Instead of providing a stable situation for renewed capital accumulation, this may lead to instability and economic and political crises. The welfare state may therefore in some cases be dysfunctional for capitalism.

The welfare state as a cost to capitalism

Welfare — cheaper than social unrest?

Offe (1984) has argued that in fact the idea of a pure *laissez-faire* capitalism as outlined by the New Right would not work because the ensuing social unrest would undermine the stability required for capital accumulation. Nonetheless he does see the welfare state as constituting a cost to the capitalist system. His conclusion is that 'while capitalism cannot coexist with the welfare state, neither can it exist without the welfare state'.

This is moving away from earlier Marxist positions – which tended to see the welfare state as unproblematically creating the conditions for continued capital accumulation – towards a position that argues that there is a cost to capitalism; a necessary cost, but a cost nonetheless. The implication is that the capitalist class may choose to, and may succeed in, dismantling most or all of the welfare state. The lack of a coordinated response to 'attacks' on the welfare state from the New Right has tended to confirm this view. Offe now argues that capitalism may be able to survive with a very minimalist welfare state for the poor and with the rest of the population surviving on private welfare.

Feminist approaches to welfare

Reinforcing women's dependency

The assumption contained in the Beveridge Report that married women would not want to seek paid employment had important implications for the way the welfare state developed. (See Section 14.3.) For example, many benefit payments are dependent on a past record of National Insurance contributions that usually come through paid employment, so women who have not worked regularly are placed at a disadvantage. This type of issue has been discussed by feminist writers. Williams (1989), for instance, argues that because the development of the welfare state after 1945 was based on this questionable view of the role of women, in many ways it served to reinforce women's dependency in the home. (See also Section 5.7.) Clearly this analysis points to the way the operation of the welfare state sought to control the activities of women and to reinforce women's traditional place and role in society.

Failure to provide childcare

Lewis (1991) is concerned to highlight the important campaigning role of women inside the Labour party in actually bringing about welfare state reforms. However, she also points out that as a result of the way it was implemented the welfare state rarely prioritized women's concerns. This can be seen, for example, in the failure to provide a comprehensive, publically funded system of childcare.

Women as cheap labour

Feminist writers have also been concerned with the welfare state as an employer, since the majority of its employees are women. Overall, therefore, while the welfare state may have led to some improvements in living standards, feminist writers have been concerned to highlight the ways in which gender assumptions remain embedded in its structure.

Activity

Make a list of the key concepts associated with each approach to welfare, and using this textbook and other resources provide your own definition of each.

C3.2, C3.3

Social control and the emergence of welfare in the UK

The middle ages – fear of social disorder

Once a centralized state machinery had been created – which in the UK occurred around the time of Henry VIII – the question of the extent to which it should intervene in the running of society became necessary. At the time there was a great fear of social disorder following the Black Death, and so questions of social control and social welfare became intrinsically linked. The early institutions set up in this period were therefore explicitly concerned with dealing with the threat of social disorder by imposing social control on the population.

There were also those who wanted state welfare on the basis of social justice. Many accepted that poverty was the result of economic forces beyond the control of any one individual, and this led to the establishment by 1536 of measures allowing parishes (i.e. local areas) to collect money for the poor, although private charities remained the main source of assistance for the poor until the 1660s.

The Poor Law

The Poor Law Act of 1601 was occasioned by fear of social disorder, there having been a large rise in the number of vagrants. The Act put into place formal classification of the poor who were to be divided up into:

- the impotent poor (the aged and the sick) who were to be provided accommodation in almshouses
- the able-bodied poor (the unemployed) who were to be provided with work in workhouses
- the persistent idlers who were to be sent to houses of correction.

The basic idea was to provide three very different policies for these three groups. Importantly, this involved the creation of three different types of institutions which were aimed at providing responses to the three types of behaviour or person who were viewed as being in need of correction. However, since it was implemented by local government, differences often occurred and in many ways the system was never fully operational.

The original Poor Law system remained in place for the next 200 years although various influences changed its mode of application:

- Owing to the rise in Puritanism, the application of the law was made much harsher. This led to poverty being seen as a sign of individual deficiency and a punishment for sin. Support for the poor by the Church began to decline.
- As a result of industrialization the numbers employed in agriculture decreased, and this led to a massive increase in unemployed labour which was not fully taken up by the new factories. Even those who did obtain work in factories faced appalling conditions and low wages.

Discussion point

Do you agree with the idea that the poor should be punished?

C3.1a

The 1834 Poor Law Amendment Act

The Poor Law Commission recommended changes to the system to reflect the idea that the poor needed to accept the economic disciplines of the emerging new order. Out of all this emerged the 1834 Poor Law Amendment Act. This change was most certainly linked to notions of social control and the view that the poor were to be encouraged through punitive action to seek their own salvation though employment. The key element of social control was the extremely harsh and punitive nature of the workhouses, as outlined in the novels of Charles Dickens.

The principle of less eligibility

The changing ideology was most clearly reflected by the 'principle of less eligibility'. This meant that conditions in the workhouses were to be made worse than the lowest-paid employment, as a conscious effort to discourage people from applying for help. Relief outside the workhouse was denied to any able-bodied person, and a strict moral order was maintained in the workhouses with clear separation of the sexes, even husbands and wives. Historian E. P. Thompson quotes Poor Law assistant commissioners as saying:

Our intention is to make the workhouses as like prison as possible ... Our object is to establish therein a discipline so severe and repulsive as to make them a terror to the poor and prevent them from entering.

(Thompson, 1968, p. 295)

Despite this, he quotes figures showing the number of workhouse inmates rose from 78 536 in 1838 to 197 179 in 1843.

The Act concentrated on the idea that people became poor through their own personal deficiencies or laziness, and that this should not be rewarded. Instead people should have their behaviour patterns modified. There was little if any recognition of the effect of societal economic and social change in causing poverty and distress. Unemployment was assumed to be caused by wilful laziness rather than lack of jobs. (See also Section 14.5.)

The workhouses as institutions of social control

The workhouses were notoriously fearful places. The treatment of the poor in these times – and revulsion at it – is one of the main sources of inspiration for the novels of Charles Dickins (1812–70). Implementation of this Act led to massive protests. Historian John Knott (1986) reports that there were riots in many areas following the setting up of the new workhouses: 1835 saw riots

in Eastbourne, Chesham and Ipswich. Later there were many cases of protesters attempting to burn down the new workhouses. The level of protest indicated the horror and revulsion that ordinary people felt against the new legislation.

Social control and the moral definition of the poor

Underlying intervention by the state in the name of welfare is an essentially moral distinction between the deserving poor and the undeserving poor:

- The deserving poor were those who society (or the dominant elements within it) defined as poor through no fault of their own, meaning essentially those suffering from old age, disability or chronic (long-standing) illness of some sort.
- The undeserving poor were seen as those who were able to work but attempted to avoid it to live off the state.

The New Right and the deserving and the undeserving poor

This distinction – albeit with changing names attached – is a fairly constant element of state intervention in the social policy arena.

It can most certainly be seen to have been resurrected by New Right approaches to welfare (see also Section 14.2) with the rise of notions of an underclass and in particular the cultural version of that, which viewed poor people as being in poverty through their own misguided actions which the state sought to discourage. While this notion of the undeserving poor used to be applied to the unemployed it has more recently been applied to single-parent families (see also Section 5.8).

Activity

Suggest examples of groups seen as 'the deserving poor' and those seen as 'the undeserving poor' in contemporary UK society. How valid do you think this distinction is?

C3.1a, C3.2, C3.3

Explanations for unemployment – blame or not?

Keynes and the failure of the free market

John Maynard Keynes (1936) was an extremely influential economist whose work had a big influence on government economic and social policies after World War II up until the mid-1970s.

Keynes argued that the experience of mass unemployment in the 1930s showed that the market left to itself did not, and would not, provide full employment as its supporters argued. More importantly he argued that an economy might reach a point of equilibrium (a position where there is no pressure to change) with mass unemployment which would therefore become a long-lasting feature of society. (See also Section 7.3.)

He therefore urged a rejection of free-market economics, and for the government to take a much more active role in the running of the economy – with the aim of achieving certain objectives including full employment. The experience of World War II was important in showing that the state could direct the economy (as happened in wartime), and this provided the basis for the radical change in government economic and social policy based on the work of Keynes and Beveridge.

Criticisms of Keynesianism

One potential problem with this schema was the worry that wage rates would rise excessively in a time of full employment. This worry resulted in successive governments attempting to effect policies of wage restraint. This led to the clash between the trade unions and the Labour government of 1974–79, an episode that came to be known as the 'Winter of Discontent'. It provided the backdrop to the general election of 1979 which brought the Conservatives and Margaret Thatcher to power. Armed with a New Right ideology, they set about reasserting the importance of the free market.

The New Right and the failure of the state

The central insight of the New Right is that the free market is inherently superior to state inter-vention. They were therefore strongly opposed to the kind of Keynesian interventionism that had characterized government over the last 30 years. They argued that the role of government was to create a stable low-inflation environment in which businesses and enterprise could flourish. Only in this way could jobs be created and unemployment thereby reduced.

New Right economist Milton Friedman (1980) argued that the state causes problems for economic growth owing to its tendency to spend more than it raises in taxes, requiring it to borrow to fund its activities. This borrowing is known as the 'public sector borrowing requirement' (PSBR). Friedman argued that this extra demand for borrowing pushes up interest rates, and therefore pushes up the costs of businesses. He argued that the level of government borrowing should be reduced and a strict control kept on the money supply to reduce inflationary pressures. This is known as 'monetarism'.

Friedman also argued that there is a natural level of unemployment, which is made higher by trade union demands for more wages and by welfare expenditure. Both of these place upward pressure on the wage rate, and as a result workers price themselves out of jobs and are reluctant to reduce their wage rates owing to the level of welfare benefits.

Unemployment under 'New Labour'

With the election of a Labour government led by Tony Blair in 1997, and the election of the Social Democrats to government in Germany in the following year, the political balance inside the European Union shifted noticeably to the left. Concerns about the rise in unemployment following the widespread application of New Right policies had already been expressed in the Delors Report published in 1993, when unemployment in the EU as a whole stood at 11 per cent. The report pointed to the need to set a target of creating 15 million new jobs by the year 2000.

Continuing growth in the jobless

Despite this, in 1998 the unemployment rate in the EU remained at 11 per cent, and the economic growth that did occur created very few new jobs – a phenomenon identified by Dahrendorf as 'jobless growth' (see Section 17.2).

Criticism of New Labour

Coates (1998) argues that one of the key problems is the way the new administrations, while nominally of the left, have in fact pursued policies that are in some instances merely continuations of the old policies of the Right. In the UK, 'New Labour' is a prime example. Coates points to an interview with Prime Minister Tony Blair in the newspaper *The European* on 19 January 1998, in which he said that 'not just socialism but social democracy as practised in most of Europe is past its sell-by date'.

Coates is unsurprised that there has been little change in employment prospects in the EU, despite the electoral victories of the left in recent years. He himself calls for a concerted campaign on unemployment, with a call for a shorter (35 hour) working week without loss of pay, and for more government intervention to deal with the problem. This view led him into conflict with New Labour, and to his deselection as a candidate for the European elections and therefore the loss of his position as an MEP.

The fall in public spending under New Labour

Further evidence of the turn away from public expenditure as a policy tool, reflecting the shift from Old Labour to New Labour, came in an article by David Brindle in the *Guardian* of 25 August 1999. This showed that public spending as a proportion of national income:

... will be sharply lower under Tony Blair than under even the Thatcher government that was vilified by Labour for draconian spending cuts.

(Brindle, 1999, p. 1)

Quoting research by the Insititute for Fiscal Studies, Brindle points out that the Labour government projections for the four years from 1997 to 2001 show public spending will average 39.4 per cent of GDP, compared with 41.4 per cent for John Major's administrations of 1990–97 and 43.0 per cent for the Thatcher administrations of 1979–90.

'Welfare to work': New Labour and social control

Central to the welfare policy of New Labour was 'welfare-to-work' – meaning that resources would be increased in areas of policy where there were attempts to shift people from reliance on benefits for income to reliance on work for income. A series of 'new deals' were set up to provide assis-

tance and 'gateways to employment'. Young people and adults unemployed for six months or more were to be offered four options:

- subsidized private-sector employment
- approved full-time education or training
- work experience in the voluntary sector
- work experience as part of a national environmental task force.

Participation in these schemes for these groups was made compulsory. There are, however, other schemes which are non-compulsory. Ruth Lister (1998) comments on these schemes as follows:

Participation will be mandatory, with harsh benefit sanctions for those who fail to comply. The other new deals – for lone parents with school-age children and the disabled – will not be compulsory, but the message is clear: for all those deemed capable of paid employment, 'work not welfare' represents the passport to social inclusion.

(Lister, 1998, p. 220)

The compulsion element of welfare to work

One of the key sources of concern and controversy over the introduction of welfare to work was over the potentially coercive nature of the scheme, and the inequality in terms of differential degrees of compulsion and being affected by compulsion. As Ruth Levitas has pointed out:

Reservations about the New Deal for those under the age of 25 concerned the quality of placements available, and the potentially coercive nature of the scheme. The pre-election version of welfare to work effectively had a gendered approach to compulsion. Coercion in the form of benefit sanctions was central to the New Deal for the young unemployed ... The programme for lone-parents – who might be in the same age group – was consistently presented as optional ... Above all, the policy was presented as an opportunity for women, 90 per cent of whom, it was claimed, wanted to work. The principally male targets of the other parts of the New Deal, potential agents of social disruption, needed to be forced into work by withdrawal of benefits.

After the election, compulsion tightened. Young people could be sanctioned by total withdrawal benefit for refusing placements under the New Deal.

(Levitas, 1998, p. 141)

Discussion point

How much compulsion do you feel is justified in relation to welfare to work?

C3.1a

Social control and welfare reform — lone parents and the disabled

Anger from lone parents and the disabled

It was the proposals relating to lone parents and disabled people that caused the greatest amount of controversy.

The row over benefits for lone parents

In 1996, the Conservative government had proposed to cut lone-parent benefit premium – that is, the extra amount paid to lone-parents in recognition of the extra costs they endure. At the time Labour attacked this suggestion, but in December 1997 the new Labour government proposed to go ahead with the cut. This caused major rows within the parliamentary Labour party, and in the actual vote 47 Labour MPs voted against the government proposal, which was nonetheless passed.

Arguments over threats to benefits for the disabled

Shortly after this, the focus moved towards proposals to change the benefits available to the disabled. This led to a protest by disabled groups outside Downing Street.

One key government concern was the rise in those claiming incapacity benefits, from 1.24 million people receiving £4.5 billion in 1989 to 1.67 million receiving £7.3 billion in 1998. A second concern was the low level of the disabled who were economically active: 59 per cent compared with a figure of 85 per cent for the non-disabled (Walker, 1998).

While the government states that it has no intention of compelling the disabled to work, it is proposing to put more resources into providing the disabled with advice about jobs, and setting up a Disability Rights Commissioner to investi-

gate cases of discrimination against disabled people.

Despite this, it was the *perception* that the government was perhaps considering changes – particularly to the definition of the notion of incapacity and related benefits – that led to an outburst of anger from disabled groups.

The centrality of work and responsibility in the New labour programme

One clear message that has come out of New Labour reforms and the welfare to work programme is the belief that the key to avoiding poverty or getting out of poverty is through work. Thus lone parents and the disabled have been encouraged to work and the availability of benefits for them has been cut (in the case of lone parents) or with eligibility criteria tightened up (in the case of disability benefits). One key problem with this approach, apart from its moralistic social control Puritanical undertones, is that it ignores the potential problem that there may be those in work who are still in poverty through the problem of low wages. Although the Labour government did introduce a minimum wage (see Section 17.2) there were and continue to be debates about whether the level was set too low to eradicate poverty wages. There is also some evidence that this is a problem in American where many of these ideas originated, as the accompanying article 'Poor show' shows.

Communitarianism, morality and social control

The 1990s have been important for a reawakening of sociological, political and policy-orientated interest in the role of community. Much of the debate stems from so-called 'communitarians'. In a similar way to Tönnies and Durkheim, communitarians feel that the individualism of the present capitalist society is isolating people and breaking up their sense of community and the stability it brings for them and society. It is clear that communitarian ideas have influenced New Labour and have given it a moralistic emphasis on social control and responsibility as an emphasis which can be seen in elements of their welfare policy. It is therefore worthwhile considering

POOR SHOW

MARTIN EVANS

GORDON BROWN'S policy of pushing more and more claimants off benefit into jobs is American-inspired. But has New Labour been listening to the people on the far side of the Atlantic who are now saying that getting tough on welfare can end up harming programmes designed to reduce poverty and improve skills?

Sure, the United States can boast a 40% reduction in the number of those claiming welfare, saving $9bn. More American lone parents are working as a result – the rates have risen from 44% in 1992 to 57% in 1998. But other evidence says that these headline results hide worrying trends.

The main reason for fewer Americans claiming welfare is that they are often not allowed to claim and/or that huge obstacles are placed in their way. Welfare is the responsibility of state governors and mayor, most of whom have implemented an approach called Work First. It puts claimants in the position where they have to actively consider taking a job even as they make a claim for welfare. ...

But while many welfare leavers get jobs and are better off, for some the move is no great progression. Around 20% of ex-welfare cases do not work at all and have no obvious signs of independent income. Nearly a third of those who do get jobs return to claim welfare within a year. Between a third and half of those who do work have incomes that are lower than their previous benefit levels.

Because work is the most common antidote to poverty we are told (by Labour ministers) that stricter welfare to work programmes will reduce poverty. Yet the American experience suggests that poverty is still common for many. Two thirds of Wisconsin's welfare leavers are living under the American poverty line. The centre for budget and policy priorities in Washington DC found that across the US, lone parents in the lowest income bracket have got poorer since welfare reform. The poorest fifth of lone parents had shown income gains during the early 90s – an extra $1000 a year on average in the two years before welfare reform. Since Clinton's reforms came in, their incomes have fallen by almost 7%. Most of this is due to the withdrawal of benefits.

Both Britain and America put great store in making work pay by rewarding work with benefits rather than paying welfare during unemployment. While this distinction between in-work benefits and out-of-work benefits is clear to policy makers, many ordinary poor people just see both as part of the system that is making their life deliberately difficult. If Gordon Brown wants his working family's tax credit to be an unequivocal success, he should think long and hard about making welfare even tougher.

Source: Adapted from *Guardian*, 6 March 2000

the ideas of communitarianism and in particular those of its American guru, Amatai Etzioni.

Etzioni's *The Spirit of Community* (1995) offers the:

... call to restore civic virtues, for people to live up to their responsibilities and not focus on their entitlements, to shore up the moral foundations of society.

(Etzioni, 1995, p. ix)

He claims that this focus has already gained the respect of key members of the UK's three main political parties. Success in the communitarian project relies on:

... building shared values, habits and practices that assure respect for one another's rights and regular fulfilment of personal, civic and collective responsibilities.

(Etzioni, 1995, p. 255)

Etzioni's focus is modern America, a nation where he says people are all too aware of their rights (and with an interest in extending them, with the help of self-interested lawyers) but who show little or no sense of their obligations to fellow citizens as a community or a nation. He feels that the same applies to the UK.

💬 Discussion point

To what extent is it true to say that politicians agree with the communitarian agenda? Can you provide specific examples?

C3.1a

Welfare and moral reconstruction

According to communitarians, the answer to the identified problems lies in 'moral reconstruction', for which Etzioni proposes a five-fold programme:

1 Families should aim to teach their offspring full moral values. This relies on *both* parents taking responsibility for childcare, but relies on workplaces offering flexible work patterns to allow it.

2 Schools need to reinforce the moral values taught at home, or make up for parents who neglect their duties in this area.

3 National governments need to allow 'social webs' to develop and to empower them to make contributions to maintaining their own communities. This would bring people of all backgrounds together, who, by expressing a

'civil commitment', would 'build community and foster mutual respect and tolerance'.

4 National society must regulate local communities and groups to ensure that conflicts do not break out and that communal obligations remain in place.

5 Fifthly, Etzioni tells us 'Don't get mad; get going' (p. 249). If we have a special interest or concern we should work through democratic processes to express it; through debate will come community-wide consensus.

In conclusion he asserts that communities will work only if people have a *commitment* to good behaviour rather than being forced. As a result citizens need educating, praising when they act well and 'frowning upon' when they don't.

🗨 Discussion point

To what extent do you agree with the five-fold programme advocated by Etzioni? Can you identify any problems with it?

C3.1a

Third sector welfare

These themes are taken up by the many contributors to Atkinson's *Cities of Pride* (1995). Prashar (1995), for example, argues for government-supported community initiatives (a 'third sector') which would 'innovate, agitate, and interrogate so that our democracy remains vibrant and responsive'. Halliday (1995) describes how this is already being done by Community Development Trusts, voluntary groups who identify shortfalls in community provisions and work to fill them (along the lines of Etzioni's 'social webs'). Being locally based they are best able to identify local needs, but are also more visible and accountable should local people be dissatisfied with their service provision. However, she appears to differ from Etzioni by noting that communities in depressed areas, with a longer road to travel, do need financial help from the government.

Criticisms of communitarian theory

Socialist and social-democratic criticism of communitarianism

Although the communitarian call to re-invoke community values has many supporters, it has also caused waves of criticism. Derber (quoted in Steele, 1995) from a Marxist standpoint, has criticized Etzioni's concentration on ordinary people while ignoring business practices which make the minority richer and create wider inequalities. He needed to make reference to 'corporate social obligations', important in a world where multinational corporations have:

... produced abandoned plants and ghost communities all over America.

(Quoted in Steele, 1995; see also Section 16.10.)

Marquand (1996), who has taken a social–democratic perspective, criticizes Etzioni's lack of political awareness, suggesting that a reliance on morals and voluntary action is a 'counsel of despair'. Self-discipline and motivation have a place but we ought not to give up on local and national government leadership and co-ordinating powers. The answer is to take 'the market' out of public policy and to ensure that wealth creation schemes also include 'community values' at their heart.

Feminist criticisms of communitarianism

Feminist theorists such as Bea Campbell (1995b) have also found fault with Etzioni's critique of the modern family – the assertion that family breakdown is linked to community breakdown – on a number of counts. Firstly, she believed his call for both parents to take responsibility for their children was a backdoor way of restating old patriarchal ideas of the woman's place being in the home. (See Chapter 5.) When a similar argument was put to Etzioni he responded by saying:

... to say we should tell both parents that it is OK to neglect children because we're afraid that, initially at least, more responsibility will fall on mothers ... disregards the needs of children and I feel very strongly that we should not do that.

(Quoted in Kelly, 1995, p. 21)

Secondly, Campbell criticized his view that lone mothers are the fault of modern society's problems. Single mothers, she said, are very active in creating self-help groups (the sort of behaviour advocated by *The Spirit of Community*) and not passive victims. Instead men are the problem:

... a war is being waged against the community itself by criminalized coteries of men and boys – 88 per cent of offenders appearing in court are male – and

community solidarity is sustained overwhelmingly by mothers.

(Campbell, 1995a, p. 31)

Generally the lack of reference to feminism, for Campbell, is indication enough of the poverty of the communitarian perspective.

The New Right, individualism and criticisms of communitarianism

Other sociologists have been concerned about the individual in communitarian theory. For the New Right – what Etzioni calls 'liberals' or 'libertarians' – the advocated programme infringes on personal choices. For them it is unlikely that the strong moral consensus, if established, would tolerate deviations according to the actions and beliefs of minority groups and individuals. As such it is too authoritarian: the type of power asserted in totalitarian, communist societies and not the sort expected from free democratic ones (see Section 15.1). As far as they are concerned people should be able to do what they want, as long as it doesn't harm others. Etzioni feels our actions always have knock-on effects, whether we perceive it or not.

Pahl (1995), although not of the New Right, developed this theme by suggesting that communitarianism was failing to take account of people's sense of individuality. They are not selfish and uncaring, but social beings operating in friendship networks, ready to help their friends whenever they are needed; yet their sense of individuality requires that they have their own identity. Therefore 'phoney communitarianism' had misread reality and if it had its way 'the spirit of community' would return us to the divided and oppressive communities of the past.

Activity

a Summarize the key arguments for and against communitarianism.

b Which ones stand up best to scrutiny?

 C3.2, C3.3

Interactionism, 'total institutions' and personal identity

'Total institutions'

Interactionism offers a critical view of institutions. A key example of this can be found in the writing of Goffman, whose most famous work in this vein was *Asylums* (1991; orig. pub. 1968). He emphasizes how institutions such as prisons and psychiatric hospitals, which ostensibly reflect the concern of society for people being treated, are in fact mechanisms of social control.

Goffman argues that we need to talk of 'total institutions' that are characterized as places where people exist cut off from wider society, and where their lives are totally regimented and controlled by bureaucratic regulations.

Institutionalization and the loss of identity

Asylums was a study of psychiatric institutions, based on observations in one such hospital (see also Section 12.2). Goffman argued that, while the inmates of such places do enter with their own culture, the process of institutionalization may result in the loss of this culture and therefore the loss of ability to deal with the everyday aspects of life outside such an enclosed environment. The clear divisions between staff and patients, and the strict regulations, result in the loss of the feeling of self (the 'mortification of the self'). In their lives in total institutions, inmates find that things they take for granted in the outside world, such as going to the toilet or sending a letter, now require permission. The feeling of being an individual is stripped away.

Responses to total institutions

Whilst emphasizing the extent of bureaucratic control exerted on individuals in total institutions, Goffman does also argue that the responses to their situation vary. Some choose to withdraw from all aspects of life in the institution beyond those that are compulsory, others challenge the institution, while still others accept the view of the institution and try to become perfect inmates and even in some cases come to prefer life inside the institution. The majority of inmates simply try to get by.

Since Goffman emphasizes that, by and large, most inmates do retain some notion of their self, the stated aims of such institutions – which is to reform people in some way – are not achieved, and he himself argues that they instead function merely as dumping grounds for people. Such a view was instrumental in the development of critiques of incarceration as the basis of treatment of the mentally ill, which fed into later debates about community care.

> **Discussion point**
>
> Should people be treated in psychiatric institutions or in the community?
>
> C3.1a

The impact of wider society

The interactionist focus on the construction of meaning through interaction within total institutions has been criticized for ignoring the impact of wider society.

On the basis of a study of prisons in California, Irwin (1970) argued that inmates' responses to imprisonment depended to a large extent on their experiences prior to imprisonment. This appears to undermine Goffman's notion of understanding institutional life as separate from that of wider society. Further, Cohen and Taylor (1971) studied inmates of Durham Prison and suggested that their behaviour showed a degree of resistance to institutionalization that went beyond the view elaborated by Goffman.

Contemporary theories of bureaucracy and institutions

Michel Foucault: The surveillance society

The notion of institutions as mechanisms of social control has more recently been taken up in the work of Michel Foucault (1967, 1977). Foucault argues that the development of modern institutions concerned with social control, such as prisons, can be traced back to the eighteenth century with the development of systematic rules of punishment and control which replaced the personal power of rulers to make arbitrary decisions. The rise of prisons is linked to the rise of new forms of knowledge and technologies, including the development of the human sciences, particularly psychology and psychiatry. (See also Section 15.6.)

> **Discussion point**
>
> Are psychology and sociology part of the solution to societal problems or part of the problem themselves?
>
> C3.1a

This, along with the innovations of modern medicine, allowed the development of a new form of disciplinary power concerned with control of human bodies. There arose an attempt to understand the reasons why people deviate from normal behaviour, and then to modify their behaviour – a process Foucault refers to as *normalization*. These new technologies of disciplinary power can be seen to underlie such developments as the workhouse, devised under the Poor Law, and psychiatric hospitals.

All of these new disciplinary powers depend on knowledge inside institutions, and this, says Foucault, can be seen in the Panoptican design of prisons, which allows warders to observe all inmates from a central viewing point. This notion is developed further into the idea of a surveillance society, where watching people and gaining information about them becomes a central facet. Thus, argues Foucault, all institutions come to resemble prisons with minute scrutiny over the activities of those within them.

> **Discussion point**
>
> In what ways and to what extent does your school or college resemble a prison?
>
> C3.1a

While this form of control may not be as painful as the pre-modern forms of punishment, Foucault argues that we should not be blinded to the fact that it allows a greater degree of social control, albeit more subtle, but nonetheless impinging even more on individual freedom.

Foucault's notion of a surveillance society has also been applied more recently in the work of Lyon (1993). He argues that the construction of large computer databases creates the basis for a greater level of surveillance, although he says that we need to consider the fact that people often actively consent to be surveyed in this way through, for example, providing their details on credit card applications.

Care in the community

One main criticism of the welfare state concerned its uniform and unresponsive nature. This criticism was particularly aimed at institutional care within the welfare state. In his famous study, *Asylums*, interactionist Erving Goffman (1968) demonstrated that care for the mentally ill within institutions had negative effects on their health. (See also Sections 12.2 and 12.6.) Similar points can be made about the negative perceptions that surround homes for the elderly.

Alternatives to institutional care for the elderly and the disabled

In response to this, an alternative framework of care has been developed which has become known as 'care in the community'. What this means is that the elderly, the mentally ill and the physically handicapped are looked after not in separate institutions but within society. It is argued that this is possible owing to the range of service providers in this age of welfare pluralism. It is also argued that such care avoids isolating people away from the rest of society, which is seen as one of the key negative effects of institutional care.

Advantages of care in the community

One major advantage of care in the community is that it is cheaper. According to *New Society* (1987), looking after a single elderly person then cost about £295 a week in an NHS hospital and roughly £135 a week in residential care, whereas the cost of care in the community was just under £100. This clearly has an appeal to those who wish to reduce public expenditure.

Despite this, it is suggested that the vast majority of local authority spending on the elderly and those with disabilities goes on residential care: Gray *et al.* (1988) quote figures of 73 per cent for residential care and 18 per cent for community services.

Problems with care in the community

A major problem is that a lack of funding and resources means there are in reality not enough community support facilities. Concerns over this have focused attention particularly on the number of suicides and homicides committed by the mentally ill.

A government report (quoted in the *Guardian* on 16 January 1996) showed that in the previous year there had been 240 suicides among mentally ill people; of these 53 were in-patients, 154 out-patients and 33 discharged within the past year. These figures appear to show that there are more suicides among those outside institutional care than inside, which has led to pressure to improve provision of care in the community.

It is precisely because of this lack of real service backup that Alan Scull (1984) refers to the policy as one not of care in the community but of 'decarceration' – emphasizing that essentially it involves removing people from institutional care but with no real notion of how then to look after them, leaving vulnerable people open to private landlords and others with no care background. It is suspected that a large proportion of the rise in the homeless in the UK can be accounted for by people who have been ejected as large institutions closed.

Towards the end of 1996 something of a sea change emerged when the then government admitted that the 'care in the community' policy had failed (reported in the *Times* on 6 November 1996). The Health Secretary outlined plans for a new debate and legislation on care for the mentally ill, based around some degree of 24-hour in-hospital provision. Whether this will satisfy all the critics of care in the community remains to be seen.

Discussion point

a To what degree can care in the community be seen as a realistic possibility rather than an aspiration?

b How do you think society should provide care for groups such as the elderly and the mentally handicapped?

C3.1a

Children in care

Kirton (1999) argues that we can trace the origins of the modern childcare system to the nineteenth-century child-savers such as Barnado and Carpenter, but that it mostly took shape after World War II. The Children Act 1948 led to the establishment of children's departments in local authorities.

While this enabled support to take the form of support to families and foster parenting, there was also the gradual development of residential homes for children. Kirton makes the point that in 1995 there were 14 400 people working in residential children's homes and 26 per cent of all local authority social services expenditure was on children and families. Clearly this has become a substantial element of the welfare state.

Children and institutional abuse

Why these residential homes are also important is that in recent years they have been the focus on a number of investigations which have revealed that widespread abuse of children occurred within these instiutions, including bullying by other residents, though also often abuse by those who were employed to protect and care for the children. Spring 2000 saw the final publication of a report into the abuse of children at residential homes in North Wales which involves large numbers of children and which led to media reports of potential other investigations being carried out.

One key aspect of abuse identified in residential homes was the operation of a policy of 'pin-down' introduced to try to control children seen as being temporarily disruptive but this was seen as being abusive.

The NHS and Community Care Act

Under the 1990 National Health Service and Community Care Act there was a move towards more provision of services in the community but also moves away from seeing the local authority social services department as the provider of all services and instead as a purchaser who could buy in provision from any number of providers. This was also an attempt to encourage the development of a quasi-market and greater private sector provision in pursuit of the idea of welfare pluralism.

Cutting the cost of residential care for the elderly

One of the key factors leading to community care was the cost of residential and institutionalized provision and concerns that this cost would rise as the number of elderly in the population continued to rise.

Table 14.7 Elderly population census figures (1901–81) and Census projections (1987–2027)

	65+	%	75+	%	85+	%
1901	1734	4.7	507	1.4	57	0.15
1931	3316	7.4	920	2.1	108	0.24
1951	5332	10.9	1731	3.5	218	0.45
1961	6046	11.8	2167	4.2	329	0.64
1971	7140	13.2	2536	4.7	462	0.86
1981	7985	15.0	3053	5.7	552	1.03
1987	8624	15.6	3699	6.7	746	1.3
1991	8838	15.8	3925	7.0	875	1.6
2001	8984	15.6	4309	7.5	1144	2.0
2011	9425	16.1	4372	7.5	1291	2.2
2021	10642	18.0	4699	7.9	1287	2.2
2027	11472	19.2	5308	8.9	1326	2.2

Source: OPCS; Government Actuary p. 2, no. 16 (Quoted in Moore, 1993, p. 151)

This issue of the rise in the elderly and the effect this will have on the cost of personal social services and the welfare state more generally has been at the centre of concerns over moves towards care in the community.

The Griffiths Report

The Griffiths Report recommended that there be changes to the system of residential care available. Instead it suggested that each individual should be treated as an individual and should have a care plan set up for them by the primary caring authority. This meant that there was a need to establish who was the primary caring authority. In the case of those with health problems there was a distinction made between health and social problems. However, this was not without problems.

The elderly, residential care and personal social services

One key area of change which has affected the elderly is changes to the provision of personal social services. The provision of residential care has moved from being largely local authority based to being largely private sector based. There have been a number of concerns about the ability of elderly people to pay their residential care bills and still maintain their home. Equally the elderly like other groups were caught in the failures of the 'care in the community' initiative.

Nonetheless, despite these problems, Evandrou and Falkingham (1998) point out that between 1973 and 1993 there was a real rise on personal social services expenditure of 3.8 per cent per annum, and that in relation to elderly people between 1986 and 1994 real spending rose by 6.4 per cent per annum. However, Sefton (1997) points out that in relation to help with residential care, it is not the poorest who receive the most help. Evandrou and Falkingham (1998) point to another area where there are problems — the provision of home help by local authorities — where they point out that whereas 62 per cent of the elderly received this support in 1980, this had fallen to 45 per cent in 1994

The long-term unemployed, welfare and identity

One key issue central to identity is your job and therefore the loss of a job not only affects your income and therefore standard of living but also your self-esteem. The effect of being long-term unemployed increases this loss of self-esteem. We therefore need to consider not only how unemployment affects society and individuals but also how welfare policies in relation to unemployment affect people.

The extent of unemployment

The claimant count

As its name suggests, this is compiled by adding together the total of people eligible for certain social security benefits, notably unemployment benefit, income support and national insurance credits. The rate of unemployment on this basis is arrived at monthly by taking the total number of the unemployed so defined as a percentage of the workforce. There are, however, questions over the validity of this as a measure of unemployment:

- This count exists only as a by-product of the administrative procedures surrounding welfare benefits.

- It is really *entitlement* to benefits that it measures, so someone who is working but nonetheless entitled to a benefit might be included.

- If the rules concerning entitlement to a benefit change, this will change these figures even

though it has no direct effect on whether someone has a job or not.

As an example of the last point, in April 1983 the government changed regulations to the effect that men over 60 who were without work were no longer required to 'sign on'. This had the effect of reducing this count of unemployment by approximately 107 000.

Labour Force Survey

The main alternative definition and measure of unemployment arises from the *Labour Force Survey*, conducted quarterly. This utilizes the definition of unemployment developed by the International Labour Office (ILO) – people without a paid job who were available to start work and had looked for work. It is thus not based on eligibility for benefits and is not affected by changes to the benefits system.

Difference between the measures

These two measures of unemployment provide very different figures. For instance, the figures for spring 1993 provided in *Employment Gazette* in October 1993 show that the total unemployment figure on the claimant count was 2.86 million, while the ILO figure was 2.81 million.

One important difference is the effect on the gender composition of unemployment. In the spring of 1993 the claimant count showed that there were 2.20 million men and 0.66 million women unemployed. In contrast, the ILO figures stated that there were 1.90 million men and 0.91 million women unemployed.

Clearly the gender balance is different. One of the key reasons for this is the lack of entitlement to benefits for some married women, who thus do not appear on the claimant count but may consider that they are looking for a job and may therefore appear on the ILO count.

Activity

a Explain in your own words the differences between the two measures of unemployment outlined above.

b Consider the effect of adopting one of these measures on the gender differences in unemployment as officially measured.

c Consider which of these two measures you think best measures actual unemployment.

C3.2, C3.3

Criticisms of unemployment statistics

If we look at figures from the national Census (see Section 9.6), then the number of people describing themselves as unemployed differs from the official count. In a critical discussion of official statistics, Miles and Irvine (1979) point out that the 1971 Census found 1 365 775 people who described themselves as unemployed, while official Department of Employment figures for that year gave a total of 773 800 unemployed. Clearly people themselves think of unemployment in ways which differ from the official definition.

The validity of the official statistics surrounding both employment and unemployment is a debate that continues to this day. January 1997 saw the issue of the December 1996 unemployment statistics. The unemployment figures for that period were 1 884 700 according to the claimant count but 230 000 according to the *LFS* (for November 1996). The one-month discrepancy would not explain much of the total discrepancy of 345 000 between the two figures, so leading politicians argued over the figures.

The then Prime Minister, John Major, claimed that the 45 100 reduction in the number out of work and claiming benefits – producing the lowest figure for six years – had 'broadened the smile' on Britain's face (quoted in the *Guardian*, 16 January 1997). The Labour employment spokesman, Ian McCartney, said figures from the OECD showed that 18.9 per cent of British households had nobody working in them, the fourth highest rate in the industrialized western countries (also quoted in the *Guardian* on the same day).

Guardian journalists Elliot and Ryle (1997) pointed out the parameters of the debate over the latest figures:

Figures from the Office for National Statistics show that claimant-count unemployment has fallen by 350,000 in the past year, with half the fall in the latest three months. ... The Treasury admitted that it, too, was skeptical, saying that the Chancellor preferred an alternative measure of unemployment – the Labour Force Survey. ... According to the LFS ... unemployment is more than 300,000 higher than on the claimant-count measure, and dropping far more slowly. ... In the year to last autumn, LFS unemployment declined 166,000 while claimant count unemployment fell by 243 000.

(Elliot and Ryle, 1997, p. 2)

Some more recent figures for unemployment using the ILO measure now adopted by the government are shown in Table 14.8.

> ### Activity
> From Table 14.8, identify the social groups with the highest and lowest rates of unemployment in the spring of 1998.
>
>

Types of unemployment

Social scientists distinguish between three broad types of unemployment:

- frictional
- cyclical
- structural.

Table 14.8 ILO unemployment, spring 1998

	Total (000s)			Rate[a]		
	All	Males	Females	All	Males	Females
All aged 16+	1766	1091	674	6.1	6.8	5.3
16–59/64	1746	1082	664	6.3	6.9	5.4
16–17	133	73	60	16.6	18.0	15.2
18–24	409	257	152	11.3	13.0	9.3
16–24	542	330	212	12.3	13.8	10.5
25–34	481	289	192	6.3	6.7	5.9
35–49	448	263	184	4.4	4.7	3.9
50–59/64	276	200	75	4.9	5.8	3.4

[a] Rate equals total ILO unemployed as a percentage of all economically active persons in the relevant age group.
Source: Labour Force Survey, spring 1998

Frictional unemployment

This refers to the fact that when workers change jobs there may be a short gap between leaving one job and starting another. Since this is short-term unemployment and occurs only because people take a break between jobs, it is not regarded as a problem.

Cyclical unemployment

This is so called because it is related to the ups and downs of the economic cycle. In periods of economic boom the number of jobs available rises and an economy may approach full employment. If the economy moves into depression, firms will usually respond by cutting their costs, most notably by making people redundant. Commenting on this phenomenon in relation to the recent experience of the UK, Madry and Kirby (1996) point out that:

... in the last 15 years the economy appears to have gone through a complete cycle, starting with a large recession between 1980 and 1983 followed by an economic boom which reached its height in 1987–8 and then another recession starting in about 1990 which appeared to be coming to a slow end by late 1994.

(Madry and Kirby, 1996, p. 119)

Structural unemployment

This occurs when there are changes to the structure of an industry or to the particular skills required within it, and the skills people actually possess are needed no longer. One of the key examples of this in the UK in recent years has been the declining demand for workers in industries such as mining and shipbuilding. Areas previously largely reliant on these industries for employment, such as Clydeside, Yorkshire, the North East of England and South Wales, have as a result of their decline suffered large levels of unemployment.

The relative balance between cyclical and structural unemployment is important. If the majority of unemployment is of a cyclical nature, the level can be expected to fall as the economy picks up. However, a return to economic prosperity will not by itself cure structural unemployment. Therefore, if most unemployment is of a structural nature, this might be expected to continue into the future unless new policies are adopted to try to reduce it, such as retraining or support for regional redevelopment.

The consequences of unemployment

Financial effects

Moving from being employed to being unemployed clearly has an adverse effect on financial income for most people. Changes to benefit rates in the 1980s made this even more true. Hutton (1996) points out that unemployment benefit as a percentage of average earnings for male workers fell from 16.3 per cent in 1979 to 12.4 per cent in 1992 for single men, and from 26.2 per cent to 20.1 per cent for married men.

However, beyond the financial problems caused by unemployment lie other issues.

Social effects

Sociologists want also to consider the possible social consequences of unemployment, for both individuals and for society as a whole.

The most notable large-scale research on these issues arises from the extensive social survey on unemployment and social change conducted by Gallie *et al.* (1994). They wanted to view the individual's experience of unemployment in the context of a wider concern over unemployment held by society:

Gallup interviewers ask a monthly quota sample of adults in Britain what they think is the 'most urgent problem' facing the country today. Unemployment dominated replies throughout the 1980s, being the issue most frequently named as either the most urgent or the second most urgent problem.

(Gallie *et al.*, 1994, p. 1)

Unemployment, or even the fear of unemployment, appears to have an effect on peoples' lives. But in order to investigate the basis of these fears it is necessary to consider some of the concrete evidence on how unemployment affects people.

Physical and psychological health
Physical health
Unemployment is bad for your health. (See also Chapter 12.) Two pieces of research in recent years have reinforced this view.

In the USA, Brenner (1979) found that societies where unemployment increased by 1 million experienced a rise in deaths from various health disorders of up to 275 000 people. In the UK, Graham (1985a) found that families living on benefits, which obviously includes the unemployed, were twice as likely as other groups to suffer from health problems.

In their book *Investigating Work, Unemployment and Leisure*, Madry and Kirby (1996) quote the following findings in relation to the UK:

According to the Observer *(27 September 1992) the British Regional Heart Survey, based on studies of 253 British towns over ten years, found that those who were unemployed at any time during the five years prior to the research were more than one and a half times as likely to die in the next five years as employed men. In relation to morbidity as opposed to mortality, the Office of Health Economics published statistics showing that the number of prescriptions issued on Merseyside was 9.7 per person in 1991 compared with 6.9 per person in the South West Thames Regional Health Authority. The respective unemployment rates in these two areas were 12.5 per cent and 4.2 per cent.*

(Madry and Kirby, 1996, p. 138)

Psychological health

There is also evidence of the psychological effects of unemployment. While the unemployed suffer higher levels of suicide and psychological ill-health, Burchell (1994) found that this was also true of those suffering economic insecurity in the form of working on casual, short-term or other flexible working arrangements (see also Section 17.2). He found that their psychological profiles were closer to the unemployed than to those in secure employment.

This finding is significant, given the major increase in the demand for flexible working conditions and the greater use of part-time and casual labour. The changes introduced into the labour market and actively promoted by the New Right governments of the 1980s and 90s are found to have damaging consequences psychologically for those involved.

The reasons for the effect of unemployment or casualization on psychological health are themselves a matter of debate. Many argue that it is a direct result of the financial stress involved. However, Jahoda *et al.* (1972) argue that it is more to do with the loss of the routine in people's lives which having a job creates, and the sense of identity associated with involvement in a certain job.

Discussion point

How important do you think jobs are as a source of personal identity for people today?

C3.1a

Women, welfare, unemployment and inequality

Martin and Roberts (1984) published one of the most important sociological findings about the distribution of unemployment. In a survey they found that wives of unemployed men were much more likely to be unemployed themselves than were the wives of employed men. In terms of households, this finding will clearly lead to the negative effects of unemployment impacting much more on some households than others.

The key reason for this relationship seems to be the feature of the benefits system whereby a couple's benefits are reduced by the level of the woman's earnings, since this creates a negative incentive to be working for women whose husbands are unemployed. (See also Section 14.3.) It clearly has implications for the distribution of income in society by creating work-rich (and therefore more income-rich) households and work-poor households with very low standards of living.

Unemployment and society

The extent of unemployment in the 1980s and 90s has made it one of, if not the, most important of contemporary social issues. The reasons for this are not hard to understand.

First there is the direct cost of unemployment to the economy, and therefore society, involving the loss of tax revenue and the cost of unemployment and other benefits.

Secondly there is the indirect cost to the standard of living of the whole economy, in the sense of the loss of the goods and services that could have been produced by the unemployed if they had been employed.

And finally there is the cost in terms of the links between poverty, deprivation and crime. Writing in the *New Statesman and Society*, Dickinson (1994) claimed to show a clear link between unemployment and crime, particularly for young males.

Further reading

Good introductory books on this topic are:

- Cole, T. (1986) *Whose Welfare?*, London: Tavistock.

- Kane, S. and Kirby, M. (2001) *Wealth, Poverty and Welfare*, London: Macmillan.

- Kidd, W. *et al.* (1999) *Readings in Sociology*, Oxford: Heinemann Educational.

- Trowler, P. (1996) *Investigating Health, Welfare and Poverty*, London: Collins Educational.

Power and control

Protest and social movements

Chapter outline

The context of political action

15.1 Defining political action
page 581
This section introduces the basic issues, concepts and themes of political action, and focuses on the concept of democracy as a major principle of political legitimation and organization in the contemporary world, together with the problems for traditional sociological analysis of contemporary voting behaviour and patterns.

15.2 Globalization and nationalism *page 600*
This section discusses the claim, made by some commentators in the West, that contemporary times are characterized by a new world order. It considers the impact of the process of globalization on the nation state, and on the operation of power within both the individual nation-state and the global political arena, and examines the strengthening of nationalism and regionalism as a reaction to globalization.

The changing patterns of political action

15.3 Forms and patterns of political action *page 604*
This section considers the major types of direct political action: riots, terrorism, demonstrations and strikes, and investigates the explanations sociologists and other social commentators have given for the forms and patterns of such political action.

Power, culture and identity

15.4 Contemporary conceptualizations of power in society *page 615*
This section looks at more contemporary ways in which power is understood to operate in society. Rather than defining power in a narrow sense to refer to the operation of élite groups and the state, an attempt is made to look at power as a broad and wide-ranging concept.

15.5 Power and the state *page 619*
This section introduces the theories of functionalism, pluralism, élite theory and Marxism. It discusses the differences between how these theories view the nature of power and the role of the state in contemporary society. It also looks at the variety of opinions within these broad traditions.

15.6 Power in everyday life
page 632
This section considers debates inspired by phenomenology, Foucault and post-modernism about how the concept of power can be applied to struggles in everyday life. It considers examples of the notion of the loss of truth and the politics of the body alongside ideas of the growth of the surveillance society.

15.1 Defining political action

In common-sense thought and language, 'politics' is usually associated with the activities of those in government (parties and individual MPs), the state in general, and sometimes with those seeking political power perhaps in a different form – such as pressure groups.

Sociologists, on the other hand, should consider 'the political' as much wider than simply the activities of elected élites: politics in its wider definition is about the exercise of power and can be seen to occur through the whole of social life on a number of different levels, both macro and micro. For example, for feminists, 'sexual politics' is about the struggles for power between men and women in many social arenas (see Section 15.6).

Basic definitions

We can draw a basic distinction between:

- *power* – getting one's own will
- *politics* – the struggles for power.

> ### Activity
> Using the definition above – that 'politics' is about the exercise of power – make a list of political struggles of a 'micro' nature that have affected your own life over the past few days.
>
> **C3.2, C3.3**

Political sociology

Although all social life is political in a sense, political sociology has traditionally focused on a number of key concerns. A distinction must be drawn between the academic activities of political sociologists and the discipline of political science.

- political science focuses on the institutions of government, political parties and voting behaviour
- political sociology takes a much more society-based approach and is concerned with investigating the effects of power in society.

> ### Discussion point
> To what extent do you think it is possible to maintain the above distinction between political science and political sociology?
>
> **C3.1a**

Varieties of political systems

Taking politics in its narrow sense to refer to the operation of government and the state, we can begin to make a distinction between the main varieties of 'political systems' in operation around the globe in contemporary social life.

Three types of political system

Totalitarianism

Carl Friedrich (1954) offers a four-fold classification of the key elements of totalitarianism:

- a single set of ideological principles which everyone must accept and follow
- a single party state led by one dictator
- the use of violence as a means of control
- total state control of all economic and social institutions.

> ### Activity
> Can you think of any examples of societies – from the past or from contemporary times – which fit the above description of a 'totalitarian' society?
>
> **C3.2, C3.3**

Oligarchy

An oligarchy means to be governed by the few, as opposed to being ruled by a single dictator.

Democracy

The term 'democracy' has a Greek origin: *demos* = the people, and *kratos* = rule. Thus democracy means 'rule by the people'. Athens, in ancient Greece, is usually associated with the birth of democracy, using popular public assemblies and law courts to make decisions by debate and discussion. In reality, however, not all those living in Athens at that time could attend public assemblies or vote at them: only the male citizens had rights of voting, whereas women and the vast slave population were excluded.

Even today the concept 'democracy' is highly problematic because many different societies of a wide variety of political systems, cultures and structures describe themselves as democratic. It must be noted that there is an important difference between *claiming* to be democratic and actually *being* democratic.

> ### Discussion point
> Why has democracy become a major legitimation claim in the contemporary world?
>
> **C3.1a**

Marxist criticisms of 'democracy'

Tom Bottomore

Bottomore (1978, 1993), adopting a Marxist perspective, is highly critical of the claims to democracy made by many societies, including those of the western world. He suggests that all the time a ruling class exists, claims of democracy are nonsense. From a Marxist perspective (see Section 15.5), the concept 'ruling class' is used to refer to those who own the means of production (i.e. all that is necessary to make a finished product). Even with a regular system of secret voting, those who have the real power remain unelected yet in control owing to their ownership of the means of production. Bottomore suggests that the popular rule associated with democracy is impossible in capitalist societies:

One must be sceptical, therefore, of the view that the extension of voting rights to the mass of the population can establish easily and effectively – or has in fact established in the short period of time in which modern democracies have existed – popular rule, and gradually erode or eliminate the power of a ruling class. What seems to have taken place in the democratic countries up to the present time is not so much a reduction in the power of the upper class as a decline in the radicalism of the working class.

(Bottomore, 1993, p. 289)

💬 Discussion point

To what extent can societies be democratic if they have great inequalities of wealth and a dominant class which enjoys the majority of that wealth?

C3.1a

Steven Box

A similar view to Bottomore's is that of Box (1983) who, also working within a Marxist perspective, suggests that claims to democracy can be used by ruling groups to hide their criminal and power-seeking behaviour. They can do this because, under a representative form of democracy, we must trust those who we vote to represent us – something they may not do properly in practice:

In a truly democratic society, the problem of power is not solved but it is contained. There is no way that people determined to behave badly, and having mastered the shameless art of deception, can be prevented from occupying positions of power. ... large sections of the public lack the inclination, ability, or power to make accountable those wielding political power, and through them, those wielding economic power. Ironically, for a nation that went to war against fascism, the democratic will to solve the problem of power has been lost; we have people in

political and economic power who are not accountable to those whose lives they control.

(Box, 1983, pp. 202 and 204)

💬 Discussion point

To what extent do you agree with this statement by Box as an assessment of government in contemporary advanced capitalist societies?

Types of democracies

At the heart of these problems in defining the concept 'democracy' lies a conflict between two opposing definitions that lead to very different types or models of democratic systems. On the one hand, democracy can mean the direct participation by all; while on the other hand, given the size of contemporary nation-states, it can also mean the election of those who are to rule. There are, then, two basic models of democracy (Held, 1993, p. 15):

- participatory democracy – where citizens are directly involved in actual decisions
- representative democracy – where 'representatives' are elected to act on behalf of the voting public.

In contemporary western societies the representative model is the most common form of political system.

The limits of democracy

A number of sociologists, philosophers, economists and others have been concerned to chart what they see as the limits of the democratic system of government.

It has been suggested that, given the size of nation-states, it is only realistic for representative style democracies to develop. Yet within this political system it is highly unlikely that the people will have all their wishes met with suitable collective decisions from full-time party officials or rulers. These representatives may themselves turn into an élite group, supported in their rule by the massive bureaucracies set up to administer the state. (See also Section 15.5.)

Discussion point

To what extent can democracy really be achieved in a society where political participation for the majority is limited to a vote in an election every four to five years?

C3.1a

Max Weber – the problems of 'party machines'

Max Weber, in his key work *Economy and Society* (1968; orig. pub. 1921), notes that 'party machines' – massive bureaucratic systems – are needed to control modern states to the extent that participation in the governing or ruling process by the people is often minimal (see also Section 15.5). Weber was concerned that, unless parties developed in nation-states standing for different interests, then democracy via the ballot box could be highly problematic. Little real choice could be given to a people to choose who to represent their interests - a very undemocratic situation.

Discussion point

To what extent would you agree that ideology has ended in contemporary politics – that the political parties are now more similar than they are different?

C3.1a

Activity

Using a suitable local library or other centre of information, obtain copies of the most recent manifestos for the main political parties in your local area. Make lists of each of the parties' main policies on a few issues that interest you. Now answer this question: To what extent do you agree with Weber, that little real choice is given to the people when deciding for whom to vote?

IT3.1, C3.2, C3.3

Political participation: elections and voting behaviour

Societies such as the UK are regarded as 'liberal democracies' – sometimes referred to as 'liberal–capitalist'. Democracy is claimed to be achieved through a system of representative democracy, whereby the general population vote in free elections for those individuals or groups whom they wish to rule over them for the time being.

Representative democracy might appear normal or natural to those who have never experienced anything else, but it is important to remember that this is just one political system among many. Equally, within the category of liberal democracy we can find important differences. In today's society, the concept of democracy is often associated with voting, and so a great deal of sociological literature exists on the nature of voting.

Problems for 'psephology'

Psephology means the study of voting behaviour and patterns. Many modern-day sociologists have suggested that the study of the outcome of voting has become even more complex and problematic since the end of World War II.

For many commentators, the post-war period in British politics has been characterized by two essential characteristics:

- alignment
- partisanship.

Until the late 1970s it was considered the norm that working-class members of society voted for the Labour party (with the backing of their trade union), while the middle classes voted Conservative or Liberal. This was voting *in line with* one's true class interests, or in alignment with one's class position. Alternatively it could be said that voters experienced a sense of *partisanship* with a particular political party: they were loyal to the goals, ideas and interests of one party and did not often change their minds or become what today are called 'floating voters'.

Voting was seen, in the past, as being relatively stable and in line with one's social position.

Butler and Stokes

Butler and Stokes (1969) conducted in-depth analyses of voting patterns and behaviours in the 1960s and 70s, and their results appeared to agree with this partisan and class-alignment image of voting. They suggested that class loyalty was ensured through the process of political socialization within the family: the sons and daughters of manual workers voted in line with their parents' Labour loyalties, while those born to middle-class families did the same with the Conservative party.

For example, Butler and Stokes suggest that even when the electorate as a body is renewed with first-time voters coming of age, it is still possible to detect:

... the electorates enduring party alignments. Support comes to any party for the most astonishing variety of reasons. But some of these will be general enough and enduring enough to be considered as bases of party alignment. Since the rise of the Labour party the foremost of these in Britain has been social class.

(Butler and Stokes, 1969, p. 4)

Contemporary voting patterns

The contemporary debate for political sociologists is between two related issues:

- Is voting aligned or dealigned?
- Is voting volatile or stable?

In other words – has voting changed dramatically since World War II? To answer this question, we need to look at the following four features of voting behaviour:

1 'deviant voting'
2 dealignment
3 the 'demise' of the deviant voter
4 the rise of volatility.

After this, we look at various modern-day models which explain voting behaviour.

1 The deviant voter

Traditionally, a great deal of psephology sought to explain the existence of deviant voters – those who did not appear to vote in line with their class interests. A number of explanations for deviant voting were put forward:

- Middle-class people might vote for Labour if they worked in 'caring professions', owing to Labour's traditional commitment to the welfare state.
- Middle-class people might vote Labour if they once were working-class themselves and have experienced upward social mobility – they might still 'feel' working-class.
- Working-class elderly people may vote Conservative as a result of pre-war traditions.
- Some working-class people may feel that the

middle-class Conservatives are their 'betters' and 'natural leaders'.

2 Dealignment

Since the 1970s and the work of Butler and Stokes, it is possible to detect a number of changes to the modern pattern of voting behaviour. It is suggested that we are experiencing a process or pattern of dealignment, whereby the traditional relationships between class and party loyalties are slowly being eroded.

In line with the foregoing discussion, there may be at least two processes involved here: class dealignment and partisan dealignment. Voters may no longer vote according to the traditional or expected fashion based on their class background, or they may have given up established loyalty to a particular party and instead may float their vote, possibly changing their mind from election to election.

3 The 'demise' of the deviant voter

The processes of dealignment almost certainly explains the observation that many working-class people must have voted for the Conservative party since the 1979 election for the party to have stayed in power for an extensive period. This has implications for the idea of deviant voting, because it seems that the majority of society have become 'deviant voters' – and if this is true, then the term 'deviant' becomes inappropriate. Perhaps this concept is no longer useful to explain voting patterns since 1979.

4 Volatility

When class and partisan dealignment occur, this makes the voting system highly volatile. Today it is becoming increasingly difficult to predict the outcomes of elections, or indeed to predict an individual's voting pattern or party loyalty (if any) from their social background:

... while the two-class, two-party model has dominated British political science, most commentators have agreed that class, both as a social and a political force, has been steadily declining in Britain. Rising levels of affluence and the break-up of traditional communities are held to have eroded class solidarity. Labour in particular, it is said, can no longer rely on working-class support in the way that it could a generation ago, and the new breed of affluent skilled manual workers in the South of

England are believed to have swung decisively to the Conservatives. The spread of home-ownership in the working class exacerbates the trend. Such changes in the character of the working class are held to explain why a left-wing ideology can no longer win the working-class vote.

(Heath *et al.*, 1985, p. 8)

Understanding how the UK votes

In their study *Understanding Political Change: The British Voter 1964–1987*, Heath *et al.* (1991) note that the general elections of 1979, 1983 and 1987 are often presented as a sea-change in popular political opinion.

Activity

Examine the statistics in Table 15.1. What trends can you see in voting behaviour since 1945?

C3.2, C3.3

'Thatcherism'

Following Margaret Thatcher's first general election victory in 1979, commentators such as Hall (1984) wrote of her deliberate project to challenge and change popular attitudes to develop what she would have described as a 'self-reliant' society. To Hall, this represented a return to hegemonic politics – the lure of Thatcherism

was its popularist rhetoric and its power lay in its ability to obtain popular consent. Hall described the shift or popular victory of New Right policies as 'The Great Moving Right Show'.

Development of the project of Thatcherism may have enabled the Conservative party to gain voters from those who would usually have voted Labour or Liberal Democrat, or traditional working-class voters. Thus the success of Thatcherism was to take advantage of the changing nature of class voting behaviour – yet in doing so, it contributed even more to the process of de-alignment. With the rise of the New Right, many started to ask the question 'Will Labour lose again?'

Thatcherism can be seen to have acted as a bridge between the libertarian and social authoritarian elements in New Right thinking. Some, however, are sceptical as to whether Thatcherism as a distinct political ideology ever existed as such. They suggest that what we now call Thatcherism was no more than an effective (in terms of gaining popular public support) set of short-term pragmatic and practical responses to changing social and economic conditions. In other words, they say it was not a premeditated and formulated social philosophy.

Stuart Hall

Others, such as Hall (1984), see Thatcher's particular brand of popular capitalism as a form of authoritarian populism – a distinctive set of political strategies which are based on strong leader-

Table 15.1 UK general election results since 1945

| | Percentage of votes | | | | Parliamentary seats | | | | |
	Con	Lab	Lib Dem	Nat	Con	Lab	Lib Dem	Nat	Total
1992	41.9	34.4	17.8	5.8	336	271	20	24	651
1987	42.3	30.6	22.5	2.0	376	229	22	6	650
1983	42.4	27.6	25.4	1.7	397	209	23	4	650
1979	43.8	36.8	13.8	2.2	339	269	11	4	635
1974 Oct.	35.8	39.2	18.3	3.5	277	319	13	14	635
1974 Feb.	37.9	37.2	19.3	2.8	297	301	14	9	635
1970	46.4	43.1	7.5	2.4	330	288	8	5	630
1968	41.9	48.0	8.6	1.1	253	364	12	1	630
1964	43.4	44.1	11.2	0.9	304	317	9	0	630
1959	49.4	43.8	5.8	0.6	365	258	6	0	630
1955	49.7	46.4	2.7	0.9	345	277	6	2	630
1951	48.0	48.8	2.6	0.4	321	295	8	3	625
1950	43.4	46.1	9.1	0.6	298	315	9	2	625
1945	39.6	48.0	9.0	1.4	210	383	12	6	640

Source: Guardian, 11 April 1994

ship from above and with a mass appeal. As Hall comments on the growth of New Right politics:

There can be no doubt about it: the move to the right no longer looks like a temporary swing of the pendulum. On the national political stages of Britain and the United States and at the international meetings, the spotlight has veered over to the ideas and rhetoric of the New Right. Nowhere has this been more apparent than in Maggie Thatcher's austere kingdom. But it would be wrong to identify the success of the British radical right solely with the personality of Mrs Thatcher and her hard-nosed cronies. Although they have given the swing to the right a distinctive personal stamp, the deeper movement is a form of authoritarian populism which has great appeal to the average punter.

(Hall, 1984, p. 24)

Labour in the 1992 general election

The 1992 general election brought another victory for the Conservative party. As with the landslide of the 1983 election, when Labour suffered their greatest losses ever, the 1992 result was seen as a bitter defeat for them (although in 1992 the Conservative majority dropped to just 21 seats, a loss of 80 seats from the 1987 result). This time, still in the aftermath of the claims of the demise of Labour and the rise of the middle ground in response to the 1987 and 1983 results, yet another rethink took place among British political commentators. The essential question now was not whether Labour would lose, but the even more pessimistic 'Can Labour ever win again?'

Ivor Crewe

Crewe (1992) suggests that Labour could have won the 1992 election. The implementation of the massively unpopular poll tax had turned many away from the Conservatives, and there was rising unemployment and concern over 'fat-cat' wages to heads of privatized companies. Given this scenario, a shift back towards traditional class voting patterns should have paved the way to a Labour victory. Yet, despite all this, Labour still lost. As Crewe asks: 'Why did Labour lose (yet again)?'

Crewe argues that Labour lost owing to the way in which the public perceived the then Labour leader, Neil Kinnock, as not competent to rule the country, and the Labour party in general as likely to mismanage the economy.

Crewe also suggests that many Liberal Democrat voters may well have returned to the Conservative party as a method to stop Labour coming to power. Therefore, the Conservatives did not so much win the election, as Labour lost it. Or, to put it another way, the Conservatives won only because the electorate did not wish Labour to do so.

Andrew Gamble

Gamble (1994), in his *Loves Labour Lost*, suggested that Labour had a real political challenge on their hands after four concurrent election defeats:

Conservative dominance will not be easily overturned. The Conservatives are entrenched and their opponents are divided. The party enjoys many advantages over its competitors in funding, membership, and press and business support. Its ideas are the ruling ideas. It has set the policy agenda for more than a decade, and it can rely on a large core vote which is concentrated in the south of England, where the bulk of the constituencies now are.

(Gamble, 1994, p. 44)

Gamble raises some very important issues here. Success at the ballot box is a much more complex process than just winning favour with the electorate. It is necessary to consider the ability a party has to attract new voters or young voters, the type and success of campaign its members can put together, and its public image in – and treatment by – the press and other media. Facing all these dimensions of a successful election campaign, Gamble did not think a Labour victory would come easily:

... Labour will do well to continue its advance at the next election. It would be an exceptional result for Labour to win the next election outright. But it is not impossible. Much depends on the ability of the leadership to unite the party around a set of policies and a political style that can give Labour a distinctive, radical profile and broaden its appeal. Labour will not win the kind of landslide it requires unless it breaks decisively with its past and helps to create a momentum for radical change which gives voters positive reasons for switching to Labour. Geography, social structure, and history all seem to be against it. But British politics remains unpredictable. The country is in a mess, and many of the solutions of the 1980s have been discredited. Labour has an opportunity to relaunch itself and become the focus of a new radical politics. Will it take it?

(Gamble, 1994, p. 44)

The 1997 general election

While the 1992 election had been held against the backdrop of changes within the Conservative party – epitomized by the transition (in 1990) from Margaret Thatcher to John Major as party leader and Prime Minister – the 1997 general election was held against the backdrop of the considerable transformation of the Labour party, enshrined in the leadership of Tony Blair.

The launch of 'New' Labour was an attempt to communicate a clear break with the party's past. The increasing importance of the ideas of ethical socialism and communitarianism (see Section 14.4) within the party are examples of this.

While it was clear this transformation had led to a resurgence in support for Labour as expressed in opinion polls, there were fears that it might lead to the danger of alienating the party's traditional base of support in the trade unions and the working class.

Despite his image as a grey man leading a government staggering from one crisis to the next, John Major's Conservative administration had managed to hold on to power for the full duration of its five-year term of office (ending in 1997). The Wirral South by-election held on 27 February 1997, won by Labour with a majority of 7888 (a massive swing of 17.2 per cent), did not provide much basis for optimism about the impending general election in the Conservative camp, thus fuelling expectations that 1997 would see the Labour party returning to power for the first time since 1979. On 1 May 1997, the general election duly arrived and the results are summarized in Table 15.2.

The long-awaited victory of the Labour party clearly undermined the idea that Labour would never govern again and that the Conservatives would hold power in perpetuity, a view often expressed in the 1980s. However, the transformation in the Labour party since 1992 means that its significance in terms of the continuing debate about class and voting are more difficult to analyse. Does the Labour victory mean class is still important, or is it an example of its demise?

Activity

Obtain reports on the 1997 general election from newspapers and magazines such as *New Statesman and Society* and the *Economist*. Use these, and any more substantial academic articles you are aware of, to consider how the result of the 1997 general election will affect the models of voting behaviour outlined in this section.

IT3.1, C3.2, C3.3

In one sense, the victory of the Labour party in 1997 meant entering new times. Nevertheless, the transformation of the Labour party under Tony Blair can certainly be seen as an example of trends which others have drawn more widely, including the notion that we now live in post-class and even post-socialist times.

Tony Blair and New Labour

In the aftermath of the 1997 election, many wondered if this so-called 'new' party was simply a change in image – or, more fundamentally, a change in thinking and direction. A few years on since this election, Tony Blair has made a number of very public announcements that New Labour represents what he and others have called a '*third way*' in UK politics: somewhere on the political spectrum between what are seen as the excesses of both the New Right and the socialism and trade unionism of 'Old' Labour. This third way is based upon the adoption of a '*communitarian*' style of politics.

Communitarianism

These ideas of communitarianism are associated with the ideas of sociologist Etzioni (1995) – who suggests that modern politics needs to be based upon:

- the responsibility for families to socialize 'correct moral values'
- the responsibility of schools to instill both discipline and a sense of 'citizenship' into the young
- the government's need to further involve the community in the business of politics on local and regional levels

Table 15.2 UK general election 1997 – summary of results

Party	MPs elected	Share of the vote (%)
Labour	419	43
Conservative	165	31
Liberal Democrat	46	17
Others	29	9

- debate – a 'critical dialogue' – which should be encouraged at all levels of society.

There are here some important differences and similarities between this New Left position and that of the New Right of Thatcherism: whereas the New Right wish to create individualism, the New Left seem more interested in the community; yet they both wish to reduce state spending and to re-enforce so-called traditional family values.

Discussion point
What do you see as the future of the role played by class in politics, in contemporary times?

C3.1a

Pressure groups, citizenship and new social movements

An essential distinction must be drawn between political parties and pressure groups – both of which, in the pluralist perspective, are seen to be important in the political process.

- *Political parties* are interested in gaining power at a governmental level. In western liberal democracies, parties compete for votes by putting candidates forward for election by the population. By their very nature, political parties are national because they wish to govern the whole nation-state, and are interested in every issue of political discussion. Nationalist parties, such as those in Northern Ireland, Wales and Scotland, obviously contest what counts as a nation-state but would, if successful, still seek to govern in a redrawn map of nation-states.

- *Pressure groups* (sometimes referred to as interest groups) are usually concerned with a single issue, or a set of related issues. They do not seek election, but rather operate in the political process by lobbying those in power for their help. They can be local, national or even international (global), but they do not wish to govern the nation-state.

Many contemporary pluralists have argued that the arena of political battles has slowly moved away from political parties and elections, towards the activities of pressure or interest groups. This is seen as the result of a rapid expansion in the number and activities of pressure groups in the post-war period. Today, pressure groups are seen as essential to western democracy.

Discussion point
a Would the existence of a ruling class owning the means of production mean that pressure groups could not be effectual?

b Can pressure groups change power differences to any significant extent?

C3.1a

Types of pressure group

A distinction can be made between pressure groups that are protective and those that are promotional.

Protective pressure groups seek to look after the interests of their members. *Promotional* groups try to achieve *change* by advocating or promoting a particular cause. Within these two categories, many pressure groups can be seen as single-issue groups, with a very narrow focus. The following are some examples from British political life:

- protective: Trade Union Congress (TUC), Confederation of British Industry (CBI), National Farmer's Union (NFU)

- promotional: Greenpeace, Amnesty International, Campaign for Nuclear Disarmament (CND).

Activity
Choose one pressure group, either from the list above or another of your own choice, and investigate its history and activities. Write up this information in the form of a short report.

IT3.1, C3.2, C3.3

In reality, it may be difficult to decide, in the final analysis, between classifying a pressure group as promotional or as protective. For example, on the one hand Greenpeace *promotes* environmental issues, but it could also be argued that in doing so it seeks to *protect* us from the hazards of environmental crisis. The same point could be made about CND.

Pressure groups in British politics

Marsh (1983) notes that sociologists' treatments of the role, effect and influence of pressure groups since the 1960s have changed. This is due, he argues, to changes in the relationships between pressure groups and society. Marsh identifies three main changes:

- The number of pressure groups has greatly multiplied.
- Groups are becoming increasingly involved in politics.
- Groups have increased their contact with the state, yet reduced their contact with political parties.

Related to these main changes, a number of other trends can be identified:

- A number of pressure groups have resumed contact with the Labour party, while at the same time reducing contact with the Conservatives.
- What Marsh calls ideological groups (those seeking to promote or defend legislation on ideological principles) have grown in number. Also, economic groups (those seeking to promote or protect the specific financial interests of their membership) have been drawn into a more formal role in the decision-making process, and as a consequence are more able than ideological groups to produce change.
- Since the 1970s there has been an increase in single-issue groups, but they have been largely unsuccessful in changing government policy, or even in obtaining government favour and help. Consequently these groups have instead tried to influence public opinion largely through the media.
- Many single-issue groups have tried to obtain the support and recognition of the TUC in an attempt to gain power, especially within the Labour party.

However, despite these major trends and their consequences, Marsh is keen to emphasize that the role of pressure groups in society is in a dynamic state: it is unpredictable and open to great change.

Activity

Figure 15.1 depicts how pressure groups have had an influence in several major controversies. Answer the following questions.

a Over what issues have people protested?

b What changes have resulted from these campaigns?

C3.2, C3.3

Activity

a Consider what pressure groups can actually do, in order to 'put pressure' on those in government and influence policy.

b Create a list of those means, and then put the list in order of effectiveness, from the most to the least.

C3.2, C3.3

Pressure groups and democracy

Grant (1989) suggests that pressure groups are vital for democracy in the western world:

There is a fundamental link between the existence of pressure groups and the very survival of a system of democratic government. Freedom of association is a fundamental principle of democracy. Democracy permits the existence of groups, but it could also be argued that groups contribute to the quality of the decision-making process. Those that have axes to grind may have something to say that is relevant to the issue under consideration.

(Grant, 1989, p. 21)

Grant contends that representative democracy in fact offers a relatively infrequent choice of political view, with elections required only every five years (in the UK). It could also be said that, with the increasing similarity of views between the major British political parties, this choice is becoming further limited, even when an election is held.

Grant therefore sees the existence of pressure groups as essential to democracy, because they often offer diverse political opinions, and a more frequent opportunity than elections for one's political voice to be heard:

Pressure groups permit citizens to express their views on complex issues which affect their lives. In systems of voting, each vote counts equally, but numerical democracy can take no account of the intensity of opinion on a particular issue. Democracy cannot be simply reduced to a head-counting exercise: it must also take account of the strength of feelings expressed, and of the quality of arguments advanced.

(Grant, 1989, p. 21)

Discussion point

What role do pressure groups play to facilitate democracy?

C3.1a

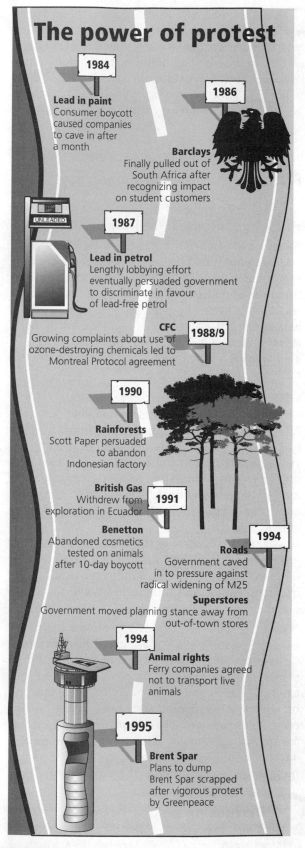

Figure 15.1 The power of protest
Source: Guardian, 22 June 1995

Citizenship

Since the 1980s the concept of citizenship has risen in significance in British political debate. What does it mean to be a person in a democratic society? To have citizenship – to be a citizen of a nation-state – means to live under the control of a state with rights that one can exercise, and duties and obligations which the state must perform.

Discussion point

What rights do the people living in the UK have?

C3.1a

Marshall

T. H. Marshall (1977) suggested that the concept of citizenship could be divided into three different, but related, sets of rights:

- civil rights
- political rights
- social rights.

Marshall argues that the contemporary concern with rights is a reflection of the development of capitalism. Since capitalist economic systems are based on the principles of freedom and consumption, the development of rights and law were, he suggests, vital to the business contract. Without these rights a fair relationship between producer and consumer could not be guaranteed.

Faulks

Faulks (1994) notes that, on the current political stage, the concept of citizenship and the concern with rights is treated differently by the Left and the Right:

For those on the Left of the political spectrum it is seen as a useful concept around which to mobilize support for egalitarian policies; for those on the Right the notion of the citizen has been utilized to encourage a greater sense of civic duty and to make public services more efficient through the operation of the government's new citizens' charter.

(Faulks, 1994, p. 2)

Turner

It is possible to identify some problems with the concept of citizenship. Turner (1986) argues that the concern with citizenship is a reflection of the rise and development of the nation-state in 'modernity' – a term used to refer to the rise of industrial societies and, in the West, the development of capitalism. However, with the onset of globalization many argue that the nation-state is no longer as important as it once was.

The individual citizenship of a nation-state can today be overruled by the global rights given to individuals by the European Court of Human Rights and the 1948 United Nations Universal Declaration of Human Rights. For Turner, citizenship is becoming problematic – national identity and the nation-state are becoming outdated tools of sociological analysis. (See also Section 15.2.)

Lister

Lister (1990) asserts that the New Right in British parliamentary politics have narrowed our understanding of being a citizen in contemporary society. She notes that being a citizen seems almost exclusively related to being a consumer, and little else. Lister points out that, for members of the New Right, citizenship is seen as the product of the free-market economy: we are given the power by the market to consume, and in doing so express our freedom from the state. For the New Right, citizenship is about breaking down the state, not being supported by it (see Section 14.2).

Hirst

Hirst (1990, 1993a), from a neo-pluralist stance, argues that in today's society citizens lack any real power to challenge the policies of government, except at the ballot box. One possible solution to this situation is to establish a Bill of Rights which specifically identifies the rights citizens are entitled to. In this way, a newly elected government would always have to operate within clear boundaries.

New social movements

Much of the contemporary sociological study of political struggle and protest has concentrated on the idea of new social movements.

A 'social movement' is – defined in simple terms – a non-institutional body or group which takes up a given cause or issue of a political nature. Use of the prefix 'new' to describe new social movements came about owing to the recent rise (or rather, return) of these movements in the late twentieth century.

For many decades sociology has been preoccupied with the relationships between power, the state, social class and voting – almost to the point of dismissal of social movements which have been seen as adding and contributing little to the political arena. However, since the 1960s there has, arguably, been a return to these types of political expression.

Why have new social movements risen?

A number of factors can be identified for this return of (new) social movements:

- disillusionment with the ability of the state to distribute welfare
- disillusionment with the choice of ideas offered by political parties
- the so-called 'death of class' in voting behaviour.

These three interrelated social developments are used by some as evidence of a post-industrial society, one where traditional class struggle and political issues no longer exist. For Hallsworth (1994) the term new social movement:

... may be viewed as a concept originally developed by commentators on the political left. It was one developed specifically to refer to the wide and diverse spectrum of new, non-institutional political movements which emerged or (as in the case of feminism) re-emerged, in western liberal democratic societies during the 1960s and 1970s. More specifically, the term is most often used to refer to those movements which may be held to pose new challenges to the established cultural economic and political orders of advanced (i.e. late twentieth century) capitalist society.

(Hallsworth, 1994, p. 7)

Identity and lifestyle

Inglehart (1990) notes that new social movements, and the modern political arenas they have created, are more concerned with non-material political issues – identity and lifestyle – and the inequalities these are subjected to, rather than economic inequality as such.

Examples of new social movements are:

- black power
- student power
- gay liberation
- greens
- women's liberation.

What these types of movement have in common is a move away from a traditional membership based on social class. The political movements of old were largely workers' movements or labour movements, whereas those of today exist separately from production-centred politics.

Whereas the old workers' movements were concerned with attacking the state, economic inequality and class struggle, the new social movements are more concerned with individual and group autonomy. Whereas the old workers' movements organized themselves through formal and hierarchical groups, such as unions, the new social movements are based much more on informal networking.

Post-modernism and 'DIY cultures'

Some post-modernists would claim that new social movements offer the individual the opportunity to reconstruct a personal identity in a post-modern society: to use identification with a wider group as a political process, to subvert how the state and other institutions attempt to control an individual's life.

The term 'DIY culture' is sometimes used to refer to the lifestyles offered to the individual by new social movements. One does not so much join a new social movement as live one. Membership (although not in the traditional sense of this word) of new social movements is based on constructing a lifestyle from a pastiche of elements – picking and choosing from a number of choices on offer, from dress codes through food-consumption codes to sexual identity (see Section 4.1). This picking and mixing has lead to some post-modernists claiming that involvement in a new social movement is an expression of a post-modern lifestyle.

New social movements and identity politics

One of the crucial bases of the new social movements is the need to establish politics on a new basis, centered on the notion of identity. This politics was about reclaiming and placing positive value on identities that had been subject to oppression, such as 'women', 'blacks', 'gays'. In contrast to older social movements, principally the labour movement, the identities involved were not based around production and therefore the job that people do. Since this latter is the basis of identification of class, it is often felt that this new form of politics grew up in opposition

to class-based politics. However, there is no logical reason why class politics cannot be analysed in the same way since it is clear that subjective class identities exist and also the extent to which they exist affects the nature and extent of political mobilization.

What is clear in all cases is that, when engaging in political protests and direct action, people are working to change the world in ways which fit in with their notion of a better or ideal society – and that this also involves some notion of who they are, who they want to be and how they want to live their lives. Notions of identity are therefore clearly central to contemporary political mobilization, leading to the use of the term 'identity politics.'

The turn away from class

It is clear that the origins of identity politics and the rise of the new social movements is based on a rejection of class-based politics. The reasons for this are diverse but include the argument that class as an economic relationship excluded consideration of a whole range of other forms of oppression not necessarily economic in nature. This argument is summarised by Aronowitz (1992):

The historically exclusive focus of class-based movements on a narrow definition of the issues of economic justice has frequently excluded gender, race, and qualitative issues, questions of worker's control over production, and similar problems. The almost exclusive emphasis on narrow quantitative issues has narrowed the political base of labour and socialialist movements which, as often as not, perceived class politics as inimical to their aims.

(Aronowitz, 1992, p. 67)

This quotation gives a flavour of the feeling that work-located class-based politics did not offer enough attention to other areas of life. It is also important to note that in the 1960s and 1970s these other areas of life were open to great change, leading to people questioning what were seen as almost natural or common sense assumptions about how people lived their life and what it meant to be a man or a woman, for instance. Equally it meant that class-based movements were unlikely to be seen as a natural basis to orient around. The quote below explains the reluctance of the gay movement to link up with class-based movements:

If gays had been left out of traditional Marxist analy-

sis – together with most aspects of sexuality, which were seen as merely superstructural and reactive in an unproblematic way to the economic 'base' of society – then class analysis itself was likely to be left at the back of the political cupboard in the general excitement which characterised the development of sexual politics in the late sixties.

(Watney, 1980, p.67)

The rise of the black civil rights movement argued that black people should be treated on an equal basis to white people and as part of this movement there was the aim of presenting positive images and identities of black people to black people and others. Slogans such as 'Black is Beautiful' express the aim of creating a positive identity.

Oppression and identity

A second aspect of this idea of the creation of a positive identity was the notion that this identity could only flourish if oppression could be overcome and this oppression could only be defined and fought against by those who suffered from that oppression. In simple terms only black people could fight against racism and only women could fight against sexism. Experience is seen as the key basis of knowledge and this leads to the creation of clusters of people sharing an identity but also sharing a commonality against the rest of the world. (See also Chapter 4.)

The rejection of class-based politics

A third element contributing to the rise in identity politics was a rejection of the possibility of class-based politics being successful. The key argument here was the post-Fordist argument (see Section 17.2) that we now live in a globalized world based on the need for a flexible workforce and that the new support for the politics of the market had meant that attacks on the trade unions and the labour movement had led to a fatal undermining of its transformative strength. This idea is perhaps best expressed in the title of Andre Gorz's book *Farewell to the Working Class* (Gorz, 1982).

Michel Foucault

The rejection of Marxist-based arguments left space for other theories to define a new politics and undoubtedly one of the most influential was Michel Foucault. Kate Nash (2000) summaries this as follows:

The influence that Foucault's work has had on the new political sociology cannot be over-estimated. His direct influence is widely acknowledged by those who work on issues in the politics of identity and difference. ... Once we begin to look at the world through the lenses Foucault provides for us, conventional politics at the level for the state is displaced to the periphery of vision and other forms of politics come into focus.

(Nash, 2000, pp. 26–7)

This quote makes the important link between the changes in political and sociological notions of power and politics and changes in the world in terms of the activities and aims of political movements. The ideas of Foucault are also examined in Section 15.6, and in this section we will now proceed to examine some examples of the rise of movements based on identity politics.

Ethnicity, action and identity

One of the key starting points for the emergence of ethnic identity politics was the way that racism defined and labelled black people. One interesting example of this can be seen by considering the definition of black and white in a dictionary:

Black, blak, a. Destitute of light; dark; gloomy; sullen; atrocious; wicked. – n. The Darkest colour; a negro. –vt. To make black.

White, whit, a. Being of the colour of pure snow; pale; pallid; pure and unsullied. n. The colour of snow; a white pigment; white of an egg, eye &c. – vt. (whiting, whited). To make white.

(*Oxford University English Dictionary*, quoted in Kirby, 1995, p. 195)

This example illustrates the way in which behaviour and character traits are imputed to a colour and through this to people creating a discriminatory racist notion of difference.

Edward Said and the 'Other'

The response to this was to criticise the way this involved definitions of the 'Other'. Edward Said (1985) pointed to the way that European encounters with the Orient led to definitions of the Other including notions of being exotic, unpredictable and mysterious. This idea of the 'exotic other' can also be used to treat people in a derogatory way. Even if it is not, it is clear that this is an identity that is not self-chosen but is imposed, and so one key aspect of identity politics is to be able to choose your own identity. This meant that black people themselves should define and determine the nature of being black.

Black nationalism

This led to the emergence of 'black nationalism', the idea that black people form a cultural nation who need to live separately from white people, and in some cases the argument that this meant there was a desire to return to Africa. Certainly it is clear that there was no role for white people in such a movement. Malcolm X, one of the key early leaders of the Black Nationalist movement, defined it as follows:

The political philosophy of black nationalism means that the black man should control the politics and the politicians of his own community.

(Quoted in Ovenden, 1992, p. 69)

This position was based on the idea that all black people have something in common and that all white people are oppressors of black people.

Martin Luther King

The Civil Rights Movement led by Martin Luther King, in contrast, argued not for separatism but instead for integration through the ending of segregation in the USA, which was at that time (the early 1960s) still very strong in parts of the nation, particularly in the southern states of the USA. Principally this was based, as the name suggests, on winning civil citizenship rights for blacks on an equal footing to whites, notably the right to vote. The principal forms of activity were demonstrations and campaigns to increase voter registration among blacks, often a dangerous business in the southern states of the USA.

Activity

To consider some of the debates and issues from these times rent copies of films such as *Malcolm X* or *Mississippi Burning*. Make notes on what message you think each film conveys and what it tells you about struggles for black identity in the USA.

C3.2, C3.3

Equality or difference?

This debate in the USA divided those who wished to campaign for inclusion and equality with white people and those who argued instead for the retention of a separate positive black identity. This notion of equality or difference is a consistent theme running through identity politics. However, it might be argued that this poses the issue in rather stark either/or terms and is also open to the criticism made by Tariq Modood (1992) that we cannot see the world in terms of a simple dualism, that is a simple division between black and white, and instead have to consider the existence of a multiplicity of ethnic identities.

The 'new ethnicities'

Stuart Hall took up this idea with his notion of the 'new ethnicities', where he argues that all identities are fluid and constantly in flux as a result of human interaction and creativity:

If the black subject and black experience are not stabilized by nature or by some other essential guarantee, then it must be the case that they are constructed historically, culturally politically – and the concept which refers to this is 'ethnicity'. The term ethnicity acknowledges the place of history, language and culture in the construction of subjectivity and identity, as well as the fact that all discourse is placed, positioned, situated and all knowledge is contextual.

(Hall, 1992, p. 257, quoted in Nash, 2000, p. 194)

Hall's article was centrally concerned with black film makers and he cites a number of examples of films which might illustrate the themes he was exploring. (See also Section 4.3.)

Activity

Watch some films that reflect these debates. One example of the complexities of identity and the relationship this involves can be seen in the film *My Beautiful Launderette* which involves the relationship between a gay Pakistani and a white ex-Paki basher. Equally you might watch *Bhaji On the Beach*, *The Buddah of Suburbia* or *Mississippi Masala*.

Write notes on what you think the film says about identity and the complexities and fluidity of contemporary ethnicities.

C3.2, C3.3

The fluidity of ethnic identities

Paul Gilroy has also added to this notion of the fluidity of ethnic identities with his argument that there is a need to combat 'ethnic absolutism' by recognising that global cultural styles are mixed together and that therefore contemporary black cultures and identities do not draw on some fixed notion of ethnic identity but instead on a fluid, flexible notion. He rejects the usefulness of class analysis in understanding this, He does, however, suggest that the black community since it still suffers from racism can use cultural elements such as music, dance and sport as a form of resistance to racism and that such resistance will be locally based. Talking about the inner-city riots in the UK in the 1980s, he argues:

In the representation of the recent riots, it is possible to glimpse a struggle, a sequence of antagonisms which has moved beyond the grasp of orthodox class analysis. Unable to control the social relations in which they find themselves, people have shrunk the world to the size of their communities and begun to act politically on that basis.

(Gilroy, 1987, p. 245)

While this clearly represents notions of local activism, it might be open to the criticism that it is political action that ignores anything that does not happen in your immediate locality and there is a question mark over whether this is a sustainable form of political mobilization.

Discussion point
Is shrinking the world to the size of your community a good thing or not?

C3.1a

Ethnic identities and nationality

While, as we have seen, notions of ethnicity have moved away from the earlier ideas of ethnic absolutisim, there are still examples of movements based on these ideas. Notably there is the Nation of Islam in the USA. Equally there is the notion of Zionism, which is the ideology behind the state of Israel and many Jewish-based movements. This is based on the idea that gentiles (non-Jews) will be inherently anti-Semitic and therefore Jewish people have to have their own homeland to ensure they do not suffer oppression. This example and the term black nationalism and some of the return to Africa movements which have been associated with this term show the link between ethnicity and nationality. We will therefore now look at an example of the way national identity has been utilised as the basis of political action and identity. (This issue is covered in more detail in Sections 4.2 and 4.3.)

Nationality, action and identity

Maps of the world show borders that divide territory up into nations. In this form of presenta-

tion, these borders can almost look natural. In some cases the borders are natural, being rivers or mountain ranges. However, if you look at a map of Africa, for example, you will see that many borders consist of straight lines. Despite the view of some sociologists such as Edward Shils (1957) that nations are natural entities, these straight lines are a clue that such borders are not natural, as indeed they are not since they were drawn up in offices in London by colonial officials. Nations can therefore be artificial constructions. However, the importance of nation-states as the key sovereign political bodies (until, and even in some ways despite, recent debates about globalization) has meant that there have always been lots of nationalist movements seeking to set up their own nation-states. In the UK recently we have seen examples of this with the setting up of devolved governmental power in Scotland, Wales and for a period Northern Ireland.

Nations as 'imagined communities'

Eric Hobsbawn (1992) and Benedict Anderson (1991) both argue that the nation is an invented concept and that there is nothing satisfactory to define what is a nation. Anderson uses the term 'imagined community'. What he means by this is that if you are British you are meant to have something in common with the 59 million other people who are British. Since you will never meet 99.9% of those people, you will be unable to know if you have anything in common, you merely imagine it. This leads to an importance being placed on symbols.

We can, however, distinguish between those symbols which are largely cultural in nature such as languages, religion and other things amenable to choice. If these are seen as the basis of nationality this is known as civic nationalism. Alternatively if the emphasis is placed on biological lineage and notions of blood line then we have the much more dangerous form of ethnic nationalism. You cannot choose or change your nationality and the biological element can lead to bloody conflict if this type of nationalism comes to prominence. (See also Section 4.2.)

Ethnic nationalism and conflict

We have seen recent examples of this in the former Yugoslavia, where there were conflicts between Croats, Serbs and Muslims in Bosnia, and between Serbs and ethnic Albanians in Kosovo. These conflicts were about ethnic nationalism and led to some of the worst human rights abuses seen in Europe since World War II.

Equally in Africa in the region around Rwanda there have been ethnically based conflicts around territory that led to large scale massacres.

These examples have shown the continuing importance of notions of nationality in relation to political mobilization and identity and also the great dangers if the particular form of nationalism invokes myths of common ethnic background and blood ties as the basis of mobilization.

Discussion point

What does it mean to be English, or Scottish, or Welsh, or Irish, or British? Which, if any, of these do you feel yourself to be and why?

C3.1a

Gender, action and identity

The women's liberation movement was, to an extent, built upon the theoretical and practical development of the USA's black nationalist movement and it also therefore adopted the notion of separatism, namely that women could not free themselves from male oppression unless they lived separately from them. This led to divisions within the women's movement between lesbians and heterosexual women, leading to notions of political lesbianism when whom you slept with and your sexuality were seen as political questions. Although there were other tensions, the divisions around sexuality illustrate some of the themes of identity and political action and can also be seen in the contemporary rise of 'Queer Nation'. (See also Section 4.1)

Queer Nation

In relation to sexuality, this is one example of a movement which illustrates this theme of identity very well. The name 'Queer Nation' is based on appropriating the language of the oppressors (queer) and creating a positive identity out of it, but it is also by using the word 'nation' suggesting that the basis of political struggle is to create communities based on sexual identity. This would in effect mean exclusively gay districts. The separatist tendencies involved here can be seen in the headline of the 'Queer Nation' manifesto: 'I Hate Straights' (quoted in Smith, 1994, p. 19).

Queer Nation was formed in New York in March 1990 by groups of gay and lesbian activists

interested in notions of direct action. In effect what this has meant is engaging in activities which assert the right to be treated the same as everyone else and to be accepted rather than merely tolerated:

In practice, queer activism is associated with 'in your face' demonstrations such as 'kiss-ins' which 'mimic the privileges of normality', the return of camp styles and other forms of irony, 'mixed' venues for men and women, and 'gender-fuck' aesthetics.

(Nash, 2000, p. 177)

One key debate that this has involved is the hostility of some elements of the gay movement to identities such as bisexuality or transexuality, which in earlier theorizations were sometimes considered as confused or not real identities at all. Again this reflects a move away from the old dualism of 'gay' and 'straight' but instead must consider the multiplicity of sexual identities all of which should be seen as acceptable and none of which should be seen as in some way natural.

Again one potential danger of this is the danger of fragmentation as more and more complex identities are created and movements split to represent these new identities. If the aim is to create a space in which you can express your identities this is fine, but if the aim is to create solidarities across movements and oppressed groups then the emphasis on identity and cultural communities may be just as likely to fragment and divide as to bring people together. As Kate Nash (2000) points out, it may also create problems in terms of discouraging the setting up of institutional forms which provide full citizenship for lesbians and gays. Here there is a tension between putting pressure on the state to gain citizenship rights and creating a space free from state interference to create identities and communities and live your life as you please.

The category of 'woman'

More recent debates inside feminism have led to argument about the need to reject the category of 'woman'. Carol Gilligan (1993) argues that women are different from men in that they have a different voice. This leads to questioning of equality with men as the aim of the women's movement and instead focuses on maintaining what are seen as the strengths and virtues of being women. This equality versus difference dilemma has arisen because of the rejection of the overarching notion of women as a result of the experience of the women's movement when there were divisions between white women and black women, lesbians and heterosexual women and middle-class and working-class women.

Such divisions led to the questioning of whether the term 'women' actually meant anything since a movement consisting of women contained so many conflicting groups. This point has led Judith Butler (1990) to argue that we should not use the term 'women', since this term represents a category that does not exist. Instead there are multiple possible ways of being a woman and therefore women are a socially constructed identity which exist only when there are actions which bring the identity into focus.

This sort of theory led to divisions inside the French women's movement. Leonard and Atkins (1996) point to the problems which arose when a group called Psychanalyse et Politique, founded after political upheaval in France in1968, based themselves on the notion that 'woman has never existed' and therefore declared themselves against feminism since this set out to liberate what for them was a non-existant object, women. There were also debates about whether the celebration of women in the form of the talk of women's cycles, rhythms, bodily fluids, insight, empathetic approach and more emotional view on life is a basis for liberation or instead a construction of a neo-femininity, which celebrates women as different from men and therefore can be seen by some as a backward step. All of this does, however, point to the potential complexities which exist around the deceptively simple question: 'What is a woman?' (See also Sections 4.1 and 17.8).

Disability, action and identity

Julia Twigg (1999) argues that we can trace the rise of the disability movement in the UK back to the 1970s and 1980s, to groups and individuals who wished to challenge the oppressive and demeaning way they were treated. Part of this movement also involved a redefinition of notions of disability away from an emphasis on individual impairment to a collective notion of disablement, which included the concept of the way that an uncaring and oppressive society treats people. Disability is therefore not something natural but, since it also involves the way some people treat other people, is a socially constructed notion. This idea is associated with the work of Michael Oliver (1990; Campbell and Oliver, 1996).

However, this idea is itself controversial since it has been subject to the criticism from authors such as Tom Shakespeare (1994) that the emphasis on the social construction of disability has led to an under-emphasis on individual impairment as an element of the experience of disability which has made it almost invisible. Equally Julia Twigg (2000) argues that greater emphasis in sociology on the body has meant that issues of body shape and impairment are now returning to the centre of the sociological and political agenda.

Arguments about what it means to be disabled and therefore the identity of disablement have come to greater prominence in recent years due to the 'care in the community' policies which impacted on the experience of disabled people and, more recently, attempts by the new Labour government to cut back on disability benefits. Equally arguments over developments in cloning and genetic science have led to notions of whether this will become a rather unpleasant version of social engineering which would threaten to remove disabled people, and the effect that this must have on the positive image that disabled people have built up through debates about the notion of disability and disability rights.

Age, action and identity

Vincent (1995) makes the point that there are a variety of ways of being old and again this illustrates the way in which conceptions of age are not biologically fixed but instead are social constructions which vary from place to place and time to time. In concrete terms, we can see one example of this in the UK at present where the age at which you retire is being changed gradually to equalise the sexes at 63. If the retirement age is seen as a key definer of being elderly then this can be seen as variable. In relation to the elderly provision of pensions and welfare benefits has been a key mobilizer of people in protest.

Johnson *et al.* (1989) argued that there was likely to be a war between the generations as less and less workers were required to pay the higher bill for the pension and welfare provisions of more and more elderly people. Clearly the changing age balance of the population has certainty created a debate about the possibility of a crisis in the welfare state. However, Hutton (1996) and Manning (1990) have both argued that there will not necessarily be a crisis and the ratio of welfare dependent to contributors will remain largely stable. Hutton (1996) also points out that with a very small rise in tax there will be the ability to keep the real value of pensions as they are. This is an important debate since the standard of living of the elderly does tend to depend on the generosity of the state and the real value of pensions fell relative to earnings in the 1980s and early 1990s. This did lead to moves to create a pensioners' movement led by the former union leader, Jack Jones.

In more recent years, there has also been a more positive image of the elderly with talk of life-long learning and the University of the Third Age. These are attempts to again change the conception of the identity of what it means to be a certain age and instead to suggest flexible interpretations of ageing.

Social class, action and identity

Although the rise of new social movements often occurred in a way that was hostile to notions of politics based on class, Alan Scott (1990) has argued that it is possible to see some similarities between the old movements such as the labour movement and the new social movements. He argues that these new social movements are best seen as part of a continuum that stretches from informal network associations to formal party-like organisations. This continuum would include new social movements but also pressure groups and political parties. On this basis it is possible to analyse class-based movements in terms of activity and identity. Equally it has been the case that the greater interest and emphasis shown in subjectivity and identity in political and sociological circles has meant a shift in class analysis away from merely assigning someone to a class to instead considering the subjective identity involved in notions of class.

Studies have found that although many have talked about the death of class, in terms of identity at least this argument may be premature. There are two key examples of this we could cite. Mackintosh and Mooney (2000) provide the following summary of the importance of class as a basis of identity:

The British Social Attitudes Survey provides one regular source of evidence of how class permeates people's understanding of society. The 1995–96 edition showed that 69 per cent of people surveyed thought that a person's social class affected his opportunities a 'great deal' or 'quite a lot' (Jowell et al., 1995). In a

different 1996 survey, two-thirds of those interviewed agreed that 'there is one law for the rich and one for the poor' and that 'ordinary people do not get a fair share of the nation's wealth' (Adonis and Pollard, 1998, p. 11).

Social class can provide us with a sense of belonging; it can tell us who 'we' are and who 'they' are and hence, how to relate to the world around us. Many people see the UK as a society sharply divided by class divisions and inequalties, but it does not follow that individuals have a strongly developed sense of class identity. Whether, or how strongly, you identify yourself as a member of social class will be shaped by your personal history, including your family background, your occuptiaon, and your personal experiences of struggle and conflict. While some people ... see 'working class' as a positive label they can identify with, others reject the term as stigmatizing or patronizing.

(Mackintosh and Mooney, 2000, pp. 95–6)

They go on to include a diagram from the *Guardian* (reproduced below) which shows that between 1966 and 1997 the proportion of 'Don't Knows' fell in terms of identity meaning the proportion defining themselves in class terms increased. It also shows that a majority defined themselves as working class. (See also Section 4.4.)

Discussion point

What do Mackintosh and Mooney mean when they say that: 'Many people see the UK as a society sharply divided by class divisions and inequalities, but it does not follow that individuals have a strongly developed sense of class identity'? What are the implications of this for political activity?

C3.1a

A second example is the results of a survey conducted for the *New Statesman* by Gallup. Gallup's long-running poll results on the British public's awareness of 'a class struggle' would seem to be further indication of growing awareness of 'the hardening of class inequalities' in modern times (see Table 15.3).

John Westergaard

As a result, there have been those who have been willing to defend the importance of class as a basis of identity and also as a potential basis for political action. John Westergaard describes the

Table 15.3 Gallup's long-running poll result

'There used to be a lot of talk in politics about a "class struggle". Do you think there is a class struggle in this country or not?'

	'Is'	'Is not'	'Don't know'
1961 (Dec)	56	22	22
1964 (Aug)	48	39	13
1972 (Jun)	58	29	13
1973 (Feb)	53	33	14
1973 (Apr)	60	29	11
1973 (Dec)	57	29	14
1974 (Jan)	58	31	11
1974 (Feb)	62	27	11
1974 (Apr)	60	29	12
1975 (May)	60	29	11
1981 (Mar)	66	25	9
1984 (Mar)	74	20	6
1986 (Feb)	70	24	6
1991 (Jul)	79	16	4
1993 (Sep)	77	17	6
1994 (Mar)	78	16	7
1995 (Nov)	81	12	7
1996 (Aug)	76	15	9

1996 percentage agreement by voting intention. Labour 81, Conservative 66, Liberal Democrat 77

Source: Gallup Organization

class-eclipse theorists as engaging in sociological fantasy rather than fact. The facts of income inequality signify a widening of consumer inequalities of choice. He concludes that all this has made for more class-divided life experiences

Activity

a Describe in your own words the overall trend suggested by the information in Table 15.3.

b Using information from this section and elsewhere, to what extent do you either agree or disagree with the claim that class still remains a key basis of identity and a potential basis for political action

C3.2, C3.3

in all respects, including illness and the risks of death. Westergaard also notes that class-denial theorists have been too quick to announce the eclipse of class politics. He contends that voters still vote as much along class lines as they did in relative terms in the 1960s and 70s. Importantly they continue to show unease about inequality generally and concentration of power at the top.

Lee and Turner concur, with the conclusion that:

... the existence of class divisions and their profound effects on people's lives is an objective finding which sociology can claim to have established.

(Lee and Turner, 1996, p. 9)

A risk society?

Beck (1992) suggests that, rather than having entered a period of post-modernity, instead we have reached a further stage of modernity – *reflective modernity*. In reflective modernity, Beck argues that we have created a *risk society*:

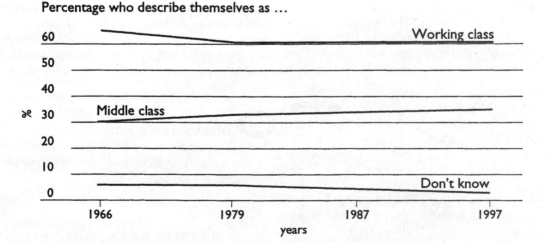

Figure 15.2 Identity in terms of class in Britain, 1999
Source: Guardian, 15 January 1999, quoted in Mackintosh and Mooney (2000, p. 96)

the fundamental organizational principle of most lifestyles is the avoidance of risk or danger. Individual identity is therefore based on the adoption of a lifestyle that avoids the problems created by capitalist production and industrialization – such as pollution, exposure to dangerous levels of ozone, etc.

Viewed in this way, modern society (as opposed to a post-modern society) poses particular problems for the individuals involved. One solution to these problems, one way to avoid the risks, is to adopt a lifestyle based on membership or association with a new social movement. Beck identifies the growth of the green movement to be a specific response to living in a risk society.

Criticisms of new social movements

Callinicos (1989), writing from a Marxist perspective, rejects a post-modern analysis of the growth of new social movements. He suggests, instead, that internationally or collectively a working class can still be identified, and class inequality does still exist. Further, this working class still retains powerful political movements which operate alongside new social movements, rather than having been replaced by them.

Hirst (1993a), from an updated pluralist (or neo-pluralist) stance, is critical of the claim made by some that the future of political struggle rests with new social movements. He suggests that they are based on such loose associations and networks that they contribute virtually nothing to political life: they are too fragmented to challenge effectively the existing nature of the distribution of power.

> ### 💬 Discussion point
> To what extent has contemporary political protest moved away from a traditional class-based notion of political struggle and inequality? What forms do contemporary political protests take, and around what issues?
>
> C3.1a

15.2 Globalization and nationalism

In contemporary sociology, few terms have been given as much importance in recent years as 'globalization'. As Waters (1995) notes:

Social change is now proceeding so rapidly that if a sociologist had proposed as recently as ten years *ago to write a book about globalization they would have had to overcome a wall of stony and bemused incomprehension. But now, just as post-modernism was the concept of the 1980s, globalization may be the concept of the 1990s, a key idea by which we understand the transition of human society into the third millenium.*

(Waters, 1995, p. 1)

For Waters, globalization can be defined as:

A social process in which the constraints of geography on social and cultural arrangements recede and in which people become increasingly aware that they are receding.

(Waters, 1995, p. 3)

> ### 📝 Activity
> Using the definition supplied by Waters, create a list of aspects of your own social life which could be seen to have been influenced by global forces.
>
> C3.2, C3.3

> ### 💬 Discussion point
> Can countries manage their own political affairs separately from other countries, or are we all inter-dependent?
>
> C3.1a

The end of ideology?

Fukuyama (1992), from a right-wing perspective, has proclaimed a forthcoming end of history – whereby a global consensus based on liberal democracy will become the ruling political system. Fukuyama's ideas echo those of earlier theorists who charted the rise of post-industrial societies in which we see the 'end of ideology' – where the East and West converge ideologically – and a new world order is established around democracy.

> ### 💬 Discussion point
> To what extent do we live in a new world order, where East and West have converged and consensus politics rule?
>
> C3.1a

Critics of this idea – particularly from a Marxist or neo-Marxist stance – point out that, rather than an equal convergence between East and

West, what in fact lies at the heart of these ideas is the belief in the process of westernization across the globe. With the collapse of the USSR and related self-proclaimed communist systems, the western 'liberal–capitalist–democratic' model of political organization is seen to have won the Cold War.

Globalization and the success of capitalism

For many of the New Right, globalization can be equated with the collapse of so-called communism and the establishment of free markets on a truly international scale. Establishment of the World Bank, the International Monetary Fund (IMF) and to a lesser extent the European Union (EU) indicates the growth of new markets – the expansion of a world economy and of world capitalism.

Equally, the growth of globalization can be seen in terms other than economic ones: growth of the United Nations (UN) as a peace-keeping force, and the European Court of Human Rights, may serve as examples of modern international politics.

For many who take a Marxist or neo-Marxist perspective, globalization – whether economic, cultural or military – is seen as yet further evidence of the Americanization of the globe.

Although the increased expansion of global free markets would be an opportunity embraced by many on the New Right, globalization also holds its more sinister side for those of this political view. If applied to the international regulation of laws, globalization is seen by some on the New Right to raise problems of national sovereignty. Global courts and their laws may have the power to veto, or block, an individual nation-state's law-making process. If this were the case, national sovereignty and citizenship may be called into question.

Multinational companies and the power of capital

Lash and Urry (1987) claim that modern societies have reached a new global stage in historical development, whereby disorganized capitalism has occurred. That is to say, multinational (or transnational) companies exist separately from a particular home country, and they can undermine the power of a national economy. These companies have shifted their manufacturing operations to the *underdeveloped world*, where labour power is cheaper (see Section 12.5). As as a result a decline in class politics is occurring, because in the West employment is changing from manufacturing to service industries – traditional working-class jobs are being lost, as are the political significance of traditional working-class movements.

Sklair (1991) suggests that sociological analysis must now rethink how it conceptualizes politics in the light of these global forces.

Is the nation-state dead?

For many commentators, then, globalization and not nationalism is the prime sociological category of the present age. However, the death of the nation-state is far from certain. For example, Hirst (1993b) argues that state intervention is still required from time to time to bail out capitalist economies from crises, and therefore a truly independent, global free-market economy is impossible.

Fukuyama (1992) claims that the new world order will be one where capitalist economics dominate the globe and consensus politics emerges between the once-opposed East and West. Others such as Van der Pijl (1989) argue that globalization brings with it the development of global class struggle. Rather than class politics dying, Van der Pijl argues that the old fight between capital and labour is transferred on to a larger, global stage, where transnational companies exploit a transnational working class – who share a common alienated experience of work.

Nationalism, globalization and self-identity

By 'globalization', sociologists usually mean the process whereby societies, communities and individuals are increasingly *interconnected* around the world (McGrew, 1992). Social processes in one part of the world impact on those in other parts. The cultural implications of globalization have been of particular interest. (The sociological arguments about globalization

ts implications are also explored in Sections
.nd 4.5.)

Globalization is sometimes portrayed as a
process in which the individual is helpless; a
process through which the multinational cultural
conglomerates come to dominate popular culture
across the world in a relentless way.

Critics, including some Marxists, would argue
that this is, indeed, happening. Cultural homogenization (the wiping out of regional and local
cultures) will accelerate as the same fast-food outlets, the same cola advertisements, the same
fashions, the same satellite television shows, and
the same popular music, proliferate around the
world. After all, Rupert Murdoch, owner of News
Corporation, with huge media interests in
America, the UK, Europe and Asia, has indicated
that his strategy is to find the cultural common
denominator that will allow him to market the
same cultural commodities through all the parts
of the globe in which he has an interest. The common formula, he thinks, is sport plus rock music.

Three scenarios on the effect of globalization

In considering the relationship between national
identity and globalization, Stuart Hall (1992b, p.
300) identifies three possible scenarios:

- *Cultural homogenization.* National identities
  and culture are eroded by the impact of global
  cultural industries and multinational media.
- *Cultural resistance.* National and local cultures
  may be strengthened if members of nations and
  local communities consciously resist the impact
  of cultural globalization. The French state, for
  example, passed legislation intended to reverse
  the creeping Americanization of its language
  and culture. In most parts of the globe there are
  cultural resistance movements of one kind or
  another, each struggling to preserve a sense of
  national, regional or local identity.
- *The emergence of 'new identities of hybridity'.*
  Globalization may encourage a circulation of
  cultural elements and images which allows
  local communities to create new 'hybrid' identities. Gillespie's study of Punjabi youth in
  Southall (see the case study in Section 4.3)
  demonstrates clearly the impact of global influences in the process of constructing a new
  youth subculture, but they are fused with
  strong traditional influences as well.

Cultural homogenization, or cultural resistance?

A number of writers favour the cultural homogenization thesis and there is considerable evidence to support their views.

In 1997, Tunstall pointed to the global dominance of American culture. More recently, the
experience of Canada has prompted writers to
conclude that global communication systems make
it very difficult for nation states to protect national
cultural identities even when they use state legislation (Perlmutter, 1993; Collins, 1985). Canada
has been anxious to limit the impact of US media
on Canadian cultural life but it has been unable to
prevent a steady movement of audience away from
the Canadian national broadcasting system
towards US satellite stations which reach across
the border, or the dominance of Canadian cinema
by US-based multinationals. This is despite the
efforts of the Canadian government in encouraging national cultural projects.

In Europe, similar fears are now being
expressed about the dominance of multinational
media conglomerates and their impact on
national cultures, particularly since many
European governments have deregulated to allow
market forces a greater influence in media markets (Petley and Romano, 1993; Blumler, 1992a).

However, there are some important criticisms
of the cultural homogenization model which
encourage a more optimistic interpretation, and
the idea of cultural resistance. As Robins (1991)
points out, even if multinational media conglomerates enjoy an increasing influence, *this may not
necessarily lead to the eradication of cultural
differences.* He argues that successful global conglomerates will exploit local cultures and identities commercially, rather than try to eradicate
them. This is what Sony, the Japanese electronic
and media corporation, calls 'global localization'.
The Coca Cola Corporation describes itself as
'multi-local', rather than multinational.

Case Study – MTV in Europe

Further evidence to support Robins' thesis is provided by a study of MTV in Europe (Sturmer,
1993). MTV, the television rock music station,
was launched in 1981 when it reached 1.5 million households. By 1991 it reached 201 million
households in 77 countries, across five continents. Given the global reach of MTV and the

nature of popular music, this example might be regarded as a good illustration of the cultural homogenization thesis.

However, as Sturmer shows, the situation is more complex. The European branch of MTV (MTVE) is based in London but broadcasts to the whole of Europe, including Scandinavia and eastern Europe. It is largely independent of its US parent company; its choice of videos and programming strategy represent a conscious attempt to avoid Americanization. There is a strong emphasis on European music, such as 'Euro pop' and 'indie', while attempts are made through audience request shows to establish a relationship with European audiences.

Sturmer does note, nevertheless, that the uneven distribution of wealth and living standards within Europe means that MTVE's marketing strategy is oriented more towards northern Europe, with less attention given to the local cultures and identities of young people in southern and eastern Europe.

Perhaps the most important evidence concerns the response of audiences. Are they embracing a 'Euro-culture'? The varying degree of success of MTVE suggests that local cultural differences are still very important in determining audience responses. MTVE is hugely popular in Sweden but less successful in Italy. Most interestingly, MTVE's rap programme *Yo!*, which *is* imported from the USA, has enjoyed a very mixed response. While it is one of the more popular shows across Europe as a whole, it is much less successful in the UK and France where there are very strong indigenous rap and jungle music scenes. This may indicate that in certain circumstances local culture can resist global influences. For Sturmer:

The differing reactions to Yo! *in Germany and the UK, or to the channel as a whole in Sweden, Poland or Italy, indicate that as MTVE strives to build its European profile it is at the same time reflecting and helping to create a range of diverse and surprising 'imaginary continents' for and with its young audience.*
(Sturmer, 1993, p. 65)

New identities of hybridity

The third possible scenario identified by Hall is the emergence of 'new identities of hybridity'. Hall points out that globalization through the spread of western cultural influences around the globe is as old as colonialization and certainly not a new phenomenon. What was new was the volume of migration from one society to another in the second half of the twentieth century. By 1990, one in every four Americans came from an African–American, Asian–American or American–Indian background.

In Europe, migration has brought strong cultural influences from, for example, North Africa, Turkey, Senegal, Zaire, the Caribbean, Bangladesh, Pakistan, India, Kenya, Uganda and Sri Lanka. These are the new post-colonial diaspora (dispersions of peoples and cultures). In this way, globalization has made much more complex the issue of national identity: there is now a 'pluralization of national cultures and national identities' (Hall, 1992b, p. 307). The simple existence of *different* cultures within one nation makes the concept of a 'national culture' much more problematic but it also makes the emergence of new cultural identities possible through a process of cross-fertilization.

However, Hall makes it clear that the emergence of new hybrid cultures is not inevitable. First, local communities may respond to the influence of globalization through a fierce reassertion of tradition and fixed ethnicity (he points to the rise of national and religious fundamentalists around the world). Secondly, cultural exchange is never an even or equal process. The cultures of minority communities will also reflect the experience of racism, and the opportunities for creating new subcultural identities will be constrained by the continuing dominance of white mainstream culture in schooling, the mass media, and so on.

Activity

a Stuart Hall identifies three possible consequences of globalization. Identify and explain each one.

b Summarize briefly some of the evidence which points to: (i) growing cultural homogenization, (ii) continuing cultural resistance, and (iii) the emergence of cultural hybridity.

C3.2, C3.3

15.3 Forms and patterns of political action

Types of direct action

For many social commentators, voting is to be the limit of political action in society that is considered. While voting and participation in electoral politics is indeed an important and, at least in relation to general elections, relatively popular activity, it is also clear that there are other actions beside voting that people consistently engage in with political aims. As the job of sociologists is to consider the whole of human society, it is important that these forms of action are considered, and also the explanations sociologists and other thinkers have developed as to the nature and the reasons for the existence of these other forms of political action.

This section will therefore consider a variety of actions that affect the political arena, including riots, terrorism, demonstrations and strikes.

Riots

Riots are large-scale, usually short-duration, outbursts usually motivated by extremely strong sentiments held by a section or sections of society. We will consider some contemporary examples of riots here, and also examine some explanations of the place and role of riots in contemporary life.

We start by looking at examples from the developing world, where interventions by western banks and attempts to convince governments of the need to cut back on public expenditure have led to some very strong riots in protest at the effect on people's lives.

The IMF, structural adjustment plans and hunger riots

In the wake of the Third World 'debt crisis', private commercial lending to these countries dried up and developing countries were left with little alternative but to ask for assistance from the World Bank and the IMF (International Monetary Fund). The World Bank is charged with promoting development, and the IMF is involved because in many cases it acts as factfinder for the Bank. Membership of the Bank is conditional on membership of the IMF. These institutions will pro-

vide help only if certain conditions are agreed to by those they are helping. It is the nature of the conditions applied that have caused controversy. New loans to help countries with debt problems were have been made conditional on the countries undertaking certain economic and social reforms.

Both the World Bank and the IMF subscribe to free-market beliefs, including the beliefs that:

- economic growth can come only from opening up national economies to the world market
- development requires governments to pursue policies of economic stabilization
- wealth will 'trickle down' from the rich to the poor.

'Structural adjustment plans' (SAPs) form the centrepiece of the demands made on borrowers. Walton and Seddon (1994) describe their introduction in 1980 and state that 37 were implemented between 1980 and 1986. Typically they involved 19 policy measures with up to 100 separate conditions. Jackson provides the following brief description of a typical set of policy requirements:

The classic IMF treatment consists of short, sharp, shock-tactics of financial belt-tightening to skim off foreign exchange for debt payment. The strategy relies on cutting imports (to save foreign currency), increasing exports (to earn more of it), and cutting government spending.

(Jackson, 1994, p. 109)

While in economic terms some of these policies would lead to some degree of stability, the overall economic effect is very recessionary. With up to 40 countries trying simultaneously to increase their exports the result is a glut of products, a fall in prices and therefore in export earnings. For example, despite increasing its exports of rubber by 31 per cent, Thailand saw its earnings from this fall by 8 per cent.

There has also been great concern at the human and social cost of SAPs. George (1988) points out that, according to one study, of 196 objectives applied by the IMF only once was the aim specifically included to protect poor people from the effects of adjustment.

It is the poor who have suffered most, often seeing their standard of living drop dramatically. Cuts in government spending often include cuts in food subsidies and in educational and health provision. Walton and Seddon (1994) estimate that in some countries the loss of real income in the 1980s varied between 10 and 40 per cent, and they also quote UN figures showing that over 1000 children a day continue to die in Africa – a grim statistic the UN puts down to the effects of the 'debt crisis' and the fall in commodity prices.

The people of the developing countries are not simply victims who passively accept this erosion of their living standards. Much of the developing world has seen food riots in response to the adjustments demanded by international financial agencies. Walton and Seddon (1994) list a total of 146 such riots in 39 different countries between 1976 and 1992. Twelve countries had a single riot in this period, including Egypt, Turkey, Tunisia, Niger and Iran. In other countries the scale of protest was much bigger, as Table 15.4 shows.

Table 15.4 Some austerity protests, 1976–92

Country	Date of first protest	Number of protests
Peru	July 1976	14
Argentina	March 1982	11
Chile	October 1982	7
Bolivia	March 1983	13
Brazil	April 1983	11
Haiti	May 1985	6
Yugoslavia	November 1986	7
Poland	March 1987	6
Venezuela	February 1989	7
India	February 1992	3

Source: Adapted from Walton and Seddon (1994, p. 39)

George has commented on this situation as follows:

Will the IMF succeed where Marx failed? Riots – which might well one day become revolutions – are more frequently set off in our time by the Fund's austerity programme, prescribed as a means to pay off debts, than by the 'communist subversion' the West claims to fear.

(George, 1988, p. 77)

Walton and Seddon (1994) argue that the two key factors which lay behind these protests were (a) urbanization and (b) the involvement of international agencies such as the IMF in domestic political and economic policy. Urbanization, they assert, results in high levels of trade union, political and community organization capable of organizing mass protests in a way that scattered

peasant communities cannot. Government implementation of structural adjustment plans was behind price rises and wage cuts that were the spur to these riots.

No more riots?

There are some sociologists who have claimed that large-scale rebellion in contemporary western society is unlikely. Cooke, for instance, makes the following claim:

Post-modern Britain looks no more collectively rebellious a society than the USA. The urban masses of both countries have been stupefied by the invasion of their relatively secure world of employment by Thatcherism, Reaganomics and world industrial recession, they are the subjects of more proficient surveillance than ever before and are policed in Britain, as in the USA, by increasingly abrasive methods of social control.

(Cooke, 1988, p. 489)

Cooke, a post-modernist, suggests that it is now likely that we will no longer see collective rebellion in urban society because the 'masses' have been 'stupefied', or ground into submission. We now consider whether such submission has been gained by the ruling élite of urban society, and if a rebellion is likely from the working classes.

Riots and urban social movements

M. Castells, a Marxist, began a debate in the 1970s to suggest that political resistance was likely to come from urban social movements, being groups based on consumption rather than production. This is the issue we take up here.

Urban riots became a major topic of debate in the 1980s, taking place in many of the UK's towns and cities during that decade (and since). However, these British riots were not without precedent. Field (1982) notes that instances such as collective attacks on the police, arson, widespread looting and the contagion of riots from town to town had all occurred previously during this century. We might also note that urban riots are not unique to the UK; the USA has also suffered similar disorders throughout this century, a recent prominent example being the riots in Los Angeles in 1992.

Communal and commodity riots

Janowitz (1979), looking specifically at the USA, offers a useful distinction between 'communal riots' and 'commodity riots' to account for changing patterns of collective racial violence.

Communal riots were the 'typical' 'race' riots during and immediately after World War I. They were the result of a clash between blacks and whites over rights of settlement in particular areas, with whites leading violent attacks on what they feared were expanding boundaries of black communities. British riots of 1959 which occurred in Nottingham and Notting Hill (London) could be seen as examples of communal riots.

According to Janowitz, commodity riots – which were large-scale outbursts within the community of black people – became more prevalent after World War II. He believes they represented a form of collective behaviour against the 'agents and symbols' of the wider society. They were described as commodity riots because they were associated with outbursts of looting and, he suggests, had their high point in the period between 1964 and 1967 (for example in the Watts area of Los Angeles in 1965).

Commodity riots lacked any conspiratorial quality. They were likely to be set off by an actual or perceived malpractice by the police. This led to stoning of the police, the development of a crowd and mounting tensions. The second phase of the riot would involve breaking of windows, a breakdown of local social control and perception of the temporary opportunity for looting. A final phase developed if the crowd was not dispersed and involved arson attacks and possible sniper fire and a military-type response by a combined force of the police and army. Initially participants were likely to be over-represented by single, young, unemployed men who formed part of the informal street community. The looters who joined the riots after they were under way were more likely to be part of the 'respectable' adult world.

Such actions could be explained by the failure of the black civil rights movement to produce social change for the populations they represented through legal/'democratic' political channels. As such they were outbursts against the perceived 'double standards' for the black and white people, the latter being seen as politically, economically and socially advantaged.

We will see that many of the riots that have taken place in the UK and the USA since this classic 'ideal type' description have followed the anticipated pattern almost directly. Yet Janowitz lacked the ability to see this application in the future as he saw blacks 'acting' rather than 'reacting'. Since the 1960s, he believes, collective violence has been characterized by 'political

racial violence', terroristic-style violence by small groups of organized blacks against whites. Certainly this has not come to popular public consciousness, although ethnic minorities in the USA and UK did, at various times, form vigilante defence groups to protect their communities.

Riots in the UK

British riots which took place in the late 1970s and early 80s – beginning with the St Paul's district of Bristol, studied by Pryce (1986) – bore a number of similarities to the US commodity riots. They virtually all started in the same way, with the spark being actual or perceived aggressive behaviour by the police. In each case the primary grievances were seen to be aggressive police practices, unemployment, poor housing conditions and the discrimination felt by the minority communities. One exception to this was in Southall in 1981, where the Asian community reacted to violence and 'violation of their community' by National Front activists – thus this was more of a 'communal riot'.

A major government enquiry led by Lord Scarman (1982) explained that young inner-city inhabitants were being raised in insecure social and economic conditions, in an impoverished environment. They shared the same desires and expectations as the society at large, but faced discrimination that caused frustration when their expectations were not met. The report called for an effective and co-ordinated approach to tackling inner-city problems: consultation of local communities, by both private and public bodies. The needs of ethnic minorities with regard to housing, education and employment needed to be more readily recognized. However, as argued by many of the contributors to Benyon's (1984) *Scarman and After*, the two years following the report saw little evidence of a response. Disadvantage and discrimination were likely to continue, was the message, unless the problems of the inner city and ethnic minorities in particular were solved.

Discussion point

Bearing in mind what the UK government has done to revitalize inner-city areas can we argue that it has finally responded to the Scarman Report and that urban riots are likely to be a thing of the past?

C3.1a

Riots in largely ethnic-minority areas such as Brixton (in 1995) and Bradford (also in 1995), as well as on council estates that have predominantly white residents like Blackbird Leys in Oxford (in 1991) and Meadow Well in Newcastle (also in 1991), suggest that violent urban protest is likely to continue, particularly if we accept the opinion of many critical commentators that their underlying structural causes have not been remedied.

The Los Angeles riot of 1992

A similar situation was evident in the USA following the trial of a group of LA policemen who were accused – and then acquitted – of unlawfully beating Rodney King, a black motorist. The beating had been captured fully on video and shown on television. The not-guilty verdict was felt to be unacceptable, not least to blacks in Los Angeles who rioted for five days before being quelled by 6000 National Guards and 1000 federal police:

Over the next few days, disturbances broke out across America as people from every background protested against the injustice of the Rodney King verdict.

(Jackson, 1992, p. 13)

Jackson reports the underlying causes as the growing polarization between wealthy whites and poor blacks, the social marginalization of the poorest blacks in inner-city ghettos, reductions in government spending on urban redevelopment, and a younger generation of black people who are not as willing to compromise as their parents had been.

Urban riots and urban social movements

The suggestion so far seems to be that urban riots are not infrequent forms of political protest. We now need to consider how we define those who riot and whether rioting is the only form of urban political protest. In general, it would appear that urban rioters are a homogeneous, yet disorganized, group of people who feel segregated and disenfranchised. Rioting appears to be the only way they have to voice their concerns and resentment. Pure Marxists might see them as part of the working-class mass; pure Weberians might note the combination of their class and ethnic status.

Such issues have come to light in the debate about 'urban social movements', a concept developed by the Marxist, Manuel Castells. He saw them as:

... organizations standing outside the formal party systems which bring people together to defend or challenge the provision of urban public services and to protect the local environment.

(Castells, 1983; quoted in Lowe, 1988, p. 456)

Although rioters are reported to be disorganized, their aim is similar so we might be able to apply some of the principles from the debate.

Castells' earlier writing was very much influenced by what he had seen in France, especially the riots and protests in Paris in 1968. Groups such as the squatter movement were geared towards stopping the massive urban renewal programmes. This led Castells to believe the protest movement was not in itself a strictly working-class movement (students had been heavily involved), based around factory production, as might have been expected by pure Marxists; but rather a movement of consumers of urban public services. Initially he saw these movements as of secondary importance to class-based ones, but after visiting the USA and noting a wide variety of social movements, he moved to the position that they arose independently of class and act as autonomous organizations 'against the logic, interest and values of the dominant class'. The importance of class-based protest had declined with the globalization of production which had reduced people's abilities to control their own lives. As Kirby (1995) notes:

... people try to control their lives by controlling their locality. The urban social movements are thus a defensive reaction to structural change in the world which has made the old forms of movement obsolete.

(Kirby, 1995, p. 76)

However, Castells' theory of urban social movements has been criticized on at least two counts. First, he sees their role as radical, trying to redress disadvantages in service provision, whereas many urban pressure groups now seek to protect their advantages. For example, middle-class 'nimby's' ('not-in-my-back-yard') may form groups to protect their residential areas from redevelopment for roads, new housing and the like (Urry, 1990a). Secondly, many recent urban protests have been about environmental issues rather than collective consumption of state services, which the theory of urban social movements cannot account for (Bagguley, 1993).

Thus the debate about 'urban social movements' has developed into a wider contemporary debate about 'new social movements'. A particularly relevant idea for us regarding new social movements comes from Beck (1992), who suggests that class inequality has been supplemented by 'risks' to which everyone, no matter what social class, is susceptible. For example, environmental hazards and pollution are 'risks' to which all people are subject, although others might argue that inner urban residents (who tend to be poorer) are more at risk than middle-class ruralites. Certainly urban environmental protest groups have become more common. Groups such as 'Reclaim the Streets' have taken to direct action like blocking streets to make their point to car-drivers and policy-makers. Bellos (1996), a journalist, noted how single-issue direct-action protest groups were beginning a process of 'cross-fertilization' (working together), and quoted P. Deluce of Corporate Watch (an organization aiming to help others campaigning against large corporations) who said:

Pick any issue and there is a multitude of issues. Newbury ... [scene of a protest over the building of a bypass] ... is not just about the environment. It is also about transport, housing and biodiversity. We are interested in jobs and local communities needs. Calling them single issues is only trying to marginalize them.

(Bellos, 1996)

Bagguley (1993), in a useful attempt to clarify the debate, offers some direct contrasts between 'old' (or 'urban') and 'new' social movements, suggesting that they might be seen on a continuum between two pure types. The former are based around economic issues, with their values stemming from their relationship to the means of production. They generally have a working-class base and are represented by officials in bureaucratic organizations who work towards discussion and compromise. New social movements differ in that they are concerned with issues beyond the workplace, such as the environment or human rights, based on the importance of each individual and their cultural identity. They are more likely to have a middle-class base, be organized around localized networks, and have no particular spokesperson or leader. They are likely to work towards an ultimate end with no compromise.

How urban rioters are classified obviously depends on how we assess their aims and whether we think they have acted as an organized mass. It is clear that they have tended to be socially disadvantaged, working class and/or from an ethnic minority, and they have been somewhat aggrieved by a lack of service provision, which might allow us to label them 'old' or 'urban social movements'. However, they do not appear to have any bureaucratic organization, leadership, or in the short term be ready to compromise (they tend to be 'controlled' into submission), which might make them a 'new social movement'. They do tend to have qualities of both new and old movements, but given their spontaneous uprising and their almost as sudden disappearance it would be worth questioning whether rioters represent a 'movement' in any real sense.

Activity

Make notes on the following using material from the above section.

a To what extent can the concept of an 'urban social movement' be applied to the recent urban rioters in the UK and the USA?

b To what extent have 'new social movements' been effective, particularly on environmental issues?

c Are there political issues in your local area that have inspired widespread opposition? Have the various viewpoints inspired urban or new social movements? How successful have they been? How can you account for that?

What is certain is that urban living does create the conditions for a variety of communal groupings or movements. How these develop in the future will continue to be the stimulus for further sociological speculation and research.

The anti-capitalism riots in December 1999

The meeting of the World Trade Organization (WTO) in Seattle in the USA in December 1999 led to mass protests including some riots. This became known as the Battle of Seattle. Protests were coordinated worldwide using the resources of the Internet and this included protests in London as the report opposite shows.

RIOTERS STILL DEFIANT

WILL WOODWARD

ORGANISERS of the rally in London that led to Tuesday night's riot at Euston station yesterday blamed the violence on capitalism.

Police said they had mounted a 'very successful operation' in controlling the riot, during which seven people were injured, a police van set alight and bus stops smashed.

Five people were charged yesterday after the violence that began at the end of the 'N30' rally, linked to worldwide protests against the world trade summit in Seattle.

Mark Sully of Reclaim the Streets, the loose 'disorganisation' behind the Euston rally and the June 18 protest that led to riots in the City of London, said last night: 'We'd say the fault was capitalism's. If you are focusing on the police and one box on wheels getting turned over, it's not very important when you consider that this economic system is responsible for the destruction of people's livelihoods.'

Mr Sully said the group had expected there would be a 'sort of street party' after the rally but that 'they came up against police'. He refused to condemn attacks on officers. 'If capitalism is to be overturned then there might be some violence as well,' he said.

Police in riot gear were brought in to fend off and separate hundreds of protesters who charged at them. Some protesters were penned in for several hours as police contained the crowd and made arrests. Euston rail terminal and five tube stations were closed for a spell.

At a press conference yesterday, the Metropolitan police deputy assistant commissioner Andy Trotter praised 'very good sharp, fast assertive policing which I think kept the injury level down and kept the damage level down.'

Three officers were injured, most seriously PC Paul Squires, who suffered spinal injuries after he was hit on the head by a metal bin.

Mr Trotter said of the violence: 'It's not terribly dissimilar to what happens on high streets on Saturday nights except this time it's attached to a demonstration.' Several of those arrested had been under the influence of drugs or drink.

Forty arrests were made on Tuesday, although four were in relation to offences at the June 18 protest. Up until the riot began just three people had been arrested in a day of mainly peaceful demonstrations against capitalism.

Source: Adapted from the *Guardian*, 2 December, 1999

Discussion point

How successful might riots be against capitalism?

C3.1a

Theories of riots and revolutions

Psychological theories

One of the most notable theories of revolutionary movements and riots was developed by Gustav Le Bon (1913, 1960). This essentially psychological theory suggests that collective political action is irrational and that therefore riots and revolutions are the result of people being in the throes of irrational moods, which may lead them to engage in large-scale acts of violence.

The key problem with this is that revolutions are not always that violent. In the Russian revolution in 1917 a total of 5 people were killed in capturing the Winter Palace in St Petersburg (Kirby, 1995, p. 116).

Functionalist theories

Given that functionalists consider that the normal or equilibrium state of society is characterized by consensus and harmony, social change through riots and revolutions are seen as abnormal anomalies.

The key cause is seen as a disequilibrium between various levels in society, notably between the economic and the moral. For Durkheim (1893), the fact that economic growth could outstrip the growth of moral regulation would lead to a period of *anomie*. He argued that such a period would be characterised by a number of things, including strikes and industrial and political conflict.

Johnson argues that technological change has a similar effect. This, combined with a loss of legitimacy by political élites and the outrunning of the societal value system, can lead to revolution.

Marxist theories

For Marxists, revolutions and direct political action are expected and predicted events in society. Marx argued that class societies break down because they each contain the seeds of their own destruction. Thus in capitalism, goods that are produced go unsold because workers cannot afford to buy them. This means there is a crisis of overproduction, not relative to needs but instead relative to profitable sale of goods.

Such crises are endemic to capitalism and over time this may lead workers to organize to campaign against and eventually to overthrow capitalism. Marxists argue that the key cause of revolutions and riots will not be abolished until capitalism is itself abolished.

Neo-Weberian theories

In contrast, Weberian thinkers have tended to argue that revolutions and riots are caused by problems in the state mechanism itself. Weberian writers have criticized Marxists for what they see as economic determinism: that is, arguing that the actions of the state are somehow effectively limited by the economic structure of society.

In contrast, Weberians argue that there is a need to view the state and indeed other structures as largely autonomous of each other.

Political actions and political crises are therefore the result of fissures or problems in the political structures of society, notably the state. This argument is best outlined in Skcopol (1979). She argues that military and economic competition which leads to the collapse of state structures for those on the losing side (and sometimes for those on the winning side) is the key cause of revolutions.

This emphasis on war and the military can also be seen in other neo-Weberian writers such as Giddens (1985) and Michael Mann (1986).

Marxists argue that the ability to wage war depends on the economic structures of society and also that the military machine is also sometimes used for internal repression as well as external aggression.

As the above demonstrates, there are many psychological and sociological theories on the cause of riots and revolutions.

Terrorism

Terrorism involves the use of force to achieve political ends. It first emerged as a political description of what went on after the French revolution (1789). The term itself tends to have a pejorative meaning in that terrorists induce terror and this is seen as a bad thing. It is usually the case, though, that one person's terrorist will be another person's freedom fighter. After all, one of the world's most famous terrorists (according to his jailers, the South African government) was Nelson Mandela. It is also the case that some people distinguish between guerrilla movements, who have specific military installations or personnel as targets, and terrorists, who are said also to operate against the civilian population. However, this distinction does not seem to be a very clear one.

Terrorism is seen as being a justified fight for freedom by people who believe there is no other possible or effective way of influencing the political process in their country other than through direct and violent methods.

The justification for terrorism in South Africa was held by many around the world to be the fact that the apartheid system denied the vote to the vast majority of the population, who were also treated dreadfully and oppressed by the state.

Lack of democracy was a feature of many colonial situations so it is not surprising to find that movements that may be described as terrorists have emerged as freedom fighters in many ex-colonies. Indeed it is as nationalist or anti-colonial movements for freedom that many terrorist organizations have emerged. Examples of such movements include the following:

- El Fatah – campaigning for a Palestinian state against Israel and those who support Israel
- Euzkadi ta Askatasuna (ETA) – campaigning for a Basque state against both France and Spain
- Front de la Liberation Nationalise Corse (FLNC) – for Corsican nationalism against the French state
- Irish Republican Army (IRA) – for Irish nationalism against the UK.

Source: Adapted from Giddens (1989, p. 366)

In the UK it is the last example that has been heard of the most. At the time of writing the peace process in Northern Ireland is moving forward and the IRA and other para-military groups have been on ceasefire for some considerable time. An elected assembly for the province has been set up and various reforms suggested to key institutions including the Royal Ulster Constabulary (RUC).

The success of political strategies by the African National Congress (ANC) in South Africa and Sinn Fein in Northern Ireland seems to have encouraged others to consider moving away from an almost exclusive reliance on violence, although unless national borders are changes it is likely that nationalist tensions and demands will remain.

Demonstrations

One of the most common forms of direct political action is participating in a demonstration. Again, this is a form of action that has a long history: the route to and from Trafalgar Square to

Hyde Park in London, for example, has been the site of many famous demonstrations.

It is clear that the importance of demonstrations has become greater in recent times. In the UK, the post World War II period saw the emergence of large-scale demonstrations, notably those surrounding the establishment of the Campaign for Nuclear Disarmament (CND).

Demonstrations became a focus of sociological concern again in the Thatcherite period. Edgell and Duke (1991) argue that one explanation for the rise in demonstrations may have been the relative ineffectiveness of orthodox political action (such as voting) in a period when the Conservatives seemed destined to continue winning elections, which led to a greater willingness to engage in other forms of action.

Table 15.5 Percentage of UK population taking part in action against spending cuts

	1981	1984
Signing a petition	2.2	5.5
Attending a meeting	4.3	1.2
Marching in a demonstration	1.8	2.8
Total (all actions)	11.2	12.3

Source: Adapted from Edgell and Duke (1991, p. 193)

Edgell and Duke also argue that another possible interpretation of this increase in activism is the greater willingness to citizens to participate in direct political action as democracies mature.

Despite this evidence of a rise in involvement in direct political action, the research of Parry, Moyser and Day (1991) based on a 1500-person sample in 1985 concluded that while only 4 per cent of their respondents were totally inactive, the only activity in which a majority of the population was involved (other than voting in general election) was signing a petition. They also argue that substantial political activism is confined to 25 per cent of the population. More active citizens on this scale tended to be more middle class, and were slightly more likely to be male.

Case Study — the poll tax demonstrations

The 1987 Conservative party manifesto pledged to abolish the then existing system of local taxation, domestic rates. The government proposed to replace it with a community charge, which became commonly known as the poll tax. This tax caused widespread anger, as many people saw it as unfair and unjust (though some were eligible for rebates and so it did find some supporters).

It was also felt that some might try to avoid paying the tax by failing to register to vote, thus losing their democratic rights. A third concern was that the new system would curb the rights of elected local councillors to determine spending in their area. Opinion polls in the *Daily Telegraph* found that 54 per cent thought it a bad idea and only 28 per cent a good idea.

Despite the opposition, the government introduced the poll tax in Scotland in April 1989 and in England and Wales from April 1990.

Almost immediately local anti-poll tax groups sprang up. They argued that people should refuse to pay the tax. There were massive demonstrations outside council chambers. Such demonstrations even occurred in areas where a majority of voters supported the Conservative party.

By February 1990 it was estimated that one in three adults in Scotland had not paid the poll tax and 145 000 people in Glasgow had not paid a single penny.

At the same time, large demonstrations were taking place in England and Wales. In February 1990, 2000 people marched against the poll tax in Maidenhead in Berkshire. In March 1990, 5000 people demonstrated against the tax in Hackney and in Bristol, 2000 demonstrated in Lambeth and 1000-strong marches took place in Barrow, Crewe, Norwich, Telford and Lancaster.

Despite opposition to the idea of non-payment, the marches and the non-payment campaign in Scotland continued to grow. Simultaneous marches against the tax were organised for 31 March 1990 in London and

Glasgow. The Glasgow march was estimated to be 40 000 strong, and in London over 200 000 marched. It was on the London march that riots broke out in Whitehall and Trafalgar Square. In response, the police arrested over 500 people in relation to alleged offences on the demonstration.

By June 1990 it was estimated that one-third of people in the country had not paid their poll tax, and in parts of London the figure rose to 80 per cent. This campaign of non-payment became one of the biggest campaigns of civil disobedience in UK history.

The evident unpopularity of the poll tax added to existing unease among Conservative MPs and was a contributory factor in the party's decision to ditch Margaret Thatcher as leader. Soon afterwards Michael Heseltine announced that the poll tax would be abandoned, and a new form of local taxation, the council tax, was introduced with effect from April 1993. The poll tax, which Margaret Thatcher had once described as her flagship, had lasted four years.

Source: Adapted from Kirby (1995, pp. 11–12)

Discussion point
Is the fact that the country can be divided into the active citizens and the not-so-active citizens a good or bad point for democratic control of the UK?

C3.1a

One of the most notable occasions in recent years involving large-scale amounts of direct political action was the introduction of the poll tax by the Conservative government in the late 1980s. The poll tax was introduced to replace the rates as the main form of local taxation. Since rates were based on housing value and mortgages were linked to income, there was a vague link to ability to pay with the rates. However the introduction of the poll tax meant a flat rate for all from the low paid to millionaires. This was seen by many to be unjust and sparked mass protests across the UK.

Strikes

In a survey of the contemporary position of trade unions, sociologist John Williams (1997) points

out that only 31 per cent of UK workers are now unionized, and for workers under 25, the figure is just 7 per cent. It is on the basis of figures like these that there has been talk of the end of trade unionism. However, while it is the case that this situation has put trade unions on the defensive, it should not be assumed that this has stopped all union protest. Indeed it is often the case that trade union activity has been instigated by the changes introduced by New Right reforms to the economy, with managers trying to reassert the right to manage and annoying workers to such an extent that they take action to defend themselves. The next two subsections will therefore consider in more detail recent examples where, despite the unfavourable legal context, workers have continued to act to defend their interests.

Discussion point
Why do you think young people seem relatively uninterested in trade unions?

C3.1a

Case Study — Lecturers in further education colleges

Strikes and industrial action are often considered to be the preserve of manual workers. However, the dispute which led to the largest number of strike days in both 1994 (63 000: 22 per cent of total) and 1995 (39 000: 9 per cent of total) was centred on a group of non-manual workers, namely lecturers in further education (FE) colleges.

The 1992 Further and Higher Education Act removed further education colleges from the control of local authorities and turned them into corporations, a form of quasi-privatization. At the same time, the funding mechanism was changed and they were subject to requirements to make efficiency gains.

The key way in which this was to be achieved was through the introduction of a new 'professional' contract for lecturers. The College Employers Forum (CEF), a grouping that brought together managers from colleges who in all other respects argued that they were individual entities, produced the model for this. The contract (compared to the existing nationally negotiated contract for college lecturers) increased the teaching load for lecturers by 26 per cent, increased their overall working hours by 23 per cent and also reduced their holiday entitlement. It was argued that this was needed to allow colleges to provide a flexible service in a new business-orientated environment.

💬 Discussion point

Should business principles operate in an educational environment?

C3.1a

Lecturers and their union, the National Association of Teachers in Further and Higher Education (NATFHE), argued that such a change would not only worsen lecturers' conditions but would also have a negative impact on the level of quality of the education provided. The new contract therefore became the central issue in a rolling conflict.

Lecturers were balloted on industrial action over the proposed introduction of the contract and a positive result was then challenged in the courts by arguing that a national strike would be illegal since it involved employees from a number of different legal entities. The court ruled that such a strike would therefore be illegal. Despite the fact that the proposed new contract to be introduced into the colleges was based on a unitary model contract produced by the CEF to which most colleges were affiliated, a similar unified response from the union was deemed to be illegal because the colleges were legally individual entities.

While this means that the defence of existing conditions has been made harder, it does not mean the end of the dispute. For six years lecturers have held out against increasing levels of pressure on them to sign the new contract. At the same time, there has been an increase in the use of part-time hourly paid lecturers and a decline in the employment of full-time lecturers as well as an increase in the number of redundancies in the colleges.

As well as the dispute over contracts, relations inside the colleges have been affected by changes in management style following their removal from local authority control. This led to fears that there now appears to be little public control over the activities of the managers of the colleges despite the fact that they are still largely publicly funded. This issue was highlighted at the end of 1996 by activities at Stoke-on-Trent College, one of the biggest colleges in the UK,

where it was revealed that the college had to cut £8 million from its budget. *Times* journalist, David Charter (1996) argued that:

A clearer picture has emerged of Stoke's descent into financial crisis. At the heart seems to lie a lack of accountability at the most senior level of the kind that further education colleges last year pledged to Lord Nolan's inquiry into standards in public life that they would strive to overcome.

(Charter, 1996, p. 37)

NATFHE members at the college had complained in a survey of the 'dictatorial and bullying style' of the Principal.

While it may be argued that this is an isolated case, the fact that it happened at all must mean that there are serious question marks placed over the level of public accountability of institutions and their managers who are spending large amounts of public money. Meanwhile, NATFHE and lecturers continue their case to resist the erosion of their working conditions, their living standards and to try to improve the quality of provision offered in the colleges.

In 1998, following a detailed investigation by the *Times Education Supplement* (TES), Roger Ward, the combative lead negotiator for the Association of Colleges (AoC, the successor body to the College Employers Forum) left the AoC, and a new approach was adopted leading to national negotiations with NATFHE, which in turn led to the production of a new proposed framework for lecturers' contracts. However, this still retained what were considered high hours of contact time and in a ballot on the new proposed framework, NATFHE members rejected this as a way forward. Negotiations continued, though, and the appointment of a new head of the AoC, David Gibson, in February 1999, led to renewed hope of an end to the dispute. Finally, in March 1999, the official end of the six-year dispute was announced with the setting up of various working parties to examine the pay and working conditions of lecturers in FE colleges.

Case Study — the Liverpool dockers

The docks have always been an important part of Liverpool and, for a time in the early part of this century, Liverpool was the leading seaport in the UK. In September 1995 the docks were the site of the start of one of the longest-running struggles in modern UK history. Dockers working for a private contractor, Torside, were ordered to work overtime at a rate they disputed. Protests followed and within 24 hours 80 dockers were sacked. The sacked workers mounted a picket line and all 329 dockers employed by the Mersey Docks and Harbour Company refused to cross it and were sacked. Since being sacked the workers have been presented with a number of final offers ranging from new jobs on individual contracts to redundancy payments, but the dockers have continued their fight to get their old jobs back. The dispute has mobilized many people and once a week the picket is composed of women and children (this picket is organized by WOW (Women on the Waterfront)) composed of partners, mothers and sisters of the sacked workers.

The dispute over overtime payments is part of concerns among the dockers that changes instituted in the 1980s are leading back to the casual labour system that operated in the past, and was the basis for a number of disputes.

Casualization has become a part of the 1990s struggle since the sacked dockers found their jobs had been taken by casual labourers employed by PDP Services. Their contract provides for an hourly rate of £4 with no overtime rate and provides that the contract can be terminated when the contractor determines. It also states that there is:

... no obligation on the contractor to provide the worker with any guaranteed number of working hours in any day or week. There will be periods when no work is available.

(Quoted in Pilger, 1996, p.16)

This type of activity has fuelled the fears of dock workers that casualization, which they fought so hard to end, is returning to the docks with all the uncertainties and indignities that that involves.

Socialist journalist John Pilger (1996) is in no doubt that the reason for this is the changes brought about by the New Right governments of the 1980s and 1990s:

The truth is that the number of dockers' jobs has spiralled down to about 300, a tiny fraction of the figure a few years ago. As for 'wealth creation', profits have soared from less than £9 million in 1989 to more than £31 million last year – the year the company jettisoned its dockers ...

It was taxpayers' money that floated Mersey Docks and Harbour Group in 1970, and taxpayers' money that wrote off £112 million in loans, and funded up to £200 million worth of redundancies, and paid out

£37.5 million for the regeneration of the dock area. Add to this £76 million of City Challenge funding. Since 1989, the company has received some £13.3 million in European Regional Development Funds. According to the Liverpool Echo, *'directors of Mersey docks have received phenomenal grants to create employment' – while unemployment has gone up. Inexplicably, the company's literature boasts of its success in something called the 'free market'.*

(Pilger, 1996, p. 16)

 Discussion point

To what extent do you agree that this dispute illustrates the return of a form of casualization to the docks?

C3.1a

Pilger points to the large sums of money made by some individuals out of the spate of privatizations in the dockyards in the 1980s and also points to the 38 per cent pay increase the managing director of Mersey Docks received just before the dockers were sacked.

The dispute is therefore a microcosm of the way the changes instituted by the government have led to changes in working conditions which make conditions for workers worse and allow a few to enrich themselves.

In their study of the dispute, Jane Kennedy and Michael Lavalette (1996), sociologists from Liverpool University, place the dispute in the context of the long-running struggles against casualization and flexible labour in the docks, and also its implications due to the widespread promotion of 'flexible working practices' throughout workplaces in the UK.

However, they are also concerned to highlight the great levels of solidarity that still exist and are illustrated by the action of the dockers in this dispute. The issue of the notion of class and who are the working class is also part of the analysis since, although dockers are manual workers, they are also service workers. This highlights the fact that we cannot equate service work with being middle class. Kennedy and Lavalette (1996) also consider the arguments over strategy within the union between those who tend towards the belief that in the context of changes to the law and earlier defeats for workers, solidarity is not a realistic option, and those who argue that this is the key to winning this dispute and thereby reasserting the importance of traditional trade union principles. In a separate article, they also comment on the effect of the dispute on relations with 'New Labour':

The Labour party have not made a single statement about either the dispute, casualization or the tactics of the MDHC. They clearly want to dissociate themselves from such working class activities and in this they have been successful. However, the consequences of this are that for many Liverpool dockers 'New Labour' means little to their lives and struggles. Repeatedly dockers told us they may still vote Labour but membership and active campaigning for the party are not part of their agenda. The central lesson of the Liverpool dock dispute would seem to be that working class communities need to rely on their own strength, via active rank and file trade unionism and strong community organisation, to protect their jobs, work conditions, communities and social and family lives

(Lavalette and Kennedy, 1996, p. 106)

15.4 Contemporary conceptualizations of power in society

All sociological theories can be seen to contain a theory of power. They have all entered into a discussion or debate as to the precise nature of power and its operation in society. However, as elsewhere in sociological analysis and discussion, we find that different theories define power in various ways. According to Westergaard and Resler:

Power ... is a rather exclusive phenomenon. Its effects are tangible. But power as such is something of an abstraction. It certainly cannot be measured in the way, for example, that the distribution of wealth can be measured. And just because it is not hard and fast, there is no simple and agreed definition of what it is.

(Westergaard and Resler, 1976, p. 142)

Authority, legitimation and coercion

In a very broad sense, engaging in politics means seeking power; or in other words, to seek one's own will at the expense of others (or to get one's own way). In this broad way, all aspects of social life are situations of power and the struggle to possess it, so all sociology is the study of power.

Taking this definition further, many sociologists draw a distinction between power based on authority and power based on coercion. For Weber (1968; orig. pub. 1921), although all power is ultimately based on domination – especially by the use of violence or force by the state – it is possible to draw a distinction between legitimate and illegitimate power:

- legitimate power = authority (winning the 'hearts and minds')
- illegitimate power = coercion (using force).

Weber and more recent commentators have suggested that coercive power is less stable than authoritative power. A ruler who wins the hearts and minds of a population can expect to enjoy a longer rule than in those societies based on force.

Frequently, coercion leads to attempts to establish authority. This may be by appealing to democracy, one of the greatest and most powerful legitimation claims of the contemporary world. Some governments, especially in relatively politically unstable areas such as eastern Europe and the developing world, obtain initial power through coercion, but quickly thereafter wish to establish themselves as legitimate in the eyes of their own population and the rest of the world.

Weber's 'ideal-types' of authority

Weber discusses types of authority in some detail. The construction and use of ideal-types is fundamental to Weber's sociology, and they enable him to discuss in pure terms the essential characteristics of a given phenomenon. Ideal-types can be understood as lists of characteristics a given social phenomenon may have, against which the sociologist compares reality.

Ideal-types are pure or abstract expressions. It is not a problem if all the characteristics of the ideal-type do not match up or conform with reality, since even in making this observation knowledge is gained of the social world. Ideal types enable sociologists to compare societies, and different time periods within the same society.

Weber identifies three pure types of authority, all of which are legitimate sources of power used by leaders or leading groups to secure the consent of the population:

- rational–legal – based on rules and laws
- traditional – based on a sense of established customs from the past

- charismatic – based on the special qualities of an individual.

In social reality, Weber argues that these pure types may well be combined together. It is perfectly possible, for example, for traditional authority to arise from charismatic authority. In this situation we may well find societies where members of a particular family are seen to have special religious or magical power (charismatic) and who therefore have always ruled and only members of this family can rule (traditional).

A radical view of power

Adopting a perspective which, while not Marxist as such, owes a great deal to left-of-centre or radical approaches in sociology, Lukes (1974) identified three dimensions of power:

- decision-making
- non-decision-making
- shaping decisions.

Lukes is critical of pluralist notions of power, especially within the work of Dahl (see page 622). Lukes notes that pluralists really focus only on the first dimension of power – they have a one-dimensional theory. He suggests that, while pluralists take at face value the notion that power can always be seen in decision-making, sometimes power is unseen, not observable. In this sense, modern western societies are far from open and democratic: they operate on a dimension of power which is hidden, closed and inaccessible to the majority. As Lukes notes:

... the pluralists assume that interests are to be understood as policy preferences – so that a conflict of interests is equivalent to a conflict of preferences. They are opposed to any suggestion that interests might be unarticulated or unobservable, and above all, to the idea that people might actually be mistaken about, or unaware of, their own interests.

(Lukes, 1974, p. 14)

In defining the precise nature of these three dimensions identified by Lukes, we can present them as follows.

The one-dimensional view: decision-making

In this dimension, power can be seen as a battle between open interests which conflict until a decision is reached. Lukes suggests that pluralism focuses solely on this aspect of power,

whereas this dimension can truly be understood only in relation to the second and third dimensions:

I conclude that this first, one-dimensional, view of power involves a focus on behaviour in the making of decisions on issues over which there is an observable conflict of (subjective) interests, seen as express policy preferences, revealed by political participation.

(Lukes, 1974, p. 15)

The two-dimensional view: non-decision-making

In the second dimension, power must be understood as operating also through a process of non-decision-making. Some issues or topics are ignored from the public agenda, and therefore they cannot be discussed openly:

... the two-dimensional view of power involves a qualified critique of the behavioural focus of the first view (I say qualified because it is still assumed that non-decision-making is a form of decision-making) and it allows for consideration of the ways in which decisions are prevented from being taken on potential issues over which there is an observable conflict of (subjective) interests, seen as embodied in express policy preferences and sub-political grievances.

(Lukes, 1974, p. 20)

The three-dimensional view: shaping decisions

In the third dimension, power can be identified in the process of shaping the wishes or desires of the population. By making some situations appear normal, natural and inevitable, the population of a society may simply go along with the rules of society and not even begin to *think* about questioning them, let alone *actually* questioning them. People's decisions can be made or shaped for them by those who rule:

... the three-dimensional view of power involves a thorough-going critique of the behavioural focus of the first two views as too individualistic and allows for consideration of the many ways in which potential issues are kept out of politics, whether through the operation of social forces and institutional practices or through individual's decisions. This, moreover, can occur in the absence of actual, observable conflict, which may have been successfully averted – though there remains here an implicit reference to potential conflict. This potential, however, may never in fact be articulated. What one may have here is a

latent conflict, which consists in a contradiction between the interests of those exercising power and the real interests of those they exclude.

(Lukes, 1974, p. 24)

Lukes therefore wishes the concept of power to be understood as multi-dimensional. He suggests that it is important for sociologists to recognize that power is related to decisions made by a ruling group from which they benefit and which are subsequently exercised over the general population – often against their interests – even if they do not actually know what their true interests are.

This view has been highly influential in much neo-Marxist sociology in recent years. Lukes work itself appears to reflect some of the ideas of Gramsci and the idea of hegemony – where rule is established in society by making such a rule appear normal, natural and beyond question. As Lukes comments concerning his third dimension of power:

Is it not the supreme and most insidious exercise of power to prevent people, to whatever degree, from having grievances by shaping their perceptions, cognitions and preferences in such a way that they accept their role in the existing order of things, either because they can see or imagine no alternative to it, or because they see it as natural and unchangeable, or because they value it as divinely ordained and beneficial?

(Lukes, 1974, p. 24)

Activity

Using the ideas of Lukes, suggest an example of each of the three dimensions of power in relation to your education.

C3.2, C3.3

Ideology, hegemony and New Social Movements

One key question that needs to be considered in relation to theories of power and control is the impact of the distribution of power and views about the legitimacy of power as a key spur to the foundation and consolidation of the New Social Movements (see also Section 15.3).

New Social Movements arose out of the Marxist tradition and tends not to adhere to pluralist views about the inclusiveness of liberal democracy (see also Section 15.1). New Social Movements do arise around notions of injustice, oppression or exclusion. Therefore they do tend to have negative views about the state as the fulcrum of power in society and tend to argue that conceptions of power need to take into account all three of the dimensions identified by Lukes (1974) in his view of power outlined above.

Since the third dimension of Lukes (1974) notion of power is about the shaping of attitudes and opinion, this also brings into play theories of ideology. New Social Movement theory does draw upon and build from the Marxist notion that there is dominant ideology (Marx and Engels, 1977) and that this means their ideas will not get a fair hearing. Later versions of theories of ideological control are based on the work of Antonio Gramsci (1971) and his theory of hegemony.

In this section we will consider how theories of ideology and power can be seen to operate in impacting upon the creation and action of New Social Movements.

The term 'New Social Movement' is somewhat unsatisfactory since there is an argument about how new they are, but nonetheless it is used to contrast movements such as the women's liberation movement, black nationalism, gay liberation and environmentalism from the older movements based on class positions, notably the Trades union and wider workers movement (Kirby, 1995).

Motivations behind the formation of New Social Movements

While the workers movement, either through trade unionism or through the creation of socialist parties, attempted to gain power through gaining control of the state and focused on the winning of economic rights such as minimum wage, better pay and working conditions and job security, the New Social Movements were based on identities that were not based around the workplace and therefore could largely not be understood in class terms.

They often aspired to the acceptance of their identities and lifestyles and instead of attempting to gain power through entering state machinery and arguing for changes to the law, they most often simply desired to be left alone to get on with their lives in peace.

This emphasis on autonomy and private life is evidence of the influence of liberalism on these types of movement and it is also clear that they tended to be based on the lifestyle of the 'new middle class'. The key base was Marxist thinkers who were alienated by the rigid bureaucracy and tyranny evident in Stalinist Russia and who felt there was a need to create libertarian Marxism.

Avoiding the dominant ideology

The Frankfurt School's most notable addition to Marxist theory was a clearer outline of the theory of dominant ideology (Marcuse, 1964; Adorno and Horkheimer, 1979). Theorists working within this school argued that the reason that capitalism had managed to survive in Western Europe was due to the rise of a dominant ideology. This was based on the mass media and the creation of a mass society through the manipulation of the wishes and desires of the population through propaganda and advertising (see also Section 6.1).

Members of the Frankfurt School had seen this is action in Germany during the time of Hitler, and in America where they had fled during WW II. They did not like what they saw and this distaste is evident in the title of the book by Herbert Marcuse (1964), *One-dimensional Man*. They believed that contemporary mass society made everyone shallow and depthless, satisfied with meaningless trinkets and baubles of consumerism.

Crucially as Marxists, they believed that the working class had been brought off by these consumer products and they agreed that there was a need to look elsewhere for ideas of change. Marcuse himself argued that there was a need to look towards the students.

The key reason for this belief was the argument that students and other groups had not yet been integrated into the dominant ideology of consumerism and would be potentially a basis for protest against capitalism. Since the dominant ideology was seen to spread itself throughout society, later writers, such as Michel Foucault (1980), argued that there was a need to look to the margins of society, to those who were not integrated into society, as a basis of looking at possible avenues for social change.

Centre or margin

One theory of how we can radically change society, end oppression and exploitation and live the good life is provided by Marxist ideas. This basically suggests that capitalism is crisis-ridden because of its economic and other structures which are full of conflict and that as a result there will be opportunities for workers and others to join together to change society over time. This will involve the need to take over and smash the central controlling mechanism of society, namely the state.

In contrast, the view presented by adherents of the New Social Movements suggests that the way to avoid domination by the capitalist state is to seek to create your own autonomous lifestyles on the margins of society. By creating your own space free from the influence of wider structures and ideas of society, it may be possible to achieve a degree of autonomy to pursue your own lifestyle.

Clearly, the Marxist vision aims at ultimately using its power to change the very centre of society, while the proponents of New Social Movements aim to use their power to create spaces on the margins of society free from the influence of the centre of society.

What both have in common is a desire to end oppression and exploitation and to encourage people to achieve their full creative potential, and a distaste for the artificiality and shallowness of life in capitalism. Therefore, they both engage in political and other struggles over ways of life. This approach came to be known as cultural politics.

The influence of the post-modern

With the demise of the regimes of eastern Europe, there was talk of the demise of socialism many Marxists started calling themselves post-Marxists. Most notably this occurred among the group that had taken Gramscianism to its heart, namely the group around the Communist party journal, *Marxism Today*. Among this group of thinkers were Hall and Jacques (1983, 1989).

This group had developed the notion of cultural politics originally as a way of supporting socialism and the workers movement, but now as a struggle in its own right. This shifted them onto the terrain of individual freedom, autonomy and creativity.

At the same time, the demise of the structural Marxist project led to renewed emphasis on individual and social action and a resurgence of interest in New Social Movements through the work or Alan Touraine (1982). Touraine argued that society was characterized by a class struggle, but he argued that the people fighting against oppression were not necessarily the workers as seen in classical socialist arguments. He argued that this was because we had now moved into an era dominated by Information Technology and it was information workers who would now be the most important group.

Cultural politics and discourse theory

However, a much wider notion of cultural politics was also in circulation, deriving from the emergence of post-modernist ideas in the work of discourse theory. As Nash (2000) points out, this rejected the idea that the key basis of struggle was to uncover ideological untruths and instead show people the truth, which was the key legacy of the Marxist tradition. Instead, it argued that there was a need to create new discourses which allowed for a diversity of ways of living:

It is not that social movements must establish the 'true' identities of their opponents, nor the 'realities' of the situation in which they are engaged. It is rather that they necessarily engage in strategic and persuasive exchanges in which they try to bring others into their project for change, redefining the terms within which the battle lines have been drawn, changing people's views of their real interests, and convincing them to see the world and themselves in a different way.

(Nash, 2000, p. 136)

If there is no truth then there is no notion of false, so clearly we cannot talk about people having false consciousness, class or otherwise. However, there is still, within many new social movements, some talk about interests, which are generally seen as objective truths independent of what people think or feel. (It could be argued that it is not in the interests of people to pay over the top prices for designer clothes with labels on it, even though some people may wish to act in this way.)

The fact that the word 'interests' does tend to depend on an objective account leads to it being viewed in generally hostile terms in postmodern circles. Instead it is presumed that people know their own desires and should be given freedom and autonomy to live their lives as they see fit.

Discussion point
What would happen if peoples' wishes clashed?

C3.1a

Beyond the State?

Critics of New Social Movements suggest that they were successful in Eastern Europe because the state structures in those societies did not have legitimacy and were unable to survive uprisings (Hirst, 1990). In contrast, the state structures in Western Europe are seen as legitimate and most people accept the results of elections and accept that they should follow the law. In this situation, there will be little possibility that the New Social Movements will be able to radically alter the way the state operates. New Social Movements will then only be able to consider creating new ways of living if they can find marginal areas of society free from state interference.

The rise of theories of the surveillance society (considered in Lyon, 1993) suggests that over time they will find this harder to achieve. On the other hand, Jurgen Habermas (1976) holds to the argument that the states of Western Europe are beginning to face a legitimation crisis and this might change the situation.

Conclusion

The New Social Movements do have a distinctive view of the state, power ideology and social change, compared to older political forms. Whether they are able to become effective in achieving their aims remains to be seen and whether their lifestyle politics is generalizable beyond the 'new middle class' will also be an issue of interest for the future. For the moment, they clearly add a level of debate to theories of power and ideology.

15.5 Power and the state

Of key importance in contemporary sociological analysis of power in society is the role of the state. In fact, the state is a relatively recent phenomenon in the overall history of humanity, but in the contemporary world it is a major feature of all developed, developing and undeveloped societies.

The state can be seen as the organization or bureaucratic mechanism through which a government exercises power in society – whether that society in question has a democratic, oligarchical or totalitarian political system. The state includes the government, the law-making and law-keeping bodies, and the civil service. It operates within a given geographical space or territory, and many commentators have focused on the state's legal monopoly of legitimate force within these territories.

The nation-state

Sociologists today usually refer to a state as a 'nation-state'. The given territory in which the state operates is whole nations or countries. In ancient Greece, and taking Athens as an early example, city-states existed where the territory of state rule was confined to much smaller geographical and political spaces.

The expansion of the nation-state across the globe is a key feature of modernity. It is seen to be the result of the legitimacy of *nationalism* as a political force. As Birch comments:

The entire surface of this planet, with the single exception of Antarctica, is now divided for purposes of government into territories known as nation-states. This is a relatively recent development in human history. Only two hundred years ago, there were fewer than twenty states with the shape and character that we should now recognize as deserving describing as nation-states ... The transformation has come about largely because the doctrine of nationalism has both triumphed in Europe and been exported to the rest of the world.

(Birch, 1993, p. 13)

Citizenship

Living under the rule of a nation-state, one may become a citizen. Citizenship is associated with a number of rights and duties, which differ according to the precise laws of each nation-state. For example, a citizen is required to pay taxes to support the state and to keep within the boundaries of its laws. If one breaks the law and is caught doing so, the state has the legitimate right to use the threat of force or actual force against that citizen.

Max Weber – state violence

For Weber (1968; orig. pub. 1921) the central defining characteristic of the state was its legitimate right to use coercion or violence within its defined territory. To this end, the state was an iron fist in a velvet glove – underpinning its rule was a systematic use of force. Weber uses the term 'political community' to refer to the social

space under the control of the state and its rules and domination through violence.

Sovereignty

Nation-states operate the right to self-rule, or to govern their affairs in an autonomous fashion within their defined territory. Nation-states are therefore *sovereign* – they have legitimate legal authority within their political space and are not answerable to outside forces.

In theory this concept of sovereignty is a clear one, but in practice the operation of nation-states in the contemporary world is not clear-cut. Some combine or give up part of their sovereignty to global political and/or economic organizations or powers, such as NATO or the European Union. Some human rights and civil rights laws and organizations cut across state sovereignties, yet are enforced differently.

Functionalism and the state

Emile Durkheim

For Durkheim, participatory democracy was an impossible ideal. Given the large scale of modern nations, democratic rule could be established only by using the state as a mechanism through which to define collective moral sentiments in law, and to ensure that these collective sentiments are followed.

In this view, the state is essential for the democratic process in society. It allows for increased communication between the masses and their rulers so as to ensure that the will of those who rule is also the will of the collective. Therefore the state is essential for social solidarity):

... solidarity comes from the inside and not from the outside. Men are attached to one another as naturally as the atoms of a mineral and the cells of an organism. The affinity which they hold for each other is based on sympathy ... Now, at each moment in its development, this solidarity is expressed externally by an appropriate structure. The state is one of these structures. The state is the external and visible form of sociability.

(Durkheim, 1988, p. 56; orig. pub. 1886)

Talcott Parsons

For Parsons (1963, 1967), power is a commodity to be shared among all those in society. It is not held by an élite group who use it in their own interests. Instead, Parsons' ideas on power focus on the traditional functionalist notions of value consensus and normative harmony and stability. For Parsons and other functionalists, social goals are collective in nature: those who rule do so because they are allowed to by the majority, but only if those who rule act in the interests of the majority, following collective sentiments.

This Parsonian functionalist image of power can be compared to modern banking. Thus politicians are like brokers or bankers, being allowed to borrow or invest the power given to them by their subjects or citizens; but if those subjects are unhappy about the uses to which this power is being put, they can withdraw their power and put their support in the hands of others.

Functionalists see the nature of the stratification system to be such that those who obtain the highest positions, with the highest rewards, are generally those who deserve to be there. Thus, power is given from the collective to a suitable set of leaders who ensure that the collective sentiments are met in a democratic fashion. If this is not the case, then power can be withdrawn at times of elections and referendums.

Criticisms of the functionalist approach

It is worth noting that the image of power central to the work of Parsons is based on a very specific set of ideological principles – in much the same way as other perspectives are political or ideological in nature, such as Marxism, feminism or the New Right. Parsons sees the model of western liberal democracy as the best or most suitable model of power in society. For this reason some critics – usually from a left-of-centre approach – have argued that functionalism, and Parsonian functionalism in particular, is nothing more than an academic justification or legitimation for western politics, and for capitalism in particular.

- Marxists would point out, as would some feminists, that in so-called western democracies the existence of elections does nothing to change those who are truly in power, who are seen to exist behind those voted for, possibly manipulating those in government for their own ends.

- Furthermore, those societies characterized as liberal democracies still contain great inequalities, whether they be based on class, gender, ethnicity, age or (dis)ability.

- Therefore, elections do nothing to solve the problems of those truly in need, who appear to be ignored from the power of collective sentiments given to political leaders to borrow.

Classical pluralism

Both sociologically and ideologically, the approach adopted by pluralism owes more to functionalism than to any other perspective. As has happened with many other perspectives in recent years, some pluralists have attempted to update the theory in the light of changes in society.

The core of all pluralist thinking – as the name suggests – is that the nature and distribution of power in western liberal capitalist societies is based on a *plurality* of power centres. Politics – the distribution of power, the conflict of wills – is based on the principles of competition, conflict and compromise.

Basic ideas of pluralism

- Pluralism does *not* assume the existence of an all-encompassing value consensus, as does functionalism. Rather than a single moral unity, society is seen as split into sections, or sectional interests.

- It is possible for an individual to have interests

represented by more than one group, and to be in harmony with other individuals over one issue, but in conflict with the same individuals over another issue.

- When it comes to voting behaviour, pluralists believe that an individual votes for the party representing the majority of his or her interests at that time.

- Other interests, not offered by the political parties on offer, are catered for by non-political party political groups, such as pressure groups, which are much wider in membership but narrower in focus.

Case Study – Who controls community power?

A classic piece of pluralist research into community power structures is provided by Dahl's work *Who Governs?* (1961), in which he studies how local politics is structured in the American city of New Haven. Dahl's central question was this:

In a political system where nearly every adult may vote but where knowledge, wealth, social position, access to officials, and other resources are unequally distributed, who actually governs?

(Dahl, 1961, p. 1)

Or, to put this in more detail:

Now it has always been held that if equality of power among citizens is possible at all – a point on which many political philosophers have had grave doubts – then surely considerable equality of social conditions is a necessary prerequisite. But if, even in America, with its universal creed of democracy and equality, there are great inequalities in the conditions of different citizens, must there not also be great inequalities in the capacities of different citizens to influence the decisions of their various governments? And if, because they are unequal in other conditions, citizens of a democracy are unequal in power to control their government, then who in fact does govern? How does a democratic system work amid inequality of resources?

(Dahl, 1961, p. 3)

Who makes decisions?

Dahl was interested in discovering whether a single élite group were responsible for decision-making, or whether – according to traditional pluralist ideas – decision-making was the product of a plurality of local power bases whereby a variety of local interests were represented. Dahl looked specifically at the election of the mayor of New Haven, the development of local land-use, and the way in which education was organized and structured.

Methodology

In order to conduct his study, Dahl adopted the method of looking at the decisions made on the above issues and at who it was making those decisions. Dahl contends that if one looks at a number of decisions made on a range of issues within a given time period, as he did, in every case where a decision has been made a number of different interests had had their say in the decision-making process. From Dahl's pluralist viewpoint, this proves the plurality of power in New Haven.

Conclusions

Dahl concludes that, rather than an élite group dominating these areas of local political life, power and the ability to influence the decision-making process was in the hands of the wider community through the representation of their interests by pressure groups. He claims that those in official governmental office – such as the mayor and other politicians – were forced to listen to and consult the local community before making major decisions. In this way, the various interests in New Haven were engaged, from the pluralist perspective, in the democratic processes of conflict, competition and compromise.

Classical pluralism and the state

A pluralist explanation of the role of the state in contemporary society rests on the ideas of competition, compromise and negotiation.

In conjunction with other non-state agencies such as pressure groups, political parties not in government, local councils, etc., a process of competition, compromise and negotiation takes place over the resources provided by the state. The power of the state is thus exercised by a variety of élites working both within the state and from without, and the various interests of the population are met.

The nature of society is such that a functionalist-style value consensus is not believed to exist. Instead there is conflict between the divided interests of the population, but a conflict which is resolved through the wider interplay of competition and conflict between élites. For pluralists the state operates for the good of all.

Elite pluralism

Commentators have drawn a distinction between:

- classical pluralist thinking, and
- the more recent, revised, élite pluralism.

In drawing this distinction, Marsh (1983) provides the following definitions.

Classical pluralist thinking

In the classical pluralist position power is seen as diffuse rather than concentrated. Society is viewed as consisting of a large number of groups, representing all the significant, different interests of the population, who compete with one another for influence over government. This competition occurs within a consensus about the rules of the game.

(Marsh, 1983, p. 10)

Elite pluralism

Elite pluralism is seen by Marsh to differ from classical pluralism in two main ways:

First, there is a greater acceptance that all individuals may not be represented by groups and that some citizens are therefore under-represented by the interest group system. ... Secondly, the élite pluralist admits that groups are less open and responsive to their members than the classical pluralists assumed because all organizations tend to be hierarchically run.

(Marsh, 1983, pp. 11 and 12)

Classical pluralism, then, tends to assume that all interests are represented – that power is shared equally. However, for élite pluralists:

- It is possible to identify some interests that are represented more readily and more successfully than others.
- Those interests which support the ideas, values and culture of élites in society – or, at least, those interests which do not expose, attack or undermine the interests of élites – hold more sway in society.
- Simply because a pressure group or interest exists does not automatically mean that it will be successful in influencing the decision-making or power-holding processes of society.
- Power is still seen as a process of competition, but now the rules of the game are recognized to be fixed in favour of some at the expense of others.

Classical élite theories

All élite theories are based on the identification of a narrow ruling group who rule over the majority in society. Whereas some élite theories are left-of-centre, and therefore are highly critical of this two-tier social arrangement, others see élite rule as necessary. The approach known as classical élite theory fits into the second of these types.

These ideas are usually associated with the writings of Niccolo Machiavelli, Vilfredo Pareto (1963) and Gaetano Mosca (1939) in Italy.

Basic ideas of classical élite theories

In this approach, élites who have the power to rule the state become so as a result of superior personal qualities. Since, therefore, they are most suited to such élite positions, their rule is natural: some people are fit to be rulers and others only fit to be ruled. This unequal situation was seen by Pareto and Mosca to be characteristic of all human societies, and therefore an inevitable consequence of social life.

Discussion point

Is it normal and natural to have élites in society?

C3.1a

Machiavelli – legal rule and rule through force

The ideas of Pareto are very similar to those of Niccolo Machiavelli (1469–1527), another Italian political scientist and philosopher. Machiavelli is most noted for his work *The Prince*, in which he outlines his recommendations for a successful élite ruler. He draws a distinction between two types of rule which an élite or élite group can adopt: rule through legal means, and rule through force. Machiavelli believed that while the development of a legal system places humanity above the animals, sometimes the law is not enough and force must be used to secure rule. He draws an analogy between two types of animals which, he argued, élite rulers would do well to mimic. These were the fox for cunning and the lion for the use of strength and force.

Machiavelli's advice for élites is that rule over a majority will be successful only for the individual who displays courage, boldness, cunning and strength – which he refers to as *virtu*. The ideas of Machiavelli are largely associated with authoritarian, right-wing political ideas.

Pareto – the 'circulation of élites'

Pareto adopts the same distinction between the fox and the lion. However he suggests that, even with the use of cunning or strength, there will probably come a time when one set of élites will be replaced by another. The nature of élite rulers is such that they are easily corruptible, giving way to a life of power and pleasure. When this happens, élite rule circulates and another set of élites come to power.

Mosca – are élites natural?

The other theorist associated with classical élite theory is Gaetano Mosca. Like Pareto and Machiavelli, he too believed that élite rule is normal, natural and inevitable, and that élites are those who possess characteristics separating them from the ordinary masses – in his case, mainly organizational skills.

Activity

Evaluate the ideas of classical élite theory from Marxist and feminist viewpoints.

C3.2, C3.3

Radical élite theory

Although another 'élite theory', this view is very different from that held by the classical élite theory discussed above.

Case Study – Who governs?

Hunter (1953), in his work *Community Power Structure: A Study of Decision Makers*, can be seen to approach the issue of 'who governs?' from a very different ideological and methodological stance from that of Dahl's pluralism. As an early example of radical élite theory, Hunter studied the number of groups involved in a local community's decision-making processes, in order to identify the existence of élites who controlled the processes and who, as a group, ruled over the population of a city.

Methodology

To conduct his research Hunter used a panel of local people to identify those who they felt were in positions of significant power in the local community. He then compared these reputations together in order to identify those considered most powerful. A common set of names was drawn up. As Hunter himself notes:

It has been evident to the writer for some years that policies on vital matters affecting community life seem to appear suddenly. They are acted on, but with no precise knowledge on the part of the majority of citizens as to how these policies originated or by whom they are really sponsored. Much is done, but much is left undone. Some of the things done appear to be manipulated to the advantage of relatively few.

(Hunter, 1953, p. 1)

Conclusions

Hunter rejects Dahl's pluralist-based notion that the community is involved in the decision-making process through the help of pressure groups. Instead, studying what he refers to as Regional City, a city with a population of about a half million, Hunter identifies the existence of a narrow group of élites who exercise power over the majority who make decisions for their own benefit and for the benefit of others like them.

Case Study – The power élite

C. W. Mills' *The Power Elite* (1956) was also written with the élite composition of America in mind. Although Mills felt he had been successful in identifying a number of élites in America, unlike some pluralists and Pareto and Mosca, he was highly critical of their existence – believing the existence of élites to be highly undemocratic. He identified three élite groups which together form what he described as the power élite:

The power élite is composed of men whose positions enable them to transcend the ordinary environments of ordinary men and women; they are in positions to make decisions having major consequences. ... For they are in command of the major hierarchies and organizations of modern society. They rule the big corporations. They run the machinery of the state and claim its prerogatives. They direct the military establishment. They occupy the strategic command posts of the social structure, in which are now centred the effective means of the power and the wealth and the celebrity which they enjoy.

(Mills, 1956, pp. 3–4)

These three sets of élite groups are:

• industry/business

• military

• political.

Between them, capitalism in America is governed, controlled and maintained in the interests of these three groups. Clearly, not everyone working in these three areas can be seen to represent an élite, but those in the top positions of the hierarchies of these three areas certainly do. Mills suggests that these people are known to each other, and so rule in conjunction with one another. However, he notes:

Despite their social similarity and psychological affinities, the members of the power élite do not constitute a club having a permanent membership with fixed and formal boundaries. It is of the nature of the power élite that within it there is a good deal of shifting about, and that it thus does not consist of one small set of the same men in the same positions in the same hierarchies.

(Mills, 1956, p. 287)

Thus, the power élite can be seen as a relatively stable set of élite positions along with which comes great influence and power. The owners or holders of these positions may change, but the positions themselves will continue to exist, so power will continue to be concentrated in the hands of a small power élite.

Mills suggests that those in each of the three strands of the power élite are similar people. He puts this down to the process of socialization within these organizations (training on the job) and the selection processes used to choose their personnel – and especially their top personnel.

Mills thus regards the top positions of American society to be based on this three-strand power élite model. What implications does this have for those members of the general population who are subject to the power held by the power élite? Mills himself asks this question:

But how about the bottom? As all these trends have become visible at the top and on the middle, what has been happening to the great American public? If the top is unprecedentedly powerful and increasingly unified and wilful; if the middle zones are increasingly a semi-organized stale-mate in what shape is the bottom, in what condition is the public at large? The rise of the power élite, we shall now see, rests on, and in some ways is part of, the transformation of the publics of America into a mass society.

(Mills, 1956, p. 297)

Discussion point

Is society a meritocracy? (Is one's position in society based upon merit – or on who you know?) Does the existence of élites make society unfair?

C3.1a

Classical Marxism

For Marx and Engels, power is based in an individual's class location in society. From this viewpoint, power will be plural or communal only in a society that is classless: where no one ruling group owns the means or forces of production, and uses this to dominate or rule over the rest of society. As Marx and Engels state in *The Communist Manifesto*:

The history of all hitherto existing society is the history of class struggles. ... But every class struggle is a political struggle.

(Marx and Engels, 1967, pp. 79 and 90; orig. pub. 1848)

Power is seen here primarily as a result of economic ownership. This power is largely accepted by those ruled over – the working classes – owing to the use of both coercion and ideology as control mechanisms. Many Marxist writers see the working class as in a state of false class consciousness, unable to see for themselves the true nature of society under capitalist control: the inequalities of power are due to inequalities of wealth. In this classical view, the state is an instrument of ruling class power.

Elite rule or ruling classes?

A distinction is usually drawn between the concept of an élite and the idea of a ruling class – particularly the Marxist notion of a ruling class. While a ruling class is an élite in one sense, since collectively its members experience power, status and prestige over and above that held by the masses, in Marxism a class is defined in terms of its ownership of the means or forces of production. Whereas the working class own nothing except their labour power which they sell to the ruling classes, the latter, by definition, own the means or forces of production.

On the other hand, an élite or élite group can still experience the lifestyle, life-chances and power of a ruling class but not actually own the means of production. The term élite, then, is a much wider term than ruling class and could refer to members of government, non-elected high state positions, etc.

Classical Marxism and the state

Like the classical élite theorists earlier, Marxists too see power to lie in the hands of a privileged few, but this situation is not seen as desirable. For Marx, the end of history will result in the establishment of a truly classless society where the means of production will be communal and serve to the benefit of all.

A tool of the ruling class?

In the classical Marxist treatment of the state, it is seen as a tool in the class struggle, supporting the interests of the ruling, capitalist class. As Marx and Engels state in *The Communist Manifesto*:

The executive of the modern state is but a committee for managing the common affairs of the whole bourgeoisie.

(Marx and Engels, 1967, p. 82; orig. pub. 1848)

Frederick Engels – the origins of the state

Frederick Engels claims, in his work *The Origin of the Family, Private Property and the State* (1972; orig. pub. 1884), that the origins of the state lie in the creation of private property. While private property did not exist, and property was collectively owned, a ruling group did not exist and therefore the state was not needed to protect and preserve their unequal rule. However, once property was established – once a surplus was produced within a society – class distinctions developed when one group claimed this property or surplus for themselves. The state is then needed to control class conflict. The newly established ruling class had created new organs to protect their interests, and:

As the state arose from the need to hold class antagonisms in check, but as it arose, at the same time, in the midst of the conflict of these classes, it is, as a rule, the state of the most powerful, economically dominant class, which, through the medium of the state, becomes also the politically dominant class, and thus acquires new means of holding down and exploiting the oppressed class.

(Engels, 1972, p. 160)

Marxist criticisms of classical pluralism

- To a certain extent, Marxist and neo-Marxist criticisms of pluralism take as their starting point the observation that only some interests are successful in their representation.

- Viewed from a Marxist perspective, the operation of pressure groups is not democratic, far from it. They may well create the illusion of democracy, but those interests which do not support the activities or interests of the ruling capitalist class will not be taken seriously, or will even be actively suppressed.

- It might even be contended that some pressure groups and their leaders will not attempt to change or promote some issues for fear of damaging their reputation or potential success in other areas.

> ### 💬 Discussion point
>
> Is the UK governed by a ruling class, by a ruling élite, or by the people?
>
>

Problems with the classical Marxist theory of the state

Parkin (1979) argued that the ideas of classical Marxism on the role of the state in society needed to be updated for contemporary times. He suggested that Marx did not have a fully developed theory of the state, just a handful of comments made about the state while in the process of discussing other issues.

Internal contradictions within Marxist theory?

Parkin argues that the few ideas on the state Marx did have contain within them what appears to be a contradiction. We can identify two views:

- VIEW ONE: On the one hand, Marx refers to the state as an instrument of the rule of the capitalist class.

- VIEW TWO: On the other hand, Marx suggested in places another, much more complicated, relationship between the state and the ruling class, where the state has a *relative autonomy* from the ruling class.

Ralph Miliband – the state as an instrument

Miliband (1973) echoes the first interpretation of

the ideas of Marx and Engels – that the state is an instrument in the hands of the ruling class. He suggests that the nature and operation of the state in society is of central importance in any understanding of the nature of political and class struggle in society:

More than ever before men now live in the shadow of the state. What they want to achieve, individually or in groups, now mainly depends on the states sanction and support. But since that sanction and support are not bestowed indiscriminately, they must, ever more directly, seek to influence and shape the state's power and purpose, or try and appropriate it altogether. It is for the state's attention, or for its control, that men compete; and it is against the state that beat the waves of social conflict. It is to an ever greater degree the state which men encounter as they confront other men. This is why, as social beings, they are also political beings, whether they know it or not. It is possible not to be interested in what the state does; but it is not possible to be unaffected by it.

(Miliband, 1973, p. 3)

Miliband is critical of élite theories and of pluralism, both of which, be believes, operate to hide the real nature of the state in society. He believes they ignore the fact that the interests of the state are the interests of capitalism, and in particular of the ruling classes themselves. Those in the state machinery operate in the interests of those who own the means of production.

Does the state have a 'relative autonomy'?

In the second view identified by Parkin, that the state has a *relative autonomy* from the ruling class, Marx appears to suggest that the state does serve the interests of the capitalist class, but is not its puppet: the state serves the interests of capitalism, but without being its executive committee *per se*.

Discussion point

Is the state merely a tool of the ruling class, or does it have some independence?

C3.1a

The idea that the state has some degree of autonomy from the ruling classes is a popular one in much contemporary Marxist and neo-Marxist theorizing.

Neo-Marxism

In the work of Antonio Gramsci, an Italian neo-Marxist, we see the second interpretation of Marx's ideas on the state.

Hegemony

Gramsci (1971), writing in a Fascist prison in the 1930s, stresses the role played by *hegemony* in class domination in capitalist societies. He notes that in order to secure their position of leadership, the capitalist class need to rule through a combination of both repressive and ideological means over all other classes – to dominate totally a class society.

Hegemony refers to rule through ideological means: to rule through the consent of the masses by manipulating and organizing this consent. The state is the tool through which this consent is manipulated and controlled – it operates to create the hegemony of the ruling group. As Gramsci suggests:

... the state is the entire complex of practical and theoretical activities with which the ruling class not only justifies and maintains its dominance, but manages to win the active consent of those over whom it rules.

(Gramsci, 1971, p. 244)

Protecting ruling-class legitimacy

However, in order to make the rule of the ruling classes seem legitimate, the state operates with a degree of relative autonomy since it makes concessions with the ruled masses and is affected by popular social-democratic struggles. In this sense, the state arbitrates between the classes, yet it is not a genuine arbitration since, at the final analysis, the ruling class hegemony is protected.

Gramsci divides the operations of the state into two areas, civil society and political society:

... it should be remarked that the general notion of the state includes elements which need to be referred back to the notion of civil society (in the sense that one might say that state = political society + civil society, in other words hegemony protected by the armour of coercion).

(Gramsci, 1971, pp. 262–3)

Collectively, the two halves of the state are referred to by Gramsci as the *integral state*. In defining the relationships between these two levels of the integral state, he writes:

What we can do, for the moment, is to fix two major superstructural levels: the one that can be called civil society, that is the ensemble of organisms commonly called private, and that of political society. ... These two levels correspond on the one hand to the function of hegemony which the dominant group exercises throughout society, and on the other hand to that of direct domination or command exercised through the state and 'juridicial' government.

(Gramsci, 1971, p. 12)

Thus, Gramsci draws a distinction between the use of force or domination by the state (political society), and the use of ideological means to secure hegemony (civil society). The majority of Gramsci's work focuses on the latter at the expense of the former.

Activity

a Compare the ideas of Ralph Miliband and Antonio Gramsci on the state – they each offer a different interpretation of a Marxist view of the state, as identified by Frank Parkin.

b Create a list of the differences and similarities between these two views.

C3.2, C3.3

Structural Marxism

A structuralist account of the role of the state under capitalism is offered by Poulantzas (1980). Like Miliband, he stresses the importance of the state in contemporary life:

Who today can escape the question of the state and power? Who indeed does not talk about it? ...
Whether overtly or not, all twentieth-century political theory has basically posed the same question: what is the relationship between the state, power and social classes?

(Poulantzas, 1980, p. 11)

However, whereas Miliband stresses the first reading of Marx, that the state is an instrument of the ruling class, Poulantzas emphasizes the second reading – that the state has a degree of relative autonomy from the ruling class.

- Poulantzas argues that the state will automatically follow the needs of those who own and control the economic base the – ruling classes.
- Unlike Miliband, he does not regard the class composition of the élites who run the state as important: regardless of who they are they are structurally predisposed to serve the interests of capitalism.
- But – while the state is determined to act out the will of the ruling class, it is not run by the ruling class on a day-to-day basis. Rather it is governed by those in government.
- Thus the state has a relative autonomy, but will always work in the interests of those for whom capitalist society is structured – the owners of the means of production.

State apparatus

In defining the state, Poulantzas follows the work of Althusser in drawing a distinction between:

- ideological state apparatus
- repressive state apparatus.

This distinction is very similar to that made by Gramsci between political society (domination) and civil society (ideology). So the state maintains the superiority of the capitalist class not only by the use of force or repression, as through the army or police and law courts, but also through ideological means – such as through the media, education, the family and other institutions of socialization.

Poulantzas suggests that too much emphasis has been given, in contemporary Marxist and neo-Marxist thought, to ideological domination. This, he argues, has been at the expense of under-stating physical domination, a feature of the state much discussed originally by Weber. While Poulantzas supports the work of Gramsci in highlighting the ideological power which keeps capitalism together in the face of economic contradictions and problems of legitimacy, we should not ignore repression altogether:

Only too often does emphasis on the state's role in ideological relations lead to underestimation of its repressive functions. By repression should be understood first and foremost organized physical violence in the most material sense of the term: violence to the body. ... The state is always rooted in its physical constraint, manipulation and consumption of bodies.

(Poulantzas, 1980, p. 29)

Concern with the physical manipulation of bodies as a form of power also surfaced in the later work of post-structuralist Michel Foucault.

Who rules the UK?

In Britain there are two sets of difficulties involved in the attempt to analyse whether there is a power élite (with or without group consciousness, coherence and conspiracy) or a ruling class. The first is lack of information. ... The second is that the interpretation of this evidence very much depends on the general picture that one has of the workings of society as a whole. ... The empirical information cannot in itself confirm or refute the hypothesis that there is a ruling class unless two other conditions exist. One is that specific criteria of this concept must be provided. The other is that a concept only makes sense and its value judged when it is placed within a whole set of other concepts which are theoretically related.

(Urry; in Urry and Wakeford, 1973, p. 8)

A Marxist perspective

Westergaard and Resler (1976) have argued that concessions made by the state operate to increase hegemony by hiding class domination, and making the activities of the state appear legitimate.

Criticisms of pluralism

In making their claims, Westergaard and Resler are critical of pluralist ideas, whereby the welfare state is seen as a clear indication of the dismantling of the power of capital and the increased redistribution of wealth to the masses. For pluralists the nature of power is such that it is becoming shared by a variety of élites who represent, democratically, a variety of interests. Westergaard and Resler comment on this:

The trouble with this thesis is twofold. First, in so far as it is right, what it says is hardly worth saying. Second, its proponents studiously avert their gaze from questions that do matter. Because they then see nothing, they draw the conclusion that there is nothing to see.

(Westergaard and Resler, 1976, p. 245)

But, from their perspective, Westergaard and Resler argue that, despite the development of a welfare state, power and wealth are still concentrated in the hands of a ruling class and class conflict against this ruling group is being dampened by the arguments produced by pluralist theories. Thus social welfare is being made to seem like the establishment of equality in society, yet it is only a piecemeal, token gesture. The state still, ultimately, serves the interests of the ruling class.

The difficulties of defining and measuring 'power'

Westergaard and Resler suggest that power is a difficult phenomenon to see in social life, but the effects of power differences are obvious:

The continuing inequalities of wealth, income and welfare that divide the population are among the most crucial consequences – the most visible manifestations – of the division of power in a society such as Britain. Those inequalities reflect, while they also demonstrate, the continuing power of capital – the power, not just of capitalists and managers, but of the anonymous forces of property and the market. They also both reflect and demonstrate the orientation of state power.

(Westergaard and Resler, 1976, pp. 141–2)

They go further, and suggest that the problem with the pluralist notion – that society is characterized by a plurality of interests and groups representing those interests – is that:

... it tells us nothing. ... There is no value, then, to the point that many pressures go to shape the outcome of events. It is obvious. The crucial questions concern the nature of the pressures and the direction of the outcome.

(Westergaard and Resler, 1976, pp. 245–6)

Thus, from a Marxist perspective, the pluralist notion that power resides in the competition between élites – who in turn represent the interests of the local community – is a dubious one. Instead, power resides in the ownership or non-ownership of the means or forces of production.

Contemporary applications of Marxism and radical élite theory

John Scott

Scott's (1986) approach to the analysis of power in contemporary society appears to draw on the traditions of both Marxism and radical élite theory. Scott claims that the UK does still have an easily identifiable upper class, despite the claims made to the contrary by other traditions. However, he wishes to redefine this concept to make it more applicable to post-war capitalist societies:

Although there is widespread agreement that Britain did once have a sharply defined upper class, many researchers have argued that the twentieth century has seen its demise. This upper class was formed in the late nineteenth and early twentieth century from the landed, commercial and manufacturing classes of earlier periods, but was unable to sustain its position in the face of the economic trends of the twentieth century.

(Scott, 1986, p. 3)

Scott, however, disagrees with this interpretation. He claims that the upper class have not become an irrelevance, they do still exist and hold considerable power (see also Section 16.6). He rejects the pluralist-based managerialist position which claims that, owing to changes in the production processes in industry and the development of shareholding of industry, the power and control of the upper classes has taken a back seat to the rising post-war power and influence of the manager. Instead, Scott claims that we have witnessed a depersonalization of the ownership of property, whereby the property owned by the modern upper class is no longer the land, factories and industrial plants of yesteryear, but the assets, pension funds and insurance funds flickering on computer screens in global money markets.

Pluralists may claim that those individuals who make up the company boards which collectively own and control these monies come from wide backgrounds and are drawn from the new middle classes. Scott argues, however, that close analysis of the types of people sitting on these company boards illustrates that, along with these salaried middle classes, there are still to be found a number of entrepreneurial capitalists who often own a majority of shares to give them control:

Top corporate decisions, therefore, are taken by a group of directors with significant shareholding interests, often with controlling blocks of shares, and with interests which are closely allied with those of the financial intermediaries. Directors and top executives are the beneficiaries of the structure of impersonal share ownership, and through their membership of the boards of banks and insurance companies are actively involved in taking decisions about the use of this impersonal institutional share ownership. Top directors are tied together through the interlocking directorships which are created whenever one person sits on two or more boards. Through these interlocking directorships a web of connections is created which ties together a large number of enterprises and casts the multiple directors in a key role as co-ordinators of the business system as a whole.

(Scott, 1986, p. 6)

Scott himself asks, although an upper class undoubtedly exists, is it also a ruling class? He notes that those in top positions – those who have the opportunity to exercise control and power over others – do still tend to be drawn from the upper class:

The various parts of the state élite cabinet, parliament, judiciary, civil service and military are recruited disproportionately from among the economically dominant upper class. This similarity of economic background is reinforced by the fact that they had studied at a small number of major public schools and at Oxford and Cambridge Universities. ... The upper class and the political élite show a similarity of social background and are, in many cases, the same people.

(Scott, 1986, p. 7)

However, for Scott, the upper class are not a ruling class *per se*. He considers, like Gramsci that the state itself is a major source of power in societies and as such can, and often does, operate separately from the government and the upper class. Scott contends that the concept of power bloc best describes the distribution of power in contemporary western societies:

Neither ruling class nor élite can be used as adequate descriptions of the British political structure. Historical patterns of class dominance must be understood in terms of the particular alliance of classes and sections of classes which constitute the power bloc. A power bloc is an informal coalition of social groups, often under the leadership of one group, which actually holds the levers of political power in a society. ... British society in the twentieth century has been ruled by just such a power bloc, headed by the upper-class members of the establishment. ... Over the course of the century the cohesion of the power bloc has weakened, but it remains the basis of upper-class political dominance. ... Britain has an upper class that dominates government, but it does not have a ruling class.

(Scott, 1986, p. 7)

Activity

First read the articles 'Three in five top civil servants land quango jobs' and 'Oxbridge retains grip on judiciary' on pages 631 and 632, and then write an answer to the following question: Which theory is supported the most by the 'evidence' supplied in these articles – pluralism, Marxism, or Scott?

 C3.2, C3.3

Is there a future left for the state?

Recent debate on the nature of the state in contemporary, western liberal democracies has focused on the future roles of the state. Notably, many theorists are becoming increasingly pessimistic, and believe that the future of the state will be dramatically different from its recent past.

State overload

Brittan (1975), and others more recently, have suggested that one way to interpret the future role of the state is to recognize that its rapid expansion since World War II will have to be reduced or stopped. In economic terms, western societies will not be able to afford to deliver the goods as promised, particularly in the areas of social welfare which cost governments vast sums each year. As the state promises more and more, in order to obtain the increasingly fragile and volatile support of the population, it can in reality afford to deliver less and less.

The New Right and the nanny state

With the rise of the New Right in western politics, there can be seen a keen awareness of the notion of the state becoming overloaded. In the UK, since the establishment of the first Thatcher government in 1979, there has been – as a core ideological feature of New Right politics and policies – the rejection of what is called the 'nanny state'. It is believed by some New Right theorists that excessive reliance on the state providing social welfare – benefits, healthcare, etc. – cannot be met by the revenue generated by the state through taxation.

These theorists go further and suggest that too much public expenditure and support leads to a nanny state in which individuals become far too dependent on the state for support. As a result a dependency culture is established whereby those asking for state support lack the necessary drive to look for work, or to take control over their lives and those of their families. This issue became a major arena for political conflict in the UK during the 1980s and early 1990s, between the New Right, the so-called New Labour opposition, and the middle ground occupied by the Liberal Democrats.

In New Right thinking, individual responsi-

bility needs to be encouraged – but only if individuals can be trusted to take moral responsibility. The state should not – and cannot afford to – care for these people, if they cannot do so for themselves.

Feminism: the patriarchical state

For feminists such as Pateman (1988) and Walby (1990), the state is seen as a patriarchical institution. By this they mean that it operates to legitimate male domination and power in society at the exclusion of women.

Three in five top civil servants land quango jobs

ANDY McSMITH

THREE out of five top-ranking civil servants in Britain receive jobs on quangos after retiring from service.

In his report Lord Nolan warned that the right to appoint or approve 10,000 quango appointments every year is giving Ministers 'considerable power of patronage'. He called for the creation of committees with independent members to advise on quango appointments, and a Commissioner for Public Appointments to monitor them.

The report added: 'Some argue that this is an unhealthy concentration of power . . . We share some of this concern, particularly about the absence of independent checks and balances.'

A survey by Labour MP Alan Milburn shows that 15 of the 25 civil servants who retired with the rank of permanent secretary in the past five years have quango posts.

He said: 'Whitehall is infested with a 'jobs for the boys' culture. Unlike the rest of the population, Sir Humphreys are finding nice little earners when they retire.'

Other former permanent secretaries have taken relatively modest positions on quangos, for instance as museum trustees. Sir Richard Lloyd Jones, former permanent secretary at the Welsh Office, agreed to take on an unpaid post as chairman of the Arts Council in addition to his paid job chairing the Staff Commission for Wales. But there has been no quango job for Sir Allan Green QC, who had to resign as Director of Public Prosecutions in 1991 after being caught soliciting near King's Cross in London.

Sir Duncan Nichol, former NHS chief executive, is also one of the 10 without a quango.

He received a £113,550 payoff and a £36,000-a-year pension when he left last year to become professor of health care at Manchester University and a £15,000-a-year director of Bupa, the private health organisation.

Source: Observer, 14 May 1995

Oxbridge retains grip on judiciary

ALAN TRAVIS

THE upper reaches of the judiciary are still dominated by those who are Oxbridge-educated, according to official figures published yesterday. This is despite the protestations of the Lord Chancellor, Lord Mackay, that the "old boy network" no longer determined the appointment of judges.

The figures, published by the Lord Chancellor's Department, show that 80 per cent of Lords of Appeal, Heads of Divisions, Lord Justices of Appeal and High Court judges were educated at Oxford or Cambridge.

More than 50 per cent of the middle-ranking circuit judges went to Oxbridge but only 12 per cent of the lower ranking district judges.

Sir Thomas Legg, the permanent secretary at the Lord Chancellor's Department, answered criticism over the Oxbridge domination of the higher courts from MPs yesterday by insisting: "It is not the function of the professional judiciary to be representative of the community."

He told the Commons Home Affairs Committee that the Lord Chancellor had to choose the senior members of the judiciary from "the most successful members of a learned profession, and from those who had been in it for at least 20 to 30 years."

But Chris Mullin, Labour MP for Sunderland South, said that the system of appointments appeared to be self-perpetuating, with all the senior judges aged between 55 and 66 and moving in limited circles.

He added that the only woman judge in the Appeal Court happened to be the sister of a previous Lord Chancellor and the daughter of a Lord of Appeal.

Mr Mullin said that a study carried out last year by Labour Research had shown that of 641 judges, 80 per cent had been to public school.

Other official figures published yesterday included a sample survey of 218 new appointments as magistrates in England and Wales. This showed that 91 were Conservative voters, 56 Labour, 41 Liberal Democrat, 24 had no political affiliation, and four voted Plaid Cymru.

Source: Guardian, 18 May 1995

claims that patriarchy – male dominance over women – exists in six spheres of society:

- paid employment
- sexuality
- the household
- violence
- culture
- the state.

For the feminists, all these structures of patriarchical control operate on women's lives in conjunction. Thus violence in the home and the exclusion of women from paid employment are related, as is the fact that overseeing all of social life is the state which, they say, turns a blind eye to the plight of women. (Walby's work and the debates surrounding it are discussed in more detail in Section 17.8.)

15.6 Power in everyday life

The dramaturgical analogy: phenomenology

Goffman, in his book *The Presentation of Self in Everyday Life* (1971; orig. pub. 1959), adopts what he describes as a 'dramaturgical approach'. By this, he compares social life to the theatre: individuals are social actors, they follow scripts, they adopt roles and give performances. Within this analogy is a micro-theory of power and the political nature of everyday life.

Goffman suggests that in any interactional encounter we seek to define the social situation. We need to understand how others perceive us, and what meanings they give to the situation. Power is exercised in everyday life through the attempt to take control of the definition of the social situation. This is achieved by 'impression management' by carefully manipulating the impression of our-'self' which we give to other social actors.

The rise of post-modern ideas of power

With the rise of post-modern theories in sociology, the conventional view of power as getting one's way is becoming seen by many as problematic. The definition of power is now a controversial area. Many seek to define *alternative spaces or sites of power*; that is to say, to identify how power operates at a number of different

For example, Pateman argues that the concentration on the definition of politics as something associated with democracy acts to exclude the private lives of women from the political process. Whereas politics is seen almost exclusively as something conducted by the business of governments (i.e. men) and states, the inequality experienced by many women in the private sphere – the family – goes unrecognized as a legitimate political struggle.

Walby offers a very similar analysis. She

levels in ordinary life as well as in the structures set up by government.

Discussion point
How is power a feature of all aspects of social life?

C3.1a

Recent approaches to sociological theorizing about power and politics in everyday life have tended to concentrate on the idea of a post-modern society. This contains the belief that contemporary times are different from those of the past, that significant changes have occurred in the nature or fabric of social life – including that of the political – so making our contemporary lives post (or after) a previous stage.

'New times' and new types of power

In these 'new' times, social theorists are still debating quite what the nature of these times are, and the directions future social change might take. These theorists differ considerably, not only with respect to what characterizes these times, but whether their characteristics are positive or not for society.

For example, some theorists have identified what they see as the development of the post-political: a significant loss in the participation, interest or confidence of populations in democracy, party politics and voting in general. Whereas, for some, the development of the post-political is treated as further evidence for the decline of hope for the future of society, others see this process as simply yet another opportunity for pastiche.

Looking at power all around us

Post-modern sites of power, rather than the traditional nation-state, are areas of social life and social living such as culture, identity, knowledge and language. The contemporary concern with these alternative conceptualizations of power is an attempt to move social theory on, to redefine traditional sociological debates.

The 'silent majorities' and political participation

Jean Baudrillard (1983b) is very pessimistic of contemporary social life. He writes of the development of the silent majorities who, disillusioned with politics, have lost the ability even to be interested in power any more, let alone fight it.

The death of politics

Baudrillard believes that politics has died: the silent majority, the masses, are indifferent to all party politics. The masses are free, but only in the sense that they are unable to be represented by anyone, anything or any set of beliefs. All that are left, in this world characterized by the death of politics, are fatal strategies (Baudrillard, 1990) – social theory is unable, any longer, to study the social, to investigate how and where the politics is in life.

'The post-modern condition'

For Jean-Francois Lyotard (1984), the 'post-modern condition' is best described as a relativity of reason. No longer, he argues, can the grand narrative of the freedom of humanity through scientific reason be sustained in the light of the contemporary fragmentation of knowledge. In other words, scientific reason – once a major form of legitimacy in the world – is now becoming understood as yet another big story, yet another claim to truth with no objective criteria through which to measure its truth.

The loss of truth

For Lyotard, there is no such thing as a universal, single truth, only *truths*. There is no such thing as reality, only *realities*. In this way, all knowledge is relative – all is as good as any other. In this post-modern condition, knowledge itself has become a site for power – a battlefield. According to Sarup:

It is widely accepted that computerized knowledge has become the principal force of production over the last few decades. ... Knowledge will be the major component in the world-wide competition for power and it is conceivable that nation-states will one day fight for control of information, just as they battled for control over territories in the past.

(Sarup, 1993, p. 133)

The power that knowledge brings

For Lyotard, knowledge itself is no longer a goal – it has become a commodity. It is something to be bought and sold, something to be consumed. Within the production of this knowledge, though, lies power. Who owns what knowledge? How much will it cost? Will everyone have equal access as consumers? According to Lyotard:

Knowledge and power are simply two sides of the same question: who decides what knowledge is, and who knows what needs to be decided? In the computer age, the question of knowledge is now more than ever a question of government. ... In the discourse of today's financial backers of research, the only credible goal is power. Scientists, technicians, and instruments are purchased not to find truth, but to augment power.

(Lyotard, 1984, pp. 8 and 46)

Language-games and power

For many contemporary thinkers, language too is a site for power. Lyotard uses the concept of a language-game to describe how the power that knowledge gives is expressed through the use of language. Communication between individuals is understood as a game between players with rules: each utterance is like a move in the game.

In this way, language is an expression of the use of power since we are in conflict with each other. Lyotard uses the metaphor of battle to describe how power operates in these language-games:

In the ordinary use of discourse – for example, in a discussion between two friends – the interlocutors use any available ammunition, changing games from one utterance to the next: questions, requests, assertions, and narratives are launched pell-mell into battle. The war is not without rules, but the rules allow and encourage the greatest possible flexibility of utterance.

(Lyotard, 1984, p. 17)

The power that institutions have over the individual bears down on these language-games and restricts our freedom within them. That is to say, institutions shape the rules of language – they define what are correct and incorrect utterances, and in doing so they exercise power over us by controlling the game in their favour. In this way, institutional and bureaucratic life functions to:

... filter discursive potentials, interrupting possible connections in the communication networks: there are things that should not be said. ... There are also things that should be said, and there are ways of saying them. Thus: orders in the army, prayer in church, denotation in the schools, narration in families, questions in philosophy, performativity in businesses.

(Lyotard, 1984, p. 17)

Post-structuralism: the politics of the body

Michel Foucault

For Foucault (1991), the key to understanding the nature of society is to study the origins of discourses. A discourse is a set of knowledge and rules, often associated with a specialized language. For example, Foucault would consider the discourse of psychology to enable psychologists to control, label and constrain some people into specialized spaces – asylums – often against their wishes. Foucault notes that discourses organize, although they are not exclusively confined to, an associated space or institution in which they operate, such as the asylum or the hospital.

Discourses and 'space'

Power in this sense is all around us, although Foucault notes that these discourses can be resisted: we can attempt to reverse the identity they give us. This fighting back or resistance is referred to by Foucault as the 'politics of space'. Power is then about the discipline and control of the body. As Foucault notes:

... the body is also directly involved in a political field; power relationships have an immediate hold on it; they invest it, mark it, train it, torture it, force it to carry out tasks, to perform ceremonies, to emit signs.

(Foucault, 1991, p. 25)

Like many other contemporary thinkers, Foucault is also concerned with the role power plays in knowledge:

We should admit rather that power produces knowledge (and not simply by encouraging it because it serves power or by applying it because it is useful); that power and knowledge directly imply one another; that there is no power relation without the correlative constitution of a field of knowledge, nor any knowledge that does not presuppose and constitute at the same time power relations.

(Foucault, 1991, p. 27)

Knowledge *is* power because it controls, labels and constrains, it limits possibilities for the subject of its gaze. Power exists everywhere like a web or maze covering all aspects of society:

Foucault argues that power is not a possession or a capacity. It is not something subordinate to or in the service of the economy. He insists that relations of power do not emanate from a sovereign or a state; nor should power be conceptualized as the property of an individual or class. Power is not simply a commodity which may be acquired or seized. Rather it has the character of a network; its threads extend everywhere.

(Sarup, 1993, pp. 73–4)

Discipline and surveillance

Foucault emphasizes the role played by social institutions in the discipline and control of the populations of western societies. He argues that the state has an overarching control over, and use of, techniques of punishment and discipline – through many and varied institutions such as prisons and asylums, and perhaps less obviously through hospitals and schools.

In his work *Discipline and Punish: The Birth of the Prison* (1991; orig. pub. 1975), Foucault notes that all these institutions use similar methods of control of the body. In making this claim he uses the concepts of discipline, punishment and control in a very broad fashion to refer to any system or set of practices which function to label, constrain, organize or regulate the human body. Of particular importance to Foucault's work is the use of timetables and taxonomies (classification systems) by institutions as instruments for the control and ordering of social actors.

Power and popular culture

Modern day theories of power and political action often look towards the daily lives of 'ordinary people' and look at power in everyday life. Politics is seen as a matter of indentity, consumption and sexuality, among others, and struggles for power are seen to exist everywhere. Even popular culture is sometimes regarded as a vast symbolic 'battle field' upon which individuals and groups exercise their control of the meaning and use of the products concerned.

The problem of 'popular culture'

In recent years, theorists of popular culture have been concerned to avoid what they regard as two great pitfalls.

1 Writers have sought to avoid the danger of 'élitism'. That is, they wished to avoid the 'mistakes' made by, for example, the advocates of the mass culture thesis and the Frankfurt School. Both the Frankfurt School and mass-culture critics, like Arnold, Eliot and Leavis, in attacking commercialism in the culture industries, implied that much popular culture was 'inferior' to other cultural forms. Such judgements were criticized for betraying a form of élitism.

2 It became unfashionable to present arguments that could be interpreted as examples of 'economic reductionism' (the attempt to explain the development of cultural patterns in terms of economic forces). Both Marxist and non-Marxist theorists tried to avoid the 'danger' of economic reductionism by employing theoretical approaches that directed attention to cultural issues (magazine content, tastes in shopping, television audiences, and so on), rather than questions of how the institutions of cultural production were organized. Culturalist approaches and those drawing on the idea of a post-modern society grew in popularity because they appeared to avoid the danger of economic reductionism.

The reaction against culturism

There is now a reaction against culturalism and similar approaches. Harris (1992) argues that the theorists who began to employ Gramsci's ideas in the 1960s and 70s (culturalists) did so in ways that tended to 'close off', rather than open up, empirical research or theoretical development.

Harris argues that other kinds of sociology have been more 'open' in the sense that researchers have been prepared to be 'surprised', or to acknowledge data and historical evidence that did not fit neatly into their theoretical frameworks. It is a little too easy, Harris suggests, to read into audience or consumer behaviour 'evidence' of 'resistance', particularly if qualitative, ethnographic methods are used. The danger is that culturalists 'find' what they assume to be the case at the beginning; and then ignore forms of popular cultural activity that are not compatible with their theoretical and political assumptions.

Little attention, Harris notes, has been given to popular but politically less palatable cultural pastimes like blood sports (for example, illegal dog-fighting) or 'consumer pathologies', such as the playground bullying of 'style fascists', who victimize those without designer clothes and trainers.

The collapse into cultural populism

McGuigan (1992) condemns what he regards as a collapse into 'cultural populism'. He reminds us that the pioneers of cultural studies, including writers like Raymond Williams and Richard Hoggart, were motivated by a desire to see ordinary people's experiences and culture taken more seriously in the curriculum offered in schools and colleges. That is not the same thing as assuming that *any* kind of popular culture should be embraced uncritically simply because it is popular amongst ordinary people.

Recent approaches, McGuigan argues, are so eager to avoid the mistakes of old mass-society or manipulation approaches that they end up offering an entirely uncritical endorsement of popular culture. This point might be applied to both culturalism and post-modernism. Any kind of popular culture is welcomed because it offers opportunities for 'resistance'. But, McGuigan points out, evidence of 'resistance' is often thin and, at the same time, the mechanisms of real political power are often ignored. Recent approaches, he argues, have also been too anxious to avoid the charge of economic reductionism:

In consequence, the economic aspects of media institutions and the broader economic dynamics of consumer culture were rarely investigated, simply bracketed off, thereby severely undermining the explanatory and, in effect, critical capacities of cultural studies.

(McGuigan, 1992, p. 41)

McGuigan suggests that what is required is an approach that tries to relate a political economy of popular culture to a sociology of consumption and identity. In other words, sociologists and cultural theorists should retain an interest in the various and diverse ways in which we all consume commodities and construct identities; but they should not lose sight of the point that many of our cultural options are shaped by the interests of cultural and media conglomerates, the working of capitalist markets, the power of the state, and the routines and professional values of workers inside the cultural industries – artists, producers, film and video directors, journalists, advertising executives, and others.

Constraints in the production of popular culture

Ferguson and Golding (1997) have recently completed a further critical review. They, too, are critical of the extent to which culturalist approaches have focused too much attention on how audiences consume popular culture and too little attention on the pressures and constraints involved in the actual production of popular culture, whether a television programme or a fashion magazine.

In particular, they are sympathetic to those who call for a return to the analysis of culture in the context of social class and structured inequality. We now know a great deal about the diverse ways in which people construct identities and derive pleasures from cultural consumption. Perhaps, the next step forward is to return to some of the traditional sociological questions about, for example, the inequalities in cultural resources and power.

Activity

a What is the danger of 'economic reductionism'?

b Summarize in your own words the criticisms made by Harris of research influenced by culturalism.

c Summarize in your own words the criticisms made by McGuigan and Fersuson and Golding. Do you agree?

C3.2, C3.3

Further reading

Accessible texts designed to introduce the key debates in this field include:

- Kirby, M. (1995) *Investigating Political Sociology*, London: Collins Educational.
- Nash, K. (2000) *Contemporary Political Sociology*, Oxford: Blackwell.
- Riley, M. (1988) *Power, Politics and Voting*, London: Harvester–Wheatsheaf.
- Woodward, K. (ed.) (2000) *Questioning Identity: Gender, Class, Nation*, London: Routledge.

The following are designed to provide more detail than the above introductory A level texts:

- Bottomore, T. (1993) *Political Sociology*, 2nd edn, London: Pluto Press.
- Lovenduski, J. and Randall, V. (1993) *Contemporary Feminist Politics*, Oxford: Oxford University Press.

Important studies which are accessible and of theoretical and empirical significance are:

- Mattausch, J. (1989) *A Commitment to Campaign: A Sociological Study of CND*, Manchester: Manchester University Press.
- Roseneil, S. (1995) *Disarming Patriarchy: Feminism and Political Action at Greenham*, Buckingham: Open University Press.

Back issues of the periodical *Sociology Review* (formerly known as *Social Studies Review*) also contain many articles on this field of sociology and many others.

Applied sociological research skills

Sociological research design and methodology

Chapter outline

The value of the claims made by sociology – the status of 'sociological knowledge' – rests ultimately on the validity of the methods used in research. The study of research design and methodology is therefore central to sociology.

16.1 Research design and sociological theory   *page 639*

This section gives a detailed introduction to sociological theory and its development from the works of Durkheim, Weber and Marx to the contemporary debates on sociological theory. From this basis, the approaches taken by the main methodological approaches towards research design can then be considered.

16.2 Context of data collection   *page 661*

This section considers some methodological debates, notably the difficulty of moving from links or correlation between variables to making cause and effect statements. It links into various methodological approaches

16.3 Techniques of data collection and recording   *page 667*

The sociological research methods of questionnaires, interviews and observation each have their strengths and limitations. This section looks at what each method entails and then moves to consider these strengths and weaknesses.

16.4 Positivism and research design   *page 682*

Positivists believe that sociology can and should be scientific, and that it is possible to be purely objective as a researcher. Furthermore it wishes sociology to study social facts, which positivists believe exist objectively.

16.5 Phenomenology and research design   *page 688*

The phenomenological tradition in sociology rests on the argument that the subject matter – human beings – are inevitably subjective. This approach argues that the role of sociology is to arrive at a truly objective account (by the researcher) of the thoughts and feelings of the human subjects under study.

16.6 Realism and research design   *page 691*

Realism argues that all theories are value-laden, so it is impossible to remove values from sociological research. As a result realists believe that, although the world *does* exist objectively, it is impossible for sociology ever to provide a truly objective picture for all times because of the subjective value-laden nature of human theories.

16.7 Post-modernism and research design   *page 699*

Post-modernists, too, believe that all theories (or 'discourses' as they call them) are value-laden. This implies that values are an integral part of sociology. The differing values of the approaches means that not only do they disagree with each other, they also talk in a variety of languages so that differences can never be resolved. Since reality is somehow constructed through these discourses, the world can have no objective existence outside of the particular discourse being examined. This presents a picture of a wholly subjective sociology, characterized by relativism.

16.1 Research design and sociological theory

Modernity and the emergence of sociology

Although thinkers have commented on the nature of society since the beginning of humanity, sociology as a distinct subject emerged only in the nineteenth century. Why was this? It can be seen to follow from two broad sets of changes that occurred in the eighteenth century:

- There were changes in the way people lived, most notably seen in the 'industrial revolution' and the French Revolution.
- There were changes in the way people thought about the world, particularly in the rise of the set of ideas known as the Enlightenment.

The industrial revolution

The first important material change was the industrial revolution, a process that began in England and spread out across Europe. This brought a profound change in the way people lived their lives. Work was concentrated in specific places built for that purpose, namely factories. This led to a split between the place of residence and the place of work. People were no longer spread out across the land growing crops, but became concentrated in towns and cities.

The Enlightenment

At the same time, traditional notions of how society should operate were being undermined by changing ideas, notably through the process known as the Enlightenment. This phrase covers a widespread development of thinking about the world, culminating in the mid-eighteenth century with the rise of science as a method of explanation – and as a result the declining importance of religion in many people's lives.

The 'new' idea that people were not merely the passive subjects of God's will, but were in some way able to comprehend and master their own world, also had political repercussions. The French Revolution of 1789 and the American Revolution of 1776 were the most important early results of this new way of thinking, and the impact of these events shook the whole world.

The world 'reborn'

In short, the world was turned upside down:

- Science replaced religion as the main basis or source of knowledge.
- Notions of 'the people' and 'democracy' replaced 'religion and the monarchy' as the main platform of government (see also Section 15.1).
- Industrial production and urbanization transformed previously agricultural, rural societies.

These developments have been seen collectively as the emergence of modern society and modernity.

For anyone interested in human affairs, this was a period of intense change. Many people were led to ask about the implications of these changes for society and the way people lived. In relation both to political authority and to more general knowledge about the world, the idea that people could understand the world and could therefore participate in the construction and administration of that world was the central theme. From being objects of the world, people now saw themselves as able to shape their own destiny. What was required was the knowledge to do so, and sociology was to be that knowledge.

The entrance of sociology

What knowledge was needed to understand the changes society had been through? Some argued that there was a need for sociology to restore a degree of *stability* to society, while others argued it was needed to ensure that future changes to society were made on the basis of *informed scientific statements*. In either case, sociology could play a central role.

We can consider contrasting reactions to this situation by two early sociologists, Auguste Comte (1798–1857) and Herbert Spencer (1820–1903).

Comte: sociology as a reforming ideology for the state

Comte is famous for actually inventing the term 'sociology' and for promoting it as the main element in his positive philosophy (Comte, 1877; orig. pub. 1830–2). He believed that society progressed through a number of stages reflecting the development of human ideas.

The first two of these stages – the theological and the metaphysical – represented eras when the clergy and philosophers, respectively, were the ultimate arbiters of knowledge; this represented Comte's view of the development of human society up to that point.

His third stage – positivism – represented the triumph of science (see Section 16.4). He argued that an understanding of human society could and should be developed on a scientific basis. This knowledge was to be used to bring about changes beneficial to society.

Comte believed that, with the growth of economic specialization and the division of labour (whereby people specialized in different tasks), the notion of community – of having something in common with others – might break down. It had been the main basis of social integration in pre-industrial society. He therefore set out to produce an outline of changes needed to avoid this situation. Central to his solution was the state, which he saw as the only real potential unifying

force in this new period of individualism. The problem was to get people to recognize the validity of the state's right to regulate their lives.

It is here that sociology comes in, since Comte argued that the authority of the state would be greater if it was backed up with a specific intellectual doctrine. Sociology was therefore assigned a central role in the reconstitution of a notion of community in society, through providing authority for state regulation over society. It might be argued that this presents a very authoritarian vision of society, with directions given by sociologists and enforced by the state.

Spencer: society as a marketplace

In contrast, Spencer argued that the state was not needed. In so far as it did intervene, it had the effect of stifling the individual initiative which was now the key basis of economic and societal development. Drawing on the ideas of Adam Smith, Spencer (1874, 1896) argued that society was now regulated merely by the mutual self-interest of individuals and all that was needed was exchange and trade between individuals. He argued that the move from military societies of the past to the industrial society had led to a decline in the need for state regulation. Societies would therefore almost automatically stabilize as long as individual self-interest was not stifled.

The individual and society

We all like our own individual freedom when it is threatened, but perhaps we are not so enamoured of individual freedom when it involves our neighbours' freedom to play loud music until four in the morning. Every day we face the problem of how we can retain individual freedom while at the same time living in some sustainable relationship with others in society. Comte and Spencer offered contrasting views on this dilemma:

- Comte worried that society might break down in the face of the new ideas of individualism. He argued for a strong state to limit this individualism.

- Spencer saw individualism not as a threat but as the hope for the future. He argued that trade and exchange (in short, the market) provided all the cement that was needed to keep people together in some sort of civilized relationship.

The relationship between society and the individuals within it forms the key continuing focus of sociological theory. Should we view society as the construction of individuals, and therefore understand it by looking at how those individuals interact to make and remake society? Or should we instead see individuals as the *product* of society, and therefore start our analysis at the level of society?

Activity

a Suggest ways in which the themes and arguments put forward by Comte and Spencer are present in contemporary debates about society. Which of these two contrasting visions of society do you think offers the best blueprint for society today?

b Draw up a list of the advantages and drawbacks of each of these two schemes.

C3.2, C3.3

The answers to these questions form the starting point for sociological analysis. The contrasting answers given by Comte and Spencer form the backdrop to the ideas developed by the three generally acknowledged founders of modern sociology – Marx, Durkheim and Weber. These in turn form the basis for all subsequent theory.

The value of classical sociological ideas

If you are wondering why we are spending time looking at how some dead sociologists reacted to events over 100 years ago, the answer is quite simple. The problems they considered, the questions they asked and the answers they provided are still relevant. As one commentator put it:

One reason we return to Marx is that there is still a class struggle, even though its form has changed. One reason we return to Durkheim is that the problem of solidarity in an individualistic society is still an issue for us. One reason we return to Weber is that power relations continue to proliferate on many other dimensions than the economic.

(Kilminster, 1992, p. 153)

Discussion point

To what extent do you agree that class struggle, power relations and debates about freedom and solidarity are present in modern society? Are there other issues which are more important today? Discuss the relative importance of all these issues in contemporary UK society.

C3.1a

The development of classical sociological theories

This section considers in some detail the key ideas of three thinkers commonly identified as the founders of classical sociology – Karl Marx, Emile Durkheim and Max Weber. We also look at some of the diverse ways in which their ideas have been later interpreted.

Karl Marx

Marx (1818–83) grew up in the Rhineland area of what is now part of Germany – a society obsessed with the implications of the French Revolution and how to stop such a thing happening in Germany. Marx himself gravitated towards a group of thinkers who developed rather more radical ideas out of Hegelian philosophy. The central insight which Marx took from Hegel was the idea that things develop through the clash of contradictions. For Hegel, this meant a clash of ideas, but Marx argued that real material existence was more important. For him the clashes were real material clashes between human beings.

Historical materialism

Marx argued that the fundamental element of human society is the need to produce the basic needs of humanity: food, shelter and clothing. All this needs to be done before people can reflect on and develop ideas. Marx therefore believed that production, combined with the social relationships people entered into to meet these needs, was the fundamental element of society.

By around 1845 Marx and his close collaborator, Friedrich Engels, were deeply involved in the growing communist movement. They wrote a number of works, such as *The German Ideology* (1974; orig. written 1845), describing an outline of their own thinking – which came to be known as 'historical materialism'. Their work considers topics which today would clearly be called 'sociology', as we can see from the following quotation from their *Communist Manifesto*:

[The] essence of man is no abstraction inherent in each single individual. In its reality it is the ensemble of the social relations.

(Marx and Engels, 1968, p. 29; orig. pub. 1848)

Class struggle and social change

Production, and the social relations it entails, are therefore central to Marx's analysis. However, what makes it distinctive is the way in which he does two things:

• He argues that the relationships created in the process of production have always entailed conflicts of interest, which lead to social conflicts between classes and to social change. Class conflict is therefore the central motor of history.

• He also argues that the relationships created in the production sphere have an effect on all other social relations in society.

In relation to the first of these, the description contained in *Communist Manifesto* provides a summary of this notion of human society developing through successive conflicts centred on production:

The history of all hitherto existing societies is the history of class struggles. ... Freeman and slave, patrician and plebeian, lord and servant, guildmaster and journeyman, in a word, oppressor and oppressed, stood in constant opposition to one another, carried on an uninterrupted, now hidden, now open fight, a fight that each time ended, either in the revolutionary re-constitution of society at large, or in the common ruin of the contending classes.

(Marx and Engels, 1968, p. 36; orig. pub. 1848)

The theory of exploitation

The important question to ask here is why these relationships were antagonistic – that is, between 'oppressor' and 'oppressed'. To answer this question, we need to examine the labour theory of value, which Marx supported. This is an abstract concept which tries to describe the fundamental relationships within production. Marx uses it to develop an analysis of actually existing society (1954, orig. pub. 1867; 1956, orig. pub. 1885; 1959, orig. pub. 1894; 1973, orig. pub. 1857). It focuses on the fact that the important thing about

production is not technological change, but change in the way it is socially organized.

The labour theory of value

The theory argues that the inherent value of anything is based on the number of socially necessary hours needed to produce it, since that is what things have in common. The term 'socially necessary' is used because otherwise a table made by an incompetent carpenter who takes a very long time would be extremely valuable, and that would be a nonsense. On the basis of this theory, it is only by being directly involved in production that people produce value.

But Marx noted that in all social relationships of production up to that time, some of the people involved in production actually did no direct work at all. Marx argued, however, that since they produced no value themselves, their money must arise from the work of others. In simple terms, part of the value created by workers was taken not by them but by the 'capitalists'. This is what Marx meant by exploitation, the expropriation of money from workers by capitalists.

Alienation

This is also the basis of Marx's notion of 'alienation'. By this, Marx meant the way in which things we make come to have a power over us. Money is a prime example, since it is not a natural thing, but a human invention which now occupies much of our thoughts and often worries. The lack of it restricts our ability to engage in certain activities. Production, which Marx saw as potentially liberating, both in terms of the goods it could provide and the satisfaction to be gained from making things, in fact became a drudge, a necessity and an arena in which one group lived by exploiting another.

Marx therefore argued that the direct producers – meaning the workers who produced things – would rise up and overthrow their oppressors, and would create a society where the surplus was shared by all, a communist society. Production and the producers (the working class) were therefore central to his analysis.

The economy and society

How does the process of production affect the rest of society? In *Capital*, Marx provides the following summary of this argument:

The specific economic form, in which unpaid surplus-labour is pumped out of direct producers, determines the relationship of rulers and ruled, as it grows directly out of production itself and, in turn, reacts upon it as a determining element. Upon this, however, is founded the entire formation of the economic community which grows out of the production relations themselves, thereby simultaneously its specific political form. It is always the direct relationship of the owners of the conditions of production to the direct producers – a relation always naturally corresponding to a definite stage in the development of the methods of labour and thereby its social productivity – which reveals its innermost secret, the hidden basis of the entire social structure, and with it the political form of the relation of sovereignty and dependence; in short, the corresponding form of the state. This does not prevent the same economic basis – the same from the standpoint of its main conditions – due to innumerable different empirical circumstances, natural environment, racial relations, external historical influences, etc., from showing infinite variations and gradations in appearance, which can be ascertained only by analysis of the empirically given circumstances.

(Marx, 1959, p. 791; orig. pub. 1894)

This has come to be known as the 'base–superstructure' model of society, since it suggests that the way production (the economic base) is organized will have a determining effect on all other relationships in society. However, the point Marx made about the varieties of society that are compatible with the same economic base leads to the conclusion that Marx believed that the way production was organized put definite limits on the way the rest of society could be organized.

Ideology and class consciousness

The implication of the 'base–superstructure' model of society is that workers engaging in struggles over production, will, if they are successful, cause changes not only in the sphere of production but in all other areas of society as well. This is the meaning of 'social revolution'. Put together, these elements provide both a view of historical changes and a vision of the future, a communist society. Marx was centrally involved in the setting up of the First Communist International, an entity dedicated to developing the struggles taking place in society to the point where a social revolution would occur. This suggests that Marx believed such a process was not automatic.

One major reason for this was his belief that the ideas in people's heads reflected the ideas of the people in charge of society. Ideologies kept the existing society going and they were an important part of the circumstances within which people struggled to change society. This idea is encapsulated in the following extract from the *Communist Manifesto*:

Men make their own history, but they do not make it just as they please; they do not make it under circumstances chosen by themselves, but under circumstances directly encountered, given and transmitted from the past. The tradition of all the dead generations weighs like a nightmare on the brain of the living.

(Marx, 1968, p. 96; orig. pub. 1872)

The idea is expressed more specifically in what has come to be known as the 'dominant ideology thesis', which states:

The ideas of the ruling class are in every epoch the ruling ideas: i.e. that class which is the ruling material force in society is at the same time its ruling intellectual force.

(Marx and Engels, *The German Ideology*, 1974; orig. written 1845; quoted in Callinicos, 1987, p. 140)

This suggests that the struggle to change society is not merely an economic one but must also engage in ideas and ideological struggle, in order first to persuade workers that the ideas in society are not correct but merely justify their treatment.

Criticisms of Marx

Economic determinism

The centrality of production in Marx's work has also been the basis of one of the most oft-repeated criticisms, namely that Marx's work is an example of economic determinism. This has led to accusations that such an approach ignores all the social relationships not directly involved in production, and indeed those people not even involved in production.

Feminists (see Section 17.8) have argued that Marxism downplays conflicts in the *domestic* sphere; and post-modernists (see Section 16.7) have argued that, in contemporary society, processes of *consumption* are more important than production in the formation of identity and social relationships.

Despite these criticisms, it seems clear that

the level of economic production does at the very least place clear *limits* on other aspects of society. Whether it is so utterly determining as some interpretations of Marx would suggest is still open to question.

Over-emphasis on class conflict

A related criticism is that 'class conflict' as a unique theory of social change does explain why other aspects of inequality, too, can operate to achieve social change. The women's movement (see Chapter 17) and black nationalism (see see Chapter 17) are the most obvious; but we can also include here the more recent new social movements (see Section 15.3) which often consciously organize themselves around identities that have nothing to do with the sphere of production.

Over-emphasis on the working class

Finally, the link between Marxism and the working class has led to criticisms along the lines that, since the working class has not as yet led a revolution in western Europe, Marx's analysis of the process of social change is flawed. This has arguably been the spur to the various interpretations of Marx that have developed in recent years.

Interpretations of Marx

Some followers of Marx, notably those leading the Second Communist International, tended towards an evolutionary view which relied on developments in technology to produce a communist society. This led to divisions, and revolutionary Marxists split from the Second International to create the Third Communist International. The leaders of this included Lenin, Trotsky and Stalin, who themselves were later to diverge in their analyses.

The revolutionary tradition continued in the period after the Russian Revolution of 1917, but the failure of the revolution to spread to western Europe led to the growth of what has been called 'western Marxism', of which there are many variants. It is undoubtedly the versions of this that are most prominent in contemporary Marxist sociology. These developments have led to a multitude of 'Marxisms'.

Structural Marxism

Marx's focus on how the structure of production

relationships has a determining effect on other aspects of society has led some to see Marxism as a version of economic determinism – a belief that the economy determines everything else. In some versions of Marxism, this entails a belief that economic and technological developments will almost automatically lead to socialism. More recently, reacting against this, Althusser (1966, 1968) developed what came to be known as 'structural Marxism' – structural because it denied any place in the theory for human action despite Marx's statements about men making history.

Humanist Marxism

In contrast, humanist interpretations of Marx say that his critique of capitalism was about dehumanizing social relationships. Further, they stress the potential for people to overcome this and create a fully free society. The various strands of this approach are examined in Section 13.4.

Marx and ideology

The comments Marx made about ideology have led to an interpretation of his arguments stressing that economic struggle alone is not sufficient to cause social change; it is necessary also to engage in ideological and cultural struggles. This interpretation can be seen in the work of Italian Marxist Antonio Gramsci (1971; orig. pub. 1929–35), as well as in the work of the Frankfurt School and the development of 'critical theory'.

Emile Durkheim

Society as a 'social fact', and the need for sociology

Durkheim (1858–1917) argued that society was in reality *sui generis* (a unified whole). Society is not reducible to the sum of individuals within it, it is exterior to them; but it is nonetheless a 'social fact' because it puts a constraint on their actions. The idea that we live a life determined for us is clear from the following extract from Durkheim's *The Rules of Sociological Method*:

When I fulfil my obligations as brother, husband, or citizen I perform duties which are defined, externally to myself and my acts, in law and custom. Even if they conform to my own sentiments, and I feel their reality subjectively, such reality is still objective, for I did not create them; I merely inherited them through my education ... the church member finds the beliefs and practices of his religious life ready made at birth; their existence prior to him implies their existence outside himself.

(Durkheim, 1938b; orig. pub. 1895; quoted in Jones, 1993b, p. 25)

Activity

a With regard to the three roles outlined by Durkheim in the quotation above, suggest what the law and customs define as the obligations of these roles.

b Provide two further examples of roles, and explain how the law and custom constrains the people in these roles to act in certain ways.

C3.2, C3.3

Durkheim goes on to set out the implications of this for sociology. While he argued that the new subject had to be scientific, he believed that economics – the social science that had most followed the methodology of the natural sciences – erred by starting from the notion of the isolated individual. Given Durkheim's definition of society, he could not accept this. Instead he argued that sociology should study 'social facts' which were exterior to individuals and were not directly observable by watching the actions of these individuals.

Discussion point

Why is society distinct from the individuals who make it up? Could we not simply understand what happens in sociology as the result of the actions and motivations of the collections of individuals within it? Durkheim's answer to this would be a clear 'No'. Do you agree with him?

C3.1a

Durkheim argued that sociology should concern itself with the causes of these 'social facts', as well as the reasons for their persistence over time. In order to study this latter aspect he argued that we needed to consider the functions served by these social facts; he reasoned that if they did not serve any function they would die out. The application of this methodology to pro-

duce a specifically Durkheimian approach can be seen in his other main works.

The division of labour in society, the moral basis of society and *anomie*

Durkheim's first book dealt with the relationship between the individual and society in the context of the transition from pre-industrial to industrial society. He argued that we could not understand society simply on the basis of agreements between individuals. *The Division of Labour in Society* (1938a; orig. pub. 1893) was dedicated to a critique of this position, and the allied theory that society resulted from a contract. Durkheim rejected this view of the origin of society, and he did so by arguing that for people to make a contract they must have a prior basis on which to do so:

In Durkheim's celebrated phrase, there is 'a non-contractual element in contract': the existence of contractual exchanges presupposes moral authority, the authority which renders contracts binding.

(Giddens, 1978, p. 10)

The conscience collective

Durkheim set out to show how the individualism of modern society, which was absent in traditional societies, could be explained in terms of changes to the moral order. He called this moral order the 'conscience collective' – emphasizing that it was both a moral and a rational outlook.

Durkheim argued that in traditional societies the conscience collective formed a strongly defined moral consensus. The usual method of transmission of this moral consensus was through the church and religion. Subject to a powerful and all-embracing moral order, people were essentially very similar and this was what kept society together. Durkheim called this 'mechanical solidarity' – emphasizing its similarity to a biological organism composed of cells very similar to each other.

Solidarity and individualism

However, modern society was very different because important changes had taken place as a result of industrialization and urbanization. Most notably, there was now division of labour – the work done in society was divided up and people had begun to specialize. Durkheim wanted to consider the social effects of this development. He argued that society was now based not on people being similar but on them being individuals.

For this to come about there needs to have been some transformation of the nature of the conscience collective. This social force needed to alter to allow for the growth of the notion of 'individualism'. Individualism was therefore not the product of individuals but of the changing moral order of society. Society created individuals and individualism. Society now survives, because individuals need each other. Since there is now specialization, no one individual can perform all the tasks needed to survive, so each is mutually dependent. This Durkheim calls 'organic solidarity'. This different type of society has a different moral basis, but it still does have a moral basis:

This is not to say, however, that the conscience collective is likely to disappear completely. Rather it increasingly comes to consist of very general and indeterminate ways of thought and sentiment, which leaves room open for a growing variety of individual differences. There is even a place where it is strengthened and made precise: that is, in the way in which it regards the individual.

(Durkheim, 1938a, p. 146; orig. pub. 1893)

Anomie

Durkheim recognized that there might be some problems in the transition from mechanical to organic solidarity. It could result in a 'forced division of labour', leading to some people failing to be properly integrated into the new society. He used the phrase '*anomie*' to indicate this state of being outside societal regulation, and he argued that this might be seen to lie behind such phenomena as industrial conflict, unhappiness and rising levels of suicide. Nonetheless, he asserted that this was an abnormal state of affairs and a result of the great transformations that had taken place. He looked forward to a return to social stability over time.

The normal state of affairs was therefore a society where there was a clear moral consensus and social stability. *Anomie* was a problem but a temporary one. This concept also illustrates another strand of Durkheim, which distinguishes him from the earlier positivism of Comte. He argued that there are forces and processes in society that are not reducible to individuals, and which therefore are not directly observable by looking at individuals. This view is known as 'realism' (see Section 16.6), and Durkheim's method is therefore arguably a combination of positivism and realism.

This can perhaps be seen most clearly in his study of suicide (1979; orig. pub. 1897).

Anomic suicide

Anomic suicide resulted when individuals were insufficiently regulated by society. This occurred when the value consensus holding society together began to break down, particularly during periods of social change that resulted in uncertainty for individuals.

While there are major debates about the validity of this piece of work as an explanation of suicide, it illustrates a number of key Durkheimian themes:

• the power of society over individuals
• the superiority of sociological analysis
• the use of science as a method – via the collection and analysis of facts, in this case statistics on suicide rates
• the belief that the key factor in society is the moral order – how this integrates individuals into society, and can explain variations in individual behaviour.

Society, religion and rituals

The final aspect of Durkheim to consider is his analysis of religion (1982; orig. pub. 1912). This is more fully examined in Section 7.8. However, some comments are required here because of its importance in the overall Durkheimian schema.

When Durkheim analysed religious rituals he came to the conclusion that their function was to facilitate people coming together. Through such rituals, people, and therefore society, were bonded together.

The importance of rituals based on Durkheim's ideas was studied by Shils and Young (1953). They viewed the coronation ceremony of Queen Elizabeth II as just such a ritual, allowing the reaffirmation of certain values and support for such values. A similar analysis was provided of the rituals surrounding the investiture of the Prince of Wales:

The feelings about the Queen and Prince Charles which the Investiture invoked, managed to fuse personal with public concerns in a symbolic fashion that Durkheim would have understood.

(Blumler *et al.*, 1971, p. 170)

C3.1a

Discussion point

How might such theorists view the divorces in the Royal Family? What might they view them as indicating, and what vision of the future might they foretell?

For Durkheim, the analysis of religion served to underline the absolute need for a moral order in society, and a secular morality was required to replace the declining religious value system. This led him to consider how the moral basis of society could be reinvigorated.

Criticisms of Durkheim's approach

The 'reification' of society

The first criticism of Durkheim concerns his notion of 'society'. He argued that it had an existence which could not be reduced to the experiences of individuals within it. This is a controversial point, since it appears to attribute life to something ('society') that is an *abstract concept*. He seemed to be presenting society as a living entity beyond the sum of individuals within it. This is known as 'reification'.

Durkheim tended to see society as similar to the human body, with interrelated elements each fulfilling a function. The danger is that this approach can lead one to see society itself as a living organism – which it isn't.

Discussion point

How much individual free will is there in society, according to Durkheim? How might his idea be applied to the choice of A level subjects by students?

C3.1a

Over-emphasis on the consensual nature of society

Durkheim has also been criticized for overstating the degree of *consensus* in society. He held that, in his mode of organic solidarity, the normal state of affairs was for society to be an integrated whole. The problem here is that anything that diverges from these modes is then discounted as 'abnormal' – or, to use Durkheim's word, 'pathological'.

In the section of *The Division of Labour in*

Society where he discusses the reality of the situation in France at the time, he presents a picture of class conflict, rising dissatisfaction and rising levels of suicide, all described by his famous concept of *anomie*.

'Normality' and 'abnormality' are subjective concepts

There appears to be a contradiction in Durkheim's analysis. He saw sociology as the study of social facts, which he defined as something present in the average of societies. In France at the time he was writing, unrest was clearly a social fact on this basis, yet he himself chose to describe it as an abnormality:

As a result, he tended to idealise societies he thought of as integrated, ignoring the tensions and conflicts within them, while seeing the realities of his own society only as the pathological deviations from its future, normal, ideally integrated state.

(Lukes, 1973, p. 30)

Discussion point

What is normal and what is abnormal, and how do we decide?

C3.1a

Lukes further argues that Durkheim's notion of rituals having a uniting force is unacceptable. It can be shown that societies do exist where there is no consensus (such as in Northern Ireland). Some rituals do not serve an integrating function – the Orange Order parades in Northern Ireland do not lead to greater social integration, but instead tend to intensify differences.

Interpretations of Durkheim

The potential contradictions in his thought are the basis of recent sociological attempts to provide a radical interpretation of Durkheim. There are arguably three differing interpretations.

Durkheim as a forerunner of functionalism

Durkheim argued that everything that survived over time did so because it served some function. His view of society as a system of interrelated parts which form a whole also leads to a functional analysis. This stress on the interrelatedness of parts and the function each fulfils in maintaining the whole became a central part of functionalist analysis.

Whilst it is clear that the notion of 'function' is central to Durkheim's sociology, whether the interpretation of Durkheim in functionalist sociology is totally justified is an area for debate. It is, however, certainly this interpretation of Durkheim which is most prevalent in sociology, though it has recently been challenged by two other contrasting versions.

Durkheim as a forerunner of structuralism

Structuralism might be defined as follows: *The whole is more than the parts, and cannot be reduced to the parts. What is important is the relationship between the parts.*

The view of Durkheim as a structuralist is clearly held by Bottomore and Nisbet (1979), who argue that Durkheim must be regarded as 'the prominent structuralist in French sociological thought' (p. 565).

Structuralism became an important component of French thought through the work of anthropologists, but became more widely used in sociology primarily through the development of 'structuralist Marxism' and the work of Althusser.

Radical Durkheimianism

Although, as a theorist, Durkheim has often been portrayed as a rather conservative thinker who was overly concerned with order and social integration, Pearce (1989) and Gane (1992) have both argued that he should be seen as a radical thinker, concerned with the inequalities of industrial society.

Max Weber

Social action and *verstehen*

Max Weber (1864–1920) is seen quite rightly as one of the originators of the approach in sociology usually known as 'social action theory'. This asserts that we need to see society as the result of the actions of human individuals. So, in contrast to the extreme structural views, Weberian sociology always starts off with the notion of an active humanity. Weber's stance on this can be grasped from the following extract where he talks about how we need to understand social phenomena:

[these] collectivities must be treated as solely the   and modes of organisation of the particu-   f individual persons, since these alone can

be treated as agents in the course of subjectively understandable action.

(Weber, 1968, p. 13; orig. pub. 1921)

The last phrase of this statement is also important because it brings us to his second point about the study of sociology – that we need to study the meanings people give to their actions, to understand the way they look at the world and how this influences their actions. Weber gave the name *'verstehen'* to this approach, meaning 'to understand'. This implies a very different theoretical and methodological approach from the positivist tradition, namely phenomenology (see Section 16.5).

The theory of rationalization

Weber's key concerns in sociological theory (1968; orig. pub. 1921) were (a) the effects of the rise of rationalization in society, and (b) his fear that the growth of bureaucracy would become a threat to individual freedom, an 'iron cage' as he put it. At the same time, Weber was clearly a German nationalist, proud of the cultural traditions of Germany. His work is therefore concerned with the development of rationalism and its potential effects on western – and more specifically German – civilization. These concerns led to a number of recurring themes that may be summarized as:

- a continuing debate with Marx, rejecting his exclusive emphasis on material and economic factors, and stressing instead the role that ideas, culture and non-economic factors can play in life
- the analysis of rationalization, both as a set of ideas and as a set of institutional processes, leading to a discussion of power and the political sphere.

Class and status

His first work was a study of peasants in eastern Germany. Following German unification in the 1870s, landowners in the eastern regions began replacing German workers with foreign migratory workers. This led Weber to study how farm workers who shared the same basic economic relationship nonetheless differed in their status, notably because of the precarious position of foreigners as guest workers in Germany

Here we can see the basis of the distinction Weber later famously drew between 'class' (a purely economic relationship) and 'status' (relating to non-economic notions of prestige, but also a basis for inequality).

Religion, ideas and social change

The 'protestant ethic' and the 'spirit of capitalism'

What also emerged out of this early study was the argument that economic conduct could be understood only by also analysing the ideas that people held and which affected the way people pursued their economic aims. When later refined and developed into an analysis of the general process of the growth of rationality, the study of ideas and their role in history can be seen to be the basis of perhaps Weber's most famous work, *The Protestant Ethic and the Spirit of Capitalism* (1930; orig. pub. 1905).

Criticism of Marx

Marx had argued that history was understandable in terms of the development of *material factors*. Weber disagreed with this. He said that ideas could also be an important basis for social change. These were seen as a crucial factor in the rise of capitalism in western Europe:

Weber had no regard for comprehensive accounts of history, seeing, instead, the contemporary developments as entirely distinctive to the history of Western Europe and the United States and unmatched elsewhere. ... Acquisitiveness and avarice are common throughout all societies. In other societies, work and the pursuit of wealth are regarded as necessary evils, as means which provide the good life; they do not in themselves make up the good life. In modern capitalism, by contrast, work has a morally positive character.

(Hughes *et al.*, 1995, p. 95)

Weber's argument

According to Weber, it is the 'spirit of capitalism' – this positive idea of hard work as a duty – which distinguishes western civilisation. Capitalism cannot be seen as pure individual acquisitiveness, since this was often greater in pre-capitalist societies. It is the idea, the ethic, the spirit that makes it distinctive. (See also Section 7.9.)

He notes that there was a correlation between the rise in commercial activity and the adoption of protestantism:

... business leaders and owners of capital, as well as the higher grades of skilled labour, and even more the higher technically and commercially trained personnel of modern enterprises, are overwhelmingly Protestant.

(Weber, 1930, p. 35; orig. pub. 1905)

He sought to explain this by examining the impact of their religious beliefs on the lives of people following Calvinism, a protestant doctrine. Calvinists argued that all people were *predestined* either to be saved or damned in the afterlife. This implied there was actually nothing they could do to change their ultimate fate. However, *uncertainty* about whether they were in fact chosen would lead people to look for a sign. This, allied with the Puritan disdain for unnecessary possessions, would lead them to work hard and reinvest any surplus rather than spend it on material goods:

The spirit of modern capitalism is thus characterised by a unique combination of devotion to the earning of wealth through legitimate economic activity, together with the avoidance of the use of this income for personal enjoyment. ... the performance of 'good works' became regarded as a 'sign' of election – not in any way a method of attaining salvation, but rather the elimination of doubts of salvation.

(Giddens, 1971, pp. 126–9)

In his study of Weber, Bendix (1963) states that Weber also made reference to material factors that were necessary for the rise of capitalism. In particular, Bendix points to Weber's analysis of the rise of the independent power of the city. Weber argued that trade in medieval cities was regulated by ethical ideas, which can therefore also be seen as precursors of the spirit of capitalism. He argues that what was different about the rise of cities in Europe was that all inhabitants were made citizens of the city, whereas elsewhere they were not. The importance of this is that the ethical regulation over trade in European cities covered all inhabitants and was therefore much more powerful.

A second important fact was that one of the requirements of citizenship (see Section 15.1) in European cities was to participate in military service. This gave European cities a basis for independent power, and this local autonomy further reinforced their power to regulate commercial activity. Thus Bendix asserts that material factors are, arguably, as important as ideas in Weber's explanation overall – though an emphasis on the ideas of Calvinism has dominated later commentary.

Comparative studies of religion

In his comparative studies of religion (1951, orig. pub. 1915; 1952, orig. pub. 1917; 1958, orig. pub. 1916), Weber further fleshed out his theory that the belief in certain ideas may have an effect on the level of development of rationality in the economic sphere, and in society in general. He argued, broadly, that differences in religious ideas could be seen as one explanation of why economic rationality developed first in Europe. Although most of the material prerequisites for capitalism were also present in China, Weber suggests that its non-emergence could be traced to the differences between Calvinism and Confucianism – or more properly to the social effects of these different theologies.

Discussion point

Bearing in mind the relatively recent rise to economic prominence of countries such as Japan, China and South Korea, how might this development question Weber's focus on religious differences as a key variable in explaining economic development?

C3.1a

Criticisms of Weber

Weber's theories about Calvinism has been subject to a number of criticisms.

A mismatch between Calvinism and capitalism

It has been pointed out that in some areas that were strongly Calvinist – notably Switzerland, Scotland and the Netherlands – capitalism did not develop early on.

The debate about what caused what

A second criticism is that capitalism predated Calvinism, which would of course eliminate all possible consideration of them having some unique causative relationship.

In a contribution to a recent debate about Weber's 'protestant ethic' thesis, MacKinnon (1994) has argued that Weber misinterpreted Calvinism. MacKinnon asserts that Calvinism also allowed for 'good works' to be merely spiritual. If true, there would be no need for adherents to engage in economic activity to look for a sign of their salvation, which would undermine the central correlation espoused by Weber.

Pessimism

Weber's rather pessimistic analysis of the effects of rationalization has been questioned, most notably by Habermas.

Activity

Weber's views about the importance of ideas, and of analysing society in terms of the meanings developed by individuals, clearly provide the basis for contrasts between his work and that of Durkheim and Marx.

a Using material from this section, suggest how Marx would respond to Weber's emphasis on the importance of ideas, and how Durkheim would respond to Weber's conception of society. Write short summaries of the differences you have identified.

b In each case, suggest which theorist you feel has the stronger argument, giving reasons. Remember that you should consider how useful these ideas are in explaining contemporary society.

Interpretations of Weber

Weber, rationalization and 'critical theory'

Weber's studies of religion were all concerned with investigating the relationship between ideas and action. This can also be seen in his major overall theme: the rise of rationality for the basis of action, and its effect on social life. Bendix argues:

Weber was preoccupied throughout his career with the development of rationalism in Western civilisation.

(Bendix, 1963, p. 9)

It is this strand in Weber's thinking that has influenced the development of 'critical theory' through the work of the Frankfurt School, as well as more recent thinkers broadly in this tradition such as Habermas (1972, 1976, 1981a). They can be seen to be engaged in a reworking of the meaning and significance of this process of rationalization. This idea has also had an influence in the Marxist tradition through the work of Lukács (1971; orig. pub. 1923).

Weber as an alternative to Marx

A common interpretation of Weber involves the idea of him engaging in a debate with the ghost of Marx – which leads to the development of a very different analysis of power and inequality in society, through 'conflict theory'. Crucially, this involved the development of his argument that not all conflicts or social developments can be explained with reference to economic factors.

'Social action theory'

It is clear that Weber saw human meaning as central to the study of sociology, and this insight is a key basis for the 'social action' tradition in sociology. This can be contrasted with versions of Durkheim and Marx who, it can be argued, see individuals almost as puppets with their lives determined by structural forces in society. Weber can be seen as providing insights that develop into the contemporary approach of phenomenology and ethnomethodology (see Section 16.5).

Activity

a Using a large sheet of paper, present the key ideas of Marx, Weber and Durkheim diagrammatically. Start at the top with their names as headings.

b Using the sections above on *interpretations* of these three writers, try to draw arrows suggesting the more contemporary ideas which show the continuing influence of these three classical sociologists.

Theoretical synthesis

In recent years a number of sociologists have attempted to synthesize approaches, and in particular to try to overcome the division between social structural approaches and social action approaches that has been evident for so long. The writers explored in this section all argue that this is something that should be considered, even though their proposed solutions differ.

Norbert Elias

The work of Elias has become more central to sociology in recent years. There are two main reasons for this. First Elias always denied that it was possible to sustain the structure/action split,

and so he fits alongside others who have sought to go beyond this conceptual split. The second reason is the influence of his work on the sociology of sport and leisure (see Section 13.5), areas of growing interest within sociology in general and post-modernist circles more particularly.

Figurations

Elias is concerned with the process whereby people and the ideas they hold are constituted through chains which stretch back through the generations. Society is seen as the result, often accidental, of all the interweavings between social actors. He used the term 'figurations' to describe this:

From the interweaving of countless individual interests and interactions – whether tending in the same direction or in divergent and hostile directions – something comes into being that was planned and intended by none of those individuals, yet has emerged nevertheless from their intentions and actions. And really this is the whole secret of social figurations.

(Elias, 1982, p. 160; orig. pub. 1939)

Dynamism and process

Central to his sociology is an examination of the processes whereby such figurations work themselves out. This emphasis on dynamism and process is central to his rejection of the structure/action dichotomy. The individual and society are not two different things, merely two different perspectives on the same thing. This leads him to examine the nature of the structure emerging from these interdependencies, and the way this leads to the formation of later structures. His work is therefore an examination of the evolution of both structures and individual personalities within sets of interdependencies.

Although he shares the idea of evolution with the functionalists, he saw their work as overly static. His work therefore emphasizes dynamism, albeit evolutionary dynamism. His attraction to post-modernist thinkers arises because of his emphasis on the way people exist as pluralities:

Since people are more or less dependent on each other first by nature and then through social learning, through education, socialisation and socially generated reciprocal needs, they exist, one might say, only as pluralities, only in figurations.

(Elias, 1978, p. 261; orig. pub. 1939)

The Weberian strand of his thinking comes across in his consideration of *power*, which he

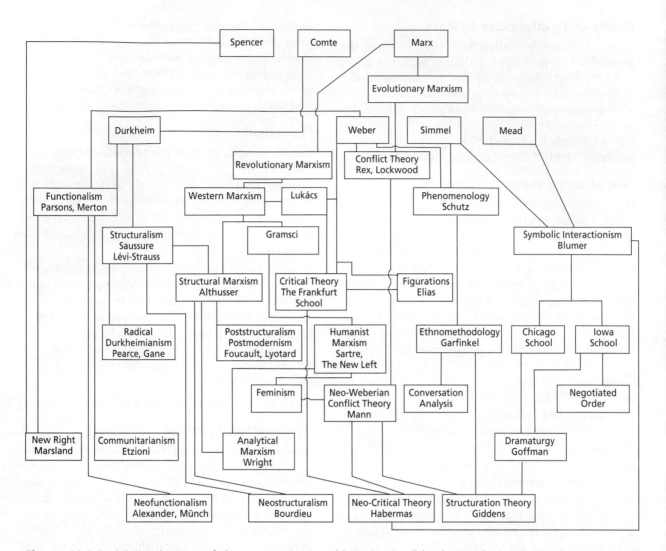

Figure 16.1 Sociology, the war of the perspectives, and bringing it all back together again: an interpretation

sees as a characteristic of all social relationships – although he differs in the consideration of the extent and meaning of the idea of the growing rationality of power.

The civilising process

Elias' central work is *The Civilising Process* (1978, 1982), originally published in German in 1939. In it he presents an analysis of the evolution of human manners and the way in which changes in the social structure change aspects of our personality structure, namely our feelings for others.

Elias studied court society (primarily in France) between the thirteenth and the nineteenth centuries. He observed that if you look at certain forms of human behaviour – such as handling food, farting, burping and spitting – these have undergone a long-term evolution, described

as the continuous civilizing of behaviour with an increase in social pressure on people to behave in certain ways. He argued that this process led to a change in psychological development, so that the constraints on the way people behaved – which were originally external – now became internal and therefore self-restraint. He emphasized that this is not to suggest that the past was totally uncivilized, since he argued that the civilizing process is a process without a beginning.

The evolution of manners and states

There is, nonetheless, a clear idea of the evolution of manners and embarrassment and shame thresholds over time. Elias argued that this cannot be explained on the basis of material changes or changes in knowledge about health, but instead is related to respect for others. The cause is changes in the social relations between people. These occurred first in the upper class and then filtered down.

Elias links this changing behaviour to the formation of states (thereby showing the way 'micro' and 'macro' issues can be linked) by arguing that it is possible to investigate the process through which states gained monopoly power in respect to taxation and the legitimate use of violence. As a result, conflicts became more a matter of who ran the state rather than whether one should exist at all, and Elias argued this had led to the progressive reduction in the use of violence. Centralization and integration are key processes here, and Elias emphasized the way competitors to state power were eliminated (thereby coming close to neo-Weberian accounts of the state which emphasize military conflicts), although he argued that the monopoly over taxation was also needed. He further argued against Marxism by saying that neither of these monopolies could be understood to arise from strictly economic processes:

Elias is emphatic that the monopolisation of the means of violence and of taxation is not reducible to an economic process.

(Mennell, 1989, p. 70)

Beyond symbolic interactionism?

Although Elias' emphasis on people interacting has similarities with symbolic interactionism, the emphasis there is always on people interacting face-to-face. Elias' idea of figurations, or chains of interdependence stretching back over time, emphasizes that our actions are also affected by the fact that we are dependent on people we have never met. While this is clearly true in one sense, it has been criticized. Layder points out that he is wrong to suppose that there is no real difference between face-to-face interaction and the other type of connections encompassed within the term 'figurations':

Dealing with someone on a face-to-face basis (say in a family, or a coffee bar) is very much influenced by the reality of the presence of other people. ... As social relations stretch away into the impersonal realm of institutional phenomena, say our connection with some government agency, we find that our ties of interdependence are based primarily upon an absence rather than a presence. We do not experience the presence of the government as such; there is no face-to-face encounter with the

institution. ... We must be aware that the defining characteristics of institutions are not to be found in the connectedness of people as such. ... It is the nature of the ties between people (rather than the fact of ties per se ...) that is the crucial defining feature.

(Layder, 1994, p. 122)

💬 Discussion point

Elias' notion of 'figurations' implies that we are affected by chains of interdependencies stretching back through the ages. To what extent do you feel that these can be analysed in the same way as face-to-face interactions?

C3.1a

Criticisms of Elias

Elias' work has been much discussed in sociology, but it is not without its critics. His emphasis on evolution has led some to argue that he is merely reasserting the ideas of some of the earlier sociologists, such as Spencer and Comte, and the whole idea of 'evolution' has been criticized as tending towards presenting a hierarchy of societies with some seen as more advanced than others. Giddens, for example, argues that:

Elias does stress certain specific characteristics of the modern West, but these are largely submerged in a generalised evolutionism. In the 'less complex societies' there is lower individual self-control, greater spontaneous expression of emotion, etc. People in such societies are rather like children, spontaneous and volatile.

(Giddens, 1984, p. 241)

Giddens points out quite clearly that he believes this view to be wrong.

The idea of a progressive growth in civilization is also open to question. Mennell (1987), although a supporter of Elias' approach, points to two key criticisms of this argument.

- First, it is argued that there was civilized behaviour in stateless societies. This criticism undermines the idea of the progressive evolution of civilization, although Elias was careful to argue that the process had no beginning – in other words, there were no societies having no civilization.

- A second line of criticism points to the way levels of barbarism have increased in recent years, and particularly to the rise of nazism and the Holocaust as key examples.

In answer to the second criticism, it is clear that Elias' work is an attempt to go beyond structure versus action, and the phrase he used to describe the level of personality characteristics people share with others is *habitus*, a word since also used by Bourdieu (see below). What they both point to, albeit in different ways, is the need to think about the process linking people and society or structure and action rather than just portraying it as an empty space between these two opposing views.

Pierre Bourdieu

The sociology of social practices

Bourdieu's (1977, 1984, 1990, 1993a) argument centres around the need to see social practices as the central subject of sociological analysis. He argues that both structural and action-based theories have produced rather one-sided accounts of human life. By 'social practices' he means the way people create and recreate the objective structure of society in certain ways. In contrast to structuralist accounts, this does take the notion of humans as agents seriously; and in contrast to action-based sociology, it retains a notion that there are objective structures beyond us which nonetheless constrain our actions. What provides the link is the social practices people engage in.

Habitus

The central concept he develops to provide a link between the structural and action aspects of society is that of 'habitus'. This term refers to the actual means by which people produce and reproduce social circumstances. In particular, Bourdieu wishes the term to refer to the way in which certain forms of behaviour become so internalized that they appear almost, though not quite, automatically:

With the notion of habitus you can refer to something that is close to what is suggested by the idea of habit, while differing from it in one important respect. The habitus ... is that which one has acquired, but which has become durably incorporated in the body in the form of permanent dispositions. ...

But then why not say 'habit'? Habit is spontaneously regarded as repetitive, mechanical, automatic, reproductive rather than productive. I wanted

to insist on the idea that the habitus is something powerfully generative. To put it briefly, the habitus is a product of conditionings which tends to reproduce the objective logic of those conditionings while transforming it. It's a kind of transforming machine that leads us to 'reproduce' the social conditions of our own production, but in a relatively unpredictable way.

(Bourdieu, 1993a, p. 86)

The knowledge gained from living in a particular culture or subculture in a sense predisposes the choices that we will make, although not entirely, and we still have to actually make a choice. The *habitus* is therefore history embodied in human bodies, rather than in objects such as books and buildings.

Activity

Suggest ways in which the *habitus* embodied in yourself has predisposed you to make choices in your life in a particular way.

C3.2

While Bourdieu's theory does therefore include a strong element of constraint, it might be said that Bourdieu is then open to the criticism that although he talks about choices, in effect he sees most of these as predetermined. This point is made by May when he says that:

The result is that the habitus may be read as a gun out of which the individual is shot, thereby determining their social trajectory.

(May, 1996, p. 127)

May goes on to say, however, that such an interpretation would be counter to Bourdieu's wish to view the *habitus* as open and flexible to some extent. He quotes Bourdieu as follows:

Habitus is not the fate that some people read into it. Being the product of history, it is an open set of dispositions that is constantly subjected to experiences ... that either reinforces or modifies its structures. ... Having said that ... most people are statistically bound to encounter circumstances that tend to agree with those that originally fashioned their habitus.

(Bourdieu; quoted in May 1996, p. 127)

Objective structures

It seems that Bourdieu believes that things *are* determined, but not totally and not passively. They are determined only in so far as people so determine them. However, he wishes to retain a clear notion of objective structures, and rejects the attempt to argue (originating in phenomenological views but also present in some post-structuralist formulations) that ideas and subjectivity are the only real basis of things. Instead:

Only by constructing the objective structures (price curves, chances of access to higher education, laws of the matrimonial market, etc.) is one able to pose the question of the mechanisms through which the relationship is established between the structures and the practices or the representations which accompany them, instead of treating these 'thought objects' as 'reasons' or 'motives' and making them the determining cause of the practices.

(Bourdieu, 1977, p. 21)

The cultural sphere

Bourdieu insists, however, that his serious attention to the cultural sphere reveals that he is interested in subjectivity and is seriously trying to avoid the determinism evident in other versions of structuralism. Despite this insistence, the criticisms remain, and in this respect his weaknesses can be seen to be the opposite of those of Giddens' theory of structuration (see below). Alexander argues that this does mean that his work ultimately falls back on a *type* of determinism. In looking at Bourdieu's work on the 1968 revolts in France, Alexander argues that:

His theoretical interest is in denying the voluntaristic, self- or value-generated dimension of critical change. ... Even in Bourdieu's efforts to make this crisis model more complex, the subjective element falls away.

(Alexander, 1995, p. 148)

The similarities and differences between Bourdieu and Giddens are examined by Layder, who argues:

Habitus is the means through which people produce and reproduce the social circumstances in which they live. This makes it similar to Giddens' idea about structures being both the medium and the outcome of activity. Bourdieu is much more inclined to view social circumstances in the more conventional 'objective' sense of structures and institutions than is the case with structuration theory.

(Layder, 1994, p. 144)

It is this attempt to retain some notion of structure which arguably causes Bourdieu some problems. In some accounts, he argues that these structures are the result of human social practices, but he also wishes to see them as embedded in power relationships.

The theory of distinction

Bourdieu's theory of distinction emphasizes the way in which social factors affect the choices we make about leisure (see Section 13.5), but also shows that these choices are affected by the degree of capital we have. He wished to move the notion of capital away from the purely economic connotation of that term evident in orthodox Marxism, and also included the idea of 'cultural capital'. This can be seen in his analysis of education (see Section 11.1), whereby some people can translate their economic capital into cultural capital (buy a good education) which then becomes the basis for the accumulation of further economic capital.

He therefore emphasizes the cultural construction of inequality and the way in which social divisions are produced and reproduced through cultural tastes and actions.

Criticisms of Bourdieu

The key problem posed is that, if Bourdieu believes all our choices are essentially rooted in a form of inequality of power, this places him very close to the notion of all knowledge being rooted in power – which underlies post-structuralist accounts. Bourdieu does not want to encompass this idea; he wishes to assert that it is possible for sociologists to gain some objective knowledge of the world, and for this his theory must require a notion of *objectivity*.

This points to a long-standing problem in social thinking. If the view of the sociologist is no more valid than any other, why should anyone listen to the sociologist? This 'relativism' is clear in post-structuralism. If, to avoid this dilemma, one suggests that there is a difference (usually seen as the more scientific nature of sociology compared with common sense), then how can one retain some notion of humans as active agents, since they clearly do not possess all the necessary information to make real choices?

💬 Discussion point

To what extent does the notion that sociology is superior to common sense undermine the other notion that humans are active knowledgeable agents? Are sociologists merely imposing their view on the world?

C3.1a

It is perhaps clear that, in trying to overcome the structure/agency division, Bourdieu tends towards the more structural type of analysis. Lash (1990) argues that Bourdieu allows humans only a minimal amount of autonomy from the power embedded in structures, and May therefore argues that Bourdieu's work has:

... the tendency, despite his wish to avoid this very problem, for an ahistorical structuralism to reassert itself.

(May, 1996, p. 133)

Anthony Giddens

Giddens' most notable contribution to sociological theory has been his development of 'structuration theory', which is an attempt to consider and go beyond the division between structural and social action approaches. Giddens (1977, 1979, 1987, 1990) has been developing some of the elements of structuration theory for some considerable time, but it is probably best developed in his book *The Constitution of Society* (1984). At its heart is his own particular conception of structure.

The 'duality' of structure

The notion of a 'social structure' has traditionally been seen as placing limits (constraints) on the extent of choice individuals have. In contrast, Giddens argues that social structures should be viewed as having a 'duality of structure':

Of prime importance in this respect is a dualism that is deeply entrenched in social theory, a division between objectivism and subjectivism. ... In spite of Parson's terminology of 'the action frame of reference', there is no doubt that in his theoretical scheme the object (society) predominates over the subject (the knowledgeable human agent). ... By attacking objectivism – and structural sociology – those influenced by hermeneutics or by phenomenology were able to lay bare major shortcomings of those views, but they in turn veered sharply towards subjectivism. The conceptual divide between subject and social object yawned as widely as ever.

Structuration theory is based on the premise that this dualism has to be reconceptualised as a duality – the duality of structure.

(Giddens, 1984, pp. xx–xxi)

Structures as 'enabling' as well as 'constraining'

In essence, Giddens' argument is that neither social structures nor social actions can exist independently of one another, and therefore accounts focusing on one or the other are deficient. Social structures should not be seen as purely *constraining* our actions, but also as *enabling* them to take place.

For example, the structure of a language, its rules of grammar and construction are clearly a structure in that they exist independently of any one individual. We can view them as constraining our action in so far as they limit the particular ways in which we communicate. This aspect of structure is familiar and conventional. It is the enabling aspect of structures that is novel. However, to use the example of language again, we can see that Giddens has a point. Without a structure of language shared between individuals, no communication would be possible. So the structure of language enables us to engage in the social activity of communication, and of course all other possible social actions are based on this ability to communicate.

To take the example further, new words emerge in languages, so not only does the structure of language enable social action to take place, but that structure is itself created, re-created and changed through social action. This is an example of what Giddens calls 'rules', by which he means the principles regulating social action. Human agents can and do transform as well as reproduce structures. The duality of structure therefore emphasizes that structures both constrain and enable social action to take place.

Structural approaches to sociology usually make reference to inequalities of power in society, but Giddens also argues that we can see power as enabling action in certain circumstances, and further as something which does not exist unless it involves human action. He argues that the resources we use can be divided into *allocative* resources, by which he broadly means raw materials such as land and technology, and *authoritative* resources, by which he broadly means systems of power and authority. His point is that in both cases neither of these exist in a usable form *unless human actions turn them into resources*. So structures of production, power and authority can also be traced back to human action, and so power too can be viewed as a resource. Here Giddens partially supports Parsons' view of power as a capacity to achieve outcomes.

Structures consist of rules and resources

In structuration theory, 'structure' is regarded as rules and resources recursively implicated in social reproduction; institutionalised features of social systems have structural properties in the sense that relationships are stabilized across time and space.

(Giddens, 1984, p. i)

However, since both rules and resources are created by humans, the clear link between structure (in Giddens' sense) and action is maintained. Structures do exist independently of individuals but only in so far as they are reproduced by human action.

Humans are viewed by Giddens as 'knowledgeable agents' and in this respect his work draws on both Goffman and Garfinkel in emphasizing how humans are active and attempt to make sense of the particular situations they find themselves in. Giddens argues that humans desire a degree of predictability in their lives, so they create institutions and structures that exist beyond the control of any one individual. However, these are created by human actions and for the purpose of facilitating and helping human life.

Choice

Since Giddens views structures as the result of knowledgeable human agents, he is very critical of the conventional structural argument that our lives are determined in some way. He argues that there are very few situations where as individuals we have *no* choice. In particular he argues that constraints often mean only a limited course of action, given aims set by ourselves. He refers to Marx's argument that propertyless labourers must sell their labour power, but comments:

... there is only one feasible option, given that the worker has the motivation to wish to survive.

(Giddens, 1984, p. 177)

The implication here is that the worker does face a choice – that of either living or dying. If the choice is to live, this may itself involve a choice between different jobs. Giddens argues further that this choice is also enabling since it does allow the worker to make a living and therefore enable existence. What appears like a constraint is seen by Giddens to result from the motivations and choices of actors.

However, whether the choice between living and dying is sufficiently real is a matter of debate. Although it is clearly true that we do have the option, this might be seen as offering only pyrrhic choice. There is a perception that Giddens' attempt to merge structure and action can operate only by redefining structure in such a way that notions of 'constraint' almost disappear.

Criticisms of Giddens

Archer (1982, 1988, 1995) argues that Giddens underplays the importance of structures and constraint. She argues that his emphasis on agents recreating the world tends to imply that if different choices are made, the world can be changed almost at will. This, she thinks, is incorrect. She points to the constraint involved in Cuba's literacy programme, based on getting one literate person to teach one illiterate person. The key constraint here was the number of existing literate persons. She further points to physical constraints such as volcanoes and floods. Although these would appear as factors in Giddens' notion of allocative resources, she argues that their effect on humanity does not depend on humans exercising a choice – although it could be argued in response to this that it might be another example of life or death being seen as a choice. She therefore argues that structure and action have to be understood as linked but distinct levels of analysis.

From a different angle, New (1993) suggests that Giddens' theory does not provide much of a conception of human agency either. She argues that although it may be technically true that people always have a choice, some people have more choice than others, and for some their options are severely limited. This means he does not address questions such as: 'Who can transform what aspects of social structure, and how?'. Her point is that by emphasizing choice as present in *all* situations, the fact that some social structures are more impervious to change than others is obscured – and so therefore is the issue of the extent to which human agency can have effects.

Activity

a Suggest a number of possible situations where it might be said that human action is constrained.

b In each instance, try to think of a list of possible choices still open to 'knowledgeable actors' in these situations.

c On the basis of these examples, summarize the relationship between freedom of choice and determinism in human society.

d Evaluate the notion of choice embodied in Giddens' structuration theory, and consider whether you think it provides effectively for sufficient real choice among human actors.

C3.2, C3.3

Jürgen Habermas

Habermas is the most recent thinker in the 'critical theory' tradition which stretches back to the writings of the Frankfurt School. Their work was influenced by a number of key social thinkers, notably Marx, Weber and Sigmund Freud. However, Habermas (1972, 1976, 1981a) has added to this tradition by making his own distinctive contribution which also weaves in the influence of Durkheim, Mead and Parsons.

Rejection of post-modernism

One controversial aspect of his work is rejection of the arguments of post-modernism (see Section 16.7). Habermas refuses to accept the post-modernist notion that it is impossible to understand the world rationally. As such he stands (along with Anthony Giddens) as a key defender in contemporary times of the inspiration behind the rise of sociology – namely that it is possible to understand the world and to use that knowledge to construct a better world.

He argues that post-structuralism and post-modernism are merely variants of the re-emergence of conservative thinking, arguing that their proponents are the 'young conservatives' who are merely recreating the nostalgic longing for a pre-capitalist order, which has for so long been a trend in social thinking. This argument illustrates his main aim, namely to reformulate the meaning of rationality to remove what he sees as distortions introduced both by positivism and by Weber's pessimism about the future. At the heart of his work is a reconsideration of the notion of 'rationalization'.

Thinkers in the Frankfurt School have long been critical of positivistic conceptions of science (see Section 16.4). They view its attempt to remove all notion of subjectivity not just a falsehood, but also almost an arrogance about the supposed power of science. Habermas builds on this by arguing that any notion of understanding something must involve both an object and a subject, so no science is able to be purely objective. In this respect, and in the importance accorded to communication in his overall theory, he is building on the insights of the interpretive tradition in German thinking, but arguably also the way in which this was incorporated into symbolic interactionism.

Rescuing rationality

Habermas' book, *Knowledge and Human Interests* (1972), is a critique of the positivist conception of science, and argues for the need to rescue the notion of rationality from such interpretations. The process of rationalization is of course a central element in Weber's work), and this shows the influence of Weber on Habermas.

However, Habermas argues that Weber's analysis, ending in the idea of a world strangled by the 'iron cage' of bureaucracy, highlights the potential downside of the growth of rationality. He feels that Weber's conclusion is overly pessimistic, and it is the attempt to rescue rationality as a positive force that underlies all his work. He argues that the central reason for Weber's pessimism was that he shifted emphasis from an early concern with the development of rational thinking by humans to a later concern with the development of rationalization as the growth of bureaucratic institutions. As a result he lost sight of the cultural process involved in the process of rationalization. Weber's analysis led to the problem of how to develop a rational critical theory if 'rationalization' was identified with 'domination'.

The theory of communicative action

Habermas argues that it is necessary to redefine the meaning of 'rationalization', so that it is not seen simply as an objective process concerned with the achievement of clearly defined goals by precise calculation, but also as an active process of the development of the subjectivity and knowledgeability of humans.

C3.2, C3.3

Activity

Consider the following passages (taken from Scott, 1995) and answer the questions that follow:

In order to build his theory of communicative action, Habermas turns to Mead's symbolic interactionism. ... He also turns to ethnomethodology for insight into communicative action. Unlike Giddens, however, he sees the ethnomethodologists as providing merely a rather extreme formulation for Mead's ideas. Ethnomethodological ideas must be reined back and consolidated into the mainstream of symbolic interactionism. (p. 194)

The claims of ethnomethodology were largely ignored by orthodox sociology until they were taken up by Giddens. It is through Giddens' work that ethnomethodology has been brought into the mainstream of sociological analysis. (p. 239)

Social development has always been seen by Habermas as a process of evolution, a directional process of change. ... This teleological view of social development differs sharply from the strictly anti-evolutionist model outlined by Giddens, though his actual description of the course taken by social development has considerable similarity to that given by Giddens. (p. 245)

a Summarize *in your own words* the differences between Habermas and Giddens as outlined in these passages.

b What similarities might be noted in the aims of Giddens and Habermas?

c Using material from this chapter and elsewhere, explain (i) what it is in Mead that Habermas uses, and (ii) what it is in Garfinkel and ethnomethodology that Giddens uses.

At the heart of this is the idea of communication and understanding, a theory he developed fully in *The Theory of Communicative Action* (1981a). He moved the discussion away from an exclusive focus on the development of 'instrumental rationality' towards a notion of 'communicative rationality'. Habermas argues that we can distinguish two types of action:

• *Instrumental* action is that orientated towards the achievement of a specific goal. The key measure of this action is in terms of success and failure. Getting promoted, pursuing a career or trying to become a millionaire might fall into this category.

• *Communicative* action is that where the aim is not a specific goal but simply understanding and the reaching of agreements.

In capitalist society, moving away from instrumental rationality towards communicative rationality involves not seeing the pursuit of profit as the only rational course, but instead seeing rationality as containing an ethical element involving the development of mutual self-understanding. In this sense rationality can be equated with freedom, since it enables people to see through falsehoods and thereby enhance their power.

Since communication is central to understanding and agreement, Habermas is also concerned with language, ideas and symbols and the role they can play in the struggle for emancipation. It is belief in the importance of agreements which allows Habermas to quote Parsons approvingly, although he is arguing that the goal of such a society is *desirable* rather than existing, as Parsons argued.

It might be argued that Habermas is attempting to construct the theory of action that Parsons set out to achieve in his early work but quickly abandoned for the structural emphasis of his later work. In this sense, Habermas is clearly in tune with one of the most notable elements of modern social theory, namely the attempt to consider human as actors and to focus on the process of action rather than simply the identification of actors.

The notion of communicative rationality and communicative action is offered as a way in which we can retain reason as a liberating force and a standard against which we can measure existing societies. Culture, norms and values are seen as of prime importance, and this leads Habermas to reject Marxist attempts to argue that they are in some way purely derived from economic phenomena. However, he recognizes the power of the Marxist criticism of capitalism, and he himself talks of the way labour relations are exploitative. In essence he sees all these phenomena as examples of how culture and structures of power both develop. His aim, of course, is to rescue rationality from the exploitative and dominating ways in which it has been applied in capitalist society.

The 'lifeworld' and the social 'system'

Habermas distinguishes between what he calls the 'lifeworld' and the social 'system'.

- The lifeworld is made up of the set of assumptions that are taken for granted in social interactions. This lifeworld is the mediation between culture, ethics and social structures. Society evolves through the rationalization of the lifeworld. What this means is that the growth of critical and reflective thinking allows us to reject traditional customs from the past. This process thereby promotes learning and the evolution of society. His concept of the lifeworld also includes institutions, norms and social practices that help to reproduce society.

- In contrast, by 'social system' Habermas refers to things not linked through shared human communication. This essentially means those areas where money and power rule, since here there is no need for agreement to be reached.

He argues that areas of the lifeworld have become subject to control through money and power, and this vision points towards the danger of the system overcoming the lifeworld.

For example, information and education are now in some respects commodities sold for profit rather than promoted for mutual understanding. Habermas (1976) calls this the 'colonization of the lifeworld', not seen as legitimate by many people and leading to crises of legitimacy that are more important than economic crises. Many people no longer see corporations and the state as acting in their interests, but instead see them as instruments of domination. Communicative action aims to rescue all aspects of the lifeworld from the stranglehold of the system, thus expanding the areas of social life governed by agreement and communication, rather than by money and power.

Positive rationality

The important implication of this is Habermas' belief that the positive features of rationalization (that is, the growth of rational standards of interpersonal behaviour, and the way we reflect on our actions and communicate through arguments judged by their logic and truth) are still evident in society and can therefore be used to create a better world. In summary, he turns around Weber's pessimistic ending to provide the opportunity for a happy ending in which rationality still has a role to play.

This focuses on the way language and communication can be used to achieve agreement and to sustain social relationships. In this, however, he faces a key problem explained by Giddens:

Truth is agreement reached through critical discussion. Here Habermas' standpoint seems to face a major difficulty. How are we actually to distinguish a 'rational consensus' – one based upon reasoned agreement – from a consensus based merely on custom, or power?

(Giddens, 1985a, p. 130)

The 'ideal speech situation'

Habermas' answer to Giddens' question is that a consensus arrives purely from the use of logical argument. He sets out a model of what would be required for such a condition to be met – which he calls an 'ideal speech situation'. There are essentially two conditions required for such a situation:

- all relevant evidence is presented
- nothing apart from logical argument is involved.

Giddens provides a summary of what this would mean:

An ideal speech situation is one in which there are no external constraints preventing participants from assessing evidence and argument, and in which each participant has an equal and open chance of entering into discussion.

(Giddens, 1985a, p. 131)

Habermas' idea is to provide a model of what would be required for society to allow for the full development of communicative rationality. Since this is based on language, it underlies all other possible forms of rationality, including instrumental rationality. Its neglect has not, therefore, meant its elimination, and the one-sided nature of the rationalization process can be rectified. The model of communicative rationality would serve as a benchmark against which we can measure existing societies. The gap also provides the key areas for campaigns for social change.

Criticisms of Habermas

It is clear that Habermas' work involves integrating elements from many thinkers, but perhaps the most notable line of criticism is that his work, in contrast to the earlier Frankfurt School, is not critical enough. Marx is less of a presence

Activity

a Draw up a list of ways in which discussion and decision-making in the UK fall short of an 'ideal speech situation'. One example might be that the UK possesses a very wide-ranging Official Secrets Act, which means that all the evidence might not be presented in all cases, particularly relating to defence. As such this means discussion might fall short of the first criterion Habermas sets for an 'ideal speech situation'.

b On the basis of your answer to (a), discuss in groups reforms that might be made to move the UK closer to the position of an 'ideal speech situation'.

C3.2, C3.3

and Weber and Parsons more of a presence, the latter particularly being the most likely basis for this criticism.

In an ideal world we should reach understanding rationally as a way of running society; but the question of how we arrive at that situation and stop the 'colonization' of the 'lifeworld' by the 'system' – to use Habermas' terminology – is a big question, and the agent of that change is not entirely evident. Habermas focuses on the new social movements (see Section 15.3), but whether they can achieve this remains to be seen.

16.2 Context of data collection

Theories, methods and types of data

The terms *quantitative* and *qualitative* have an important meaning in this context. Both words refer to types of data:

- Quantitative refers to data that are largely numerical in form or contain large amounts of numbers and/or statistical data.

- Qualitative refers to data consisting of words – that is, verbal descriptions.

Whilst it is important to note that sociologists of all persuasions may produce their evidence in terms of both types, there is a link between a particular theoretical outlook and the likelihood of producing a certain type of data. For example:

- Positivist sociologists (who believe that sociology should be scientific and precise in nature) tend to be more likely to want evidence in the form of quantitative data – and therefore to use methods that provide such data.

- Phenomenologically inclined sociologists (who believe the job of sociology is to report the way people see and understand the world) are more concerned to understand the point of view of the people they are researching – and this leads them to report their respondents' views in their own words, leading to a desire for qualitiative data and the use of methods that provide such data.

Positivism, quantitative methods, and causes and effects

The positivists' desire for quantitative data has several roots.

1 They hold the belief that humans are in essence subject to the *laws of society*.

2 This vision of humanity implies that it does not really matter what individual people think, because their views can have no real influence on the direction society will take. This leads to a concern with delineating the *structures of society*.

3 Their belief in the superiority and precision of the *scientific method* is a further factor influencing them to move in the direction of quantitative research. This will lead to the production of data in the form of numbers – essentially statistics that can then be manipulated easily to consider *trends over time* or *differences between various social groups* according to certain criteria.

4 This in turn leads them to seek *connections* – and ultimately causal connections – *between variables*.

Cause and effect: the problem of correlation and causation

Demonstrating a link (correlation) between two variables is merely evidence that there *might* be a relationship between them. It is important to remember that the link is *not* evidence that one *causes* the other. Unfortunately this is often the basis for dubious interpretations of statistical findings.

For example, in looking at the statistics relating to number of marriages and number of wedding rings purchased one would expect to find that they were linked – when one rises, so does the other. However, it would be foolish to argue that the reason people get married is because they have bought a wedding ring. Clearly some *other* factor is here causing a change in people's behaviour such that they (a) buy a wedding ring and (b) get married. It might be said that the causal factor was 'falling in love', or 'a baby due to be born'. Here a third factor – which can be debated – causes changes in the first two factors.

Another important example of this is the economic doctrine of 'monetarism'. On the basis of studies of the American economy, monetarist economists noted that there was a link between the rise in the level of money in circulation and the rate of inflation. They demonstrated that the two variables were *correlated*. However, monetarists then went on to argue that this was a *causal* link whereby increases in the supply of money in circulation were the cause of inflation. This argument is hotly disputed by other economists, but this economic doctrine was behind much of the economic policy of the New Right in the 1980s and 90s.

In summary, *never confuse correlation with causation* – one does not prove the other. When reading accounts of sociological research, always be careful to check that this confusion of thought is not occurring.

Strengths of quantitative methodology

Statistics play an important role in sociology because they do allow us to consider trends over time. Since numbers provide a common currency with which to compare social groups in relation to certain issues, quantitative research remains very popular.

Secondly, quantitative data can be analysed quite easily using standard statistical techniques. This attractive feature has been enhanced in recent years by the availability of computers and software that can process data rapidly, allowing sociologists to derive findings from social surveys with large samples with relative ease.

Computers also permit one to re-analyse data easily, so later sociologists can go back and re-use primary data that was collected earlier.

Problems with quantitative methodology

Those influenced by phenomenology would suggest that at the heart of all problems is the nature of humanity espoused by positivism – namely the way humans are viewed as puppets subject to forces and laws external to themselves.

The construction of questionnaires and interview schedules often reveals this problem, with a limited number of options being offered and no space being given to allow people to explain in detail the reasons behind their choices. This reflects the positivists' belief, but it is rejected by phenomenological sociologists. The latter argue that it is precisely in the process of *interaction* that humans not only have choices, but make the choices that determine the world the way it is. This is central to sociology, they argue, and it is largely missed out in quantitative methodology, *which instead imposes its own framework of meaning on those being researched.*

It is therefore argued by phenomenologists that, although quantitative methods can be shown to be reliable (in the sense that if repeated they will produce the same result), this reliability is of no use because the findings, although constant, are not valid. Rather, they represent the 'reality' imposed on people by the researcher. Furthermore, it is this which also accounts for the data's reliability, since the findings are a reflection of the methodology used rather than the superiority and accuracy of the method.

Those who criticize quantitative methods thus say they lack *validity*, in that the findings do not really represent the reality of those being studied.

The belief that facts are value-free and theory-free is at the heart of positivist methodology, and this is of course rejected by those who argue that facts only make sense in the context of theories. The danger is of generating reams of 'facts' without any coherent theoretical framework with which to make sense of it all.

Phenomenological approaches, qualitative methods and interpretive theories

For research sociologists, the central defining aspect of methodological approaches is that reality is the result of human interactions, and the way people interpret their world and try to construct meanings out of it.

So the key concern is a wish to describe and analyse how people interact. Although it is possible to do this using quantitative methods, these are largely rejected because they impose a frame of meaning on the subject being researched – as explained above.

For example, a questionnaire framed to elicit quantitative data will allow only responses picked from a preselected number of alternative answers. People might be forced to place themselves within a category that does not really represent their true situation, and it is also possible that two people with widely differing views might end up in the same statistical mass.

For instance, in a survey asking people whether they are (a) impressed or (b) unimpressed with the current leader of the Labour party, the group of responses in the second category might include Conservatives, Liberal Democrats and left-wing socialists. This category would thus include a very diverse range of people who made their choices for divergent reasons. Conservative supporters might be unimpressed because they see the Labour leader as a socialist, while left-wing socialists might be unimpressed because they see the same person as not enough of a socialist.

To explore more deeply the meanings and attitudes behind responses like these requires the asking of further questions, leading towards a qualitative methodology. Those adopting a qualitative methodology argue that research should be approached without any preconceptions or structures, and should treat people as conscious, active subjects in order to capture the full depth and detail of how people interact meaningfully to create the world. This reality, they say, is far too complex to be captured by pigeon-holing people into the categories associated with quantitative methodology.

Strengths of qualitative methodology

The key advantage claimed for qualitative methods is that they allow a deeper – and therefore more valid – picture to emerge of the particular set of social relationships under investigation. By focusing on interactions, they allow sociologists to look at the dynamic and fluid nature of society; and by focusing on the meanings people construct they concentrate on the active nature of humanity.

Secondly, in so far as social researchers wish to view people in this way and to focus on the cultural and social processes by which they live their lives, then this approach has clear advantages over the more static fixed pictures emerging from quantitative methods.

This is seen as much more important than defining so-called objective variables that are seen merely as the imposition of researchers on a somewhat more fluid, subjective reality.

Ultimately the advantages of qualitative methods are related to the methodological theories out of which they flow, and if one disagrees with the theories then the approach will seem subjective and unreliable. Justification of such criticism relies on a more positivistic view of the world than those undertaking qualitative research will accept.

Problems with qualitative methodology

The key criticism, resting implicity on positivistic notions, is that qualitative approaches are subjective. The implied charge is that data produced using such approaches should not, ultimately, be taken too seriously. Sometimes this criticism is extended to say that qualitative methods tend to be applied towards the more trivial aspects of life – but obviously this depends very much on your own point of view.

A potentially more serious criticism made of qualitative methods is that they are unreliable. By this is meant that a second researcher repeating the research using the same techniques – or even the same researcher repeating the research at a later date – will not be guaranteed to achieve the same results. While it is clearly the case that techniques such as observation as a participant do rely very heavily on the personal characteristics and skills of the researcher – and therefore another researcher is unlikely to be able to repeat the research precisely – this may be missing the point:

It might be that the positivist's research tool consistently and reliably measures the variables, but if what is being researched is invalid then the whole process is rather pointless. ... For example, intelligence tests are reliable measures of intelligence quotients but whether this has anything to do with intelligence is debatable.

(Harvey and MacDonald, 1993, p. 188)

In other words, a method that consistently measures things inaccurately or wrongly in some sense can still be considered reliable, but ought to be considered rather pointless and arguably dangerous in certain contexts.

Positivistic research uses preset categories of answers. However, one criticism of this is that respondents are forced to pigeonhole themselves into answers imposed by the researchers. Proponents of qualitative research claim that it overcomes this imposition problem. Ray Pawson, however, argues that there is nonetheless an imposition problem involved in qualitative methods. As an example he cites the large amount of material generated by Ann Oakley in her study of the experiences of motherhood (see also Section 5.7), which involved 233 interviews and produced 545 hours of tape-recorded data. It is clear that not all of this material appears in the final report of her research project. (This is a general problem with all research that produces qualitative data.) In the final report, the data are represented by quotations from the material, but not by production of the whole data set. The problem with this is outlined by Pawson:

The phenomenological schools as a whole have traditionally been very tough on quantitative methods for imposing meaning. ... This very familiar anti-positivistic missile has now been trained inwards and applied to participant observation. 'Field research' in general, and by its very nature, tends to produce findings which are anecdotal and massively selective in terms of the ratio of events reported to those witnessed. In this process of the selection and packaging of evidence, the possibility of imposition of meaning again looms large.

(Pawson, 1989, p. 161)

Discussion point

To what extent do you agree with the argument that both positivist and phenomenological approaches suffer from the imposition problem? Do they suffer from it in exactly the same way, or differently?

C3.1a

Realism and methodological approaches

In terms of methodology, the distinction between 'qualitative' and 'quantitative' as a broad dividing line is inapplicable to realism. This is because the latter argues that, while it is indeed necessary to take seriously the idea that people are conscious human agents, *there is also the need to uncover objective truths about the underlying causal mechanisms of society*.

Thus realism seeks to understand the meanings that people arrive at, *but within the context of the existence of real underlying structures that help to generate those meanings*. This leads to a desire to place studies of society in an overall historical context and, using theories and concepts abstracted from the reality of everyday society, to try to illustrate the underlying mechanisms.

'Cultural reproduction' theory is an example of this type of study, as is the more recent work by Paul Willis (1977). He was concerned to show how what takes place in school leads to working-class children getting working-class jobs. His study adopted primarily an ethnographic method. Harvey and MacDonald explain the methodological implications of this in the context of Willis' study:

Critical Ethnography usually starts by examining the social structure rather than taking it for granted. The ethnographic enquiry provides detailed data that helps to assess the structural analysis. However this is not done by testing a hypothesis with a view to falsifying a theory (as a falsificationist might). There is a two-way development of understanding. The ethnographic material is used to re-examine the structural relationship and, at the same time, the

Activity

Select the correct words from the list below to fill the gaps in the extract that follows (each word is used only once):
reliability; ethnographer; representative; survey; bias; sample; validity

Where the _____ researcher may claim _____ and representativeness, the ethnographer will claim _____. The survey enthusiast will point out the dangers of _____ and unreliability in ethnography, and stress how the representativeness of a _____can be calculated precisely. The _____ may concede all this, but would point out that it is not much use being able to produce the same results over and over again, and to say how _____ they are, if they are invalid in the first place.
(McNeill, 1985, p. 114)

C3.2, C3.3

structural analysis will help to make sense of the ethnographic data.

(Harvey and MacDonald, 1993, p. 185)

Realism, therefore, does not fit very easily into a quantitative/qualitative split, precisely because it denies the validity of the methodological theories behind this distinction and which tend to pose it as an either/or choice.

Using more than one method (triangulation)

Triangulation refers to the use of more than one method, to try to counter the weaknesses of one particular method by combining it with another that is strong in that area. So, for example, structured interviews might be combined with participant observation. It is also possible to use both structured and unstructured interviews, the logic behind doing so being to try to gain the highest levels of both validity and reliability.

Eileen Barker – The Moonies

The classical sample of this approach is in Barkers' (1984) study of the Unification Church, better known as the Moonies. In her study, Barker used participant observation, questionnaires and interviews. Information from the participant observation (which lasted six years) and from the interviews (which consisted of 30 interviews lasting between six and eight hours) was used to gain a detailed picture of the Unification Church, and this information was then used to enable the researcher to draw up more detailed hypotheses for later investigation using questionnaires.

Barker argued that by combining these methods her study of the Moonies gained greater validity and reliability than would have been the case if she had conducted the study using only qualitative or only quantitative methods.

Since research methodology allows us to be fairly sure about the relative strengths and weaknesses of the various techniques, and since this information is now widely available, more and more sociologists are seeking to use triangulation – or 'methodological pluralism' as it is sometimes called.

Pierre Bourdieu, *Distinction*

As another example we can look at the points made by Pierre Bourdieu when being interviewed about his book *Distinction* (Bourdieu, 1984):

Q: I'd now like to turn to the question of the relationship between sociology and the neighbouring sciences. Your book Distinction *opens with the sentence: 'Sociology is rarely more akin to a social psychoanalysis than when it confronts an object like taste.' Then come statistical tables, and accounts of surveys – but also analyses of a 'literary' type, such as one finds in Balzac, Zola or Proust. How do these two aspects fit together?*

A: The book results from an effort to integrate two modes of knowledge – ethnographic observation, which can only be based on a small number of cases, and statistical analysis, which makes it possible to establish regularities and to situate the observed cases in the universe of existing cases. So you have, for example, the contrasting description of a working-class meal and a bourgeois meal. ... On the working-class side, there is a declared primacy of function, which appears in all the food that is served: the food has to be 'filling, body-building' ... to give strength (conspicuous muscles). On the bourgeois side, there is the primacy of form, or formality, which implies a kind of censorship and repression of function, an aestheticization, which is found in every area, as much in eroticism, functioning as sublimated or denied pornography, as in pure art which is defined precisely by the fact that it privileges form at the expense of function. In fact, the analyses that are described as 'qualitative' or more pejoratively, 'literary', are essential for understanding, that's to say fully explaining, what the statistics merely record, rather like rainfall statistics. They lead to the principle of all the practices observed, in the most varied areas.

(Bourdieu, 1993a, p. 14)

Problems and solutions

While it might be seen that this approach can allow research strategies to be developed that avoid the problems associated with using only one method, it should be noted that it does not eliminate these problems – it merely covers them over by utilizing other methods with strengths in the areas of weakness in the first method. Rather than a unified overall methodology, it is a form of using complementary methods. As Tim May has pointed out:

While triangulation might appear attractive, it is not a panacea for methodological ills.

(May, 1993, p. 90)

(A panacea is a cure-all so clearly May feels triangulation cannot solve all problems.)

Nonetheless it is clear that triangulation can offer real benefits and is leading to more and more sociologists adopting the principles that lie behind it. Case studies focusing on specific issues but using more than one methodological technique, or even methodology, have risen in popularity in sociology recently. While this might put a spotlight on the issues of validity and reliability, it could also impact on the issue of representativeness.

For instance, the famous study by Goldthorpe and colleagues, *The Affluent Worker* (1968), chose to study workers in Luton, not because they were representative, but because this seemed the most likely place to find 'affluent workers'. In this sense an extreme case was picked rather than a representative sample.

Whether a unified methodological toolkit can be devised which would go beyond triangulation remains to be seen.

Most of the sections in the remainder of this chapter contains extracts from sociologists talking about their research, and more than one method was used in many instances.

Further factors impacting on the research selection process

This part of the chapter would be redundant if we lived in a world where sociologists were allowed to put forward their theoretical arguments (positivism *versus* phenomenology *versus* realism) and then choose research methods solely on that basis. Of course, we do not live in such a world. Structures of power exist, and these impinge upon – and are created by – sociologists in the world of sociology just as in every other sphere of society. These structures therefore have an impact upon how research is done.

Obvious constraints are *money* and *time*. Funding is not always easy to come by, and awarding bodies may require the sociologist to undertake research using specific methods as a condition of their funding. Equally, if a research

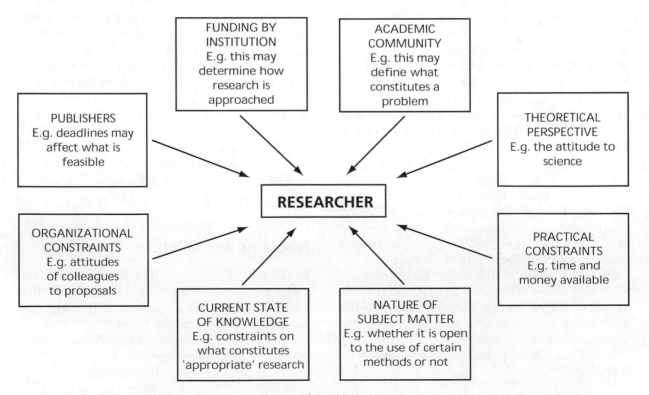

Figure 16.2 Influences on the researcher's choice of method
Source: Lawson (1986, p. 40)

report is required in four months one is unlikely to have the luxury of choosing in-depth participant observation. Lawson (1986) has provided a useful summary of possible constraints on researchers (see Figure 16.2).

Lawson points to how the subject matter itself can constrain choices:

Interactionists are likely to be highly disposed towards observational techniques. But if you are a fifty-year-old female sociologist interested in football hooliganism, it is going to be difficult to perform a participant observation study of that topic! Similarly, if you are a positivist wishing to investigate illiteracy, a written questionnaire is not an option you can easily take.

(Lawson, 1986, p. 41)

Activity

Suggest *two* examples of your own of how
(i) the nature of the subject matter, and
(ii) practical constraints such as time and money, may serve to affect choices over research methods to be employed.

C3.2, C3.3

The points made above about resources serve as a reminder that sociological research (as opposed to reading about it) operates in a world where the people with power might not care much for your preference for qualative methods. They might want just the bare statistics, and they could withdraw funding if they do not get their way. Of course, it is likely that such a project would be entrusted to a sociologist already quantitatively inclined, but this would leave our qualitative sociologist without a grant and therefore possibly unable to do research. The nature of what is researched, and how it is researched, would therefore still be influenced.

16.3 Techniques of data collection and recording

The founder of sociology, Auguste Comte, was one of a number of thinkers clearly influenced by the achievements of the natural sciences who set out to emulate these sciences. Comte even considered calling sociology 'social physics' – which would have made this connection even clearer. Nonetheless, this link to science remains in the name since the literal meaning of 'sociology' is

the science of society. This obviously leads to the question of exactly how it is a science.

That is a question which can be approached on many levels – for instance, in terms of philosophy and epistemology. For the moment, however, we will consider the extent to which the key scientific method – the *experiment* – can be used in sociological research. It is clear that Comte believed that human behaviour could be analysed in terms of laws, just as the natural world could be, and this led to consideration of whether the key method of the natural sciences could be used to discover these laws.

We can divide experiments into two main approaches: namely laboratory experiments and field experiments.

Laboratory experiments

A laboratory experiment enables a natural scientist to test a prediction and to come to a conclusion as to whether his or her hunches (hypotheses) are correct.

Experimental and control groups

The classical scientific experiment works by dividing an identical sample into two groups, one known as the experimental group and one known as the control group. The variable being tested is then varied for the experimental group but not for the control group. Since this is the only difference between the two groups, any difference in outcome between the two groups after the experiment has been conducted can reasonably be assumed to relate to this variable.

For example, scientists might test the proposition that light is necessary for plants to grow by taking two identical samples of plants and placing one in an area illuminated by sunlight and one in an area of complete darkness, but at the same temperature and humidity. On this basis a single variable (light) is varied to consider the effects. Since the plants without light would eventually die and those with light might live, this experiment would confirm the importance of light to the life of plants.

The key question is whether this methodology is applicable to the study of human behaviour. Thinking about the outcome of the plant experiment might lead to some justifiable doubts, since quite clearly the experimental process, in order to work, has to have some effect on the subjects – for example, the plants in the dark died.

Ethics

This clearly leads to an extremely important ethical issue. Can sociologists justify affecting and changing the lives of other people purely for the purposes of doing their research? If the effect on the people were dramatic, detrimental and permanent, most thinkers would agree that the experiment was not ultimately ethical. This clearly places wide constraints on the use of experiments in the social sciences, while not ruling them out entirely. There are, for instance, a number of examples of its use in psychology and social psychology.

Milgram's study

One of the most famous of these was the study conducted by Milgram (1974). Milgram wished to test the hypothesis that cruelty is not committed by cruel individuals who are different from the rest of us, but by ordinary men and women who will use cruelty if they feel it is appropriate in the circumstances they find themelves in.

To test this, he got volunteers to play 'teachers' or 'learners'. The 'teachers' were told to administer electric shocks to the 'learners' when they got questions wrong. In fact, the experiment was set up so that no shocks took place, but the 'teachers' did not know this.

Milgram found that most were prepared to administer what they believed were painful electric shocks: 30 per cent of the sample continued until the end of the experiment, and if the victims were hidden and their fake 'screams' made inaudible, the proportion willing to administer the shock shot up to 65 per cent. Milgram argued that this showed it is easier to be cruel if the victim is hidden and we neither see nor hear their distress.

Zimbardo's study

Another experiment that looked at willingness to commit cruelty and authoritarin behaviour was conducted by Zimbardo (1972). Here volunteers played the role of 'prisoners' and 'prison guards' in a make-believe prison, used as a laboraory setting. This was purposely set up as realistically as possible, involving appropriate dress, behaviour and rules and regulations. Originally the experiment was supposed to run for two weeks, but was stopped after one week for fear that permanent damage might be done.

The study found that the volunteers very enthusiatically took up their respective roles. The 'guards' indulged in a wide variety of dominance over the 'prisoners', who in turn seemed to adopt a submissive role. Ordinary volunteers became, in the role of a prison guard, sadistic and bullying. Zimbardo and colleagues said that this was caused by the social situation they found themelves in and the social expectations of them in these roles, rather than revealing any cruel or vicious streak inherent in the individuals themselves.

The study by Bandura and others

The theme of violence and cruelty has been a continuing concern, and this experimental method has been applied also to studies that have tried to look at the effect of violent images in the media on the behaviour of people. One of the most famous of these was a series of experiments carried out by Bandura *et al.* (1963).

They divided a group of children into four sub-groups. The first sub-group saw real-life adults using a mallet to attack a self-righting inflatable doll; the second saw a film of adults attacking the doll; the third saw a film of cartoon characters attacking the doll; and the fourth (the control group) were shown no violence at all. After viewing these images the children were deprived of being allowed to play with toys – to induce mild frustration – and then placed in a room for 20 minutes with a doll similar to the one featured in the images shown to the first three groups.

The finding of the study was that aggression towards the doll was markedly higher in each of the three groups that had experienced prior violent imagery, compared with the control group. This piece of research was the key element in the popularisation and then acceptance of the notion of the 'hypodermic syringe' model of the effect of the media (see Section 6.7) and led to great concerns over the need to control the actual content of the media.

Drawbacks of laboratory experiments

Further research on the effects of the media has undermined support for the hypodermic syringe model, suggesting that the rather automatic relationship between viewing violence in the media and acting violently implied by this model was overly simplistic. One of the key reasons for this was the suggestion that in real-life, unlike in the experiment, we do not view media images in isolation.

This points to the second practical criticism made of laboratory experiments, namely that they are incapable of providing a realistic context for the study of human behaviour. Firstly this is because we do not live our lives in laboratories, and therefore when placed in one we may behave differently. This criticism would certainly apply to the use of laboratory experiments in psychology and social psychology.

In addition to this, sociologists would point out that laboratory experiments often work with an isolated individual and the whole point of sociology is that our behaviour is affected by others, namely peer groups, our community or our society. Since it is impossible to place a whole society or even a small community inside a laboratory, even if that were ethically possible, it is virtually impossible to measure the effect of social influences on personal behaviour through laboratory experiments.

Perhaps not surprisingly, therefore, owing to both ethical and practical limitations, the laboratory experiment is virtually unused in sociology.

Field experiments

Since sociology is concerned with how people behave in the real world, sociologists have sought to adapt the experimental method to a realistic context ('the field'). Without the confinement of a laboratory, sociologists can seek to overcome the practical (but not always the ethical) objections to the use of the laboratory method. By adjusting variables they can then hope to consider the effect of these variables.

The study by Rosenthal and Jacobson

A famous example of this occurred in the context of education, when Rosenthal and Jacobson (1968) tested how teachers responded to pupils with differing abilities.

They selected randomly a number of pupils and informed the teachers that these pupils were 'intellectual bloomers' whose performance would increase significantly in the next year. When the researchers revisited the school a year later, they found that the improvement of these particular students was indeed significantly higher than that of the other pupils. This study led to a concentration on the effect of *teacher expectations* on pupil performance.

One important issue to consider is the ethics of this study. Clearly, in order to undertake their experiment the researchers were untruthful to the teachers about the abilities of certain pupils.

Secondly, since the teachers seemed to have acted on this information, the experiment will almost certainly have affected (presumably adversely in some cases) the educational performance of some students for a year.

Drawbacks of field experiments

One key problem is the impossibility of controlling *all* the possible variables, and therefore of being able to identify the actual variable that causes the observed changes. Such criticisms were made of Rosenthal and Jacobson's study of teachers, and this point can be generalised to all field experiments.

The Hawthorne effect

A second problem occurs with field experiments when the subjects know they are being watched, leading to the phenomena of 'the Hawthorne effect'. This arose out of a series of studies by Elton Mayo and colleagues at the Hawthorne works of the Western Electricity Company.

The study (which today might be called a time-and-motion study) was concerned with attempting to find the optimum working conditions to enhance productivity performance. It was conducted by adjusting a whole series of variables in the workplace – such as lighting level, room temperature and the duration of work breaks. However, whatever the experimenters did – whether it made the working conditions better or worse – productivity increased. The conclusion arrived at was that this effect was due to the interest shown in the workers by the researchers – *whose presence was therefore the key factor*.

The Hawthorne effect is named after this study because it demonstrates that people will probably change their behaviour if they are aware of being watched – so an accurate picture of their normal behaviour is not obtained. This has led to debate over whether researchers should let subjects know they are being studied and risk them changing their behaviour, or instead not inform them (covert research). The latter approach is considered unethical by some because it undermines people's privacy and does not allow them to choose whether they wish to be involved in the research – thus breaching the principle of *informed consent*.

The examples above demonstrate that there are ethical and practical problems surrounding the use of both laboratory and field experiments in sociological research. For these reasons, the methodology is not one that is highly favoured today. Certainly the laboratory experiment is almost unknown within sociology, and field experiments have little usage.

Questionnaires and social surveys

The term 'social survey' refers to a study which aims to gain data from large numbers of people, generally through the use of various types of questionnaire and interview methods. A questionnaire, which is a list of organized questions, is the primary research tool in much sociological research.

The basic questionnaire method involves providing respondents with a printed list of questions to be answered. If, on the other hand, the questions are asked verbally by the researcher, then this situation becomes an interview. Many interviews involve some kind of questionnaire and must take into account the methodological rules devised for drawing up, administering and analysing questionnaires.

Questionnaires are most commonly used when there is a desire to gain information from a large sample of people. There is a minimum number which must be reached if the sample is to stand a chance of being representative – though this is a necessary but not sufficient basis for representativeness.

By ensuring that each respondent is faced with an identical stimulus – that is, an identical questionnaire – the method aims to be reliable. Variations in answers will not be the result of any variations in the questions, or the order in which they were asked, or the manner in which they were asked. As May comments:

The theory is that if all respondents are asked the same questions in the same manner, and if they express a difference of opinion in reply to those questions, these variations result from a 'true' difference of opinion, rather than as a result of how the question was asked or the context of the interview.

(May, 1993, p. 67)

The validity of findings from a social survey using a questionnaire is related to the actual wording of the questions, so extreme care must be taken at the stage of designing and wording the document. If questions are ambiguous, or if the instructions on how to complete the question-

naire are unclear, it might be that the answers given do not reflect the true situation. The design of a questionnaire and its testing through a *pilot study* are therefore very important.

Piloting a questionnaire

A pilot study is a small initial study conducted with an early draft of a questionnaire. Its sole aim is to test whether it is worded clearly and contains questions that are both understandable and answerable. At this stage it is hoped that any sociological jargon will show up, and any questions that remain unclear can be rectified.

In a pilot study, therefore, respondents may be asked to comment on the questionnaire itself. On the basis of this study, careful consideration must be given to any possible need to rewrite or reorder the questions.

This stage is important because once questionnaires have been issued it is unlikely that they can be reissued if any problems emerge. The finalized questionnaire must be clear of any technical blemishes.

Administering a questionnaire

There are a number of ways of asking people questions, and consideration must be given to the choice of method of administration of a questionnaire. There are four main methods:

- respondents' self-completion
- delivery by mail
- delivery by telephone
- administration by an interviewer.

In the first two cases the questionnaire will be completed by the respondents, so there is a particular need for the wording of the questions to be as clear as possible. Instructions on how to complete the questionnaire have to be drawn up and attached to the front.

The other two forms of administration involve the researcher, or interviewers working on his or her behalf, filling in the answers. Here, careful training is needed to ensure that the interviewers apply the questionnaire in a standardized way and record the answers accurately. There is a degree of personal interaction, and so issues relating to interviewing technique are involved.

Respondents' self-completion

This occurs when questionnaires are handed to respondents who are then asked to complete the document themselves. Such delivery requires that the sample be concentrated in one area and be accessible to the researcher. This is most likely to occur when the questionnaire is being administered to people in an institutional setting, such as workers in a factory or students in college.

Delivery by mail

Mailed questionnaires are sent via the postal system to the sample selected, with a reply-paid envelope for return of the document. Because there is no obvious reason why the sample should complete the questionnaire, such surveys require the researcher to draw up a covering letter explaining the purpose of the research and asking for the co-operation of the respondent.

Since the researcher and the respondent will in this case be geographically distant, it is impossible for the researcher to clarify any questions or instructions that are unclear. It is vitally important that careful attention be paid to the design and piloting of the questionnaire.

Mailed questionnaires are popular for surveys because they allow researchers to select a sample from a geographically disparate population, and they are cheaper to administer than those conducted by an interviewer. Catherine Hakim (1987) estimated that their cost was about half that of interview-administered questionnaires.

However, a major problem with postal questionnaires is the often low response rates. May (1993) suggests that a figure of 40 per cent is not uncommon. This creates a difficulty because the people who *do* respond to the questionnaire cannot be said to be representative of the sample as a whole (they are clearly unusual in one sense, in that they chose to respond). May provides the following example of the problems that can result:

It is possible that only some groups will reply and not others. The replies might then be systematically biased towards one part of the population. For instance, in one health survey, people appeared more healthy than was generally thought the case. An examination of replies found that those in more deprived areas had a low response rate. As there is a relationship between health and income, this biased the results showing a more healthy population than was actually the case.

(May, 1993, p. 72)

Clearly such issues need to be considered and possible solutions suggested. It is likely that it will be necessary to send reminders, probably enclosing a second copy of the questionnaire, to non-respondents to try to ensure that a high response rate is achieved. However, there are also a number of problems with this. First, if the questionnaire is anonymous, the researcher will not be able to tell which members of the sample have responded and which have not. Secondly, the cost of the survey is increased if two letters have to be sent to some respondents.

Delivery by telephone

Although the researcher in this case is not involved in face-to-face interaction, it is necessary to consider issues relating to the manner and tone of the conversation.

A key problem with using the telephone is the potential for the sample to be unrepresentative. May (1993) points out that in many households it is a male in whose name the telephone is registered, and whose name will therefore appear in the telephone directory. It is also the case that some people choose to be ex-directory. The sample will therefore miss representative females, and those who choose to be unapproachable by strangers.

> ### 💬 Discussion point
> What other problems might arise from the use of a telephone directory to obtain a research sample, and the telephone to administer a questionnaire?
>
>

As a result of these problems, telephone administration is considered the most likely to be problematic with regard to representativeness – although, as May points out, if one is studying a *particular* population, with virtually 100 per cent ownership of a phone, this problem is likely to be less. Telephone surveys are often used by private research organizations, but they are rare in sociological research.

Administration by an interviewer

In this case, all the points about the need for questions and instructions to be clear still apply, and in addition there is the need to train interviewers.

Closed versus open-ended questions

Closed questions allow only a limited number of possible responses. Often these responses are written on the questionnaire, where a space or box is allocated for a tick or a cross. Another variety of closed question is that attempting to elicit the attitudes of people by providing them with a set of scales – ranging from, say, 'strongly agree' to 'strongly disagree'. Other scales are possible.

Alternatively, questions may be open-ended. Here the respondents are provided with spaces in which they can construct their own answers.

Some questionnaires contain a mixture of closed and open-ended questions, with closed questions used to identify the person on a set of social variables such as gender, occupation (and thereby class), age, and locality. If statistical information is needed then it is likely that the vast majority of the rest of the questions will also be closed.

There is a link between the choice of type of question and a sociologist's theoretical and methodological beliefs, since closed questions will result in quantitative data and open-ended questions will result in qualitative data. *Whether or not statistics are required will therefore be a consideration in the design and construction of the questionnaire, and methodological beliefs are likely to play a part in this decision* (although they are unlikely to be the only factor).

Aspects of closed questions

By limiting the number of possible responses, closed questions allow the data to be produced in quantitative form, which is ideal for statistical analysis. The advent of computers has meant that large amounts of data can be compiled into statistical tables and graphs easily and quickly. This has to some extent led to a resurgence in interest in quantitative social surveys.

The main criticism of this type of question is that, since the researcher constructs the possible answers, this forces people to pigeon-hole themselves, and the possible responses may not in fact cover all possibilities. Further, the meanings of the possible responses may vary between respondents, and so what looks like a homogeneous block of people who all respond in the same way might in reality not be such. Sociologists influenced by the phenomenological approach therefore argue that closed questions do not reveal in-depth insights into the people being studied, and the results can be an artifact of the way the survey was constructed. McNeill summarizes this view as follows:

The questionnaire may produce the same statistics whenever it is used, but this may be just a matter of repeating the same distortions. The survey style of research imposes a structure on that which is being researched, rather than allowing the structure to emerge from the data as it is collected.

(McNeill, 1985, p. 114)

The choice of categories can attempt to minimize this problem, by ensuring that all possible alternatives are included and by adding an 'Other' category. These are issues to address at the pilot stage.

However, this will not eliminate the fact that the researcher is imposing a structure, albeit possibly a looser one than a poorly designed questionnaire would impose. In essence, at the heart of this is a philosophical and theoretical debate about whether sociologists can use categories at all. Some would argue that, for example, social classes do not exist in any real sense and are merely constructions of researchers.

There are definite practical advantages in the use of closed questions. Generally they are very quick to administer, and are therefore correspondingly cheaper than other methods. If proper attention is paid to issues of questionnaire design they will produce a reliable research instrument. However, their key weaknesses remains a question-mark over their validity and the imposition of the researcher's framework through the pre-set selection of possible answers.

Aspects of open-ended questions

Open-ended (or simply 'open') questions are designed to avoid the problems of closed questions. By allowing respondents to speak for themselves, they are not limited in their possible responses.

However the great problem with this is, of course, that it becomes extremely difficult to make comparisons between the answers because there is no way of ensuring that all respondents interpret the questions in exactly the same way. There is no guarantee that there will be any overlap in their answers which would allow comparisons. In effect, results can be reported only by quoting the comments of the people who have responded.

Can it be claimed that the conclusions are valid if in reality only a sample of all the answers is quoted in the final report or book, and the decision over which bits to include lies with the researcher? Questionnaires conducted using open-ended questions can therefore be criticized over their validity and representativeness, unless all the answers are included in the final research report (which is unlikely).

So, while in the use of closed questions a researcher imposes a meaning on the situation *prior to* the answers being given, a similar process happens with open-ended questions *after* the questions have been answered.

Case Study – Age barriers at work

In one of the contributions to Arber and Ginn's study of the connections between gender and ageing, Miriam Bernard *et al.* (1995) looked at how processes in the workplace impact on women in later life.

As part of this they commented on the findings of a piece of research (known as the METRA study) conducted by two of their number, Catherine Itzin and Chris Phillipson (1993). This sought to look at how age barriers might operate in the context of local government employment. The following draws on their comments on the methodology employed in this research:

The ... Metropolitan Authorities Recruitment Agency study ... was a large-scale national survey examining the position of mature and older male and female workers in the context of local government. ... The METRA study had three major phases. The first phase involved a postal questionnaire to all local authorities in England and Wales and was carried out in the spring of 1992. Of 449 authorities, 221 completed the questionnaire, a response rate of 49 per cent. The second phase involved case-study fieldwork in a representative sample of 11 local authorities. Each case study looked at the corporate policies and practices of the authority and then focused on the particular situations within different service departments. Tape-recorded in-depth interviews were held with managers, and group interviews were held with older employees in senior management, in administrative and clerical work, and in manual work. Group interviews were also carried out with women aged 35–50 in middle management. Overall, around 350 people were interviewed in one form or another in the case studies. The third phase involved a self-completion questionnaire sent to 476 senior managers in 8 of the 11 service departments selected for the case-study research. Three-hundred and three questionnaires were completed, giving a response rate of 64 per cent.

(Bernard *et al.*, 1995, pp. 59–60)

Activity

a What were the response rates achieved in the two questionnaires mentioned in the extract?

b Explain why the researchers feel it is important to mention this.

c Apart from questionnaires, what other methods were used in this research?

d Identify the distinct sample used in each phase and suggest how these samples were arrived at.

C3.2, C3.3

Interviews

While all research involves asking questions in some way, if a questionnaire is administered face to face then this becomes an interview. The design of the questionnaire remains important, but many other issues arise from the fact that an interview involves interpersonal interaction. The relative importance of these issues varies according to the type of interview conducted.

Types of interview

All interviews involve communication between people, but the way in which this occurs can vary. One key issue is the degree of *structure*, leading to three different types of interview: structured, unstructured and semi-structured.

Structured interviews

These occur when the interviewer is not allowed to deviate from the wording of the questions, nor the order in which they are asked. The aim is to *standardize* the experience so that variations in the answers given reflect real variations. Since this type of interview is used mainly by those interested in obtaining quantitative data, the questions will usually be of the closed type.

Structured interviews were used by Marshall *et al.* (1988) in their study of social class in modern Britain. The methodological issues surrounding this piece of research are considered in detail later in this section.

Unstructured interviews

These occur when there is no rigid format imposed on the interviewer, although there will almost certainly be a checklist of topics to be covered. The interviewer may thus decide the order in which questions are asked, and indeed may modify the questions themselves to suit the flow of the interview. It is unlikely that a detailed list of questions would be drawn up beforehand. Instead the researcher uses interviewing skills to frame questions to cover all chosen areas.

The questions are likely to be much more open than those used in structured interviews. The aim is to try to make the interview feel as natural as possible, almost like a conversation. The lack of structure permits the interviewer to react to the actual answers given by the respondent.

Semi-structured interviews

As their name suggests, these fall in between the above two extremes. The questions are not set down in detail beforehand, thus allowing the interview to proceed in a natural way. The interview will focus on certain predetermined topics, but without preset questions. Alternatively it could be that some questions *will* be preset, especially those relating to the social characteristics of the interviewee which the interviewer has deemed to be possible significant variables. This allows consideration of the way responses might vary according to these social characteristics, whilst also ensuring that the overall sample is representative of the population to be studied in respect of the social variables identified.

The extent of the structuring of the interview will be affected by the general methodological beliefs of the researcher. The more structured interviews are likely to be part of social surveys aimed at producing quantitative data, whilst less structured interviews tend to be favoured by those seeking qualitative data and looking for a more natural interview process.

Number of interviewees

Should people be interviewed individually or as a group? Group interviews allow the researcher to consider the views of a lot of people in a shorter time than it would take to interview them individually, and in certain circumstances this might also be seen to be more natural.

For example, Paul Willis (1977) adopted the group-interview method in his study of working-class male pupils because he interviewed some of the 'lads' together (see Section 8.7). He argued that since they acted together as a group, interviewing them as a group would create a more natural setting which would also allow him to observe interactions between them while conducting the interview.

A potential problem with this is that people are required to respond in the presence of others, and this can affect the accuracy of the answers they are prepared to give. If, for example, a group of workers were interviewed together with their boss, they might be reluctant to be openly critical of the management. The question of whether people should be interviewed individually or in a group is therefore an issue requiring careful thought.

Discussion point

What would be the advantages and disadvantages of interviewing students from the same group in a joint interview? To what extent might this depend on the topic being researched?

C3.1a

The depth of interview

Ethnographers have developed what are called 'in-depth interviews', which are now used more widely in sociology to uncover the cultural meanings perceived by individuals. Rather than talking to a large range of people, the aim here is to focus on one person or a few people (possibly seen as key individuals). Thus by talking to a few people over a long period of time, issues can be considered in detail and points emerging can be followed up.

Such information may then be used as the basis of interview schedules for more standard samples, or the method may stand on its own as a distinctive approach concerned more with depth than with breadth.

The interview process

An interview is similar to (though not the same as) a conversation in that it involves interaction between at least two people. In order to make an interview work it is necessary to build up some form of relationship with the person being interviewed, if only to encourage them to participate. The role of the interviewer also involves making contact with potential interviewees and gaining their co-operation. The interview process clearly involves the use of interpersonal skills.

The interviewer effect

A problem may arise over *objectivity* if the personality of an interviewer intrudes into the research process. This is particularly true if more than one interviewer is used, since the intrusion of their *different* personalities will mean that the interview experience varies between the interviewees. Then the actual experience of the interviewees will not be the only variable involved, so the research experience will not have been standardized. This would place a question-mark over the reliability of the research findings.

This issue has been investigated by looking at the outcome of interviews conducted with variations in the characteristics of the interviewers. May (1993) quotes a study of the levels of satisfaction of black Americans with their social, economic and political lives, showing that the answers given differed according to whether respondents were interviewed by white or black interviewers. Given that the interviews were conducted in the southern US state of Tennessee, it is likely that the overall context of racial relations there had an effect, but it was manifested in variations in response according to the social characteristics of the interviewer.

Labov (1973) found that black children responded very differently when interviewed by white or black interviewers. In this case the findings from the sessions with white interviewers had been used to define the black children as linguistically deprived, and such a conclusion was the basis of special programmes of education for them. Labov clearly showed this finding to be invalid; instead the interviews reflected the extent to which black children in a country with high levels of racism would respond openly to white people.

That is a clear example of what is called the 'interviewer effect'. The characteristics and behaviour of the interviewer can be hugely important factors affecting the answers that respondents give. It is in order to minimize this problem that surveys using more than one interviewer often involve training (sometimes of many days' duration), covering in detail how the interviewers are to approach their task. This issue is of extreme importance if the research findings are to be used for practical social reform.

The interview problem

When choosing both interviewers and the location of the interviews, researchers must be aware of the potential for these to affect the research findings. This can be called the 'interview problem'.

Oakley (1979) highlighted this by pointing out that an interview is an artificial situation. It is therefore likely that, however hard the interviewer tries to create a naturalistic environment, respondents may choose not to reveal certain things. This is particularly true of any questions relating to sensitive issues. Thus we can be fairly certain that an interview reveals only what respondents are willing to say – which may not be the same as what they actually think or say in other circumstances.

Conducting the interview

A non-directive approach

Precisely because an interview is an artificial situation, with the need to develop a continuing rapport with the respondent, there have been a number of debates relating to the actions and stance the interviewer should take within it.

One early position on this stressed that the interviewer should adopt a neutral role and avoid any commentary on the answers respondents gave, to avoid affecting the answers to later questions. This is known as a *non-directive interview*.

This view was rejected by Becker (1971), who felt that in certain circumstances a more directive and aggressive style of interviewing is needed. The aim here is to arrive at the truth, rather than simply be satisfied with the information the respondent is apparently willing to provide. Becker most famously used his method when interviewing 60 Chicago teachers about their attitudes to pupils. He argued that a non-directive interview would have provided information only on what teachers thought they were *supposed* to think about pupils. Since he was aiming to discover the reality of how teachers actively labelled pupils, he adopted a sceptical stance to their answers. This, he says, allowed him to discover the reality of the views they held of pupils.

Clearly, research into events that do happen but which are not officially meant to happen could require such an approach to break through the bland responses that might result from a non-directive interview.

Feminist approaches

Another debate about interviews was sparked off by Oakley's (1979) work on the experience of motherhood, and her further reflections (1990) on issues arising out of the interview process.

She argues that textbook models of interviewing tend to stress the need for the interviewer to remain detached and neutral (the classic non-directive interview). The interview is totally controlled by the interviewer, but she argues that this tends to set up a hierarchical relationship where only the interviewer is allowed to ask questions, while remaining aloof from the respondent beyond the minimal need to establish rapport.

Her argument is that this style of interviewing results from a desire to be seen as *scientific* and to remain the detached researcher. She rejects this model on the basis of her experiences of interviews about motherhood. She argues that there is a need to include values such as *subjectivity* and *equality* in the research process, and sees the objective detached model as infused with patriarchal values linked to science.

In her research Oakley conducted repeat interviews with women, and the relationship she built up with them involved her answering their questions as well as them answering hers. She sees this as a more equitable and therefore non-oppressive form of interviewing. A similar approach was taken by Kelly (1988) when interviewing women about domestic violence.

The importance of *personal experience* in feminist sociological views leads them to reject *im*personal interviews; the latter tend to undervalue the personal experiences of the interviewees. It is also sometimes argued that to operate as 'the detached researcher' is to strengthen what is seen as a patriarchal structure in society.

This points towards the idea that there is a distinctly feminist approach to methodology. Exactly what this might involve is a matter of debate. For instance, another feminist-inspired sociologist, Angela McRobbie (1991a), has been critical of Oakley by arguing that all research involves some degree of power relationship, and that Oakley's research methods did not in fact overcome this. She points out that pregnant women in hospital were to some extent in a posi-

tion of powerlessness, particularly *vis-à-vis* the doctors, and it may have been this that contributed to their willingness to participate in Oakley's research:

Their extreme willingness to participate in the research could also be interpreted as yet another index of their powerlessness.

(McRobbie, 1991a, p. 79)

Oakley presumed that her stance would at least not add to this sense of powerlessness because of her common identification as a woman with the respondents. However, McRobbie suggests that this assumes that *all* women have a shared sense of oppression, a view she rejects since it rests on a unified notion of women. Although they may share gender, there are still other bases for power inequalities.

Evaluating interviews as a research method

In essence, the advantages and disadvantages of interviews depend on the degree of structure imposed.

Structured types

Advantages

One advantage here is that it is possible to make *direct comparisons* between the responses given by interviewees, given the commonality of questions asked and the attempt to standardize the interview experience. In so far as this is done successfully, such interviews can be said to have a high degree of reliability.

In this respect they are similar to self-administered closed-question questionnaires. However, an advantage they have over those is the fact that there is someone present to clarify the meaning of any confusing questions. Also, the response rate from social surveys using the interview method tends to be much higher (around 65–80 per cent) than is the case with mailed questionnaires.

Disadvantages

A disadvantage of this method is that the structure of the interview is preset, and it is argued – particularly by qualitative researchers – that this precludes the respondent providing full and detailed responses. This results in a lower degree of validity than would be achieved by, for example, an unstructured interview.

Unstructured types

Advantages
Here, since respondents can respond in their own words, it is argued that this provides a more in-depth valid picture of reality. The interviewer can follow up issues arising in the course of the interview. The more naturalistic setting is also likely to make the respondent relaxed and willing to continue participating.

Disadvantages
The key disadvantage is that there is no guarantee there will be any great level of comparability between interviews within a research project. It is possible for two interviews which start at the same point to go off in different directions, making comparisons difficult if not impossible. This lack of similarity undermines the reliability of the approach.

Interviews of all types

Interviews as a whole tend to gain a greater response rate than mailed questionnaires, but they also tend to be roughly twice as expensive to conduct. This will affect the number of people it is possible to interview.

Time constraints also limit the number of people it is possible to interview, and therefore the size of the sample in interview programmes tends to be smaller than in mailed questionnaires. In particular the sample size in unstructured interviews tends to be between only 30 and 150, which means that careful consideration needs to be given to the sampling procedure to ensure that something approximating a representative sample is achieved. The smaller the actual sample, the more difficult this is.

Finally, with all interviews the skill of the interviewer is paramount. The selection and training of interviewers must be undertaken carefully to minimize the 'interview effect'. All of this adds to the time and cost of the method.

Nonetheless, conducting interviews remains a very popular method of social research, with the potential to provide both qualitative and quantitative data.

Case Study – Social class in modern Britain

Marshall *et al.* (1988) used the social survey method in their investigation of social class in modern Britain. Thus the study obtained sizeable amounts of quantitative data from a large number of people in a relatively short time. This was done using a large questionnaire administered by interviewers.

The questionnaire contained some 136 questions, though not every respondent was asked all of them. Sampling and training of interviewers were both key issues. The following lengthy quotation is provided here to reveal the various methodological decisions that were taken in relation to this piece of research:

AGENCIES
The Project Directors ... were Gordon Marshall, Howard Newby, and David Rose. Carolyn Vogler was Senior Research Officer from January 1983 until August 1985. The Survey Research Centre at Social and Community Planning Research assisted with the questionnaire design, carried out the fieldwork, edited and coded the data, under the Research Directorship of Patricia Prescott-Clarke.

THE SAMPLE
The sample was designed to achieve 2000 interviews with a random selection of men aged 16–64 and women aged 16–59 who were not in full-time education. The Electoral Register was used as a sampling frame. ...

A three-stage design was employed. This involved the selection of parliamentary constituencies, polling districts, and finally individuals. ... One hundred parliamentary constituencies, then two polling districts from each sampled constituency, were selected with probability at both stages proportionate to size of electorate. ...

Nineteen addresses from each sampled polling district were then selected by taking a systematic sample through the list of elector names and noting the address of the elector on which the sampling interval landed. ... One person at each address was then selected from those eligible for the survey. This selection was made by interviewers who were given the set of rules laid out in the respondent selection sheet that forms the frontispiece of the questionnaire. ...

When deciding on the size of the starting sample of addresses two forms of sample loss, in addition to non-response, had to be taken into account. The smaller of these losses is the 'deadwood' contained in a sample of addresses selected via electoral registers. This comprises addresses which are found to be no longer occupied as residential properties. The usual allowance of 4 per cent was made for this factor. The other form of loss was related to the population to be surveyed – persons of working age who were not in full-time education. It was known that a proportion of sampled addresses would contain no such persons and therefore no interviews could be conducted at these addresses. (Some addresses, for example, would contain only persons of pensionable age.) Data from the 1981 Census were used as a basis for estimating the number of such ineligible households. These suggested that around 20 per cent of sampled addresses would be outside the scope of the survey and this too was allowed for in the sample size selected. It was decided, on the basis of these estimates and an anticipated net response rate of 70 per cent, to issue 3800 addresses (19 in each of the 200 selected polling districts).

Of the addresses issued, 165 were found to be non-residential, vacant, or demolished. At 805 of the 3635 occupied residential addresses in the starting sample, interviewers established that none of the occupants was eligible for the survey. A successful interview was conducted at 1770 of the remaining addresses (a response rate of 62.5 per cent). ...

FIELDWORK AND QUALITY CONTROL

Fieldwork was carried out during the period 1 March to 3 July 1984. One hundred and twenty-three interviewers were employed on the survey. Six full-day briefing sessions were held, all of which were attended by a member of the Essex team, and interviewers were also given a full set of written instructions. The first three interviews conducted by each interviewer were subjected to an immediate thorough checking in order that critical comments, where appropriate, could be conveyed. During the course of fieldwork the work of interviewers was subject to personal recall. Ten per cent of issued addresses were re-issued for recall (13 per cent of productive interviews). In addition, 36 interviewers were accompanied in the field by supervisors, as part of SCPR's standard supervision process. The mean length of interviews was 77 minutes.

(Marshall *et al.*, 1988, pp. 288–291)

Activity

a Explain the meaning of the terms 'population', 'sampling frame' and 'response rate'.

b What was used as a sampling frame in this study?

c Suggest reasons why this sampling frame was used.

d Bearing in mind the target population of the research, what problems might be involved in using the electoral register as a sampling frame?

e Apart from the example mentioned in the quotation, suggest one other type of household which would have fallen into the category of having no occupants eligible for interview.

f How did the researchers try to ensure that interviews were standardized?

C3.2, C3.3

Observational methods

Participant and *non-participant* observation are two important methods in sociology which arise from the ethnographic methods developed by anthropologists. The term 'ethnography' refers to the study of small-scale communities. It derives in particular from researchers such as Bronislaw Malinowski who, in order to study the Trobriand Islanders, actually lived in their society as a member and a researcher. He observed while participating. (See also Section 7.8.)

While the term 'ethnography' is strictly wider than participant observation and includes a number of other possible approaches, such as interviews and document analysis (see Section 9.6 on Hey's research), it is undoubtedly true that participant observation is the most important legacy of ethnography in sociology.

The central idea is to study life 'as it really is', and to observe the interactions people engage in. In order to do this, it is argued that the best way to obtain the most natural and most valid picture is to use a naturalistic setting, observing life in as undisturbed a way as possible. What differentiates it as a sociological research method from purely journalistic descriptive accounts of lifestyles is that it is used to develop and test theories in a systematic way.

The key aim behind observational methods is to avoid the construction of an artificial research environment, which would occur if one approached somebody with a clipboard or even sent a questionnaire through the post. The latter methods provide only a static snapshot of social reality, and as a result miss out the most important fact about societies – namely that they consist of people interacting in a dynamic way.

Non-participant observation

This involves a sociologist observing without actually participating in the events being studied. The method is used both to capture the reality of a dynamic situation without affecting it by intrusive research situations (such as conducting structured interviews), because it is believed that any such intrusion would actually affect the situation being observed. It is therefore a non-obtrusive method.

The most obvious way to observe something without affecting what happens is to do it from a distance or from behind a barrier such as a two-way mirror – then those being observed are not aware of their status. This is to avoid the infamous 'Hawthorne effect' (discussed earlier in Section 9.4). That effect was observed in an example of a 'field experiment' in which variables were changed systematically, and the results observed were explained on the basis that workers responded in a certain way precisely *because* they were being watched – they knew the experiment was taking place. Unobtrusive measures seek to avoid this drawback.

This may mean that researchers choose not to be visible to the group being observed; or alternatively not to announce that they are conducting research.

The most famous examples of this type of research are the various interactionist-inspired studies of education. In David Hargreaves' (1967) study, for example, observation occurred by the researcher sitting in on classes, and there is some evidence that his presence affected what subsequently happened. Some teachers and pupils clearly modified their behaviour whilst under observation.

However, although this method has been used, one of its key drawbacks is the virtual impossibility of eliminating totally any trace of the Hawthorne effect. It is for this reason that participation is considered as a cover for the observation. Such research then becomes a form of participant observation.

Participant observation

There are a variety of possible approaches to participant observation, reflecting the level of participation involved and whether or not the group being observed is made aware of the research being undertaken. Any one study may involve a variety of these subtypes, though it is usual for one to predominate.

The degree of involvement

It is possible to envisage either complete participation in all the activities of a group, or only partial involvement. Ned Polsky (1971), for example, in his study of poolroom hustlers, was involved in their activity in the poolroom (where his prowess as a pool player helped him) but was not involved in other activities of the group. In contrast, William Foote Whyte (1943) lived as a lodger in an Italian house with the group he was studying, even becoming a member of their street gang.

Is total participation possible?

One important consideration concerns the extent to which total participation is possible. Clearly in order to participate the researcher has to share some particular social characteristics of the group. It would not be possible, for example, for a male middle-aged sociologist to engage in complete participant-observation research of the Girl Guides, nor would a white sociologist be able to join the Black Panthers as a participant.

It also tends to place a limit on the type of groups than can be studied by this method. One obvious thing that is characteristic of researchers is that they are adults, and this limits the extent to which they can become complete participants in the activities of youths and children. Since the method has been popular in the study of juvenile delinquents, this issue has frequently surfaced, and the general response has been to try to achieve an accepted status which means that one can hang around and observe.

Paul Willis' (1977) study of male subcultures in a school environment (see Section 8.7) might fit into this category, since as an adult he clearly could not be a complete participant but was allowed to hang around with the youths. Similarly, Howard Parker (1974), in his study of juvenile delinquents in Liverpool, used his position as a community worker to hang around and therefore observe.

Safety issues

Even if it is possible to participate, it might be decided against on the grounds of personal safety. As mentioned, many studies have used this method to study juvenile delinquents who engage in illegal activities. Clearly to be a complete participant involves the danger of being called upon to participate in such acts.

'James Patrick' (1973) found this was the case with his study of a juvenile gang in Glasgow: he was eventually forced to flee and abandon his research when he refused to carry a weapon and turn up to a gang fight. Another member of the gang, at that time in prison, threatened him with retaliation and the researcher was forced to leave and change his name – with the result that the real name of the author of *A Glasgow Gang Observed* is not known and he is referred to as 'James Patrick'.

Laud Humphreys (1970) was on occasions arrested by the police during his study of gays, and Michael Haralambos (1974) recounts episodes of being threatened with a gun several times while researching music and culture in Chicago.

It is essentially because of these dangers that Polsky argued against *covert* participant observation when studying criminal groups, since he believed that such observers would invariably be found out and would then face violent retribution.

This leads on to the question of whether the researcher should inform the subjects of what is going on, and thereafter engage in *overt* participant observation, or whether covert observation is the better choice. It might be argued that unannounced (covert) observation is the only effective way to engage in research on certain activities because some groups are unwilling to be observed openly. This is, of course, particularly true of any activities of a sensitive or criminal nature, and why therefore the research by Humphreys and 'James Patrick' illustrate this point so well.

Ethical issues

Again, even if it is possible to participate, it might be decided against on ethical grounds. There is clearly an ethical question surrounding *covert* participant observation. Should sociologists *ever* engage in research on people without their knowledge, since this involves a breach of privacy?

This method of research receives special mention in the British Sociological Association's (1991) ethical guidelines:

There are serious ethical dangers in the use of covert (or secret) research, but in some circumstances covert methods may avoid certain problems. Covert methods violate the principles of informed consent and may invade the privacy of those being studied. Participant or non-participant observation in non-public spaces or experimental manipulation of participants without their knowledge should be resorted to only where it is impossible to use other methods to obtain essential data. Inexperienced researchers are strongly advised to avoid covert research. ... Covert researchers should: (1) safeguard the anonymity of research participants, and (2) ideally obtain consent to the research after it has been concluded (prior to publication).

(BSA, 1991, p. 2)

Activity

a Explain in your own words the principle of informed consent.

b Suggest some problems that covert methods might avoid in certain circumstances.

c To what extent do you agree with the view that this method should be resorted to only where it is impossible to use other methods?

C3.2, C3.3

Structured obsrvation

As well as forms of observation that allow the researcher to collect qualitative data, there is also a form of observation that allows you to collect quantitative data. This is known as structured observation. It works as follows. The researcher will observe a group of people interacting and will make a note of who speaks, who speaks to whom, and how many times each person speaks. The data can then be constructed into a diagram that shows the frequency of involvement in discussion and the level of contact between each individual.

This method is often used to analyse small-scale interactions between groups of people, such as a classroom or a committee meeting for instance.

Case Study – The Greenham Common 'peace camp'

Sasha Roseneil (1995) presents a specifically feminist portrayal of the actions of the women at the Greenham Common 'peace camp'. She was first involved with the camp as a participant but later went back to study it using the methods of observation, interviews and documentary sources. These methods, and some of the issues which arise out of them, are discussed by her in the extract below:

Three main sources provide the data on which the book is based; my own 'retrospective auto-ethnography', interviews with Greenham women, and documentary sources.

RETROSPECTIVE AUTO-ETHNOGRAPHY

In effect, the research for this book began back in December 1982, when I first visited Greenham for the 'Embrace the Base' demonstration. But this was not a conventional research trip; I was sixteen, and went to Greenham wholly as a participant. A year later I had left school and moved to Greenham, where I lived for ten months. During this time, I had a whole range of 'Greenham experiences' – actions, arrest, court appearances, prison, evictions, harassment from police, soldiers and vigilantes, and, above all, being part of the camp, contributing to its daily re-creation and transformation. I kept a diary only sporadically and untrained and uninterested in the niceties of sociological research methods, I did not systematically gather 'data' on Greenham whilst there. However, my memories and reconstruction of experiences at Greenham have been plundered continually in the course of the formal research process.

Whilst 'insider research' is rarely discussed in texts on research methods, I am certainly not the first sociologist to use her personal experiences and unique life history for research purposes. Long before feminists were advocating this, Mills argued that the sociological imagination thrives on inward reflection: '[You] must learn to use your life experience in your intellectual work, continually to examine and interpret it. In this sense craftsmanship is the centre of yourself and you are personally involved in every intellectual product upon which you work (Mills 1958: 196). ...

My own involvement with Greenham locates me as anything but the unbiased, objective researcher required by the positivist tradition in sociology, or even of mainstream interpretive qualitative research.

... Rather than 'bracketing' (Schutz 1967) my pre-existing experiences and politics, I sought to engage with them reflexively, to interrogate them, and to locate myself on the same critical plane as the women I interviewed and the archives I trawled. Indeed, I claim a high level of validity for my findings because of, not despite, my own involvement in Greenham. I do not claim that this work is in any way definitive, but I do believe that it is better than that produced by an outsider could have been.

That said, insider research is not without problems. The most obvious of these is the danger of being too close to the subject matter, either to see the sociological significance of that which appears completely normal, or to be able to frame criticisms – the 'rose tinted spectacles' problem. Had I started researching Greenham very soon after living there, with little time for reflection, desensitization through familiarity may have been a more serious issue. As it was, beginning four years after Greenham had last been my home, I came back to the subject matter refreshed. Throughout the formal period of my research I made a conscious effort to 'make the familiar strange', to attempt to see things as if for the first time and then to compare these observations with my immediate 'gut feelings'. As far as criticising Greenham is concerned, the proof of the pudding is in the reading – I have attempted to tell 'the truth' about Greenham as I understand it, warts and all. Here again the length of time between my living at Greenham and formally beginning my research, and my subsequent engagement with individual feminists and a feminist literature hostile to Greenham have, I believe, afforded me a certain degree of critical distance.

Activity

a Explain what Roseneil means by 'auto-ethnography'. How convincing do you find her defence of this method against the criticisms she herself notes?

b What are the advantages and disadvantages of 'insider research'?

c To what extent do you agree with her assertion that her findings were more valid precisely because of her status as a participant in what she was researching?

C3.2, C3.3

16.4 Positivism and research design

Sociology and science

The basic starting point for positivists is a belief that sociology should be scientific – meaning that when considering evidence it should use, as far as possible, the procedures developed by the natural sciences.

Positivists believe that the relationship between evidence and explanation is based on the notion that concepts that try to describe classes of phenomena are not real in the same sense that individual things are real. This position is known as 'nominalism'. One important variant of this is the doctrine of 'empiricism', which stresses that science can proceed only by the collection of facts, by which is meant observable phenomena only.

Not all positivists are empiricists in this sense, though the two terms have often been confused. Bryant particularly emphasizes this when he states:

Comte condemned theory without observation as 'mysticism', and observation without theory as 'empiricism' (1844, p. 25). The latter in particular cannot be overstressed given that many contemporary social scientists simply equate positivism with a crude empiricism.

(Bryant, 1985, p. 14)

This point serves to underline the fact that sociologists disagree about the meaning of 'positivism'. This section considers the three major variants of positivism in sociology, based largely on distinctions elaborated by Bryant, namely:

- classical positivism
- logical positivism
- instrumental positivism.

Classical positivism

Classical positivism derives from the work of Saint-Simon (1819, 1825) and Auguste Comte (1830, 1851), who saw sociology's role as providing information that would inform the new enlightened rulers of society.

Sociology and natural science

In order to do this, Comte (see also Section 16.1)

argued that sociology should use the methods of the natural sciences. It is this belief which is the central defining aspect of positivism, as Bryant makes clear:

Positivism in sociology has come to be associated with the very idea of a social science and the quest to make sociology scientific.

(Bryant, 1985, p. 1)

The reason for this was the important role the natural sciences played in the period known as the Enlightenment, being seen as the epitome of the new form of knowledge which offered tremendous possibilities and benefits for humanity. If sociology could imitate the methodology of the natural sciences, Comte reasoned, then it would be able to provide information of a calibre required to fulfil the role he defined for it.

Comte's most famous notion is the idea that society – or more specifically the human mind – has evolved through three stages of development. This is his 'law of the three stages of human knowledge'.

Comte's law of three stages

- *The theological.* In this stage everything is assumed to be caused by some *super*natural being. Humanity wants to search for the origin and purpose of everything, in some wish to know this supernatural being.
- *The metaphysical.* In this stage, deities (gods) are replaced by abstract forces of some nature present in all things, and debate is about the nature and correct identification of these forces through speculation and philosophical reasoning.
- *The positive.* Here, knowledge is characterized by the abandonment of the search for absolute causes:

In the final, positive stage, the mind has given over the vain search after Absolute notions, the origin and destination of the universe, and applies itself to the study of their laws – that is, their invariable relations of succession and resemblance. Reason and observation, duly combined are the means of this knowledge.

(Comte, 1853, vol. 1, p. 1)

Positive science

The quotation above demonstrates Comte's belief that there are *laws* which explain how society works. Secondly, through reasoning and observation, particular *facts* can be linked to these laws, allowing us to gain knowledge of them. The facts, however, exist whether we know about them or not. In other words, the world has an *objective existence*.

As science progressed, society could be fully explained by these laws. This would allow knowledge to be used for *positive* reasons – that is, for social reform. Comte believed that science in this sense implied abandoning any metaphysical or philosophical speculations about the origin of things, and instead confining oneself to theories about accessible (that is, observable) phenomena.

In simple terms, the positivists believed that sociology should seek to adapt the methods of the natural sciences so that the scientific method becomes the basis of a positivist methodology. That which cannot be known scientifically cannot be known at all, as science becomes the only basis of knowledge. Positivism in sociology might therefore be summarized as:

... the assertion that the concepts and methods employed in the natural sciences can be applied to form a 'science of man', or a natural science of sociology.

(Giddens, 1974, p. 3)

Can sociology imitate the natural sciences?

The central approach of the natural sciences – experiments based in a laboratory – was mentioned by Comte as one possible method, but it was not something sociology could easily utilize (see Section 9.5). One cannot literally put society in a laboratory. Whilst it is possible to test human behaviour in a laboratory, the unnatural environment was most likely to lead to unnatural behaviour – which would undermine the whole enterprise. However, the aim of making sociological findings scientific could still be approached even though the exact mechanisms of the techniques to be used needed to be worked out.

As well as experiments, Comte argued that the methods of observation, comparison and the historical method could be used. Comparison allows us to look at two different societies or different phenomena and, by observing similarities and differences, gain knowledge of how they operate. Furthermore, comparison of societies at different periods in history allows us to look at the way things change.

Sociology, positivism and the end of individual choice

It is perhaps with the implications and use of this knowledge that Comte's beliefs become more controversial. He argued that the adoption of the scientific method would ensure that the laws of the universe were uncovered, thus ending the need for choices to be made. Bryant spells out the implications of this:

Once such laws are presumed to obtain, there can be no more justification, as Comte pointed out, for freedom of opinion in social matters than there is in astronomy. Instead the laws of social statics and dynamics provide applied sociology with the means to determine all moral and political questions scientifically.

(Bryant, 1985, p. 32)

Sociology and social policy

As sociology was the highest science, sociologists would determine policy. It is this approach which led Comte later in his *System of Positive Polity* (1851) to see sociologists as the priests in his 'religion of humanity'. Saint-Simon had earlier emphasized the need for a 'new Christianity' (1825) – meaning a new set of ethics – because he believed that, while the educated would accept the findings of science and would comply, the ignorant might still need some form of religion. Similarly Comte argued that such a 'religion of humanity' was needed to instil correct behaviour in the working class, through festivals emphasizing adherence to humanity rather than God and underlining their social duties.

Evaluating classical positivism

While the notions of 'religion' were dismissed by other social thinkers, and later by Durkheim, they do offer an insight into the possible realization of the limitations of the development of science and positivism which undermines the earlier confidence of Comte and Saint-Simon. However, what both the earlier and later versions share is a view of sociologists telling people how to live their lives – a fairly authoritarian view. This aspect of positivism has led to later criticism, notably from the Frankfurt School (see Section 16.9).

Although notions of a 'religion of humanity' would not be taken particularly seriously today, the question of how sociology can use the scientific method is clearly still an important one. A number of questions flow out of this. Most importantly, how can sociology adapt the methods of the natural sciences?

Problems in using the natural scientific method

Since the object of research is different, we cannot simply apply without modification the methods of the natural sciences, since this would entail the banal conclusion that society and people within it can be investigated by means of pouring acid on them, heating them up or putting them in a test-tube to see what would happen. Clearly this is not what is meant. However, it leads to the question of how far a modification creates not an adaptation but a new qualitatively different methodology.

So exactly how much adaptation is allowed before we are dealing with something else altogether? The basic point to be adapted seems to boil down to the notion that all knowledge derives from observation and reasoning, and that all such knowledge must be verified by reference to the real world, which operates according to laws or law-like generalizations which are discoverable by application of this method of observation and reasoning. This general view is applicable to any object (either natural or social), and this, then, is what is meant by the adoption of the methods of the natural sciences.

Positivism and its emphasis on laws

The emphasis on laws is perhaps the weakest aspect of positivism, since this seems to lead to a contradiction. If society is governed by laws that operate independently of our awareness of them (it is not necessary for you to be aware of the law of gravity for the apple to fall), then why should we need a priesthood of sociologists or sociology at all, since whatever was going to happen according to the laws of society would happen anyway? If laws of society are held to operate in the same way as the laws of the natural world:

… it would make no difference whether positivist sociologists succeeded or not in the accumulation of positive knowledge.

(Bryant, 1985, p. 17)

Humans as puppets?

Some theories do indeed present humans as being like puppets who are simply determined by the operation of laws. The presence of this notion of laws (not only of sociology but of society) is the most problematic aspect of positivism.

Comte did believe that such knowledge could help us in some way to predict the future; but that implies that the laws are in a sense not laws, or that we might know when something was going to happen but not be able to do anything about it. All the time this comes back to the fundamental question of sociological theory: are humans' experiences totally determined for them, or can they make real choices and so affect the course of human development?

Discussion point
To what extent do you think sociology can help humankind to predict the future? Would such knowledge be of any use?

C3.1a

Society as a reality *sui generis*

Today, few would accept Comte's rather rigid belief in the laws of society (arguably few did even in Comte's time). This does not necessarily entail disavowal of the scientific method, though it does mean we cannot accept the full-blown version of Comtean positivism.

Emile Durkheim (1938a; orig. pub. 1893), for example, does not seem to argue that society is based on the operation of inviolable laws, since his analysis of the 'division of labour' (see Section 16.1) at least allows for the possibility of society developing in normal or abnormal ways – and therefore the need for action in the form of reforms to avoid abnormality. This is clearly not a totally determinist view, but Durkheim (1938b; orig. pub. 1895) shares with Comte the idea that society is a reality *sui generis* (whole in itself) and therefore independent of the actions of the individuals within it. There is still, therefore, a degree of determinism in his views which would certainly be unacceptable to sociologists in the social-action tradition influenced by phenomenological views (see Section 16.5).

The variety of positivisms

Thus, while positivists share the idea that the social sciences should seek to be scientific – and that this involves adapting in some way the methods of the natural sciences – the actual way in which that view is worked out differs. In other words there is more than one variety of positivism, and these variants developed by thinking about the problems in Comte's schema. In terms of the development of sociology in the UK, it is arguably *logical positivism* that has had the greatest influence, and which people are generally referring to when they talk of 'positivism'.

Logical positivism

The 'verification principle'

Logical positivism grew out of attempts in the 1920s and 30s – by analytical philosophers known as the Vienna Circle (1929) – to define a universal method for science. This endeavour was supported by three representatives of the scientific world, namely Albert Einstein, Bertrand Russell and Ludwig Wittgenstein. They argued that there were really only two bases for science, namely:

- empirical statements
- analytical statements of logic.

This implied that only empirical data could serve as a basis for acquiring knowledge, and in considering such data scientists must apply the rules of logic to their theories:

The logical positivists went much further than Comte in that they demanded something he opposed, the identification of positivism with empiricism.

(Bryant, 1985, p. 112)

Hypotheses

The aim was to resolve age-old philosophical debates by rendering them into statements (known as hypotheses) which could then be tested through empirical investigation. There were to be no things unamenable to such testing, since they were be simply unknowable or unobservable. Such hypotheses existed merely because methods to observe and test them had not yet been properly worked out.

Verification

Once the data have been collected, the question arises of whether a hypothesis is confirmed or not. In relation to this, the Vienna Circle argued that the issue was of *verification*. If the hypothesis is confirmed or verified by the data, then it counts as scientific knowledge. Otherwise, not only is the hypothesis not scientific knowledge, it is utterly without any meaning.

Understanding or explanation?

The implication of this was that statements had meaning only in so far as they referred to observable experience in the world. Everything – even the meanings people construct – is a physical event located in a particular space and time. Thus the social sciences could use the same method and verification test as the natural sciences, and there was no justification for the argument (associated most famously with Max Weber, and the basis for the whole social-action tradition in sociology – see Section 16.5) that there was a need for a separate notion of social research based on 'understanding', as opposed to the natural scientific notion of 'explanation'.

The key problem with this idea is that it set up a standard, the verification principle, which cannot itself be verified – the so-called 'paradox of positivism'.

'Falsification'

Karl Popper (1959), philosopher of science, wrestled with the verification paradox by arguing that it was necessary to set a different standard. He suggested that instead of seeking to verify their hypotheses, scientists should seek to *falsify* them.

He argued that it was not true to say that statements that are not verifiable are meaningless, and he instead argued that they are simply statements that have not yet been falsified. If we wish to develop these into scientific knowledge, we must recast them in terms that would allow of the *possibility* that they could be falsified. The importance of this is the rejection of the idea implicit in the original positivist formulation that it is possible to approach universal knowledge.

Popper argued that just because something has been verified lots of times, this is no proof that it will always be true (thus identifying the central problem of inductive reasoning) – it is possible it might be falsified at some point in the future. The true test of knowledge is whether it is formulated in ways that *allow* of this falsifiability, and the true test of science is that it should seek to falsify things. It is knowledge if it has resisted falsification so far, despite being framed in such a way as to allow falsification. This does not, however, imply that it will be knowledge for all time.

The hypothetico-deductive method

This means that science needs to start with statements that can be tested – 'hypotheses'. To ensure that a statement can be tested, it should be as precise as possible. The inspiration for a hypothesis might come from observation, but equally it might come from thinking about something. Sense-experience is therefore not seen as the sole basis of scientific knowledge. This is the basis of the approach known as the 'hypothetico-deductive' method, the stages of which are illustrated in Figure 16.3.

The impossibility of absolute knowledge

Because statements may be falsified at some point in the future, Popper's argument points towards the impossibility of ever arriving at absolute knowledge – since this depends on being able to count something as true for all time and gradually adding to such statements until everything is known. An important implication of this is that the kind of grand schemas for wholesale societal reform outlined by Comte (see Section 16.1) are undermined. According to Popper, science cannot predict the future, merely know something about what is true today. In practical policy terms this points towards the advocacy of piecemeal social reform and gradual evolution, a view which also led Popper to be critical of Marxism.

Was Popper a positivist?

The distinction between verification and falsification means that, although Popper had some connections with the logical positivists, he is not really a positivist in this sense – and he himself rejected the label. Actually his ideas tend to point

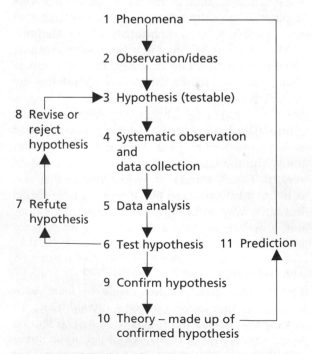

Figure 16.3 The hypothetico-deductive model
Source: McNeill (1985, p. 42)

towards a realist view of science. This is because he rejected the idea of induction, and because he argued that as a consequence all scientific statements are intrinsically theory-bound. However, his argument that the facts (theory-bound though they are) could be tested empirically at least left him associated in many eyes with positivism, as widely defined.

Evaluating logical positivism

Uncritical ideology

Popper was attacked as a positivist by those in the 'critical theory' tradition who argued that, if facts were theory-bound, then so were the tests designed to falsify or verify those facts. Thus science was not a method capable of escaping the theories out of which its statements emerged. Positivism was necessarily adopting concepts which promoted the interests of powerful groups, since these arose from the existence of a 'dominant ideology' in society (see Section 6.2). By disavowing criticism as value-laden, positivists did not arrive at a scientific truth, merely a form of ideology which justified the existing state of society.

Kuhn and scientific revolutions

This line of argument has also been taken up by another philospher of science, Thomas Kuhn, whose book *The Structure of Scientific Revolutions* (1970) emerged out of a series edited by two members of the Vienna Circle.

Basically Kuhn argued that scientists work within sets of ideas or paradigms that do not derive from, and are not sustained by, their proximity to facts alone. Because their careers depended on it, they were unlikely to take risks most of the time. This idea undermined the notion of the scientist as a detached observer, concerned with the careful testing of hypotheses – and therefore ultimately undermined the notion of science the logical positivists had sought to build on.

Instrumental positivism

This version of positivism grew up in the USA in the late 1930s, and has dominated American sociology. The term 'instrumental positivism' to describe this school originates with Bryant (1985). It is positivist in the sense that it is based on the idea that we should generate knowledge through empirical research; but its key distinguishing characteristic is the belief that research should be confined to areas where research techniques which would provide such evidence already exist.

Limitations of instrumental positivism

There is here a clear limiting of the areas of social scientific investigation, and implicitly this pushes instrumental positivism much more towards empiricism than can be found in either logical or classical positivism. There is an almost complete reliance on quantitative data in the form of statistics (see Section 9.6), and the development of ever more elaborate statistical techniques to analyse data. This can be seen in the book *The People's Choice* by Lazersfeld *et al.* (1944), which was an empirical investigation into political decision-making through refinement of the opinion poll technique.

Value-free facts?

This overall approach meant that sociology was to be based on the gradual accumulation of knowledge, primarily through statistical analysis. It was to be scientific in the sense of not being concerned overtly with the question of the uses to which the data were to be put, or indeed with any attempt to argue that sociological knowledge could help create a better society. 'Taking a stand' was seen to undermine objectivity, leading to their promotion of value-freedom as a key element in the instrumental approach. Equally, theory was rejected as not being based on data and as such effectively excluded from what counts as sociology.

That said, it did appear that instrumental positivists acted on an implicit theory of society, since they believed that knowledge could be based on the findings generated by questionnaires administered to individuals, summarized as:

... the development of a total portrait of man derived from the combination of discrete questionnaires, surveys and other 'atomic' facts.

(Horowitz, 1968, p. 200)

The individualistic view of society

This points to a view which believes that society is merely the sum of the individuals within it, fitting in with the individualistic ethos of the society in which this variant of positivism was born. An important implication is that any notion of social structures, which cannot be measured by such methods, disappears.

Such an approach in American sociology contrasts with the attempt by Talcott Parsons (1937, 1951), the key theorist of the functionalist approach in sociology, to arrive at a 'grand theory' of society. Functionalism most certainly does rely on a notion of social structures, and does believe theory is a necessary part of sociology. Social science cannot therefore be based merely on adding together the views and attitudes of lots of individuals (or 'abstracted empiricism' as C. Wright Mills called it), which the instrumental positivists tended towards. The rise of functionalism to prominence in sociology undermined the appeal of instrumental positivism's attack on theory, but did not necessarily undermine the use of the approach they identified. Statistical analysis remained dominant.

Evaluating instrumental positivism

Abstracted empiricism

The disdain for theory and social structures in this approach led to it being criticized in the 1960s and 70s. In his book *The Sociological Imagination*, C. Wright Mills (1959) described it as 'abstracted empiricism' – whereby sociology became merely a matter of considering individuals abstracted from their place in wider social structures. Thus he argued that Lazersfeld and colleagues had tried to examine American politics merely by reference to the voters' choices and the media, without examining the wider structures of power within which they operated.

Value-neutrality as indifference or complicity

Other radical sociologists also suggested that the notion of value-neutrality held by these researchers in effect meant that sociologists became merely empirical researchers up for hire to the highest bidder. This, it was argued, made them complicit with various questionable operations undertaken by the American government, notably in Latin America. The key example of this is the notorious Project Camelot. The nature of this project and the issues surrounding it have been summarized by Bilton *et al*:

In its natural concern for social order in the lower half of the continent, the Pentagon wished to discover the causes of revolt and remove them. In order to achieve this, they planned to spend up to six million dollars and recruit a huge team of political scientists and sociologists to work in the countries concerned. Their employer made the aims clear in a recruiting letter: 'The US Army has an important mission in the positive and constructive aspects of nation-building in less-developed countries as well as a responsibility to assist friendly governments in dealing with active insurgency problems.' The aims were equally clear to the South American governments concerned, and they rapidly forced the abandonment of the project, with accusations of spying and covert intervention by the United States. All this came as a shock to those who agreed to take part, for they believed they were aiding those countries by advocating policies such as land reform which would remove the need for revolution. It is a sad comment on social scientists that they could be so naive about the intentions of the powerful.

(Bilton *et al.*, 1987, p. 607)

Activity

Suggest elements of Project Camelot which identify it as being derived from the ideas of instrumental positivism.

C3.2

16.5 Phenomenology and research design

While positivists stress that sociology can in some sense adapt the methods of the natural sciences to its own purposes – since the social world, just like the natural world, is an objective reality existing independently of our awareness and knowledge of it – it is the denial of this point that marks out phenomenological and hermeneutic approaches. This leads to an approach that stresses the importance of *interpretation* and the way knowledge is socially constructed.

- *Hermeneutics* arose originally as a way of interpreting texts and other static representations of human life. It is this approach which lies behind Max Weber's famous notion of *verstehen* as the central aim of sociology, since this is a German word meaning 'to understand'.

- *Phenomenology* equally seeks to understand, but in this case the concern is with understanding how that order and regularity are actively created by humans through the construction of meanings. It is further concerned with explaining how these constructions come

to be seen as natural. This brings it into clear conflict with positivism, which believes the world is a reality external to individuals.

These insights have had various implications for discussions about methodology which will be examined here.

Humans as conscious thinking subjective beings

The key point of phenomenology is that humans think about things: they are conscious beings and their actions are therefore not equivalent to those of atoms or rocks. The ideas that a person has in his or her head as part of this consciousness are a crucial part of being human. Thus any study of humanity cannot rest on a notion of an objective world existing in isolation from our awareness of it. In fact our awareness of the world is an important part in its construction, and any notion of human society – and the study of it – must start from this insight.

It follows, say the phenomenologists, that we cannot utilize the methods of the natural sciences because one of the key differences between the natural and the social sciences relates to their subject matter. The social sciences are interested in the actions, motives and intentions of human beings: 'intentional explanation is the feature that distinguishes the social sciences from the natural sciences' (Elster, 1983, p. 69).

Choices, not laws

People make choices, and this makes the social world to some extent unpredictable and not therefore amenable to law-like statements, unlike the natural world. This has a further important implication for the question of whether we can simply observe a world that exists separately from our observations of it. Anthony Giddens (1976) wrote his book *The New Rules of the Sociological Method* partly as a conscious refutation of the positivistic elements to be found in Durkheim's earlier *Rules of the Sociological Method* (see Section 16.1). Giddens explains this in his later book on positivism and sociology:

Durkheim proposed that social phenomena should be treated like things: we should regard ourselves as though we were objects in nature. Thereby he accentuated the similarities between sociology and natural science. ... although this type of standpoint has been very pervasive in sociology, it is one I reject. ... We cannot approach society, or 'social facts', as we do objects in the natural world, because societies exist in so far as they are created and re-created in our own actions as human beings. ... It follows from this that the practical implications of sociology are not directly parallel to the technological uses of science, and cannot be. Atoms cannot get to know what scientists say about them, or change their behaviour in the light of that knowledge. Human beings can do so.

(Giddens, 1986, pp. 11–12)

💬 Discussion point

What are the implications of Giddens' arguments for the actual methods of research adopted by sociologists, and for whether sociology can be a science?

C3.1a

The inapplicability of the natural scientific method

This view leads on to the phenomenological and hermeneutical approaches in sociology, centred on the idea that it *does* matter crucially that the object of analysis is qualitatively different from that of the natural sciences. This is not an excuse to reject rigour in methodology, but instead a belief that sociologists cannot simply adapt the methods of the natural sciences. So, reflections on the nature of humanity lead to the rejection of positivism.

Max Weber and *verstehen*

The most notable classical contribution to this approach came in the work of Max Weber (see also Section 16.1). In particular he made two important points in relation to the issue of sociological methodology:

- Sociology must start from an understanding of the subjective meanings people use in interactions. Thus subjectivity is an intrinsic part of the subject matter for research

- Sociologists should seek to obtain an objective understanding of these subjective meanings since it is important to distinguish between facts and values. However, this does not mean that sociologists can be morally indifferent. Their values will affect what they choose to

study, but should not affect *how* they study social phenomena.

Sociology and subjective meaning

Weber argued that the starting point for any sociology was an understanding of the subjective meanings that people use in the process of interaction. Thus, social research cannot exclude consideration of the subjective feelings of people, as positivists had suggested, since in reality the object of sociological research *is* a subjective being.

The reality that we wish to investigate is in fact made by people through the active construction of meanings which people engage in when they interact. Weber argued that it was necessary to reject the notion that there could be any universal causal laws governing society, which was a key element of classical positivism. He argued instead that it was necessary to understand the *motives* behind any particular action in order to arrive at an understanding of a situation. He said this should be the task of sociology, starting from a recognition of the importance of seeing humans as engaging in subjectively meaningful actions, and therefore as different from the objects of research in the natural sciences. McNeill provides the following summary of Weber's approach:

If we are to explain some event in the social world, our explanation has to take into account what the people involved think and feel. We must not regard them simply as helpless puppets.

(McNeill, 1985, p. 111)

Sociology as an art form?

The reasons for human behaviour are therefore internal to people, not external as classical positivism claimed. Following this line of criticism of positivism, Georg Simmel – a contemporary of Weber – even went so far as to argue that sociology should be seen almost as an art form.

💬 Discussion point

To what extent does the fact that human beings are subjective conscious actors undermine the idea that sociology can be a science? Should it be seen as an art form? What do you think sociology as an art form would involve?

C3.1a

In contrast, Weber did wish to retain some notion of sociology as a science, by which he meant it must have methodological rigour. He rejected the particular version of sociology as a science embodied in positivism because of his views on the centrality of human subjective consciousness to an explanation of human action.

Weber and objectivity: the search for value freedom

A second element of Weber's argument has been the subject of much later controversy. While rejecting positivism, he asserted that there needed to be a clear distinction between facts and values in social research. He argued that it was possible to arrive at an objective understanding of the subjective meanings people attribute to their actions in the world.

Value freedom is not moral indifference

It is important at this point to distinguish Weber's position from the rather cruder versions of this idea present in instrumental positivism (see Section 16.4). That view of sociology – almost merely as a technique – meant that instrumental positivists saw it in principle as usable by anyone, and they further felt that to let values enter into decisions about who or what is studied was not objective. As we have seen, this led them to fail to avoid becoming the handservants of the US military in various pieces of 'social research'.

This is not at all what Weber wanted to say, since he argued that:

- scientists should be responsible in their approach and have a concern for the consequences of their work: 'An attitude of moral indifference has no connection with scientific "objectivity"' (quoted in Giddens, 1971, p. 138); and

- values do enter into the choices of subject matter to be researched.

The reason for this rests on his rejection of the possibility of ever arriving at an overall universal theory of society. Instead he argued that the problems arise in particular historical circumstances. Since these particular circumstances will also affect the values individuals hold, and so dictate what will be of interest to them, the choice of topics for study is inherently value-relative, that is governed by people's values.

This did *not* mean that Weber was willing to reduce science merely to values, since he did believe it was possible ultimately to arrive at an objective understanding of society. He thought it

was not possible to arrive at statements of policy from statements of fact; that is, one cannot derive *evaluative* statements about what should or should not be by starting from statements about *what is*. (This comes from the philosophical argument that one cannot derive an 'ought' statement from an 'is' statement.)

Duties of sociologists and duties of citizens

Weber contended that while it was the duty of sociologists to outline to the best of their competence the facts, they should not – as the classical positivists had suggested was possible – argue that this negates the need for moral and political choices to be made. Indeed Weber was insistent that such responsibilities not only could not, but should not, be lifted from the citizens by sociologists. The contrast with classical positivism can be seen in the comparison of statements by Weber and Comte:

It can never be the task of an empirical science to provide binding norms and ideals from which directives for immediate practical activity can be derived.

(Weber, 1949a, p. 52; orig. pub. 1904)

The social sciences, which are strictly empirical sciences, are the least fitted to presume to save the individual the difficulty of making a choice, and they should therefore not create the impression that they can do so.

(Weber, 1949b, p. 18; orig. pub. 1917)

Science would ensure that correct policy was followed whatever the situation; indeed it would make moral and political 'choice' a misnomer insofar as man possessed of positive knowledge has only the choice between compliance with what the laws of succession and resemblance require or non-compliance, which has as its inevitable consequence eventual failure accompanied by the generation of unnecessary social costs.

(Bryant, 1985, p. 20 – describing the views of Comte)

Ideal-types

Weber's attempt to create some more general notion of society led him to construct 'ideal-types'. By these, Weber effectively meant simplified abstract notions of what exists in the ideal world of thought, rather than actually representing something which concretely exists in the world. The ideal-types would not in all likelihood exist in their full-blown versions: they represent Weber's attempt to argue that, while it should be recognized that we are imposing order on a rather more complex reality through the methods of science, nonetheless this is a necessary stage in ensuring coherence and direction to sociological enquiries.

This highlights Weber's rather ambiguous position. While wishing to start from the basis of subjective experiences, he nonetheless wants to cling to some notion of objective understanding.

Activity

a Explain *in your own words* the difference between Comte and Weber over the issue of whether sociology can be used to determine policy choices.

b Suggest the key distinct problems associated with each of these two contrasting views.

c Evaluate the relative merits of each position in relation to contemporary social policy debates.

C3.1a, C3.2, C3.3

The phenomenological critique

Avoiding the imposition of meaning

The ambivalence of Weber's position presents a problem. Schutz (1972) argues that the attempt to understand human subjective behaviour scientifically was flawed, because the interpretation of events and meanings given by the social scientist could differ from those of the person being studied. Schutz therefore argued that sociology should confine itself to the actual methods people used to construct meanings, rather than trying to impose meanings. It is this insight which led to the development of phenomenology and ethnomethodology.

Observing behaviour in its natural setting

The methodological implications of this line of argument are:

- that sociologists should observe behaviour in its natural setting
- that the overall aim must be to achieve an understanding of the thought processes of humans which direct their actions.

The approach of the Chicago School which developed out of the insights of George Herbert Mead (1934) and 'symbolic interactionism' can be seen as an important example, providing a clear contrast to the statistically driven view of sociology as a technique presented by instrumental positivism, but arising at broadly the same time.

Naturalistic methods with no prior assumptions

The Chicago School argued that the key problem with the questionnaires and opinion polls used by instrumental positivists was that they were written by the researchers, and were therefore based on *assumptions* about what was important. The Chicago School asserted that no assumptions should be made beforehand, and so they advocated the use of observation techniques (see Section 9.5) to allow researchers to get involved with people engaged in everyday activities. The belief that people should be studied in their natural environments also contained a critique of positivism, since it was argued that all other forms of research, including questionnaires (see Section 9.5), were an unnatural form of communication. Thus there was no guarantee that such methods would arrive at a valid – that is to say, accurate – portrayal of human action and thought.

The whole tradition of 'social-action sociology' therefore rests on statements concerning human consciousness, and the implication that the methods of the natural sciences are not appropriate to the study of human interactions (or society).

Realist criticisms of phenomenology

While this approach stressed the need to study human subjectivity in a naturalistic setting, it did nonetheless assume that the facts generated by such observation were available to be collected and did represent reality. Against this it has been argued that what are considered 'facts' are mediated by our theories of the world, and so there is no such thing as a natural fact waiting to be gathered. This is the basis of realist criticisms of phenomenologically inspired methodologies, which are examined in Section 16.6.

16.6 Realism and research design

Realism defined

The distinguishing characteristic of positivism and empiricism is that sociology is a science, and this has most often been interpreted as meaning it should confine itself to analysis of things that can be observed directly. Phenomenological views suggest that this is in fact all there is, since the idea is rejected that there is an objective truth behind the various subjective accounts research can generate.

Realism rejects both those positions. It holds that there *are* real structures beneath surface phenomena. These may be unobservable directly, but that does not prove they do not exist; and realists argue that such entities do exist.

In contrast to the positivists, it is argued that it is essential that these real material bases of society be included in an overall analysis if we are to claim to give a full account of society.

Realism can therefore be summarized as the belief that there are real structures of society which exist, but which are not necessarily open to observation. The implication of this is that the pure empiricist position, which is to go out and collect facts and to consider only these as scientific, must be rejected as presenting an incomplete view of the world: it cannot account for the fundamental structures of society. Theory and method are therefore intrinsically linked together, since sociologists need a theory of society couched in theoretical terms which provides the basis for empirical research.

Scientific revolutions

The appeal of realism arises partly from the failure of natural and social scientists to be able to prove that what they did in actuality matched up to the rules of science as defined by empiricism and positivism. This can be seen in the work of Kuhn (1970). In *The Structure of Scientific Revolutions*, Kuhn argued that there is a need to consider what it is that scientists actually do in the course of their work, and this led him to devise the term 'normal science'.

Kuhn argued that all such normal science operated within a paradigm, by which he meant a set of concepts, theories and methods which define both areas of research and methods to be adopted. As such, the paradigm effectively provides both the questions and the answers – and therefore frames and limits the reality of scientific investigation. Furthermore, since the paradigm is laid down by the scientific community, its acceptance or rejection is not a purely objective matter but involves social considerations and conflict. Scientists have a vested interest in main-

taining their academic careers, and this leads them to argue for the retention of the paradigm within which they work.

Kuhn asserted that it is only occasionally that discoveries occur which cause the replacement of one paradigm by another. When this happens 'scientific revolutions' occur:

Paradigm changes do cause scientists to see the world of their research-engagement differently. In so far as their only recourse to that world is through what they see and do, we may want to say that after a revolution scientists are responding to a different world.

(Kuhn, 1970, p. 110)

He outlines how one such revolution occurred with the rise of Copernicus' discovery in 1543 that the sun, not the earth, is at the centre of our universe. More recent examples of 'scientific revolutions' include the impact of Newton's theory of gravity in 1648 and the way this revolutionized physics – only to be overcome by the paradigm shift initiated by Einstein's 'general theory of relativity' in the 1920s and Heisenberg's 'uncertainty principle' in the 1930s. Once these scientific revolutions have taken place, 'normal science' is resumed until the next paradigm shift occurs.

Realist accounts of natural science

According to Kuhn's line of reasoning, natural scientists do not proceed solely by empirical testing which yields new knowledge, but instead new knowledge flows out of the theoretical breakthroughs which initiate paradigm shifts and therefore scientific revolutions. These occur because existing theories begin to break down under the weight of evidence, but it requires new theories to initiate the paradigm shift. This further underlines the theory-laden basis of scientific knowledge.

A second implication for the social sciences is that, since natural scientists are not as 'scientific' (as conventionally defined) as was thought, it is possible for social science to be similar to the natural sciences – as long as the reality of the natural sciences is recognized along the lines set out by Kuhn.

Clearly such a view undermines the basis of most variants of positivism (see Section 16.4), since science is considered no longer to rest purely on observation. However, in integrating the notions that scientists hold their views for non-scientific reasons, Kuhn's approach created support for those who argued that science was a social construction (see Section 16.5). Ultimately this leads to a relativist position, since scientific theories constructed in different paradigms cannot be tested against each other, and the history of science could therefore be seen as a succession of paradigms none of which could ultimately be tested against another.

Realism against relativism

It is the relativist conclusion set out above that realists seek to avoid. In this lies the importance of their idea that there is an independent reality to which our theories are answerable, even though this reality cannot be grasped by the empirical testing posed by positivism.

Lakatos (1975), another philosopher of science, criticizes Kuhn's notion of 'scientific revolutions' by arguing that it is not the case that a single paradigm is all-powerful at any one time, and in fact in reality many paradigms compete all the time. He goes on to say that the truth of these statements cannot be proved by reference to empirical testing alone, but he nonetheless argues that it is possible to arrive at an objective standard by which to judge the relative merits of different theories:

One cannot prove statements from experiences. ... all propositions of science are theoretical and, incurably, fallible.

(Lakatos, 1975, vol. 1, p. 16)

This link to the theory-bound nature of science, and the idea that nonetheless we can and should seek to arrive at objective measures of the truth, builds towards the realist argument that rejects empirical testing as the sole criterion of truth:

The rejection of empiricism is the basic trend which marks the distinctiveness of modern realism from earlier variants.

(Outhwaite, 1987, p. 27)

Realism and classical sociology

The most obvious candidates for inclusion in the category of realist among the classical sociologists are Emile Durkheim and Karl Marx (see Section 16.1). Durkheim is often thought of as a positivist, though he himself rejected the term

and was critical of Comte's claim to have found a way of explaining all societies on the basis of one universal law. While he can clearly be seen as a positivist in his belief that we can view society as being similar to the human organism, and his adoption therefore of the organic analogy, his writings reveal an interest in things which could not be directly observed. Bryant describes his work as follows:

The strength and penetration of the currents which impel us to marry, have children or commit suicide, for example, are reflected in the level and stability of the marriage, fertility and suicide rates for different groups. The rates serve as indicators of phenomena whose dimensions are not immediately graspable.

(Bryant, 1985, p. 35)

Durkheim the realist?

In his choice of subject matter (notably in the case of suicide), Durkheim was interested to discover more than simply the surface 'facts' about these phenomena as revealed in the statistics; instead he saw such 'facts' as indicators of more deeply-lying 'social facts'. Positivism is involved since he looks for something observable and measurable (suicide statistics), but his analysis is also realist since these statistics are held to indicate something else – that is, the level of social integration or the lack of it. His explanation for the variations in the levels of suicide was squarely in terms of the power of society over individuals. In other words, he was using suicide as an example to demonstrate the power of the social.

Realism is the belief that there are certain processes (or forces) which are real, and Durkheim used suicide rates as an indicator of these forces. While his use of official statistics has therefore led to him being labelled and criticized as a positivist by phenomenological writers such as Douglas (1966) and Atkinson (1978), realist accounts point quite clearly to the idea that Durkheim saw these statistics as indicators of deeper structures in society.

One cannot, for example, find any statistics or hope to measure something like *anomie* directly, which is one of the key concepts Durkheim developed and applied to his study of suicide. Merely because *anomie* is not directly measurable or observable, however, does not mean it does not exist.

Taylor (1982), in his study of suicides and deaths on the London Underground, argues that in order to understand suicide we cannot rely simply on empirical evidence, but instead need to outline the underlying unobservable structures and causal processes which contribute to suicide. He argues that this approach is realist – and points to his view that Durkheim's original study of suicide was as well – which undermines phenomenological criticisms of it based on the question of empirical data.

Criticisms of the view that Durkheim was a realist

On the other hand, Bryant asserts that some accounts of the attempt to define Durkheim as a realist succeed only by presenting a caricatured version of positivism. He includes Taylor's work in this category. Bryant argues that this problem arises because the main view of positivism in some realist approaches is that of logical positivism. While this type of positivism is clearly incompatible with realism, since it insists that anything which is not observable is meaningless, Bryant argues that:

... although some positivisms are incompatible with realism, that of the French tradition is not.

(Bryant, 1985, p. 55)

This leaves open the view of whether we should see Durkheim as a positivist or a realist, or possibly as veering between one and the other.

Clarke and Layder (1994), like Taylor, see Durkheim's suicide analysis as a key example of a realist approach, as Figure 16.4 indicates. Clarke and Layder summarize the main points of realism as follows:

1. *Firstly, realism concentrates on the nature of society as a whole rather than the smaller elements that make it up.*

2. *Realism tries to combine an interest in the analysis of human activity as it occurs in face-to-face encounters with an interest in the institutional elements of society, such as economic and political organization, or religious ideas.*

3. *Realism is interested in aspects of society which may not always be apparent to an observer or even a trained researcher.*

4. *Realism searches for explanations in terms of underlying causes.*

(Clarke and Layder, 1994, pp. 7–8)

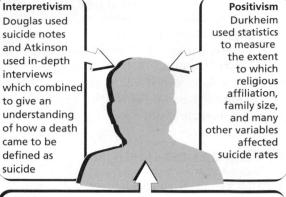

Understanding suicide

Interpretivism
Douglas used suicide notes and Atkinson used in-depth interviews which combined to give an understanding of how a death came to be defined as suicide

Positivism
Durkheim used statistics to measure the extent to which religious affiliation, family size, and many other variables affected suicide rates

Realism
From his findings Durkheim conceived that an excess or lack of social integration or moral regulation in society would result in higher suicide rates

Figure 16.4 Theorizing suicide
Source: Clarke and Layder (1994, p. 8)

Activity

a Write out Clarke and Layder's summary of realism *in your own words*.

b Suggest criticisms of this view that might be made by a positivist sociologist.

c Suggest criticisms of this view that might be made by a phenomenological sociologist.

C3.2, C3.3

As an example of something which exists and is important, but which is not directly observable, Clarke and Layder cite racism. They argue that racism and similar doctrines are:

... not easily observed since it is their 'low profile' which serves to maintain and enforce them in the first place. ... In this respect it is important to accept that underlying causes ... may not be readily observable in the way that other aspects of social life are.

(Clarke and Layder, 1994, p. 8)

Discussion point

a If something is not easily observed, how do we know it really exists?

b How might we set out to test the existence of things not easily observed?

 C3.1a

Marx as a realist

With regard to Marx, the picture is also of someone who accepted the need for science to go beyond surface observations in order to understand the real nature of society. In fact Marx saw the existence of such entities as the key reason for the need for a scientific approach, since:

... all science would be superfluous if the outward appearance and the essence of things directly coincided.

(Marx, 1959, p. 817; orig. pub. 1894)

He labelled as 'the philistines' those who believe that things can be understood simply by looking at surface appearances (the empiricists of their day).

> ### Discussion point
>
> Marx here provides a particular view of how science can be distinguished from other forms of thinking, and of its uses. To what extent do you agree with this as a view of what science is?
>
> C3.1a

Scientific realism

While the theories espoused by Durkheim and Marx provide the basis for the emergence of realism, only in recent times has it emerged as a distinct view of how social research should be conducted. Writers who have developed the notion of realism significantly are Bhaskar (1978, 1979, 1986), Keat and Urry (1975) and Sayer (1979, 1984). There are differences between the approaches of these writers, but they have all contributed to the development of what is now known as 'scientific realism'.

Essentially, scientific realism arose out of a dissatisfaction with the positivist view that anything that could not be verified or falsified purely through empirical testing could not count as evidence or knowledge. Such a view is certainly associated with logical positivism and instrumental positivism, though arguably not with classical positivism (see Section 16.4).

The underlying structures of society

Realists claim that in order to examine phenomena in both the natural and the social world, it is necessary to take account of the underlying realities of society (hence 'realism'). Bhaskar argues that it is possible to use the methods of the natural sciences, but not in the way advocated by positivists. The important thing to remember, he says, is that although humans create their world, they do not enter into a vacuum so their actions need to be understood in relation to an already existing underlying structure of society. In order to fully understand things, therefore, sociologists need to concentrate not on static visions of either individuals in society or of structures impinging on individuals, but instead on the social relations that exist and which both constrain and enable action to take place.

Not everything is directly observable (*alienation* and *anomie*, for example), but since realists argue that they exist they need to be incorporated into explanations. This requires the construction of models of society that account for and can explain phenomena that are observable. These explanations should then be subjected to empirical research, and the results will provide further issues for debate and research. The important thing is to test the usefulness of different theories and explanations. Testing these theories allows us to identify how the underlying structures of society work, and thereby design effective research methods.

It is important to recognize that, while classical empiricist research sought simply to identify relationships between observable variables, realists seek to establish links between observable phenomena and the underlying generative mechanisms which are not necessarily directly observable. This requires that researchers engage in theory first in order to establish detailed explanations of these generative mechanisms, which can then be tested. A second implication of this is that all variables need to be considered in a particular context, and cannot be viewed as true for all times.

Realism versus positivism

This leads to two key ways in which such an approach differs from positivism:

- In rejecting the belief that theory arises from empirical data and consists of statements made only about such observable data, realists can be distinguished from both logical positivists and instrumental positivists.

- In rejecting the idea that sociology can discover laws that are applicable for all times, realists reject elements of the Comtean version of positivism (see Section 16.1). Precisely because they view society as a dynamic set of relations, such iron laws do not exist. Things may generate effects, but whether those effects take place or not depends on a whole series of complex relations which also need to be taken into account.

The picture of society offered is therefore much more complex than the original positivist view based on the notion of unchanging causal laws.

In essence, this means that all empirical statements are theory-dependent – that is, they can make sense only in the context of an overall theory. This does *not* mean that empirical research is rejected, as Outhwaite explains:

The realist emphasis on the legitimacy and the importance of theoretical argument should not be understood to imply the depreciation of empirical research. What it does suggest, I think, is that such research cannot achieve useful results in the absence of theoretical reflection on the structuration of empirical data and a rejection of empiricism, understood as an exclusive focus on social phenomena which are empirically observable and measurable.

(Outhwaite, 1987, p. 60)

Empirical research and empiricism

We therefore need to underline the point that empirical research, meaning the collection of data, should not be confused with empiricism. Empiricism is based on the notion that data exist independently of theories and therefore leads to the belief that theories can be empirically tested, and indeed that this is the only way theories can be tested.

The use of the word 'structuration' is not accidental since Bhaskar makes conscious use of Giddens' 'theory of structuration', in showing the need to go beyond positivism and phenomenology and their links to exclusively structural or action sociologies. However, although realists argue that it is necessary to study both structures and social actions, they are also critical of Giddens' approach – as Archer (1995) makes clear in her argument that what is needed is:

... a theoretical approach which is capable of linking structure and agency rather than sinking one into the other. The central argument is that structure and agency can only be linked by examining the interplay between them over time. ... When discussing 'structure' and 'agency', I am talking about a relationship between two aspects of social life which,

however intimately they are intertwined ... are nonetheless analytically distinct.

(Archer, 1995, p. 65)

This debate further underlines the link between theoretical developments and methodological developments.

Realism versus phenomenology

The key claim of realism is that, while rejecting the positivist characteristics of empiricism and attempts to discover the laws of humanity, we should nonetheless seek to establish sociology on a scientific footing. This leads realists into clashes with phenomenologically inspired versions of sociological methodology.

The key difference here is the realist's insistence that there are deeper structures in society than the merely surface phenomena, which is all that phenomenologists claim there ever is. However, realists take from the phenomenological tradition the idea that the active nature of humanity must be taken into account in any conception of social science. They hold that this does not mean that sociologists cannot learn from the natural sciences, and here they draw on reflections on the actuality of the way natural scientists work, as opposed to the textbook model of natural science.

Realism and science

Here it is possible to identify a number of elements, the first being the importance of *theory* in natural sciences. Natural scientists do not confine themselves to that which is observable. Keat and Urry (1975) cite biological and medical sciences, where the idea of viruses existed before they were identified empirically. The idea was used to explain diseases for which bacterial agents could not be found. Later the idea was of course found to be empirically valid. However, the theory came before the empirical validation.

A second important point about natural sciences is that the classical laboratory experiment cannot be applied in many instances. Sayer (1984) points to the important distinction between closed and open systems as subjects of scientific enquiry. A laboratory is set up as a closed system where everything apart from one variable is controlled. Although this is seen as the epitome of natural scientific research, it has limited application. In particular, certain sciences – such as meteorology – have to operate with open systems where such controls are not available. Meteorologists have to work with the weather in the real world, rather than in a laboratory, so their findings are much less precise. It is no accident that the recent emergence of 'chaos theory' in natural sciences came originally from meteorology.

Chaos theory: realism in science?

The impact of chaos theory is instructive. In attempts to arrive at certain scientific laws, small changes were ignored as being insignificant. The neatness of the laboratory is, however, undermined by the real world, where meteorologists found that tiny changes do have an effect and so cannot be ignored. This is best summed up in the famous phrase:

A butterfly stirring the air today in Peking can transform storm systems next month in New York.

(Gleick, 1987, p. 8)

Recognition of this meant that laboratory approximations were simply no longer good enough and would in any case never be able to predict accurately. Since small differences matter, explanations have to be for particular circumstances and have to be put in the context of an overall theory. In this sense, natural sciences (as opposed to the traditional image of them) are similar to what social scientists do, in that both in reality are often faced with open systems where the laboratory experiment is inapplicable or useless.

Chaos theory has major implications for the natural sciences, since it posits that small changes cannot be ignored. However, it nonetheless argues that there is an underlying order to all this. Chaos theory is not, therefore, similar to post-modernism (see Section 16.7) but is in fact its opposite. The ideas of chaos theory may be applicable to sociology in that societies can be viewed as chaotic systems.

🗨 Discussion point

a To what extent do you agree that societies might be chaotic systems?

b What implications does this have for sociology as a science of society?

C3.1a

The importance of structures

A second point of similarity between the natural and the social sciences is that both suggest that things are affected by underlying structures. So realists suggest that the social sciences can be like the natural sciences as long as we have a realistic understanding of the way natural scientists operate. In this respect, the work of both Popper and Kuhn in explaining exactly how natural scientists operate is relevant.

Popper was in effect a scientific realist. He said that the Vienna Circle was wrong to reject as 'nonsense' everything except that which could be verified:

A metaphysical position, though not testable, might be rationally critisable or arguable. I had confessed to being a realist, but I had thought that this was no more than a confession of faith.

(Popper, 1976, p. 150; quoted in Outhwaite, 1987, p. 29)

It is also the case that Kuhn's work on scientific revolutions was instrumental in getting recognition of the reality of exactly what natural scientists did. Although he and Popper disagreed on some points, Kuhn himself pointed to the fact that he was largely in agreement with Popper:

On almost all the occasions when we turn explicitly to the same problems, Sir Karl's view of science and my own are very nearly identical.

(Kuhn, 1974; quoted in Derry, 1996, p. 18)

In conclusion it can be re-stated that a realist's account of natural sciences is very different from the model presented by positivists. Exactly what sociology has to do to be scientific is thus very different.

Case Study – A realist investigation of CCTV

The failure of quasi-experimental methods

An example of realism is the work of Pawson and Tilly (1996) on closed-circuit television (CCTV) and crime detection. They argue that quasi-experiments, aimed at measuring the effects of such initiatives as community policing, fail precisely because they try to keep everything constant except one variable and then measure the difference between an area where community policing has been applied and one where it has not:

Our point is that programmes are the products of skilled action by human agents, not reducible to the 'facticity' of a given event. It is not programmes that 'work' as such, but the practitioners' attempt to change the reasoning processes of their subjects. It is not contact patrols that 'work' as such, but something about the character of the contact. Quasi-experimentation gazes past these vital issues, since the experimental/control comparison, which is at the heart of the logic, demands that we see the programme as a kind of binary dosage which is simply 'present' or 'absent'.

(Pawson and Tilly, 1996, p. 38)

Studying crime detection scientifically

However, they say that this does not mean that we cannot come to scientific conclusions. They wish therefore to arrive at a scientifically valid study of crime detection, but one which avoids the problems of the experimental method – namely that it ignores the whole network of events and sequences, including human action, which needs to be considered if an adequate explanation is to be provided.

This requires a look at the overall context in which CCTV might be employed since it is never employed in a social vacuum (precisely why experimental methods fall down):

Just as there is nothing about police patrols which intrinsically reduces fear of crime, so too there is nothing about CCTV in car parks which intrinsically inhibits car crime. It certainly does not create a physical barrier making cars impenetrable. The scientific realist begins by pondering the rather different mechanisms through which CCTV may, nevertheless, lead to a reduction of car crimes and the contexts needed, if these potentials are to be realised.

(Pawson and Tilly, 1996, p. 45)

The mechanisms by which CCTV works

They suggest nine mechanisms by which CCTV might work. These include the idea that CCTV may deter potential offenders; it may reduce crime by making the apprehension of actual offenders more likely; or it may, by the use of notices, jog drivers' memories about the potential for car crime and lead them to be more careful in securing vehicles. They also say that the use of CCTV needs to be considered in specific contexts, and they identify five in which CCTV might be used. These include whether the car park is long-stay or short-stay; whether the CCTV

in one place merely leads to increased car crime elsewhere; and the extent to which it is deployed in conjunction with other security measures.

They argue that a full study of the effect of CCTV needs to take into account these variations in both the context of its applications and the actual mechanism of its usage. Such an approach widens enquiry out from a simple consideration of the use of CCTV to a whole series of networks of connections with wider features of society – thus illustrating the classical realist themes that:

- things need to be considered as parts of networks of connections

- empirical research needs to be informed by the theoretical reasoning that allows one to come up with a number of potential contexts and mechanisms.

Although these researchers found that CCTV does tend to reduce car crime, they conclude that it does not do so by catching offenders. They go on to point to further lessons learned:

Most else remains unclear. It does so, so to speak, because the scientific realism entered too late. That which would need to be measured could not be reconstructed after the event with the data available. Consider, for example, the possibility that the 'appeal to the cautious' mechanism may play a part in certain contexts. In relation to this, a survey of cars parked before and after installation of CCTV, together with signs indicating its operation, could ascertain changes in the numbers left locked and in the extent to which attractive goods were left on display. ... It is by no means transparent at first sight that looking inside parked cars would comprise part of the evaluation process. This needs early thought and pre-planning.

(Pawson and Tilly, 1996, p. 49)

The limits of empiricism

It is the need to consider, identify and theorize about all the possible contexts and mechanisms in which CCTV might contribute to a reduction in car crime that marks this out as a study conducted using a scientific realist approach. As the researchers admit, this entered late into their study, which meant the data were not necessarily collected to enable a full realist evaluation to take place. Here is an illustration of the pitfalls of a purely empiricist strategy of merely going out and collecting the facts: it is first necessary to theorize about exactly what data are needed, some of which may not be obvious.

16.7 Post-modernism and research design

Post-modernists see the concepts of reason and of the free individual as the key legacies of modernist thinking (see also Section 16.1). This led to the notion that rational thinking individuals can gain insights into the real nature of the world, an idea that clearly lies behind all theories of methodology. It is this which post-modernists reject.

Instead they argue that the notion of gaining control over the natural world, and the attempt to arrive at a total theory of society, leads to authoritarian ends. This is because of their belief that all forms of knowledge are merely forms of power (Foucault, 1980), which seek to arrive at a uniform truth only by denying the differences that are an important aspect of humanity. The search for truth is therefore something that can never be finally solved, for two reasons:

- there is no ultimate truth, and

- what are presented as truths are merely the ideas that are the most powerful at any one time, but not necessarily for ever.

Science is therefore the form of knowledge which is presently winning the power-struggle, but that is all it is.

Clearly in contrast to Comte's notion of the evolution of human knowledge, which saw science (positivism) as a superior form of thinking which would replace other modes, post-modernists argue that science is merely one form of thinking among others. There is a clear implication that it is not necessarily superior, merely popular at the moment and for that reason powerful.

Post-structuralism

The theory of language

The key element in post-structuralism is a critique and modification of Saussures' structuralist theory of language. In essence, Saussure argued that the link between an object and the symbol (word/image) that represented it was arbitrary. Although arbitrary, there was still a link. The importance of this is that all attempts to explain the truth about the world (which underlies all methodological approaches) are conducted in language, so the question of the link between objects (either natural or social) in the world and the symbols used to describe them is fundamental to all methodological issues.

Post-structuralism and language

Post-structuralists argued that not only was the link between objects and the symbols that represent them arbitary, but that there are more symbols than objects in the real world. In simple terms there is always more than one word to describe something. If this can cause confusion it means that there can never be one totally absolute true way of describing something. While this is difficult enough if we are talking about just one word, Foucault argued that whole languages reflect specific ways of thinking and talking about objects in the world, and that there are therefore many ways of thinking about things which operate like languages – that is to say they may present a view of the same thing very differently.

Discourses

One potential example of this might be that it is possible to identify religious explanations of the origin of the world, or the meaning of life, and scientific explanations. While both focus on the same questions, the answers they give are not only different but are framed in entirely different sets of concepts, ideas and thoughts. What this means effectively is that it is not possible to use one approach to criticize another. Foucault calls these sets of knowledge discourses, leading to the term 'discourse theory' being used to describe post-structuralist approaches. Since each discourse has its own set of concepts, all we can effectively say is that they are different.

The key implication of this is to deny it is possible ever to arrive at an absolute truth. There are essentially two key tests that are applied to any theory, and these are:

1 Is it internally coherant?

2 Is it consistent with the external reality of the world?

In essence, since post-structuralism implies that it is not possible to gain clear unequivocal knowledge about the external reality of the world, either we use only criterion 1, or we say that in relation to criterion 2 all theories may possibly be an explanation of the real world, but it is impossible to decide finally in absolute terms. Instead everything is relative. As Jones explains:

A relativist believes there is no such thing as 'objective' truth; there are only competing ways of looking at things and competing ways of knowing about things.

(Jones, 1997, p. 16)

Foucault and discourse theory

For Foucault, the key question is trying to work out why particular discourses came to prominence at particular times. This leads to the conclusion that conflict over methodologies and theories is not a question of the truth conquering over evil, but of power struggles where one particular approach becomes popular at a particular time. Again this argument is well summarized by Jones:

Believing in the notion that the world is as it is because God made it that way, or that witchcraft causes misfortune, or that the conjunction of the planets can cure warts or whatever, is not believing in falsehoods except from the point of view of another definition (in this case scientific) of truth. So just because we live in a world where scientific discourse prevails does not mean it is therefore superior to other claims for truth. For relativists, it is the other way round: scientific knowledge is not powerful because it is true: it is true because it is powerful; thus the question is not 'What is true?' but 'How did this version of what is true come to dominate in these social and historical circumstances?'

(Jones, 1997, p. 16)

One key implication of this is that all views are continually in a struggle to achieve dominance. These competing, contradictory and irreconcilable discourses all exist as part of our struggle for subjective identity. In simple terms, what we think is true we will believe to be true, but the number of possible truths offered to us gets more and more as time goes on and therefore thinking about the world and indeed about our own identity becomes ever more complex.

Applications of discourse theory

In contrast to earlier interactionist and phenomenologically inspired approaches to subjectivity, what is different in discource analysis is the key importance of the concept of *power* and the idea that different views on living and different claims to the truth are in constant conflict and struggle with each other for dominance. Those that do achieve dominance for a time are said to enjoy 'hegemony', so much post-structuralist analysis

is concerned to uncover the elements of the prevailing hegemonic discourses.

Feminist post-structuralism

One key example of this is the way many feminist-inspired writers, and feminist post-structuralists, have seen masculine codes as a hegemonic form which suppresses the alternative female voice. For example, Hey writes:

Gramsci's notion of hegemony remains central to an understanding of how the cultural is implicated in the maintenance or disruption of forms of power. It underpins the radical theorization of youth collective forms as counter-hegemonic – it has been argued that youth subcultures were 'symbolic forms of resistance ... spectacular symptoms of a wider and more generally submerged dissent (Hebdige, 1979: 80). There is nothing inherently masculine in the definition of culture which underpinned subcultural ethnographies, 'that level at which social groups developed distinct patterns of life and give expressive form to their social and material life-experience' (Hall and Jefferson, 1980: 10). The definition of 'group' and 'expressive forms' however was operationalized through masculine cultural codes which obscured the fact that, as McRobbie (1980: 45) says 'it's different for girls. Those public leisure cultures of the streets and the "lads" were not only less available to girls, girls were also significantly less interested in occupying them.'

(Hey, 1997, p. 16)

Here we have a comment not only about male and female experiences of life and the ways in which they differ, but also about the methodologies adopted by sociologists and how the particular approaches they take informed by particular hegemonic discourses leads to only a one-sided presentation of reality. This makes invisible other alternative and different views and experiences of reality. One of the key ways in which methodology has developed in relation to this is the growth in studies based on ethnographic analysis (as Hey's research quoted above was).

Ethnographic analysis

The key emphasis on subjectivity has led to the growth of ethnographically based studies (of particular ways of living). It carries the implication that there are multiple ways of living and that we must understand these in terms of how people themselves understand the world.

Hence the need to uncover the multiplicity of lifestyles and, using ethnographic analysis, reveal the complexity and multi-faceted nature of reality or realities. The rejection of the truth/falsehood distinction is often made by reference to post-structuralist sociologists referring positively to the power of novels (i.e. fiction). This comparison of fact and fiction is based on rejecting the idea that they are fundamentally different, and instead judging ideas on the basis of the quality and style of the writing; in which case it is probably valid to argue that novelists produce work with more style than at least some sociological writings.

Post-modernism

If the idea that there is a universal, true-for-all-times-and-places truth is rejected as a result of the development of the post-structuralist theory of language, then we are left with a multiplicity of irredeemable discourses. However, the centrality of power in the post-structuralist analysis does not lead it to reject the idea of the truth totally – merely to say that what is the truth, or deemed to be the truth at any one time, because it is powerful, may not necessarily be the truth in another time and place.

Post-modernist analysis goes one step further and denies all possibility of their ever being a truth. The key reason for this is the rejection of any possibility of considering a link between symbols and the objects in the real world they represent. Since 'objectivity' is based on the idea that symbols (ideas, words, languages) must represent *something* in the real world against which to judge their accuracy, once this connection is broken any possibility of objective knowledge – and therefore of sociology being a science – disappears.

The media-saturated world

A notable contribution to post-modernist thinking comes from Baudrillard (see also Section 6.5). He argues that we now live in a media-saturated world where we are bombarded with so many images and where images are created from images in an almost never-ending series of copies of copies that any connection to objects outside this media world are lost or are impossible to trace.

For Baudrillard, therefore, the media images do not represent reality, they *are* reality. Thus the perennial debate in the sociology of the media about whether there is bias becomes meaningless in post-modernist terms, since the answers to this question depend upon comparing the content of the media against the real world to see the extent to which media images and symbols accurately represent this world.

Popularity as truth, sociology as common sense

If there is no reality outside of the media, then all we can say is that there are different views and we have no means of telling which is true; indeed, none can be seen to be true or false, merely different. This means that the truth is established through popularity – the ideas that are popular are seen as true. This raises the important question of the extent to which sociology provides a superior form of knowledge to common sense. Since common sense means a set of ideas that are popular or popularly held, then clearly here there is no real distinction between sociological knowledge and common sense. All ideas are valid if people believe in them, and no ideas can claim to be more truthful than any other – each is relative. Sweetman (1995) summarizes the implications of this for sociological methodology:

Relativism appears to represent a direct challenge to the project of modernity, with its reliance on objective reason, scientific neutrality and absolutist conceptions of unfolding progress. Against this latter view, postmodernity posits multiplicity, plurality, a mix of competing world-views, and a relative rather than absolute notion of 'truth' and 'reason'.

(Sweetman, 1995, p. 10)

Culture rather than political economy

The whole post-structuralist and post-modernist tradition does have some methodological ideas that flow out of its origins in post-1968 Maoist and libertarian Marxist French thought.

The rejection of technological methods of solving social problems led to a focus on grass-roots struggle. With the defeat of 1968 and other left-wing upsurges, there then arose the belief that the state had managed to gain greater control. The desire to escape the control of the state, along with the emphasis on culture (from Mao's 'cultural revolution'), led away from an emphasis on political economy and instead into a study of cultural lifestyles.

Interest was focused on groups at the margins of society. The key reason for this was the belief that the hegemony of dominant ideas might be weaker there, offering the best chance to achieve social change. Clearly, such a view held an appeal to those groups who had traditionally faced oppression, and post-modernist ideas flourished among the feminist and women's movements, and among movements based on sexual orientation and ethnic identity.

Rejection of scientific rationalism

Post-moderism thus provides a basis for rejecting the dominance of scientific rationalism as seen most clearly in positivist sociology. This has led to the argument that there are alternative ways of thinking that are equally valid, notably the feminist argument that malestream versions of scientific rationality ignore the importance of emotions in understanding human behaviour, and the whole range of spiritual and mystic beliefs that go under the heading of 'New Age'.

Post-modernism and Weberian sociology

The themes that emerge out of post-structuralist analysis of language have enabled the bringing together of trends that have been in evidence for a long time in French and German sociology, namely the influence of relativism and phenomenological ideas. In simple terms, this has meant an opposition to positivism's one-sided and simplistic presentation and celebration of science.

Weber's notion of 'disenchantment' is a central element here. Weber used this term to denote the way in which, although the growth of rationality made things more efficient, it also made things more 'depersonalized'. The clear importance and centrality of subjective meanings in Weberian-influenced sociology has meant that it has been relatively easy for proponents to adopt the key emphasis on culture and identity that flows from post-modernist analysis.

Criticisms of post-modernist approaches

Critics argue that post-modernist approaches lead straight to a very strong form of relativism – which ultimately leads to the proposition 'anything goes'. In terms of social theory it is criticized as being a cowardly response to contemporary society by giving up on any prospects of human emancipation, instead becoming a celebration of the expression of difference through consumption – again seen as an excuse for the excesses offered to some in the era of late capitalism (Callinicos, 1989).

Post-post-modernism

One of the key problems with post-modernist analysis is its total relativism – ideas have no universal validity for all times and places. Although this undermines authoritarian impulses, it clearly does not offer a very satisfactory basis for sociology – which is motivated to have an impact on the world, either in the form of social policy analysis or the more politically oriented forms of Marxism and feminism.

Holland (1995) has therefore talked about the growth of a form of post-post-modernism. This attempts to look both at the generation of meaning through experience and at the experience of difference (in this case mainly gender difference), and how these experiences are located in actual material spaces – people or other material aspects of society. In essence, this seems to be a way to try to ground post-modernist analysis and creates a new kind of structure–agency debate.

16.8 Sociology and science: the ongoing debate

The aim of Sections 16.4 to 16.7 has been to provide a detailed consideration of the question of whether sociology can, and whether it should, seek to be scientific. The answer ultimately rests on various notions of what being 'scientific' implies, and these have altered over time – from the view of natural sciences held by classical positivism, through to the criticisms of this position in the work of Kuhn.

Is objective knowledge possible?

Here the criticisms made by phenomenology and hermeneutics are relevant, and the later argument of the post-modernists (see Section 16.7) that all forms of knowledge are inevitably subjective and reflect power relations in society. Thus it is argued that it is not possible to distinguish between objectivity and subjectivity in a way that allows us to distinguish truth from opinion.

Some (including feminist sociologists) have argued that the use of science as a model for sociological methodology is problematic because science rests on a particular form of knowledge, which denies the importance of personal experience and emotions. In this view, if sociology tries to mimic science it risks becoming subject to the oppressive structures science itself is part of. It risks becoming part of the problem rather than part of the solution.

This denial of the possibility of objectivity is rejected by realists. The latter nevertheless argue that we cannot rely on purely empirical testing, since all empirical statements are theory-laden and not everything that is relevant is directly observable. Thus, while sociologists can still attain an objective – and therefore scientific – methodology, what is meant by science and scientific testing is very different from the notions developed by positivism.

Activity

Use the material in Sections 16.4 to 16.7 (and Lawson's article 'In the shadow of science' (1986) if you can locate it in your library) to answer the following questions.

a On what basis did positivists argue that sociology could be a science?

b What are the key strengths and weaknesses of this approach?

c What are the key points of phenomenological criticisms of positivism?

d What are the implications of these criticisms for the methods sociologists should use?

e What are the criticisms of the phenomenological position made by realist sociologists?

f What are the key strengths and weaknesses of post-modernist approaches to sociological methodology?

g Which of these four positions do you think provides the best basis for a sociological methodology? Should sociology seek to be scientific?

C3.1a, C3.2, C3.3

Theory and methods: making the link

Positivism and phenomenology

It is important to realize that the questions of:

• how we know things, and

• how statements are tested

are the basic starting point for the development of sociological methodology. These issues were at the heart of debates about sociological theory and methodology, and were crystallized in the contrast which was drawn between positivist and phenomenological sociologists in relation to these issues. As Lawson has written:

Positivists believe that only by adopting a position of total objectivity towards the subject matter or phenomena can unbiased knowledge or theories be produced. ... adopting a positivist perspective towards the search for knowledge implies a certain type of methodology. But the social sciences will clearly have difficulty in putting such ideas into practice, if only because, unlike rocks, plants and animals of the natural sciences, the subject matter of the social sciences – human beings – think. This awareness, or consciousness, about what is happening to them makes the subject matter of the sociologist extremely difficult to control. ... These obvious difficulties have led some sociologists to question whether it is possible to adopt positivistic procedures or methods, and others to suggest that the subject matter of sociology is so different from the natural sciences that is it not desirable to follow them at all. ...

However, many natural scientists have themselves dismissed the idea that research into chemistry, physics, biology and the rest is carried out in the way that the positivists suggest. ...

If neither the social, nor the natural, sciences measure up to positivistic standards in the search for 'truth', are they both equally non-scientific? ...

Science, therefore, casts a shadow over sociological research, and it is in the context of the positivistic model that the relationship between theories and methods in sociology must be understood.

(Lawson, 1986, pp. 37 and 38)

The debate about whether sociology can or should be a science goes on today.

Beyond positivism versus phenomenology

Until the 1980s, most sociology textbooks focused on the notion of sociological theory and method based on a set of dichotomies:

• In relation to theory, this rested on the distinction between structural approaches (notably functionalism and Marxism) and social-action based approaches (notably symbolic interactionism and phenomenology/ethnomethodology).

• In relation to methodology, there was the distinction between positivism and phenomenology. It was suggested that there was a broad

– although not perfect – link between them in that structuralist-minded sociologists tended to adopt a positivist approach and social-action based sociologists tended to adopt a phenomenological approach.

Although this broad dichotomy had some degree of truth to it, it was something of a simplification because it suggested that structurally minded sociologists tended to see the world as a mechanical clockwork one, as modelled by the positivists. For Marxism, in particular, this did not fit – since otherwise why would Marx, Lenin and others in the Marxist tradition spend their time engaging in action if everything was predetermined?

A model of the four methodological approaches

It is possible to present a more complex view of methodological theories incorporating all four of the main approaches identified above, and to consider how they relate to the main sociological theories. If we first of all consider a simple box summarizing sociological theory it would look something like Figure 16.5.

Although we can fill out four boxes in relation to theory, when it comes to methodology we are usually presented with only two approaches, namely positivism and phenomenology (sometimes called anti-positivism). The distinct views of realists and post-modernists do not appear, and it is therefore difficult to see how they are similar to, or different from, the earlier approaches of positivism and phenomenology.

However, it is possible to construct a box for methodological approaches as well, and thus be able to have a much clearer ability to see the link between theories and methodological theories. Richard Kilminster (1992) outlines the work of Johnson *et al.* (1984) who argued that there are

in fact four key approaches in methodological terms: empiricism, subjectivism, rationalism and substantialism. Positivism in sociology is an example of rationalism, and phenomenology is an example of empiricism. Marxist realism is an example of substantialism, and post-structuralism and post-modernism are examples of subjectivism.

What distinguishes these four positions is:

- whether they believe that reality is defined solely internal to the individual (subjectivism), or whether there is a real world which exists outside the individual (objectivism)
- whether they believe that the most important source of knowledge is ideas and people's thoughts (idealism), or people's lives and real experiences (materialism).

Using these categories we can produce a summary of sociological methodology that is similar to the one produced above for sociological theory. This is only really an approximation, but at least it includes the new methodological approaches of realism and post-modernism (see Figure 16.6). We can therefore provide links between theories and methodologies as shown in Table 16.1.

Basis of knowledge:	**Objective** (reality exists external to the individual)	**Subjective** (reality limited to and defined by the individual)
Idealism (priority given to ideas)	POSITIVISM	POST-MODERNISM
Materialism (priority given to existence and experience)	REALISM	PHENOMENOLOGY

Figure 16.6 A diagramatic representation of sociological methodology

Table 16.1 Links between theories and methodologies

Methodology	Sociological theory	Methodological approach in sociology
Rationalism	Functionalism	Positivism
Substantialism	Marxism	Realism
Subjectivism	Symbolic interactionism	Post-modernism
Empiricism	Phenomenology	Phenomenology

Believe society is characterized by:	**Social structures**	**Social actions**
Consensus	FUNCTIONALISM	SYMBOLIC INTERACTIONISM
Conflict	MARXISM	PHENOMENOLOGY

Figure 16.5 A diagramatic representation of debates in sociological theory

Another way to try to comprehend this is to consider the notion of 'enquiry' at its simplest. This involves a researcher (the subject) trying to gain knowledge of something (the object) – see Table 16.2.

Table 16.2 Objectivity and subjectivity of methodologies

Methodology	Nature of subject's understanding	Content of description of object
Positivism	Objective	Objective
Phenomenology	Objective	Subjective
Realism	Subjective	Objective
Post-modernism	Subjective	Subjective

Clearly, in recent years the belief that it is possible to arrive at an objective knowledge of human behaviour has fallen from favour to be replaced by the idea that theories and methods in sociology are inevitably subjective, that is to say value-laden. There is, however, a debate about whether an objective world exists independently of the perception of the observer, as realists believe, or whether this is not the case, as subjectivists such as post-modernists believe.

This debate has implications for the issues considered in the following section, namely whether sociology can arrive at objective knowledge, and whether it is possible or desirable for the values of the sociological researchers to be excluded from their research.

16.9 Values in sociological research

A key issue is the extent to which sociology and sociological research can be carried on independently of the values (that is to say the ideas, attitudes, political and moral views) of either the subjects being studied or the researcher personally.

This issue has become more important with the rise of methodologies based on subjectivism (notably feminist standpoint methodology and post-modernism) and methodologies based on the rejection of the idea of the objective value-free researcher (namely realism and post-modernism). However, the debate can be traced back a long way to differences between those who thought the subject matter of sociology was *objective* or *subjective*. This debate was between positivists and phenomenologists and was long-standing in German sociology in particular. The views of the Frankfurt School attempted to avoid the problems they saw implicit in both versions of methodology.

The Frankfurt School and 'critical theory'

In relation to methodology, the Frankfurt School (a group of German Marxists) criticized Weber's argument that sociology could be both value-relative and value-free, which was later developed into the doctrine of logical positivism. The context of this criticism was a debate between the logical positivists and the 'critical theorists' of the Frankfurt School (see Section 13.2). 'Critical theorists' reject positivism for two main reasons.

The first rejection of positivism: opinions are not necessarily facts

Critical theorists reject the idea (most prominent in logical and instrumental positivism) that empirical data are the key element of science. Bearing in mind that the Frankfurt School had been located in America between 1934 and 1950, its leading lights had had the opportunity to witness American social science at first hand, and by and large they did not like what they saw. What was presented as social science was, in essence, large amounts of opinion polls. Social surveys, no doubt technically correct in relation to sampling and the wording of questions, simply elicited people's opinions on a wide range of subjects. Pollack rejected the idea that these findings could be seen as scientific:

The concept of opinion held by current opinion ... operates with a subjective concept of truth, without even a glance at the problem of the objective. Objectivity, on which it prides itself so much, is nothing but a generality abstracted from subjectivities of this kind – the common denominator of opinions, as it were, unrelated to their objective validity.

(Pollack, 1955, p. 85; quoted in Bryant, 1985, p. 122)

To clarify what Pollack meant, consider a hypothetical finding of a social survey. If it asked people whether the earth was flat and found that 70 per cent did believe that the earth was flat (admittedly an unlikely result, but certainly not impossible), what could one conclude? Does this present objective proof that the earth is flat, or merely objective demonstration that the subjective beliefs of most people are wrong?

💬 Discussion point

If 70 per cent of people in a survey thought the earth was *not* flat, would that make the findings more scientific, or not? What can this tell us about notions of objectivity and science?

C3.1a

In case you are thinking that this example is too far-fetched, let us look at a real example:

The age of the American hero is dead and most Americans can no longer tell right from wrong, according to a new study. Based on 1800 question interviews with 2000 Americans held simultaneously at 50 locations, with privacy and anonymity guaranteed, 'The Day America Told the Truth' found that 91 per cent of Americans lie regularly both at work and at home.

(*Guardian*, 2 May 1991)

✏️ Activity

a What exactly did the *Guardian* survey reveal, if anything? (Think carefully before you answer.)

b How would Pollack respond to such research? Would he consider it objective?

c What do you think about this piece of research?

C3.2, C3.3

The second rejection of positivism: there is no value-free methodology

Critical theorists also reject the fact/value distinction leading to the notion that sociology should be value-free. The ideas they are attacking can best be found in American social research and the work of Weber.

The Frankfurt School argued that it is impossible to be value-neutral, since this implies that social scientists cannot really have any say in the way society develops. Weber argued that sociology could not arbitrate over questions of ethical, moral and political choices, and he

makes a clear distinction between 'science' and 'politics'. However, the Frankfurt School argued that this meant that sociology would, for example, have nothing to say about the advent of Hitler to power – since that was a political rather than a scientific choice. Even worse, it can be argued as a development of this position (and certainly was in the USA) that sociologists can advise governments and societies on the means to a predetermined end, but not about which end to adopt.

Against an uncritical sociology

In other words, Weber's distinction actually does not work in practice. Certainly the Frankfurt School saw this idea of a value-free sociology as a way of creating an uncritical science, because it did not effectively ask questions of the uses to which its knowledge was put.

Furthermore, they argued that this was not simply a question of some errors by particular sociologists, but that such positions necessarily arose from the nature of positivism itself. What they meant by this is that the concentration on 'objective knowledge' in positivism was linked to a desire to control nature. Herbert Marcuse in *Reason and Revolution* (1955) argues that positivism was a reaction to Hegelianism, seen as negative in the context of conservatives frightened by the French Revolution. Positivism thus set about restoring order:

The laws positivist science discovered, and that distinguish it from empiricism, were positive in the sense that they affirmed the prevailing order as a basis for denying the need to construct a new one. ... Observation instead of speculation means, in Comte's sociology, an emphasis on order in place of any rupture in the order; it means the authority of natural laws in place of free action, unification in place of disorder. The idea of order, so basic to Comte's positivism, has a totalitarian content in its social as well as its methodological meaning.

(Marcuse, 1955; orig. pub. 1941, p. 348)

Interests and truths

Thus it is people's interests that will necessarily dictate what is to count as objective knowledge. In a society riven with conflict, ideas will inevitably be distorted. As Harvey puts it:

At the heart of critical social research is the idea that knowledge is structured by existing sets of social relations. The aim of a critical methodology is to provide knowledge which engages the prevailing social structures. These social structures are seen by critical social researchers, in one way or another, as oppressive structures.

(Harvey, 1990, p. 2)

The focus on universal laws in positivism denied this possibility and denied people the possibility of making choices, an aim the critical theorists saw as central to their whole approach. This issue did, however, also bring them into conflict with Weber's value-relative stance on methodology.

Can choices be objective?

Critical theorists say that it is not possible, as Weber arguably tried to do, to stand outside such conflicts and retain an objective stance. Weber's position was that, while science could contribute to policy by informing debate, it could not actually make choices for people. The problem with this is that it says nothing about how such choices are to be made, and his support for the need for strong leaders has been seen as leaving little defence against force as the ultimate decision-maker. This issue was of importance in Germany, owing to the rise of Hitler. Weber's position appeared to offer no defence against this sort of decision-making.

Habermas has focused on how decisions can be reached. He argues that what is needed is a reformulation of rationality to allow for the development of communicative action – by which he means a situation wherein we can all freely talk and arrive at agreement, thus reaching a consensus of truth (see Section 16.1).

Feminist criticisms of positivism and science

Comte argued that science would eventually make all other forms of knowledge redundant. In the positive age, science would become the only *acceptable* form of knowledge. He saw science as based on reasoning and observation, the use of humankind's rational faculties to understand the world.

However, he also believed that men were superior to women in terms of their intellectual capacity while women were superior to men in terms of affectivity and emotionality. Put simply,

this suggests that men are rational and women are emotional. A similar view of women can be seen in Durkheim's writings. It implies two things:

- Women can never be as good as men at understanding science.
- Since science was to be the exclusive basis of knowledge, such knowledge would be exclusively defined by men.

The feminist rejection of positivism

Not surprisingly, Comte's position is one that feminists and other contemporary sociologists reject. However, the feminist rejection is complicated by the division among feminists over their views on the nature of women (discussed in detail in Chapter 17). Put simply:

- Some feminists see women and men as *essentially similar*, and they explain inequalities between them on the basis of social constructions which can be changed to achieve equality.
- Other feminists say that women and men are *essentially different* and that women are more in touch with their emotions (see Section 4.1).

Men and male science as inferior

While the second of those two positions mirrors Comte in arguing that there is an essential difference between men and women, some feminists argue that the fact that women can be both rational and emotional while men cannot suggests that it is men who are inferior.

Feminist true knowledge

Feminists go on to suggest that a true knowledge of society needs to recognize both the rational and the emotional aspects of behaviour, and so science (as conceived by positivists) is not and cannot provide a complete picture of society. Furthermore, the general acceptance of science as the highest form of knowledge perpetuates the oppression of women since it is a form of knowledge based on a way of thinking in which men are perceived to be the strongest.

Scientific thinking therefore leads to domination by men both as researchers and as subjects of research, since science concentrates on the study of measurable phenomena and ignores 'emotionality and values'. Science is therefore not only an inadequate model for sociology, it is also a model that furthers the oppression of women.

In this sense, feminist criticisms mirror the critique of positivism put forward by the Frankfurt School, though they apply the notion of science as oppressive to women in particular.

Feminist standpoint methodology

This approach can be seen in the work of Stanley and Wise (1990, 1993), who draw on elements of phenomenology and ethnomethodology to suggest that science is a social construction, just like everything else. The search for a 'feminist science' is therefore rejected, and instead it is argued that feminists should adopt a reflexive attitude to research – uncovering the variety of forms of knowledge that women have. This can be done only by women because only they share the experience of oppression:

Thus there is no way of moving outside of experience to validate theories 'objectively' – nothing exists other than social life, our place within it and our understanding of all this.

(Stanley and Wise, 1993, p. 193)

Criticisms of feminist methodology

Pawson (1992) is critical of claims that there is a need for a specific 'feminist methodology'. He argues that even though one can find views about women in Durkheim and others which are clearly wrong, this does not in itself mean that all Durkheim's insights can be set aside (although it does point to the fact that there did exist for a long time a blind-spot about gender in sociological research). Further, the claim to base research solely on experience is invalid since it leads to a form of relativity where all experiences are true, but this leaves no way to judge between which of the different and contrasting accounts of experience are valid.

Sociology, expertise and common sense experience

At the heart of methodological debates is the argument over whether we need specialized trained sociologists (or others) in order to understand and interpret reality for us, or whether this knowledge is accessible to all and

therefore the work of sociologists and others is merely to gather together the views of 'ordinary' people.

The idea of the expert

It is quite clear that one version of the 'expert' argument can be traced back to Plato's notion of the 'philosopher kings'. This idea can be seen to be reworked in Comte's notion of the ability of a 'priesthood of sociologists' to be able to predict the future and therefore remove the need for free choice. Arguably a more recent example can be found in the Marxist tradition, and in particular the Leninist notion of the vanguard party who are the most advanced section of the working class.

Such views might be seen as dividing the population into two, one section of which have more knowledge than the other and therefore assumes the right to 'lord it' over the others.

It was in reaction to these assertions that subjectivist notions of sociology arose, with ethnographic attempts to 'tell it as people saw it', and centring on how people thought and felt regardless of whether these views were scientifically proven.

The recent influence of psychoanalysis in various brands of social thinking (see Kirby, 1999c) can be seen as the latest move in a tradition that presents something beyond common comprehension – in this case in the form of the Freudian notion of the unconscious, which needs an expert, the psychoanalyst, to interpret.

Against this it might be said that, since the unconscious is by its nature unknowable, it is merely a newer instance of Comte's metaphysical stage with psychoanalysis as the new religion (See also Section 16.1).

Science as common sense?

On the other hand, if science is simply the sum total of ordinary everyday common sense, why do we need a methodology at all, and on what basis can we claim that scientific sociological understanding is superior to common sense?

A clear implication of much post-modernist thinking is that science is not superior, except that its seems powerful at the moment because it is the predominant discourse. However, as can be seen in various areas of social life, the old scientific certainties are being rejected as either failures or even positively dangerous, and many people are grappling for alternative ways of understanding the world. Examples are the growth of interest in alternative medicine, and 'New Age' thinking, and each of these might also be seen as discourses that are equally internally coherant and as valid as science.

If this point of view is accepted, the introductions to earlier textbooks which pointed out the massive differences between sociological thinking (good) and commonsense thinking (bad) need to be understood simply as a power struggle, in which, not surprisingly, sociologists stand up for sociology. However, it is no more or less valid than commonsense thinking. This total relativism or perspectivism is a key implication of post-modernist methodologies.

One big problem with this line of reasoning rests in a quite simple logical flaw. If post-modernists insist that there are no truths, then this surely also covers their own doctrines – leading to the paradoxical conclusion that post-modernists cannot believe post-modernism to be true, merely a view or one truth among many truths.

This will be a continuing debate, but it is no longer one that can be glibly answered by arguing that sociologists use rigorous methods like questionnaires and sampling and that therefore this is superior to common sense. Methodological debates have moved on and we are now definitely in the post-positivist age.

Discussion point

Is sociology superior to common sense? What implications does your answer have for our view of 'society' and notions of 'expertise'?

C3.1a

16.10 Reporting reflexive research

The nature and content of sociological knowledge changes over time as existing theories are questioned and new explanations come into favour. Since there can never be a theory that is true for all places and all times, sociological knowledge will always be conditional and subject to revision. We should, therefore, consider the way in which knowledge comes to be revised and, while we have considered some of the theoretical debates

about this in relation to the argument of Thomas Kuhn and others, in this section we wish to briefly consider some of the practical steps sociological researchers and students doing their coursework project have to take if their work is to be able to contribute to the ongoing construction, reproduction and reconstruction of sociological knowledge. This involves issues both of a practical nature, relating to the production of a research report, and also the responsibilities that go along with research, both in the sense of responsibilities towards the individuals who have helped you in your research and also to yourself and to society due to the reflexive nature of the sociological research.

Producing a research report

Students who opt to take Module 2538 as part of their OCR A Level in Sociology need to conduct a Personal Study (See also Section 1.1). This will involve the application of research methods in a real world context bearing in mind the points made in Chapter 9. Assuming that you have successfully navigated the state of data collection, you now need to sit down to analyse your data (again in relation to this, you should also consult Section 9.7) and then begin to put your findings together to form the report of your Personal Study. It is essential that in doing this you adhere to the regulations specified in the OCR A Level Sociology specification, summarized here.

The Personal Study for OCR Sociology

The first thing the Board specifies is that your Personal Study should be no more than 2500 words.

The actual terms of the Personal Study require candidates to choose an area of interest to them, to develop a research proposal in relation to a topic in this area and then pilot this topic. Throughout this whole process candidates are required to keep in mind legal matters and ethical principles of research as outlined in the British Sociological Association's 'Statement of Ethical Practice' (BSA, 1991).

The OCR specification provides the following summary of the three main sections of the requirements for the Personal Study Report:

The emphasis of the Personal Study is on the design of the research, on trialing or piloting the design, and on evaluating the trial or pilot. Candidates and their teachers must recognise that credit will be given for the quality or the design of the investigation, and for its evaluation, rather than for the quantity and type of any data collected.

(OCR, 2000, pp. 16–7).

The main body of the Report consists of:

- the rationale
- the research
- the evaluation.

The content and suggested length of each of these sections is as follows:

The rationale

Here candidates are required to provide a statement of the central research issue, question or hypothesis, a statement of the reasons for carrying out the study and a description and justification of the research design and procedures. It is suggested this be between 500 and 750 words.

The research

Here candidates provide a report on the testing or piloting of the actual research design, to include an analysis and interpretation of their findings and the conclusions that can be drawn from the Personal Study. It is suggested this section be between 750 and 1000 words.

The evaluation

Here candidates are required to provide an evaluation of the research method employed, an assessment of the research findings and suggestions for further areas of development of the research.

It is suggested this section be between 750 and 1000 words.

The above outline provides the basic structure for your report. However, it is important to be aware of a number of issues relating to the detail of the reporting to ensure that your report achieves consistency and that your findings are reported in accordance with accepted conventions.

Practical issues in reporting your findings

Conventions of reporting research

In Chapter 9 we included a whole section devoted to the issues surrounding the interpretation and presentation of data, both quantitative and qualitative. This section is to be read in conjunction with a re-reading of Section 9.7, since the points relating to the presentation and reporting of quantitative and qualitative data there are very relevant in the construction of your report.

Although you are not required to type up your report, it is clear nonetheless that word-processing your work and the possible use of spreadsheets and graphics packages to create tables and graphs in your report would enable you to create evidence towards Key Skills qualifications. (More information on this is included in the OCR specifications on pages 42–53.)

Clearly you will be able to, and indeed will have to, write the three key sections of your report at different stages since they in effect ask you to tell us what you are going to do, tell us what you did, and tell us how you think you did.

The rationale will therefore be written prior to any actual research and is an important element in ensuring that your project has focus and is manageable. You should therefore ensure that you regularly discuss this with your teacher and amend your aims and rationale in the light of discussions with him or her. This will mean that your rationale will go through many versions and it will therefore be vital to keep a copy on computer somewhere to avoid having to type the whole thing out every time. As Barzum and Graff (1977) pointed out, in capital letters:

NO ONE, HOWEVER GIFTED, CAN PRODUCE A PASSABLE FIRST DRAFT. WRITING MEANS REWRITING.

(Quoted in Bell, 1993, p. 132)

So, one key convention that you will need to get used to very quickly is that all sections of your research report will be continuously modified in the light of new evidence or thoughts that come to light. This means that you are constantly monitoring your own activities through consideration of the need to amend or modify your report and the research project it is based on. This a key element in what is known as being reflexive. One key implication of this is that your schedule should include plenty of time for revision of your report before it is needed to be submitted for marking.

The time available for this research report is obviously something you will need to discuss with your teacher but we feel that this should also include the question of drawing up a work schedule that explicitly includes reference to time for revision of sections of the report as you reflect on your experiences.

Conventions of the report

How do you construct a report? The key thing is that it includes the three key sections outlined above and that it meets the criteria laid down in the OCR specification. It will therefore include:

1 a separate title page
2 a list of contents on a separate page
3 the rationale
4 the research
5 the evaluation
6 a bibliography
7 an appendix
8 your research diary
9 annexe.

We will now consider some issues to be borne in mind when finally completing your report.

Headings

Above we have provided a list of the sections that are needed. These are, if you like, similar to the chapter titles in this book. However, you will notice that there are other headings in this book which, we hope, make it easier for the reader to navigate through. You should therefore include headings in your work. This also requires you to think about the structure of your report and where material should go.

References

In the body of your report it is inevitable that you will wish to make reference to the published work of others. The most popular way of doing this (and the method we have adopted in this book) is to cite the authors followed by the date of publication of the book or article we are referring to in brackets after their names. You can see what we mean by flicking through this book and looking at the way authors are referred to in chapters. However, a few examples might be:

McNeill (1990)
Dunsmuir and Williams (1991)
Acker (1989)
Hall (1991a)
Hall (1991b)

Notice that in the last example we have an author who has been cited for two pieces of writing, both of which were published in 1991. In this instance we use letters a, b, etc., to differentiate between the articles.

Tables, graphs and figures

It is likely that at least some of these will be included in your report. Tables and graphs are different ways of reporting quantitative data, while figures may be anything else including extracts of text, pictures, cartoons or diary extracts. They should be placed in an appropriate place, given a title and numbered in order. Tables and graphs can use one series and diagrams another series such that you may end up with a list of tables and a list of diagrams. Again, one way to get an idea of how to include these in your report is to consider the examples of tables and diagrams included in this book. Always remember that tables and diagrams need to be directly referred to and commented on in the text. They do not stand on their own.

Quotations

It seems likely that you may want to include a few short quotations from the work of others. This should be consistently done. Again, one way to consider how to do this is to look at the procedures adopted in this book (or others). The first thing to note in relation to this is the absolute necessity of making a clear note of the source of any quotations at the time you locate them. The danger if you don't is that you will have to spend hours flicking through books trying to track down some wonderful quote which you found but did not write the details down for immediately. This can be an intensely frustrating and annoying process (we speak from experience!) so we suggest you try to avoid it.

The rules are generally this: quotations from others should be placed in inverted commas, or set off from the main text in italics in the case of longer quotes, and they must be exact – that is to say you cannot change the wording. The only possible exception to this is where you wish to leave some text out as compared to the original source. This should be indicated by three dots as follows […]. The name of the author plus the date of publication of the book or article and the page number must all be provided in brackets after the end of the quote. We can provide an example. In his book on religion, John Bird (1999) makes the following comment on historical evidence and the secularization debate:

The historical evidence does not, however, clinch the argument one way or the other, for two main reasons. First, the evidence itself is simply not comprehensive enough. … Second, when there is firm evidence for a fall in church attendance, for example, disagreement about secularization only starts up again: those who support the thesis see this evidence as conclusive; those who do not either question the data, or claim that a fall in attendance is only part of the issue, and often go on to point to the importance of the continued significance of religious belief ..., and the growth of religious sects and other new religious movements.

(Bird, 1999, p. 83)

You will see that there are two sets of dots [...] in this quote. The first is because there was detail included that I did not want to include and the second is because John Bird at that point provides a cross-reference to Chapter 3 of his book, which is of no significance to the quote in this context. If you want to check this out see Bird (1999) p. 83. Always check that you are quoting people accurately. I just did and found that I had missed a comma out. Hopefully, no one will write in to tell me of any other mistakes. However, if they do, and their point is correct, I would have a duty to try to correct the mistake at the earliest opportunity and to apologise to John Bird.

Bibliography

You will need to provide a comprehensive bibliography which lists the full details of all books, articles or other documents that you have directly referred to in your report. It should be the case that if you use material or ideas from a book you must make explicit reference to the source of that material. You will therefore end up with quite a few references in your report. You must include all of these in the bibliography.

The first point that is important to remember here is that you must make a note of the full details of all books or articles you refer to. If you do not do this you are in danger of scrabbling about in your school/college library trying to remember exactly what you meant when you wrote 'Smith, article about media'. So make a note of the full details at the time you first consult the book or article.

There are several ways of actually including material in bibliographies and again we would suggest that you look at the bibliography in this and other books to get a general idea. The system being used in this book has the following features for books and articles:

Books are referenced as follows:

• Author surname, initial(s) (date of publication) *title of book*, edition number if not first edition, place of publication: publisher.

Articles are referenced as follows:

• Author surname, initial(s) (date of publication) 'Title of article', *title of journal or magazine*, volume number and edition number [or] month or season.

To illustrate this we include the full bibliography entries of the works included in the References section above. However, one final point: references should be included in your bibliography in alphabetical order by author surname, so we have placed the references in the order they would appear in a bibliography:

Acker, J. (1989) 'The problem with patriarchy', *Sociology*, vol. 23., no. 2.

Dunsmuir, A. and Williams, L. (1991) *How to do Social Research*, London: Collins Educational.

Hall, S. (1991a) 'And not a shot fired', *Marxism Today*, December.

Hall, S. (1991b) 'The local and the global: globalisation and ethnicity', in King, A. D. (ed.), *Culture, Globalisation and the World System: Contemporary Conditions for the Representation of Identity*, Basingstoke: Macmillan.

McNeill, P. (1990) *Research Methods*, 2nd edn, London: Routledge.

Appendix, diary and annexe

The OCR specifications require that these sections are part of your research report. Their usage is as follows. Firstly, the appendix is to be used to include a copy of the research proposal, a single copy of any research materials used, such as questionnaires or letters.

Secondly, you need to keep a research diary which fully documents all your activities and includes your reflections and comments upon how your research is going, and what you have learnt from any experiences you encounter. Material from the diary is likely to be drawn upon in the section when you evaluate your research project.

Finally, the annexe should include all the raw data that your research project generated.

In relation to these and all other sections, you should consult your teacher and the relevant pages of the OCR specifications for further clarification.

Checklist for putting together your report

The following is a selection of points made by Judith Bell in relation to writing up your research report:

1 set deadlines

2 write regularly

3 create a rhythm of work

4 write up a section as soon as it is ready

5 stop at a point from which it is easy to resume writing

6 leave space for revisions

7 check that all essential sections have been covered

8 check length is according to requirements

9 don't forget the title page

10 include headings where possible

11 number tables and figures and provide titles

12 make sure all quotations are acknowledged

13 provide a full list of references in a bibliography

14 use the appendix and annexe for material not needed in the main report. Do not clutter the report with irrelevant items.

15 remember to leave sufficient time for revision and rewriting

16 try to get someone to read the report. Fresh eyes will often see errors you have overlooked.

Source: Adapted from Bell (1993, pp. 133–5)

Transparent reporting

Tables and graphs must be clearly labelled with all axes identified and explanations given of what measures are being used in the table. One example is the term average, which is often used without much thought. We know that there are in fact three different averages, namely the mean, the median and the mode. If you are using average figures anywhere it is important that you are transparent about their usage and explain to potential readers and examiners exactly which type of average you are using. Any other measures that may have more than one meaning need to be clarified so that the exact meaning of any information you present is transparent, that is to say, it is quite clear to the reader with no possible ambiguity in the interpretation of what you are showing. (This does not mean that there will be no ambiguity in the interpretation of the significance or meaning of what your research report shows, merely that it should be clear what you are trying to show.)

A table or diagram often allows the meaning to be grasped more easily than many pages of text, though it is important to be aware of the need to explain in the body of the text exactly what you feel the diagram or table shows. Tables or diagrams should not be just left in the air. If you have spent time on a computer package carefully generating them, then we can certainly agree that they look pretty but they do not explain themselves. Explain what they show and the relevance of this information to the research project overall.

The reflexive researcher

Reflexivity ... involves two things. First, it requires that researchers reflect upon the research process in order to assess the effect of their presence and their research techniques on the nature and extent of the data collected. Crudely put, researchers must consider to what extent respondents were telling them what they wanted to hear; did the researcher(s) inhibit respondents; did the format of the data collection restrict the kind of data being collected, and so on? Second, ethnographic reflexivity requires that researchers critically reflect upon the theoretical structures they have drawn out of their ethnographic analysis. In effect, researchers are expected to reconceptualize their evidence in terms of other possible models – to think laterally. Ethnographers should not just fit details into a preformed schema but try to reform the schema to see if the details have different meanings.

(Harvey, 1990, p. 11)

A key element of your research report is your own evaluation of how the research experience went. In essence, this is what is meant in this context by the term 'reflexive researcher', meaning that you are always considering the fact that research takes place in an interactive setting, that your own actions may affect the process and that your own views and interpretations of data may not be the only possible interpretations and you need to consider others.

Crucially this means that you need to think and rethink every stage of the process bearing in mind your own experiences and your reflections on them (which should be continuously recorded in your research diary) and to be aware of the potential effect of utilizing certain methods of research on the actual process. One clear issue that comes through in relation to all methods is that people who are being researched do not necessarily act naturally and therefore you need to think about the effect of your presence in the research process on the actual data you collect. Clearly the way you deal with this issue will depend on the actual methods you have chosen to use and you should therefore consult in detail books referring to the particular methods you have chosen to use (see also Section 9.5).

It is also clear that in your evaluation and conclusions sections you need to consider a variety of theoretical explanations for the data you have collected.

Reflexivity and accountability to research participants

A further aspect of reflexivity is an awareness that research is not some clinical process cut off from real life and having no effect on it. It is the case that the process of research does have an effect on real-world life. Sociology is often criticized for being seen as common sense. However, this should not really be viewed as a criticism since it reflects the way that sociological findings and research both drawn up the society in which they take place and also affect what is considered to be common sense in those societies. Thus the terms 'moral panic' and 'labelling' could now be said to be a part of the common sense but it took sociological research to have this effect. It is important therefore to realise that research does have effect and you therefore need to think of the implications of your actions and reflecting on everything you have done in terms of its impact on you, your research participants and society more generally. At this level, it is unlikely that your efforts would have any major effect on society as a whole (although this is not impossible) but it is most certainly the case that your efforts could have drastic effects on your research correspondents and indeed yourself. It is therefore vital that you continuously think about, reflect on and discuss with others including your teacher, every stage of the research process. Always question anything that you feel is taken for granted either by you or by anyone else.

Accountability to research participants

No one can be required to help you out in your research so all research is reliant on the willingness and co-operation of others to make themselves, their lives and possibly personal and intimate details about themselves available to us. The fact that we are reliant on others and that we delve into sometimes sensitive and personal topics means that we have a clear responsibility to think carefully about the effects of our actions on our research participants and indeed other researchers. (See also Section 9.3.)

If you manage to annoy a group of people or some organizations in your area at the very least it is going to make it difficult for other A level students to conduct coursework in your area or indeed for professional researchers to do so.

This means that permission must be sought from your research participants to ensure that you comply with the principle of informed consent. This means you need to make clear the purpose of your research and the people who will read your final report. You must also make clear whether you are able to offer people anonymity or not.

Discussion point
Does referring to someone as the 'head of sociology' at the local college offer them anonymity?

C3.1a

The question of anonymity is potentially fraught with problems if the role or position that someone occupies is unique but reference to that position is an essential part of explaining the dynamics of whatever you are researching.

Equally you need to consider whether you will allow your informants to check what you say about them and whether it is accurate or not.

Activity
Think of the potential problems involved in offering people anonymity or the right to check the accuracy of your statements about them in your research report. Discuss this with other students in your class.

C3.1a C3.2 C3.3

Finally, you need to think about the effect of the research on the respondents and indeed the effect of the research process on yourself. A passing familiarity with the work of James Patrick and his Participant Observation studies is enough to tell you that there are clear dangers involved in covert research and why the BSA (1991) suggests that it is left to experienced researchers. Clearly you are accountable to yourself and your teacher to ensure that your research proposal and actions are safe, legal and ethical and in relation to this you should also consult the specifications produced by the OCR.

However, you also have responsibilities to your respondents. Let us say your wonderful piece of research gets published in *Sociology Review* after winning a sociology coursework award but the head of your school does not find your research subject, 'Are teachers lazy?', very amusing. In particular she is not amused by accounts of the way the head of sociology behaves. Could this lead to someone losing their job? Because the answer is yes, we are sure that you would not dream of allowing such an outcome to arise, but the dangers are not always obvious and that is why a key part of the project is to continually reflect upon and think about the potential consequences of your action. Being reflexive about the potential consequences of your research on your respondents is a key responsibility placed on you in moral and ethical terms as part of being a researcher and a sociology student.

We therefore advise you to think carefully and to discuss and to re-discuss every stage of this process with your teacher or lecturer. As long as you do this and act in a mature and responsible fashion, we are sure that this project will provide scope for you to engage in some interesting research pilots. We also look forward to reading about the coursework students complete and are continually amazed at the good quality of work that is produced. Make your teacher proud of the work you do!

Further reading

The following is a very useful introductory text:

- Chignall, H. (1996) *Theory and Methods*, Lewes: Connect.
- Stephens, P., Leach, A., Taggart, L. and Jones, H. (1998) *Think Sociology*, Cheltenham: Stanley Thornes.

Original readings in relation to this topic appear in:

- Kidd, W. *et al.* (1999) *Readings in Sociology*, Oxford: Heinemann Educational.

The following are excellent videos which consider issues relating to sociological theory and theories of methodology:

- Taylor, S. (1996) Theory and Methods, London: Vine Video.
- Taylor, S. (1998) Making Sense of Sociological Theory, London: Vine Video.

A clear and comprehensive overview of the social research process can be gleaned from:

- May, T. (1993) *Social Research*, Buckingham: Open University Press.

Back issues of the periodical *Sociology Review* (formerly known as *Social Studies Review*) also contain many articles on this field of sociology and many others.

Social inequality and difference

17.1 Contemporary changes in the distribution of income and wealth

Income

The most important statistics relating to the distribution of income came from the Royal Commission on the Distribution of Income and Wealth which reported periodically until 1980 (when it was abolished by the government). Statistics from its research show some degree of redistribution of income from the top one-tenth to the next six-tenths, but little change overall for those at the bottom of society (the bottom 30 per cent – despite some improvement in the 1950s and 60s (see Table 17.1).

Activity

Write your own summary of what the information presented in Table 17.1 shows in terms of the changing distribution of income between 1949 and 1979.

C3.2, C3.3

The shift towards greater inequality

Since 1979 there has been a definite move back to greater inequality. The main reason for this has been the preference for the 'free market'. Markets operate on the basis of reward and sanction and thus serve to create greater inequality. The level of inequality rose faster in the UK than anywhere else, except New Zealand, between the late 1970s and the early 1990s, according to research by the Joseph Rowntree Foundation (Hills, 1995). This can be seen in Figure 17.1.

Activity

a Identify countries in Figure 17.1 that are members of the European Union.

b To what extent are UK trends out of step with other members of the EU? Justify your answer.

C3.2, C3.3

One facet of this is that, while the average income rose by 36 per cent between 1979 and 1992, income for the poorest one-tenth (after housing costs are deducted) fell by 17 per cent (Mann, 1995). One important element of this has been changes in the labour market. Unemployment has more than doubled since 1979, but it has been unequally experienced. Also, changes to the tax and benefits system – such as the cutting of income tax and the matching increase in indirect taxes – have benefited those at the top while disadvantaging those at the bottom.

Kirby (1999) quotes research from the Social Exclusion Unit at the London School of Economics which shows that, in 1977, the top one-tenth of earners had an income 2.29 times that of the bottom one-tenth of earners, but by 1997 this ratio had increased to 3.32. This occurred because in that 20-year period the income of the top earners rose by 91 per cent in real terms, while that of the bottom earners rose by only 32 per cent in real terms. The clear effect of this is that the gap between rich and poor has widened considerably over the period.

Table 17.1 Historical trends in percentage shares of total income

	Before tax			After tax		
	Top 30%	Next 10%	Bottom 60%	Top 30%	Next 10%	Bottom 60%
1949	33.2	54.1	12.7	27.1	58.3	14.6
1954	29.8	59.3	10.9	24.8	63.1	12.1
1959	29.4	60.9	9.7	25.2	63.5	11.2
1964	29.0	61.4	9.6	25.1	64.1	10.8
1967	28.0	61.6	10.4	24.3	63.7	12.0
1974	26.8	62.3	10.9	23.6	63.6	12.8
1979	26.1	63.5	10.4	23.4	64.5	12.1

Source: Atkinson (1983, p. 63)

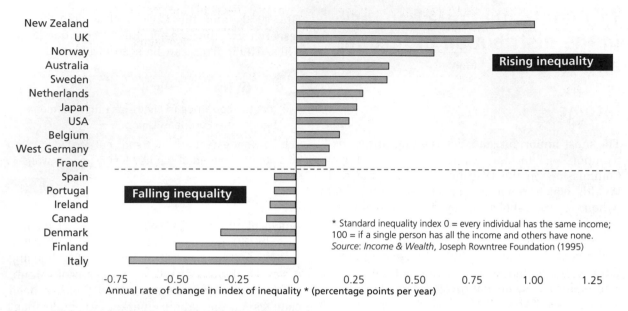

Figure 17.1 International income inequality trends.
Source: Mann (1995, p. 7)

New Labour and income inequality

One controversial aspect of New Labour is the way it appears to have rejected the idea of large-scale redistribution of income, preferring instead to try to raise economic performance in a way that echoes some elements of the New Right 'trickle-down' theory. This has caused some antagonism from old Labour supporters.

David Piachard (1999), in an analysis of poverty under the Labour government, argues that current policies involve redistribution by stealth. In a reply to this, David Walker (1999) says that it is precisely the argument that redistribution is occuring by stealth that underlines the abandonment of open policies of redistribution. He asserts that this reflects the acceptance of the argument that inequality is not offensive any more:

Asked if the state should be responsible for cutting differences between rich and poor, 48 per cent assented in 1985 but only 36 per cent in 1996. Assault on inequality is yesterday's politics, a relic from the time when socialism had a future. ... If there is no alternative to capitalism, and capitalism's rocket fuel is inequality, you can ameliorate the lot of the worst off by state transfers, but that is about it.

(Walker, 1999, p. 17)

He therefore argues that the government, in accepting this view of things, is left with little alternative but to pursue redistribution by stealth. However, as Piachard (1999) points out, this will mean that the amount of redistribution will not be enough to reduce poverty to its 1979 levels.

The New Earnings Survey 1999

This survey showed that the average gross weekly earnings of an adult in April 1999 was £400, a rise of 3.7 per cent on the figure in April 1998. A more detailed breakdown can be seen in Table 17.2.

Activity

From Table 17.2, identify which income inequalities reduced between 1998 and 1999 and which increased.

C3.2, C3.3

Regional inequalities in income

Paul Baldwin (1999) points out that there is a growing regional income divide in the UK. This analysis was based on a survey of income by postcodes by the market research group CACI (see Table 17.3). It found that nine of the 20 poorest postcode areas are in Liverpool, while high incomes are concentrated in central London areas such as Belgravia, Blackfriars and Barbican.

Table 17.2 Average gross weekly earnings (adults whose pay was not affected by absence) (£ per week)

	Full-time			Part-time	All
	Manual	**Non-manual**	**All**		
April 1999					
Men	335	526	442	155	420
Women	222	347	327	128	244
All	315	443	400	132	337
April 1998					
Men	328	508	429	150	408
Women	211	331	310	120	232
All	307	427	386	125	325
Increase (%)					
Men	2.1	3.4	3.2	3.2	3.0
Women	5.4	4.9	5.2	6.3	5.3
All	2.6	3.8	3.7	5.7	3.6

Source: New Earnings Survey 1999, reported by the Government Statistical Service, ONS press release (99) 360, October 1999

Table 17.3 Average annual household incomes, 1999

By county

Top 5		*Bottom 5*	
Surrey	£29,700	Tyne & Wear	£17,400
Berkshire	£28,100	Cornwall and Isles of Scilly	£17,400
Buckinghamshire	£27,900	South Yorkshire	£17,500
Hertfordshire	£26,900	Isle of Wight	£17,700
Outer London	£25,600	Mid-Glamorgan	£17,700

By postcode

Top 5		*Bottom 5*	
Temple, EC4Y 7	£51,900	Bootle, L59	£8,200
Blackfriars, EC4V 3	£49,900	Leicester, LE1/2	£8,800
Barbican, EC1A 4	£47,800	Middlesbrough, TS11	£9,000
Belgravia, SW1X 7	£47,800	Belfast, BT1/3	£9,000
Gerrards Cross, SL98	£46,500	Birkenhead, L4/17	£9,000

Source: Paul Baldwin, 'Postcodes chart growing income divide', *Guardian*, 25 October 1999

Wealth

The twentieth century (or at least its first 70 years) saw a gradual redistribution in wealth. The richest 1 per cent of the population owned 69 per cent of wealth in 1911, but this had reduced to 42 per cent by 1960. Equivalent figures for the richest tenth are 92 per cent down to 83 per cent.

Limited redistribution

A similar trend emerges with later figures. The most wealthy 1 per cent fell from 21 per cent in 1976 to 18 per cent in 1991. What is most notable is the limit of the redistribution of this wealth. While the very wealthy appear to have lost out, they appear to have lost out to the not-quite-so-wealthy. The rest do not seem to have increased their level of wealth at all. The least wealthy 50 per cent of the population owned 8 per cent of wealth in 1976 and this was unchanged in 1991.

A major reason for the redistribution of wealth noted above appears to have been the transfer of assets among family members to avoid death duties, so it is unclear whether these are 'real' redistributions. Inheritance still constitutes an important source of wealth. Harbury and

Hitchens (1979) found that, among the top 0.1 per cent of the population in property-holding terms, 51 per cent were inheritors in 1957 but this had fallen to 36 per cent in 1973. However, among the extremely wealthy (those left more than £1 million), the fall was less marked – from 9 per cent in 1957 to 7 per cent in 1973.

> ### Discussion point
> Emile Durkheim argued for a law to effectively abolish inheritance. Do you agree that such a change should be made?
>
> **C3.1a**

Forms of wealth

One form of wealth that increased in the 1980s was the ownership of company shares: by 1988, 21 per cent of people owned some shares, often the result of the privatizations of the period. However, Scott (1994) points out that the richest 1 per cent of the population owned 75 per cent of all privately owned shares.

The other main area of growing wealth is in housing. The growth of owner-occupation in the 1980s increased the stock of wealth. Scott sees this as one of the main reasons why there was a degree of redistribution of wealth in the early 1980s, but it is debatable whether this constitutes marketable wealth since the money can be realized only by selling one's house and thus making oneself homeless.

Marketable wealth

Westergaard (1995) is another to claim that the trend for wealth to be less unequally distributed was stopped or reversed in the 1980s. Using material from *Social Trends*, he argues that if we exclude the value of personal dwellings, the share of the richest 1 per cent of the population in marketable wealth rose from 26 to 28 per cent, and of the richest 5 per cent of the population from 45 to 53 per cent. Even with the value of personal dwellings included, the share of the richest remained constant throughout the 1980s.

Quantifying extreme wealth

Kirby (1999) quotes research by the *New Internationalist* magazine which shows that, in the late 1990s, the total wealth of the ten richest men in the world (they are all men) was 1.5 times the total wealth of the combined population of the 48 poorest countries, some 560 million peo-

ple. This points to the massive extremes of global inequality that now exist.

Research by *Forbes Magazine 1997*, quoted in the *Human Development Report* (UNDP, 1998), showed that the world's 225 richest people had a combined wealth equal to the annual income of the poorest 47 per cent of the world's population. It is estimated that the cost of achieving and maintaining basic social services, education, healthcare and food and safe water for all of the world's population is $40 billion a year, less than 4 per cent of the combined wealth of these 225 richest people. The wealthy are unequally distributed around the world, with most in the countries of the Organisation for Economic Cooperation and Development (OECD) – which comprises the world's advanced industrial economies. There are, however, some ultra-rich people even in sub-saharan Africa and in Eastern Europe, and in members of the Confederation of Independent States which comprises those countries formerly part of the USSR. This can be seen in Table 17.4.

> ### Activity
> Obtain further detail and updating of this information by visiting the *Forbes Magazine* website at: www.forbesmagazine.com.
>
> **C3.2, IT3.1**

Table 17.4 Distribution of the 225 richest people of the ultra-rich in 1997 (monetary figures are in billions of US dollars)

Region or country group	No. of the ultra-rich	Combined wealth	Average wealth
OECD of which:	143	637	4.5
USA	(60)	(311)	(5.1)
Germany	(21)	(111)	(5.2)
Japan	(14)	(41)	(2.9)
Asia	43	233	5.4
Latin America and Caribbean	22	55	2.5
Arab States	11	78	7.1
Eastern Europe and CIS	4	8	2.0
Sub-Saharan Africa	2	4	2.0
Totals	225	1015	

Source: Forbes Magazine 1997, quoted in *Human Development Report*, UNDP (1998, p. 30)

3rd	Richard Branson (£2400m)		530th	James Caan (£61m)
22nd	Mohammed Al-Fayed (£1000m)		531st	Sean Connery (£60m)
41st	Sir Paul McCartney (£550m)		531st	Lennox Lewis (£60)
58th	Lord Andrew Lloyd-Webber (£420m)		531st	Jimmy Page (£60m)
106th	The Queen (£275m)		531st	Robert Plant (£60m)
183th	Sir Elton John (£160m)		595th	Mark Knopfler (£55m)
198rd	Mick Jagger (£150m)		595th	Ronnie Wood (£45m)
292nd	David Bowie (£100m)		623rd	Tom Jones, (£50m)
292ndt	Phil Collins (100m)		623rd	Brian May (£50m)
292nd	Sting (£100m)		747th	Nigel Mansell (£35m)
338th	George Harrison (£90m)		747th	Jim Kerr (£40m)
439th	Eric Clapton (£75m)		747th	Anita Roddick (£40m)
438th	Chris Evans (£75m)		832rd	Van Morrison (£35m)
447th	Barbara Taylor Bradford (£70m)		914th	Chris De Burgh (£30m)
447th	Ringo Starr (£70m)		914th	Engelbert Humperdinck (£30m)
508th	Charlie Watts (£60m)			

Figure 17.2 Some famous names on the *Sunday Times'* 1000 richest list

The 2000 *Sunday Times* survey of the richest people in the UK

Beresford and Boyd (2000) comprises the 12th annual *Sunday Times* list of the richest individuals in the UK, now expanded to cover 1000 people. Their total wealth reached £146bn, up £31bn on the previous year. The top two are in retail and property management, namely Hans Rausing (£4,000m), the inventor of milk cartons, and the Duke of Westminster (£3,750m). However, the list shows the rise of high-technology including 63 multi-millionnaires who made their money from the Internet, as well as those in computing, telecommunications or mobile phones.

Looking at the top 1000 as a whole, inherited wealth has fallen as a proportion of the total but still constitutes 26 per cent of the richest individuals (258 out of 1000, of which 129 are titled aristocrats) in contrast with 57 per cent in 1989. 64 people on the list were educated at Eton and 11 at Harrow. 53 went to Oxford University and 46 to Cambridge University.

The list contains 64 women compared to 71 in 1999 and 6 in 1989. The ethnic minority group most represented are Asians with 54 entries. In terms of regional location, Southeast England dominates with over half (506) being resident in that area.

Activity

The *Sunday Times'* reports of the UK's richest people can be found on the Internet at www.sunday-times.co.uk. Locate a copy of the latest edition of the survey and calculate the following as percentages:

a those who are women

b those who are titled aristocrats

c those who were educated at a public school

d those who were educated at an Oxford or Cambridge college

e those who currently live in (i) the south-east of England or (ii) Wales.

17.2 Contemporary workplace inequalities

In order to discuss sociological theories of work, it is first of all necessary to discuss exactly what we mean by work, since without clearly differentiating it from other activities the sociology of work is in danger of becoming the sociology of everything.

Defining work: money or effort?

Although the term 'work' has a commonsense meaning, as in the phrase 'I'm off to work', when we delve a little deeper it becomes clear that the meaning of the word can be contested.

Himmelweit and Costello (1995) provide the following examples and discussion of the problem of defining work:

One could say, for example, that it depends who the children are as to whether looking after them is to count as work or not. When you look after your own children that is not seen as work, but if you employ a child minder to look after them that is her job and it is her work … a market gardener who grows flowers to sell is more likely to see it as work than an amateur pursuing gardening as a hobby for its own sake. Similarly, some onerous tasks may count as work in some contexts but not in others. Writing lists and filling in forms is part of a clerical worker's job but it is also a chore most of us have to do at various times without considering it as work … it is not what you are doing but the social context in which it is done which determines whether we see a particular activity as work or not.

(Himmelweit and Costello, 1995, p. 10)

Discussion point

What are the problems involved in defining 'work'?

C3.1a

The construction of work as paid effort

Work is often associated with paid labour, but we need to note that there is nothing natural or universal about this. Therefore, at some point, for some reason, the exchange of money must have achieved its present degree of prominence. While the exchange of money is a key feauture of capitalist societies, in order for capitalism to exist it is possible to identify a whole range of activities that are essential but which nonetheless are not based on the exchange of money. Are these activities work?

Housework: work in reproducing society

The most obvious and important example is the work performed largely by women in the domestic sphere, i.e. housework – without which the whole social and economic system we live under would very quickly grind to a halt. (See also Section 5.7.)

Why, if this is essential, is it differentiated from other activities by not leading to the exchange of money? This is a very good question and one which feminist sociologists have raised increasingly in the last 20 years. It is also a question which leads to the consideration of a very different way of conceptualizing work. Again Himmelweit and Costello (1995) summarize the differences between the two possible meanings of work that may arise out of this:

We have two meanings of the term 'work': one of them refers just to work done for money whereas the other usage of the term encompasses all activities necessary for the reproduction of society whether paid or not. Both correspond to ways in which the term 'work' can be used in everyday speech.

By the first definition, the content of the activity is irrelevant; it is the social context in which it is done that defines it as 'work'. This is underlined by the tendency in our society for clear distinctions of time, place and attitude to be drawn between 'work' and 'non-work' in this first sense.

In the second sense, 'work' includes a number of activities that bring in no money to the person doing it, but are nevertheless important or necessary to society. Here it is the content of the work done that is significant and it may be done in different social contexts, for example be paid or unpaid, and still count as work.

(Himmelweit and Costello, 1995, p. 13)

Sociologists have been concerned to study the relationships between the two possible definitions of work to uncover the mechanisms by which one or the other is actually applied in concrete circumstances.

Discussion point

Is work only that which we are paid for?

C3.1a

The three economies in society

Sociologists Gershuny and Pahl (1985) used the phrase the 'three economies' to try to capture all the possible different social relationships covering the expending of human effort.

First they talk about the *formal economy*, by which is meant effort that leads to monetary reward and which is officially recognized as contributing to the economy.

Secondly there is an *informal economy* which

also involves effort but does not always lead to monetary reward or official recognition as work. This informal economy can be further subdivided into two aspects:

- the household/communal economy
- the underground or hidden economy – 'the black economy'.

Gershuny and Pahl further argue that it is possible to identify ways in which specific tasks have moved from one economy to another over time; for example, they point to the way washing clothes started out in the home, then moved to the laundry, but now with the development of washing machines has moved back to the home (arrows 1 and 2 on Figure 17.3). Equally:

The current prevalence of household construction work paid for in cash may indicate a shift from formal to underground, or 'black' production (arrow 3 on Figure 17.3), and if unemployment levels rise, the cost of black work will drop and some jobs, now DIY, will move across (arrow 6 on Figure 17.3)'.

(Gershuny and Pahl, 1985, p. 250)

Activity

Suggest an example of a change in economy location for each of the arrows numbered 4 and 5 in Figure 17.3.

C3.2, C3.3

By *communal economy*, Gershuny and Pahl (1985) mean work done outside the household but without money exchanging hands. This covers the whole of what is normally called voluntary work (see also Section 7.2). It also covers

kinship and neighbourhood-based networks providing services reciprocally.

By the *hidden/underground economy*, Gershuny and Pahl (1985) mean what is often called the 'black' economy. This is where work is done in exchange for money but is not officially declared, particularly to the tax authorities. This is of course illegal and therefore poses the question of whether this should be considered as work or deviance. Interactionists might argue that it depends on whether you get caught.

One aspect of the household/communal economy is housework. The amount of effort expended here can be gauged from figures which appeared in the *Daily Telegraph* in 1993.

These showed that the total number of hours worked by housewives, at 70.7 per week, was considerably higher than the number worked by those in full-time work. Since the cost of providing these services through paid labour (£348.75) was considerably higher than average earnings (£316.90 in 1993), we can begin to understand why some feminists campaigned for wages for housework.

It is of course important to say that cost should not necessarily be the criterion on which these things are decided, and that since housework is not paid, it is just as easy to point to the cost in terms of paid employment income lost to all the women who do, and have, engaged in housework. (See also Section 8.3.)

The total social organization of labour

In a further attempt to consider the way we define work, Glucksmann (1995) has developed the concept of the 'total social organization of labour'. This argues that we need to consider the way in which labour in a society is divided up and allocated to structures, institutions and activities in society. By using this concept, the fact that labour takes different forms and is utilized in different ways and contexts is highlighted; and by considering the organization and utilization of labour in a total way, all sorts of activities which go well beyond the arena of paid work can be analysed, using the approaches developed by sociologists examining work in society.

The concept was originally developed to consider gender and work, reflecting the continuing importance of the debate about how we analyse

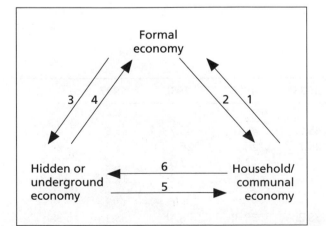

Figure 17.3 The three economies
Source: Gershuny and Pahl (1985, p. 250)

the various labour activities traditionally more likely to be undertaken by women.

This approach highlights the continuing trend towards the acceptance among sociologists of using *effort* rather than money-based approaches to the definition of work – even though this may not be true of society as a whole at present, where notions of work continue to tend towards being linked with paid employment.

Work and non-work

A consideration of some of the issues surrounding the definition of work therefore leads to the identification of a number of different ways in which it is possible to define work, and by extension, non-work. Non-work could be defined as those areas or aspects of society which are not included in the notion of work. Of course altering the definition of work will alter the definition of non-work too.

One important component of non-work is leisure activities (see Section 13.5), comprising those things we do for enjoyment. But depending on the definition of work adopted, there are a number of other activities that, while not really leisure activities, might fit into the category of non-work – notably housework, crime and voluntary activities. Why these have in certain respects come to be defined as non-work is an interesting sociological question in itself, and one which exists as a backdrop to the rise and changing nature of the sociological study of work – most evidently in the case of arguments about the activities of women.

While much of the rest of the chapter is concerned with the arena of paid employment, it must be remembered that exactly what this is cannot be taken for granted. Paid employment must itself be seen as a *social construction* and therefore open to debate concerning the possibility of change.

We will now look at recent evidence about the experience of work. This evidence will be used as the basis for considering how patterns of employment are structured in contemporary Britain, and how important work remains for diverse groups of people. We will focus largely on gender and ethnic issues.

Measuring work participation in contemporary Britain

There are two official measures of employment used in the UK today (see Section 9.6).

The *Labour Force Survey* (LFS) is based on interviews of people in households, and is produced quarterly. The summer 1998 *Labour Force Survey* showed that in the spring there were a total of 26.9 million persons in employment in the UK, of whom 20.2 million were in full-time employment and 6.7 million in part-time employment (see Table 17.5).

Secondly there are the quarterly *Workforce in Employment* (WiE) statistics, derived from surveys of employers. These measure employment that contributes to economic output as judged by gross domestic product (GDP), and the data are therefore a measure of jobs rather than people. One important implication of this is that people who have two jobs (800 000 people in 1995 for example) would be counted only once on the LFS but twice on the WiE. This will mean that the calculation for the number of part-time jobs is higher on the WiE statistics than the LFS statistics.

Table 17.5 Features of employment in the UK (millions)

	1984	1990	1994	1995	1996	1997	1998
No. of people aged 16 and over	43.8	45.1	45.5	45.6	45.7	45.9	46.1
People in employment	24.0	26.9	25.7	26.0	26.2	26.7	26.9
ILO unemployed[a]	3.2	2.0	2.7	2.5	2.3	2.0	1.8
Economically inactive	16.6	16.2	17.0	17.1	17.2	17.2	17.3
Average usual hours worked per person per week (all)	38.3h	39h	38.2h	38.3h	38.1h	38.1h	38h

[a] International Labour Office.
Source: Labour Force Survey, summer 1998

In the summer of 1995, for example, according to the WiE measure, there were a total of 25 million persons in employment – 18.1 million full-time and 7.0 million part-time. In contrast for the same period, the LFS showed a total of 25.5 million in employment – 19.3 million full-time and 6.2 million part-time. Since the level of those in part-time employment is a central element in contemporary debates about work, it is important for you to be aware of the effect of using different measures.

Problems with employment statistics

The Times' labour correspondent Philip Bassett (1996) argued thus:

Not only does the government not know how many people are out of work in the UK, it doesn't even know how many people are in work ... Does this matter? Well, yes. In terms of knowing about what is going on in both the labour market and the economy more generally, the number of people in productive work is clearly a key factor. Politically, job growth is a key goal: ministers proclaim the growth of jobs as a key indicator of the claimed success of government policy.

(Bassett, 1996, p. 27)

Keith Perry (1996) of the then Central Statistical Office (now the Office for National Statistics, ONS) argues that in the 1980s the two series of measures showed similar trends, but that since 1992 they have diverged:

Although the WiE was thought by some to more accurately reflect the 1992 fall in economic activity, the LFS seemed to be the more consistent measure during the early stages of the economic upturn.

(Perry, 1996, p. 20)

Perry argues that the technical differences between the two measures might explain some of the discrepancy (for example, the LFS includes unpaid family workers – i.e. people who work in a family business – while these are excluded from the WiE).

However, Bassett analysed figures from both the LFS and the WiE and argued that, while the technical differences would mean that the actual numbers would differ, if they are both to be regarded as valid, the trends they reveal should be the same. However:

... analysis of the figures over a year to last summer shows that in many cases they are not. The LFS, for instance, shows employment up by 1.2 per cent. WiE figures show a fall of 0.4 per cent. Male employment is rising twice as fast in the LFS than in the WiE, while part-time work is increasing twice as rapidly in the WiE measure compared with the LFS.

(Bassett, 1996, p. 27)

He concludes that there is no evidence to show that one series is more reliable than the other, and this leaves us with a still unexplained gap of 500 000 in the figures for the number of people in work.

The decline of permanent full-time employment?

Dahrendorf (1999a) sees the demise of permanent full-time employment and the growth of part-time, temporary or seasonal employment as a Europe-wide and arguably worldwide phenomenan. He points out that men in particular are retiring earlier, such that by 1995 only 56 per cent of men aged 55–64 were in full-time paid employment. A further factor is the ending of the link between employment growth and economic growth which seems to have had most effect in the UK. Between 1970 and 1995, while the economy grew by 60 per cent, total employment fell by 4 per cent.

However, despite the potential lack of growth of jobs, this has not been accompanied by any significant reduction of the number of hours worked (see Table 17.6), which might provide one explanation of the rise of jobless growth.

Table 17.6 Average weekly paid hours of work (adults whose pay was not affected by absence)

| | Full-time | | | Part-time |
	Manual	Non-manual	All	
April 1998				
Men	45.0	39.1	41.7	19.0
Women	40.2	37.1	37.6	19.4
All	44.1	38.2	40.2	19.3
April 1999				
Men	44.4	39.0	41.4	19.2
Women	39.9	37.0	37.5	19.4
All	43.6	38.1	40.0	19.4

Source: New Earnings Survey, April 1999

Activity

From Table 17.6, which social groups saw their average weekly paid hours of work decrease between 1998 and 1999, and which groups saw their hours increase?

C3.2, C3.3

The belief in the all-conquering nature of part-time work is, however, slightly contradicted by figures from the Organisation for Economic Cooperation and Development (OECD, 1997). OECD is an organization including all major industrial countries. Its figures for the UK show that, while the proportion of the workforce working part-time grew slightly between 1985 and 1995 (from 21.2 to 24.1 per cent), among women a smaller proportion of those employed worked part-time in 1995 than in 1985 (44.3 compared with 44.8 per cent).

In neither total employment nor in female employment has there been the massive rise in part-time work often alluded to, and in neither case do part-time workers constitute a majority of the workforce.

Activity

a Calculate the percentage of male employees working part-time, and the percentage of female employees working part-time in 1998, according to the figures in Table 17.7.

b Summarize the differences between males and females in terms of their distribution between full- and part-time employment.

c How might sociologists explain these patterns of employment?

C3.2, C3.3

There has, however, been a significant change in male working patterns. In 1985, only 4.4 per cent of employed males worked part-time, but by 1995 this had nearly doubled to 7.7 per cent. By 1998 it had risen even further to 8.9 per cent (see Table 17.7).

These figures do indicate that some changes are taking place, and in particular they tell us about how work is divided between the genders. But it is also important to emphasize the limits of these changes in the face of notions of total and complete change. We will now move on to examine in more detail some of the issues about gender divisions in work alluded to in this section.

Gender and work

Increasing participation of women in paid employment

Women are increasingly involved in paid employment, and indeed it is likely that at some point in the near future women will constitute a majority of the workforce. In certain areas of the UK, for example in the north, the south-west of England and in Scotland, this is already the case (Roberts *et al.*, 1996).

In the UK overall in 1995, women formed 49.3 per cent of employees, according to the Department of Employment's *Annual Employment Survey*. Frances Sly (1996) points out that in 1995, 67 per cent of single women and 73 per cent of married and cohabiting women were economically active. This trend towards greater participation in paid employment has continued, with the total number of women in employment rising from 9.9 million in 1984 to 12 million in 1998 (see Table 17.8).

Table 17.7 Full- and part-time employment in the UK, by gender (millions)[a]

	1986	1988	1990	1992	1994	1996	1997	1998
Males								
Full-time	13.45	13.94	14.39	13.30	13.05	13.20	13.39	13.56
Part-time	0.71	0.85	0.92	1.01	1.12	1.24	1.33	1.34
Females								
Full-time	5.83	6.28	6.64	6.45	6.35	6.46	6.59	6.64
Part-time	4.52	4.74	4.97	5.04	5.16	5.31	5.37	5.40

a Full-part-time is based on respondent's self-assessment.
Source: Labour Force Survey, 1986–98

Table 17.8 Gender and paid employment in the UK (millions)

	1984	1990	1994	1995	1996	1997	1998
Men in employment	14.1	15.3	14.2	14.4	14.4	14.7	14.9
ILO unemployed	1.9	1.2	1.8	1.6	1.5	1.3	1.1
Economically inactive	5.1	5.3	6.1	6.2	6.2	6.3	6.4
All aged 16 and over	21.1	21.8	22.1	22.1	22.2	22.3	22.4
Women in employment	9.9	11.6	11.5	11.6	11.8	12.0	12.0
ILO unemployed	1.3	0.8	0.9	0.8	0.8	0.7	0.7
Economically inactive	11.5	10.9	11.0	11.0	10.9	10.9	10.9
All aged 16 and over	22.8	23.3	23.4	23.4	23.5	23.6	23.6
Average usual hours worked per person per week							
Men	44.3	45.1	44.4	44.4	44.2	44.1	44.0
Women	30.0	31.0	30.6	30.7	30.6	30.8	30.8

Source: Labour Force Survey, spring 1998

Factors affecting women's involvement in paid employment

Perhaps the most important factor in determining whether a woman is economically active is the presence or otherwise of children, and more specifically the age of the youngest child. Sly (1996) reports that only 52 per cent of women with a child under 4 years are economically active, compared with 78 per cent of women with children aged 11–15.

Childcare obligations also seem to explain why so many women work part-time, allied to the very low level of publicly funded childcare support in the UK. Crompton and Le Feuvre argue that the differences in the level of such support are the key reason for the fact that, while in France only 20 per cent of women work part-time, the equivalent figure for the UK is 40 per cent:

Before the Second World War, British social policy in respect of child welfare worked so as to keep women out of the labour market in the interests of both the health of their infants and the national economy. In general, British women have been treated for social policy purposes as mothers, rather than as workers and, moreover, as mothers who will be provided for by a man.

(Crompton and Le Feuvre, 1996, p. 430)

They argue that there is still the expectation that women will concern themselves primarily with the household in support of their male partner's career (see also Section 5.7). They also point out that if women wish to get on they are almost required to adopt 'masculine' patterns of work, meaning full-time continuous work. Obviously given the lack of childcare this in effect means women choosing between career and children.

Women and the workplace: segregated experiences

It is clear that women's involvement in paid employment is increasing, but we need to ask what types of job women are filling – in order to consider the extent to which such involvement provides a degree of economic autonomy:

- The first point is the much greater level of part-time working among women. In 1995, about 43 per cent of women in employment worked part-time and women comprised 84 per cent of all part-time workers. In comparison, 6 per cent of men in employment worked part-time (Sly, 1996).

- However, since 1985 both full-time employment and part-time employment for women have risen by 10 per cent, so the rise in employment of women cannot be accounted for solely by changes in the structure of the labour market with the growth of part-time jobs. Indeed there is evidence that the growth of temporary jobs has affected men more than women. Between 1985 and 1995, the number of women in permanent jobs rose by 12 per cent, while the equivalent figure for men fell 5 per cent. Both groups experienced a large rise in the number of temporary employment (fixed-term or casual work), with a 21 per cent rise for women and a 71 per cent rise for men.

- It is also the case that the gender differential in pay levels is much lower in part-time work than in full-time work; and perhaps surprisingly, the average earnings of part-time workers are lower for men than for women. Women earn 78.6 per cent of average male earnings if they work full-time, but they earn 104.0 per cent of male earnings if they work part-time (although this might be affected by the fact that most male part-time workers tend to be young). Age is clearly a factor that affects this, as can be seen from Table 17.9.

Table 17.9 Hourly gross earnings (£s) from full-time employment, by gender and age

	Male	Female
Under 18	3.47	3.31
18–20	4.77	4.51
21–24	6.89	6.32
25–29	8.50	7.97
30–39	10.62	9.28
40–49	11.69	8.76
50–59	11.07	8.07
60–64	8.77	6.78

Source: New Earnings Survey, April 1998

Activity

Among which age group is the difference between male and female earnings the greatest, and in which age group is it the least? What explanations might sociologists offer for these patterns?

C3.2, C3.3

Types of segregation

While these statistics indicate something of the nature of the changes that are often described as the 'development of the flexible labour market' (see also Section 17.2), and while they indicate that some men may be suffering the effects of this, this does not necessarily mean that women are gaining at the expense of men.

In order to look at this we need to look at the type of jobs that women are involved in. Two concepts developed by feminist sociologists to explain the gender divisions in paid employment are useful here: horizontal segregation and vertical segregation.

Horizontal segregation refers to the way in which men and women are separated into different occupations. Vertical segregation refers to the way in which men and women tend to hold jobs at different levels in hierarchical structures.

Horizontal segregation

Evidence on horizontal segregation is a standard feature of *Labour Force Surveys*. In their survey of women and employment using statistics for 1980 from the Department of Employment, Martin and Roberts (1984) reported that 63 per cent of women worked only with other women. In relation to the husbands of these women, 81 per cent worked only with other men. This clearly underlines the extent to which workplaces are horizontally segregated. More recent information on this can be found in the figures for spring 1995 which are shown in Figure 17.4.

The spring 1995 *Labour Force Survey* found that the employment of men was roughly equally divided between manual and non-manual work, but that 70 per cent of women employees worked in non-manual jobs. Furthermore it found that 51 per cent of all women in employment worked in four occupational groups: clerical, secretarial, sales and personal service. By looking in even more detail at horizontal segregation, that is at the level of individual occupations, we find that 92 per cent of receptionists are female, as are 87 per cent of nurses, 75 per cent of clerks and secretaries and 63 per cent of teachers. In contrast, the occupations which are most male-dominated are in engineering, mechanics and agriculture.

The fact that there are no occupations where the gender division is equal (teaching is perhaps the nearest, although issues of vertical segregation matter here as we shall see) means that horizontal segregation continues to be relevant.

Vertical segregation

Vertical segregation is the grade at which people are located within occupations. While teaching is the occupational category closest to being equally divided between men and women, male and female teachers can be clearly differentiated in terms of the grade at which they work. A National Union of Teachers (NUT) (1988) survey found that, while 50 per cent of male primary school teachers were headteachers, only 15 per cent of female primary school teachers were.

In relation to the effect of labour market segregation on pay, Webb (1982) points to the following factors as explaining pay differences between males and females: 7 per cent could be accounted for by the differential distribution of men and women among occupations, 13 per cent by differences in hours worked, and almost 80 per cent by differences within occupations.

In their research into the issue of work in five localities, Bagguley and Walby (1988) found that between 1971 and 1981 there had been a decline in the degree of vertical segregation between men and women as women gained access to the higher level jobs, but there had also been an increase in the extent of horizontal segregation.

Explaining the segregation by gender

Crompton and Le Feuvre provide the following summary of feminist arguments on this issue:

Feminists have seen the restrictions on women's participation in paid employment ... as reflecting the patriarchal control of women by denying them access to the kinds of employment which would generate a sufficient income to live independently.

(Crompton and Le Feuvre, 1996, p. 427)

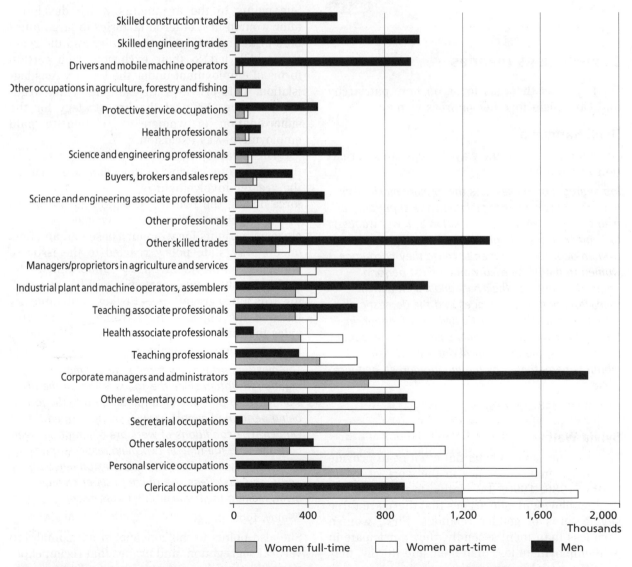

Figure 17.4 Numbers of women and men of working age in employment by occupation, Great Britain; spring 1995 (not seasonally adjusted)
Source: Labour Market Trends, (March 1996, p. 97 data from Labour Force Survey)

This still leaves open to debate the actual mechanisms by which such patriarchy operates.

Activity

a From the information in Figure 17.4, identify the two industries with the highest proportion of women workers, and the two with the highest proportion of male workers.

b Identify the two industries with the highest proportion of women part-time workers, and the two with the lowest proportion of women part-time workers.

c Write a short summary of any patterns you see in Figure 17.4.

C3.2, C3.3

Dual-systems theories

Dual-systems theorists focus on how patriarchy and capitalism together oppress women.

Heidi Hartmann

Hartmann points to the way this operates in relation to employment:

Job segregation by sex ... is the primary mechanism in capitalist society that maintains the superiority of men over women, because it enforces lower wages for women in the labour market. Low wages keep women dependent on men because they encourage women to marry. Married women must perform domestic chores for their husbands. Men benefit then, from both higher wages and the domestic division of labour. This domestic division of labour, in turn, acts to weaken women's position in the labour market. Thus, the hierarchical domestic division of labour is perpetuated by the labour market, and vice versa.

(Hartmann, 1982, p. 448)

Sylvia Walby

Perhaps the most substantial attempt to provide a dual-systems theory lies in the work of Sylvia Walby (1986, 1990). In relation to the sphere of paid employment, she argues that there are three key features of gender relations. First, women earn less than men; secondly, they participate in paid employment less than men; and thirdly, they do different jobs from men.

Although she agrees with Hartmann that we need to consider the interplay between capital-

ism and patriarchy, Walby argues that Hartmann does not pay enough attention to the way in which there is a degree of tension between these two structures, and she sets out to consider this.

First she argues that the emphasis on the family wage (meaning the idea that men on their own should earn enough to keep themselves and their family) is overplayed since many households do not operate on this basis. She points to the way in which the two demands on women's time, namely as workers for capitalists and as providing domestic work for husbands (see Section 5.7), potentially come into conflict, since time spent on one leads to less time for the other.

From exclusion to segregation

She points to the arguments which developed after women first entered factories in large numbers in the mid-nineteenth century and the reaction which led to their exclusion from certain forms of employment under the Factory Acts legislation. This provides an example of her argument that in the past the key strategy for the subordination of women in relation to paid employment was exclusion.

This strategy is, however, no longer seen as the crucial one, owing to developments such as the greater involvement of women in the workforce during the two world wars and the political campaigns that were waged to gain citizenship rights for women. These had an effect on the way state policy reacted to the issue of women's employment. They undermined the basis of exclusionary strategies and led to a shift towards job segregation as the key contemporary basis of the oppression of women. Walby provides the following summary of what she means by segregation approaches:

The most important new form of labour market segregation in Britain since the 1940s is that of the division between part-time and full-time work, the former being performed almost exclusively by married women. The conditions of work are different between part-time and full-time in two main respects: part-time jobs pay less than full-time ones on average; part-timers have less secure contracts of employment, making them vulnerable to dismissal.

(Walby, 1990, p. 54)

She also points to the concepts of horizontal and vertical segregation, and argues that recent experience in the UK has been for a decline in vertical segregation to be matched with a rise in horizontal segregation.

So in the context of her overall argument about the changing nature of patriarchy, Walby argues that in relation to the sphere of paid employment this has taken the form of a shift from exclusionary strategies to segregation strategies as ways of enforcing gender inequalities in the paid employment sphere. These obviously have an effect on other areas of life. She concludes her arguments on paid employment with the following three points:

1. The Labour market is more important and the family less important as the determinant of women's labour force participation than is conventionally assumed.
2. Women's lesser participation in paid work is a result of material constraints rather than a matter of 'choice' or of cultural values, as is frequently argued.
3. Politics and the state are much more important in the structuring of the sexual division of labour than is often recognized; we need an analysis not merely of economy, but of political economy.

(Walby, 1990, p. 56)

Women, work and choice: Catherine Hakim

The idea that the reasons for the unequal position of women in the paid employment sphere are material and structural constraints rather than personal choice has recently surfaced as the basis of an argument raised in various publications by Hakim (1991, 1995, 1996b).

She argues that it is primarily a question of choice that women have a different and unequal position in the paid employment sphere. Such an approach is clearly contrary to that of Walby and other feminists.

Hakim argues that the idea that inequalities in the workplace are the result of structural determination (whether capitalism or patriarchy) is wrong, and suggests instead that gender inequalities result from the differential behaviour and attitudes to work of men and women. To put it in simple terms, she argues that women have less commitment to work, and it is this which is the basis of their inferior pay rewards.

First she argues that, looked at in terms of the hours of paid employment:

... there was absolutely no increase in the volume of female employment, measured in full-time equivalent numbers, from World War Two up to 1987 in Britain. Rather than underlining the increase in women's employment, we should be seeking to explain the long-

term stability of female employment despite dramatic social and economic change over the past century.

(Hakim, 1995, p. 431)

Her own explanation for the pattern of stability she has outlined is basically that men and women do hold different attitudes towards paid employment, and men have higher levels of commitment to work. She argues that when asked if they would continue to work, even if they did not *need* to financially, men outscore women, with two-thirds of women still preferring to have a job, compared with three-quarters of men.

She finds there is little difference among men and women working full-time, and that the overall difference emerges when looking at part-time working. She further asserts that the difference in the level of commitment between full-time and part-time workers is not merely quantitative but qualitative as well (see also Section 9.3). This leads her to argue that we can identify two groups of women: first career women and secondly those women who:

... give priority to the marriage career, do not invest in what economists term 'human capital', transfer quickly and permanently to part-time work as soon as a breadwinner husband permits it, choose undemanding jobs 'with no worries or responsibilities' when they do work, and are hence found concentrated in lower grade and lower paid jobs which offer convenient working hours with which they are perfectly happy.

(Hakim, 1995, p. 434)

She further argues that childcare problems cannot be the main reason affecting women's work since part-time working and not working at all extends well beyond those with childcare responsibilities.

To summarize, Hakim suggests that the lower commitment to paid employment by women is the key reason why part-timers, and therefore women, are treated differently in the labour market. In essence, it is women's choices about orientation to work which lead to gender inequalities in relation to paid employment.

Criticisms of Hakim

Crompton (1997) argues that there are flaws in Hakim's argument.

First she disputes the division between committed and uncommitted women workers developed by Hakim, pointing out that Hakim herself says that women will switch between these groups, which rather questions their existence as

Table 17.10 Job status of people of working age in Great Britain, by gender and ethnic group, spring 1995 (percentages)

	White	Black[a]	Indian[b]	Pakistani/ Bangladeshi	Other[c]	All ethnic groups
Males						
Working full-time	72	49	65	41	51	71
Working part-time	5	8	7	8	8	5
Unemployed	8	21	10	18	12	9
Inactive	15	22	18	33	29	15
All (=100%)(thousands)	16 993	273	306	216	224	18 017
Females						
Working full-time	38	37	36	12	30	38
Working part-time	29	15	19	6	16	28
Unemployed	5	14	7	7	8	5
Inactive	28	34	38	75	46	29
All (=100%)(thousands)	15 420	296	279	191	238	16 428

[a] Includes Caribbean, African and other black people of non-mixed origin.
[b] Includes Chinese, other ethnic minority groups of non-mixed origin and people of mixed origin.
[c] Includes ethnic group not stated
Source: Labour Force Survey, quoted in *Social Trends*, 1996

separate clear groups. Her evidence points to the fact that women want to be able to combine both domestic and market commitments and do therefore make choices.

However, Crompton argues that Hakim consistently underplays the structures within which such choices have to be made. In particular she cites the development of the 'male breadwinner' model and the way this has been enshrined in welfare state and other social policy developments (see Section 14.3), meaning that explanations based purely on notions of choice cannot explain all inequalities:

To be sure, women can and do make choices – although in aggregate, their relative lack of power and resources relative to men means that both today and in the past, they have been less able to do so than the opposite sex. Women – and men – can choose but are also constrained, a fact which lies at the root of sociological explanations of human behaviour. The tension between 'structural' and 'action' explanations is a long-standing one in sociological theory and research, and has not yet been satisfactorily resolved. ... However I am concerned that Hakim's oversimplified rendering of the complexities of the structuring of the gender division of labour, with its emphasis on one 'side' (choice) to the exclusion of the other, might focus the argument

on the sterile dichotomies of choice or constraint, structure or action.

(Crompton, 1997, pp. 4–5)

Ethnic minorities and employment

There are clear differences in the economic status of people in ethnic groupings, and these differences are reinforced by gender differences. This can be seen in Table 17.10.

Church and Summerfield (1996), in *Social Focus on Ethnic Minorities*, point out that in the spring of 1995, while 82 per cent of black Caribbean men and 70 per cent of black Caribbean women were economically active, only 66 per cent of Bangladeshi men and 20 per cent of Bangladeshi women were. While white males had an unemployment rate of 8 per cent, the rate for Pakistani/Bangladeshi men was 18 per cent and that for black men was 21 per cent. These differences will have an important effect on inequality, given the importance of paid employment as a source of income.

The employment of ethnic minorities also appears to show the characteristics of segregation explored earlier in the section on gender:

- Employment in distribution, hotel and catering is higher among South Asian groups than among whites, but both groups are likely to be employed in manufacturing industry; whereas for blacks the most likely sectors of employment are public administration, health and education.

- Nursing is one occupation with a large proportion of ethnic minority workers. But while 34 per cent of whites and 35 per cent of Asian nurses were charge nurses or senior nurses, only 29 per cent of black nurses were in these grades.

- The employment of ethnic minorities in the civil service also shows that they are clearly under-represented among all but the lowest clerical grades.

Table 17.11 and other statistics show that ethnicity is a clear factor in determining the type and level of job occupied, generally meaning that ethnic minorities suffer worse working conditions and worse standards of remuneration.

Statistics show that people from ethnic minority groups are much more likely to be temporary workers. In the spring of 1995, 7 per cent of white workers were temporary, compared with 8 per cent of Indian workers, 9 per cent of black workers and 13 per cent of Pakistani/Bangladeshi workers. Three-quarters of workers from Pakistani/Bangladeshi groups said this was because no permanent work was available, compared with fewer

Table 17.11 Percentages of UK civil service staff belonging to ethnic minorities, by grade level

	1989	1995
AA	6.5	7.6
AO	5.6	6.7
EO	2.9	4.3
HEO	1.7	2.4
SEO	1.2	2.1
Grade 7	1.2	2.6
Grade 6	2.2	2.8
Grade 5	1.8	2.5
Grade 4	0.6	0.4
Grade 3	0.0	0.2
Grade 2	0.0	0.0
Grade 1	0.0	0.0
All grade levels (thousands)	18.0	23.0

Source: Cabinet Office, and Church and Summerfield (1996, p. 43)

Table 17.12 Average gross hourly pay (£s) of full-time employees in Great Britain, by gender, 1994/95

	Males	Females	All
Black	7.01	6.71	6.88
Indian	8.01	5.75	7.12
Pakistani/ Bangladeshi	6.87	4.78	6.43
Other ethnic minorities	7.70	6.66	7.32
White	8.34	6.59	7.73

Source: Labour Force Survey, Church and Summerfield (1996, p. 47)

than half giving this reason among white workers. This ethnic difference is important in the context of the debates about the spread of flexible working practices. (See Section 17.2.)

These points contribute to the differences in hourly pay rates as shown in Table 17.12.

Explaining labour market inequalities between ethnic groupings

These inequalities have sometimes been explained by the idea that ethnic minorities, along with women, occupy a secondary labour market. This idea is explained by Webb as follows:

It is often argued that the 'secondary workforce' is composed of a number of groups which when needed can be channelled into jobs of low status and pay, and that ethnic minorities as well as the majority of women are such groups. Ethnic-minority women in the labour market may have a double handicap and form a very distinct segment in terms of levels of participation and types of occupation.

(Webb, 1982, p. 166)

Dual labour market theory

The notion that secondary labour markets exist is a development of the broadly Weberian notions of Rex and Tomlinson (1979). They argued that there are dual labour markets, with a primary labour market consisting of well-paid secure jobs, and a secondary labour market with low wages and poor working conditions. They asserted that this, along with discrimination in housing, meant that ethnic minorities did not identify with the white working class. This analysis has latterly been developed into the structural version of the underclass thesis.

Reserve-army-of-labour thesis

Marxist theorists have argued that ethnic minorities constitute a reserve army of labour, forming a distinctive strata within the working class because of the discrimination they face from racism.

They argue that this position derives from the fact that capitalism faced labour shortages, having exhausted the supply of indigenous women, and therefore turned to immigration as a source of a reserve pool of cheap labour which could be exploited.

The issue of whether this means that they constitute a part of the working class distinctly separate from white workers, or merely a disadvantaged part of the working class, is a source of debate among Marxists, with Castles and Kosack (1973) taking the former position and Phizacklea and Miles (1980) taking the latter.

Mason (1995), in his book *Race and Ethnicity in Modern Britain*, points out that the position of ethnic minorities has been affected by the fact that large-scale migration in the 1950s (see Section 17.9) occurred because there were labour shortages. This meant that white workers could move up into higher level jobs, leaving the worst jobs for the new immigrants. This, and continuing racism, affects their position today.

One contemporary example of the argument that racism contributes to the ethnic composition of the workforce arose in relation to a dispute at Ford UK where racism was alleged. *Guardian* journalist Seamus Milne (1997) reported that, while 45 per cent of Ford shop-floor workers are from ethnic minorities, only 2 per cent of prized jobs as drivers in Ford's truck fleet are.

Contemporary theories of changes in the workplace

We will now consider the debates surrounding the notion of a growth of flexibility in labour markets, and the transition to post-industrial and post-Fordist societies that has been suggested ('the second industrial revolution').

Theories of the post-industrial society suggest that we are moving from a period dominated by manufacturing industry and manual workers, to one where the service sector and non-manual workers dominate. This has implications for debates about the class composition of the workforce.

The more recent theories of a transition to post-Fordism also have implications for class analysis, since they invariably also suggest either a decline in manual work, or the creation of important divisions within the working class. In effect, therefore, both these theories by implication consider the changing class composition of the workforce.

The reason such a notion has arisen is the observation that the way we organize work has undergone a number of dramatic changes in recent years. The first element of this concerns the changing distribution of employment in terms of the three sectors of the economy, namely the primary, secondary and tertiary sectors:

- By *primary* sector is meant employment in agriculture and extraction, mainly mining.
- By *secondary sector* is meant employment in manufacturing – making things. It is the shift from predominance of the first of these to predominance of the second which is the central process underlying the industrial revolution.
- The *tertiary sector* means employment in service industries such as banking, hotel work or cleaning. One of the important trends noticed in recent years has been the rise of jobs in the service sector and the decline (both absolute and relative) in manufacturing industry, both in the UK and in other western advanced industrial economies.

The move to a service economy?

Ian Marsh *et al.* (1996) point to the change taking place in the distribution of the workforce in the UK as follows:

In the UK in 1946 the manufacturing, construction and mining industries employed about 45 per cent of the labour force. By 1990 this had dwindled to around 20 per cent. The teaching profession now employs more people than mining, the steel industry and shipbuilding combined.

(Marsh *et al.*, 1996, p. 160)

Looking at even more recent figures, Roberts *et al.* (1996) point out that the 1995 *Annual Employment Survey* in Great Britain showed that 75 per cent of employees worked in the services sector and 18 per cent in manufacturing. We can also look at the distribution of employees divided into men and women, and whether they have full-time paid employment or part-time paid employment.

The post-industrial economy thesis

The notion that advanced economies were moving from an industrial to a post-industrial stage first arose in sociology in the 1960s and 1970s. Daniel Bell (1973) argued that we were witnessing such a change characterized, as he saw it, by the change from jobs based on physical strength to mental agility. He argued that this would lead to the growth of a knowledge-based society, and as a result the arena of work would become much more pleasant since the dirty, dangerous jobs associated with industry would be replaced with safer, more pleasant and satisfying jobs which gave scope for the use of one's brain.

Discussion point

Would such a change necessarily make people happier?

C3.1a

Convergence theory

These ideas were also present in 'convergence theory' (Kerr *et al.*, 1973; orig. pub. 1960). This argued that the needs of industrial society meant inevitably that similar levels of inequality and social structure were produced in both capitalist and self-proclaimed communist societies.

The functional imperatives of industrial society would dominate, according to this theory, meaning communist societies would converge with capitalist societies. This would then show that it was not capitalism but *industrialism* that was the key determinant of social structures.

This line of thinking led to the idea that capitalism had now changed its spots and would in the future act as a benevolent mechanism in society, one that would produce a more caring, democratically controlled form of capitalism. This rather optimistic picture of the emergence of post-industrial society has not held up very well in an historical perspective.

Criticisms of the post-industrial economy thesis

In *Prophecy and Progress*, Kumar (1978) argued that the notion of a 'great transformation' was not backed up by the facts. He pointed out that as long ago as 1900 the majority of workers in Scotland were in the service sector, and that for the UK as a whole manufacturing employees were never in a majority, reaching a peak of 48 per cent in 1955.

Webster (1995) has argued that no capitalist economy has ever had a majority of its workforce employed in manufacturing industry. The obvious point is that the image of industrial society against which the theories of post-industrial society were counter-posed was a severe exaggeration. We should also consider the nature of those service sector jobs that have emerged and see whether they measure up to Bell's notion of a knowledge-based society.

Deindustrialization

In fact what appears to have happened is not the emergence of nice well-paid technologically-based jobs, but instead the emergence of service sector jobs that in many respects are similar to or even worse than the manufacturing jobs they have to some extent replaced.

Callinicos, a Marxist social theorist, provides the following description of the process in California:

Deindustrialization has been a painful process, with socially regressive results. Nowhere is this better illustrated than in California, the paradigmatic 'postindustrial society', strategically located on the Eastern edge of the dynamic Pacific economy, with 70 per cent of its workforce employed in services in 1985, ideally suited, thanks to Hollywood and Silicon Valley, to supply the world market with entertainments and information. The 1979–82 recession virtually wiped out the state's car, steel, tyre and other basic industries. High unemployment combined with an influx of (often illegal) immigrants to push down wages. Labour-intensive low-wage industries consequently expanded, in manufacturing as well as services. Employment in textiles, where California can now compete with Hong Kong and Taiwan, grew. As Mike Davis commented, 'LA industry has been turned back from "Fordism" to "Bloody Taylorism" of an almost East Asian standard.' A similar pattern can be observed in service industries, whose wages are on average 40 to 50 per cent lower than in basic manufacturing. Consequently, despite California's fabled wealth and dynamic growth rates, the state's per capita income fell from 123 per cent of the US average in 1960 to 116 per cent in 1980 and 113 per cent in 1984.

(Callinicos, 1989, p. 125)

The promise of high-quality lifestyles emerging from the shift to a service economy does not seem to have been fulfilled. However, while it is clear that service sector jobs have grown and manufacturing jobs have declined in some countries, this is far from being true on a global level. There is evidence of some manufacturing industry shifting to parts of the newly industrializing countries; and furthermore, in the advanced economy showing the most economic success in the 1980s and 1990s, Japan, the proportion of service sector workers actually fell between 1960 and 1982.

The idea that shifting to a post-industrial service economy will provide economic success and growing prosperity does not seem to have universal support, and the service sector jobs that have been created do not appear to adhere to the vision outlined by Bell in 1973.

It seems that we need to seek alternative explanations for the shifts that are occurring, and this leads on to a consideration of arguments that focus on the growth of flexibility in the period after the 1970s.

Flexible production methods and post-Fordism

It was against the backdrop of problems in the system of mass production characterized as Fordism that the foregoing theories developed. But what is meant by this term?

Fordism

The term was coined by Antonio Gramsci (1971a) writing in his prison notebooks on Americanism and Fordism in the early 1930s. Gramsci highlighted how the adoption of mass production techniques by Henry Ford in 1913, utilizing some of the ideas of 'scientific management', changed the face of work. Such production required economic stability, and mass consumption changed other aspects of society, notably government economic policy and the advent of advertising and marketing on a mass level. Gramsci also argued that there was a clear element of social control involved in Fordism:

In America, rationalization of work and prohibition are undoubtedly connected. The enquiries conducted by the industrialists into the workers' private lives and the inspection services created by some firms to control the 'morality' of their workers are necessities of the new methods of work.

(Gramsci, 1971a, p. 302)

The crisis of Fordism, leading to post-Fordism

The Fordist system fell into crisis in the 1970s, and the possible consequences of this led to talk of a transition from Fordism to post-Fordism.

The proponents of post-Fordism argue that the economic changes in the 1970s signalled the end of Fordism. This was partly because the economic stability it required was undermined, but also because consumers were no longer happy to put up with the mass-produced range of goods Fordism offered and were looking for more choice. The system therefore lost legitimacy and was no longer able to operate either as a mode of production or as a mode of regulation.

This led to the emergence of firms operating on 'post-Fordist principles', described by Watson (1995) as follows:

The post-Fordist regime of accumulation replaces the Fordist one with an emphasis on quality-competitive production for shifting and differentiated markets using qualified and highly skilled flexible labour, and is supported by a post-Fordist mode of regulation in which there is reduction in state intervention in labour markets, a shift of responsibility for welfare provision from the state to the employers or private individuals, and a more flexible and varied approach to employment relations.

(Watson, 1995, p. 343)

Within this argument about the end of Fordism, a number of propositions have emerged with slightly differing conclusions. We will therefore look at each in turn before going on to evaluate the whole debate about flexibility in the workplace.

Flexible specialization

The key work here is that of Piore and Sabel (1984). They argue that when technological choices are at issue we are in a period of industrial divides, and these choices affect the social development of society for decades afterwards.

The first such industrial divide occurred with the development of mass production techniques at the end of the nineteenth century, and the central argument of their book is that we are now at the threshold of a second industrial divide. They outline the choice this involves:

The reactions of firms and nations to the economic dislocations of the 1970s point to two contrasting ways out of the crisis. The world-car strategy suggests that one way is multinational Keynesianism:

the extension of the principles of institutional organization that gave rise to the corporation and to macroregulation. ... By contrast, the spread of flexible specialization suggests that the way out of the crisis requires a shift of technological paradigm and a new system of regulation. If recovery proceeds by this path, then the 1970s and 1980s will be seen in retrospect as a turning point in the history of mechanization: a time when industrial society returned to craft methods of production regarded since the nineteenth century as marginal – and proved them to be essential to prosperity.

(Piore and Sabel, 1984, pp. 251–2)

Although they argue that either outcome is possible, they themselves seem to prefer the move to flexible specialization, largely because they feel this offers the prospect of jobs that are satisfying. The advent of computers is a key component of this:

The computer is ... a machine that meets Marx's definition of an artisan's tool: it is an instrument that responds to and extends the productive capacities of the user. ... The advent of the computer restores human control over the production process; machinery again is subordinated to the operator.

(Piore and Sabel, 1984, p. 261)

The Third Italy

In studies of how this operates, commentators point to what has been called the Third Italy – 'third' because it is not the mass production industrial north, nor the still agriculturally dominated south. It broadly encompasses the areas of Tuscany and Emilia-Romagna, where production is dominated by small firms and workshops. The small workshops and factories in these areas produce high-quality sophisticated design-conscious products. Cooperation with other firms was also part of the set-up, based on sub-contracting, which built relationships between these small firms, as did their tendency to group together to obtain specialist services such as accountancy and marketing. These local traditions were underpinned by the role of socialist and communist councils in the area.

As a result of this flexible specialization the area has experienced good economic growth and high standards of living, all combined with stable employment and social provision.

Flexible specialization in the USA

Piore and Sabel consider it possible to identify certain areas in the USA that might also become areas of flexible specialization, notably Boston and Palo Alto in California. However, this would require the setting up of the social infrastructure which is a part of the Italian example.

The example of Benetton

The example most often quoted of flexible specialization, Benetton, might also be seen as a negation of this form of organization. Benetton is a company employing only about 1500 people directly, but working with a number of sub-contractors. Their outlets are franchised but with an on-line link allowing them to make immediate note of trends in consumption which, it is claimed, allows them to respond to market trends in 10 days. However, while Benetton might have started out as a small firm, it is now a multinational giant and therefore might be seen as coming:

... ever closer to the 'world car model' that is the very antithesis of the post-Fordist concept.

(Kumar, 1995, p. 62)

In summary, the notion of flexible specialization offers an optimistic view emphasizing the possibilities of an end to alienating work on mass production assembly lines and the return of craftwork.

Flexibility: the 'new capitalism'?

Sennett (1998) provides a resounding critique of the effects on people's lives of the demands of flexibility in the workplace. He argues that the term 'flexibility' is used today as the latest way of avoiding the notion of oppression present in the phrase 'capitalist system'. His argument is, however, that flexibility is oppressive by impinging on the lives of people caught up in the way work is organized today. This is what he calls the 'new capitalism':

In work, the traditional career progressing step by step through the corridors of one or two institutions is withering; so is the deployment of a single set of skills through the course of a working life. Today, a young American with at least two years of college can expect to change jobs at least eleven times in the course of working, and change his or her skill base at least three times during those forty years of labour.

(Sennett, 1998, p. 22)

The most important consequence of this is that there is no 'long term', and this impacts on other areas of a person's life. For instance, Sennett points to the way it impacts on family life, where it leads to patterns of 'keep moving, don't commit and don't sacrifice'. This, he argues, means that children do not see commitment from their parents, and this will feed through into their family habits. Ultimately, therefore, the emphasis on flexibility at work leads to the corrosion of the human character and has negative consequences for society as a whole:

Questions about flexibility address matters of political economy proper, and do find contrasting formulations today in America and Europe. Are there any limits to how much people are forced to bend?

(Sennett, 1998, p. 53)

He points to the contrast between:

- the form of organization common in continental Europe (what he calls the 'Rhine model'), where management and trade unions share power, and where strong welfare states provide a safety net; and

- the form of organization emphasized in the Anglo-American model based on flexibility, neo-liberal free-market economics with only a minimal role for the state and reductions in the role of the welfare state.

He argues that, contrary to some assertions, both models can provide the advantages of flexibility in the workplace (quoting the work of Piore and Sabel discussed above) but that the social effects of the two models are very different:

- The Anglo-American model leads to relatively low levels of unemployment, but a massive rise in income inequality.

- The Rhine model avoids these excesses of income inequality, but it suffers from high unemployment.

The rise of flexibility has led to changes which have undermined the social obligations and institutions of the post-World War II world. Sennett points to the development of flexitime which rose with the entry of women into the workforce in large numbers. This does have advantages in terms of juggling work and domestic responsibilities, but the new freedom it promised is largely illusory:

In the revolt against routine, the appearance of a new freedom is deceptive. Time in institutions and for individuals has been unchained from the iron cage of the past but subjected to new, top-down controls and surveillance. The time of flexibility is the time of a new power. Flexibility begets disorder, but not freedom from restraint.

(Sennett, 1998, p. 59)

He thinks that this has effects on the whole of society, often leading to defensive calls for the restoration of community to avoid feeling totally alone in the perpetually changing world. He argues that this is reinforced by the neo-liberal attacks on the welfare state, presenting those who rely on it as parasites and talking of a dependency culture.

However, the notion of community embodied in communitarian arguments is not one he finds very appealing, since it emphasizes unity and sees conflict as a wholly negative and threatening thing. He argues instead that through conflict we learn and may eventually learn to work together. This allows us to feel needed, since there are others who need help. It is this deep sense of belonging which is being eroded by the new capitalism, and Sennett believes this may lead to its downfall:

... a regime which provides human beings no deep reasons to care about one another cannot long preserve its legitimacy.

(Sennett, 1998, p. 148)

Jobless growth and the new face of work

A similar focus on the major change in present-day work patterns can be found in the work of Dahrendorf (1999). He argues that debates about the welfare state have often assumed work to be a constant, but that is not the case, with what was regarded as the typical work pattern about to become a minority phenomenon. He points to six key changes that will impact on social policy in the future:

- The relationship between economic growth and growth in employment no longer holds. Since the 1970s we have had growth but this has been jobless growth. He cites figures for Japan, where between 1970 and 1995 the economy (measured by GDP per head) grew by 150 per cent, but employment rose by only 2 per cent. In the USA in the same period the economy grew by 50 per cent and employment by only 25 per cent; while in the UK the economy grew by 60 per cent and employment actually fell by 4 per cent.

- While employment opportunities may continue in the public sector, in the market sector of the economy, such as financial services, the trend to jobless growth is at its greatest. The emphasis on the market sector in recent years has therefore exacerbated this trend.

- The number of people in permanent full-time employment has seen a significant decline since the 1970s. In Germany, 84 per cent of those in employment had such 'typical' contracts in 1970, but by 1995 this had fallen to 68 per cent.

- The key areas of employment growth have been in part-time, temporary or time-limited contracts as well as in unpaid voluntary work. A welfare state set up on the premise that most people are sustained by income from full-time employment will therefore no longer meet the needs of people.

- The age at which people retire is falling. In the UK only 56 per cent of 55- to 64-year-old men were in paid employment in 1995. Equivalent figures for other European countries are 49 per cent in Germany, 42 per cent in Italy, and 38 per cent in France.

- Changes in what work means also imply changes in what unemployment means.

All these changes imply that there is a need to reconsider how the tax and benefits system and the wider welfare state should operate. The classic welfare state set-up (for instance that based on the Beveridge Report of 1942; see Section 14.3) is based on the assumption that men work full-time and provide for their womenfolk, who remain at home to look after the children. The assumptions about the family in this model have been challenged:

We no longer assume that the nuclear family is the only model. It is time to make a similar leap of understanding with respect to jobs and employment. What used to be typical is about to become a minority phenomenon.

(Dahrendorf, 1999, p. 11)

The minimum wage

In 1999 the Labour government introduced legislation to enforce a minimum wage for most workers. The level of this was set at £3.60 an hour for those aged over 21, £3.00 an hour for those aged 18–21, and £3.20 per hour for those aged 22 or over in the first six months of employ-

ment if they are receiving training. While this will raise the pay of many workers (Table 17.13 shows the going rates before the legislation came into force), there have been criticisms from trade unionists that the minimum levels were set too low.

Table 17.13 The worst-paid job categories

For women	For men
Childcare (£2.83 per hour)	Waiter (£3.00 per hour)
Hairdresser (£2.95)	Kitchen porter (£3.01)
Bar staff (£3.01)	Bar staff (£3.25)
Waitress (£3.06)	Shelf filler (£3.34)
Care assistant (£3.15)	Catering assistant (£3.37)
Kitchen porter (£3.16)	Security guard (£3.45)
Cleaner (£3.17)	Cleaner (£3.53)
Food preparation (£3.23)	Care assistant (£3.53)
Dry cleaner (£3.24)	Car park attendant (£3.55)
Shoe repairer (£3.25)	Dry cleaner (£3.65)
	Hotel porter (£3.65)

Source: Guardian, 29 March 1999, based on New Earnings Survey figures

Disorganized capitalism

Lash and Urry (1987, 1994) argue that we have moved on from an era of organized capitalism, characterized by high levels of state intervention and regulation of the economy, the domination of production by a professional, managerial and technical service class, and the cultural domination of modernism, rationalism and nationalism. The new era is one of 'disorganized capitalism', characterized by the growth of multinational capital, the further growth of a service class, the shift of manufacturing industry to the Third World, and the fragmentation of cultural life with the decline of modernism and the rise of postmodernism.

What differentiates Lash and Urry's analysis from other views is their argument that there are a number of causes of this change, notably the various processes identified by the phrase 'globalization' (on this see Sections 4.2, 6.9 and 15.2). The implication for Lash and Urry is that:

The power of a mass industrial working class to shape society in its own image is for the foreseeable future profoundly weakened.

(Lash and Urry, 1987, p. 311)

The term 'disorganized capitalism' was also used

by Offe (1985a). He means by it that the mechanisms which supposedly organize socio-political systems in welfare state capitalism no longer seem able to fulfil this task (see also Section 14.5). Principally this applies to the trade union movement, which he argues is no longer able to act as the representative of unified working-class interests, owing to the growth of economic and cultural divisions within the working class, and because a number of groups such as the young appear to be turning their backs on the trade union movement.

Offe argues that the trade unions can restore their claim to act as a universal voice only by extending their concerns beyond a consideration of people as employees. Again an implication of this is that the working class and its representatives can no longer be seen as the key component of groups arguing for social change.

Neo-Fordism

The notion of 'Fordism' was most fully developed by the French neo-Marxist 'regulation school', whose notable members were Michel Aglietta (1979) and Alain Lipietz (1987). It is this idea which forms the starting point for post-Fordist theories.

However, the 'regulation school' themselves are skeptical of post-Fordism, arguing instead that what we are witnessing is really a form of 'neo-Fordism' – which is merely the development of new strategies on the part of capitalism to try to survive. Fordism, in its classical form, no longer brings in the profits, so new ways have been developed.

Crucially, they argue, this has involved the development of 'global Fordism'. This means that labour-intensive parts of work have been shifted to parts of the developing world, where the conditions resemble classical Fordism or worse, while the adoption of flexible strategies in the developed world have been aimed at breaking trade unions and labour organizations.

Overall then, on a global level enough remains of the old Fordist methods to talk of neo-Fordism. Therefore, although the crisis of profitability may be staved off by the use of cheap labour in the developing world, the problems which led it into crisis in the 1970s have not been overcome.

Activity

Draw up a table summarizing the main views on a post-Fordist economy considered above. This should contain the names of writers associated with the debate, and an outline of differences between the views. A column can be used to make notes of criticisms of these theories.

C3.2, C3.3

17.3 Workplace change and class formation

In his book *The State We're In*, Will Hutton (1996) considers changes to industrial relations in the UK affected by the Conservative administrations of the 1980s. He comments:

Fifteen years after the Conservatives' election the scope of labour reform exceeded even the wildest dreams of the New Right in the 1970s. There was no regulation of working time; no legally-protected conditions for labour hired under fixed term contracts; no minimum wage legislation; minimal employment protection; and employees had no legal right to representation at the workplace. The OECD, compiling a composite index of these measures, could by the summer of 1994, rank Britain at zero – the lowest, apart from the US, in the industrialized world. With the lack of legislation there was no obligation on employers to treat their workers other than as disposable commodities, or even to pay them fairly.

(Hutton, 1996, p. 95)

There have been major changes in this area, reflecting both the ideology of the New Right concerning trade unions, and the policies by which that ideology has been implemented.

The New Right and industrial relations

The New Right believe that the free market works, and that without any imperfections the wage rate will settle at a level that leads to full employment. Their explanation for unemployment therefore centres on those institutions which attempt to limit the operation of the free market, notably the welfare state (see also Section 14.4) and trade unions.

Discussion point

To what extent do you agree that trade unions are the chief cause of unemployment?

C3.1a

As a result, trade unions came under critical fire from the very first Conservative administration in 1979. That pattern continued, leading to the situation described by Hutton above, where to be a worker in the UK was to be totally bereft of rights.

The New Right's assault on trade unions

The implementation of legislative changes impacting on employment and trade unions shows how this ideology was actually enacted.

The 1980 and 1982 Employment Acts

In 1980 an Employment Act was passed which placed restrictions on picketing by making it illegal to picket anywhere other than at your own place of work, and by outlawing secondary action (i.e. action against other companies). A further Employment Act in 1982 made it possible for employers to sue trade unions for damages, and to take out court injunctions to stop trade unions taking certain actions.

The miners' strike, 1984–85

The effect of trade union legislation can be seen in perhaps the most important dispute of recent years, the miners' strike of the mid-1980s. In March 1984, miners at Cortonwood pit came out on strike when their mine was threatened with closure. This escalated into a national miners' dispute as other areas joined in to support the protest – as allowed under the union rules. However, it became clear that the government had put in place plans to defeat the miners (including the stockpiling of vast amounts of mined coal), and part of the reason for this appeared to be a desire to get even for the defeat the miners had inflicted on the previous Conservative government in 1974.

The miners received tremendous levels of support from around the country and inspired the setting up of a number of support groups, most notably Women Against Pit Closures which helped to break down the level of sexism evident in certain parts of the mining community.

The police were quickly called upon, and the following year witnessed a major restriction of free movement, which was described by James Anderton, then Chief Constable of Greater Manchester, as being in some respects like that in totalitarian states. The level of violence inflicted by police in riot gear on protesting miners was broadcast to the whole nation in news reports from Orgreave in South Yorkshire in June 1984.

The miners remained on strike for a year, but their dispute was lost. As a result, the level of pit closures increased.

Subsequent industrial relations legislation

Although it would be possible to say that at this stage the organized trade union movement was somewhat on the defensive, the legal barrage against it continued:

- The Trade Union Act 1984 introduced a requirement that there be secret ballots before any industrial action, and there were new rules for the election of union leaders.

- The Employment Act 1988 provided employees with the right to ignore union ballot results, and not to be disciplined by their union.

- The Employment Act 1989 placed restrictions on paid time off for trade union representatives.

- The Employment Act 1990 made unions liable for the actions of their members, and effectively outlawed the 'closed shop' (only union members allowed at the particular workplace).

- The Trade Union Reform and Employment Rights Act 1993 made it possible for ordinary members of the public to sue unions for losses arising from disputes. Unions now had to provide notice of any industrial action, and all strike ballots had to be conducted by post, to avoid intimidation of the voters.

In 1834 the so-called Tolpuddle Martyrs had been punished by transportation to Australia because of their attempt to form a trade union. The particular forms of democracy and representation which workers had fought for ever since were now being systematically undermined in pursuit of the idea that workers should behave as individuals. The initial impetus for the formation of trade unions was the acknowledgement by workers that as individuals they would always be less powerful than employers, and that their only way to seek to improve their conditions would be to join together in collective representation. This clearly went against the individualistic philosophy of the New Right and the legislation described above is the result.

Activity

a Construct a table summarizing all the pieces of legislation mentioned in the preceding pages. Place them in date order.

b Note the year and title and then summarize its effect in your own words.

c Use this information to evaluate the effect of legislative change on the trade unions in the 1980s and 1990s.

C3.2, C3.3

Trade unionism today

John Williams (1997) points out that, overall, only 31 per cent of UK workers are now a member of a union. For workers under 25 the figure is just 7 per cent. It is on the basis of figures like these that there has been talk of the end of trade unionism.

However, while it is true that trade unions have been put on the defensive, it should not be assumed that all protest has stopped. Indeed it is often the case that trade union activity has been instigated by the changes introduced by New Right reforms to the economy, with managers trying to reassert the right to manage and annoying workers to such an extent that they take action to defend themselves. The next sub-section will therefore consider in more detail recent examples where, despite the unfavourable legal context, workers have continued to act to defend their interests.

Discussion point

Why do you think young people seem relatively uninterested in trade unions?

C3.1a

Union strategy in contemporary Britain

Debate about trade union strategy as a whole has tended to be divided between the broadly Weberian approach of Batstone (1984, 1988) and the Marxist approach of Darlington (1994).

Eric Batstone

Batstone noted that the onslaught on the unions by the Conservatives in the 1980s did not destroy them. There were important levels of continuity in terms of shop-steward and local union organization. In other words, unions were able to continue to represent their members. This point is not at issue in the debate, however, which concerns the reasons why unions have continued to be effective in some instances, and by implication, the choices to be made over strategy for the future.

Batstone argues that the success of trade union shop stewards now and in the future depends on leading stewards adopting a realistic stance towards bargaining with management. Such bargaining should allow them to improve their members' conditions. In essence, the point here is that successful trade unionism will depend on the development of sophisticated bargaining skills, rather than traditional industrial action.

Ralph Darlington

On the basis of his study of trade unionism on Merseyside, Darlington (1994) is critical of the foregoing idea:

My aim is to put Batstone's resolute endorsement of a 'sophisticated' shop steward organization that engages in 'strong bargaining relations' with management to the test of empirical research through the prism of an alternative Marxist theoretical framework.

(Darlington, 1994, p. 5)

Darlington therefore argues instead that the development of these sophisticated shop stewards, which did involve reforms in the 1970s – for instance increasing the level of paid time off for union officials and providing them with more facilities – could be seen as an indicator of the *bureaucratization* of grassroots trade union organization. At its worst, these developments also involved trade union representatives almost acting to police their members, diffusing their potential to take action by talk of the way strikes could harm their negotiations.

In other words, while some gains might have come from negotiations, in the long run the divisions between union members and union representatives that this entailed would lead to a reduction in the ability of the unions to fight if the need arose.

Darlington's solution is for a return to rank and file unionism, with a renewed emphasis on industrial action as the basis for negotiations so that workers are all part of the union action.

'New realism'

In the 1980s and 90s, the development of 'new realism' in the Labour party and the trade unions led to a number of instances in which ordinary union members felt that their union was acting with a concern to secure negotiations rather than to get involved in industrial action. The resulting tension between and within local union representatives is a reflection of the arguments identified by Batstone and Darlington. These tensions were evident in the 1984–85 miners' strike, and it is also clear that they played a role in the Liverpool dockers' strike, as Kennedy and Lavalette (1996) make clear in their book describing the dispute. (See also Section 15.3.)

Class formation and class action

In one major respect, neo-Marxist and neo-Weberian theories are united: they are both based around an 'employment-aggregate' model of class analysis. The main principle of this empirical approach is the statistical analysis of large national datasets which are then grouped into 'social classes'. Crompton (1993), in a review of debates between the various approaches to class, says that this employment-aggregate approach can be located within the broader sociology of class and stratification. The employment-aggregate approach is thus only one strand of class analysis as a whole. During the 1970s the 'action' approach which was emerging in sociology could be seen within class analysis as a range of studies that sought to focus on class processes; that is:

... the mechanisms through which the class structure changed and developed, and how different groups of class actors struggled for advantage within it.

(Crompton, 1996b, p. 20)

The class formation approach

A further approach is known as 'class formation'. The way in which class formation differs from class structure is described as follows:

If class structure refers to the system of positions in the division of labour, class formation, on the other hand, tends to refer to the way in which these groups of people who occupy a common position in

the division of labour may form as a social collectivity on the basis of these positions.

(Savage *et al.*, 1992, p. 226)

Class consciousness and class action

According to Crompton, studies of class formation involve studies of class consciousness and action. These, she says, have often overlapped with level-1 type studies of particular occupational groups, but are often supplemented with contemporary empirical research. Her own joint research (Crompton and Jones, 1984) was one such example of empirical research into the 'proletarianization' of clerical, administrative and managerial workers.

Crompton (1996a) notes that by the 1970s and 80s within the area of empirical approaches to class analysis there had developed a divergence between case studies of class formation on the one hand, and the more quantitative employment-aggregate approach on the other hand.

A recent example of the class-processes approach can be seen in the work of Savage *et al.* (1992). They argue that the 'middle classes' constitute classes in that they form cohesive social entities. Borrowing from Wright they look at how organizational assets can be seen as a source of power for those in middle-class positions. These can be used in conjunction with cultural assets – such as educational credentials – to secure and maintain their position. This study still relies on the use of quantitative class structure data, which is indicative of the difficulty of testing the findings of case studies on which class-formation analysis is based.

It seems that nowhere in sociology is the debate between structure and action more pertinent than in considerations of their relative merits for class analysis. Here perhaps Giddens' structuration thesis provides some hope, on the basis that structure and action are seen as 'two sides of the same coin' – which in terms of class analysis implies the need for study of the dynamic interrelationship between class structure and class processes. The findings based on the former tend to indicate the stability of the class structure and its enduring effects, while studies of class processes tend to portray changes, some of which seem to be undermining the very notion of class.

Rationality

McDonaldization

Rather than penal institutions, Ritzer (1993) believes that fast-food restaurants are the current model for organizations. For him, 'McDonaldization' is:

... a process by which the principles of the fast-food restaurant are coming to dominate more and more sectors of American society as well as the rest of the world.

(Ritzer, 1993, p. 1)

McDonald's, for Ritzer, is the epitome of how consumer culture can be seen as an extension of Weber's rationalization thesis, whereby things are produced for consumers according to strict calculation and predictability, utilizing the material environment to control the behaviour of human beings with, for example, fixed menus, limited options, spartan seats and queue control barriers. Food is therefore produced bureaucratically and dispensed in rational, modernist, Fordist ways:

The fast-food restaurant is Fordist in various ways, most notably in the degree to which it utilises assembly-line principles and technologies. ... While there may be changes in the economy which support the idea of a post-industrial society, the fast-food restaurant and the many other elements of the economy that are modelled after it do not.

(Ritzer, 1996, p. 443)

Thus rationality is alive and well, though the key model now is fast-food restaurants rather than government bureaucracies.

> ### 💬 Discussion point
>
> Do you agree that more and more areas of society are becoming dominated by the principles of McDonaldization? Is this a good thing?
>
> **C3.1a**

Disneyization

Bryman (1999) argues that his notion of 'Disneyization' can serve as a compliment to Ritzer's notion of McDonaldization in allowing us to understand processes at the heart of social and organizational change today.

He argues that Ritzer's key criteria of efficiency, calculability, predictability and control can be found in Disney and other theme parks. This sort of argument has led to the further development of the concept of McDonaldization as outlined in Ritzer and Liska (1997).

However, Bryman argues that this concept really considers Disney as an example only of McDonaldization in the leisure industry, whereas he is interested in how Disney has developed certain phenomena that have achieved significance outside the leisure sphere itself since the first park opened in 1955. He identifies four trends he associates with Disneyization, which are: theming, de-differentiation of consumption, merchandising, and the development of 'emotional labour'.

- *Theming*. From its origins in Disney theme parks, the idea of theming is now spreading wide into restaurants, pubs, hotels and cruise ships. In Las Vegas virtually everything is themed, with hotels depicted as Ancient Egypt, Ancient Rome or Olde England, for instance. As well as these arenas, theming is now spreading to shopping centres, airports and other environments. Themed amusements have therefore spread leading to permanent themed environments.

- *De-differentiation of consumption*. By this is meant the way in which forms of consumption become locked together and are hard to separate: 'Thus we see in the Disney parks a tendency for shopping, eating, hotel accommodation and theme park visiting to become inextricably interwoven' (Bryman, 1999, p. 34). Most leisure attractions now include shops of some sort, and increasingly shopping centres are including leisure facilities of some sort, such as activities for children in school holidays.

- *Merchandising*. Copyrighted goods are promoted and sold. The sale of Mickey Mouse merchandise is perhaps the best example of this, and the sale of merchandise is what financed Disney's improved cartoon animation techniques. More recently, with films such as *Lion King* and *Jurassic Park*, there has been a vast outpouring of merchandised products, sometimes making more in profits than the original commodity. This process has now spread far and wide, with products linked to Thomas the Tank Engine, Wallace and Gromitt, and Noddy.

- *Emotional labour*. In relation to work in these new areas, Bryman argues that McDonaldization was analysed largely using the categories of deskilling developed by Braverman. However, Ritzer pointed to one new feature, namely the scripting of interaction – the 'Have a nice day!' phenomenon. Bryman argues that it goes further than this, involving manipulating the way workers view themselves and feel about themselves. This internal aspect is not a feature of McDonaldization in the way that overt behaviour is. Bryman argues that the point is to control employee behaviour both through scripted interaction and through emotional labour, to try to show that workers are having fun too and therefore not really having to work.

Rationalization and consumerism

It is important to note that there are clear differences between the concepts of McDonaldization and Disneyization. Ritzer's McDonaldization suggests that rationalization is still the key process in society, and McDonaldization is seen as the latest stage in a process outlined in Max Weber's work on rationality.

The concept of Disneyization, on the other hand, derives from an emphasis on consumerism and consumer culture:

The identification of Disneyization with theories of consumer culture seems to imply that whereas McDonaldization is a modern phenomenon, Disneyization is a post-modern one. ... Certainly there are many features of Disneyization that are frequently associated with post-modernity: the proliferation of signs, de-differentiation of institutional spheres, depthlessness, cultivated nostalgia, and the problematisation of authenticity and reality. However it is important not to fall headlong into an immediate association with postmodernity.

(Bryman, 1999, p. 43)

Bryman argues that this is because consumers still look for reassuring aspects of modernity – such as security, comfort, hygiene and reliability – in the Disneyized world. Nonetheless, Bryman does point to the fact that, since the concepts come from very different theoretical traditions, the way they do or do not fit together is problematic.

Defining and operationalizing the concept of class

Alongside the protracted debates both within and between neo-Marxist and neo-Weberian schools of thought about the theoretical meaning of class and its empirical applications, there have been other – less theoretically informed – attempts to operationalize the concept. These have tended to be based on the defining characteristics of occupations, such as skill or prestige.

Objective definitions of class

The Registrar-General's definition of social class

The Registrar-General's classification was devised:

... so as to secure that as far as possible, each category is homogeneous in relation to the general standing in the community of the occupations concerned. This criterion is naturally correlated with ... other factors such as education and economic environment, but it has no direct relationship to the average level of remuneration of particular occupations.

(HMSO, 1966; quoted in Crompton, 1993, p. 53)

This indicates that the Registrar-General's social class (RGSC) scale is based on the assumption of a hierarchy of occupational status, reflecting relative 'standing in the community' but closely related to educational credentials and skill requirements. Thus many have seen this as more accurately described as a status classification rather than a class one.

However, apart from a shift in emphasis from occupational prestige to skill as the basis of ranking in 1980, from 1911 until the 1991 Census (see also Section 9.6) this was the main way in which social class was measured in official statistics as well as in sociological research.

The RG model

The RG model divides the population into six classes (since 1971) as in Table 17.14, which also shows their distribution.

Table 17.14 Social class distribution of the economically active population, by RG category (percentages)

Class	Description	1971	1981	1991
I	Professional	4	4	5
II	Managerial and technical	18	22	28
IIINM	Skilled non-manual	21	22	23
IIIM	Skilled manual	28	26	21
IV	Semi-skilled manual	1	19	15
V	Unskilled manual	8	7	6

Sources: Censuses 1971, 1981, 1991

Activity

a According to the Registrar-General's classifications in Table 17.14, which class has experienced the biggest percentage point increase in size since 1971?

b Identify the classes that have increased in size and those that have decreased.

C3.2, C3.3

The key division, as with most occupationally based schemes, is between the manual and non-manual categories. Thus classes I, II and IIINM are said to be non-manual and are also taken to represent the 'middle classes', while the remaining (IIIM, IV and V) consist of manual workers and are taken to represent the 'working classes'.

Since the scheme assumed that the hierarchy accurately reflected the regard in which each group was held, the belief that manual workers were inferior resulted in them being placed at the bottom of the class structure. The assumption of shared values is integral to this idea of a mutually agreed status hierarchy, and it places the RG scale within a functionalist perspective to stratification, as does the notion of the naturalness and necessity of inequality.

Problems with the RG model

A number of problems flow from the fact that the RG scale does not bear a direct relationship to the relative earning power of the various occupations. There are anomalies, such as the fact that priests (placed in class I) have an income which is considerably less than others placed lower down the scale.

As it is based on 'general standing in the community' the RG scale owes more to ideas of inequality based on status than to social class. Since assessments of status are essentially subjective, this might be thought of as undermining the RG scale's claims of objectivity.

Finally, the reliance on occupation as the determinant of class membership means that those without paid employment do not feature in it in their own right. This has proved particularly troublesome in terms of locating women in the class structure, as the unit of class analysis is taken as 'male head of household'. Although it is still used widely for long-term comparisons in socio-medical data, the RGSC is now seldom used for most professional sociological purposes.

A new definition of class from Census 2001

Because of the problems with the RGSC, the Office of Population Censuses and Surveys (as it was then called – now the Office for National Statistics, ONS) commissioned the Economic and Social Research Council (ESRC) to review the existing classifications.

The ensuing report, *Constructing Classes: Towards a New Social Classification for the UK* (Rose and O'Reilly, 1997), states that occupationally based classifications will continue to be important tools for policy analysis, despite the problems with the current classifications. On practical grounds, they are based on routinely and widely collected data; and on theoretical grounds they are useful in that a person's employment situation is a key determinant of life chances.

The *Times* article 'Class tightens its grip on Britain' gives a fair view of what the new class structure will be (see also Figure 17.5).

This scheme can in some ways be seen as an extension of Goldthorpe's class schema shown in Figure 17.5 (he was a consultant to the ESCR committee). It is still subject to a number of criticisms, not least of which is the issue of the appropriateness of such a scheme for the classification of women, and the apparent incongruities involved in placing certain occupations in the same class, as for instance in the case of lorry drivers and traffic wardens.

Evaluation of occupationally based classifications of class

Some of the advantages and disadvantages of these schemes are given below:

Class tightens its grip on Britain

MARK HENDERSON

A report published today recommends increasing the number of classes used to categorise the public in government documents. The report finds that the current classification of people according to six occupational groups is out of date and misleading. It proposes eight social classes, still based on on occupation but with tighter descriptions and new categories.

The system takes into account the "underclass" of people who have never worked or are long-term unemployed or ill. It also splits one of the most visible social groups in 1980s Britain, the skilled manual workers known by market researchers as C2s.

David Rose, Professor of Sociology at Essex University, said "if anything, occupational class has become more significant as we learn to live with the flexible labour market. The demise of the unions and a job for life mean a person's relationship to their job is a defining part of who they are." Professionals, employers and managers still had much greater job security than employees, leading to crucial class distinctions.

If the statistics office approves the changes, the revised structure should be ready for the 2001 census. It suggests eight classes [see Figure 19.5], with new ones for the self-employed and the long-term unemployed, and dividing up skilled manual workers between several groups. Employers and managers in large firms would join professionals in Class 1, with smaller employers and "associate professionals" such as nurses and law firm staff going in Class 2.

Class 3 would largely replicate the present class IIIN, including sales staff and secretaries, while Class 4 would be for self-employed non-professionals, such as driving instructors and carpenters. Class 5 would represent employed skilled manual workers and supervisors, with Class 6 made up of "routine occupations" such as lorry-drivers and traffic wardens. At the bottom will be "elementary occupations" such as waiters, labourers and cleaners in Class 7, and the underclass in Class 8.

Professor Rose said that the self-employed and the non-employed could not fairly be included with any other category, and the poor employment rights experienced by waiters, labourers and cleaners, many of whom work on a casual basis, set them apart from other manual workers.

Source: Adapted from the *Times*, 15 December 1997

Advantages

- Such schemes are reasonably easy to understand.

- They are used regularly in research and are therefore familiar.

- They allow comparisons over time where a standard measure is repeated, and thus facilitate replication.

- For most people their occupation provides virtually all their income, and so this is a potent indicator of inequality.

Disadvantages

- Occupational dynamics make comparisons over time difficult or misleading.

- It is debatable whether a single criterion such as occupational status can capture the full significance of class, particularly in the Marxist sense of the word.

- Occupational scales are essentially descriptive, saying little about class processes or class relations. In particular they deny the existence of the capitalist class and are unable to explain the inequalities that arise from the ownership of capital.

- It is difficult to classify those who do not have a paid job. Classification on the basis of a previous job is unsatisfactory as it implies that an unemployed sales representative has the same command over resources as an employed teacher.

- Married women are not classified by social class according to their own occupation.

- There are anomalies between occupational class and income. Someone who earns less than someone else may well be placed in a higher class.

- The class position of people is based on their current position in the occupational class hierarchy. This does not indicate either their class origins or their future aspirations.

Overall, then, while the use of 'occupation' as a proxy for 'social class' has some advantages these tend to be administrative rather than theoretical. Edgell (1993) describes how reviews of the history of official occupational classification schemes have concluded that they are an obsolete and simplistic, arbitrary and crude, but well used, measure of social inequality.

Class	Description	Examples
1	Professionals Employers Administrators Managers in companies employing 25 or more people[1]	Doctor, lawyer, scientist, company director
2	Associate professionals Employers Administrators Managers in companies employing fewer than 25 people Supervisors	Nurse[1], sales manager, laboratory technician
3	Intermediate occupations in administrative, clerical, sales and service work	Secretary, nursery nurse, salesman, computer operator
4	Self-employed non-professionals	Plumber[3], driving instructor
5	Other supervisors Craft and related workers	Factory foreman, joiner
6	Routine occupations in manufacturing and services	Lorry driver[2], traffic warden, assembly-line worker
7	Elementary occupations	Fast-food waiter, supermarket cashier, cleaner, labourer[1]
8	Never worked Long-term unemployed Long-term sick	

Figure 17.5 The new classification of class
Source: Times, 15 December 1997
[1]Moves up a class; [2]Moves down a class

Discussion point

'It is difficult to conduct credible sociological research into class without using some sort of occupational-based scheme to categorize people, but the existing ones all seem to have their drawbacks.' Discuss this proposition. If it has any truth, should we still use these schemes?

C3.1a

Subjective definitions of class

In most of the objective class schemes noted above, people are assigned to a class according to the criterion of what job they do. But many people thus defined as middle class might well describe themselves as working class. The implication of this is that we can tell very little about levels of *class consciousness* from objective classifications alone. An example of the complexity of the relationship between objective and subjective data can be seen from Table 17.15.

The anomalies produced by using objective and subjective classifications are dramatically illustrated also by the following example. In 1989 a MORI poll showed that 30 per cent of people described themselves as middle class and 67 per cent described themselves as working class. This contrasts with the objective data from the 1991 Census which showed that, of the economically active population, 56 per cent were middle class and 42 per cent were working class.

Table 17.15 How a sample of people saw themselves, compared with their objective classification (percentages)

Subjective social class	Objective social class					
	I	II	IIINM	IIIM	IV	V
Middle class	74	71	48	37	21	29
Working class	11	23	42	56	66	62

Source: Reid (1989)

There have to be doubts about the wisdom of relying on objective measurements of class. This suggests the need for greater understanding of the *perceptions* of various groups of 'class actors'.

17.4 Concepts and measures of poverty

The distinction between absolute and relative poverty centres around whether our conception of human need is based on biological notions or social notions. Oppenheim and Harker of the Child Poverty Action Group provide the following definitions of absolute and relative poverty:

A definition of absolute poverty assumes that it is possible to define a minimum standard of living based on a person's biological needs for food, water, clothing and shelter. ... [Relative] poverty is defined in relation to a generally accepted standard of living in a specific society at a specific time and goes beyond basic biological needs.

(Oppenheim and Harker, 1996, pp. 7 and 9)

Absolute poverty: Seebohm Rowntree

Application of the idea of a subsistence or absolute approach to poverty is seen clearly in the work of Seebohm Rowntree (1901) in York.

In order to derive a measure of poverty in York, he devised a *subsistence poverty line* based on the monetary value of subsistence needs. In relation to food this led him to calculate the cost of a standard diet similar to that offered in the workhouse – though as John Scott (1994) points out, as he did not include provision for fresh meat his 'diet' was even harsher than that offered to paupers in the York workhouse.

In his original survey in 1899, Rowntree found that a total of 28 per cent of the population of York were in poverty. Since the main cause of poverty identified by Rowntree was low wages, his work undermined the idea behind the Poor Law – which was that the main cause of poverty was indolence and laziness. This fed into pressure for social reform, leading towards establishment of the welfare state.

Rowntree (1937, 1941; and Lavers, 1951) conducted follow-up surveys in later years. These showed that the proportion in poverty had fallen to 18 per cent in 1936 and 1.5 per cent in 1950. This situation was also seen as a success story for the welfare state.

Rowntree's work is important for the effect it had on sociological and governmental thinking on the issue of poverty. The suggestion that the problem of poverty had been solved certainly fitted in with the notion of affluence which became influential in both popular and sociological thinking in the 1950s and early 60s.

Defining relative poverty

Not everyone was convinced that the problem of poverty had been solved by the 1960s. That period witnessed the rediscovery of poverty largely through the work of Abel-Smith and Townsend (1965). In a study comparing the incidence of poverty in 1960 with that in 1954, they found that there had been an increase, from 7.8 per cent of people in 1954 to 14.2 per cent in 1960. Abel-Smith and Townsend demonstrated that, far from the welfare state removing poverty, the levels of benefits paid out were so low and required such strict behaviour of the recipients that poverty could still exist and grow despite the welfare state.

The rediscovery of poverty

The trend identified is completely the reverse of that seen in the series of studies undertaken by Rowntree, and at first sight this seems a contradiction. It is not, however, because Abel-Smith and Townsend were using a very different definition of poverty – which came to be known as 'relative poverty'. *This rests on the idea that our needs in contemporary society are more than simply biological needs, but include the need to be able to participate in the normal activities of society.* Townsend outlined the condition of relative poverty as follows:

Poverty can be defined objectively and applied consistently only in terms of the concept of relative deprivation. ... Individuals, families and groups in the population can be said to be in poverty when they lack the resources to obtain the types of diet, participate in the activities and have the living conditions and amenities which are customary ... in the societies to which they belong.

(Townsend, 1979, p. 31)

An important implication of this is that what

counts as poverty differs from society to society and from time to time, as social experiences and social expectations change in a way that biological needs generally do not. Deprivation consists of more than simply biological want; it means lacking the resources to meet socially expected ways of living and therefore to make choices about how to live one's life.

Townsend's surveys on poverty – the deprivation index

Townsend followed up his early work with a national survey on poverty and a later survey of poverty in London, allowing comparisons with Charles Booth's (1902) pioneering social survey of London.

In order to operationalize his definition of poverty to conduct this empirical work, Townsend constructed a 'deprivation index'. This consisted of a list of 60 items that acted as indicators of lifestyle, the absence of which would constitute evidence of deprivation. He felt these items both reflected a range of lifestyles and allowed him to test the sort of lifestyles that are common to the majority of the population.

To create his deprivation index, Townsend selected 12 items the lack of which were all linked to low income. He then set out to discover the percentage of households who lacked these items (see Table 17.16).

The question arises of how many items a household must lack in order to suffer from dep-

rivation and be classed as in poverty. Townsend used statistical techniques to show that there is a point at which lack of household resources leads to a qualitative reduction in social participation. This he found occurred when there was a household income of less than 140 per cent of the 'supplementary benefit' level. This level of income constituted the threshold of deprivation. As a result he concluded that 22.9 per cent of the population were in poverty.

Townsend asserted that this statistical measure of deprivation constituted an *objective measure of relative poverty*. This reinforced the earlier claims by Abel-Smith and Townsend that it was possible for poverty to exist even given the existence of the welfare state and its associated benefits.

Other indicators identified by Townsend

Townsend's work also calculated the extent of poverty using two other indicators. Although Townsend himself did not favour these measures, they have continued to play a part in the ensuing debate. They are:

- *the state's effective standard of poverty*, simply measured by calculating the number of people living below an income, achieved by adding together the existing levels of supplementary benefit (now income support) and an amount for housing costs – on this basis 6.1 per cent of the population were in poverty

Table 17.16 Townsend's deprivation index

Characteristic	Percentage of population
1 Has not had a week's holiday away from home in last 12 months	53.6
2 *Adults only*. Has not had a relative or friend to the home for a meal or snack in the last 4 weeks	33.4
3 *Adults only*. Has not been out in the last 4 weeks to a relative or friend for a meal or snack	45.1
4 *Children only* (under 15). Has not had a friend to play or to tea in the last 4 weeks	36.3
5 *Children only*. Did not have party on last birthday	56.6
6 Has not had an afternoon or evening out for entertainment in the last two weeks	47.0
7 Does not have fresh meat (including meals out) as many as four days a week	19.3
8 Has gone through one or more days in the past fortnight without a cooked meal	7.0
9 Has not had a cooked breakfast most days of the week	67.3
10 Household does not have a refrigerator	45.1
11 Household does not usually have a Sunday joint (3 in 4 times)	25.9
12 Household does not have sole use of four amenities indoors (flush WC; sink or washbasin and cold-water tap; fixed bath or shower; and gas or electric cooker)	21.4

Source: Townsend (1979, p. 250)

- *the relative income measure*, which calculates the number of people living on less than half average income – on this basis 9.2 per cent of the population were in poverty.

 Activity

Write out your own definitions of absolute and relative poverty and then make a list of the various ways these have been operationalized by the various researchers discussed above.

C3.2, C3.3

Absolute versus relative: the continuing debate

Arising from the different definitions, estimates of the extent of poverty in the UK in the period after the 1960s vary widely, from 1.5 to 22.9 per cent. This discrepancy clearly has implications because poverty is seen as a serious social problem which governments must address.

The adoption of a *relative* definition of poverty is explicitly a critique of the adequacy of an absolute definition. So far, in order to provide a clear contrast we have not delved into the details. This subsection will highlight the points of argument.

Points in favour of an absolute definition of poverty

1   It provides an easily understandable and universal notion of a poverty line.

2   The absolute definition of poverty fits in with many people's everyday conception of what poverty is. For instance, a recent British Social Attitudes survey (Taylor-Gooby, 1990) found that 60 per cent of people thought of poverty basically in subsistence terms.

3   The methodology behind the absolute approach to poverty was very influential in the development of the Beveridge Report (see Section 14.3) and therefore in the construction of welfare state policies to deal with poverty.

Points against an absolute definition of poverty

1   The construction of a subsistence existence to define a poverty line has most often been done by 'experts', and without consistency. Rowntree included the price of tea in his original survey, though it is clear that the nutritional value of this is negligible. The notion of a 'changing absolute' is contradictory.

2   There is the real problem of attempting to arrive at one measure of subsistence which is applicable universally. For instance, the cost of living may vary from one part of the UK to another and from one social group to another.

3   It is clear that a set of value judgements entered into the work of the early researchers. Beveridge himself stated that the issue of what was needed for human subsistence was ultimately a matter of judgement, and in many cases judgements have more often been made on the basis of moral rather than scientific distinctions.

Points in favour of a relative definition of poverty

1   Such a measure is more able to reflect accurately the way in which poverty is a social construction, since such conceptions are rooted in notions of the normal standard of living, which will obviously vary from society to society and from time to time.

2   Such conceptions link discussion of poverty to other areas of social life rather than treating poverty as an isolated phenomenon. Debates about poverty are therefore linked into notions of citizenship which affect everyone, not just the poor.

3   Since they do not rely on building up a single subsistence line, they are better able to reflect the diversity of lifestyles found in contemporary advanced industrial societies such as the UK.

Points against a relative definition of poverty

1   Relative poverty definitions still tend to operate with a poverty-line. Townsend, for instance, created an effective poverty-line in terms of a point where normal participation gives way to deprived participation. The reason for doing this is his argument that it is possible to arrive at an objective measure of poverty. This view has been subject to much

criticism, notably from Dorothy Wedderburn (1974) who argues that the list of items which made up his deprivation index were chosen arbitrarily. As such, the index represents his subjective view and this therefore undermines its claim to objectivity.

2 Townsend's index does not take choice into account. Vegetarians would choose to go without meat on a Sunday (or indeed on any other day), but this would appear as a deprivation in Townsend's index. By definition, vegetarians do not feel deprived if they do not eat meat.

3 Much of Townsend's empirical work has in fact investigated the extent of poverty measured by using fixed empirical measures – such as the level at which benefits are paid. His survey of London, for example, found that 7 per cent of Londoners were living on incomes below the level at which benefits were paid. The term 'living in the margins of poverty' is more often used to describe those living below Townsend's theoretically derived poverty line (i.e. on income above the benefit level but less than 140 per cent of that level).

4 Sen (1983) has argued that all relative definitions have an absolute core in that they use fixed measures such as nutritional requirements to measure relative living standards.

5 Using an absolute measure is easier for propaganda purposes as it is more easily understood by the general population.

6 Relative poverty is simply a measure not of poverty but of inequality. New Right thinkers argue that if we take the measure of relative poverty based on those who earn less than 50 per cent of average earnings, such people will always exist unless we achieve a society with nearly even distribution of income. As an example, Marsland argues that:

The so-called relative concept of poverty is a pure nonsense designed to keep alive the guttering flame of Marxist and socialist critique of capitalism. Its implication, which is self-evidently ludicrous, is that there is worse poverty in Britain than in Uganda. ... As John Moore put it, in commenting on the poverty lobby manipulations of income data, 'It is utterly absurd to speak as if one in three people in Britain today is in dire need. These claims are false and they are dangerous'.

(Marsland, 1996, p. 47)

7 The indicators used to measure relative poverty (namely income less than 50 per cent of average income or below 140 per cent of the benefit level) are open to the criticism that the percentages chosen are arbitrary and subjective.

8 It has been argued by Roll (1992) that a relative definition would deny the existence of poverty in a country where everyone was starving and/or where there was a drastic but evenly spread fall in everyone's living standard.

Activity

Outline the policy implications of the choice between defining poverty in absolute or relative terms. You could do this by listing the kind of policies each definition would lead to for a government attempting to alleviate 'poverty'.

C3.2, C3.3

Contemporary definitions of poverty

Budget standards

Piachard showed in 1979 that amounts allowed for children in supplementary benefit payments covered only about 66 per cent of the actual cost of raising a child, and child benefit for working parents covered about 50 per cent of such cost. Bradshaw *et al.* (1992; quoted in Oppenheim, 1993, p. 50), using a budget standard drawn up using actual patterns of expenditure, showed that income support would provide 34–39 per cent of the cost of their modest but adequate budget. Similarly a study conducted in 1993 to estimate the cost of a modest but adequate family budget and a low-cost budget using methods similar to Rowntree's showed that benefit levels did not meet such basic subsistence needs. A two-adult, two-child family received 31 per cent less in state benefits than the survey suggested was needed on their low-cost budget.

It seems, therefore, that contrary to popular belief the levels of benefits paid out by the welfare state are often far from generous, and in many instances fall below what is deemed necessary by studies conducted using methodology similar to the originators of the notion of absolute poverty.

A consensual definition of poverty

In the two Breadline Britain studies conducted in 1983 and 1990 by Mack and Lansley (1985, 1992), the authors accepted that poverty should be defined in relative terms and therefore centre on the notion of deprivation. However, in order to avoid the criticism levelled at Townsend – namely that his list of items was selected arbitrarily by himself – they set out to arrive at a consensual measure of need by asking a sample of respondents whether they thought items on a list were necessities. This allows them to argue that their standard of necessity is not one set by themselves but by the prevailing societal norms, shown by the results of their survey.

In order to ensure that the items in their 'deprivation index' were considered necessities, Mack and Lansley included only those felt to be necessities by at least 50 per cent of their respondents. Having constructed an index, they could then set out to discover the number of households of various sizes lacking such items. The findings from their first survey are set out in Table 17.17.

Table 17.17 Multiple deprivation, 1983: percentage lacking necessities

No. of necessities lacked	All adults	Bottom 10% income	Top 30% income
0	66	29	82
1 or more	34	71	18
2 or more	19	52	7
3 or more	12	39	4
4 or more	10	34	3
5 or more	8	29	2
6 or more	5	21	1
7 or more	4	19	0

Source: Mack and Lansley (1985, p. 107)

Clearly from this table the question then arises of how many items one needs to lack in order to be in deprivation. Mack and Lansley's answer is that lacking three or more necessities represented a point where deprivation had a pervasive impact on people's lives, and this therefore became their cut-off point.

From Table 17.17 we can see that 12 per cent of the population were in poverty in 1983 according to this definition, a total of 7.5 million people. This even includes 4 per cent of those in the top 30 per cent of income earners.

In 1990 Mack and Lansley found that the number in poverty had increased to 11 million people (20 per cent of the population), including more than 3 million children. They comment:

These are much higher than the equivalent figures for 1983. They present a stark alternative to images of universal gains in prosperity.

(Mack and Lansley, quoted in Frayman, 1991, p. 10)

Some findings from the 1990 survey

- Roughly 10 million people in the UK today cannot afford adequate housing; for example, their home is unheated or damp or the older children have to share bedrooms.
- About 7 million go without essential clothing, such as a warm waterproof coat.
- There are approximately 2.5 million children who are forced to go without at least one of the things they need, like three meals a day, toys, or out-of-school activities.
- Around 5 million people are not properly fed by today's standards – they don't have enough fresh fruit and vegetables, or two meals a day, for example.
- About 6.5 million people cannot afford one or more typical household good, like a fridge, a phone, or carpets for living areas.
- At least one of the necessities which 'make life worth living' – hobbies, holidays, celebrations, etc. – are too expensive for about 21 million people.
- More than 31 million people – over half the population – live without minimal financial security. They say they cannot save £10 a month, or insure the contents of their homes, or both.

The innovative use of a questionnaire designed to elicit what people themselves (as opposed to panels of experts) considered to be necessities has led to this being called the 'consensus' notion of necessities and of the level of goods needed to avoid 'being in poverty'. This approach has been more recently applied in research by the Child Poverty Action Group (Middleton *et al.*, 1994).

Discussion point

To what extent are definitions of poverty now determined by political ideologies rather than by scientific objective evidence? Will this always be the case?

C3.1a

The social indicators approach

One new approach that emerged in the late 1990s is the use of *multiple social indicators* to consider the level of poverty and social exclusion, and to predict how this will change in the future on the basis of government policy changes and other economic and social trends.

What are the social indicators?

The New Policy Institute has produced a set of 46 key indicators, each capable of regular updating. These indicators cover a wide variety of social and economic situations and allow researchers to analyse changes over time by updating the indicators. The indicators are concerned with six headings, namely:

1   income
2   children
3   young adults
4   adults aged 25 to retirement
5   older people
6   communities.

They cover a whole range of statistics, including:

- long-term recipients of benefits
- low-birthweight babies
- pupils gaining no GCSEs at grade C or above
- births to girls conceiving under age 16
- unemployment rates
- suicide statistics
- criminal records
- long-standing illness or disability
- without a telephone
- spending on travel
- non-participation in civic organizations
- vulnerability to crime
- overcrowding.

The Joseph Rowntree Foundation (1998) outlined the benefits of this new system in a briefing, by arguing that:

Social exclusion has become an issue of central policy interest. Growing inequality in the 1980s led to renewed concern about not just poverty itself, but the degree to which groups of people are being excluded from participation in work, lack full access to services and in other ways find themselves outside the mainstream of society. The setting up of the Social Exclusion Unit in 1997 symbolised a desire by

government to address the problems facing the most disadvantaged in this wider context.

Howarth *et al.* (1998) produced figures using the 46 indicators outlined by the New Policy Institute. The main findings of their research were as follows:

- The number living on low incomes relative to the average was far higher than it was 20 years previously. Households with below half average earnings rose from 4 million in 1982 to 10.5 million in 1997.

- More than 2.5 million children live in workless households. Children born in the bottom two social classes are 25 per cent more likely to be underweight as babies.

- Young adults have twice the average rate of unemployment. Young men with no known occupation are four times more likely to commit suicide than young men in social classes 1 and 2.

- Over four million working-age adults would like to work but do not.

- Thirty per cent of pensioners are in the bottom fifth of the income distribution.

- Disadvantage is concentrated in certain communities. Eighty per cent of households in social housing have a weekly income of less than £200, and in 70 per cent of such household the head of household is not in paid work.

17.5 Contemporary trends in poverty

Precisely because there is no fundamental agreement about definitions of poverty, there is no one universally accepted measure of the extent of poverty today.

An ideological edge was given to the debate when recent Conservative governments reversed their earlier acceptance of the notion that poverty should be measured in relative terms and moved back towards an absolutist approach. As a result, the extent of poverty today can vary from the 'negligible amount' seen to exist in the statement made by John Moore in 1989 (then a Conservative cabinet minister) announcing the shift back to absolute measures, up to approximately 22 per cent of the population according to the findings of the Breadline Britain 1990s survey discussed in Section 17.4.

Main measures of poverty used

Although there has never been an official 'poverty-line' in the UK, because governments have consistently failed to devise one, benefits are calculated to provide for a person's basic needs and to avoid creating a disincentive to work. The level at which benefits are paid might therefore arguably be seen as a proxy for such a poverty line. The main alternative choice is to measure the proportion of the population living below 50 per cent of average income, after housing costs. Using this measure, Oppenheim and Harker (1996) provide a summary of recent trends in the extent of poverty (see Figure 17.6).

It is clear that, on this measure, the extent of poverty has risen quite dramatically in recent decades. In his book on poverty and wealth, Scott argues that this reflects:

... a marked reduction in inequality between 1968 and 1979, followed by a sharp rise over the following decade.

(Scott, 1994, p. 92)

The picture of a marked rise in the number in poverty is still true even if we use the alternative measure of the proportion of the population below the level of income support. Statistics show that this number has risen from 6 per cent of the population in 1979 to 8 per cent in 1992 – some 4.7 million people.

Since income support is paid at a level which meets basic needs, it is sometimes difficult to see how people living below this level survive. The

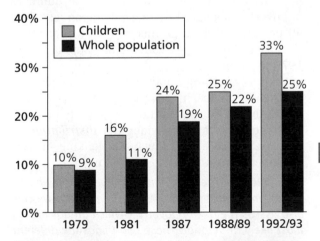

explanation for this rests on the evidence that means-tested benefits are not claimed by all of those eligible to receive them. Oppenheim and Harker (1996) reveal that about £2 billion worth of means-tested benefits to which people were entitled went unclaimed in 1992, which underlines the scale of this problem. As a result their actual income falls below that set out in the benefits legislation. This can be seen in Table 17.18.

Table 17.18 Take-up rates for various benefits (the percentage of those eligible actually claiming)

Name of benefit	Nature of benefit	Take-up rate (%)
Income support	Means-tested	81
Family credit	Means-tested	51
Housing benefit	Means-tested	80
Retirement pension	Not means-tested	100
Child benefit	Not means-tested	100

Source: Department of Social Security (1992), *Social Security Statistics* London, HMSO, p. 349

Official statistics on poverty

Two important series of data are published by the government which provide indications of the level of poverty. Until 1988 the government provided statistics on low-income families (LIFs), but since then this measure has been replaced by statistics on households below average income (HBAI). While these provide a rich source of data, they have one problem in common: both are derived from the annual *Family Expenditure Survey* (FES) which omits from its sample the homeless and people living in institutions. (See also Section 9.6.) Since these are groups likely to contain many people with little money, statistics derived from this source are bound to under-estimate the extent of poverty.

Low-income families

Until 1988, LIF statistics used to measure the extent to which there were families surviving on incomes less than the value of basic state benefit: income support (IS), previously supplementary benefit (SB). Using both the officially published statistics and the later calculations of the extent of LIF produced by independent researchers, Oppenheim (1990, 1993) and Oppenheim and Harker (1996) conclude that the

Figure 17.6 Proportion of children and population living in poverty between 1979 and 1992/3 (living below 50% average income after housing costs)
Source: Oppenheim and Harker (1996, p. 37) using data from DSS, *Households below average income, 1979–1988/9* and *1979–1992/3*, HMSO, 1992 and 1995

numbers in poverty increased from 6 million in 1979 (12 per cent of the population), to 10 million in 1987 (19 per cent), 11.3 million in 1989 (20 per cent), and 13 million in 1993 (25 per cent).

Households below average income

From 1989 the government replaced the LIF statistics with HBAI. One of the reasons for this was the then government's opposition to the use of the IS/SB scales as a poverty benchmark, and the suggestion that households are more appropriate measures of income since they often share resources. It has been pointed out (Alcock, 1993) that this is a contested claim since families rather than households are more likely to share resources. (See also Section 5.7.)

Nevertheless, since one of the commonly used measures of poverty is those households on less than 50 per cent of average income, this has been used to provide such a measure. The Child Poverty Action Group has published figures derived from these statistics and argues that they present similar results.

Despite their different approaches, what both methods reveal is that:

- In 1992, 4 740 000 people (8 per cent of the population) were living *below* income support level. In 1979, 6 per cent of the population were living *below* the supplementary benefit level.

- In 1992, 13 680 000 people (24 per cent of the population) were living *on or below* the income support level. In 1979, 14 per cent of the population were living *on or below* the supplementary benefit level.

- In 1992/93, 14.1 million people (25 per cent of the population) were living *below* 50 per cent of average income after housing costs. In 1979, 9 per cent of the population were living *below* 50 per cent of average income after housing costs.

So, whichever way you measure it, poverty has grown significantly over recent years. By 1992/93, between 13 and 14 million people in the UK – around a quarter of our society – were living in poverty.

(Oppenheim and Harker, 1996, p. 24)

Using DSS publications, Alcock argues that these trends show that:

Despite government claims of growing affluence for all over this period, the 1988–9 figures also show a decline in real terms (against inflation) of 6 per cent in the incomes of the bottom 10 per cent of the population.

(Alcock, 1993, p. 17)

The extent of this growth in inequality can be further glimpsed through statistics from the *Family Expenditure Survey*. These show that, between 1979 and 1994, the highest earners (the top one-tenth) increased their income in real terms by 62 per cent while the income of the poorest tenth fell (again in real terms) by 17 per cent. (See also Section 17.1.)

The distribution of poverty

In the 1980s the number of poor households in the UK increased dramatically. A European Commission report stated that almost 25 per cent of poor households in Europe were in the UK. It went on to show that the number of poor people, defined as those who spend less than 50 per cent of the national average, had increased in the UK from 1980 to 1985, reaching 10.3 million people, while the number in other EU countries remained broadly static.

A report by the Joseph Rowntree Foundation (1995) claims that, since the late 1970s, income inequality has been growing more rapidly in the UK than in any other country with the exception of New Zealand. (See also Section 17.1.)

Narrowing the focus to look at the numbers in poverty (measured by those living on less than 50 per cent of average income) shows that they increased from 9 per cent of the population in 1979 to 25 per cent in 1993. However, this does not tell us anything about who these people are, or whether those in poverty in 1993 were significantly different from those in poverty in 1979. This requires us to consider the *distribution* of poverty. There are two ways of looking at this, as Oppenheim and Harker explain:

We can look at the composition of the poor – which groups make up the bulk of those in poverty; we can also assess the risk of poverty – which groups are most likely to be poor. These two things are different – e.g. lone parents make up only a small proportion of the total number of people in poverty as they are a small group; however, they have a high risk of poverty.

(Oppenheim and Harker, 1996, p. 34)

Activity

Study Figures 17.7 and 17.8 and identify the following social groups:

a the social group by family status which comprises the smallest proportion of the poor

b the social group by economic status which comprises the largest proportion of the poor

c the social group by economic status which has the smallest risk of being in poverty

d the social group by family status which has the largest risk of being in poverty

e one social group by economic status which comprises a fairly small proportion of the poor but with a moderately high risk of being in poverty

f one social group by family status which comprises a relatively large proportion of the poor but with a fairly low risk of being in poverty

g two social groups in each of the status diagrams with the highest risk of being in poverty (excluding 'others').

C3.2, C3.3

Changes in the distribution of poverty

In contrast with the earlier figures produced by Oppenheim (1993), a few changes can be highlighted. The elderly now comprise a smaller proportion of the poor than in 1989, while lone parents and the unemployed comprise a larger proportion. Equally, pensioners now face a lower risk of being in poverty (40 per cent of households with head/spouse aged 60+ were in poverty in 1989) and the unemployed and lone parents face a greater risk (69 per cent of households with head/spouse unemployed were in poverty in 1989, and 50 per cent of lone-parent families were in poverty in 1989).

Groups who are consistently at risk of poverty

A number of social groups have consistently appeared in studies and commentaries about poverty because they have always constituted a great proportion of the poor. These groups are pensioners, the sick and disabled, single parents and the unemployed.

This shows that vulnerability to poverty is not equally spread but is affected by gender, age, disability and class. Those social divisions which lie at the heart of all social stratification therefore perhaps unsurprisingly lie at the heart of the construction and distribution of poverty. However, as Oppenheim (1990, 1993), Oppenheim and Harker (1996) and Alcock (1993) point out, the relative importance of these groups among the poor has changed dramatically over the last 25 years. As a proportion of the poor, pensioner couples and single pensioners have fallen, while couples with children, lone-parent families with children and single people have risen as a proportion of the poor. Clearly this has pushed a greater focus on to concern with children and poverty.

The extent of income inequality and social exclusion

Howarth *et al.* (1998), using the set of 46 social indicators for poverty and social exclusion devised by the New Policy Institute, provide a picture of the extent of poverty and social exclusion in 1997, giving a picture of the inheritance of the new Labour government in this area.

The massive rise in inequality and its effect on poverty

They point out that there was a massive rise in income inequality, leaving 10.5 million households on below half the average income in 1997. Lone-parent familes are the household type with the greatest risk of being in this situation, with over 50 per cent of such households having less than half the average income in 1997. A third of children, nearly three million, live in households with less than half average earnings. Young people are twice as likely as adults to be out of work, and even when in work suffer from low pay. A third of 16- to 24-year-olds earned less than £3.65 per hour, half the average male wage. Twenty-five per cent of adults in the hotel and catering trade earned less than £3.65 per hour, 20 per cent of the poorest fifth of the population lacked a bank account, and over half had no home contents insurance – even though they were twice as likely to be burgled as those who did have it.

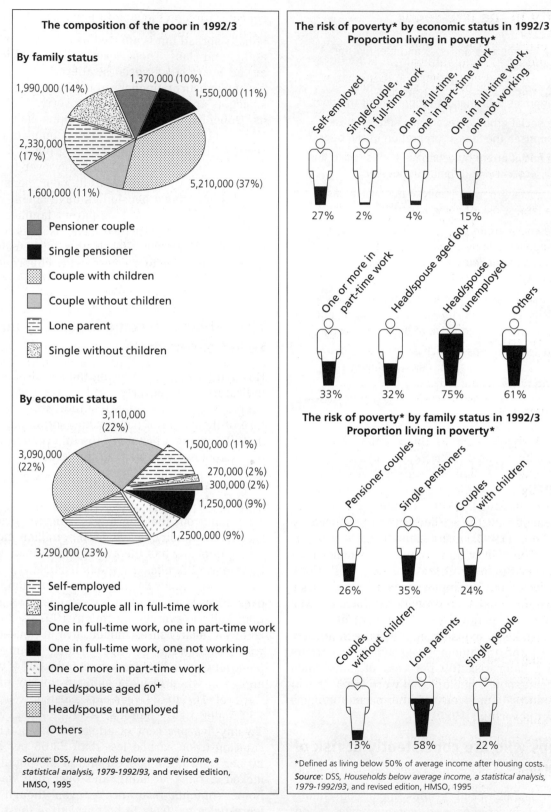

The composition of the poor in 1992/3

By family status

1,990,000 (14%)   1,370,000 (10%)
1,550,000 (11%)

2,330,000 (17%)

1,600,000 (11%)   5,210,000 (37%)

- Pensioner couple
- Single pensioner
- Couple with children
- Couple without children
- Lone parent
- Single without children

By economic status

3,110,000 (22%)
1,500,000 (11%)
3,090,000 (22%)
270,000 (2%)
300,000 (2%)
1,250,000 (9%)
1,2500,000 (9%)
3,290,000 (23%)

- Self-employed
- Single/couple all in full-time work
- One in full-time work, one in part-time work
- One in full-time work, one not working
- One or more in part-time work
- Head/spouse aged 60+
- Head/spouse unemployed
- Others

Source: DSS, *Households below average income, a statistical analysis, 1979-1992/93,* and revised edition, HMSO, 1995

The risk of poverty* by economic status in 1992/3 Proportion living in poverty*

Self-employed — 27%
Single/couple, in full-time work — 2%
One in full-time, one in part-time work — 4%
One in full-time work, one not working — 15%

One or more in part-time work — 33%
Head/spouse aged 60+ — 32%
Head/spouse unemployed — 75%
Others — 61%

The risk of poverty* by family status in 1992/3 Proportion living in poverty*

Pensioner couples — 26%
Single pensioners — 35%
Couples with children — 24%

Couples without children — 13%
Lone parents — 58%
Single people — 22%

*Defined as living below 50% of average income after housing costs.
Source: DSS, *Households below average income, a statistical analysis, 1979-1992/93,* and revised edition, HMSO, 1995

Figure 17.7 The composition of the poor, defined as living below 50 per cent of average income, after housing costs
Source: Oppenheim and Harker (1996, p. 35)

Figure 17.8 The risk of poverty
Source: Oppenheim and Harker (1996, p. 40)

Poverty in the late 1990s

David Piachard (1999) points out that, between 1979 and 1997, the number of individuals in poverty – defined on the basis of living below half average income level – rose from 5 million to 14 million, a quarter of the population (see Table 17.19).

Table 17.19 The bottom line: people in poverty by personal, economic and family status, 1996/97

	Total number (millions)	Proportion who are poor (%)	Number in poverty (millions)
Adult women	22.0	24	5.3
Children	13.0	35	4.5
Adult men	21.1	20	4.2
Elderly	9.8	31	3.0
Lone-parent family	4.3	63	2.9
Unemployed	4.6	78	2.3
All	56.1	25	14.1

Source: Department of Social Security figures, 1998, quoted in Piachard (1999, p. 2)

Alternatively, looking at the number receiving benefits, he points out that by February 1999 this had reached 3.8 million receiving income support, rising to 6.7 million if partners and dependents are included. With another 1.3 million receiving job seeker's allowance, this means a total of 8 million people depended on the state's minimum benefits.

Piachard points out that the Labour government elected in 1997 has made some changes that are designed to reduce these figures, such as:

- increasing the value of child benefit
- reducing unemployment
- introducing the national minimum wage
- introducing the working families tax credit
- introducing the children's tax credit.

He argues that this will help families with children, but that other groups such as families without children or pensioners will see less benefit. However, he believes that the effect of the changes will be to reduce the numbers in poverty by two million, down to 12 million by 2002. To reduce poverty down to 1979 levels, he argues there needs to be more redistribution and more concentration on the long-term causes of poverty, particularly unemployment and low pay.

Child poverty in the late 1990s

Gregg *et al.* (1999) examined the effect of family poverty on children. They found that a third of children lived in households with below half average earnings, and most poor children live in workless households. These comprise two main types: lone-parent households and those with two parents but both without work. They found that worklessness was a greater contributor to child poverty than lone-parent status:

One-fifth of the overall rise in child poverty can be attributed specifically to the rise in the proportion of children with lone parents, from 6 per cent to 22 per cent of all children. But a bigger factor has been the rising chance of either one- or two-parent families being out of work.

(Gregg *et al.*, 1999, p. 2)

They also point out that, while child poverty (based on those living in households with below half average earnings) fell in the 1970s, it barely fell at all between 1979 and 1996, despite a substantial increase in general living standards. This meant that in real terms the amount spent on toys, children's clothing, shoes and food for the bottom fifth of the population was no higher in 1996 than in 1968.

It is certainly true that the late 1990s saw a renewed emphasis on the problem of child poverty, since there are more children in poverty than adults and 40 per cent of children are born poor. As a result child poverty has been a priority area for the Labour government elected in 1997.

Discussion point

Read the two articles from the *Guardian* and the *Observer* (the latter is obviously written by a government representative). To what extent will the initiatives suggested in the above articles lead to a reduction in child poverty and overall poverty?

C3.1a

Work gets started on promised fairer land

YVETTE COOPER

SUDDENLY EVERYONE is talking about child poverty. The Prime Minister set a target of abolishing it within a generation. Then the treasury produced a new report full of gory details about the extent and causes of poverty today.

The real revelation in last week's treasury document is how far poverty and inequality are still embedded in the British class system. Consider the facts. The chances of making it into the top 25 per cent of earners are four times as high if your father was a top earner than if his earnings fell in the lowest 25 per cent. John Major's waffle about a classless society didn't make much difference. Past Labour governments have achieved much by reducing absolute poverty, but they have had surprisingly limited impact on class-based inequalities.

In fact, academics Swift and Marshall (*Prospect*, November 1995) found the relative chances of rich children compared to poor children have hardly changed in 100 years.

If we are to end child poverty within 20 years, we must shatter the link between the parents' disadvantages and the children's chances as they grow.

Improving the educational opportunities for children from low-skill backgrounds is a vital start. Over twenty years we must go further, with a national crusade to raise the educational achievement of disadvantaged children.

Alongside educational reform, that means financial help too. As new research from the Rowntree Foundation shows, poverty lowers children's aspirations across the board, from birthday presents to careers.

Raising the income of families with children was a central element of the Budget, and as the treasury research shows, the most powerful way to do it is to get parents into jobs or help them raise their skills. Where work isn't an option, it must mean raising benefit levels for families with children. The government's decision to raise child benefit and substantially increase the income support premium for under-11s is the right way forward.

Source: Adapted from the *Guardian*, 5 April 1999

We'll Get Rid of the Poor

ALISTAIR DARLING

TODAY, as every other day, 2000 children will be born in Britain. And a third of these children will be born into poverty. It is that injustice which the government is determined to end. Between 1979 and 1997 the number of working-age, workless households more than doubled.

It was the divisions and the waste of the Tory years that led many people to support us. And we have made a significant start.

By the end of this Parliament one and a quarter million people will be lifted out of poverty, 700,000 of them children. This is not happening by accident, or despite a Labour government, but because of it.

We have introduced Britain's first ever minimum wage. The biggest rise in child benefit – £250 a year. More help for the poorest pensioners – this year's Winter Fuel Payment has increased fivefold to £100.

And from October the Working Families Tax Credit will provide extra help to 1.4 million families, targeting those who earn below £235 per week.

We are increasing the amount of help that goes to disabled children – worth in some cases an extra £37 per week. We are spending £800m on the poorest housing estates, more than £140m to tackle homelessness.

By the end of this Parliament we will have spent over £5bn on families and children, £4bn on pensioners and more than £2bn on help for disabled people.

The Social Exclusion Unit, another innovation, is helping find new solutions to homelessness, truancy, teenage pregnancies and the poorest housing estates.

But our policy is not just about investing more money. It is to change the philosophy and culture of the system. We are not prepared to see people written off and, just as important, we are not prepared to allow people to write themselves off.

First we must make sure that money and opportunity is fairly distributed and that the greatest help goes to those most in need. That's what people expect. And the right to benefit and support must be accompanied by the responsibility to take up the opportunities provided. Second, we want to prevent poverty before it happens. Our reforms are as much about housing, education and support for young children as they are about benefit changes.

Third, we are in for the long-term. We are not into short-term fixes. It will take time to turn around housing estates where generation after generation has been stuck in poverty.

We want to be remembered because we had the courage to reform the welfare state for the better and because we had the same courage as Attlee's government of the forties. The same courage but with different solutions. The right solutions for people in the twenty-first century. Something that will improve people's lives now and in the 50 years to come.

Source: Adapted from the *Observer*, 22 August 1999

Our children are the worst off in Europe

By Kirsty Walker

THE UNITED KINGDOM is the worst place in Europe to grow up, a major new study reveals today.

It suffers from the worst child poverty rates, has the highest number of households where no parent works and has substantially more teenage pregnancies than any other EU country.

The UK's record for the number of 16-year-olds in education and the maths results of 14-year-olds are also below the average of other countries.

The study, by Labour think tank the Institute of Public Policy Studies, paints a bleak picture of life for British children. Researchers examined seven key areas and found that the UK was the worst in three and below average in five.

Their report says: 'The overall picture provides much cause for concern, with the UK emerging as a serious contender for the title of worst place in Europe to be a child.

'At the same time, the UK's performance on several indicators is presenting an obstacle to the goal of greater social cohesion in the Union. One in five households with children in the UK had no adult in work - the highest rate in the EU. In Spain, where unemployment rates are high, the worklessness rate is little more than half that in the UK.'

The report's authors say the Government has recognised the problems – which have mostly been inherited – and has committed itself to stamping out child poverty.

Lisa Harker, research director of the IPPS, said: 'These figures, the latest available, show the Government is right to prioritise on child poverty. Yet we should not underestimate the enormity of the task ahead. Child poverty is not a problem that can be resolved overnight, nor in one single Budget. The Government will need to be bold to hold its head up high in Europe.

'It is a very concerning situation. While our figures are for 1997, and we recognise that there have been some improvements, it is still striking how far we have to go.

'The rise in the number of children in poverty has been very rapid and I believe it is now one of the biggest challenges facing this Government.'

The report found that nearly a third of children live in poor households in the UK, compared with only 13 per cent in Germany, 12 per cent in France and 24 per cent in Italy. In terms of the percentage of children who live in workless households, the UK also leads the field with nearly 20 per cent. The EU average is nearly half this.

Almost every European country has seen a rise in the number of single parents, but the UK has witnessed the largest increase.

In the 1980s and early 1990s, the numbers of children living in poverty increased by 40 per cent. The report is not all bleak. Children are safer on British roads, for example. The UK has the second lowest numbers of deaths among five to 14-year-olds.

Source: the *Daily Express*, 17 March 2000

The continuing problem of child poverty

Child poverty increased considerably in the UK during the 1980s and 1990s and the Labour government elected in 1997, despite making tackling child poverty a priority and working to take a million children out of poverty, still faced a massive task. This was exemplified in an article in the *Daily Express* on 17 March 2000 which talked of 'our children' as the 'worst in Europe' and an article in the *Observer* of 11 June 2000 which talked of the shame of child poverty in the UK. These articles have been reproduced.

Activity

a Identity and outline two measures of poverty used in the articles on this and the following page.

b Draw up a table of the evidence of child poverty referred to in the articles.

c Use the internet or other resources to try to update these statistics.

d You could try the website of the Joseph Rowntree Foundation at www.jrf.org.uk.

C3.2, C3.3, IT3.1

As well as these reports, a further report from UNICEF outlined the fact that there are 47 million children living in poverty in the rich industrialized nations. The UNICEF Innocenti Report Card (UNICEF, 2000) concludes that one in six of the rich world's children is poor – a total of 47 million. The report shows that the rates of child poverty vary greatly from under 3 per cent in Sweden to a high of over 22 per cent in the USA. The UNICEF report challenges the common assumption that large numbers of lone-parent families cause child poverty, showing that those countries with a high proportion of children living in lone-parent families include some with the lowest rates of child poverty. For example, Sweden boasts the highest share of children living in lone-parent families but has the lowest child poverty rate.

Discussion point

Should the UK follow the USA or Sweden in its development of policies to deal with child poverty?

C3.1a

Shame of child poverty in UK:

Almost one in five children is poor, reveals UN report

KAMAL AHMED

Britain's shameful record on childhood poverty is laid bare today in a damning United Nations report revealing that millions of young people are trapped in conditions among the worst in Europe.

The Observer has obtained a report by Unicef, the children's arm of the UN, which says that Britain has one of the worst records on childhood poverty in the industrialised world. Nearly 20 per cent of young people live in families which are below the official poverty line – judged as household income below half median earnings.

The report, which will prove an acute embarrassment to Tony Blair's government, puts Britain below countries such as Turkey, Poland and Hungary, which suffer less relative poverty than the UK.

Countries such as Sweden, Norway and Finland suffer rates below 5 per cent.

'It is a question this country must face,' said David Piachaud, expert in childhood poverty at the London School of Economics. 'Do we want another generation of children who are brought up in poverty, who have worse health, worse education, worse housing and deficient lifetime prospects? Children are supposed to be the innocents.'

The report, which will be published on Tuesday, says that even when it comes to absolute poverty - households with an income below the US official poverty line - Britain still languishes in the bottom quarter of the child poverty league.

Out of 19 countries surveyed, the UK came 14th, just above Italy. Nearly every European country has fewer children living in poor households and estimates say that anywhere between three and four million children live in British households affected by poverty.

The report says that the UK fails on five key indicators of childhood poverty. The childhood poverty rate is high, the number of lone parent families suffering from poverty is high, and the number of workless households is high, as is the number of people who suffer from low wages or have low benefits.

The report, to be published on Tuesday, will reignite the debate on Britain's poor. Although it will praise the Government for taking action to lift more than one million children out of poverty, it will reveal the huge amount still to be done.

Inquiries by *The Observer* have discovered the true cost to children of living in households without enough money.

Children are eating main meals which consist of little more than toast and beans and rice pudding. Many live in terrible surroundings, with damp running down the walls and inadequate heating. Parents often cannot afford to buy new clothes as the little money they have is spent on food. Some lone parents have less than £100 a week with which to bring up their children and pay the bills.

Poor nutrition leads to bad performance at school and worse health, with associated costs to the National Health Service.

It is estimated that it would cost Britain £10 billion to eradicate the problem.

The chancellor, Gordon Brown, has been briefed on the contents of the report and is set to enter the poverty debate to mark its publication. Treasury sources said that Brown believes childhood poverty is one of the most serious problems affecting Britain.

He is planning a raft of new measures to tackle the issue. A multi-million pound package will be announced in summer's comprehensive spending review.

Funding for the sure start programme, which helps children up to the age of three, will be increased so that the number of programmes will be doubled to 400. A children's fund will also be set up to help people up to the age of 19. Brown has set up a task force with the education secretary, David Blunkett, and the social security secretary, Alistair Darling, to look at the issue. The prime minister has said he wants to see poverty eradicated 'in a generation'.

The fund will be used to give children better drugs education and health advice. It will also be used to help parents find jobs and cheap childcare so that their wages will not be soaked up by high childcare costs.

Brown has also asked Maeve Sherlock, the director of the National Council for One Parent Families, to sit on the influential Council of Economic Advisers to guide policy formulation.

The Government has faced criticism that, although it has put millions of pounds into relieving child poverty which it says is a priority, it still needs to do more.

'Gordon Brown cut the rate of income tax by 1p,' said Jonathan Bradshaw of York University. 'That money could have been used to help the most vulnerable people. That would have shown a real commitment.'

Source: The Observer, 11 June 2000

Hope is a luxury she can't afford

KAMAL AHMED and NICK PATON WALSH

LIKE MILLIONS OF BRITONS, Margaret will collect her benefits cheque tomorrow. The cash – £96.30 – is not much for one week, not in Newtown, north Birmingham. Not anywhere, in fact.

Since she moved there a year ago, the council has taken to sealing off the alleyways to stem the tide of 'snatch and run' muggings. There has been a shooting every week. Each evening, at the parade of shops at the bottom of the street, the gutters are filled with litter and the local kids sit around the phone box, a little stoned and a little angry.

Margaret doesn't go to the shops very often, partly through fear, partly because she can't afford to. She shops once a week, hoping it will last until the next cheque. Last week it didn't, and she had to live on £2.18 for three days. Her two children, aged six and four, sometimes eat pizza and sausages, but mostly live on beans and toast. Last month the family sat down to eat two tins of rice pudding for dinner. There was nothing else left.

This is a story of everyday life in Britain. As the chattering class sits around its collective coffee table and argues about who should go to Oxford or Cambridge, or about whether the Women's Institute was rude when it heckled Tony Blair, a whole sector of society simply gets on with harsh lives in hidden places, rarely given the oxygen of media publicity.

This week a damning report by the children's arm of the United Nations, Unicef, will reveal the real plight of Britain and the world's poor. Leaked to *The Observer*, it makes sobering reading. One in six children in the rich, industrialised nations lives in poverty. In terms of relative poverty – the number of families living on less than half median earnings – Britain finds itself in the bottom four, below Turkey, Poland and Hungary. Of the 23 countries surveyed, only Italy, the US and Mexico have a worse record on poverty.

Nearly 20 per cent of Britain's children live in poverty, between three and four million people. That compares to 2.6 per cent in Sweden and 3.9 per cent in Norway, the two countries which could teach our stratified, wealth-obsessed country a thing or two about being a caring and equitable nation.

Blair has made the eradication of childhood poverty one of the key planks of his Government's term of office. He says he wants to see an end to children eating beans for tea while the damp runs off the walls. He wants childhood poverty to end 'in a generation'. It is a tall order.

The report makes much of what the Government has done in the past three years. It agrees with the claim that policies aimed at the problem – increases in child benefit, the working families tax credit, the new deal to get more poor parents into jobs – are working. To an extent. More than a million children have been lifted out of the poverty gap. But that still leaves three million too many languishing in a world of tinned rice pudding and few life chances.

Child poverty experts, such as Jonathan Bradshaw from the University of York, say that much of the problem can be tracked back to the years of Margaret Thatcher when redistribution of wealth was a swear word, not a policy.

The economics of trickle-down and rampant unemployment created an underclass against which Britain is still struggling. Bradshaw says that, despite progress, the problems run so deep that the country still finds itself in the position of the heartless man of Europe.

To tackle the problem seriously will need a huge redistribution of wealth. And that needs political guts and political action, action which critics say the Government is reluctant to undertake fully, aware as it is of the important audience of Middle England. Experts estimate that it will cost another £10 billion to heave Britain up to the position enjoyed by Sweden or Norway.

'It begs the question whether there is the political support for that,' said David Piachaud, child poverty expert at the London School of Economics. 'Can you make such fundamental changes if you continue on this policy of redistribution by stealth? At some point people are going to notice it.'

Gordon Brown, the Chancellor, will use this summer's spending review to announce further measures worth hundreds of millions of pounds. But as Brown gets up on Thursday evening to face the serried ranks of black-tied businessmen for his Mansion House speech, he will do so with the uncomfortable knowledge that each week, once Margaret has paid the bills - gas, electricity, telephone and water – her family has £25 to live on.

Margaret's youngest daughter 'celebrated' her fourth birthday yesterday. But Margaret won't be able to get to the shops to buy her anything as simple as a present until tomorrow's money rolls in. Her daughter's shoes are falling apart, and she sleeps on a mattress some friends had thrown out. Their house has no television or carpets.

Last week there was food enough in the cupboard – Margaret had budgeted carefully – but the bills she has paid means she calculates that she's already spent £4.14 of next week's money.

Theresa, a mother of three from Acomb in York, remembers the moment when she felt most hopeless, about a year ago. She and her three children had just moved into a long-awaited council house. There were no carpets, and the walls were filthy. Her son, Lewis, nine at the time, was too scared to sleep in his room, the walls defaced with graffiti and stained black from a recent house fire. He clambered into his mother's bed for comfort. Theresa found it hard to soothe him: she was just as scared herself.

Theresa's family have lived on the breadline since her husband left six years ago. In 1992 she received around £80 a week with which she had to pay her bills and feed the four of them. Now, she gets £93. Once the bills are paid, she has £45 a week to buy food and clothes. It's taken her a long time to learn how to budget it well.

'I'm allowed to earn an extra £15 a week from cleaning. I end up spending whatever's in my purse. My daughter asked me for 20p last week. I had to say no. I hope that she understands. I hate the pettiness that poverty brings – I'm always on at the kids to turn off the bathroom light,

continued on next page

continued

as every penny counts. This week has been particularly bad. I'm two months behind on the sewage and water bills.'

Two hundred miles away, in the shadow of London's Canary Wharf, a group of four tower blocks are known collectively as Will Crook Estate. On the top floor of Devitt House lives Moriom Begum. She is 44 and was born in Bangladesh. In 1991, her family of five moved into a two-bedroomed flat. Her son, 21, and daughter, 16, share one room, and the youngest, who is six, sleeps with her husband in their bed. The room was not even big enough for a cot.

Her husband has recently become unemployed and the family claim a Jobseekers Allowance of £179 every 14 days. From this they must pay their gas, electricity and telephone bills, which leaves them with £57 to spend on food for five each week. Moriom buys a big bag of rice at the beginning of the week to feed the family. Within 10 days, the money is exhausted, and four days pass during which they eat whatever is left. She can't afford to purchase clothes for her daughters costing more than £5.

Margaret in Newtown can see no way out. 'The council are trying to get me to go back to work at the moment,' she says. 'But it's impossible with the kind of childcare available. People don't seem to value family life any more.'

Source: The Observer 11 June 2000

Activity

a Draw up diaries of your own life and compare it to the lives outlined in this article

b What does the article tell us about the experience of poverty and how it is affected by class, gender and ethnicity.

C3.2, C3.3

In a further report produced by UNICEF (part of the United Nations) John Micklewright and Katie Stewart (2000) argue that the lives of 10,000 children across Europe could be saved if conditions of care for children were raised to the standard that exists in Sweden and Luxembourg. Their work reveals that Belgium and Portugal are at the bottom of the league of under five mortality rates with 9.6 deaths per 1,000 live births. The UK falls mid-table with a rate of 7.2 deaths per 1,000 and Luxembourg and Sweden come out best with only 4.4 and 4.7 respectively. Such variations prove that reductions in child death rates are not automatic outcomes of strong economic performance.

This report shows that child poverty can be a matter of life and death.

Table 17.20 Childhood poverty and mortality in Europe

Country	Children (0–15) in poor households (%)	Households with children (0–14) without working adult (%)	Under-5 mortality (rate per 1000)	Births per 1000 to 15–19 year olds
UK	32	19.5	7.2	28.5
Ireland	28	15.4	7.3	15.1
Portugal	27	3.3	9.6	20.2
Spain	25	10.1	7.6	8.3
Italy	24	7.6	8.5	7.0
Luxembourg	23	3.8	4.4	10.6
EU	20	10.5	7.5	10.7
Greece	19	4.5	9.0	12.9
Netherlands	16	9.3	6.8	5.8
Belgium	15	11.0	9.6	9.2
Germany	13	8.6	7.1	13.0
France	12	8.8	7.1	9.6
Denmark	5	–	6.3	8.7
Finland	–	11.8	5.0	9.8
Austria	–	4.9	6.7	17.5
Sweden	–	–	4.7	8.6

Source: Adapted from John Micklewright and Katie Stewart (2000)

Activity

a List all the countries in rank order in relation to each of the indicators listed above.

b In which areas is the UK relatively bad in terms of child poverty and in which areas is it relatively good?

c Discuss with other students which of these indicators you feel is most important and therefore most urgent in terms of social policy and government action

C3.1b, C3.2, C3.3

Reasons for the changing composition of the poor

We can identify two major reasons for the changing composition of the poor: changes in the labour market and family structure (see Chapter 5).

Labour market changes

The end of the Beveridge-inspired commitment to full employment, and the reassertion of the ideas of the free market with a greater emphasis on flexibility, has led to the return of mass unemployment. In April 1994, official unemployment figures showed there were 2 734 400 out of work, representing 9.7 per cent of the workforce. This is extremely high compared with annual averages of 1.7 per cent for 1951–64 and 2.0 per cent for 1964–70.

The result is higher levels of poverty since income for the unemployed is well below average income. For instance, Micklewright (1985) estimated that for a single man with no children, unemployment benefits would equal 27 per cent of the average male manual wage. (See also Section 14.6.)

Family structure changes

The number of single-parent families has increased over the period. Eight per cent of families with children had a lone parent in 1971, but this rose to 12 per cent in 1979, 16 per cent in 1989 and 20 per cent in 1991. The vast majority of these (over 90 per cent) are headed by women. It is also the case that the proportion of single mothers in employment has decreased from 49 per cent in 1979 to 41 per cent in 1993. (See also Section 5.4.)

As a result these two groups (the unemployed and lone parents) constitute a much greater proportion of the poor than in the past, and consequently other groups have fallen as a proportion of the total poor. One of the most important outcomes is a shift from those groups traditionally seen as part of the deserving poor (the elderly, the sick and disabled) to groups often seen as part of the undeserving poor (the unemployed and single-parent families). As a result the extent to which consideration of poverty and the poor is burdened with moralistic distinctions has grown.

Gender and poverty

Women appear in a number of the groups most likely to suffer poverty. Women's life expectancy is longer, so they are more likely to feature among pensioners in poverty. Also, about 90 per cent of single-parent families are headed by a woman. Changes to family structures – in particular the rise in divorce, which is the most common cause of single-parent families – have led to greater numbers of women being identified among those in poverty.

In 1992, 5.4 million women and 4.2 million men were living in poverty (on or below the income support level), according to Oppenheim and Harker (1996).

The feminization of poverty

In their studies of women and poverty from a broadly feminist perspective, Glendinning and Millar (1987, 1992) refer to the growth in usage of the term the 'feminization of poverty'. By this is sometimes meant that the extent of poverty suffered by women has increased. However, one problem with this notion is that it can serve to hide the extent to which women have *always* experienced poverty. Lewis and Piachard (1992) pointed out that 61 per cent of adults on poor relief at the beginning of the twentieth century were women, while Oppenheim (1993) calculates that 62 per cent of those dependent on state benefits in 1991 were women.

Glendinning and Millar therefore argue that the only consistent usage for the term must be a growing awareness of the extent to which women suffer from poverty.

Women and the labour market

One of the main reasons for the majority of the poor being women relates to their secondary position in the labour market (see also Section 17.2). Glendinning and Millar say that, although women are participating in greater numbers in the labour market, they have not achieved equality of pay, and many have found themselves in insecure, low-paid, part-time work: something like 80 per cent of part-time workers are women.

Callender (1992) says that, despite the fact that unemployment remains higher for men than women, the insecurity of such jobs has made women much more susceptible to unemployment.

She points out that between 1979 and 1986 male unemployment rose by 146 per cent and female unemployment by 276 per cent.

In a study looking at the interrelationship between gendered employment and pension entitlements, Bernard *et al.* (1995) say that the increasing phenomenon of early retirement may lead to increased risk of poverty among older women owing to their interrupted career patterns and low earnings during their employed lives, since this will largely determine their financial circumstances in retirement.

Women and the social security system

A second area of concern is the treatment of women in the social security system and the effect this has on their likelihood of being poor. Because the British welfare system is based largely on an insurance model where contributions made by those in work count towards their benefit, the historical lesser involvement of women in the labour market has had the effect of reducing their eligibility for benefits. Women are less likely than men to have made full National Insurance contributions and therefore are more likely to be ineligible for a number of benefits.

Changes in the nature of the welfare state have exacerbated these divisions. The re-emergence of an emphasis on care in the community has in many cases meant care by women (see also Sections 5.3, 12.6 and 14.4): this has further reduced their ability to enter the labour market. Also, the change to greater amounts of welfare being dispensed via occupational pensions has meant that women have less access to these, again owing to their secondary position in the labour market.

Gender and age

Arber and Ginn (1991, 1995) have written extensively about the situation faced by women and the interrelationship between gender and age. They consider the extent to which there is pressure on women to retire if their husbands retire early. Although they point out that such situations do exist, and such pressures may lead women to retire early with negative financial consequences, in some ways the pressure on women to fit in with the employment pattern of their male partner may be less among those in their fifties since the male is more likely to have a pension and therefore not be reliant on means-tested ben-

efits. It is the rules concerning partner's earnings within these benefits that lead to women of unemployed men being much more likely to be unemployed themselves among younger age groups.

In another piece of work on this issue, Groves (1992) points out that, while pensions often make provision for widows based on their husbands' contributions, such rights may well be lost to the wife when couples divorce, though the man would retain such rights. Given that the divorce rate is increasing and that women have the greater life expectancy, this will increase the likelihood of a woman falling into poverty in retirement.

Women and lone-parent families

The increasing numbers of lone-parent families also largely affects women. The need to provide childcare and the problems of doing so on the lower wages women get make this group particularly susceptible to the risk of poverty.

While married mothers were participating in larger numbers in paid employment in the 1980s, the proportion of lone mothers (with children under 15) in paid employment declined from 45 per cent in 1981 to 39 per cent in 1990 (Bartholomew *et al.*, 1992). A government plan to end the lone-parent benefit – on the grounds that it encourages single-parenthood – met with a barrage of criticism. (See also Sections 14.5 and 14.6.) Critics of the plan argued that this would mean that single parents became even more dependent on the state because it would adversely affect only those in employment (see Figure 17.9).

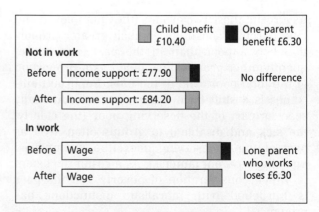

Figure 17.9 The effects of scrapping one-parent benefit on a family with one child
Source: The Guardian, 5 September 1995

Ethnicity and poverty

A specific question on ethnicity was included in the national Census only in 1991, owing to fears about the use to which such data might be put. It is also the case that the DSS does not classify claimants by ethnic origin. There is therefore a paucity of official information on this issue.

However, Alcock (1993) says there is evidence to show that black people are likely to feature among many of the social groups who are known to suffer a greater risk of poverty. Here again it is both the employment structure and the institutions of the welfare state which seem to be the main culprits.

Ethnicity and employment

Amin and Oppenheim (1992), in a survey of poverty and ethnicity produced for the Child Poverty Action Group and the Runnymede Trust, point out that unemployment for black people is much higher than for whites. Table 17.21 provides recent figures on such divisions.

Table 17.21 Unemployment rates in the UK in 1994, by sex, age and ethnic origin (ILO rates, percentages)

	Men		Women	
	All aged 16+	16–24	All aged 16+	16–24
Whites	1	18	7	12
Ethnic minorities	25	37	16	27
Ratio W/EM	2.27	2.05	2.28	2.25

Source: Adapted from Oppenheim and Harker (1996, p. 116)

Activity

a From Table 17.21, identify the social group where the ratio of the unemployment rate for ethnic minorites compared with white people is highest, and the social group where it is lowest.

b What does the information in this table suggest about the relative importance of ethnicity and the other social divisions shown in the table?

C3.2, C3.3

It is also evident that ethnic minorities have employment prospects that are skewed towards the lower-paid jobs (see also Section 17.2). In the third Policy Studies Institute research report on ethnic inequality in the UK, Brown (1984) found that while only 3 per cent of white men were in unskilled manual jobs, 9 per cent of West Indians were and 6 per cent of Asians were. A survey in the city of Leicester found that average pay for full-time workers among both ethnic minority men and women was 82 per cent of that for white men and women.

The higher levels of unemployment and lower pay makes it much more likely that ethnic minority groups will need the support of the welfare state. Here, however, there are a number of problems.

Ethnic minorities and the welfare state

The difficulties range from outright racism towards claimants from ethnic minorities, to a number of requirements in the legislation which make it less likely that ethnic minorities groups will be eligible.

Alcock (1993) points out that their life-experience of immigration to this country as adults, and possibly spending periods abroad, means they are less likely to qualify for full benefits based on NI contributions. This makes them more dependent on means-testing, but it has been shown that they are less likely to claim such benefits. In a study of Batley in West Yorkshire, Gordon and Newnham (1985) found that 39 per cent of immigrant families were not claiming benefits to which they were entitled, compared with 23 per cent of the indigenous population. Possible reasons for such reluctance are racism, and problems of language and/or cultural differences.

Differences within ethnic minorities in relation to poverty

Berthoud (1998) provided material relating to poverty and ethnicity, resulting from an in-depth study of 2500 ethnic-minority households. He found that in terms of ethnicity, Pakistani and Bangladeshi households are easily the poorest and are four times as likely to be living on low incomes as white households. The key reasons include high unemployment among men, low levels of economic activity by women, and large family sizes.

- Sixty per cent of Pakistani and Bangladeshi households in the study had an income below the poverty threshold of half average earnings. Among the elderly, Pakistani and Bangladeshi pensioners were much less likely to benefit from occupational pensions and many were existing on means-tested benefits.

- In contrast, Indian and Chinese people had high levels of employment, and their average income was actually above that of white people. Nonetheless, they still suffered from much higher rates of poverty in their households. Poverty affected 22 per cent of Indian households and 28 per cent of Chinese households.

- While there was high unemployment among people of Caribbean origin, with low wage rates and higher levels of lone-parent families, the level of household poverty was found to be only slightly higher than that among white households.

The study highlights the diversity of experience in relation to poverty among ethnic minorities. The author argued that there were a number of factors which might explain these differences, such as differential education and training; different religious and cultural factors, particularly in relation to Islamic views on female employment; family size; and finally economic factors such as the decline of the textile industry which has hit particularly Pakistani and Bangladeshi communities relatively hard.

The inner city

Some common themes are evident in the various theories of the development of the 'world city', 'post-modern city' or 'post-industrial city'. In particular they have all noted how migrants from developing countries have been attracted to the urban regions of richer countries to perform unskilled jobs in the newer service and high-tech industries (see Section 17.2). As subcontracted (or officially 'self-employed') workers on short-term and/or part-time contracts, they have been used flexibly by companies in order to maximize profits. Long periods of unemployment are likely. Many theorists see these migrants being separated, geographically and socially, from other communities; although Jencks (1996) suggests this is not exclusively so.

Contemporary sociologists have been keen to study this situation, theoretically and empirically, particularly in terms of quality of life (deprivation, policy initiatives to alleviate the problems and the consequences of both) and the potential consequences for society as a whole.

A classic study from the 1980s is that on Hackney by the critical journalist Harrison (1985). This provides an illustration of Jencks'

point that areas flicker like 'pulsating stars'. In the past Hackney was a successful area, but in recent times its traditional manufacturing base has largely been lost, owing to cheaper and more technologically advanced bases in the UK and abroad, resulting in a life of unemployment and surviving on 'the dole' for people in the area. The people Harrison interviewed reported a lack of control over their own lives because decisions that affected the area were made beyond it – they had little chance of altering them. They also felt frustrated at being deprived of basic 'life chances' such as decent homes, environment and schools. A major consequence, as people lost hope, was a falling population as people who could move sought a better life elsewhere.

This section now looks at a number of more recent case studies which develop these themes, in an attempt to explain them in terms of the global restructuring of capital and industry that Harrison had pointed to.

Case Study – Chicago

Wacquant's study of Chicago in 1989 aimed to explain what he saw as 'hyperghettoization': the 'undeveloping' of an inner area in a short space of time, owing to a complex of factors:

The plight of the ghetto is the outcome of a complex interaction of economic, social and political factors and no monocausal theory will ever satisfactorily account for it.

(Wacquant, 1995, p. 419)

The economic reasons for 'hyperghettoization' were, according to Wacquant, based around the restructuring of the capitalist economy that we considered in the previous section. Sectorally, the economy moved from the old industries, destroying the jobs previously taken up by inner-city dwellers. Occupational changes meant that what jobs they could get were poorly paid or short-term. Spatial changes in the economy meant that jobs had moved away from the city to the suburbs and regions beyond. However, these were not neutral processes, but based on:

... the new 'hegemonic–despotic' phase of American capitalist development – one which pacifies workforces by uprooting itself or threatening to do so, leaving workers the choice of a poor job or no job.

(Wacquant, 1995, p. 419)

Socially, Wacquant identifies institutional and individual racism as a cause of the 'hyperghettoization'. White employers (in both an organizational and an individual sense) tended to see black inner-city inhabitants as lazy, poorly qualified and unable to assume a 'work-first' mentality. This led them to overlook black applicants, or to locate away from the black inhabitants of the inner city. This further segregated the 'wealthy' whites and the 'poor' blacks.

Politically based interference was seen as the third cause of 'hyperghettoization'. Road-building policies helped the de-industrialization process and the flight to the outer regions. They also acted as buffers to prevent spatial expansion of the ghetto. The outward flight of industry, and the wealthy, was helped by government subsidies for factory and home building in the outer regions. Slum clearance programmes making way for new centrally-based commerce resulted in displaced residents being forced into the remaining ghetto, making for a more concentrated, homogeneous form. Welfare policy became penal policy:

[the] War of Poverty of the 1960s [became] the ... War on the Poor of the 1980s.

(Wacquant, 1995, p. 438)

The poor were blamed for the making of the ghetto through the 'New Right's' underclass agenda which claimed that the lifestyle of the inner-city poor, who were too lazy to work and who couldn't be bothered to help themselves, had brought the problems on their own localities. This allocation of blame allowed reductions in welfare programmes – which were accused of creating a dependent culture – and led to the development of policies criminalizing the poor, resulting in them being put in prison. Wacquant was angered by the direction in policy:

Since ghetto poverty is the product of economic and political forces and struggles, not the result of the aggregation of free individual choices or moral failures, remedies to it must likewise be economic and political.

(Wacquant, 1995, p. 435)

17.6 Poverty and theory: Culture, structure and the underclass debate

Proposed solutions to the problem of poverty depend on the various explanations of its causes. These tend to fall into two broad camps: the indi-

vidualist/cultural and the structural. What differentiates them is the abiding moral element to British social policy – should those in poverty be viewed as unfortunate victims requiring help, or as profligate idlers requiring motivation or punishment? The notion of the deserving and the undeserving poor is still alive and well, as Lister points out:

There has always been a tendency to categorize poor people ... according to their respectability or 'deservingness', i.e. according to moral rather than economic or demographic characteristics.

(Lister, 1991, p. 194)

Activity

If the term 'poverty' carries with it the implication and moral imperative that something should be done about it, then the study of poverty is only justifiable if it influences individual and social attitudes and actions.
(Piachard, 1987, p. 61)
Make a list of the arguments for and against this statement.

C3.2, C3.3

This can perhaps best be seen in the growth of the notion of an 'underclass', certain versions of which contain the implication that the reason people are poor is because of their own behaviour.

However, one of the problems the poor face is that the cost of unhealthy food is cheaper than more healthy food, and the growth of out-of-town supermarkets has confined the poor without private transport to using local shops which tend to be more expensive. This can be seen in Figure 17.10.

Structural and cultural views on poverty

The political implications for social policy are clear. If we adopt a structural explanation of poverty, then the government should do something to alleviate the distress. On the other hand, a cultural approach implies less the need for governmental financial assistance than for campaigns to get the poor to change their behaviour. These campaigns need not necessarily imply spending more money. Indeed, some writers in the tradition of the New Right argue that

£14	£9.80
Weekly cost per person of a healthy diet – 1986	**Weekly spending in a low income family – 1986**

Increase in food price (1982–86)

Healthy food		**Not so healthy food**	
Wholemeal bread	17%	White bread	15%
Green vegetables	17–51%	Biscuits	19%
Salad vegetables	29–37%	Sugar	13%
Root vegetables	22–42%	Beef, lamb, pork	9–14%
Fresh fruit	16–45%	Bacon	13%
Fruit juice	64%	Sausages	13%
Poultry	26%	Whole milk	17%
White fish	44%	Butter	9%

Figure 17.10 The rising cost of eating well
Source: The Observer, October 1995

spending more to help those in poverty is actually part of the problem, not a solution.

Structural approaches to poverty

This term covers a variety of perspectives, ranging from Marxist and feminist approaches through to social democratic arguments.

Social democratic perspectives

Social democracy encompasses a wide spectrum of people who broadly share the belief that a market economy left to its own devices will create large income inequalities and therefore poverty, but that such a situation can be changed through government intervention acting through the parliamentary system. Clearly this is one motivation for setting up the welfare state based on the principle of full employment and universal provision of certain benefits.

Poverty and the labour market

The key cause of poverty, according to writers in this tradition, is the operation of the labour market, and in particular the creation of high levels of unemployment (see Section 14.6). Townsend (1979) certainly sees the operation of the labour market as a central cause of poverty. Since par-

ticipation in the labour market is seen to be the main source of income for most people, exclusion from work is likely to be a weighty factor.

Changes to the labour market in the 1980s and 90s under the impact of the New Right promotion of a 'flexible' enterprise economy (see Section 17.2) led to a rise in the numbers unemployed and to the creation of a whole raft of new jobs, often part-time and often poorly paid. Opportunities for the unemployed to remove themselves from poverty by finding well-paid jobs were reduced. Changes to the taxes and benefits system have also meant the widening of inequalities (see Section 17.1) and a reduction in the real value of benefits, leaving worse off those dependent on them for their income.

One example of this is the shift from grants to loans in the social fund, which has led to some in need being refused assistance precisely because they are poor. In relation to the Social Fund, Timmins (1995) pointed out that between 1992/93 and 1995/96 almost 250 000 claimants were refused help on the grounds that they were judged too poor to repay the loans.

Discussion point

To what extent do you think the refusals outlined in the article 'Poorest claimants are refused help' are justified?

C3.1a

The poverty trap

A second example of how government operation of the social security system affects the level of poverty is the 'poverty trap'. This affects those in low-paid employment: a large proportion of any increase in earnings is clawed back in reduced entitlement to social security benefits. In the past this meant that for some, for every extra £1 earned, they lost more than £1 in benefits and therefore lost out overall.

Oppenheim and Harker (1996) point out that in 1985/86 there were some 290 000 familes who stood to lose between 70p and 99p out of every extra £1 earned because of this, and by 1993/94 this figure had increased to 640 000 familes.

Townsend argues that there is a need for government intervention through policies aimed at reducing inequalities in income and wealth, greater industrial democracy to give workers more say in how companies operate, the abolition of unemployment through a right to work, and the institution of incomes to dependants such

Poorest claimants are refused help

NICHOLAS TIMMINS

Almost a quarter of a million applications for a loan to the Social Fund have been turned down because those seeking help were judged too poor to be able to repay, according to official figures.

The fund, set up in 1986, provides the emergency safety net for people on income support who take the interest-free loans to buy furniture, cookers or other capital items, with the repayments deducted from their benefit. However, those with existing loans or who already have direct deductions to meet fuel or other debts can be refused a loan on the grounds that they have too little benefit left to make the repayments.

Refusals on the ground of inability to pay have more than doubled since 1992–93, up from 44,890 to 116,095 last year, according to figures provided by Ian Magee, chief executive of the Benefits Agency, to Alan Milburn, Labour MP for Darlington. Precise comparisons are difficult due to a switch from counting applications for loans to counting the number of items refused. But refusals on one count or the other now total almost 250,000 over the past three years.

Mr Milburn said the figures showed that Peter Lilley, Secretary of State for Social Security, was betraying his pledge to target help on the most needy. "The very people that the Social Fund was designed to help now find they are too poor to qualify," he said. "Even before ministers take the axe to social security spending again, thousands of vulnerable people are being left without a vital lifeline."

Source: The Independent, 16 October 1995

as children and housewives so that involvement in the labour market is not a precondition for a decent income.

The idea that the social security system is based on outdated notions of how people live their lives is also expressed by Oppenheim and Harker:

Designed for a full-time male workforce, it discriminates against those who have been low paid or unemployed, against those who have worked part-time and people who have come to this country from abroad.

(Oppenheim and Harker, 1996, p. 4)

Marxist perspectives

Capitalism and poverty

Marxists agree with social democratic thinkers that the cause of poverty is to be located in the nature of free-market capitalism. Marxists dis-agree with social democratic thinkers about the solution because they do not believe that the welfare state and notions of citizenship can overcome the inequalities created by capitalism. Since, they say, poverty is a permanent feature of capitalism, the only solution is the revolutionary overthrow of capitalism and the institution of a communist society where production is based on human needs, not profit.

Surplus value

Central to the writings of Marx was the idea that capitalism operated by workers producing more in value than they were paid in wages, leaving this 'surplus value' to be accumulated by the capitalists. The lower the wages, the higher the income of the capitalists. The creation of poverty is thus the obverse of the creation of great stocks of wealth.

Marx's 'immiseration thesis' predicted that, over time, more and more people would become poor relatives to the capitalist class with their wealth at the top of society. Competition between capitalists would largely be solved by pressures for cuts in wages or greater productivity from workers, all of which would be backed up by the threat of unemployment if workers resisted. Such a threat existed, argued Marx, because the capitalists maintained a permanent reserve army of unemployed labour. (See also Section 14.6.)

The reserve army of labour

Since capitalism requires this permanent phenomenon of a reserve army of labour, there is a need to provide basic subsistence payments to enable such people to survive while they are not wanted. All capitalist states will therefore develop basic welfare systems. These will serve not to eliminate poverty, but merely to ensure that the poor can survive physically.

The limits of the welfare state

The Marxist approach to the welfare state does not accept the possibility outlined by social democratic thinkers that it can overcome the inequalities created by capitalism. The reasons for this are perhaps best explained by neo-Marxist writer Claus Offe. He points out that the welfare state faces a number of key structural limits to its powers. The most important of these is its reliance on tax revenue from private production and borrowing from private financial institutions to fund its activities. This means that in order to fund its activities it needs to ensure the continued profitable operation of capitalism:

The welfare state, rather than being a separate and autonomous source of well-being which provides incomes and services as a citizen's right, is itself highly dependent upon the prosperity and continued profitability of the economy.

(Offe, 1984, p. 148)

Marxist theorists are not greatly impressed by the social democratic vision of the possibility of the welfare state creating universal citizenship and being able to effect the kind of reforms. What is needed is a social revolution to overthrow the capitalist basis of society.

Feminist perspectives

The gendered division of labour and the welfare state

Feminists have also been critical of the welfare state for the way in which the gendered division of labour between the male breadwinner and a dependent full-time housewife is reinforced in its structures. This means effectively that most of the benefits it dispenses require participation in the labour market; and this serves to exclude large numbers of women, or at best confine them to a secondary status. The operation and construction of the welfare state therefore serves to reinforce exiting gender inequalities and as such can be described as operating in a patriarchal way.

Removing barriers to women's involvement in the labour market

For feminists the solution to poverty would be an end to such assumptions. This would involve a variety of changes, some of which might concentrate on removing barriers to the involvement of women in the labour market – such as the provision of state-financed childcare facilities – plus the institution of greater benefits for those who do not want to participate in the market. This would enable women (and indeed men) to make choices about the way they lived their lives and remove the risk that women would fall into poverty either through having to take responsibility for bringing up children or through being economically dependent on a male.

Individualistic (cultural) approaches to poverty

The key reason for poverty identified by individualistic thinkers is the behaviour and culture of the individuals in poverty. This was perhaps first expressed in the notion of 'the undeserving poor' which formed part of the Poor Law legislation. More recently it has been expressed in 'the culture of poverty' and in the cultural version of the 'underclass thesis'.

The culture of poverty

On the basis of his studies of the urban poor in Mexico and Puerto Rico, Lewis (1961, 1968) argued that the poor have a distinctive set of attitudes, norms and values which include a sense of resignation and fate. This cultural attribute makes them different from the rest of the population. His list of attributes of this culture of poverty runs to some 62 traits, including things such as feelings of helplessness and marginality, early sexual experience and violence in the household.

Lewis argued that, although middle-class researchers might find it hard to understand, such a way of life provided something positive for poor people and therefore it would be perpetuated. The culture of poverty is passed on from generation to generation. Lewis argued that in the USA something like 20 per cent of those in poverty could be said to live in this 'culture of poverty'.

Since that time the concept has come into more general usage, and often tends to be presented as the *reason* for poverty: these people are in poverty because of their own behaviour and attitudes, or at best, that of their parents. Their fatalistic attitude to life leads them to fail to take up opportunities and so they remain poor. They tend to live life for the moment, spending rather than saving, and not getting involved in political or community groups who are campaigning for change. Even if some of their poverty is due to the structure of society, their failure to get involved in any attempt to change it is due to their culture, not to structural factors.

The cycle of deprivation

Although Lewis was sympathetic to the people he studied, the idea that culture was central to the causes of poverty has been most notably taken up by the political Right, notably by Sir Keith Joseph in the UK. He argued that there was a cycle of deprivation, and he saw culture as the key element which kept the cycle going. Since this appears to let society off the hook for poverty, and instead labels the poor as essentially cultur-ally deficient, this viewpoint has attracted criti-cism for at least two reasons:

- The notion of a culture of poverty is deficient because it is not precisely specified, and fur-thermore culture is a consequence – not a cause – of poverty (e.g. Bilton *et al.*, 1988).

- Evidence shows that the children of those in poverty are not necessarily likely to remain in poverty, as the culture of poverty thesis would suggest.

An example of the second criticism can be found in the work of Brown and Madge (1982). In a study set up to test the 'cycle of deprivation the-sis', they found no evidence to support the idea that deprivation is culturally transmitted. This clearly questions the extent to which a culture is passed on through the generations.

A further criticism is based on the idea of sit-uational constraints: that the behaviour of poor people is to be explained on the basis of social and economic constraints which keep them in their present situation. If the poor express fatal-ism, it is because of the way these constraints are a reality, not because they are failing to take up opportunities that really exist. The poor have the same aspirations as everyone else but these situational constraints stop them from achieving them (Liebow, 1967).

The dependency culture

A more widespread concept in the individualis-tic approach today is that of the 'dependency cul-ture'. This is similar to the 'culture of poverty', but the explanation of the source of that culture is distinctive.

Here, the origin of the culture of dependency is the welfare state. New Right thinkers argue that the welfare state, by providing the poor with money for doing nothing, removes their incentive to go out and find work. They therefore stay unemployed and become dependent on their benefit payments. This leads to a loss of dignity and pride and to failure to take up new opportunities.

Against universal welfare provision

Marsland (1992) asserts that the idea of a 'dependency culture' provides the basis for argu-ing against universal welfare provision. He says that the cause of poverty is the socialist ideology underlying the setting-up of universal welfare benefits, since this saps people of the need to strive to survive. Socialism, by ridiculing compe-tition and the competitive market, undermines the pursuit of excellence and the ability of capi-talism to produce the increased living standards it undoubtedly is capable of.

The solution, it is argued, is that benefits must be made more selective and people should be encouraged to rely more on family and com-munity support if they fall into difficulties. Further, the benefits system should seek to encourage people to improve themselves by, for example, providing training schemes which help to keep people in tune with the skills required to obtain a job. Reducing the cost of social welfare would also allow a reduction in taxes, which would provide a spur to further economic growth and create more job opportunities.

Critics of this approach point out that when we last had unfettered capitalism the levels of poverty were high, largely owing to low wages. Having a job in an unfettered capitalist economy is therefore not a guarantee that one will not suf-fer poverty. A further criticism is that all the evi-dence shows that in means-tested benefits the poor are least likely to apply, either because of the stigma attached or because they do not understand the system. Middle-class applicants are more likely to benefit. (See also Section 14.1.)

The underclass debate

Cultural explanations of poverty have been given a further twist by discussion of the idea that there is an 'underclass'. This term has been the sub-ject of intense debate owing to the two very dif-ferent meanings attached to the word. Pilkington (1992) identifies a cultural and a structural view of the underclass.

The cultural view of the underclass

The cultural view is very much, though not exclu-sively, associated with New Right thinkers and has been very influential in the USA, most promi-nantly through the work of Murray (1984, 1989, 1994). This type of argument continues the line developed by the 'culture of poverty' thesis; although in contrast to Lewis, these writers are very unsympathetic and in some cases overtly hostile to the people they are describing.

Murray argues that the key cause of such an underclass is the growth of illegitimacy, which led to the growth of groups with distinct value systems. Again the emphasis is on the idea that people are poor because of their distinct values and behaviours and it is therefore their fault.

This view has been subjected to numerous critiques. Heath (1992) collected data on the attitudes of those defined as being in the underclass and found no evidence to support the idea that they held distinct cultural values. In fact, they seemed more likely to want to work than those in households where someone already had a job, and in all other respects held attitudes very similar to the rest of the population.

There seems to be an absence of hard evidence to support the notion of a distinct culture among the poor.

The structural view of the underclass

The structural view is associated with Weberian sociology since it argues that we cannot understand poverty and deprivation simply on the basis of the class structure alone: we need also to consider the way status divisions interact.

This view also highlights the fact that structural constraints in society may lead to the growth of the poor who are more or less permanently dependent on benefits, not because they do not wish to find a job, but because mass unemployment means there are not jobs for everyone. The distinction is to pointedly divide them off from the working class. Runciman (1990), a neo-Weberian sociologist, therefore includes the underclass as a separate class in his schema, and Labour MP Frank Field (1989) has concentrated on the way changes to welfare state provision have excluded certain groups from the standard of living and citizenship rights obtained by others.

The clear implication of this view is that the underclass are the victims of changes beyond their control, usually changes in the job market and welfare benefits.

Concluding comments

The distinction between the cultural and the structural views of the underclass has been blurred by recent interventions. Dahrendorf (1987) argues that, although structural factors play the major part in the *creation* of an underclass, this then develops its own culture. This idea has been shared by Frank Field (1996). Writing for the right-wing think-tank, the Institute for Economic Affairs, he says that the welfare system created after World War II does contain incentives for bad behaviour. In particular he

argues that means-testing, by treating the poor badly, lays the ground for the emergence of a 'yob culture'. He is still mainly focusing on the structural deficiencies of means-tested benefits, but the notion of a yob culture brings him closer to the cultural view of the underclass.

The concept of an underclass has been strongly rejected by Marxist thinkers. They contend that the poor are a part of the working class and exhibit no cultural differences from them.

Discussion point

To what extent is it possible to identify distinct structural and cultural approaches to the idea of the existence of an underclass?

C3.1a

17.7 Concepts of class

Karl Marx and social class

Virtually all discussions of social class can be traced back to the writings of Karl Marx (1818–83) (see also Section 16.1), in the sense that his analysis of class and class conflict retain their relevance in contemporary society.

Class conflict

Marx believed that all societies beyond the most primitive are characterized by conflict between two main classes; though he recognized that in certain historical circumstances intermediate class 'fractions' may exist.

The relationship between the two classes is based on conflict over the economic exploitation of the oppressed by the oppressor – whether it be master versus slave in the ancient epoch, noble versus peasant in the feudal, or the bourgeoisie versus the proletariat in capitalist society. This antagonism or class conflict was, for Marx, 'the motor of history' because it contained the contradictory forces that ultimately lead to the transformation of society from one stage to another.

Class and class conflict under capitalism

Much of Marx's writing was devoted to an explanation of the economics of the capitalist system, its impending demise and its ultimate replacement by a communist order.

In capitalist society the two great classes defined in terms of their relationship to the means of production are (a) the bourgeoisie, the owners of capital, and (b) the proletariat, those who have little choice but to sell their labour power. (But see Giddens on this in Section 16.1.) According to Marx's theory of surplus value, workers are not paid the true value of what they produce. Increases in productivity mean that more is produced than is required to provide a basic subsistence living to all under capitalism. Part of this surplus production is appropriated by the bourgeoisie.

Employers are in a position to exploit owing to their power to hire and fire workers. Workers have little choice but to sell their labour power in return for wages, and will only be employed for as long as their labour power produces profit for capital. Marx believed that the exploitation of the proletariat would lead to entrenched conflict between two increasingly polarized classes in a context of widening inequality between rich and poor. (See also Section 17.1.)

The role of the proletariat

The role of the proletariat, or 'working class', in Marx's theory of social change was to become a revolutionary class. However, he realized that it would not occur automatically: it depended on the establishment of 'radical class consciousness' on the part of the working class. In Marx's terms the proletariat had to be transformed from being a 'class in itself' (a group of people who objectively share a common position in relation to the means of production), to a 'class for itself' (one with subjective awareness of its common interests and an intention to ovrthrow the oppressors – the bourgeoisie).

The Marxist conception of class cannot be reduced simply to income level or even occupation, because class is fundamentally an expression of a social relationship between people *vis-à-vis* the production process – in which differences in income and work performed are secondary to the basic relationship of *ownership* or *non-ownership* of the means of production.

Furthermore, even occupation itself cannot be equated simply with social class in the full Marxist sense of the word. There are significant differences between two people doing essentially the same work if one of them is self-employed and the other is not. What is important is not so much the work done as the degree of autonomy and control that flows from ownership of the means of production.

The Marxist view of capitalist society portrays a dichotomous class structure (arranged on two sides) in which two polarized, antagonistic classes coexist in a relationship until such time as the proletariat overthrow their counterparts, thereby bringing about the transformation of society and simultaneously abolishing themselves as a social class.

Criticisms of Marx

Criticisms of Marx's theory of social class centre on two main issues:

- the likelihood of a class ever becoming fully class-conscious
- the inapplicability of his analysis to concrete historical situations generally, and in particular to capitalist society in the twentieth century.

Class consciousness

Class consciousness is for Marx's critics an improbability, though not an impossibility. Max Weber, in particular, took issue with the Marxist assumption that radical class consciousness would occur. He suggested that it might be possible to envisage social circumstances that would facilitate its development, but was of the opinion that it does not readily occur.

The dichotomy of classes

A frequent criticism is that Marx's dichotomous view of class is far too simplistic to be applicable to any real situation. Clearly any theory is an abstraction from the real world; and Marx, in his primary concern to point out the fundamental class division in society, was aware of the numerous anomalies in such a classification. Many groups or individuals are in an ambiguous position, unable to identify their interests with either bourgeoisie or proletariat. However, according to Marx, eventually polarization would occur whereby more and more people would come to identify their interests with one class or the other.

Middle classes

While some of the intermediary classes which Marx saw as transitional have disappeared, there has been an increase in the number of so-called 'middle classes'. This development tends to undermine Marxist theory as an explanation of the class structure of advanced industrial society.

The 'managerial revolution'

A further criticism of Marx's original theory claims that, as a result of the 'managerial revolution', control of capital has now become separated from, and more important than, its ownership. Thus the notion of class based around ownership/non-ownership is no longer relevant and does not take into account the rise of the so-called 'managerial élite'.

Max Weber: class, status and power

Class and class consciousness

Unlike Marx, Weber was less concerned to link the analysis of class to a general theory of history. (See also Section 16.1.) While agreeing that class conflicts occur frequently, Weber denied them the central place accorded by Marx. Weber's main criticism of Marx was that he confused what is *sometimes* the case with what is *necessarily* the case.

Though not using the same terminology, Weber implicitly agreed with Marx's distinction between class 'in itself' and class 'for itself'. Weber pointed to a variety of class actions that could result from a particular class situation, and he stressed that in capitalist society class consciousness resulting in class conflict was by no means inevitable.

Three dimensions of power and stratification

Weber argued that stratification has three conceptually distinct dimensions which relate to different spheres of power. 'Power' for Weber refers to the ability of an individual or group to get what they want even against the opposition of others. Weber's three spheres of power are the *economic*, the *social* and the *political*. Power in the economic system is stratified into classes, in the social sphere into status groups, while the political is based on parties and interest groups. Weber noted that, of the three, 'class situation is by far the predominant factor' (1961, p. 190).

Class

Weber agreed with Marx that class is an economic phenomenon: a person's class situation is a function of their position within the economic structure. It is position within the market that determines a person's 'life chances', so for Weber class exists to the extent that a number of persons share a common chance in the market for the possession of goods and other opportunities for income. Weber claimed that 'property' and 'lack of property' were the 'basic categories of all class situations' (1961, p. 182).

Thus for Weber, as for Marx, class situation pivots on ownership or non-ownership of capital; but for Weber it will also vary within and between these categories according to 'market situation'. In turn a person's market situation will depend on the skills and services they can offer in the labour market. In return for what people bring to the labour market (skills, qualifications, etc.) they are rewarded differently in terms of income, job security, benefits, and opportunities for social mobility. The effect of these factors, according to Weber, is to discourage the development of class consciousness.

Weber's theory of class specifically allows for a multiplicity of classes. In an attempt to establish a definition of the concept, Weber argued that a social class is comprised of a 'constellation' or grouping of class situations which share a number of commonalities. There were four such constellations:

1 The dominant ownership and commercial class.

2 The propertyless white-collar workers and intelligentsia.

3 The petty bourgeoisie (owners of small businesses).

4 The manual working class.

Activity

Suggest one example of a status group which demonstrates cross-class allegiance, and one example which illustrates a potential for internal class conflict.

C3.1a

Status

As part of his overall theory of power, Weber's analysis of class went beyond the economic dimension by linking it to status. If class reflects differences in economic power, status marks differences in the social sphere of prestige or honour. According to Weber, 'classes' are stratified according to their relationship to the production and acquisition of goods; whereas 'status groups' are stratified according to the principles of their consumption of goods as represented by 'special styles of life'. Status groups, unlike classes, tend *de facto* to have a sense of identity and common purpose.

According to Hamilton (1990, p. 194), Weber's main concern in defining these concepts is to characterize the stratification systems of societies as either class-based or status-based. Industrial capitalist society is predominantly class-based. Earlier forms of society have often been status-based.

Evaluations of status depend on a subjective, consensual notion by which they can be measured. Status thus involves a personal element which contrasts with the impersonality of class and which has implications for the kind of collective action that can arise from status groups as distinct from class action. Action based on status is concerned with 'social inclusion' and 'exclusion', status groups are concerned with maintaining social distance and exclusivity.

Discussion point

To what extent do you agree that New Labour's emphasis on 'social inclusion' and 'social exclusion' relies most on a Weberian status conception of inequality, and underplays the purely economic class-based elements of inequality?

C3.1a

Party

Parties are groups that pursue political power in the broadest sense. Thus they include political parties, trade unions, pressure groups and professional associations. In Weber's view, the holders of power may not be the most wealthy or have the highest status. Parties are related to, but distinct from, class and status groups and represent a further dimension of Weber's overall discussion of power, his primary concern.

Activity

a Try to think of (i) indicators of *status* that have universal significance, and (ii) those indicators that are of relevance only to the members of a particular subcultural group. Draw up two lists and note any similarities and differences.

b Which list is most significantly linked to the possession of *power*?

c Assess the extent to which status indicators in each list correlate with *social class*.

d Describe the relationship between *class* and *status,* and assess their relative importance in sociological analysis.

e Describe the relationship between *status* and *power*.

C3.2, C3.3

Comparing Weber with Marx

Weber's view of class can be contrasted with that of Marx on a number of grounds.

- Weber's is a pluralistic classification rather than a dichotomous one.

- It suggests that industrialization complicates patterns of stratification rather than simplifying them in the direction of two great classes confronting each other. For Weber the complexity of market relations generated by the division of labour in capitalism creates a variety of different and overlapping interests often making for cross-class allegiances and internal conflicts within classes.

- Class is seen as an objective fact about a person's life chances, but it does not follow that people in common situations always see that situation in the same way. In line with Weber's general sociological position (see Section 16.1), he gives a much greater role to subjectivity and meaning in the relationship between economic interests and class consciousness, seeing the development of class action as a voluntaristic process and as a result far from inevitable.

- Class is seen primarily in terms of market situation (the means of consumption) rather than in terms of the relationship to the means of production. Marx placed much greater emphasis on the latter.

- Weber places much more emphasis on the

advantages that stem from the possession of knowledge.

- Weber stresses the importance of status as a basis of group formation.

- Weber rejects what is seen as Marx's economic determinism, by questioning the primacy of economic factors in shaping social life over others, such as political ones.

- Essentially, then, while Marx predicted class conflict and polarization, Weber highlighted the problematic nature of class action and predicted a fragmentation of the class structure.

🗪 Discussion point

Discuss the proposition that there are as many similarities as differences between Marx's and Weber's theories of social stratification.

C3.1a

The inheritance from Marx and Weber has continued to inform virtually all subsequent accounts of class analysis. This section considers ways in which neo-Marxist and neo-Weberian theory attempted to adapt to changes in the class structure during the twentieth century.

A neo-Marxist approach

Wright: contradictory class locations

Wright (1976, 1985, 1997), an American Marxist, has developed neo-Marxist class analysis further. Wright devised a classificatory scheme which included the higher non-manual occupations – which he described as being in a 'contradictory class location'. They are said to be in a contradictory location within class relations because they are located immediately between two other classes in a hierarchy based on differential access to control, one of which has more control while the other has less. Wright adds the dimension of 'organizational control' to the more conventional one of ownership/non-ownership. He divides possession of organizational control into three types:

- control over investment
- control over the means of production
- labour power.

While the bourgeoisie possess all three, the contradictory classes show a mixed pattern –

controlling some elements but not others, and having control over some while being controlled by others. This is illustrated in Figure 17.11.

A class map

Wright devised four degrees of control which generated a four-fold classification of contradictory classes between the bourgeoisie and the proletariat. He also distinguishes between two sections of the bourgeoisie, the 'traditional capitalists' and the 'corporate executives'. When the proletariat, the semi-autonomous workers, the petty bourgeoisie and small employers are added to the picture, Wright's original class map contained ten classes. This was hailed as a significant development in dealing with the intermediate propertyless classes. But there were problems with trying to differentiate the proletariat from semi-autonomous workers.

Exploitation

Wright also went on to question the notion of 'contradictory classes', on the basis that it placed too much emphasis on the concept of *domination* and took little account of *exploitation*. Wright revised his analysis with central emphasis on the concept of exploitation. He argues that it is not only the bourgeoisie who are able to exploit workers; some non-owners are able to exploit other non-owners owing to the fact that they possess capital in the form of educational credentials and strategic managerial control, rendering them at one and the same time exploiters and exploited.

Wright thus constructs a class schema which is based around the Marxist notion of exploitation, while also making the distinction between owners and non-owners and accommodating the complexity of twentieth-century class relations (see Figure 17.12).

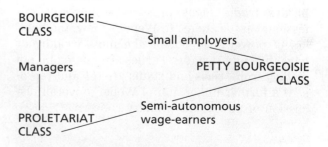

Figure 17.11 Wright's class map 1 (basic version): the relationship of contradictory class locations to the basic class forces in capitalist society
Source: Wright (1976)

Relationship to means of production

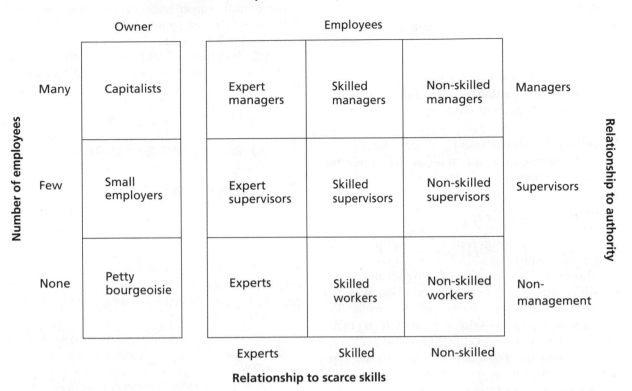

Figure 17.12 Wright's elaborated class typology
Source: Wright (1997)

An elaborated class typology

Wright's second map is to be read as follows. First, the distinction between owners and non-owners of the means of production is clear. Each class category is further differentiated. In the case of the *owners* the distinction is between those working for themselves and those who hire and fire others. Among *employees* the two key criteria are: firstly their location in the authority structure of the organisation (i.e. the degree to which they possess managerial authority) and secondly their possession of skills (including educational credentials). This generated six 'new' categories in the propertyless category.

Wright is clear about the fact that the people in the propertyless middle-class category have interests opposed to those of workers, so he describes them as being in contradictory locations within exploitative relations. Wright acknowledges, therefore, that his scheme implies that the process of class formation and class struggle is a far more complex process than Marx's original theory allowed.

Criticisms

Wright developed doubts about some aspects of his theory, notably the idea that managers are *necessarily* exploiters, that control is the basis of their exploitation, and that exploitation may be the basis for intra-class divisions rather than inter-class divisions. Others such as Savage *et al.* (1992) point out that it is unclear how a person with skill exploits the unskilled.

The most common criticism against Wright has been that his approach moves away from Marx towards Weber. This he denies, making the point that he has adhered to the Marxist notion that material interests in processes of exploitation are objective regardless of the subjective states of the actors.

Defining characteristics of a Marxist theory of class

Wright outlines the three defining characteristics of a Marxist theory of class as follows:

1   Class is defined in relational rather than gradational terms (i.e. the one significant class

division that matters is between owners and non-owners of the means of production).

2   Class relations are fundamentally shaped by the organization of production, not by the market.

3   The analysis of class relations is rooted in the processes of exploitation rather than in the technical division of labour.

Relational or gradational?

Wright has defended his Marxist orthodoxy by arguing that his class map (Figure 17.12) is 'relational' and not 'gradational'. In other words he claims that his map still contains the fundamental Marxist antagonistic dichotomy – capitalists and workers with different relationships to the means of production.

However, once he starts to discuss the internal differentiation of the non-owning category he resorts to gradational measures. So, while his description of ownership exploitation is relational, differences in organizational and skill/credential assets are gradational. It is not clear, for instance, why the possession of organizational skills and/or credentials should lead to the exploitation of non-experts by experts. The possibility arises that the propertyless middle classes do not constitute a distinctive, relationally defined class.

Production or the market?

With regard to Wright's second defining characteristic of Marxist class theory – its production-centred nature – he accepts that both Marx and Weber used production-based definitions of class. The main difference between them was that, where Weber looked to the market exchange of assets, Marx looked at production in terms of the exploitation it generates.

Edgell (1993) has commented that on close inspection of Wright's scheme it is difficult to see how it differs from Weber's in practice: as well as using property, Wright suggests that other factors – such as skill – can create class differences among the propertyless.

Exploitation or division of labour?

Wright's final defining characteristic of Marxist class theory is the distinction between *class* and *occupation*, which is the source of the Marxist thesis of class relationships being inherently antagonistic. In his analysis of the contradictory 'middle class' locations, he identifies them by reference to the occupational hierarchy. Therefore occupational considerations are not excluded from Wright's class analysis.

It might be concluded that, even in terms of his own definition of Marxist class theory, neither of his two class maps are purely Marxist as they contain gradational as well as relational elements.

A neo-Weberian approach

Goldthorpe: a new class map

Goldthorpe (1987), following Lockwood's (1989; orig. pub. 1958) expression of Weber's two elements in terms of the distinction between *work* and *market* situation, attempted to combine both components into a single class scheme – which can thus be described as a neo-Weberian approach:

We combine occupational categories whose members would appear, in the light of available evidence, to be typically comparable, on the one hand, in terms of their sources and levels of income, their degree of economic security and chances of economic advancement [i.e. market situation]; and on the other in their location within the systems of authority and control governing the process of production in which they are engaged [i.e. work situation].

(Goldthorpe, 1987, p. 40)

Thus the Goldthorpe class map aggregates together those occupations that share broadly similar market and work situations and results in a seven-fold class scale.

Market and work situations

The logic of this is extended to the arrangement of these seven into three broad groupings – 'service', 'intermediate' and 'working' – according to the commonality of their market and work situations. Goldthorpe argues that his employment-based class scheme is 'relational' – that is as reflecting the actualities of class relations based around property ownership. However, to the extent that it is based on a distinction between manual and non-manual work it is also said to be gradational (hierarchical ranking by occupation).

Thus in Goldthorpe's scheme a single class can include both the propertied and the propertyless (market situation) and manual as well as non-manual occupations (work situation). Those

Service class

I   Higher-grade professionals; higher-grade administrators and officials; managers in large establishments; large proprietors

II Lower-grade professionals and higher grade technicians; lower-grade administrators; managers in small establishments; supervisors of non-manual workers

Intermediate class

III Routine non-manual workers (largely clerical) in administration and commerce; sales personnel; other rank-and-file employees in services

IV Small proprietors, including farmers and small-holders, self-employed, artisans; other 'own account' workers (except professionals)

V   Lower-grade technicians; supervisors of manual workers

Working class

VI Skilled manual wage-workers

VII All manual wage-workers in industry in semi-skilled and unskilled grades; agricultural workers

Figure 17.13 Goldthorpe's model of the British class structure (Nuffield Mobility Study)
Source: Goldthorpe (1987)

Activity

a Within Goldthorpe's three broad categories – service, intermediate and working – identify which ones contain a mixture of propertied and propertyless people.

b Which contain a mixture of both manual and non-manual workers?

c Describe briefly what is distinctive about the working class according to these criteria, and in what sense does this make them a 'pure' class?

d Which class would be described as the most heterogeneous (containing the most diverse elements)?

e Explain what you understand to be the distinction between relational and gradational class elements.

classes that include such a mixture are said to contain gradational as well as relational elements. These can be seen in Figure 17.13.

Criticisms of the Goldthorpe scheme

Criticisms have centred around the problem of trying to resolve the use of relational (ownership and non-ownership dimension) and gradational (occupational dimension) in one overall scheme and within class groupings.

The relational definition implies the Marxist dichotomous model of two antagonistic groups, while a gradational definition tends at the very minimum to have three groups. Thus the merging of the two definitions is seen to be incompatible. Goldthorpe asserts that the scheme does primarily reflect the structure of class relations and is not consistently hierarchical.

Neo-Marxists such as Wright argue that, because it is based on occupational class rather than social class, the scheme obscures the fundamental social cleavage in a capitalist society – the conflict of interest between owners and non-owners of capital. Indeed, definitions which emphasize occupational groupings ultimately appear to exclude the capitalist (employer) class altogether.

A second and related point is that Goldthorpe's description of the 'service class' elevates their status by merging them with large proprietors, implying that they share similarities in income and power. However, this view is questioned on the basis that the impersonalization of control of capital has not reduced the privileged position of the capitalist class (Scott, 1991).

Other criticisms relate to the problem of including disparate occupational groups within the same category. This is seen in the placement of routine white-collar employees in the same ('intermediate') class as small proprietors.

Finally, there have been feminist objections to the use of a male head of household as the unit of class analysis, on the basis that this is no longer a salient measure of 'household class' owing to the increase in female employment and the growth in female-headed one-parent families. On the other hand it is also argued that, because women are concentrated in different segments of the workforce, especially routine non-manual work, then these classes need to be revised to make them more suited to the class allocation of women (Walby, 1986). Goldthorpe has responded to this by suggesting that in his scheme the routine white-collar jobs could be combined with the semi- and unskilled manual category.

Comparison of neo-Marxist and neo-Weberian positions

There has been a tendency to see an emerging convergence between the neo-Marxist and neo-Weberian versions of class analysis. However, Edgell identifies a number of important differences between them, as summarized in Figure 17.14.

So, despite similarities between neo-Marxist and neo-Weberian theoretical approaches to class, they retain significant differences in their approaches to the problem of how to combine relational and gradational elements in a single classification.

Social mobility

Social mobility is of central concern to sociologists for a number of reasons. It is important in the sense that the prospect of upward mobility may help to legitimize the existing social structure in the eyes of individuals, thereby reducing the potential for class conflict. But it is also important at a structural level, since according to Weberian sociologists it is related to class formation, the sense of class cohesion and the possibility of class conflict. Where there is considerable social mobility there tends to be a blurring of the edges between classes.

Ascribed and achieved status

Sociologists have distinguished between different systems of stratification according to whether they can be described as relatively open or closed:

- A 'closed' system is one in which social positions are determined at birth and a person's status is said to be 'ascribed'. Each social stratum is closed in that there is no possibility of movement between the various strata through either marriage or merit. Each stratum is thus totally recruited from within its own ranks.

- At the other extreme, a totally 'open' society would be one in which there is 'perfect' social mobility according to which class origins are completely unrelated to eventual class destinations. This implies fluidity of movement between the classes to the extent that those in the top stratum should contain by origin roughly equal proportions of people from each of the other strata. In such a society social positions would be said to be achieved – the true meritocracy – in which people would be totally responsible for where they end up. This arrangement might result in dysfunctional consequences – such as arrogance on the part of those at the top and demoralization of those at the bottom – with attendant possibilities for conflict (Young, 1961). However, it is still seen as a desirable direction in which to be moving.

Neo-Marxist class analysis	Neo-Weberian class analysis
• Contains an occupational dimension to class which is essentially relational	• Contains an occupational dimension to class which is essentially gradational
• Incorporates the idea of a distinctive capitalist class	• Obscures the existence of a small but powerful class
• Sees the main 'fault line' in advanced societies as between employers and employees	• Sees the main division as between non-manual and manual workers
• Main advantage is ability to differentiate capitalists from non-capitalists	• Main advantage is ability to differentiate between a variety of non-capitalist classes
• Main disadvantage is that the proletariat is seen to include disparate groups such as routine white-collar workers and unskilled manual workers	• Main disadvantage is that the service class is seen to include disparate groups such as employers and employees

Figure 17.14 Comparison of neo-Marxist and neo-Weberian positions
Source: Adapted from Edgell (1993)

Discussion point

If class conflict might occur even in a truly meritocratic society, is it still an ideal wor... striving for?

Problems with measuring s... mobility

In attempts to measure the extent of mobility, a complicating factor is that th... pational structure is changing; so mol... related to the changing nature of jobs (s... Section 17.2) as well as to the fluidity of the ture at any given time.

Sociologists have distinguished b... *absolute* mobility, on the one hand, which... to the total amount of movement going on... class structure and the net changes in the each class, and *relative* mobility on the ou... hand, which refers to the chance of an individual from each class going up or down by a certain distance.

Both types of mobility need to be measured by comparing class status over successive generations – this is known as *inter-generational* mobility. The three main factors which affect social mobility are the number of positions to be filled, the methods of access and entry to positions, and the number of offspring to fill these positions.

Payne (1987) says that the occupational transition that has occurred in post-war Britain has helped to generate upward mobility, because there are more professional and managerial posts to fill. Most of these jobs require educational qualifications. It has also been the case that the fertility rates of those in the highest classes have been too low to fill all the new posts with their own offspring, so opportunities for upward mobility from below have arisen.

Figure 17.15 shows the importance of educational credentials for achieved status (in this case measured by income). As a result of the growth of educational opportunities, a debate has arisen as to whether a meritocracy has been established in Britain.

...toric working class appeared to be diminishing... towards less than two-fifths of the Brit... population.

When they compared the jobs of th... men with those of their fathers, they... that there had been substantia... mobility over the 60 years to 19...

Service class almost dou...

What had happened w... had almost doubled... recruit new mem... working classe... this was th... are more a... has a...

...sample surveys. (See also Section 8.5.) Glass (1954) and his LSE colleagues carried out the first major twentieth-century British survey of social mobility in 1949. The main finding was that the class structure was fairly static, with the number who rose roughly equaling the number who fell.

More recent studies have been undertaken: those carried out by Nuffield College, Oxford, in 1972, and the follow-up re-analysis of data collected in 1983 as part of the British General Election Study (Goldthorpe, 1987); and the Essex University Class Project in 1984 (Marshall *et al.*, 1988). The first two of these concentrated entirely on males for reasons of cost, while the latter included both male and female mobility.

Absolute social mobility

The Nuffield study was based on a survey of 10 000 men aged between 20 and 64 and was based on the Hope–Goldthorpe classification (see Figure 17.13). The picture that emerged was significantly different from that found by Glass in 1949. In terms of absolute mobility, the proportion of people in the top two classes (Goldthorpe's service class – S) had increased. Of those men born in the period 1908–17, only 22 per cent were in the service class in 1972 while the figure for those born in 1938–47 was nearer 30 per cent. The less well-off classes (intermediate and working – I and W) had declined, and the his-

10 000 ... discovered ... net upward ... 72.

... led

... as that the service class ..., and inevitably it had to ... ers from the intermediate and ... s. One important consequence of ... fact that the sons of the service class ... likely to stay where they are – which ... impact on relative mobility – and this is ... ussed later. In terms of the degree of openness of the top classes, while the service class still contained a majority who were born into it, there had also been an influx from other classes. Thus there has been a widening of its recruiting base and a consequent decline in the extent to which it is self-recruited.

Long-range upward mobility

Also in contrast to Glass, the Nuffield team found evidence of 'long-range' upward mobility. This contrast is illustrated by the fact that in the 1949 survey the percentage of people of class 7 origins who had reached a class 1 destination in 1949 was 0 per cent, while the equivalent figure in 1972 was 7.1 per cent. There was clearly 'more room at the top' and the survey found about 750 who had moved from the bottom to the top.

The 1983 study confirmed the strong upward trend of absolute social mobility. In 1972, just under half the respondents said they had manual jobs; by 1983 the figure was nearer one in three. And one in three had service class jobs, compared with about one in four eleven years previously. The one note of change was that long-term unemployment (see also Section 14.6) had increasingly come into the picture, but as might be expected its effects were felt most by the manual working class. So, while in 1972 sixteen per cent of the men from working-class backgrounds aged between 20 and 34 had moved up the ladder into the service class, and 60 per cent had stayed in the working class, by 1983 twenty-two per cent had moved up and only 40 per cent had stayed there. But 11 per cent of these were unemployed.

Working class more homogeneous

Goldthorpe also noted that it was becoming increasingly difficult to escape from the working class later in life, and as a result those who stayed in the working class were becoming more homogeneous. This point is salient to debates about developments in the working class and the 'underclass'. So the overall picture continued to be one of a growing heterogeneous middle class underpinned by an increasingly tight self-recruited working class. Rose (1988) has argued that the growth of middle-class jobs has ended, and points out that even if more were created – which is unlikely – they would most probably go to the children of this new expanded middle class.

The 1984 survey

The 1984 survey produced quite similar results, as can be seen from Table 17.22, which has been simplified by omitting the data on the intermediate class. Payne summarizes the 1980's findings thus:

Moves up from manual to service class tend to be higher by the 1980s. ... people born in the service class are able to retain their position ... and fewer of those born in the working class remain there.

(Payne, 1991, p. 13)

Table 17.22 Absolute male social mobility in three British studies (percentage of origin)

Origin	Destination	1972	1983	1984
Service	Service	58	62	60
Manual	Service	16	24	20
Service	Manual	19	16	20
Manual	Manual	61	53	51

Source: Payne (1991)

Occupational transition as the basis of increased absolute social mobility

Such findings on the increase in absolute social mobility might be seen by some as evidence that the UK has become a more open society and even a 'classless' one. However, Goldthorpe (1987) and Marshall *et al.* (1988) have argued that the increased levels of social mobility are not necessarily indicators of equal opportunity or a classless society, but are instead to be explained by changes in the occupational structure.

More recent evidence on changes in the occupational structure from 1971 to 1991 based on national census data is illustrated in Figure

17.16. This shows clearly the changes in the numbers of people in each class and the net result of social mobility.

Goldthorpe (1987) and Halsey (1980) conclude that the upward mobility was wholly explained by the UK's general post-war economic expansion, social reforms such as the 1944 Education Act having contributed nothing. Goldthorpe says:

Even in the presumably very favourable context of a period of sustained economic growth ... the general underlying processes of inter-generational class mobility – or immobility – have apparently been little altered.

(Goldthorpe, 1987, p. 86)

Halsey shows that the main effect of educational reform was in fact to increase the proportion of middle-class children going on to university. (See also Section 11.3.) The message is that policies of social democracy had not brought about greater equality of opportunity. The middle classes managed to be the prime beneficiaries of welfare services provision (see also Sections 12.3 and 14.5), and this is evidenced by continued differences in relative opportunities for upward mobility.

Relative social mobility

While it is clear that absolute levels of mobility have increased, this does not necessarily mean that inequalities of access based on social class background have been eliminated. What really matters are the chances that, say, two children from very different class backgrounds have of reaching the top. This is what is measured by *relative* social mobility, and it emerged that, despite the general opening-up of chances, the odds were still stacked against the sons of working-class fathers.

The 1972 study found that the service-class children were three-and-a-half times as successful (in ending up in the service class) as children of manual workers. By 1984 this had fallen to a still significant 3 to 1 advantage. If the effects of occupational transition are controlled for (using statistical techniques), then according to Goldthorpe (1987, p. 252) 'no significant reduction in class inequalities has in fact been achieved'. Marshall *et al.* concluded that 'there have been no changes in social "fluidity" – that is, in the direction of greater equality of opportunity' (1988, p. 137).

Odds ratios

The Essex mobility findings on relative mobility have been presented in the form of 'odds-ratios'. Marshall explains the principle of this technique by reference to the example of betting odds. A very good horse and jockey may be expected to win a race and be given odds of 2 to 1, whereas an outsider might be given odds of 20 to 1. Then the odds ratio – that is the difference in their *relative* chances – is 20/2, or 10. The Essex team worked out such ratios for mobility chances and these are shown in Table 17.23.

In order to understand this table, examine the transition for men from service- and working-class backgrounds competing to end up in a service-class rather than a working-class destination. The odds ratio here is 7.35 to 1, which is the measure of the advantage held by the former over the latter in this particular competition.

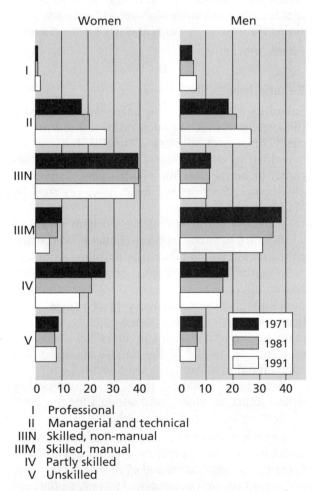

Figure 17.16 Social class mobility: percentage of the UK population by social class and sex
Source: Census/*Guardian*, 25 February 1995

Legend:
- I   Professional
- II   Managerial and technical
- IIIN   Skilled, non-manual
- IIIM   Skilled, manual
- IV   Partly skilled
- V   Unskilled

Table 17.23 Transition from class of origin to present class position

Pairs of origin classes 'in competition'	Pairs of destination classes 'competed for'					
	Men			Women		
	S vs I	**S vs W**	**I vs W**	**S vs I**	**S vs W**	**I vs W**
S vs I	2.75	3.09	1.12	1.67	3.75	2.23
S vs W	4.00	7.35	1.82	3.77	12.95	3.43
I vs W	1.47	2.37	1.62	2.23	3.45	1.54

Note: S = service class; I = intermediate class; W = working class
Source: Marshall *et al.* (1988, p. 105)

In other words, the chances of someone starting in the service class being found in the service class rather than the working class are over 7 times greater than the same chances for someone starting in the working class in the case of men, and almost 13 times greater in the case of women. If there were no class inequality in this respect then the odds ratio in any given comparison would be simply 1. All the figures in the table are over 1. What is more, these relative mobility chances do not vary much over time, so the odds ratios have remained remarkably constant.

Activity

From Table 17.23, identify those 'competitions' where the odds ratio is greatest and smallest in the case of men. Repeat the exercise for women.

C3.2, C3.3

Criticisms of the notion of relative mobility

Saunders (1990a) has accused Goldthorpe, Marshall *et al.* of being unrealistic, on the grounds that it is inappropriate to expect the odds ratios to be identical and it is wrong to ignore the occupational transition effect. He says that they will not accept that there is equality of opportunity until destination is completely unrelated to origin. He argues that greater affluence has been significant in causing large numbers of people to experience upward mobility and this cannot simply be ignored on the grounds that we are not yet totally equal in access to opportunity.

Marshall and Rose, on the other hand, argue that Saunders is wrong to simply assume that because considerable numbers of people have experienced upward mobility it follows that they have done so meritocratically. Payne sheds light on this debate with the following example:

Suppose that 70 per cent of today's service class are recruited from origins in other classes; is this high or low, good or bad? If 85 per cent of the population started in the other classes, then 70 per cent is not too bad, but it means that the other classes are not achieving their share (i.e. 85 per cent) of the best occupations. Saunders is stressing that the 70 per cent is quite good, while Marshall and Rose are saying the missing 15 per cent is what really matters.

(Payne, 1991, p. 13)

Genetic inequality?

Saunders (1996) has also been associated with the argument that the odds ratios are not necessarily the result of class inequality but can be explained by other factors, such as genetic superiority or better parenting on the part of the middle classes. Such views have been rejected by Marshall and colleagues.

Table 19.5 shows that class origins *do* make a difference to social mobility chances, even when educational level is taken into account. Saunders believes that IQ ('intelligence quotient' or ability) has an effect over and above the effect of educational qualifications and has replaced social privilege as the major factor determining where a child is likely to end up in the class structure. (For further details of the debate about IQ and educational achievement, see Section 11.6.)

Saunders believes that in contemporary Britain there is widespread support for the ideal of meritocracy according to which:

... there is a strong and shared sense of fairness and justice which demands that there be some link between individual talent and effort on the one hand, and reward through occupational success on the other.

(Saunders, 1996, p. 88)

For him, Britain can be described as a truly meritocratic system because, though unequal in outcome ('end-state' inequality), it is essentially fair in terms of the operation of equality of opportunity. He rejects the notion that social advantages and disadvantages determine where people end up in the class system. He claims that the notion of impenetrable social barriers which blocks the rise and blights the lives of millions of people was, despite their own experiences of upward mobility, a fiction created by novelists, playwrights, television producers and left-wing sociologists.

Saunders has in turn been criticized by members of the Nuffield College Oxford Sociology Group who argue that his data have serious flaws to which he is blinded by his own ideological position and political dogma.

Education and 'natural talent'

The crux of the debate seems to revolve around the question of how far the outcome of the competion for educational credentials and occupational positions is simply a result of 'natural talent' and effort which will somehow 'out' regardless of social privlege or deprivation. The converse position is that social environmental factors are vital and that equality of opportunity is not possible until children come from more or less the same class backgrounds in the first place.

Goldthorpe has continued to research 'mcritocratic' social selection in present-day Britain. Polly Toynbee (1999) quotes the findings of recent research by sociologists at Nuffield College, including Goldthorpe's. Studying two cohorts of children, one born in 1958 and the other in 1970, he found that the earlier group had slightly more class mobility than the latter. He argues that ability and effort play only a limited part in ultimate class destination. The paradox is that the more peple who become educated, the smaller part credentials in themselves play in the operation of class mobility.

According to Goldthorpe, in a free market employers decide what constitutes merit, and he believes that class lays heavily with employers. In other words, people may be promoted on qualities other than intelligence or qualifications. To an extent, less bright middle-class children have improved their chances of at least maintaining the class position of their birth by taking a disproportionate amount of the new university places. Such an argument goes some way towards providing an explanation for the data in Table 17.23.

In the *Times Higer Education Supplement* of 10 October, 1997 Adonis and Pollard (1997) argued that Britain's top universities are dominated bt students from private or grammar schools, leading to a situation of virtual educational apartheid. There is further evidence for this in the form of a 1995 BMA study quoted by Adonis and Pollard. The BMA found that 55% of medical students were educated at private schools or state schools and one in five even had a doctor as a father or mother, making medicine a partly hereditary profession. On the same lines, a third of Eton pupils are the sons of Etonians.

Even more recent support for the continuing importance of inequalities in access to education and its impact on wider inequalities came from research funded by the Sutton Trust (Lampl, 2000). This showed that while the less affluent make up half the nation's families, they only make up a quarter of the university population, and students from the third of families who live in poor neighbourhoods make up only 18 per cent of the university population.

When attention is focused on the 13 top universities, the inequalities become even greater as can be seen from the *Times* editorial of 10 April 2000 printed below.

Activity

Read the editorial the *Times*.

a Summarize the findings on entrance to university.

b On what basis does the editorial argue that 'things are getting worse, not better'?

c How does this bit of research fir in with social mobility figures quoted earlier in this section?

d How night Peter Saunders respond to this editorial?

C3.2, C3.3

Female mobility

Most of the material discussed in this section has related to male mobility. As can be seen, the Essex Class Project also included an investigation of female mobility. In order to overcome the automatic sexism in most social mobility studies, they used the term 'chief childhood supporter'.

Most of the findings confirmed the view that women experience sex segregation in employment, which disadvantages them. This probably explains the most striking fact about women's class trajectories: regardless of starting point, any-

Universities should be far more meritocratic

If anyone still doubted that the class system remains entrenched in British education, today's analysis by the Sutton Trust proves the point. Britain's top universities should be admitting the brightest 18-year-olds; instead their intake is heavily skewed towards rich intelligent pupils, particularly those from private schools.

Of course, the best private schools are highly selective, so one would expect their pupils to win a disproportionate number of places. but, even taking account of A-level results, the study finds that the top five universities admit 50 per cent or more privately educated students than would be expected, and 40 per cent fewer than expected from lower social classes.

When the study widened its focus to the top 13 universities, it found that the probability of winning a place was some 25 times greater for those educated privately than those from a low social class or a poor area. These discrepancies cannot be explained away by differential ability.

The Sutton Trust's findings confirm an earlier study by Bristol University, which tracked 600 young people who scored similar marks in a test at 11, but who took contrasting educational paths. Nearly 40 per cent of those who went to private schools (half of them on assisted places) won a place at Oxford, Cambridge or one of the other top universities, compared with fewer than 30 per cent from grammar schools and fewer than 10 per cent from comprehensives. In Britain, it is still clear that money can buy educational success.

You do not have to be a class warrior to believe that this is wrong; simply a meritocrat. Bright working-class children are not given enough chance to better themselves through education, and it is not just they who lose out, but society too.

Unfortunately, things are getting worse, not better. In the 1960s, the proportion of state-education children going to Oxford and Cambridge was far higher, thanks to the existence of direct-grant and grammar schools. Now most of the direct-grant schools have joined the private sector, and most of the grammar schools have been abolished. Since Labour took power, there are no longer even assisted places at private schools for the less affluent but highly intelligent children.

The Sutton Trust's study looks at the chances of gaining a place based on equal A-level grades. But it is much harder to win three A grades from an inner-city comprehensive than from Eton. Universities such as Bristol, which have offered slightly lower entrance requirements to students from schools with poor A-level averages, have found that they quickly catch up, and often overtake their peers when it comes to degree results.

Ideally, British universities would look for aptitude as well as achievement in their prospective undergraduates. This is what happens in America, where all applicants sit a Scholastic Aptitude Test (in effect, a sophisticated IQ test). University admissions officers trawl the results to try to identify potential in students from under-achieving schools.

They also work far harder at persuading students from poorer backgrounds to apply. So far in Britain, such effort has been undertaken almost single-handedly by Peter Lampl, the philanthropist who set up the Sutton Trust. It is time that universities took more seriously their obligation to offer the best education in the country to the best pupils in the country.

Source: Editorial in *The Times*, 10 April 2000

---

thing from a third to a half end up in class III (by their own occupation). Table 17.24 indicates the different trajectories of men and women when controlling for level of educational attainment. The social fluidity among men and women is virtually the same; that is, taken as separate entities the internal characteristics of their mobility patterns are similar. But equality of opportunity for women appears to be limited because their destinations (jobs) have in the past tended to be less advantageous than those of men.

Activity

a State *in your own words* how the information in Table 17.24 demonstrates that differences in social mobility chances cannot be explained by superior educational attainment alone.

b To what extent does the evidence in the table support the claim that male and female patterns of mobility are different?

C3.2, C3.3

Table 17.24 Mobility trajectories (percentages)

Educational attainment			Male destinations			Female destinations			All destinations		
			S	I	W	S	I	W	S	I	W
HIGH	origins	S	92	3	5	78	22	0	86	11	3
		I	90	5	5	63	35	2	75	21	3
		W	91	9	0	57	39	4	76	22	2
MEDIUM	origins	S	43	32	26	30	61	9	39	41	20
		I	31	41	29	22	63	16	27	49	24
		W	15	37	43	21	60	19	17	47	36
LOW	origins	S	33	27	40	0	57	43	23	36	41
		I	13	33	54	13	37	50	13	34	53
		W	11	25	64	2	43	56	7	33	60

Source: Marshall and Swift (1993)

Conclusion

If a classless society is one where there are only weak links between people's origins and where they end up, then even on this definition the UK cannot be said to be classless. It has a far from perfectly mobile society, and studies of social mobility demonstrate the continuing effects of class origins on eventual class destination. In the words of Heath, 'silver spoons continue to be distributed' (1981, p. 77). Marshall and colleagues sum up the situation thus:

Such upward mobility as has existed is the result of changes in the shape (rather than the openness) of the class structure.

(Marshall *et al.*, 1988, p. 137)

Activity

Explain the last statement from Marshall *et al.* (1988), and evaluate its validity using information from this section.

 C3.2, C3.3

17.8 Feminist theories

Many social scientists are critical of the view that there are naturally occurring behavioural and psychological differences between men and women. They argue instead that whilst there are certainly visible differences in the life-chances and life-courses of men and women, these should be seen as the product of social and economic inequalities, not as the inevitable consequence of natural forces. Arguments like this are based on the assumption that equality between men and women is desirable, although the means of achieving that equality may differ. Arguments emphasizing inequalities are summarized below.

Marxism: 'nature' versus history

The work of Marx and his successors has offered a challenge to biological theories which claim that inequalities between women and men are 'natural'. Rather than being 'natural', argue Marxists, all inequalities are products of particular historical conditions – what happened at a particular time, in a particular place.

Marxists suggest that human beings have no 'natural' tendency to behave in particular ways. If gender relations the world over appear similar

– with men dominant – this is because it suits the capitalist economic system to keep it so.

It is the course of history rather than the course of nature that determines the existence of such inequalities. Crucially, the course of history can change, and quickly, where tensions over inequalities between classes, in particular, become too much for a society to bear. This is in contrast to biological and evolutionary theories which give scope to conceive only gradual social change, in tune with biological evolution.

Engels: *Origins*

Marxists have argued that women's oppression is generated, like other sets of exploitative relations, through the workings of capital. Friedrich Engels (1972; orig. pub. 1884) identified the cause of inequalities between women and men in his 1884 pamphlet *The Origins of the Family, Private Property and the State*.

Engels wrote of an historical phase, early in the development of all societies, in which men and women carried out work tasks according to a division of labour by sex. But while men were hunters and women were responsible for domestic work, men did not dominate women, and women were not subordinate to men. Furthermore, no restrictions were placed on sexual activity – monogamous marriage, as today's western societies would understand it, did not exist – and men and women could have sexual intercourse with many partners if they so wished. This meant that the male parentage of children was uncertain, and so private property, of which there was very little – tools, cooking pots and so on – was handed on through the maternal line.

But as humankind began to herd animals, rather than simply to stalk them in the wild, the concept of private property took on greater importance. This was because a trade in meat and skins emerged. As this trade developed, so did men's power relative to women: men controlled the animal herds, and thus the key to early economic success. Not wishing to relinquish control of their own animal herds to a child of uncertain parentage, men found ways to restrict women's sexual choices. As they did so they created the patriarchal family, in which men dominate and control women and children (see Section 5.7). In this way, women suffered what Engels called a 'world-historic' defeat. Furthermore, the subsequent development of the capitalist economic system has meant that they have been unable to correct the imbalance in power.

Contemporary Marxism

All Marxist theorists share Engels' assumption that inequalities between men and women have arisen historically. Marxist theorists also argue, as did Engels, that women's subordination is basically a product of economic circumstances in a capitalist economy. Contemporary Marxists might also argue that the way in which inequalities act on the lives of men and women changes over time.

Marxist theorists have attempted to correct Engels' anthropological assumptions, focusing on more recent data in order to underscore the complexity of class and gender relationships (Coontz and Henderson, 1986).

Marxism and feminism

Many of the most compelling modern accounts of women's subordination do not base themselves on Marxist theory alone. Rather they draw on feminist theory too. In this way it has been possible for theorists to separate class exploitation and women's subordination, allowing questions about whether economic conditions and historical circumstances are solely to blame for gender-related inequalities, and allowing theorists to look closely at inequalities between women.

While Marxist theorists have offered explanations for women's subordination and racial subjugation, both black writers and feminist writers have argued that Marxism cannot satisfactorily explain the complex entirety of inequalities. They suggest that Marxism is effectively gender-blind and 'race'-blind.

Feminist sociology and patriarchy

Feminist sociologists – and other feminist writers – have argued that the social and economic odds are almost always stacked against women, so that they may face inequalities in all areas of their lives. Contemporary British society, many have argued, is a patriarchal one in which men have tended to determine the broad patterns of women's lives and choices. The term 'patriarchy' is used by most feminists to describe and analyse the unequal distribution of power between women and men. Broadly speaking, the term means 'male dominance of women'.

The theory of patriarchy

The theory of patriarchy is central to feminist arguments about sex and gender. This is because it provides a lens through which to view all the everyday ways in which feminists might argue that men are dominant over women. Patriarchy as an idea helps to make links between what might appear to be isolated instances – say, one man in one household never cleaning the bathroom – and other instances of the same occurrence – many men in many households, none of whom clean the bathroom. Maggie Humm, a professor of women's studies, has suggested that the concept 'patriarchy' is:

... crucial to contemporary feminism, because feminism needed a term by which the totality of oppressive and exploitative relations which affect women could be expressed.

(Humm, 1995, p. 200)

When patriarchy the theory is seen in action it is variously called 'subordination', 'oppression', or 'exploitation'. Feminists argue about the exact meaning of these terms, but each of them broadly suggests women's relative lack of power and status.

An example of patriarchy in action

Here is an example of how patriarchy appears to work. If it is assumed in theory, for example, that women are 'naturally' weaker than men, then it might also be assumed that women cannot work in jobs requiring physical strength (e.g. a warehouse packer). These assumptions may play themselves out in practice in various ways: that girls are discouraged from applying for warehouse jobs because they are 'dirty' and 'unsuitable' and positively encouraged to think about more 'feminine' jobs, such as hairdresser or beautician, or working in the office at the warehouse, instead; and that girls applying for warehouse jobs are not hired as packing is 'man's work'.

The overall result is likely to be that, as a result of such subordination, oppression or exploitation – call it what you will, for now – there are relatively few women working in manual jobs in warehouses. This example serves to illustrate the point, although it may be over-exaggerated for the purpose. In another version of the same

example, warehouse packers may be either men or women – but women pack smaller, lighter goods, whilst men deal with the larger, heavier ones or those on high shelves. Some women workers may actively seek to pack smaller goods in order not to be seen as 'unfeminine'.

Activity

a The 1975 Sex Discrimination Act made discrimination between men and women illegal in matters of employment, education, housing and the provision of other services. It banned recruitment advertising that sought applicants of a particular sex, for example, except in special circumstances. Check the job advertisements in the *Guardian*. Can you find any that refer to workers of a specific sex? What sort of jobs are they recruiting for?

b Study Table 17.25 and suggest ways in which its information supports the idea of the existence of patriarchy in the practices of everyday life.

C3.2, C3.3

Varieties of feminism

Several schools of feminist thought emerged in the 1970s and 80s as part of feminism's so called 'second-wave', a burst of activity in which women tried to right the imbalance of power between the sexes that they had identified (see later). Each school developed their own theory of patriarchy.

Radical feminists, like Firestone (1979) and Millett (1970), argued that the primary oppression women suffered was based around an entrenched gendered social divide. Men, they said, benefited both individually and collectively from women's unpaid cleaning and caring work in the home. In their view, a male-dominated society would tend to deny women access to positions of power, in order to maintain and consolidate their own standing.

In the opposite corner, early Marxist feminists like Rowbotham (1973) contested radical feminists' views, instead laying emphasis on the exploitative nature of the capitalist economic system. Like radical feminists, Marxist feminists focused on women's unpaid work in the home, but suggested that the owners of the means of production were the primary beneficiaries of this free labour: benefits accrued to men as a by-product of capitalism.

Table 17.25 How people spent their time (in hours) in May 1995

Weekly hours spent on:	In full-time employment		In part-time employment		Retired		All adults
	M	F	M	F	M	F	
Sleep	57	58	62	60	67	66	61
Free time	34	31	48	32	59	52	40
Work, study and travel	53	48	28	26	3	4	32
Housework, cooking and shopping	7	15	12	26	15	26	16
Eating, personal hygiene and caring	13	13	13	21	15	17	15
Household maintenance and pet care	4	2	6	3	9	3	4
Free time per weekday	4	4	6	4	8	7	5
Free time per weekend day	8	6	8	6	10	8	8

Source: ESRC Research Centre on Micro-social Change, from *Omnibus Survey/Social Trends* (1996, p. 216)

Early radical feminism and patriarchy

Firestone argues that the difference between men and women structures every aspect of human social life. In *The Dialectic of Sex* (1970) she suggests that men are able to oppress women because their physical strength is often superior and because women are disadvantaged by their childbearing and childrearing roles. Based in biology, men's power is inevitably reflected in culture and patterns of socialization.

What would be her solution? She would want to see social institutions, like the nuclear family (see Section 5.1), restructured so that women would no longer be dependent and subordinate, and – with a utopian vision presaging the advanced reproductive technology 25 years away – to 'end the tyranny of reproduction' (1970, p.

221) so that women were freed from the biological process of giving birth. This, Firestone argues, would mean an end to patriarchy, as women became men's biological equals, and were also able to control their participation in childrearing.

While many radical feminists did not share Firestone's views on childbearing, and have subsequently disagreed over the extent and nature of necessary social transformation, their assessment of the causes of women's oppression has remained broadly similar: women are categorized 'as an inferior class to the class "men" on the basis of ... gender' (Humm, 1995, p. 231). Patriarchy, for radical feminists, is society's defining principle and the primary explanation for gender stratification.

Early Marxist feminism and patriarchy

By contrast, early Marxist feminists like Rowbotham (1973) argued that patriarchy operated within the capitalist economic system. Rowbotham's evidence for this claim was drawn from her analysis of men's and women's work. She showed how the taken-for-granted division between work, which takes place outside the home, and leisure, which takes place inside the home, was a division which exists only for men. Far from being a place of rest for women, argued Rowbotham, the home was a place of work. In fact, women's unpaid work in the home – childcare, domestic labour, giving of emotional care – enabled capitalist and patriarchal social relations to reproduce themselves, as male and female children learned their behaviour by example. It was said that men exploited women within the environment of home and family, from whence a new generation of workers would come, fully socialized into the ways of capitalism and patriarchy. (See Section 5.7.)

Early socialist feminism and patriarchy

Many feminists argued that Marxists – who claimed to be able to explain all social, political and economic relationships – viewed the exploitation of women as ultimately less important than the class struggle. For this reason, feminists wishing to make use of Marxist insights, but certain that Marxism could not wholly explain women's oppression, developed what they called a 'dual-systems theory', distinguishing this perspective from Marxist feminism by calling it 'socialist feminism'.

Socialist feminist dual-systems theory was intended to show how capitalism and patriarchy acted together, infusing and moulding a social structure which created women as subordinate to men, both at work and at home. Feminists found it difficult to construct a dual-systems perspective that made complete sense, however. They argued that this was because Marxist theory, with its emphasis on 'class', could not easily accommodate feminist ideas.

The 'class' of Marxism and the 'gender' of feminism

Barrett, a feminist social theorist, explored the troubled relationship between Marxism and feminism in *Women's Oppression Today* (1989; orig. pub. 1980), as did Marxist feminist theorist Hartmann (1981) in an article 'The unhappy marriage of marxism and feminism'.

Hartmann argues that the relationship between Marxism and feminism is tense but necessary, and only a combination of both sets of ideas can unpick the role women play in reproducing capitalist relations. Barrett's tone is less certain that the two theories could co-exist. Reflecting almost ten years later in a revised edition, she writes that her book was part of an attempt:

... to bring together two world-views that have continued to go their separate ways in spite of our efforts at marriage guidance.

(Barrett, 1989, p. v)

Activity

Read the extract 'The unhappy marriage of marxism and feminism: towards a more progressive union'.

a Explain *in your own words* the limitations Hartmann identifies with respect to marxist analyses of relations between men and women.

b Why does Hartmann feel that a feminist analysis alone cannot account for inequalities between men and women?

C3.2, C3.3

Early black feminism and patriarchy

Feminists writing from black perspectives have criticized both radical feminist and Marxist/socialist feminist theories of patriarchy because they do not address the problems of racism that some women face. Black feminists like Anthias and Yuval-Davies (1983) have pointed out that radical feminists and Marxist feminists – in the main white women – have tended to 'forget' ethnicity in their analyses. Black feminists have called this forgetfulness 'ethnocentrism'. To be 'ethnocentric' means to focus on issues and problems specific to your own ethnic group, claiming that they are representative of the concerns of all, whilst failing to recognize the differing concerns of other ethnic groups.

Black feminists have argued that some white feminist theorists claim to speak on behalf of all women, but fail to notice the dissimilarity between some aspects of the experiences of white women and black women. Mama (1989) points out, for example, that social policy impacts differently on black women and white women. She argues that:

Black women with British-born children are

The unhappy marriage of marxism and feminism: towards a more progressive union

The 'marriage' of marxism and feminism has been like the marriage of husband and wife depicted in English common law: marxism and feminism are one, and that one is marxism. Recent attempts to integrate marxism and feminism are unsatisfactory to us as feminists because they subsume the feminist struggle into the 'larger' struggle against capital. To continue our simile further, either we need a healthier marriage or we need a divorce.

The inequalities in this marriage, like most social phenomena, are no accident. Many marxists typically argue that feminism is at best less important than class conflict and at worse divisive of the working class. This political stance produces an analysis that absorbs feminism into the class struggle. Moreover, the analytic power of marxism with respect to capital has obscured its limitations with respect to sexism.

While marxist analysis provides essential insight into the laws of historical development, and those of capital in particular, the categories of marxism are sex-blind. Only a specifically feminist analysis reveals the systemic character of relations between men and women. Yet feminist analysis by itself is inadequate because it has been blind to history and insufficiently materialist. Both marxist analysis, particularly its historical and materialist method, and feminist analysis, especially the identification of patriarchy as a social and historical structure, must be drawn upon if we are to understand the development of western capitalist societies and the predicament of women within them. We suggest a new direction for marxist feminist analysis.

Source: Adapted from Hartmann (1981, p. 30)

---

threatened with deportation when they leave violent husbands. Or Black women rehoused under the domestic violence policies fought for by feminists in some Local Authorities can find themselves housed in accommodation which had to be abandoned by the previous Black family because of racial harassment.

(Mama, 1989, p. 35)

Many black feminists have argued that the concept 'patriarchy' is unlikely to be able to include 'race'. They suggest that 'patriarchy' is a fully formed concept already and has no room for 'race' under its umbrella. Black feminists have pointed out that a black woman is both 'black' and 'female' at the same time, not primarily 'female' and then 'black' (or vice versa). James and Busia (1993) have spoken of the principle of the 'simultaneity of oppression' as a way of understanding how 'race', 'gender' and 'class' operate together to construct women's lives. They suggest that 'race', 'class' and 'gender' are relational categories – that is, they do not operate separately on the lives of individual women, and they should not be conceived of as separate analytical categories or abstract concepts.

Aziz (1997) agrees that the work of black feminists has tended to focus on the suppression by feminism of black/white difference. At the same time, where black women have been central to research they have often been presented as 'deviant' from a white norm. Whilst white women have been able to speak with authority on behalf of the whole female sex, black women have been seen as only able to speak for other black women, not for all women. Aziz points out that 'race' is not an issue that affects just black women. She argues:

... white-ness is every bit as implicated as black-ness in the workings of racism. Thus, whether or not they are aware of it, racism affects white women constantly.

(Aziz, 1997, p. 71)

Walby: updating the theory of patriarchy

Walby (1989, 1990, 1997), a feminist sociologist, has tried to link together feminists' competing explanations of women's oppression. She says that 'patriarchy' is too useful a concept to be abandoned: rather, it needs rethinking, in particular so that it can incorporate the experiences and analyses of black women. Hence she has developed what Roseneil (1994, p. 92) has called a 'triple-systems theory' of patriarchy.

Three interlinked structures

Walby proposes that patriarchy should be understood as a system of abstract relationships between women and men – but a system that intersects with capitalism and racism. For example, sociologists making use of triple-systems theory might undertake a study of black women's employment. (See also Section 17.2.) Having found that the majority of working black women occupy low-paying jobs that are relatively worse-paid than the low-paying jobs occupied by the majority of white working women, triple-systems theorists would then refer to Walby's system of abstract relations – explaining black women's position of relative disadvantage according to the manner in which patriarchy, capitalism and racism act on women as a group, and on individual women.

The six structures of patriarchy

Walby's theory does not understand patriarchy itself in terms of a single ultimate cause-and-effect mechanism. Instead Walby argues that patriarchy consists of six social structures which can act independently of each other or together. Roseneil (1994, p. 92) has summarized these six social structures as follows (see Figure 17.17):

1 *The patriarchal mode of production*, which refers to the exploitation of women's labour by husbands/cohabitees within the household – housework and caring work (See also Section 5.7.)

2 *Patriarchal relations in paid work*, which serve both to exclude women from high-status well-paid jobs, and to segregate women in particular low-status low-paid jobs. (See also Section 17.2.)

3 *Patriarchal relations in the state*, which means that the state tends to operate in the interests of men rather than in those of women. Examples of this include the policy of community care, which has returned, largely to women, the responsibility for caring for sick and elderly relatives; and the weakness of equal-pay legislation and the lack of investment in the machinery to implement the leg-

islation, which means that women still earn about £0.75 for every £1.00 earned by men.

4 *Male violence against women*, which takes the form of rape, sexual assault, wife-beating and sexual harassment. (See also Section 5.9.)

5 *Patriarchal relations in sexuality*, exemplified by the almost compulsory nature of heterosexuality and the stigmatization of lesbianism, and the sexual double standard, which values multiple partners and sexual encounters for men, yet labels women who behave similarly as 'slags' (Lees, 1986). (See also Section 4.1.)

6 *Patriarchal relations within cultural institutions*, such as the media, the education system and religion, which help to create masculine and feminine identities. (See also Sections 6.5, 8.8 and 11.5.)

Activity

a Suggest an example of patriarchy 'in practice' for each of the six structures identified in the list and Figure 17.17. 'Sexuality' has been done for you.

b Consider whether you would add any further structures to Walby's six. What would they be? Explain your choices.

C3.2, C3.3

Walby acknowledges that inequalities between men and women vary over time and in intensity, pointing, for example, to changes such as the fact that young women are on average attaining better educational qualifications than young men (Walby, 1990, p. 23). (See also Section 11.5.)

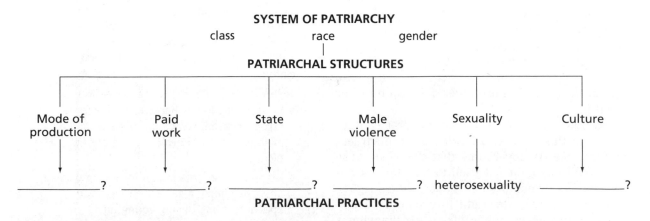

Figure 17.17 Patriarchy as a three-tier system of oppression: Walby's triple-systems theory

*'That's an excellent suggestion, Miss Triggs. Perhaps one of
the men here would like to make it.'*

From private patriarchy to public patriarchy

These variations in inequalities are linked to changes in the form of patriarchy itself. Walby points to a shift from private patriarchy to public patriarchy in the last 100 years, arguing that prior to the twentieth century the household was the main site of women's oppression. During the nineteenth century middle-class women in Britain were increasingly restricted to the home; and even while most unmarried working-class women were engaged in paid work, an ideology of domesticity (see Section 5.7) restricted their access to a variety of jobs, education and other forms of public life. No woman could hold a legitimate place in the public sphere, and she had no voting rights and few property rights, while her husband had the legal right to beat her. Women tended to exist under the control of their fathers and then their husbands, residing within the home, with few opportunities for economic or social independence.

At the beginning of the twenty-first century in Britain this picture of patriarchy is much less recognizable. Walby claims that this is because patriarchy has adjusted itself to fit women's relatively recently acquired civil and political rights. Women have won the right to vote and participate as citizens in public life, while enjoying a greater degree of freedom and independence than ever before. At the same time, they are poorly represented at higher levels within the state and private-sector businesses, tending to be concentrated in lower-paying, lower-status occupations (see Section 17.2).

Furthermore, women are culturally represented in what is arguably an increasingly sexist manner: television, film and advertising in the main portray women as sexual objects (see Sections 6.5 and 13.6). Evidence like this points to the existence of a public patriarchy that controls women's lives, even as they have become more independent of individual men.

Activity

Lara Croft, cartoon superheroine of computer game *Tomb Raider*, uses an Uzi machine gun to flatten her enemies, whilst wearing very few clothes, all the better to show off her exaggerated figure.

a View this fictional character at the *Tomb Raider* website: www.tombraider.com. You might be able to download and print a picture.

b Is Lara a feisty role model for young women, or is she simply a sex object created to appeal to game-buying young men?

C3.2, C3.3, IT3.1

Criticisms of Walby

Although Walby's theory of patriarchy represents an attempt to address some of the problems of earlier theories, and thus to answer feminists' questions about male dominance over women more effectively, some critics have suggested that her modern reworking of patriarchy is still inadequate.

Acker, for example, has pointed out that the search to 'theorize male dominance as a systemic process at the societal level' (Acker, 1989, p. 236) was stilled in the late 1970s and early 80s as feminist theorists realized that they had perhaps bitten off more than they could chew at that time. Three points in particular can be cited:

1 Feminist theorists had not compiled a full-enough record of women's histories and experiences to be able to formulate a theory that spoke to all women.

2 The territory to be encompassed was enormous and complex'.

3 The more general theories of society on which feminists had drawn to create their own large-scale understanding of male dominance claimed to be gender-neutral, but

[feminist] theorists understood that standing behind [concepts like] the gender-neutral human-being and gender-neutral societal processes were assumptions based on men's experiences.

(Acker, 1989, p. 237)

Acker admits that a move away from the unambiguity of a theory of patriarchy to the more fuzzily defined 'gender' means that what she calls 'critical-political sharpness' is lost. A theory of patriarchy like Walby's is a way of stating male domination and women's subordination unequivocally.

Hakim: the feminist 'myth' of patriarchy

Feminist theories have influenced contemporary sociology to a degree that has led some critics to suggest feminism constitutes a new and unwelcome orthodoxy in sociological thinking. Hakim is one such critic.

She suggests that feminists have over-emphasized their research findings in order to corroborate their strongly held beliefs. While she does not deny that in the past women have been subject to discrimination, she argues that feminists' theories of patriarchy are misleading, in the face of evidence showing women making rational choices about their day-to-day lives, and about the longer term.

Feminist myths about women's employment

In a controversial article entitled 'Five feminist myths about women's employment', Hakim demonstrates that far from being victims of unfair employment practices, women actively choose part-time work in order to manage the domestic responsibilities with which they actively wish to be engaged. (See also Section 17.2.) While she takes issue with feminist claims about women's participation in the labour market, her argument, by extension, is critical of a spectrum of feminist assumptions in other areas of sociological study. Hakim's claims are listed below:

1 There has been no substantial increase in women's labour market participation, contrary to feminists' perceptions and claims. Whilst the economic activity rates for women of working age have increased in the last 50 years, this increase can be explained mainly in terms of the substitution of part-time for full-time jobs and the substitution of married women for single women workers.

2 Women part-time workers are less 'committed' to their jobs than their male full-time counterparts. Hakim writes:

[The] commitment of a part-time worker to a part-time job is not equal to the commitment of a full-time worker to a full-time job. At the minimum the two levels of commitment differ in degree, and arguably they differ qualitatively as well.

(Hakim, 1995, p. 434)

This is because many more women working part-time have traditional attitudes towards women's role in the home and at work, than do their full-time women counterparts. Hakim suggests that while some women give priority to careers and training, others choose to give priority to what she calls the 'marriage career' (ibid.).

3 A lack of available and affordable childcare is not a major barrier to women's employment. This is because women with access to birth control can choose whether or not to have a

Feminist fallacies: a reply

Extract A 'The reasons for women's shorter job tenure (whether they leave for job-related reasons, for childbirth or for other domestic reasons including their partner's job moves) and the extent to which job quits reflect job changes or interrupted employment are important. ... Recent work confirms that the gender difference in turnover rates is attributable to the occupation rather than the person and that, once factors such as occupation, sector, firm size and age are controlled, women employed part-time are *less* likely to leave their jobs than those working full time (Elias, 1994).

Hakim's rejection of childcare as a major explanation of women's shorter job tenure is unconvincing. First, her data shows that women with dependent children have shorter job tenure than those without. Second, although women without dependent children also have shorter job tenure than men, they need to be disaggregated into women who are childless and those whose children are no longer dependent' (Ginn *et al.*, 1996, p. 171).

Extract B 'It is well known that part-time jobs are not only worse than full time, in terms of hourly pay, training opportunities, fringe benefits and statutory rights, but are also at a lower level in Britain than in other western countries (Dale and Joshi, 1992). ...

Expressed 'satisfaction' by part-timers with their job is likely to reflect their lack of alternatives and weak bargaining position with employers because of having to accommodate domestic responsibilities. Rubery *et al.* (1994) show that women part-timers are overqualified for their jobs and that their initial 'satisfied' response in surveys is not confirmed on examination. For example, they were less likely than women full-timers to say their current job was the one they liked best: over half women part-timers, compared with a third of full-timers (women and men), said that given their qualifications and experience they could expect a better job. ...

A key issue is whether women prefer part-time *jobs* or jobs with *short hours*. If women were able to stay in the same job, with the same employment conditions, status and level of responsibility, but reduce their hours to accommodate family commitments, would they choose to switch to jobs in the part-time sector of the labour market, with all the disadvantages characteristic of such jobs? Evidence from Sweden and Denmark, where working hours can be reduced in this way, suggests that they would not (Ginn *et al.*, 1996, p. 170).

Extract C 'Hakim points out that the total hours of female employment, in terms of full-time equivalents (FTEs), have increased little in the postwar period up to 1987 in spite of the dramatic rise in the number of women employed. We are unaware that recent feminist writing has claimed

otherwise. But FTEs are not necessarily the most relevant measure of women's employment and oversimplify a complex set of changes.

For many research purposes, the proportions of women employed, either full time or part-time, are more useful than FTEs. ... Even if two part-time jobs are comparable with one full-time job for statisticians, this is not so for those who hold the jobs nor for their employers' (Ginn *et al.*, 1996, p. 167–8).

Extract D 'Hakim reports evidence of gender equality since the late 1980s in non-financial commitment to work, which is confirmed by her own data. However, in spite of this evidence, and the equal proportions of women in full- and part-time employment who show non-financial work commitment, Hakim remains unconvinced that women and men are equally committed to work and dismisses what is surely a most impressive change in employed women's attitudes.

Curiously, Hakim states that commitment to a part-time job 'is not equal to the commitment of a full-time worker', without explaining how equating commitment with hours can be justified. She suggests that the women working part-time may well express greater commitment to their families than full-timers, but this is likely to reflect differences in their family situation. It is possible to be highly conscious of the needs of one's family and at the same time to care deeply about maintaining employment. As Dex observes, 'Most women ... want to enjoy both work and home life to the full' (Dex *et al.*, 1994 p. 168)'. (Ginn *et al.*, 1996, p. 168).

Extract E Hakim cites studies 'showing that part-time work is chosen voluntarily by women' (e.g. Hakim, 1991), claiming this refutes the view that childcare problems are a major barrier to women's full-time employment.

Where women state a preference for part-time work, this must be understood in the context of demands on their time and childcare costs, which limit their employment options more than men's. ...

Clearly other factors besides current childcare responsibilities influence women's employment. Breaks in employment and part-time work while children are young tend to confine women to a narrow segment of the labour market, reducing their chance of returning to their previous full-time occupation. In addition, having adult children in the household increases the likelihood that mid-life women work part time, suggesting that the domestic workload associated with non-dependent children restricts women's capacity to take full-time employment (Ginn and Arber, 1994). ...The evidence that childcare is a major factor in restricting British women's full-time employment seems undeniable (Ginn *et al.*, 1996, p. 169).

child. If a woman chooses to have a child, rather than simply having a child by default, it is likely that she will prioritize childrearing over employment.

4 Female part-time workers are not 'exploited'. Hakim responds to writers who have argued that part-time jobs should accrue the same benefits as full-time jobs, pointing to evidence which shows that part-time workers make a qualitatively different compromise between market and non-market activities. She argues that part-time workers are adequately protected by law and have adequate rights at work.

5 Women and part-time workers have higher absentee rates and higher instability rates than do their male and full-time counterparts, owing to differing 'work orientations' (Hakim, 1995, p. 448).

It can be seen that Hakim thinks that feminist sociologists have skewed the evidence on women's employment and women's labour market participation to suit their own ends. She writes:

In each of the five cases examined, feminist orthodoxy has replaced dispassionate social scientific assessment of the evidence on women's position in the labour market, effectively dictating a narrow range of acceptable conclusions (broadly, that women are victims who have little or no responsibility for their situation) and even eliminating certain topics from the research agenda.

(Hakim, 1995, p. 448)

Hakim argues that, while feminists have contributed much to knowledge about women's position in society, they have also:

... creat[ed] a new set of feminist myths to replace the old patriarchal myths about women's attitudes and behaviour.

(Hakim, 1995, p. 430)

Her point that women are capable of making intelligent choices emphasizes the discomfort many feel on learning from feminist theory that they are the victims of a patriarchal society.

Responses to Hakim

Hakim's work has been called provocative by those feminist sociologists and economists seeking to defend themselves against her accusations.

Breugel (1996), a feminist social scientist, suggests that Hakim caricatures feminist ideas in order to shore up her argument, deliberately understating the complexity of much feminist work. At the same time, says Breugel, Hakim uses statistics to suit her own purposes, reading from a set of figures that best match her own thesis, rather than surveying all the available evidence, including that pointing in another direction. An extract from Breugel's response is reproduced here as 'Whose myths are they?'

In another response, ten writers (Ginn *et al.*, 1996) respond to her claims, closely examining the evidence that she cited, and finding it possible to make further, contradictory interpretations. Extracts from their article are reproduced here as 'Feminist fallacies: a reply'.

Activity

a Referring to 'Whose myths are they?', summarize Breugel's argument in no more than 50 words.

b From 'Feminist fallacies: a reply', match Ginn *et al.*'s refutations of Hakim's five claims to the appropriate myths in the earlier list.

c To what extent do you think that taking issue with the statistical evidence cited by Hakim, as Ginn *et al.* and Breugel do, refutes Hakim's argument?

C3.2, C3.3

Whose myths are they?

Hakim's attempt to re-establish the myth of women as unstable, unreliable workers is the most disturbing part of her paper. It is, of course, true that, taken as a whole, women have higher turnover rates and shorter job tenure durations than men. The results of a regression analysis of job duration for all those employed and living in South East England in 1993, suggests that the effects of gender are relatively small once occupation, age and type of job are controlled for. Though job duration rose by about 4 months for every extra year of age, women without dependent children had on average been in their jobs just 1 year less than men without children. The average duration of current jobs for mothers was *ceteris paribus* 2 years and 8 months less than fathers, which is hardly surprising given the norm that it is women not men who leave their jobs when starting a family. ... In some occupations – catering and routine assembly, for example – women tend to have been in jobs longer than men, in each age group. Of course there is considerable room for discussion about what is and what isn't an appropriate control. It is possible to follow human capital theorists in arguing that women choose occupations in which high turnover is not penalized; equally the same data can be used to argue that employers select women for occupations where high turnover is not costly. Either way, higher turnover amongst women workers is not inherent, but the result of an interaction between occupation and gender.

Source: Breugel (1996, p. 176)

Feminism in action

Whilst sociologists have adopted a number of theoretical approaches to gendered inequalities, it is feminists' theories that have proved the most influential in reshaping sociology's traditional concerns, and in delineating new areas for sociological investigation.

How feminism has changed sociology

Maynard (1990), herself a feminist sociologist, has argued that feminists' theories of gender have changed the overall shape of empirical sociology in two main ways. The first she calls the 'additive approach'. This, says Maynard, is:

... designed to bring women's lives into view, take seriously the female experience and compensate for their previous neglect.

(Maynard, 1990, p. 270)

Feminist sociologists have added women to already-existing areas of sociological research – education, employment, crime and deviance, and so on.

Secondly, argues Maynard, feminism has introduced new areas of study to the discipline of sociology, focusing, for example, on housework and resource allocation in households, motherhood, childbirth and pregnancy, and issues regarding sexuality – none of which had previously been thought to be central sociological concerns (see Sections 4.1 and 5.7). She writes:

These areas of concern were previously ignored, either because they were regarded as inconsequential or because it was not recognised how significant they were in the structuring of women's lives.

(Maynard, 1990, p. 270)

Just as feminists have suggested new avenues for sociological research, they have also developed a set of research methods which, they claim, are better able to take account of women's experiences and ideas than more traditional ways of asking sociological questions (see also Section 16.9). They point to much sociological research conducted prior to 1970 to support their case.

Until that time, they suggest, the bulk of sociological research was firmly 'malestream'. Using this pun on the word 'mainstream', feminists have been able to show how sociology had privileged men and male concerns as it sought research subjects, and how it subsequently generalized the findings of such research to account for the actions of both men and women. This sort of practice, say feminists, has produced sociological knowledge which is misleading and inaccurate. Thus, feminist research has conceived of itself as a corrective to sociological inaccuracy, as much as it has sought to establish a new sociological paradigm.

Middle-range feminist theory

Currently feminist work in sociology includes empirical research and fieldwork, as well as what Maynard (1990) has called the 'middle-range' theory generated by such work. At the same time feminists are producing theory based on their assumptions about 'capitalism', say, or 'patriarchy' – theory which is derived from material observation and which expects to generate feminist political activity. Lastly, feminists are questioning the assumed relationships between feminist theory and feminist activity made by feminist sociologists working in the first two areas.

It is through considering feminism as a body of ideas with a history and a particular terrain that we are able to assess critically the extent of its impact on sociology. Therefore the remainder of this section concentrates on explaining what feminism *is*.

What is 'feminism'?

Journalist Rebecca West said in 1913:

I myself have never been able to find out precisely what feminism is. I only know that people call me a feminist whenever I express sentiments that differentiate me from a doormat or a prostitute.

(West, 1982, p. 219)

Humm affirms the difficulty of defining feminism, pointing out that feminists have widely different concerns and analyses. She has, however, suggested that all feminists share a 'woman-centred perspective' (1995, p. 95).

But while feminism means paying attention to the particular experiences of women where they have previously been rendered invisible, or differently understood, feminists do not agree on the precise nature of the political, social and economic changes that will be required to improve women's lives. In fact, change is an imprecise term which speaks differently to feminists depending on the way they view women's subordination. So while *Marxist* feminists might envisage change as an end to capitalism's exploitation of women and men, *radical* feminists are likely to imagine a change in the nature of sexual and family relations as patriarchal domination is eroded.

Changing men?

Certainly men are implicated in any proposed changes to the established order, given that they have been deemed to be responsible, intentionally or unconsciously, individually or collectively, for the subordination of women. Thus, feminists have been critical of individual men when they think and behave in a sexist manner. Feminists have also been critical when male-dominated institutions have excluded or marginalized women. But many men and male-dominated institutions have been slow to change their ways in response to feminists' demands. This has meant that feminists have used, and continue to use, a variety of tactics to persuade them that change is necessary (see Section 4.1).

Feminist activism

Feminist activists have often used very familiar mechanisms of protest to state their demands for change – organizing meetings and marches, petitions and letter-writing campaigns in order to express their views. For example, feminists concerned with women's safety issues periodically organize 'Take Back the Night' marches. Such a march is intended to reflect women's (and men's) collective strength in precipitating a change to established norms and material circumstances. Activists may request, say, that their local authority installs more effective street-lighting in a particular area, which will in turn allow women to feel safer if they are walking alone after dark. If better lighting is subsequently installed then feminist activists have enjoyed a measure of success because change has occurred.

'Liberal feminism'

Those feminists who have been wedded to the use of 'official' political mechanisms – like meetings and letter-writing campaigns to voice their concerns about women's status – are often referred to as liberal feminists. This is because liberal feminists' concerns are focused on fitting women into existing social and political structures – the structures of liberal democracy.

Liberal feminists wish to bring women into the decision-making processes of all public institutions on an equal basis with men, so that those bodies will take account of women's issues.

Liberal feminists are closely associated with the rhetoric and practice of equal opportunities. While they seek to improve women's access to work and education, and to codify their legal rights, subsequently an individual woman can choose to take advantage of the opportunities that have been created for her – or not. Thus, any changes in women's status and conditions tend to occur on an individual basis rather than for women *en masse*.

Most importantly, liberal feminists do not seek to reshape liberal democracy fundamentally. For this reason they have been criticized by other feminists who argue that their position cannot lead to the attainment of equality for most women.

Feminist journalist Natasha Walter's recent book *The New Feminism* provides useful examples of the liberal feminist case. For example:

Women want power for their own security and freedom, because unless women are more accepted and less exceptional in powerful positions, every individual career will always be more vulnerable, every individual woman's presence always an anomaly that might be smoothed out. They will always be unsure about whether they are there as tokens or on their own merit; or about what part their looks play in their success. They will always be slightly ill at ease in an alien culture. They want women both above and below them so that they don't find their presence questioned. ...

Justice will not come for women without power. In an unequal society all inequalities bolster and mirror one another. The discrimination that a female doctor encounters personally (there are twice as many suspensions of women doctors as men, but only half as many are finally upheld) mirrors the discrimination that a female patient suffers personally (women must be much iller than men to get hospital treatment for heart disease). ...

Similarly fewer young women in law courts and police stations mean that women find themselves disadvantaged when they come into contact with the criminal justice system because their voice and their experiences are those of an outsider; fewer women in the media mean that priorities associated with women are still made peripheral and that women are the object rather than the subject of debate; few women in business and the City mean that power and money are always seen as masculine attributes, and that a woman who demands them is seen to be rocking the boat. More women in power will mean a better deal for women throughout society. ...

So the battle for greater equality in the corridors of power is a battle worth fighting, partly for the individual woman facing up to her future, partly for the interests of women more generally and partly for society at large.

(Adapted from Walter, 1998, pp. 183–3)

💬 Discussion point

Do you think that having more women in high places, as Walter suggests, will mean a better deal for all women or a better deal for the individual woman who has 'done well'? Can an individual woman who has 'made it' really improve conditions for the majority of women?

C3.1a

Feminist forms of action

Although marching, petitioning and letter-writing have served feminists well, they are very traditional forms of protest. Increasingly feminists have used their imaginations to think up newer ways of drawing attention to sexism, oppression, exploitation and inequality. Often these forms of protest have served other causes simultaneously. When feminist peace activists camping outside the nuclear weapons base at Greenham Common in the 1980s adorned miles of the fence surrounding the base with ribbons, children's toys and photographs, they had established as much a peace movement-derived protest as a feminist protest.

Protests that do not fit the familiar letter-writing and marching mould, but involve a non-violent presence that disrupts the usual activities of the institution that is the target of the protest, are often referred to as 'direct action' (see also Section 15.3). Thus, feminists living at the women's 'peace camp' at Greenham Common nuclear base often climbed the fence to enter the base, forcing military workers to eject them. The act of entering the base was a constant reminder for the military of the women's feminist, anti-nuclear stance.

Alongside their direct actions or more familiar forms of protest, feminists have also pressed into service what have been seen as women's traditional skills – sewing and knitting, for example – to create decorative banners for display.

Banners are historically associated with movement-based protests. They symbolize the strength and solidarity of the group they represent. The banners pictured in Figure 17.18 demonstrate feminist strength and solidarity using emblems of women's traditionally ascribed concerns.

✎ Activity

Suggest reasons why feminists have used symbols of 'traditional' womanhood to represent their cause, as in the banners in Figure 17.18.

C3.2, C3.3

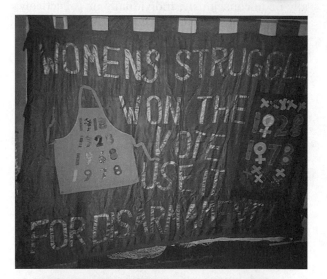

Figure 17.18 Banners in support of a cause, using 'traditional' images of womanhood

Thinking about activism

Just as feminists have worked to expand their repertoire of methods of activist-style protest, many have suggested that thinking and writing are forms of action too. When feminists write books or articles in which they try to explain their ideas about the need for change, they are in a very real sense 'speaking out'. The term 'feminist activity' refers to *all* feminists' efforts to bring about change – grassroots activism as well as thinking and writing.

Griffin, a professor of women's studies, has suggested that feminist activity is currently characterized by:

... a discontent with the present, and possibly the past; a desire for improvement in the future; and a (self-)questioning in the face of struggle.

(Griffin, 1995, p. 1)

While this section has already dealt with Griffin's first two claims, her third statement speaks to the ambivalence with which feminists have always determined their allegiances. For example, many feminists have necessarily 'blamed' men as a group for the subordination of women. At the same time, those feminists each have male friends who may be consciously acting to frame their personal behaviour in a non-patriarchal way. In this way a feminist analysis which apportions 'blame' to men is problematized: men are not as similar as some feminists' theories would suggest (see Section 4.1).

Neither are all women as similar as might be supposed. Lesbian feminists, for example, have criticized the heterosexist nature of some feminists' assumptions about women's lives. In the same way, working-class women active in the feminist movement have been critical of the assumptions of their middle-class counterparts. Thus differences between women are emphasized as part of a process in which feminists take issue with each other's answers to the questions 'What is a woman?' and 'What is a feminist?'

Feminists' agendas for change are invariably redrawn when lesbian feminists point out that those agendas are heterosexist, or working-class women point out that middle-class values are inscribed into statements about what women and feminists want.

'I'm not a feminist, but ...'

There are, however, many women who are broadly in agreement with feminists' objectives but are not prepared to call themselves a femi-

nist. Some women live in circumstances which make it difficult for them to speak out, finding themselves ostracized by family and friends if they openly criticize, say, the unequal distribution of household duties between their male partners and themselves.

Activity

Read through the following quotations, which are adapted from an article in the *Guardian* of 12 November 1998. Would you describe yourself as a feminist? Why, or why not?

- 'I'm proud to think of myself as a feminist, but the term has become *passé*. Promoting women's issues is a nicer way of saying it.' – Sarah Pyper, editor, *Sugar* magazine

- 'These feminists are doing themselves a lot of harm. It's damned ridiculous objecting to men opening doors and giving up their seats. They're ruining standards.' – Harry, 66, a -pensioner

- 'A feminist is someone who believes women should be able to live the way they choose. That's fine by me.' – Jimmy, 27, a butcher

- 'I used to consider myself a feminist because I thought it was about equality. Now I'm wary of the term. Feminists are extremists who hate men.' – Trevor Berry, president of Families Need Fathers

- 'It's all changed since my day. It was all about burning your bra then, now it's about wearing your short skirt and getting the job.' – Marie, 54

- 'It's when men act more feminine ... like girlie, isn't it?' – Greg, 16

- 'They're usually more manly than men, aren't they? No make-up, short hair and all that. But it's important to fight for women's rights, particularly when in some places like the Saudi, where I was born, women aren't allowed to drive, let alone work. There's no point in having an education if you can't use it, is there?' – Asha, 16

C3.2, C3.3

Furthermore, popular culture has constructed a negative stereotype of 'the feminist'. While caricatures of crop-haired, man-hating feminists are only the most recent incarnation of a centuries-old attempt to 'keep women in their place', those who have no sources of information about feminism bar, say, the tabloid press are likely to be wary.

Feminism: a brief history

Women have been protesting about their unequal condition for hundreds of years. The rest of this section provides a brief outline of feminist concerns, campaigns and ideas.

Mary Wollstonecraft

Mary Wollstonecraft (1759–97) was one of the earliest writers to espouse principles similar to those of modern feminists. Wollstonecraft was part of a group of radical, forward-thinking intellectuals who supported the principles of the Enlightenment and the French Revolution. She saw no reason why the principles of 'equality' and 'freedom' should not be extended to women.

In a book, *A Vindication of the Rights of Woman* (1792), she claimed that women should be educated properly. Educating women, she argued, had indisputable social benefits. Wollstonecraft focused her concern around the social role of mothers.

Wollstonecraft's work – which at the time amounted to little less than a revolutionary statement – attracted ferocious criticism from the British conservative establishment. But her ideas were welcomed by supporters of the revolution in France, even though most did little to practically advance her cause.

Feminist activity from the mid-nineteenth century

Assumptions about 'equality' and 'difference' have generated currents of thought which are clearly traceable in the feminist activity of the last 150 years, but particularly in the twentieth century. Feminist activity in the twentieth century is often characterized as having occurred in two waves, 'the first sweeping over Europe and America in the mid- to late-nineteenth century, the second crashing against the post-war consensus a hundred years later' (Phillips, 1991, p. 121).

- First-wave feminists, campaigning for change round about the start of the twentieth century, were very much concerned with attaining legal and political rights – the vote, access to higher education, and so on – in an effort to become socially and financially independent of men.
- Feminists in the second wave began to emphasize what they identified as women's ways of thinking and living and the curtailment of these in a male-dominated society.

Without wishing to suggest that feminist activity occurs in isolated bouts as women formulate a series of demands which are then granted, the rest of this section focuses on first- and second-wave activity in an attempt to explain the relationship between feminist theory and feminist activism, and the relationship of these to the recent reshaping of sociology.

The first wave: suffragettes and suffragists

Women campaigning for the vote – the 'suffrage' – and other reforms were known as 'suffragettes' or 'suffragists', depending on their views as to how their aims could be achieved.

The Women's Social and Political Union (WPSU)

Those who were prepared to take direct action through civil disobedience, and who were concerned with enfranchisement above all else, joined the WSPU. Calling themselves suffragettes, these women were prepared to use unorthodox means to get attention. Thus, some women famously chained themselves to the railings outside Downing Street and others smashed windows and stormed public meetings. Some were prepared to go to prison for the cause, having been caught perpetrating acts of violence against property, for example.

The WSPU were not alone in campaigning for the vote and attendant reforms. Feminist historians Liddington and Norris (1978) point out that conventional histories of the suffrage movement almost invariably portray a middle-class, London-based campaign. But in fact, campaigns led by working-class women, particularly in the Lancashire area, had a tremendous impact on the popular consciousness, and played an important part in the suffrage movement as a whole. Women involved in such campaigns were known as 'radical suffragists'.

Radical suffragist movements

Radical suffragists called for the vote for all adults over the age of 21. This would mean enfranchisement for women and for the small number of white working-class men who were still disenfranchised. Their demands existed in contrast to the position adopted at one stage by the WSPU leadership, who had suggested that giving the vote only to those women who owned property would be acceptable as a prelude to total enfranchisement. Clearly, such a partial enfranchisement would mitigate against poorer women – the very women who most needed a legitimate political voice in the eyes of the radical suffragists.

Working women, trade unionism and Empire

Women began to organize against poor working conditions towards the end of the nineteenth century – particularly in the textile industry where many were employed. A major focus of their concern was an exploitative outworking system known as 'sweating'. Factory owners had found that they could produce goods more cheaply if they employed women and children working from home or in cramped workshops that were not restricted under existing governmental guidelines on employment. They often paid piecework rates (remunerating workers per finished item and not per hour), forcing them to keep up production or lose income.

Women trade unionists

Women workers made up a large part of the sweated labour force. Women trade unionists like Emma Paterson (1848–86) – founder of the first women worker's organization, the Women's Trade Union League (WTUL) in 1874 – argued that the Factories Acts, which legislated to 'clean up' factories by requiring higher safety standards and better cleanliness, had pushed women out of factory-based employment and into the unregulated labour market because employers hired men in preference to women. Thus, said Paterson and her supporters, the Factories Acts benefited men, but not women, and they lobbied against the introduction of further legislation. In 1875 Paterson was one of two women delegates to the Trades Union Congress (TUC). At this and at subsequent congresses she opposed the Factories Acts, calling them 'man-made' restrictive legislation on women's employment.

The second wave

After all women aged over 21 had been given the franchise in 1928, some suffrage groups dis-

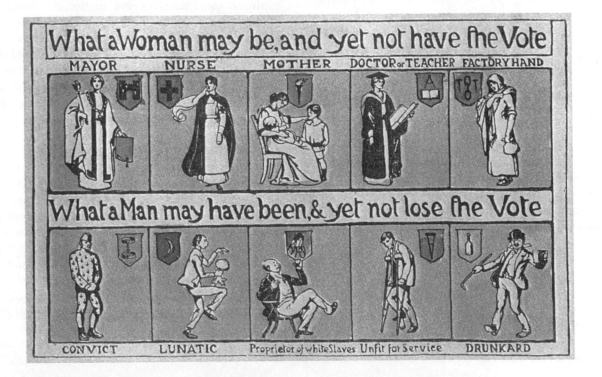

banded. This did not mean that women stopped writing, thinking and campaigning for change, however. Feminist campaigns continued across the world through the mid-century period. But what has been called a 'second wave' of concentrated feminist activity gathered momentum in the UK in the late 1960s, taking some of its inspiration from an earlier burst of similar activity in the USA.

Second-wave feminism flourished in a time of political ferment, from the late 1950s and mid-60s onwards, in the USA and Europe, respectively. The relative success of the 'civil rights' movement in securing new freedoms for black US citizens fuelled other groups' desire to express their widespread disillusionment with political systems as they stood. An explosion of political activity across the USA and western Europe emerged from opposition to US involvement in the Vietnam War, while 1968 saw a Europe-wide wave of student-led protests and demonstrations. In the UK a politics of anti-racism was developing, as was a fledgling lesbian and gay-liberation movement. (See also Section 4.1.)

Simultaneously, economic and technological changes had acted to make women feel a little more sure of themselves. Innovations in reproductive technology, and in particular the introduction of the contraceptive pill, meant that for the first time women were able to control their own fertility, while more women than ever before were entering the labour market (see Section 17.2). However, employment opportunities for women were still very restricted, and they were paid less than men. The following pages show how these issues and others were of primary concern to particular groups of women as they participated in second-wave feminist campaigns.

The women's liberation movement

During the late 1960s and early 70s, small women's liberation groups appeared in many large towns. These groups often met in members' homes to discuss issues of women's rights. The groups arguably had a dual function – consciousness-raising and campaigning. The extract reproduced here from a promotional leaflet for Women's Liberation Workshop shows the idea.

What was consciousness-raising?

Women felt that they needed to be able to discuss the difficulties that they faced on a day-to-day basis, with other women. That way, they argued, they would be able to find a collective strength to solve their problems. At the same time, they argued, the minutiae of women's lives should no longer be seen as trivial and unimportant. Instead women's feelings were worth exploring and addressing. Kathie Amatniek, a member of a US consciousness-raising group, suggested that: 'Our feelings will lead us to ideas and then to action' (quoted in Rowbotham, 1989, p. 246).

Activity

a Explain *in your own words* why Women's Liberation Workshop is closed to men.

b What criticisms of the 'leaderless' structure of meetings might be made by activists and sociologists from other perspectives, such as Marxism?

C3.2, C3.3

Campaigning

Women were able to share their knowledge with other women outside the groups, via newsletters and magazines, as well as larger meetings and conferences. This often led to the mounting of protest marches and demonstrations as well as smaller, well-orchestrated direct actions. In November 1969, for example, women entered the BBC studios where the Miss World beauty contest was being transmitted live and disrupted the broadcast. In 1970, during a similar demonstration, a bomb exploded under a BBC outside-broadcast van. Five women were subsequently arrested (Rowbotham, 1989, p. 248).

Women's liberation groups worked with the belief, above all, that 'the personal is political'. They argued that daily life tended to be thought of as taking place either in the public sphere or the private sphere. Feminists argued that any distinction made between public and private was artificial and acted to prevent women from speaking out. As Rowbotham has put it:

The separation of personal and public spheres was seen as a way of restricting women's articulation of grievances.

(Rowbotham, 1989, p. 246)

WOMEN'S LIBERATION WORKSHOP

Women's Liberation Workshop believes that women in our society are oppressed. We are economically oppressed: in jobs we do full work for half pay, in the home we do unpaid work full time. We are commercially exploited by advertisements, television and press; legally we often have only the status of children. We are brought up to feel inadequate, educated to narrower horizons than men. This is our specific oppression as women. It is as women that we are, therefore, organizing.

The Women's Liberation Workshop questions women's role and redefines the possibilities. It seeks to bring women to a full awareness of the meaning of their inferior status and to devise methods to change it. In society women and girls relate primarily to men: any organization duplicates this pattern: the men lead and dominate, the women follow and submit.

We close our meetings to men to break through this pattern, to establish our own leaderless groups and to meet each other over our common experience as women. If we admitted men, there would be a tendency for them, by virtue of their experience, vested interests, and status in society, to dominate the organization. We want eventually to be, and to help other women to be, in charge of our own lives; therefore, we must be in charge of our own movement, directly, not by remote control. This means that not only those with experience in politics, but all, must learn to take their own decisions, both political and personal.

For this reason, groups small enough for all to take part in discussions and decisions are the basic unit of our movement. We feel that the small group makes personal commitment a possibility and a necessity and that it provides understanding and solidarity. Each small group is autonomous, holding different positions and emerging in different types of activity. As a federation of a number of different groups, Women's Liberation Workshop is essentially heterogeneous, incorporating within it a wide range of opinions and plans for action.

The magazine, *Shrew*, is produced by a different group each month. Thus, to a certain extent, it reflects the preoccupations of the group producing it. WLW meets monthly, the small groups weekly. We come together as groups and individuals to further our part in the struggle for social change and the transformation of society.

Source: Peckham Rye Women's Liberation Workshop Collective (1971)

Women in the early second wave were adamant that their concerns should be heard in the public arena, and furthermore that they should have some input into public decision-making processes. Their voices had been absent for too long.

National women's conference, 1970

Some of the women attending liberation groups, and a number of other women working in universities, decided that they would hold a general conference on women's liberation in order to develop their ideas about the freedoms women wanted. Rowbotham describes what happened:

We thought perhaps a hundred women would come. In fact more than 500 people turned up, 400 women, 60 children and 40 men. ... I'd never seen so many women looking so confident in my life before.

(Rowbotham; quoted in Wandor, 1990, p. 22)

The conference lasted a weekend and formulated four demands (see the box). These represented some of the early aims and objectives of the women's movement.

At subsequent similar women's conferences, further demands were added, including legal and financial independence for women, an end to discrimination against lesbians, and freedom from intimidation by emotional abuse or sexual violence.

Activity

a Identify any links between the areas of women's lives referred to in 'The four demands'.

b Suggest how you would modify or add to the original demands if you were writing them today. Provide reasons for any changes you would make.

C3.2, C3.3

Strike at Ford, 1968

The women's liberation movement was not exclusively the preserve of middle-class women. But it did not always focus on issues that were at the forefront of working-class women's feminist agenda. Women trade unionists and factory workers were very much occupied with the question of equal pay for work of equal value. Working women had been lobbying business and government on this issue for years with no success.

In 1968, women workers at the Ford car plant in Dagenham, East London, went on strike. As sewing machinists who stitched car upholstery, they were angry that the company refused to acknowledge their skills and reward them with a higher level of pay. Audrey Wise, a trade-union

The four demands

At the first national women's conference at Ruskin College, Oxford, in February/March 1970, the following four demands were formulated.

EQUAL PAY
We have to understand *why* we don't have equal pay. It's always been said that a woman's place is in the home. We don't want to do equal work and housework as well. We don't want to do equal work when it's shit-work. Equal pay means not just the same money for the same work, but also recognising how many women work not because they want to, but because they *have* to, either for money or for friends. Equal pay is the first step not just to more money, but to control over how, why, and for whom we work.

EQUAL EDUCATION AND OPPORTUNITY
We don't want to demand an education equally as bad as that of men – we want equal resources, not equal repression. We want to fight for real education, to make our own jobs and opportunities.

24-HOUR NURSERIES
We need somewhere for the kids, but we have to choose as to whether the kids will be kept out of the way or given their own space, and whether, freed from children, we just manage to survive through working or make the time to discover who stops us from living.

FREE CONTRACEPTION AND ABORTION ON DEMAND
We want to be free to choose when and how many kids to have, if any. We have to fight for control over our own bodies, for even the magic pill or (in the case of mistakes) abortion on demand only gives us the freedom to get into a real mess without any visible consequences. We still can't talk of sex as anything but a joke or a battle-ground.

Source: Women's Newspaper, 6 March 1971
Reprinted in Wandor, 1990, pp. 242–3

activist involved with the women's campaign, remembers the strike's effects:

'What is really central in my mind is the fact that they stopped the whole factory. Everybody thought of cars as being about the track, about engines and metal, and here you had women working with soft materials, sewing, and they could stop a huge car factory. So it was an indication to those women and lots of other people of the power in their hands. Women are not used to feeling powerful, so it had a very great effect on them.'

(Wise; quoted in Wandor, 1990, p. 202)

The Ford women formed an action committee along with other trade unionists from across the country – both men and women – to help them decide how to run the strike and to plan further campaigns of action. In May 1969 the committee organized an 'equal pay and equal rights' rally in Trafalgar Square. This was one of the very first large protests organized by women in the early second wave of feminist activity. Wise further comments:

The first women's liberation demonstration in 1971 is usually referred to as being the first big demonstration after the suffragettes, and it just isn't true, because it's got to do with this idea that only middle-class women are interested in feminism.

(Wise; quoted in Wandor, 1990, p. 204)

Black women organizing

Many black women involved with the women's liberation movement noted that its agenda did not seem to reflect their concerns, and that some of its ideas – about the nature of family life, for example, and about reproductive rights – explicitly excluded their experiences. In response to these omissions, and alongside their developing politics of anti-racism, black women began organizing independently.

Black women in Brixton, London, formed one of the earliest second-wave African–Caribbean women's organizations in 1974. Initially a study group, members met in a back room at a book-shop or at each other's houses, although by 1980 they had their own black women's centre. At the same time Asian women were active in campaigning from the late 1970s. One of the earliest Asian women's groups, Awaz, drew attention to immigration issues, highlighting the so-called 'virginity testing' occurring at airports as Asian women affianced to British Asian men attempted to gain entry to the UK.

Organization of Women of Asian and African Descent (OWAAD)

Asian and African–Caribbean women worked together through OWAAD. This was formed from a 1978 conference of 250 black women, at which topics for discussion included immigration rights and the law as it appeared to discriminate against black people. OWAAD spawned a number of other black women's organizations, and attempted to maintain links between them. But as feminist political scientists Lovenduski and Randall (1993) have pointed out, OWAAD's very attempt to bring black women together was bound to draw attention to the differences between them. Successive conferences in the early 1980s ended in bitter divisions (mirroring arguments similarly occurring at women's liberation movement conferences at this time).

Contemporary feminist debates

Sisterhood: women working together for change

Women working for change in the second wave have often had an uneasy relationship with each other. While some feminists have wanted to emphasize the togetherness of women in the face of male oppression – their 'sisterhood' as described in the extract from *Shrew* – others have argued that it is not easy for women from different backgrounds to metaphorically link hands. Women, it is said, have such varied and different life experiences that attempts by some feminists to present the movement as a united front must be doomed to failure.

The early women's liberation movement operated on the assumption that women had a set of common demands that could be identified and then realized. The 'four demands' statement of 1970, reproduced above, might seem to suggest that all women in the UK in 1970 shared a common bond by virtue of their oppression and could be read as a demonstration of feminists'

Sisterhood is ...

Sisterhood becomes possible when, at last, we become aware of ourselves as women in common plight with other women. It is, for the individual, a consciousness of her situation *vis-à-vis* men and society.

However it seems to us that Sisterhood really only exists when the individual goes out and relates to and acts with other women in the light of this consciousness. We identify with other women in terms of our common oppression and servitude and we have a solidarity between us born from this.

In our discussions, in our minute examination of how we see ourselves and how we really feel towards our sisters, and towards men, is formed a bond of communication and understanding. This is the confidence of Sisterhood, which is constantly confirmed through our action in the workshops.

Source: Shrew, vol. 3, no. 5 (1971)

---

agreement about what needed to be done to end the oppression of women.

It is easy to see why some feminists might have wanted to suggest that all women have a common bond. It could be argued that their sisterhood claim gave legitimacy to all feminist activity. The notion of sisterhood suggests that feminist campaigns operate for the good of all women, and furthermore that all women will benefit in a similar way from any changes that are made in legislation, in attitudes, in employment practices, and so on. However, is this really the case?

> ### Discussion point
> To what extent might the concept of 'sisterhood' mitigate against the recognition of differences between women? Does this matter?
>
> C3.1a

Case Study – The Equal Pay Act

Do all women benefit in the same way from changes in legislation? An examination of the impact of the Equal Pay Act 1970 might suggest that this is not so.

The Act legitimized the principle of equal pay for work of equal value. Introduced to Parliament by Labour MP Barbara Castle, it was intended to end wage discrimination on the grounds of sex. In 1984, following a European court ruling, its scope was extended to allow claims for equal pay on the basis of equivalence of skill, effort and decision-making.

Criticisms of the Act

Critics argued that it would do little, in practice, to alter the imbalance between men's and women's pay. If employers could not discriminate against women overtly, then they would do it covertly, by regrading work tasks within a firm, so that they could suggest women were undertaking less-skilled work than men. Thus they could evade the Act.

Other critics argued that, while it might be effective where women were doing jobs that could be directly compared to the type of jobs that men did, it could do nothing to change the low pay received by women in largely gender-segregated occupations like cleaning and catering. Cleaning and catering work was – and continues to be – performed almost exclusively by women. (See also Section 17.2.)

Feminists monitoring the immediate effects of the Act noted that it had seemed to have little impact in the large. Snell commented:

Although most women received some increase in pay as a result of the Equal Pay Act, many are still underpaid in relation to the men they work with, and in relation to their level of skill and effort. ... Most women are still concentrated in low-grade, low-paid women's jobs with little prospect of better-paid jobs or promotion.

(Snell, 1986, p. 34)

Although feminists welcomed the Act, many considered that it had a very limited scope. As Snell has commented:

The women's movement has always been ambivalent about the value of legislation in bringing about real change. On the one hand women have campaigned vigorously for legislation to improve women's domestic, economic and political positions. On the other hand, women inevitably find that laws, once passed, are unsatisfactory and that the inequalities they were intended to remove still remain.

(Snell, 1986, p. 12)

Activity

Study the evidence presented in Tables 17.26 and 17.27 on this and the next page. Does it support the claims outlined by critics of the Equal Pay Act, above? Have there been any noteworthy changes in the relative positions of men and women since 1991?

Case Study – Feminisms

In order to better address the inequalities noted above, feminists changed tack. Where previously they had attempted to present a united front, now feminism became 'feminisms', as women joined together in smaller, identity-based groups in which they could discuss issues and plan campaigns.

Black women formed groups in which they could consider feminism and racism at the same time – something that the mainly white women's liberation movement was not doing. Some lesbian women met together to consider feminism alongside the homophobia and heterosexism of the movement and wider society.

'Feminisms' have thus emerged as a series of often-conflicting ideas and arguments, based around the differences between women, rather than as a unified and universally agreed-upon set of principles and demands.

Women at Greenham Common

Roseneil's (1995) research (see also Section 9.5) on the women's 'peace camp' at Greenham Common focuses on the differences and resultant productive tensions between women activists at the camp. Women peace activists maintained a constant presence outside the nuclear air base at Greenham Common, near Newbury in Berkshire, from 1981 to 1994. Ostensibly, they were protesting at the deployment of US cruise missiles to the UK. But importantly the protest

Table 17.26 How men and women in the UK occupied jobs in 1991 and 1998 (percentages)[a]

	Men		Women	
	1991	**1998**	**1991**	**1998**
Managers and administrators	16	19	8	11
Professional	10	11	8	9
Associate professional and technical	8	9	10	11
Clerical and secretarial	8	8	29	26
Craft and related	21	17	4	2
Personal and protective services	7	8	14	17
Selling	6	5	12	12
Plant and machine operatives	15	15	5	4
Other occupations	8	8	10	8
All employees[b] (millions)	11.8	12.2	10.1	10.6

[a] At spring each year; males aged 16 to 64, females aged 16 to 59
[b] Includes a few people who did not state their occupation (percentages are based on totals which exclude this group)
Source: Social Trends 29 (ONS)

Table 17.27 How men and women workers in the UK were distributed in industry in various years (percentages)[a]

	Men				Women		
	1981	1991	1998		1981	1991	1998
Manufacturing	33	26	25		18	12	10
Distribution, hotels, catering and repairs	16	19	20		25	25	26
Financial and business services	10	15	16		12	16	19
Transport and communication	9	9	9		3	3	3
Construction	8	8	8		1	1	1
Agriculture	2	2	2		1	1	1
Energy and water supply	5	3	1		1	1	–
Other services	17	19	19		39	41	40
All employee jobs (millions)	12.6	11.5	11.7		9.3	10.7	11.5

[a] At June each year
Source: Social Trends 29 (ONS)

Compulsory heterosexuality and lesbian existence

When we look hard and clearly at the extent and elaboration of measures designed to keep women within a male sexual purlieu, it becomes an inescapable question whether the issue feminists have to address is not simple 'gender inequality', nor the domination of culture by males, nor mere 'taboos against homosexuality', but the enforcement of heterosexuality for women as a means of assuring male right of physical, economical, and emotional access.

One of many means of enforcement is, of course, the rendering invisible of the lesbian possibility, an engulfed continent which rises fragmentedly into view from time to time only to become submerged again. Feminist research and theory that contribute to lesbian invisibility or marginality are actually working against the liberation and empowerment of women as a group.

The assumption that 'most women are innately heterosexual' stands as a theoretical and political stumbling block for feminism. It remains a tenable assumption partly because lesbian existence has been written out of history or catalogued under disease, partly because it has been treated as exceptional rather than intrinsic, partly because to acknowledge that for women heterosexuality may not be a 'preference' at all but something that has had to be imposed, managed, organized, propagandized and maintained by force, is an immense step to take if you consider yourself freely and 'innately' heterosexual.

Yet the failure to examine heterosexuality as an institution is like failing to admit that the economic system called capitalism or the caste system of racism is maintained by a variety of forces, including both physical violence and false consciousness. To take the step of questioning heterosexuality as a 'preference' or 'choice' for women – and to do the intellectual and emotional work that follows – will call for a special quality of courage in heterosexually identified feminists, but I think the rewards will be great: a freeing-up of thinking, the exploring of new paths, the shattering of another great silence, new clarity in personal relationships.

Source: Rich (1994)

was organized and carried out by women, many of whom were informed by feminist ideas.

Initially women had camped at 'Yellow Gate' or 'Main Gate' near the main entrance to the base. But as more women arrived and differences of outlook began to assert themselves, those who shared common interests or attitudes set up camp at other gates. This affected the nature of the camp as a whole, as Roseneil comments:

[There was] a discourse at Greenham which constructed the gates as different from each other in important respects. In the case of Blue Gate, for example, this meant that working class women living there felt an enhanced sense of identity and community with the women around them, and were able to distance themselves from some of the aspects of Greenham which they found oppressively middle class. Similarly, many women, aware that

Greenham was often thought of as 'spiritual' and 'earth-motherly', and rejecting that aspect of Greenham, were able to construct the 'cosmic' as other, by locating it at Green Gate. There were two women, both visitors, who in the course of their interviews expressed disapproval of the behaviour and high visibility of lesbians at Greenham, and sought to disassociate themselves from the 'militant feminism' (which is frequently a euphemism for lesbianism) of some of the women. They were, in part, able to do this by pinpointing gates which they did not visit ... and thus separating themselves from those features of Greenham which they disliked.

(Roseneil, 1995, p. 79)

Activity

Read the extract 'Compulsory heterosexuality and lesbian existence'.

a To what extent do you agree that heterosexuality is 'imposed, managed, organized, propagandized and maintained by force'?

b Suggest examples which might illustrate each of these points.

C3.2, C3.3

Evidence of changing gender roles

A plausible case can be made for the view that changes in gender roles are impacting on both the production and consumption of popular culture. At least four issues can be identified:

1 As women participate more extensively in labour markets (see Section 17.3), so they also should gain more recognition as significant consumers of popular culture. There is some evidence to suggest that this is the case. More magazines, books and television programmes are targeted at key female audiences, and more services are available in the market to support female cultural participation, from women's minicab firms, to pubs with male strippers.

2 On the production side, there is some evidence to suggest that women are, at last, securing positions of seniority within the cultural industries. The BBC, for example, set itself the objective of filling 40 per cent of its senior managerial positions with either female staff or staff recruited from ethnic minority backgrounds by the year 2000. Women's magazines have long represented a sector in which female journalists have occupied a majority of the senior editorial positions.

3 Changes in values and the expectations associated with traditional gender roles have opened up more opportunities for women to participate as creative artists in such areas as drama, music, film and literature. The days when girls were allowed to 'decorate' pop bands as 'singers' but were denied opportunities to write or play music have gone.

4 Changes in gender role expectations have impacted on youth subcultures. Club and dance culture appears to open up more opportunities for girls.

17.9 Definitions of 'race' and ethnicity

All human beings are born free and equal in dignity and right. They are endowed with reason and conscience and should act towards one another in a spirit of brotherhood.

(United Nations Declaration of Human Rights, Article 1)

It is widely recognized that although individuals enter this world on an equal basis, society constructs labels, based on physical differences, which are used to differentiate unequally between people. There is no scientific basis for 'race' as a classification, yet 'race' and the related concept of ethnicity exist as frames of reference in contemporary society. Individuals, groups, institutions and the government perpetuate meanings associated with an ideology of 'race' and ethnicity.

The consequences of this in the UK are far-reaching, resulting in continued and widespread prejudice and discrimination. Despite legislation outlawing racial discrimination, people have failed to act towards each other in a 'spirit of brotherhood'. Racial and ethnic disadvantage was prevalent in the 1990s; for example, 60 per cent of Bangladeshis and 47 per cent of Pakistanis were reported to be living in overcrowded conditions, as opposed to 3 per cent of whites (Anthias and Yuval-Davis, 1993).

Defining key terms

Before we begin it is necessary to examine the key terms used in any discussion of 'race' and ethnicity. Generally sociologists have tried to use terms in their studies of 'race relations' which are preferred by members of the various groups themselves. For example, in the UK 'black' was adopted as a political identity by people of African–Caribbean and Asian descent (Bradley, 1996) and sociologists used this as a term to describe those groups.

However, Modood (1992) claims that all-encompassing terms such as 'black' conceal the differences of distinct groups. As an alternative frame of reference it has been proposed that each group should be referred to by its cultural identity, be it Pakistani, Bangladeshi or whatever. Yet it must be remembered that differences of experience exist even within these identities. Sociologists remain divided on this issue, but for the purposes of this book it is important to account for existing definitions within the sociology of 'race' and ethnicity.

'Race'

'Race' has been used to refer to real or perceived biological differences which have been given a social meaning, such as skin colour (phenotype). As Mason explained:

... race is a social relationship in which structural positions and social actions are ordered, justified and explained by reference to systems of symbols and beliefs which emphasize the social and cultural relevance of biologically rooted characteristics.

(Mason, 1995, p. 9)

'Race' as a biological characteristic is seen as a delusion based on unsubstantiated scientific research. As Donald and Rattansi noted:

... the physical or biological differences between groups defined as 'races' have been shown to be trivial. No persuasive empirical case has been made for ascribing common psychological, intellectual or moral capacities or characteristics to individuals on the basis of skin colour or physiognomy.

(Donald and Rattansi, 1992, p. 1)

Despite this, discrimination based on 'racial' assumptions is widespread in the UK. Whether 'race' exists or not, the racial frames of reference do and these have social consequences. People act as if 'race' is an objective category, and this is reflected in political discourse. As O'Donnell acknowledged:

'Race', understood in biological terms, has proved remarkably unsuccessful as a basis for categorising people and of explaining differences in their behaviour. However, this has not stopped people seeking explanations of others' behaviour in terms of their supposed race.

(O'Donnell, 1991, p. 3)

'Race' as a social construct to which meanings are attached is very real, as are its effects. Consequently it has been argued that 'race' could be seen as the construction of differences based upon non-existent biological differences which are expressed, or believed to be expressed, in cultural activities (Anthias and Yuval-Davis, 1993). 'Race' is therefore grounded, as Anthias and Yuval-Davis noted, 'on the separation of human populations by some notion of stock or collective heredity of traits' (p. 2).

Ethnicity

'Ethnicity' as a concept is more social and rooted in self-definition than 'race'. There is no single definition of ethnicity, but it has been suggested that the most important factor that creates an ethnic group is culture.

Ethnic groups may be defined (or define themselves) on the basis of language, religion or nationality, but the idea of shared culture is perhaps the crucial issue.

(Bradley, 1996, p. 121)

Therefore, ethnicity becomes a characteristic of social groups based upon a shared identity (real or perceived) rooted in common cultural, historical, religious or traditional factors, and who are regarded so by others.

'Ethnicity' as a term used to be treated cautiously, because it was suspected that its links with culture would carry connotations of failure: for example, the under-achievement of 'black' pupils being linked to cultural deprivation through ethnicity. (See also Section 11.4.) However, ethnicity can be a useful concept in many ways, such as allowing for conflicts within groups not distinguishable on racial grounds (e.g. Indian Sikhs and Hindus), or to refer to a sense of belonging within a community. It must be remembered that, as with 'race', the notion of ethnicity is still a differentiating force within society:

RACE – THE FACTS

VIOLENCE
Racist attacks are on the increase in many parts of the world.
- Indigenous Canadians are six times more likely to be murdered than other Canadians.[1]
- In the UK Asians are 50 times and West Indians 36 times more likely than Whites to be victims of racial violence.[14]
- In the US, 6 out of every 10 hate crimes had a racial motivation and a further 1 in 10 an ethnic motivation. 36% were anti-black, 21% anti-white and 13% anti-Jewish.[15]

IMPRISONMENT & EXILE
Belonging to the 'wrong' group increases the chances of imprisonment and asylum rejection.

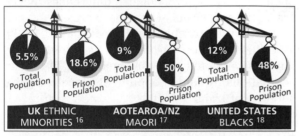

UK ETHNIC MINORITIES [16]	AOTEAROA/NZ MAORI [17]	UNITED STATES BLACKS [18]
5.5% Total Population / 18.6% Prison Population	9% Total Population / 50% Prison Population	12% Total Population / 48% Prison Population

- Most of the world's 15 million refugees come from the South and seek refuge in neighbouring countries. One person in 10 was a refugee in Malawi in July 1993, compared to one in 5000 in the UK. The rate of asylum refusal on appeal in the UK has risen from 14% to 72%.[19]

WORK
Racial prejudice affects access to jobs.
CANADA – indigenous people are twice as likely to be jobless as the rest of the population.
US – blacks are twice as likely to be jobless as whites.[1]
UK – ethnic minorities are twice as likely to be jobless. Ethnic minority women are three times as likely to be jobless as other women.
AUSTRALIA – Aboriginal people are more than three times as likely to be jobless as the general population.[3]
But in **INDIA** 10% of higher level jobs in the public sector now go to people from the Scheduled Castes (more than 16% of the total population) compared with only 3.5% in 1972.[4]

STRIFE & GENOCIDE
Half of the world's states have recently experienced inter-ethnic strife.
The result has been:
- In Afghanistan 1 in 6 people have been disabled by a landmine.
- In Zaire more than 800,000 people have been displaced.
- In Sri Lanka more than 14,000 have died in clashes between Tamils and the Sinhalese.
- In former Yugoslavia more than 130,000 people have been killed since 1991.[1]
- Up to 50,000 people were killed in Burundi in 1993.[20]
- In Rwanda the attempted genocide of Tutsis has resulted in an estimated 200,000–500,000 deaths.
- In Brazil an average of one tribe a year has been wiped out since 1990.[10]

HEALTH, WEALTH & HOUSING
How we live, where we live and how long we may live may often be determined by race.
In the **US**
- Nearly 50% of the black population live in polluted areas, compared to 30% of the white population.[1]
- 40% of Native Americans live below the poverty line. 37% die before the age of 45.[10] They are 10 times as likely to die of alcohol abuse.[11]

In **AUSTRALIA**
- Aboriginal people's life expectancy is 15 years lower than the rest of the population. Infant mortality is three times higher.[3]
- The suicide rate is six times higher.[10]
- Aboriginal family income is about half the Australian average.[12]

In **SOUTH AFRICA**
- The white 14% of the population owns almost 90% of the land.
- Life expectancy for whites is 73 years, for blacks 57. Infant mortality among whites is 13 per 1,000; among blacks, 57 per 1,000.[9]

In the **UK**
- People from ethnic minorities are four times more likely to be homeless in London than whites.[15]

EDUCATION
Discrimination affects the languages we speak and the education we get.
Fewer than 5% of the world's languages are given official recognition by governments.[5] No more than 100 people can speak Japan's indigenous Ainu language fluently.[6]

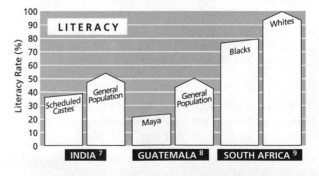

LITERACY — Literacy Rate (%): INDIA [7] Scheduled Castes / General Population; GUATEMALA [8] Maya / General Population; SOUTH AFRICA [9] Blacks / Whites

1 UNDP *Human Development Report*, 1994. **2** 1991 Census; Crown copyright. Through NEMDA. **3** NSW Task Force on Aboriginal Health, 1987. **4** *India Today*, 30 April 1994. **5** Minority Rights Group. **6** *COLORS* 4, 1993. **7** Indian Census 1991. **8** Phillip Wearne, *The Maya of Guatemala*, MRG, London, forthcoming. **9** *Choices*, UNDP, June 1994. **10** Survival International. **11** *Talking Stick* 1, 1993. **12** 1986 Census, Australian Bureau of Statistics. **13** *Race through the 90's*, Council for Racial Equality and BBC, 1993. **14** Institute of Race Relations. **15** *Uniform Crime Report*, March 1994, FBI, reported by Center for Democratic Renewal. **16** Home Office Statistical Bulletin 9/91. Through NEMDA. **17** Julian Berger *The Gaia Atlas of First Peoples*, 1990. **18** Bureau of Justice Statistics, in *New Statesman and Society*, 1 April 1994. **19** *WUS Update*, June 1994. **20** UNHCR *Information Bulletin*, 10 December 1993.

'Race' and ethnicity are social categories used in reference to divisions within a particular society.

(Bradley, 1996, p. 122)

In contemporary society the term 'ethnic' is quite often used as a synonym for someone seen as culturally different. This may possibly result in 'ethnocentrism' which has been defined as:

... the practice of evaluating other groups, and their cultures and practices, from the perspective of one's own.

(Mason, 1995, p. 10)

Judgements (good or bad) are made of another group based on our own subjective experiences, and Mason argues that these usually entail misunderstanding and possibly result in racism. The term 'ethnic minority' has also been seen to have potential problems, because it is used in reference to a group of people in a population whose cultural origins lie in another country and are therefore 'different'. However, not all 'ethnic' or 'minority' groups are perceived as 'ethnic minorities' – consider Polish (white European) immigrants.

'Ethnicity' as a concept has gained credibility because it recognizes the shortcomings of assimilationist assumptions (that all ethnic minorities should absorb themselves into the culture of the country in which they live) and accepts the permanence of these communities. It also avoids the biological determinism of 'race' by concentrating on culture and diversity.

Racism and racialism

'Race' and ethnicity as terms and concepts have the potential to clarify, yet also foster, racism and racialism. The concept of racism was first used as the title of a German book by Hirschfield in 1933 (Miles, 1993). However, it was not defined until the 1940s when Benedict (1943) used the term in reference to nazi Germany:

... the dogma that one ethnic group is condemned by nature to congenital inferiority and another group is destined to congenital superiority.

(Solomos, 1993, p. 97)

Racism therefore involves racial prejudice, which is the holding of preconceived attitudes and beliefs about others and prejudging them on that basis, usually in a negative way. Racism is an ideology based on non-existent biological divisions (Miles, 1990). Mason saw it as:

... situations in which groups of people are hierarchically distinguished from one another on the

basis of some notion of stock difference and where symbolic representations are mobilised which emphasise the social and cultural relevance of biologically rooted characteristics.

(Mason, 1995, p. 11)

This definition of racism brings in a notion of action, a concept involved more usually in racial discrimination or racialism, which is the behavioural manifestation of racial prejudice. Cashmore defined racialism as:

... the action of discriminating against particular others by using the belief that they are racially different, and usually inferior. It is the practical element of the race concept.

(Cashmore, 1983, p. 37)

Mason, however, has used the term 'racism' to encompass both racial prejudice and discrimination. In this sense racism becomes a relative concept, changing according to time, place and situation. As Cohen noted:

Racism has always been multi-dimensional and specific to different contexts.

(Cohen, 1988, p. 136)

It has been argued that a distinction between 'racism' and 'racialism' should be retained, because if 'racism' incorporates theory and ideology, while 'racialism' involves practice and behaviour, then each requires combating in different ways – possibly through socialization to change racism, or legislation to prevent racialism. 'Institutional racism' as a concept utilizes

Activity

Consider these two reported cases, cited by Jacobs (1988, pp. 116–17):

Five Asians were arrested following clashes between Asians and white youths in Spitalfields in London's East End. The fighting started after a white man was reported to have sprayed Bengali children with beer and called them 'Pakis'. Following disturbances, a number of shops in the area were damaged.

Two white youths were reported to have thrown a petrol bomb into an Asian family's home in Bradford. The youths, aged 16 and 15, told police that they had thrown the missile 'for fun' and admitted arson.

To what extent could the actions in these cases be perceived as racist?

C3.2, C3.3

a general idea of racism, involving belief and behaviour, when it is seen as racial inequality within the structure of society. It involves treating ethnic minorities differently in social situations, such as employment, just because they are members of that minority group.

Activity

First read the article 'Black student killed "out of racist hatred"'. Just over a week after this article appeared, the *Observer* (28 April 1996) reported that the Crown Prosecution Service (CPS) official, Howard Youngerwood, who withdrew murder charges against the alleged killers of Stephen Lawrence was later accused of 'covering up racism where the CPS paid damages to a black manager'.

Taking into account the article and the later revelations about Youngerwood, evaluate the neo-Marxist belief that racism can be examined only autonomously.

C3.2, C3.3

The Macpherson Report

On 24 February 1999, the Macpherson Report into the police investigation of Stephen Lawrence's murder branded the Metropolitan police 'institutionally racist'. Stephen Lawrence had been murdered by a gang of white youths in an unprovoked attack in 1993. The police had failed in their duty to investigate the case fully, the assailants remaining free. The Lawrence family's determination to find justice for their son's murder acted as a catalyst for the Macpherson investigation. The main recommendations of the report are displayed here in a box.

Metropolitan Police Commissioner Sir Paul Condon had at first rejected the idea of institutional racism within the force, stating that it would brand all his officers bigots. However, he later claimed that institutional racism may apply to his police force, depending on how it was defined. Macpherson defined institutional racism as:

The collective failure of an organisation to provide an appropriate and professional service to people because of their colour, culture or ethnic origin. It can be seen or detected in processes, attitudes and behaviour which amount to discrimination through unwitting prejudice, ignorance, thoughtlessness and

Main recommendations of the Macpherson Report

- The Home Secretary should give priority to improving relations between police and ethnic minorities.

- There should be an immediate review of racism-awareness training throughout the police force.

- There should be an immediate inspection of the Metropolitan Police Force by HM Inspectorate of Constabulary to restore public confidence in the service.

- There should be a shake-up in the structure of the metropolitan force to put it on the same footing of accountability with its police authority as other forces.

- The National Curriculum for schools should be changed so that it 'values cultural diversity' and reflects society.

- Any police officer found to have acted in a racist manner should be dismissed.

- Investigations into complaints against police should be carried out independently.

Source: Independent, 25 February 1999

Activity

... there are aspects of national and international processes that have an indirect but fundamental impact on black people's housing situation, notably government immigration and housing policies, the structure and workings of the labour market, and the interactions between 'race' and other major lines of stratification, particularly class and gender. These processes may be described as structural racism, because they are not tangibly institutionalized in the local housing scene; they are institutionalized in the socio-economic structure beyond immediate housing institutions.

(Ginsberg, 1992, p. 109)

a Explain 'structural racism' *in your own words*.

b Investigate how Marxists and Weberians would explain the disadvantaged position of black people in relation to housing.

C3.2, C3.3

racist stereotyping which disadvantages minority ethnic people.

(Macpherson Report, 1999)

Black student killed 'out of racist hatred'

MICHAEL STREETER

A black student was murdered by a gang of white youths simply because of the colour of his skin, a court heard yesterday. Stephen Lawrence, 18, died from two stab wounds inflicted by racist attackers, motivated by a "deep-felt hatred" of blacks, the Old Bailey was told.

Michael Mansfield QC, prosecuting, told the all-white jury: "There can be no mistaking that it was an unprovoked, unwarranted attack by those who hold not just racist views but racist views which involve the desecration of those who are black by injury and possibly death. Whoever did this was someone who had a deep-felt hatred of black people existing."

Later, Mr Lawrence's friend, Dwayne Brooks, described seeing the A-level student stabbed and then collapsing on the ground "with blood running on the floor".

Three men are the subject of a private prosecution brought by the Lawrence family. All deny murder.

Mr Mansfield outlined the events leading up to the killing on 22 April 1993, almost exactly three years ago. Mr Lawrence, who attended Bluecoat School in south-east London, was an "ordinary" young man who started that day not knowing it was to be his last. He and Mr Brooks were on their way home from an evening with Mr Lawrence's uncle when they stopped at a bus stop in Wellhall Road, Eltham, after 10pm, said Mr Mansfield. Soon afterwards, they were approached by a group of four to six white youths – whom the prosecution says included the defendants – one of whom shouted "What, what, nigger" to them. When approached, the black men tried to run but Mr Lawrence was not as quick to escape as his friend, Mr Mansfield said.

Mr Lawrence was surrounded and struck by an overarm blow with a weapon such as a "rather large, kitchen knife". Two wounds, on either side of his chest severed vital arteries and he was pronounced dead on arrival at hospital.

Mr Mansfield said the jury might think that the white youths, who fled into the night, had only one object on their minds that evening, which was to cause serious injury to one or other of the black youths. "This attack was swift, merciless and vicious. They approached together, attacked together and disappeared together."

The case continues.

Source: Independent, 19 April 1996

Based on this definition, Condon accepted, with a 'sense of shame', that institutional racism was indeed evident in the metropolitan force, but that it existed at an unconscious level, rather than as calculated racialism.

Nationalism

The term 'nationalism' also implies thoughts and actions when it suggests that national boundaries should coincide with ethnicity; that is, all those, and only those, who belong to an ethnic group should share a common territory. This incorporates racial prejudice and racial discrimination, because it relies on beliefs about national identity and ultimately on behaviour which reinforces boundaries.

In the UK, nationalism has been intensified by the rise of 'new racism', which has focused on the cultural incompatibility of ethnic minorities and indigenous populations. It stems from the idea of 'nation', which implies distinct political territory linking people together, even though most of the population of a community do not know each other. This sense of 'nation' has been employed by Bradley (1996) as an explanation of 'race' and ethnicity in general:

'Race' and ethnicity are two of the social categories which have evolved to explain lived relationships which emanate from territorially based groups around the world.

(Bradley, 1996, p. 114)

It is argued that migration (by coercion and/or exploration) has mixed up groups of people from different territorial groupings and resulted in 'social pluralism', where a multitude of ethnic groups co-exist. However, the term 'immigrant' (any person who has recently arrived from another society in which he or she has habitually lived) still carries the negative associations developed when the UK was a colonial power, quite often resulting in unequal treatment for the immigrant. (You will also find discussion of the sociological implications of nationalism in Section 15.2.)

'Black'

Racial and ethnic disadvantage has common themes, and it is argued that it is appropriate to use the term 'black' for those who are victims of white racism/racialism. This idea has been challenged.

Brah (1992) has argued that black people may have a similar structural position in post-war Britain (e.g. the lowest stratum in the socioeconomic system), and experience similar racism, but the ideologies which racialized them were different. In other words the experiences of

African–Caribbeans was very different from those of Asians. Brah concluded that the term 'black' falsely homogenizes diverse groups.

Modood (1988) and Hazareesingh (1986) both stated that black should be used only in reference to people of sub-Saharan African descent, because it has no cultural meaning to southern Asians. However, it might be proved that on this basis the term 'black' would also ignore differences within African groups.

'Black' has varying meanings both historically and in a contemporary context. In the nineteenth century the colour black was a representation of evil; in the 1960s it represented political pride; and in a contemporary context being 'black' provides homogeneity as a political force or represents a basis for dividing ethnic minority groups. Consequently the notion of being black has been interpreted differently by sociologists, either as a tool for unifying oppressed ethnic minorities, or conversely as a way of concealing their differences. Brah realized that changing the term 'black' would have few structural ramifications:

It is unlikely that replacing black by some other politically neutral description will secure more equitable distribution of resources.

(Brah, 1992, pp. 129–30)

Sociologists are therefore faced with the problem of occasions that necessitate a generic term to describe general processes of exclusion for certain sections of society.

In this chapter the term 'black' will be used to refer to all ethnic minorities who are not white when reference to historic countries of origin are not possible. The term will not, however, henceforth appear in inverted commas because it is argued that it has been adopted by some ethnic minorities as a political identity (see Section 4.3) and should not be viewed in the same sense as 'race'. The term 'racism' will be used to refer to both racial prejudice and racial discrimination, unless otherwise stated.

Activity

In Britain there were no legal definitions of a black person, or legal restrictions on mixed marriages. This may have been in part because until the mid-1950s the number of black people in Britain was very small – never more than 15,000, often less. The few 'half-castes' were generally recognised by both black and white people as different from black. But they were stigmatised as much in Britain as elsewhere, perhaps more so, since they were usually born into the poorest sector of society, whilst in other countries they tended to be part of the intermediate class. ... Since the 1960s there have been major changes in both Britain and the USA that seem likely to have led to both black and mixed-parentage people developing more positive identities. The scientific discrediting of theories about the superiority of the white race, and the increasing liberalisation of white attitudes, have tended to reduce the stigma attached to being black or of mixed parentage.

(Tizard, 1994, p. 3)

Explain *in your own words* why Tizard thinks that black or 'half-caste' people are more likely to be stigmatized in the UK than elsewhere. In what ways does Tizard think this situation has changed since the 1960s?

C3.2, C3.3

Theories and research on 'race' and ethnicity – an overview

Theories and research in the USA

Academic enquiry into 'race' and ethnicity began by focusing on scientific differences, but when these were discredited social scientific investigations started to take place. Bradley concluded that:

There has been a growing interest in the study of 'race' and ethnicity in Britain over the course of the twentieth century.

(Bradley, 1996, p. 143)

'Race relations'

In the USA in the 1920s, Robert Park established the study of 'race relations'. He focused on the social and economic inequalities experienced by black people, their cultural and psychological backgrounds, their family relationships and political isolation. In 1944, Gunnar Myrdal foresaw, through documenting the history of inequality in the United States, the assimilation of the

American black population into mainstream society. Assimilation is defined by Lawson and Garrod as:

... a view of 'race relations' which sees the host community as culturally homogeneous and the task of the immigrant community is to be absorbed into the host community as quickly as possible, by adopting host features. Sensitivity to cultural differences is minimal so that ethnic minority culture is disparaged.

(Lawson and Garrod, 1996, p. 14)

This work developed ideas on racial conflict and their origins and became known as the 'assimilation model'. It enabled social scientists to see that 'race' became important only after cultural and social meanings were attached to the physical traits of a particular group.

Theories and research in the UK

Theorizing and research into 'race' and ethnicity in the UK began in the 1940s. It then concentrated on immigration and the role of colonialization in creating popular conceptions on colour and 'race' (Glass, 1960). Marxist and Weberian perspectives were developed to examine these areas, focusing largely on concepts of class.

In the 1950s and 60s, Glass (1960), Rex and Moore (1967) and Patterson (1963) carried out studies into 'race relations', concentrating on interactions between minority and majority communities in employment, housing and other social contexts. However, it has been noted that there was a lack of clear theoretical perspective about the object of analysis (Solomos, 1993). Consequently, in the 1960s problematic 'race relations' became the dominant area of research.

The 1970s

As all good students of sociology know, a theoretical perspective can dictate how re search is carried out. Therefore, the absence of a clear theoretical approach can make research confusing or ambiguous. In the 1970s the work of John Rex provided a theory of 'race relations' in the UK, defining it in a structural sense based on conflict over scarce resources and conditions of exploitation and occupational segregation.

Later, Rex and Tomlinson's (1979) study of Handsworth discovered that immigrants held a place outside that of the working class in employment; they were seen as an 'underclass' who occupied the lowest stratum in society, resulting in discrimination in education and housing. Their examination of blacks as an 'underclass' established a model of political action, raising the issue of politics and racism. (The 'underclass' debate is examined also in Section 17.6.)

The 1980s

The 1970s saw class and social differentiation on racial/ethnic grounds as the major theoretical theme. However, in the 1980s criticism of Marxist ideology began to emerge based on three factors:

1 Marxism's reliance on class obscures any analysis of racial/ethnic phenomena in their own right. This issue became the focus of important debates.

2 It provided little historical or theoretical reflection on the role of slavery/colonialism, etc. in the capitalist mode of production.

3 Marxists' work showed use of dormant racial stereotypes and uncritical use of racist imagery.

Marxist views on 'race' and ethnicity

Miles (1984) offered a debate on the Marxist framework, initiating a more theoretical investigation into 'race' and ethnicity. He viewed the analysis of racism as integral to capitalism and examined it via its political, class and ideological relationships. He concluded that 'race' is a human construct which hides real economic relationships. Therefore racism is a consequence of:

... on the one hand the need of the capitalist world economy for the mobility of human beings, and on the other the drawing of territorial boundaries and the construction of citizenship as a legal category which sets boundaries for human mobility.

(Miles, 1988, p. 438)

For Miles, 'racial identities' are ideologically constructed by the state in order to fragment the working class racially and reduce class conflict.

Neo-Marxism and the Centre for Contemporary Cultural Studies

Concern with the ideological and cultural dimensions of 'racism' opened the way for the Centre for Contemporary Cultural Studies (CCCS) in Birmingham, which offered a contemporary analysis of 'race' and ethnicity. The CCCS was concerned with the changing nature of politics and 'race', and *The Empire Strikes Back* (1982) analysed the social and political construction of 'race'. This type of investigation into 'racism' did not occur in the United States for another decade, when Omi and Winant (1994) examined the processes of 'race formation' and the influence of political and legal relations on these.

Collecting data about ethnic minorities and ethnicity

The 1980s also saw the development of national quantitative data on ethnic minorities in the UK, which had not been freely available before, as Gordon acknowledged:

Until the mid 1980s relatively little statistical information about minority ethnic group people in Britain was collated at a national level or, indeed, in any systematic way.

(Gordon, 1996, p. 22)

Before the 1980s virtually no relevant national data were collected regularly on education, health, housing, welfare, social services, the criminal justice system, policing or racial violence. Therefore it was virtually impossible to know the extent of racial disadvantage or discrimination. The available sources were:

- the national Census, carried out every ten years but only providing direct data on ethnicity since 1991

- immigration data

- the Labour Force Survey, carried out every two years.

Organizations within the fields of 'race relations' wanted statistical data to back up their arguments on racial inequalities in the UK.

The problem of racialized data

It must be remembered that 'racial groups' which are used in statistics are social constructions, rather than objective scientific categories, and that this can affect the collection of 'racialized data'.

For example, the 1991 Census gave respondents nine 'race' categories to choose from, resulting in very different information based on changed perceptions of 'race groupings'

This problem of creating suitable categories has been impossible to overcome, with some institutions appearing to produce racial identifications in a racist manner. For example, Anthias and Yuval-Davis (1993) argued that the police have carried out ethnic monitoring using a visual assessment of 'racial' physical characteristics, such as colour of skin, type of hair and nose shape. Therefore their 'monitoring' is neither objective (country of origin), nor a classification based on the people's own perception of their ethnic identity. However, researchers have generally attempted to improve categories by including a mixture of 'racial', national and ethnic classifications. The 1991 Census referred to 'race' (skin colour), nationality (Indian/Pakistani, etc.) and ethnicity.

Activity

In March 1982, the Metropolitan Police issued its statistics on crimes recorded in London in 1981. The figures highlighted two things. First, an 8 per cent rise in serious crime over the previous year and, second, an increase in 'mugging' and the alleged disproportionate involvement of black people in this crime. The figures stated that the 'appearance of the assailant' had been described as white by just under 5000 victims, but as 'coloured' by more than 10,000. This was the first occasion on which police statistics had been racialized in this way.

(Gordon, 1996, p. 29)

Prepare the arguments for *both* sides of the following debate: 'We believe that the police perpetuate racist beliefs by issuing statistics on crime and "race".'

This activity will involve your sociological understanding of 'race' and ethnicity in relation to crime, deviance and research methods.

 C3.2, C3.3

The uses of data on ethnicity

It has been argued that data on ethnicity, despite the usual methodological problems, is useful on three levels:

1 *Fact-finding* – General observations can be made about 'race' and ethnicity.

2 *Informing government policy* – Data collected can assist in creating legislation.

3 *Social reform* – Using the data, areas can be identified where ethnic minorities may be subject to discrimination. Then policies can be implemented to promote equal opportunities.

However, it must be remembered that *all* statistics are open to misuse by way of an alternative interpretation. A government, for example, could use secondary data for purposes other than for which it was intended – information on client problems during migration could be used to tighten immigration controls. Gordon is clear

to point out both the advantages and the disadvantages of collecting racialized data, but concludes that it is justifiable as a route to removing racial disadvantage:

The collection of ethnic data is not an end to itself but a means to an end: that of implementing equal opportunities and racial equality.

(Gordon, 1996, p. 41)

The 1990s

A key concern of studies in the UK on 'race' and ethnicity has been the need to develop ideas of racialization and its effects on politics and ideology. New theories are emerging, such as post-Marxism and post-modernism (see Section 13.9), which avoid a homogenous conceptualization of 'race' and ethnicity, with the differences within ethnic minority groups being emphasized. These

---

Surveys of ethnic minorities in the UK

• **[1968] W. W. Daniel,** *Racial Discrimination in England* There were fewer than one million ethnic minorities in the UK. The survey focused on racial discrimination following the passing of the Race Relations Act 1966. It was based on interviews, to record peoples' perceptions and experiences of discrimination, and also objective tests on discrimination. Daniel devised an experiment to find out whether racial discrimination was 'real' in the UK by getting both white and ethnic minority actors to apply for the same job vacancy with the same qualifications and experience. The response of employers to the ethnic minority applicants showed that discrimination was a feature of British social life. Daniel's discoveries encouraged the outlawing of direct discrimination with the Race Relations Act 1967.

• **[1974] D. J. Smith,** *Racial Disadvantage in Britain* This survey was conducted under the realization that ethnic minority groups faced structural disadvantage and therefore indirect discrimination, such as poorer qualifications resulting in fewer employment opportunities. Smith found that there was a great deal of inequality between whites and ethnic minorities in employment and housing, which motivated the government into introducing the Race Relations Act 1976 to ban indirect discrimination.

• **[1982] C. Brown,** *Black and White in Britain* The third survey was conducted during a period that displayed evidence of some ethnic minority upward mobility. Ethnic groups were still disadvantaged compared with whites, but some ethnic groups were improving their position in employment. Brown showed the differences between

whites and ethnic minority groups, but also showed how some ethnic groups were having experiences different from others in the UK.

• **[1994] T. Modood and colleagues,** *Ethnic Minorities in Britain: Diversity and Disadvantage* There were three million ethnic minorities in the UK. This most recent survey focused on education, employment and housing, interviewing a representative sample 5196 people of Caribbean and Asian origin and a comparison sample of 2867 white people. South Asian children have achieved above-average qualifications, but Caribbean boys are not doing as well as white boys. Some ethnic groups are represented well in high-level jobs, while others remain in lower-level employment or unemployment and experience low income. Income was directly related to poverty, and white and Chinese families were found to be the most prosperous families, while Pakistani and Bangladeshi families were found to be the poorest.

The first two surveys were undertaken by Political and Economic Planning (PEP), which became the Policies Studies Institute (PSI) following a merger in 1978.

The first survey covered six towns with significant minority populations. The second covered all enumeration districts with more than 2.2 per cent minority population. The third and fourth were fully representative of England and Wales.

Despite the national Census counting three million ethnic minorities in the UK, the PSI surveys remain the only large-scale national studies comparing ethnic minority circumstances with the white population.

Source: Adapted from Modood, T. *et al.* (1997, pp. 1–8)

contemporary theories have broadened studies on ethnicity, focusing on identities, the interconnections between 'race' and nationhood, nationalism, cultural practices and racial discourses in post-colonial society (Gilroy, 1987; Phizacklea, 1983; Anthias and Yuval-Davis, 1993.

The study of 'race relations' is politically charged and results in different theories 'making imperialist demands to command the whole field to the exclusion of all other theories' (Rex, 1988, p. 64). However, as Solomos notes 'not one theoretical perspective is dominant at the present time' (Solomos, 1993, p. 36).

This could be attributed to the way in which the separate theories complement each other, rather than discredit each other. Rex (1988) highlighted three areas where potentially contradictory theories could support general investigation into 'race' and ethnicity:

- Different theories deal with different kinds of issues.
- Different perspectives may see the same issue in a different way.
- Different approaches may operate on different levels of abstraction, such as macro and micro levels.

Sociological approaches to 'race' and ethnicity are complex and variable. Contemporary perspectives may have arisen from previous theories, but they have progressed a great deal from the classical approaches which concentrated mainly on biology, industrial development and cultural assimilation – although a recent resurgence in biological examinations of 'race' and ethnicity has stunned the social scientific world (Herrnstein and Murray, 1994).

Contemporary approaches to 'race' and ethnicity

Neo-Marxism

Classical interpretations of Marxism have tended to reduce 'race' to a facet of class exploitation. However, since the 1960s Marxist sociologists have relied less on economic reductionism, focusing instead on areas such as the extent of autonomy in the field of 'race relations'. As with early Marxism, neo-Marxism consists of competing schools of thought. Two of the main approaches

are the 'relative autonomy model' and the 'autonomy model'.

The relative autonomy model

This approach was developed by the Centre for Contemporary Cultural Studies (CCCS, 1982). The CCCS aimed to establish an analysis of racism which:

- accepted the relative autonomy of 'race' from class-based social relations
- acknowledged its specific historical position in relation to capitalism.

Their approach has also been termed 'cultural Marxism' (Bradley, 1996), because of its emphasis on imperialism and the use of racism in strengthening cultural hegemony in the UK.

The CCCS began examining racism in the early 1970s (Hall *et al.*, 1978) when attempting to explain 'moral panics' on mugging. The construction of 'race' as a social problem and political issue was investigated and paved the way for the influential CCCS publication *The Empire Strikes Back* (1982). This book suggested the following:

- Previous sociological/Marxist accounts of 'race relations' have not furthered our knowledge of racism and may even have reproduced ethnocentrism.
- A greater emphasis should be placed on 'state racism'.
- The relationship between 'class' and 'race' should be reconceptualized as relatively autonomous. This was initiated by Gilroy, who more recently has presented a post-Marxist, post-modernist approach.

The CCCS's approach is based on a theory of racism which deals with the economic and structural features, but also with its historical and social distinctiveness. Hall (1980) suggested three main areas which critical Marxist analysis of 'race' should involve:

- an attempt to understand what causes racism in a particular society, because it is an historical phenomenon
- an understanding of racism being relatively autonomous from other social relations – working separately from, but at the same time affecting, social relations
- an understanding that 'race' and class have to be analysed together.

The work of Hall and the CCCS has influenced later sociological developments in the study of 'race' and ethnicity. The idea that 'racisms' rather than 'racism' should be considered results in an understanding of racism as a multi-faceted phenomenon that develops in specific situations. The CCCS has been criticized for neglecting the economic context when emphasizing relative autonomy. This criticism, however, appears trivial in the wake of post-modernist reactions to studies of 'race relations', which remove 'racial' and ethnic relations from part of the class structure, replacing them in an analysis based on cultural diversity.

Activity

Another major influence in recent debates about the politics of race can be traced to the work of authors who have at one time or other been associated with the Birmingham Centre for Contemporary Cultural Studies. This research was stimulated in many ways by the publication of Hall's programmatic essay on 'Race, articulation and societies structured in dominance' (1980). Hall's most important argument was that while racism cannot be reduced to other social relations, neither can it be explained autonomously from them. Thus, racism commands a relative autonomy from economic, political and other social relations.

(Solomos and Back, 1995, p. 25–6)

What do you understand by Solomos and Back's conclusion that, in Hall's approach, 'racism commands a relative autonomy from economic, political and other social relations'?

The autonomy model

The autonomy model criticizes relative autonomy as still being ultimately 'reductionist', because it reduces 'race' to one aspect of class. This does not allow racial inequality or discontent to form a separate issue in political struggles, as it is seen as part of class conflict in general. Gabriel and Ben-Tovim (1979) analysed 'race' not separately from its social and class relations, but as a product of contemporary and historical struggles, which could not be reduced to wider economic and social relations. Therefore they perceived 'race' and racism to be autonomous from other social relations.

Gabriel and Ben-Tovim started by examining various struggles – local, national, political and ideological conflicts – in which 'race' was socially constructed. They were aware that wider structural constraints could affect these struggles, but they argued that it was not known to what extent. Gabriel and Ben-Tovim therefore concluded that 'race' could not be reduced to class on any level, and that all Marxist analysis of racism should start by examining the ideological and political practices which work autonomously to produce this phenomenon.

An overview of neo-Marxism

The autonomy model was a breakthrough theoretically from normal Marxist concerns, but it has resulted in the following irreconcilable rift within neo-Marxism on 'race' and ethnicity (Solomos, 1988):

1 It cannot be agreed whether 'racial' and ethnic categorizations are 'relatively autonomous' or 'autonomous' of economic and class determination.

2 The role of political institutions and the state in reproducing racism in capitalist society cannot be agreed upon.

Marxism has moved on from the days when it was seen as just a deterministic theory of social development. Many neo-Marxists challenge determinism (Wright, 1980) and analyse specific areas of industrial society. This has complicated neo-Marxist analysis, making it impossible to construct an acceptable framework of 'racism' for all to follow. Solomos (1988), however, has proposed a Marxist approach that shows how racism is interconnected with wider social relations, but also has autonomy:

• 'Race relations' form part of the structural features of capitalist society.

• Each historical situation needs to be examined in its own specific context, and therefore no general Marxist theory can be applied.

• Structural contradictions cannot totally explain 'race' and ethnic divisions.

Solomos believes that economic and social conditions do play a role in structuring racism as an ideology and as a specific set of practices. He concludes that Marxism may involve diverse perspectives, but in relation to the analysis of 'race' it has homogeneity on two levels:

Marxist theories of 'race' are heterogeneous in approach, though it can be argued that they are unified through a common concern with (a) the material and ideological basis of racism and racial oppression, however it may be defined, and (b) the role that racism plays in structuring the entire social, political and economic structures of societies.

(Solomos, 1988, p. 107)

Neo-Marxism has made the debate over 'race' more challenging, touching areas of concern to non-Marxists (e.g. the origins of racist ideologies) and thereby stimulating further investigations. As Solomos wrote:

... a sizeable and growing body of theory and research in the area of 'race' and ethnic relations is based on or draws inspiration from Marxism.

(Solomos, 1988, p. 86)

The New Right and 'new racism'

Unlikely as it may seem, the theoretical work of Italian Marxist Antonio Gramsci, particularly his concept of hegemony, has been appropriated by the New Right.

(Seidel, 1986, p. 107)

The New Right in the UK is associated with the right-wing politics of Conservative administrations since 1979. As a sociological perspective it utilizes conservative traditions, and:

... insists on the freedom of the individual and the primacy of the free market in all social and economic arrangements.

(Lawson and Garrod, 1996, p. 178)

This emphasis on capitalist free enterprise is where Seidel (1986) has made the connection to Gramsci. Hegemony (class domination) has two aspects, coercion and consensus. Thus the state has the apparatus to force procedures or produce and diffuse its chosen ideology. It is argued that the New Right is attempting to construct their own dominant ideology – in market relationships as the basis of social life – replacing post-war liberal democracy:

[The New Right] is engaged in a cultural battle to unsettle and displace the dominant ideology which constructed the post-war liberal and social democratic consensus.

(Seidel, 1986, p. 107)

Nation and a common culture

In order to do this, language has to be manipulated and cultural and political history redefined. Seidel argues that Roger Scruton and the New Right publication *The Salisbury Review* have been vehicles for the construction of a new political language, the focus of which has been 'nation' and the construction of racist ideologies.

Casey (1982), in *The Salisbury Review*, based the idea of 'nation' in authority and an assumed common culture. He argued that West Indians are a 'problem' because they are different, not accepting authority and therefore prone to criminality. This led Seidel to observe:

... the New Right's racism does not require the hypothesis of innate superiority, only that of cultural difference.

(Seidel, 1986, p. 114)

'New racism'

The New Right is seen to support some elements of the 'new racism' (a term first coined by Barker, 1981). This is based on supposedly fixed cultural differences between ethnic groups, in contrast to 'old racism' which was based on the supposed biological superiority of whites. However, the Conservative party deny that they support racism, as did Enoch Powell in 1969 after his 'Rivers of Blood' speech. Yet in 1979, Prime Minister Margaret Thatcher claimed that 'people are really rather afraid that this country might be swamped by people of a different culture'.

Mason outlined what he perceived to be the basis of 'new racism':

Proponents of the idea that there is a 'new racism' draw attention to the increasing frequency with which political arguments in favour of the exclusion of migrants, or the segregation of members of different population groups, appeal to notions of cultural incompatibility and to the allegedly mutually disruptive and negative consequences.

(Mason, 1995, p. 10)

It is argued that language and discourse create values and ways of thinking, which channel our political behaviour and action in certain directions. Discourse which involves racism rests on institutional support; for example, immigration legislation and nationalism is both ideological and institutional. Gilroy (1992) states that this is incorporated into 'new racism' via three main concepts:

1 'Race' is central to political discourse, but is never used as a term. Seidel (1986) explains this as part of a larger New Right strategy – if 'race' has no meaning then agendas such as repatriation cannot be seen as racist.

2 It identifies 'race' with culture and identity, rather than biology.

3 It links 'race' with notions of nationalism, presenting an imaginary definition of the nation as a unified cultural community.

However, Mason (1995) is clear to point out that while 'new racisms' focus on cultural rather than biological differences, this has not altered popular conceptions on 'race'. In fact on 30 August 1992 the *Independent on Sunday* included an article by a sports commentator who explained that Pakistani fast-bowler success in a Test Match against England was based on the distinctiveness of their sweat in polishing the ball! Also, the recent work of Herrnstein and Murray (1994) has argued that cultural incompatibility is part of the biological view of 'race'.

'New racism' and nationalism

Nationalism in the UK today is tied up in its history of colonial conquest, jingoism and the construction of the national identity built on racist definitions about who is British. (Nationalism is also discussed in Section 10.6.) In Europe, essentialism, which involved each individual being assigned a specific ethnicity or situational ethnicity (Barker, 1981), was linked to fascism in nazi Germany and has been associated with the increase in neo-fascist movements in recent years.

Essentialist ideas have been attractive to fascism because ethnic difference is assumed by this concept to make a difference. These differences are used as the basis for, and justification of, racial prejudice and discrimination against ethnic minority groups. As Solomos (1993) notes, the 1990s were showing a rapid change in the politics of 'race', which included the rise of racist social and political movements in western and eastern Europe. Neo-fascists and right-wing political parties used popular issues, such as immigration, to attract support and perpetuate the myth of 'us' and 'them'.

Education

Education has been a recent tool of the New Right for attracting anti-anti-racist support (Gilroy, 1992). It is argued by the New Right that:

Activity

Twenty years ago attitudes were overtly racist, with the assumption that immigrants should 'fit in' with British cultural expectations. The British media today is on the whole less racist, although nationalism bordering on racism can occasionally be found in the tabloids. The article below discusses the changing attitude of the media towards the UK's ethnic minority population. Using your sociological understanding, take words from the list below and place them in the most appropriate gaps.

racialist	immigration
racists	fierce
increase	media
host community	black
demands	

Some 20 years ago the BBC ran a series called The Editors. *One day, July 13 it was, they invited a group of _____ editors on. Gurdip Singh Chaggar, a young Sikh from Southall, had been murdered by a group of _____ whites. And Southall had exploded. We, a group of black and Asian editors of London papers, were called to the BBC's studios to discuss the issues.*
We laid heavy blame at the doors of the national _____ for helping to create a climate in which racial murders were taking place. We identified the major perpetrator as a programme in the BBC's Open Door *series which had been made by the 'Campaign against _____'. Then, as now, we had no illusions about attitudes and personnel which that campaign conceals. Our criticisms were _____. But the specific _____ that we made – for black programmes, black reporters, black feature writers, black columnists – ended up on the cutting room floor ...*
Today I doubt very much whether any access series on the BBC would allow _____ disguised as decent Britons to putrefy our screens with the garbage of 20 years ago. And there has certainly been an _____ in the numbers of black programmes broadcast ... [however] It is difficult to avoid the conclusion that there is a tendency among the _____ to balk at a concentration of blacks. The readiness to disperse us has, in fact, been a constant feature of our presence in this country, something that no one should feel particularly proud of.
(Darcus Howe, 'Black, white and yellow journalism', *New Statesman*, 6 September 1996)

C3.2, C3.3

- schools are repositories of the authentic national culture
- multi-culturalism in the curriculum is a 'bastardization of genuine British culture'.

Therefore education is seen as an area where anti-racist policies should be abolished and a clear 'British identity' established. (This issue is also discussed in Sections 4.2 and 11.4)

💬 Discussion point

What do you think has caused the recent resurgence of neo-fascism in Europe?

C3.1a

📝 Activity

Ray Honeyford, former head teacher of Drummond Middle School, Bradford, is well known for his outspoken views on 'race relations' issues and education. Using the following statement by Mr Honeyford, and knowledge you have attained elsewhere, outline and evaluate his views on multi-cultural education.

A 'racist' is to the race relations lobby what 'Protestant' was to the inquisitors of the Counter-Reformation, or witches to the seventeenth-century burghers of Salem. It is a totem of the new doctrine of anti-racism. Its definition varies according to the purpose it is meant to achieve. It is a gift to the zealot, since he can apply it to anyone who disagrees with him – and he often ejaculates the word as though it were a synonym for 'rapist' or 'fascist'. It takes force not from its power to describe but from its power to coerce and intimidate. It is attached to anyone who challenges the arguments or rhetoric of the race relations lobby. It is more a weapon than a word.

(Honeyford; quoted in Lewis, 1988, p. 1)

C3.2, C3.3

The media

The New Right has put 'new racism' on the political and academic agenda. It has linked national identity with culture, with black people being perceived as having a different culture and therefore constituting a threat. However, as Gilroy points out, no culture is completely segregated from others, so:

There is no neat or tidy pluralistic separation of racial groups in this country.

(Gilroy, 1992, p. 57)

In 1996 the *Daily Mirror* newspaper printed a controversial front page with the headline 'Achtung! Surrender' (Figure 17.19) the day before England were due to play Germany in a football match during the Euro 96 championship. It was accompanied by a note from the editor issuing a 'declaration of war' against the Germans on the football pitch. The language was reminiscent of Neville Chamberlain's announcement of the outbreak of World War II and was intended to evoke feelings of patriotism, using lines such as 'Wherever there is a television set, loyal English hearts shall beat with pride and the Cross of St George shall wave in all its glory'.

📝 Activity

Suggest ways in which newspaper articles might support the idea that there is a link between nationalism and racism.

C3.2, C3.3

It is useful to note the responses to the *Daily Mirror*'s actions the following day by the quality newspapers. The *Times* wrote that:

The Editor of the Daily Mirror *has apologised after hundreds of people protested about yesterday's front page.*

The jingoism was not confined to the *Daily Mirror*. The *Sun*, which in common with the *Times* is owned by News International, ran the headline 'Let's Blitz Fritz' on an inside page. The *Independent* noted on its front page that:

The British still seem obsessed by Nazism and the War – more so than the occupied countries of Europe still are – and resentful of post-war German prosperity.

The next day, 26 June 1996, the *Independent* published on its front page the following poem by Martin Newell, entitled '1966/1996':

Oasis aren't the Beatles
And Blur are not the Kinks
As Double D. and Watney's Pale
Were not designer drinks
And aerials weren't dishes
And football songs weren't hip
As monocles and spiky hats
Weren't German football strip
And Mitchell wasn't Garnett

Figure 17.19 The front page of the *Daily Mirror* on the eve of the England–Germany football match in the Euro 96 football championship

As Heath was not a fool

And Hamburg found the Mersey Sound
As much as Liverpool
And Klinsmann isn't Haller
As Shearer isn't Hurst
And Ramsey was as much revered
As Venables is cursed

But mad old Tommy Tabloid
Still hammers at the hun
A powdered egg-bound xenophobe
Marooned in '41
He hears the grainy wireless
Across the sun-parched lawn

"4–2, 4–2." He must be true
To lion and unicorn
And younger generations
For whom his cant is meant
Will dress alike and dance alike
With or without consent
As sons of Thames or Tyneside

The Elbe, Rhine and Spree
Will only speak in footballese
Upon the field of play.

Activity

Newell's poem is about Euro 96, but what is it saying in relation to nationalism and 'race relations'?

C3.2, C3.3

Post-modernism

The notion of 'post-modern' evokes images of something that comes after the modern age. Modernity, according to Lyon (1994), was a social order that developed after the decline of medieval European society. As it progressed it became industrial, capitalist, bureaucratic with a central state apparatus and adopted, on a cultural level, the values of enlightenment (secularism, materialism, rationalism, individualism and progression).

A new social order

Sociologists and cultural theorists have claimed, however, that the modern age is being replaced by a new social order – post-modernity. The post-modern society contains, as Richardson notes:

... more flexible (post-Fordist) forms of technology, new communication systems (e.g. global networks) and new social and political institutions (e.g. grouping of nation states in to larger units such as the European Union.

(Richardson, 1996, p. 72)

As part of the post-modern society a new set of values, lifestyles and art forms have emerged (post-modernism), creating a whole new cultural ethos (see Figure 17.19). Post-modernism challenges former doctrines of objectivity, great art and seriousness, finding value in relativity, popular culture and superficiality:

Where the modern age bred uniformity, post-modernism revels in diversity, fragmentation and rapid social change.

(Richardson, 1996, p. 70)

In relation to the study of 'race' and ethnicity, post-modern perspectives offer a critique of one-dimensional modernist theories such as Marxism, which claims that 'race' and ethnicity are secondary aspects of stratification determined by capitalist relations:

... a post-modern approach allows for the development of a multi-dimensional account of inequality, in which each dimension can be accorded equal weight. 'Race' and ethnicity are considered crucial aspects of social differentiation in their own right.

(Bradley, 1996, p. 130)

Synoptic Assessment

The synoptic module, *Social Inequality and Difference*, is the final module you will take if you are studying for the full A level. In this module you will be required to demonstrate your ability to connect issues of methodology as well as social inequality across the whole specification. Therefore, whatever options you have taken during the course you must ensure you make note of possible links to the synoptic module.

The assessment for this synoptic module will test your understanding of the connections between sociological thought and methods of enquiry as they apply to the study of social inequality and difference. You should therefore take every opportunity to include references to aspects of social inequality that you have studied throughout your course, including AS modules studied as part of you're a level.

Chapter 17 is concerned with the synoptic issues. The empirical material from the chapters listed in the table should be read in the context of the theories and methodological points outlined in Chapter 17 but also in the sections listed.

The table below highlights those sections which may help you to prepare for the synoptic module.

Chapter Sections useful for synoptic module

3	**3.1** Introducing the individual and society
	3.2 Socialization: values, norms and culture
4	**4.1** Gender identities
	4.2 National identities
	4.3 Ethnic identities
	4.4 Class identities
	4.5 Social change and identities
5	**5.3** Social policy and the family
	5.4 Recent trends in family life

	5.7 The distribution of power between men and women . . .
	5.8 The relationship between parents and children
6	**6.1** Trends in the ownership and control of the mass media
	6.2 Ownership and trends in production and consumption
	6.5 Media stereotypes
	6.6 Theories of media content
	6.7 The effects of the mass media on audiences
7	**7.3** The appeal of religious institutions
	7.4 The secularization debate
	7.5 Religion and control
	7.7 Religion, ideology and conflict
8	**8.1** Youth culture and subcultures
	8.2 Youth and class, gender and ethnicity
	8.7 Experiences of schooling
	8.8 Femininity, masculinity and subject choice
9	All of this chapter is relevant
10	**10.3** Measuring crime and the fear of crime
	10.4 Patterns of crime and victimization by social profile
	10.6 Social control and the role of the law
11	**11.2** Institutional processes in education
	11.3 Social class and educational attainment
	11.4 Ethnicity and educational attainment
	11.5 Gender and educational attainment
	11.6 Educational participation . . .
12	**12.3** Social class, region and health inequalities
	12.3 Gender, ethnicity and health inequalities
	12.8 The sociology of the body, mind and sexuality
13	**13.3** The political economy of culture
	13.4 Consumption, lifestyle shopping and popular culture
	13.6 Femininity, masculinity and the culture industries
14	**14.4** Contemporary welfare provision
	14.5 Welfare, social control and stratification
	14.6 The welfare state as social control
15	**15.3** Forms of and explanations for political action
	15.6 Power in everyday life
16	All of this chapter is relevant

Further reading

The following books cover the topic of workplace inequality at an appropriate level for A level students:

- Deem, R. (1988) *Work, Unemployment and Leisure*, London: Routledge.
- Kidd, W. (ed.) (1998) *Readings in Sociology*, Oxford: Heinemann.
- Madry, N. and Kirby, M. (1996) *Investigating Work, Unemployment and Leisure*, London: Collins Educational.

The following books offer more detailed analysis of some of the debates covered in this chapter:

- Grint, K. (1991) *The Sociology of Work*, Cambridge: Polity.
- Sennett, R. (1998) *The Corrosion of Character*, London: Norton & Co.
- Watson, T. (1995) *Sociology, Work and Industry*, 3rd edn, London: Routledge.

Poverty

- Alcock, P. (1993) *Understanding Poverty*, London: Macmillan.
- Oppenheim, C. and Harker, L. (1996) *Poverty: The Facts*, 3rd edn, London: Child Poverty Action Group.
- Scott, J. (1994) *Poverty and Wealth*, London: Longman.

General accounts of inequality and difference

- Bradley, H. (1996) *Fractured Identities*, Cambridge: Polity Press.
- Kirby, M. (1999) *Stratification and Differentiation*, London: Macmillan.

Books on class

- Crompton, R. (1993) *Class and Stratification: An Introduction to Current Debates*, Cambridge: Polity Press.
- Lee, D. and Turner, B. (eds.) (1996) *Conflicts About Class*, Harlow: Longman.

- Westergaard, J. (1995) *Who Gets What?*, Cambridge: Polity Press.
- Wright, E. O. (1997) *Class Counts*, Cambridge: Cambridge University Press.

Feminist theories and gender inequality

The following are two short books on gender written specifically for A level study:

- Garratt, S. (1987) *Gender*, London: Routledge.
- Mayes, P. (1986) *Gender*, London: Longman.
- Abbott, P. and Wallace, C. (1997) *An Introduction to Sociology: Feminist Perspectives*, 2nd edn, London: Routledge.

Suzanne Franks' very readable book tracks optimistic young women entering the labour market to face discrimation and a lack of opportunities.

- Franks, S. (1999) *Having None of It*, London: Granta.

Books on 'race' and ethnicity

A useful book concentrating on the UK is:

- Jones, T. (1993) *Britain's Ethnic Minorities*, London: Policy Studies Institute.

The following is a very good introductory text:

- Mason, D. (1995) *Race and Ethnicity in Modern Britain*, Oxford: Oxford University Press.

The following is an interesting collection of essays for students who want a more detailed approach to specific areas of 'race' and ethnicity:

- Donald, J. and Rattansi, A. (eds.) (1992) *'Race', Culture and Difference*, London: Sage.

A very useful text for those wanting more detailed information on 'race' and ethnicity is:

- Solomos, J. (1993) *Race and Racism in Britain*, London: Macmillan.

Back issues of the periodical *Sociology Review* (formerly known as *Social Studies Review*) also contain many articles on this field of sociology and many others.

Bibliography

Abbott, D. (1994) 'Family, conjugal roles and the labour market', *Sociology Review*, vol. 4, no. 1.

Abbott, P. and Wallace, C. (1990) *An Introduction to Sociology: Feminist Perspectives*, London: Routledge.

Abbott, P. and Wallace, C. (1992) *The Family and the New Right*, London: Pluto Press.

Abbott, P. and Wallace, C. (1997) *An Introduction to Sociology: Feminist Perspectives*, 2nd edn, London: Routledge.

Abel-Smith, B. and Townsend, P. (1965) *The Poor and the Poorest*, London: Bell & Sons.

Abercrombie, N. and Turner, B. S. (1978) 'The dominant ideology thesis', *British Journal of Sociology*, vol. 29, no. 2.

Abercrombie, N. and Warde, A. (eds) (1994) *Family, Household and the Life-Course*, Lancaster: Framework.

Abercrombie, N., Hill, S. and Turner, B. S. (1980) *The Dominant Ideology Thesis*, London: Allen & Unwin.

Abercrombie, N. and Warde, A., with Soothill, K., Urry, J. and Walby, S. (1994) *Contemporary British Society*, 2nd edn, Cambridge: Polity Press.

Abrams, M. Gerard, D. and Timms, N. (eds) (1985) *Values and Social Change in Britain*, London: Macmillan.

Acheson, Sir Donald (chairman) (1998) *Independent Inquiry into Inequalities in Health*, London: Department of Health on behalf of the Controller of HMSO.

Acker, J. (1973) 'Women and social stratification: a case of intellectual sexism', *American Journal of Sociology*, vol. 78.

Acker, J. (1989) 'The problem with patriarchy', *Sociology*, vol. 23, no. 2.

Actionaid, Bond, Cafod, Christian Aid, Intermediate Technology, Oxfam, Save the Children, Voluntary Service Overseas, Unicef, World Development Movement, World Wildlife Fund (1996) *The Case For Aid: A Manifesto*, London: Actionaid.

Adams, B. (1993) 'Sustainable development and the greening of development theory', in Schuurman, F. J. (ed.), *Beyond the Impasse: New Directions in Development Theory*, London: Zed.

Adonis, A. and Pollard, S. (1997) *A Class Act*, London: Hamish Hamilton.

Adorno, T. W. (1991) *The Culture Industry*, London: Routledge.

Adorno, T. W. and Horkheimer, M. (1979) *The Dialectic of Enlightenment*, London: Verso (orig. pub. 1944).

Adorno, T. W. and Horkheimer, M. (1993) 'The culture industry: enlightenment as mass deception', in During, S. (ed.), *The Cultural Studies Reader*, London: Routledge (orig. pub. 1944).

Adorno, T. W., Albert, H., Dahrendorf, R., Habermas, J., Pilot, H. and Popper, K. (1976) *The Positivist Dispute in German Sociology*, London: Heinemann.

Aggleton, P. (1987) *Rebels without Cause: Middle Class Youth and the Transition from School to Work*, London: Falmer Press.

Aggleton, P. (1990) *Health*, London: Routledge.

Aglietta, M. (1979) *A Theory of Capitalist Regulation*, London: Verso.

Ahmad, W. I. U. (ed.) (1993) *'Race' and Health in Contemporary Britain*, Buckingham: Open University Press.

Ainley, P. and Cohen, P. (1999) 'In the country of the blind: youth studies and cultural studies', in Ainley, P. *et al. Studies in Learning Regeneration*, University of East London: Centre for New Ethnicities Research.

Albrow, M. (1970) *Bureaucracy*, London: Pall Mall.

Alcock, C., Payne, S. and Sullivan, M. (2000) *Introducing Social Policy*, Harlow: Pearson Education.

Alcock, P. (1993) *Understanding Poverty*, Basingstoke: Macmillan.

Aldrich, R. (1988) 'The National Curriculum: an historical perspective', in Lawton, D. and Chitty, C. (eds), *The National Curriculum* (Bedford Way Papers 33), London: Institute of Education, University of London.

Alexander, J. (ed.) (1985) *Neofunctionalism*, London: Sage.

Alexander, J. (1987) *Sociological Theory Since 1930*, New York: Columbia University Press.

Alexander, J. (1995) *Fin de Siècle Social Theory*, London: Verso.

Allan, G. (1985) *Family Life*, Oxford: Basil Blackwell.

Allan, P., Benyon, J. and McCormick, B. (eds) (1994) *Focus on Britain*, Deddington: Philip Allan.

Allen, H. (1987) *Justice Unbalanced*, Buckingham: Open University Press.

Allen, J. (1994) 'Foucault and special educational needs: developing a framework for analysing children's experiences of mainstreaming'. Unpublished paper given at the BERA Symposium on aspects of integration policy and provision for children with special educational needs.

Allen, S. (1982) 'Gender inequalities and class formation', in Giddens, A. and Mackenzie, G. (eds), *Social Class and the Division of Labour*, Cambridge: Cambridge University Press.

Allen, T. and Thomas, A. (eds) (1992) *Poverty and Development in the 1990s*, Oxford: Oxford University Press.

Althusser, L. (1968) *Reading Capital*, London: New Left Books.

Althusser, L. (1971a) *Lenin and Philosophy and Other Essays*, London: New Left Books.

Althusser, L. (1971b) 'Ideology and ideological state apparatuses', in *Lenin and Philosophy and Other Essays*, London: New Left Books.

Althusser, L. with Balibar, E. (1966) *For Marx*, London: Allen Lane.

Amin, K. and Oppenheim, C. (1992) *Poverty in Black and White*, London: CPAG/Runnymede Trust.

Amin, S. (1974) *Accumulation on a World Scale*, London: Monthly Review Press.

Amin, S. (1976) *Unequal Development*, Brighton: Harvester.

Amin, S. (1977) *Imperialism and Unequal Development*, Brighton: Harvester.

Amos, V. and Parmar, P. (1984) 'Challenging imperial feminism', *Feminist Review*, no. 17.

Anderson, A. and Gordon, R. (1978) 'Witchcraft and the status of women: the case of England', *British Journal of Sociology*, vol. 29, no. 2.

Anderson, A. and Gordon, R. (1979) 'The uniqueness of English witchcraft: a matter of numbers?', *British Journal of Sociology*, vol. 30, no. 3.

Anderson, B. (1983) *Imagined Communities*, London: Verso.

Anderson, J. and Ricci, M. (eds) (1994) *Society and Social Science: A Reader*, Buckingham: Open University Press.

Anderson, M. (ed.) (1971) *Sociology of the Family*, Harmondsworth: Penguin.

Andrews, A. and Jewson, N. (1993) 'Ethnicity and infant death: the implications of recent statistical evidence for material explanations', *Sociology of Health and Illness*, vol. 15, no. 2.

Andrews, G. (1997) 'The inclusive society', *New Times*, 21 June.

Ang, I. (1985) *Watching 'Dallas': Soap Opera and the Melodramatic Imagination*, London: Methuen.

Ang, I. (1991) *Desperately Seeking the Audience*, London: Routledge.

Angell, I. (1995) *The Information Revolution and the Death of the Nation State*, London: Libertarian Alliance.

Annandale, E. and Clark, J. (1996) 'What is gender? Feminist theory and the sociology of human reproduction', *Sociology of Health and Illness*, vol. 18, no. 1.

Anthias, F. (1990) 'Race and class revisited: conceptualising race and racisms', *Sociological Review*, vol. 38, no. 1.

Anthias, F. and Yuval-Davis, N. (1983) 'Contextualising feminism: gender, ethnic and class divisions', *Feminist Review*, no. 15.

Anthias, F. and Yuval-Davis, N. (1993) *Racialized Boundaries*, London: Routledge.

Anyon, J. (1983). 'Intersections of gender and class: accommodation and resistance by working class and affluent females to contradictory sex-role ideologies', in Walker, S. and Barton, L. (eds), *Gender, Class and Education*, Lewes: Falmer Press.

Apple, M. (1986) *Teachers and Texts: A Political Economy of Class and Gender Relations in Education*, London: Routledge.

Apter, D. and Rosberg, C. (1994) 'Changing African perspectives', in Apter, D. and Rosberg, C. (eds), *Political Development and the New Reality of Sub-Saharan Africa*, Charlottesville: University Press of Virginia.

AQA (1999) *GCE Sociology Specification*, 2001/2, Guildford: AQA.

Arber, S. and Ginn, J. (1991) *Gender and Later Life: A Sociological Analysis of Resources and Constraints*, London: Sage.

Arber, S. and Ginn, J. (eds) (1995) *Connecting Gender and Ageing*, Buckingham: Open University Press.

Arblaster, A. (1984) *The Rise and Decline of Western Liberalism*, Oxford: Blackwell.

Archer, M. S. (1982) 'Morphogenesis versus structuration: on combining structure and action', *British Journal of Sociology*, vol. 33.

Archer, M. S. (1988) *Culture and Agency*, Cambridge: Cambridge University Press.

Archer, M. S. (1995) *Realist Social Theory: The Morphogenetic Approach*, Cambridge: Cambridge University Press.

Arensberg, C. M. and Kimball, S. T. (1968) *Family and Community in Ireland*, 2nd edn, Cambridge, MA: Harvard University Press.

Argyle, K. and Shields, R. (1996) 'Is there a body in the Net?' in Shields, R. (ed.), *Cultures of the Internet*, London: Sage.

Aries, P. (1973) *Centuries of Childhood*, Harmondsworth: Penguin.

Armstrong, D. (1995a) 'The rise of surveillance medicine', *Sociology of Health and Illness*, vol. 17, no. 3.

Armstrong, D. (1995b) *Power and Partnership in Education: Parents, Children and Special Educational Needs*, London: Routledge.

Arnold, M. (1960) *Culture and Anarchy*, Cambridge: Cambridge University Press.

Aronson, J. (1977) *Money and Power*, London: Sage.

Aronson, N. (1984) 'Comment on Bryan Turner's "The government of the body: medical regimes and the rationalization of diet"', *British Journal of Sociology*, vol. 35, no. 1.

Ashcroft, B. *et al.* (eds) (1995) *The Post-Colonial Studies Reader*, London: Routledge.

Assiter, A. (1996) *Enlightened Women: Modernist Feminism in a Postmodern Age*, London: Routledge.

Atkinson, A. B. (1983) *The Economics of Inequality*, Oxford: Oxford University Press.

Atkinson, J. M. (1977) 'Societal reactions to suicide: the role of coroners' definitions', in Cohen, S. (ed.), *Images of Deviance*, Harmondsworth: Penguin.

Atkinson, J. M. (1978) *Discovering Suicide*, Basingstoke: Macmillan.

Atkinson, J. M. and Heritage, J. (eds) (1984) *Structures of Social Action: Studies in Conversation Analysis*, Cambridge: Cambridge University Press.

Atkinson, P. (1985) *Language, Structure and Reproduction: An Introduction to the Sociology of Basil Bernstein*, London: Methuen.

Avalos, B. (1982) 'Neocolonialism and education in Latin America', in Watson, K. (ed.), *Education in the Third World*, Beckenham: Croom Helm.

Ayres, R. (ed.) (1995) *Development Studies*, London: Greenwich University Press.

Aziz, R. (1997; orig pub. 1992) 'Feminism and the challenge of racism', in Safia Mirza, H. (ed.), *Black British Feminism*, London: Routledge.

Bagguley, P. (1993) 'Urban sociology', in Haralambos, M. (ed.), *Developments in Sociology*, vol. 9, Ormskirk: Causeway Press.

Bagguley, P. and Mann, K. (1992) 'Idle thieving bastards: scholarly representations of the underclass', *Work Employment and Society*, vol. 6, no. 1.

Bagguley, P. and Walby, S. (1988) *Women and Local Labour Markets: A Comparative Analysis of Five Localities*, Lancaster: Lancaster Regionalism Group, University of Lancaster.

Bakx, K. (1991) 'The "eclipse" of folk medicine in western society', *Sociology of Health and Illness*, vol. 13, no. 1.

Baldock, J., Manning, N., Miller, S. and Vickerstaff, S. (eds) (1999) *Social Policy*, Oxford: Oxford University Press.

Ball, S. (1981) *Beachside Comprehensive: A Case Study*

of Secondary Schooling, Cambridge: Cambridge University Press.

Ball, S. (1994) *Education Reform: A Critical and Post-structuralist Approach*, Buckingham: Open University Press.

Ball, S. J., Bowe, R. and Gerwitz, S. (1996) 'School choice, social class and distinction: the realization of social advantage in education', *Journal of Educational Policy*, vol. 11, no. 1.

Ball, J. S. and Gerwirtz, S. (1997) 'Girls in the education market: choice, competition and complexity', *Gender and Education*, vol. 9, no. 2.

Ballard, C. (1979) 'Conflict, continuity and change: second generation south Asians', in Khan, V. S. (ed.), *Minority Families in Britain*, Basingstoke: Macmillan.

Ballard, R. (1982) 'South Asian families', in Rapoport, R. N., Fogarty, M. P. and Rapoport, R. (eds), *Families in Britain*, London: Routledge & Kegan Paul.

Balls, E. (1994) 'East Asian experience shows link between growth and equality', *Guardian*, 4 July.

Bandura, A., Ross, D. and Ross, S. A. (1963) 'The imitation of film-mediated aggressive models', *Journal of Abnormal and Social Psychology*, vol. 66, no. 1.

Banton, M. (1955) *The Coloured Quarter: Negro Immigrants in an English City*, London: Routledge.

Banton, M. (1983) *Racism and Ethnic Competition*, Cambridge: Cambridge University Press.

Banton, M. (1987) *Racial Theories*, Cambridge: Cambridge University Press.

Banton, M. (1994) *Discrimination*, Milton Keynes: Open University Press.

Barak, G. (ed.) (1994) *Varieties of Criminology*, Westport: Praeger.

Barber, B. (1963) 'Some problems in the sociology of professions', *Daedalus*, vol. 92, no. 4.

Barbour, R. S. (1990) 'Health and illness', in Haralambos, M. (ed.), *Developments in Sociology*, vol. 6, Ormskirk: Causeway Press.

Barker, E. (1984) *The Making of a Moonie: Choice or Brainwashing*, Oxford: Blackwell.

Barker, M. (1981) *The New Racism*, London: Junction Books.

Barnes, C. (1992) *Disabled People in Britain and Discrimination: A Case for Anti-Discrimination Legislation*, London: Hurst & Co. in association with the British Council of Organizations of Disabled People.

Barnett, T. (1988) *Sociology and Development*, London: Hutchinson Educational.

Barrat, D. and Cole, T. (1991) *Sociology Projects: A Student's Guide*, London: Routledge.

Barrett, M. (1980) *Women's Oppression Today: Problems in Marxist Feminist Analysis*, London: Verso.

Barrett, M. (1989) *Women's Oppression Today*, 2nd edn, London: Verso.

Barrett, M. and McIntosh, M. (1982) *The Anti-Social Family*, London: Verso.

Barrett, M. and McIntosh, M. (1991) *The Anti-Social Family*, 2nd edn, London: Verso.

Barrow, J. (1982) 'West Indian families: an insider's perspective', in Rapoport, R. N., Fogarty, M. P. and Rapoport, R. (eds), *Families in Britain*, London: Routledge & Kegan Paul.

Barthes, R. (1973) *Mythologies*, London: Paladin.

Bartholomew, R., Hibbert, A. and Sidaway, J. (1992) 'Lone parents and the labour market', *Employment Gazette*, November.

Bartley, M., Carpenter, L., Dunnell, K. and Fitzpatrick, R. (1996) 'Measuring inequalities in health: an analysis of mortality patterns using two social classifications', *Sociology of Health and Illness*, vol. 18, no. 4.

Barton, L. (1988) *The Politics of Special Educational Needs*, Lewes: Falmer Press.

Bassett, P. (1996) 'Will Britain's workforce ever stand up and be counted?', *The Times*, 17 January.

Bates, I. and Riseborough, G. (eds) (1993) *Youth and Inequality*, Buckingham: Open University Press.

Batstone, E. (1984) *Working Order: Workplace Industrial Relations Over Two Decades*, Oxford: Blackwell.

Batstone, E. (1988) *The Reform of Workplace Industrial Relations*, Oxford: Clarendon Press.

Baudrillard, J. (1981) *For a Critique of the Political Economy of the Sign*, St Louis: Telos.

Baudrillard, J. (1983a) *Simulations*, New York: Semiotext(e).

Baudrillard, J. (1983b) *In the Shadow of the Silent Majorities – or, The End of the Social and Other Essays*, New York: Semiotext(e).

Baudrillard, J. (1988) *Selected Writings*, Poster, M. (ed.), Cambridge: Polity Press.

Baudrillard, J. (1990) *Fatal Strategies*, New York: Semiotext(e).

Baudrillard, J. (1993a) 'Game with vestiges', in Gane, M. (ed.), *Baudrillard Live: Selected Interviews*, London: Routledge.

Baudrillard, J. (1993b) 'Baudrillard: the interview', in Gane, M. (ed.), *Baudrillard Live: Selected Interviews*, London: Routledge.

Baudrillard, J. (1993c) 'The evil demon of images and the precession of the simulacra', in Doherty, T. (ed.), *Postmodernism: A Reader*, Hemel Hempstead: Harvester Wheatsheaf.

Baudrillard, J. (1995) *The Gulf War Did Not Take Place*, Sydney: Power Publications.

Bauer, P. (1991) *The Development Frontier*, Hemel Hempstead: Harvester Wheatsheaf.

Baugh, W. E. (1987) *Introduction to the Social Services*, 5th edn, Basingstoke: Macmillan.

Bauman, Z. (1990) *Thinking Sociologically*, Oxford: Blackwell.

Bauman, Z. (1991) *Modernity and Ambivalence*, Cambridge: Polity Press.

Bauman, Z. (1992) *Intimations of Postmodernity*, London: Routledge.

BBC (1995) *Report and Accounts*, London: BBC Publications.

BBC (1998) *Report and Accounts*, London: BBC Publications.

Beardsworth, A. and Keil, T. (1993) 'Hungry for knowledge: the sociology of food and eating', *Sociology Review*, vol. 3, no. 2.

Beauvoir, S. de (1972) *The Second Sex*, Harmondsworth: Penguin (orig. pub. 1953).

Beck, U. (1992) *Risk Society*, London: Sage.

Becker, D. and Sklar, R. (eds) (1987) *Postimperialism: International Capitalism and Development in the Late Twentieth Century*, London: Lynne Rienner.

Becker, H. S. (1951) 'Role and career problems of the Chicago public school teacher', doctoral thesis, University of Chicago.

Becker, H. S. (1971) 'Social-class variations in the teacher–pupil relationship', in Cosin, B. R., Dale, I. R., Esland, G. M. and Swift, D. F. (eds), *School and*

Society, London: Routledge & Kegan Paul (orig. pub. 1952).

Becker, H. S. (1973) *Outsiders: Studies in the Sociology of Deviance*, New York: Free Press.

Beckerman, W. (1974) *In Defence of Economic Growth*, London: Jonathan Cape.

Beckford, J. A. (1985) *Cult Controversies: The Societal Response to the New Religious Movements*, London: Tavistock.

Beechey, V. (1977) 'Some notes on female wage labour in capitalist production', *Capital and Class*, no. 3.

Beharrell, P. (1993) 'AIDS and the British Press', in Eldridge, J. (ed.), *Getting the Message: News, Truth and Power*, London: Glasgow University Media Group/Routledge.

Bell, D. (1973) *The Coming of Post-Industrial Society*, New York: Basic Books.

Bell, D. (1977) 'The return of the sacred? The argument on the future of religion', *British Journal of Sociology*, vol. 28, no. 4.

Bell, N. W. and Vogel, E. F. (eds) (1968) *A Modern Introduction to the Family*, revised edn, New York: Free Press.

Bellah, R. N. (1970) *Beyond Belief*, New York: Harper & Row.

Bellos, A. (1996) 'Action marks move beyond "single issue" campaigning', *Guardian*, 8 August.

Ben-Tovim, G. and Gabriel, J. (1982) 'The politics of race in Britain, 1962–1979: a review of the major trends and recent debates', in Husband, C. (ed.), *'Race' in Britain: Continuity and Change*, London: Hutchinson.

Bendix, R. (1963) *Max Weber: An Intellectual Portrait*, London: Methuen.

Benedict, R. (1943) *Race and Racism*, London: Routledge.

Bennett, A. (1999) 'Subcultures or neo-tribes: rethinking the relationship between youth, style and musical taste', *Sociology*, vol. 33, no. 3.

Benthall, J. (1995) *Disasters, Relief and the Media*, London: I. B. Tauris & Co.

Ben Tovim, G. and Gabriel, J. (1979) 'The politics of race in Britain: A review of the major trends and of recent literature', *Sage Race Relations Abstracts*, vol. 4, no. 4.

Benyon, J. (ed.), (1984) *Scarman and After: Essays Reflecting on Lord Scarmans's Report, the Riots and their Aftermath*, Oxford: Pergamon Press.

Benyon, J. (1986) 'Turmoil in the cities', *Social Studies Review*, vol. 1, no. 3.

Benyon, J. and Denver, D. (1990) 'Mrs Thatcher's electoral successes', *Social Studies Review*, vol. 5, no. 3.

Beresford, P. and Boyd, S. (2000) 'The *Sunday Times* rich list 2000', *Sunday Times Magazine*, 19 March.

Berger, P. L. (1966) *Invitation to Sociology*, Harmondsworth: Penguin.

Berger, P. L. (1987) *The Capitalist Revolution*, Aldershot: Gower.

Berger, P. L. (1990) *The Sacred Canopy: Elements of a Sociological Theory of Religion*, New York: Anchor Books.

Berger, P. L. and Kellner, H. (1981) *Sociology Reinterpreted*, Harmondsworth: Penguin.

Berger, P. L. and Luckmann, T. (1967) *The Social Construction of Reality: A Treatise in the Sociology of Knowledge*, Harmondsworth: Penguin.

Berle, A. A. and Means, G. C. (1968) *The Modern Corporation and Private Property*, New York: Harcourt, Brace and World Inc. (orig. pub. 1932).

Bernard, M., Itzin, C., Phillipson, C. and Skucha, J. (1995) 'Gendered work, gendered retirement', in Arber, S. and Ginn, J. (1995) (eds), *Connecting Gender and Ageing*, Buckingham: Open University Press.

Bernardes, J. (1997) *Family Studies: An Introduction*, London: Routledge.

Bernstein, B. (1977) *Class Codes and Control*, vol. 3, London: Routledge & Kegan Paul.

Bernstein, E. (1961) *Evolutionary Socialism*, New York: Schoken Books (orig. pub. 1899).

Bernstein, H., Crow, B. and Johnson, H. (eds) (1992) *Rural Livelihoods: Crises and Responses*, Oxford: Oxford University Press.

Berthoud, R. (1998) *The Incomes of Ethnic Minorities*, Colchester: Institute for Social and Economic Research, University of Essex.

Beveridge, W. (1942) *Social Insurance and Allied Services*, London: HMSO.

Beyer, P. (1994) *Religion and Globalization*, London: Sage.

Beynon, H. (1973) *Working For Ford*, Harmondsworth: Penguin.

Bhaskar, R. (1978) *A Realist Theory of Science*, 2nd edn, Brighton: Harvester Wheatsheaf.

Bhaskar, R. (1979) *The Possibility of Naturalism*, Brighton: Harvester Wheatsheaf.

Bhaskar, R. (1986) *Scientific Realism and Human Emancipation*, London: Verso.

Billington, R. *et al.* (1991) *Culture and Society*, Basingstoke: Macmillan.

Bilton, T., Bonnett, K., Jones, P., Stanworth, M., Sheard, K. and Webster, A. (1987) *Introductory Sociology*, 2nd edn, Basingstoke: Macmillan.

Bilton, T., Bonnett, K., Jones, P., Skinner, D., Stanworth, M. and Webster, A. (1996) *Introductory Sociology*, 3rd edn, Basingstoke: Macmillan.

Birch, A. H. (1993) *The Concepts and Theories of Modern Democracy*, London: Routledge.

Bird, J. (1999) *Investigating Religion*, London: Collins Educational

Blackburn, C. (1991) *Poverty and Health*, Buckingham: Open University Press.

Blair, T. (1996) 'My radical task', *Observer*, 15 September.

Blake, A. (1992) *The Music Business*, London: Batsford.

Blakemore, K. and Boneham, M. (1994) *Age, Race and Ethnicity*, Buckingham: Open University Press.

Blakemore, K. and Symons, A. (1993) 'Health policy in Britain', in Taylor, S. and Fields, D. (eds), *Sociology of Health and Health Care*, Oxford: Blackwell Science.

Blanch, M. (1979) 'Imperialism, nationalism and organised youth', in Clarke, J. *et al.* (eds), *Working Class Culture*, London: Hutchinson.

Blanchard, S. and Morley, D. (1982) *What's This Channel Fo(u)r*, London: Comedia.

Blau, P. (1955) *The Dynamics of Bureaucracy*, Chicago: University of Chicago Press.

Blauner, R. (1964) *Alienation and Freedom*, Chicago: University of Chicago Press.

Blumer, H. (1969) *Symbolic Interactionism: Perspective and Method*, Englewood Cliffs, NJ: Prentice-Hall.

Blumler, J. G. (1991) 'The new television marketplace:

imperatives, implications, issues', in Curran, J. and Gurevitch, M. (eds), *Mass Media and Society*, New York: Edward Arnold.

Blumler, J. G. (ed.) (1992a) *Television and the Public Interest: Vulnerable Values in Western European Broadcasting*, London: Sage.

Blumler, J. G. (1992b) 'Vulnerable values at stake', in Blumler, J. G. (ed.), *Television and the Public Interest: Vulnerable Values in West European Broadcasting*, London: Sage.

Blumler, J. G., Brown, J. R., Ewbank, A. J. and Nossiter, T. J. (1971) 'Attitudes to the monarchy: their structure and development during a ceremonial occasion', *Political Studies*, vol. 19.

Blumler, J. G. and Katz, E. (eds) (1974) *The Uses of Mass Communication: Current Perspectives on Gratifications Research*, Beverly Hills: Sage.

Blumler, J. G., Katz, E. and Gurevitch, M. (1974) 'Utilization of mass communication by the individual', in Blumler, J. G. and Katz, E. (eds), *The Uses of Mass Communication: Current Perspectives on Gratifications Research*, Beverly Hills: Sage.

Bly, R. (1991) *Iron John*, Shaftesbury: Element Books.

Boaler, J. (1997) 'When even the winners are losers: evaluating the experiences of "top set" students', *Journal of Curriculum Studies*, vol. 29, no. 2.

Boaler, J. (1998a) *Experiencing School Mathematics: Teaching, Styles, Sex and Setting*, Buckingham: Open University Press.

Boaler, J. (1998b) 'Sets maniacs', *Guardian*, 24 November.

Bocock, R. (1974) *Ritual in Industrial Society. A Sociological Analysis of Ritualism in Modern England*, London: George Allen & Unwin.

Bocock, R. (1985) 'Religion in modern Britain', in Bocock, R. and Thompson, K. (eds), *Religion and Ideology*, Manchester: Manchester University Press.

Bocock, R. (1993) *Consumption*, London: Routledge.

Bogenhold, D. and Staber, U. (1991) 'The decline and rise of self-employment', *Work, Employment and Society*, vol. 5, pp. 223–39.

Bone, A. (1983) *Girls and Girls-Only Schools: A Review of the Evidence*, Report of the Equal Opportunities Commission, UK.

Bonger, W. (1916) *Criminality and Economic Conditions*, Boston: Little Brown.

Booth, C. (1902) *The Life and Labour of the People*, London: Williams & Northgate.

Booth, D. (1985) 'Marxism and development sociology: interpreting the impasse', *World Development*, vol. 13.

Booth, D. (1993) 'Development research: from impasse to a new agenda', in Schuurman, F. J. (ed.), *Beyond the Impasse: New Directions in Development Theory*, London: Zed.

Bordo, S. (1990) 'Feminism, postmodernism and gender-scepticism', in Nicholson, L. (ed) *Feminism/Postmodernism*, London: Routledge.

Bott, E. (1971) *Family and Social Networks*, 2nd edn, London: Tavistock.

Bottomore, T. (1973) 'Ruling élite or ruling class?', in Urry, J. and Wakeford, J. (eds), *Power in Britain: Sociological Readings*, London: Heinemann.

Bottomore, T. (1978) *Classes in Modern Society*, London: George Allen & Unwin (orig. pub. 1965).

Bottomore, T. (1993) *Elites and Society*, 2nd edn, London: Routledge (orig. pub. 1964).

Bottomore, T. and Nisbet, R. (1979) 'Structuralism', in Bottomore, T. and Nisbet, R. (eds), *A History of Sociological Analysis*, London: Heinemann.

Bourdieu, P. (1977) *Outline of a Theory of Practice*, Cambridge: Cambridge University Press.

Bourdieu, P. (1984) *Distinction: A Social Critique of the Judgement of Taste*, London: Routledge.

Bourdieu, P. (1990) *In Other Words: Essays Towards a Reflexive Sociology*, Cambridge: Polity Press.

Bourdieu, P. (1993a) *Sociology in Question*, London: Sage.

Bourdieu, P. (1993b) *The Field of Cultural Production*, Cambridge: Polity Press.

Bourdieu, P. and Haacke, H. (1995) *Free Exchange*, Cambridge: Polity Press.

Bourdieu, P. and Passeron, J. C. (1977) *Reproduction in Education, Society and Culture*, London: Sage.

Bourke, J. (1994) *Working Class Cultures in Britain 1890–1960*, London: Routledge.

Bowe, R., Ball, S. with Anne Gold (1992) *Reforming Education and Changing Schools: Case Studies in Policy Sociology*, London: Routledge.

Bowlby, J. (1965) *Childcare and the Growth of Love*, 2nd edn, Harmondsworth: Penguin.

Bowles, S. and Gintis, H. (1976) *Schooling in Capitalist America*, London: Routledge & Kegan Paul.

Box, S. (1981) *Deviance, Reality and Society*, 2nd edn, London: Holt, Rinehart & Winston.

Box, S. (1983) *Power, Crime and Mystification*, London: Routledge.

Box, S. (1995) *Power, Crime and Mystification*, 2nd edn, London: Routledge.

Bradley, H. (1989) *Men's Work, Women's Work*, Cambridge: Polity Press.

Bradley, H. (1996) *Fractured Identities: Changing Patterns of Inequality*, Cambridge: Polity Press.

Bradshaw, J. and Holmes, H. (1989) *Living on the Edge*, Newcastle: Tyneside Child Poverty Action Group.

Bradshaw, J., Hicks, L. and Parker, H. (1992) *Summary Budget Standards for Six Households*, York: Family Budget Unit, working paper 12.

Brah, A. (1992) 'Difference, diversity and differentiation', in Donald, J. and Rattansi, A. (eds), *'Race', Culture and Difference*, London: Sage.

Braidotti, R. (1991) *Patterns Of Dissonance*, Cambridge: Polity Press.

Braithwaite, E. R. in Wambu, O. (ed.) (1998) *Empire Windrush*, London: Victor Gollancz.

Brandt Commission (1980) *North–South: A Programme for Survival*, London: Pan.

Brandt Commission (1983) *Common Crisis*, London: Pan.

Braverman, H. (1974) *Labor and Monopoly Capital*, New York: Monthly Review Press.

Brenner, H. (1979) 'Mortality and the national economy', *The Lancet*, 15 September.

Brenner, R. (1986) 'The social basis of economic development', in Roemer, J. (ed.), *Analytical Marxism*, Cambridge: Cambridge University Press.

Breugel, I. (1996) 'Whose myths are they anyway: a comment', *British Journal of Sociology*, vol. 47, no. 1.

Brierley, P. and Hiscock, V. (eds) (1993) *UK Christian Handbook: 1994-5 Edition*, London: Christian Research Association.

Brindle, D. (1999) 'Public spending lowest for 40 years', *Guardian*, 25 August.

British Medical Association (1993) *Complementary Medicine: New Approaches to Good Practice*, London: BMA.

British Sociological Association (1991) *Statement of Ethical Practice*, London: BSA.

Brittan, S. (1975) 'The economic contradictions of democracy', *British Journal of Political Science*, vol. 15.

Brittan, S. (1989) 'The case for the consumer market', in Veljanovski, C. (ed.), *Freedom in Broadcasting*, London: Institute of Economic Affairs.

Brody, M. (ed.) (1975) *Mary Wollstonecraft: 'Vindication of the Rights of Woman'* (orig. pub. 1792), Harmondsworth: Penguin.

Brown, A. (1994) 'Thalidomide's horrors plague poor of Brazil', *Observer*, 23 October.

Brown, A. (1997) 'Examination matters: note-taking', *Sociology Review*, vol. 6, no. 3.

Brown, C. (1984) *Black and White in Britain: The Third PSI Survey*, Oxford: Heinemann Educational.

Brown, D. (1991) *Bury My Heart at Wounded Knee: An Indian History of the American West*, London: Vintage.

Brown, G. and Harris, T. (1978) *The Social Origins of Depression*, London: Tavistock.

Brown, M. (1990) *TV and Women's Culture*, London: Sage.

Brown, M. and Madge, N. (1982) *Despite the Welfare State*, London: Heinemann.

Brown, P. (1990) 'The "third wave": education and the ideology of parentocracy', *British Journal of Sociology of Education*, vol. 11.

Brown, P., Halsey, A. H., Lauder, H. and Wells, A. S. (1997) 'Introduction to the State and the restructuring of teachers work', in Halsey, A. H., Lauder, H., Brown, P. and Wells, A. S. (eds) *Education: Culture, Economy, Society*, Oxford: Oxford University Press.

Brown, P. and Scase, R. (eds) (1991), *Poor Work, Disadvantage and the Division of Labour*, Buckingham: Open University Press.

Browne, K. (1992) *An Introduction to Sociology*, Cambridge: Polity Press.

Bruce, S. (1995) *Religion in Modern Britain*, Oxford: Oxford University Press.

Bruce, S. and Wallis, R. (1989) 'Religion: the British contribution', *British Journal of Sociology*, vol. 40, no. 3.

Bruntland, G. *et al.* for World Commission on Environment and Development (1987) *Our Common Future*, Oxford: Oxford University Press.

Bryan, B., Dadzie, S. and Scafe, S. (1985) *The Heart of the Race: Black Women's Lives in Britain*, London: Virago.

Bryant, C. (1985) *Positivism in Social Theory and Research*, Basingstoke: Macmillan.

Bryant, C. and Becker, H. (eds) (1990) *What has Sociology Achieved?*, Basingstoke: Macmillan.

Brydon, L. and Legge, K. (1996) 'Gender and adjustment: pictures from Ghana', in Thomas-Emeagwali, G. (ed.), *Women Pay the Price: Structural Adjustment in Africa and the Caribbean*, New Jersey: Africa World Press.

Bryman, A. (1999) 'The disneyization of society', *Sociological Review*, vol. 47, no. 1.

Bryson, L. (1992) *Welfare and the State: Who Benefits?* Basingstoke: Macmillan.

Buchanan, K. (1975) *Reflections on Education in the Third World*, Nottingham: Spokesman.

Budge, I. and McKay, D. (eds) (1993) *The Developing British Political System: The 1990s*, 3rd edn, London: Longman.

Bull, M. (1990) 'Secularization and medicalization', *British Journal of Sociology*, vol. 41, no. 2.

Bulmer, M. (ed.) (1982) *Social Research Ethics: An examination of the Merits of Covert Participation Research*, Basingstoke: Macmillan.

Burawoy, M. (1979) *Manufacturing Consent*, Chicago: University of Chicago Press.

Burawoy, M. (1985) *The Politics of Production*, London: Verso.

Burchardt, T. and Hills, J. (1997) *Private Welfare Insurance and Social Security: Pushing the Boundaries*, York: Joseph Rowntree Foundation.

Burchell, B. (1994) 'The effects of labour market position, job insecurity, and unemployment on psychological health', in Gallie, D., Marsh, C. and Vogler, C. (eds), *Social Change and the Experience of Unemployment*, Oxford: Oxford University Press.

Burgess, R. (1984) *In the Field: An Introduction to Field Research*, London: Unwin Hyman.

Burghes, R. and Roberts, C. (1995) 'Lone parents', *Community Care*, 6–12 July.

Burkitt, I. And Tester, K. (1996) 'Identity', in Haralambos, M. (ed) *Developments in Sociology*, vol. 12, Ormskirk: Causeway Press.

Burnham, J. (1945) *The Managerial Revolution*, London: Pelican.

Burns, T. and Stalker, G. M. (1966) *The Management of Innovation*, 2nd edn, London: Tavistock.

Burrows, R. and Butler, T. (1989) 'Middle mass and the pit: a critical review of Peter Saunders' sociology of consumption', *Sociological Review*, vol. 37, no. 2.

Burrows, R. and Loader, B. (eds) (1994) *Towards a Post-Fordist Welfare State?*, London: Routledge.

Busfield, J. (1996) *Men, Women and Madness: Understanding Gender and Mental Disorder*, Basingstoke: Macmillan.

Butler, T. and Savage, M. (eds) (1995) *Social Change and the Middle Classes*, London: UCL Press.

Butler, D. and Stokes, D. (1969) *Political Change in Britain: Forces Shaping Electoral Choice*, Basingstoke: Macmillan.

Butler, J. (1990) *Gender Trouble: Feminism and the Subversion of Identity*, London: Routledge.

Butler, J. (1993) 'Imitation and gender insubordination', in Abelove, H., Barale, M. A. and Halpin, D. (eds) *The Lesbian and Gay Reader*, London: Routledge.

Butterworth, E. and Weir, D. (eds) (1975) *The Sociology of Modern Britain*, revised edn, Glasgow: Fontana.

Byrne, E. (1978) *Women and Education*, London: Tavistock.

Byrne, T. and Padfield, C. (1985) *Social Services Made Simple*, 3rd edn, London: Heinemann.

Callender, C. (1992) 'Redundancy, unemployment and poverty', in Glendinning, C. and Millar, J. (eds), *Women and Poverty in Britain: The 1990s*, Hemel Hempstead: Harvester Wheatsheaf.

Callinicos, A. (1982) *Is There a Future for Marxism?*, Basingstoke: Macmillan.

Callinicos, A. (1987) *Making History*, Cambridge: Polity Press.

Callinicos, A. (1989) *Against Postmodernism: A Marxist Critique*, Cambridge: Polity Press.

Callinicos, A. (1995) *Theories and Narratives*, Cambridge: Polity Press.

Campbell, A. (1981) *Girl Delinquents*, Oxford: Basil Blackwell.

Campbell, B. (1995a) 'Granddaddy of the backlash', *Guardian*, 1 April.

Campbell, B. (1995b) 'Old fogeys and angry young men', *Soundings*, no. 1, autumn.

Campbell, B. (1988) *Unofficial Secrets*, London: Virago.

Campbell, C. (1972) 'The cult, the cultic milieu and secularization', in Hill, M. (ed.), *A Sociological Yearbook of Religion in Britain*, London: SCM Press.

Campbell, C. (1977) 'Clarifying the cult', *British Journal of Sociology*, vol. 28.

Campbell, C. (1995) 'The sociology of consumption', in Miller, D. (ed.), *Acknowledging Consumption*, London: Routledge.

Campbell, D. (1995c) 'Cameras key weapon in fight against crime', *Guardian*, 30 December.

Carby, H. (1982) 'White women listen: black feminism and the boundaries of sisterhood', in *The Empire Strikes Back*, London: CCCS/Hutchinson.

Cardoso, F. H. (1973) 'Associated dependent development', in Stepan, A. (ed.), *Authoritarian Brazil*, New Haven: Yale University Press.

Carnoy, M. (1974) *Education as Imperialism*, New York: David McKay.

Carter, B. (1995) 'A growing divide: Marxist class analysis and the labour process', *Capital and Class*, vol. 55, spring.

Cartwright, A. and O'Brien, M. (1976) 'Social class variations in health care', in *The Sociology of the NHS*, *Sociology Review*, vol. 22.

Carver, T. (1991) *Engels*, Oxford: Oxford University Press.

Casey, J. (1982) 'One nation: the politics of race', in *The Salisbury Review*.

Cashmore, E. (1983) *Introduction to Race Relations*, London: Routledge & Kegan Paul.

Cashmore, E. and Troyna, B. (1990) *Introduction to Race Relations*, London: Sage.

Cassell, P. (ed.) (1993) *The Giddens Reader*, Basingstoke: Macmillan.

Castells, M. (1983) *The City and the Grassroots*, London: Edward Arnold.

Castles, S. and Kosack, G. (1973) *Immigrant Workers and Class Structure in Western Europe*, Oxford: Oxford University Press.

Centre for Contemporary Cultural Studies (1982) *The Empire Strikes Back: Race and Racism in 70s Britain*, London: CCCS/Hutchinson.

Centre for Research in Education Marketing (1996) *Student Decision-making and the Post-16 Market Place*, Southampton: CREM, University of Southampton.

Chandler, J. (1991) *Women Without Husbands*, Basingstoke: Macmillan.

Chandler, J. (1993) 'Women outside marriage', *Sociology Review*, vol. 2, no. 4.

Charles, N. and Kerr, M. (1988) *Women, Food and Families*, Manchester: Manchester University Press.

Charles, N. and Kerr, M. (1994) 'Gender and age differences in family food consumption', in Anderson, J. and Ricci, M. (eds), *Society and Social Science: A Reader*, 2nd edn, Buckingham: Open University Press.

Charmaz, K. (1983) 'Loss of self: a fundamental form of suffering in the chronically ill', *Sociology of Health and Illness*, vol. 5, pp. 168–95.

Charsley, S. R. (1986) ' "Glasgow's miles better": the symbolism of community and identity in the city', in Cohen, A. P. (ed.), *Symbolising Boundaries: Identity and Diversity in British Cultures*, Manchester: Manchester University Press.

Charter, D. (1996) 'The college in crisis', *Times*, 13 December.

Cheal, D. (1991) *Family and the State of Theory*, Hemel Hempstead: Harvester Wheatsheaf.

Cheal, D. (1993) 'Unity and difference in postmodern families', *Journal of Family Issues*, vol. 14, March.

Chen, K. H. (1992) 'Post-Marxism: critical postmodernism and cultural studies', in Scannel, P. *et al.* (eds), *Culture and Power*, London: Sage.

Chen, R. S. (ed.) (1990) *The Hunger Report*, Providence, RI: Alan Shawn Feinstein World Hunger Program.

Chester, R. (1985) 'The rise of the neo-conventional family', *New Society*, vol. 9, May.

Chibnall, S. (1977) *Law-and-Order News: An Analysis of Crime Reporting in the British Press*, London: Tavistock.

Childline (1999) *Annual Review 1999*, London: Childline.

Chodorow, N. (1978) *The Reproduction of Mothering: Psychoanalysis and the Sociology of Gender*, Berkeley, CA: University of California Press.

Chomsky, N. (1999) *Profits Over People: Neoliberalism and Global Order*, New York: Seven Stories Press.

Church, J. and Summerfield, C. (1996) *Social Focus on Ethnic Minorities*, London: HMSO.

Citizen's Advice Bureaux (1996) *A Right to Family Life: CAB Client's Experience of Immigration and Asylum*, London: Association of Citizens Advice Bureaux.

Clark, J. (1996) 'Insights: gender and education revisited', *Sociology Review*, vol. 5, no. 4.

Clark, T. N. and Lipset, S. M. (1991) 'Are social classes dying?', *International Sociology*, vol. 6, no. 4.

Clarke, J. and Critcher, C. (1985) *The Devil Makes Work*, Basingstoke: Macmillan.

Clarke, J. and Langan, M. (1993) 'Restructuring welfare: the British welfare regime in the 1980s', in Cochrane, A. and Clarke, J. (eds), *Comparing Welfare States*, London: Sage.

Clarke, J. and Layder, D. (1994) 'Let's get real: the realist approach', *Sociology Review*, vol. 4, no. 2.

Clarke, R. (1980) 'Situational crime prevention: theory and practice', *British Journal of Criminology*, vol. 20.

Clarricoates, K. (1978) 'Dinosaurs in the classroom: a re-examination of some aspects of the "hidden" curriculum in primary schools', *Women's Studies International Quarterly*, vol. 1.

Clegg, S. R. (1990) *Modern Organizations*, London: Sage.

Clegg, S. R. (1992) 'Modern and postmodern organizations', *Sociology Review*, vol. 1, no. 4.

Cloward, R. A. and Ohlin, L. E. (1960) *Delinquency and Opportunity: A Theory of Delinquent Gangs*, Glencoe, CA: Free Press.

Cloward, R. A. and Ohlin, L. E. (1989) 'Differential opportunity and deliquent subcultures', in Kelly, D. H. (ed.), *Deviant Behaviour: A Text-Reader in the Sociology of Deviance*, 3rd edn, New York: St Martin's Press.

Coates, D. (1984) *The Context of British Politics*, London: Hutchinson.

Cochrane, A. and Clarke, J. (eds) (1993) *Comparing Welfare States*, London: Sage.

Cockburn, C. (1983) *Brothers: Male Dominance and Technological Change*, London: Pluto Press.

Cohen, A. (1955) *Deliquent Boys: The Culture of the Gang*, Glencoe, CA: Free Press.

Cohen, M. D., March, J. G. and Olsen, J. P. (1972) 'A garbage-can model of organisational choice', *Administrative Science Quarterly*, vol. 17, no. 1.

Cohen, M. (1998) 'A habit of healthy idleness: boys' under-achievement in historical perspective', in Epstein, D. *et al.* (eds), *Failing Boys? Issues in Gender and Achievement*, Buckingham: Open University Press.

Cohen, P. (1972) 'Subcultural conflict and the working class community', in *Working Papers in Cultural Studies*, no. 2, Birmingham Centre for Contemporary Cultural Studies.

Cohen, P. (1988) 'The perversions of inheritance: studies in the making of multi-racist Britain', in Cohen, P. and Bains, H. (eds), *Multi-Racist Britain*, Basingstoke: Macmillan.

Cohen, P. (1992) 'It's racism what dunnit: hidden narratives in theories of racism', in Donald, J. and Rattansi, A. (eds), *'Race', Culture and Difference*, London: Sage.

Cohen, P. S. (1968) *Modern Social Theory*, London: Heinemann.

Cohen, S. (ed.) (1977) *Images of Deviance*, Harmondsworth: Penguin.

Cohen, S. (1980) *Folk Devils and Moral Panics: The Creation of the Mods and Rockers*, Oxford: Basil Blackwell.

Cohen, S. (1994) *Visions of Social Control: Crime, Punishment and Classification*, Cambridge: Polity Press.

Cohen, S. and Taylor, L. (1971) *Psychological Survival: The Experience of Long-Term Imprisonment*, Harmondsworth: Penguin.

Cole, T. (1986) *Whose Welfare?*, London: Tavistock.

Coleman, J. (1958) 'Relational analysis: the study of social organisations with survey methods', *Human Organisation*, vol. 16, no. 4.

Coles, B. (1995) *Youth and Social Policy*, London: UCL Press.

Collins, R. (1985) 'Broadcasting policy in Canada', in Ferguson, M. (ed.), *New Communication Technologies and the Public Interest*, London: Sage.

Communist Party of Great Britain (1990) *Manifesto for New Times: A Strategy for the 1990s*, London: Lawrence & Wishart.

Comte, A. (1830/77) *Cours de Philosophie Positive*, Paris: Bachelier/Ballière & Sons.

Comte, A. (1844) *A Discourse on the Positive Spirit*, London: William Reeves (transl. 1903).

Comte, A. (1851) *System of Positive Polity*, London: Longmans Green.

Comte, A. (1853) *The Positive Philosophy of Auguste Comte* (edited by Harriet Martineau), 2 vols, London: Chapman.

Connell, R. W. (1987) *Gender and Power*, Cambridge: Polity Press.

Connell, R. W., Ashenden, D. J., Kessler, S. and Dowsett, G. W. (1982) *Making the Difference*, Sydney: George Allen & Unwin.

Connor, S. (1989) *Postmodernist Culture*, Oxford: Basil Blackwell.

Connors, J. (1992) *Manual on Violence Against Women in the Family in Commonwealth Countries*, London: Commonwealth Secretariat.

Cook, L. (1983) 'Popular culture and rock music', *Screen*, vol. 24, no. 3.

Cooke, P. (1988) 'Modernity, postmodernity and the city', *Theory, Culture and Society*, vol. 5, nos. 2 and 3.

Coontz, S. and Henderson, P. (eds) (1986) *Women's Work, Men's Property*, London: Verso.

Cope, J. (1987) *Business Taxation*, Wokingham: Van Nostrand Reinhold.

Corbett, J. (1994) 'Challenges in a competitive culture: a policy for inclusive education in Newham', in Riddell, S. and Brown, S. (eds), *Special Educational Needs Policy in the 1990s: Warnock and the Market Place*, London: Routledge.

Corbett, J. (1995) *Bad Mouthing: The Language of Special Needs*, Lewes: Falmer Press.

Corbridge, S. (1993) 'Ethics in development studies: the example of debt', in Schuurman, F. J. (ed.), *Beyond the Impasse: New Directions in Development Theory*, London: Zed.

Cornell, D. L. (1992) 'Gender, sex and equivalent rights', in Butler, J. and Scott, J. W. (eds), *Feminists Theorise the Political*, London: Routledge.

Coser, L. (1956) *The Functions of Social Conflict*, London: Routledge & Kegan Paul.

Coser, L. (1977) *Masters of Sociological Thought*, 2nd edn, New York: Harcourt Brace Jovanovich.

Coverley, B. (1996) *Successful Step-parenting*, London: Bloomsbury.

Cox, O. (1970) *Caste, Class and Race*, New York: Monthly Preview Books.

Craib, I. (1992) *Modern Social Theory*, 2nd edn, Hemel Hempstead: Harvester Wheatsheaf.

Cressey, P. G. (1932) *The Taxi Dance Hall: A Sociological Study in Commercialised Recreation and City Life*, Chicago: University of Chicago Press.

Crewe, I. (1985) 'Can Labour rise again?', *Social Studies Review*, vol. 1, no. 1.

Crewe, I. (1987) 'Why Mrs Thatcher was returned with a landslide', *Social Studies Review*, vol. 3, no. 1.

Crewe, I. (1992) 'Why did Labour lose (yet again)?', *Politics Review*, September.

Crippen, T. (1988) 'Old and new gods in the modern world: toward a theory of religious transformation', *Social Forces*, vol. 67, December.

Critcher, C. (1979) 'Football since the war', in Clarke, J. *et al.* (eds), *Working Class Culture*, London: Hutchinson.

Croland, M. (1985) *One in Five: The Assessment and Incidence of Special Educational Needs*, London: Routledge & Kegan Paul.

Croll, P. and Moses, D. (1985) *One in Five: The Assessment and Incidence of Special Educational Needs*, London: Routledge.

Crompton, R. (1993) *Class and Stratification: An Introduction to Current Debate*, Cambridge: Polity Press.

Crompton, R. (1996a) 'Gender and class analysis', in Lee, D. and Turner, B. (eds), *Conflicts About Class*, Harlow: Longman.

Crompton, R. (1996b) 'Is class dead?', *Sociology Review*, vol. 5, no. 2.

Crompton, R. (1997) 'Gender and employment: current debates', *Social Science Teacher*, vol. 26, no. 2.*

Crompton, R. and Jones, G. (1984) *White Collar Proletariat*, Basingstoke: Macmillan.

Crompton, R. and Le Feuvre, N. (1996) 'Paid employment and the changing system of gender relations: a cross-national comparison', *Sociology*, vol. 30, no. 3.

Cross, M. (1992) 'Introduction', *New Community*, vol. 19, no. 1.

Cross, M. and Keith, M. (1993) *Racism, the City and State*, London: Routledge.

Crow, B. (1992) 'Understanding famine and hunger', in Allen, T. and Thomas, A. (eds) *Poverty and Development in the 1990s*, Oxford: Oxford University Press.

Crozier, G. (1996) 'Empowering the powerful: a discussion of the inter-relation of government policies and consumerism with social class factors and the impact of this upon parent interventions in their children's schooling', *British Journal of Sociology of Education*, vol. 18, no. 2.

Cuff, E. C., Sharrock, W. W. and Francis, D. W. (1990) *Perspectives in Sociology*, 3rd edn, London: Routledge.

Culley, L. and Dyson, S. (1993) '"Race", inequality and health', *Sociology Review*, vol. 3, no. 1.

Curran, J. (1991) 'Mass media and democracy: a reappraisal', in Curran, J. and Gurevitch, M. (eds), *Mass Media and Society*, New York: Edward Arnold.

Curtice, J. (1997) 'Anatomy of a landslide', *Politics Review*, vol. 7, no. 1.

Curtis, L. R. (1968) *Anglo-Saxons and Celts*, Connecticut: University of Bridgeport.

Dahl, R. A. (1961) *Who Governs?*, New Haven: Yale University Press.

Dahrendorf, R. (1959) *Class and Class Conflict in an Industrial Society*, London: Routledge & Kegan Paul.

Dahrendorf, R. (1987) 'The erosion of citizenship and its consequences for us all', *New Statesman*, 12 June.

Dahrendorf, R. (1999a) *Equality and the Modern Economy*, London: Smith Institute.

Dahrendorf, R. (1999b) 'It's work Jim, but not as we know it', *New Statesman*, vol. 15, January.

Dale, R. (1969, 1971, 1974) *Mixed or Single Sex School?*, vols 1–3, London: Routledge & Kegan Paul.

Dalla Costa, M. and James, S. (1972) *The Power of Women and the Subversion of the Community*, Bristol: Falling Wall Press.

Dallos, R. and Sapsford, R. (1995) in Muncie, J., Wetherell, M., Dallos, R. and Cochrane, A. (eds), *Understanding the Family*, London: Sage.

Darlington, R. (1994) *The Dynamics of Workplace Unionism*, London: Mansell.

David, M. (1993) *Parents, Gender and Education Reform*, Cambridge: Polity Press.

David, M. (1986) 'Moral and maternal: the family in the Right', in Levitas, R. (ed.), *The Ideology of the New Right*, Cambridge: Polity Press.

Davidoff, L. (1979) 'The separation of home and work? Landladies and lodgers in nineteenth century England', in Burman, S. (ed.), *Fit Work For Women*, London: Croom Helm.

Davidoff, L. and Hall, C. (1987) *Family Fortunes: Men and Women of the English Middle Class 1780–1850*, Chicago: University of Chigaco Press.

Davies, B. (1989) *Frogs and Snails and Feminist Tales: Pre-school Children and Gender*, Sydney: Allen & Unwin.

Davies, G. (1994) *Religion in Britain Since 1945*, Oxford: Blackwell Publishers.

Davies, T. (1994) 'Disabled by society', *Sociology Review*, vol. 3, no. 4.

Davis, K. and Moore, W. E. (1945) 'Some principles of stratification', *American Sociological Review*, vol. 10.

Davis, K. and Moore, W. E. (1967) 'Some principles of stratification', in Bendix, R. and Lipset, S. M. (eds), *Class Status and Power*, 2nd edn, London: Routledge.

Davis, M. (1995) 'Fortress Los Angeles: the Militarization of Urban Space', in Kasinitz, P. (ed.), *Metropolis: Centre and Symbol of Our Times*, Basingstoke: Macmillan.

Dawkins, R. (1976) *The Selfish Gene*, Oxford: Oxford University Press.

Dawkins, R. (1989) *The Selfish Gene*, 2nd edn, Oxford: Oxford University Press.

Daye, S. (1994) *Middle Class Blacks in Britain*, Basingstoke: Macmillan.

Deakin, C. (1998a) 'Exam matters: active learning', *Sociology Review*, vol. 8, no. 1.

Deakin, C. (1998b) 'Exam matters: continuing active learning', *Sociology Review*, vol. 8, no. 2.

Dearing, R. (1993) *The National Curriculum and its Assessment – Final Report*, London: Schools Curriculum and Assessment Authority.

Dearing, R. (1996) *Review of Qualifications for 16–19 Year Olds: Full Report*, London: Schools Curriculum and Assessment Authority.

Deedes, W. (1968) *Race Without Rancour*, London: Conservative Party Political Centre.

Deem, R. (1988) *Work, Unemployment and Leisure*, London: Routledge.

Deem, R. (1990) 'Women and leisure', *Social Studies Review*, vol. 5, no. 4.

Dejevsky, M. (1999) 'Welfare reforms deprive US poor', *Independent*, 23 August.

Delamothe, T. (1989) 'Class dismissed', *British Medical Journal*, vol. 299, 1356.

Delphy, C. (1979) 'Sharing the same table', in Harris, C. (ed.), *The Sociology of the Family*, Keele: University of Keele.

Delphy, C. (1977a) *The Main Enemy*, London: Women's Research and Resource Centre.

Delphy, C. (1977b) 'Women in stratification studies', in Roberts, H. (ed.), *Doing Feminist Research*, London: Routledge.

Delphy, C. (1984) *Close to Home: A Materialist Analysis of Women's Oppression*, London: Hutchinson.

Delphy, C. and Leonard, D. (1993) *Familiar Exploitation*, Cambridge: Polity Press.

Dennis, M. (1975) 'Relationships', in Butterworth, E. and Weir, D. (eds), *The Sociology of Modern Britain*, revised edn, Glasgow: Fontana.

Dennis, N., Henriques, F. and Slaughter, C. (1956) *Coal is our Life*, London: Eyre & Spottiswoode.

Dennis, N. and Erdos, E. (1992) *Families Without Fatherhood*, London: IEA Health and Welfare Unit.

Denny, E. (1994) 'Liberation or oppression? Radical feminism and *in vitro* fertilisation', *Sociology of Health and Illness*, vol. 16, no. 1.

Denscombe, N. (1993) *Sociology Update 1993*, Leicester: Olympus Books.

Denscombe, N. (1995) *Sociology Update 1995*, Leicester: Olympus Books.

Department of Employment (1995) *Labour Force Survey*, London: HMSO.

Department of Employment (1996) *Labour Market and Skill Trends 1995/6*, London: HMSO.

Department of Health (1995) *Child Protection: Messages from Research*, London: HMSO.

Derrida, J. (1977) *Of Grammatology*, Maryland: John Hopkins University Press.

Derrida, J. (1978) *Writing and Difference*, London: Routledge & Kegan Paul.

Derry, J. (1996) 'Teaching the sociology and philosophy of science', *Social Science Teacher*, vol. 25, no. 2.*

Devine, F. (1992) *Affluent Workers Revisited: Privatism and the Working Class*, Edinburgh: Edinburgh University Press.

Dewey, J. (1972) 'Communication, individual, and society', in Manis, J. and Meltzer, B. (eds), *Symbolic Interaction: A Reader in Social Pschology*, Boston: Allyn & Bacon.

Dex, S. (1987) *Women's Occupational Mobility*, Basingstoke: Macmillan.

DfEE (1997) *Excellence in Schools*, Cm3681, London: Stationery Office.

Dickinson, D. (1994) 'Criminal benefits', *New Statesman and Society*, 14 January.

Dobash, R. E. and Dobash, R. P. (1980) *Violence Against Wives: A Case Against Patriarchy*, Shepton Mallett: Open Books.

Donald, J. and Rattansi, A. (eds) (1992) *'Race', Culture and Difference*, London: Sage.

Dopson, S. and Waddington, I. (1996) 'Managing social change: a process–sociological approach to understanding organisational change within the National Health Service', *Sociology of Health and Illness*, vol. 18, no. 4.

Dore, R. (1987) *Flexible Rigidities: Industrial Policy and Structural Adjustment in the Japanese Economy, 1970–80*, London: Athlone.

Douglas, J. (1967) *The Social Meanings of Suicide*, Princeton: Princeton University Press.

Douglas, J. W. B. (1964) *The Home and the School*, London: Macgibbon & Kee.

Douglas, M. (1966) *Purity and Danger*, London: Routledge.

Downes, D. and Rock, P. (1995) *Understanding Deviance: A Guide to the Sociology of Crime and Rule Breaking*, 2nd edn, Oxford: Oxford University Press.

Doyal, L. (1995) *What Makes Women Sick? Gender and the Political Economy of Health*, Basingstoke: Macmillan.

Doyal, L. and Pennell, I. (1979) *The Political Economy of Health*, London: Pluto Press.

Drew, D. and Gray, J. (1990) 'The 5th year examination achievements of black young people in England and Wales', *Educational Research*, vol. 32, no. 3.

Drew, D. Fosam, B. and Gillborn, D. (1995) 'Statistics and the pseudo-science of "race" and IQ: interrogating the Bell Curve'. Unpublished paper presented at the annual conference of the Royal Statistical Society, July 1995.

Dummett, M. and Dummett, A. (1982) 'The role of government in Britain's racial crisis', in Husband, C. (ed.), *'Race' in Britain: Continuity and Change*, London: Hutchinson.

Dumont, T. (ed.) (1993) *Channels of Resistance*, London: BFI Publishing.

Duncombe, J. and Marsden, D. (1993) 'Love and intimacy: the gender division of emotions and "emotion work"', *Sociology*, vol. 27, no. 2.

Duncombe, J. and Marsden, D. (1995) *Sociology Review*, vol. 4, no. 4.

Dunleavy, P. and Husbands, C. (1985) *Democracy at the Crossroads*, London: George Allen & Unwin.

Dunleavy, P. and O'Leary, B. (1987) *Theories of the State: The Politics of Liberal Democracy*, Basingstoke: Macmillan.

Dunning, E. (ed.) (1971) *The Sociology of Sport*, London: Frank Cass.

Dunning, E., Murphy, P. and Williams, J. (1988) *The Roots of Football Hooliganism*, London: Routledge.

Dunsmuir, A. and Williams, L. (1991) *How to do Social Research*, London: Collins Educational.

Durham, M. and O'Shaughnessy, H. (1994) 'UK in secret £2bn arms bid', *Observer*, 13 November.

Durkheim, E. (1938a) *The Division of Labour in Society*, Glencoe, CA: Free Press (orig. pub. 1893).

Durkheim, E. (1938b) *The Rules of the Sociological Method*, Glencoe, CA: Free Press (orig. pub. 1895).

Durkheim, E. (1979) *Suicide: A Study in Sociology*, London: Routledge & Kegan Paul (orig. pub. 1897).

Durkheim, E. (1982) *The Elementary Forms of the Religious Life*, London: George Allen & Unwin (orig. pub. 1912).

Durkheim, E. (1988) *Selected Writings* (edited by A. Giddens), Cambridge: Cambridge University Press (orig. pub. 1886).

Dworkin, A. (1997) *Life and Death: Unapologetic Writings on the Continuing War against Women*, London: Virago.

Eadie, T. and Morley, R. (1999) 'Crime, justice and punishment', in Baldock, J., Manning, N., Miller, S. and Vickerstaff, S. (eds) *Social Policy*, Oxford: Blackwell Publishers.

Ealing Women's Liberation Workshop Collective (eds) (1971) 'Sisterhood is ...', *Shrew*, vol. 3, no. 6.

Eatwell, J. and Taylor, L. (1998) *International Capital Markets and the Future of Economic Policy: The Performance of Liberalised Capital Markets*, London: IPPR.

Eco, U. (1987) *Travels in Hyper-reality*, London: Picador.

Eco, U. (1995) *Apocalypse Postponed*, London: Flamingo.

Edgell, S. (1980) *Middle Class Couples*, London: George Allen & Unwin.

Edgell, S. (1993) *Class*, London: Routledge.

Edgell, S. and Duke, V. (1991) *A Measure of Thatcherism*, London: Routledge.

Edholm, F. (1991) in Loney, M., Bocock, R., Clarke, J., Cochrane, A., Graham, P. and Wilson, M. (eds), *The State or the Market*, London: Sage.

Education and Training for the 21st Century (1991), London: DfEE.

Edwards, T., Fitz, J. and Whitty, G. (1989) *The State and Private Education: An Evaluation of the Assisted Places Scheme*, Lewes: Falmer Press.

Egerton, M. and Halsey, A. H. (1993) 'Trends by social class and gender in access to higher education in Britain', *Oxford Review of Education*, vol. 19, no. 2.

Eggleston, S. J., Dunn, D. K. and Anjoli, M. (1986) *Education for Some: The Educational and Vocational*

Experiences of 15–18 Year Old Members of Minority Ethnic Groups, Stoke-on-Trent: Trentham Books.

Ehrlich, P. R. (1972) *The Population Bomb*, London: Ballantine.

Eisenstadt, S. N. (1956) *From Generation to Generation*, Chicago: Free Press.

Eldridge, J. (1971) *Sociology and Industrial Life*, London: Michael Joseph.

Eldridge, J. (1991) 'Whose illusion, whose reality? Some problems of theory and method in mass media research', in Eldridge, J. (ed.), *Getting the Message: News, Truth and Power*, London: Routledge.

Eldridge, J. (1993) 'News, truth and power', in Eldridge, J. (ed.), *Getting the Message: News, Truth and Power*, London: Routledge.

Elias, N. (1978) *The Civilising Process, Vol 1*, Oxford: Blackwell (orig. pub. 1939).

Elias, N. (1982) *The Civilising Process, Vol 2*, Oxford: Blackwell (orig. pub. 1939).

Eliot, T. S. (1948) *Notes Towards a Definition of Culture*, London: Faber & Faber.

Elliot, C. and Ellingworth, D. (1997) 'Assessing the representativeness of the 1992 British Crime Survey: the impact of sampling error and response biases', *Sociological Research Online*, vol. 2, no. 4.

Elliot, F. R. (1996) *Gender, Family and Society*, Basingstoke: Macmillan.

Elliott, L. and Ryle, S. (1997) 'Fall in dole queue "fiddled"', *Guardian*, 16 January.

Elliott, L. (1999) 'East is Eden', *Guardian*, 7 December.

Ellsworth, E. (1989) 'Why doesn't this feel empowering? Working through the repressive myths of critical pedagogy', *Harvard Educational Review*, vol. 59, no. 3.

Elsted, J. I. (1996) 'How large are the differences – really? Self-reported long-standing illness among working class and middle class men', *Sociology of Health and Illness*, vol. 18, no. 4.

Elster, J. (1983) *Explaining Technical Change*, Cambridge: Polity Press.

Elwood, J. (1995a) 'Gender, equity and the gold standard: examination and coursework performance in the UK at 18'. Unpublished paper presented at the AERA conference, San Francisco, USA.

Elwood, J. (1995b) 'Undermining gender stereotypes: examination and coursework performance in the UK at 16', *Assessment in Education*, vol. 2, no. 3.

Elwood, J. (1999) 'Gender achievement and the gold standard: differential performance in the GCE A-level examination', *Curriculum Journal*, vol. 10, no. 2.

Elwood, J. and Gipps, C. (1999) *Review of Recent Research on the Achievement of Girls in Single-Sex Schools*, London: Institute of Education, London University.

Emmanuel, A. (1972) *Unequal Exchange: A Study of the Imperialism of Free Trade*, New York: Monthly Review Press.

Engels, F. (1972) *The Origins of the Family, Private Property and the State*, London: Lawrence & Wishart (orig. pub. 1884).

Engels, F. (1984) 'On the history of early Christianity', in Feuer, L. S. (ed.), *Marx and Engels: Basic Writings on Politics and Philosophy*, Aylesbury: Fontana (orig. pub. 1895).

Engels, F. (1986) 'Anti-Dühring', in Marx, K. and Engels, F., *Collected Works*, vol. 25, Moscow: Progress Publishers (orig. pub. 1878).

Epstein, D. (1993) *Changing Classroom Cultures: Anti-racism, Politics and Schools*, Stoke-on-Trent: Trentham Books.

Epstein, D. (1995) ' "Girls don't do bricks": gender and sexuality in the primary classroom', in Siraj-Blatchford, J. and I. (eds), *Educating the Whole Child: Cross-Curricular Skills, Themes and Dimensions*, Buckingham: Open University Press.

Epstein, D. *et al.* (eds) *Issues in Gender and Achievement*, Buckingham: Open University Press.

Eribon, D. (1992) *Michel Foucault*, London: Faber & Faber.

Erikson and Goldthorpe, J. (1992) *The Constant Flux: A Study of Class Mobility in Industrial Societies*, Oxford: Clarendon Press.

Esping-Andersen, G. (1990) *The Three Worlds of Welfare Capitalism*, Cambridge: Polity Press.

Esping-Andersen, G. (ed.) (1993) *Changing Classes*, London: Sage.

ESRC (1989) *Unequal Jobs, Unequal Pay: The Social Change and Economic Life Initiative*, ESRC working paper 6.

Etzioni, A. (1995) *The Spirit of Community*, London: Fontana.

Evans, J. and Lunt, I. (1994) 'Dilemmas in special educational needs: some effects of local management of schools', in Riddell, S. and Brown, S. (eds), *Special Educational Needs Policy in the 1990s – Warnock and the Market Place*, London: Routledge.

Evans, J. and Vincent, C. (1996) 'Parental choice and special education', in Glatter, R., Woods, P. and Bayley , C. (eds), *Choice and Diversity in Schooling: Perspectives and Prospects*, London: Routledge.

Eversley, D. and Bannerjea, L. (1982) 'Social change and indications of diversity', in Rapoport, R. N., Fogarty, M. P. and Rapoport, R. (eds), *Families in Britain*, London: Routledge & Kegan Paul.

Eysenck, H. J. (1970) *Crime and Personality*, London: Paladin.

Faludi, S. (1992) *Backlash: The Undeclared War Against Women*, London: Chatto & Windus.

Faulks, K. (1994) 'What has happened to citizenship?', *Sociology Review*, vol. 4, no. 2.

Featherstone, M. (1991a) *Consumer Culture and Postmodernism*, London: Sage.

Featherstone, M. (1991b) 'The body in consumer culture', in Featherstone, M., Hepworth, M. and Turner, B. S. (eds), *The Body: Social Process and Cultural Theory*, London: Sage.

Featherstone, M., Hepworth, M. and Turner, B. S. (eds) (1991) *The Body: Social Process and Cultural Theory*, London: Sage.

Ferguson, M. (1983) *Forever Feminine: Women's Magazines and the Cult of Femininity*, London: Heinemann.

Ferguson, M. (1990) 'Electronic media and the redefining of time and space', in Ferguson, M. (ed.), *Public Communication: The New Imperatives*, London: Sage.

Ferguson, M. and Golding, P. (eds) (1997) *Cultural Studies in Question*, London: Sage.

Ferri, E. and Smith, K. (1998) *Parenting in the 1990s*, London: Family Policy Studies Centre/JRF.

Field, D. (1976) 'The social definition of illness', in Tuckett, D. (ed.), *An Introduction to Medical Sociology*, London: Tavistock.

Field, D. (1992) 'Elderly people in British society', *Sociology Review*, vol. 1, no. 4.

Field, F. (1989) *Losing Out: The Emergence of Britain's Underclass*, Oxford: Blackwell.

Field, F. (1993) *An Agenda for Britain*, London: HarperCollins.

Field, F. (1996) *Stakeholder Welfare*, London: IEA.

Field, S. (1982) 'Urban disorders in Britain and America', in Field, S. and Southgate, P. (eds), *Public Disorder: A Review of Research and a Study in One Inner City Area*, London: HMSO.

Fielding, A. J. (1995) 'Migration and middle class formation in England and Wales 1981–91', in Butler, T. and Savage, M. (eds), *Social Change and the Middle Classes*, London: UCL Press.

Filakti, H. (1997) 'Trends in abortion', *Population Trends 87*, London: ONS.

Finch, J. and Mason, J. (1991) 'Obligations in kinship in contemporary Britain: is there normative agreement?', *British Journal of Sociology*, vol. 42, no. 3.

Finch, J. and Mason, J. (1993) *Negotiating Family Responsibilities*, London: Routledge.

Fine, B. (1995) 'From political economy to consumption', in Miller, D. (ed.), *Acknowledging Consumption*, London: Routledge.

Finegold, D. *et al.* (1990) *A British 'Baccalaureat': Ending the Division Between Education and Training*, London: Institute for Public Policy Research.

Firestone, S. (1970) *The Dialectic of Sex*, London: Women's Press.

Firestone, S. (1979) *The Dialectic of Sex*, 2nd edn, London: Women's Press.

Fiske, J. (1989a) *Understanding Popular Culture*, London: Unwin Hyman.

Fiske, J. (1989b) *Reading the Popular*, London: Unwin Hyman.

Fiske, J. (1990) *Introduction to Communication Studies*, 2nd edn, London: Routledge.

Fiske, J. (1991) 'Postmodernism and television', in Curran, J. and Gurevitich, M. (eds), *Mass Media and Society*, London: Edward Arnold.

Fitzpatrick, T. (1999) 'Cash transfer', in Baldock, J., Manning, N., Miller, S. and Vickerstaff, S. (eds), *Social Policy*, Oxford: Oxford University Press.

Fletcher, R. (1966) *The Family and Marriage in Britain*, Harmondsworth: Penguin.

Florida, R. and Kenney, M. (1996) 'Japanese automotive transplants and the transfer of the Japanese production system', in Deyo, F. C. (ed.), *Social Reconstructions of the World Automobile Industry*, Basingstoke: Macmillan.

Foot, P. (1996) 'A lack of principal', *Private Eye*, 27 December.

Foote Whyte, W. (1943) *Street Corner Society: The Social Structure of an Italian Slum*, Chicago: University of Chicago Press.

Foote Whyte, W. (1981) *Street Corner Society: The Social Structure of an Italian Slum*, 3rd edn, Chicago: University of Chicago Press.

Ford, J. (1990) 'Households, housing and debt', *Social Studies Review*, vol. 5, no. 5.

Foster, J. (1990) *Villains*, London: Routledge.

Foster-Carter, A. (1978) 'The modes of production controversy', *New Left Review*, vol. 107.

Foster-Carter, A. (1985) 'The sociology of development', in Haralambos, M. (ed.), *Sociology: New Directions*, Ormskirk: Causeway Press.

Foster-Carter, A. (1995) 'A tiger's eye', *New Statesman and Society*, 17 March.

Foucault, M. (1967) *Madness and Civilization*, London: Tavistock.

Foucault, M. (1970) *The Order of Things*, London: Tavistock.

Foucault, M. (1972) *The Archaeology of Knowledge*, London: Tavistock.

Foucault, M. (1974) *The Birth of the Clinic: An Archaeology of Medical Perception*, London: Tavistock.

Foucault, M. (1977) *Discipline and Punish: The Birth of the Prison*, Harmondsworth: Penguin.

Foucault, M. (1979a) *The History of Sexuality*, vol. 1, London: Allen Lane.

Foucault, M. (1979b) 'Governmentality', *Ideology and Conciousness*, vol. 6, autumn.

Foucault, M. (1980) *Power/Knowledge: Selected Interviews and Other Writings 1972–1977*, Brighton: Harvester.

Foucault, M. (1989a) *The Birth of the Clinic: An Archaeology of Medical Perception*, new edn, London: Routledge.

Foucault, M. (1989b) *Madness and Civilization: A History of Insanity in the Age of Reason*, new edn, London: Routledge.

Foucault, M. (1990a) *The History of Sexuality. 1: An Introduction*, new edn, Harmondsworth: Penguin.

Foucault, M. (1990b) *The History of Sexuality. 3: The Care of the Self*, new edn, Harmondsworth: Penguin.

Foucault, M. (1991) *Discipline and Punish: The Birth of the Prison*, new edn, Harmondsworth: Penguin.

Foucault, M. (1992) *The History of Sexuality. 2: The Use of Pleasure*, new edn, Harmondsworth: Penguin.

Frank, A. G. (1969) *Capitalism and Underdevelopment in Latin America*, New York: Monthly Review Press.

Frank, A. G. (1979) *Dependent Accumulation and Underdevelopment*, New York: Monthly Review Press.

Frank, A. G. (1991a) 'Latin American development theories revisited', *Scandanavian Journal of Development Alternatives*, vol. 10, no. 3.

Frank, A. W. (1991b) 'For a sociology of the body: an analytical review', in Featherstone, M., Hepworth, M. and Turner, B. S. (eds), *The Body: Social Process and Cultural Theory*, London: Sage.

Fraser, D. (1973) *The Evolution of the British Welfare State*, Basingstoke: Macmillan.

Fraser, S. (ed.) (1995) *The Bell Curve Wars*, London: Basic Books.

Frayman, H. (1991) *Breadline Britain 1990s*, London: LWT.

Friedman, M. (1980) *Free To Choose*, Harmondsworth: Penguin.

Friedrich, C. (1954) *Totalitarianism*, Cambridge, MA: Harvard University Press.

Friedson, E. (1974) *The Profession of Medicine: A Study of the Sociology of Applied Knowledge*, New York: Dodd Mead.

Friere, P. (1982) *Pedagogy of the Oppressed*, Harmondsworth: Penguin.

Friere, P. and Macedo, D. (1987) *Literacy: Reading, the Word and the World*, London: Routledge & Kegan Paul.

Friere, P. and Shor, I. (1987) *A Pedagogy for Liberation:*

Dialogues on Transforming Education, Basingstoke: Macmillan.

Frisby, D. (1984) *Georg Simmel*, London: Tavistock.

Frith, S. (1984) *The Sociology of Youth*, Ormskirk: Causeway.

Frith, S. (1988) *Music For Pleasure*, Cambridge: Polity Press.

Fröbel, F., Heinrichs, J. and Kreye, O. (1980) *The New International Division of Labour*, Cambridge: Cambridge University Press.

Fryer, P. (1984) *Staying Power: The History of Black People in Britain*, London: Pluto Press.

Fukuyama, F. (1992) *The End of History and the Last Man*, Harmondsworth: Penguin.

Fulcher, J. and Scott, J. (1999) *Sociology*, Oxford: Oxford University Press.

Fuller, M. (1980) 'Black girls in a London Comprehensive school', in Deem, R. (ed.), *Schooling for Women's Work*, London: Routledge & Kegan Paul.

Gallie, D. (1991) 'Patterns of skill change: Upskilling, de-skilling or the polarization of skills?', *Work, Employment and Society*, vol. 5.

Gallie, D. (1994) 'Are the unemployed an underclass? Some evidence from the social change and economic life initiative', *Sociology*, vol. 28, no. 3.

Gallie, D., Marsh, C. and Vogler, C. (eds) (1994) *Social Change and the Experience of Unemployment*, Oxford: Oxford University Press.

Galloway, P., Armstrong, D. and Tomlinson, S. (1994) *The Assessment of Special Educational Needs: Whose Problem?*, London: Longman.

Galtung, J. and Ruge, M. (1981) 'Structuring and selecting news', in Cohen, S. and Young, J. (eds), *The Manufacture of News: Deviance, Social Problems and the Mass Media*, London: Constable.

Gamble, A. (1994) 'Loves labour lost', in Perryman, M. (ed.), *Altered States: Postmodernism, Politics, Culture*, London: Lawrence & Wishart.

Gamman, L. (1988) 'Watching the detectives: the enigma of the female gaze', in Gamman, L. and Marshment, M. (eds), *The Female Gaze: Women as Viewers of Popular Culture*, London: Women's Press.

Gamman, L. and Marshment, M. (eds) (1988) 'Introduction', in *The Female Gaze: Women as Viewers of Popular Culture*, London: Women's Press.

Gane, M. (ed.) (1992) *The Radical Sociology of Durkheim and Mauss*, London: Routledge.

Gannon, K. (1995) 'Killing of Pakistan's boy activist draws demands for banning of child labour', *Guardian*, 21 April.

Gans, H. (1962) *The Urban Village*, New York: Free Press.

Gans, H. (1974) *Popular Culture and High Culture*, New York: Basic Books.

Gardner, H. (1995) 'Cracking open the IQ box', in Fraser, S. (ed.), *The Bell Curve Wars*, London: Basic Books.

Garfield, S. (1986) *Expensive Habits: The Darker Side of the Music Industry*, London: Faber & Faber.

Garfinkel, H. (1967) *Studies in Ethnomethodology*, Englewood Cliffs, NJ, Prentice-Hall.

Garfinkel, H. (1984) *Studies in Ethnomethodology*, new edn, Cambridge: Polity Press.

Garrett, A. (1996) 'Census sensibility on trial', *Observer* (Business Section), 24 November.

Garrett, S. (1987) *Gender*, London: Tavistock.

Gellner, E. (1983) *Nations and Nationalism*, Oxford: Blackwell.

George, S. (1976) *How the Other Half Dies*, Harmondsworth: Penguin.

George, S. (1988) *A Fate Worse than Debt*, Harmondsworth: Penguin.

George, V. and Wilding, P. (1994) *Welfare and Ideology*, London: Harvester Wheatsheaf.

Geraghty, C. (1991) *Women and Soap Opera*, Cambridge: Polity Press.

Gerry, C. (1985) 'Small enterprises, the recession and the "disappearing" working class', in Rees *et al.* (eds), *Political Action and Social Identity*, Basingstoke: Macmillan.

Gershuny, J. and Pahl, R. (1985) 'Britain in the decade of the three economies', in Littler, C. R. (ed.), *The Experience of Work*, Aldershot: Gower.

Giddens, A. (1969) 'Georg Simmel', in Raison, T. (ed.), *The Founding Fathers of Social Science*, revised edn, London: Scolar Press.

Giddens, A. (1971) *Capitalism and Modern Social Theory*, Cambridge: Cambridge University Press.

Giddens, A. (1973) *The Class Structures of the Advanced Societies*, London: Hutchinson.

Giddens, A. (ed.) (1974) *Positivism and Sociology*, London: Heinemann.

Giddens, A. (1976) *The New Rules of the Sociological Method*, London: Hutchinson.

Giddens, A. (1977) *Studies in Social and Political Theory*, London: Hutchinson.

Giddens, A. (1979) *Central Problems in Social Theory*, Basingstoke: Macmillan.

Giddens, A. (1980) *The Class Structure of the Advanced Societies*, 2nd edn, London: Hutchinson.

Giddens, A. (1984) *The Constitution of Society: An Outline of the Theory of Structuration*, Cambridge: Polity Press.

Giddens, A. (1985a) 'Jürgen Habermas', in Skinner, Q. (ed.), *The Return of Grand Theory in the Human Sciences*, Cambridge: Canto.

Giddens, A. (1985b) *Capitalism and Modern Social Theory: An Analysis of the Writings of Marx, Durkheim and Max Weber*, Cambridge: Cambridge University Press.

Giddens, A. (1985c) *The Nation State and Violence*, Cambridge: Polity Press.

Giddens, A. (1986) *Sociology: A Brief but Critical Introduction*, 2nd edn, Basingstoke: Macmillan.

Giddens, A. (1987) *Social Theory and Modern Sociology*, Cambridge: Polity Press.

Giddens, A. (1988) *New Rules of Sociological Method*, London: Hutchinson.

Giddens, A. (1989) *Sociology*, Cambridge: Polity Press.

Giddens, A. (1990) *The Consequences of Modernity*, Cambridge: Polity Press.

Giddens, A. (1991) *Modernity and Self-Identity: Self and Society in the Late Modern Age*, Cambridge: Polity Press.

Giddens, A. (1993a) *Sociology*, 2nd edn, Cambridge: Polity Press.

Giddens, A. (1993b) *The Consequences of Modernity*, Cambridge: Polity Press.

Giddens, A. (1997) 'Goodnight, Mr Average', *Observer*, 26 January.

Giddens, A. (1997) *Sociology*, 3rd ed, Cambridge: Polity Press.

Giddens, A. (1998) *The Third Way*, Cambridge: Polity Press.

Giddens, A. (2000) *The Third Way and its Critics*, Cambridge: Polity Press.

Giddens, A. and Turner, J. (eds) (1987) *Social Theory Today*, Cambridge: Polity Press.

Gilbert, N. (1995) 'Official social classifications in the UK', *Social Research Update*, July.

Gill, S. and Law, D. (1988) *The Global Political Economy*, Hemel Hempstead: Harvester Wheatsheaf.

Gillborn, D. (1990) *'Race', Ethnicity and Education: Teaching and Learning in Multi-ethnic Schools*, London: Unwin Hyman.

Gillborn, D. and Gipps, C. (1996) *Recent Research on the Achievements of Ethnic Minority Pupils*, London: Ofsted.

Gillborn, D., Youdell, D. and Kirton, A. (1999) 'Government policy and school effects: racism and social justice in policy and practice', *Multicultural Teaching*, vol. 17, no. 3.

Gillespie, M. (1995) *Television, Ethnicity and Cultural Change*, London: Routledge.

Gilligan, C. (1982) *In a Different Voice: Essays on Psychological Theory and Women's Development*, Cambridge, MA: Harvard University Press.

Gillis, J. R. (1985) *For Better, For Worse: British Marriage 1600 to the Present*, Oxford: Oxford University Press.

Gilroy, P. (1982) 'The myth of black criminality', *The Socialist Register*, London: Merlin Press.

Gilroy, P. (1982a) 'Police and thieves', in *The Empire Strikes Back: Race and Racism in 70s Britain*, London: CCCS/Hutchinson.

Gilroy, P. (1982b) 'Steppin' out of Babylon: race, class and autonomy', in *The Empire Strikes Back: Race and Racism in 70s Britain*, London: CCCS/Hutchinson.

Gilroy, P. (1987) *There Ain't No Black in the Union Jack*, London: Unwin Hyman.

Gilroy, P. (1990) 'The end of anti-racism', *New Community*, vol. 17, no. 1.

Gilroy, P. (1992) 'The end of antiracism', in Donald, J. and Rattansi, A. (eds), *'Race', Culture and Difference*, London: Sage.

Gilroy, P. (1993) *The Black Atlantic: Modernity and Double Conciousness*, London: Verso.

Ginn, J. *et al.* (1996) 'Feminist fallacies: a reply to Hakim on women's employment', *British Journal of Sociology*, vol. 47, no. 1.

Ginsburg, N. (1991) 'The wonderful world(s) of welfare capitalism', *Critical Social Policy*, summer.

Ginsberg, N. (1992) 'Racism and housing: concepts and reality', in Braham, P., Rattansi, A. and Skellington, R. (eds), *Racism and Antiracism: Inequalities, Opportunities and Policies*, London: Sage/Open University Press.

Ginsburg, N. (1998) 'Postmodernity and social Europe, in Carter, J. (ed.) *Postmodernity and the Fragmentation of Welfare*, London: Routledge.

Gipps, C. and Murphy, P. (1994) *A Fair Test? Assessment, Achievement and Equity*, Buckingham: Open University Press.

Giroux, H. (1989) *Schooling for Democracy: Critical Pedagogy in the Modern Age*, London: Routledge.

Gittins, D. (1985) *The Family in Question*, Basingstoke: Macmillan.

Gittins, D. (1993) *The Family in Question*, 2nd edn, Basingstoke: Macmillan.

Glaser, B. G. and Strauss, A. L. (1965) *Awareness of Dying*, Chicago: Aldine.

Glasgow University Media Group (1976) *Bad News*, London: Routledge & Kegan Paul.

Glasgow University Media Group (1980) *More Bad News*, London: Routledge & Kegan Paul.

Glasgow University Media Group (1982) *Really Bad News*, London: Writers and Readers Cooperative.

Glass, D. V. (ed.) (1954) *Social Mobility in Modern Britain*, London: Routledge.

Glass, R. (1960) *New Comers: West Indians in London*, London: Allen & Unwin.

Gledhill, C. (1997) 'Genre and gender: the case of soap opera', in Hall, S. (ed.), *Representation: Cultural Representations and Signifying Practices*, London: Sage/Open University.

Gleick, J. (1987) *Chaos*, London: Cardinal.

Glendinning, C. and Millar, J. (eds) (1987) *Women and Poverty in Britain*, Hemel Hempstead: Harvester Wheatsheaf.

Glendinning, C. and Millar, J. (eds) (1992) *Women and Poverty in Britain: The 1990s*, Hemel Hempstead: Harvester Wheatsheaf.

Glennerster, H. (1995) *British Social Policy Since 1945*, Oxford: Blackwell.

Glock, C. Y. (1958) *Religion and the Face of America*, Berkeley: University of California Press.

Glock, C. Y. and Bellah, R. N. (eds) (1976) *The New Religious Consciousness*, Berkeley: University of California Press.

Glock, C. Y. and Stark, R. (1965) *Religion and Society in Tension*, Chicago: Rand McNally.

Glock, C. Y. and Stark, R. (1968) *American Piety: The Nature of Religious Commitment*, Berkeley: University of California Press.

Glucksmann, M. A. (1985) 'Why work? Gender and the "total social organization of labour"', *Gender, Work and Organization*, vol. 2, no. 2.

Glyptis, S. (1989) *Leisure and Unemployment*, Buckingham: Open University Press.

Goffman, E. (1971) *The Presentation of Self in Everyday Life*, Harmondsworth: Penguin (orig. pub. 1959).

Goffman, E. (1991) *Asylums: Essays on the Social Situation of Mental Patients and Other Inmates*, Harmondsworth: Penguin (orig. pub. 1968).

Golding, P. and Murdock, G. (1991). 'Cultural communication and political economy', in Curran, J. and Gurevitch, M. (eds), *The Mass Media and Society*, London: Edward Arnold.

Goldthorpe, J. (1987) *Social Mobility and Class Structure in Modern Britain*, Oxford: Clarendon/Oxford University Press.

Goldthorpe, J. (1982) 'On the service class: its formation and future', in Giddens, A. and MacKenzie, G. (eds), *Social Class and the Division of Labour: Essays in Honour of Ilya Neustadt*, Cambridge: Cambridge University Press.

Goldthorpe, J. (1983) 'Women and class analysis: In defence of the conventional view', *Sociology*, vol. 17, no. 4.

Goldthorpe, J. and Marshall, G. (1992) 'The promising future of class analysis: A response to recent critiques', *Sociology*, vol. 26, no. 3.

Goldthorpe, J., Lockwood, D., Platt, J. and Bechhofer, F.

(1968) *The Affluent Worker*, Cambridge: Cambridge University Press.

Gomm, R. and McNeill, P. (1982) *A Handbook for Sociology Teachers*, Oxford: Heinemann Educational.

Goode, W. J. (1963) *World Revolution and Family Patterns*, New York: Free Press.

Gordon, D. M. (1988) 'The global economy: new edifice or crumbling foundations?', *New Left Review*, no. 168.

Gordon, P. (1996) 'The racialization of statistics', in Skellington, R. (ed.), *'Race' in Britain Today*, London: Sage.

Gordon, P. and Newnham, A. (1985) *Passports to Benefits: Racism in Social Security*, London: CPAG/Runnymede Trust.

Gorz, A. (1982) *Farewell to the Working Class*, London: Pluto Press.

Goss, M. E. W. (1969) 'Influence and authority in an outpatients clinic', in Etzioni, A. (ed.), *A Sociological Reader on Complex Organizations*, 2nd edn, New York: Holt, Rinehart & Winston.

Gough, I. (1979) *The Political Economy of the Welfare State*, Basingstoke: Macmillan.

Gough, K. (1972) 'An anthropologist looks at Engels', in Glazer-Malbin, N. and Waeher, H. Y. (eds), *Woman in a Man Made World*, Chicago: Rand-McNally.

Gould, S. (1981) *The Mismeasure of Man*, Harmondsworth: Penguin.

Gould, S. (1995) 'Curveball', in Fraser, S. (ed.), *The Bell Curve Wars*, London: Basic Books.

Gouldner, A. (1954) *Patterns of Industrial Bureaucracy*, Glencoe, CA: Free Press.

Gouldner, A. (1957) *Wildcat Strike*, London: Routledge & Kegan Paul.

Gouldner, A. (1975) *For Sociology*, Harmondsworth: Penguin.

Gouldner, A. (1979) *The Future of Intellectuals and the Rise of the New Class*, Basingstoke: Macmillan.

Graham, A. (1985a) 'Bearing the weight of unemployment', *Community Care*, vol. 7, March.

Graham, H. (1985b) *Health and Welfare*, Walton-on-Thames: Nelson.

Graham, H. and Oakley, A. (1981) 'Competing ideologies of reproduction: medical and maternal perspectives on pregnancy', in Roberts, H. (ed.), *Women, Health and Reproduction*, London: Routledge.

Graham-Brown, S. (1991) *Education in the Developing World*, London: Longman.

Gramsci, A. (1971) *Selections from the Prison Notebooks* (edited by Q. Hoare), London: Lawrence & Wishart (orig. written 1929–35).

Gramsci, A. (1977) *Selections From Political Writings, 1910–1920* (edited by Q. Hoare), London: Lawrence & Wishart.

Gramsci, A. (1978) *Selections From Political Writings, 1921–1926* (edited by Q. Hoare), London: Lawrence & Wishart.

Grant, W. (1989) *Pressure Groups, Politics and Democracy in Britain*, Hemel Hempstead: Philip Allan.

Gray, A. M., Whelan, A. and Norman, C. (1988) *Care in the Community: A Study of Services and Costs in Six Districts*, York: University of York Centre for Health Economics.

Green, A. (1990) *Education and State Formation: The Rise of Education Systems in England, France and the USA*, Basingstoke: Macmillan.

Green, A. (1993) 'Post-16 qualification reform', *Forum*, vol. 35, no. 1.

Green, D. G. (1988) *Everyone a Private Patient*, London: Institute for Economic Affairs.

Green, E., Hebron, S. and Woodward, D. (1990) *Women's Leisure, What Leisure?*, Basingstoke: Macmillan.

Greer, Germaine (1984) *Sex and Destiny: The Politics of Human Fertility*, London: Picador; in associations with Secker and Waring Limited.

Gregg P., Harkness, S. and Machin, S. (1999) *Child Development and Family Income*, London: YPS/JRF.

Gregory, M. (1994) 'Flight into a minefield', *Guardian*, 30 August.

Griffin, C. (1985) *Typical Girls? Young Women from School to Job Market*, London: Routledge.

Griffin, G. (1995) 'Introduction', in Griffin, G. (ed.), *Feminist Activism in the 1990s*, London: Taylor & Francis.

Grint, K. (1991) *The Sociology of Work*, Cambridge: Polity Press.

Groves, D. (1992) 'Occupational pension provision and women's poverty in old age', in Glendinning, C. and Millar, J. (eds), *Women and Poverty in Britain: The 1990s*, Hemel Hempstead: Harvester Wheatsheaf.

Habermas, J. (1972) *Knowledge and Human Interests*, London: Heinemann.

Habermas, J. (1976) *Legitimation Crisis*, London: Heinemann.

Habermas, J. (1981a) 'New social movements', *Telos*, no. 49.

Habermas, J. (1981b) *The Theory of Communicative Action*, London: Heinemann.

Habermas, J. (1988) *Legitimation Crisis*, new edn, Cambridge: Polity Press.

Habermas, J. (1989) *The New Conservatism*, Cambridge: Polity Press.

Hakim, C. (1987) *Research Design*, London: George Allen & Unwin.

Hakim, C. (1991) 'Grateful slaves and self-made women: fact and fantasy in women's work orientations', *European Sociological Review*, vol. 7.

Hakim, C. (1995) 'Five feminist myths about women's employment', *British Journal of Sociology*, vol. 46, no. 3.

Hakim, C. (1996a) 'The sexual division of labour and women's heterogeneity', *British Journal of Sociology*, vol. 47, no. 1.

Hakim, C. (1996b) *Key Issues in Women's Work*, London: Athlone Press.

Hall, S. *et al.* (1979) *Policing the Crisis*, London: Macmillan.

Hall, C. (1982) 'The butcher, the baker, the candlestick maker: the shop and the family in the industrial revolution' and 'The town turned upside down? The working class family in textiles 1790–1850', in Whitelegg, E. *et al.* (eds), *The Changing Experience of Women*, Buckingham: Martin Robertson/Open University Press.

Hall, S. (1980) 'Race, articulation and societies structured in dominance', in *Sociological Theories: Race and Colonialism*, Paris: Unesco.

Hall, S. (1984) 'The great moving right show', *New Internationalist*, March.

Hall, S. (1985) 'Religious ideologies and social movements in Jamaica', in Bocock, R. and Thompson, K. (eds), *Religion and Ideology*, Manchester: Manchester University Press.

Hall, S. (1991a) 'And not a shot fired', *Marxism Today*, December.

Hall, S. (1991b) 'The local and the global: globalisation and ethnicity', in King, A D. (ed.), *Culture, Globalisation and the World System: Contemporary Conditions for the Representation of Identity*, Basingstoke: Macmillan.

Hall, S. (1992a) 'New ethnicities', in Donald, J. and Rattansi, A. (eds), *Race Culture and Difference*, London: Sage.

Hall, S. (1992b) 'The question of cultural identity', in Hall, S. *et al.* (ed.), *Modernity and its Future*, Cambridge: Polity Press.

Hall, S. (1995) *Fantasy, Identity and Politics*, in Carter, E., Donald, J. and Squires, J. (eds), *Cultural Remix: Theories of Politics and the Popular*, London: Lawrence & Wishart.

Hall, S. and du Gay, P. (eds) (1996) *Questions of Cultural Identity*, London: Sage.

Hall, S. and Jacques, M. (eds) (1983) *The Politics of Thatcherism*, London: Lawrence & Wishart.

Hall, S. and Jacques, M. (eds) (1989) *New Times*, London: Lawrence & Wishart.

Hall, S. and Jefferson, T. (eds) (1976) *Resistance Through Rituals*, London: Hutchinson.

Hall, S., Critcher, C., Jefferson, T., Clarke, J. and Roberts, B. (1978) *Policing the Crisis: Mugging, the State and Law and Order*, Basingstoke: Macmillan.

Hallam, S. and Toutounji, I. (1996) *What Do We Know About the Grouping of Pupils by Ability? A Research Review*, London: Institute of Education, London University.

Hallsworth, S. (1994) 'Understanding new social movements', *Sociology Review*, vol. 4, no. 1.

Halsey, A. H., Heath, A. and Ridge, J. M. (1980) *Origins and Destinations*, Oxford: Clarendon Press.

Ham, C. (1992) *Health Policy in Britain*, 3rd edn, Basingstoke: Macmillan.

Hamilton, M. (1990) 'Inequality and stratification', *Social Studies Review*, vol. 5, no. 5.

Hamilton, M. and Hirszowicz, M. (1993) *Class and Inequality*, Hemel Hempstead: Harvester Wheatsheaf.

Hamilton, P. (1992) 'The Enlightenment and the birth of social science', in Hall, S. and Gieben, B. (eds), *Formations of Modernity*, Cambridge: Polity Press/Open University.

Hammond, P. E. (ed.) (1985) *The Sacred in a Secular Age: Toward Revision in the Scientific Study of Religion*, London: University of California Press.

Hancock, G. (1989) *Lords of Poverty*, London: Mandarin.

Hansen, A. (ed.) (1993), *The Mass Media and Environmental Issues*, Leicester: Leicester University Press.

Haralambos, M. (1974) *Right On: From Blues to Soul in Black America*, Ormskirk: Causeway Press.

Haralambos, M. and Holborn, M. (1995) *Sociology: Themes and Perspectives*, 4th edn, London: Collins Educational.

Haralambos, M. and Holburn, M. (2000) *Sociology: Themes and Perspectives*, 5th edn, London: Collins Eduacational.

Haraway, D. (1990) 'A manifesto for cyborgs: science technology and socialist feminism in the 1980s', in Nicholson, L. (ed) *Feminism/Postmodernism*, London: Routledge.

Harbury, C. and Hitchens, D. (1979) *Inheritance and Wealth Inequality in Britain*, London: George Allen & Unwin.

Hardiman, M. and Midgley, J. (1982) *The Social Dimensions of Development: Social Policy and Planning in the Third World*, Chichester: John Wiley.

Harding, L. (1996) *Family, State and Social Policy*, London: Macmillan.

Hargreaves, A. (1989) 'Decomprehensivisation', in Hargreaves, A. and Reynolds, D. (eds), *Education Policies: Controversies and Critiques*, Lewes: Falmer Press.

Hargreave, D., Hestar, S. and Mellor, F. (1975) *Deviance in Classrooms*, London: Routledge & Kegan Paul.

Hargreaves, D. H. (1967) *Social Relations in a Secondary School*, London: Routledge & Kegan Paul.

Harman, C. (1996) 'Tories steal benefits from low paid', *Socialist Worker*, 23 November.

Harris, D. (1992) *From Class Struggle to the Politics of Pleasure: The Effects of Gramscianism on Cultural Studies*, London: Routledge.

Harris, G. (1989) *The Sociology of Development*, London: Longman.

Harris, L. (1993) 'Postmodernism and Utopia', in Cross, M. and Keith, M. (eds), *Racism, the City and State*, London: Routledge.

Harris, N. (1983) *Of Bread and Guns*, Harmondsworth: Penguin.

Harris, N. (1986) 'Theories of unequal exchange', *International Socialism*, autumn.

Harris, N. (1987) *The End of the Third World*, Harmondsworth: Penguin.

Harris, S. *et al.* (1993) 'School work, home-work and gender', *Gender and Education*, vol. 5, no. 1.

Harris, S. (1994) *Sociology Revise Guide*, London: Longman.

Harrison, P. (1985) *Inside the Inner City: Life Under the Cutting Edge*, Harmondsworth: Penguin.

Harrison, P. (1993) *Inside the Third World*, 3rd edn, Harmondsworth: Penguin.

Harriss, K. (1989) 'New alliances: socialist-feminism in the eighties', *Feminist Review*, no. 31.

Hart, A. (1991) *Understanding the Media: A Practical Guide*, London: Routledge.

Hart, N. (1976) *When Marriage Ends: A Study in Status Passage*, London: Tavistock.

Hart, N. (1985) *The Sociology of Health and Medicine*, Ormskirk: Causeway Press.

Hartley, R. E. (1966) 'A developmental view of female sex-role identification', in Biddle, B. J. and. Thomas, E. J. (eds), *Role Theory*, London: John Wiley.

Hartmann, H. (1981) 'The unhappy marriage of Marxism and feminism: towards a more progressive union', in Sargent, L. (ed.), *The Unhappy Marriage of Marxism and Feminism: A Debate on Class and Patriarchy*, London: Pluto Press.

Hartmann, H. (1982) 'Capitalism, patriarchy and job segregation by sex', in Giddens, A. and Held, D. (eds), *Classes, Power and Conflict*, Basingstoke: Macmillan.

Hartmann, P. and Husband, C. (1974) *Racism and the Mass Media*, London: Davis-Poynter.

Hartmann, P. and Husband, C. (1976) 'The mass media and racial conflict', in Cohen, S. and Young, J. (eds),

The Manufacture of News: Deviance, Social Problems and the Mass Media, London: Constable.

Hartsock, N. (1990) 'Foucault on power: a theory for women?', in Nicholson, L. J. (ed.), *Feminism/Postmodernism*, London: Routledge.

Harvey, D. (1989) *The Condition of Postmodernity*, Oxford: Blackwell.

Harvey, L. (1990) *Critical Social Research*, London: Unwin Hyman.

Harvey, L. and MacDonald, M. (1993) *Doing Sociology: A Practical Introduction*, Basingstoke: Macmillan.

Hay, D., Linebaugh, P., Rule, J. G., Thompson, E. P. and Winslow, C. (1988) *Albion's Fatal Tree: Crime and Society in Eighteenth Century England*, Harmondsworth: Penguin.

Hayek, F. (1944) *The Road to Serfdom*, London: Routledge.

Hayek, F. (1960) *The Constitution of Liberty*, London: Routledge.

Hayter, T. (1971) *Aid As Imperialism*, Harmondsworth: Penguin.

Hayter, T. (1985) 'Introduction', in Hayter, T. and Watson, C. (1985) *Aid: Rhetoric and Reality*, London: Verso.

Hayter, T. and Watson, C. (1985) *Aid: Rhetoric and Reality*, London: Verso.

Hazareesingh, S. (1986) 'Racism and cultural identity: an Indian perspective', *Dragons' Teeth*, no. 24.

Hearn, G. (1987) *The Gender of Oppression: Men, Masculinity and the Critique of Marxism*, London: Pluto Press.

Heath, A. (1981) *Social Mobility*, Glasgow: Fontana.

Heath, A. (1992) 'The attitudes of the underclass', in Smith, D. J. (ed.), *Understanding the Underclass*, London: Policy Studies Institute.

Heath, A., Curtice, J., Jowell, R., Evans, G., Field, J. and Witherspoon, S. (1991) *Understanding Political Change: The British Voter 1964–1987*, Oxford: Pergamon.

Heath, A., Jowell, R. and Curtice, J. (1985) *How Britain Votes*, Oxford: Pergamon.

Heath, A., Jowell, R. and Curtice, J. (with B. Taylor) (eds) (1994) *Labour's Last Chance?*, Aldershot: Dartmouth Publishing.

Hebdidge, D. (1979) *Subculture: The Meaning of Style*, London: Methuen.

Hebdidge, D. (1988) *Hiding in the Light: On Images and Things*, London: Comedia.

Hebdidge, D. (1996) 'The impossible object: towards a sociology of the sublime', in Curran, J. *et al.* (eds), *Cultural Studies and Communications*, London: Arnold.

Heidensohn, F. (1989) *Crime and Society*, Basingstoke: Macmillan.

Heidensohn, F. (1996) *Women and Crime*, 2nd edn, Basingstoke: Macmillan.

Heisler, B. (1991) 'A comparative perspective on the underclass', *Theory and Society*, vol. 20, 455–83.

Held, D. (1987) *Models of Democracy*, Cambridge: Polity Press.

Held, D. (1991) 'Democracy, the nation state and the global system', in Held, D. (ed.), *Political Theory Today*, Cambridge: Polity Press.

Held, D. (1993) 'Democracy: from city-states to a cosmo-politan order?', in Held, D. (ed.), *Prospects for Democracy: North, South, East, West*, Cambridge: Polity Press.

Hencke, D. (1994) 'MP reveals £20m of overseas aid funds went to firms with links to ex-Ministers', *Guardian*, 12 December.

Hencke, D. and Norton-Taylor, R. (1992) 'Taxpayers meet bill for Baghdad forces', *Guardian*, 17 November.

Herberg, W. (1956) *Protestant, Catholic, Jew*, New York: Doubleday.

Heritage, J. (1987) 'Ethnomethodology', in Giddens, A. and Turner, J. (eds), *Social Theory Today*, Cambridge: Polity Press.

Herrnstein, R. and Murray, C. (1994) *The Bell Curve: Intelligence and Class Structure in American Life*, New York: Free Press.

Herskovits, M. J. (1958) *The Myth of the Negro Past*, Boston: Beacon Press.

Herzlich, C. (1973) *Health and Illness*, London: Academic Press.

Hester, S. and Eglin, P. (1996) *A Sociology of Crime*, London: Routledge.

Hetherington, K. (1998) 'Vanloads of uproarious human-ity: New Age travellers and the utopics of the coun-tryside', in Skelton, T. and Valentine, G. (eds), *Cool Places: Geographies of Youth Culture*, London: Routledge.

Hewitt, T., Johnson, H. and Wield, D. (eds) (1992) *Industrialization and Development*, Oxford: Oxford University Press.

Hey, V. (1994) *Elderly People and Community Care*, London: SSRU, Institute of Education, University of London.

Hey, V. (1997) *The Company She Keeps: An Ethnography of Girls' Friendships*, Buckingham: Open University Press.

Hick, D. (1982) 'Colonialism and education: Vietnam', in Watson, K. (ed.), *Education in the Third World*, Beckenham: Croom Helm.

Hicks, C. (1988) *Who Cares: Looking After People At Home*, London: Virago.

Hicks, N. and Streeten, P. (1981) 'Indicators of develop-ment: the search for a basic needs yardstick', in Streeten, P. and Jolly, R. (eds), *Recent Issues in World Development*, Oxford: Pergamon.

Higgins, A. (1997) 'The boom that backfired', *Guardian*, 16 January.

Higginson Committee (1988) *Advancing A levels*, London: HMSO.

Hill, S. (1976) *The Dockers*, London: Heinemann.

Hills, J. (ed.) (1990) *The State of Welfare*, Oxford: Oxford University Press.

Hills, J. (1995) *Inquiry into Income and Wealth*, York: Joseph Rowntree Foundation.

Hills, J. with Gardiner, K. (1997) *The Future of Welfare*, York: Joseph Rowntree Foundation.

Himmelweit, H. T., Humphreys, P. and Jaeger, M. (1985) *How Voters Decide*, Buckingham: Open University Press.

Himmelweit, S. and Costello, N. (1995) 'Work and the economy', in *Society and Social Science: Foundation Course D103*, Buckingham: Open University Press.

Hirschfield, M. (1938) *Racism*, London: Victor Gollancz.

Hirst, P. (1990) *Representative Democracy and its Limits*, Cambridge: Polity Press.

Hirst, P. (1993a) *The Pluralist Theory of the State*, London: Routledge.

Hirst, P. (1993b) 'Globalization is fashionable but is it a myth?', *Guardian*, 22 March.

Hirst, P. and Thompson, G. (1995) 'Globalisation and the future of the nation state', *Economy and Society*, vol. 24, no. 3.

Hirst, P. and Thompson, G. (1996) *Globalisation in Question*, Cambridge: Polity Press.

Hobsbawn, E. J. (1990) *Nations and Nationalism Since 1870: Programme, Myth and Reality*, Cambridge: Cambridge University Press.

Hobson, D. (1989) 'Soap operas at work', in Seiter, E. *et al.* (eds), *Remote Control: Television, Audiences and Cultural Power*, London: Routledge.

Hochschild, A. (1989) *The Second Shift*, New York: Avon.

Hodgson, A. and Spours, K. (1999) 'Curriculum and qualifications reform from 14+: the context for New Labour's approach to qualifications reform', in Hodgson, A. and Spours, K. (eds), *Labour's Educational Agenda*, London: Kogan Page.

Hodkinson, P., Sparkes, A. and Hodkinson, P. H. (1996) *Triumphs and Tears: Young People, Markets and the Transition from School to Work*, London: David Fulton Publishers Ltd.

Hoggart, R. (1958) *The Uses of Literacy*, Harmondsworth: Penguin.

Hoggart, R. (1996) *The Way We Live Now*, London: Pimlico.

Hoggart, R. *et al.* (1995) *Rural Europe: Identity and Change*, London: Arnold.

Holmwood, J. (1996) *Founding Sociology? Talcott Parsons and the Idea of General Theory*, London: Longman.

Holland. J. (1995) *Proposal for Nuffield Research Fellowship*, London: Social Science Research Unit, Institute of Education.

Holton, R. J. and Turner, B. S. (1988) *Talcott Parsons on Economy and Society*, London: Routledge.

hooks, b. (1982) *Ain't I A Woman?: Black Women and Feminism*, Boston: South End Press.

Horne, J. (1987) *Work and Unemployment*, London: Longman.

Horowitz, I. (1968) *Professing Sociology*, Chicago: Aldine.

Horrocks, R. (1992) *Masculinity in Crisis*, Basingstoke: Macmillan.

Hoselitz, B. (ed.) (1960) *The Sociological Aspects of Economic Growth*, New York: Free Press.

Hout, M., Brooks, C. and Manza, J. (1993) 'The persistence of classes in post-industrial societies', *International Sociology*, vol. 8, no. 3.

Howarth, C., Kenway, P., Palmer, G. and Street, C. (1998) Monitoring Poverty and social exclusion: Labour's inheritance, York: JRF.

Howe, D. (1996) 'Black, White and Yellow Journalism', *New Statesman*, 6 September.

Howe, N. (1994) *Advanced Practical Sociology*, Walton-on-Thames: Nelson.

Hughes, J. A., Martin, P. J. and Sharrock, W. W. (1995) *Understanding Classical Sociology: Marx, Weber, Durkheim*, London: Sage.

Humm, M. (ed.) (1992) *Feminisms: A Reader*, Hemel Hempstead: Harvester Wheatsheaf.

Humm, M. (1995) *The Dictionary of Feminist Theory*, Hemel Hempstead: Prentice-Hall/Harvester Wheatsheaf.

Humpheries, J. (1977) 'Class struggle and the persistence of the working class family', *Cambridge Journal of Economics*, vol. 3.

Humphreys, L. (1970) *Tearoom Trade*, London: Duckworth.

Hunt, I. (1999) 'Education now!', *Guardian*, 23 March.

Hunt, L. (1986) *The GLC Women's Committee: A Record of Change and Achievement for Women in London:* London: Greater London Council Women's Committee.

Hunt, S. (1995) 'The "race" and health inequalities debate', *Sociology Review*, vol. 5, no. 1.

Hunter, F. (1953) *Community Power Structure: A Study of Decision Makers*, Chapel Hill: University of North Carolina Press.

Huntington, S. (1968) *Political Order in Changing Societies*, New Haven: Yale University Press.

Hustwitt, M. (1984) 'Rocker boy blues', *Screen*, vol. 25, no. 3.

Hutson, S. and Liddiard, M. (1994) *Youth Homelessness: The Construction of a Social Issue*, Basingstoke: Macmillan.

Hutton, W. (1987) 'Thinking aloud', Channel 4, 12 November.

Hutton, W. (1995) 'Is there a new underclass in British society?', Benjamin Meaker Lecture, University of Bristol, February.

Hutton, W. (1996) *The State We're In*, London: Vintage.

Hyden, G. (1983) *No Shortcut to Progress*, London: Heinemann.

Ignatieff, M. (1995) 'The ideological origins of the penitentiary', in Fitzgerald, M., McLennan, G. and Pawson, J. (eds), *Crime and Society: Readings in History and Theory*, London: Routledge.

Illich, I. (1990) *Limits to Medicine – Medical Nemesis: The Expropriation of Health*, Harmondsworth: Penguin.

Illsley, R. (1986) 'Occupational class, selection and the production of inequalities in health', *Quarterly Journal of Social Affairs*, vol. 2, no. 2.

IMF (1998) *World Economic Outlook*, Washington, DC: IMF (December).

Independent Television Commission (1999) *ITC Annual Report and Accounts*, London: ITC.

Inglehart, R. (1990) 'Values, ideology and cognitive mobilization in new social movements', in Dalton, R. J. and Kuechler, M. (eds), *Challenging the Political Order*, Cambridge: Polity Press.

Ingleheart, I. (1971) 'The silent revolution in Europe: intergenerational change in post-industrial societies', *American Political Science Review*, pp. 991–1017.

Irwin, J. (1970) *The Felon*, Englewood Cliffs, NJ: Prentice-Hall.

ITEM (1995) *The Third World Guide 1994/95*, Montivideo: Instituto del Tercer Mundo (ITEM).

IT Online (1999) 'North-south divide widens', 3 December.

Itzin, C. and Phillipson, C. (1993) *Age Barriers at Work: Maximising the Potential of Mature and Older People*, Solihull: METRA.

Jackson, B. (1968) *Working Class Community: Some General Notions Raised by a Series of Studies in Northern England*, Harmondsworth: Penguin.

Jackson, B. (1994) *Poverty and the Planet: A Question of Survival*, Harmondsworth: Penguin.

Jackson, P. (1992) 'The dark side of LA', *Politics Review*, vol. 2, no. 1.

Jacobs, B. (1988) *Racism in Britain*, Cambridge: Cambridge University Press.

Jahoda, M. (1958) *Current Concepts of Positive Mental Health*, New York: Basic Books.

Jahoda, M., Lazersfeld, P. and Zeisel, H. (1972) *Marienthal: The Sociography of an Unemployed Community*, London: Tavistock.

James, C. L. R. (1963) *The Black Jacobins: Toussaint L'Overture and the San Domingo Revolution*, New York: Vintage.

James, S. and Busia, A. (eds) (1993) *Theorising Black Feminisms: The Visionary Pragmatism of Black Women*, London: Routledge.

James, W. (1993) 'Migration, racism and identity', in James, W. and Harris, C. (eds), *Inside Babylon: The Caribbean and the Black Diaspora*, London: Verso.

Jameson, F. (1991) *Postmodernism*, London: Verso.

Jamrozik, A., Hoey, M. and Leeds, M. (1981) *Employment Benefits: Private or Public?*, Sydney: Social Welfare Research Centre.

Janowitz, M. (1979) 'Collective racial violence: a contemporary history', in Graham, H. D. and Gurr, T. R. (eds), *Violence in America: Historical and Comparative Perspectives*, New York: Bantam.

Jardine, A. (1985) *Gynesis: Configurations of Women and Modernity*, London: Cornell University Press.

Jary, D. and Jary, J. (1991) *Collins Dictionary of Sociology*, London: HarperCollins.

Jeffs, T. and Smith, M. (1998) 'Youth', in Haralambos, M. (ed) *Developments in Sociology*, vol. 14, Ormskirk: Causeway Press.

Jeffs, T. and Smith, M. (1999) 'The problem of youth for youth work', *Youth and Policy*, no. 62, winter.

Jencks, C. (1996) 'The city that never sleeps', *New Statesman and Society*, 28 June.

Jenkins, J. (1991) 'Passions of crime', *New Statesman and Society*, 17 May.

Jenkins, R. (1992) 'Theoretical perspectives', in Hewitt, T., Johnson, H. and Wield, D. (eds), *Industrialization and Development*, Oxford: Oxford University Press.

Jenkins, R. (1994a) 'Capitalist Development in the NICs', in Sklair, L. (ed.), *Capitalism and Development*, London: Routledge.

Jenkins, R. (1994b) 'Rethinking ethnicity: identity, categorization and power', *Ethnic and Racial Studies*, vol. 17, no. 2.

Jenks, C. (1993) *Culture*, London: Routledge.

Jensen, A. R. (1969) 'How much can we boost IQ?', *The Harvard Educational Review*, 1969.

Jesson, D., Gray, J. and Tranmer, M. (1992) *GCSE Performance in Nottinghamshire 1991: Pupil and School Factors*, Nottinghamshire County Council Education, Advisory and Inspection Service.

Jessop, B. (1994) 'The transition to post-Fordism and the Schumpeterian workfare state', in Burrows, R. and Loader, B. (eds), *Towards a Post-Fordist Welfare State*, London: Routledge.

Jewson, N. (1976) 'The disappearance of the sick man from medical cosmology 1770–1870', *Sociology*, vol. 10, no. 2.

Jewson, N. (1990) 'Inner city riots', *Social Studies Review*, vol. 5, no. 5.

Jewson, N. (1994) 'Family values and relationships', *Sociology Review*, vol. 3, no. 3.

Johnson, P. and Webb, S. (1990) *Counting People with Low Incomes*, London: Institute for Fiscal Studies.

Johnson, R. (1979) 'Really useful knowledge', in Clarke, J. *et al.* (eds), *Working Class Culture*, London: Hutchinson.

Johnson, T. J. (1972) *Professions and Power*, Basingstoke: Macmillan.

Johnson, T., Dandeker, C. and Ashworth, C. (1984) *The Structure of Social Theory*, London: Macmillan.

Johnston, P. (1999) 'Sometimes it's hard to be a new man in Rochdale', *Daily Telegraph*, 16 June.

Johnson, P., Conrad, C. and Thomson, D. (eds) (1989) *Workers Versus Pensioners: Intergenerational Justice in an Ageing World*, Manchester: Manchester University Press.

Jones, A. (1993a) 'Becoming a "girl": post-structuralist suggestions for educational research', *Gender and Education*, vol. 5, no. 2.

Jones, L. and Moore, R. (1993) 'Education, competence and the control of expertise', *British Journal of Sociology of Education*, vol. 14.

Jones, P. (1997) 'Post-modernism', in Barter, J., Gomm R. and Madry, N. (eds), *The Best of Social Science Teacher*, London: ATSS.*

Jones, P. (1993b) *Studying Society: Sociological Theories and Research Practices*, London: Collins Educational.

Jones, S. (1991) 'We are all cousins under the skin', *Independent*, 12 December.

Jordan, W. D. (1974) *The White Man's Burden*, Oxford: Oxford University Press.

Jorgensen, N. (1995) *Investigating Families and Households*, London: Collins Educational.

Jorgensen, N. (1996) 'Coming to terms with the family?', *Sociology Review*, vol. 5, no. 3.

Joseph Rowntree Foundation (1998) 'Monitoring poverty and social exclusion', *Findings* D48, York: JRF.

Jowell, R., Brook, L., Prior, G. and Taylor, B. (eds) (1992) *British Social Attitudes* (9th report, 1991), Aldershot: SCPR.

Jowell, R., Curtice, J., Brook, L. and Ahrendt, D. (1995) *British Social Attitudes* (11th report, 1994–95), Aldershot: SCPR.

Joyce, P. (ed.) (1995) *Class*, Oxford: Oxford University Press.

Kamata, S. (1984) *Japan in the Passing Lane*, London: Unwin.

Kamin, L. (1974) *The Science and Politics of IQ*, New York: John Wiley.

Kaplan, E. A. (1987) *Rocking Around the Clock: Music Television, Postmodernism and Consumer Culture*, London: Methuen.

Kaplan, G. (1992) *Contemporary Western European Feminism*, New York: NY University Press.

Karabel, J. and Halsey, A. H. (1977) *Power and Ideology in Education*, Oxford: Oxford University Press.

Karpf, A. (1988) *Doctoring the Media: The Reporting of Health and Medicine*, London: Routledge.

Kasinitz, P. (1995) *Metropolis: Centre and Symbol of Our Times*, Basingstoke: Macmillan.

Kasler, D. (1988) *Max Weber: An Introduction to His Life and Work*, Oxford: Polity Press.

Kearney, M. C. (1998) '"Don't need you": rethinking identity politics and separatism from a grrrl perspective', in Epstein, J. S. (ed.), *Youth Culture in a Postmodern World*, Oxford: Blackwell Publishers.

Kearney, R. (1993) *Modern Movements in European Philosophy*, Manchester: Manchester University Press.

Keat, R. and Urry, J. (1975) *Social Theory as Science*, London: Routledge & Kegan Paul.

Keddie, N. (ed.) (1973) *Tinker, Tailor: The Myth of Cultural Deprivation*, Harmondsworth: Penguin.

Kellner, D. (1989) *Jean Baudrillard: From Marxism to Post-Modernism and Beyond*, Cambridge: Polity Press.

Kelly, E. (1988) *Surviving Sexual Violence*, Cambridge: Polity Press.

Kelly, G. (1995) 'Off-the-self sociology', *Times Higher Educational Supplement*, 24 March.

Kennedy, J. and Lavalette, M. (1996) *Solidarity on the Waterfront: The Liverpool Docks' Lock-out*, Liverpool: Liver Press.

Kerr, C., Dunlop, J., Harbison, F. and Myers, C. (1973) *Industrialism and Industrial Man*, Harmondsworth: Penguin (orig. pub. 1960).

Key Data 95 (1995) London: HMSO.

Keynes, J. M. (1936) *The General Theory of Employment, Interest and Money*, Basingstoke: Macmillan.

Kidd, W. *et al.* (1998) *Readings in Sociology*, Oxford: Heinemann Educational.

Kidd, W. (1999) 'Family diversity in an uncertain future', *Sociology Review*, vol 9, no 1.

Kidron, M. (1975) *Capitalism and Theory*, London: Pluto Press.

Kiely, R. (1995) *Sociology and Development: The Impasse and Beyond*, London: UCL Press.

Kiernan, K. (1992) 'The impact of family disruptions in childhood on the transitions made in adult life', *Population Studies*, vol. 46.

Kilminster, R. (1992) 'Theory', in Haralambos, M. (ed.), *Developments in Sociology*, vol. 8, Ormskirk: Causeway Press.

Kimmel, A. (1988) *Ethics and Values in Applied Social Research*, London: Sage.

Kingdom, J. (1992) *No Such Thing as Society?* Buckingham: Open University Press.

Kirby, M. (1995) *Investigating Political Sociology*, London: Collins Educational.

Kirby, M. (1999a) *Stratification and Differentiation*, London: Macmillan.

Kirby, M. (1999b) 'New approaches to social inequality', *Sociology Review*, February.

Kirby, M. (1999c) 'Structure and agency in the wake of the time and space of Diana', *Social Science Teacher*, vol. 28, no. 2.

Kirby, M., Madry, N. and Koubel, F. (1993) *Sociology: Developing Skills Through Structured Questions*, London: Collins Educational.

Kirton, D. (1999) 'The care and protection of children', in Baldock, J., Manning, N., Miller, S. and Vickerstaff, S. (eds), *Social Policy*, Oxford: Oxford University Press.

Kitching, G. (1989) *Development and Underdevelopment in Historical Perspective*, London: Routledge.

Knapp, M. (1989) 'Private and voluntary welfare', in McCarthy, M. (ed.), *The New Politics of Welfare*, Basingstoke: Macmillan.

Knott, J. (1986) *Popular Opposition to the 1834 Poor Law*, London: Croom Helm.

Knowles, C. and Mercer, S. (1992) 'Feminism and antiracism: an exploration of the political possibilities', in Donald, J. and Rattansi, A. (eds), *'Race', Culture and Difference*, London: Sage.

Kohn, M. (1995) *The Race Gallery*, London: Jonathan Cape.

Kruse, A. M. (1992) ' "We have learnt not just to sit back, twiddle our thumbs, and let them take over": single-sex settings and the development of a pedagogy for girls and a pedagogy for boys in Danish schools', *Gender and Education*, vol. 4, no. 1.

Kübler-Ross, E. (1970) *On Death and Dying*, London: Tavistock.

Kuhn, T. (1970) *The Structure of Scientific Revolutions*, 2nd edn, Chicago: University of Chicago Press.

Kuhn, T. (1974) 'Logic of discovery or psychology of truth?', in Schilpp, P. A. (ed.), *The Philosophy of Karl Popper*, La Salle, IL: Open Court.

Kumar, K. (1978) *Prophecy and Progress*, Harmondsworth: Penguin.

Kumar, K. (1986) *Prophecy and Progress: The Sociology of Industrial and Post-Industrial Society*, Harmondsworth: Penguin.

Kumar, K. (1995) *From Post-Industrial to Post-Modern Society*, Oxford: Blackwell.

Kuper, A. and Kuper, J. (1989) *The Social Science Encyclopedia*, London: Routledge.

Kuzmics, H. (1988) 'The civilising process', in Keane, J. (ed.), *Civil Society and the State*, London: Verso.

Labour Party (1996) *Aiming Higher: Labour's Proposals for the Reform of the 14–19 Curriculum*, London.

Labov, W. (1973) 'The logic of nonstandard English', in Keddie, N. (ed.), *Tinker, Tailor: The Myth of Cultural Deprivation*, Harmondsworth: Penguin.

Lacan, J. (1977) *Ecrits: A Selection*, London: Tavistock.

Lacey, C. (1970) *Hightown Grammar: The School as a Social System*, Manchester: Manchester University Press.

Laclau, E. (1971) 'Feudalism and capitalism in Latin America', *New Left Review*, vol. 67.

Laing, R. D. and Esterson, A. (1964) *Sanity, Madness and the Family*, Harmondsworth: Penguin.

Laing, R. D. and Esterson, A. (1970) *Sanity, Madness and the Family*, new edn, Harmondsworth: Penguin.

Lakatos, I. (1975) *Philosophical Papers*, 2 vols, Cambridge: Cambridge University Press.

Lal, B. (1988) 'The "Chicago School" of American sociology, symbolic interactionism, and race relations theory', in Rex, J. and Mason, D. (eds), *Theories of Race and Ethnic Relations*, Cambridge: Cambridge University Press.

Lal, D. (1983) *The Poverty of 'Development Economics'*, London: IEA.

Land, H. (1991) 'The confused boundaries of social care', in Gabe, J., Calnan, M. and Bury, M. (eds), *The Sociology of the Health Service*, London: Routledge.

Land, H. (1995) 'Families and the law', in Muncie, J., Wetherell, M., Dallos, R. and Cochrane, A. (eds), *Understanding the Family*, London: Sage.

Lane, P. (1979) *British Social and Economic History*, Oxford: Oxford University Press.

Langley, P. and Corrigan, P. (1993) *Managing Sociology Coursework*, Lewes: Connect.

Lappé, F. M. (1975) *Diet for a Small Planet*, New York: Ballantine Books.

Lappé, F. M. and Collins, J. (1980) *Food First: The Myth of Scarcity*, London: Souvenir Press.

Lash, S. (1990) *The Sociology of Postmodernism*, London: Routledge.

Lash, S. and Urry, J. (1987) *The End of Organised Capitalism*, Cambridge: Polity Press.

Lash, S. and Urry, J. (1994) *Economies of Signs and Space*, London: Sage.

Laslett, P. and Wall, R. (eds) (1972) *Household and Family in Past Time*, Cambridge: Cambridge University Press.

Lather, P. (1991) *Getting Smart: Feminist Research and Pedagogy with/in the Postmodern*, London: Routledge.

Laurance, J. (1999) 'Preventable deaths grow as health gap widens', *Independent*, 2 December.

Lawler, J. (1991) *Behind the Screens: Nursing, Somology and the Problem of the Body*, London: Churchill Livingstone.

Lawson. T. (1986) 'In the shadow of science', *Social Studies Review*, vol. 2, no. 2.

Lawson, T. (1993a) 'Question and answer special: action planning your revision', *Sociology Review*, vol. 4, no. 2.

Lawson, T. (1993b) *Sociology for A Level: A Skills-Based Approach*, London: Collins Educational.

Lawson, T. and Garrod, J. (1996) *The Complete A–Z Sociology Handbook*, London: Hodder & Stoughton.

Layard, R. and Nickell, S. (1986) *How to Beat Unemployment*, Oxford: Oxford University Press.

Layder, D. (1994) *Understanding Social Theory*, London: Sage.

Lazersfeld, P., Berelson, B. and Gaudet, H. (1944) *The People's Choice*, New York: Columbia University Press.

Lea, J. and Young, J. (1993) *What is to be Done about Law and Order? Crisis in the Nineties*, London: Pluto Press.

Le Bon, G. (1913) *The Psychology of Revolution*, New York: Putnams.

Le Bon, G. (1960) *The Crowd*, New York: Viking.

Lechner, F. (1990) 'Fundamentalism revisited', in Robbins, T. and Anthony, D. (eds), *In Gods We Trust*, New Brunswick: Transaction.

Leder, D. (ed.) (1992) *The Body in Medical Thought and Practice*, London: Kluwer Academic.

Lee, D. (1990) *Scheming for Youth*, Buckingham: Open University Press.

Lee, D. and Newby, H. (1983) *The Problem of Sociology*, London: Hutchinson.

Lee, D. and Turner, B. (eds) (1996) *Conflicts About Class*, Harlow: Longman.

Lees, C. and Hindle, S. (1995) 'Scandal of football's child slavery', *Sunday Times*, 14 May.

Lees, S. (1986) *Losing Out: Sexuality and Adolescent Girls*, London: Hutchinson.

Legge, K. and Kirby, M. (1999) 'The fall of neo-liberal development theory: causes and consequences', in Haralambos, M. (ed.), *Developments in Sociology*, vol. 15, Ormskirk: Causeway Press.

Le Grand, J. (1982) *The Strategy of Equality*, London: Allen & Unwin.

Le Grand, J. (1990) 'The state of welfare', in Hills, J. (ed.), *The State of Welfare: The Welfare State in Britain Since 1974*, Oxford: Oxford University Press.

Le Grand, J. (1996) 'Knights, knaves or pawns? Human behaviour and social policy', unpublished paper quoted in Whitty, G. (1997) 'Marketization, the State and the re-formation of the teaching profession', in Halsey, A. H., Lauder, H., Brown, P. and Wells, A. S. (eds), *Education: Culture, Economy, Society*, Oxford: Oxford University Press.

Le Grand, J. and Winter, D. (1987) *The Middle Classes and the Welfare State*, London: LSE.

Le Grand, J., Winter, D. and Woolley, F. (1990) 'The National Health Service: safe in whose hands?', in Hills, J. (ed.), *The State of Welfare: The Welfare State in Britain Since 1974*, Oxford: Oxford University Press.

Lemert, E. M. (1989a) 'Primary and Secondary Deviation', in Kelly, D. H. (ed.), *Deviant Behaviour: A Text-Reader in the Sociology of Deviance*, 3rd edn, New York: St Martin's Press.

Lemert, E. M. (1989b) 'Paranoia and the dynamics of exclusion', in Kelly, D. H. (ed.), *Deviant Behaviour: A Text-Reader in the Sociology of Deviance*, 3rd edn, New York: St Martin's Press.

Leonard, D. and Hood-Williams, J. (eds) (1988) *Families*, Walton-on-Thames: Nelson.

Leonard, E. (1982) *Women, Crime and Society*, New York: Longman.

Leonard, M. (1995) 'Masculinity, femininity and crime', *Sociology Review*, vol. 5, no. 1.

Lévi-Strauss, C. (1963) *Structural Anthropology*, New York: Basic Books.

Lévi-Strauss, C. (1989) *The Savage Mind*, London: Weidenfeld & Nicholson (orig. pub. 1962).

Levitas, R. (1996) 'The concept of social exclusion and the new Durkheimian hegemony', *Critical Social Policy*, vol. 46, February.

Lewis, J. (1991) *Women, Family, Work and the State Since 1945*, Oxford: Blackwell.

Lewis, J. and Piachard, D. (1992) 'Women and poverty in the twentieth century', in Glendinning, C. and Millar, J. (eds), *Women and Poverty in Britain: The 1990s*, Hemel Hempstead: Harvester Wheatsheaf.

Lewis, O. (1950) *Five Families*, New York: Basic Books.

Lewis, O. (1951) *Life in a Mexican Village*, Illinois: Illinois University Press.

Lewis, O. (1961) *The Children of Sanchez*, New York: Random House.

Lewis, O. (1968) *La Vida*, Harmondsworth: Penguin.

Lewis, R. (1988) *Anti-Racism: A Mania Exposed*, London: Quartet Books.

Leys, C. (1996) *The Rise and Fall of Development Theory*, London: James Currey.

Liddington, J. and Norris, J. (1978) *One Hand Tied Behind Us*, London: Virago.

Liebow, E. (1967) *Tally's Corner*, Boston: Little Brown.

Lipietz, A. (1987) *Mirages and Miracles: The Crisis of Global Fordism*, London: Verso.

Lister, R. (1989) 'Social security', in McCarthy, M. (eds) *The New Politics of Welfare*, London: Macmillan.

Lister, R. (1990) *The Exclusive Society: Citizenship and the Poor*, London: Child Poverty Action Group.

Lister, R. (1991) 'Concepts of poverty', *Social Studies Review*, vol. 6, no. 5.

Lister, R. (1998) 'From equality to social inclusion: new Labour and the welfare state', *Critical Social Policy*, vol. 18, no. 2.

Little, I. (1981) 'The experience and causes of rapid labour-intensive development in Korea, Taiwan province, Hong Kong and Singapore, and the possibilities of emulation', in Lee, E. (ed.), *Export-Led Industrialisation and Development*, Bangkok: ILO.

Lloyd, C. (1993) 'Universalism and difference: the crisis of anti-racism in Britain and France', in Rattansi, A. and Westwood, S. (eds), *Racism, Modernity, Identity*, Cambridge: Polity Press.

Lloyds Bank (1995) *Economic Bulletin*, London, February.

Lockwood, D. (1964) 'Social integration and system integration', in Zollschan, G. K. and Hirsch, W. (eds), *Explorations in Social Change*, London: Routledge & Kegan Paul.

Lockwood, D. (1981) 'The weakest link in the chain?', in Simpson, S. and Simpson, I. (eds), *Research in the Sociology of Work*, Greenwich, CT: JAI Press. Reprinted in Rose, D. (ed.) (1988) *Social Stratification and Economic Change*, London: Hutchinson.

Lockwood, D. (1989) *The Black Coated Worker*, 2nd edn, Oxford: Oxford University Press (orig. pub. 1958).

Lockwood, D. (1992) *Solidarity and Schism*, Oxford: Clarendon Press.

Lombroso, C. (1876) *L'Uomo Delinquente*, Milano: Hoepli.

London Docklands Development Corporation (1994) *Attitudes to London Docklands: A Survey of Local Residents,* London: LDDC.

Loney, M., Bocock, R., Clarke, J., Cochrane, A., Graham, P. and Wilson, M. (eds) (1991) *The State or the Market*, London: Sage.

Long, N. and Van den Ploeg, J. (1991) 'Heterogeneity, actor and structure: towards a reconstitution of the concept of structure'. Unpublished paper quoted in Booth (1993).

Lonsdale, S. (1990) *Women and Disability: The Experiences of Physical Disability among Women*, Basingstoke: Macmillan.

Lovell, T. (ed.) (1990) *British Feminist Thought: A Reader*, Oxford: Blackwell.

Lovenduski, J. and Randall, V. (1993) *Contemporary Feminist Politics: Women and Power in Britain*, Oxford: Oxford University Press.

Lovibond, S. (1990) 'Feminism and postmodernism', in Boyne, R. and Rattansi, A. (eds), *Postmodernism and Society*, Basingstoke: Macmillan.

Lowe, R. (1993) *The Welfare State in Britain Since 1945*, Basingstoke: Macmillan.

Lowe, S. (1986) 'Urban social movements: the city after Castells', in O'Donnell, M. (ed.), *New Introductory Reader in Sociology*, Walton-on-Thames: Nelson.

Luckmann, T. (1967) *The Invisible Religion: The Transformation of Symbols in Industrial Society*, Basingstoke: Macmillan.

Luckmann, T. (1996) 'The privatization of religion and morality', in Heelas, P., Lash, S. and Morris, P. (eds), *Detraditionalization: Critical Reflections on Authority and Identity*, Oxford: Blackwell.

Luhmann, N. (1982) *The Differentiation of Society*, New York: Columbia University Press.

Lukács, G. (1971) *History and Class Consciousness*, London: Merlin (orig. pub. 1923).

Lukes, S. (1973) *Emile Durkheim: His Life and Work*, Harmondsworth: Penguin.

Lukes, S. (1974) *Power: A Radical View*, Basingstoke: Macmillan.

Lukes, S. (1984) 'The future of British socialism?', in Pimlott, B. (ed.), *Fabian Essays in Socialist Thought*, London: Heinemann.

Lull, J. (ed.) (1987) *Popular Music and Communication*, London: Sage.

Lull, J. (1995) *Media Communication Culture*, Cambridge: Polity Press.

Lunt, I. and Evans, J. (1994) 'Dilemmas in special educational needs: some effects of local management of schools', in Riddell, S. and Brown, S. (1994) *Special Educational Needs Policy in the 1990's: Warnock and the Market Place*, London: Routledge.

Lyon, D. (1993) 'An electronic panoptican? A sociological critique of surveillance theory', *Sociological Review*, vol. 41, no. 4.

Lyon, D. (1994) *Postmodernity*, Buckingham: Open University Press.

Lyon, M. and West, B. (1995) 'London Patels', *New Community*, vol. 21, no. 3.

Lyotard, F. (1993) 'Answering the question: what is postmodernism?', in Doherty, T. (ed.), *Postmodernism: A Reader*, Hemel Hempstead: Harvester Wheatsheaf.

Lyotard, J. (1984) *The Postmodern Condition: A Report on Knowledge*, 2nd edn, Manchester: Manchester University Press (orig. French edn 1979).

Mac an Ghaill, M. (1988) *Young, Gifted and Black: Student–Teacher Relations in the Schooling of Black Youth*, Buckingham: Open University Press.

Mac an Ghaill, M. (1991) 'Black voluntary schools: the "invisible private sector"', in Walford, G. (ed.), *Private Schooling: Tradition, Change and Diversity*, London: Paul Chapman Publishing.

Mac an Ghaill, M. (1994) *The Making of Men: Masculinities, Sexualities and Schooling*, Buckingham: Open University Press.

MacDonald, D. (1957) 'A theory of mass culture', in Rosenberg, B. and Manning White, D. (eds), *Mass Culture: The Popular Arts in America*, Basingstoke: Macmillan.

Macdonald, I., Bhavani, R., Khan, L. and John, G. (1989) *Murder in the Playground: The Burnage Report*, London: Longsight Press.

Macionis, J. J. and Plummer, K. (1997) *Sociology: A Global Introduction*, New Jersey: Prentice Hall.

MacKinnon, M. H. (1994) 'The longevity of the thesis: a critique of the critics', in Lehman, H. and Roth, G. (eds), *Weber's Protestant Ethic: Origins, Evidence, Contexts*, Cambridge: Cambridge University Press.

Macpherson Report (1999) London: HMSO.

McAllister, F. (ed.) (1995) *Marital Breakdown and the Health of the Nation*, 2nd edn, One plus One – The Marriage and Partnership Charity.

McCarthy, M. (ed.) (1989) *The New Politics of Welfare*, Basingstoke: Macmillan.

McClelland, D. (1961) *The Achieving Society*, New York: Van Nostrand.

McCracken, E. (1993) *Decoding Women's Magazines: From Mademoiselle to Ms*, Basingstoke: Macmillan.

McDonnell (1990) 'The beginning and end of social class', *Social Science Teacher*, vol. 20, no. 1.*

McGrew, A. (1992) 'A global society?', in Hall, S. *et al.* (eds), *Modernity and Its Futures*, Cambridge: Polity Press.

McGuigan, J. (1992) *Cultural Populism*, London: Routledge.

McInnes, J. (1972) *The Western Marxists*, London: Alcove Press.

McInnes, J. (1987) *Thatcherism at Work*, Buckingham: Open University Press.

McKeown, T. (1979) *The Role of Medicine: Dream, Mirage or Nemesis*, Oxford: Blackwell.

McKinley, J. (1977) 'The business of good doctoring or doctoring as good business: reflections on Friedson's view of the medical game', *International Journal of Health Services*, vol. 17, no. 3.

McLuhan, M. (1964) *Understanding Media*, London: Routledge.

McNeill, P. (1985) *Research Methods*, London: Tavistock.

McNeill, P. (1990) *Research Methods*, 2nd edn, London: Routledge.

McQuail, D. (1983) *Mass Communication Theory: An Introduction*, London: Sage.

McQuail, D. and Windahl, S. (1993) *Communication Models*, 2nd edn, New York: Longman.

McRae, S. (1993) *Cohabiting Mothers*, London: Policy Studies Institute.

McRobbie, A. (1978) 'Working class girls and the culture of femininity', in *Women Take Issue: Aspects of Women's Subordination*, Birmingham: Women's Study Group/Centre for Contemporary Cultural Studies.

McRobbie, A. (1983) 'Teenage girls, *Jackie* and the ideology of adolescent femininity', in Waites, B., Bennett, T. and Martin, G. (eds), *Popular Culture: Past and Present*, London: Croom Helm.

McRobbie, A. (1991a) 'Settling accounts with youth sub-cultures', in McRobbie, A., *Feminism and Youth Cultures*, Basingstoke: Macmillan.

McRobbie, A. (1991b) *Feminism and Youth Cultures*, Basingstoke: Macmillan.

McRobbie, A. (1994) *Postmodernism and Popular Culture*, London: Routledge.

Mack, S. and Lansley, J. (1985) *Poor Britain*, London: George Allen & Unwin.

Mack, S. and Lansley, J. (1992) *Breadline Britain*, London: LWT.

Madry, N. and Kirby, M. (1996) *Investigating Work, Unemployment and Leisure*, London: Collins Educational.

Maffesoli, M. (1996) *The Time of the Tribes: The Decline of Individualism in Mass Society*, London: Sage.

Mahmood, S. (1996) 'Cultural studies and ethnic abso-lutism: comments on Stuart Hall's "Culture, Community, Nation"', *Cultural Studies*, vol. 10, no. 1.

Mair, A. (1994) *Honda's Local Global Corporation*, Basingstoke: Macmillan.

Malinowski, B. (1954) *Magic, Science and Religion and Other Essays*, New York: Anchor Books.

Malthus, T. H. (1986) *Essay on the Principle of Population*, Harmondsworth: Penguin (orig. pub. 1798).

Mama, A. (1989) 'Violence against black women: gender, race and state responses', *Feminist Review*, no. 32.

Mama, A. (1992) 'Black women and the British state: race, class and gender analysis for the 1990s', in Braham, P., Rattansi, A. and Skellington, R. (eds), *Racism and Antiracism: Inequalities, Opportunities and Policies*, London: Sage/Open University Press.

Mann, K. (1995) 'Work, dependency and the underclass', in Haralambos, M. (ed.), *Developments in Sociology*, vol. 11, Ormskirk: Causeway Press.

Mann, M. (1973) *Consciousness and Action Among the Western Working Class*, Basingstoke: Macmillan.

Mann, M. (1986) *The Sources of Social Power*, vol. 1, Cambridge: Cambridge University Press.

Mann, M. (1988) *States, Wars and Capitalism*, Oxford: Blackwell.

Mann, M. (1993) *The Sources of Social Power*, vol. 2, Cambridge: Cambridge University Press.

Mann, N. (1995) 'Britain "second among equals"', *New Statesman and Society*, 10 February.

Mannheim, K. (1960) *Ideology and Utopia: An Introduction to the Sociology of Knowledge*, London: Routledge.

Manning, P. (1993) 'Consumption, production and popu-lar culture', *Sociology Review*, vol. 2, no. 3.

Manning White, D. (1957) 'Mass culture in America: another point of view', in Rosenberg, B. and Manning White, D. (eds), *Mass Culture: The Popular Arts in America*, Basingstoke: Macmillan.

Mansfield, P. and Collard, J. (1988) *The Beginning of the Rest of Your Life*, Basingstoke: Macmillan.

March, J. G. and Simon, H. A. (1958) *Organizations*, New York: Wiley.

Marcuse, H. (1955) *Reason and Revolution*, new edn, London: Routledge & Kegan Paul (orig. pub. 1941).

Marcuse, H. (1964) *One-Dimensional Man*, London: Routledge & Kegan Paul.

Mares, P., Larbie, J. and Baxter, C. (1987) *Training in Multi-Racial Health Care*, Cambridge: National Extension College.

Marks, J. (1991) *An Appraisal of the Assisted Places Scheme*, London: Independent Schools Information Service.

Markham, F. (ed.) (1952) *Henri Comte de Saint-Simon: Selected Writings*, Oxford: Blackwell.

Marmot, M. G., Shipley, M. J. and Rose, G. (1984a) 'Inequalities in death: specific explanations of a gen-eral pattern', *The Lancet*, vol. i, 1003–6.

Marmot, M. G., Adelstein, A. M. and Bulusu, L. (1984b) *Immigrant Mortality in England and Wales, 1970–78*, OPCS Studies on Medical and Population Subjects, no. 47 (HMSO).

Marsh, D. (1983) 'Introduction – Interest groups in Britain: their access and power', in Marsh, D. (ed.), *Pressure Politics: Interest Groups in Britain*, London: Junction Books.

Marsh, I., Keating, M., Eyre, A., Campbell, R. and McKenzie, J. (1996) *Making Sense of Society: An Introduction to Sociology*, Harlow: Longman.

Marshall, G. (1987) 'What is happening to the working class?' *Social Studies Review*, vol. 2, no. 3.

Marshall, G. (ed.) (1994) *Concise Oxford Dictionary of Sociology*, Oxford: Oxford University Press.

Marshall, G. and Swift, A. (1993) 'Social class and social justice', *British Journal of Sociology*, June.

Marshall, G., Newby, H., Rose, D. and Vogler, C. (1988) *Social Class in Modern Britain*, London: Hutchinson.

Marshall, T. H. (1963) 'Citizenship and social class', in Marshall, T. H. (ed.), *Sociology at the Crossroads*, London: Heinemann.

Marshall, T. H. (1977) *Class, Citizenship and Social Development*, Chicago: University of Chicago Press.

Marsland, D. (1992) 'The roots and consequences of col-lectivist paternalism', *Social Policy and Administration*, vol. 26, no. 2.

Marsland, D. (1996) *Welfare or Welfare State?*, Basingstoke: Macmillan.

Martin, D. (1978) *A General Theory of Secularization*, Oxford: Blackwell.

Martin, D. (1990) *Tongues of Fire*, Oxford: Blackwell.

Martin, D. (1991) 'The secularization issue: prospect and retrospect', *British Journal of Sociology*, vol. 42, no. 3.

Martin, E. (1989) *The Woman in the Body: A Cultural Analysis of Reproduction*, Buckingham: Open University Press.

Martin, J. and Roberts, C. (1984) *Women and Employment: A Lifetime Perspective*, London: HMSO.

Marx, K. (1954) *Capital*, vol. 1, London: Lawrence & Wishart (orig. pub. 1867).

Marx, K. (1956) *Capital*, vol. 2, London: Lawrence & Wishart (orig. pub. 1885).

Marx, K. (1959) *Capital*, vol. 3, London: Lawrence & Wishart (orig. pub. 1894).

Marx, K. (1968) 'The Eighteenth Brumaire of Louis Bonaparte', in Marx, K. and Engels, F., *Selected Works*, Moscow: Progress Publishers (orig. pub. 1852).

Marx, K. (1969) 'The Eighteenth Brumaire of Louis Bonaparte', in Feuer, L. (ed.), *Marx and Engels: Selected Writings*, London: Collins Fontana (orig. pub. 1852).

Marx, K. (1973) *Grundrisse*, Harmondsworth: Penguin (orig. pub. 1939).

Marx, K. (1984a) 'Excerpts from "The Eighteenth Brumaire of Louis Bonaparte"', in Feuer, L. S. (ed.), *Marx and Engels: Basic Writings on Politics and Philosophy*, Aylesbury: Fontana (orig. pub. 1852).

Marx, K. (1984b) 'Excerpt from "Toward the critique of Hegel's philosophy of right"', in Feuer, L. S. (ed.), *Marx and Engels: Basic Writings on Politics and Philosophy*, Aylesbury: Fontana (orig. pub. 1844).

Marx, K. and Engels, F. (1977) *The German Ideology*, (edited by C. J. Arthur), London: Lawrence & Wishart (orig. written 1845).

Marx, K. and Engels, F. (1967) *The Communist Manifesto*, Harmondsworth: Penguin (orig. pub. 1848).

Marx, K. and Engels, F. (1968) 'Manifesto of the Communist Party', in Marx, K. and Engels, F., *Selected Works*, Moscow: Progress Publishers (orig. pub. 1848).

Mason, D. (1995) *Race and Ethnicity in Modern Britain*, Oxford: Oxford University Press.

Matthews, R. (1993) 'Squaring up to crime', *Sociology Review*, vol. 2, no. 3.

Matza, D. (1969) *Becoming Deviant*, New Jersey: Prentice-Hall.

Matza, D. (1990) *Delinquency and Drift*, New Brunswick: Transaction.

May, T. (1993) *Social Research: Issues, Methods and Processes*, Buckingham: Open University Press.

May, T. (1996) *Situating Social Theory*, Buckingham: Open University Press.

Mayes, P. (1986) *Gender*, London: Longman.

Maynard, M. (1990) 'The reshaping of sociology? Trends in the study of gender', *Sociology*, vol. 24, no. 2.

Mayo, E. (1933) *The Human Problems of an Industrial Civilisation*, New York: Macmillan.

Mead, G. H. (1934) *Mind, Self and Society*, Chicago: University of Chicago Press.

Meadows, D., Randers, J. and Behrens, W. W. (1972) *The Limits to Growth*, New York: Universe.

Mears, R. (1994) 'Why have sociologists neglected nationalism?', *Social Science Teacher*, vol. 23, no. 2.*

Mennell, S. (1989) *Norbert Elias: Civilisation and the Human Self-Image*, Oxford: Blackwell.

Meredith, P. (1993) 'Patient participation in decision-making and consent to treatment: the case of general surgery', *Sociology of Health and Illness*, vol. 15, no. 3.

Merton, R. K. (1952) 'Bureaucratic structure and person-ality', in Merton, R. K., *Reader In Bureaucracy*, New York: Free Press.

Merton, R. K. (1968) *Social Theory and Social Structure*, New York: Free Press.

Merton, R. K. (1989) 'Social structure and anomie', in Kelly, D. H. (ed.), *Deviant Behaviour: A Text-Reader in the Sociology of Deviance*, 3rd edn, New York: St Martin's Press (orig. pub. 1938).

Michel, J. H. (1996) 'Partnerships in development', *OECD Observer*, February/March.

Micklewright, J. (1985) 'Fiction versus fact: unemployment benefits in Britain', *National Westminster Bank Quarterly Review*, May.

Micklewright, J. and Stewart, K. (2000) *Is Child Welfare Converging in the European Union?*, Florence: UNICEF Innocenti Research Centre.

Middleton, S., Ashworth, K. and Walker, R. (1994) *Family Fortunes: Pressures on Parents and Children in the 1990s*, London: Child Poverty Action Group.

Midwinter, E. (1994) *The Development of Social Welfare in Britain*, Buckingham: Open University Press.

Mies, M. (1986) *Patriarchy and Accumulation on a World Scale*, London: Zed.

Miles, I. and Irvine, J. (1979) 'The critique of official statistics', in Irvine, J., Miles, I. and Evans, P. (eds), *Demystifying Social Statistics*, London: Pluto Press.

Miles, R. (1982) *Racism and Migrant Labour*, London: Routledge.

Miles, R. (1984) 'Marxism versus the "sociology of race relations?"', *Ethnic and Racial Studies*, vol. 7, no. 2.

Miles, R. (1988) *Racism*, London: Routledge.

Miles, R. (1989) 'Racism, Marxism and British politics', *Economy and Society*, vol. 17, no. 3.

Miles, R. (1990) 'Racism, ideology and disadvantage', *Social Studies Review*, vol. 5, no. 4.

Miles, R. (1993) *Racism After 'Race Relations'*, London: Routledge.

Milgram, S. (1974) *Obedience to Authority*, London: Harper & Row.

Miliband, R. (1973) *The State in Capitalist Society: Analysis of the Western System of Power*, London: Quartet Books.

Mill, J. S. (1982) *On Liberty*, Harmondsworth: Penguin (orig. pub. 1959).

Millar, J. (1989) *Poverty and the Lone Parent Family: The Challenge to Social Policy*, Aldershot: Gower.

Miller, D. and Williams, K. (1993) 'Negotiating HIV/AIDS information: agendas, media strategies and the news', in Eldridge, J. (ed.), *Getting the Message: News, Truth and Power*, London: Glasgow University Media Group/Routledge.

Miller, E. (1992) *Men at Risk*, Jamaica: University of the West Indies Press.

Millett, K. (1970) *Sexual Politics*, New York: Doubleday.

Mills, C. W. (1956) *The Power Elite*, Oxford: Oxford University Press.

Mills, C. W. (1959) *The Sociological Imagination*, New York: Oxford University Press.

Milne, S. (1997) 'Ford in last minute talks to settle race row', *Guardian*, 27 January.

Mirrlees-Black, C. and Allen, J. (1998) 'Concern about crime: Findings from the 1998 British Crime Survey', Home Office Research, Development and Statistics Directorate, *Research Findings*, No. 83.

Mirza, H. S. (1992) *Young, Female and Black*, London: Routledge.

Mirza, H. S. (ed.) (1997) *Black British Feminism*, London: Routledge.

Mishra, R. (1984) *The Welfare State in Crisis*, Brighton: Wheatsheaf.

Modood, T. (1988) ' "Black" racial equality and Asian identity', *New Community*, vol. 14, no. 3.

Modood, T. (1989) 'Religious anger and minority rights', *Political Quarterly*, July.

Modood, T. (1992) *Not Easy Being British*, Stoke on Trent: Trentham Books.

Modood, T. (1994) 'Political blackness and British Asians' *Sociology*, vol. 28, no. 4.

Modood, T. *et al.* (1997) *Ethnic Minorities in Britain: Diversity and Disadvantage*, London: Policy Studies Institute.

Moir, A. and Jessel, D. (1989) *Brain Sex: The Real Difference Between the Sexes*, London: Macmillan.

Moir, A. and Jessel, D. (1995) 'A cure for murder?', *Guardian*, 30 September.

Mommsen, W. J. and Osterhammel, J. (eds) (1987) *Max Weber and his Contemporaries*, London: Unwin Hyman.

Momsen, J. H. (1991) *Women and Development in the Third World*, London: Routledge.

Moore, H. (1994) 'Divided we stand: sex, gender and sexual difference', *Feminist Review*, no. 47.

Moore, M. (1995) 'India's consumerism fuels sharp rise in dowry deaths', *Guardian*, 13 April.

Moore, S. (1988) 'Here's looking at you kid', in Gamman, L. and Marshment, M. (eds), *The Female Gaze: Women as Viewers of Popular Culture*, London: Women's Press.

Moore, S. (1988) *Investigating Crime and Deviance*, London: Collins Educational.

Moore, S. (1993) *Social Welfare Alive*, London: Stanley Thornes.

Moores, M. (1995) 'Examination matters special: asking awkward questions', *Sociology Review*, vol. 3, no. 2.

Morgan, D. H. J. (1975) *Social Theory and the Family*, London: Routledge & Kegan Paul.

Morgan, D. H. J. (1996) *Family Connections: An Introduction to Family Studies*, Cambridge: Polity Press.

Morgan, M., Calnan, M. and Manning, N. (1985) *Sociological Approaches to Health and Medicine*, London: Routledge.

Morley, D. (1980) *The Nationwide Audience: Structure and Decoding*, London: British Film Institute.

Morley, D. (1992) *Television, Audiences and Cultural Studies*, London: Routledge.

Morris, D. (1968) *The Naked Ape*, London: Corgi.

Morris, L. and Irwin, S. (1992) 'Employment histories and the concept of the underclass', *Sociology*, vol. 26, no. 3.

Morris, J. and Winn, M. (1990) *Housing and Social Inequality*, London: Hilary Shipman Ltd.

Morris, L. (1987) 'Constraints on gender: the family wage, social security and the labour market', *Work, Unemployment and Society*, vol. 1, no. 1.

Morris, L. (1993) 'Household finance management and the labour market: a case study in Hartlepool', *Sociology Review*, vol. 4. no. 3.

Morris, L. (1994) *Dangerous Classes: The Underclass and Social Citizenship*, London: Routledge.

Morris, M. D. (1979) *Measuring the Conditions of the World's Poor: The Physical Quality of Life Index*, New York: Pergamon.

Mort, F. (1996) *Cultures of Consumption: Masculinities and Social Space in Late Twentieth Century Britain*, London: Routledge.

Mortimore, P. (1981) 'Achievement in schools', *Contact*, London: ILEA, November.

Mount, F. (1982) *The Subversive Family*, London: Jonathan Cape.

Mouzelis, N. (1986) *Politics on the Semi-Periphery: Early Parliamentarianism and Late Industrialization in the Balkans and Latin America*, Basingstoke: Macmillan.

Mouzelis, N. (1993) 'The poverty of sociological theory', *Sociology*, vol. 27, no. 4.

Mouzelis, N. (1995) *Sociological Theory: Whatever Went Wrong?*, London: Routledge.

Mukherjee, S. (1994) 'Question and answer special: evaluation', *Sociology Review*, vol. 3, no. 3.

Mullard, C. (1982) 'Multiracial education in Britain: from assimilation to cultural pluralism', in Tierney, J. (ed.), *Race, Migration and Schooling*, London: Holt, Rinehart & Winston.

Mulvey, L. (1975) 'Visual pleasure and narrative cinema', *Screen*, vol. 16, no. 3.

Münch, R. (1987) 'Parsonian theory today: in search of a new synthesis', in Giddens, A. and Turner, J. (eds), *Modern Social Theory*, Cambridge: Polity Press.

Munchau, W. (1995) '"Sweatshop" Britain works the longest', *Times*, 24 January.

Muncie, J. and Sapsford, R. (1995) 'Issues in the study of the family', in Muncie, J., Wetherell, M., Dallos, R. and Cochrane, A. (eds), *Understanding the Family*, London: Sage.

Muncie, J., Wetherell, M., Dallos, R. and Cochrane, A. (eds) (1995) *Understanding the Family*, London: Sage.

Murdock, G. P. (1949) *Social Structure*, New York: Macmillan.

Murdock, G. P. (1965) *Social Structure*, 2nd edn, New York: Free Press (orig. pub. 1949).

Murray, C. (1984) *Losing Ground*, New York: Basic Books.

Murray, C. (1989) 'Underclass', *Sunday Times Magazine*, 26 November.

Murray, C. (1990) *The Emerging British Underclass*, London: Institute for Economic Affairs.

Murray, C. (1994) *Underclass: The Crisis Deepens*, London: Institute for Economic Affairs.

Myers, K. (1986) *Understains: The Sense and Seduction of Advertising*, London: Comedia.

Myrdal, G. (1969) *An American Dilemma: The Negro Problem and Modern Democracy*, New York: Harper & Row.

Narasimham, S. (1993) 'The unwanted sex', *New Internationalist*, February.

National Union of Teachers (1988) *Women: What Does the NUT Offer You?*, London: NUT.

Navarro, V. (1976) *Medicine Under Capitalism*, London: Croom Helm.

Navarro, V. (1978) *Class Struggle, the State and Medicine*, London: Martin Robertson.

Navarro, V. (ed.) (1982) *Imperialism, Health and Medicine*, London: Pluto Press.

Nayak, A. (1999) ' "White English ethnicities": racism, anti-racism and student perspectives', *Race, Ethnicity and Education*, vol. 2, no. 2.

NCH Action for Children (1997) *Family Forum, Family*

Life: The Age of Anxiety, London: NCH Action for Children.

Negrine, R. (1994) *Politics and the Mass Media in Britain*, 2nd edn, London: Routledge.

Nelson, D., Pillai, M. G. G. and Durham, M. (1994) 'How Thatcher aid deal's golden fruit turned sour', *Observer*, 27 February.

Nettleton, S. (1995) *The Sociology of Health and Illness*, Cambridge: Polity Press.

Nettleton, S. (1996) 'Women and the new paradigm of health and medicine', *Critical Social Policy*, vol. 24, London: Sage.

New, C. (1993) 'Structuration theory revisited: some reflections on agency', *Social Science Teacher*, vol. 22, no. 3.*

New Earnings Survey (1995) London: HMSO.

New Internationalist (1994) 'The new globalism', August.

New Society (1987) 'The crisis in community care', 18 September.

New Statesman and Society (editorial) (1993) 'A free market for crime', 26 February.

Newby, H. (1977) 'In the field: reflections on the study of Suffolk farm workers', in Bell, C. and Newby, H. (eds), *Doing Sociological Research*, London: Allen & Unwin.

Newby, H. (1987) *Country Life: A Social History of Rural England*, London: Cardinal.

Nicholls, D. (1999) 'Yes, to a minister of youth', *Youth and Policy*, no. 63, spring.

Nichols, T. and Beynon, H. (1977) *Living With Capitalism*, London: Routledge & Kegan Paul.

Nicholson, L. (ed) (1990) *Feminism/Postmodernism*, London: Routledge.

Niebuhr, H. R. (1957) *The Social Sources of Denominationalism*, New York: World Publishing Co.

Nietzsche, F. (1969) *Thus Spake Zarathustra: A Book for Everyone and No One*, Harmondsworth: Penguin.

Nisbet, R. (1976) *Sociology as an Art Form*, London: Heinemann.

Noddings, N. (1984) *Caring: A Feminist Approach to Ethics and Moral Education*, Berkeley: University of California Press.

Nordlinger, E. A. (1981) *On the Autonomy of the Democratic State*, Massachusetts: Harvard University Press.

Norris C. (1990) *What's Wrong With Post-modernism: Critical Theory and the Ends of Philosophy*, Hemel Hempstead: Harvester Wheatsheaf.

Norris, C. (1992) *Uncritical Theory: Postmodernism, Intellectuals and the Gulf War*, London: Lawrence & Wishart.

Norris, C. (1993) *The Truth about Postmodernism*, Oxford: Blackwell.

Northcott, M. (1993) 'Identity and decline in the Kirk', in McCrone, D., Storrar, W., Northcott, M., Shanks, N., Harvey, J. and Swanson, I., *Seeing Scotland: Seeing Christ*, Edinburgh: Centre for Theology and Public Issues.

Norton, C. (1999) 'Chances of free abortions "rely on postcode lottery"', *Independent*, 2 December.

Oakley, A. (1972) *Sex, Gender and Society*, London: Temple Smith.

Oakley, A. (1974a) *The Sociology of Housework*, Oxford: Martin Robertson.

Oakley, A. (1974b) *Housewife*, London: Allen Lane.

Oakley, A. (1979) *From Here to Maternity*, Harmondsworth: Penguin.

Oakley, A. (1984) *The Captured Womb: A History of the Medical Care of Pregnant Women*, Oxford: Blackwell.

Oakley, A. (1990) 'Interviewing women: a contradiction in terms', in Roberts, H. (ed.), *Doing Feminist Research*, London: Routledge.

Oakley, A. (1997) 'A brief history of gender', in Oakley, A. and Mitchell, J. (eds), *Who's Afraid of Feminism?*, Harmondsworth: Penguin.

Oakley, R. (1982) 'Cypriot families', in Rapoport, R. N., Fogarty, M. P. and Rapoport, R. (eds), *Families in Britain*, London: Routledge & Kegan Paul.

O'Brien, M. and Jones, D. (1996) 'Revisiting family and kinship', *Sociology Review*, vol. 5, no. 3.

O'Brien, P. and Roddick, J. (1983) *Chile: The Pinochet Decade*, London: Latin America Bureau.

O'Connell, H. (1994) *Women and the Family*, London: Zed Books.

O'Connor, J. (1973) *The Fiscal Crisis of the State*, London: St Martin's Press.

O'Connor, J. (1984) *Accumulation Crisis*, Oxford: Blackwell.

ODA (1994a) *British Aid Statistics 1989/90–1993/94*, London: HMSO.

ODA (1994b) *Aid That's Really Going Places*, London: ODA.

O'Day, R. (1983) 'Women in the household: an historical analysis (Unit 7: U221)', Buckingham: Open University Press.

O'Donnell, M. (1987) 'Ideology, social policy and the welfare State', *Social Studies Review*, vol. 2. no 4.

O'Donnell, M. (1991) *Race and Ethnicity*, London: Longman.

O'Donnell, M. (1992) 'Your good health?', *Sociology Review*, vol. 2, no. 1.

O'Donnell, M. (1993) *A New Introduction to Sociology*, 3rd edn, Walton-on-Thames: Nelson.

Offe, C. (1984) *The Contradictions of the Welfare State*, London: Hutchinson.

Offe, C. (1985a) 'New social movements: challenging the boundaries of institutional politics', *Social Research*, vol. 52, no. 4.

Offe, C. (1985b) *Disorganised Capitalism*, Cambridge: Polity Press.

Omi, M. and Winant, H. (1994) *Racial Formation in the United States*, London: Routledge.

ONS (1996) *Social Focus on Ethnic Minorities*, London: ONS.

ONS (1997a) *Living in Britain: General Household Survey*, preliminary findings 1996. London: ONS.

ONS (1997b) *Social Focus on Families Family Law Act 1996*, London: ONS.

ONS (1999) *Social Trends* 29, London: ONS.

OPCS (1995) *Marriage and Divorce Statistics in England and Wales*, London: HMSO.

Oppenheim, C. (1990) *Poverty: The Facts*, London: Child Poverty Action Group.

Oppenheim, C. (1993) *Poverty: The Facts*, 2nd edn, London: Child Poverty Action Group.

Oppenheim, C. and Harker, L. (1996) *Poverty: The Facts*, 3rd edn, London: Child Poverty Action Group.

Ortner, S. (1974) 'Is female to male as nature is to culture?', in Rosaldo, M. and Lamphere, L. (eds), *Woman, Culture and Society*, Stanford: Stanford University Press.

Osbourne, K. and Nichol, C. (1996) 'Patterns of pay:

results of the 1996 New Earnings Survey', *Labour Market Trends*, November.

O'Sullivan, T. and Jewkes, Y. (1997) 'Introduction to extract from the work of Anne Karpf', in O'Sullivan, T. and Jewkes, Y. (eds) *The Media Studies Reader*, London: Arnold.

Our Healthier Nation: A Contract for Health (a consultation paper) (February 1998), Norwich: Stationery Office.

Outhwaite, W. (1987) *New Philosophies of Social Science*, Basingstoke: Macmillan.

Outhwaite, W. (1989) 'Theory', in Haralambos, M. (ed.), *Developments in Sociology*, vol. 5, Ormskirk: Causeway Press.

Outram, S. (1989) *Social Policy*, London: Longman.

Oxfam (1995) *The Oxfam Poverty Report*, Oxford: Oxfam.

Oxfam (1996) *Sweat Shirt, Sweat Shop*, Oxford: Oxfam.

Pahl, J. (1989) *Money and Marriage*, Basingstoke: Macmillan.

Pahl, J. (1993) 'Money, marriage and ideology', *Sociology Review*, vol. 3, no. 1.

Pahl, R. (1984) *Divisions of Labour*, Oxford: Blackwell.

Pahl, R. (1995) 'Friendly society', *New Statesman and Society*, 10 March.

Pahl, J. (1999) 'The family and the production of welfare', in Baldock, J. *et al.* (eds), *Social Policy*, Oxford: Oxford University Press.

Pareto, V. (1963) *A Treatise on General Sociology* (edited by A. Livingstone), New York: Dover Publications.

Park, R. (1950) *Race and Culture*, New York: Free Press.

Parker, H. (1974) *View From The Boys*, Newton Abbott: David & Charles.

Parkin, F. (1972) *Class Inequality and Political Order*, St Albans: Paladin.

Parkin, F. (1979) *Marxism and Class Theory: A Bourgeois Critique*, London: Tavistock.

Parkin, F. (1986) *Max Weber*, London: Routledge.

Parmar, P. (1982) 'Gender, race and class: Asian women in resistance', in *The Empire Strikes Back*, London: CCCS/Hutchinson.

Parry, G., Moyser, G. and Day, N. (1991) *Political Participation and Democracy in Britain*, Cambridge: Cambridge University Press.

Parry, N. and Parry, J. (1976) *The Rise of the Medical Profession*, London: Croom Helm.

Parry, O. (1996) 'Equality, gender and the Caribbean classroom', in *21st Century Policy Review Special Issue: Institutional Development in the Caribbean*, Baltimore.

Parsons, T. (1937) *The Structure of Social Action*, Glencoe, CA: Free Press.

Parsons, T. (1951) *The Social System*, London: Routledge & Kegan Paul.

Parsons, T. (1955) 'The Amercian family: its relation to personality and the social structure', in Parsons, T. and Bales, R. F. (eds), *Family Socialisation and the Interaction Process*, New York: Free Press.

Parsons, T. (1959) 'The social structure of the family', in Anshen, R. (ed.), *The Family: Its Function and Destiny*, London: Harper & Row.

Parsons, T. (1963) 'On the concept of political power', *Proceedings of the American Philosophical Society*, vol. 107.

Parsons, T. (1967) *Politics and Social Structure*, New York: Free Press.

Parsons, T. (1977) *The Evolution of Societies*, Englewood Cliffs, NJ: Prentice-Hall.

Parsons, T. and Bales, R. F. (1956) *Family, Socialization and the Interaction Process*, London: Routledge & Kegan Paul.

Pateman, C. (1988) *The Sexual Contract*, Cambridge: Polity Press.

Pateman, C. (1992) 'Equality, difference, subordination: the politics of motherhood and women's citizenship', in Bock, G. and James, S. (eds), *Beyond Equality and Difference: Citizenship, Feminist Politics, Female Subjectivity*, London: Routledge.

Patrick, J. (1973) *A Glasgow Gang Observed*, London: Eyre Methuen.

Patterson, S. (1963) *Dark Strangers*, Harmondsworth: Penguin.

Pauk, W. and Fiore, J. P. (1989) *Succeed in College*, Massachusetts: Houghton Mifflin.

Pawson, R. (1989) 'Methodology', in Haralambos, M. (ed.), *Developments in Sociology*, vol. 5, Ormskirk: Causeway Press.

Pawson, R. (1992) 'Feminist methodology', in Haralambos, M. (ed.), *Developments in Sociology*, vol. 8, Ormskirk: Causeway Press.

Pawson, R. and Tilly, N. (1996) 'How (and how not) to design research to inform policy-making', in Samson, C. and South, N. (eds), *The Social Construction of Social Policy*, Basingstoke: Macmillan.

Payne, G. (1987) *Economy and Opportunity*, Basingstoke: Macmillan.

Peacock Committee (1986) *Report of the Committee on Financing the BBC* (Peacock Report), London: HMSO.

Pearce, D., Markanda, A. and Barbier, E. (1989) *Blueprint for a Green Economy*, London: Earthscan.

Pearce, F. (1976) *Crimes of the Powerful*, London: Pluto Press.

Pearce, F. (1989) *The Radical Durkheim*, London: Unwin Hyman.

Pearce, N. and Hillman, J. (1998) *Wasted Youth: Raising Achievement and Tackling Social Exclusion*, London: Institute for Public Policy Research.

Pearson, G. (1983) *Hooligan: A History of Respectable Fears*, Basingstoke: Macmillan.

Pearson, R. (1992) 'Gender matters in development', in Allen, T. and Thomas, A. (eds), *Poverty and Development in the 1990s*, Oxford: Oxford University Press.

Peckham Rye Women's Liberation Workshop Collective (eds) (1971) 'Women's Liberation Workshop', *Shrew*, vol. 3, no. 5.

Perlmutter, T. (1993) 'Distress signals', in Domunt, T. (ed.), *Channels of Resistance*, London: BFI Publishing.

Perrow, C. (1970) *Complex Organizations*, 2nd edn, Glenview: Scott, Foresman & Co.

Perrow, C. (1986) *Complex Organizations*, 3rd edn, New York: Random House.

Perry, K. (1996) 'Measuring employment: comparison of official sources', *Labour Market Trends*, January.

Pesticides Trust (1994) 'The international medical appeal for Bhopal', *Guardian*, 3 December.

Petley, J. and Romano, G. (1993) 'Public service television in Europe', in Dumont, T. (ed.), *Channels of Resistance*, London: BFI Publishing.

Phillips, A. (1987) *Feminism and Equality*, Oxford: Blackwell.

Phillips, A. (1991) *Engendering Democracy*, Cambridge: Polity Press.

Phillips, A. (1992) 'Universal pretensions in political

thought', in Barrett, M. and Phillips, A. (eds), *Destabilising Theory: Contemporary Feminist Debates*, Cambridge: Polity Press.

Phillips, A. (1996) 'What has socialism to do with sexual equality?', *Soundings*, no. 4.

Phillips, A. (1999) *Which equalities matter?*, Cambridge: Polity Press.

Phillips, M. (1995) 'We've fiddled the figures, thank you', *Guardian*, 29 January.

Philo, G. (1990) *Seeing and Believing: The Influence of Television*, London: Routledge.

Philo, G. (1994) 'Politics, media and public belief', in Perryman, M. (ed.), *Altered States: Post-modernism, Politics, Culture*, London: Lawrence & Wishart.

Phizacklea, A. (ed.) (1983) *One Way Ticket: Migration and Female Labour*, London: Routledge & Kegan Paul.

Phizacklea, A. and Miles, R. (1980) *Labour and Racism*, London: Routledge & Kegan Paul.

Piachard, D. (1979) *The Cost of a Child*, London: CPAG.

Piachard, D. (1987) 'Problems in the definition and measurement of poverty', *Journal of Social Policy*, vol. 16, no. 2.

Piachard, D. (1999) 'Wealth by stealth', *Guardian*, 1 September.

Pilger, J. (1995) 'Natural born partners', *New Statesman and Society*, 10 March.

Pilger, J. (1996) 'They never walk alone', *Guardian*, 23 November.

Pilkington, A. (1984) *Race Relations in Britain*, Slough: University Tutorial Press.

Pilkington, A. (1992) 'Is there a British underclass?', *Sociology Review*, vol. 1, no. 3.

Piore, M. and Sabel, C. (1984) *The Second Industrial Divide*, New York: Basic Books.

Plowden Report (1967) *Children and their Primary Schools*, London: HMSO.

Plummer, K. (1975) *Sexual Stigma*, London: Routledge.

Plummer, K. (1976) 'Men in love: observations on male homosexual couples', in Corbin, M. (ed.), *The Couple*, Harmondsworth: Penguin.

Plummer, K. (1983) *Life Documents*, London: Unwin Hyman.

Plummer, K. (1984) 'Sexual diversity: a sociological perspective', in Howells, K. (ed.), *Sexual Diversity*, Oxford: Blackwell Publishers.

Plummer, K. (1995) *Telling Sexual Stories: Power, Change and Social Worlds*, London: Routledge.

Pollack, F. (1955) 'Empirical research into public opinion', in Connerton, P. (ed.), *Critical Sociology*, Harmondsworth: Penguin.

Pollack, O. (1961) *The Criminality of Women*, New York: A. S. Barnes.

Pollert, A. (1988) 'Dismantling flexibility', *Capital and Class*, vol. 34.

Pollert, A. (ed.) (1991) *Farewell to Flexibility*, Oxford: Blackwell.

Polsky, N. (1971) *Hustlers, Beats and Others*, Harmondsworth: Penguin.

Popper, K. (1959) *The Logic of Scientific Discovery*, London: Hutchinson.

Popper, K. (1976) *Unended Quest*, Glasgow: Fontana.

Porter, S. (1992) 'Women in a woman's job: the gendered experience of nurses', *Sociology of Health and Illness*, vol. 14, no. 4.

Poulantzas, N. (1978) *State, Power, Socialism*, London: New Left Books.

Poulantzas, N. (1980) *State, Power, Socialism*, new edn, London: Verso.

Power, S., Whitty, G., Edwards, T. and Wigfall, V. (1998) 'School boys and school work: gender identification and academic achievement', *International Journal of Inclusive Education*, vol. 2, no. 2.

Prebisch, R. (1959) 'Commercial policy in the underdeveloped countries', *American Economic Review*, vol. 44.

Prest, A. R. and Barr, N. A. (1985) *Public Finance in Theory and Practice*, 7th edn, London: Weidenfeld & Nicholson.

Pringle, J. (1995) *Men, Masculinities and Social Welfare*, London: UCL Press.

Pryce, K. (1979) *Endless Pressure*, Harmondsworth: Penguin.

Pryce, K. (1986) *'Endless Pressure': A Study of West Indian Lifestyle in Bristol*, Bristol: Bristol Classical Press.

Pusey, M. (1987) *Jürgen Habermas*, London: Tavistock.

Quinney, R. (1973) *Critique of Legal Order*, Boston: Little Brown.

Quinney, R. (1977) *Class, State and Crime*, New York: McKay.

Rabinow, P. (ed.) (1991) *The Foucault Reader: An Introduction to Foucault's Thought*, Harmondsworth: Penguin.

Randall, V. (1987) *Women and Politics: An International Perspective*, 2nd edn, Basingstoke: Macmillan.

Rapoport, R. N., Fogarty, M. P. and Rapoport, R. (eds) (1982) *Families in Britain*, London: Routledge & Kegan Paul.

Rattansi, A. (1994) '"Western racisms", ethnicities and identities in a postmodern frame', in Rattansi, A. and Westwood, S. (eds), *Racism, Modernity and Identity*, Cambridge: Polity Press.

Reay, D. (1998) 'Setting the agenda: the growing impact of market forces on pupil grouping in British secondary schooling', *Journal of Curriculum Studies*, vol. 30, no. 5.

Redclift, M. (1987) *Sustainable Development: Exploring the Contradictions*, London: Methuen.

Redclift, M. (1994) 'Development and the environment: managing the contradictions', in Sklair, L. (ed.), *Capitalism and Development*, London: Routledge.

Redfield, R (1930) *Tepotzlan: A Mexican Village*, Chicago: University of Chicago Press.

Redhead, S. (1990) *The End of the Century Party*, Manchester: Manchester University Press.

Redhead, S. (1993) *Rave Off: Politics and Deviance in Contemporary Youth Culture*, Aldershot: Avebury.

Regional Trends 34 (1999)London: ONS.

Reiner, R. (1996) 'Crime and control: an honest citizen's guide', *Sociology Review*, vol. 5, no. 4.

Rentoul, J. (1987) *The Rich Get Richer*, London: Unwin Hyman.

Rex, J. (1961) *Key Problems of Sociological Theory*, London: Routledge & Kegan Paul.

Rex, J. (1973) *Race, Colonialism and the City*, London: Routledge & Kegan Paul.

Rex, J. (1983) *Race Relations in Social Theory*, London: Routledge & Kegan Paul.

Rex, J. (1986) *Race and Ethnicity*, Buckingham: Open University Press.

Rex, J. (1988) 'The role of class analysis in the study of race relations: a Weberian perspective', in Rex, J. and Mason, D. (eds), *Theories of Race and Ethnic Relations*, Cambridge: Cambridge University Press.

Rex, J. and Moore, R. (1967) *Race, Community and*

Conflict: A Study of Sparkbrook, London: Institute of Race Relations/Oxford University Press.

Rex, J. and Tomlinson, S. (1979) *Colonial Immigrants in a British City: A Class Analysis*, London: Routledge & Kegan Paul.

Rich, A. (1972) *Of Woman Born: Motherhood as Experience and Institution*, New York: Norton.

Rich, A. (1994) *Blood, Bread and Poetry*, New York: W. W. Norton.

Richards, A. (1993) 'Korea, Taiwan and Thailand: trade liberalisation and economic growth', *OECD Observer*, October.

Richards, A. (1994) 'Hong Kong, Singapore and Malaysia and the fruits of free trade', *OECD Observer*, January.

Richardson, J. (1996) 'Race and ethnicity', in Haralambos, M. (ed.), *Developments in Sociology*, vol. 12, Ormskirk: Causeway Press.

Richardson, J. and Lambert J. (1985) *The Sociology of Race*, Ormskirk: Causeway Press.

Riddell, S. and Brown, S. (1994) *Special Educational Needs Policy in the 1990s: Warnock and the Market Place*, London: Routledge.

Ridley, M. (1993) *The Red Queen: Sex and the Evolution of Human Nature*, Harmondsworth: Penguin.

Rist, R. C. (1977) 'On understanding the processes of schooling: the contributions of labeling theory', in Karabel, J. and Halsey, A. H. (eds), *Power and Ideology in Education*, Oxford: Oxford University Press.

Ritzer, G. (1993) *The McDonaldization of Society*, Thousand Oaks, CA: Pine Forge Press.

Ritzer, G. (1996) *Modern Sociological Theory*, 4th edn, New York: McGraw-Hill.

Ritzer, G. and Liska, A. (1997) '"McDisneyization" and "post-tourism": complementary perspectives on contemporary tourism', in Rojek, C. and Urry, J. (eds), *Touring Cultures*, London: Routledge.

Roberts, H. (ed.) (1990) *Doing Feminist Research*, London: Routledge & Kegan Paul.

Roberts, K. *et al.* (1977) *The Fragmentary Class Structure*, London: Heinemann.

Roberts, M., McGee, N. and Payne, M. (1996) 'Results of the 1995 Annual Employment Survey', *Labour Market Trends*, November.

Robertson, R. (1992) *Globalisation: Social Theory and Global Culture*, London: Sage.

Robins, K. (1991) 'Tradition and translation: national culture in its global context', in Corner, J. and Harvey, S. (eds), *Enterprise and Heritage: Crosscurrents of National Culture*, London: Routledge.

Robins, K. (1997) 'What is globalisation?', *Sociology Review*, vol. 6, no. 3.

Rock, P. (1989) 'New directions in criminology', *Social Studies Review*, vol. 5, no. 1.

Rodgers, B. and Pryor, J. (1998) *Divorce and Separation: The Outcomes for Children*, York: Joseph Rowntree Foundation.

Roethlisburger, F. and Dickson, W. (1939) *Management and the Worker*, Cambridge, MA: Harvard University Press.

Rogers, E. M. and Dearing, D. W. (1987) 'Agenda-setting research', in Anderson, J. (ed.), *Communication Yearbook*, vol. 11, London: Sage.

Rojek, C. (1985) *Capitalism and Leisure Theory*, London: Tavistock.

Rojek, C. (1993) *Ways of Escape*, Basingstoke: Macmillan.

Roll, J. (1992) *Understanding Poverty: A Guide to the Concepts and Measures*, London: Family Policy Studies Centre.

Rosaldo, M. (1974) 'Woman, culture and society: a theoretical overview', in Rosaldo, M. and Lamphere, L. (eds), *Woman, Culture and Society*, Stanford: Stanford University Press.

Rose, D. (1995) *A Report on Phase 1 of the ESRC Review of Social Classifications*, Swindon: ESRC.

Rose, D. and O'Reilly (eds) (1997) *Conducting Classes: Towards a New Social Classification for the UK*, London: ONS.

Rose, G. and Marmot, M. G. (1981) 'Social class and coronary heart disease', *British Medical Journal*, vol. 45.

Rose, R. (1989) *Politics in England: Change and Perspective*, 5th edn, Basingstoke: Macmillan.

Rose, R. and McAllister, I. (1990) *The Loyalties of Voters: A Lifetime Learning Model*, London: Sage.

Rose, S., Kamin, L. J. and Lewontin, R. C. (1984) *Not in Our Genes: Biology, Ideology and Human Nature*, Harmondsworth: Penguin.

Rosenberg, B. and Manning White, D. (eds) (1957) *Mass Culture: The Popular Arts in America*, New York: Macmillan.

Roseneil, S. (1994) 'Gender', in Haralambos, M. (ed.), *Developments in Sociology*, vol. 10, Ormskirk: Causeway Press.

Roseneil, S. (1995) *Disarming Patriarchy: Feminism and Political Action at Greenham*, Buckingham: Open University Press.

Rosenthal, R. and Jacobson, L. (1968) *Pygmalion in the Classroom*, London: Holt, Rinehart & Winston.

Rosser, R. and Harris, C. (1965) *The Family and Social Change*, London: Routledge & Kegan Paul.

Rostow, W. W. (1960) *The Stages of Economic Growth: A Non-Communist Manifesto*, Cambridge: Cambridge University Press.

Routh, G (1987) *Occupations of the People of Great Britain, 1801–1981*, London: Macmillan.

Rowbotham, S. (1973) *Woman's Consciousness: Man's World*, Harmondsworth: Penguin.

Rowbotham, S. (1989) *The Past is Before Us: Feminism in Action since the 1960s*, Harmondsworth: Penguin.

Rowland, R. (1985) 'A child at any price?', *Women's Studies International Forum*, vol. 8, no. 6.

Rowntree, B. S. (1901) *Poverty: A Study in Town Life*, London: Macmillan.

Rowntree, B. S. (1937) *The Human Needs of Labour*, London: Longmans Green.

Rowntree, B. S. (1941) *Poverty and Progress*, London: Longman.

Rowntree, B. S. and Lavers, G. R. (1951) *Poverty and the Welfare State*, London: Longmans Green.

Rowntree, D. (1997) *Learn How to Study: A Guide for Students of All Ages*, London: Warner.

Rowntree Foundation (1995) *Inquiry into Income and Wealth*, York: Joseph Rowntree Foundation.

Roxborough, I. (1979) *Theories of Development*, Basingstoke: Macmillan.

Rubin, G. (1975) 'The traffic in women: notes on the "political economy" of sex', in Reiter, R. R. (ed.), *Toward an Anthropology of Women*, New York: Monthly Review Press.

Ruggiero, V., Ryan, M. and Sim, J. (eds) (1995) *Western European Penal Systems: A Critical Anatomy*, London: Sage.

Runciman, W. G. (1990) 'How many classes are there in contemporary British society?', *Sociology*, vol. 24, no. 3.

Runnymede Trust (1994) *Multi-Ethnic Britain: Facts and Trends*, London: Runnymede Trust.

Russell, G. (1983) *The Changing Role of Fathers*, Buckingham: Open University Press.

Rutherford, J. (1988) 'Who's that man?', in Chapman, R. and Rutherford, J. (eds), *Male Order: Unwrapping Masculinity*, London: Lawrence & Wishart.

Rutherford, J. (1997) *Forever England: Reflections on Masculinity and Empire*, London: Lawrence & Wishart.

Sabel, C. (1989) 'Flexible specialisation and the re-emergence of regional ecomomics', in Hirst, P. and Zeitlin, J. (eds), *Reversing Economic Decline?*, London: St Martin's Press.

Sacks, H. (1984) 'Methodological remarks', in Atkinson, J. M. and Heritage, J. (eds), *Structures of Social Action: Studies in Conversation Analysis*, Cambridge: Cambridge University Press.

Sacks, H. (1992) *Lectures on Conversation, 1965–1972*, Oxford: Blackwell.

Said, E. (1978) *Orientalism*, New York: Random House.

Saint-Simon, Henri de (1819) 'The organiser', in Markham, F. (ed.), *Henri Comte de Saint-Simon: Selected Writings*, Oxford: Blackwell (pub. 1952).

Saint-Simon, Henri de (1825) 'The new Christianty', in Markham, F. (ed.), *Henri Comte de Saint-Simon: Selected Writings*, Oxford: Blackwell (orig. pub. 1952).

Sanderson, J. (1994) *LLB Criminology Textbook 1994–1995*, 5th edn, London: HLT.

Sarah, E., Scott, M. and Spender, D. (1980) 'The education of feminists', in Spender, D. and Sarah, E. (eds), *Learning to Lose: Sexism and Education*, London: Women's Press.

Sarantakos, S. (1993) *Social Research*, Basingstoke: Macmillan.

Sarlvick, B. and Crewe, I. (1983) *Decade of Dealignment*, Cambridge: Cambridge University Press.

Sartre, J-P. (1960) *Critique of Dialectical Reason*, London: New Left Books.

Sartre, J-P. (1974) *Existentialism and Humanism*, London: Eyre Methuen.

Sarup, M. (1993) *An Introductory Guide to Post-Structuralism and Postmodernism*, 2nd edn, Hemel Hempstead: Harvester Wheatsheaf.

Saunders, P. (1978) 'Domestic property and social class', *International Journal of Urban and Regional Research*, vol. 2, no. 2.

Saunders, P. (1987) *Social Theory and the Urban Question*, London: Unwin Hyman.

Saunders, P. (1990a) *A Nation of Homeowners*, London: Unwin Hyman.

Saunders, P. (1990b) *Social Class and Stratification*, London: Routledge.

Saunders, P. (1995) *Capitalism: A Social Audit*, Buckingham: Open University Press.

Saunders, P. (1996) 'A British Bell curve? Class, intelligence and meritocracy in modern Britain', *Sociology Review*, vol. 6, no. 2.

Saussure, F. de (1974) *Course in General Linguistics*, London: Fontana (orig. pub. 1915).

Savage, M. (1995) 'The middle classes in modern Britain', *Sociology Review*, vol. 5, no. 2.

Savage, M., Barlow, J., Dickens, P. and Fielding, T.

(1992) *Property, Bureaucracy and Culture*, London: Routledge.

Savage, M. and Warde, A. (1993) *Urban Sociology, Capitalism and Modernity*, Basingstoke: Macmillan.

Sayer, A. (1979) 'Science as critique: Marx versus Althusser', in Mepham, J. and Ruben, D-H. (eds), *Issues in Marxist Philosophy –3: Epistemology, Science, Ideology*, Brighton: Harvester.

Sayer, A. (1984) *Method in Social Science*, London: Hutchinson.

Sayer, A. (1989) 'Postfordism in question', *International Journal of Urban and Regional Research*, vol. 13, no. 4.

Scannel, P. (1989) 'Public service broadcasting and modern public life', *Media, Culture and Society*, vol. 11, no. 2.

Scannel, P. (1990) 'Public service broadcasting: the history of a concept', in Goodwin, A. and Whannel, G. (eds), *Understanding Television*, London: Routledge.

Scarman, Lord (1982) *The Scarman Report*, Harmondsworth: Penguin.

Scase, R. (1999) *Britain Towards 2010*, London: ESRC.

Schacht, R. (ed.) (1993) *The Great Philosophers: Nietzsche Selections*, New York: Macmillian.

Schlesinger, P. (1992) *Putting 'Reality' Together*, London: Routledge.

Schultz, T. (1961) 'Investment in human capital', *American Economic Review*, vol. 51, March.

Schumacher, E. (1973) *Small is Beautiful*, London: Abacus.

Schumpeter, J. A. (1992) *Capitalism, Socialism and Democracy*, London: Routledge (orig. pub. 1943).

Schutz, A. (1972) *The Phenomenology of the Social World*, London: Heinemann.

Schuurman, F. J. (ed.) (1993) *Beyond the Impasse: New Directions in Development Theory*, London: Zed.

Scott, A. (1990) *Ideology and the New Social Movements*, London: Unwin Hyman.

Scott, Allen J. (1988) *Metropolis: From the Division of Labour to Urban Form*, Berkeley: University of California Press.

Scott, J. (1985) *Corporations, Classes and Capitalism*, 2nd edn, London: Hutchinson.

Scott, J. (1986) 'Does Britain still have a ruling class?' *Social Studies Review*, September.

Scott, J. (1991) *Who Rules Britain?*, Cambridge: Polity Press.

Scott, J. (1994) *Poverty and Wealth*, London: Longman.

Scott, J. (1995) *Sociological Theory: Contemporary Debates*, Aldershot: Edward Elgar.

Scott, J. (1996) *Stratification and Power*, Cambridge: Polity Press.

Scraton, S. and Bramham, P. (1995) 'Leisure and post-modernity', in Haralambos, M. (ed.), *Developments in Sociology*, vol. 11, Ormskirk: Causeway Press.

Scruton, R. (1986) 'Authority and allegiance', cited in 'New ethnicities', in Donald, J. and Rattansi, A. (eds) (1992), *Race, Culture and Difference*, London: Sage.

Scruton, R. (1991) Speaking on the Radio 4 programme, 'Punters', 8 August.

Scull, A. (1979) *Museums of Madness*, Harmondsworth: Penguin.

Scull, A. (1984) *Decarceration: Community Treatment and the Deviant, a Radical View*, Cambridge: Polity Press.

Seabrook, J. (1993) *Victims of Development: Resistance and Alternatives*, London: Verso.

Sedgwick, P. (1982) *Psycho Politics*, London: Pluto Press.

Seedhouse, D. (1986) *Health: The Foundations for Achievement*, Chichester: John Wiley.

Segal, L. (1987) *Is the Future Female? Troubled Thoughts On Contemporary Feminism*, London: Virago.

Segal, L. (1989) 'Slow change or no change: feminism, socialism and the problem of men', *Feminist Review*, no. 31.

Seidel, G. (1986) 'Culture, nation and "race" in the British and French New Right', in Levitas, R. (ed.), *The Ideology of the New Right*, Cambridge: Polity Press .

Seidler, V. (1989) *Rediscovering Masculinity*, London: Routledge.

Selfe, P. (1995) *Work Out Sociology*, Basingstoke: Macmillan.

Selfe, P. and Starbuck, M. (1998) *Religion*, London: Hodder & Stoughton.

Selznick, P. (1957) *Leadership in Administration: A Sociological Interpretation*, New York: Harper & Row.

Sen, A. (1983) 'Poor, relatively speaking', *Oxford Economic Papers*, no. 25.

Sender, J. and Short, S. (1986) *The Development of Capitalism in Africa*, London: Methuen.

Senior, M. (1996) 'Health, illness and postmodernism', *Sociology Review*, vol. 6, no. 1.

Sennett, R. and Cobb, J. (1977) *The Hidden Injuries of Class*, Cambridge: Cambridge University Press.

Sewell, T. (1997) *Black Maculinities and Schooling: How Black Boys Survive Modern Schooling*, Stoke-on-Trent: Trentham Books.

Shaiken, H. (1979) 'Numerical control of work: workers and automation in the computer age', *Radical America*, vol. 1, no. 6.

Sharma, U. (1992) *Complementary Medicine Today: Practitioners and Patients*, London: Routledge.

Sharpe, S. (1976) *Just Like a Girl: How Girls Learn to be Women*, Harmondsworth: Penguin.

Shaskolsky, L. (1970) 'The development of sociological theory: a sociology of knowledge interpretation', in Reynolds, L. T. and Reynolds, J. M. (eds), *The Sociology of Sociology*, New York: McKay.

Shaver, S. and Bradshaw, J. (1995) 'The recognition of wifely labour by welfare states', *Social Policy and Administration*, vol. 29, no. 1.

Shaw, C. (1931) *The Natural History of a Delinquent Career*, Chicago: University of Chicago Press.

Shaw, C. (1966) *The Jackroller*, Chicago: University of Chicago Press.

Shearer, A. (1981) *Disability: Whose Handicap?*, Oxford: Blackwell.

Sheeran, Y. (1995) 'Sociology, biology and health: is illness only a social construction?', *Sociology Review*, vol. 4, no. 4.

Sherlock, H. (1991) *Cities Are Good For Us*, London: Paladin.

Shields, R. (ed.) (1996) *Cultures of the Internet*, London: Sage.

Shilling, C. (1993) *The Body and Social Theory*, London: Sage.

Shils, E. (1961) 'Mass society and its culture', in Jacobs, N. (ed.), *Culture for the Millions*, New Jersey: Van Nostrand.

Shils, E. and Young, M. (1953) 'The meaning of the coronation', *Sociological Review*, vol. 1.

Shortall, S. (1994) 'Farm women's groups: feminist, farming or community groups, or new social movements?', *Sociology*, vol. 28, no. 1.

Shorter, E. (1977) *The Making of the Modern Family*, London: Fontana.

Showalter, E. (1987) *The Female Malady*, London: Virago.

Shutz, A. (1967) *The Phenomenology of the Social World*, Evanston: Northwestern University Press.

Simmel, G. (1890) *On Social Differentiation*, Berlin: Dünker & Humblot.

Simmel, G. (1968) *Sociology*, Berlin: Düncker & Humblot (orig. pub. 1908).

Simmel, G. (1978) *The Philosophy of Money*, London: Routledge & Kegan Paul (orig. pub. 1900).

Simon, H. A. (1957) *Models of Man*, New York: John Wiley.

Simon, R. (1982) *Gramsci's Political Thought: An Introduction*, London: Lawrence & Wishart.

Simons, M. (1988) 'The red and the green: socialists and the ecology movement', *International Socialism*, winter.

Sivanandan, A. (1976) 'Race, class and the state: the black experience in Britain', *Race and Class*, vol. 17, no. 4.

Sivanandan, A. (1982) *A Different Hunger*, London: Pluto Press.

Sivanandan, A. (1990) *Communities of Resistance*, London: Verso.

Sivanandan, A. (1995) 'La tratison des clercs', *New Statesman and Society*, 14 July.

Skeggs, B. (1991) 'Postmodernism: what is all the fuss about?', *British Journal of Sociology of Education*, vol. 12, no. 2.

Skellington, R. (1996) *'Race' in Britain Today*, London: Sage/Open University Press.

Skidmore, P. (1995) 'Just another moral panic? Media reporting of child sexual abuse', *Sociology Review*, vol. 5, no. 4.

Skinner, Q. (ed.) (1990) *The Return of Grand Theory in the Human Sciences*, Cambridge: Canto.

Sklair, L. (1989) *Assembling for Development*, London: Unwin Hyman.

Sklair, L. (1991) *Sociology of the Global System*, Hemel Hempstead: Harvester Wheatsheaf.

Sklair, L. (ed.) (1994) *Capitalism and Development*, London: Routledge.

Skocpol, T. (1979) *States and Social Revolutions*, Cambridge: Cambridge University Press.

Slattery, M. (1985) 'Urban sociology', in Haralambos, M. (ed.), *Sociology: New Directions*, Ormskirk: Causeway Press.

Slattery, M. (1986) *Official Statistics*, London: Tavistock.

Slattery, M. (1991) *Key Ideas in Sociology*, Basingstoke: Macmillan.

Sly, F. (1996) 'Women in the labour market: results from the spring 1995 Labour Force Survey', *Labour Market Trends*, March.

Smaje, C. (1996) 'The ethnic patterning of health: new directions for theory and practice', *Sociology of Health and Illness*, vol. 18, no. 2.

Small, S. (1994) *Racialised Barriers*, London: Routledge.

Smart, B. (1985) *Michel Foucault*, London: Routledge.

Smart, B. (1994) *Postmodernity*, London: Routledge.

Smart, C. (1976) *Women, Crime and Criminology*, London: Routledge & Kegan Paul.

Smart, C. (1991) 'Securing the family? Rhetoric and policy in the field of social security', in Loney, M. *et al.* (eds), *The State or the Market*, London: Sage.

Smith, A. (1999) *Accelerated Learning in the Classroom*, Stafford: Network Educational Press.

Smith, D. (1988a) 'Crime prevention and the causes of crime', *Social Studies Review*, vol. 3, no. 5.

Smith, D. J. (ed.) (1992a) *Understanding the Underclass*, London: Policy Studies Institute.

Smith, G. (1986) 'Pluralism, race and ethnicity in selected African countries', in Rex, J. and Mason, D. (eds), *Theories of Race and Ethnic Relations*, Cambridge: Cambridge University Press.

Smith, J. (1989) *Misogynies*, London: Faber & Faber.

Smith, M. (1994a) 'Police accused of "dirty tricks" war on BA passenger', *Daily Telegraph*, 31 August.

Smith, M. (1994b) 'BA is sued over "intimidation"', *Daily Telegraph*, 24 September.

Smith, M. and Kollock, P. (eds) (1998) *Communities in Cyberspace*, London: Routledge.

Smith, M. G. (1962) *West Indian Family Structure*, Seattle: University of Washington Press.

Smith, P. (1992b) 'Industrialization and environment', in Hewitt, T., Johnson, H. and Wild, D. (eds), *Industrialization and Development*, Oxford: Oxford University Press.

Smith, R. T. (1988b) *Kinship and Class in the West Indies*, Cambridge: Cambridge University Press.

Smith, S. (1995) 'The ideas of Samir Amin: theory or tautology?', in Ayers, R. (ed.), *Development Studies*, London: Greenwich University Press.

Smithers, A. and Robinson, P. (1995) *Post-18 Education: Growth, Change and Prospect*, London: Council for Industry and Higher Education (executive briefing).

Smithers, R. (1994) 'Near miss denied as inquiry starts into airliner's aborted landing', *Guardian*, 31 August.

Smyth, G., Jones, D. and Platt, S. (eds) (1994) *Bite the Ballot: 2500 Years of Democracy*, London: Channel 4/New Statesman and Society.

Snell, M. (1986) 'Equal pay and sex discrimination', in *Feminist Review* (ed.), *Waged Work: A Reader*, London: Virago.

Social Trends 1998 (1998) London: ONS.

Solomos, J. (1988) 'Varieties of Marxist conceptions of "race", class and the state: a critical analysis', in Rex, J. and Mason, D. (eds), *Theories of Race and Ethnic Relations*, Cambridge: Cambridge University Press.

Solomos, J. (1993) *Race and Racism in Britain*, Basingstoke: Macmillan.

Solomos, J. (1993) 'Constructions of black criminality: racialisation and criminalisation', in Cook, D. and Hudson, B. (eds). *Racism and Criminology*, London: Sage.

Solomos, J. and Back, L. (1995) *Race, Politics and Social Change*, London: Routledge.

Solomos, J. *et al.* (1982) *The Organic Crisis of British Capitalism and Race: The Experience of the Centre for Contemporary Cultural Studies*, Birmingham: Race and Politics Group.

Spelman, E. (1990) *Inessential Woman: Problems of Exclusion in Feminist Thought*, London: Women's Press.

Spencer, H. (1874) *The Study of Society*, London: Appleton.

Spencer, H. (1896) *The Principles of Sociology*, London: Appleton.

Spencer, H. (1971) *Structure, Function and Evolution*, London: Nelson.

Spender, D. and Sarah, E. (eds) (1980) *Learning to Lose: Sexism and Education*, London: Women's Press.

Spiro, M. E. (1968) 'Is the family universal?', in Bell, N. W. and Vogel, E. F. (eds), *A Modern Introduction to the Family*, revised edn, New York: Free Press.

Spours, K. and Young, M. (1990) 'Beyond vocationalism', in Gleeson, D. (ed). *Training and it's Alternatives*, Milton Keynes: Open University Press.

Spurgeon, P. (ed.) (1993) *The New Face of the NHS*, Edinburgh: Churchill Livingstone.

Stacey, M. (1988) *The Sociology of Health and Healing*, London: Unwin Hyman.

Stanko, E. (1988) 'Fear of crime and the myth of the safe home', in Borad, M. and Yuo, K. (eds), *Feminist Perspectives of Wife Abuse*, London: Sage.

Stanley, L. (ed.) (1990) *Feminist Praxis: Research, Theory and Epistemology in Feminist Sociology*, London: Routledge.

Stanley, L. and Wise, S. (1983) *Breaking Out*, London: Routledge & Kegan Paul.

Stanley, L. and Wise, S. (1990) 'Method, methodology and epistemology in feminist research processes', in Stanley, L. (ed.), *Feminist Praxis: Research, Theory and Epistemology in Feminist Sociology*, London: Routledge.

Stanley, L. and Wise, S. (1993) *Breaking Out Again*, London: Routledge.

Stanworth, M. (1983) *Gender and Schooling: a Study of Sexual Divisions in the Classroom*, London: Hutchinson.

Stanworth, M. (ed.) (1987) *Reproductive Technologies: Gender, Motherhood and Medicine*, Cambridge: Polity Press.

Stanworth, P. and Giddens, A. (eds) (1974) *Elites and Power in British Society*, Cambridge: Cambridge University Press.

Starbuck, M. (1995) 'Figuring out the sociology of Norbert Elias', *Social Science Teacher*, vol. 24, no. 2.*

Stark, R. and Bainbridge, W. S. (1985) *The Future of Religion: Secularization, Revival and Cult Formation*, Berkeley: University of California Press.

STATLAS UK (1995) Ordnance Survey (HMSO).

Stead, M. (1991) 'Women, war and underdevelopment in Nicaragua', in Ashar, H. (ed.), *Women, Development and Survival in the Third World*, London: Longman.

Steele, J. (1995) 'Clinton policies are caught in the communitaran crossfire: commentary', *Guardian*, 12 April.

Steele, J., Mortimer, E. and Jones, G. S. (1989) 'The end of history?', *Marxism Today*, November.

Sternberg, R. J. (1995) 'Interview with *Skeptic* magazine, *Skeptic*, vol. 3, no. 3.

Sternberg, R. J. (1996) 'Myths, mythical countermyths, and truths about intelligence', *Educational Researcher*, vol. 25, no. 2.

Stewart, A., Prandy, K. and Blackburn, R. M. (1980) *Social Stratification and Occupations*, Basingstoke: Macmillan.

Stille, A. (1997) *Excellent Cadavers*, London: Vintage.

Stoller, R. (1968) *Sex and Gender: On the Development of Masculinity and Femininity*, New York: Science House.

Stone, M. (1981) *The Education of the Black Child in Britain: The Myth of Multiracial Education*, London: Fontana.

Storey, J. (1993) *An Introductory Guide to Cultural Theory and Popular Culture*, Hemel Hempstead: Harvester Wheatsheaf.

Sturmer, C. (1993) 'MTV's Europe: an imaginary continent', in Dowmunt, T. (ed.), *Channels of Resistance*, London: BFI/Channel 4.

Strinati, D. (1995) *An Introduction to Theories of Popular Culture*, London: Routledge.

Stryker, S. (1981) *Symbolic Interactionism: A Social Structural Version*, Englewood Cliffs, NJ: Prentice-Hall.

Sugrue, B. (1995) 'Question and answer: interpretation and application', *Sociology Review*, vol. 4, no. 4.

Sugrue, B. (1996) 'Examination matters: knowledge and understanding', *Sociology Review*, vol. 5, no. 4.

Sumner, C. (1994) *The Sociology of Deviance: An Obituary*, Buckingham: Open University Press.

Swann, W. (1991) *Variations Between LEAs in Levels of Segregation in Special Schools: Preliminary Report*, London: CSIE.

Swatridge, C. (1995) *General Studies A Level*, London: HarperCollins.

Sweetman, T. (1995) 'Aspects of relativism', *Social Science Teacher*, vol. 24, no. 3.*

Swift, R. (1994) 'Squeezing the south', *New Internationalist*, July.

Swingewood, A. (1977) *The Myth of Mass Culture*, Basingstoke: Macmillan.

Sykes, G. M. and Matza, D. (1989) 'Techniques of neutralization: a theory of delinquency', in Kelly, D. H. (ed.), *Deviant Behaviour: A Text-Reader in the Sociology of Deviance*, 3rd edn, New York: St Martin's Press.

Szasz, T. (1970) *The Manufacture of Madness*, New York: Harper & Row.

Szasz, T. (1973) *The Myth of Mental Illness*, New York: Paladin (orig. pub. 1961).

Tame, C. R. (1991) 'Freedom, responsibility and justice: the criminology of the New Right', in Stenson, K. and Cowell, D. (eds), *The Politics of Crime Control*, London: Sage.

Tang Nain, G. (1991) 'Black women, sexism and racism: black or antiracist feminism', *Feminist Review*, no. 37.

Tarling, R. (1993) *Analysing Offending*, London: HMSO.

Taylor, F. W. (1911) *The Principles of Scientific Management*, New York: Harper & Row.

Taylor, F. W. (1964) 'Shop management', in Taylor, F. W. (ed.), *Scientific Management*, New York: Harper & Row (orig. pub. 1903).

Taylor, I., Walton, P. and Young, J. (1973) *The New Criminology: For a Social Theory of Deviance*, London: Routledge & Kegan Paul.

Taylor, J. G. (1979) *From Modernisation to Modes of Production*, Basingstoke: Macmillan.

Taylor, P. M. (1992) *War and the Media: Propaganda and Persuasion in the Gulf War*, Manchester: Manchester University Press.

Taylor, P., Richardson, J., Yeo, A., Marsh, I., Trobe, K., Pilkington, A., Hughes, G. and Sharp, K. (1995) *Sociology in Focus*, Ormskirk: Causeway Press.

Taylor, S. (1982) *Durkheim and the Study of Suicide*, Basingstoke: Macmillan.

Taylor, S. (1990) 'Beyond Durkheim: sociology and suicide', *Social Studies Review*, vol. 6, no. 2.

Taylor, S. (1994) 'Beyond the medical model: the sociology of health and illness', *Sociology Review*, vol. 4, no. 1.

Taylor, S. and Field, D. (eds) (1993) *The Sociology of Health and Health Care*, Oxford: Blackwell Science.

Taylor-Gooby, P. (1990) 'Social welfare:the unkindest cuts', in Jowell, R. *et al.* (eds), *British Social Attitudes: The Seventh Report*, Aldershot: Gower.

Taylor-Gooby, P. (1991) *Social Change, Social Welfare and Social Science*, Hemel Hempstead: Harvester Wheatsheaf.

Thomas, A., Crow, B., Frenz, P., Hewitt, T., Kassam, S. and Treagust, S. (1994) *Third World Atlas*, 2nd edn, Buckingham: Open University Press.

Thomas, H. and Klett-Davies, M. (1995) 'Unequal pay for equal parts: a survey of performers in the theatre and the electronic media', London: Equity/Goldsmith's College, University of London.

Thomas, W. I. (1909) *The Child in America*, New York: Alfred Knopf.

Thomas, W. I. and Znaniecki, F. (1919) *The Polish Peasant in Europe and America*, Chicago: University of Chicago Press.

Thompson, E. G. (1995) Letter on *Social Trends*, *Guardian*, 13 February.

Thompson, E. P. (1968) *The Making of the English Working Class*, Harmondsworth: Penguin.

Thompson, E. P. (1978) *The Poverty of Theory and Other Essays*, London: Merlin Press.

Thompson, K. (1998) *Moral Panics*, London: Routledge.

Thompson, P. (1988) *The Voice of the Past: Oral History*, Oxford: Oxford University Press.

Thompson, P. (1989) 'The end of bureaucracy?', in Haralambos, M. (ed.), *Developments in Sociology*, vol. 5, Ormskirk: Causeway Press.

Thompson, P. (1993) 'The labour process: changing theory, changing practice', *Sociology Review*, vol. 3, no. 2.

Thornton, S. (1995) *Club Cultures: Music Media and Subcultural Capital*, Cambridge: Polity Press.

Thorogood, N. (1992) 'Private medicine: "You pay your money and you get your treatment"', *Sociology of Health and Illness*, vol. 14, no. 1.

Tiger, L. and Fox, R. (1972) *The Imperial Animal*, London: Secker & Warburg.

Tipton, S. (1982) *Getting Saved From the Sixties*, Berkeley: University of California Press.

Tizard, B. (1994) *Black, White or Mixed Race? Race and Racism in the Lives of Young People of Mixed Parentage*, London: Routledge.

Tomlinson, J. (1994) 'A phenomenology of globalization? Giddens on global modernity', *European Journal of Communications*, vol. 9, pp. 149–72.

Tomlinson, S. (1982) *A Sociology of Special Education*, London: Routledge & Kegan Paul.

Tong, R. (1989) *Feminist Thought*, London: Unwin Hyman.

Tönnies, F. (1955) *Community and Association*, London: Routledge & Kegan Paul.

Tooley, J. (1995) 'Can IQ tests liberate education?,' *Economic Affairs*, vol. 15, no. 3.

Touraine, A. (1982) *The View and the Eye*, Cambridge: Cambridge University Press.

Townsend, P. (1979) *Poverty in the United Kingdom*, Harmondsworth: Penguin.

Townsend, P. and Davidson, N. (1982) *Inequalities in Health: The Black Report*, Harmondsworth: Penguin.

Townsend, P., Davidson, N. and Whitehead, M. (1987) *Inequalities in Health and the Health Divide*, Harmondsworth: Penguin.

Toynbee, P. (1999) 'Look under the comfy middle-class perches and see what lies there', *Guardian*, 25 January.

Travis, A. (1995) '10,000 spy cameras for high streets', *Guardian*, 23 November.

Travis, A. (1996a) 'Straw seizes on fall in convictions', *Guardian*, 6 February.

Travis, A. (1996b) 'Muggings mar third year's fall in crime', *Guardian*, 27 March.

Travis, A. (1996c) 'Deportation list hits record total of 17,800', *Guardian*, 25 October.

Trist, E. L., Higgin, G. W., Murray, H. and Pollack, A. B. (1963) *Organisational Choice*, London: Tavistock.

Troeltsch, E. (1981) *The Social Teachings of the Christian Churches*, vols 1 and 2, Chicago: University of Chicago Press.

Trowler, P. (1985) 'Social policy and administration', in Trowler, P., *Further Topics in Sociology*, Slough: University Tutorial Press.

Trowler, P. (1989) *Investigating Health, Welfare and Poverty*, London: Unwin Hyman.

Trowler, P. (1996) *Investigating Health, Welfare and Poverty*, 2nd edn, London: Collins Educational.

Trowler, P. with Riley, M. (1987) *Topics in Sociology*, London: Bell & Hyman.

Tuchman, G. (1981) 'The symbolic annihilation of women', in Cohen, S. and Young, J. (eds), *The Manufacture of News*, London: Constable.

Tudor-Hart, J. (1971) 'The inverse care law', *The Lancet*, 27 February.

Tulloch, J. (1990) 'Television and Black Britons', in Goodwin, A. and Whannel, G. (eds), *Understanding Television*, London: Routledge.

Tunstall, J. (1977) *The Media are American*, London: Constable.

Turner, B. S. (1984) *The Body and Society*, Oxford: Basil Blackwell.

Turner, B. S. (1982) 'The government of the body: medical regimes and the rationalization of diet', *British Journal of Sociology*, vol. 33, no. 2.

Turner, B. S. (1985) 'More on the government of the body: a reply to Naomi Aronson', *British Journal of Sociology*, vol. 36, no. 2.

Turner, B. S. (1986) *Citizenship and Capitalism*, London: Allen & Unwin.

Turner, B. S. (1987) *Medical Power and Social Knowledge*, London: Sage.

Turner, B. S. (1989) *The Body and Society: Explorations in Social Theory*, new edn, Oxford: Basil Blackwell.

Turner, B. S. (1990) *Medical Power and Social Knowledge*, 2nd edn, London: Sage.

Turner, B. S. (1991) *Religion and Social Theory*, 2nd edn, London: Sage.

Turner, B. S. (1992) *Regulating Bodies: Essays in Medical Sociology*, London: Routledge.

Twigg, J. (1999) 'Social care', in Baldock, J., Manning, N., Miller, S. and Vickerstaff, S. (eds), *Social Policy*, Oxford: Oxford University Press.

UNDP (1995) *United Nations World Development Report 1995*, Oxford: Oxford University Press.

UNDP (1998) *United Nations Human Development Report 1998*, Oxford: Oxford University Press.

Ungerson, C. (1991) *Gender and Caring*, Hemel Hempstead: Harvester Wheatsheaf.

Ungerson, C. (1995) 'Gender, cash and informal care', *Journal of Social Policy*, vol. 24, no. 1.

Urry, J. (1990a) 'Urban sociology', in Haralambos, M. (ed.) *Developments in Sociology*, vol. 6, Ormskirk: Causeway Press.

Urry, J. (1990b) *The Tourist Gaze*, London: Sage.

Urry, J. and Wakeford, J. (eds) (1973) *Power in Britain: Sociological Readings*, London: Heinemann.

Useem, M. (1984) *The Inner Circle*, New York: Oxford University Press.

Van den Berghe, P. (1978) *Race and Racism: A Comparative Perspective*, New York: John Wiley.

Van den Berghe, P. (1988) 'Ethnicity and the sociobiology debate', in Rex, J. and Mason, D. (eds), *Theories of Race and Ethnic Relations*, Cambridge: Cambridge University Press.

Van den Haag, E. (1975) *Punishing Criminals*, New York: Simon & Schuster.

Van der Pijl, K. (1989) 'The international level', in Bottomore, T. and Brym, R. (eds), *The Capitalist Class*, Hemel Hempstead: Harvester Wheatsheaf.

Van Dijk, T. A. (1991) *Racism and the Press: Critical Studies in Racism and Migration*, London: Routledge.

Van Every, J. (1995) *Heterosexual Women Changing the Family: Refusing to Be a 'Wife'!*, London: Taylor & Francis.

Van Zoonen, L. (1991) 'Feminist perspectives on the media', in Curran, J. and Gurevitch, M. (eds), *Mass Media and Society*, New York: Edward Arnold.

Veal, A. J. (1993) 'The concept of lifestyle', *Leisure Studies*, vol. 12.

Veblen, T. (1953) *The Theory of the Leisure Class: An Economic Study of Institutions*, New York: Mentor Books (orig. pub. 1912).

Veljanovski, C. (1989) 'Competition in broadcasting', in Veljanovski, C. (ed.), *Freedom in Broadcasting*, London: Institute of Economic Affairs.

Vidal, J. (1991) 'Aid', *Education Guardian*, 12 March.

Vidler, C. (1998) 'The sick tiger syndrome', *Business Review*, September.

Vienna Circle (1929) 'The scientific conception of the world', in Neurath, O. (ed.), *Empiricism and Sociology*, Boston: Reidel (orig. pub. 1929).

Vincent, J. (1995) *Inequality and Old Age*, London: UCL Press.

VSO (1996) *Aid Counts: Don't Cut It*, London: VSO.

Wade, R. And Veneroso, F. (1998) 'The Asian crisis: the high-debt model versus the Wall Street–Treasury–IMF complex', *New Left Review*, no. 231, September/October.

Wadsworth, M. E. J. (1986) 'Serious illness in childhood and its associations with later life achievement', in *Class and Health: Research and Longitudinal Data*, London: Tavistock.

Walby, S. (1986) *Patriarchy at Work*, Cambridge: Polity Press.

Walby, S. (1989) 'Theorising patriarchy', *Sociology*, vol. 23, no. 2.

Walby, S. (1990) *Theorizing Patriarchy*, Oxford: Blackwell.

Walker, A. (1989) 'Community care', in McCarthy, M. (ed.), *The New Politics of Welfare*, Basingstoke: Macmillan.

Walker, B. and Waddington, I. (1991) 'Aids and the doctor–patient relationship', *Social Studies Review*, vol. 6, no. 4.

Walker, D. (1999) 'Kinds of equality', *Guardian*, 3 September.

Walkerdine, V. (1981) 'Sex, power and pedagogy', *Screen Education*, vol. 38.

Walkerdine, V. and Waldon, R. (1982) *The Practice of Reason*, London: Institute of Education (Bedford Way Series).

Walklate, S. (1994) 'Crime victims: another 'ology'?

Sociology Review, vol. 3, no. 3.

Wallerstein, I. (1974) *The Modern World-System*, London: Academic Press.

Wallerstein, I. (1991) in King, A. D. (ed.) *Culture, Globalisation and the World System: Comtemporary Conditions for the Representation of Identity*, Basingstoke: Macmillan.

Wallis, R. (1984) *The Elementary Forms of the New Religious Life*, London: Routledge & Kegan Paul.

Wallis, R. and Bruce, S. (1986) *Sociological Theory, Religion and Collective Action*, Belfast: Queen's University.

Walsh, D. (1972) 'Functionalism and systems theory', in Filmer, P., Phillipson, M., Silverman, D. and Walsh, D. (eds), *New Directions in Sociological Theory*, Basingstoke: Macmillan.

Walter, N. (1998) *The New Feminism*, London: Little, Brown.

Walton, J. and Seddon, D. (1994) *Free Markets and Food Riots: The Politics of Global Adjustment*, Oxford: Blackwell.

Wambu, O. (ed.) (1998) *Empire Windrush: Fifty Years of Writing About Black Britain*, London: Victor Gollancz.

Wandor, M. (ed.) (1990) *Once a Feminist: Stories of a Generation*, London: Virago.

Ward, R. and Jenkins, R. (eds) (1985) *Ethnic Communities in Business*, Cambridge: Cambridge University Press.

Warde, A. and Abercrombie, N. (eds) (1994) *Stratification and Social Inequality: Studies in British Society*, Lancaster: Framework Press.

Warnock Report (1978) *Report of the Committee of Enquiry into the Education of Handicapped Children and Young People*, London: DES/HMSO.

Warren, B. (1980) *Imperialism: Pioneer of Capitalism*, London: New Left Books.

Warwick, D. (1982) 'Tearoom trade: means and ends in social research', in Bulmer, M. (ed.), *Social Research Ethics: An Examination of the Merits of Covert Participation Research*, Basingstoke: Macmillan.

Waters, M. (1995) *Globalisation*, London: Routledge.

Watkins, K. (1996) 'Zimbabwe "miracle cure" fails to save the poor', *Guardian*, 27 July.

Watkins, K. (1999a) *Education Now: Breaking the Cycle of Poverty*, Oxford: Oxfam Publications.

Watkins, K. (1999b) 'Riderless horses and a third world handicap', *Guardian*, 19 April.

Watson, K. (ed.) (1982) *Education in the Third World*, Beckenham: Croom Helm.

Watson, T. (1995) *Sociology, Work and Industry*, 3rd edn, London: Routledge.

Webb, M. (1982) 'The labour market', in Reid, I. and Wormald, E. (eds), *Sex Differences in Britain*, London: Grant McIntyre.

Weber, M. (1930) *The Protestant Ethic and the Spirit of Capitalism*, London: Allen & Unwin (orig. pub. 1905).

Weber, M. (1949a) '"Objectivity" in social science and social policy', in *The Methodology of the Social Sciences*, Glencoe, CA: Free Press (orig. pub. 1904).

Weber, M. (1949b) 'The meaning of "ethical neutrality" in sociology and economics', in *The Methodology of the Social Sciences*, Glencoe, CA: Free Press (orig. pub. 1904).

Weber, M. (1951) *The Religion of China*, New York: Macmillan (orig. pub. 1915).

Weber, M. (1952) *Ancient Judaism*, New York: Macmillan (orig. pub. 1917).

Weber, M. (1958) *The Religion of India*, New York: Macmillan (orig. pub. 1916).

Weber, M. (1961) *From Max Weber: Essays in Sociology*, London: Routledge & Kegan Paul.

Weber, M. (1968) *Economy and Society: An Outline of Interpretive Sociology* (edited by G. Roth and C. Wittich), New York: Bedminister Press (orig. pub. 1921).

Weber, M. (1985) *The Protestant Ethic and the Spirit of Capitalism*, new edn, London: Unwin Paperbacks (orig. pub. 1905).

Webster, A. (1990) *Introduction to the Sociology of Development*, 2nd edn, Basingstoke: Macmillan.

Webster, F. (1995) *Theories of the Information Society*, London: Routledge.

Wedderburn, D. (1974) *Poverty, Inequality and Class Structure*, Cambridge: Cambridge University Press.

Weeks, J. (1977) *Coming Out: Homosexual Politics in Britain From the Nineteenth Century to the Present*, London: Quarto.

Weeks. J. (1986) *Sexuality*, London: Tavistock.

Weinberg, G. (1973) *Society and the Healthy Homosexual*, New York: Doubleday.

Weiner, G. (1994) *Feminisms in Education: An Introduction*, Buckingham: Open University Press.

West, R. (1982) *The Young Rebecca* (edited by J. Marcus), Basingstoke: Macmillan.

Westergaard, J. (1995) *Who Gets What? The Hardening of Class Inequality in the Late Twentieth Century*, Cambridge: Polity Press.

Westergaard, J. and Resler, H. (1976) *Class in a Capitalist Society: A Study of Contemporary Britain*, Harmondsworth: Penguin.

Wheelock, J. (1990) *Husbands at Home*, London: Routledge.

Whitehead, M. (1988) 'The health divide', in Townsend, P., Davidson, N. and Whitehead, M. (eds), *The Health Divide*, Harmondsworth: Penguin.

Whitty, G. (1992) 'Integrated humanities and world studies: lessons from some radical curriculum initiatives of the 1980s', in Rattansi, A. and Reeder, D. (eds), *Radicalism and Education: Essays for Brian Simon*, London: Lawrence & Wishart.

Whitty, G., Rowe, G. and Aggleton, P. (1994) 'Subjects and themes in the secondary school curriculum', *Research Papers in Education*, vol. 9, no. 2.

Whitty, G. (1997) 'Marketization, the State and the re-formation of the teaching profession', in Halsey, A. H., Lauder, H., Brown, P. and Wells, A. S. (eds), *Education: Culture, Economy, Society*, Oxford: Oxford University Press.

Whyte, W. F. (1943) *Street Corner Society*, Chicago: University of Chicago Press.

Wiles, R. and Higgins, J. (1996) 'Doctor–patient relationships in the private sector: patients' perceptions', *Sociology of Health and Illness*, vol. 18, no. 3.

Wilkinson, H. and Mulgan, G. (1995) *Freedom's Children: Work, Relationships and Politics for 18–34 Year Olds in Britain Today* (pamphlet), London: Demos.

Wilkinson, R. G. (ed.) *Class and Health: Research and Longitudinal Data*, London: Tavistock.

Willetts, D. (1992) *Modern Conservatism*, Harmondsworth: Penguin.

Williams, F. (1989) *Social Policy: A Critical Introduction*, Cambridge: Polity Press.

Williams, F. (1993a) 'Gender, "race" and class in British

welfare policy', in Cochrane, A. and Clarke, J. (eds), *Comparing Welfare States*, London: Sage.

Williams, F. (1994) 'Social relations, welfare and the post-Fordism debate', in Burrows, R. and Loader, B. (eds), *Towards a Post-Fordist Welfare State*, London: Routledge.

Williams, J. (1986) 'Football hooliganism', *Social Science Teacher*, vol. 15, no. 3.*

Williams, J. (1997) 'In focus: work and the trade unions', *Sociology Review*, vol. 6, no. 3.

Williams, J. (1998) 'Crime trends and fear of crime', *Sociology Review*, vol. 7, no. 4.

Williams, J. (1999) 'The 1998 British Crime Survey', *Sociology Review*, vol. 8, no. 4.

Williams, K. (1993b) 'The light at the end of the tunnel: the mass media, public opinion and the Vietnam War', in Eldridge, J. (ed.), *Getting the Message: News, Truth and Power*, London: Glasgow University Media Group/Routledge.

Williams, L. and Dunsmuir, A. (1991) *How To Do Social Research*, London: Collins Educational.

Williams, R. (1961) *The Long Revolution*, Harmondsworth: Penguin.

Williams, R. (1963) *Culture and Society 1780–1950*, Harmondsworth: Penguin.

Williams, R. (1983) *Towards 2000*, London: Verso.

Williams, R. (1990) *Television, Technology and Cultural Form*, 2nd edn, London: Routledge.

Williams, S. J. (1995) 'Theorising class, health and lifestyles: can Bourdieu help us?', *Sociology of Health and Illness*, vol. 17, no. 5.

Williamson, J. (1978) *Decoding Advertisements*, London: Marion Boyers.

Willis, P. (1977) *Learning to Labour*, Farnborough: Saxon House.

Willis, P. (1990) *Common Culture*, Buckingham: Open University Press.

Willmott, P. (1987) *Friendship Networks and Social Support*, London: PSI.

Willmott, P. (1988) 'Urban kinship past and present', *Social Studies Review*, vol. 4, no. 2.

Willmott, P. and Young, M. (1971) *Family and Class in a London Suburb*, London: New English Library.

Wilson, B. R. (1966) *Religion in a Secular Society: A Sociological Comment*, London: C. A. Watts and Co.

Wilson, B. R. (1970) *Religious Sects: A Sociological Study*, London: Weidenfeld & Nicholson.

Wilson, B. R. (1985) 'A typology of sects', in Bocock, R. and Thompson, K. (eds), *Religion and Ideology*, Manchester: Manchester University Press.

Wilson, J. (1975) *Thinking About Crime*, New York: Basic Books.

Wilson, W. J. (1987) *The Truly Disadvantaged*, Chicago: University of Chicago Press.

Wimbush, E. (1986) *Women, Leisure and Wellbeing*, Edinburgh: Centre for Leisure Research.

Winship, J. (1986) *Inside Women's Magazines*, London: Pandora.

Winterton Report (1992) *Report of the Social Services Select Committee on Maternity Services*, London: HMSO.

Witcher, S. (1994) 'Introduction' to Oppenheim, C., *The Welfare State: Putting the Record Straight*, London: CPAG.

Witz, A. (1992) *Professions and Patriarchy*, London: Routledge.

Wolf, N. (1990) *The Beauty Myth*, London: Vintage.

Wolpe, H. (ed.) (1980) *The Articulation of Modes of Production*, London: Routledge.

Women in Journalism Research Committee (1996) *Women in the News: Does Sex Change the Way a Newspaper Thinks?*, London: Women in Journalism.

World Bank (1986) *Poverty and Hunger*, Washington, DC: World Bank.

World Bank (1993) *World Development Report 1993*, Oxford: Oxford University Press.

World Bank (1996) *Social Indicators of Development 1996*, Baltimore: Johns Hopkins University Press.

World Bank (1998) *World Development Report*, New York: World Bank.

World Development Movement (1996) *Corporate Giants*, London: WDM.

Woronoff, J. (1992) *The Japanese Economic Crisis*, Basingstoke: Macmillan.

Worsley, P. (1984) *The Three Worlds*, London: Weidenfeld & Nicolson.

Wright, E. O. (1976) 'Class boundaries in advanced capitalist societies', *New Left Review*, no. 98.

Wright, E. O. (1978) *Class, Crisis and the State*, London: Verso.

Wright, E. O. (1985) *Classes*, London: Verso.

Wright, E. O. (1994a) 'What is analytical Marxism?', in Wright, E. O., *Interrogating Inequality*, London: Verso.

Wright, E. O. (1994b) *Interrogating Inequality*, London: Verso.

Wright, E. O. (1997) *Class Counts*, Cambridge: Cambridge University Press.

Wrong, D. (1969) 'The oversocialised concept of man in modern sociology', in Coser, L. and Rosenberg, B. (eds), *Sociological Theory: A Book of Readings*, London: Collier Macmillan.

Young , J. (1977) 'The role of the police as amplifiers of deviancy, negotiators of reality and translators of fantasy', in Cohen, S. (ed.), *Images of Deviance*, Harmondsworth: Penguin.

Young, M. (1961) *The Rise of the Meritocracy*, Harmondsworth: Penguin.

Young, M. F. D. (1971) 'An approach to the study of the curriculum as socially organised knowledge', in Young, M. (ed.), *Knowledge and Control: New Directions for the Sociology of Education*, London: Macmillan.

Young, M. and Willmott, P. (1957) *Family and Kinship in East London:* London: Routledge & Kegan Paul.

Young, M. and Willmott, P. (1975) *The Symmetrical Family*, Harmondsworth: Penguin.

Zaretsky, E. (1976) *Capitalism: The Family and Personal Life*, London: Pluto Press.

Zimbardo, P. (1972) 'Pathology of imprisonment', *Society*, vol. 9.

Zweig, F. (1961) *The Worker in an Affluent Society: Family Life and Industry*, London: Heinemann.

Social Science Teacher is the journal of the Association for the Teaching of the Social Sciences. For further information write to: ATSS, PO Box 61, Watford WD2 2NH.

Copyright Acknowledgements

AEB for the cartoon on p. 15; Ashgate Publishing Limited for the figure from *The Experiences of Work*, Littler, C. R. 1985 on p. 723; *Bedfordshire on Sunday* for the article on p. 508; Blackwell Publishers for the table from *The Sociology of Housework*, Oakley, A. 1974 on p. 119; for the figure from *Girl Delinquents*, Campbell, Dr A. 1981 on p. 328; for the table from *The Role of Medicine*, McKeown, T. 1979 on p. 428; for the table from *The Three Worlds of Welfare Capitalism*, Esping-Andersen, Prof. G. 1993 on p. 537; for the table from *Free Markets and Food Riots: The Politics of Global Adjustments*, Walton, J. & Seddon, D. 1994 on p. 605; Blackwell Science Ltd for the figure from *The Sociology of Health and Health Care*, Taylor & Field, 1993 on p. 463; Cambridge University Press for the figure from *Class Counts*, Wright, 1997 on p. 779; Cath Tate Cards/Grizelda Grislingham for the cartoon on p. 62; Childline for the tables on p. 130; Christian Research Association for the figure from *UK Christian Handbook, 1994-5 Edition*, Brierley, P. & Hiscock, V. (eds) 1993 on p. 197; CPAG and HMSO for the figures on pp. 755 and 758; for the tables on pp. 562, 759 and 767. Crown Copyright is reproduced with the permission of the Controller of Her Majesty's Stationery Office; The Department of Health for the figure on p. 432; for the table on p. 131; Reprinted from *Child Abuse and Neglect*, vol. 9, Baker, A. and Duncan, S. 'Child sexual abuse: a study of prevalence in Great Britain', pp. 457-67. Copyright 1985, with permission from Elsevier Science on p. 130; Express Newspapers for the articles on pp. 505 and 761; Goldsmiths College for the figure from *Unequal Pay for Equal Parts: A Survey of Performers in the Theatre and the Electronic Media*, Thomas, H. & Klett-Davies, M. 1995 on p. 510; Goldthorpe, J. for the figure from *Social Mobility and the Class Structure in Modern Britain*, 1987 on p. 781; Greenwood Publishing Group, Inc. for the figure from *Varieties in Criminology*, Barak. © 1993, reproduced with permission of Greenwood Publishing, Inc., Westport, CT on p. 242; *The Guardian* for the material on pp. 48, 51, 70, 107, 116, 145, 168, 170, 187, 203, 208, 239, 241, 266, 306, 334, 350, 351, 352, 355, 405, 423, 455, 491, 493, 544, 547, 569, 585, 590, 599, 609, 632, 719, 760, 766 and 785; HarperCollinsPublishers for the figure from *Investigating Health, Wealth and Poverty*, 2nd edn, Trolwer, P. 1996 on p. 452; for the table from *Topics in Sociology*, Trowler, P. and Riley, M. 1987 on p. 460; for the table from *Social Class Differences* in Britain, Reid, I. 1989 on p. 748; Hip-Hop Connection for the material by Andy Cowan on p. 488; HMSO for the figure from 'Recent research on the achievements of ethnic minority pupils', *Educational Researcher*, vol. 32, no. 3 on p. 377; for the table from *Health and Personal Social Statistics for England*, 1986 on p. 446; for the tables from *Inequalities in Health: The Black Report and the Health Divide*, Townsend, Davidson & Whitehead, 1988 on pp. 430, 450 and 452; for the extracts from *The Stephen Lawrence Inquiry: Report of an Inquiry* on p. 816; for the tables on pp. 235, 337, 550, 733 and 755; for the figures on pp. 336 and 464. Crown Copyright is reproduced with the permission of the Controller of Her Majesty's Stationery Office; The Home Office for the material on pp. 234, 323, 324, 326, 327, 335, 338 and 339; Independent Newspapers (UK) Ltd for the material on pp. 384, 388, 411, 439, 473, 771 and 817; Independent Television Commission for the table on p. 509; The Institute for Social and Economic Research (incorporating the ESRC Research Centre on Micro-social Change) for the table from the *British Household Panel Survey* on p. 103; for the table on p. 792; The Joint Council for General Qualifications for the Inter-Board Statistics on pp. 256 and 389; for the Inter-Group Statistics on p. 387; The Joseph Rowntree Foundation for the figure on p. 718; Klein, R. for the article on p. 520; Jane Lindsey Management and Promotion and Newell, M. for the poem on p. 827-6. Martin Newell is *The Independent*'s regular poet and this poem first appeared on the paper's front page on 26 June 1996; Little, Brown & Co (UK) for the diagram from *Life and Death: Unapologetic Writings on the Continuing War Against Women*, Dworkin, A. Virago Press, 1997 on p. 11; for the extract from *Blood, Bread and Poverty*, Rich, A. Virago Press, 1994 on p. 811; Macmillan Press Ltd for the table from *Values and Social Change in Britain*, Abrams, M. et al. (eds) 1985 on pp. 197, 198 and 199; Mirror Syndication for the front cover of the *Daily Mirror* on pp. 141, 156 and 827; National Centre for Social Research for the tables from the *British Social Attitudes Survey*, 1991 on pp. 197 and 198; *New Internationalist* for the article on p. 814; News International Newspapers Limited, 28 February 1994, on p. 268; *New Left Review* for the figure from *Class Boundaries in Advanced Capitalist Societies*, Wright, E. O. on p. 778; *New Statesman* for the figure on p. 173; OCR for the extracts on pp. 23 and 42; the *Observer* for the material on pp. 105, 115, 263, 264, 408, 631, 760, 762, 763 and 770; ONS for the Census data on p. 574; for the material from the 1991 Census on p. 746; for the material from the *Employment Gazette*, 1995 on p. 783; for the material from the *Labour Force Survey*, 1996 on pp. 729 and 733; for the material from the *Labour Force Survey*, 1998 on pp. 576, 724 and 727; for the material from the *Labour Force Survey*, 1986-98 on p. 726; for the material from *Le Grand*, 1982 on p. 554; for the material from *Living in Britain: General Household Survey, Preliminary Findings*, 1995 on pp. 104 and 107; for the material from *Living in Britain: General Household Survey, Preliminary Results*, 1996 on pp. 103 and 306; for the material from *Living in Britian: General Household Survey*, 1998 on p. 96; for the material from the *New Earnings Survey*, 1995 on p. 306; for the material from the *New Earnings Survey*, 1998 on pp. 728 and 739; for the material from the *New Earnings Survey*, 1999 on pp. 719 and 725; for the material from *Population Trends*, 1997 on p. 473; for the material from *Regional Trends 34*, 1999 on pp. 437, 438, 441, 442, 443, 444 and 445; for the material from the *Royal Commission on* the *Distribution of Income and Wealth* (1979a) on p. 717; for the material from *Social Trends 22*, 1992 on p. 304; for the material from *Social Trends 25*, 1995 on p. 555; for the material from *Social Trends 26*, 1996 on pp. 96, 97, 103, 108, 109, 111, 202, 302, 431 and 732; for the material from *Social Trends 28*, 1998 on pp. 98, 103 and 125; for the material from *Social Trends 29*, 1999 on pp. 98, 108, 810 and 811. © Crown Copyright 2000; Open University Press for the figure from *Doing Your Research Project*, Bell, J. 3rd edn. 1993 on p. 305; for the extracts from *Disarming Patriarchy*, Roseneil, S. 1995 on pp. 681 and 811-12; Material from *Which Picture?* information leaflet, 1994, reproduced with permission of Oxfam Publishing, 274 Banbury Road, Oxford, OX2 7DZ on p. 162; Oxford University Press for the table from 'Gender and crime', Heidensohn, F. (1994), in Maguire, M., Morgan, M. and Reiner, R. *The Oxford Handbook of Criminology* on p. 234; From *Human Development Report*, 1998 by United Nations Development Program © 1998 by the United Nations Development Program. Used by permission of Oxford University Press, Inc. on p. 720; © Denis McQuail and Sven Windahl. Reprinted by permission of Pearson Education, the figure from *Communication Models for the Study of Mass Communication* on pp. 148 and 150; Philip Allan Publishers for the extracts from *S Magazine* on pp. 4 and 22; for the material from 'Money marriage and ideology: holding the purse strings?', Pahl, J. *Sociology Review*, vol. 3, no. 1, 1993 on p. 120; for the figure from 'The world's religions', *General Studies Review*, 1991 on p. 186; for the figure from 'In the shadow of science', Lawson, T. *Social Science Review*, vol. 2, no. 2, 1986 on p. 278 and 666; for the figure from 'Squaring up to crime', Matthews, R. *Sociology Review*, vol. 2, no. 3, 1993 on p. 354; for the extract from 'Insights: gender and education revisited', Clark, J. *Sociology Review*, vol. 5, no. 4, 1996 on p. 387; for the material from 'Let's get real: the realist approach to sociology', Clark, J. and Layedr, D. *Sociology Review*, vol. 4, no. 2, 1994 on p. 694 Pluto Press for the figure from *What is to be Done About Law and Order?*, Lea, J. and Young, J. 1993 on pp. 358 and 359; for the extract from *Women and Evolution: A Discussion of the Unhappy Marriage of Marxism and Feminism*,

Hartmann, 1981 on p. 794; *Police*, May 1981 for the cartoon on p. 334; Policy Studies Institute for the extracts from *Ethnic Minorities in Britain: Diversity and Disadvantage*, Modood, T. 1997 on p. 821; Punch Library and Archive for the cartoons on pp. 238 and 796; Rex Features for the front cover of *The Sun* on p. 141; Routledge for the figure from *What's This Channel Fo(u)r?*, Blanchard & Morley, 1982 on p. 149; for the figure from *Introduction to Communication*, Fiske, 1990 on p. 177; for the material from *Social Class in Modern Britain*, Marshall et al. 1988 on pp. 283, 677-8 and 786; for the figure from *Reforming Education and Changing Schools: Case Studies in Policy Sociology*, Bowe, Ball & Gold, 1992 on p. 401; for the table from *A Measure of Thatcherism*, Edgell, S. & Duke, V. 1991 on p. 611; for the figure from *Research Methodology*, McNeill, P. on p. 686; for the table from *Poor Britain*, Mack & Lansley, 1985 on p. 753; for the figure from *Class*, Edgell, S. 1993 on p. 782; Sage Publications for the table from *Medical Power and Social Knowledge*, Turner, B. S. 1987 on p. 421; Taylor & Francis Ltd., PO Box 25, Abingdon, Oxford, OX14 3UE for the table from 'Social class and social justice', Marshall and Swift, *British Journal of Sociology*, 1993 on p. 789; for the extracts from 'Five feminist myths about women's employment', Hakim, C. *British Journal of Sociology*, vol. 46, no. 3, 1995 on pp. 797-9; for the extracts from 'Feminist fallacies: a reply to Hakim on women's employment', Ginn et al. *British Journal of Sociology*, vol. 47, no. 1, 1996 on p. 798; for the extracts from 'Whose myths are they anyway: a comment', Breugel, *British Journal of Sociology*, vol. 47, no. 1, 1997 on p. 799; © Telegraph Group Limited for the article of p. 331; © Times Newspapers Limited, 22 May 1994, on p. 384; © Times Newspapers, 6 March 1996, on p. 384; © Times Newspapers Limited, 15 December 1997, on pp. 747 and 748; © Times Newspapers Limited, 19 March 2000, on p. 721 © Times Newspapers Limited, 10 April 2000, on p. 788; ©Times Supplements Limited for the material on pp. 382 and 384; Wallis, V. for the figure from *The Elementary Forms of the New Religious Life*, Wallis, R. 1984 on p. 193; Wandor, M. for the extract from *Once A Feminist: Stories of a Generation* on p. 808.

Name Index

Subject Index

employment 767–9
health and illness 440–56
health and illness definitions 451
IQ testing 365, 393–5
leisure participation 502
Marxism 819
masculinity 518–19
maternal health 452
moral panics 152–3, 333
'new' 71–3, 594
poverty 767–9
religion 199
representations 71–3, 159–63
schooling 251–2
television and identity 72
theories 818–22
UK theories and research 819–22
U.S.A. theories and research 818–19
white tribes 69
women 515–16
ethnography 249, 301, 700–1
everyday life
power 632–6
see also interactionism;
phenomenology; symbolic interactionism
examinations
A Levels 385–6, 388, 389, 412–13
gender subject choices 255–8
skills 18–19
Excellence in Cities (DfEE report) 398
Excellence in Schools (DfEE report) 398
excorporation 499–500
experience
first generation migrants 67–8
learned 320
schooling 248–52
expertise 708–9
exploitation theory 642, 778
extended family 91

F
facts
'social' 644–5
value-free 687
facts/opinions 705–6
fairness, welfare 533
Falklands conflict 178–9
false consciousness 138–9
falsification 685–6
family 86–136
African-Caribbean 110
ageing population 100
alternative terms 87
birth rates 99–100
black feminism 133
child abuse 129–32
childlessness 126–7
cohabitation 102–4
conjugal 95
critical views 89
Cypriot 109–10

definition of term 86
diversity 108–112
East London 95
election manifesto 1997 113
emotional labour 121
employment 125
Family Allowances 542
fathers 114
feminism 89–90, 118–19, 132
financial control within 120
functionalism 88–9
functions 88
household size 122
ideology 90, 345
industrialization 93–5
late-modern views 116–17
low-income 755–6
Marxism 89
Marxist-feminism 89
middle-class 110–11
parenting 124–5
parents and children 122–6
political positions on 113–17
post-modern views 115–16
poverty 765
power inequalities 119
pre-industrial societies 93
recession 120–1
reconstituted 104
remarriage 104
same-sex 105–6
single-parent 106–8, 766
social policy 101–2
South Asian 109
state 101–2
statistical patterns 95–6
step-parenting 104
structure and function 88–90
symmetrical 118–19
violence in 127–8
welfare provision 545–6
working-class 111
family agenda, New Labour 114–15
Family Allowances Act 1945 542
family concepts 86–95
family diversity 108–17
The Family Expenditure Survey 295, 298
family groups 122
Family Law Act 1996 98
family life 117
full-time employment 125
recent trends 102–8
family and marriage in East London 95
Family Policy Studies Centre 122
family responsibilities 121
family structures, alternative 91–3
family types, parenting 124–5
family welfare responsibilities, women 546
famine reporting 161–3
fantasy, translation 321
fashion, male 512–13

fathers
families 114
New Labour agenda 114–5
FE college lecturers, industrial action 612–13
fear of crime
female 360
measurement 322–9
female
fear of crime 360
misogyny 169
oppression 37–8
pupils 250
social mobility 787–8
teachers 252
see also feminism; women
femininity
construction 52–4
cult 158
gendered hierarchy 163
women 515
feminism 37–8
activism 800–4
anti- 60–1
black women 522
category of 'woman' 596–7
consciousness-raising 806
contemporary debates 809–12
definitions 800–1
dual-systems theory 730–1
Empire 805
Greenham Common peace camp 810–12
history 804–9
liberal 157, 801–2
male theorists 60
and Marxism 790
Marxist/socialist 157
'middle-range' theory 800
myth of patriarchy 797–9
National Women's Conference 1970 807
Organization of Women of Asian and African Descent 808–9
popular culture 486–7
radical 157
'sisterhood' 809
sociology 800–4
trade unionism 805
types 810–12
women's liberation movement 806–8
see also female; women
feminist fallacies 798
feminist methodology 708
feminist perspectives 789–812
the body 447–8
citizenship 800
class 518
communitarianism 570–1
culture 486–7
culture industries 508–10
domestic abuse 132
education 372
the family 89–90
family 118–19
gender role changes 812